The Palgrave Handbook of Popular Culture as Philosophy

David Kyle Johnson
Editor-in-Chief

Dean A. Kowalski • Chris Lay • Kimberly S. Engels
Editors

The Palgrave Handbook of Popular Culture as Philosophy

Volume 1

With 1 Figure and 2 Tables

Editor-in-Chief
David Kyle Johnson
King's College
Wilkes Barre, PA
USA

Editors
Dean A. Kowalski
University School of Milwaukee
Waukesha, WI, USA

Chris Lay
Young Harris College
Young Harris, GA, USA

Kimberly S. Engels
Molloy University
Rockville Centre, NewYork, NY, USA

ISBN 978-3-031-24684-5   ISBN 978-3-031-24685-2 (eBook)
https://doi.org/10.1007/978-3-031-24685-2

© Springer Nature Switzerland AG 2024
This work is subject to copyright. All rights are reserved by the Publisher, whether the whole or part of the material is concerned, specifically the rights of translation, reprinting, reuse of illustrations, recitation, broadcasting, reproduction on microfilms or in any other physical way, and transmission or information storage and retrieval, electronic adaptation, computer software, or by similar or dissimilar methodology now known or hereafter developed.
The use of general descriptive names, registered names, trademarks, service marks, etc. in this publication does not imply, even in the absence of a specific statement, that such names are exempt from the relevant protective laws and regulations and therefore free for general use.
The publisher, the authors, and the editors are safe to assume that the advice and information in this book are believed to be true and accurate at the date of publication. Neither the publisher nor the authors or the editors give a warranty, expressed or implied, with respect to the material contained herein or for any errors or omissions that may have been made. The publisher remains neutral with regard to jurisdictional claims in published maps and institutional affiliations.

This Palgrave Macmillan imprint is published by the registered company Springer Nature Switzerland AG.
The registered company address is: Gewerbestrasse 11, 6330 Cham, Switzerland

If disposing of this product, please recycle the paper.

For my wife and son, who demonstrated exceptional patience with me during the five years this project took to complete.

Preface: A Brief Defense of Pop Culture as Philosophy

If you want to tell people the truth, make them laugh, otherwise they'll kill you.
—George Bernard Shaw[1]

Abstract

This introductory chapter articulates the overarching objectives and methodology of the Palgrave Handbook of Popular Culture as Philosophy. Its primary aim is to treat works of popular culture as philosophical works, essentially considering them to be works of art that aspire to articulate philosophical arguments or provoke profound philosophical inquiries. The chapter also defends the concept that creative works, including but not limited to films, possess the capacity to do philosophy – an idea characterized by Paisley Livingston as the "Bold Thesis." A persuasive case in favor of the Bold Thesis is articulated and objections to it are considered and answered.

Introduction

William Irwin started the "Pop Culture and Philosophy" craze with *Seinfeld and Philosophy* in 1999; the second volume of the series, *The Simpsons and Philosophy (2001)*, ended up selling over 200,000 copies. (Because it was published in 2001, at the time it might have been the best-selling philosophy book of the twenty-first century.) Later volumes, like *The Matrix and Philosophy* (2002) and *The Lord of the Rings and Philosophy* (2003), were also highly successful (and impeccably timed with popular movie sequels). And it was around that time, at a point when Irwin started to bring in other editors to help with the workload (Eric Bronson and Greg Bassham were volume editors of the *Lord of the Rings* book), that the series really took off. Regardless of how you count, to date, there are at least 200 "pop and phil" books.

Although I had taught a "Simpsons, South Park, and Philosophy" class at the University of Oklahoma as a graduate student ca. 2004, my first published chapter was in Robert Arp's *South Park and Philosophy* in 2006; the first words I ever published were "Cartman is an ass." I went on to write almost 30 pop culture chapters, attend multiple pop-culture conferences, and edit three books in Irwin's

Blackwell *Philosophy and Pop Culture* series: *Heroes and Philosophy* (2009), *Inception and Philosophy* (2011), and *Black Mirror and Philosophy* (2019). Irwin also graciously asked me to co-edit his textbook *Introducing Philosophy Through Pop Culture* (2010), which is a collection of select chapters from his Blackwell series, organized by subject so that it can be used in the classroom. We published an updated edition in 2022, and I have used chapters from it, and other chapters from the series, in my classroom for many years.

I mention all this not to demonstrate my "bona fides" (others have certainly edited and published on pop culture more) but to emphasize that this current project – *The Palgrave Handbook of Popular Culture as Philosophy* – is *NOT* a continuation of that series. As should be obvious, I am a big fan of the "pop and phil" approach; but it is decidedly not the approach that this handbook takes. The astute reader might have noticed the difference in its title – it's "*as*" philosophy, not "and." It's subtle, but that "as" makes a lot of difference.

The Difference Between "As" and "And"

The goal of the "pop *and* phil" approach is to use popular culture as a kind of springboard to introduce and discuss philosophical concepts and arguments. If the show has an android – like *Data* from *Star Trek* – we can introduce the reader to the philosophical debate about artificial intelligence by discussing whether Data has a mind. If the show has characters waging war and vying for political power – like *Game of Thrones* – we can examine their actions to introduce the reader to just war theory and political philosophy. *The Matrix* can be used to explain Descartes' dream problem, *Inception* can be used to discuss the acceptability of faith, and *The Good Place* can be used to explore ethical theories and the possibility of an afterlife. I'm oversimplifying, of course, and the number of philosophical issues explored in any one "pop and phil" book is broad and diverse. But the "and philosophy" approach treats the pop culture it engages as a kind of thought experiment – one that is already known and loved and so makes the task of introducing the reader to philosophy easier. As Irwin has often said about his series, "A spoonful of sugar helps the medicine go down" (Written Voices n.d.).

The "as philosophy" approach is different. The basic idea is that the creators of popular culture – the directors, the writers – can actually *do* philosophy while playing at their craft. They can not only be inspired by philosophy, or use ideas they learned in philosophy class, but they can convey philosophical points, raise philosophical questions, and even make philosophical arguments.[2] Consequently, the works they produce can *be* philosophy, and as a result are worth philosophical examination. Ruppert Read and Jerry Goodenough's *Film as Philosophy: Essays on Cinema after Wittgenstein and Cavell* (2005), Murry Smith and Thomas Wartenberg's *Thinking through Cinema: Film as Philosophy* (2006), Thomas Wartenberg's *Thinking on Screen: Film as Philosophy* (2007), and Bernd Herzogenrath's *Film as Philosophy* (2017), all embrace the "as philosophy" approach.

Preface: A Brief Defense of Pop Culture as Philosophy

Of course, not all pop culture is philosophy; but quite a bit is, with some examples greatly standing out in this respect – like *The Matrix* and *Inception*. In fact, these two movies are perfect examples. While both movies could be used to explain Descartes' dream problem, they seem to argue for completely different conclusions. *The Matrix*, by making a villain out of the one character (Cypher) who willfully embraces ignorance, seems to be arguing that one should care for and strive to embrace reality – to obtain objectively true beliefs. *Inception* on the other hand, by having Cobb turn away from his spinning top (his test of reality) in the final scene and instead choose to believe that his children are real, seems to suggest that, in the end, it is only "your truth" that matters. Other examples of obviously philosophical films include *2001: A Space Odyssey, Lord of the Rings, Star Wars, Blade Runner, Groundhog Day, The Shawshank Redemption, Tenet, Ex Machina, Don't Look Up, AI: Artificial Intelligence, Fight Club,* and *Gattaca*, all of which (and much more) are covered in this handbook.

Going Beyond Films

It's not only films, of course. Most people recognize that series (what used to be relegated to television but now also exist on streaming services) like *Star Trek, South Park, Black Mirror, House of Cards, Doctor Who, The Handmaid's Tale,* and *The Good Place* can do something similar. (All of these and more are also covered in this handbook.) But one thing that generally goes unappreciated, even by philosophers, is that other kinds of popular culture can be philosophy as well – like graphic novels and video games. Both have long since ceased being "for kids only," and the creators of both enjoy certain kinds of creative freedom that make them an especially welcome medium for philosophical reflection. The graphic novel *V for Vendetta*, for example, does a much better job of articulating exactly when violent political rebellion is warranted than the movie it inspired. And modern video games, with their interactive features and story-telling, can make points about, say, political choice and free will that their strictly scripted movie counterparts cannot. (The game *Papers Please*, where you choose whether to cooperate with a fascist regime or resist it – and can "win" the game either way – is most notable in this regard.) What's more, while common wisdom will tell you that graphic novels and video games aren't as "popular" as TV series and films, graphic novels serve as the groundwork for some of the most popular movies and TV of all time (*The Avengers, X-Men, Justice League, Watchmen, 300, The Walking Dead,* etc.) and the video game industry dwarfs all other entertainment industries in terms of profit (grossing $160 billion in 2020).

Because of its reliance on spoken word, another medium that is prime for the doing of philosophy is stand-up comedy. On the *Comedy Gold Minds* podcast (2021), Hasan Minhaj elaborated on how his experience with competitive debate – the same thing that helped prepare me for a career in philosophy – helped prepare him for his career as a comedian. "Comedians," he says, are "just normal philosophers," tasked with turning "coffee into espresso" (i.e., taking what's difficult to understand and compressing it into something comprehensible). In an interview with Khan Academy (2020), he elaborated a bit more: "Stand-up comedy is just funny speech and debate ... The most important thing for comedy is the argument. You are making a funny joke, but at the core, what is your argument? So great jokes at their essence are great philosophical positions said in a funny way."

Some comedians, like Jerry Seinfeld, shy away from this responsibility. "Ok, fine, fine." he said on the HBO special *George Carlin's American Dream*, "you want the comedian to be your lens on society. Go. . .enjoy it. But, for me, I never heard a comic bit that changed my opinion on anything" (Apatow & Bonfiglo 2022). But the promotional featurette for the very special in which Seinfeld speaks these words begins with multiple comedians not only saying that George Carlin was the smartest man they ever met, but that he was also a "genius at making you laugh and *changing your mind*" (HBO 2022). In the special itself, Chris Rock was more specific.

> I remember one time Carlin said to me, "I'm not in show business, I'm a comedian." ... I took it to mean that comedians were thinkers. But, when you think about the history of [hu]man[ity], [hu]man[ity] used to love philosophers. We don't really have philosophers anymore. But we have comedians. So, Carlin encompassed all those things; that's what he meant. Like, this is what we do, this is the life we've chosen, we're, you know, a kind a secret society in a sense. (Apatow & Bonfiglo 2022)

In his last comedy special, "Nothing Special," Norm McDonald (2022) was a bit more kind to living philosophers.

> Like nowadays, I've heard ... "The comedian is the modern-day philosopher," you know? Which, first of all, it always makes me feel sad for the actual modern-day philosophers, who exist, you know.

Thanks for the shout-out Norm; indeed, we do exist. But what Rock was getting at still stands: the public doesn't listen to philosophers anymore – at least not like they used to. Don't get me wrong, philosophers still influence society; but the public doesn't crowd event halls to go listen to philosophers speak, as they used to do with academics in the past. But they *do* watch comedians; and many comedians – from George Carlin and Dave Chappell to Amy Schumer and Hannah Gadsby – are presenting philosophical arguments that change people's minds. (Sometimes they are explicit, like Carlin's arguments against religion; other times they are implicit, like Schumer's arguments about feminism. But the arguments are there.) They may not always mean to. Carlin himself said that "try[ing] to make people think ... would be the kiss of death" for a comedian; he only aims "to let them know I'm thinking." But they are doing it, nonetheless – comedians are making people think. And so, it should be worth the real-world (existing) modern philosopher's time to examine what comedians are saying, and the arguments they are making, to see whether they are onto something – or whether they are full of (sh)it.

The same holds for philosophy that is being done in movies, television/streaming series, graphic novels, and video games. While the people who make these things are doing philosophy, they usually are not professional philosophers; they don't always have a philosophy degree; they might not have even had a philosophy class. So, they

Preface: A Brief Defense of Pop Culture as Philosophy

may be getting things wrong.[3] They might also be getting them right; but how can we know unless those who know the subject best take a closer look, identify what argument being made, and evaluate whether it is any good – or identify the question being raised and explore the answers it might have? That is what I tried to do in my course for *The Great Courses* (now known as *Wondrium*) *Sci-Phi: Science Fiction as Philosophy*, and that's what I tried to have my authors do in *Exploring The Orville* (which I edited with Michael Berry) and in *Black Mirror and Philosophy* (even though it was in an "and philosophy" series). And that is what this handbook aims to do: identify and evaluate the philosophy that is being done in and by popular culture.

This is important to do not only because pop culture can be very influential, but because it can be easily misinterpreted and misused. Think of how the term "snowflake" has become ubiquitous in right–wing political circles, to describe those who they think are easily offended. They stole the term from the mouth of Tyler Durden in *Fight Club*; but those who use it today don't seem to recognize that (a) Durden is the villain of the film, not the hero and (b) he uses the term to solidify obedience in his communistic commune – and communism is something that the right decries. (For more on *Fight Club*, see Alberto Oya's magnificent chapter in this volume. For more on how snowflakey (easily offended) many in right-wing political circles are, see the second half of my chapter on *South Park*.)

Speaking of *South Park,* almost every episode of *South Park* is some kind of argument on some social or political issue – and a lot of young impressionable viewers think Matt Stone and Trey Parker make good points. And sometimes they do. *South Park: Bigger, Longer, and Uncut* effectively argues that parents skirt responsibility for their children's behavior by blaming cartoons, and their film *Team America: World Police* effectively criticizes America's militaristic role as "world police" (while also arguing, through a very vulgar (but seemingly accurate) analogy, that it is sometimes necessary). When I was younger, Matt and Trey definitely changed my view about a few things. But Matt and Trey also get things very wrong. In season 10's *ManBearPig* (2006) they made fun of Al Gore (and his 2006 film *An Inconvenient Truth*) and equated his concerns about climate change with concerns about a mythical creature called ManBearPig that didn't actually exist. Their argument was that Gore just wanted attention. But in Season 22, Stone and Parker admitted they were wrong with two episodes, "Time to Get Cereal" and "Nobody Got Cereal?," that revealed that ManBearPig was indeed real, is now murdering and destroying the town, and thus that Al Gore was right (about climate change) all along (see Miller 2018).

Perhaps one might argue that this is more of a scientific, rather than a philosophic, issue. But a scene in "Time to Get Cereal" makes clear that they have a philosophical point in mind. A patron at Red Lobster tries to mansplain to his wife why ManBearPig is not real – "What you need to understand, Susan, is that everyone has an agenda, mmmkay?" – as ManBearPig actively kills the other patrons in the restaurant and his wife yells "he's real!" The patron eventually turns around – yet when he sees ManBearPig with his own eyes, he only begrudgingly admits he was wrong and immediately shifts to "What are we going to do about it now, huh? What are we going to do that's going to make any difference now, Susan? What can we do that everyone else will also do?," only to then be eaten alive by ManBearPig.[4] Matt and Trey go on to show townhall meetings where, as ManBearPig destroys the town, the people calmly agree that, perhaps, they should, maybe, begin to consider thinking about possibly being worried. And when it's revealed that ManBearPig is attacking because Stan's grandpa and his generation made a deal with ManBearPig (for cars and premium boutique ice cream because they "didn't think they would have to live with the consequences"), and Stan tries to renegotiate the contract, Stan goes to the townspeople with the new terms of the deal:

Stan (to the townspeople)	Um, [ManBearPig] says he'll never come back again, but, we have to give up soy sauce and *Red Dead Redemption 2.*
Townspeople (in unison, disappointed)	Ohhh. . . . A long silence
A single townsperson	Just plain rice?
Stan (pauses, but is unsurprised)	Yeah, that's what I thought.

The scene is hilarious and so on the nose that it's depressing. Stan has to strike another deal.

Lawyer	Sign here that ManBearPig has rights to the lives of all children in third world countries.
Stan	Ok, got it.
Lawyer	And you agree to ignore ManBearPig until he returns in five years, in which time the carnage will be a thousand-fold.
Stan	Ok, where do I sign that?

Parker and Stone are not known for being subtle, and clearly they are making a philosophical point; yet one might still struggle to put it into words so that it can be examined – hence the need for professional philosophers to step in. A chapter on these episodes would show that the Red Lobster scene is making a philosophical point about how climate change denial is epistemically bankrupt; no matter how obvious the evidence is, or how imminent the threat, their denial and excuses will continue. Such a chapter would point out that the townhall meeting scene is making the point that, because of people's epistemic tendency toward self-denial when it comes to things so overwhelmingly unpleasant, even those who recognize the severity of the threat are afraid to say that people should be even worried for fear of being labeled "alarmist." And it would point out that the negotiation scene shows how human selfishness makes us collectively incapable of giving up even the most basic comforts for the good of others (like children in third world countries), future generations, or even ourselves five years from now. (My chapter on *South Park* in this volume covers a different topic, but check out this handbook's chapter on *Don't Look Up* to see that Parker and Stone are essentially right on these topics.)

The Handbook's Approach

I've divided the handbook into five sections – cinema, series, comedians, video games, and graphic novels – but the basic approach of each chapter will be similar.

1. A short introduction to the pop culture work and the philosophical issue it raises
2. A quick summary of the work itself
3. An attempt to identify exactly what argument the work is making or what question it is raising
4. An evaluation of that argument or an attempt to answer the relevant philosophical question

Now, there is a lot of variation; I tried to give the author of each chapter the freedom to evaluate the philosophy being done by their selected piece of pop culture in the most appropriate way. But each has the goal of treating the pop culture in question as philosophy – or, in the case of a comedian, as a philosopher.

Another thing I tried to make consistent throughout is the writing style. Each author, of course, has their own flair and approach – but while this handbook is more academic in nature, and some of its chapters are quite long, I intended the handbook for classroom use. So, each chapter is written with the goal of being understandable to the average college student. (If the chapter is long, its sections make it divisible into readable parts.) What's more, the reason that I made sure that each chapter contains a summary of the pop culture in question is so the instructor does not have to assign it or spend valuable class time screening it. That's not to say that doing so wouldn't enhance the student's experience; but a familiarity with the pop culture in question is not required to understand, learn from, or enjoy any chapter.

Defending a Bold Thesis

Despite the popularity of viewing films as philosophy, the notion that films can do philosophy, which of course would entail that popular culture (e.g., TV, graphic novels, etc.) can do philosophy, has its detractors. I, however, have never found the arguments against the notion very convincing. After all, my guess is that most readers would agree that the novels *To Kill a Mockingbird* and *1984* are arguments against racism and fascism – so why can't the movies based on them be the same? And why couldn't something that is even more overtly philosophical, like *The Matrix,* be presenting an argument?

Bruce Russell (2000) would argue that *The Matrix* (and *To Kill a Mockingbird* and *1984* for that matter) doesn't do philosophy but merely inspires viewers (or readers) to do their own philosophy – to construct their own arguments and raise their own questions. I have three responses to this charge. First, even if Russell's claim is true and pop culture can't do philosophy (but instead merely inspires people to do philosophy), this handbook is still warranted, as it essentially contains the philosophy that pop culture inspired professional philosophers to do. Second, inspiring others to do philosophy can be (and often is) philosophy itself. Philosophy is often aimed at simply changing our perspective, making us think about the world or a situation in a way that we have not before. As any philosophy instructor will tell you, that is the goal of nearly every philosophy class. So, even if inspiring others to do philosophy is all a piece of popular culture does, that work of popular culture is still doing philosophy.

The third response is that this claim is simply false. Films can do more than inspire philosophy; they can do philosophy. To take a rather obvious example (anticipated by Smuts 2009), suppose someone took one of Plato's dialogues and turned it into a movie – which, of course, could be done because they are dialogues complete with characters and settings. Wouldn't it undeniably be philosophy? And couldn't the story of Plato's cave be made into a movie; and if it was, wouldn't it have just as much of a philosophical point as the story does in Plato's *Republic*? Or take the article, "A Debate Between a Theist and a Santa Clausist," that Ruth Tallman and I divided into two "acts" and published in the journal *Think* in 2015. It was written (and originally delivered at a conference) as a sketch, and could easily be turned into a short film that has the express purpose of convincing the audience that many of the arguments given in favor of theism could be given in defense in Santa Claus – and thus that theistic belief is on shaky ground. The quality of such a film might be questionable, but such a film would undoubtedly be philosophy.

In reply, skeptics might insist that a film can't be philosophy by simply putting philosophical arguments in the mouths of characters. But, again, I would object. First, why not? I mean, it would be one thing for a painter to say that he had a painting that "did philosophy," only to find out that he had just written a philosophical treatise on a canvas with a paint brush. That's not a painting. In the same way, just recording a video of someone giving a philosophy lecture wouldn't count as an example of "film as philosophy." That's not really a film; it's not cinema. (A recorded lecture lacks certain defining features of cinema at both an aesthetic and technical level.) But to have a character give a philosophical argument at a crucial moment that delivers the film's philosophical message doesn't disqualify a piece of media from being cinema. Take the film *God's Not Dead* for example. It not only contains a student – on three separate occasions – presenting formal arguments for God's existence, but it has the conclusion the movie is arguing for in the damn title! It may have lazy writing and be a really bad movie – and as one chapter in this handbook will show, the arguments it presents are pretty bad – but that doesn't mean it's not philosophy. (Bad philosophy is still philosophy.)

At this point in the debate, skeptics might argue that *good* film can't be philosophy. "Without just putting arguments in characters' mouths, films can't do philosophy. A *real* film would be able to show the argument without having a character 'spell it out' for the audience." There are two problems with claims like this. First, such a line of argument would be fallacious, something akin to the no-true-Scotsman fallacy. If I say that no Scotsmen lie, and then you produce a clear, obvious example of a lying Scotsman, I can't refute your counter example by simply claiming "he's not a *true* Scotsman." That's a fallacy. That's just me claiming, arbitrarily, that your example doesn't count so I don't have to admit I'm wrong. In the same way, those skeptical of the idea that films can be philosophy can't just say that movies like *My Dinner with Andre,* which involves two people having a philosophical dinner conversation, don't count "as philosophical films" because they contain people bluntly making philosophical arguments and thus aren't *true* films. In fact, *My Dinner with Andre* is frequently regarded as a masterpiece of a film – in part *because* of its philosophical content.

What's more, there seem to be clear examples of films, even very good films, doing philosophy without simply putting the argument for the film's thesis in the mouths of its characters. My favorite example might be *Contact,* the movie based on Carl Sagan's novel of the same name, in which aliens (seem to) make contact with Earth and give us instructions for building a device to visit them. Carl Sagan was a famous skeptic and science communicator who was labeled as an atheist by religious conservatives but who was, in reality, merely agnostic. In 2021, in chapter six of William Anderson's *Film, Philosophy and Religion,* I showed how *Contact* is an argument for a thesis that Sagan often defended in public: science and religion are compatible. The film has Dr. Arroway dismiss Rev. Palmer's belief in God because it is based solely on his personal experience, only to have Dr. Arroway turn around and believe that she visited aliens based solely on her personal experience. The argument Dr. Arroway uses against Rev. Palmer (based in Occam's razor) is turned back on her, and she answers it in almost the same way he answered her: "Everything I am tells me it was real. It changed me forever." The movie is an argument from analogy that it never formally states: if Arroway's beliefs based in her personal experience about aliens are justified, and they are, then Palmer's beliefs (and the beliefs of those like him in the real world) in God, based in personal experience, are justified as well. And such beliefs are as compatible with science as Dr. Arroway's are. As I try to explain in my aforementioned chapter, it's not a good argument – Dr. Arraoways' belief is not scientific and science and religion are not compatible in the way that Sagan or the movie suggests – but it is an argument, the kind that are made by philosophers every day. To deny that *Contact* is doing philosophy seems ludicrous.

Or take an even better example: *No Exit,* the play by Jean Paul Sartre that everyone agrees conveys very clearly his intended message: "Hell is other people." Although those words are spoken by the character Garcin, no formal argument for that thesis is put forth; yet the message is clearly there and the play (and thus the movie based on it) is very clearly doing philosophy. A film must do more than just illustrate a position or worldview to be philosophy; after all, mysticism and religion can merely state positions. But when films actually argue for a position, whether it be directly or indirectly, they seem to be doing philosophy.

Now, to be fair, pop culture may not be able to explore every nuance philosophers can in print; but (a) that is what projects like this handbook are for and (b) they might be able to explore other nuances in a way that philosophers can't in print. Think of how *Contact* is able to make the viewer experience Dr. Arroway's contact with her deceased "father" (or the alien she believes is taking his form) and thereby make them feel the same emotions she does – all to make the analogy stick in a way that the mere printed word can't. Or think of how a videogame – because of its immersive qualities and choice-making – can provide the player with a phenomenological experience that reading an argument simply cannot.

When Paisley Livingston (2006) entered the debate on this issue, he argued that doing philosophy in film required some very specific conditions. For film to really be considered philosophy, it must make an innovative, independent contribution to philosophy using only means "exclusive to the cinematic medium" – sounds, images, camera angles, visual setting, and the like – no spoken words (at least, not to convey the philosophical message). He called the idea that films could do this the "Bold Thesis." Since it seems that arguments and questions can only be made and raised with words, it seems that the Bold Thesis is false; film doing philosophy, in the way that Livingston says is must, would seem to be an impossible task. But, again, I have objections.

First, even if pop culture isn't making independent, innovative contributions to philosophy and instead is just putting already existing philosophical arguments into another form, so what? Pop culture has brought those arguments to the public's attention, so the arguments are still worth identifying and evaluating. Even if that's all this handbook does, it's still something that needs to be done.

Second, why use the restrictive definition that Livingston demands? Why must film be making *innovative, independent* contributions to philosophy to be doing philosophy? My introduction to philosophy course doesn't do that, yet I and my students are still doing philosophy. If a film makes an argument, then it is doing philosophy, even if someone else made that argument first. Further, why must a film only use elements unique to film to do philosophy? Yes, one might argue that there is no good way to disentangle the language from the cinema-exclusive elements, so there's no way to determine if the philosophy we find in a film gets its philosophical worth from the language the film uses or from its specifically cinematic elements. So, one might argue, the film isn't doing the philosophical work – it's just a delivery vehicle for language to do philosophy. But language is still an essential part of film; so why must language be excluded as a means by which filmmakers can do philosophy? Wouldn't that be like demanding that, if a song is going to rhyme (like poetry rhymes), it has to do with only with musical notes? "It can't use lyrics to rhyme, since notes are unique to songs but words are not!" That's ridiculous. Sure, musical notes can't rhyme, but musical notes are not all that is essential to a song. In the same way, maybe camera angles can't do philosophy – but that is just one element of a film.

Or think of it this way: Are comedians not doing philosophy when they use words to tell a joke with a philosophical point because words are not unique to comedy? Wouldn't this be like saying that philosophers can't make jokes while doing philosophy because jokes are not something unique to philosophy? Comedians aren't the only ones who get to use jokes to make people laugh, so why are philosophers the only ones who get to use language to do philosophy?

What's more, it seems that Livingston's burden can be met. In his defense of the bold thesis in his book *Joss Whedon as Philosopher*, Dean Kowalski (2017) persuasively argues that the *Buffy the Vampire* episode "Hush" coveys a message about the limitations inherent in propositional knowledge while containing not only

Preface: A Brief Defense of Pop Culture as Philosophy

no formal argument but almost no dialogue at all (p. 144-8). Now Livingston might object because the philosophical message of the episode can be put into words (e.g., "there are inherent limitations to propositional knowledge"), and (Livingston would argue) it is only once an argument is put into words that it has any value, or is even an argument to begin with. But notice that I have only been able to put the conclusion of the argument into words, not its premises. If the episode can make a conclusion arise within my mind without using language or any articulable premises, this seems to not only be a prime example of a film doing philosophy well, but doing it in exactly the way that Livingston says it must (to be philosophy). If Livingston would still insist that it "doesn't count" simply because I can understand the episode's non-linguistic argument well enough to put its conclusion into words, he has arbitrarily selected standards that would make film doing philosophy impossible. (This is something Livingston seemed to later acknowledge, in that he eventually admitted that Ingmar Bergman's films do philosophy; see Livingston 2009.)

Other criticisms of the "film as philosophy" thesis are answerable as well. Does the fact that works of popular culture are open to interpretation mean that they can't be doing philosophy? Why would it? The works of continental philosophers (such as Hegel, Schopenhauer, Nietzsche, Sartre, Foucault, and Deleuze) are definitely open to interpretation – as are the works of, say, Kant and Spinoza. But even as frustrating as some (like myself) find their works to be, no one will say that they aren't philosophy. Even if film always does its philosophy implicitly, rather than explicitly, well, so do a lot of philosophers. Does the fact that films are fictional while philosophy is supposed to reveal truth about the world mean that films can't do philosophy? Again, why would it? Philosophical thought experiments are fictional, but philosophers use them all the time – not only to reveal our intuitions but also philosophical truths about the world. Nozick's experience machine thought experiment, for example, is thought to be an effective refutation of hedonism. And wouldn't that mean that famous written philosophical works like *No Exit*, *The Stranger,* or *The Metamorphosis* are not philosophy just because they are works of fiction?

What's more, while the arguments against pop culture being philosophy seem to be aimed at preserving the integrity of philosophy, in reality they seem to undercut it. Consider *Saving Private Ryan*, Steven Spielberg's World War II movie that preceded his creation of the landmark HBO series *Band of Brothers*. After depicting the horrors of the war, including D-Day, and how a band of soldiers sacrificed themselves to save another – Private Ryan (Matt Damon), whose three brothers have all died in the war – Spielberg has Capt. Miller (Tom Hanks) simply give Ryan two dying words: "Earn this." An elderly Ryan then stands above Miller's grave in the present day and asks his wife to assure him that he led a good life. It's an obvious ethical call for Americans to (better) appreciate "the greatest generation," because of the sacrifices it made in its fight against fascism, and to better appreciate the life free of the influences of fascism that they earned us – to appreciate it both intellectually and emotionally and also in how they live. Given the rise of fascism in America and around the world more than 20 years later, the film takes on a new significance. But in 1998, it fundamentally changed my perspective on, and my appreciation of (and my relationship with), my (now) late grandfather, who earned a bronze star serving in the war's European theater. To insist that the ethical argument the movie makes is not actually a case of Spielberg doing philosophy seems to suggest that film can do better what philosophy is supposed to do best: affect people's beliefs and change the way they live.

Let me put it another way; this is an important point. Since the time of the ancients, the stated goal of philosophy has been to lead those who do it to "the good life" and an appreciation of what really matters. And philosophy is supposed to do this like nothing else; it is unique in that respect. But as Julian Baggini (2003) points out, fictional stories can and do accomplish this as well (p. 18). If film can do this without doing or being philosophy, then philosophy not only fails to be unique, it is superfluous: it's not really needed. If, instead, we recognize that when films do this, they are doing philosophy, then the uniqueness and indispensability of philosophy are preserved. Films can only change people's lives in this way because they can do philosophy. Yes, they can change my life in a raw, phenomenological way, by appealing to my emotions. But what makes media like film, games, and graphic novels so beautiful is that they can combine that kind of affective response with an intellectual (philosophical) one, so as to have a more genuine and long-lasting effect.

In the end, those who deny works of popular culture can be philosophy may simply have too rigid and inflexible a view of what philosophy is. Just like there are many ways for something to be a religion, and no one definition of religion captures them all, there are many different ways to do philosophy, many of which popular culture can and does engage in. How a piece of pop culture is philosophy may not always be obvious, but we can discern whether and how it is by taking a closer look at what is being conveyed – which is exactly what this handbook intends to do with nearly 100 pieces of pop culture that, I think, most readers will come to agree, are obviously doing philosophy.

"Let's Go to Work"

My goal here is not to give a detailed review of the debate surrounding the bold thesis or even a full defense of it. Christopher Falzon (n.d.) already has a well-informed overview of the debate on *The Internet Encyclopedia of Philosophy*, and much more knowledgeable philosophers than myself – like Stephen Mulhall (2008) and Dean Kowalski (2017), the latter of whom helped edit numerous chapters in this handbook – have elsewhere done a much better job of defending it. Instead, my goal here is to merely defend the idea that pop culture can be philosophy enough to justify the existence of this handbook. If you remain unconvinced, I highly recommend Mulhall (2008) and chapters six and seven of Kowalski's 2017 book. If you still remain unconvinced, I guess this handbook is not for you. But if you are – or if you didn't need convincing in the first place – you will find this handbook worthwhile. At least I hope so. While it was a labor of love, it took over five years to complete!

Preface: A Brief Defense of Pop Culture as Philosophy

But before we begin, many thanks are in order. I'd like to thank Ruth Lefevre and Rekha Sukumar at Palgrave, the former of which set up this little project, and the latter of which helped with the logistics of pulling it off. I'd like to thank the other editors of the project – Chris Lay, Kimberly S. Engels, and Dean Kowalski – who helped out with the enormous workload, especially in the latter years of the project (after I finally realized that, without help, I couldn't complete it). You are all wonderful philosophers, careful editors, and great persons; the handbook is ten times better thanks to your involvement. I can't express enough my gratitude for your time, wisdom, and efforts. I'd also like to thank numerous colleagues that I roped into giving feedback on certain chapters, as well as many student aides and others who helped with formatting and proofing over the years. I'd also like to thank King's College for granting me a sabbatical to finally complete the project. I couldn't be more thankful to work at such a wonderful institution.

Finally, but most importantly, I'd like to thank every last one of the authors who contributed to this handbook, for their tireless efforts and for their patience in putting up with me as their editor. Much of the work on this handbook was done during the COVID pandemic; COVID even cost it a few chapters, as the pressures the pandemic brought made it impossible for some potential authors to complete their work. Indeed, even though the handbook has nearly 100 chapters, there are countless pieces of pop culture and comedians that I wanted covered but couldn't find an author for. But to those who did contribute, you all have my heartfelt thanks. Your work was fantastic! Although I know it took a long time to finally see the handbook in print, I hope that it was worth the wait.

Notes

1. The original source of this quote is debatable, but it is credibly attributed to Shaw. See https://quoteinvestigator.com/2016/03/17/truth-laugh/.
2. They can even take you on confusing but potentially enlightening philosophical journeys, like the continental philosophers Deleuze or Derrida do in their works. Admittedly, this volume does not deal with continental philosophy to a large degree. Perhaps that topic deserves its own volume.
3. I don't mean to imply that professional philosophers always get things right; only that non-professional philosophers doing philosophy are more likely to make philosophical mistakes, and thus the philosophical works of non-philosophers deserve an expert eye.
4. You can watch the clip here – and you should: https://southpark.cc.com/video-clips/mqwfxt/south-park-it-s-right-there

April 2024

David Kyle Johnson

References

Apatow, Judd, and Michael Bonfiglo. 2022. *George Carlin's American Dream.* HBO.

Arp, Robert. 2006. South Park and philosophy. Wiley-Blackwell.

Baggini, Julian. 2003. Alien ways of thinking: Muhall's on film. *Film-Philosophy* 7 (24).

Basham, Greg, and Eric Bronson. 2003. *The Lord of the rings and philosophy.* Open Court.

Comedy Gold Minds (podcast, hosted by Kevin Hart). 2021. Hasan Minhaj. 18 Feb. https://comedy-gold-minds-with-kevin-hart.simplecast.com/episodes/hasan-minhaj-Lb_YEYiw

Falzon, Christopher. n.d. Philosophy through film. *Internet Encyclopedia of Philosophy.* https://iep.utm.edu/phi-film/

HBO (YouTube). 2022. *George Carlin's American dream: What George meant to me, featurette.* 20 May. https://www.youtube.com/watch?v=T_L3mDG9r4I

Herzogenrath, Bernd. 2017. *Film as philosophy.* Minneapolis/London: University of Minnesota Press.

Irwin, William, ed. 1999. *Seinfeld and philosophy.* Open Court.

———, ed. 2001. *The Simpsons and philosophy.* Open Court.

——— (ed.) 2002. The matrix and philosophy.

Irwin, William, and David Kyle Johnson, eds. 2022. *Introducing philosophy through pop culture: From socrates to star wars and beyond.* 2nd ed Wiley-Blackwell.

Johnson, David Kyle. 2009. *Heroes and philosophy.* Wiley-Blackwell.

———. 2011. *Inception and philosophy.* Wiley-Blackwell.

———. 2019. Black mirror and philosophy.. Wiley-Blackwell.

———. 2021. Contact and the incompatibility of science and religion. In *Film, philosophy and religion*, ed. William Anderson's. Vernon Press.

Khan Academy. 30 July 2020. Hasan Minhaj on finding your gifts, being authentic, & understanding yourself, Homeroom with Sal. YouTube video, 32:26. https://youtu.be/mm0Y3ym-JUg.

Kowalski, Dean. 2017. *Joss Whedon as philosopher.* Lexington Books.

Livingston, Paisley. 2006. Thesis on cinema as philosophy. In *Thinking through Cinema: Film as philosophy*, ed. Murry Smith and Thomas E. Wartenberg, 11–18. Hoboken: Wiley-Blackwell.

———. 2009. *Cinema, philosophy, Bergman: On film as philosophy.* 1st ed. Oxford University Press.

MacDonald, Norm. 2022. Nothing special. *Netflix.*

Miller, M. 2018. In a rare move, South Park admits it was wrong about climate change. *Esquire*, 15 Nov. https://www.esquire.com/entertainment/tv/a25127458/south-park-climate-change-manbearpig-apology-season-22-episode-7/

Mulhall, Stephen. 2008. *On Film.* New York: Routledge.

Read, Ruppert, and Jerry Goodenough. 2005. *Film as Philosophy: Essays on Cinema after Wittgenstien and Cavell.* Palgrave Macmillan.

Russell, Bruce. 2000. The philosophical limits of film. *Film and philosophy* (special edition): pp. 163–167.

Smith, Murry, and Thomas E. Wartenberg, eds. 2006. *Thinking through cinema: Film as philosophy*. Hoboken: Wiley-Blackwell.

Smuts, Aaron. 2009. Film as philosophy: In defense of a bold thesis. *The Journal of Aesthetics and Art Criticism* 67 (4): 409–420.

Tallman, Ruth, and David Kyle Johnson. 2015a. A debate between a theist and a Santa Clausist: Act I (co-authored with Ruth Tallman). *Think* 14 (40): 9–25. https://doi.org/10.1017/s147717561500010x.

Tallman, R., and D.K. Johnson. 2015b. A debate between a theist and a Santa Clausist: Act II (co-authored with Ruth Tallman). *Think* 14 (40): 27–41. https://doi.org/10.1017/s1477175615000111.

Wartenberg, Thomas. 2007. *Thinking on screen: Film as philosophy*. Routledge.

Written Voices. (n.d.) *About William Irwin with George A. Dunn and Rebecca Housel*. http://mail.writtenvoices.com/author_display.php?auth_id=Dunn

Contents

Volume 1

Part I Television and Streaming **1**

1 *The Good Place* as Philosophy: Moral Adventures in the
Afterlife 3
Kimberly S. Engels

2 **Twilight Zone as Philosophy 101** 23
Mimi Marinucci

3 *Star Trek* as Philosophy: Spock as Stoic Sage 41
Massimo Pigliucci

4 *Star Trek: The Next Generation* as Philosophy: Gene
Roddenberry's Argument for Humanism 65
Kevin S. Decker

5 *Battlestar Galactica* as Philosophy: Breaking the Biopolitical
Cycle 93
Jason T. Eberl and Jeffrey P. Bishop

6 *Black Sails* as Philosophy: Pirates and Political Discourse 113
Clint Jones

7 *Doctor Who* as Philosophy: Four-Dimensionalism and Time
Travel 135
Kevin S. Decker

8 *Breaking Bad* as Philosophy: The Moral Aesthetics
of the Anti-hero's Journey 163
David Koepsell

9 *The Handmaid's Tale* as Philosophy: Autonomy and
Reproductive Freedom 185
Rachel Robison-Greene

xxiii

Contents

10 *Mister Rogers' Neighborhood* as Philosophy: Children as Philosophers 211
David Baggett

11 *Futurama* as Philosophy: Wisdom from the Ignorance of a Delivery Boy 233
Courtland D. Lewis

12 *Firefly* as Philosophy: Social Contracts, Political Dissent, and Virtuous Communities 259
Dean A. Kowalski

13 *Arrested Development* as Philosophy: Family First? What We Owe Our Parents 283
Kristopher G. Phillips

14 The Doctor as Philosopher: The Collectivist-Realist Pacifism of the Doctor and the Quest for Social Justice 311
Paula Smithka

15 *Grey's Anatomy* as Philosophy: Ethical Ambiguity in Shades of Grey 341
Kimberly S. Engels and Katie Becker

16 *House of Cards* as Philosophy: Democracy on Trial 361
Brendan Shea

17 *Last Week Tonight* as Philosophy: The Importance of Jokalism ... 383
Christelle Paré

18 *Russian Doll* as Philosophy: Life Is Like a Box of Timelines 407
Richard Greene

19 *The Orville* as Philosophy: The Dangers of Religion 425
Darren M. Slade and David Kyle Johnson

20 *Westworld* as Philosophy: A Commentary on Colonialism 453
Matthew P. Meyer

21 *Black Mirror* as Philosophy: A Dark Reflection of Human Nature 479
Chris Lay

22 *Rick & Morty* as Philosophy: Nihilism in the Multiverse 503
Sergio Genovesi

23 *The X-Files* as Philosophy: Navigating the "Truth Out There" ... 519
Dean A. Kowalski

24 *Game of Thrones* as Philosophy: Cynical Realpolitiks 541
Eric J. Silverman and William Riordan

Contents

xxv

25 *The Mandalorian* as Philosophy: "This Is the Way" 555
Lance Belluomini

26 *Midnight Mass* as Philosophy: The Problems with Religion 581
David Kyle Johnson

27 *Squid Game* as Philosophy: The Myths of Democracy 609
Leander Penaso Marquez and Rola Palalon Ombao

28 *South Park* as Philosophy: Blasphemy, Mockery, and (Absolute?)
Freedom of Speech 633
David Kyle Johnson

29 *Frank Herbert's Dune* as Philosophy: The Need to Think for
Yourself 673
Greg Littmann

30 *The Boys* as Philosophy: Superheroes, Fascism, and the
American Right 703
David Kyle Johnson

Volume 2

Part II Films **751**

31 *Inception* as Philosophy: Choose Your Dreams or Seek Reality ... 753
David Kyle Johnson

32 *Okja* as Philosophy: Why Animals Matter 773
Randall M. Jensen

33 *2001* as Philosophy: A Technological Odyssey 795
Jerold J. Abrams

34 *The Lord of the Rings* as Philosophy: Environmental
Enchantment and Resistance in Peter Jackson and
J.R.R. Tolkien 827
John F. Whitmire Jr and David G. Henderson

35 *Star Wars* as Philosophy: A Genealogy of the Force 855
Jason T. Eberl

36 *The Godfather* as Philosophy: Honor, Power, Family, and Evil ... 873
Raymond Angelo Belliotti

37 *Groundhog Day* as Philosophy: Phil Connors Says "No" to
Eternal Return 897
Kimberly Blessing

38 *The Big Lebowski*: Nihilism, Masculinity, and Abiding Virtue 917
Peter S. Fosl

39 *Harry Potter* as Philosophy: Five Types of Friendship 951
James M. Okapal

40 *Deadpool* as Philosophy: Using Humor to Rebel Against the System 967
Matthew Brake

41 *Blade Runner* as Philosophy: What Does It Mean to Be Human? 983
Timothy Shanahan

42 *Up in the Air* as Philosophy: Buddhism and the Middle Path 1005
Leigh Duffy

43 *Ex Machina* as Philosophy: Mendacia *Ex Machina* (Lies from a Machine) 1025
Jason David Grinnell

44 *Gattaca* as Philosophy: Genoism and Justice 1043
Jason David Grinnell

45 *A.I.: Artificial Intelligence* as Philosophy: Machine Consciousness and Intelligence 1061
David Gamez

46 *The Shawshank Redemption* as Philosophy: Freedom and Panopticism 1091
Alexander E. Hooke

47 *Snowpiercer* as Philosophy: The Danger to Humanity 1109
Leander Penaso Marquez

48 *The Matrix* as Philosophy: Understanding Knowledge, Belief, Choice, and Reality 1131
Edwardo Pérez

49 *A Serious Man* as Philosophy: The Elusiveness of Moral Knowledge 1151
Shai Biderman

50 *The Cabin in the Woods* as Philosophy: Cinematic Reflections on Ethical Complexity, Human Nature, and Worthwhile Horror 1169
Dean A. Kowalski

51 *Magnolia* As Philosophy: Meaning and Coincidence 1193
Bart Engelen

Contents

xxvii

52 *Fight Club* **as Philosophy: I Am Jack's Existential Struggle** 1217
Alberto Oya

53 **Tarantino as Philosopher: Vengeance – Unfettered, Uncensored,
but Not Unjustified** 1235
David Kyle Johnson

54 *The Man from Earth* **as Philosophy: The Desirability of
Immortality** 1271
Kiki Berk

55 *Avatar* **as Philosophy: The Metaphysics of Switching Bodies** 1289
Joshua L. Tepley

56 *Pulp Fiction* **as Philosophy: Bad Faith, Authenticity, and the
Path of the Righteous Man** 1311
Bradley Richards

57 *Tenet* **as Philosophy: Fatalism Isn't an Excuse to Do Nothing** 1327
Lance Belluomini

58 **Tom Sawyer as Philosopher: Lying and Deception on the
Mississippi** 1349
Don Fallis

59 *Don't Look Up* **as Philosophy: Comets, Climate Change, and
Why the Snacks Are Not Free** 1373
Chris Lay and David Kyle Johnson

60 *Little Women* **as Philosophy: Death or Marriage and the
Meaning of Life** 1411
Kimberly Blessing

61 *God's Not Dead* **as Philosophy: Trying to Prove God Exists** 1435
David Kyle Johnson

Volume 3

Part III Comedians **1467**

62 **Hannah Gadsby as Philosopher: Is Comedy Really Such a
Good Thing?** 1469
Mark Ralkowski

63 **Amy Schumer as Philosopher: Fuck the Feminine Mystique** 1491
Charlene Elsby

64 **George Carlin as Philosopher: It's All Bullshit. Is It Bad
for Ya?** 1511
Kimberly S. Engels

65 Louis CK as Philosopher: The King and His Fall 1533
Jennifer Marra Henrigillis

**66 Marc Maron as Philosopher: Comedy, Therapy, and
Identification** 1563
Steven S. Kapica

**67 Hari Kondabolu as Philosopher: Enacting a Philosophy of
Liberation** 1583
Brandyn Heppard

**68 Richard Pryor as Philosopher: Stand-Up Comedy and Gramsci's
Organic Intellectual** 1603
Cori Hall Healy

69 Larry David as Philosopher: Interrogating Convention 1619
Noël Carroll

**70 Jerry Seinfeld as Philosopher: The Assimilated Sage of
New Chelm** 1631
Stephen Stern and Steven Gimbel

71 Dave Chappelle as Philosopher: Standing Up to Racism 1643
Steven A. Benko and Reagan Scout Burch

72 Ricky Gervais as Philosopher: The Comedy of Alienation 1669
Catherine Villanueva Gardner

**73 Hasan Minhaj as Philosopher: Navigating the Struggles of
Identity** 1685
Pankaj Singh

74 Stephen Fry as Philosopher: The Manic Socrates 1701
Christopher M. Innes

**75 Phoebe Waller-Bridge as Philosopher: Conscious Women
Making Choices** 1719
Neha Pande and Kimberly S. Engels

Part IV Video Games **1739**

**76 *The Last of Us* as Moral Philosophy: Teleological Particularism
and Why Joel Is Not a Villain** 1741
Charles Joshua Horn

**77 *Journey* as Philosophy: Meaning, Connection, and the
Sublime** 1757
Russ Hamer

78 *The Witness* as Philosophy: How Knowledge Is Constructed 1771
Luke Cuddy

Contents   xxix

79   *Cyberpunk 2077* **as Philosophy: Balancing the (Mystical) Ghost in the (Transhuman) Machine** 1789
Chris Lay

80   *Detroit Become Human* **as Philosophy: Moral Reasoning Through Gameplay** 1811
Kimberly S. Engels and Sarah Evans

81   *Papers, Please* **as Philosophy: Playing with the Relations between Politics and Morality** 1833
Juliele Maria Sievers

82   *Planescape: Torment* **as Philosophy: Regret Can Change the Nature of a Man** 1847
Steven Gubka

83   *Disco Elysium* **as Philosophy: Solipsism, Existentialism, and Simulacra** 1865
Diana Khamis

84   *The Legend of Zelda: Breath of the Wild* **as Philosophy: Teaching the Player to Be Comfortable Being Alone** 1883
Chris Lay

85   *Persona 5 Royal* **as Philosophy: Unmasking (Persona)l Identity and Reality** 1907
Alexander Atrio L. Lopez and Leander Penaso Marquez

86   *God of War* **as Philosophy: Prophecy, Fate, and Freedom** 1929
Charles Joshua Horn

Part V   Graphic Novels **1947**

87   **Frank Miller's Batman as Philosophy: "The World Only Makes Sense When You Force It To"** 1949
Steve Bein

88   *Watchmen* **as Philosophy: Illustrating Time and Free Will** 1969
Nathaniel Goldberg and Chris Gavaler

89   **The Joker as Philosopher: Killing Jokes** 1987
Matthew Brake

90   *From Hell* **as Philosophy: Ripping Through Structural Violence** 2003
James Rocha and Mona Rocha

91   *Deadpool's* **Killogy as Philosophy: The Metaphysics of a Homicidal Journey Through Possible Worlds** 2025
Tuomas W. Manninen

**92 *V for Vendetta* as Philosophy: Victory Through the Virtues of
     Anarchy** 2043
Clara Nisley

93 Asterios Polyp as Philosophy: Master of Two Worlds 2065
Bradley Richards

94 *Yes, Roya* and Philosophy: The Art of Submission 2085
Nathaniel Goldberg, Chris Gavaler, and Maria Chavez

**95 *The Walking Dead* as Philosophy: Rick Grimes and Community
     Building in an Apocalypse** 2103
Clint Jones

Index 2119

About the Editor-in-Chief

David Kyle Johnson is Professor of Philosophy at King's College (PA) who earned his Ph.D. at the University of Oklahoma and specializes in metaphysics, philosophy of religion, and scientific/critical reasoning. He also produces lecture series for Wondrium's *The Great Courses* (such as *Sci-Phi: Science Fiction as Philosophy*, *The Big Questions of Philosophy*, and *Exploring Metaphysics*) and has published in journals such as *Sophia*, *Religious Studies*, *Think*, *Philo*, *Religions*, *SHERM (Socio-Historical Examination of Religion and Ministry)*, and *Science, Religion, and Culture*. In addition to other duties, he regularly contributes chapters to and edits volumes for Blackwell's Philosophy and Pop Culture series (such as *Black Mirror and Philosophy: Dark Reflections*), and also co-edited *Introducing Philosophy Through Popular Culture* with the series editor William Irwin. He maintains two blogs for *Psychology Today: Plato on Pop* and *A Logical Take*.

About the Editors

Dean A. Kowalski is Professor of Philosophy and Chair of the Arts and Humanities Department in the College of General Studies at the University of Wisconsin-Milwaukee. He earned his Ph.D. in Philosophy from the University of Wisconsin-Madison. He specializes in the Philosophy of Religion and Metaphysics and has published articles in such academic journals as *Religious Studies* and *Philosophy and Theology*. He regularly teaches philosophy of religion, Asian philosophy, and ethics.

Prof. Dean has written extensively on philosophy and popular culture – both philosophy in popular culture and popular culture as philosophy – specializing in film and television. He has published articles in *The Journal of Whedon Studies* and *Film and Philosophy*, and more than 30 book chapters in volumes dedicated to popular culture. He is the author of *Joss Whedon as Philosopher* (2017), *Classic Questions and Contemporary Film*, 2nd edition (2016), and *Moral Theory at the Movies* (2012). He is the editor of *Indiana Jones and Philosophy* (2023), *The Big Bang Theory and Philosophy* (2012), *The Philosophy of The X-Files*, revised edition (2009), and *Steven Spielberg and Philosophy* (2008), and he is the co-editor of *The Philosophy of Joss Whedon* (2011).

Chris Lay earned his Ph.D. from the University of Georgia in 2018 and has held teaching positions at UGA, the University of Texas at El Paso, and Young Harris College in northeast Georgia. Currently, he runs the YHC philosophy program as Assistant Professor of Philosophy, offering courses like Science Fiction and Philosophy, Video Games as Philosophy, and Feminism in Horror Films. Professor Lay specializes in metaphysics – especially issues of personal identity and mereology – and the philosophy of popular culture generally, and he has published numerous "pop culture" volumes that bring the two subjects together.

Kimberly S. Engels is Associate Professor of Philosophy at Molloy University. She received her Ph.D. in Philosophy from Marquette University in 2017. Her research interests include existentialism, Native American philosophy, philosophy and pop culture, and UAP studies. She is the editor of *The Good Place and Philosophy: Everything Is Forking Fine!* and co-editor of *Westworld and Philosophy: If You Go Looking for the Truth, Get the Whole Thing*.

Contributors

Jerold J. Abrams Creighton University, Omaha, NE, USA

David Baggett School of Christian Thought, Houston Baptist University, Houston, TX, USA

Katie Becker Greensboro, NC, USA

Steve Bein Philosophy Department, University of Dayton, Dayton, OH, USA

Raymond Angelo Belliotti The State University of New York, Emeritus, Fredonia, NY, USA

Lance Belluomini San Francisco Bay Area, CA, USA

Steven A. Benko Meredith College, Raleigh, NC, USA

Kiki Berk Southern New Hampshire University, Manchester, NH, USA

Shai Biderman Beit-Berl College, Kfar Saba, Israel
Tel Aviv University, Tel Aviv, Israel

Jeffrey P. Bishop Center for Health Care Ethics and Department of Philosophy, Saint Louis University, St Louis, MO, USA

Kimberly Blessing Philosophy, SUNY Buffalo State, Buffalo, NY, USA

Matthew Brake Northern Virginia Community College, Manassas, VA, USA

Reagan Scout Burch Meredith College, Raleigh, NC, USA

Noël Carroll Philosophy Program, The Graduate Center, City University of New York, New York, NY, USA

Maria Chavez Charlottesville, VA, USA

Luke Cuddy Southwestern College, Chula Vista, CA, USA

Kevin S. Decker Eastern Washington University, Cheney, WA, USA

Leigh Duffy SUNY Buffalo State College, Buffalo, NY, USA

Jason T. Eberl Center for Health Care Ethics, Saint Louis University, St Louis, MO, USA

Charlene Elsby University of Ottawa, Ottawa, ON, Canada

Bart Engelen Tilburg Center for Moral Philosophy, Epistemology and Philosophy of Science (TiLPS), Tilburg University, Tilburg, The Netherlands

Kimberly S. Engels Molloy University, Rockville Centre, NY, USA

Sarah Evans Molloy University, Rockville, NY, USA

Don Fallis Philosophy, Northeastern University, Boston, MA, USA

Peter S. Fosl Transylvania University, Lexington, KY, USA

David Gamez Department of Computer Science, Middlesex University, London, UK

Catherine Villanueva Gardner University of Massachusetts Dartmouth, North Dartmouth, MA, USA

Chris Gavaler W&L University, Lexington, VA, USA

Sergio Genovesi University of Bonn, Bonn, Germany

Steven Gimbel Gettysburg College, Gettysburg, PA, USA

Nathaniel Goldberg W&L University, Lexington, VA, USA

Richard Greene Weber State University, Ogden, UT, USA

Jason David Grinnell Philosophy Department, SUNY Buffalo State, Buffalo, NY, USA

Steven Gubka Florida Atlantic University, Boca Raton, Florida, United States

Cori Hall Healy Bowling Green State University, Bowling Green, OH, USA

Russ Hamer Mount St. Mary's University, Emmitsburg, MD, USA

David G. Henderson Western Carolina University, Cullowhee, NC, USA

Brandyn Heppard Raritan Valley Community College, Somerville, NJ, USA

Alexander E. Hooke Stevenson University, Stevenson, MD, USA

Charles Joshua Horn University of Wisconsin-Stevens Point, Stevens Point, WI, USA

Christopher M. Innes Philosophy Department, Boise State University, ID, Boise, USA

Randall M. Jensen Northwestern College, Orange City, IA, USA

David Kyle Johnson Department of Philosophy, King's College, Wilkes-Barre, PA, USA

Clint Jones Plover, WI, USA
Capital University, Columbus, OH, USA

Steven S. Kapica Keuka College, Keuka Park, NY, USA

Diana Khamis Nijmegen, Netherlands

David Koepsell Department of Philosophy, Texas A&M, College Station, TX, USA

Dean A. Kowalski Arts and Humanities Department, University of Wisconsin-Milwaukee, College of General Studies, Waukesha, WI, USA

Chris Lay Young Harris College, Young Harris, GA, USA

Courtland D. Lewis Philosophy, Pellissippi State Community College, Knoxville, TN, USA

Greg Littmann Southern Illinois University Edwardsville, Edwardsville, IL, USA

Alexander Atrio L. Lopez University of the Philippines Diliman, Quezon City, Philippines

Tuomas W. Manninen Arizona State University, Glendale, AZ, USA

Mimi Marinucci Eastern Washington University, Cheney, WA, USA

Leander Penaso Marquez College of Social Sciences and Philosophy, University of the Philippines Diliman, Quezon City, Philippines

Jennifer Marra Henrigillis St. Norbert College, De Pere, WI, USA

Matthew P. Meyer University of Wisconsin–Eau Claire, Eau Claire, WI, USA

Clara Nisley Atlanta, GA, USA

James M. Okapal Missouri Western State University, Saint Joseph, MO, USA

Rola Palalon Ombao College of Social Sciences and Philosophy, University of the Philippines Diliman, Quezon City, Philippines

Alberto Oya IFILNOVA – Instituto de Filosofia da Nova (Universidade Nova de Lisboa), Lisboa, Portugal

Neha Pande Royal Roads University, Victoria, BC, Canada

Christelle Paré Department of Communication, University of Ottawa, Ottawa, ON, Canada
École nationale de l'humour, Montréal, Québec, Canada

Edwardo Pérez Tarrant County College, Fort Worth, TX, USA
The University of Texas at Arlington, Arlington, TX, USA

Kristopher G. Phillips Southern Utah University, Cedar City, UT, USA
Eastern Michigan University, Ypsilanti, MI, USA

Massimo Pigliucci Department of Philosophy, The City College of New York, New York, NY, USA

Mark Ralkowski George Washington University, Washington, DC, USA

Bradley Richards Department of Philosophy, York University, Toronto, ON, Canada

William Riordan Christopher Newport University, Newport News, VA, USA

Rachel Robison-Greene Utah State University, Logan, UT, USA

James Rocha California State University, Fresno, CA, USA

Mona Rocha Clovis Community College, Clovis, CA, USA

Timothy Shanahan Department of Philosophy, Loyola Marymount University, Los Angeles, CA, USA

Brendan Shea Rochester Community and Technical College, Rochester, MN, USA

Juliele Maria Sievers Federal University of Alagoas, Maceió, Brazil

Eric J. Silverman Christopher Newport University, Newport News, VA, USA

Pankaj Singh School for Life (SFL), University of Petroleum and Energy Studies, Dehradun, India

Darren M. Slade Global Center for Religious Research (GCRR), Denver, CO, USA

Paula Smithka University of Southern Mississippi, Hattiesburg, MS, USA

Stephen Stern Gettysburg College, Gettysburg, PA, USA

Joshua L. Tepley Saint Anselm College, Manchester, NH, USA

John F. Whitmire Jr Western Carolina University, Cullowhee, NC, USA

Part I

Television and Streaming

The Good Place as Philosophy: Moral Adventures in the Afterlife

1

Kimberly S. Engels

Contents

Introduction 4
Summary and Plot 4
The Link Between Ethics and the Afterlife: Human Morality and Human Mortality 7
What Would a Just Afterlife Reward System Look Like? 13
Is an Eternal Afterlife Desirable? 17
Conclusion 21
References 21

Abstract

The Good Place was a historical landmark in the field of pop culture as philosophy, as it was the first mainstream sitcom to explicitly tackle the works of philosophers in its content. In addition to exposing its viewers to the works of famous philosophers, *The Good Place* makes its own philosophical arguments. The show is ultimately about the concept of the afterlife – what it might look like, how it would operate, and if it is even desirable. The show also explores the relationship between morality and the afterlife. Essentially, *The Good Place* explores three focal questions: (1) Are there reasons to be morally good, irrespective of how that plays out in an afterlife? (2) What would a fair system for gaining admission to a merit-based afterlife look like? And (3) is an eternal afterlife even desirable? Ultimately the show argues that yes, virtue is worthwhile for virtue's own sake, irrespective of the consequences in an afterlife. Second, it argues that a fair merit-based system would allow people the chance to improve and get better, given the right circumstances. Third, it argues that an eternal afterlife, in which you maintain your identity and live forever, is not desirable.

K. S. Engels (✉)
Molloy University, Rockville Centre, NY, USA
e-mail: kengels@molloy.edu

© Springer Nature Switzerland AG 2024
D. K. Johnson et al. (eds.), *The Palgrave Handbook of Popular Culture as Philosophy*,
https://doi.org/10.1007/978-3-031-24685-2_1

Keywords

The Good Place · Virtue theory · Aristotle · Kant · Rawls · Afterlife · Justice · Immortality · Hinduism · *Moksha*

Introduction

The Good Place tells the story of Eleanor Shellstrop, a woman who has died, as she navigates the afterlife with three fellow humans. There are many plot twists throughout the series, like Eleanor realizing she isn't actually in the Good Place, rather a deceptive Bad Place designed to make her and her friends torture each other. Throughout four seasons, the show tells a highly entertaining story about morality and the afterlife, explicitly utilizing the works of various famous philosophers in its episodes. While many shows have utilized philosophical concepts and themes that made philosophical arguments, *The Good Place* stands out as a work that integrated the direct discussion of philosophical questions and theories into its plot.

At the 2018 North American Sartre Society conference, show creator Michael Schur said, "The goal is to try to ask the question of what it meant to be a good person. That was the one line source of the show" (Engels 2021, p. xvii). This question about what it means to be a good person is explored through various scenarios related to the afterlife. This forces viewers to ponder what, exactly, the link is between morality and the afterlife. For example, is the only reason we should care about morality is that we are worried about our immortal souls? Or are there other reasons to be moral? Or, is it fair for our afterlife to be connected to how good we were during our time on earth? How could we make such a connection as fair as possible? And last, is an eternal afterlife desirable? Would it actually be rewarding to live forever?

The show makes an argument in response to each of these questions. I will show that, first, it argues that there are, indeed, reasons to be moral that aren't tied to an afterlife. When a plot twist keeps the protagonists from being able to earn points to go to the Good Place, the characters decide it is still worth it to pursue virtue, "for virtue's sake." Second, the final two seasons take up the theme of the fairness of the afterlife's point system, which is based primarily on the consequences of one's actions, and devise a new system that would give people a chance to improve and become good enough for the Good Place. *The Good Place* argues that a fair system cannot be solely dependent on luck, and must offer the possibility of rehabilitation and improvement. Last, when the characters finally make it to the real Good Place, they realize that they wouldn't want to live forever, at least not in their conscious human form.

Summary and Plot

Eleanor Shellstrop has died. She is told by the Good Place's archangel host Michael that she is one of the select few to make it to the Good Place. As Michael praises her life and good deeds as an ACLU lawyer who worked to get innocent people freed

1 The Good Place as Philosophy: Moral Adventures in the Afterlife

from Death Row, it becomes clear that there's been a mix up. These aren't Eleanor's memories, and she doesn't actually belong in the Good Place, which is reserved for the world's most praiseworthy human beings.

Eleanor keeps quiet about the mistake and is introduced to her "soulmate" Chidi Anagonye. Chidi lived his life on Earth as an extremely indecisive philosophy professor who taught ethics and moral philosophy. Eleanor confides in him that she does not actually belong in the Good Place, sending Chidi into a moral conundrum about whether or not to give her up. He decides not to and instead agrees to teach her ethics so she can become a better person and become truly worthy of the Good Place. If she is able to improve and become Good Place material, Chidi won't have to feel guilty about harboring her. Plus, he gets to put his philosophical training to work.

Eleanor meets her neighbors, Tahani, an extremely attractive though slightly narcissistic philanthropist, and Tahani's soulmate Jianyu, a Buddhist monk who has taken a vow of silence. Eventually it is revealed that there's been another mistake and Jianyu is really an obnoxious Florida DJ and Blake Bortles fan named Jason Mendoza. Jason, like Eleanor, isn't quite up to Good Place standards. So, he too joins in on Chidi's ethics lessons. Other vital characters include the Good Place neighborhood designer and host, Michael, and his A.I. helper Janet, who has access to all the knowledge in the universe. Janet is available whenever Good Place residents call on her to provide them with any needed information.

The end of Season One serves up an epic twist, when Eleanor realizes, after a series of debacles that lead to the characters driving each other crazy, that they are not in the Good Place at all, and rather are occupying the Bad Place. Michael, to the audience's surprise, confirms that Eleanor is correct, and that this is actually the Bad Place. It is revealed that Michael is not an angelic guide of the Good Place but a demon who helped create a new torture system, "The Good Place" in which humans would torture each other without demonic intervention (a move straight from Sartre's *No Exit*). The end of Season One has Michael wiping the four humans' memories clean, to start over from scratch, hoping that through a reboot he can get his new torture system to work.

Season Two begins with Michael trying over and over again to get the humans to torture each other, but each time he is unsuccessful because Eleanor is always able to figure out the secret. After over 800 tries, Michael is forced to admit that he has to try something new. He confesses to the humans that if his "Good Place" neighborhood fails, he will be tortured for eternity. Thus, the gang suggest a plan: Michael could take Chidi's ethics lessons so he too can improve enough to make him worthy of getting into the real Good Place. Michael's improvement is slow; for instance, during an ethics lesson on the Trolley Problem, Michael simulates various Trolley Problem scenarios as an alleged learning aid, although he really just intends to torture Chidi. In one of the show's most comedic and philosophical moments, Michael makes the Trolley Problem real, putting himself and Chidi on a real train, and forcing Chidi to make split second decisions about who should be saved. Chidi, whose entire character is defined by indecisiveness, ends up failing the task repeatedly, resulting in gruesome simulated deaths ("The Trolley Problem"). Despite these early challenges, eventually Michael grows fond of his human friends and also begins to show a genuine desire to change his evil ways. Michael eventually helps the humans escape through multiple levels of the Bad Place to be able to face the "judge," the ultimate decision-maker regarding Good Place and Bad Place affairs. Although the judge determines that none of the humans (except Eleanor) have actually improved enough to make it into the Good Place, the judge makes a deal: The humans can be sent to Earth to try again to earn enough points to make it into the Good Place. This sets up the plot for Season Three.

Season Three sees our characters returning to Earth, where Michael plots to get them connected with each other again so they can grow and improve together. Eventually he hatches a plan by getting Chidi to conduct a research project on near-death experiences, and gives Eleanor, Tahani, and Jason clues that lead them to apply. Eventually the four humans meet up again in the real world. But a twist happens: Eventually Michael and his plans are exposed – he and Janet are observed through a portal to the Bad Place, and the gang realizes who he is and that he is trying to guide them to earn enough points for the Good Place. Now that they know, their motivations for their actions will be tainted, and they can never earn enough points to get into the Good Place. This leads Eleanor to eventually approach Chidi and suggest that maybe it is still worth it to try to be good. Maybe virtue is worth pursuing for virtue's sake alone, without any anticipated reward.

Season Three also sees Michael beginning to learn something about the point system that is used to determine whether humans make it into the Good Place or not. It seems the system is unfair, because no human has made it into the Good Place for 521 years. At first Michael believes the Bad Place demons have been tampering with the points system, but eventually he realizes the real problem is the unforeseen consequences of one's actions. Life on Earth has gotten so complicated that even the small act of purchasing a tomato has a long chain of unexpected negative effects. Michael sees an urgent need to talk to the judge and the Good Place committee to remedy the problem. Eventually the judge and the committee see eye to eye with Michael and agree that the system is unfair, but only after the judge takes her own trip to Earth and sees the extent of the problem. When she returns, she admits "Earth stinks, y'all. It's hot, and it's crowded but somehow also cold and lonely. I thought it was going to be so easy to make good decisions. The first thing I did was I Googled 'big, juicy natural tomatoes,' which led me to a porn site that was for people with a sunburn fetish or... I kind of never recovered" ("Chidi Sees the Time-Knife"). Michael begs the judge to consider that humans really can get better when given the right circumstances. The judge agrees, and proposes an experiment with four people who are roughly the "same general level of badness" as Eleanor, Chidi, Tahani, and Jason, putting them in a similar "Good Place" neighborhood and seeing if, under the right conditions, they too can improve ("Chidi Sees the Time-Knife"). This sets up the plot for Season Four.

Season Four sees the introduction of the new neighborhood, with the introduction of four new characters who are being secretly helped by Michael and the humans to get better. Eventually the judge agrees the experiment is a success and that it is possible for humans to improve. Another plot twist is introduced when the judge decides that the solution is to cancel Earth and start over because the system is unfair. But there is still time for Chidi to step in and to devise a new system – a fair one, which would take into consideration the fact that humans can improve when given the right circumstances. After Chidi convinces the judge of the fairness of his new system, the humans are finally allowed to go to the real Good Place. They get there to discover that the Good Place residents are actually extremely unhappy, as life in the Good Place becomes unbearably boring and mundane after several thousand years. A life of goodness without contrast eventually leads to simply being tired of life. The gang must unite one more time to solve the problem and devise a new system that allows residents of the real Good Place to leave and simply be at peace when they are ready to.

As we see in this summary, a key theme throughout the entire series is the link between morality and the afterlife, and the questions this chapter seeks to answer are introduced: Are reasons to be good linked to a potential afterlife? What is an actually fair system of judgment for deciding what kind of afterlife you experience? Last, is an eternal afterlife rewarding?

The Link Between Ethics and the Afterlife: Human Morality and Human Mortality

One question or theme taken up by *The Good Place* throughout all of its seasons is the relationship of being good or moral to some type of reward in the afterlife. The question is basically this: Should we be good for the sake of a future punishment or reward? Or are there reasons to be moral that aren't linked to some future consequence for us? Many people in modern society assume there is a link between being good and reward/punishment. This is reinforced in our legal system, which punishes us for crimes society has agreed are immoral, as well as in most dominant religious systems. Christianity and Islam link the underlying reasons for morality to God's will, and Eastern religions Buddhism and Hinduism believe our choices in this life have karmic repercussions that affect our reincarnation in future lives.

In philosophical discussion, the idea that morality is dependent on some cosmic order is usually expressed in a moral system called divine command theory. This approach to morality says it is God's will alone that determines what is moral or immoral. Thus, if we want to know right or wrong, we must simply look to religious texts to see what God says. There are multiple practical problems with this assertion: First, there are multiple religious texts from which to choose. Even if we settle on the Bible, there is little concrete moral advice, and there often are conflicting passages, leaving almost everything up for interpretation. But assume we could confidently decipher what God wills. There are still philosophical complications. The Euthyphro Dilemma is a famous dilemma posed in Plato's dialogue *Euthyphro.* Either God commands things *because* they're moral, or things are moral *because* God commands them. If we accept the former, it seems that God is commanding a standard that even He (in the Christian tradition) cannot change. This would mean morality is independent of God's will, and that He is unable to change it, meaning he is not omnipotent. If we accept the latter proposition, it seems God's commands are then arbitrary, based on nothing, and He could just have easily willed something different than He did. For example, most religious people believe that God has commanded us not to commit murder. But if God's commands are arbitrary, then God could just as easily have commanded the opposite, for us to murder each other. This seems to diminish God's greatness. If God can simply command *anything* and it's good, we seem to have no reason for praising God as an omnibenevolent being (Plato 2007, 10a–16a; Rachels 2011, pp. 51–54). These difficulties have led most moral philosophers to separate morality from some kind of divine will. Instead, they look for reasons to be moral that aren't linked to religious belief, or any kind of afterlife system.

Immanuel Kant, for example, argued that we should not be moral because we are afraid of going to hell but because we are rational human beings, and fully exercising our rationality entails being moral. Kant argued that all morality is based on one's intentions, irrespective of the consequences of the actions that occur. Kant says the only true moral motive is to act *from* a sense of moral duty, out of respect for the moral law. He argues that the moral law is discoverable from the use of reason alone, so that we may know the moral thing to do before we act. Two formulas, or categorical imperatives that he introduces are: (1) act only according to a maxim that you can will to be a universal law and (2) treat every person as an end in themselves, never as a means only (Kant 1997, pp. 31 & 38). The first maxim means that we should never act in ways that make exceptions for ourselves. For example, keeping our promises and commitments to others is usually seen as the moral thing to do. This is because, according to Kant, we should ask if we can will the maxim "Everyone should break promises." We can't do that, because then the very notion of making a promise would make no sense. No one would trust anyone who was making a promise. Thus, you cannot make an exception for yourself by making false promises. The second formulation involves treating every person as a rational being deserving of respect, not as an object that you can use for your own gain. Making a false promise to someone is giving them false information, manipulating them into doing what you want rather than treating them as a decision-maker who deserves full information.

Most important for this discussion, though, is that Kant's conception of morality is independent of any type of afterlife system. The moral law is independent of a creator God's will, and the reasons we should be moral are independent of this self-interested end. In fact, for Kant, if you are acting morally because you don't want to go to hell instead of *out of moral duty*, this is not truly a right motivation and cannot be considered a moral act. Kant identifies two different kinds of motivations, those that are heteronomous and those that are autonomous. Heteronomous motivations are those in which we are bound to obey the rule or law due to something outside of ourselves: punishment or reward, God, being socially ostracized or socially adored. Autonomous motivations come from inside of us – we choose to *bind ourselves* to these laws because we think this is how humans ought to act, and thus choose to act this way ourselves. He writes,

1 *The Good Place* as Philosophy: Moral Adventures in the Afterlife

> Thus the principle of every human will as *a will giving universal law through all its maxims* provided it is otherwise correct, would be very well suited to be the categorical imperative by this: that just because of the idea of giving universal law *it is based on no interest* and therefore, among all possible imperatives, can alone be *unconditional*; or still better, by converting the proposition, if there is a categorical imperative (i.e., a law for every will of a rational being) it can only command that everything be done from the maxim of one's will as a will that could at the same time have as its object itself as giving universal law; for only then is the practical principle, and the imperative that the will obeys, unconditional, since it can have no interest as its basis. (Kant 1997, p. 40 emphasis in original text)

Kant argues that truly moral acts must have autonomous motivations, that is to say, we must do them because we think this is the consistent way humans should act. Proper use of our reason shows that we should not make exceptions for ourselves, and that we should respect the rationality and decision-making of others. The essence of all human beings is to be rational, and we should desire a rational community in which all people are respected as decision-makers. For Kant, acting morally because we are concerned about our soul's eternal salvation would be a heteronomous motivation, and thus any behavior done for this reason cannot be considered moral.

Aristotle, too, thought morality was independent of a human afterlife. Aristotle's ethics is known as virtue ethics and shifts the moral focus from thinking about the morality of acts to instead thinking about one's moral character. Instead of asking the question "what makes an action morally right?" Aristotle asks, "what does it mean to live a good human life?" or "What does it mean to flourish as a human being?" Aristotle's view is rooted in his teleological worldview, that is to say, his view that everything in the natural world has a *telos. Telos* can be considered the goal, purpose, or end of every natural thing. A flower that fulfills its telos takes in water, grows petals, offers pollen for bees, reproduces, and looks beautiful. A squirrel that fulfills its *telos* grows strong, can climb trees well, collect acorns, and reproduce and take care of its young (Aristotle 1999, p. 3). Like flowers and squirrels, humans too have a *telos*. The human telos is to make use of our reason. But Aristotle identified a type of reason called *practical reason*, which he characterized as activity of the soul in accordance with virtue.

In other words, a vital part of our human flourishing, or telos, is to develop virtues, or desirable character traits, throughout our lives. Examples of such traits include honesty, loyalty, courage, friendliness, patience, generosity, and wit. Developing these character traits is a matter of finding the golden mean between two extremes. This means that hitting the virtue is the middle point between excess and deficiency. For example, an excess of courage becomes foolhardiness. If, in an attempt to be courageous, I jump in the water to try to save someone even though I cannot swim myself, we would both drown and Aristotle would consider this foolishness. But if I was too cowardly to try to do anything at all to help and just sat watching the person drown, that would be a deficit of courage (Aristotle 1999, pp. 20–33).

For Aristotle, we should develop virtuous traits "for virtue's sake." A virtuous actor chooses virtuous action intentionally, and for its own sake. Virtues are intrinsically valuable, then, and not valuable for the sake of something else. Aristotle writes,

> [I]f the acts that are in accordance with virtues have themselves a certain character it does not follow that they are one justly or temperately. The agent also must be in a certain condition when he does them: in the first place he must have knowledge, secondly he must choose the acts, and choose them for their own sakes, and thirdly his actions must proceed from a firm and unchangeable character. (Aristotle 1999, p. 25)

Aristotle's point is that a person may perform actions that can be described as just or temperate, however if a person is doing them unknowingly or only because they seek some reward, they cannot be considered moral acts. Virtues should be chosen for their own sake. The virtuous person is able, with minimal effort, to know the right reason for their action, has the desire to do so because based on the right reason, and possesses a consistent internal character from which virtuous actions flow naturally. In other words, a virtuous person is able to consistently act in ways that are temperate, honest, loyal, and just without much effort, because through practice they have developed a self that is naturally inclined to act virtuously. The virtuous agent rarely has to deliberate long between options, because they intuitively know the right thing to do.

We see here two models of thinking about morality that divorce the concept from a creator God or from a divine system of getting what one deserves. For Kant and Aristotle, actions must be done because they are moral, not because the acting agent has a self-interested goal of going to Heaven or the Good Place. The fundamental premise of *The Good Place* links morality to the afterlife – the whole show is about four individuals who weren't good enough on Earth to make it into Heaven. But in Season Three, the show takes a different turn and directly explores the question of whether virtuous actions are worth pursuing for the sake of themselves, independent of any specific reward we may receive from completing them. In "Jeremy Bearimy" Chidi, Eleanor, Jason, and Tahani stumble upon Michael's plan to give them little pushes to help them meet up and improve each other. Michael and Janet are forced to give up their identities when the gang see them through a Bad Place portal and must tell them about their (now forgotten) experiences in the Bad Place. It is then revealed that since the characters know about the afterlife system, all of their actions now have the wrong motivation (getting to the Good Place), and thus they cannot earn any points for them. (Paradoxically, although there *is* an afterlife and you *do* go there based on your actions, the actions are only judged as moral if you have a motive other than self-interest.)

Chidi So, to sum it up, we've been to hell, and now, no matter how good we are, for the rest of our lives, we're going back to hell?

Michael Again, it's not the classic Christian hell, but...that's the gist, yes. As soon as you learned about the afterlife, your motivation to be good was corrupted. So you can't earn points anymore. So sorry for eternally dooming you. ("Jeremy Bearimy")

1 *The Good Place* as Philosophy: Moral Adventures in the Afterlife

This realization throws Chidi into a complete nihilistic funk. His students find him making chili with M&M's and marshmallow peeps in it, clearly going through a mental struggle. When they ask him to please teach them something, he briefly describes the three major ethical systems in Western philosophy and then states:

> But here's the thing, my little chili babies: all three of those theories are hot, stinky, cat dookie. The true meaning of life, the actual ethical system that you should all follow is nihilism. The world is empty. There is no point to anything and you're just gonna die. So, do whatever! And now, I'm gonna eat my marshmallow candy chili in silence and you all can jump up your own butts. ("Jeremy Bearimy")

Chidi seems convinced that, without the promise of an afterlife, there is no reason for him to be good anymore. This seems counterintuitive for an ethics professor who was an expert in both Kantianism and virtue ethics, but it shows that at his core, Chidi thought being good would pay off for him. It is Eleanor who comes to the rescue, when she convinces the gang that even though they can never go to the Good Place, maybe there is still a reason to be good after all – just for the sake of being good.

> That stupid little voice in my head told me to do something good today and it was so annoying, but it also made a dork and his very untalented daughter super happy. Me trying, just a little bit, put some good out into the world. The six of us are not getting in to the Good Place. But there are still people in this world that we care about. So I say we try and help them be good people. Try and help them get in. I mean, why not try? It's better than not trying, right? ("Jeremy Bearimy")

She suggests that there are still reasons to be good – they could help other people become moral and increase others' chances of getting into the Good Place. To this end, she suggests they team up and become the "Soul Squad," dedicated to saving souls. Tahani, for one, comes around, and, after doing some charitable work with Jason, says,

> Well, I was thinking about why I was sent to hell, as one is wont to do when one has recently been told that one had been sent to hell. And it occurred to me, I have always been held captive by my desire for attention. Now that I know how it all ends, I just want to be virtuous for virtue's sake. ("Jeremy Bearimy")

Tahani expresses that now that she knows her fate and is no longer concerned with trying to control it, her reasons for doing good things have changed. She admits to being narcissistic and having the wrong motivations for her charity work in the past. Now that she knows this was a path that led her, literally, straight to hell, she realizes morality might be about more than that.

Another episode that directly explores the link between morality and the afterlife is found in Season Two, titled "Existential Crisis." Michael is failing Chidi's ethics lessons, and Chidi is struggling to understand why. He decides this must be because Michael has always been immortal, and thus has never had to feel the weight of the consequences of his actions. Here, Chidi links the concept of life having an end to what makes actions matter. Chidi prompts Michael to get into the human mindset and asks him if he could die and no longer exist. Michael says he cannot die, but he can "retire." "It's an extreme form of punishment. We call it 'The Eternal Shriek.' My soul will be disintegrated, and each molecule will be placed on the surface of a different burning sun" ("Existential Crisis"). Michael continues that his essence will be scooped out of his body and poured over hot diamonds, and whatever is left of him will be beaten for eternity with a titanium rod. When Chidi suggests he ponder the full gravity of this possibility, the exercise forces him into an existential crisis, contemplating the random and absurd nature of the universe. "You mean there would be...no...me?" he asks, before slumping over in existential dread.

It is Eleanor who is able to snap Michael out of it, telling him that he is simply having a very human experience. She says, "All humans are aware of death. So we're all just a little bit sad. All the time. That's just the deal." After Michael accepts that it is okay to feel a little bit sad about his own mortality, he has entered what the show considers the proper mindset for learning ethics and understanding why our actions matter. If life does not go on forever, we have a deeper obligation to make the best of the time we do have. The existentialist thinker Simone de Beauvoir argued that the fact that there is no divine judge who will reconcile everything is what makes humans completely responsible for what we do, writing:

> Existentialism alone gives – like religions – a real role to evil, and it is this, perhaps, which make its judgments so gloomy. Men do not like to feel themselves in danger. Yet, it is because there are real dangers, real failures and real earthly damnation that words like victory, wisdom, or joy have meaning. Nothing is decided in advance, and it is because man has something to lose and because he can lose that he can also win. (De Beauvoir 1980, p. 34)

Here Beauvoir is arguing that the absence of a divine creator and cosmic system of justice means there are real stakes, real risks, and failures. Simultaneously, it is because of the very real possibility of failing, of doing bad in the world, that ethics becomes so important, and that we have the real opportunity to succeed in our moral strivings. (Here again, there is a bit of a paradox afoot, as Chidi suggests that our actions only have meaning in a temporary construct with death as a conclusive end, while at the same time it has been revealed that all the characters are, in fact, immortal and learning ethics in the afterlife.)

Thus, *The Good Place* makes a two-sided argument about the link between morality and the afterlife. While its fundamental premise is that there is an afterlife that judges us for what we do, particular episodes and plot lines suggest that this afterlife system should not be the motivating factor behind our actions. The statement by Chidi in "Existential Crisis" that human mortality matters for human morality suggests that it is the temporal nature of our lives that gives our actions true consequences. Further, the fact that it is revealed that according to the points system your actions only have moral worth if they have the right motivation reflects a Kantian sentiment that actions done out of self-interest are not truly moral acts. So, the existence of the Good Place and Bad Place still cannot be the grounding reasons

1 *The Good Place* as Philosophy: Moral Adventures in the Afterlife

for morality. Last, the decisions of the gang in Season Three when they decide to be good even though they know they can never make it to the Good Place suggests an Aristotelian account of virtue, where human flourishing in the present life matters, independent of what happens when you die. Ironically, a show about the afterlife argues that morality is not actually about the afterlife.

What Would a Just Afterlife Reward System Look Like?

Another question posed throughout the series is what an actually just or fair judgment system would look like? Except for Mindy St. Claire, the sole human being to be sent to the Medium Place, the Good Place system presents only two polar options: either you go to paradise, or you are tortured forever. From the very beginning of the series, Eleanor finds this unfair. In the pilot, when Chidi tells her she needs to face the fact that she doesn't belong in the Good Place, she responds,

> Well, then this system sucks. What, one in a million gets to live in paradise and everyone else is tortured for eternity? Come on. I mean, I wasn't freaking Gandhi, but I was okay. I was a medium person. I should get to spend eternity in a medium place! Like Cincinnati. Everyone who wasn't perfect but wasn't terrible should get to spend eternity in Cincinnati. ("Everything is Fine!")

Indeed, a system where you either have to be the cream of the crop or get tortured forever doesn't seem very fair at face value.

A second problem is that the ability to earn points seems to be influenced considerably by *luck* – for example, one's upbringing, one's financial means, and one's general ability to have influence on others. Having a good upbringing would definitely influence one's ability to earn points, at least earlier in life. Additionally, the consequences-focused nature of the points system means that those who have the financial means to influence society (like Tahani) have a greater advantage, as long as their motivations were in the right place. While luck dominates most of our social landscape – for instance, the socioeconomic class you belong to is almost entirely dependent on luck – most people would agree that the question of where you spend eternity really should be independent of luck. Advantages gained by life's lotteries shouldn't determine your eternal fate.

The third problem is that it is revealed in Season Three that no human has made it into the Good Place for over 521 years ("Janet[s]"). This is because the Good Place's points system considers the effects of actions into its calculations – including the unintended consequences. Modern life has gotten so complicated that you cannot predict the full scope of the consequences of your actions. Thus, humans are left in a bind where even engaging in modern life in any way makes them ineligible for the Good Place. Even the extremely virtuous Doug Forcett, who has dedicated his life to earning enough points, is falling considerably short of the threshold, having earned only half the points required ("Don't Let the Good Life Pass You By").

> Life now is so complicated, it's impossible for anyone to be good enough... These days, just buying a tomato at the grocery store means you are unwittingly supporting toxic pesticides, exploited labor, contributing to global warming. Humans think they're making one choice, but they're actually making dozens of choices they don't even know they're making. ("Chidi Sees the Time Knife")

Clearly a system in which *no one* is able to earn enough points to get into the Good Place due to circumstances outside their control cannot be considered just.

To explore what a just afterlife might look like, we have to introduce competing accounts of justice. The Good Place system focuses on a form of justice known as retributive justice – giving one what one deserves, even if no further good comes from that punishment. In other words, being tortured forever in the Bad Place because of their behavior on Earth does no further good to the individuals being punished, nor to the people they may have harmed during their lifetimes. The objective is to give them what they deserve, not to produce any further good from the situation. But almost all accounts of retributive justice argue that the punishment one deserves should be proportionate with the moral offense. Being tortured for eternity seems a disproportionate retribution for the moral crimes of the protagonists on Earth. Eleanor's main moral failing was that she was selfish, Tahani was narcissistic, Chidi was indecisive, and Jason was chaotic. An eternity of torture seems to be a disproportionate response to the main character's levels of badness.

Additionally, the fact that how many points individuals earn for their actions is entirely out of their control also reflects a lack of justice. While we can certainly be held morally responsible for outcomes we did not intend, the fact that the full scope of completely unknown consequences is impossible to calculate makes it impossible for actors to be aware of the morality of their actions. Additionally, as shown by Doug Forcett, there seems to be no way that a human can exist in the modern world without earning negative points. A system which is set up so that *no one* has the ability to be good enough cannot be considered just, under a purely retributive framework.

There also seem to be concerns of *procedural justice*, in other words, the procedures used for determining how different benefits and burdens will be distributed. The Good Place point system bases quite a bit of the point system on *luck* since no one can know the full outcomes of their actions. As mentioned, given that so much of what gives an individual opportunities to earn points (such as having access to money that would allow them to produce actions with positive outcomes) is out of their control, the procedures for determining who goes to the Good Place and who goes to the Bad Place do not appear to be just. John Rawls, a theorist of justice, argued that society should be designed behind a Veil of Ignorance, meaning that the designers would make decisions about how society would operate without having any knowledge of what their place in society would be. Rawls calls this the "original position." Rawls argues that no one inherently "deserves" to be born into a rich or poor family, to have more or less abilities than others, to be a certain race, or to be male or female. Thus, it isn't right for individuals to have less access to societal goods based on undeserved characteristics. Behind the Veil of Ignorance, the architects would choose policies that would not disadvantage certain members of society based on life's lotteries. Rawls writes:

> For example, if a man knew that he was wealthy, he might find it rational to advance the principle that various taxes for welfare measures be counted unjust; if he knew that he was poor, he would most likely propose the contrary principle. To represent the desired restrictions one imagines a situation in which everyone is deprived of this sort of information. One excludes the knowledge of those contingencies which sets men at odds and allows them to be guided by their prejudices. (Rawls 1999, p. 17)

For example, not knowing if they would be born with a learning disability or not, the architects would want to ensure that the education system was designed to include the needs of children with a variety of learning styles. Additionally, not knowing what their sex or gender would be, the architects would choose policies that ensured individuals of all sexes and genders were fairly compensated for their labor. Rawls argues that policies resulting in inequalities are only acceptable if they make those least well off in society better off than they otherwise would be.

Applied to the Good Place afterlife system, we can ask the question: If the designers of the points system were put behind a Veil of Ignorance, would they choose to have the system operate the way it does? It seems the answer to this question is no. One's economic status, social upbringing, and opportunities for producing good consequences are dependent almost entirely upon luck. Architects would not know who their parents would be, how they would raise them, and how that would affect their moral motivations and the points they could earn. They would not know what monetary means they would have and whether that would allow them to do charitable work. And, given the complications of modern life, a system in which no one could accurately calculate the effects of their actions would not be appealing no matter what your status in life. The points system, thus, fails the test of the Veil of Ignorance.

The characters recognize this lack of justice, leading Michael and the gang in the third season to plead with the judge to give the humans another chance. Jason makes perhaps the best plea, explaining a past issue he had with a member of his dance crew:

> I used to yell at Big Noodle 'cause he always showed up late to rehearsal. Then one day, the swamp under my house flooded. I needed a place to crash, so I slept at Big Noodle's house. Turns out that he had to juggle three jobs to take care of four grandparents who all lived in the same bed just like in Willy Wonka. I never yelled at Big Noodle for being late after that 'cause I knew how hard it was for him to be there. And he definitely didn't have time to research what tomatoes to buy. Even if he wanted to, possession of a non- fried vegetable is a felony in Jacksonville. The point is, you can't judge humans 'cause you don't know what we go through. ("Chidi Sees the Time-Knife")

The gang point out to the judge that even if one does have the time to Google where their vegetables come from, the unintended consequences of actions are often impossible to calculate. And, as Eleanor points out, contemporary life seems set up to encourage us to be bad, making a reference to Chic Fil-A. "There are booby traps everywhere. Like, there's this chicken sandwich that if you eat it, it means you hate gay people. And it's delicious" ("Chidi Sees the Time-Knife"). Not only does modern life make it impossible for the point system to work, Michael says it's clear that humans can get better given the right conditions for doing so. After consulting with the Bad Place demon Shawn, the judge agrees to let Michael set up another experimental neighborhood, with individuals who are about the same level of badness to see if the humans help each other improve. This will determine whether Michael's original experiment was a fluke or whether humans truly can get better given the right conditions.

After the experiment in Season Four is a success, the judge decides the only solution is to cancel Earth and start over. To avoid this, Chidi, having had all 800 of his afterlives downloaded at once, designs a new system: In the new system, the points total on Earth will serve as a baseline to "determine how hard or easy your test is." Each person is then given individually tailored tests. After each one, each person will be evaluated and then rebooted for a new scenario, keeping a vague memory of what they learned from the previous times, through the "little voice in their head." Individuals can take the test as many times as they need to until they pass – and gain entry to the Good Place ("You've Changed Man"). This new system is focused on what may be called rehabilitative justice. In a rehabilitative justice framework, the focus is not primarily on giving someone what they deserve but on giving the offender the possibility and tools to improve themselves and get better. Rehabilitative justice is sometimes thought of as *utilitarian justice*, meaning that the rehabilitation of offenders leads to more happiness and better outcomes for society as a whole.

Chidi's new system seems fair or just for several reasons. First, each person is treated equally. Every person must pass their test, and everyone gets the same unlimited chances to do so. Second, there is an element of retributive justice still at play: Everyone must go through the test as many times as necessary for them to improve, meaning that each is getting what they deserve if they choose not to change and get better. Third, the system is rehabilitative, and gives every person the opportunity to improve.

However, the possibility of unforeseen circumstances and consequences outside of their control still influences their path to getting into the Good Place, as the point total on Earth determines the baseline for how hard their designed test will be. Thus, individuals working to pass their afterlife tests would not all have the same "baseline." Examining the new system behind the Veil of Ignorance, there may still be concerns of procedural justice, then, as some people will have much easier tests that allow them admission into the Good Place based solely on luck. The important question to pose would be if this particular system results in the least well off being better off than they would otherwise be. There doesn't immediately seem to be a better option that wouldn't result in a complete restructuring of Earth in which issues of luck simply don't exist. This would, in essence, amount to what the judge wanted to do: cancel Earth. Given that the protagonists believe Earth is worth saving as it is, it seems Chidi's proposed system would still pass the test of the Veil of Ignorance. Acknowledging that it is better for everyone that Earth continues to exist without getting canceled and restarted, the architects would choose the system that resulted in the maximum amount of fairness, leaving as little to luck as possible. While there are still inequalities in the new system, these inequalities result in the least well off (those unlucky in life and forever doomed to the Bad Place) being better off than they otherwise would be. The alternatives are a system that is even more unfair (like the previous points system), or Earth being destroyed, making everyone worse off.

The Good Place thus makes an argument that an afterlife system that does not consider the particular needs and circumstances of individuals cannot be considered fair. Moreover, the focus on the chance of improvement shows that a just system must allow every person the same opportunity to change and improve. Thus, an afterlife system must include some kind of utilitarian end, aimed at increasing welfare for each individual person. While retribution or what each person deserves is reflected in the system in which each person must continue as many times as it takes, the system is not based on retribution alone, but aimed at giving individuals the possibility to improve. While it's not entirely free of unfairness, perhaps that's the best an afterlife system based on an unjust human society can look like. Since we are considering the afterlife judgment system under the Veil of Ignorance and not all of human society, it passes the test of the Veil of Ignorance, since rational, self-interested people would agree it results in the fairest distribution of burdens and benefits.

Is an Eternal Afterlife Desirable?

The third major question explored by *The Good Place* also appears in Season Four: Is an eternal afterlife is really desirable? Most people desire some kind of afterlife because they are afraid to lose their sense of self, to be separated from their loved ones, for their personality to be gone, and to simply no longer exist. While it is intuitively comforting to think of an afterlife where we could be reunited with loved ones and live in paradise, deeper reflection on this idea reveals such a situation may not be as desirable as we may originally think.

A vital part of life seems to be challenge, change, growth, and temporality. The things we do each day matter because we have limited time to do them. We seem to derive meaning from the things we cherish, accomplish, and enjoy because, as humans, we know they are temporary. Thus, we are thankful for the time we get to spend with family, thankful for a meaningful project we are passionate about, and thankful for time we get to relax, because we know these things will end one day. A two-week vacation in a beach paradise only feels like paradise because it is a temporary break from our everyday lives. If we lived at the beach paradise all the time, it would lose its meaning. We can return to Chidi's comment in "Existential Crisis" that actions only matter when you can think about life having an ending. If we only have limited time, the time we do have becomes more important, and thus, the actions we take within it matter more. The obligation to do good in the world, to improve it, and to improve yourself all seem tied-up in space-time. When everything lasts forever, nothing is of vital importance.

There seem to be two reasons, then, that an eternal afterlife is undesirable: First, in the Good Place, everything is good, so there is no pain or suffering. Again, at first glance this seems like an awesome deal, but we also realize that we have lost any sense of *contrast*. When everything is good, eventually nothing is. Good and joyful experiences require less enjoyable ones in order for us to understand the contrast. Second, there is an objection raised by the philosopher Bernard Williams: the lack of any determined ending seems to be, simply, boring (Williams 1973, p. 88). Even if we could spend 1000 years finding things to enjoy and explore, eventually it seems we would simply run out of things to enjoy. Williams explores the possibility that perhaps the afterlife could strip you of the possibility of experiencing boredom. In other words, souls in the afterlife lose the conscious ability to be bored. But he ultimately argues this really amounts to a form of being psychologically altered – and no one truly wants to experience this. Williams introduces two conditions he says must be met in order for an afterlife to be desirable: (1) the afterlife scenario has to be the kind of life I would actually want to live and (2) the person living the life has to actually be me. Even if stripping someone of their ability to be bored could lead to this scenario being one we would actually like to experience, it simultaneously would strip us of core parts of our identity that make us who we are (Williams 1973, pp. 90–91, see also Johnson 2021).

Both of these critiques are leveled against the afterlife system proposed in *The Good Place*, in which essentially carbon copies of our souls (we have the same personalities, memories, continuity of identity, etc.,) live on for eternity. However, this is not the only conception of an afterlife that one may have. Reincarnation, or being reborn into a different life, is another possibility for an afterlife. This avoids both critiques, as future lives would still have contrast and be meaningful, and forgetting each life when you start the next one means that you would never get bored of living. This would not, however, meet Williams' identity condition, because you would not retain your sense of self after you die. However, it would mean that this isn't the end of conscious experience, either.

There is an alternative conception about the afterlife in which you do not retain your individual personality from Earth, but rather return to a state of unified consciousness or oneness. In Hinduism, for example, everything that exists is part of the one divine thing, known as *Brahman*. Each person's soul is an individuated expression of *Brahman*, known as *atman*. The individual soul, or atman, goes through a cycle of birth life, death, decay, and rebirth, experiencing good or bad *karma* in each subsequent life as a result of their behavior on Earth during each incarnation. Eventually, the atman can be released from the cycle if it realizes that no material pursuits will every truly satisfy a person and will always lead to being reborn. Through meditation, yoga, and other spiritual practices, individuals can remember themselves as manifestations of the divine. The final goal of life is *moksha*, which is the release from the endless cycle of rebirth. To achieve *moksha*, the person must realize the unity of all existence and see themselves in all other souls. In reaching *moksha*, the individual self, or atman, realizes it is one with the higher, cosmic self, or Brahman. This results in a release from the reincarnation cycle and a unification with God or the source of all life. For

1 *The Good Place* as Philosophy: Moral Adventures in the Afterlife

Hinduism, every single person is an individuation of *Brahman*, and we ultimately all know this, we just have to remember it. The goal of Hinduism is not to find or worship God so one can go to Heaven but rather to realize the inner divinity found inside oneself.

> A Brahmana (a knower of Brahman) enjoys a life of peace and tranquility while still on earth and, upon his departure from this world, obtains *moksha* and his soul (*atman*) completely merges into the Supreme Soul like a lump of salt in the ocean, never to be separated again. (Ma'Sumian 1995, p. 8)

As we have only ever experienced the universe from the perspective of our human form, we cannot conceive what it would be like to realize ourselves as Brahman (Ma'Sumian 1995, pp. 1–8, see also McGowan 2021).

When the gang finally make it to the Good Place, they find the residents there in exactly the conundrum described above. Chidi finally fulfills his dream of meeting a famous philosopher when he meets Hypatia of Alexandria, who tells him to call her Patty. When Patty learns that Chidi, too, is a philosopher, she begs him for help.

Hypatia	Wait, wait, wait, wait. Are you... What's it called, um, a think-book-man? No, um... a think-read-book-man.
Chidi	A philosopher, yes.
Hypatia	Sorry! It's been so long, my brain is foggy. Listen carefully before I forget how to say this. You gotta help us, we are so screwed. ("Patty")

Patty explains that experiencing all good all the time has taken all meaning out of living, and, as she says, turned her into a "mush person." Lacking the contrast and ups and downs of life, nothing is interesting, nothing is challenging, and nothing is exciting.

> This is how I spend most of my time. Sitting in beautiful places, drinking my milkshake, slowly peeing into my pants, which instantly evaporates and leaves no trace. . .On paper, this is paradise. All your desires and needs are met, but it's infinite, and when perfection goes on forever, you become this glassy-eyed mush person. ("Patty")

The Good Place has grown meaningless and boring after the residents have been there so long. The souls there no longer experience any sense of enjoyment, having lost all contrast in life and lived on far too long. Eleanor refers to the Good Place residents as having become "happiness zombies." To solve the dilemma, Michael and Eleanor again return to the point made in "Existential Crisis": It seems to be the fact that our lives are temporary and eventually end that not only makes ethics important, but ultimately what makes life meaningful.

Michael	You said that every human is a little bit sad all the time, because you know you're gonna die. But that knowledge is what gives life meaning.
Eleanor	The way to restore meaning to the people in the Good Place is to let them leave. ("Patty")

An eternal paradise eventually turns into no paradise. In order to make the Good Place an actual, meaningful place where the residents want to be, there has to be an ending point, something that makes their time there ultimately a temporary experience.

So, once more, the protagonists help revise the afterlife system. They agree on this: After spending as much time there as they wish, experiencing everything they want to experience, souls can make a request to leave the Good Place and be at peace.

Chidi	We're gonna set up a new kind of door. Um, somewhere peaceful, so that when you feel happy and satisfied and complete, and you want to leave the Good Place for good, you can just walk through it, and your time in the universe will end.
Tahani	You don't have to go through it if you don't want to, but you can. And hopefully, knowing that you don't have to be here forever will help you feel happier while you are.
Paltibaal	What will happen when we go through it?
Janet	Well, we don't really know, exactly. All we know is, it will be peaceful, and your journey will be over. ("Patty")

The finale of *The Good Place* shows the characters finally living meaningful, joyful lives in the Good Place, growing powerful bonds between them. Eleanor and Chidi, who began their relationship in the afterlife, finally get to have happy time together as real soulmates. AI Janet and Jason similarly bond and grow their friendship, building on the connection they too developed in the original Good Place neighborhood. But gradually, each character begins to feel an existential tiredness, and a feeling that they have experienced everything they wish to experience in their current form. Each eventually makes the decision to cross the barrier and be "at peace," leaving their current form as a human soul. These scenes between the characters are quite powerful and sad, as there is an element of grief to the end of an incarnation – the end of an individual perspective and experience and the relationships that had been built with others. But that sadness is accompanied by a deep sense of inner peace and love, knowing that the life was beautiful, and sometimes things need to end in order to stay beautiful.

In a final scene with Eleanor, Chidi assures her that while he will no longer live on as "Chidi," he is returning to the oneness of the universe and will not be completely gone. In comforting Eleanor, he says,

Picture a wave in the ocean. You can see it, measure it – its height, the way the sunlight refracts as it passes through – and it's there, you can see it, and you know what it is, it's a wave. And then it crashes on the shore and it's gone. But the water is still there. The wave was just... a different way for the water to be for a little while. ("Whenever You're Ready")

Chidi likens this sentiment to Buddhist thought, but it has distinctly Hindu origins. We can recall the distinction between *atman*, the individual self, and *Brahman*, the cosmic or God-self, the One or the All. The introduction of the new door leads to the possibility of a return to Oneness or a state of being that has been inside us all along.

While it wouldn't be accurate to say the option to leave the Good Place is equivalent to *moksha* in Hinduism (we simply don't have enough information about what happens after the residents exit the door to make that case), there is a sense that leaving the Good Place is an end to an individual soul's journey but that it could also be the beginning of something new and perhaps greater than an individual incarnation. Additionally, the humans are able to spend time in the afterlife improving themselves until they feel at peace with the decision to leave. While this isn't the same as the Hindu cycle of birth and rebirth, there is a similarity in that the individuals eventually cultivate a feeling of deep inner peace within themselves in order to be released from their individual journey.

Thus, *The Good Place* argues that an eternity as our current selves is not actually a desirable afterlife. We would ultimately become insufferably bored, life having lost all contrast and meaning. The introduction of the possibility of leaving the Good Place so one's individual soul can return to oneness and be at peace has more in common with Asian religious traditions, such as Hinduism.

Conclusion

The Good Place is a groundbreaking work of pop culture that explicitly made use of the arguments of famous philosophers throughout the series. As Pamela Hieronymi and Todd May say, it successfully "makes philosophy cool" (Hieronymi and May 2021, p. xxvii). By exploring the question of what it means to be a good person alongside the possibility of an afterlife, it offers viewers an intricate exploration of fundamental ethical and metaphysical questions. Throughout the story it tells, it makes an argument that the afterlife is not ultimately what morality should be about but rather that we should do good actions for the sake of themselves. It also argues that a just afterlife system would not punish people for circumstances outside of their control, would give all people equal opportunity to enter the Good Place, and would give souls the chance to grow and improve. Last, it argues that an afterlife in which we retain our identity as individual souls forever is not desirable.

References

Aristotle. 1999. *Nicomachean Ethics, 2nd edition*. Trans. Terrence Irwin. Indianapolis: Hackett.
De Beauvoir, Simone. 1980. *The Ethics of Ambiguity*. Trans. Bernard Frechtman. Secaucus: Citadel Press.
Engels, Kimberly, ed. 2021. *The Good Place and Philosophy: Everything is Forking Fine!* Hoboken: John Wiley and Sons.
Hieronymi, Pamela, and Todd May. 2021. Introduction. In *The Good Place and Philosophy: Everything is Forking Fine!* ed. Kimberly S. Engels, xxii–xxvii. Hoboken: John Wiley and Sons.
Johnson, David. 2021. Why it wouldn't be rational to believe you're in the good place (and why you wouldn't want to be anyway). In *The Good Place and Philosophy: Everything is Forking Fine!* ed. Kimberly S. Engels, 270–282. Hoboken: John Wiley and Sons.

Kant, Immanuel. 1997. *Grounding for the Metaphysics of Morals*. Trans., and ed. Mary Gregor. Cambridge: Cambridge University Press.

Ma'Sumian, Farnaz. 1995. *Life after Death: A Study of the Afterlife in World Religions*. Los Angeles: Kalimat Press.

McGowan, Michael. 2021. Conceptions of the Afterlife: *The Good Place* and Religious Tradition. In *The Good Place and Philosophy: Everything is Forking Fine!* ed. Kimberly S. Engels, 189–201. Hoboken: John Wiley and Sons.

Plato. 2007. *Euthyphro*. Trans. Cathal Woods and Ryan Pack. San Francisco: Creative Commons.

Rachels, James. 2011. *The Elements of Moral Philosophy*. Boston: McGraw Hill.

Rawls, John. 1999. *A Theory of Justice*. Cambridge, MA: Belknap Press of Harvard University.

Williams, Bernard. 1973. The Makropulos case: Reflections on the tedium of immortality. In *Problems of the self*. Cambridge: Cambridge University Press.

Twilight Zone as Philosophy 101

2

Mimi Marinucci

Contents

Introduction	24
A Land of Both Shadow and Substance, of Things and Ideas	24
A Dimension Not Only of Sight and Sound, but of Mind	26
A Dimension as Vast as Space and as Timeless as Infinity	28
Curiosity	29
Depth	29
Abstraction	30
Controversy	31
Your Next Stop Is *The Twilight Zone*	33
What (and How) Can We Know?	33
Who (or What) Are We?	34
What Should We Do (and Why)?	36
References	38

Abstract

This is a threefold introduction: an introduction to philosophy, to *The Twilight Zone*, and to the rest of the handbook. This chapter begins with a discussion of the advantages of using examples, salient features, and an immersive approach when introducing new subject matter. This is then followed, first, by an examination of some of the salient features of philosophy, particularly those features that are also features of *The Twilight Zone*, and then, second, by a detailed discussion of the philosophical content of specific episodes of *The Twilight Zone*, particularly those topics that are also addressed in other chapters of this book. This immerses the reader in the process of doing exactly what philosophers often do, which is engaging with philosophical texts, and with the purpose of this handbook: to treat works of popular culture as philosophy.

M. Marinucci (✉)
Eastern Washington University, Cheney, WA, USA
e-mail: mmarinucci@ewu.edu

© Springer Nature Switzerland AG 2024
D. K. Johnson et al. (eds.), *The Palgrave Handbook of Popular Culture as Philosophy*,
https://doi.org/10.1007/978-3-031-24685-2_14

Keywords

Introductory philosophy · *The Twilight Zone* · Rod Serling · Meaning of philosophy · Socrates · The unexamined life · Plato · Necessary and sufficient conditions · Definition · Bertrand Russell · Value of philosophy · Questioning · Saliency · Wittgenstein · Family resemblance · MacIntyre · Practice · Epistemology · Ethics · Metaphysics · Descartes · Robots · Artificial intelligence · Egoism · Altruism

Introduction

The Twilight Zone was an anthology television series, featuring a different cast and a different story each episode. The one constant was the producer of the show, Rod Serling, who also served as the narrator for each episode. The series aired on CBS for five seasons from 1959 to 1964. In 1983, *The Twilight Zone* was made into a feature film by Steven Spielberg and John Landis. In 1985, another version of the television series was created, again for CBS. It ran for 2 years, followed by a third season in syndication. Yet another version of the show began airing on UPN in 2002 and lasted only one season. Most recently, Jordan Peele, along with Simon Kinberg and Marco Ramirez, created a version for CBS All Access. This incarnation, introduced in 2019, was renewed for a second season before getting canceled in 2020. In each of these versions, *The Twilight Zone* presents far-fetched or thought-provoking stories, usually in the science fiction genre, but occasionally incorporating features of horror or fantasy. Much of the following discussion would be generalizable to other versions of *The Twilight Zone*, but this chapter is focused exclusively on the original series.

The purpose of this chapter is threefold insofar as it aims to serve, not only as an introduction to the classic television series, *The Twilight Zone*, but also as an introduction both to the study of philosophy and to the rest of this handbook. An introduction is an opportunity to convey a rudimentary understanding of whatever it is that is being introduced, while simultaneously making something unfamiliar seem more familiar. As such, this introduction attempts to provide some idea of what *The Twilight Zone* is all about, as well as what philosophy and this handbook are all about.

A Land of Both Shadow and Substance, of Things and Ideas

There are various ways to explain the nature of ideas and concepts. One way is to supply a definition that articulates the criteria for including or excluding things from the category in question. In philosophy, such criteria are sometimes referred to as necessary and sufficient conditions. A condition is necessary if something cannot be included in the category without satisfying that condition; the criterion is required for category membership. A condition is sufficient if anything that satisfies that condition is included in the category; the criterion is enough for category membership. Note that a condition might be necessary but not sufficient and a condition might be sufficient but not necessary. For example, being four-sided is a necessary (but not sufficient) condition of squares; being a square is a sufficient (but not necessary) condition of rectangles. This method of definition is often used to introduce formal terminology. Within geometry, the term triangle refers unambiguously to closed figures with exactly three sides and internal angles that equal a sum total of 180°. If something is a triangle, then it will match this description, and if something matches this description, then it is a triangle; if something is not a triangle, then it will not match this description, and if something does not match this description, then it is not a triangle. This description establishes criteria for determining, in all cases and without exception, what is properly categorized as a triangle and what is not.

Outside of geometry and other formal systems, necessary and sufficient conditions are often difficult or impossible to articulate. Consider, for instance, the concept of linguistic fluency. There does seem to be a real difference between knowing and not knowing a language, but that boundary is not sharp, and sometimes the question of fluency depends on context. Someone who is fluent in specialized settings, perhaps within a professional environment such as medicine, may lack fluency in social situations. Someone might be fluent but illiterate, and someone might have written fluency but lack verbal abilities. While geometric concepts (like square, rectangle, and triangle) are readily reduced to defining criteria, other concepts (like fluency and literacy) are not. Category boundaries are often blurry, and there can be much discussion, debate, and disagreement about what does and does not belong.

For better or worse, philosophy invites discussion, debate, and disagreement about pretty much everything, including how to define philosophy. Although different courses and textbooks often have some content in common, there is remarkable variety of interpretation among philosophy instructors and textbook authors. Similarly, there is no shortage of conference sessions, and even entire conferences, devoted to providing opportunities for professional philosophers to disagree among themselves about the answer to some version of the question, "What is philosophy?"

This unresolved quality, which is at least part of what makes philosophy so difficult to define, has been identified, rather ironically, as a defining feature of philosophy. Socrates, who is often regarded as a founder of the western philosophical tradition, apparently believed that "The unexamined life is not worth living" (Plato in West 1979). This is consistent with the incessant questioning for which Socrates was well known, and which ultimately led to a death sentence for (among other things) unapologetically challenging (and, by example, leading others to challenge) the gods recognized by the ancient city of Athens. More recently, Bertrand Russell has suggested that philosophy is unlike other disciplines in that it is focused more on asking questions than on answering them with any degree of finality. According to Russell, various academic disciplines, all of which are rooted in philosophy, make the transition from philosophy to science when there is consensus around a collection of facts accepted by all, or at least most, practitioners of the emerging discipline. In contrast, "The value of philosophy is, in fact, to be sought largely in its very uncertainty" (Russell 1912, p. 141).

In suggesting that philosophy consists of questions without answers, Russell does not seem to be posing this as a definition in the sense of necessary and sufficient conditions. After all, not all instances of questioning are regarded as examples of philosophical inquiry. Someone may wonder about the nutritional content of a fast-food menu item without thereby engaging in what would normally be considered philosophy. Similarly, not all fields of study that go unresolved are regarded as philosophical fields of study. Medical research may never reach its apparent goal of preventing or treating all human ills, but it is not thereby considered philosophy. Additionally, some of what happens in philosophy, particularly in academic settings, includes learning accepted details about various philosophical concepts and schools of thought, sometimes with very little opportunity to question the material that is presented. Because questions, including unanswered questions, can exist outside of philosophy, questioning is not a sufficient condition for philosophy. Because factual content can exist inside of philosophy, uncertainty is not a necessary condition for philosophy. Nevertheless, the speculative aspect of philosophy that Russell identifies does seem to capture something central to what philosophy is all about. To put it another way, this speculative quality is a salient feature of philosophy, even if, strictly speaking, it does not define it.

A Dimension Not Only of Sight and Sound, but of Mind

According to Ludwig Wittgenstein, salient features often contribute to something like a family resemblance among the various members of a given category. The notion of a family resemblance provides an alternative to the idea of categories that are neatly defined by necessary and sufficient conditions (Wittgenstein 1968, §§ 66–81). People who are biologically related often resemble one another, and there are often specific features that are common among individuals who resemble one another, but there is rarely a single characteristic or set of characteristics that applies to all family members while simultaneously differentiating them from people to whom they are unrelated. For Wittgenstein, it is this sort of similarity, or family resemblance, rather than necessary and sufficient conditions, that unites different members of the same category. Wittgenstein uses the concept of games to demonstrate this idea:

> Consider for example the proceedings that we call "games." I mean board-games, card-games, ball-games, Olympic games, and so on. What is common to them all? – Don't say: "There must be something in common, or they would not be called "games"" – but look and see whether there is anything common to all. – For if you look at them you will see nothing that is common to all, but similarities, relationships, and a whole series of them at that. (Wittgenstein 1968, §§ 66)

There are salient features common to many games, such as competition among or between players, amusement, rules, athleticism, intellectual ability, luck, and so forth, but there is no single property common to all games (Wittgenstein 1968, §§ 66–68). An understanding of the general concept of games can be gained or advanced, however, by becoming familiar with the commonalities among specific examples of games. Competition may not be a necessary or sufficient condition for something to be considered a game, but it is nevertheless a salient feature of many games and therefore worthy of attention by those seeking to understand gaming. Similarly, although asking questions without answering them is neither necessary nor sufficient for something to be considered an example of philosophy, it is a salient feature of philosophy and therefore worthy of attention by those seeking to understand philosophy.

Getting to know something by way of salient features is one alternative to rigid definitions. Another closely related alternative is to become familiar with as many examples of that thing as possible. To understand, say, a particular musical genre, a playlist would be at least as helpful as any list of words or string of sentences anyone might offer instead. These two methods of introducing new things are closely related: While familiarity with the salient features of a certain kind of thing can help one identify specific examples of it, familiarity with specific examples of a certain kind of thing can in turn help to identify its salient features. Yet another way to get to know something, particularly something that constitutes what Alasdair MacIntyre refers to as a practice, is to become immersed in it. MacIntyre explains the concept of a practice as follows:

> By a practice I am going to mean any coherent and complex form of socially established cooperative human activity through which goods internal to that form of activity are realized in the course of trying to achieve those standards of excellence which are appropriate to, and partially definitive of, that form of activity, with the result that human powers to achieve excellence, and human conceptions of the ends and goods involved, are systematically extended. (MacIntyre 1997, p. 187)

Some of the examples of practices supplied by MacIntyre include certain professions, such as architecture and farming, as well as certain games, such as football and chess. The idea behind an apprenticeship or an internship is that valuable knowledge about the nature of certain professions, or practices, can be gained by actually doing some of the work involved in those fields. In other words, doing something is a way of learning something. This will likely resonate with anyone who, frustrated with the tedious process of learning a new board game, has finally suggested setting the instructions aside and just learning the game by playing it. This is how people usually learn their first language, and, in many cases, it is also how they become proficient in additional languages as well.

Much like the rule booklets included with board games, dictionaries and grammar guides are useful for sorting out specific details, such as whether to use "boardgame," "board-game," or "board game" in a piece of scholarly writing, or when encountering terminology that is completely unfamiliar. In general, however, an effective introduction generates familiarity, not strictly through formal definitions and rules, but by identifying salient features, providing plenty of examples, and immersing the student in the relevant practice. This approach is often used in introductory philosophy courses and textbooks, where students learn what philosophy is by doing what philosophers frequently do – namely, reading, writing, and discussing philosophical texts – which exposes them to examples of philosophical work and introduces them to some of its more salient features.

This book adopts a similar approach, featuring essays by a number of contemporary philosophers on a wide range of philosophical topics. What distinguishes it from so many other texts is that the examples of philosophy addressed throughout this book are all taken from popular culture. Material aimed at a general audience avoids much of the scholarly jargon found in more conventional philosophy texts and hopefully makes the content feel more familiar and more accessible than it might otherwise seem, especially to uninitiated readers.

The accessibility and familiarity of their source material notwithstanding, the analyses in this book are philosophically rigorous. As a preliminary to delving directly into these analyses, what follows is, first, an examination of some salient features of philosophy, particularly those that are also features of *The Twilight Zone*, followed by a discussion of the philosophical content of specific episodes of *The Twilight Zone*, particularly those that are also covered in other chapters of this book.

A Dimension as Vast as Space and as Timeless as Infinity

As addressed in preceding sections, Bertrand Russell characterizes philosophy as endless questioning. This characterization is consistent with much of what has emerged throughout the history of philosophy as an academic discipline, dating back at least as far as Socrates. One salient feature of philosophy, then, is that philosophy is often, for lack of a better word, *curious*. Recall that identifying something as a salient feature of philosophy is not the same as saying it is present in all instances of philosophy, nor is it the same as saying that it is present only in instances of philosophy. Instead, it is an acknowledgment that, generally speaking, the feature is common within and characteristic of philosophy. There are also other salient features. Not only is philosophy curious, but it is also *deep*, and it is also *abstract*. In addition, it is frequently *controversial*. This is not intended as an exhaustive or exclusive list of the salient features of philosophy. This means that the features listed may overlap, such that something can be an example of more than one feature from the list, and it also means that there are more features than the ones listed. Because these salient features of philosophy are also salient features of *The Twilight Zone*, familiarity with philosophy can contribute to understanding *The Twilight Zone*, and familiarity with *The Twilight Zone* can contribute to understanding philosophy.

Curiosity

Many episodes of *The Twilight Zone* pose questions or identify possibilities without committing to a particular set of beliefs with regard to those questions or possibilities. For example, the episode "Five Characters in Search of an Exit" depicts a soldier, a dancer, a clown, a bagpiper, and a hobo all struggling to escape from a large metal bin in which they are mysteriously trapped. In an unexpected twist, the ending reveals that they are not actually humans, but dolls that have been tossed into a Salvation Army donation bin. This episode does not seem to be making a specific point or advancing a particular philosophical position. Rather, it simply seems to ask the audience to entertain the notion of consciousness in inanimate objects, in this case dolls. Indeed, living dolls is a recurring theme in *The Twilight Zone*. In the aptly titled episode, "Living Doll," a family is terrified by a child's *Talky Tina* doll who, as luck would have it, is not merely alive, but apparently evil. Similarly, in "The After Hours," department store mannequins take turns living like regular human beings for 1 month at a time before returning to their usual, lifeless existence.

A closely related theme is that of robots so lifelike that people begin to relate to them as humans. "The Lonely" features an inmate, James Corry, who is serving a life sentence of solitary confinement on a distant asteroid. Out of sympathy, the person who delivers Corry's supplies also delivers a robot designed to look like a beautiful woman for companionship and possibly more. Predictably, Corry falls in love with the robot, despite initially feeling mocked by her feminine appearance and referring to her as "a hunk of metal with arms and legs instead of wheels." Similarly, in "I Sing the Body Electric," a family purchases a custom robot to fulfill the role of grandmother and, eventually, comes to accept her as a beloved family member. There are also episodes, such as "The Monsters Are Due on Maple Street" and "Will the Real Martian Please Stand Up?" which introduce the possibility of beings from space living undetected among humans. In "The Monsters Are Due on Maple Street," people are overly paranoid about this possibility and turn against one another when they really should not, while in "Real Martian," the fear of space aliens turns out to be warranted. It seems, then, that the point of such episodes is not so much to assert a belief that there actually are (or are not) robots and space aliens living among humans. Instead, the point seems to be that things may not always be what they appear to be. It is a reminder to probe beyond the surface of how things seem.

Depth

Quite literally, probing beyond the surface of something means delving more deeply into it. Often, the ideas that get characterized as deep are those that seem to be beyond the limits of human understanding. These are also the kinds of concepts addressed in philosophy, and they are the kinds of topics presented in *The Twilight Zone*. Consider, for instance, episodes that explore the role of evil, personified in the form of Satan, in the lives of human beings. Notably, in "The Howling Man," the devil has been trapped and imprisoned by a group of monks in a remote abbey, thereby keeping humankind safe from unimaginable evil. The episode ends, of course, with a well-meaning visitor releasing the prisoner, quite possibly unleashing hell on Earth. In "Escape Clause," Walter Bedeker makes a deal with the devil in exchange for immortality. Immortality ends up being less appealing than anticipated, however, and Bedeker is eventually driven by a series of unfortunate circumstances to implement the *Escape Clause*, trading immortality for death after all. "One for the Angels" does not depict the devil, but rather a personification of death, who is convinced to spare the life of a street vendor long enough for one great, final, sales pitch. Death returns in "The Hitch-Hiker," this time to pursue an unsuspecting woman taking a solo drive across the country. Similarly, in "Nothing in the Dark," an elderly woman refuses to open the door for fear that any visitor could be death.

In "Last Stop Willoughby," death plays a much different role. In this episode, death is a welcome escape out of the miserable modern world inhabited by Gart Williams, and into the nostalgic old town this exhausted advertising executive discovered, apparently in a dream, on the train home from work. The full weight of the decision to make a permanent move to Willoughby is finally revealed when Williams' lifeless body is found in the snow by the tracks where it hit the ground after Williams jumped from the speeding train. In "Walking Distance," yet another advertising executive stumbles upon a nostalgic old town while waiting for car repairs. In this episode, a middle-aged Martin Sloan visits a much younger Martin Sloan and attempts to offer advice for the sake of their collective future. This does not go well, however, and Sloan must return to the present time. In another time travel episode, "No Time Like the Past," a scientist who travels back in time to change the past, including Hitler's rise to power, also learns that the past belongs in the past. These are just a few examples of episodes that delve deeply into subjects that seem inevitably and eternally beyond human understanding, such as good and evil, death and dying, the meaning of life, time, fate, and the like.

Abstraction

Related to depth is abstraction, which is another salient feature of philosophy. While some philosophical approaches, including some feminist and pragmatist approaches, emphasize specificity, philosophy very often deals with general concepts rather than focusing on particular instances and individuals. What are often referred to as thought experiments are common in philosophy as a way to explore how things could be, apart from the specific details of how things actually are. Thought experiments present scenarios, often improbable or impossible scenarios, to test the conceptual limitations of various ideas or reveal our intuitions and beliefs.

An early example of a thought experiment is Plato's so-called "allegory of the cave" (Plato 1973, Book VII), in which readers are invited to imagine a group of people imprisoned and bound in such a way that the only thing they are able to see is the cave wall in front of them, which displays shadows reflected by objects passed in front of a fire that is positioned behind them. If their whole lives were spent this way, the prisoners would likely take the shadows on the cave wall for reality, and it would be difficult to convince them that these shadows were mere reflections of something more substantial. This thought experiment offers an abstract way of exploring the distinction between reality and appearance. While it can be difficult for people to imagine that they themselves are mistaken about reality, it is easier to imagine that others, like the imaginary prisoners, could be. In a thought experiment about the ring of Gyges (Plato 1973, Book II), Plato invites readers to imagine themselves to be in possession of the magical ring from a myth about a shepherd named Gyges who was able to become invisible by turning this magic ring, thereby gaining the ability to do pretty much anything without getting caught. This offers an abstract way of exploring the extent to which public scrutiny and the risk of punishment factor into moral decisions.

The use of thought experiments is not unique to Plato. They are common in contemporary philosophy as well. A more recent example is found in the question posed by Thomas Nagel, who asks, "What is it like to be a bat?" (Nagel 1974). By asking this question, Nagel is suggesting that, even if literally every scientific detail about bats could be revealed, there would nevertheless be something leftover to explain. According to Nagel, this reveals that there is a subjective, experiential component, or phenomenal aspect, that is not subject to scientific explanation, and thus purely physical explanations of the mind are therefore inadequate.

Likewise, many episodes of *The Twilight Zone* function as thought experiments by providing opportunities to explore issues in the abstract. The aforementioned episodes involving lifelike dolls and robots, for example, invite the audience to consider conceptual possibilities, such as machine consciousness, apart from practical limitations and logistical constraints. Episodes that involve manipulating the passage of time invite audiences to wonder whether the universe is deterministic or whether, instead, it is susceptible to intervention and free will. Episodes involving complicated relationships between human beings and intelligent beings from other planets invite audiences to reflect on the complicated relationships between people of different races and cultural backgrounds.

Challenging racism is difficult even today and was even more so when *The Twilight Zone* initially aired. Explicit references to the oppression of people of color by white America would have violated censorship rules and likely would have alienated mainstream white audiences of that era. Imaginary examples of prejudice and inequality, however, provided *The Twilight Zone* with a point of entry for social commentary and criticism, as discussed below.

Controversy

Although *The Twilight Zone* had to work around conservative values and media censorship, Rod Serling was nevertheless committed to addressing racism: "I happen to think that the singular evil of our time is prejudice. It is from this evil that all other evils grow and multiply. In almost everything I've written there is a thread of this: a man's seemingly palpable need to dislike someone other than himself" (Quoted by May 1967). Initially, Serling pitched a show about race relations as a reaction to the racist lynching of Emmett Till. In 1955, at just 14 years old, Emmett Till was brutally murdered for allegedly intimidating a white woman in a Mississippi grocery store. The white men who murdered Till were acquitted by a jury of white men, and more than 60 years later, the white woman who made the initial allegation admitted to lying about it in court. At the time, this topic was deemed too controversial for television:

> During the 1950s and 1960s, the networks and advertisers measured the viewing audience as an undifferentiated mass. Despite the lumping together of all viewers, broadcasters structured programming content around the "normal," dominant, values of white, middle-class Americans. Therefore, content centered around the concerns of the nuclear family. Topics such as racism or sexuality which had little direct impact on this domestic setting were excluded from content. Indeed, ethnic minorities were excluded, for the most part, from the television screen because they did not fit into the networks' assumptions about the viewing audience. (Newcomb 2004, p. 483)

Serling finally developed *The Twilight Zone* to address social problems like racism in more subtle ways. In addition to making episodes that focused on equality, Serling also sought to achieve racial diversity in casting the show, explaining that "Television, like its big sister, the motion picture, has been guilty of the sin of omission" (Quoted by Zicree 1992).

The Twilight Zone also dealt with other controversial topics, such as war, capitalism, greed, and so forth. In a particularly poignant episode about war, "A Quality of Mercy," a US soldier is suddenly transported into the body of a Japanese soldier prior to an attack on the USA. In a similarly poignant episode about capitalist greed, "The Brain Center at Whipple's," a business executive introduces automation technologies that leave thousands of workers unemployed and dehumanized. In another episode about greed, "The Fever," a reluctant Las Vegas tourist ends up getting obsessed with gambling and losing everything.

Social conformity is another controversial theme in *The Twilight Zone*. "Eye of the Beholder" and "Number 12 Looks Just Like You" focus specifically on conformity to seemingly impossible beauty standards, particularly for women. Both episodes depict social worlds in which people are forced to undergo surgery in order to look the way society expects them to look. These are just a few examples of controversial subject matter in *The Twilight Zone*. In philosophy, no subject is off limits, regardless of how controversial it is. Indeed, controversy has surrounded philosophy at least since the trial of Socrates, for whom that controversy ultimately carried a death sentence. Like philosophy in general, and like Socrates and many other philosophers in particular, *The Twilight Zone* is often curious, deep, abstract, and controversial.

Your Next Stop Is *The Twilight Zone*

Each chapter of this handbook depicts a philosophical problem, position, question, or argument as it is addressed, raised, or made by a piece of popular culture. Individually, these chapters provide an opportunity to delve deeply into the ideas they cover. Collectively, they provide an explanation, by way of example, of what philosophy is all about. In a similar manner, the individual episodes of *The Twilight Zone*, taken together, present a broad introduction to philosophy by posing philosophical questions and positing philosophical positions – including some questions and positions that are also covered in this book. Just as philosophers display a wide variety of perspectives regarding the definition and salient features of philosophy, they also offer multiple ways of organizing its subject matter into different areas of study. Although different ways of organizing the relevant material may be equally legitimate, it is nevertheless helpful to employ some system for sorting through the otherwise overwhelmingly vast subject matter of philosophy. This discussion organizes the material around three basic questions, and these questions loosely correspond to epistemology, metaphysics, and ethics. Noting once again that definitions are negotiated and negotiable, epistemology usually refers to the study of knowledge, metaphysics to the study of reality, and ethics to the study of morality.

What (and How) Can We Know?

The first question, "What can we know," along with such follow-up questions as "How can we know it?" and "How can we know that we know it?" addresses knowledge and certainty. In the pilot episode of *The Twilight Zone*, "Where Is Everybody?" a person with no memory of the past suddenly wanders alone into an otherwise ordinary town that was recently abandoned. Despite evidence that people have just been there, like running faucets and burning cigarettes, they are nowhere to be found. The audience eventually learns that the confused person is actually an astronaut, Mike Ferris, who has been deprived of human interaction for nearly 3 weeks in preparation for space travel, and the town is an elaborate hallucination Ferris created in order to cope with the lack of stimulation. Like Plato's allegory of the cave, this episode of *The Twilight Zone* invokes the possibility that things are not the way they seem.

This possibility has preoccupied many philosophers concerned with the study of knowledge, particularly Rene Descartes. Descartes developed a skeptical method, aptly dubbed the "Method of Doubt," of rejecting any potential belief that has even a remote possibility of being false (Descartes 1993). The idea behind this method is that adhering only to carefully vetted beliefs should eliminate uncertainty, even if it reduces the overall number of beliefs adopted. Using this method, Descartes quickly determined that empirical knowledge, or knowledge acquired through the senses, is susceptible to radical doubt, given that anything perceived by the senses could be an illusion, a hallucination, a dream, or even the work of a powerful demon who enjoys tricking people into false perceptions. Much like the films *Inception* and *The Matrix*, both of which are covered in later chapters of this book, the pilot episode of *The Twilight Zone* invites the sort of skepticism with which Descartes' philosophy begins. *Inception* and *The Matrix do* this by demonstrating just how real dreams and computer simulations can seem, while this episode of *The Twilight Zone* does it by making the same point about hallucinations.

There are many other episodes that soften the boundary between reality and imagination. In "A World of His Own," for example, a novelist brings people into and out of existence simply by recording descriptions of them, or, alternatively, by destroying the tapes that contain those recordings. This raises the possibility that there may be at least some situations in which observation involves an element of imagination. The credibility of direct observation is addressed again in "The Arrival," in which different Federal Aviation Agency investigators discover factual discrepancies in their descriptions of a plane that has mysteriously landed with no crew and no passengers. They seem to have parallel, but different, experiences, again acknowledging the possible connection between imagination and observation. This in turn raises questions about how knowledge is acquired. How knowledge is acquired is an enduring question within philosophy and popular culture. Again, films such as *Inception* and *The Matrix*, raise questions about the acquisition of knowledge by depicting people struggling to differentiate fact from fiction after recognizing that the world they inhabit may be an illusion. The relationship between observation, belief, and certainty is also addressed in some detail in a later chapter of this book, using the example of the video game *The Witness*, in which players, much like the astronaut in the *Twilight Zone* pilot episode, attempt to make sense of an unfamiliar world with no preliminary knowledge of how they got there or what they are expected to accomplish. As demonstrated by these and other examples, human knowledge is subject to uncertainty both in general and in its specific details.

Who (or What) Are We?

Related to questions about the relationship between imagination and observation are broad questions about the human condition. Referring again to the pilot episode of *The Twilight Zone*, "Where is Everybody?" the medical officer explains the astronaut's hallucination as follows:

> You see, we can feed stomachs with concentrates. We can supply microfilm for recreation, reading, even movies of a sort. We can pump oxygen in, waste material out, but there's one thing we can't simulate. That's a very basic need. Man's hunger for companionship, the barrier of loneliness. That's one we haven't licked yet.

This expresses two ideas about the human condition. First, by indicating that science is incapable of fully understanding and predicting human needs, it suggests that human actions are not completely determined. Determinism entails everything, including human behavior, is the result of a previous event and is therefore predictable, at least in principle. Determinism is often thought to be incompatible with free will. By suggesting that some aspects of human behavior are outside the scope of science, this episode thereby suggests that people are capable of acting freely. Second, by suggesting that people are dependent on one another, this episode suggests that human nature is fundamentally social. Questions about human freedom and human nature are common within philosophy, within *The Twilight Zone*, and within popular culture. Chapters in this volume that address such issues include the chapters on the video games *Legend of Zelda: Breath of the Wild* and *God of War.*

Related to the topic of freedom and determinism is the idea that people are basically machines – albeit very complex machines. Determinism suggests that robots with artificial intelligence could, in principle, function in ways that are indistinguishable from and interchangeable with human beings. In *The Twilight Zone* episode, "Uncle Simon," a woman is tormented, first, by a wealthy but verbally abusive uncle and, eventually, by a robot designed to continue the abuse even after the uncle has died. In this example, the uncle lives on, so to speak, through the robot. The episode *The Mighty Casey* depicts a baseball pitcher who outperforms all of the other players in the league. The episode takes an interesting turn when, after Casey is discovered to be a robot and disqualified from the game, he is equipped with a biological heart and gets reclassified as human. With this heart, however, comes human emotions, and Casey is no longer willing to strike players out for fear that it will ruin their careers and make them unhappy. The robots in both episodes have something like free will – though in the first case, it is merely an extension of the will of its creator, and in the second case, it is the very basis for reclassifying the machine as human.

As already discussed "The Lonely" depicts a lonely prisoner who falls in love with a robot that was designed for human companionship, and "I Sing the Body Electric" portrays a family that adopts a robot to take on the role of grandmother. Similarly, in "The Lateness of the Hour," a family lives with a staff of servants, all of whom are robots. After the daughter pleads to have the robots dismantled, however, arguing that the family is becoming too dependent on them, the plot takes a turn and the daughter discovers that she is a robot herself. All three of these episodes suggest that it might be impossible to determine whether other people are actually robots. "The Lateness of the Hour" is especially interesting, however, insofar as this episode suggests that it might also be impossible for people to determine whether they are actually robots themselves.

The possibility of robots passing as human is an extension of what is often referred to in philosophy as the problem of other minds. The problem associated with other minds is that there is no direct way to verify that others have any conscious experience at all, nor to obtain knowledge of the felt quality of any mental experience they do have. Using the example of robots and artificial intelligence extends this problem by demonstrating that it is likewise impossible to verify that someone or something lacks conscious experience. In the above examples, the robots behave in ways that are consistent with human consciousness. In yet another example, the "replicants" depicted in the film *Blade Runner* and the "hosts" depicted in the television series *Westworld* are extremely advanced manufactured beings who are nearly indistinguishable from biological born "natural" human beings. Similarly, the films *AI: Artificial Intelligence* and *Ex Machina* both depict robots that seem capable of having hopes, dreams, and possibly even the ability to feel love. These examples are explored more fully in later chapters.

While the pilot episode of *The Twilight Zone* implied that human nature is beyond the scope of science, later episodes presented a more deterministic account. There is a similar discrepancy between the pilot episode and later episodes regarding the depiction of human nature. Such discrepancies can be recognized, not as an internal inconsistency of the show, but rather as evidence of a commitment to exploring themes rather than dogmatically advocating a particular position. *The Twilight Zone* does not pretend that there are easy answers to enduring philosophical questions, and it does an especially good job of demonstrating the tension between two opposing accounts of human nature. "Where is Everybody?" suggests that people are interdependent and social. Other episodes, however, describe people as comparatively solitary or selfish. Other examples include "The Shelter," in which a group of neighbors fight to access the limited space and resources inside a bomb shelter, and "The Masks," in which a group of people assembled to collect their inheritance from a wealthy relative are given masks that become the outward expression of their selfishness and greed. In philosophy, this is often discussed in terms of the distinction between altruism (i.e., selflessness) and egoism (i.e., selfishness). These concepts are addressed in many examples throughout popular culture. Notable examples addressed in this volume include the South Korean television series, *Squid Game*, and the video game, *The Last of Us*, which pit the interests of different characters against one another.

What Should We Do (and Why)?

As a description of human nature, egoism maintains that people are basically selfish. There is also a prescriptive version of egoism, ethical egoism, which maintains that morality consists in people behaving in their own self-interest. The distinction here is between description and prescription, or between what is the case and what ought to be the case. The two positions are different, but they are not unrelated. If human nature precludes the possibility of behaving altruistically, for example, then it will not make sense to say that this is what people should do. *The Twilight Zone* episode "Where Is Everybody?" suggests that people are fundamentally social. In this example, and in many others, *The Twilight Zone* challenges individualistic conceptions of human nature in favor of the notion that people need people. In "Time Enough At Last," Henry Bemis takes joy in being the last survivor of an H-bomb attack because it provides an opportunity for endless, uninterrupted reading. Ironically, however, Bemis' eyeglasses get broken, leaving the avid reader with nothing to do and nobody to do it with. Similarly, in "The Mind and the Matter," a misanthropic Archibald Beechcroft is endowed with the ability to make things happen simply by willing them to occur. After wishing everyone else out of existence, Beechcroft quickly learns that, regardless of how annoying they may be, the world would be lonely and boring without other people. And in what is perhaps the most scathing indictment of egoism in any episode of *The Twilight Zone*, "It's a Good Life" depicts a young child, Anthony Fremont. Much like Archibald Beechcroft in "The Mind and the Matter," Anthony Freemont can turn wishes into reality, thereby forcing the few people who have not yet been wished away to the cornfield to conform to the whims of this demanding child. Messages favoring cooperation and compassion are not hard to come by in popular media. An especially wholesome example, as discussed in a later chapter, is the children's television series, *Mister Rogers' Neighborhood*.

The tension between the solitary self and the social self was depicted by Arthur Schopenhauer through a story about porcupines in the cold, simultaneously drawing together for warmth and pulling apart because of their sharp quills, alternately moving back and forth (Schopenhauer 2015). This metaphor suggests that human society offers both comfort and danger. Whereas many episodes of *The Twilight Zone* emphasize the necessity of human connection, many others depict the dangers of social conformity. Both "Eye of the Beholder" and "Number 12 Looks Just Like You" depict societies with rigid expectations, including expectations for how people should look, and people are required to undergo surgery to conform to these expectations. The central characters in these episodes are women, which highlights the disproportionate impact of social demands on marginalized people.

Various aspects of feminism are discussed in later chapters of this handbook including ► Chap. 9, "*The Handmaid's Tale* as Philosophy: Autonomy and Reproductive Freedom." *The Handmaid's Tale* delves deeply into the repression of women in patriarchal society. This topic is touched upon in more subtle ways in the *Twilight Zone*. It is noteworthy that the episode "The After Hours," in which the audience learns about the secret lives of department store mannequin, first aired in June of 1960, which is just a little more than a year after Mattel released the first Barbie doll. Barbie has been wildly popular and widely criticized ever since she was first introduced in March of 1959, and the timing of "The After Hours" suggests that this episode was, at least in part, a nod to the image of womanhood represented by Barbie. Nearly the entire episode consists of Marsha White, who does not yet realize that she is just a mannequin, shopping for a thimble, purchasing a thimble, discovering that the thimble is damaged, attempting to return the thimble, and then fainting. It is fitting that a life-size doll would engage in trivial activities and display physical weakness, and it is no coincidence that women were, and often still are, stereotyped as trivial and weak.

An episode that is particularly interesting from a feminist perspective is "Twenty Two," in which a professional dancer, Liz Powell, hospitalized for exhaustion, is summoned to the mysterious room 22 each night by a sinister nurse who is never there during the day. The dismissive hospital staff, along with Liz's condescending manager, Barney, insists that this must be a dream or the product of Liz's imagination, thereby engaging in what is often referred to as gaslighting. At its worst, gaslighting is a form of emotional abuse in which people, usually women, are manipulated by others, usually men, into thinking they are mentally unstable or incompetent, usually as a way to control them. More casually, gaslighting is when people find it easier to question women's sanity than to believe what they say about their own experiences. The staff knows that room 22 is the location of the hospital morgue, but they do not acknowledge the significance of this detail in their conversations with Liz. After leaving the hospital, Liz attempts to board a flight to a dance gig in Miami. Noticing that it is flight number 22 and that the flight attendant looks just like the sinister nurse, Liz decides not to board the plane after all. The plane explodes shortly after taking off, and Liz's sanity is no longer suspect. This episode acknowledges that people, particularly those in positions of power or authority, have a tendency to disregard and dismiss the experiences of others, particularly those in marginalized social positions.

Like many of the popular culture examples discussed throughout this book, *The Twilight Zone* addresses philosophical questions and invites the audience to think critically and reflectively. Examples drawn from literature, film, and television can give life to abstract questions and concepts. As demonstrated throughout this volume, however, some examples from popular culture do not just reiterate existing philosophical perspectives but instead offer their own contribution to the pursuit of philosophy by asking new questions or providing new answers to some of the old ones. While other examples addressed in this collection, such as *Star Trek*, explore a wide range of philosophical topics, a virtue of *The Twilight Zone* is that, as an anthology series, each episode tells a single, self-contained story, thereby eliminating the need for any background knowledge about continuing plot or recurring characters. This is also the case for more recent series, such as *Black Mirror*, which is also addressed in this collection, but what is unique about *The Twilight Zone* is that it is a classic series that has already withstood the test of time. It offers the appeal of nostalgia without seeming irrelevant or outdated.

References

Descartes, René. 1993. *Discourse on method; and, meditations on first philosophy.* Indianapolis: Hackett Publishing Company.

MacIntyre, Alasdair. 1997. *After virtue.* 2nd ed. Notre Dame: Notre Dame University Press.

May, Ellen Cameron. 1967. "Serling in creative mainstream" (interview). *Los Angeles Times*, June 25, 1967, pp. C22–23.

Nagel, Thomas. 1974. What is it like to be a bat? *The Philosophical Review* 83 (4): 435–450.

Newcomb, Horace, ed. 2004. *Encyclopedia of television.* 2nd ed. New York: Fitzroy Dearborn Publishers.

Plato. 1973. *The republic and other works.* Trans. Benjamin Jowett. New York: Anchor Books Random House.

Russell, Bertrand. 1912. The problems of philosophy, Ch. XV: "The value of philosophy."

Schopenhauer, Arthur. 2015. *Parerga and Paralipomena: Short philosophical essays*, vol. 2. Ed. Christopher Janaway. Cambridge: Cambridge University Press.

West, Thomas G. 1979. *Plato's "apology of Socrates": An interpretation, with a new translation*. Ithaca: Cornell University Press.

Wittgenstein, Ludwig. 1968. *Philosophical investigations*. Trans. G.E.M. Anscombe. New York: Macmillan Publishing.

Zicree, Marc Scott. 1992. *The twilight zone companion*. 2nd ed. Silman-James Press.

Star Trek as Philosophy: Spock as Stoic Sage

3

Massimo Pigliucci

Contents

Introduction: Spock as the Positive Image of a Stoic 42
Stoicism, the Basics 44
Stoic Sagehood 101 47
Mr. Spock as *Prokoptôn* 56
Conclusion: So, Is Spock a Stoic, and Should *We* Be? 62
References 63

Abstract

It has been suggested that Gene Roddenberry, the creator of the original *Star Trek* series (TOS), more or less consciously built the equivalent of a philosophical argument in favor of Stoic philosophy by centering his story lines on the interacting and exquisitely complementary characters of Mr. Spock, Captain Kirk, and Doctor McCoy. Spock in particular was apparently purposefully meant by Roddenberry to represent Stoicism as he understood it. Modern practitioners of Stoicism, however, tend to see Spock as a "stoic" (lower-s) in the vernacular sense of the term: going through life constantly sporting a stiff upper lip and suppressing his emotions. I argue in this chapter that, on the contrary, the evolution of Spock from the young officer serving on the *Enterprise* NCC-1701 to ambassador to the Romulans in the last movie based on TOS can be understood as the story of someone entering the path to sagehood in the Stoic sense. And yes, Stoicism definitely is about far more than stiff lips and the suppression of emotions.

M. Pigliucci (✉)
Department of Philosophy, The City College of New York, New York, NY, USA
e-mail: mpigliucci@ccny.cuny.edu

© Springer Nature Switzerland AG 2024
D. K. Johnson et al. (eds.), *The Palgrave Handbook of Popular Culture as Philosophy*,
https://doi.org/10.1007/978-3-031-24685-2_2

Keywords

Stoicism · Virtue ethics · Cosmopolitanism · *Star Trek: The Original Series* · Spock

Introduction: Spock as the Positive Image of a Stoic

Star Trek is one of the most beloved television and movie franchises in the history of movies and television. (Throughout this I will use material drawn from the original three series of Star Trek, as well as from the first six movies. I will intentionally ignore the "alternative timeline" created by J.J. Abrams with his 2013 reboot.) While there certainly is a lot of variance in the quality of both *The Original Series* (TOS), which comprised 3 seasons and 79 episodes, and the 6 movies that followed it (not to mention the various spin-off series and related movies), it is hard to deny its lasting impact on popular culture, as well as the richness of its implied philosophical material.

The number of recognitions TOS gathered is impressive, including Emmy nominations for outstanding dramatic series in 1967 and 1968; outstanding supporting actor (Leonard Nimoy as Spock) in 1967, 1968, and 1969; eight episodes named for the Hugo Award, one of science fiction's top prizes; as well as ratings of the show as "greatest cult show ever" (*TV Guide* – The 25 Top Cult Shows Ever! May 30 – June 5, 2004 issue) and as one of "the greatest shows of all time" (Fretts and Roush 2013). Even the iconic sci-fi writer Isaac Asimov wrote that Star Trek was a "fresh and intellectually challenging" show (Letters of Note 2012).

While the series is known for Roddenberry's progressive and optimistic view of the future, as well as for an unusually diverse cast (with major roles for a black woman, a gay Japanese-American, and a Russian), arguably the epicenter of the early *Star Trek* universe was organized around the three main characters of Captain James Tiberius Kirk (played by William Shatner), Doctor Leonard "Bones" McCoy (DeForest Kelley), and first science officer Mr. Spock (Leonard Nimoy). Their adventures on the starship *Enterprise* NCC-1701, set to "boldly go where no man has gone before," are often used as a captivating device to explore humanity's foibles, magnified either by encountering alien races that are portrayed as having hyper-developed along a particular tendency already present in human history (like in the episode "Bread and Circuses," set on a planet with modern technology but where the Roman empire never collapsed) or by way of Spock's dry observations on humans in general and of McCoy in particular (like this quip at McCoy's expense in "Errand and Mercy": "It is curious how often you humans manage to obtain that which you do not want.")

From the original series through the six movies, we follow Spock's career and personal development. He begins, as noted, as the *Enterprise*'s first and science officer, eventually becoming commanding officer and finally, after his retirement, ambassador for the United Federation of Planets. Spock is the son of the Vulcan Sarek and the human Amanda Grayson, and it is this mixed genetic and cultural heritage that sets him to be so unique and philosophically fascinating (as he would

3 *Star Trek* as Philosophy: Spock as Stoic Sage

say). What makes him an ideal candidate to explore the concept of the Stoic sage is that, while he appears to embody the classical inaccurate stereotypes used to describe Stoics – suppression of emotions and going through life with a stiff upper lip – a closer analysis, as I will argue, shows him to be a far more nuanced and good exemplar of Stoic character.

Modern Stoics (Pigliucci 2017; Irvine 2019; Robertson 2019) tend to distance themselves from Spock as they, rightly, reject the abovementioned stereotype. Stoics are *not* in the business of suppressing emotions (as we shall see in the next section), and, although endurance certainly is a Stoic value, there is a lot more to it than the stiff upper lip caricature allows. In fact, Farren (2014) argues in detail that Spock should *not* be considered a Stoic model. While conceding that there may be ways in which Spock *appears* to be a Stoic, she ultimately rejects the suggestion:

> All in all, Spock is hardly the Stoic sage. Although he has some Stoic leanings, he consistently falls short of being the man of action. Furthermore, in completely suppressing his emotions, he conforms to the stereotype of the Stoic, in contrast to the real Stoic who aims to cultivate positive emotions such as joy and wishing others well. (2014, p. 198)

Surprisingly, Farren actually concludes that Captain Kirk is a better candidate:

> Kirk tries to balance emotion and reason, but he never loses sight of taking action. His choices and actions make him take risks for the common welfare, even when the purely logical thing might be to do nothing. Perhaps he, as the perfect mixture of good emotions and ethical imperatives, a mixture, as it were, of the best of Spock and McCoy, is Star Trek's real Stoic: *the man of both action and contemplation*. In the words of Captain Kirk himself: "Gentlemen, we're debating in a vacuum, let's go get some answers." (2014, p. 200)

Farren concludes that Roddenberry – while deliberately setting up Spock as a Stoic character – in almost Platonic fashion "took the perfect person and divided him into three, the administrative courageous part in the Captain (Kirk), the logical part in the Science Officer (Spock) and the humanist part in the Doctor (McCoy)" (2014, p. 200). (The obvious problem with this analogy being that, in Plato's Republic, it would be Spock, not Kirk, that should be in charge of things, since Plato said that it was the logos – the logical part of the "tripartite soul" – that should be in charge.)

In what follows, by contrast, I will argue for the thesis that – just like Roddenberry himself intended – Spock really is *Star Trek*'s Stoic. And moreover that, throughout his long career, he develops along a path similar to the one that the Stoics thought leads to sagehood. While I remain agnostic on whether Spock actually does become a sage or not by the time the sixth and last movie comes around, I think he certainly gets very close when he famously declares to a stunned young Vulcan officer: "Logic is the beginning of wisdom, not the end."

To arrive at my conclusion, I will proceed first by briefly summarizing the basic tenets of Stoicism, with particular emphasis on the Stoic treatment of emotions and the concept of acceptance/endurance – i.e., the two sources of the common stereotype. I will then discuss the notion of the Stoic sage as it emerges from modern scholarship on the topic. After that, I will explore the character of Spock at various stages of his life and career, through his own words. We will then have all the pieces of the puzzle in front of us, and we will be able to connect them to decide whether Spock is a good model of Stoic practitioner, if not, perhaps, an actual sage.

Stoicism, the Basics

Stoicism is a philosophy of life that began with Zeno of Citium around 300 BCE (Inwood 2003; Sellars 2016; Pigliucci 2019). A good way to understand it is to see that it is based on one fundamental theoretical axiom and two pillars to guide practice. The axiom is that we should "live according to nature," and the practical pillars are known as the "dichotomy of control," and the four "cardinal virtues." Let us consider them in turn.

Living according to nature was a slogan common to a number of Hellenistic philosophies, including Stoicism's close cousin, Cynicism, but also its main rival, Epicureanism. The phrase meant that we should live in accordance with a proper understanding of human nature, though the different schools disagreed on what, precisely, such understanding should consist of. The standard account is given by Diogenes Laertius:

> When reason by way of a more perfect leadership has been bestowed on the beings we call rational, for them life according to reason rightly becomes the natural life. For reason supervenes to shape impulse scientifically. This is why Zeno was the first (in his treatise *On the Nature of Man*) to designate as the end "life in agreement with nature" (or living agreeably to nature), which is the same as a virtuous life, virtue being the goal towards which nature guides us. So too Cleanthes in his treatise *On Pleasure*, as also Posidonius, and Hecato in his work *On Ends*. Again, living virtuously is equivalent to living in accordance with experience of the actual course of nature, as Chrysippus says in the first book of his *De Finibus*; for our individual natures are parts of the nature of the whole universe. And this is why the end may be defined as life in accordance with nature, or, in other words, in accordance with our own human nature as well as that of the universe, a life in which we refrain from every action forbidden by the law common to all things, that is to say, the right reason which pervades all things . . . Diogenes [of Babylon] then expressly declares the end to be to act with good reason in the selection of what is natural. Archedemus says the end is to live in the performance of all befitting actions. (Lives VII.85–88)

The Stoics, in other words, believed that the most important aspect of human nature is that we are social animals capable of reason. It follows that our natural "function," or best propensity, is to use reason to improve human society. This is why the Stoics were explicitly cosmopolitan and accepted that every creature endowed with reason is capable of arriving at, and acting upon, the same conclusion (including, unusually for the time, women). In modern terms, we would say that human beings are naturally prosocial animals and that a lot of cultural evolution is the result of conscious attempts to improve the structure and function of our society (admittedly, with more than mixed results) (de Waal et al. 2009; Laland 2018).

It is worth noting in passing, at this preliminary stage, that Mr. Spock not only works for what can fairly be described as a cosmopolitan organization (the United Federation of Planets) but invariably acts in the most rational and prosocial fashion

3 *Star Trek* as Philosophy: Spock as Stoic Sage

allowed by the circumstances. I will return to the notion of living according to nature when discussing the Stoic sage below.

Moving from theory to practice, the first pillar of Stoic philosophy is the dichotomy of control, famously summarized by Epictetus:

> Some things are within our power, while others are not. Within our power are opinion, motivation, desire, aversion, and, in a word, whatever is of our own doing; not within our power are our body, our property, reputation, office, and, in a word, whatever is not of our own doing. (Enchiridion I.1)

This is interpreted by modern Stoics as a call to internalize our goals, because our judgments and decisions to act are "up to us," but the outcomes of our actions are not. So, for instance, I should not desire to obtain that new job for which I am going to interview tomorrow; rather, I should desire to do my best in order to get that job. Let the chips fall where they may. Spock, it turns out, acts very much as if guided by the dichotomy of control. He knows very well that he can only try to do his best but that the outcomes of his actions are not under his complete control. (As a side note, apparently so does the chief engineer, Mr. Scott, at least when he says things like "I canna change the laws of physics! I've got to have 30 minutes [Captain]!," in *The Naked Time*.)

The second practical pillar that I mentioned is constituted by the cardinal virtues, which are to be used as a moral compass to navigate life the Stoic way. These are practical wisdom (the knowledge of what really is and is not good for us), courage (in the moral sense of standing up for the right thing), justice (knowing what the right thing is), and temperance (acting always in a manner proportionate to the occasion).

So let's say I witness a coworker being harassed by my boss. I immediately consult my inner moral compass and determine that it is good to help others in distress (practical wisdom) and harassment is unacceptable (justice). I therefore ought to intervene (courage), though in proportion to the situation (temperance), neither by just whispering an inaudible complaint nor by punching my boss on the nose. Again, even though Spock does not explicitly mention the four virtues (which modern empirical research suggests are near-universal: Dahlsgaard et al. 2005), episode after episode, and movie after movie, he seems to act precisely in this fashion. He tends to know what the right thing to do is, has the courage to do it, and does it with resolve while being ready to suffer the consequences. For instance, in the double episode The Menagerie, Spock takes the apparently extreme but necessary actions of abducting his former commander, Christopher Pike, and of locking the *Enterprise* on course. However, he then turns himself in for court-martial, ready to face the consequences of his decisions.

Now that we have a basic grasp of Stoic philosophy, let us address the two common criticisms that may induce us to think that Mr. Spock is a *caricature* of a Stoic, but not an actual *prokoptôn* (practitioner): the twin notions that Stoicism is about suppressing emotions and going through life with a stiff upper lip.

As often with misconceptions, there is a grain of truth to be had. Margaret Graver (2007) makes clear in her definitive treatment of Stoic emotions that the Stoics did not try to suppress this natural aspect of human psychology. Rather, they distinguished between *pathē* (disruptive emotions, or "passions") and *eupatheiai* (positive emotions). The idea was to move away from the first group (which includes fear, anger, and hatred) and to actively cultivate the second one (which includes love, joy, and a sense of justice). I will argue below, perhaps counterintuitively, that Spock too is not attempting to suppress emotions, despite his own occasional overt protestation to the contrary, and that he in fact does cultivate what the Stoics called *eupatheiai*.

As for the "stiff upper lip" business, the grain of truth lies in the fact that the Stoics did consider endurance to be a positive value. Here is one of my favorite, uncharacteristically humorous, quotes from Marcus Aurelius:

> "A cucumber is bitter." Throw it away. "There are briars in the road." Turn aside from them. This is enough. Do not add, "And why were such things made in the world?" (Meditations VIII.50)

The notion, as made clear in countless other Stoic writings, is to endure without complaint what cannot be avoided, because there is no sense in complaining about the inevitable, which doesn't mean one cannot (and should not) at the same time be positively engaged in other pursuits. Again, a humorous quote, this time from Epictetus, will make the point:

> I have to die. If it is now, well then I die now; if later, then now I will take my lunch, since the hour for lunch has arrived – and dying I will tend to later. (Discourses I.1.32)

There are many examples of a similar attitude in *Star Trek*, particularly in the interactions between Spock and the hyper-emotional Dr. McCoy.

Spock   It is more rational to sacrifice one life than six.
McCoy   I'm not talking about rationality.
Spock   You might be wise to start. (TOS: "The Galileo Seven")

Or:

Spock   Logic and practical information do not seem to apply here.
McCoy   You admit that?
Spock   To deny the facts would be illogical, Doctor. (TOS: "A Piece of the Action")

What I am claiming in this essay is not just that Spock's behavior is compatible with Stoic philosophy, but that he is, in fact, a *prokoptôn* who, by the end of his life and career, is getting pretty close to becoming a sage. Our next order of business, therefore, is to take a look at how the Stoics articulate the notion of sagehood.

Stoic Sagehood 101

In order to explore my fundamental thesis that *Star Trek*'s Mr. Spock is on the path to Stoic sagehood and that therefore his prominence in TOS and related movies amounts to an implicit argument for Stoicism on the part of Gene Roddenberry and his writers, we need to explore what exactly the Stoics meant by "sage" within the broader context of their philosophy. For this I will draw on the best analysis of the subject to date, René Brouwer's *The Stoic Sage: The Early Stoics on Wisdom, Sagehood and Socrates* (Brouwer 2014).

According to Brouwer, the Stoics thought of wisdom as (i) "knowledge of human and divine matters" and (ii) "fitting expertise." The first definition became commonplace in the ancient world, but Brouwer says that the Stoics were the first ones to use that particular articulation, and he begins his discussion with it: "the three elements in it — i.e. knowledge, human matters and divine matters — can be connected to the three parts of philosophical discourse as distinguished by the Stoics — i.e. logic, ethics and physics" (2014, p. 7). In other words, there is a direct connection between the Stoic concept of wisdom and the three fields (*topoi*) of Stoic philosophy.

A major source for attributing the first definition of wisdom to the Stoics is Plutarch (2013), who provides us with a near perfect summary of the basic Stoic ideas about wisdom, the nature of philosophy, and the *topoi*:

> The Stoics said that wisdom is knowledge of human and divine matters, and philosophy exercise of fitting expertise; the single and supremely fitting expertise is excellence, and excellences at their most general are three: in nature, in behavior, in reasoning. For this reason philosophy is also divided into three parts: physical, ethical and logical. Physical is when we investigate the world and the matters in the world, ethical is that which is occupied with human life, logical is that concerned with reasoning — the last they also call dialectical. (Stoicorum Veterum Fragmenta 2.35)

The division of philosophy in the three *topoi* is quintessentially Stoic and is found especially in Diogenes Laertius' (2015) commentary: "They say that philosophical discourse has three parts: the physical, the ethical and the logical part" (Lives of the Eminent Philosophers 7.39).

As is well-known, physics is concerned with the study of how the world is, logic with the study of reason, and ethics with the study of how to live. But how, exactly, are the three *topoi* related to the first Stoic definition of wisdom? Here is Brouwer:

> With ethics as the part concerned with life and the things that relate to us, human matters [in the definition] can easily be understood as a reference to ethics. With regard to physics as "the part concerned with [the] cosmos and the things in it," the link with the divine matters in the definition of wisdom may at first seem more obscure than in the case of ethics. This is not so, though: according to standard Stoic doctrine nature or the cosmos is divine or even identified with god. Dialectic and knowledge are perhaps at first sight less easy to connect [but] the Stoics included the theory of knowledge in dialectic, even agreeing among themselves that the theory of knowledge should be "placed first." (2014, p. 21)

So to recap, knowledge [logic] of human [ethics] and divine [physics] matters.

Brouwer then engages in an interesting discussion concerning the relationship between Stoic physics and ethics, dissecting the available sources about the famous Stoic dictum, "live according to nature," that I discussed briefly above. Diogenes Laertius, in this regard, says that:

> Zeno in his *On the Nature of Man* was the first to say that the end was to live in consistency with nature. (SVF 1.179)

The book title itself clearly singles out human nature, though Epictetus later on said that Zeno was talking about universal nature. Cleanthes, Zeno's successor as the head of the Stoa, spoke of living "in consistency with nature," by which he seems to have understood cosmic nature. As for Chrysippus, the third head of the Stoa, DL says that:

> By the nature with which our life ought to be in accord Chrysippus understands both common nature and in a special sense human nature. (SVF 3.4)

Either way, Stoic physics is obviously relevant to its ethics, because at a minimum the idea is that in order to figure out the best way to live, one has to have some understanding of how the world works, including a good comprehension of human nature. The emperor Julian the Apostate wrote about this:

> That [the students of the man from Citium] made "know thyself" into the main point of their philosophy, you may believe, if you will, not only from the things which they brought up in their writings, but even more so by the end of their philosophy: for they made the end living in consistency with nature, which cannot be achieved if one does not know who one is, and of what nature one is; for someone who does not know who he is, will surely not know what he ought to do. (Orations 6.6)

Or, as contemporary Stoic Larry Becker (2017) puts it in his *A New Stoicism*, living according to nature can simply be understood in modern terms as "follow the facts [about the world and humanity]."

I find what Brouwer says immediately afterward rather interesting and departing from what I think is common understanding among most modern Stoics:

> As with knowledge, the Stoics understood excellence both in cognitional and in dispositional terms, and they furthermore placed human excellence, as a character, in the wider context of the nature of the whole. ... The standard modern translation of *arete* as "(moral) virtue" is often less appropriate, as it suggests a restriction of its usage to ethics. The Stoics also used the term in a broader sense, and did not restrict its usage to the moral virtues. (2014, p. 38)

This being the case, then, Stoic excellence is to be understood both in the specific moral sense and in the broader human sense, outside the moral sphere. Brouwer elaborates: "Logic as an excellence, according to Cicero, provides a method of reasoning that guards against assenting to incorrect impressions. ... Physics is an excellence, too: without an explanation of the natural world justice towards other

3 *Star Trek* as Philosophy: Spock as Stoic Sage

human beings and piety towards the gods is impossible" (2014, p. 39). So a good Stoic does not want to excel only at the moral virtues, or in the practice of ethics, but also in the other two *topoi*, if nothing else because those are instrumental for the pursuit of the third one. Mr. Spock is clearly keen on practicing good logic and understanding science (he is the science officer on the *Enterprise*, after all!), all in the service of ethical (in the broad sense) behavior.

Brouwer then shifts to considering more in detail the second definition of wisdom given above: fitting expertise. He begins by citing Galen:

> Others defined philosophy as the exercise of fitting expertise of the best life for human beings, saying that philosophy is exercise, and calling wisdom fitting expertise, which is also a cognition of human and divine matters. (On the History of Philosophy, 5, 602.19-3.2)

It is interesting, as Brouwer notes, to recall that early definitions of philosophy, as in Herodotus and Heraclitus (Waterfield 2009), framed it as loving wisdom, whereby the "lover" (i.e., the philosopher) already possesses it. It is Plato that shifts to what then became the standard take, philosophy understood more modestly as striving *toward* wisdom. Going back to the (second) definition of wisdom itself, Brouwer goes along with Long and Sedley's interpretation, that it is a shorthand for "expertise of what is really useful." A further elaboration is found in Seneca (2017, Letter 88.26.7) where he presents a picture of different types of expertise as instances of "knowing how" (to play an instrument, to solve a geometrical problem, etc.), with wisdom being a superior type of "knowing why," that is, knowing when and how to use every other kind of knowledge.

A further explanation of what "fitting expertise" means is given by Olympiodorus:

> Cleanthes, then, says that an expertise is "a tenor that accomplishes everything methodically." But this definition is considered to be incomplete, for nature is also a tenor that does methodically all it does. Accordingly Chrysippus, after adding the phrase "with impressions," said "an expertise is a tenor that proceeds methodically with impressions." (SVF 1.490)

"Tenor," explains Brouwer, has nothing to do with opera, but is rather a technical term that refers to an enduring disposition. What Chrysippus is saying, then, is that wisdom is the ability to correctly interpret impressions. That is why, centuries later, Epictetus (2014) insisted that the most important thing to do for a student of Stoicism is to improve her faculty of judgment (*prohairesis*), i.e., the very faculty by which we assess (and give or refuse assent to) impressions:

> What decides whether a sum of money is good? The money is not going to tell you; it must be the faculty that makes use of such impressions — reason. (Discourses I, 1.5)

In the end, Brouwer concludes that the two Stoic definitions of wisdom are remarkably convergent and that "the activity that goes with the exercise of (or the search for) this expertise is called physics when we investigate the world and the things in the world, ethics when we occupy ourselves with human life, and logic (or dialectic) when we deal with reason as such" (2014, p. 50).

But is it really possible to become a sage? Plutarch (who was not particularly sympathetic to the Stoics, and whose writings need, therefore, to be interpreted with caution) comments with barely veiled sarcasm on the transition to sagehood in "How a man may become aware of his progress in wisdom":

> The sage changes in a moment or a second of time from the lowest possible inferiority to an unsurpassable character of virtue; and all his vice, of which he has not over a long time succeeded in removing even a small part, he instantaneously flees forever. (Stoicorum Veterum Fragmenta, 3.539)

If taken seriously, this makes the transition to sagehood sound very much like revelation for a Christian (say, on the way to Damascus), or enlightenment for a Buddhist, with the difference that the source of the Christian transformation is external, while for both Stoics and Buddhists is internal. It is also irreversible, as I think it is in Buddhism, but not necessarily in Christianity (where one can lose one's way; perhaps precisely because the transformation was triggered from the outside in the first place).

Much about the attributes of the sage is found in the synopsis of "The Stoics Talk More Paradoxically Than the Poets," again by Plutarch. According to Plutarch's synopsis, two things immediately characterize the transition to sagehood: its speed and the fact that it is a change between opposite states (vice and virtue). The synopsis also states that the sage may be ugly rather than beautiful and a beggar rather than a rich king. So don't expect wisdom to correspond to external attributes, such as beauty and wealth or power. One cannot help but be reminded of the fact that CBS had trouble with the figure of Spock because his pointed ears made him look too "satanic" for certain segments of the American viewership – something the series itself even refers to in "The Apple."

Spock   Precisely, Captain, and in a manner of speaking, we have given the people of Vaal the apple, the knowledge of good and evil if you will, as a result of which they too have been driven out of paradise.

Kirk   Doctor, do I understand him correctly? Are you casting me in the role of Satan?

Spock   Not at all, Captain.

Kirk   Is there anyone on this ship who even remotely looks like Satan? (McCoy and Kirk walk around Spock. McCoy is gazing intently at his ears.)

Spock   I am not aware of anyone who fits that description, Captain.

Kirk   No, Mister Spock. I didn't think you would be.

The sage does not hold "opinions" (*doxa*), meaning changeable convictions about whatever matters he contemplates. That is because he has reached the pinnacle of

3 *Star Trek* as Philosophy: Spock as Stoic Sage

human epistemic power: he does not have superhuman knowledge, but does have the best knowledge any human being can possibly achieve. His cognition, so to speak, is stable. Interestingly, Plutarch says that the Sage is not "like" Zeus, he actually is divine. As Sextus Empiricus puts it, in his non-Stoic friendly "Against the Professors" (SVF 7.423):

> According to them [i.e. the Stoics] the sage possesses an infallible criterion, which makes him in all respects divine because he never holds opinions, that is assents to what is false, wherein lies the height of unhappiness and the ruin of the inferior person.

This may strike the modern reader as just bizarre, until we remember that the Stoics did not literally believe in the Olympian gods; for them god (they only believed in one) was the same as nature itself. And human beings participate in the logos, so they are, in a sense, divine (this, of course, applies to Vulcans as well). Brouwer says:

> Chrysippus explains in allegorical fashion that not only the Olympian gods such as Zeus, Ares and Hephaistos are to be "assimilated" to, respectively, reason that rules over everything, war or the principle of order and disorder, and fire, but also that the sun and moon are gods. What we thus seem to have is an interpretation of the gods of traditional religion in terms of natural phenomena and an interpretation of natural phenomena in terms of the divine. (2014, p. 66)

Ancient Stoicism, in other words, was pantheistic.

A further characteristic of the transition to sagehood is its radical nature. That is because the ancient Stoics maintained that there is nothing between vice and virtue and that all bad deeds are equally unvirtuous. One way to explain this is summarized by Brouwer in this fashion: "According to Chrysippus in his fourth book *Ethical Questions* [see Diogenes Laertius 7.120, SVF 3.356], just as it does not matter whether the pilgrim is a hundred or a few miles away from Canopus [a sanctuary in the Nile delta which flourished in the third century BCE], as they are both not in Canopus, so it does not matter whether one makes a big or a small mistake: in either case, one is not virtuous" (2014, p. 70). Well, yes, technically, but really, the only charitable interpretation we can give of this, and the only reason we may entertain retaining this notion in modern Stoicism, is as a call for humility, along the Christian lines of "we are all sinners." If taken literally, the analogy has very little force. Obviously, lying to someone to avoid spending time with them is not as bad as killing them to avoid spending time with them. Though they are, indeed, both unvirtuous acts.

What about logic and knowledge? As we have seen, the transition to sagehood also means that the sage no longer holds to mere opinions; he actually has knowledge based on stable cognition. But even this is open to dispute, as Brouwer reminds us of the famous (and actually useful, I think) analogy of the hand: "Zeno is said to have compared the open palm of his hand with an impression, the fingers of his hand a bit contracted with assent to the impression, his fingers made into a fist with a cognition and the tight and forceful gripping of his other hand over the fist with knowledge" (2014, p. 71). It's a "handy" (literally!) reminder, worth spelling out in sequence:

Open palm = Impression
Contracted fingers = Assent to the impression
Fist = cognition (which, however, may be unstable, if one is not a sage)
Other hand over fist = knowledge (i.e., stable cognition, typical only of the sage)

And there is yet another weird thing about the Stoic sage: he may be unaware of actually having achieved sagehood! Philo of Alexandria writes:

> They [the Stoics] say that it is impossible that those people who have reached the highest wisdom and touched upon its borders for the first time, know their own perfection; for the two things do not happen at the same time, namely the arrival at the border and the cognition of arrival; in between the two there is ignorance of such a sort that is not far removed from knowledge, but close to it and on its doorstep. (SVF 3.541)

Brouwer elaborates: "wisdom consists in the special disposition of character. As this disposition is the (only) condition for wisdom, the virtuous (or expert) disposition of the Sage need not be accompanied by the awareness of the fact that it is a virtuous disposition" (2014, p. 84). This sounds to me rather odd, but I do wonder whether a Buddhist practitioner knows he has achieved enlightenment at the very moment he has, or whether a Christian mystic is aware of a state of divine bliss as it begins. Perhaps, again, the difference lies in whether the transition is triggered externally or is the result of an internal change? Be that as it may, Spock does not seem to be aware of being a sage, even later on in his life. Of course this could be either because he isn't one yet or because the sage really doesn't realize that he has achieved sagehood – at least not immediately.

The Stoics tried to explain this odd situation by way of an analogy. Let's say you have been practicing for a long time a particular craft, for instance, playing the flute. It is possible that you achieve "perfection" (whatever that means) at that craft without – again, initially – realizing it. Does it matter? No, because the earliest known characterization of wisdom, which goes back to Homer, implies that it is the mastery that counts, not the awareness of it.

Despite all the problematic aspects of the transition to sagehood outlined so far, Brouwer concludes that in a very important sense (and contra both Plutarch and Sextus Empiricus), the sage remains a human being: "the sage is in a way ordinary, in the sense that he remains doing what he did before, that is judging each impression and placing it in the overall scheme of things. As it turns out, Stoic wisdom is very much a this-worldly affair: the person who becomes a sage, will continue to live life as he did before, dealing with judging impressions" (2014, p. 86).

Becoming a sage is, in effect, a type of initiation. In the Great Etymological Dictionary edited in 1848 by T. Gaisford, and cited by Brouwer, we find:

> Chrysippus says that the doctrines [logoi] on divine things are rightly called initiations: for these should be the last things to be taught, when the soul has found its stability and has become in control, and is capable of keeping silent [amuetous] towards the uninitiated. For it is a great reward to hear the correct things about the gods and to gain control. (Brouwer 2014, p. 87)

Notice the reference to "keeping silent to the uninitiated," which sounds very much like it reflects some mystical approach to knowledge. Brouwer's comment is intriguing: "Chrysippus apparently considered it prudent that the real truth about the nature of the gods should be kept secret. Chrysippus does not tell us why, but a suggestion is that bringing out truths that reduce the traditional gods to a force in nature did not go down well with the traditional supporters of Athenian civic religion" (2014, p. 88). This is a tantalizing hint that the Stoics, while not atheists, were potentially considered "impious" by the standards of their culture. And we all know what happened to Socrates when that charge was raised against him: he was executed!

The next obvious question is: was there ever a sage? Did the ancient Stoics actually consider themselves sages? According to the nineteenth-century scholar S. Hirzel, Zeno and Cleanthes – the first and second head of the Stoa – did, but Chrysippus distanced himself from such claims and came to consider both his predecessors as very wise, but not quite sages. We shall see below that there is ample doubt that Hirzel got it right about Zeno and Cleanthes, but regarding specifically Chrysippus here is what Plutarch (remember, a critic of Stoicism) says:

> What is more, Chrysippus does not proclaim himself or any of his own acquaintances or teachers a sage. (On Stoic Contradictions, Stoicorum Veterum Fragmenta 3.662)

A lot of what we know about how the early Stoics thought of sagehood comes from Sextus Empiricus' *Against the Professors* (again, also hostile to Stoicism, and thus his pronouncements need to be taken with a grain or two of salt). Here is a taste:

> According to the Stoics themselves, Zeno and Cleanthes and Chrysippus and the others from their school are reckoned among the inferior persons [i.e., non-sages], and every inferior person is ruled by ignorance. ... Chrysippus either knew this dogma, being a Stoic one, I mean "The inferior person is ignorant of all things," or he did not know this. And if he knew it, then it is false that the inferior person is ignorant of everything; for Chrysippus, being an inferior person, knew this very thing — that the inferior person is ignorant of all things. (434)

The second part of this is a straightforward attempt at a logical "gotcha!" on the part of Sextus, but of course it is not wise to interpret the Stoics' "dogma" (a word used to mean philosophical tenet, or belief) in a literal sense. To say that we are all ignorant is something very akin to the Socratic idea that we are all unwise. It is more charitable, and useful, to treat it as a call to epistemic modesty. Diogenes of Babylon, a Stoic, says in fragment 32 that while gods (i.e., nature, the cosmos) are of such a nature that they necessarily exist, this does not apply to the nature of the sage. In a sense, then, the sage is a theoretical possibility, but does not have to be realized in any specific instance. Sextus confirms this, when he says: "up till now their sage has not been found" (SVF 3), all of which would seem to flatly contradict Hirzel's conclusions about Zeno and Cleanthes mentioned above, as they were based on guesswork and a psychological argument about how Zeno could most convincingly present his new philosophy to the public (as in "hey, come over here! I'm a sage!). Cicero (2014) too doubts the existence of the sage:

> It happens more often that a mule begets than that a sage comes into existence. (On Divination 2.61)

And he states the same opinion again while providing a description of the sage in his Tusculan Disputations:

> The man in whom there shall be perfect wisdom — whom until now we have not seen, but what he will be like, if he will come into existence one day, has been described in the doctrines of the philosophers — this person then or such reason that will be perfect and absolute in him. (2.51)

And here is Seneca (2014), also disputing the existence of sages:

> Yet I would not prescribe that you are to follow, or attach to yourself, no one but a sage. For where do you find him, whom we sought for so many centuries? Choose as the best the least bad. (On Tranquillity 7.4)

Then again, Seneca (2014) seems to hedge his bets a bit:

> There is no reason for you to say, Serenus, as your habit is, that this wise man of ours is nowhere to be found. He is not a fiction of us Stoics, a sort of phantom glory of human nature, nor is he a mere conception, the mighty semblance of a thing unreal, but we have shown him in the flesh just as we delineate him, and shall show him — though perchance not often, and after a long lapse of years only one. For greatness that transcends the limit of the ordinary and common type is produced but rarely. But this self-same Marcus Cato, the mention of whom started this discussion, I almost think surpasses even our exemplar. (On Constancy 7.1)

Marcus Cato is, of course, Cato the Younger, Seneca's favorite role model, whom he mentions frequently in his writings. There are other reports that seem to state that the sage is rare but real; take, for instance, this bit from the Aristotelian Alexander of Aphrodisias:

> There have been just one or two good men, as is fabulously related by them, like some absurd and unnatural creature rarer than the Ethiopians' phoenix. (SVF 3.658)

Seneca had also, previously, compared the frequency of the sage to that of the phoenix:

> For one of the first class [i.e., a sage] perhaps springs into existence, like the phoenix, only once in five hundred years. (Letter 42.1)

Socrates and Diogenes the Cynic are often held up as sages, but there is no straightforward evidence that the Stoics themselves thought so. For instance, Diogenes Laertius writes rather ambiguously:

> Posidonius in his first book *On Ethics* says that evidence for virtue existing is the fact that (those around?) Socrates, Diogenes and Antisthenes got to a state of progress. (Lives 7.91)

The fact that those "around" Socrates, Diogenes, and Antisthenes made progress doesn't mean that these three were actually sages. There is, however, evidence that the Stoics identified some mythological characters with the sage (and notice, again, the reference to Cato):

> The immortal gods had given us in Cato a more assured example of the wise man than Odysseus and Hercules in earlier centuries. For we Stoics have proclaimed that these were wise men, not being conquered by effort, despising pleasure, and victorious over the whole world. (Seneca, On Constancy 2.1)

As far as Spock is concerned, though Vulcans abound in the Federation, his unique blend of practical philosophy (he is, after all, a Vulcan-human hybrid! would certainly make him about as rare as the phoenix).

We also need to consider the relation between sagehood and truth. The Stoics, subtle logicians and dialecticians that they were, made an interesting distinction according to Brouwer: "The Stoics said that truth belonged to the sage exclusively, whereas the true can belong to the sage and the inferior person alike" (2014, p. 113). This is interesting because it says that we mere mortals can aspire to discovering true things, even though only the perfectly wise person has unshakable knowledge. The rest of us will have to be content with propositions that we believe are true but may need to be revised. I'll take it! Brouwer summarizes the idea in this way:

> [T]he Stoics distinguished sharply between cognitions, on the one hand, and stable cognitions or knowledge, on the other. Just as an inferior person can at times say something true, he can at times have a cognition. Just as an inferior person has no truth, he has no stable cognitions. (2014, p. 113)

Here is another passage that further elucidates early Stoic thought, this time by Quintilian, in his Institutions:

> I will respond to those who ask if they [Cicero and Demosthenes] were orators, in the manner in which the Stoics would reply, if asked whether Zeno, Cleanthes and Chrysippus themselves were sages. I shall say that these men were important and worthy of our veneration, but that they did not achieve what is the highest in the nature of man. For did not Pythagoras desire that he should not be called a wise man, like the sages who preceded him, but rather a lover of wisdom (studiosum sapientiae)? (SVF 1.44)

This, incidentally, is one of the early references to the very definition of a philosopher as lover of wisdom, or *studiosum sapientiae* in Latin. And here is an Epicurean telling us that the Stoics didn't think of themselves as Sages:

> [The Stoics described] him [Zeno] as great, as the founder of their school, but not wise. (Philodemus, On the Stoics col. 14.19–22)

Note, incidentally, that Epicurus did consider himself a sage, so Philodemus here is making a dig at the Stoics for not having any sages in their ranks. Finally, the next quote is one of my favorite stories in Stoic lore, and it comes to us from Diogenes Laertius:

> One day a conversation took place on whether the wise man would hold opinions, and Sphaerus said that he would not. Wishing to refute him, the king ordered wax pomegranates to be placed before him. Sphaerus was deceived and the king cried out that he had given his assent to a false impression. Sphaerus gave him a shrewd answer, saying that his assent was not [to the impression] that they were pomegranates but [to the impression] that it was reasonable that they were pomegranates. He pointed out that the cognitive impression is different from the reasonable one. (Lives 7.177)

This is both very shrewd, as Diogenes observes, and in fact an excellent explanation of the Stoic doctrine that there is a difference between reasonable judgments on impressions and truth. Again, the latter is obtained only by the (possibly mythological) sage. Sphaerus here has cognition, but not "stable" cognition, i.e., knowledge. Given that, then there is hope for the rest of us too.

Mr. Spock as *Prokoptôn*

In order to substantiate my argument that Spock should be seen as a *prokoptôn*, I need to make two interpretive moves concerning how to see the *Star Trek* character. I believe these moves are reasonable and do not force (too much of) a distorted reading of what Roddenberry and his writers meant. And of course, we have to allow for the obvious caveat that Spock is not a real person but a fictional construction that has itself been reinterpreted by different script writers and directors over decades. For instance, the famous moment in "Amok Time" when Spock had to pull back his joy at seeing that Kirk is still alive may be interpreted either as an instance of incoherence by the writers or as something that the young Spock, but not the more mature one, would do.

The two moves in question are (i) to interpret Spock's talk of "emotions" in the Stoic sense of referring to the *pathē* (the disruptive emotions, like hatred and anger), not the *eupatheiai* (the constructive emotions, like joy and love), and (ii) to interpret Spock's talk of "logic" in the broad Stoic sense of the study (and practice) of everything that has to do with improving one's reasoning, as opposed to the strict sense of formal logic. With these two moves firmly in the background, let us see how Spock himself holds out a practitioner of Stoicism.

To begin with, let me draw some direct parallels between Spock's behavior and standard Stoic concepts, as understood in the scholarly literature and in Stoic lore. Take the scene in "Charlie X," for example, when Kirk and Spock try to stop the superhuman Charlie from sexually assaulting Yeoman Rand and Charlie drops them to the ground with his superpowers. When Spock can't get up, he calmly reports why. "My legs. They're broken."

This scene is reminiscent of the story of young Epictetus, who was a slave in the town of Hierapolis (modern Pamukkale, Western Turkey). His master one day kept beating him hard on one leg, and Epictetus matter-of-factly told his tormentor that if he insisted with the beating, the leg would surely break. When it did break, Epictetus calmly said something along the lines of "I told you so." He remained lame for the rest of his life. The point of the anecdote is not to highlight Stoic invulnerability to pain, since there is no such thing. We can assume that both Epictetus and Spock did feel excruciating pain. The point, rather, is that Stoics strive to look at the world objectively and to abstain from value judgments (such as "my legs are broken, it's horrible!") while reminding themselves that the only truly bad thing that can happen to them is to exercise bad judgments.

Along similar lines, when Spock says "Insults are effective only where emotion is present," in "Who Mourns for Adonais?" he may as well being quoting Epictetus:

> Remember that it is we who torment, we who make difficulties for ourselves – that is, our opinions do. What, for instance, does it mean to be insulted? Stand by a rock and insult it, and what have you accomplished? If someone responds to insult like a rock, what has the abuser gained with his invective? (Discourses I, 25.28-29)

Marcus Aurelius was famously inspired – like other Stoics – by the Presocratic philosopher Heraclitus, who insisted that *panta rhei*, everything changes, which is why one cannot step into the same river twice (as he famously put it). Marcus often reminds himself of this principle in the *Meditations*, using it to put things, and his own life and struggles, into perspective:

> Is any man afraid of change? What can take place without change? What then is more pleasing or more suitable to the universal nature? And can you take a hot bath unless the wood for the fire undergoes a change? And can you be nourished unless the food undergoes a change? And can anything else that is useful be accomplished without change? Do you not see then that for yourself also to change is just the same, and equally necessary for the universal nature? (Meditations, VII.18)

In "Let That Be Your Last Battlefield," in response to Commissioner Bele's insistence that his prisoner Lokai cannot change because he belongs to "an inferior breed," Spock echoes the same sentiment. "Change is the essential process of all existence." Spock is well aware that he has adopted a whole philosophy of life, which requires an ethical commitment, just like Stoicism. As he puts it in "Journey to Babel," when explaining to his mother, Amanda Grayson about being a Vulcan, "It means to adopt a philosophy, a way of life, which is logical and beneficial. We cannot disregard that philosophy merely for personal gain, no matter how important that gain might be."

Notice that his philosophy is not just logical but also "beneficial." As David Hume famously remarked: "'Tis not contrary to reason to prefer the destruction of the whole world to the scratching of my finger" (Hume, 1739/40, book 2, part 3, section 3), meaning that reason, by itself, does not discriminate between those two events. What *does* make us prefer by far to scratch a finger to the destruction of the world is our (positive) emotional connection to fellow human beings, a necessary and acknowledged component of Stoic (and Vulcan) cosmopolitanism (Sellars 2007). Relatedly, Stoics (like their cousins, the Epicureans) put a lot of emphasis on friendship as a crucial human relationship. While the Stoic sage, according to Seneca, *can* live without friends, he does not choose to do that, if he can help it:

> If you consider any man a friend whom you do not trust as you trust yourself, you are mightily mistaken and you do not sufficiently understand what true friendship means. (Letters to Lucilius, III.2)

Spock displays a similar sentiment in *Star Trek IV: The Voyage Home*, where the now former crew of the *Enterprise* has to go back to Earth and face trial for their previous actions. At one point, Spock's father, Sarek, acknowledges his mistake in opposing Spock's wish to enlist in Starfleet when he was young:

Sarek   As I recall, I opposed your enlistment in Starfleet. It is possible that judgment was incorrect. Your associates are people of good character.

Spock   They are my friends.

In "Dagger of the Mind" the *Enterprise* visits a facility for the rehabilitation of the criminally insane, and Spock has an enlightening exchange with Doctor McCoy regarding the Stoic (and Vulcan) approach to emotions:

Spock   Interesting. You Earth people glorify organized violence for 40 centuries, but you imprison those who employ it privately.

McCoy   And, of course, your people found an answer.

Spock   We disposed of emotion, Doctor. Where there's no emotion, there's no motive for violence.

Here it seems to me that Spock is clearly referring not to "emotions" in general, but specifically to the *pathē*, the disruptive emotions that include fear, anger, and hatred, all things Spock truly is striving to control. But he also very clearly cultivates what the Stoic called *eupatheiai*, the positive emotions, as in a famous example in *Star Trek II: The Wrath of Khan*. In the movie, the *Enterprise* encounters anew Kirk's archenemy, the genetically engineered tyrant Khan Noonien Singh. During an exchange with Kirk, Spock at the same time explains the logic of his philosophy and reminds the Captain of their bond of affection:

Spock   Were I to invoke logic, logic clearly dictates that the needs of the many outweigh the needs of the few.

Kirk   Or the one.

Spock   You are my superior officer. You are also my friend. I have been and always shall be yours. (*Star Trek II: The Wrath of Khan*)

3 *Star Trek* as Philosophy: Spock as Stoic Sage

In "Spock's Brain" the crew manages to save Spock's life at the last minute, by retrieving his thinking organ, which had been stolen by the alien Kara. Spock's comment to Kirk is revealing that he does experience positive feelings connected to their friendship: "Spock Captain, there is a definite pleasurable experience connected with the hearing of your voice."

Spock is also capable of sympathy, if not downright empathy. In "Where No Man has Gone Before," a crew member develops powerful psychic abilities as a result of an accident. He begins to use such abilities destructively and becomes a danger to the *Enterprise*. By the end of the episode, Kirk has to kill the man but enters a positive comment in his log on behalf of the crew member. When he explains this to Spock, the science officer's response is yet another indication that he is capable – and not ashamed – of positive emotions:

Kirk   He didn't ask for what happened to him.
Spock   I felt for him, too.
Kirk   I believe there's some hope for you after all, Mr. Spock.

Spock is also well aware of the pitfalls of giving oneself to (negative) emotional responses. In "Plato's Stepchildren," the crew encounters a race of sadistic immortals endowed with telekinetic powers, who like to play with human emotional responses. Predictably, Doctor McCoy strikes one in defense of emotions, but without making a distinction between positive and negative ones. Our favorite Vulcan sarcastically reminds him of the consequences of that unqualified endorsement:

McCoy   The release of emotions, Mr. Spock, is what keeps us healthy – emotionally healthy, that is.
Spock   That may be, Doctor. However, I have noted that the healthy release of emotion is frequently very unhealthy for those closest to you.

This sentiment could have been lifted from Seneca when he talks about anger:

> No plague has cost the human race more dear: you will see slaughterings and poisonings, accusations and counter-accusations, sacking of cities, ruin of whole peoples, the persons of princes sold into slavery by auction, torches applied to roofs, and fires not merely confined within city-walls but making whole tracts of country glow with hostile flame. (*On Anger*, I.2)

And Spock (and, in this case, his father) clearly has a sense of humor. In "Journey to Babel," the *Enterprise* is transporting dignitaries to a diplomatic conference. At one point Amanda Grayson, Spock's mother, attempts a mediation between Sarek – Spock's father – and his son, who have often been at odds in the past, by taking advantage of the fact that Spock has just saved Sarek's life by way of a blood transfusion:

AG	And you, Sarek. Would you also say thank you to your son?
Sarek	I don't understand.
AG	For saving your life.
Sarek	Spock acted in the only logical manner open to him. One does not thank logic, Amanda.
AG	Logic! Logic! I am sick to death of logic! Do you want to know how I feel about your logic?!
Spock	Emotional, isn't she?
Sarek	She has always been that way.
Spock	Indeed? Why did you marry her?
Sarek	At the time, it seemed the logical thing to do. [She smiles, realizing they're teasing her]

Interestingly, in the above dialogue, Sarek and Spock aren't just teasing Amanda, but pretty clearly implying that *of course* Vulcan life and philosophy is not limited to logic, but very much encompasses love. Indeed, Spock's sense of humor can border on subtle sarcasm. Near the end of *Star Trek VI: The Undiscovered Country*, after the crew has preempted an attempt on the life of the President of the United Federation of Planets:

| Commander Nyota Uhura | Captain, I have orders from Starfleet Command. We're to put back to Spacedock immediately... to be decommissioned. *[long pause as Kirk contemplates the order]* |
| Spock | If I were human, I believe my response would be "go to Hell." *[Kirk looks at Spock; to Kirk]* If I were human. |

This is just how Epictetus engages in downright funny pronouncements to make his point, as we saw above in my quote from Discourses I.1.32. When the *Enterprise* encounters the entity known as V'Ger, in *Star Trek: The Motion Picture*, Spock correctly diagnoses its biggest limitation, from which he does not appear to suffer, again confirming that he does have (positive) emotions: "This simple feeling, is beyond V'Ger's comprehension."

And when Captain Kirk remarks, in "The Menagerie" (TOS), that "A Vulcan can no sooner be disloyal than he can exist without breathing," he is referring to what can be characterized as a positive emotion embedded into Vulcan character by way of cognitive reflection and mindful practice, which is more or less the way the Stoics described the process of virtue becoming second nature by practice. This, in turn, is the goal of the entire discipline of assent articulated by Epictetus (Hadot 1998, Chap. 6).

In "The Immunity Syndrome" (TOS), Spock makes a very important point to his sparring partner Dr. McCoy, who is always praising human empathy and sneering at "cold logic":

> I've noticed that about your people, Doctor. You find it easier to understand the death of one than the death of a million. You speak about the objective hardness of the Vulcan heart, yet how little room there seems to be in yours.

Similarly, the Stoics made a distinction between what we today refer to as sympathy and empathy, emphasizing the former over the latter, precisely on the ground that too much emotional involvement clouds one's judgment, even about ethical matters. Sympathy is an emotion, but has a significant cognitive component, whereby one is able to "understand" (as much as such a thing is possible) the death of a million. Modern psychologist Paul Bloom (2016) has produced empirical research backing up the Stoic (and Vulcan) insight, and Jesse Prinz (2011) has added modern philosophical arguments to the same effect.

Spock even has a sense of aesthetic, which again is psychologically rooted in emotions and is not something "purely" logical (whatever that means). In "Catspaw," when the landing party is greeted by their alien captors with what appears to be floating witches spouting rhymes:

Kirk   Spock, comment.
Spock   Very bad poetry, Captain.
Kirk   A more useful comment, Mr. Spock.

In fact, Spock refers to both meaning and beauty in "Is There in Truth No Beauty?," an episode featuring an alien ambassador whose appearance induces madness (appropriately, from a species called Medusans).

Dr. Miranda Jones   The glory of creation is in its infinite diversity.
Spock   And the way our differences combine to create meaning and beauty.

That sort of comment would fit well with the Stoic concept of an orderly cosmos permeated by a logos, a rational principle that is responsible for beauty and from which we derive meaning.

And, surprisingly given his reputation, Spock even admits to being (emotionally, one presumes) disturbed by certain kinds of beauty. In "The Cloud Minders," one of the key characters is Droxine, who is attracted to Spock ("I have never met a Vulcan, sir"), who seems to reciprocate the interest to the point of chivalry ("Nor I a work of art, madam"). Indeed, Spock openly acknowledges his turmoil: "Extreme feminine beauty... is always... disturbing."

As for the concept of logic, again a careful reading of what Spock actually says is compatible with the Stoic understanding of the term, meant to encompass not just the narrow study of the soundness and validity of arguments but more broadly all aspects of sound reasoning. In "The Galileo Seven," Spock finds himself in dire straits with some of his companions, quickly running out of options before their shuttlecraft crashes on a planet. He decides to jettison fuel and ignite it, hoping that the burst would be seen from the *Enterprise*, which would then come to the rescue. That's exactly what happens, of course, and Kirk interprets the decision as an "act of desperation" and an "emotional outburst." However, Spock explains that – having being left with no viable options – the *reasonable* thing to do was to take that particular course of action, despite the fact that the odds against it succeeding were vanishingly small. A computer deploying straightforward analytic logic may not have done the same, thus condemning itself to a quick end.

Finally, as we have seen earlier, Spock – at a later stage in his career – makes it explicit that logic is only part of what he is after, and in doing so he sounds very much like a Stoic. In *Star Trek VI: The Undiscovered Country*, the situation is dire as conspirators are attempting to undermine the sudden decision of the Klingon Empire to sue for peace with their long-time enemy, the Federation. Spock has a revealing conversation with the young Vulcan Valeris, who obviously looks up to him as a role model (another crucial Stoic concept!). When Spock says that sometimes one needs to "have faith" about the unfolding of things in the universe, Valeris is taken aback by such an odd comment for a Vulcan, but Spock explains: "Logic, logic, logic. Logic is the beginning of wisdom, Valeris, not the end."

Conclusion: So, Is Spock a Stoic, and Should *We* Be?

The preceding analysis comes, as mentioned earlier, with a fairly large and obvious caveat: Spock is a fictional character, one that has been authored by different writers and that has had at least two major incarnations. So to expect "him" to exhibit a completely coherent philosophy of life and moreover one that is consistent across more than half a century of "existence" would be preposterous. Then again, not many actual people adopt coherent philosophies or maintain the same philosophy for their entire life either.

That said, my argument has been that, contra even popular understanding among modern Stoic practitioners, Spock is indeed a *prokoptôn*, i.e., someone who espouses a Stoic-like philosophy and makes progress in the understanding of its theory and, especially, the application of its practice. Indeed, particularly later in life (meaning, in the most recent movies based on *The Original Series*), Spock can be said to approach the status of a Stoic sage, as we have seen the concept being articulated above. Specifically (i) he often arrives at correct judgments about the best course of action to take, nearing the epistemic limits of what a human (or Vulcan-human) can be expected to do (remember that sages are not superhuman, infallible individuals); (ii) he has good mastering of his negative "passions" (he does not yield to anger, fear, and other negative emotions); (iii) he actively cultivates positive "emotions," including love (of friends, but also of humanity at large), a sense of justice and duty, and joy at being with friends and striving to do the right thing (including a sense of awe for the beauty of the universe and the creatures contained in it); and finally, (iv) he adopts an explicitly cosmopolitan (in his case, literally, as in encompassing the whole cosmos) attitude that leads him to strive for peace and prosperity not just of his own people, but of all races of sentient beings.

The more important question, of course, is whether we find *Star Trek*'s implicit argument for Stoicism, as I've tried to present it, compelling. Certainly Stoic philosophy is not to everyone's liking, and I can't imagine Dr. McCoy, or even,

3 *Star Trek* as Philosophy: Spock as Stoic Sage

for that matter, Captain Kirk, going for it. And yet there is a reason why the character of Mr. Spock is so attractive to so many, arguably making him not only the most popular character in *Star Trek* but a recognizable icon in the culture at large.

Once stripped of the cartoonish "only logic-no emotion" caricature, Spock becomes someone who is compassionate toward other sentient beings; who has a deep sense of duty, honor, and loyalty toward his friends and the causes he endorses; and who attempts to use empirical facts and sound reasoning to tackle problems. It is hard to say what one could possibly object to in such a model. True, Spock does not indulge what has been referred to as the "Dionysian" aspect of human nature – the very reason why Nietzsche, though admiring the Stoics, ultimately rejected their philosophy. But it is not at all clear why engaging in highly emotional behaviors, which can easily lead to either self- or other destruction, should be such an obvious positive. At the very least, it ought to be questioned, in the way the Stoics themselves did.

We often hear that we should go "beyond reason" in making our judgments, and yet the people making such pseudo-profound pronouncements seem to be at a loss to explain what, exactly, that means, or what positive track record such an attitude has in terms of personal happiness or progress for humanity. Being a critic of reason is trendy among philosophers and other intellectuals these days, as if somehow we lived in a world plagued by the strange problem of being too reasonable. (For more on this, and for a modern broad treatment of what it means to be reasonable, see Baggini 2016.) Not to mention that such critics use reason to make their anti-reason *argument* in the first place! This reminds me of an exchange Epictetus had with one of his students:

> When one of his audience said, "Convince me that logic is useful," he said, Would you have me demonstrate it? "Yes." Well, then, must I not use a demonstrative argument? And, when the other agreed, he said, How then shall you know if I impose upon you? And when the man had no answer, he said, You see how you yourself admit that logic is necessary, if without it you are not even able to learn this much — whether it is necessary or not. (Discourses II, 25)

Sounds like something that Spock would have told McCoy, with an amused Kirk smiling in the background.

References

Baggini, J. 2016. *The edge of reason: A rational skeptic in an irrational world.* Yale, CT: Yale University Press.

Becker, L. 2017. *A new stoicism.* Princeton, NJ: Princeton University Press.

Bloom, P. 2016. *Against empathy: The case for rational compassion.* New York, NY: Ecco.

Brouwer, R. 2014. *The stoic Sage: The early stoics on wisdom, sagehood and socrates,* Cambridge classical studies. Cambridge, UK: Cambridge University Press.

Cicero. 2014. *Delphi complete works of Cicero,* Delphi ancient Classics. Vol. 23. East Essex, UK: Delphin Classics.

Dahlsgaard, K., C. Peterson, and M.E.P. Seligman. 2005. Shared virtue: The convergence of valued human strengths across culture and history. *Review of General Psychology* 9 (3): 203–213.

de Waal, F., S. Macedo, and J. Ober. 2009. *Primates and philosophers: How morality evolved.* Princeton, NJ: Princeton University Press.

Diogenes Laertius. 2015. *Delphi complete works of diogenes laertius,* Delphi ancient classics. Vol. 47. East Essex, UK: Delphin Classics.

Epictetus. 2014. *Discourses, fragments, handbook.* Oxford World Classics. (Trans: Hard, R.). Cambridge, UK: Oxford University Press.

Farren, J. (2014) Stoicism and star trek. In: P. Ussher (9ed.) Stoicism today: Selected writings, Volume 1, pp. 196–200. London, UK.

Fretts, Bruce, and Matt Roush. 2013. The greatest shows on earth. *TV Guide Magazine* 61 (3194–3195): 16–19.

Graver, M. 2007. *Stoicism and emotion.* Chicago, IL: University of Chicago Press.

Hadot, P. 1998. *The inner citadel: The meditations of Marcus Aurelius.* Cambridge, MA: Harvard University Press.

Hume, D. 1739. *A treatise of human nature.* Online at https://davidhume.org/texts/t/3/. Accessed 4 June 2019.

Inwood, B., ed. 2003. *The Cambridge companion to the stoics.* Cambridge, UK: Cambridge University Press.

Irvine, W. 2019. *The stoic challenge: A philosopher's guide to becoming tougher, calmer, and more resilient.* New York, NY: W.W. Norton & Company.

Laland, K. 2018. *Darwin's unfinished symphony: How culture made the human mind.* Princeton, NJ: Princeton University Press.

Letters of Note. 2012. *Getting Star Trek on the air was impossible.* June 25. Online at http://www.lettersofnote.com/2012/06/getting-star-trek-on-air-was-impossible.html. Accessed on 23 Apr 2019.

Pigliucci, M. 2017. *How to be a stoic: Using ancient philosophy to live a modern life.* New York, NY: BasicBooks.

———. 2019. Stoicism. Internet Encyclopedia of Philosophy. Online at https://www.iep.utm.edu/stoicism/. Accessed 25 Apr 2019.

Plutarch. 2013. *Delphi complete works of Plutarch,* Delphi ancient classics. Vol. 13. East Essex, UK: Delphin Classics.

Prinz, J. 2011. Against empathy. *The Southern Journal of Philosophy* 49 (1): 214–233.

Robertson, D. 2019. *How to think like a roman emperor: The stoic philosophy of Marcus Aurelius.* London, UK: St. Martin's Press.

Sellars, J. 2007. Stoic cosmopolitanism and Zeno's Republic. *History of Political Thought* XXVIII (1): 1–29. Abingdon-on-Thames, UK.

———., ed. 2016. *The Routledge handbook of the stoic tradition.* Routledge.

Seneca, L.A. 2014. *Hardship and happiness.* (Trans: Fantham, E., H.M. Hine, J. Ker, and G.D. Williams). Chicago, IL: University of Chicago Press.

———. 2017. *Letters on ethics: To Lucilius.* (Trans: Graver, M.). Chicago, IL: University of Chicago Press.

Waterfield, R. 2009. *The first philosophers: The presocratics and sophists,* Oxford world's classics. Oxford, UK: Oxford University Press.

Star Trek: The Next Generation as Philosophy: Gene Roddenberry's Argument for Humanism

4

Kevin S. Decker

Contents

Introduction 66
Humanism in Theory 67
    How Not to Characterize Humanism 67
    Do We Need Religion? A Purpose? 69
    Science or Faith? 70
    Questions of Ethics 72
Roddenberry, Secular Humanism, and Agonism 74
Humanism, Virtue, and Character 79
Humanism and Religion 81
Humanism and Social Ethics 86
Conclusion 89
References 91

Abstract

Star Trek: The Next Generation (*TNG*, 1987–1994) is a very close second to *Star Trek* (TOS, 1966–1969) in the hearts and minds of fans of televised science fiction. Although both series are examples of space opera that focus on the exploration of the cosmos by a group of Starfleet officers and their crew, TNG is notably different in execution. It explores the interests and backgrounds of its ensemble cast more thoroughly, for example. It also entertains inter-season story arcs and fleshes out the cultural background and politics of alien races (both new and old) in a much more grandiose way.

In many ways, *The Next Generation* is also a more robust example of *Star Trek* creator Gene Roddenberry's humanistic vision of the future than its progenitor. Ironically, this is partly because he had less personal creative control on TNG.

K. S. Decker (✉)
Eastern Washington University, Cheney, WA, USA
e-mail: kdecker@ewu.edu

© Springer Nature Switzerland AG 2024
D. K. Johnson et al. (eds.), *The Palgrave Handbook of Popular Culture as Philosophy*,
https://doi.org/10.1007/978-3-031-24685-2_3

This chapter will explore the various historical faces worn by humanists through history as well as Roddenberry's distinctive contribution to that history. To humanize the philosophy of humanism in TNG, the chapter will look at the philosophical implications of the series-spanning antagonism and verbal sparring between Captain Jean-Luc Picard and the powerful, arrogant entity Q. It will then demonstrate, through a detailed look at representative TNG episodes, the arguments that support the credibility and value of humanism against other competing worldviews in the areas of virtue and character, religious belief, and social ethics.

Keywords

Humanism · Secular humanism · Christian humanism · Agonism · Religion · Christianity · Theism · Atheism · Virtue · Ethics · Morality

Introduction

> ...[S]ecular humanism is only secondarily secular; it is primarily humane.
> —Philip Kitcher (Life After Faith)

> Men may keep busy in a variety of ways, making money, acquiring facility in laboratory manipulation, or in amassing a store of facts about linguistic matters, or the chronology of literary productions. Unless such activity reacts to enlarge the imaginative vision of life, it is on the level with the busy work of children. It has the letter without the spirit of activity.
> —John Dewey (*Democracy and Education*)

> So far you reach the rank of deity/As you accept your own humanity.
> —Montaigne ("On Experience")

Star Trek – The Next Generation (*TNG*, 1987–1994) is a very close second to *Star Trek* (TOS, 1966–1969) in the hearts and minds of fans of televised science fiction. Although both series are examples of space opera that focus on the exploration of the cosmos by a group of Starfleet officers and their crew, TNG is notably different in execution. It explores the interests and backgrounds of its ensemble cast more thoroughly, for example. It also entertains inter-season story arcs and fleshes out the cultural background and politics of alien races (both new and old) in a much more grandiose way.

In many ways, *The Next Generation* is also a more robust example of *Star Trek* creator Gene Roddenberry's humanistic vision of the future than its progenitor. Ironically, this is partly because he had less personal creative control over TNG; the executive producers and writing staff made TNG the vehicle for humanist ideas that it became. This chapter will explore the various historical faces worn by humanists through history as well as Roddenberry's distinctive contribution to that history. To humanize the philosophy of humanism in TNG, this chapter will examine the personal influence of Roddenberry's life and values on both TOS and TNG. It will look at the philosophical implications of the series-spanning antagonism and verbal sparring between Captain Jean-Luc Picard and the powerful, arrogant entity Q. It will then demonstrate, through a detailed look at representative TNG episodes,

4 *Star Trek: The Next Generation* as Philosophy: Gene Roddenberry's Argument...

the arguments that support the credibility and value of humanism as against other competing worldviews in the areas of virtue and character, religious belief, and social ethics.

Humanism in Theory

How Not to Characterize Humanism

Humanists tell stories about humanity that they hope other humans will find inspiring and empowering. Some humanists think these stories are based in explanations of human nature; others see them only as interpretations of plastic and fluid characteristics determined by conditions of associated human life. In other cases, they offer cautionary tales of universal human vices, like greed and *hubris*. If Rod Serling's *The Twilight Zone* demonstrates the latter, then *Star Trek: The Next Generation*, a distinct and lasting contribution by Gene Roddenberry to science fiction, exemplifies the optimistic and inspirational type of stories. The contemporary cultural movement of secular humanism shares with these television series the power of human imagination harnessed to a vision of what the good life for human beings might be.

"Humanism," Corliss Lamont writes,

> believes in a naturalistic metaphysics or attitude toward the universe that considers all forms of the supernatural as myth; and that regards Nature as the totality of being and as a constantly changing system of matter and energy which exists independently of any mind or consciousness. (Lamont 1990)

It is the position of humankind in this naturalistic matrix that is most debated: does the dissolution of the apparent difference between humanity – with its rationality, art, and culture – and the rest of nature reduce human efforts to a series of statistical averages? Or does our recognition that we can rise beyond being determined by our mythologies in some way elevate the human condition?

These questions have led to significant misunderstandings of humanism, two of which I will consider before looking more closely at the nature of humanist beliefs in the next subsection. To striking and critical effect, the post-structuralist Michel Foucault makes such a mistaken claim when he writes,

> One thing is most certain in any case: man is neither the oldest nor the most constant problem that has been posed for human knowledge. Taking a relatively short chronological sample within a restricted geographical area—European culture since the sixteenth century—one can be certain that man is a recent invention within it. (Foucault, in Norman 2015)

Insofar as humanists claim to base their views on universal traits of a supposed "human nature," Foucault says, they overlook the fact that these traits are historically conditioned and culturally dependent: there is a "dislocation between 'humanism' and 'humanity' that guarantees anti-Enlightenment scholars a limitless field of opportunities for critique...." (Relke 2006). Foucault's criticism that humanism is unaware of its own contingent place in a context set by the European Enlightenment is analogous to the Klingon Azetbur's accusation, in *Star Trek VI: The Undiscovered Country*, that the very idea of "inalienable human rights" is "racist," the Federation being "little better than a *homo sapiens*-only club."

Making a different point within the same framework of thinking, skeptic and materialist George Santayana expressed distaste for the term "humanism," saying that it:

> ...has this moral defect in my opinion, that it seems to make all mankind an authority and a compulsory object of affection for every individual. I see no reason for that. The limits of the society that we find congenial and desirable is determined by our condition, not by the extent of it in this world. (Santayana, in Lamont 1990)

Both these views mischaracterize what humanism is. Foucault ignores the degree to which humanists self-consciously embrace the historicity of their creed. Although cultural resources for later humanists existed in the Greek and Roman civilization, there was no self-conscious movement of humanism before the Italian Renaissance. Charles Nauert has argued that we can trace the beginnings of this movement to two Renaissance luminaries: first, to Petrarch's (1304–1374) idea of historical disconti-nuity and his privileging of classical Greek and Roman achievement over cultural conditions of the Middle Ages. Second, we can isolate the basic principle of Lorenzo Valla's (1407–1457) textual hermeneutics, the idea that "human language, like everything else outside of the material world, is a cultural artifact, so that language undergoes historical development and changes with the passage of time" (Nauert 2006). Both these ideas still underwrite the normative "master idea" of humanism: that because "man is a recent invention," the human condition is plastic and can be improved.

Santayana's criticism misses the fact that humanism is not a philosophical theory, but an interpretive meta-perspective that can be levelled at theories from a diverse number of fields, including political science, anthropology, theology, and philoso-phy. For the same reason that self-consciously historicized humanists are suspicious of a "foundation" for human nature, they also eschew foundationalism in arguing for humanism. Christian humanists such as Desiderius Erasmus were, against the background of the Protestant Reformation, "seekers of concord, promoters of plu-ralism, believers in the Bible as a fallible document open to multiple interpretations, and advocates of the view that man is a fully autonomous moral agent" (Massing 2018). Humanists like David Hume and William James assert that efforts to expunge the human element from human study of the natural and physical sciences is bound, by definition, to fail. Both also offered early warnings about scientism, the view that there is no realm of human life in which scientific methods and concepts do not belong. The humanistic pathos of Charles Darwin hesitated to address in print how his theory of natural selection impacted our understanding of the human animal for fear of what it would do to our self-image. And the humanistic stories of those who never created theories whatsoever, like Virginia Woolf and her *To the Lighthouse*, speak to "...the continuity between life and death and the significance which a person's life can have after they are dead" (Norman 2015). For if there is a

4 *Star Trek: The Next Generation* as Philosophy: Gene Roddenberry's Argument... 69

basic claim that all humanist stories share, it is that the obstacles and resources, the stability and the precariousness upon which visions of the good life for humans depend, are wholly in "this world," in its past, present, and future possibilities.

The values of the good life that fall out of their stories are eminently *Star Trek* values: freedom, risk, self-actualization, and pluralism. In the TNG episode "Ethics," we even have a response from Captain Picard in the face of Azetbur's claim from *Star Trek VI* about Starfleet respecting only human values. Lt. Worf, the only Klingon aboard the *Enterprise*, has been severely injured in a cargo bay mishap, and Riker and Picard are weighing human, Klingon, and humanistic values in responding to Worf's request for assisted euthanasia:

Riker   Worf isn't dying and he is not in pain. He could live a long life.
Picard   You or I could learn to live with that disability, but not Worf. His life ended when those containers fell on him. We don't have to agree with it, we don't have to understand it, but we do have to respect his beliefs.
Riker   I can respect his beliefs, but he is asking me to take an active role in his committing suicide.
Picard   He's asking for your help because you're his friend. That means that you're going to have to make your decision based on that friendship.

While humanism is not a philosophical theory itself, this is not to deny that its force rests on a number of such theories. Now in its eighth edition, Corliss Lamont's *The Philosophy of Humanism* continues to be an excellent synthesis of the origins and central meanings of humanism. Lamont explains how a diverse set of cultural contexts and scientific attitudes underlie humanistic philosophy. These include Renaissance humanism, the history of the sciences and scientific method, democracy and civil liberties, the philosophies of naturalism and materialism, ethical thought from different religions and philosophies, themes from literature and the arts, and finally, the Freethought, Rationalist, and Ethical Culture movements (Lamont 1990).

In the rest of this section, I want to use Lamont's "ten central propositions" of humanism to explain and enlarge upon the movement's meaning and the structure of the rest of this chapter. Note that I am proposing these ten as a structure for discussing the value of humanism, not offering them as a checklist of beliefs.

Do We Need Religion? A Purpose?

Who, in the future, is a humanist? One might say that the *Enterprise* bridge crew in TNG – with the possible except of the Klingon, Lt. Worf – are either atheists (those who say they have good reasons to believe no god(s) exist) or agnostics (those who say they have equally good reasons for and against the existence of god(s)). More accurately, however, the average Starfleet officer of the twenty-fourth century has a stance toward religious belief that we do not have a word for – although perhaps "apathetic (about religion)" will serve. Supernatural issues, except when they bear on a mission, simply *do not matter* to them; they are a nonissue in the same way that, for twenty-first century Christians, the question "Was a whole pantheon of gods birthed from Zeus' head or was it just Athena?" is a nonissue.

Yet humanists are also accused of antagonism toward religious belief. With the introduction of fan favorite villain and omnipotent alien entity Q in the series premiere, "Encounter at Farpoint," Roddenberry clearly wanted to underscore an old lesson from TOS: space explorers might become acquainted with life-forms that, although are exquisitely powerful, lack common wisdom. These creatures do not inspire worship; instead, they invite critique. This attitude, which also showcases Roddenberry's deep commitment to human development through struggle (discussed in detail in the next section), foregrounds an atheistic humanist view that is often lost in philosophical discussions of theism. It is not *just* that the theist and the atheist take opposing views on the proposition of the existence of god(s); the atheistic humanist also considers the religious believer – and especially institution-alized religion – to be part of an intricate and deceitful *fabrication*. Its leadership gains power, money, and adoration by lying to people. Their efforts are instances of, as Picard puts it in the episode "Devil's Due," "the con game."

Lamont also offers two other relevant central propositions to making a secular life meaningful:

> Humanism believes that the individual attains the good life by harmoniously combining personal satisfactions and continuous self-development with significant work and other activities that contribute to the welfare of the community. . .. Humanism believes in a far-reaching social program that stands for the establishment throughout the world of democ-racy, peace, and a high standard of living on the foundations of a flourishing economic order, both national and international. (Lamont 1990)

The future United Federation of Planets, as we see consistently in TNG, has made significant and lasting progress toward implementing both these goals without a hint of religious fervor.

Science or Faith?

To a piece of fan mail questioning why the alien races of the Federation were almost universally humanoid in appearance, Roddenberry replied:

> We depict humanoid aliens because we (along with Cal Tech studies and others) do believe that parallel evolution is a distinct possibility. Natural laws govern life development just as other natural laws govern time, space and atoms. There are no "accidents" in nature, probably not even in social development. Every effect has a cause. It is our misfortune on Earth today that our understanding of cause and effect in life and social evolution is almost nil. (Alexander 1994)

Of course, the bottom line regarding humanoid aliens was production cost; but it was important to Roddenberry that the rational *Star Trek* future be represented as one in which knowledge of "cause and effect in life and social evolution" was

4 Star Trek: The Next Generation as Philosophy: Gene Roddenberry's Argument...

sufficiently advanced beyond ours. Just as the suggestion that there might be apodictic laws of social development might raise philosophical hackles, a further three of Lamont's central propositions about human nature and human agency seem to conflict with each other and deserve some attention if their apparent tension is to be resolved. Lamont writes:

> Humanism, drawing especially upon the laws and facts of science, believes that man is an evolutionary product of the Nature of which he is a part; that his mind is indivisibly conjoined with the functioning of his brain; and that as an inseparable unity of body and personality he can have no conscious survival after death.
>
> Humanism, having its ultimate faith in man, believes that human beings possess the power or potentiality of solving their own problems, through reliance primarily upon reason and scientific method applied with courage and vision.
>
> Humanism, in opposition to all theories of universal determinism, fatalism, or predestination, believes that human beings, while conditioned by the past, possess genuine freedom of creative choice and action, and are, within certain objective limits, the masters of their own destiny. (Lamont 1990)

These humanistic propositions are the heart of the dynamic narrative of *Star Trek*. But like Roddenberry's fan mail response, they raise the issue of how humanists can consistently argue for the human condition being "an evolutionary product of...Nature" while at the same time affirming "genuine freedom of creative choice and action"? That is a question that would take many encyclopedias the size of this one to answer, but evolutionary psychology and evolutionary cognitive science have made great strides in the last half-century in creating problem-solving models and even accounts of the origins of freedom of choice and action – such as they are – that pass the naturalistic test of evidential support and predictive power (two accessible, but not uncontroversial accounts can be found in Pinker 1997 and Dennett 2003).

Humanism opposes, however, an effort to reframe the issues of origins, of the mind or soul, of human power and creative choice and action in terms of transcendent beings or powers. These substitute faith-based I.O.U.s for valid explanations. It cannot escape the attention of the informed religious believer, living in a culture informed by multiple religious traditions, that there are counter-narratives to her explanations for life's purpose and where the world came from that have just as much justification as their own. As Philip Kitcher, synthesizing 200 years of "careful investigation of religious traditions and their evolution," explains:

> The Christian *knows* that Christ was the son of God: but the Muslim who denies this and the Hindu who asserts the divinity of Vishnu are both deceived. How exactly is the difference to be explained? ....Muslims and Hindus may, with equal justice, contend that *their* favored scriptures are the media of enlightenment. No available pieces of everyday lore enable anyone to test the rival claims and thus adjudicate the dispute. (Kitcher 2014)

"Explanation" in terms of empirically transcendent beings or powers in these matters has always relied on methods of tradition, authority, hegemony, and when these fail, on force. Humanists find it surprising and perhaps depressing – as H.L. Mencken illustrated in his obituary for dead gods, "Memorial Service" – that Christians and Muslims typically are atheists with reference to *every other god but their own* (Mencken 2010).

Questions of Ethics

TNG distinguishes itself from other long-running science fiction television shows such as *Doctor Who* and *The X-Files* in that each of its episodes contain either compelling moral issues or potentially conflicting ethical visions of the good life, or both. Episodes such as "Justice" and "The Masterpiece Society" grapple with the intersection of theology, morality, and social organization. In the former, Picard grapples with an alien death sentence served on Wesley Crusher for a minor infraction, declaring, "There can be no justice so long as laws are absolute." In "The Masterpiece Society," the *Enterprise* comes to the aid of a colony of genetically engineered humans who are threatened by a stellar core fragment. Here, Picard sounds most like Kirk when he claims, "They've given away their humanity with this genetic manipulation. Many of the qualities that they breed out – the uncertainty, self-discovery, the unknown – these are many of the qualities that make life worth living. Well, at least to me. I wouldn't want to live my life knowing that my future was written, that my boundaries had been already set." The criticism is very much in the mode of Roddenberry's agonistic humanism.

Other episodes, like "Ethics" and "The Quality of Life," are provocative secular meditations on thorny moral issues that deserve multiple viewings. "Ethics," which as Lt. Worf consider euthanasia when facing the prospect of a life of disability, presents coherent and persuasive moral arguments about biomedical issues from utilitarian, deontological, virtue, and even relativist positions. In "The Quality of Life," mobile, adaptive computers are developed by a project lead on planet Tyrus VII and soon exceed their own programming, leading to a standoff between Data and Riker about whether artificial life-forms should be compelled to sacrifice their existence for the good of others. Indeed, there are few television series so well-suited to viewing in high school and college discussions of morality and ethics than TNG.

Humanists believe that being moral is about consistency, rationality, and recognizing the significance and even knowledge brought to our deliberations by our emotions. As Socrates in Plato's dialogue *Euthyphro* argues, rational morality need not rest on the authority of religion, and indeed, normative authority may be devalued by subjugating it to the will of a divinity. Humanists generally are not ethical skeptics; instead they believe that in practice, people have psychological resources to live a good life without divine commands. For them, morality is one part of the more general question of how to live a good life, and moral rules often need to be re-evaluated for how they fit into a particular ethical vision.

Aiding the search for answers to this question is the fact that there are shared human values grounded in human nature that overlap with religious commitments, such as the injunction "thou shalt not murder" and Jesus of Nazareth's preaching of equality among persons. However, humanists will typically reject moral injunctions that have nothing but a religious defense (as is often the case with contraception, abortion, and homosexuality, for example). Humanists see human rights (as they were defined by the Enlightenment) as essentials in the search for freedom and well-being; they must be guaranteed by sovereign powers. But the humanist's commitment to individual self-determination also reminds them that people are free to choose *not* to exercise their rights when they see fit – like, for example, when one gives up one's right to life in the case of voluntarily euthanasia.

Finally, humanists recognize the complexity of many moral situations: the values shared across cultures and between the secular and the sacred are "appropriately complex," not reducible to simple general rules. There is not always a single right answer to every moral dilemma, and moral tragedies exist (Norman 2015). According to Corliss Lamont, humanists are guided in their deliberations with others and in their normative judgments by three principles:

Humanism believes in an ethics or morality that grounds all human values in this-earthly experiences and relationships and that holds as its highest goal the this-worldly happiness, freedom, and progress—economic, cultural, and ethical—of all mankind, irrespective of nation, race, or religion.

Humanism believes in the widest possible development of art and the awareness of beauty, including the appreciation of Nature's loveliness and splendor, so that the aesthetic experience may become a pervasive reality in the life of men.

Humanism believes in the complete social implementation of reason and scientific method; and thereby in democratic procedures, and parliamentary government, with full freedom of expression and civil liberties, throughout all areas of economic, political, and cultural life. (Lamont 1990)

Even while being chased by the Borg in the feature film *Star Trek: First Contact*, Picard is able to convey the humanist essence of living in the Federation to Lily, the assistant to Zefrem Cochrane, inventor of warp drive: "The acquisition of wealth is no longer the driving force in our lives. ...We work to better ourselves ...and the rest of humanity. Actually, we're rather like yourself and Doctor Cochrane." Ever the poet-captain, Picard links his reason to live through the latest Borg attack to the strivings that made humanity worthy of continuing to exist in the years after the third World War.

Finally, according to Lamont, "Humanism, in accordance with [the] scientific method, believes in the unending questioning of basic assumptions and convictions, including its own. Humanism is not a new dogma, but is a developing philosophy ever open to experimental testing, newly discovered facts, and more rigorous reasoning" (Lamont 1990). As Q puts it in "All Good Things," the series finale, "The trial never ends" (TNG 1994, dir. Winrich Kolbe).

Roddenberry, Secular Humanism, and Agonism

Gene Roddenberry (1921–1991) was many things, but he was not a philosopher. So, it might seem odd to portray his work as a "philosophical argument for humanism." However, it would be wrong to assume that only philosophers can offer philosophical arguments. Furthermore, as the success of many of the "Philosophy and Popular Culture" texts cited in this chapter's list of references demonstrate, many television shows and films can be textual correlates ("artifacts") for philosophical analysis and clarification of ideas.

This having been said, Roddenberry – nicknamed "the Great Bird of the Galaxy" during the production of TOS by Associate Producer Robert Justman – had many traits of a good philosopher. David Alexander, Roddenberry's official biographer, notes that "The roots of the humanistic philosophy that would prove so appealing on *Star Trek* began … with Gene's attempt to understand his father's contradictory behavior—Papa's love for his family and his professed intolerance of certain minorities" (Alexander 1994).

Roddenberry's father, Eugene Edward Roddenberry, was a Los Angeles cop – just as the younger Roddenberry would become after leaving the Army Air Force – and was a study in contradictions. Roddenberry Senior enforced Prohibition rules on the job, but was a social drinker and had a drink every night (often homemade beer) at home during the Prohibition years of 1919–1933. Beyond this,

> While intelligent and far-sighted in many ways, Gene's father was a child of the South, who brought his ingrained cultural and racist viewpoint with him to Los Angeles. African Americans were "niggers," Jews were "kikes," and, of course, the worst of them all were the detested Republicans. [Prior to Nixon's and Goldwater's "southern strategy," "Republican" meant "liberal."] In their home, the word "Republican" was banned entirely. Papa's attitude was not something that was open for debate. It was, for him, a cultural norm—not how things should be, but how they were and would continue to be. (Alexander 1994)

Education, travel, and open-hearted interaction with diverse peoples and cultures spared Roddenberry Junior from inheriting his father's bigotry, but still left him with a task that he was to work out through his creative side:

> To see and accept Papa Roddenberry as a complete but flawed human being is a first step towards understanding his son's philosophy. To recognize Papa's ingrained decency to his family is another. Papa was a man who, in twenty years of police work, never became calloused to the suffering of children. Often he would come home and be unable to eat dinner because an incident involving a child had upset him. (Alexander 1994)

There can be little doubt that this struggle in Roddenberry's mind was projected onto encounters with god-like characters in *Star Trek*, like Apollo in the TOS episode "Who Mourns for Adonais" and the Metrons in the TOS episode "Arena." Roddenberry's vision of the future rejected, in his view, the monstrous moral implications of a creation myth in which "an all-knowing all-powerful God … creates faulty Humans, and then blames them for his own mistakes" (Guillen 2006).

4 Star Trek: The Next Generation as Philosophy: Gene Roddenberry's Argument...

The complexity of the human condition has often been plumbed through the genre of science fiction; Roddenberry admitted to being a fan of science fiction since he had been a child, and that "most of the ideas [in *Star Trek*] were a combination of things I had read and heard about. . ." from pulp magazines like *Amazing Stories* and *Astounding Science Fiction* (Gross & Altman 2016a). Throughout the development of TOS and his correspondence with giants of literary science fiction like Isaac Asimov and Harlan Ellison, Roddenberry often stated his main intention was to put on television good, dramatic science fiction aimed at adults, with all that meant in the way of novel yet credible visions of future technology, future strife, and future economic, political, and social relations (Alexander 1994).

Roddenberry's early rejection of religion also put him in a position to use his creativity to think about human nature and human foibles without dogma and hierarchy. From around age 16, Roddenberry confessed,

> [I]t was clear to me that religion was largely nonsense, was largely magical, superstitious things. . .. I stopped going to church as soon as it became possible to do things on my own as a teenager. . .. If people need to do that, ignore them and maybe they will ignore you and you can go on with your own life. (Alexander 1994)

As it turned out, Roddenberry's lack of religious spirit would be tested. As a junior pilot for Pan Am after getting out of the Army Air Force, Roddenberry was involved in a Lockheed Constellation crash between Karachi and Istanbul in 1947. Deadheading on the trip and so with no duties in the control cabin, Gene was sent back to calm the passengers after an engine caught fire and the pilot put the plane into a steep dive. He notes:

> Something happened to me during that crash that had a big influence on my life. As we were coming down, and death was absolutely certain, I was thinking all sorts of things—should I scratch a message to my wife on the metal of the side of the plane? What was I going to say—"I love you?" She already knew that. I thought, maybe I just ought to pray. I remember thinking, "Wait a minute." I didn't ordinarily pray and I would have much respect for a god that would accept prayers when I was in dire straits like this. He would be bound to judge you, if he's judging you, on what you did in ordinary times. He just wouldn't accept prayers at time like this. I remember making up my mind not to pray. I thought, "OK, take me as I am." I've always been rather proud of that. If you believe something in a dire emergency, that is probably what you truly believe. (Alexander 1994)

The pilot made a "perfect crash landing" in the Syrian desert, but the passengers in the forward section and the flight crew were killed. Roddenberry survived with two broken ribs. He was the only surviving flight officer. Roddenberry saw himself as a common sense nonbeliever; he thought that the onus was on the believer to justify what were otherwise fantastic claims, and he did not think that the evidence theists had provided was enough to change his mind. Much later in 1984, he would write to a cousin:

> . . .[I]t seems to me more and more with each passing year and each new massacre (as many perpetrated by Christians as anyone else) that the real villain is *religion*—at least, religion as

generally practiced by people who somehow become sure that they and they only know the "real" answer. . ..

At any rate, I've elected to believe in a God which is so far beyond our conception and real understanding that it would be nonsense to do anything in its name other than perhaps to revere all life as being part of that unfathomable greatness. (Alexander 1994)

As a result of reflecting on the character-building consequences of surviving the 1947 crash and other harrowing adventures in the air and on the beat as an LA cop, Roddenberry injected TOS with themes of ethical *agonism* – the view that the truth about one's character emerges from the contestation of one's values with others. This contestation cannot simply be a matter of private deliberation for Roddenberry: in a supplement written in 1966 to the "Writer-Director Information Guide" to TOS, he noted that in early script submissions, he had ". . .had some interesting analysis of possible alien civilizations, socio-economic speculation which seemed brilliant. . .," yet many of these stories failed "what we call our 'Gunsmoke-Kildare-Naked City Rule'—would the *basic story*, stripped of science fiction aspects, make a good episode for one of those shows?" In other words, a space fight or phaser battle between our heroes and monsters or aliens were something that energized the late-60s desire for action on television dramas.

In the thinking of Captain James T. Kirk, ethical agonist, calling a utopian halt to such a ceaseless contestation would be death itself for human nature. In "This Side of Paradise," Kirk and Chief Medical Officer Dr. McCoy share this exchange:

McCoy   That's the second time man's been thrown out of paradise.
Kirk   Oh no, this time he walked out of his own accord. Perhaps man wasn't meant for paradise. Maybe he was meant to claw, to scratch all the way.

Kirk here is saying that comfortable social arrangements do not bring out the best in humanity, an implicit criticism of the welfare state. In "Return to Tomorrow," Kirk waxes poetic about agonism and the *Enterprise*'s mission:

Do you wish that the first Apollo mission hadn't reached the moon, or that we hadn't gone on to Mars and then to the nearest star? That's like saying you wish that you still operated with scalpels and sewed your patients up with catgut like your great-great-great-great-grandfather used to. I'm in command. I could order this. But I'm not, because Doctor McCoy is *right* in pointing out the enormous danger potential in any contact with life and intelligence as fantastically advanced as this. But *I* must point out that the possibilities, the potential for knowledge and advancement is equally great. Risk...risk is our *business*. That's what this starship is all about. *That's why we're aboard her.*

The human struggle in Roddenberry's future is, of course, mediated by technology. Since the creation of TOS, Roddenberry had been in constant communication with Isaac Asimov, the prolific science fiction, mystery, and nonfiction author who wrote or edited more than 500 books. Roddenberry seemed to agree with Asimov that "SF is the branch of literature which deals with the response of human beings to changes in the level of science and technology" (Ingersoll 1987). Roddenberry's widow, Majel Barrett Roddenberry, wrote in a 1995 elegy to her late husband: "Gene believed the role of science fiction was not merely to entertain but to engage the imaginations of viewers, to generate ideas which would help solve humanity's current problems—and by attempting to turn dreams into reality for the future, progress would result today" (Roddenberry 1995). "In *The Next Generation*, technology moves to the fore," writes F.S. Braine:

> ...reflecting the advances in computers, telecommunications, medicine, etc. that were altering daily life in the 1980s.... The ubiquitous gadgetry of the ship, more sophisticated and user-friendly than on the first show, was replete with back-up systems and redundancies. the series became justly famous for its "technobabble," quasi-scientific repartee for the new age, as well as for its convoluted "tech" plots and "tech" solutions. (Braine 1994)

But again, it is impossible to understand the role of technology in the *Star Trek* series without interpreting it in terms of agonistic humanism. While every new *Trek* series introduces new technologies, what is key to the testing and correction of these technologies is the unique moral dilemmas they create for the series' characters. It is as if the writers and showrunners of the various *Star Trek* series were channeling German philosopher and poet Friedrich Schiller, who claimed, "Civilization, far from setting us free, in fact creates some new need with every new power it develops in us" (Schiller 1993). The notable exception to this theme is TNG's *Enterprise* NCC 1701-D itself, which encapsulates "...the idealized world of the 24th century, where the technology of the future preserves the best of the past," where "your neighbors are your co-workers, where everyone walks to work, and where most contact is face-to-face" (Braine 1994).

But it is also worth noting that Roddenberry founded the optimistic future of TOS on the wreckage of a massive human tragedy – a fictional World War III that began in 2026. The early years of the war produced the breakdown of nation-states and the rise of regional warlords as well as the eco-terrorism of the infamous Colonel Green. When nuclear bombs were finally dropped in 2053, between 37 and 600 million humans died worldwide (Okuda & Okuda 2016). In the real world of 1966, it was feared this would be the result of tension between China or Russia and the democratic west, not the result of terrorist and rogue state action as might be more credible today.

Roddenberry's influence on the backstories of TOS's main characters and situations is clearly indicative of his continuing struggle to make sense of his father as both compassionate and prejudiced. In late 1967, John Meredyth Lucas, writer, producer, and director for TOS wrote to Desilu Business Affairs regarding a draft of a *Star Trek* novel for children,

> ...Mr. Reynolds refers to Sulu as a bland faced, small oriental; to Uhura as a negress and compounds this by having her break into a spiritual. We run a totally integrated ship in an integrated century and it would seem we should avoid these particular stereotypes for a juvenile market. (Alexander 1994)

In his own memo, Roddenberry wholeheartedly agreed. George Takei, who played Lt. Hikaru Sulu in TOS, realized that his casting was a "breakthrough opportunity," since "...until then, any regular series roles for an Asian or an Asian-American character were either servants, buffoons, or villains, so it was a breakthrough" (Gross & Altman 2016a). In some ways, the persistent subtext to every iteration of *Star Trek*, from TOS to *Discovery*, has centered on personal and cultural dynamics of alienation, resistance, and integration as experienced by both individuals and groups of humans, aliens, and even nonorganic creatures like Data and the *Voyager*'s Emergency Medical Hologram Doctor.

After TOS's third and final season, Roddenberry was pinning his hopes for a reintroduction of his original vision of the values and mission of a *Star Trek* vehicle on a new television series. Much of the writing work done by Roddenberry for the *Enterprise*'s first film outing in 1979 was based on an abortive effort to produce a sequel TV series to TOS, tentatively entitled *Star Trek: Phase II*, or simply *Star Trek II*. By August 1977, these plans were dropped, but several characters developed for *Phase II*, as well as the script for the pilot, "In Thy Image" by Alan Dean Foster, were retained for *The Motion Picture (TMP)*. By extension, a number of plot and character ideas from TMP informed the development of *Star Trek: The Next Generation*, which premiered September 28, 1987, in an innovative direct-to-local-markets syndication arrangement created by Paramount Domestic Television.

Roddenberry was not lured or even drafted into his creative role on TNG. "I really feared doing it until I got angry enough to try it," he admitted (Gross & Altman 2016b). Rick Berman, executive producer for the new show, was assigned to "handle" Roddenberry. The preproduction work for TNG was fraught with technical, personal, and professional problems, partly brought on by the clash between those Roddenberry had brought along from the production of TOS – including writers Dorothy "D.C." Fontana and David Gerrold and associate producer Robert Justman – and new staff from Paramount. In particular, Roddenberry's firm attitude that there should be no interpersonal conflicts between the *Enterprise* crew was both his own projection of how far Starfleet personnel might have come since TOS as well as a nonstarter for executive producers like Maurice Hurley and Jeri Taylor. Ultimately, it was these individuals and not Roddenberry who argued for healthy conflicts and a wider pluralism in the characters and scripts of the new show.

But Roddenberry's personal attitudes had also changed because of his declining health, attributable to cerebrovascular disease and encephalopathy brought on by alcoholism and drug abuse since the making of *Star Trek: The Motion Picture*. "Back on the original show, Gene was a true liberal in the sense of women, race, and that kind of thing," Fontana recalled. "But since then it seemed that things had gone sour for Roddenberry" (Gross & Altman 2016b). Roddenberry was overheard by many colleagues making sexist and racist comments and his language was often laced with cursing and invective. His 1968 divorce had scarred him to the point of rejecting the idea of having a female officer who might be in charge of the saucer section when the new *Enterprise* separated, according to David Gerrold.

The Great Bird of the Galaxy had, it seemed, failed to fully come to terms with the contradictions embodied in his father. Or perhaps he had succeeded by coming to see that he had become his father, and now had to live within the realistic constraints of time, mortality, and the limits of personal influence.

> For twenty-two years there had been a collection of people who have said, "He didn't really do it [*Star Trek*]. It was me or my brother or my friend or this or that person." I found myself thinking, "They could be right. . .." The net result of all this made me mad, very angry.

> *Star Trek*, I said to myself, may be an ego-bent dream, and the rumormongers may be right, but at least I'm going to have the courage to say "Fuck you" as I go back to it. . . . If someone could create *Star Trek* more easily, why didn't more people do something like it in the twenty-two years since we did the original series? (Gross & Altman 2016b)

Humanism, Virtue, and Character

"In 1987, *Star Trek: The Next Generation* was launched into the teeth of a storm," claims Diana Relke. The storm she refers to was generated by the cross-currents of academic postmodernism and postcolonial theory, now "starting to creep into the work of a more widely read community of critics of popular culture," mixing with resurgent conservatism of the Reagan-Bush brand (Relke 2006). "The uniquely American brand of liberal humanism that had made Roddenberry's vision so popular among the hardcore fans of the original *Trek* would have to renegotiate a space for itself between these two cultural currents," she says, pointing to the character of Q, a "member of an omnipotent species with seemingly unlimited powers" as occupying the space at the convergence of postmodernism and conservatism:

> To Captain Picard and his crew, Q's motives and methods are as obfuscating as any postmodern text, while his arrogance and indifference to the plight of "inferior species" echo the elitism of ultra-conservatism's spiritual ancestors, the privileged classes of pre-Enlightenment Western culture. (Relke 2006)

Roddenberry added the Q narrative to the TNG pilot as a framework for Dorothy Fontana's mystery at Farpoint Station (Alexander 1994). From the very start, Q serves as a foil for human "grand narratives" about progress and liberation. He can be seen as an analogue to those in the western philosophical tradition like St. Augustine, Michel de Montaigne, and Ludwig Wittgenstein, who cautioned against *hubris* and pointed out the epistemological, natural, and theological obstacles to human self-transcendence. At his best, however, Q does not just "test" sentient beings but instead gives them an opportunity to transcend the limits of their conception of moral *virtue*.

Ethical theories based on character and virtue have certain advantages over modern ethical theories that are often stressed by secular humanists, like utilitarianism and Kantian deontology (MacIntyre 1984). Aristotle's virtue ethics encompasses both intellectual and moral virtues and extends a framework of rational evaluation to both actions and emotions (Aristotle 1999). Virginia Held's ethics of care treats the framing of ethical problems as women tend to see them, which is differentially from justice-based accounts that are traditionally male, and demonstrates how virtue ethics are not simply tied to being part of a small, homogenous community (Held 2007).

The term "ethics" comes from the Greek *ethos* which, as Corliss Lamont argues, stands for the way in which customs achieve wider normative status:

> [E]thical values and standards evolve in the interaction between individual and individual, between the individual and the group, and between group and group. The sympathetic impulses in human nature, such as the parental, the sexual, and the gregarious, become socially transformed and broadened in human association. (Lamont 1990)

Unfortunately, however, aggression and out-group prejudice are also enhanced through the development of an *ethos*, as Q-the-judge-of-humanity's bailiff demonstrates in "Encounter at Farpoint":

Bailiff Before this gracious court now appear these prisoners to answer for the multiple and grievous savageries of their species. How plead you, criminal?

Data If I may, Captain? Objection, your honor. In the year 2036, the new United Nations declared that no Earth citizen could be made to answer for the crimes of his race or forbears.

Q Objection denied. This is a court of the year 2079, by which time more *rapid progress* had caused all United Earth nonsense to be abolished.

Although Picard refuses to acknowledge the authority of Q's brutal kangaroo court, his actions and those of his crew in the premiere episode solve the puzzle at Farpoint through mercy and liberation rather than violence and retaliation. Q is not a good loser, however, saying, "I see now it was too simple a puzzle. Generosity has always been my weakness," as he disappeared. . .until next time.

And there are many next times. In "Hide and Q," Riker rather than Picard is the target of Q's attentions. Q offers Riker the god-like powers of the Q Continuum, in effect replicating Plato's famous thought-experiment of the Ring of Gyges in the *Republic*:

Riker We're growing. Something about us compels us to learn, explore.

Q Yes, the human compulsion. And unfortunately for us, it is a power which will grow stronger century after century, eon after eon.

Riker Eons. Have you any idea how far we'll advance?

Q Perhaps in a future that you cannot yet conceive, even beyond us. So you see, we must know more about this human condition. That's why we've selected you, Riker, to become part of the Q, so that you can bring to us this human need and hunger, that we may understand it.

Riker I suppose you mean that as a compliment, Q. Or maybe it's my limited mind. But to become a part of you? I don't even like you.

4 *Star Trek: The Next Generation* as Philosophy: Gene Roddenberry's Argument... 81

The question in both cases is, can a good person resist the use of unlimited power to do immoral things in a consequence-free setting? Riker passes the test, but not easily. In "Q Who?" Q tests the crew's dedication to the task of exploration in the face of the unknown. "They don't have a clue as to what's out here," he muses; and when they find out what he means is the Borg, the implications change the nature of the twenty-fourth century Federation forever.

In "Déjà Q," the tables are turned as Q is stripped of his powers by the Q Continuum and begs Picard for sanctuary and a purpose in life:

Q	I have no powers. Q the ordinary.
Picard	Q the liar. Q the misanthrope.
Q	Q the miserable. Q the desperate. What must I do to convince you people?
Worf	Die.
Q	Oh, very clever, Worf. Eat any good books lately?
Picard	Fine. You want to be treated as a human?
Q	Absolutely.
Picard	All right. Mister Worf, throw him in the brig.
Worf	Delighted, Captain.

Q discovers that the secret to being reinstated in the Continuum is feeling shame for his own actions and his eventual willingness to self-sacrifice, which he had never previously understood in his immortal state.

In the sixth season episode "Tapestry," a white-garbed Q greets Picard in a featureless environment, welcoming him to "eternity." It seems Picard's artificial heart (which was replaced by Dr. Kate Pulaski in "Samaritan Snare") has given out. In a variation on the plot of the film *It's a Wonderful Life*, Q is able to show Picard the lusterless life he would have led if he had "played it safe" early in his career, leading to a complex lesson: "Who you are now ... is a delicate balance of who you essentially are ... and the person that your choices and circumstances have made you into. In this, there is an awareness that many possible identities exist for any individual—a point with complex implications" (Barrett & Barrett 2017). Further, this is a lesson that becomes richly thematized in the J.J. Abrams *Star Trek* reboot universe, which takes place in an alternate universe to the "Prime" one of Picard and Q.

Humanism and Religion

"*Star Trek*, in its most 'modern' rational incarnation in *The Next Generation*, is militantly secular" (Barrett & Barrett 2017). Most humanists are secular rather than religious, since they do not believe in its doctrinal pillars of divine powers including the creation of the world, of an immortal soul, an afterlife, or providence. Yet a large portion of these also believe that spirituality is an important part of a fulfilling human life. Despite its main characters' lack of religiosity, *Star Trek: The Next Generation* is a prolific source of examples of pursuit of the "secular sacred." Data pursues excellence in music, painting, and acting. Picard takes a break to ride horses, fence and explore his hobby, archaeology. Everyone on the ship enjoys beautiful, if simulated worldscapes on the holodeck and R&R on Risa, the Federation pleasure planet (do *not* forget your Horga'hn!)

Many humanists think that conventional theism does not hold a monopoly on the concept of "spirituality," the Latin root of which, *spiritus*, simply refers to the "breath of life." Surely it cannot be the case that only card-carrying theists can be "inspired," in this sense. Humanists can firm up this move by placing the emphasis, as did philosophers at the turn of the twentieth century such as William James and Rudolf Otto, on religious *experience* rather than on doctrinal creeds or membership in institutionalized religious sects. Therefore, as Leon Seltzer explains,

> The non-religious quest for spirituality also includes identifying oneself as part of a larger community, as well as developing a vital, enthusiastic involvement with nature, the arts, and science. Here spiritual fulfillment equates with feeling fully, vibrantly alive and connected to others, as well as to our broader environment. (Seltzer 2013)

Humanists cannot, however, make the claim that a society would have been better off without religion, for the simple fact that we have no deep knowledge of any human culture that has evolved without it. In the *Star Trek* universe, religion is also pervasive – even the ultra-materialistic Ferengi believe in the "Blessed Exchequer" and "Celestial Auctioneers" in the afterlife. Although *Star Trek: Deep Space Nine* is the first of the sequel series to weave religion (in the form of Bajoran Emissaries and Prophets) intimately into its characters' lives, TNG presents us with a number of episodes that revolve around the humanist engagement with religion.

But humanists have claimed that we would be better off, all things being equal, without religion *now*. "Who Watches the Watchers" is a particularly important episode that turns the dynamic of humans-confronting-gods familiar from TOS on its head by placing Picard in the role of ersatz deity to the proto-Vulcan Mintakan people. Scrambling to undo the cultural damage wrought by the exposure of a Federation "duck blind" cultural observatory, the *Enterprise* crew returns one of the injured natives, Liko, to the surface after a failed memory wipe. Liko believes he has been to the Mintakan equivalent of heaven, which is governed by "the Picard" who also gave him back his life. After Liko tells his story, both enthusiasm and skepticism about the return of the gods is raised in his primitive but secular community. When Counselor Troi, posing as a Mintakan native, is seized, Picard must decide, with the aid of anthropologist Dr. Barron, whether to risk further cultural contamination by beaming down to rescue her.

Barron	The Mintakans wish to please the Overseer, but they can only guess what he wants. They need a sign.
Picard	Are you suggesting…
Barron	You must go down to Mintaka Three.
Riker	Masquerading as a god?
Picard	Absolutely out of the question. The Prime Directive…

Barron	Has already been violated. The damage is done. All we can do now is minimize it.
Picard	By sanctioning their false beliefs?
Barron	By giving them guidelines. Letting them know what the Overseer expects of them.
Picard	Doctor Barron, I cannot, I will not impose a set of commandments on these people. To do so violates the very essence of the Prime Directive.
Barron	Like it or not, we have rekindled the Mintakans' belief in the Overseer.
Riker	And are you saying that this belief will eventually become a religion?
Barron	It's inevitable. And without guidance, that religion could degenerate into inquisitions, holy wars, chaos.
Picard	(*quietly*) Horrifying. Doctor Barron, your report describes how rational these people are. Millennia ago, they abandoned their belief in the supernatural. Now you are asking me to sabotage that achievement, to send them back into the Dark Ages of superstition and ignorance and fear? No! We will find some way to undo the damage we've caused.

Some theists delight in pointing out that secular regimes from Stalin to Mao to Pol Pot have also been guilty of sowing chaos and death. But the root cause here, of course, is devout authoritarianism, not secularism. And the secular humanist may not jump to the drastic conclusions that Barron does, but they might reasonably share Picard's concern. Reasonable people, as David Hume indicated, proportion their belief to the evidence. They, as Francis Bacon noted, take responsibility for being aware of universal human psychological obstacles (like confirmation bias) to thinking reasonably in this way. In denying there is a *sui generis* transcendent divine power or providential plan, the humanist aligns himself with the views of William James, who writes, "Truth thus means, according to humanism, the relation of less fixed parts of experience (predicates) to other relatively more fixed parts (subjects); and we are not required to seek it in a relation of experience as such to anything beyond itself" (James 2000). The reasonable humanist recognizes the fallibility of human designs and must "take his lumps" when things go wrong. On the other hand, those who would inject a narrowly-framed "religious liberty" into public affairs will fall back on the hierarchical, authoritarian tendencies of institutionalized religion, on the most nebulous interpretations of sacred scripture and, unfortunately, on personal charisma of evangelical leaders when things go badly. As Philip Kitcher writes:

> Precisely because religious commitments typically pervade the lives of the devout, they are not insulated from actions with serious consequences for others. As the most vocal contemporary atheists rightly recognize, to believe [in religion] in earnest is a spur to proselytizing, to efforts at persuasion, even to coercion, punishment, and campaigns to eradicate the party of evil. (Kitcher 2014)

In "Who Watches the Wathers?" Picard's criticisms have teeth because they demonstrate the basic commitment by Roddenberry and his production teams to

"...not accept the myth, that the television audience has an infantile mind" (Roddenberry 1976). This view, incidentally, is what is missing in the newer *Star Trek* films from 2009 to 2013. Compare Picard's serious, thoughtful reaction to this situation in "Who Watches the Watchers?" to the way in which the sight of the *Enterprise* by the Nibiru in the teaser for *Star Trek Into Darkness* is just played for laughs. This comparison makes sense of James Hunt's critical comment. It is very difficult to imagine J.J. Abrams' mainstream incarnation of *Trek* as engaging thoughtfully with serious issues of religion and culture.

"Devil's Due" was an episode that had originally been proposed for the abortive *Star Trek: Phase II* series and was recycled and rewritten for TNG's fourth season. In it, The USS *Enterprise*-D receives a distress call from a Federation science station on Ventax II. The planet's population is in the grip of mass hysteria, as they believe that the cost of a deal made by their ancestors a millennium before to transform their polluted, warlike planet to a sustainable one. A powerful being named "Ardra" (whom the *Enterprise* crew initially suspect is from the Q Continuum) "returns" to claim her prize for saving Ventax II: she will lay claim to the planet ("and anything in orbit around it") and enslave its people. Ardra can appear and disappear at will, cause planetary tremors, and while she commonly takes the form of a beautiful humanoid woman, she also hints through devilish transformations that she is others – like the grotesque Klingon demon Fek'lhr, who torments dishonored warriors after they die, as well as the archetypal horns-and-barbed-tail Lucifer from Earth.

Jonathan Frakes (William Riker) claimed of this episode, "It was like an old Star Trek. It's ironic that it was an old Star Trek story, because it's really a Kirk story. It was so 60's" (Gross & Altman 1995). However, it is also a humanist broadside against so-called "god of the gaps" arguments (which proclaim god to be the explanation of anything that is not currently explained) that is much more satisfying than the one provided by 1989s *Star Trek V: The Final Frontier* and Kirk's famous line, "What does God need with a starship?" To explain the relationship between two phenomena that, by themselves, can be empirically described or naturalistically explained, theists have traditionally utilized "god of the gaps" arguments, which insert a supernatural causal power into such gaps.

The teaser for "Devil's Due" showcases this dramatically. It takes place in the *Enterprise* holodeck, which showcases the setting for Dickens' *A Christmas Carol*. Data is playing the role of Ebenezer Scrooge and has just been confronted by the ghost of his dead partner, Marley. Picard is an appreciate audience:

Marley	You don't believe in me.
Data	I don't.
Marley	What evidence would you have of my reality beyond that of your senses?
Data	I don't know.
Marley	Why do you doubt your senses?
Data	Because a little thing affects them. A slight disorder of the stomach makes them cheats. You may be an undigested bit of beef, a blot of mustard, a crumb of cheese, a fragment of an underdone potato. Why, there's more of

> gravy than of grave about you, whatever you are. Humbug, I tell you.
> Humbug. (*the ghost roars, and Scrooge cowers*)
>
> Picard Freeze program. Very well done, Data. Your performance skills really are improving.

Johnson says such arguments commit the "mystery therefore magic" fallacy (Johnson 2018). The examples are many: without God, how can we explain the ultimate reason for what exists today (Decker 2015)? Without an intelligent designer, how could something as useful as an eyeball have evolved (Behe 1996)? Humanists, however, with their respect for scientific inquiry (and in situations in which scientific expertise is appropriate) respond to "mystery therefore magic" arguments with patience: rather than accepting less simple and often supernatural theistic rationalizations, they are content to wait for valid naturalistic explanations that cohere with other physical, biological, or psychological theories about the world.

On Ventax II, Picard performs exactly the same kind of dissection of Ardra's claim to the planet, its people, and the *Enterprise* in orbit in front of Data, who serves as an arbitrator. At first, Ardra gets the upper hand in questioning Ventaxian planetary administrator Jared:

> Picard There is no conclusive evidence that this woman ever visited the planet a thousand years ago.
>
> Ardra I suppose you want a thousand year old witness?
>
> Picard That would be acceptable.
>
> Ardra Jared. In the contract, does it specify how you would know me when I return?
>
> Jared Yes by the date.
>
> Ardra Anything else?
>
> Jared By the shaking of the cities, and by the visions.
>
> Ardra And all of these occurred on schedule?
>
> Jared Yes.
>
> Ardra Thank you. Your honor, I submit that I have established my identity as stated by the contract. ("Devil's Due")

Picard has LaForge searching for a science-based solution to Ardra's power, but with time running out, he jokes, "My reputation as a litigator, not to mention my immortal soul, is in serious jeopardy." When LaForge discovers that Ardra has a cloaked ship in orbit that contains the technology behind her powers, Picard engages in some courtroom drama, even projecting an image of the demon Fek'lhr over himself, to demonstrate that not all is what it seems. Data declares the "contract" between Ventax II and Ardra null and void, and she is escorted out by Ventaxian security. But it is the part of the episode in which Picard questions administrator Jared that is of most interest to the humanist:

Picard	Jared, you've described quite thoroughly the history of your people before and after Ardra's first visit. But I am a little unclear about the change itself. Did Ardra simply snap her fingers and transform the planet into this paradise?
Jared	No, the changes occurred gradually over a long period of time.
Picard	Did she personally form the government that so peacefully ruled this planet for a millennium?
Jared	No, historical records indicate a council was convened to assess our options. They drew up a new constitution which the population later ratified.
Picard	I see. So she advised this council?
Jared	No.
Picard	No? Then she must have destroyed all the weapons on the planet.
Jared	No, our leaders did that. And they signed a treaty of non-aggression.
Picard	Well then, let's move on to the environmental gains on Ventax Two. How were those accomplished?
Jared	We shifted our economy from an industrial to an agrarian base. It was more ecologically sound.
Picard	But Ardra must have purified the polluted water and air?
Jared	No, the record shows there were a series of initiatives covering everything from atmospheric contaminants to waste disposal.
Picard	Did she not even pick up one piece of trash?
Jared	Ardra had left Ventax Two before the environmental reforms began.
Picard	Forgive me, but it sounds as if with a great deal of hard work and courage, your ancestors changed this world all by themselves. ("Devil's Due")

"Devil's Due" provides a new take on the old saw that "God helps those who help themselves." Once we have helped ourselves, there is nothing left for a god – or a devil – to do.

Humanism and Social Ethics

Quite a bit of ink has been spilled in recent times on the degree to which *Star Trek* and George Lucas' *Star Wars* franchise are examples of the American appropriation of Joseph Campbell's "monomyth" (Campbell 2008). Robert Jewett and John Shelton Lawrence explain the monomyth in this way:

> A community in a harmonious paradise is threatened by evil; normal institutions fail to contend with this threat; a selfless superhero emerges to renounce temptations and carry out the redemptive task; aided by fate, his decisive victory restores the community to its paradisal condition; the superhero then recedes into obscurity. (Jewett & Lawrence 1977)

But unlike TOS and *Star Wars*, TNG is *not* an example of the "American monomyth," and the reason why is one of TNG's most significant contributions to

4 Star Trek: The Next Generation as Philosophy: Gene Roddenberry's Argument...

humanism. TNG is an ensemble drama, emphasizing the relationships between the crew and their support of each other through problems and achievements both personal and cosmic in extent. Like its successors *Deep Space Nine* and *Voyager*, and unlike TOS and *Enterprise*, the communitarian spirit of the crew was by design. The bottom falls out of the American monomyth when its commitment to the individualistic "superhero" at its heart is challenged. Roddenberry, in creating the ethos for TNG, judged that the "...armaments and militarism [should] be deemphasized over previous *Star Trek* series and very much deemphasized over the *Star Trek* movies" but also supported a renewed sense of *esprit de corps* among the crew (Gross & Altman 2016b).

Roddenberry's production "bible" for TNG established an enlightened pretext for the crew's relationships with each other: "Show a somewhat better kind of human than today's average. Our continuing characters are the kind of people that the 'Star Trek' audience would like to be themselves. They are not perfect, but their flaws do not include falsehood, petty jealousies and the banal hypocrisies common in the 20th Century" (Teitelbaum 2019).

It is noteworthy that Roddenberry birthed this idea from a group of professionals, who were also a kind of family, from well before his television writing days. In September 1952, Roddenberry had published his first article in *The Beat*, the Los Angeles police department's in-house magazine. Utilizing the meta-level thinking that had so often stigmatized him as an intellectual in the military, Roddenberry framed and explored the philosophical aspects of "professionalism." As his biographer David Alexander points out, "Doubtless, these were concepts foreign to many policemen, ideas that many policemen, including the brass, had never been exposed to or never thought of applying to their own work" (Alexander 1994). Roddenberry listed seven characteristics that distinguished professionals at work from private citizens on the one hand and salaried or work-for-hire employees on the other:

1—A duty to serve mankind generally rather than self, individuals or groups.

2—A duty to prepare as fully as practicable for service before entering active practice.

3—A duty to continually work to improve skills by all means available and to freely communicate professional information gained.

4—A duty to employ full skill at all times regardless of considerations of personal gain, comfort or safety, and at all times to assist fellow professionals upon demand.

5—A duty to regulate practice by the franchising of practitioners, setting the highest practicable intellectual and technical minimums; to accept and upgrade fellow professionals solely upon considerations of merit; and to be constantly alert to protect society from fraudulent, substandard, or unethical practice through ready and swift disenfranchisement.

6—A duty to zealously guard the honor of the profession by living exemplary lives publicly and privately, recognizing that injury to a group serving society, injures society.

7—A duty to give constant attention to the improvement of self-discipline, recognizing that the individual must be the master of himself to be the servant of others. (Alexander 1994)

These ideas may have seemed new to the LAPD in 1952, but they are rooted in a very old argument made by Socrates against the Sophist Thrasymachus in Plato's *Republic*. When Thrasymachus advances the notion that leaders in a society construct the laws and institutions of that society in ways to benefit themselves, Socrates disagrees. When a citizen takes on a role as a leader, Socrates says, they should not be expected to do the job for free. However, we do not judge a doctor's skill level by the amount of money she makes but rather by her abilities in doing what is essential to her job – that is, in fostering her patients' health.

Thus the lack of professional behavior or apparent abrogation of "the duty to serve mankind [or species] generally" is often the first tip-off for the crew of the *Enterprise* that something is wrong. In the episode "Allegiance," for instance, the bridge crew does not realize that Picard has been whisked away to a holding cell on an unknown planet and replaced by an oddly behaving duplicate:

Riker	We're a mission that has no apparent purpose. In itself, I can accept that. All of us can, because the Captain says it's important and we trust him. Then he runs the crew through efficiency drills for the first time in my tour of duty, but he says we need them, so we need them, because we trust our Captain. But we also have a captain singing drinking songs with his men.
LaForge	A Captain who's come to the poker game for the first time.
Troi	And he was very odd with me afterwards. He wanted me to warn him if the crew started to lose confidence in him.
Riker	Any signs of mental stress or trauma?
Crusher	He came in for a physical with no word from me.
Worf	Anything unusual, Doctor?
Crusher	Every test result identical to his last physical, which is kind of unusual in itself, actually.
Riker	Almost as though he wanted to establish that there was nothing wrong.

Another scene, and one with significantly more moral weight, occurs in the 1999 feature film *Star Trek: Insurrection* when Admiral Dougherty spearheads a dubious Starfleet alliance with the warlike Son'a to remove 600 native Ba'ku from a planet ringed by metaphasic particles that can promise longer lives to billions in the Federation. Dougherty justifies the action by claiming, "On Earth, petroleum once turned petty thugs into world leaders. Warp drive transformed a bunch of Romulan thugs into an Empire. We can handle the Son'a. I'm not worried about that." Challenging him to take the moral high ground, Picard replies, "Someone probably said the same thing about the Romulans a century ago."

And just as Roddenberry envisioned that human reconstruction after a devastating nuclear war would be toward a society that would never allow such a conflict to happen again, he saw the twenty-fourth century evolution of professional ethics as leading to a form of social organization that dissolved traditional tensions of class, race, ethnicity, ability, age, and religion. Is this just a utopian pipe-dream? No, because very clear evidence is given through all the *Star Trek* series – though often as political or legal background information – as to how these dissolutions occurred, presenting us with ideals that could be compared to our own practices and beliefs.

First contact with the Vulcans was significant here; the realization that humans were not alone in the universe united humanity in a way no one thought possible after the Eugenics Wars and World War III. Within 50 years of the latter apocalypse, humanity was finally able to eliminate poverty, disease, war, and hunger, as evidenced by episodes and films such as "Time's Arrow, Part II, TNG"; *Star Trek: First Contact*; and "Broken Bow," "Demons," ENT.

Immediately prior to the founding of the Federation of Planets in 2161, humanistic philosophical ideals of equality and interdependence were tested by the Babel Crisis, when the Romulans attempted to sow dissent between humans, Andorians, Tellarites, and Vulcans by using two Romulan drone ships that were able to camouflage themselves as various other vessels. The terrorist actions of the xenophobic, humans-only Terra Prime organization were also a challenge to humanistic affirmations of pluralism but were defeated by the crew of the *Enterprise* NX-01.

The Prime Directive, which forbids inference into pre-warp cultures, is the best-known of Starfleet's humanistic respect for non-Federation cultures. Picard summarizes it by saying, "The Prime Directive is not just a set of rules; it is a philosophy... and a very correct one. History has proven again and again that whenever mankind interferes with a less developed civilization, no matter how well intentioned that interference may be, the results are invariably disastrous" ("Symbiosis" TNG). The later series *Enterprise* shows how the Prime Directive, or Starfleet General Order Number One, was a development of Vulcan noninterference policies. Early human space exploration in this show showcased both the good and the bad of collaboration with the Vulcans: on the one hand, inclusiveness and cultural humility was fostered by the Vulcan IDIC philosophy of pluralism, "Infinite Diversity in Infinite Combinations" ("Is There in Truth No Beauty?" TOS). On the other hand, the paternalistic treatment of humans by the Vulcan High Command during Captain Jonathan Archer's tenure on the NX-01 *Enterprise* was a dominant influence on Archer's command style, and by extension, his role in the creation of the United Federation of Planets ("These are the Voyages..." ENT). Societies seeking entry into the Federation faced a number of criticisms having to do with their respect for sentient rights ("The Hunted" TNG) and the repudiation of caste-based discrimination ("Accession," DS9).

As Picard told Lily in *First Contact*, the development of replicator technology spelled the end of money in the Federation and moved its planets into a post-scarcity economy. This seems to have been linked both with the increased popularity of the ethic of self-actualization that animates much of the *Enterprise* crew's free time as well as the rise of a philosophy of justice along meritocratic lines, with "merit" being defined by effort. This may explain why DNA resequencing of sentient beings for any reason other than addressing serious birth defects was made illegal by the Federation, with Starfleet forbidding the admission of young people who might have an unworked-for advantage through "accelerated critical neural pathway formation" ("Dr. Bashir, I Presume?" DS9).

Conclusion

Is a humanistic society such as that portrayed in *Star Trek* achievable? Is it even desirable? These questions are much more poignant today than when *The Next Generation* premiered in 1987. According to Gallup polls, the significance of religion in the lives of citizens of the United States has been waning since about 1965, and in 2018, while religion was still seen as very important to a slim majority of Americans, there was further evidence of the long-term decline in waning church attendance and self-identification with a particular religion (Brenan 2019). To be clear, the pluralistic, IDIC-like ideals of humanism do not target spirituality, but rather institutionalized religion, particularly as it affects public policy. But as we have seen, humanism is about far more than simply rejecting the supernatural. Politically, the rise of "competitive authoritarianism" as an alternative to liberal democracy in states that are nominally democratic is more of a threat to humanistic values than organized religion in the twenty-first century. Levitsky and Way distinguish democracy from "competitive authoritarian" regimes, like those in contemporary Russia, many sub-Saharan African states, and (increasingly) the United States, by citing authoritarian "abuse of the state" that violates "at least one of three defining attributes of democracy: (1) free elections, (2) broad protection of civil liberties, and (3) a reasonably level playing field" (Levitsky and Way 2010). A refreshed yet still ugly nationalism in the United States and across central Europe stands in the way of establishing universal human rights as guaranteed by the fictive United Federation of Planets.

None of this is good news for humanism, but there are signs that Roddenberry's basic commitments still have force. In relatively well-developed social democracies of fairly homogenous cultural communities like the Scandinavian countries, residents score at the top of the "happiness index" and enjoy their healthy societies, which boast some of the lowest rates of violent crime in the world (along with some of the lowest levels of corruption), excellent educational systems, strong economies, well-supported arts, free health care, and egalitarian social policies (Zuckerman 2010). These communities share one salient belief (besides their almost complete lack of religiosity). This is their political commitment to opening up positive freedoms for their citizens through the use of the state to mitigate the worst effects of events in life we cannot control: circumstances of our birth, health, gender, sexuality, and death. This social ethic of responsibility, each for each other, resounds throughout the world's major religions and its most sustainable ethical systems.

In TOS and TNG, Gene Roddenberry sought to place humanistic ideals like the notion of a social ethics of responsibility at the heart of an intelligent and lively science fiction television program. It should be clear that these visions were not the product of one television series, one cast, one set of writers, or one crew. The humanism embodied in the fictive twenty-fourth century society is explained and justified by series both before and after *The Next Generation*, with legions of writers, directors, crew, regular and guest cast contributing to the big picture. Similarly, while this chapter has discussed TNG as "Gene Roddenberry's argument for humanism," it would be a mistake to say that only the Great Bird of the Galaxy deserves credit for its ultimately optimistic picture of humankind's future. When it comes to affirming the philosophical value of this modern TV classic, we all say, "Engage."

References

Alexander, David. 1994. *Star Trek creator: The authorized biography of gene Roddenberry*. New York: ROC Books.

Aristotle. 1999. *Nicomachean ethics*, 2nd ed. Trans. T. Irwin. Indianapolis: Hackett Publishing,

Barrett, Michèle, and Duncan Barrett. 2017. *Star Trek: The human frontier*. 2nd ed. New York: Routledge.

Behe, Michael. 1996. *Darwin's black box*. New York: Free Press.

Braine, F.S. 1994. Technological Utopias: The future of the next generation. *Film & History* 24 (1–2): 2–18.

Brenan, Megan. Religion considered important to 72% of Americans. Gallup website. https://news.gallup.com/poll/245651/religion-considered-important-americans.aspx. Accessed 6 Aug 2019.

Campbell, Joseph. 2008. *The hero with a thousand faces*. 3rd ed. Novato: New World Library.

Decker, Kevin S. 2015. Science and nature without god. In *Revisiting Aquinas' proofs for God's existence in the 21st century*, ed. Robert Arp. Amsterdam: Brill/Rodopi.

Dennett, Daniel. 2003. *Freedom evolves*. New York: Viking.

Grech, Victor. 2013. *Star Trek*'s Picard: Humanity's conscience. *The New York Review of Science Fiction* vol. 25, no. 6 (February 2013), 20–23.

Gross, Edward, and Mark A. Altman, eds. 1995. *Captains' logs: The unauthorized complete Star Trek voyages*. New York: Little, Brown & Co.

———, eds. 2016a. *The fifty-year mission: The first 25 years*. New York: Thomas Dunne Books.

———, eds. 2016b. *The fifty-year mission: The next 25 years, from the next generation to J.J. Abrams*. New York: Thomas Dunne Books.

Guillen, Michael. 2006. *Can a smart person believe in god?* Nashville: Thomas Nelson.

Held, Virginia. 2007. *The ethics of care: Personal, political, and global*. New York: Oxford University Press.

Ingersoll, Earl G. 1987. A conversation with Isaac Asimov. *Science Fiction Studies* 41, vol 14, part 1. https://www.depauw.edu/sfs/interviews/asimov41interview.htm. Accessed 30 May 2019.

James, William. 2000. Humanism and truth. In *Pragmatism and other writings*. New York: Penguin.

Jewett, Robert, and John Shelton Lawrence. 1977. *The American Monomyth*. New York: Anchor Press.

Johnson, David Kyle. 2018. Mystery therefore magic. In *Bad arguments: 100 of the most important fallacies in Western philosophy*, ed. Robert Arp, Steven Barbone, and Michael Bruce. Malden: Wiley-Blackwell.

Kitcher, Philip. 2014. *Life after faith: The case for secular humanism. The Terry lectures*. New Haven: Yale University Press.

Lamont, Corliss. 1990. *The philosophy of humanism*. 7th ed. New York: Continuum.

Levitsky, Steven, and Lucan A. Way. 2010. *Competitive authoritarianism: Hybrid regimes after the cold war*. New York: Cambridge University Press.

MacIntyre, Alasdair. 1984. *After virtue*. 2nd ed. Notre Dame: Notre Dame University Press.

Massing, Michael. 2018. *Fatal discord: Erasmus, Luther, and the fight for the Western mind*. New York: Harper.

Mencken, H.L. 2010. Memorial service. In *Prejudices, first, second and third series*, ed. Marion Elizabeth Rodgers. New York: Library of America.

Nauert, Charles. 2006. *Humanism and the culture of renaissance Europe*. New York: Cambridge University Press.

Norman, Richard. 2015. *On humanism*. 2nd ed. New York: Routledge.

Okuda, Michael, and Denise Okuda. 2016. *The Star Trek encyclopedia*. 2 vols. New York: Harper Design.

Pinker, Steven. 1997. *How the mind works*. New York: W.W. Norton & Co.

Relke, Diana M.A. 2006. *Drones, clones and Alpha Babes: Retrofitting Star Trek's humanism, post-9/11*. Calgary: University of Calgary Press.

Roddenberry, Gene. 1976. *Inside Star Trek*. Audio LP, Columbia Records.

Roddenberry, Majel Barrett. 1995. The legacy of 'Star Trek'. *The Humanist* 55 (4): 9–11.

Schiller, Friedrich. 1993. *Letters on the aesthetic education of man*. Trans. E. M. Wilkinson and L.A. Willoughby. In *Friedrich Schiller: Essays*, eds. Walter Hinderer and Daniel O. Dahlstrom. New York: Continuum Press.

Seltzer, Leon F. Contemporary humanism and spirituality, Part 1. *Psychology Today* online, June 24, 2013. https://www.psychologytoday.com/us/blog/evolution-the-self/201306/contemporary-humanism-and-spirituality-part-1. Accessed 13 June 2019.

Teitelbaum, Sheldon. How gene Roddenberry and his brain trust have boldly taken 'Star Trek' where no TV series has gone before: Trekking to the top. *Los Angeles Times*, May 5, 1991. https://www.latimes.com/archives/la-xpm-1991-05-05-tm-2100-story.html. Accessed June 10, 2019.

Zuckerman, Phil. 2010. *Society without god: What the least religious nations can tell us about contentment*. New York: New York University Press.

Battlestar Galactica as Philosophy: Breaking the Biopolitical Cycle

5

Jason T. Eberl and Jeffrey P. Bishop

Contents

Introduction	94
Four Phases of the *BSG* Saga	95
Before the Fall: *Caprica*	97
Biopolitical Inertia: Fall of the Twelve Colonies to Baltar's Election	100
Gang on the Run: New Caprica to Baltar's Trial	103
Reconciliation and Rebirth: From Earth to Earth	107
Conclusion	111
References	112

Abstract

The reimagined *Battlestar Galactica* series (2003–2009) and its prequel series *Caprica* (2009–2010) provoked viewers to consider anew perennial philosophical questions regarding, among others, the nature of personhood and the role of religion in culture and politics. While no single philosophical viewpoint encapsulates the creators' vision as a whole, the theory of *biopolitics*, as formulated by Michel Foucault, Giorgio Agamben, and others, is a fruitful lens through which various points of story and character development may be analyzed. Two noteworthy areas of attention are, first, whether a race of intelligent, self-aware beings, who have been artificially created, should be considered "persons" with attendant

---

J. T. Eberl (✉)
Center for Health Care Ethics, Saint Louis University, St Louis, MO, USA
e-mail: jason.eberl@slu.edu

J. P. Bishop
Center for Health Care Ethics and Department of Philosophy, Saint Louis University, St Louis, MO, USA
e-mail: jeffrey.bishop@slu.edu

© Springer Nature Switzerland AG 2024
D. K. Johnson et al. (eds.), *The Palgrave Handbook of Popular Culture as Philosophy*,
https://doi.org/10.1007/978-3-031-24685-2_4

moral and legal status, and second, whether the purported ontological division between the "biological" and the "artificial" has moral import concerning the degree of control one class of beings may legitimately exercise over another.

Keywords

Battlestar Galactica · *Caprica* · Cylons · Personhood · Biopolitics · Biopower · Michel Foucault · Giorgio Agamben · *Homo sacer* · Bare life · Transhumanism · Apotheosis · Embodiment · Procreation · Religion · Roberto Esposito · Hannah Arendt · Totalitarianism · Justice · Technologies of the self · Lee Adama · Laura Roslin · Zoe Graystone · Caprica Six · Gaius Baltar

Introduction

Are you alive?
—Cylon Model Number Six

The first words spoken in the *Battlestar Galactica* [*BSG*] miniseries are by a sexy woman in a tight-fitting red dress to a middle-aged family man. More than a little confused by the question, the man responds meekly and almost as a question, "Yes (?)" Practically in his lap now, the woman challenges him to "prove it" and passionately kisses him. In any other context, one would think she might be proposing an unforgettable night of sexual awakening from the man's presumably sleepy life. In this case, however, the "woman" is a Cylon, an artificial being whose progenitors had been created by humans. The man is an officer in the fleet that defends the Twelve Colonies of humanity from the threat of a Cylon attack in reparation for the years in which Cylons were utilized as household servants, mine workers, and cannon fodder by their human creators, who did not recognize them as *persons*, with moral rights, who should not be used as mere instruments for human benefit. Instead of a night of carnal bliss, death comes for the Colonial officer, as well as for billions of human beings across the 12 planetary colonies on the receiving end of Cylon nuclear bombs. A little over 50,000 humans survive and flee under the protection of the battlestar *Galactica* and its squadron of hotshot pilots, with the Cylons in close pursuit.

As the *BSG* story unfolds over four television seasons, a one-season prequel series, *Caprica*, and three tele-movies – *Razor*, *The Plan*, and *Blood and Chrome* – multiple philosophical themes emerge, such as whether artificial beings can count as persons, what relationship should there be between religion and politics, whether deception can be a justifiable tool for instilling hope in desperate circumstances, and what moral limits there are in warfare: torture, suicide bombing, suspension of civil liberties (Eberl 2008). But underlying these and other issues raised within the *BSG* saga are persistent *biopolitical* themes.

Biopolitics, as an idea, sits at the intersection of two traditional academic disciplines – biology and politics – and was popularized by the work of philosopher

5 *Battlestar Galactica* as Philosophy: Breaking the Biopolitical Cycle

Michel Foucault, who used the concept of *biopower* to refer to various, often subtle, ways in which control over life and death is exercised upon individuals or groups of persons (typically by the state or other socially dominant groups). Foucault saw biopolitics as primarily an extension of Enlightenment reason over the governance of life and death, focusing on the diffusion of power circulating through the nation-state facilitated by political economy. While at first, Foucault understood biopower to be primarily the oppressive power of the state, toward the end of his life he understood it as a kind of power that also enabled a modicum of freedom.

Throughout this chapter, we will draw on Foucault's notion of biopolitics, as well as Giorgio Agamben's slightly different notion. Where Foucault understood biopower to be the product of Enlightenment philosophy, Agamben sees it as a concept operative from the very beginning in the West, particularly in ancient Roman law. He thus understands biopower to be part of the very nature of human political organization, an inevitable feature of our animality and our sociality. In this chapter, we will explicate how various biopolitical themes emerge throughout four phases of the *BSG* saga. As these themes emerge, we will show how the space-opera depicts potential ways to escape such biopolitical forces. We conclude that *BSG* offers reasons for both hope and cynicism: one the one hand, the surviving protagonists who make it to Earth have learned the hard lessons of having lived out a recurring narrative of creation, destruction, and rebirth and the need to break the cycle; on the other hand, when the finale flash forwards 150,000 years to contemporary society, it is apparent that humanity has forgotten those lessons and is about to perpetuate the same cycle as our progenitors.

Four Phases of the *BSG* Saga

Within the *BSG* timeline, the story begins with the creation of the first Cylon, as depicted in the prequel series *Caprica*, set 58 years before "The Fall" – when the Cylons obliterate the Twelve Colonies. Daniel Graystone, a worlds-famous cyberneticist – a sort of Steve Jobs/Bill Gates/Elon Musk combo – is attempting to secure a military contract for a robotic super-soldier: a "cybernetic life-form node." The problem is that while his engineers have developed a sophisticated and sturdy hardware chassis, the software "intelligence" is sorely lacking. He then discovers that his daughter, Zoe, "a bit of a chip off the old block," has created an artificial avatar of herself that can learn from the virtual world created by her father's Holoband technology and also think independently. When Daniel combines his daughter's software with his hardware, the first Cylon is born: a being that can learn, think, and solve problems.

The second phase of the *BSG* saga begins where the series picks up after The Fall. The surviving humans are on the run as the Cylons' plan for furthering their evolution starts to become apparent. There are many copies of various Cylon models and death is a nonissue for them: assuming there is a "resurrection ship" nearby, if a Cylon's body is destroyed, their consciousness is uploaded to the ship and then downloaded into an identical body. They even carry the memories of their previous lives such that "death becomes a learning experience" ("Scar"). The Cylons, however, are not content simply to keep resurrecting themselves. Inspired by their belief in an all-powerful, all-knowing God – inherited from their progenitor, Zoe Graystone – and that "procreation is one of God's commandments" ("33"), the Cylons seek to discover how to *reproduce* new kinds of Cylons and not merely resurrect members of existing models. This procreational experiment, as we will discuss later, takes different forms, including pairing a Cylon Model Number Eight – who goes by the human name "Sharon Valerii" – with a human, Karl "Helo" Agathon; together, they produce a Cylon/human hybrid child through their love-making. The Cylons also create a series of "farms" in which human women are artificially inseminated and utilized as biological incubators in an evidently failed attempt to create Cylon/human hybrids.

The second phase culminates with the election of Gaius Baltar as Colonial President. Baltar, unbeknownst to the other human survivors, was instrumental in The Fall after he fell in love with a Cylon Model Number Six – known as "Caprica Six" – and gave her access to the Colonial Defense mainframe computer. Baltar's election platform against incumbent President Laura Roslin involves the question of whether to settle permanently a newfound planet dubbed "New Caprica." About a year after Baltar signs his first executive order to settle New Caprica, the Cylons arrive. Instead of immediately wiping out the humans, however, they have had a change of heart and wish to coexist peacefully. The Cylons, though, implement *totalitarian* measures to control the human populace and quell a growing insurgency, all the while giving lip-service to "cooperation" with Baltar's puppet-administration. The third phase that begins on New Caprica, and the Colonials' escape once again from Cylon clutches, ends with Baltar's eventual trial for his seemingly duplicitous role in selling out humanity to Cylon tyranny. Baltar's trial is a significant turning-point for the series as the, now even fewer, human survivors must engage in serious introspective soul-searching as to what sort of society they've become.

The final phase of the *BSG* saga begins and ends with *Earth*. From the beginning of the series, the survivors of The Fall have sought the mythical home of a "thirteenth tribe of humanity." After many twists, turns, advances, and setbacks, the Colonial fleet and a group of rebel Cylons arrive at Earth. In true *BSG* style, however, Earth is not the longed-for paradise populated by humans uncorrupted by the sins of their Colonial brethren. Rather, it is a barren, nuked wasteland that, it is soon discovered, was actually populated by Cylons who had fled from humanity's original home, Kobol, thousands of years prior. The Cylons of Earth, apparently forgetting their own history, had created their own robotic servants who – no surprise! – turned on them, annihilating all but just five survivors. So, to make sure we're keeping track: Kobol is humanity's origin-planet where the first Cylons are created; civil war ensues; humanity flees Kobol and founds the Twelve Colonies, while Kobol's Cylons leave to found Earth; thanks to Daniel and Zoe Graystone, the Colonials create Cylons anew, who in turn nearly annihilate them; in the meantime, the Cylons who fled Kobol create their own Cylons who in turn annihilate all but five of them. Got it? Okay, so now we have a mixed group of homeless humans and Cylons. In an ensuing series of fortunate, unfortunate, and downright miraculous events, our wayward human/Cylon compatriots arrive at a habitable planet populated by a primitive hominid species. They decide to settle there, calling the planet "Earth" in deference to the dream they've been pursuing since The Fall, and soon begin interbreeding with the native hominids. The child of Karl Agathon and Sharon Valerii – the Cylon/human hybrid named Hera – becomes known 150,000 years later as "mitochondrial Eve," the most common ancestor of all human beings living on Earth (our planet) in the twenty-first century.

Before the Fall: *Caprica*

> A difference that makes no difference is no difference.
> —Daniel Graystone

What does it mean to be *alive*, to be a *person*? This is the most fundamental metaphysical question explored throughout the *BSG* saga. It is first raised in the pilot episode of *Caprica*, when Zoe Graystone and several others are killed in a terrorist bombing by the religiously zealous monotheists who call themselves "Soldiers of The One." Although a monotheist herself, Zoe is not a member of the STO. But unlike all the other victims, whose lives and stories end abruptly, Zoe has left a piece of herself behind in the form of a virtual avatar she created. An innovative aspect of Zoe's program is a "biofeedback protocol" that allows her avatar not only to possess Zoe's memories and personality characteristics, but also to feel what Zoe feels in real-time. Hence, when Zoe's best friend, Lacy Rand, enters "v-world" to meet with the avatar not long after Zoe's death, she finds to her horror that the avatar is covered in blood as if the avatar herself had been in the bombing. The avatar reports that she "felt [Zoe] die." On her own now, the avatar considers herself what Derek Parfit (1984) would call Zoe's "psychological survivor." Zoe's dead, but her avatar proclaims, "I know I'm not a person, but I feel like one." It is arguable that only something that actually *is* a person could report feeling like one. Yet, taking the avatar's claim at face-value as an independent assertion, and not merely a pre-programmed response, Zoe's avatar evidently has what Lynne Baker (2000) considers to be the essential capacity of persons; she possesses a "strong first-person perspective." Furthermore, though initially skeptical, both Lacy and Zoe's father, Daniel, come to accept the avatar as *Zoe*. While Daniel admits that the avatar is "a copy" of his biological daughter, he immediately asserts that she's "a *perfect* copy" and that he *knows* she's his daughter "in the only place that matters": his heart. So, in addition to exhibiting a first-person perspective, the avatar is also *recognized* as a person, and specifically as Zoe, in the *second-person relations* she bears to Lacy, Daniel, and later others. Philosophers such as Martin Buber (1970) have promoted the essential requirement of *interpersonal recognition* – "I-Thou" relations – for one's personhood to be realized.

For the avatar to be both a person and a psychological continuant of Zoe, Zoe's life would need to be reductively definable in purely "informational" terms so that it could be uploaded, copied, downloaded, etc. – from Zoe, to her avatar in v-world, and eventually into a Cylon body. When Daniel first meets the avatar and denounces her as merely a "digital image," she retorts with a litany of data-points that Zoe's program used to reconstruct her personality in her duplicate virtual self:

> People leave more than footprints as they travel through life: Medical scans. DNA profiles. School records. Email. Recordings. Video. Audio. CAT scans. Talent shows. Ball games. Traffic tickets. Restaurant bills. Phone records. Music lists. Movie tickets. TV habits . . . even prescriptions for birth control. ("Pilot")

All of Zoe's consumer choices, her interactions with the state and with the market, the expression of her choices and desires have left a residue of her life, a trace of her being-in-the-world. Yet, as we know from the political economic theories of the early- to mid-twentieth century, state and economic forces shape both the being and the residue that is left behind. Foucault (2008) notes that *neoliberalism*, which is a theory of political economy, is really the birth of biopolitics. The hallmark of biopolitics is that we are, in our being, really just the series of choices we have made. Yet, the question remains: in a world where neoliberal economics plays the game of shaping our desires, are we truly making our own choices?

Foreshadowing the second season of HBO's *Westworld*, as well as some people's concerns over what they fear may be the darker ambitions of giant tech companies such as Google, Facebook, Amazon, etc., *Caprica* depicts a means by which life might not only be (re)created, but also how it might be *controlled* insofar as it is now a "technological artifact." This is perhaps the subtlest contemporary form that biopolitics has taken, having evolved from – as discussed below – the right of sovereigns to give or take life, to the manipulation of life by those who arguably possess greater socioeconomic control over ordinary citizens than bona fide political authorities.

Giorgio Agamben (1998) distinguishes three types of *life*, starting with two foundational Greek terms. The first, *zoe*, refers to "simple natural [biological] life," like that of the wild animal or even the simplest of organisms that exists outside the *polis* – the civilized, politically governed city-state – in the disorganized, ungoverned "state of nature." The second, *bios politicos*, refers to the "political life," which, following the exhortations of Socrates, is aimed at not merely living but *living well,* and, for Aristotle, to live well requires a *polis*, a *community*. In between lies "bare life," which Agamben construes as a "politicized form of natural life." Bare life is exposed to "the force of the law in abandonment," ultimately expressed in "the sovereign's right of death" (Mills 2018, p. 45). Put differently, all living beings have *zoe* – natural life. Bare life is by nature a form of *zoe*, but when human life is brought under the regulation of the *polis* in order to promote the good life, it becomes *bios politicos*. When, though, it has been abandoned from the protections afforded those who live in the *polis*, it becomes once again bare life, placed in a situation in which its *zoe* cannot achieve the good life and even its *zoe* is at stake.

To see clearer what Agamben is describing, consider the evolution of v-world in *Caprica*. The real world is like the state of nature, where the drudgery of everyday existence is lived out in work – such as Heracles's working for a food vendor ("Know Thy Enemy"). V-world is a haven of entertainment, the safe space of communal engagement, where some version of happiness exists: a *bios politicos*. Yet, in the kingdom eventually built by the avatars of Zoe and Tamara Adama – the "Avenging Angels" – if one crosses the line, one can be abandoned from the protections afforded by the rulers, and their avatar lives can be taken from them as a form of punishment or on a whim, which parallels how the totalitarian Tauron government ruthlessly meted out death to those who stood against them ("The Dirteaters").

The exercise of political authority over life and death, while perhaps the starkest expression of biopolitical control, is by no means the only expression insofar as various other societal agents may exercise more profound, if more subtly expressed, forms of control over bare life. The power of "abandonment" to which Agamben refers is the founding condition for political life, which is the founding condition for the good life. Once one is abandoned, even *zoe* can be taken. Consider Tamara, the daughter of Joseph Adama, who was killed in the bombing that killed Zoe. Tamara and Zoe did not know each other, but after their deaths, Joseph and Daniel meet and later Tamara's and Zoe's avatars meet and become the "Avenging Angels." When Joseph first meets the avatar of his daughter that Daniel created from Zoe's program, he rejects her as "an abomination" who can't even "feel her own heartbeat." To his horror, Joseph later discovers that the avatar was not deleted when he rejected her. Eventually, the Zoe and Tamara avatars join forces to reshape v-world into their own vision of paradise. "New Cap City" represents the state of nature, a battleground of (as Thomas Hobbes (1994) aptly describes) "all against all." For Hobbes, freedom exists in the state of nature only insofar as one is free to kill in order to survive. Yet, the state of nature is not the good life, which must be carved out of the state of nature to create the conditions of security, as a suspension of the law of kill or be killed. The monarch, the one who holds sovereign power, has a foot in the state of nature and thus retains the right to kill in order to maintain the borders of the *polis* – the state which enables the good life. Zoe and Tamara replace the chaos of the state of nature in New Cap City with their version of the perfect *polis* with forests and mountains ("The Heavens Will Rise"; "Here Be Dragons"). They do so with the force of a sovereign, where any who threatens their *polis* can be killed, abandoned from the *bios politicos*. They no longer represent bare life subject to the authority of others – at least within the confines of v-world.

The confluence of technology, economics, and politics comes to the fore in *Caprica* as Daniel steals his daughter's program, engages in industrial theft with the help of Tauron mobsters, and installs the program into a Cylon chassis, resulting in a successful demonstration of the first Cylon super-soldier to government officials who offer his company a contract that will ensure its long-term financial success. While this accomplishment seems to have led Daniel to the fullest realization of his own *bios politicos*, he remains trapped within limits imposed by the socioeconomic and political exigencies of his society: he needs to make good on his contractual obligations to deliver 100,000 functional Cylon units, confront the vengeful takeover plot by Tomas Vergis – from whom he stole the "metacognitive processor" needed to download Zoe's avatar into a Cylon body – and along with his wife, Amanda, reconcile himself to his fellow Capricans who believe his daughter was a STO terrorist. Even at the pinnacle of success, Daniel is subject to the exigencies of bare life.

Agamben defines those who transcend bare life, and the biopolitical forces that manipulate it, as *Homo sacer*: the human as "sacred." He differentiates *Homo sacer* from the mythical creature known as the *wargus* or "wolf-man," who represents the "threshold or point of indistinction between 'the animal and man, *physis* and *nomos*, exclusion and inclusion ... precisely neither man nor beast, and who dwells paradoxically within both while belonging to neither'" (Mills 2018, p. 46; quoting Agamben 1998, p. 105). *Physis* refers to one's merely *physical* being, which, as we have seen, may be reducible to "informational" terms and thereby made vulnerable to biopolitical and *biotechnological* manipulation. *Nomos* refers to the "law," specifically, in terms defined by Immanuel Kant, the capacity of persons as rational, autonomous beings to come to recognize the moral imperative that binds us and self-legislatively act in accord with it. When Joseph Adama declares the avatar of Tamara to be "an abomination," he is contending that her existence violates the *nomos* that ought to govern the exercise of biotechnological power. Daniel emphatically rejects that notion and, at least initially, shares a similar vision with STO-leader Sister Clarice of a technologically driven "apotheosis," which echoes that of contemporary *transhumanists* such as Ray Kurzweil (2005, p. 9), who proclaims the inevitable evolution of A.I. technology toward what he terms "the Singularity":

> The Singularity will allow us to transcend these limitations of our biological bodies and brains. We will gain power over our fates. Our mortality will be in our own hands ... The Singularity will represent the culmination of the merger of our biological thinking and existence with our technology, resulting in a world that is still human but that transcends our biological roots. There will be no distinction, post-Singularity, between human and machine or between physical and virtual reality.

The Singularity promises a form of *bios politicos*, a version of the good life. Transhumanism generally, and Kurzweil specifically, offers a vision of ever greater movement toward the heights of the good life – an immanentized, vertical apotheosis. The biopolitical, however, asks the horizontal question of who is permitted to enter into the kingdom of the Singularity and who or what forces police that boundary. On the surface, *Caprica* depicts this vision of the good life as a group of religious fanatics; yet, the deeper we see, it might be the neoliberal political economists that subtly enact the vision of the "good" life.

Biopolitical Inertia: Fall of the Twelve Colonies to Baltar's Election

Why are we, as a people, worth saving?
—Commander William Adama

Following the miniseries that depicts the near-total annihilation of humanity by the Cylons, the first episode of *BSG*, "33," superbly draws viewers into the survivors' desperate attempt to flee the pursuing Cylons, who materialize precisely every 33 minutes as the two fleets leapfrog through a series of hyperspace jumps; this situation

5 *Battlestar Galactica* as Philosophy: Breaking the Biopolitical Cycle

is precisely the terror of the state of nature, knowing that at any moment *zoe* can be taken from you. To create a sense of realism in this sci-fi realm, the director and cinematographer utilize *cinema verité* camerawork, not only in handheld panoramic, tracking, and close-up shots of the actors on claustrophobic, darkly-lit sets, but even in visual effects shots of space combat – such as a piece of debris from an exploding ship striking the "camera" and cracking its lens. This has the effect of the audience feeling as stressed out, unkempt, hungry, and sleep-deprived as the fleeing Colonials. This first episode ends with a clear expression of primordial biopower as the newly sworn-in Colonial President, Laura Roslin – previously the Secretary of Education and 43rd in line of succession – orders pilot Lee "Apollo" Adama to destroy one of the fleet's civilian ships, the *Olympic Carrier* with over 1300 souls aboard, as there is reason to believe the Cylons are somehow tracking it through the hyperspace jumps. Although her decision is apparently justified given the circumstances, this is also an opportunity for President Roslin to assert her authority as more than just "a school-teacher" insofar as a fundamental expression of biopower concerns *taking life* versus *allowing to live*. As Foucault characterizes it, in its historical foundation, sovereign power functions as a "subtraction mechanism" that culminates "in the privilege to seize hold of life in order to suppress it" (Foucault 1990, p. 136).

As history progresses, however, the sovereign's "right of death" transfigures to "align itself with the exigencies of a life-administering power": "The ancient right to *take* life or *let* live was replaced by a power to *foster* life or *disallow* it to the point of death" (Foucault 1990, p. 138). In other words, it's not merely the case that the sovereign has a right to kill, but assumes the power to *promote* or *enable* life. In her first face-to-face meeting with Commander Adama, whose initial inclination after The Fall is to return to the Twelve Colonies to fight the Cylons, Roslin asserts her presidential authority, stating that the fleet needs to run away, survive, and "start having babies." Later, Roslin is pressured by her own words to outlaw abortion for the sake of proliferating the dwindling human species. As sovereign, she controls, through administration, the life of her subjects; they are subjected to her will.

"Having babies," of course, involves sex, and Roslin is not the only one concerned with exercising power over sex or in utilizing sex to gain power. The Fall of the Twelve Colonies is largely precipitated by sex, specifically Caprica Six's seduction of Baltar so that he will give her access to the Colonial Defense main-frame. Foucault is again instructive here:

> Sexuality is the name of a "historical construct ... a great surface network" that links the body and its pleasures to the operation of power and knowledge, in continual circuits of incitement, intensification, regulation and discursive elaboration ... sexuality is deployed not simply as a means of prohibition and control, but as a means of harnessing the forces of the body, both of the individual and the population. (Mills 2018, p. 14; quoting Foucault 1990, p. 105)

The Cylons "weaponize" sex – the origin of *zoe* – to gain the ultimate control over their creators: the "power to *foster* life or *disallow* it to the point of death."

Returning to the humans on the run in "33," we witness two primary forms Foucault identifies in which biopower manifests itself. The first involves treating "the human body as a machine in order to optimize and control its capacities through the 'parallel increase of its usefulness and its docility'" (Mills 2018, p. 15; quoting Foucault 1990, p. 139). This expression of biopower is evident in the limits to which the bodies of *Galactica*'s crew and pilots are being pressed each time the Cylons show up over the course of several days. It gets to the point that Viper and Raptor pilots are ordered to ingest stimulants in order to stay alert on virtually no sleep. Lee, as Commander of the Air Group (CAG), has not learned to actualize the biopower afforded by his position and has to be schooled by Kara "Starbuck" Thrace:

Lee   Hey, did you see the note from the XO?
Kara   I saw it. No way.
Lee   Kara, everyone else–
Kara   I don't fly with stims. They fudge with your reflexes, your reaction time.
Lee   Come on, Kara, give me a break. Just–
Kara   Why are we arguing about this?
Lee   I have no idea.
Kara   Neither do I. You're the CAG, act like one.
Lee   What does that mean?
Kara   It means that you're still acting like everyone's best friend. We're not friends. You're the CAG ... And one of your idiot pilots is acting like a child and refusing to take her pills. So she either says "Yes, sir" and obeys a direct order, or you smack her in the mouth and drag her sorry ass to sickbay and you make her take those pills.

The second form of biopower is found in the "biopolitics of the population," which focuses on the "species-body and its biological characteristics of mortality, birth rates, morbidity, longevity et cetera in order to subject them to measurement and regulatory control" (Mills 2018, p. 15; citing Foucault 1977). This form of biopolitical control is evident in Roslin's count of how many survivors are left among the fleet. Her sorrow every time she has to erase and write a lesser number, along with her joy when she gets to add one when a child is born (on the aptly-named *Rising Star*) anticipates further biopolitical measures she will adopt to ensure humanity's long-term survival.

As noted above, the Cylons are engaged in their own biopolitical project that involves controlling the bodies of human women at multiple "farms" and manipulating at least one human man, Helo, in order to find a way to fulfill God's command to procreate. As an interpretation of this command, the Cylons have come to reject their current mode of technologized reproduction by means of "resurrection," which involves downloading one's consciousness into a new, qualitatively identical body. Although there is disagreement among the various Cylon models on this score, at least some of them, the Sixes and Eights primarily, recognize that only biological procreation through *love* will provide what has been missing in previous reproductive attempts. One of the benefits of biological procreation is that the child who results is not merely a *copy* of their progenitor, but manifests *unique* qualities due to the uncontrolled interaction of their parents' respective genomes. As Roberto Esposito (2008, p. 181) notes, "[i]f one thinks about it, life and birth are both the contrary of death: the first synchronically and the second diachronically. The only way for life to defer death isn't to preserve it as such ... but rather to be reborn continually in different guises." Hera manifests Cylon and human identity in a continuous but yet distinct guise than her parents, which serves to explain why her "damned odd" blood is able to send Roslin's cancer into remission ("Epiphanies") and immunize her mother against a virus fatal to Cylons ("A Measure of Salvation"). And just as Sharon is able to carry a Cylon/human hybrid child, which has feedback benefits to her own body, Hera – the fruit of conflict between the two species whose essence she bears in her own body – becomes the progenitor for a brand new species that evolves over the next 150,000 years on Earth.

Gang on the Run: New Caprica to Baltar's Trial

> We're not a civilization anymore. We are a *gang*, and we're on the run!
> —Lee Adama

It has been said that "desperate times call for desperate measures," and the first two seasons of *BSG* certainly bear witness to the truth of this axiom: states of danger require the state of exception. The times are never so desperate, however, as when the Colonials are living under Cylon rule on New Caprica. The four-episode arc that begins the third season draws explicit parallels with the US-led occupation of Iraq and its attempt at nation-building after having toppled the dictator Saddam Hussein. For many Iraqis, however, the constant presence of heavily armed foreign troops patrolling their streets, raiding their homes, and having no evident timetable for withdrawing from their country was too much to bear. Some engaged in a violent insurgency, utilizing improvised explosive devices (IEDs) and even suicide-bombing to disrupt the occupational forces and destabilize the post-Saddam government, whom they perceived as a puppet-regime under US control. As is one of the hallmarks of great sci-fi, *BSG* turns the comparative metaphor on its head and subverts expectations by having the Colonials – the putative protagonists/heroes of the story – cast as the violent insurgents, blowing up Cylon Raiders and even engaging in suicide-bombing, in order to drive the Cylons away or at least make them suffer; as Seelix says to the Cylon Cavil after he's shot, "I hope it hurts a long, long time till you go to download city" ("Exodus, Part 1").

Through their desperate measures, the New Capricans are not only attacking the Cylons and the puppet-regime of President Baltar, they are asserting their *subjectivity*, affirming their self-identity as *Colonials*, as *humans*, as *persons* whose right to exist and to live free of the Cylons is fundamental and inalienable. As Hannah Arendt (1968b, pp. 145–155) notes, one of the primary goals of *totalitarianism*, necessary for it to succeed, is to destroy the human subject, to deny the humanity of those under its rule, to depersonalize both individuals and whole groups. This process occurs in three stages, all of which are witnessed in the Cylon occupation of New Caprica.

The first stage involves the "destruction of the juridical person, by virtue of which a human being is both constrained and protected by the law" (Mills 2018, p. 66). The first time we see Saul Tigh after the Cylons arrive, he has been in prison for an indefinite amount of time on suspicion of being the leader of the insurgency. Although he's tried to keep track of how long he has been in his cell with hash-marks on the wall made with his thumbnail, Cavil gleefully informs him that they routinely alter them and so he really has no idea how long he's been imprisoned. At one point, the Cylons remove one of his eyes and show it to him before crushing it on the ground. Indeterminate imprisonment without any formal charges, physical and psychological torture, and other forms of manipulation – consider Leoben's pseudo-domestic games with Starbuck – all contribute to depersonalization, both juridically – since all such acts are outside the bounds of typically recognized laws governing the treatment of prisoners – and existentially: the removal of Saul's eye is particularly depersonalizing as it evinces that, like the Cylons, the human body is merely a machine that can be taken apart piece by piece. (We'll set aside for the moment that Saul [SPOILER ALERT!] is actually one of the "final five" Cylons from the first Earth, as neither he nor the Cylons (except Cavil) know his true identity at this point.)

The next stage follows from the first insofar as, once juridical personhood has been suspended, the "moral dimension of personhood" also comes under threat in a couple of ways. First, it comes under threat by violating the foundational Kantian imperative always to treat a person as an "end in themselves" through the "anonymization of death" (Mills 2018, p. 66). It's bad enough to execute an individual on mere suspicion without the due process of law, but on New Caprica we witness a nighttime round-up of suspected insurgents, who are then driven out by trucks to a nearby quarry to be executed *en masse*. The second way in which moral personhood is violated can be seen in who does the rounding-up and transport to the execution site: *humans* who have joined the "New Caprica Police." Mass execution and the "mass production of moral complicity" (Mills 2018, p. 66), in distinct but complementary ways, serve to negate one's moral identity, including the moral identity of those humans who participate with the Cylons in killing their comrades.

All of this culminates in the final stage, which involves the "destruction of personal uniqueness, and along with it, the absolute suppression of spontaneity" (Mills 2018, p. 67). Totalitarianism's victims, having lost their juridical status, along with their moral identity, have been reduced from being *producers*, freely exercising their intellectual and creative talents, to being mere *reactors* in an environment in which they are constantly under threat. Akin to Thomas Hobbes's "state of nature," humans subject to totalitarianism cannot pursue cooperative projects of philosophy, art, or industry; mere survival is all one can realistically strive for:

> ... to destroy individuality is to destroy spontaneity, man's power to begin something new out of his own resources, something that cannot be explained on the basis of reactions to environment and events. Nothing then remains but ghastly marionettes with human faces, which all behave like the dog in Pavlov's experiments, which all react with perfect reliability even when going to their own death, and which do nothing but react. (Arendt 1968b, p. 153)

5 *Battlestar Galactica* as Philosophy: Breaking the Biopolitical Cycle

Laura Roslin's chronicle of the events on New Caprica is not only a means for history to be able to judge who stood up to the Cylons and who collaborated, but also a defiant expression of her own creativity insofar as it represents *her* subjective perception of the events recorded. When she sits down in the presidential chair on Colonial One as it departs the surface of New Caprica, she gently lays down her unbound diary and declares, "I'm ready." Even when she's nearly a victim of a mass execution, Roslin exerts her authentic authoritative leadership – she is no mere Pavlovian reactor.

The long-term fallout from New Caprica isn't easily settled in the boxing ring during "the dance" *Galactica* hosts a few months later ("Unfinished Business"); in fact, the Cylon occupation has only served to exacerbate humanity's sociopolitical devolution. Testifying during Baltar's trial for his alleged collaboration with the Cylons during the occupation, Lee Adama makes an impassioned speech in which he claims that the Colonials are no longer a *civilization*, but rather a "gang … on the run" ("Crossroads, Part 2"). To prove his point, he recites a litany of occasions predating New Caprica in which the standards of law and morality that had previously characterized Colonial civilization have been ignored, suspended, or violations forgiven. Lee's point is that collective survival has come to trump individual freedoms.

Lee's journey to this epiphanic moment began with the warning he received from the convicted terrorist – or "freedom fighter," depending on how you look at it – Tom Zarek when he questions the leadership of President Roslin:

Tom Who voted for Laura Roslin? You? Did you vote for her?
Lee She was sworn in under the law.
Tom The answer is, no one voted for her. And yet she's making decisions for all of us, deciding who lives and who dies. Is that democracy? Is that a free society?
Lee What is it you want from me? You want me to say she shouldn't be president? We need a government. We need rules, we need a leader.
Tom We need to be free men and women. If we're not free, then we're no different than Cylons.

Zarek's warning presages a number of instances in which Roslin, Adama, or Tigh fail to protect civil rights guaranteed under the Articles of Colonization. This is most clearly evident when Colonel Tigh, in military command of the fleet after Adama is shot, declares martial law and takes steps to enforce military priorities that result in the deaths of civilians aboard the *Gideon* ("Resistance"). This example is one of the state of emergency being exercised, when the sovereign suspends the protections afforded by the *polis* in order to protect the *polis*. As noted above, the sovereign always has a foot in the state of nature, where it is kill or be killed, and a foot in the civilized *polis*. Perhaps the most explicitly biopolitical example, however, is when Roslin, against her own personal advocacy of a woman's right to control her body, decides to outlaw abortion after Adama reminds her that one of the first things she said to him after humanity was reduced to a little over 50,000 survivors was that they needed "to start having babies" ("The Captain's Hand").

No less a measure of biopolitical control is that exercised over laborers in the "ragtag fleet." Onboard the plush *Cloud Nine* for the inauguration of the new

Quorum of Twelve, Zarek notes in an interview a civilian who is watering the grass ("Colonial Day"). While the officers and crew of *Galactica* have sworn oaths that mandate their continued service, none of the civilian survivors are bound by such an oath and, yet, they continue to show up for work and contribute to the well-being of the fleet. While watering the grass isn't too onerous or dangerous a job, the workers on the tylium refinery ship – who provide fuel for all the ships of the fleet, including the Vipers and Raptors that defend them – are laboring in dirty, exhausting, and dangerous conditions with no respite ("Dirty Hands"). In neo-Marxist, Agambean fashion, Baltar – languishing in a cell awaiting his trial – contends in his "manifesto" that capitalism, as inherently involving the instrumentalization of labor for ends over which the laborer has no investment or control, leads to the "'*zoe*-fication' of *bios*" (Mills 2018, p. 121).

Like Lee, Arendt (1968a, p. 77) sees such examples as linked together insofar as they all stem from an essential change that has occurred in the nature of political society:

> Not the loss of specific rights, then, but the loss of a community willing and able to guarantee any rights whatsoever, has been the calamity which has befallen ever-increasing numbers of people. Man, it turns out, can lose all so-called Rights of Man without losing his essential quality as man, his human dignity. Only the loss of polity itself expels him from humanity.

It's not just that Roslin, Adama, Tigh, or others change or bend a few rules now and then – as we conclude, their doing so on certain occasions is actually a sign of humanity's potential redemption, of being "worth saving." Rather, Lee's (and Arendt's) point is that there's been a fundamental change in human society since The Fall, to the point that they can no longer rightly call themselves a "civilization" – any "rights" that continue to be asserted are merely arbitrary.

Baltar's trial is a case in point. Although he's been granted a trial in line with his putative rights as a Colonial citizen, Admiral Adama (one of three empaneled judges) has already prejudged the outcome, stating that the "traitorous" Baltar doesn't even deserve a trial and thus should become "bare life," life set outside the normal protection and benefits of the *polis*; a member of the gallery shouts out that Baltar should be thrown out the airlock (which would literally make him into "bare life"). Felix Gaeta perjures himself as a witness against Baltar with impunity; Tigh and Roslin both testify under the influence of mind-altering substances; and, as Lee effectively shows, there are many others, including himself, who should be put on trial for equally egregious crimes but only Baltar has to pay as the *scapegoat* for everyone else's sins because "we don't like you" ("Crossroads, Parts 1 and 2"; see Girard 1989). Only in the context of an uncivilized gang, the state of nature, in which "we make our own laws now, our own justice," would such a show-trial be permitted, would Roslin conspire to steal a democratic election ("Lay Down Your Burdens, Part 2"), would Tigh declare martial law ("Fragged"), would Adama imprison union leaders and threaten to shoot Cally Tyrol ("Dirty Hands"), could the torture of Cylon prisoners be rationalized ("Flesh and Bone"; "Pegasus"; "Razor"), and could racial genocide be contemplated ("A Measure of Salvation").

5 *Battlestar Galactica* as Philosophy: Breaking the Biopolitical Cycle

Humanity has truly *fallen*, not because of Cylon bombs, but in its efforts to establish *bios politicos*.

Reconciliation and Rebirth: From Earth to Earth

> Earth is a dream, one we've been chasing for a long time.
> —Admiral William Adama

Is it possible to "break the cycle" of biopolitical machinations that continually entrap individuals and whole groups of people in power dynamics that dehumanize the "other" and subvert attempts to create and sustain just systems of social cooperation? *BSG's* final season depicts a few potential optimistic pathways.

One potential pathway ironically involves the exercise of biopower actually being productive of *autonomous individual selves*. In order to actualize the ultimate expression of biopower in control over the life and death of an entire species, the Cylons have to empower certain individuals to accomplish extraordinary tasks: Caprica Six has to seduce Baltar and infiltrate the Colonial Defense mainframe; Boomer (a Model Number Eight) must operate as a "sleeper agent" onboard *Galactica*; and Athena (another Model Number Eight) is paired with Helo in order to seduce him and become impregnated. In their respective assignments, each of them transcends their models' identity and reaches a point at which they assert their *individuality*. In "Downloaded," Number Three notes how the Six who seduced Baltar has become famous as "Caprica Six." Boomer searches for her authentic identity until she finally realizes it when she rescues Hera and delivers her to Athena, admitting "Today I made a choice. I think it's my last one" ("Daybreak, Part 2"). Athena, on the other hand, asserted her choice-making capacity early on when she points a gun at Commander Adama's head:

> I need you to know something. I'm Sharon but I'm a different Sharon. I know who I am. I don't have any hidden protocols or programs lying in wait to be activated. I make my own choices. I make my own decisions and I need you to know that this is my choice. ("Home, Part 2")

The narrative arc of these three Cylons exemplifies Foucault's (2003, pp. 29–30) thesis of how biopower produces autonomous selves:

> [It is] a mistake to think of the individual as a sort of elementary nucleus, a primitive atom or some multiple inert matter to which power is applied, or which is struck by a power that subordinates or destroys individuals. In actual fact, one of the first effects of power is that it allows bodies, gestures, discourses, and desires to be identified and constituted as something individual. The individual is not, in other words, power's opposite number; the individual is one of power's first effects. The individual is in fact a power-effect, the individual is a relay: power passes through the individuals it has constituted.

Whereas, with liberalism, the individual acts as a source of power to counterbalance the oppressive power of the sovereign state – the sovereign having the power over life and death – Foucault articulates a different version of power that enables the individual to be free by a kind of political suspension of the sovereign's power to kill.

Inspired by such examples, some of the Cylon models – though not including Boomer, who becomes disillusioned by the New Caprica experience – assert their independence from the totalitarian control of Model Number One, Cavil. As part of their rebellion, they unlock the cognitive capacity of the more robotic Centurions, allowing them to exercise what Foucault (1993, p. 203) refers to as "technologies of the self":

> techniques which permit individuals to effect, by their own means, a certain number of operations on their own bodies, on their own souls, on their own thoughts, on their own conduct . . . so as to transform themselves, modify themselves, and to attain a certain state of perfection, of happiness, of purity, of supernatural power and so on.

The Centurions are now able to constitute themselves as "ethical subjects," which interestingly also involves *aesthetic* transformation – notice how shiny the Centurions become after they're unlocked: they care both about the value of their behavior and of their appearance!

Simply asserting one's self-identity does not suffice to break the cycle of biopolitical control, however. For, now that one has been constituted as an "ethical subject," one is thereby subject to moral evaluation of one's actions and, if *BSG* shows us anything, it's that the universe is morally gray and no one is a "true blue" hero – even Hot Dog and Cally strayed! ("A Disquiet Follows My Soul"). But is the point of ethics to generate a list of merits and demerits? Agamben does not think so; like Aristotle, Mill, and many others, he sees ethics primarily concerning how one attains *happiness*. Life beyond biopolitical systems of ethical assessment, with consequent rewards and punishments – which Agamben (1999, p. 24) sees as the realm of *law* – thus requires the expiation of *guilt*: "ethics is the sphere that recognizes neither guilt nor responsibility; it is . . . the doctrine of happy life. To assume guilt and responsibility . . . is to leave the territory of ethics and enter that of law."

Baltar taps into this wisdom as he finally realizes why he's been drawn into leading a monotheistic religious cult:

> I am not a priest. I've never even been a particularly good man. I am in fact a profoundly selfish man. But that doesn't matter, you see. Something in the universe loves me. Something in the universe loves the entity that is me. I would choose to call this something "God," a singular spark that dwells in the soul of every living being. If you look inside yourself you will find that spark too. You will. But you have to look deep. Love your faults. Embrace them. If God embraces them, then how can they be faults? Love yourself. You have to love yourself. If we don't love ourselves, how can we love others? And when we know what we are, then we can find the truth out about others, seek what they are; the truth about them. And you know what the truth is? The truth about them? About you? About me? Do you? The truth is, we're all perfect. Just as we are. God only loves that which is perfect and he loves you. He loves you because you are perfect. You are perfect. Just as you are. ("Escape Velocity")

Expiating guilt requires seeing error as intrinsic to life, a fact to which Cavil is blind. When certain Cylon models begin to assert their autonomous self-identity, Cavil degrades them as broken machines in need of repair. He further laments the inherent limitations of having been created in human form as he confronts one of the "Final Five" who created him:

Cavil	In all your travels, have you ever seen a star go supernova?
Ellen Tigh	No.
Cavil	No? Well, I have. I saw a star explode and send out the building blocks of the universe. Other stars, other planets and eventually other life. A supernova! Creation itself! I was there. I wanted to see it and be part of the moment. And you know how I perceived one of the most glorious events in the universe? With these ridiculous gelatinous orbs in my skull! With eyes designed to perceive only a tiny fraction of the EM spectrum. With ears designed only to hear vibrations in the air.
Ellen Tigh	The five of us designed you to be as human as possible.
Cavil	I don't want to be human! I want to see gamma rays! I want to hear X-rays! And I – I want to – I want to smell dark matter! Do you see the absurdity of what I am? I can't even express these things properly because I have – I have to conceptualize complex ideas in this stupid limiting spoken language! But I know I want to reach out with something other than these prehensile paws and feel the solar wind of a supernova *flowing* over me. I'm a machine, and I can know much more. I can experience so much more. But I'm trapped in this absurd body. And why?! Because my five creators thought that "God" wanted it that way.

Foucault (1998, p. 476), on the other hand, sees limitation and error as not only endemic to humanity's biological and social nature, but also as the incontrovertible driver of history:

> if one grants that the concept is the reply that life itself has given to that chance process, one must agree that error is the root of what produces human thought and its history. The opposition of the true and the false, the values that are attributed to the one and the other, the power effects that different societies and different institutions link to that division – all this may be nothing but the most belated response to that possibility of error inherent in life … with man, life has led to a living being that is never completely in the right place, that is destined to "err" and to be "wrong."

It's thus no wonder that Cavil's "plan" for the ultimate biopolitical control over not only humanity, but also his creators and his fellow Cylon models falls apart as, one by one, each of them engages in some sort of "programming error" that furthers their path towards humanization: Boomer shoots, but doesn't kill, Commander Adama due to her internal personality conflict; a Model Number Four, Simon, kills himself rather than blowing up his ship and killing the family he's come to love; and Leoben becomes religiously infatuated with Starbuck as he perceives her to have a "special destiny" (*The Plan*).

The final step in releasing oneself from the exigencies of biopolitical control is to break the identity between the "human" and the "citizen"; for the latter is subject to the powers of the state, whereas the former is free to assert their self-identity. Agamben describes the "state-less" as breaking "the link between state, natality and territoriality, and thus inaugurate the possibility of a new 'aterritorial' or 'extraterritorial' space of topological indeterminacy … thereby liberating politics from the nation-state formation and allowing every citizen to recognize the refugee that he or she is" (Agamben 2000, pp. 23–25). Having been a "gang on the run" as "state-less refugees" for quite a while, Lee Adama comes to recognize the potential value in the Colonials owning their current mode of existence and how it provides an opportunity for them to carve out a new way of being on the lush planet they've found:

Lee	We break the cycle. We leave it all behind and start over.
Admiral Adama	You're talking about a little over 38,000 people, the entire human race, with nothing but the clothes on their backs and some provisions.
Lee	It's not the entire human race. There are people already here.
Admiral Adama	Tribal. Without language, even.
Lee	Well, we can give them that. I mean, we can give them the best part of ourselves. And not the baggage, not the ships, the equipment, the technology, the weapons. If there's one thing that we should have learned it's that, you know, our brains have always outraced our hearts. Our science charges ahead, our souls lag behind. Let's start anew.

Back on Caprica, Sister Clarice and other members of the STO attempted to technologically engineer an "afterlife" by utilizing Zoe's avatar program to recreate virtual versions of individuals when they die. Lee, on the other hand, envisions the potential for an authentic *apotheosis* of humans and Cylons who have both passed through periods of *inhumanity*. In so doing, they've embodied Agamben's (1999, p. 82) concept of the *Muselmann*, which he devises after reflecting upon the dehumanization experienced by Jews during the Holocaust: "the non-human who obstinately appears as human: he is the human that cannot be told apart from the inhuman." Catherine Mills (2018, p. 53) elaborates:

[B]eing human is fundamentally conditioned by an indefinite potentiality for being non-human, for being capable of everything and of enduring the inhuman. Being human is a question of enduring, of "bearing all that one could bear," and surviving the inhuman capacity to bear everything.

Humans and Cylons alike have borne centuries of dehumanizing enslavement, war, genocide, and lost hopes – think of Dualla's suicide after the discovery that the first Earth is a nuked-out "worthless cinder" ("Sometimes a Great Notion"). Only those who've experienced such inhumanity, and thereby understand the ever-present potential of repeating that cycle, could hope to find a way to break it.

Conclusion

> All of this has happened before, and will happen again.
> —The Sacred Scrolls of the Twelve Colonies

Does Lee's plan work? Is the cycle of creation and destruction broken? *BSG*'s creators offer reasons to be both hopeful that changes can be made that break the biopolitical cycle, but also pessimistic that such changes will actually be made on a sufficient scale. One of the final shots of *BSG*, as envisioned from the beginning by series co-creator Ronald D. Moore, is Number Six in her famous "red dress" walking through present-day Times Square in New York City. This shot would be innocuous if not for the subsequent shots of various types of robots, one of which – presumably designed in East Asia – forebodingly calls to mind Number Eight. All that has happened before, despite the best efforts of those who lived through it, will seemingly inevitably happen again. And the issues at hand do not apply only to the creation of potentially sentient robots. The same biopolitical forces of neoliberalism that shaped Colonial society are active today: "Commercialism, decadence, technology run amok. Remind you of anything?" ("Daybreak, Part 2"). So the question is thus put to us as we enter the era of emergent A.I., genetic engineering, and sundry forms of sociopolitical manipulations: can the cycle be broken?

The apparent pessimism with which *BSG* ends notwithstanding, we see peppered throughout the series moments of hope where the cycle is broken, at least for a time. Typically, these moments are when kindness is extended to a perceived threat. For instance, the Cylons abandon their original plan to exterminate humanity and attempt to live with them on New Caprica after Caprica Six and Boomer acknowledge their love for certain human individuals: Baltar and Galen Tyrol, respectively. They thus permit Samuel T. Anders to escape even after he and his "band of Bucs" blow up a Cylon café ("Downloaded"). Another example is when someone arguably deserving of death is granted mercy, as when Commander Adama stays his hand from killing Sharon ("Home, Part 2") and Lieutenant Palladino refrains from killing Tigh for the *Gideon* massacre ("Final Cut"), in contrast to Admiral Cain's lawful but unmerciful executions (*Razor*; "Pegasus"). A final case is a suspension of what the law or morality requires, such as Roslin's granting of a general amnesty to anyone who may have collaborated with the Cylons on New Caprica ("Collaborators") or the Final Five's offer to give the Cylons resurrection technology in exchange for an ultimate truce ("Daybreak").

We even see hope when the Colonials and rebel Cylons finally arrive at the inhabitable and unevolved planet that will become the Earth we know. The survivors are trying to decide how to live in a planet fecund with life, and full of *grace* as there's evidently been a divine hand guiding their destiny. The choice it seems is whether to see life as a scarce resource that must be conquered – a possession to be mastered and protected, owned and commodified, bought and sold like the children in which Phelan trades ("Black Market") – or as a *gift* of such great value that one must be willing to give it up, to give it back in self-sacrifice and a suspension of one's power to lord it over all the Earth. As Lee notes, the good life might be possible if one is willing to give away the best parts of it. We agree with such hopefulness, but only if humanity collectively remembers the hard-won wisdom from our past and continually reinforces proper attitudes towards life, the Earth, and each other. The fragility of our collective consciousness of the past and any shared sense of moral responsibility supports *BSG*'s ambivalent ending.

Acknowledgments We are grateful for feedback from participants in the Philosophy and Culture Area of the Popular Culture Association annual meeting in April 2019, particularly Jim Okapal, George Dunn, and David Kyle Johnson.

References

Agamben, Giorgio. 1998. *Homo Sacer: Sovereign power and bare life*, trans. D. Heller-Roazen. Stanford: Stanford University Press.
———. 1999. *Remnants of Auschwitz: The witness of the archive*, trans. D. Heller-Roazen. New York: Zone Books.
———. 2000. *Means without end: Notes on politics*, trans. C. Casarino and V. Binetti. (Minneapolis: University of Minnesota Press.
Arendt, Hannah. 1968a. *Imperialism: Part two of the origins of totalitarianism*. San Diego: Harcourt.
———. 1968b. *Totalitarianism: Part three of the origins of totalitarianism*. San Diego: Harcourt.
Baker, Lynne Rudder. 2000. *Persons and bodies: A constitution view*. New York: Cambridge University Press.
Buber, Martin. 1970. *I and Thou*, trans. Walter Kaufmann. New York: Charles Scribner's Sons.
Eberl, Jason T., ed. 2008. *Battlestar Galactica and philosophy: Knowledge here begins out there*. Malden: Wiley-Blackwell.
Esposito, Roberto. 2008 *Bios: Biopolitics as philosophy*, trans. T. Campbell. Minneapolis: University of Minnesota Press.
Foucault, Michel. 1977. *Discipline and punish: The birth of the prison*, trans. A. Sheridan. London: Penguin.
———. 1990. *The history of sexuality: An introduction, Volume 1*, trans. R. Hurley. New York: Vintage Books.
———. 1993. About the beginning of the hermeneutics of the self: Two lectures at Dartmouth. *Political Theory* 21 (2): 198–127.
———. 1998. Life: Experience and science. In *Aesthetics, method and epistemology: Essential works of Foucault 1954–1984, Volume 2*, ed. J. Faubion, trans. R. Hurley et al. London: Penguin Press.
———. 2003. *Society must be defended: Lectures at the Collège de France, 1975–6*, ed. M. Bertani and A. Fontana, trans. D. Macey. London: Palgrave Macmillan.
———. 2008. *The birth of biopolitics: Lectures at the Collège de France, 1978–9*, ed. M. Senellart, trans. G. Burchell. London: Palgrave Macmillan.
Girard, René. 1989. *The Scapegoat*, trans. Yvonne Freccero. Baltimore: Johns Hopkins University Press.
Hobbes, Thomas. 1994. *Leviathan*, ed E. Curley. Indianapolis: Hackett.
Kurzweil, Ray. 2005. *The singularity is near: When humans transcend biology*. New York: Penguin.
Mills, Catherine. 2018. *Biopolitics*. New York: Routledge.
Parfit, Derek. 1984. *Reasons and persons*. New York: Oxford University Press.

Black Sails as Philosophy: Pirates and Political Discourse

6

Clint Jones

Contents

Introduction	114
Series Summary	114
History, Fiction, and Philosophy	116
Social Contract Theory	118
Hobbes and Locke	118
Rousseau and Rawls	122
Democracy and Equality	125
Tolerance	129
Justice	131
Conclusion	132
References	133

Abstract

The Starz series *Black Sails*, while serving as a prequel to *Treasure Island* and thus providing intriguing backstories for such characters as James Flint, Billy Bones, and (of course) Long John Silver, portrays a realistic account of early eighteenth century pirate life in the Caribbean. In doing so, the show conveys intriguing insights into and applications of social contract theory reasoning, and both explicitly and implicitly asks questions about how those applications, especially as they pertain to the nature of government, democracy, equality, tolerance, and justice, help us understand our own society more fully.

C. Jones (✉)
Plover, WI, USA

Capital University, Columbus, OH, USA
e-mail: cjones354@capital.edu

© Springer Nature Switzerland AG 2024
D. K. Johnson et al. (eds.), *The Palgrave Handbook of Popular Culture as Philosophy*,
https://doi.org/10.1007/978-3-031-24685-2_9

> **Keywords**
>
> *Black Sails* · *Treasure Island* · Pirates · Golden Age Piracy · Thomas Hobbes · John Locke · Jean-Jacques Rousseau · John Rawls · Social Contract Theory · Democracy · Equality · Tolerance · Justice

Introduction

The Starz television show *Black Sails* (2014–2017) is a blending of fact and fiction set in the early eighteenth century, the heyday of piracy in the Caribbean often referred to as the Golden Age of Piracy. More than just a cinematic reimagining of this era in history, *Black Sails* is intended as a prequel to the iconic pirate tale *Treasure Island* (1883), which allows Robert Louis Stevenson's fictious characters to sail, scheme, and carouse alongside actual Golden Age pirates.

The action begins with Captain Flint's discovery of vital information about the magnificent Spanish treasure galleon *Urca de Lima*. Captain Flint, of course, in *Treasure Island*, is only referenced in the past tense, so if Flint successfully obtains the *Urca's* gold, we can surmise that the show will culminate with his burying of the treasure – the hunt for which is chronicled in *Treasure Island*. This allows the show to provide backstory for Stevenson's characters in the context of the world they would have inhabited alongside renowned pirates in realistic settings.

Like most historical dramas, *Black Sails* takes liberties with the historical facts, but important socio-political themes remain. The show's producers and writers masterfully weave together the historical and the fictional to provide viewers – and philosophers – with insights into Golden Age pirate life as a democratic, anti-establishment, and potentially utopian alternative to both Colonial politics and government as well as Imperial morality. Indeed, as we will see, *Black Sails* offers novel applications of classic social contract theory reasoning, and, as its pirates struggle to establish their own society, it both explicitly and implicitly asks intriguing questions about those applications regarding democracy, equality, tolerance, and justice.

Series Summary

Black Sails begins with a British merchantman attempting to flee the *Walrus*, a much faster pirate ship. The *Walrus* is captained by the notorious Captain Flint whose story is at the center of *Black Sails*. The merchantman is not Flint's primary goal, rather he seeks to obtain information recorded in the merchantman's log books about the *Urca de Lima* and its cargo of 5 million in gold destined for Spain. Capturing that haul, Flint intends to establish a New World Order, with the city of Nassau as its capital, and himself as its first pirate-king. Though Flint's grandiose ambitions remain largely hidden, he promises his friend and close confidante, the Quartermaster Mr. Gates, to make his crew "princes of the new world" he envisions.

Flint does whatever he must to obtain the *Urca*. He kills crewmembers, makes an unsteady alliance with new crewman John Silver, and forms a partnership with

6 *Black Sails* as Philosophy: Pirates and Political Discourse 115

Nassau's leading port merchant, Eleanor Guthrie. He desperately engages, at different times, an English and a Spanish man-of-war, the latter badly damaging the *Walrus*. Marooned, following his fight with the Spanish man-of-war, he and many of his crew somehow survive. Stranded on the beach they locate the *Urca* broken by a storm upon the shallow shoals of the Florida Coast and its gold spread across the beach.

Through a series of flashbacks, season two introduces Flint's backstory as an upstart British naval officer named James McGraw and his unconventional intimate relationship with Thomas Hamilton and his wife Miranda. They are mired in the politics of their day, including England's various efforts to reclaim New Providence Island; like other European powers, England jockeys for position in the New World.

Flint's past, present, and (perhaps) future unexpectedly converge when pirate captain Ned Lowe boards a merchant ship bound for Charles Town (Charleston). When Lowe learns that Abigail Ashe – daughter of Lord Peter Ashe the current governor of the Carolina Colony – is sequestered below deck, he ruthlessly kills the crew and begins plans to ransom Abigail. Captain Charles Vane eventually kills Lowe, however, and presents Abigail to his former lover, Eleanor. But Eleanor betrays Vane by delivering Abigail to Flint and Miranda. His hopes for Nassau dashed upon a Florida beach with the *Urca*, Flint and Miranda hatch a plan to return Abigail to Lord Ashe who was once part of their inner circle in London. Although Thomas was disgraced and is presumed dead, they believe Peter would be receptive to reconsidering Thomas's previous plan to reconcile England and the pirates, thereby securing a stable future for Nassau.

Peter receives Flint and Miranda, but Miranda soon discerns that Peter's governorship was bought by his betrayal a decade ago – an act that ruined Thomas and sent James and Miranda to Nassau. The negotiations sour and Flint is apprehended and put on trial for piracy. Vane rescues him, but as the two captains decimate Charles Town, in the Caribbean Captain Jack Rackham collects the *Urca's* gold while Eleanor is arrested by the Royal Navy.

Season three opens with Rackham in Nassau coordinating pirate efforts to fortify New Providence Island, but Nassau's new-found prosperity is a complication. Further complicating matters are Blackbeard's return to New Providence Island and the arrival of Woodes Rogers, who (ironically) intends to implement Thomas Hamilton's plan to civilize Nassau by offering the pirates a royal pardon. Rogers enlists Eleanor's help, offering her a pardon in return for intel about and counsel regarding Nassau. Captain Benjamin Hornigold, once Blackbeard's peer, also aligns himself with Rogers, accepting a new role as a pirate hunter for the British Royal Navy.

Rogers' plans for Nassau required financing from the Spanish Crown; in return for Spanish support, Rogers must return the stolen *Urca* gold. But Rackham and his partner, Anne Bonney, have slyly converted a portion of the gold into gemstones and have hidden it away from the rest of the treasure in Nassau (this becomes the fabled treasure chest sought in Stevenson's *Treasure Island*). Because well-funded pirates and an angry Spain will only frustrate his budding governorship, Rogers works to prevent both outcomes at all costs.

Surviving a terrible storm, the *Walrus* is becalmed in the Sargasso Sea. Flint and Silver, the latter now the *Walrus's* quartermaster, struggle to keep the crew alive. Arriving on Maroon Island, they are captured by its escaped slave and refugee inhabitants. Flint, following Silver's wise counsel, convinces the Maroon Queen to enter an alliance with the pirates; promising that together they will rid themselves of England's yoke forever.

Season four opens with Rogers reeling, his forces depleted, and Flint's ragtag army of pirates, maroons, and former slaves sailing into the harbor to retake Nassau. Rogers, however, has strategically sabotaged the bay with sunken ships. The pirates are routed and sent swimming for the beach. The surviving pirates, led by Flint, and Maroon Island slaves, led by the Queen's daughter Madi, gain footholds in the island's interior. The pirate-maroon alliance retakes Nassau, driving Eleanor and all those remaining loyal to Rogers into the fort.

Learning of Nassau's fall, Rogers returns from his desperate attempt to find allies in nearby colonies; however, he is unexpectedly driven away by the fort's guns at Eleanor's behest. Rogers, distraught and desperate, sails to Havana. Using the treasure held by the pirates as bait, he enlists Spanish aid to quell the pirate rebellion. Rogers and a formidable Spanish fleet sail into Nassau and a massacre ensues, driving the pirates from the island.

Pirate Billy Bones, feeling betrayed by Flint and Silver, seeks revenge. He informs Rogers that Madi is among those taken prisoner. Billy also informs him that Madi and Silver are lovers. Rogers then offers the pirates an exchange: Madi for the chest of gemstones. At Billy's urging, Rogers leads the pirates to a remote place, Skeleton Island, to make the exchange, but Rogers ultimate goal is his own revenge. At odds with Silver over Rogers offer, Flint absconds with the treasure and buries it on Skeleton Island.

Silver, trying to secure Madi's safe return, pleads with Rogers for time to locate Flint, kill him, and return with the treasure. Rogers agrees but then launches a devastating surprise attack on the pirate ship. Flint and Silver return in time to see help arrive in the form of Jack Rackham. However, recently returned from Philadelphia, Rackham's motives are complex. He and his business partner, Max, Nassau's formidable brothel madam, have reached an unlikely agreement with Eleanor's grandmother, Marion, to secure Nassau's future – one that does not include Captain Flint. Nevertheless, Rackham still detests Rogers, and is loath to do anything that will help him, which puts him in a difficult position. An epic battle ensues. Rogers is defeated, loses everything, and is thrown into debtors' prison. Silver puts into action his scheme to "unmake" Captain Flint, allowing him an opportunity to become James McGraw once again. As part of the agreement with Marion, a new figurehead governor, one beneficial to all parties' interests, is installed in Nassau. Meanwhile, Max and Jack subtly, but attentively, work behind the scenes to manage Nassau's affairs – at least when Jack isn't searching for Flint's buried treasure – and a precarious peace returns to Nassau.

History, Fiction, and Philosophy

From *Treasure Island's* Long John Silver to *Pirates of the Caribbean's* Jack Sparrow, pirates have long been romanticized in popular culture. Perhaps *Black Sails* romanticizes piracy in some ways, but it also acknowledges its history. Through the series'

6 *Black Sails* as Philosophy: Pirates and Political Discourse

opening graphic, we are told: "1715, West Indies. The pirates of New Providence Island threaten maritime trade in the region. The laws of every civilized nation declare them *hostis humani generis*. Enemies of all mankind. In response, the pirates adhere to a doctrine of their own—war against the world" (Chapter I). Moreover, *Black Sails* includes historical pirates – Benjamin Hornigold, Charles Vane, Jack Rackham, Anne Bonney, and Edward "Blackbeard" Teach – and former pirate (or "privateer") Woodes Rogers who served as Nassau's governor.

Interestingly, early eighteenth century world powers – including England and Spain – are (arguably) guilty of unduly denigrating Golden Age pirates and their efforts in the New World. At the very least, the declaration that pirates are *merely* brutal and debaucherous criminals – "universal outlaws, with no native legal or civil protections" – prone to all manner of moral transgressions, only obscures the serious challenges they represented for a just society in the age of Colonialism and Imperial rule. (And let's not forget that the navies of England and Spain also tended to be just as violent and prone to moral transgression as the men they hunted as pirates.)

So, yes, Golden Age pirates disrupted Caribbean maritime trade, but England's fear of losing Nassau was not just about losing a vital commercial asset in the New World; it was also about the prospect of inviting further open rebellion into the realm. Golden Age pirates were uniquely positioned to not only challenge prevailing Colonial authority, but to institute a social order directly opposed to it. Golden Age pirates formulated agreements among themselves, held each other accountable, punished transgressions among their rank, and in the process built a community in opposition to those powers that declared them outlaws. Moreover, there were pirates at the time with designs on doing more than opposing the encroachment of civilization, such as it was; instead, they wanted to establish a functional pirate community – transformed by legitimacy, but also free. Pirates, therefore, represent a community engaged in the same type of dialogue that would soon emerge among the leading men of the American Colonies.

Because pirates were poor record keepers, preventing us from discerning their real motivations and thoughts, we may never fully know all the historical details of their struggles toward independence of Colonial rule. However, *Black Sails* provides us plausible (even if stylized) scenarios regarding those struggles and, in the process, shines light on philosophical issues corresponding to them. It accomplishes this most vividly through its fictional characters, particularly Captain Flint (and eventually Long John Silver and the interactions between the two).

As early as episode one, Flint helps us understand the plight of Golden Age pirates who attempt to free themselves of Colonial rule. He informs Billy: "When a king brands us pirates, he doesn't mean to make us adversaries. He doesn't mean to make us criminals. He means to make us monsters. For that's the only way his God-fearing, taxpaying subjects can make sense of men who keep what is theirs and fear no one. When I say there's a war coming...I don't mean with King George or England. Civilization is coming and it means to exterminate us" (Chapter I). Flint believes their only hope to stave off extermination is to form their own civilization: "If we are to survive, we must unite behind our own king." When Billy reminds him that pirates have no king – in fact, they repudiate the political oppression monarchies invariably incur – Flint desperately replies, "I am your king!" *Black Sails*, in effect, asks: Are there limits to how a pirate community may overcome opposition to its existence? Could it succeed without sacrificing the ideals upon which that community is to be founded?

Throughout the series, Flint goes to great lengths to motivate, fuel, and secure his war against England – and all Colonial powers – to establish a free pirate community founded upon its own principles. He seeks this end throughout the series, bemoaning the obstacles to challenging a world power. In the series finale, he laments to Silver: "They paint the world full of shadows... and then tell their children to stay close to the light. Their light. Their reasons. Their judgments. Because in the darkness, there be dragons. But it isn't true. We can prove that it isn't true. In the dark, there is discovery, there is possibility, there is freedom in the dark once someone has illuminated it. And who has been so close to doing it as we are right now?" (Chapter XXXVIII). Here, *Black Sails* implicitly asks: How might an upstart community achieve respectability and viability in a world where world powers control the narrative? What if members of that community were deemed "monsters" that must be exterminated? How should those members respond?

Pirates of the Golden Age undoubtedly represent intriguing examples of philosophy in action; they sought to actualize various principles of ethical and political philosophy (and plausibly serve as *non-hypothetical* agents utilizing social contract reasoning). This chapter explores *Black Sails's* attempts to bring this historical period to life via its compelling storylines. That the pirates of *Black Sails*, even those based on historical figures, are fictional does not detract from their engaging the philosophical process. As we shall see, the same ethical and political philosophy principles apply, and *Black Sails* offers noteworthy insights about their application.

Social Contract Theory

Social contract theories are a way for us to conceive of how communities might have arisen; that is, how early humans would have chosen to organize themselves socially to the benefit of all. The primary thinkers identified with this tradition are Thomas Hobbes, John Locke, Jean-Jacques Rousseau, and John Rawls. Most contract theories are predicated on hypothetical assumptions about early human interactions and social needs – Rousseau being the obvious outlier in this regard. It will be useful to review the major formulations of social contract theory to better enable us to recognize and appreciate how *Black Sails* asks questions about it and conveys its own insights into this venerable piece of philosophy.

Hobbes and Locke

Thomas Hobbes was one of the first philosophers to argue for a contract-based understanding of social organization. In his seminal work, *Leviathan* (1660), Hobbes paints a horrific picture of early humanity. Hobbes believed that our natural egoistic tendencies put pre-government humans in a state of war, all against all, all the time.

Hobbes famously described the lives of these people as solitary, poor, nasty, brutish, and short. Solitary because each individual was locked in mortal combat with all other people destined to fight and die alone. Poor because being in possession of any kind of wealth or advantage made you a bigger target for others. Nasty because taking time to care for oneself rendered one vulnerable to attack. Brutishness resulted from the fact that being engaged perpetually in mortal struggle left little, if any, time to elevate oneself above the base necessities needed to continue living – essentially, humans were no better than non-human animals. Finally, lives were short, as a result of the conditions such a state of being would create.

The resulting life is obviously undesirable, and that undesirability acted as a motivator to cooperate to ensure the survival of a small band of confederates (to use Hobbes's term). According to Hobbes, at some point an individual made an agreement with another person – perhaps, something as simple as, you sleep while I stand guard and then we'll switch. After all, as Hobbes notes, sleep is the great equalizer, and even the strongest people would have lived in constant fear of needing rest. Once an agreement was struck – and honored – the twosome become stronger than any individual and, clearly, would have made joining them more desirable than confronting them. The confederacy would eventually grow, requiring the development of rules, norms, and mores to govern the group until they elected the strongest among them to act as sovereign and enforce the rules.

For Hobbes, this account explains not only how and why early communities formed, but also why a strong sovereign is desirable. Hobbes supported the monarchy of his time and sought to provide an explanation for its existence, but also to show why sovereignty is above or outside the rule of law. Hobbes believed that unless the sovereign's power was (virtually) limitless and irrepressible, we would soon return to the state of nature. We cannot be trusted to keep our agreements; a strong sovereign must be enabled to assure our compliance.

In his *Second Treatise of Government* (1689), John Locke disagrees with Hobbes' views about human nature and the resulting need for a sovereign with limitless political power. Locke did not believe that humans, if reduced to a natural condition, would fall into a state of perpetual war. Locke contends that early humans are akin to non-animals in nature, not completely docile but not overly hostile toward each other either; co-existence is common in the animal kingdom. Consequently, Locke offered an alternative account of the social contract, one that arises from an economic perspective and is regulated by democratic processes. The key for Locke is the possession of things that were advantageous to a successful life and instituting and empowering a political system that regulated how one was to possess them, under what conditions they could be taken away, and what happens when they are taken unjustly (including when the sovereign is the one acting unjustly).

Locke argues, for instance, if there is an apple tree, any person can take as many apples as they like; but one should not take more than they need. However, if someone controls access to the apple tree, then they can trade those apples for other goods or services. Reasonably, one can see how recognizing that certain things have greater trade value would motivate someone to try to control access to that thing regardless of whether it was water, food, or security. In this way, trade develops, standards are set, and, just as in the version told by Hobbes, individuals are needed to enforce the rules. In place of a sovereign, Locke postulates the development of markets, courts, etc., and the result is the formation of society rooted in the complex and stable systems of trade necessary to supply individuals with the things they need to survive, or more aptly, thrive.

Flint intriguingly conveys elements of both Hobbes's and Locke's respective formulations of social contract theory reasoning. That Flint believes Nassau survives the "coming of civilization" only if the pirates enable a sovereign, and that he is willing to assume that role, favors Hobbes's interpretation. That Flint is willing to do almost anything for a pirate commonwealth in Nassau, including those things that seem inconsistent with accepted pirate practices or are otherwise simply impermissible, only bolsters the connection to Hobbes (even if Flint's reasons and motivations are not always exactly analogous to Hobbes'). Furthermore, by the end of the series, Silver interprets Flint's unrelenting pursuit of his war as attestation of a Hobbesian state of nature. Silver queries, "Assume your war begins... spreads throughout the New World.... There's nothing in Nassau but horror. You said it was just a transition. That something better lay beyond it, something meaningful. But what if that isn't so? What if the result of this war isn't beyond the horror? What if it is the horror itself?" (Chapter XXXVI). That Flint is willing to participate, if not encourage, a constant state of war – what can only be deemed a horror – serves to further connect Flint to Hobbes's view.

Yet there are other reasons for believing that Flint also embodies Locke's formulation. This begins with his choice to leave all his British belongings behind and settle in Nassau, that is, a new community more to his liking, because, as he later tells Rogers, "England has shown herself to me. Gnarled and gray... and spiteful of anyone who would find happiness under her rule." (Hobbes disagreed with Locke about whether subjects may leave their commonwealth for another.) Furthermore, in response to Silver's query about the alleged horror of his war, he states:

> If we are to truly reach a moment where we might be finished with England...there most certainly lies a dark moment between here and there. A moment of terror...where everything appears to be without hope.... But I cannot believe that that is all there is. I cannot believe we are so poorly made as that. Incapable of surviving in the state to which we are born. Grown so used to the yoke that there can be no progress without it. (Chapter XXXVI)

Here, Flint affirms a Lockean conception of human beings, the state of nature, and the proper role of government. We are such that we can thrive if left to our devices (even if we must struggle to reach this state of affairs).

Perhaps cognizant of his inner philosophical conflict about proper government, Flint offers Silver a possible resolution, one that implicitly synthesizes his Hobbesian and Lockean sympathies. A careful read of the show reveals that Flint's solution is grounded in his overall character arc, including his deepening camaraderie with Silver (and what he's seen of Silver's budding relationship with Madi). When Silver replies to Flint's beliefs about human nature, "It's a lot to ask...to wager so much suffering on blind faith," Flint retorts, "We'll have the right people in place to lead us through it...while it finds its balance.... You and Madi.... There isn't a man or woman in Nassau who'd argue that she isn't the best of them all. . . .. I think that you are the best of us. The two of you together are the world in balance" (Chapter XXXVI). Flint's response is significant because it signals a radical break from his initial view that he alone can lead a pirate community to independence from England. Having become more fully aware of the rage within him, Flint now admits that others should lead.

Flint chooses Madi because she is a proper leader of the Maroon Island community; she is "as strong as her father" and "as wise as her mother," making her crucial to the pirate-maroon alliance struggling for independence. He chooses Silver because he finally agrees with Silver's season three assessment of proper leadership, as he tells Flint:

> I once thought that to lead men in this world, to be liked was just as good as feared, and that may very well be true. But to be both liked and feared all at once is an entirely different state of being... in which, I believe, at this moment, I exist alone. The men need to know they're in good favor with me. They need it, and there is nothing they won't do to make sure they have it. (Chapter XXIII)

Flint, violent and cunning, was feared, but never liked, let alone loved as Madi is with the escaped slaves of Maroon Island. Perhaps Flint remains the best candidate to defend Nassau Bay from naval threats, but Silver is the best candidate for leading the pirate community to independence. Madi and Silver together will bring balance to a free Nassau, serving as proper political leaders.

Flint's evolving views over the course of the series engages the philosophical process insofar as it (implicitly) attempts to combine a Hobbesian view of a politically irrepressible sovereign to ensure the safety and stability of the commonwealth with Lockean views about citizens thriving within its democratic processes. Worries about a Hobbesian sovereign with unchecked political power are deflected by empowering not the strongest among its members (Flint or perhaps Teach), but those who commendably garner respect, love, and admiration, allowing for community members to thrive of their own accord. Whether Flint's implicit theory is viable or open to serious objection remains to be seen, but it is an interesting synthesis of two venerable social contract theory perspectives, and thereby engages the philosophical process.

As it turns out, *Black Sails* opts for more of a Lockean resolution to Flint's war with England. In the first two seasons (or so), Locke's version of social contract is exemplified by Eleanor, her father, and Max. The Guthrie Trading Company exists not as an extension of piracy, but as a function of it. Pirates, no matter what waters they call home, need markets to turn their material goods into liquid assets – cash or credit. Pirates bring goods to Eleanor, she buys them at cut rates, and then sells them back to legitimate markets for a profit. The regulation of markets and market-based economies are at the heart of Locke's contract theory. But it must be remembered that Locke's focus is on who can control assets that are *marketable*, about which Max excels. She regularly trades in information and her ability to acquire information is the basis of her partnerships with Anne Bonny and Jack Rackham. In any case, the roles played by English investors, colonial agents, and plantation owners (among others) regularly factor into the decision-making about determining Nassau's future.

Indeed, in season four, Jack, Anne, and Max travel to Philadelphia to strike a deal with Eleanor's grandmother, Marion, the quiet matriarch of the Guthrie family empire. They agree that once Flint and Rogers are removed from influence, Nassau can return to stable commerce without seeking complete independence from England. There will be no strong Hobbesian sovereign, as Flint's war and the pirate-maroon alliance are circumvented. Rather, with Marion's blessing and vast financial assistance, arrangements will be made to institute a figure-head former pirate governor (Featherstone), with the real power subtly wielded by Max (perhaps under Marion's tutelage). Piracy will be (very) publicly outlawed, but in practice, will continue under Jack's judicious watch, ironically to spur the island's economy. While these arrangements, at least for now, seem advantageous to all the major players and Nassau as a whole, the series implicitly leaves the viewer to question which solution to the existential threat of civilization coming to Nassau is better: Flint's or Max's, with Madi siding with the former and Jack (obviously) with the latter. This is, again, to engage the philosophical process, reminiscent of the doubt occasioned by Socratic dialogue.

Rousseau and Rawls

In *The Social Contract* (1762), Jean-Jacques Rousseau recognizes a serious flaw in social contract theories generally – one that Locke is equally guilty of: namely, people don't exist as individuals. People are born into systems of support: families. Rousseau offers a social contract grounded in mutual support among families in a given geographic area. It is for this reason that different cultures exist, people in the mountains have different needs and expectations of their neighbors than do people living along the seacoast, and how people are organized is determined by these factors.

What makes Rousseau interesting in terms of Golden Age piracy generally, but *Black Sails* specifically, is the fact that the pirates often cast their relationships in familial terms. For instance, when Gates refers to Billy as being like a son or when Billy tells Rogers his brothers broke their oaths to him, we get the sense that these men do not think of each other as *merely* crewmates or colleagues. Familial concerns sit at the heart of *Black Sails* in other important ways as well. Flint's relationship with Miranda and Thomas, Thomas's relationship with his father, the Guthrie family issues that exist from Nassau's jetty to Boston Harbor, Vane's relationship with Blackbeard and, in parallel to that, Vane's relationship with Rackham and Bonny, as well as John Silver and Madi, and Madi's parents especially exemplify the issue of choosing one's family and the organization of society that follows. If Nassau is home and the pirates that live there think of each other as family, then Rousseau's contract theory can be very helpful in parsing out how an intentional social community forms, develops, and establishes the norms and more that will guide it.

Still, *Black Sails* implicitly asks questions that Rousseau must address, especially as it becomes clear that individual families must somehow cooperate to form larger social groups for social stability. This is poignantly conveyed in Mr. Scott's heart-felt exchange with Madi upon his being fatally wounded and returned to Maroon Island. Madi admits, "You're my father, and I love you... but I do not know you. Those men, they are your life. I wanted to know it, at least a little" (Chapter XXIII). In the next episode, Mr. Scott attempts to explain, "I wish... you and I had not been so separate all those years. I wish I could have found a way to be a better father to you. But over time, I was determined to...give you the one thing that no one could ever take away... and that would make you strong enough to understand their world, interact with their world" (Chapter XXIV). Mr. Scott was forced to leave his family and become Eleanor's surrogate father – causing resentment in his own daughter – in the hope that Madi might have a place in the world. Furthermore, the ersatz family relationships among the pirates, while real, were often strained and sometimes unruly. Jack and Anne joining Blackbeard's crew upon Vane's death serves as a microcosm. When Anne reminds Jack, "A few weeks ago, we had a chance to sail with him. You said you'd always be looking over your shoulder," Jack replies, "Charles was, in some sense, a son to him, and Charles was, in some sense, a brother to us. I couldn't tell you what that makes us to him, but something, perhaps" (Chapter XXVIII). As the pirate crews – the various ersatz pirate-families – strive toward a community strong enough to withstand the coming onslaught of civilization (as Flint might say), they must find ways to come together as such. Perhaps Rousseau would be ready to answer these sorts of questions, but *Black Sails* again enters into the philosophical conversation by (implicitly) reminding us that they must be answered.

John Rawls, in *Justice as Fairness* (2001), argues that we cannot know how society began but that we can evaluate the social contract and make adjustments to it. The first thing that is necessary is the recognition that we adhere to a basic set of principles and that we have a reasonable expectation that others are going to adhere to these principles as well. From that acknowledgment, it is easy to see a social contract underlying the organization of society – not just the whole of civilization, but our communities, social groups, states, etc. We are born into circumstances defined by a social contract, and we are raised to adhere to it even before we are given the chance to choose it. This raises an obvious question: what aspects of society would you change if you could? We do this slowly over time though voting, shifting moral positions, or more immediately through revolution, war, and diplomacy. Rawls's argument is that we can develop a hypothetical set of circumstances and use that to evaluate the social contract.

To that end, Rawls proposes the "Veil of Ignorance." Rawls asks us to assume that we are behind the Veil, say in the moment right before you are born, and in that moment, you have a choice about the kind of world you will be born into. Prior to making this choice, however, you are completely ignorant of what your life will be like after you are born. How would you arrange society? If, for instance, there was a good chance you might be born a female person of color, otherly abled, in poverty conditions, would you choose to be born in the United States the way our current society is structured? Using Rawls's Veil of Ignorance we ought to see what we would choose to make different and, hopefully, reveal a little about why we would choose such things as well. The reason Rawls positions his argument this way is so that we can clearly identify both what inequalities exist and our unwillingness to accept them. That is, if we determine that certain inequalities would be intolerable, then we have a morally justifiable reason to change those social circumstances.

Through a Rawlsian lens, we better see that many people who filled out the rank and file of pirate culture were responding to social inequities and injustices and the life of a pirate offered a viable alternative. This is captured nicely by *Black Sails* in multiple ways, but two instances stand out.

The first example pervades the series in the form of Flint's war. Being humiliated and disenfranchised by England for entering a consensual relationship with the Hamiltons, one that harmed no one and arguably benefitted themselves and others, McGraw resolutely leaves to start anew. In Nassau, he strives to follow Thomas's example (admittedly in his own way) to change the world; as he tells Rogers, "I'm through seeking anything from England except her departure from my island," regardless of England's protestations (Chapter XXV). And Flint's determination inspires the escaped slaves of Maroon Island to join his cause. Flint explains that the maroons are confronted with the harsh realities of the times, "chief among them being that England takes whatever, whenever, however it wants." Rather than merely preventing England from taking away anything more, Flint entreats the Queen: "No, I am suggesting that we help each other start taking things back, and it starts with Nassau. What does a colonial power do when the men whose toil powers it lay down their shovels, take up swords, and say, 'No more?' Bring down Nassau, maybe you bring it all down" (Chapter XXIII). The maroons, personified by Madi (Julius notwithstanding), would rather die with Flint than continue living in chains. The alliance they form with the pirates is to end unjust oppression, thereby changing the world.

The second example is more contained, but no less poignant. Prior to being publicly hanged for his crimes against the Crown, Vane is asked if he has any last words. He defiantly announces, "They know that my voice, a voice that refuses to be enslaved, once lived in you. And may yet still. They brought me here today to show you death and use it to frighten you into ignoring that voice" (Chapter XXVII). Vane sees his death as an opportunity to challenge Colonial rule and oppression. Billy also recognizes this and, in turn, uses Vane's example – his martyrdom – to invigorate the pirate revolution in Nassau. After all, per Charles's last words: "They can't hang us all." *Black Sails* vividly brings Rawls's ideas to life, implicitly challenging each of us to reexamine our own beliefs about the inequities that beset society – a crucial first step to doing philosophy.

In order to formulate a social contract that will bind people together, those people have to have something in common: for Hobbes, it is a shared need for security from constant threats to it; for Locke, it is commerce and the social stability it garners; for Rousseau, it is a supportive thriving community grounded in family-like relationships; for Rawls, it is minimal inequality. Flint's proposal to the Maroon Queen is predicated on the construction of a new identity rooted in the reclamation of Nassau

6 *Black Sails* as Philosophy: Pirates and Political Discourse

and the establishment of a new society. What that society will look like and how it will function sit at the heart of the negotiations between the two groups but those negotiations signal that the groups have accepted that identity which allows them to formulate a social contract. Furthermore, Pirates come from disparate backgrounds and have a wide variety of personal goals, but, as we'll see, as part of a crew they share an identity, and through it form their own community founded upon the principles of democracy and equality.

Democracy and Equality

Although social contract theorists invariably hold that only through hypotheticals can we shape our understanding of how society arose, pirates offer practical examples of social contract theory at work (see Jones 2018). Known as "going on the account," pirates employed articles that would govern pirate behavior *especially* aboard ship. Going on the account was required of every person that agreed to join a pirate crew whether that happened prior to the voyage or joining from a captured ship's crew. The articles varied from ship to ship, could be changed when the captain was changed, were agreed to prior to setting out for plunder, had to be adhered to for the entire voyage, and every pirate was made explicitly aware of what they were agreeing to. Universal acceptance was important because the articles included everything from the division of plunder, to insurance payments for injuries incurred at sea, to consequences for violating the articles. Because each pirate had a stake in the endeavor, each pirate was allowed a say in how the articles were drawn up.

In *Black Sails,* pirates regularly refer to the articles, the oaths they took to uphold those articles, and take seriously any offence that violates them. For example, when Rackham and Featherstone are negotiating with the crew about the articles before they set sail, Featherstone tells Jack there is an issue: Bonny and Max. The crew does not want to take a woman to sea, even one as fearsome as Anne, nor do they fancy giving a share of their plunder to Max who, though she is providing the insider tips on prizes, is not risking her life to earn her share. The crew, via Featherstone, tells Jack he can have one or the other but not both (Chapter XIII). It is possible that Jack could have approached his new crew, made an impassioned plea for both, but he instead makes a choice. This is likely because he is a newly elected captain of a crew that does not know him and he stands to lose more by rocking the boat than by making a difficult decision. This example, however, demonstrates the negotiations that were the backbone of building crew consensus prior to a voyage.

In pirate culture the captain could be deposed through a popular vote – one person, one vote among the crew. The captain could be challenged for any number of reasons from cowardice, poor seamanship, abuse of power, or an inability to locate or capture prizes, among a plethora of other concerns. Once challenged, the captain and his challenger would make their case to the crew, the crew would vote, and if unsuccessful at gaining the crew's favor, the captain would be replaced. Flint's captaincy of the *Walrus* was challenged twice. The first time Singleton had the votes to depose him, but because Flint accused Singleton of theft, the articles allowed for trial by combat. The second time Flint was deposed upon his crew learning of his treacherous actions, including Billy's suspicious disappearance.

The articles in tandem with the ability of a crew to recall a captain ensured that everyone was treated equally on the ship and, unlike their naval and merchant counterparts, no one was above the law. This idea is clearly explained by the Bosun of the *Walrus*, Billy Bones, when he is explaining to John Silver what is expected of him as the ship's cook. Bones explains matter-of-factly that no one is to get special treatment from the cook. This includes no extra portions or privileged access to the choicest cuts of meat and this rule applies to everyone, as Billy specifies, even the captain and first mate (Chapter I).

There was thus an inclusiveness that sets pirates apart from everyone else in their opposition to the various monarchies they were often fleeing. Relying on the democratic process for decisions – all decisions outside of battle – meant that no person could arbitrarily establish themselves as superior to any other person. This type of equality did not exist in the Western world until pirates established themselves in the New World. It did not matter where a person came from, the color of one's skin, one's gender or sex, or what one's aspirations were, everyone was treated equally.

Radical democracy of this type goes even beyond other historical examples, like Greek society, because the pirates excluded no one from participation once that person was a part of the crew. Of course, pirates were products of their socio-cultural milieu and could still be racist, sexist, Catholic or Protestant, or any number of problematic personality types we recognize today, but still managed to be somewhat progressive. For instance, individuals were not necessarily abandoned by a crew because of disabilities – especially those incurred during combat. This is highlighted in the show through the cook aboard the *Walrus*, Randall, who is believed by his crewmates to have been struck dumb by blow during combat. It is further explored in the development of the fictional Long John Silver as the show provides an origin story for his peg leg which is only possible because pirates managed a system of insurance whereby pirates were paid additional money for injuries received during battle or while at sea generally. Long John Silver can easily exist alongside pirates in our imaginations because his peg leg would not have been an insurmountable obstacle to his belonging to a pirate crew.

The use of radical democratic principles among the crew is on display several times throughout the show. In one scene, as the crew is preparing to pursue the *Urca*, Captain Flint explains that the ship needs to be careened and cleaned. Careening is the tedious task of tipping the ship to expose the bottom of the vessel that sits below the waterline. This is done to remove barnacles, reapply pitch, and make any necessary repairs. Flint wants to careen on a beach that the ship's master, Mr. de Groot, deems to be unsafe. Each of them makes their case to the crew and then the crew votes whether to careen at Flint's location or find a different spot (Chapter IV). Every major or minor decision that will affect the crew (presumably while not at sea or not explicitly addressed in the articles) is filtered through this process and any crewmember may contribute to the conversation attempting to sway the decision one way or another.

The only exception to such democratic processes is when the crew is at battle. During times of combat the captain assumed total control and commanded

6 *Black Sails* as Philosophy: Pirates and Political Discourse

unquestionable loyalty from the crew. This point is expressly stated by Mr. Gates during the crews' struggles to dislodge Captain Bryson and his crew from the midship bunker. After Logan refuses to accept his selection for what amounts to a suicide mission, Mr. Gates interjects, "Mr. Logan makes a valid point. Unfortunately, now is not the time," and reinforces his point by summarily beating Logan. Gates consequently exclaims to the crew, "While we are in battle the captain's orders are the law! That is what we signed up to!" (Chapter VI). Presumably, then, the articles dictate that the crew follow the captain's orders during battle; nevertheless, this suspension of the democratic process is undoubtedly made because it is in the best interest of the ship and its crew.

Again, *Black Sails* relies upon the history of "going on the account" and its corresponding articles to not only weave compelling fictional narratives about them, but also put them in a philosophical light. The first issue stems from the insight that the democratic process can be circumvented if doing so better serves the greater good. Consider Flint's season one plan to sequester a portion of the *Urca's* prize without crew consent. He believes doing so best solidifies the future of Nassau, and thus is in the best interests of all the pirates involved. He argues his case to Gates by claiming the men will just squander the prize by drinking, whoring, and pissing it away (and interestingly the show in season three bolsters Flint's position when a drunken pirate misplaces two bags of gold on successive days, despite Featherstone's admonishments before issuing the second bag). Flint believes they have a chance at something better – much better than leaving 500 pieces of eight in the privy – but that something won't happen unless *someone* makes it happen. Flint admits that his plan includes being less than honest to the crew, but he argues that his non-democratic plan is justifiable: "If no one knows, everyone wins. Who loses? Absent their worst instincts, their pride, their greed, their suspicion, in the light of pure reason, who says no to this? They'll be rich men in a safe place rather than dead thieves on a long rope…. I'm gonna deliver them into something better" (Chapter VII). If the democratic process can be suspended in times of battle, why not now given that civilization intends to exterminate them? Both are for the greater good. However, Gates believes Flint goes too far. In the past, he had acquiesced, believing that Flint's dissembling was, in the end, best for everyone, but not this time. Still suspicious about Billy's disappearance, Flint is akin to a sovereign levying a tax, and as Billy once said, pirates have no kings. Gates intends to turn Flint over to the crew once the *Urca's* gold is secured.

Interestingly, there are (at least) two instances where important questions are purposely *not* brought forward for democratic consideration. The first occurs in season three where Flint entreats Blackbeard to resume their compact about defending Nassau from further British incursion. Flint wishes to resume command of the pirate fleet, most of which is now under Blackbeard's command. Blackbeard, disgusted with so many Nassau pirates accepting Rogers's pardon, demurs: "Nassau is dead. It doesn't deserve anything else from me or the men on this beach. …And I think you know that I would never allow you to call a vote to settle the matter of who this fleet follows and risk you depleting my force by luring away some misguided minority" (Chapter XXIV). Rather than enter democratic discussion with the fleet, Flint and Blackbeard duel with pistols and swords for control. Here, *Black Sails* reminds the viewer that even in settings where democracy is prized, sometimes those in power inhibit it for personal reasons, typically to preserve that person's power or status. In doing so, it reminds us to be vigilant about protecting our ideals.

The second example contains elements of Flint's respective discussions with Gates and Blackbeard. When the Maroon Queen learns that Rogers wishes to ransom Madi for the cache of gemstones, she is unsurprisingly conflicted and consults with Flint and Silver alone. Silver contends that they should bring the question to the pirate-maroon alliance and make the argument that paying the ransom is the proper course. This would be in accordance with the democratic process. Although sympathetic, Flint argues for discretion; he states, "If we even introduce this question to the men in this camp, lines will be drawn, fighting will ensue. This alliance is far too fragile at this stage to withstand that kind of turmoil. We can pay the ransom or we can have our war, but we cannot have both" (Chapter XXXV). The Queen remains silent, representing her difficulty in siding with Sliver or Flint, but she nevertheless agrees that the way forward ought to be decided by the three of them. Although Sliver protests, his objection is not nearly as vehement as was Gates's, and he acquiesces to Flint's alternative plan. Yet Flint's argument to demur from the democratic process here is very similar to the one he gave Gates. The viewer is left to explore whether this version of Flint's argument for the greater good is better than the previous one and, if so, why? The careful viewer, furthermore, is invited to contemplate under what conditions, then, is it permissible to circumvent the democratic process and the principle of equality that underwrites it?

Black Sails also effectively conveys a perennial difficulty besetting radical democracy: the process by which people enact it is not always rational. Given the pirates' deep commitment to democracy, outright emotional manipulation is sometimes the surest way to secure an individual's desired ends when putting a question to the group – something Flint excels at. He swayed the crew – embodied by Billy's compliance – via his confrontation with Singleton by making him appear to be a thief when he was not (and then killed him to cover up his ploy). Even when the question is faithfully put forth, as it was when Flint and De Groot provided reasons for and against careening the *Walrus*, Flint successfully appealed to the crew's baser inclinations for wealth, food, and (a distinctive form of carnal) leisure. Furthermore, as things played out, De Groot had the stronger argument; had they chosen a different location, the ship wouldn't have broken free of its beach moorings and lives would not have been lost.

Even when Flint is not being overtly manipulative, *Black Sails* conveys other equally troubling difficulties about radical democracy failing rationality. Recall the struggle between Flint and Hornigold revolving around a strategic decision to storm the fort when it was being held by Captain Charles Vane. Hornigold puts the question to the various crews assembled for the assault and asks them to choose who they will follow – him or Flint. As the time for the vote draws near. Flint discusses where the unofficial votes are with Billy. Billy tells Flint he lost one of his expected votes because two men got into an argument about a game of chance and one of the men, to spite the other, a supporter of Flint as well, changed his vote to Hornigold (Chapter XV). Furthermore, even when decisions are not switched as

6 *Black Sails* as Philosophy: Pirates and Political Discourse 129

mindlessly as this, rarely are voters fully informed about an issue and votes are often purchased through bribes and personal alliances rather than considerations of what is best overall. This is conveyed in the first episode as Gates visits various factions of the crew, some of which are *always* for sale, for example Nelson's men. Gates also visits Mosiah, the leader of the African contingent; the Africans vote how Mosiah votes, no questions asked. If Gates can sway Mosiah, then Singleton no longer has the votes required to depose Flint. Mosiah agrees only if Gates rewards them with extra shares of the next haul, which only makes them a target for factions loyal to Singleton (and implicitly raises an additional issue about democracy and marginalized social factions).

By providing us vivid depictions of how committed Golden Age pirates were to the democratic process, *Black Sails* provides important insights into how difficult the process of radical democracy must have been given that it could be manipulated by the raw passions and egoistic motivations of the people involved. This, in turn, invites us to consider the nature and value of democracy, whether it can be permissibly curtailed, and the safeguards that might be put in place to ensure it serves citizens properly. And these insights pertain to our time as well the early eighteenth century, spurring us to further philosophical exploration of these important issues.

Tolerance

For radical democracy to work it would have to go beyond any political theory available during the Golden Age of Piracy, which included expanding the notion of who got to participate in it. We know of at least two women who sailed with pirates and participated fully in the life of piracy expected of any member of the crew. The existence of Anne Bonny and Mary Read, along with other notable historical examples of women who dressed as men to join military actions throughout history, suggests that it is possible other women were pirates at the time as well. Clearly, there were not likely to have been an abundance of them, and some crews explicitly forbade women aboard ship in their articles, but it does highlight nonetheless that pirates were a community where a woman *could* participate fully as an equal. In *Black Sails* this is explored more fully in the character of Anne Bonny especially as she is juxtaposed against Eleanor Guthrie and Max.

Recall that Jack's first crew is reluctant to allow Anne aboard ship and they are uneasy giving a share of their plunder to Max who is neither sailing with them nor assuming any risk. It is clearly a tough choice – take his partner, a capable pirate in her own right, with him or risk losing his silent partner and the information she provides. Nevertheless, Jack's predicament highlights how crews understood women and their willingness to include them in their dealings. Jack complains about the short-sightedness of the crew, and it is entirely possible such a choice was at some point put to the historical Jack Rackham, but outside of pirate society no such choice would have been offered because women were summarily excluded from such discussions. Only in a society built upon a principle of radical democracy, where everyone is ostensibly afforded equal status, could such political discourse naturally emerge.

The inclusion of women raises an immediate and obvious parallel concern about the inclusivity of minorities among the pirates. This is especially vital given that slavery was a booming business and pirates, like everyone, were influenced by the societies they grew up in. Not all pirates were accepting of slaves among their crews just as not all crews were accepting of women, but many crews did have former slaves – either escaped or liberated – among them. There were also people from local indigenous tribes and, though it would have been unusual, it would not have been unheard of for there to be pirates of Asian origin among the crews as well. New minority crew members could be picked up in any of numerous locations around the world and few pirates lingered in one place too long. Even before the pirate-maroon alliance, Captain Flint's *Walrus* crew included numerous African crewmen, beginning with the first episode, as well as English, French, and presumably crewmen of other European origins; there is also Joji, a sailor of clearly Asian descent.

As *Black Sails* conveys, tolerance for minority crewmembers and escaped slaves generally was sometimes tenuous. Upon the pirate-maroon alliance, the *Walrus* included new African crewmembers among its ranks. But when a rigging comes loose from its lashing, nearly killing some crewmembers, some are quick to blame an African crewmember's incompetence. Flint diffuses the situation: "If he tied it wrong, then you instructed him wrong" (Chapter XXIV). Two episodes later, Mr. Dobbs savagely beats an African crewman in retaliation for deaths caused prior to their alliance; Silver and Madi work together to quell further rifts among the crew. Furthermore, Maroon Island inhabitant Julius serves as an example of someone who is wary of the pirates and their motivations. He chides Flint: "What happens when our enemy realizes that all it needs to do to defeat us is to take away that common cause? Turn one against the other. And when that happens...as it is all but certain to do... which of us standing here are likely to be the ones who benefit and which the ones sold back into their chains?" (Chapter XXXV). The Maroon Queen attempts allay his suspicions, by vouching for Flint, Silver, and their men, and then tells Julius, "No one has ever been this close, this near a chance to change the world." Julius remains unconvinced: "No one changes the world. Not like this. Not all at once. The world is too strong for that" (Chapter XXV).

Again, not all pirates opposed slavery. In *Black Sails*, Charles Vane is presented as being staunchly anti-slavery having been, according to the show, a slave himself. Others, like Captain Flint, are much more pragmatic, and Flint's resolve to free slaves grows throughout the show as he begins to see them as allied soldiers for his brewing conflict with England. These characterizations may reflect a certain truth about the historical pirates that operated in the West Indies, but it is also true that historical pirates understood the realities of civilization at the time. For instance, in an attempt to evade capture and bribe the governor of Carolina, the historical Blackbeard sold all of his African crewmembers referring to them as "black gold." Such a thing certainly paints Blackbeard as a treacherous turncoat, but it provides a necessary counterbalance to the idea that pirates were of one mind when it came to the equality of others. Still, it is necessary to understand pirate culture as one that was

6 *Black Sails* as Philosophy: Pirates and Political Discourse

more expansive and inclusionary than the civilizing forces it was opposed to during the Golden Age.

Black Sails mirrors the historical complexities of race relations and tolerance within communities struggling for equality. By raising up that mirror, it allows us to contemplate why the world might be "too strong to change all at once" and invites each of us to look carefully at ourselves in terms of now being more tolerant and improving race relations. This, in turn, encourages us to look at the world more philosophically.

Justice

Black Sails offers extensive dialogue about what is just, where one's duty lies, how to determine what is right or best, and what is permissible both in the enactment of war and in the execution of punishments. Though Captain Flint's reasoning is often colored by his desire for vengeance, especially early in the series, he does analyze his rationale and argue for his decisions throughout the series separate from that desire. Flint engages Mr. Gates, Billy, Silver, Elenore, and her father, as well as Miranda on matters large and small in an effort to parse out what is "right." Because pirate society was fluid, lacking any reliably stable reference points for what was acceptable beyond what a group may choose in a given moment, considerations about what was right, best, or just are constantly at the fore of pirate decision-making. An extreme example of this is Vane's punishment of Max after she is determined to be responsible for the loss of the pearls Rackham was using to try to secure the *Urca* schedule from Silver in season one. Similarly, Billy Bones routinely references his oath to his "brothers" and argues that living up to that oath requires him to do certain things. For instance, though he is offered the chance at a pardon, because the pardon only extends to a total of ten men, Billy refuses to accept it on the grounds that doing so would violate his commitments to *all* his fellow pirates. And again, when Billy seeks retribution for the perceived wrongs he has suffered, he explains to Woodes Rogers that his brothers have betrayed him – that is, they violated their oaths to him.

The examples running throughout *Black Sails* raise important questions about justice – can you break the laws of a society you don't belong to? That is, do the English, or Spanish for that matter, have the authority to punish pirates as criminals? They clearly have the *power* to do so, and historically did just as they do in the show; but as the pirates correctly wonder, is it right that they do so? Obviously, we can say stealing is wrong. But if belligerents in an acknowledged conflict steal from one another in the context of that conflict, granting for the time being the conflict is justified, how should punishment for that act be handled? Who should enforce the law in that case? Once European monarchies declared pirates to be enemies of all humankind, they placed those pirates beyond the reach of their laws while still applying those laws to pirates as if they were still sovereign citizens.

A similar argument could made for murder. In *Black Sails*, Woodes Rogers solicits aid from the governor of Havana in quelling the pirate uprising in Nassau. The Spanish soldiers are given free rein to rape, pillage, and murder everyone in the town as pirates or pirate sympathizers. This action is presented as a justified course of action solely on the premise that Rogers is an agent of the English Crown. How is such an action different than that of pirates who capture non-military targets, merchant vessels, and kill and maim their way to victory? If one is unjustifiable, then surely the other is as well. If, however, pirates plundering their enemies is wrong, then certainly it is equally wrong for the agent of European monarchies to plunder native communities using similar arguments.

Outside the theaters of warfare, *Black Sails* pursues questions of right and wrong in other circumstances as well. As mentioned previously, Charles Vane forces Max to work off her debt to his crew, a loss caused by her scheming, in a horrific way. Does something being horrible render it unjust? To the viewer it may seem immediately true that Max's treatment by Vane is wrong, obviously there were other ways to recover the loss, but Vane's crew thinks the punishment fits the crime – well, not all the crew, at least not over time, as some of them, including Vane, begin to see the punishment as excessive; however, in a culture of radical democracy, if the majority of the crew believe the punishment is just, what recourse can there be to bring it to an end? When Eleanor Guthrie turns the table on Vane and exacts a terrible punishment on him for allowing the treatment of Max, Vane challenges the correctness of her having done so. The relationship between Eleanor and Max is fraught with instances of double-dealing, betrayal, shifting loyalties, and while there are numerous questions embedded in this relationship regarding the right thing, and justifications for it, their relationship also raises key questions about friendship. These questions are equally salient not only because they are raised in the context of pirate culture, but also because they are salient for all of pirate culture – especially where Rousseau's ideas are being applied or interrogated.

Paralleling the difficult relationship of Eleanor and Max, trading on similar questions of duplicity, honor, commitment, etc., is the relationship between Flint and Silver. In fact, several of Flint's relationships bear the strain of questions of justice, right, what is good, and who should decide these things. Flint's relationships with various other pirates like Mr. Gates, Billy Bones, Rackham, Vane, and even Singleton, as well as his relationships with Miranda, his lover, Eleanor, his partner in crime, and Woodes Rogers, are all imbued with questions of justice regarding Nassau, life aboard ship, the fate of England, the role of civilization, and moral goodness. *Black Sails* asks these questions effectively, providing vivid glimpses into Golden Age piracy, but they also transcend the boundaries of the show to highlight their continued relevance today. The show invites us to answer them for ourselves, encouraging us to be more philosophical.

Conclusion

We can no longer reject our social origins, opting for the possibilities of creating our own community, because there is nowhere left to go. The world is too full; all frontiers have been reduced to assimilated cultural amalgamations, and the world is

6 *Black Sails* as Philosophy: Pirates and Political Discourse

too closely and strictly policed from satellites to CCTV cameras on every corner. How society might have started is left to theory.

This wasn't the case in the Golden Age of Piracy. Far removed from the hypothetical nature of social contract theory to date, pirate communities in the Golden Age were able to achieve in practice what has mostly only been done in theory. The questions raised by eighteenth century pirate culture persist especially at the level of what the content of the social contract should be, who should determine it, how it should be determined, and under what conditions or circumstances the applicability of the social contract can be deferred. Learning to articulate those things is vital to the success of society but can only be achieved through the rigorous application of radical democratic principles of inclusion, egalitarianism, participation, and tolerance. That is, everyone who chooses to abide by the social contract must be included in its creation, equally and fairly, and everyone must participate. These standards require that we cultivate a strong sense of tolerance for other views, beliefs, and moral standards. This is much to learn from this historical era, and you are invited to research it yourself.

Yet, as we've seen here, there is also a great deal to learn from exploring a fictional rendering of Golden Age piracy, not the least of which is how film engages the philosophical process. This insight, in conjunction with the one about historical pirates, fittingly harkens back to the closing lines of *Black Sails*. Jack Rackham, deep in his cups, waxes philosophically with another historical pirate Mary Read. Jack states, "A story is true. A story is untrue. As time extends, it matters less and less. The stories we want to believe... those are the ones that survive, despite upheaval and transition and progress. Those are the stories that shape history. And then what does it matter if it was true when it was born? It's found truth in its maturity, which if a virtue in man ought to be no less so for the things men create" (Chapter XXXVIII). Even if historians (or philosophers) might take offense at Jack's perspective, he suggests that truth can be found in the stories we tell, even if those stories are not (completely) true. Perhaps those truths are woven into the story and its construction. When such stories convey insights into the human condition, philosophers should take note. *Black Sails* is one of those stories. By carefully studying it, we can glean insights into ethics, political philosophy, and, indeed, how a story can engage the philosophical process, thereby becoming philosophy in action.

References

Hobbes, Thomas. 1660/1969. *The leviathan.* London: Penguin Classics.
Jones, Clint. 2018. Piratical societies as the blueprint for social Utopia. In *Pirates in history and popular culture*, ed. Antonio Sanna, 25–36. Jefferson: McFarland.
Locke, John. 1689/2004. *The second treatise of government.* New York: Barnes & Noble.
Rawls, John. 2001. *Justice as fairness: A restatement.* Cambridge, MA: Belknap Press.
Rousseau, Jean-Jacques. 1762/1968. *The social contract.* London: Penguin Classics.
Stevenson, Robert Louis. 1883. *Treasure Island.* London: Cassell & Company.

Doctor Who as Philosophy: Four-Dimensionalism and Time Travel

7

Kevin S. Decker

Contents

Introduction	136
Touring the TARDIS and Related Dimensions	137
"Lots of impossible things happen when you pass through time": Time Travel and the Space-Time Vortex	138
"Bigger on the inside": The Widening Significance of Relative Dimensions	141
"I can foresee oodles of trouble": Problems and Paradoxes	143
Time Travel in Theory: "First things first, but not necessarily in that order"	147
Four-Dimensional Realism	154
Conclusion	156
References	159

Abstract

Doctor Who is the longest-running science fiction program on television, having been in continuous production between 1963 and 1989. "Classic" Doctor Who was widely syndicated around the world and appeared to many US viewers on their local Public Broadcasting System channel. The show was rebooted with continuity to the original program on BBC One in 2005. The success of the show rests on the appeal of its central character and his/her traveling companions, the creativity of its bizarre locations and alien adversaries, and, of course, the diversity of destinations that its time travel format allows it. This chapter is about the apparent nature of time in Doctor Who and, by extension, what the nature of "our" universe would have to be like if time travel were actual. After looking over infamous paradoxes and philosophical arguments and rehearsing

---

K. S. Decker (✉)
Eastern Washington University, Cheney, WA, USA
e-mail: kdecker@ewu.edu

© Springer Nature Switzerland AG 2024
D. K. Johnson et al. (eds.), *The Palgrave Handbook of Popular Culture as Philosophy*,
https://doi.org/10.1007/978-3-031-24685-2_18

135

some traditional philosophical approaches to the nature of time travel and the problem of changing history, I outline the theory that best accords with the reality of time travel in Doctor Who, that of "Four-Dimensional Realism."

Keywords

Doctor Who · Time · Time travel · Time machine · Hypertime · Personal versus external time · *Flatland* · Uncanniness · Bootstrap paradox · Grandfather paradox · Eternalism · Presentism · Four-Dimensional Realism

Introduction

Let me get this straight. A thing that looks like a police box, standing in a junkyard...it can move anywhere in time and space?
—Ian Chesterton ("An Unearthly Child" 1963)

Well, I thought it'd be a bit more impressive than that.
What did you expect? Some kind of space rocket with Batman at the controls?
—Greg Sutton and the Doctor ("Inferno" 1970)

Doctor Who is the longest-running science fiction program on television, having been in continuous production between 1963 and 1989. "Classic" *Doctor Who* has been widely syndicated around the world and appeared to many US viewers on their local Public Broadcasting System channel. Nine years after a one-off BBC/Universal tele-movie broadcast in 1996, the show was rebooted on BBC One in 2005 and, with the advent of cable channel BBC America and streaming availability of both the classic and new iterations, now reaches more viewers than ever before. Supplemented by hundreds of hours of professional documentaries made for DVD and Blu Ray episode releases, fan-made interviews, and dozens of reference books, "*Doctor Who* is probably the most documented television show in history" (Burk and Smith 2012, n.p.).

It is somewhat difficult to draw conclusions about certain facts about the *Doctor Who* universe. This is because "a total adherence to continuity has always been rather less important to the successive *Doctor Who* production teams than the main order of business: writing exciting stories, telling good jokes and scaring small children with big monsters" (Pearson and Parkin 2019, vol. 3, p. 3001).

Yet for its more than 850 episodes, the success of *Doctor Who* has essentially rested on three things. First is its central character, the eccentric humanoid alien known as "the Doctor" (often credited as "Doctor Who"), a character kept fresh for viewers since 1963 by the process of "regeneration," which has allowed a series of actors to portray the role in succession. Philosophically, the idea of regeneration poses intriguing questions about personal identity, questions that cannot be raised in this forum (see Johnson 2010). Second, given its origins as an adventure drama for children, *Doctor Who* has offered up an impressive variety of "monsters" – most famously represented by adversary alien races like the Daleks, the Cybermen, the

Silence, and the Weeping Angels. Third, the program is about time travel, showcasing different destinations, threats, and problems week by week. The Doctor usually welcomes new companions on board by saying something like, "We can travel anywhere and everywhere in that old box... Regardless of space and time" ("The Rescue," 1964). The Doctor's trusty time-and-space craft, the TARDIS (Time and Relative Dimension(s) in Space), is a character in its own right, often taking the Doctor where he is needed, if not always where he wants to go. Bigger on the inside than its external guise of a mid-twentieth-century British Police Call Box, the TARDIS is a product of the advanced technology of the Doctor's people, the Time Lords.

This chapter is about the apparent nature of time in *Doctor Who* and, by extension, what the nature of "our" universe would have to be like if time travel were actual. It considers a number of infamous paradoxes and philosophical arguments. In the first part, I assemble the fictive elements of what in *Doctor Who* continuity is called "Time Travel Law" from episodes of the classic program. We'll also look at the significance of the "and Relative Dimension(s)" part of the TARDIS' moniker. In the second part, I'll rehearse some traditional philosophical approaches to the nature of time and the possibility of traveling through it – and changing history. Some of these approaches have promise for understanding the nature of time in our own universe, while others don't accord with what science now tells us about the fabric of space-time. In the third part, I'll outline the theory that best accords with the reality of time travel in *Doctor Who* – a theory called "Four-Dimensional Realism" (4DR). In the conclusion, I'll point out some problems implied by 4DR as they impact our understanding of free will and moral responsibility – always central concerns of the subgenre of time travel stories – and make a few suggestions as to how those problems might be resolved.

Touring the TARDIS and Related Dimensions

Unlike popular science fiction franchises like *Star Wars*, *Star Trek*, and *Firefly*, there is no George Lucas, Gene Roddenberry, or Joss Whedon of *Doctor Who*. "Always seen as the brainchild of an ever-changing committee of early 1960s BBC staff members and freelancers, it has seemed impossible to lay the honor, or indeed the blame, for the creation of this slice of hectic nonsense at the door of any single individual" (Gillatt 1998, p. 11). The mutability of its recurring actors and its production crew between 1963 and 1989 also meant that, even within its subgenre of time travel science fiction, *Doctor Who* has worn many hats: science fiction, military action, fantasy, Gothic horror, dark comedy, and tragedy.

Original briefs, however, emphasized the Doctor's time machine as a kind of Narnia-like "magic door" to exciting but also educational adventures into history as well as yet-unrealized future civilizations. The Doctor's TARDIS, also referred to as a Type 40 TT capsule or (in the early years of the program) simply as "the Ship," was roundly criticized by other time travelers as being inefficient and out-of-date. A recurring theme of many episodes focuses on the Doctor struggling to control, repair, or augment the TARDIS, which suffers from – among other problems – a faulty "chameleon circuit" that fails to allow it to blend into destination environments, as it was originally designed. As *Doctor Who*'s first Story Editor David Whitaker says, "Everyone expects. . .to see large, gleaming spaceships orbiting planets. But what if the spaceships were here already, disguised as ordinary artifacts? And what if their occupants were already walking among us, keeping cautiously in the background to avoid notice and suspicion. . .[?]" (Bentham 1986, p. 61).

In a pivotal episode that introduced the first Time Lords, giving us a glimpse of the Doctor's home planet Gallifrey, it was revealed that the Doctor had stolen the TARDIS while attempting to escape his people in a hurry ("The War Games," 1969). In turn, the new version of the program that premiered in 2005 has performed retroactive continuity adjustments on this legendary revelation: in 2011's "The Doctor's Wife" (screen-written by Neil Gaiman), the intelligence of the TARDIS, anthropomorphized in a woman's body, claims that she stole the Doctor just as much as he stole her; in 2013's "The Name of the Doctor," companion Clara Oswald appears to deflect the First Doctor from taking the wrong TARDIS when fleeing Gallifrey, telling him, "Don't steal that one, steal this one. The navigation system's knackered, but you'll have much more fun."

In a fantastical universe of Time Tunnels, Cosmic Treadmills, DeLoreans, Time Turners, and WABAC machines, what are the unique features of TARDIS design, and how does *Doctor Who*'s canonical continuity explain its workings?

"Lots of impossible things happen when you pass through time": Time Travel and the Space-Time Vortex

The series is neither fantasy nor space travel nor science fiction. The basic premise is that four characters are projected into real environments based on the best factual information of situations in time and space and in any material state we can realize in practical terms. Using unusual, exciting backgrounds or ordinary backgrounds seen unusually, each story will have a strong informational core based on fact. (BBC WAC T5/647/1)

At base, any time travel story must involve what David Lewis called "a discrepancy between time and time." He explains:

Any traveler departs and then arrives at his destination; the time elapsed from departure to arrival. . .is the duration of the journey. But if he is a time traveler, the separation in time between departure and arrival does not equal the duration of his journey. He departs; he travels for an hour, let us say; then he arrives. The time he reaches is not the time one hour after his departure. It is later, if he has traveled toward the future; earlier, if he has traveled toward the past. (Lewis 1986, p. 67)

The discrepancy here is between the *personal time* that elapses for the traveler from start to finish of his journey and the *external time* that elapses for every other, non-time traveling being or event. In the 25th anniversary episode "Silver Nemesis" (1988), companion Ace asks the Seventh Doctor, "How can a statue destroy the

7 *Doctor Who* as Philosophy: Four-Dimensionalism and Time Travel

world?" "I'll tell you three hundred and fifty years ago," he replies, evoking external time, and just moments later in their personal time, the TARDIS materializes in a Tudor house in the year 1638.

In the wide world of time travel narratives, it is by no means necessary to use a machine to bridge swathes of external time with the comparably shorter passage of personal time. For example, in Mark Twain's 1889 novel *A Connecticut Yankee in King Arthur's Court* and in Jack Finney's *Time and Again*, psychological means are used – a bang on the head in the first case and hypnosis in the second. These kinds of "time slip" stories, in which characters often travel unintentionally through time, are contrasted with those that depend upon *time machines*, of which there are two distinct notions.

The *Wellsian* time machine was introduced in 1895's *The Time Machine*, where H. G. Wells described what has become science fiction's paradigmatic conception of a time machine: the intrepid operator dials a target date – past or future – throws a lever, and sits back while time rewinds or fast forwards until the target date is reached. Such a time vehicle treats time as a dimension to be moved through just as conventional land and air vehicles move through space's three dimensions and is probably the most common type of machine to appear in fiction. The TARDIS is a Wellsian time machine, the hexagonal central console of the TARDIS, key to all the machine's functions, represents the spirit of scientific positivism – a faith in the power of rationality to overcome limitations through scientific solutions – that is embodied in the Wellsian time machine (Decker 2005, p. 52ff).

Since the late 1980s, however, astrophysicists have been outlining the possibilities for a *Thornian* time machine, named after Nobel Laureate Kip Thorne. With his collaborators, Thorne has written a series of papers exploring how an advanced civilization could, without violating the laws of general relativistic physics, manipulate concentrations of matter-energy to deform the fabric of space-time in order to produce "closed time-like curves" (CTCs). Thornian machines would, however, only have the ability to project chrononauts into the future, not the past (Earman et al. 2016, n.p.). Consequently, they would not only disappoint fans of *Doctor Who*, but they would lack the ability to return chrononauts to their "home time" as well.

Since Einstein, it has been clear that the primary obstacle to the development of time travel – if the ontology of the universe even allows for it – is the staggering amount of energy that would be required. For example, in a 1974 proposal by Frank Tipler, then a physics graduate student, Tipler claimed, "In short, general relativity suggests that if we construct a sufficiently large rotating cylinder, we create a time machine" (Nahin 1993, p. 92). Such a "Tipler Cylinder" would have to be impossibly dense, of infinite length, and have a surface acceleration two hundred billion times faster than the acceleration of Earth's surface gravity in order to create CTCs that would allow time travel to the past or future. Furthermore, Tipler warned in 1977 that any attempt to create a time machine from "normal" matter would create singularities in space-time – points of ultra-dense matter such as exist at the heart of black holes (Nahin 1993, p. 94).

The energy requirements and presence of singularities are no problem for an advanced civilization like *Doctor Who*'s Time Lords, though. In fact, they have their own singularity, a "tamed" black hole called the "Eye of Harmony." According to show history, control over the Eye was engineered by the ancient Time Lord pioneer Omega from a star in the Sector of Forgotten Souls ("The Three Doctors," 1973). The Eye was brought to Gallifrey and stabilized against the mass of the planet. And the Eye not only powers each and every TARDIS; a "subset" of the Eye exists within each TARDIS (*Doctor Who: The Movie*).

Despite the capacity of the TARDIS to travel everywhere and everywhen, the "personal time" within Gallifreyan time machines seems to be synchronized with the "external time" of Gallifrey.

Although we have glimpsed some exceptions in the new (2005–) *Doctor Who*, it seems that in the classic show, Time Lords do not and perhaps *cannot* travel into their own past. While depictions of civilization on Gallifrey inevitably look futuristic, it is not until 2015 and the ninth series of the new show that we find out that Gallifrey's "present" is at least 4.5 billion years in the future and that Gallifrey (perhaps bereft of any Time Lords save the Doctor) still exists in the final moments of the universe ("Heaven Sent," "Hell Bent," 2015).

Gallifreyan time machines travel through a fictive "space-time vortex," the appearance, and properties of which were established in a number of early *Doctor Who* stories, including "The Chase" (1965), "The Enemy of the World" (1967–1968), and "The Time Monster" (1972). In the novelization for "The Chase," the third classic era story to feature the Daleks in a touch-and-go race lighting on different planets and in varied times, the author John Peel writes:

> The Space/Time Vortex exists outside of any normal frame of reference. Within it, light, darkness, matter and energy all blend, divide, shift and change. It underlies the whole of Creation, touching the normal Universe only slightly. Its pathways are twisted, unstable and hard to follow. A journey through these strange dimensions might take a moment and carry a traveler a million years and a billion light years from his/her/its origin. Alternatively, a journey of months in the Vortex might end in a shift of six feet and ten days in conventional space. Without being able to calculate the pathways, there was simply no telling. (Peel 1989, p. 11)

A TARDIS must dematerialize to enter the Vortex – it later rematerializes back in space-time – so the process of travel through the Vortex is not instantaneous, and therefore the Vortex represents something that some philosophers and scientists have called "hypertime." The relationship, from David Lewis, between "external" and "personal" time reflects this kind of hypertime relationship. But the very concept of hypertime is problematic, notes Theodore Sider. If we use "v-" to represent measures of time in the Vortex, and say that for each v-second spent in the Vortex, 100 years pass in "external" space-time, then we can say that time flows in external space-time respective to v-time flowing – at a different rate – in the Vortex (Sider 2016). But to explain what v-time flows in respect to, as both Sider and J.J.C. Smart recognized, is to have to postulate an "external" time to that in the Vortex – effectively, a hyper-hypertime. And for that time dimension, the question of a hyper-hyper-hypertime would be raised. The only way out of this infinite regress is to deny that seconds in space-time flow respective to v-time flow in the Vortex, or – more radically – to deny that time flows at all. (This will be the subject of section "Four-Dimensional Realism," and I discuss more *Doctor Who*-specific puzzles about time travel in "I can foresee oodles of trouble": Problems and Paradoxes" below.)

7 *Doctor Who* as Philosophy: Four-Dimensionalism and Time Travel

"Bigger on the inside": The Widening Significance of Relative Dimensions

A cross between [H.G.] Wells's Time Machine and a space age [Dickensian]
—Old Curiosity Shop... (BBC WAC T5/638/1 1963)

The Doctor has always treated the TARDIS not just as a vehicle but as his "abode...but not [a] fixed [one]" ("The Talons of Weng-Chiang," 1977). Every so often, he suggests that the TARDIS is a living thing, or at least an organic device. In the 20th anniversary special "The Five Doctors," he tells companion Tegan Jovanka, "The TARDIS is more than a machine..., it takes coaxing, persuading, encouraging." But it would only be in the 2005 series that we learn the facts behind these comments, since it turns out that TARDISes are grown, not built ("The Impossible Planet," 2006) and that "the 'living soul' of each TARDIS is an eleven-dimensional matrix" ("The Doctor's Wife," 2011).

The TARDIS is also famously "bigger on the inside than on the outside," thanks to Time Lord trans-dimensional engineering. In a cheeky bit of dialog from the novelization of the 1977 serial "The Face of Evil," the Fourth Doctor explains to a companion how this trick is accomplished:

Leela sighed. "There is no such thing as magic."
"Exactly," said the Doctor grandly. "To the rational mind, nothing is inexplicable, only unexplained."
Then explain to me how this—TARDIS of yours is larger on the inside than on the outside.
For a moment the Doctor was taken aback. Far more sophisticated minds than Leela's had been baffled by the Time Lord technology that had produced the TARDIS.
Well, it's because inside and outside aren't in the same dimension.
Leela looked blank.
"All right, Leela, I'll show you." The Doctor rooted inside the storage locker set into the TARDIS console and produced two boxes, one large, one small.
The Doctor held up the boxes, one in each hand. "Now, which box is larger?"
Leela pointed. "That one."
The Doctor nodded, put the smaller box on the console in the forefront of Leela's vision, and carried the larger one to the far side of the control room, holding it up in line with the first. "Now, which is the larger?"
Leela pointed to the box in the Doctor's hands. "Still that one."
But it looks smaller, doesn't it?
Leela looked. The small box, perched on the console just before her eyes, seemed to loom larger than the more distant box in the Doctor's hands. "That's only because it's farther away."
The Doctor came back to her side. "Exactly! If you could keep that box exactly the same distance away, and have it here..." He tapped the box. "Then the large box would fit inside the small one!" He beamed triumphantly at her.
That's silly!
"That's trans-dimensional engineering," said the Doctor severely. "A key Time Lord discovery!" (Dicks 1979, pp. 5–6)

Steve Tribe, in *Doctor Who: A Brief History of the Time Lords*, parses the theory like this: the two ancient founders of Time Lord civilization and its technical prowess, Omega and Rassilon, recognized that they would need colossal amounts of energy to create a time field large enough for a vehicle to travel into past or future. They realized that the smaller the vehicle, the less energy would be needed to displace it from their present; they envisioned something the size of a cupboard. But if it could simultaneously have an expansive interior, it could be useful for travel, research, and war. "To achieve this, the real space-time event (the exterior) needed to be mapped onto a separate continuum (the interior)" (Tribe 2017, pp. 27–28). Thus, the birth of trans-dimensional engineering enables TARDISes to contain – among many other things – bedrooms, labs, wardrobes, food machines, swimming pools, art galleries, and boot cupboards.

In this regard, it is not only *The Time Machine* that stands as an important literary antecedent to *Doctor Who* but also Edwin Abbott's 1884 *Flatland*. In constructing this allegorical two-dimensional world, Abbott asked us to imagine "straight Lines, Triangles, Squares, Pentagons, Hexagons, and other figures, instead of remaining fixed in their places, move freely about, on or in the surface, but without the power of rising above or sinking below it, very much like shadows" (Rucker 2014, n.p.). The narrative of *Flatland*, just like *Doctor Who*, works at a variety of levels, depending on the audience (Tulloch & Alvarado, 15). Rudy Rucker has identified three levels in *Flatland*: (1) it functions as Victorian social satire; (2) in dealing with the central character A Square's difficulties understanding the third dimension, it is analogous to our own problems thinking about the fourth dimension; and finally, (3) it can be read as the author's ". . .circuitous way of trying to talk about some intense spiritual experiences. A Square's trip into higher dimensions is a perfect metaphor for the mystic's experience of higher reality" (Rucker 2014, n.p.).

From its very first story, *Doctor Who* has been asking its viewers to consider how different the life would be of a central character who stands in a different relationship to time, the fourth dimension. After Coal Hill School science teacher Ian Chesterton pushes his way into the TARDIS in search of a mysterious pupil, Susan Foreman, he tells the First Doctor that the dimensionally transcendent interior of the TARDIS is an illusion.

DOCTOR	You don't understand, so you find excuses. Illusions, indeed? You say you can't fit an enormous building into one of your smaller sitting rooms.
IAN	No.
DOCTOR	But you've discovered television, haven't you?
IAN	Yes.
DOCTOR	Then by showing an enormous building on your television screen, you can do what seemed impossible, couldn't you?
IAN	Well, yes, but I still don't know
DOCTOR	Not quite clear, is it. I can see by your face that you're not certain. You don't understand. And I knew you wouldn't. Never mind. ("An Unearthly Child," 1963)

The TARDIS is, from the outside, a perfectly mundane object (or at least, police boxes were familiar enough when the show premiered), but the revelation of its potentially infinite interior is an unexpectedly wrenching, visceral experience in reconciling two things that cannot both be true. In short, it is the first and finest example of what *Doctor Who* does best, and what the Third Doctor actor Jon Pertwee has been quoted as saying, "There's nothing scarier than coming home and finding a Yeti on your loo in Tooting Bec," the idea being "there's nothing more unsettling than seeing your own recognizable world turned upside down" (Jeffery 2018).

In my book *Who Is Who? The Philosophy of Doctor Who*, I follow the analysis of Tulloch and Alvarado (1983) in identifying this key element in the *Doctor Who* formula as the *uncanny*, what Kingsley Amis generally calls "a non-rational sense of insecurity" (Amis 1960, p. 69) or what is alien yet also strangely familiar to us. The existential phenomenology of Martin Heidegger frequently returns to the idea of the uncanny, the original German word *unheimlich* suggesting "not being at ease" or "not feeling at home" – an existential disconnect. The very first episode of *Doctor Who* trades on the uncanny with the words of Coal Hill School history teacher Barbara Wright as she waits in the fog outside a lonely junkyard: "It's silly, isn't it? I feel frightened. . .as if we're about to interfere in something that is best left alone...." ("An Unearthly Child," 1963). Barbara's fear is intriguing, Heidegger might say, because it has no object – it is *of the unknown*. "All fear finds its ground in dread," he claims, and "dread can 'befall' us right in the midst of the most familiar environment" (Heidegger 1985, pp. 284, 289).

This move of making the familiar seem unfamiliar and even threatening – in both classic and new *Doctor Who* (with its statues that kill and evil Wi-Fi) – is a crucial narrative element, allowing the show to transcend its origins as a children's program whose audience watched it from "behind the sofa." However, uncanniness is also the show's signature approach to depicting time as the fourth dimension, an approach characterized by "oppositions and contradictions" rather than the clarity demanded, for example, by hard science fiction (Tulloch & Alvarado, p. 16).

The Doctor himself can be an uncanny figure inasmuch as he often baffles companions (and enemies) in his ability to "see the threads that join the universe together and mends them when they break" ("Meglos," 1981). This renegade Time Lord, we are told, is a "perpetual outsider," standing "in a special relationship to time" ("City of Death," 1979), a human-like figure who nonetheless "walks in eternity" ("Pyramids of Mars," 1975).

"I can foresee oodles of trouble": Problems and Paradoxes

Doctor Who's first Story Editor, David Whitaker, worked to a brief from the original creative team that stories set in the past would alternate with those set in the future. This eased the narrative choice of disciplines for the Coal Hill School teachers who, with the Doctor's granddaughter Susan, would be the original "TARDIS team": Barbara Wright is a history expert, while Ian Chesterton teaches science. James Chapman writes, "Historical *Doctor Who* tended to focus on periods of the past that were taught in schools and would, therefore, be familiar to children, but the series did not exclusively privilege British history" (Chapman 2013, p. 33). And although Barbara and Ian were included in the cast to ask the questions and express the concerns of the present-day (1963) audience, one thing that the program did not make particularly clear was what the difference between "the past" or "the future" represented to the Doctor and Susan. In the scrapped pilot (not viewed on UK television until 1991), Susan says she was "born in the 49th century," a line changed in the transmitted version of "An Unearthly Child" to "I was born in another time, another world. . .." Both she and her grandfather would therefore see events even in Barbara and Ian's distant future (e.g., "The Dalek Invasion of Earth" (1964), which takes place in the twenty-second century) as having occurred in their personal past. This is a problem, as we will see momentarily, with the so-called arrow of time.

In the beginning, *Doctor Who*'s attitude toward changing history was uncompromising: no character should be allowed to do it. Perhaps the most famous dialog about this occurs already in the first series between the Doctor and Barbara Wright. Taken as a reincarnation of the goddess Yetaxa by the Aztecs after emerging from a tomb in 15th century Mexico, Barbara decides to use her power over them, together with her historical knowledge, to make things better:

DOCTOR   There is to be a human sacrifice today at the rain ceremony. . . And you must not interfere. Do you understand? . . ..
BARBARA   Well, they've made me a goddess. And I forbid it!
DOCTOR   Barbara, no!
BARBARA   There'll be no sacrifice this afternoon, Doctor, or ever again. The reincarnation of Yetaxa will prove to the people that you don't need to sacrifice a human being to make it rain. . ..
DOCTOR   What are you talking about?
BARBARA   Oh, don't you see? If I could start the destruction of everything that's evil here, then everything that is good would survive when Cortez lands.
DOCTOR   But you can't rewrite history, not one line! . . .Barbara, one last appeal. What you are trying to do is utterly impossible. I know, believe me, I know.
BARBARA   Not Barbara. *Yetaxa*. ("The Aztecs," 1964)

The Doctor's vehemence in this scene suggests that he is not discussing the *logical* or even *physical* impossibility of "rewriting history," that is, changing the past. After all, there is no reason to get heated up when someone suggests squaring the circle or trying to make water boil at 32 degrees Fahrenheit. In a later story by the same scriptwriter, John Lucarotti, the Doctor tells companion Steven Taylor, ". . .[W]e're all too small to realize [history's] final pattern. Therefore, don't try and judge it from where you stand" ("The Massacre of St. Bartholomew's Eve," 1966).

Yet even in the earliest years of the show, the idea that time travelers could – and inevitably *did* change history – was also introduced. Both broadcast in 1965, "The Romans" and "The Time Meddler" were playful and light-hearted stories. In the former, the Doctor is conversing with Nero about the Emperor's big plans to

7 *Doctor Who* as Philosophy: Four-Dimensionalism and Time Travel

reconstruct Rome when he absent-mindedly sets his eyeglasses on a map of the city; refracted light sets the map to burning. Nero takes the hint: "So the Senate wouldn't pass my plans, eh? Wouldn't let me build my New Rome? But if the old one is burnt, if it goes up in flames, they will have no choice! Rome will be rebuilt to my design! Brilliant!" In "The Time Meddler," we meet another of the Doctor's people – a time-traveling "Monk" with a TARDIS of his own. The Doctor opposes him as the defender of established world history while companion Steven struggles to keep up:

STEVEN   Look, I take it you both come from the same place, Doctor?

DOCTOR   Yes, I regret that we do, but I would say that I am fifty years earlier. Now when are you going to answer my questions?

MONK   Which questions?

DOCTOR   The reason for this deliberate destruction.

MONK   I want to improve things.

DOCTOR   Improve things? Improve things, yes, that's good. Very good. Improve what, for instance?

MONK   Well, for instance, Harold, King Harold, I know he'd be a good king. There wouldn't be all those wars in Europe, those claims over France went on for years and years. With peace the people would be able to better themselves. With a few hints and tips from me they'd be able to have jet airliners by 1320! Shakespeare would be able to put *Hamlet* on television.

DOCTOR   He'd do what?

MONK   The play *Hamlet* on television.

DOCTOR   Oh, yes, quite so, yes, of course, I do know the medium.

Can they change history or not? The fact remains that time travel narratives aren't very interesting when the answer is "no," but this fact stands in tension with the role of the show's main character as a protector of the "web of time," as well as the running subtext authored by writers and producers that has Earth's history as portrayed in *Doctor Who* track very closely to "our" own history.

One notable departure from this is "Inferno," starring Jon Pertwee as the Third Doctor; it is a remarkable story that was well ahead of its time when broadcast in 1970. Ostensibly a cautionary tale about "Project Inferno's" goal of breaching the Earth's crust in search of alternative fuels, "Inferno" embraces the "Multiple Worlds" interpretation of quantum theory that only caught fire in writings by Brandon Carter and G.F.R. Ellis years *after* the episode aired. Settling into his exile on twentieth-century Earth, the Doctor experiments with the non-functional TARDIS console and manages, entirely by accident, to cross over into a parallel world of the "Republic of Great Britain," a fascist country in which the royal family has been executed. The Doctor is tortured, interrogated, and jailed by the brutal, parallel-world counterparts of his UNIT (United Nations Intelligence Taskforce) colleagues and friends. Despite this, the Doctor is fascinated by the differences between events in his own universe and those at the end of the Project Inferno of fascist Britain, running on a faster timetable. "Yes, of course, of course," he muses after returning from the cataclysm on the alternate Earth caused by their version of Project Inferno. "An infinity of universes, ergo an infinite number of choices. So free will is not an illusion after all. The pattern can be changed." It's unclear how the Doctor draws such a conclusion about free will from a complex, causally undetermined set of circumstances in "Inferno," but we'll have occasion to revist the topic of free will in the conclusion of this article.

Another exceptional Third Doctor episode – one that reaffirms the notion that those who know their history can avoid repeating it – is 1972's "Day of the Daleks." In addition to being the first outing for the Doctor's nemeses from Skaro since the program switched to color in 1970 – and a cracking good time paradox story – it is also the first time that the Doctor meets himself (although not a different incarnation of himself) through a complication in time introduced (again) by his experimenting with the TARDIS console. The physics of the *Doctor Who* universe (in the classic era) seems to either rule out the possibility of other non-Time Lord characters meeting earlier or later versions of themselves or at least predicts disastrous effects should such a meeting occur. This fictive physical law behind this restriction, the "Blinovitch Limitation Effect," was first mentioned in "Day of the Daleks" and attributed to an "Aaron Blinovitch." He supposedly wrote about it in his 1928 book *Temporal Mechanics*, but it is not entirely clear what the law specifies.

"Day of the Daleks" involves the Doctor, companion Jo Grant, and UNIT in what the new *Who* calls a "bootstrap paradox" ("Before the Flood," 2015). In it, Sir Reginald Styles, organizer of a world peace conference at Auderley House, is menaced by a camouflage-wearing guerilla. To complicate matters, the guerilla is himself attacked by huge, ape-like creatures called Ogrons and found unconscious near the house by UNIT soldiers. The Doctor finds the guerilla's box-like personal time machine and deduces that he comes from about two centuries in the future. As Jo Grant is accidentally cast into that dystopic future, in which the Daleks rule Earth with support from the Ogrons and human collaborators, the Doctor falls in with the guerrillas from the future who explain that they are trying to kill Styles because he caused an explosion at his own peace conference, starting a series of wars that left humanity vulnerable to Dalek conquest. But, as the Doctor realizes upon returning to the present day, it was not Styles but Shura, one of the guerrillas, who blew up Auderley House. Unbeknownst to them, the time terrorists created the future that they wished to change. By evacuating Auderley House and allowing a force of Daleks and Ogrons – who want the future Earth to remain under Dalek control – into the mansion before it is destroyed, the Doctor stops the dystopic future timeline from ever coming about. "Your conference has been saved, Sir Reginald," the Doctor says at the end of the story. "Now it's up to you and your friends to make sure it's a success. You still have a choice." Styles replies, "Don't worry. We all know what will happen if we fail." The Doctor nods: "So do we. We've seen it happen, haven't we, Jo?" What is ironic and goes unmentioned is that, based on a common-sense view of time as a linear flow from present to future, the source of their knowledge doesn't exist – and indeed, never did.

As *Doctor Who*'s fan base increased and it found new viewers in the USA, continuity-minded producers like Graham Williams and John Nathan-Turner took over in the 1970s and 1980s. A number of plots began to rely on the power that the Time Lords – and enemy aliens like Daleks and Cybermen – possessed to manipulate linear, "one-damned-thing-after-another" time through technology like *time loops* ("Image of the Fendahl," 1977; "The Armageddon Factor," 1979), *time scoops* ("The Five Doctors," 1983), and *time corridors* ("Resurrection of the Daleks," 1984; "Timelash," 1985). Perhaps the most bizarre example of the use of time technology occurs in "Attack of the Cybermen" (1984) when the Doctor's cyborg enemies attempt to capture a time-ship that has crashed on the planet of their stasis "tombs," Telos, in 2495. Rather than desiring to change Earth history with the time-ship (as they inadvertently did when they killed off the dinosaurs of prehistory in "Earthshock," 1982), the Cybermen are intent on changing *Doctor Who* canon – namely, to go back to 1986 and prevent the destruction of their original home planet, Mondas – an event the First Doctor was partially responsible for.

Throughout its 26 seasons, classic *Doctor Who* raised philosophical questions about the "arrow of time" – why is it that, unlike travel in the spatial three dimensions, "movement" in the fourth dimension is restricted to the direction of the future only? The show also weighed in on both sides of the question, "Could travelers to the past change history?" It occasionally involved the Doctor and his companions in potential paradoxes, like the bootstrap paradox in "Day of the Daleks." And it considered – from the perspective of space fantasy, if not hard science fiction – what it would take for an advanced civilization to manipulate time. How often did *Doctor Who* get it right? And what, conversely, was (to use one of the Fourth Doctor's favorite neologisms) "bafflegab"? In the next two sections, we will find out.

Time Travel in Theory: "First things first, but not necessarily in that order"

Recall the basic distinction for considering the possibility of time travel offered in the section "'Lots of impossible things happen when you pass through time': Time Travel and the Space-Time Vortex" from David Lewis. For Lewis, the logical possibility of time travel involves "a discrepancy between time and time.... Any traveler departs and then arrives at his destination: the time elapsed from departure to arrival ... is the duration of the journey. But if he is a time traveler, the separation in time between departure and arrival does not equal the duration of his journey" (Lewis 1986, p. 68). Lewis then introduced two useful terms that can aid us in making some sense of this discrepancy: *personal* time and *external* time. In the ordinary world of everyday experience, external time and personal time coincide and the "flow" of time presents itself as linear, arrow-like, and irreversible. In this flow, we find experiences occurring to us at a moment we call "the present," which is constantly being superseded by "the past" yet seems to draw on an inexhaustible supply of minutes and days in "the future." According to Adrian Bardon, this one-way flow manifests itself in three ways: in *psychological* terms, according to *thermodynamic* regularities, and in our experience of *causes and effects*.

1. The psychological arrow of time "just refers to the familiar fact that we remember (and never anticipate) the past, and anticipate (but never remember) the future. . .. We know things about the past but not about the future; we feel we can affect our future but cannot change our past" (Bardon, p. 113). Aristotle was one of the earliest philosophers to note the impact of the psychological arrow on philosophical thinking. In *De Interpretatione*, he mulls the idea that once a change has occurred and is in the past, it is unalterable. One version of Aristotle's "principle of non-contradiction" is that "'what was' in the past and 'what was not' are so *necessarily*." For Aristotle, this is more a truth from logic and language than from metaphysics. "With regard to what is and what has been it is necessary for the affirmation or the negation [of a claim about what happened] to be true or false. . .," he writes. "For if every affirmation or negation is true or false it is necessary for everything either to be the case or not to be the case" (Aristotle 18a29-35, p. 28). And Aristotle makes an equally strong claim regarding statements about the future: they are true or false *now*, we're simply not aware which. In fact, these statements were *always* true or false, whether they were uttered in the past, present, or will be uttered in the future. "Again if [a thing] is white now it was true to say earlier that it would be white, so that it was always true to say of anything that has happened that it would be so. But if it was always true to say that it was so, or would be so, it could not *not* be so, or not be going to be so" (Aristotle 18b10-13, p. 29). But as both Aristotle and Bardon emphasize, the psychological arrow of experience, oriented from present to future, is not what determines *events* to have a particular order; instead, the influence runs in the other direction. "There is a perfect correlation between the psychological orientation of our lives and the direction of time," Bardon says (Bardon, p. 113).

2. Regularities in thermodynamic changes also seem to have a "direction" and can be summed up by the slogan "entropy increases." Systems almost always move from a state of overall orderliness to one of disorderliness, primary because there are far more ways or chances for a system to be disordered than for it to be ordered (compare this to shooting an arrow at a target of concentric rings; there is one way to hit a bull's-eye yet many, many ways to hit an outer ring, and even more ways to miss the target completely!). As Bardon claims, "Simple chance thus dictates that, over time, any orderliness that we do not spend energy to create or maintain will tend to transition into a much, much more likely state of disorder" (Bardon, p. 114). These definitions of the thermodynamic arrow use words like "tend to" and "almost always" because the laws of statistical mechanics that explain the arrow are probabilistic only – strictly speaking, there is no law of nature in the universe preventing, for example, a broken glass from rearranging itself full of spilled water and leaping back into one's hand (as happened to companion Vicki in "The Space Museum," 1965 when the TARDIS "jumps a time track"). Such an event is extraordinarily unlikely, though. Although thermodynamics is not the most fundamental physical science, the fundamental physics that undergird it are said to be "time reversal invariant" – that is, basic physical laws don't require a reference either to the passage of time from present to future or present to past. So it would be entirely possible, as Paul Nahin

suggests, that "at some instant, somehow, every particle in the world suddenly reverse[s] its velocity vector," leading to the result that "the world would then run backward in time along the same path it had followed up until the instant of reversal..." (Nahin, pp. 186–187).

So a question that continues to hang over the philosophy of physics is, "Where does the asymmetry of thermodynamic system changes come from?" Intriguingly, this question and the theme of entropy increasing have recently been noted as a thematic arc in the final season of the Fourth Doctor (Tom Baker) – thematic arcs being very rare in classic *Doctor Who*. The common theme of social and physical systems running down in Season 18 (1980–1981) "would eventually foreshadow and culminate in the Doctor's regeneration at the end of the season" (TARDIS Wikia, n.p.). As the end of the Fourth Doctor's still-unmatched 7-year reign on television his final story "Logopolis" is an adventure that has the Doctor discover that the universe has long ago passed the point of its "heat-death," or total entropic collapse. The manner in which his arch-enemy and fellow Time Lord, the Master, exploits the mathematicians of the planet Logopolis, who have been stabilizing reality since that point, makes for a noble and grand send-off for Baker's Doctor.

3. In our experience, causes always precede their effects in time. This provides an excellent explanation for why each of us experiences psychological asymmetry between the (future) objects of anticipation and the (past) objects of remembrance: "on this account, memories pertain to the 'past' just because they are caused by the events of which they are memories" (Bardon, p. 118). However, it is debatable how much the "causal arrow" helps explain time. Aristotle distinguished between time as a unit of measurement and that which it measures – namely, change. Yet we do not experience change without the passage of time, and vice-versa; in fact, as David Hume would later point out, we do not *experience* causal relations at all; we only experience events that are associated regularly in terms of "earlier" and "later." Hume conjures the image of a billiard ball that strikes another: we see the movement of the first, hear and see the contact between it and another ball, and watch as the second ball moves away from the first. From this he concludes:

> And though none but a fool or madman will ever pretend to dispute the authority of experience, or to reject that great guide of human life, it may surely be allowed a philosopher to have so much curiosity at least as to examine the principle of human nature, which gives this mighty authority to experience, and makes us draw advantage from that similarity which nature has placed among different objects. From causes which appear similar we expect similar effects. This is the sum of all our experimental conclusions. (Hume 1993, p. 23)

Aristotle argues that experience is required to find "first principles" and causal relationships, and Hume says that we can never reach a conclusion about "matters of [empirical] fact" simply through reasoning about them. Yet the empiricism that underlies both Aristotle's confident scientific categorization of the world and Hume's skeptical view about causation raises a serious issue for our understanding of the nature of time's arrow. We know that effects may follow their causes not immediately, but much later: for example, insignificant patches of erosion on a stone may eventually accumulate to cause it to roll down a hill, years later. We also know, now that physicists have been able to study photons separated from each other by a considerable distance, that an impact on one photon can *instantaneously* affect another photon; this is "quantum non-locality" or what Einstein called "spooky action at a distance" (Zimmerman, p. 235).

But if time travel to the past is not impossible, then travels like the Doctor's could produce relations of *effects* that are actualized *before* their causes. Call this "backward causation" or "retro-causation." In "Day of the Daleks," discussed in I.C above, a future version of the Third Doctor and Jo Grant accidentally pop into existence in the UNIT lab days earlier; in "Timelash" (1984), as rebels of the planet Karfel rescue companion Peri from a plesiosaur-like Morlox, the hulk of a burning android inexplicably appears in the cave they are fighting in. It is only much later in the episode that we find out that this feat of retro-causation was the work of the Doctor, whose quickly constructed gadget based on a "Kontron crystal" was used as a weapon against one of the villain's androids. "I was hoping to use the energy absorbed by the machine to project our attackers into the past," the Sixth Doctor says. "As yet, I can't guarantee a change of location as well." Yet the rebels with him, who witnessed the apparently uncaused materialization of the destroyed android hours earlier during Peri's rescue, *can* confirm the spatial as well as temporal displacement he seeks to produce.

Inevitably, time travel would produce disruptions in the perceived flow of time for travelers – that is, in terms of the disconnection of personal from external time (though TARDIS travelers do not seem to suffer from jet lag, maybe they should). More importantly, it would force us to accept a much more complicated notion of causality that allows effects which occur before their causes. This, in turn, would allow for exceptions to the apparent asymmetry of the psychological and thermodynamic arrows of temporal flow.

Such exceptions abound in the reboot *Doctor Who* – where episode plots or entire series arcs rest on them – but careful inspection of classic episodes reveals some as well. In "The Five Doctors" (1983), a Gallifreyan time scoop is used to remove the First, Second, and Third Doctors from their respective timelines. The current Doctor at the time – the Fifth, played by Peter Davison – suffers from a loss of psychological continuity each time this happens, complaining at first of "just a twinge of cosmic angst," but what turns out to have debilitating effects in his present. "Great chunks of my past, detaching themselves like melting icebergs," he complains to companions Turlough and Tegan, just before he begins to fade from reality. And although the thermodynamic arrow says that systems will almost always go from ordered to disordered states, anytime the Doctor takes his assistants into the past to "build another Troy" on the ashes of Ilium ("The Myth Makers," 1965) or to make "over the whole world" of Victorian Earth in apparent aid of the Daleks to help them discover "the human factor" and augment their original programming, he is, in a very real sense, borrowing energy from the future to create order in the past.

7 *Doctor Who* as Philosophy: Four-Dimensionalism and Time Travel

Conceivably, the most serious challenge to the possibility of time travel is embodied in an "inconsistency paradox" such as the infamous *grandfather paradox*. During the events of "The Awakening" (1984), we are introduced to the maternal grandfather of the Fifth Doctor's long-standing companion, Tegan Jovanka. *Suppose that* after that adventure, the Doctor offers to take Tegan back 40 years in time to 1944, when her grandfather, Andrew Verney, was a teenager. She arrives, meets his younger self next to a busy street, and accidentally steps in the way of a speeding lorry, and in saving her from being killed, Verney pushes her aside only to fall under the wheels himself. The Doctor and Tegan try to resuscitate him, but he dies. Tegan is shocked and grief-stricken, but more than that, one of the undoubtable conditions for her being born years later no longer exists. Does she pop out of being, not dying but never having existed? Does the Doctor or fellow companion Turlough remember her? And are their lives substantially different, in a twinkling of an eye, because they never met Tegan?

The Doctor himself has suggested she would not just pop out of existence. In "The Two Doctors" (1985), the Sixth Doctor and Peri arrive at a space station where, just days before, the Second Doctor and Jamie MacCrimmon had arrived with the intention of investigating unauthorized time travel experiments. Now the station is in ruins, having been attacked by the clone army of the Sontarans. The Sixth Doctor finds evidence that his second incarnation was killed days ago on the station, and when they find Jamie hiding in the station infrastructure, the Highlander confirms his death. The Sixth Doctor is shaken to the core:

DOCTOR	Peri, it's possible!
PERI	What?
DOCTOR	That I was killed! It's why I collapsed, the weakness that I felt.
PERI	But you said you couldn't be dead then and here now.
DOCTOR	Yes, but if I arrived here during a time experiment, caught in an embolism and therefore outside the time flow. But if I were dead then and here now, it means that I was at the very epicenter of the engulfing chaos.
PERI	I don't understand.
DOCTOR	It means the collapse of the universe has started and nothing can stop it.
PERI	How long will it take?
DOCTOR	For everything to end? A very few centuries.
PERI	Centuries? Well, if it's going to take that long, I'll go and see if Jamie's any better.

Here is an example of a grandfather paradox involving not generations of a family, but the very same person. The Doctor implies a correlation between the amount that one has time traveled (measured in the program by one's "artron energy") and the catastrophic effects of that person being removed from time – although the effect is slow to materialize. As it turns out in "The Two Doctors," the evidence of the Second Doctor's death has been manufactured, and no paradox emerges.

A grandfather-type paradox apparently violates the *principle of non-contradiction*, which was mentioned above in the context of the psychological arrow of time. Aristotle's principle of contradiction says that, for any fact that can be expressed by a meaningful proposition, that fact either is or is not the case, and is so necessarily. At the moment of the death of Tegan's grandfather, it is the case that he continued to live and had grandchildren (Tegan is evidence of this), and *not* the case that he continued to live, because of the lorry accident (Tegan and the Doctor can confirm this). As a result, this paradox can be expressed as a logical contradiction: both A ("Andrew Verney is alive") and not-A ("Andrew Verney is not alive") are true at the same time – but logical contradictions are always false. What is going on here?

Typically, we do not see empirical effects of logical contradictions, because these are the most watertight of false statements: they cannot obtain in reality any more than a police box could be both blue and pink all over, both at the same time. To achieve "a circle that is also a square" or find that "Ian married Barbara but Barbara did not marry Ian" is impossible. For a clear case of retro-causation in which an actual fact is contradicted – like in the grandfather paradox – what are the possible ways to make sense of this situation? Let's consider three possibilities.

1. The first possibility is our own ignorance of the actual facts about the past. It could be that Andrew Verney isn't Tegan's grandfather at all, but this does not change the fact that a day before, she just interacted with Verney in the village of Little Hodcombe in 1984. Verney's death in 1944 removes a causal condition for the latter adventure – so how did it happen?

2. The second possibility is that some force – physical, intelligent, or both – either prevents retro-causation by (a) making travel to the past impossible or (b) if a journey back to Andrew Verney's youth does work, that force deflects any attempt to change established history. Option (a) has been suggested by the late Stephen Hawking in the form of a "Chronology Protection Agency." This would be something like a group of intelligent, time-sensitive agents similar to the non-interference-minded Time Lords, Poul Anderson's "Time Patrol," or Isaac Asimov's Eternity organization in the novel *The End of Eternity*. However, Hawking's original suggestion was merely as a metaphor for actual physical laws of the universe that would make time travel, like unaided human flight, impossible (Hawking 1992).

   Option (b) for preventing retro-causation implies that time travel to the past could be possible, but interference in established affairs would produce some interesting effects that could be likened, some would say, to miracles. It would be very strange, for example, in the case of young Andrew Verney if the steering wheel of the oncoming lorry was suddenly wrenched in a direction counter to the driver's intentions, thus avoiding the fatal accident. David Deutsch and Michael Lockwood write that the laws of physics seem to operate according to what they call the "autonomy principle." It states that "it is possible to create in our immediate environment any configuration of matter that the laws of physics permit locally, without reference to what the rest of the universe may be doing" (Deutsch and Lockwood 1994, p. 71). No forces other than gravity and kinetic energy are at work on the lorry's steering wheel. Nothing like "historical inertia" is going to push Verney out of the way of the lorry as he saves Tegan. Deutsch and Lockwood explain:

> When we strike a match, we do not have to worry that we might be thwarted because the configuration of the planets, say, might be inconsistent with the match being lit. … [Autonomy] underpins all experimental science: we typically take for granted that we can set up our apparatus in any configuration allowed by physical law and the rest of the universe will take care of itself. (Deutsch and Lockwood 1994, p. 71)

If the "autonomy principle" holds in physics, then it seems there is nothing stopping Tegan's grandfather from being killed, thanks to the intervention of time travelers, before he becomes a father. But because a time traveler is part of the reason for this change, the "autonomy principle" will conflict, Deutsch and Lockwood say, with John L. Friedman's "consistency principle," which states that "the only configurations of matter that can occur locally are those that are self-consistent globally." They continue:

> Under this principle, the world outside the laboratory can physically constrain our actions inside, even if everything we do is consistent, locally, with the laws of physics. Ordinarily, we are unaware of this constraint, because the autonomy and consistency principles never come into conflict. (Deutsch and Lockwood 1994, p. 71)

Time travel that changes the past would allow this conflict to happen, they claim, and so we are left not *just* with a logical contradiction, but a contradiction between laws of physics, *autonomy* says there is nothing stopping Tegan from bringing about her grandfather's death, while *consistency* says that if Tegan's life – and thus ability to be in 1944 thanks to the TARDIS – is contingent on Verney not dying before he is a father, then she cannot be involved in his death, which cannot happen at the time the lorry swerves (for an intriguing variation on this paradox in the new *Doctor Who*, see Paul Cornell's "Father's Day," 2005).

3. These contradictions can be avoided; however, if we look past, the constraints of classical (Newtonian) physics and embrace an Einsteinian universe of space-time in which Thornian time machines and closed time-like curves (CTCs) – as mentioned above in I.A – are possible. Indeed, "quantum mechanics may necessitate the presence of closed time like curves," at least at the submicroscopic level (Deutsch and Lockwood 1994, p. 72). CTCs might allow a chrononaut to travel forward in their own personal time but arrive earlier than their departure – but such travel would entail the creation or exploitation of a tear-like deformation in the fabric of space-time. (In new *Who*, during the 2013 episode "The Name of the Doctor," the Eleventh Doctor confirms that time travel "is like a tear in the fabric of reality" as he confronts "the scar tissue of [his] journey through the universe" on the planet Trenzalore.) But what is beyond this rip in space-time? Deutsch and Lockwood counterpoise travel by CTC with the "many worlds" (MW) interpretation offered by Hugh Everett III in 1957. According to Everett's view of quantum mechanics, if something physically *can* happen, it *does* happen – in

some universe or the other. According to MW quantum theory, "physical reality consists of a collection of universes, sometimes called a multiverse" (Deutsch & Lockwood 1994, p. 72). On this view, when the Doctor takes Tegan back to 1944, there is a branching moment when young Verney pushes Tegan out of the way of the lorry, and he is killed. But this event represents the creation of a new and parallel "B" universe. However, the time travelers are from the "A" universe, where Tegan's grandfather lived to see his grandchildren grow up – some of them even moved to Australia! In effect, the autonomy principle is satisfied in the B universe, while the consistency principle in the original "A" universe, so there is no conflict.

But it makes sense to reject the suggestion that this view applies to the *Doctor Who* universe. MW quantum mechanics cannot explain where the staggeringly huge amounts of matter and energy would come from in order to create a new universe at *every* crux of possibility. And the space-time vortex through which TARDISes travel is not a tear in the basic fabric of the universe; further, when he travels by TARDIS, the Doctor seems to be aware of when he outside his home universe ("Full Circle," "Warrior's Gate," "Logopolis," 1981) and doesn't imply in his adventures that there is an infinitely diverse multiverse, so there could be just a handful of different universes in *Who*, contrary to what MW posits.

So if these three options do not allow us to explain temporal paradoxes like the grandfather paradox, then perhaps we should consider that something more basic than a physical or intelligent force prevents paradoxes. What if time travel were possible, but its consequences were already "baked into" the fourth dimension of the universe, past, present, and future?

Four-Dimensional Realism

To begin to consider a solution to the problems and paradoxes posed by time travel, let's first consider one crucial fact necessary for any fictive universe that admits such travel. Any time traveler, in going from point A in space-time to point B elsewhere and elsewhen, must have a destination – *a place and time to go*. Past and future must be as real as the present. More than this, unless we assume that past and future are coequally as real as the present, many of *Doctor Who*'s moral crises have no teeth: after all, if from the perspective of Paris in 1979, the "table wine" year that is the setting for "City of Death" (written by Douglas Adams), the events of the year 400 million BCE no longer exist (being past), then why do the Fourth Doctor, and friends run so quickly into the TARDIS to stop Scaroth's space-ship? Clearly, they all believe that the event in question is taking place in that far-distant era and that, if it's not stopped, it will mean that the essential spark which allowed life on Earth to evolve from inorganic elements will never occur. (Of course, if there had been no rush and no crisis, we would have been deprived of one of the funniest scenes in classic *Doctor Who* – the scene where the TARDIS, with the Doctor, Romana and Duggan onboard, dematerializes from an art gallery in front of "art critics," and the

7 *Doctor Who* as Philosophy: Four-Dimensionalism and Time Travel

famous British comedians John Cleese and Eleanor Bron exclaim, "Exquisite. Absolutely exquisite.")

In short, time travel implies that the Doctor's universe is one of "Four-Dimensional Realism" (4DR), or as David Lewis puts it, that "the world—the time traveler's world, or ours—is a four-dimensional manifold of events." Adrian Bardon notes that this unchanging world – which, of course, from the presentist's perspective of "flow," seems full of change – is sometimes referred to as a block universe: "This refers to the notion of a four-dimensional block depicting everything happening in space over time. Observers in different reference frames will produce different representations of the block; that is to say, they will locate events in space and time somewhat differently" (Bardon, 92). And it takes a *very* long time – indeed it doesn't happen until quite late in the reboot *Doctor Who* – for the (Twelfth) Doctor to admit to this:

> Time! Time doesn't pass. The passage of time is an illusion, and life is the magician. Because life only lets you see one day at a time. You remember being alive yesterday, you hope you're going to be alive tomorrow, so it feels like you're travelling from one to the other. But nobody's moving anywhere. Movies don't really move. They're just pictures, lots and lots of pictures. All of them still, none of them moving. Just frozen moments. But if you experience those pictures one after the other, then everything comes alive. ("The Pilot," 2017)

The Doctor's ability to understand space-time from outside life "one day at a time" makes him an *eternalist*, one who holds the idea that the view that "events exist timelessly in an eternal, unchanging order" (Bardon, p. 88). This should come as no surprise, given the hints dropped in I.B above that the Doctor's perspective on the world is a fundamentally uncanny one. This contrasts starkly with the sense of the "flow" of experiences that we – and the Doctor's companions – quite rightly take as basic to our sense of time. Commonsensically, we are all *presentists*, who deny the reality of past and future in favor of the time frame that *can* actually be experienced at any moment: the present one. What is true is true now, and not at any other time, because other times simply do not exist. Presentism does have a way to deal with the psychological asymmetry of time: we can only anticipate events in the future because they don't presently exist in any cogent sense. But the presentist must also confront the question of whether any memories of (or statements about) the past can be said to be "true" or to be pieces of knowledge, if the truth-makers for such things (e.g., past events) no longer exist.

For St. Augustine of Hippo, a paradigmatic eternalist, the crystallized order of events is comprehensible in its entirety only by God, who is also its creator. In the Whoniverse, though, gods typically want to devour us ("The Time Monster," 1972; "The God Complex," 2011) or sometimes turn out to be the Doctor himself ("The Face of Evil," 1977). Eternalists like David Lewis will maintain that there must be an objective past, present, and future ("external time") in order for time travel to be possible. Within the dimension of external time, certain temporal parts of the time traveler (Lewis calls them "stages") that exist *later* in his personal timeline may actually exist earlier than other temporal parts that are *earlier* in his own personal timeline. Lewis writes:

> The time traveler's life is like a mountain railway. The place two miles due east of here may also be nine miles down the line, the west-bound direction. Clearly we are not dealing with two independent dimensions. Just as distance along the railway is not a fourth spatial dimension, so a time traveler's personal time is not a second dimension of time. (Lewis 1986, p. 71)

The aforementioned Blinovitch Limitation Effect – the *Doctor Who* in-continuity reason why time travelers cannot simply go into their own past to clean up mistakes or "try again," at the peril of being trapped in a time loop ("Day of the Daleks," 1972) – also specifies that earlier incarnations of the same time traveler will lose their memories of events that occur while crossing their timestream. Despite this, episodes of *Doctor Who* that hinge on the latest incarnation of the Doctor meeting his predecessors invoke the possibility that the Doctor can use travel through external time to allow earlier and later stages of his personal time to meet – providing more evidence for 4DR. Despite the fact that "crossing his own timestream" is expressly forbidden by Gallifrey's "First Law of Time" ("The Three Doctors," 1973), the Doctor seems to constantly be bumping into his other selves ("The Five Doctors," 1983; "The Two Doctors," 1985; and in new *Who*, the Children in Need short "Time Crash," 2007 "Day of the Doctor," 2013 and "Deep Breath," 2014).

So while *Doctor Who* has seldom been based on scientific fact and is not designed to have a consistent philosophy of the nature of time, at least in the classic iteration of the program, there is little evidence that challenges the applicability of the 4DR theory to the Whoniverse (one exception may be "Father's Day," 2005). In the beginning, in episodes like "The Aztecs," the Doctor's view that history could not be rewritten is confirmed by the thwarting of his companions' efforts to do so – not by "historical inertia" or any other occult force but rather by plausible yet unaccounted factors. In late 1960s stories, the idea is introduced (in episodes like "The Massacre") that the actions of the time travelers themselves are already part of the past, as their actions more often than not save "our" history (as when the Doctor prevents the creation of six additional "genuine" Mona Lisa paintings in "City of Death"). In fact, in the vast majority of *Doctor Who* stories, there are few if any worries about changing history. As the Doctor gains more control over the TARDIS's destination settings, time travel can be likened to a form of tourism in which the Doctor can catch up with famous people like Leonardo da Vinci, Harry Houdini, or Marie Antoinette. If it's true that the effects of any travel from one era to another is already accounted for in the 4DR structure, then perhaps the Doctor realizes that his interference will have no long-term effect.

Conclusion

Four-Dimensional Realism underwrites the impossibility of logical contradictions and conflicts between principles of physics (autonomy vs. consistency), while at the same time overcoming the limited perspective of presentism to assure the budding chrononaut that yes, Sarah Jane, there *is* a past and a future! Unfortunately, the reasons that make 4DR the most attractive theory for explaining the nature of a universe in which time travel is real are also counterbalanced by a central fact about the Doctor's universe: he is always racing around to save it.

Now, the 4DR picture, properly understood, notably levels out the asymmetries discussed in II above. If the Twelfth Doctor is correct that time is "just pictures, lots and lots of pictures. All of them still, none of them moving," then in principle, there is nothing preventing a Time Lord or some other time-sensitive viewing the pictures in reverse order, forming memories about what those in the pictures call "future" and anticipating events that have already happened to them in the "past." When it comes to the thermodynamic arrow, it seems like the block universe picture leaves us with a question that is more difficult to answer than ever before: why exactly *do* systems tend to move from orderliness to disorder when the laws of physics don't prevent them from doing the opposite? We currently have no answer to this. The same question can be asked for causes and effects. Perhaps the four-dimensional universe exists in some kind of "hypertime," as mentioned earlier, that determines these asymmetries as an external cause.

But the biggest problem for the 4DR picture is what it makes of free will and moral responsibility (see Johnson 2009 and 2016). The events of my decision A and action B, from the God's eye perspective *sub specie aeternitatis* ("under the aspect of eternity"), are – *when I choose and when I act* – already followed by consequence C, even though (with my presentist "glasses" on), I cannot yet see where my decision and action will lead. Realizing this is likely to lead to a kind of quietism about moral action – or at least fatalism. The point is that my decisions and actions are *like every other event* in the world, inexorably framed by a closed past and an equally closed future. From an episode quoted earlier, the Doctor consoles his friend Stephen about when bad things happen to good people in history by saying, "We're all too small to realize [history's] final pattern." That sounds like a 4DR world. But then the Doctor says, "I was right to do as I did. Yes, that I firmly believe." It seems strange to use the word "right" when the Doctor is merely following a pattern of history that cannot be changed. It's equivalent to saying "I was right to put one foot down after another while running through a corridor" – which, by the way, there is a tremendous amount of in *Doctor Who*!

But it might be possible that, even in a 4DR block universe, "free will is not an illusion." A traditional approach to reconciling causal determinism, in which effects follow on from their causes with lockstep necessity, is to posit a compatibilist view of free will. The compatibilist distinguishes between two types of causes that can make creatures like us decide, believe, or act in a certain way. External causes originate from "outside" an agent, as when a stranger jostles me and causes me to drop my wallet of Slightly Psychic Paper. Internal causes aren't clearly traceable to outside forces – so that when, for example, the Doctor tells her latest enemy that it has "given her no choice" but to retaliate, this is wrong if it's meant to eliminate free will on the Doctor's part. She *chooses* to retaliate under coercive circumstances. Compatibilists will then say that as long as her actions originate from the latter type of cause, the Doctor is free.

The new *Doctor Who*, while not explicitly endorsing the 4DR picture, would also make an effort to justify the Doctor's moral crusading through the concept of "fixed points." "Fixed points in history" are *Doctor Who*'s way of isolating events or situations that are causally significant because, as the Tenth Doctor explains, "There is no way of stopping [them]" ("The Fires of Pompeii," 2008). In the same episode, the Doctor informs companion Donna Noble that preserving fixed points in time is "the burden of the Time Lords" and even seems to simply walk away from significant tragedies, such as the destruction of Bowie Base One on Mars in 2059 ("The Waters of Mars," 2009).

However, neither compatibilism nor this theory of fixed points seems to be plausible given the version of 4DR we've been considering. For accepting eternalism demands that we reevaluate our thinking about causality, physical laws, and scientific explanation. This is because we typically think of a set of causes and a set of effects as having a relation of *production*, cause to effect, past to future. A 4DR universe is, however, like a block in which past and future co-exist with an experienced present. Theoretically, if we could "slice" the four dimensions of the block universe – with each slice being just a fraction of a second "thick" in time – you would have a universe-wide cross section of all events occur at that fraction of a second. But the relationship between each of these slices is neither governed by natural laws nor causality at all. They stand in a relationship of *succession*, like the Twelfth Doctor's "lots and lots of pictures"; they do not entail a relation of *production* (see Sider 2003, Zimmerman 2011, and Bardon 2013). So any theory of free will that depends upon a theory of causal agency – wherever that causal chain begins, internal or external to a moral agent – will be incompatible with 4DR.

Three possibilities present themselves as ways to "save" free will in a 4DR universe, but the question will be raised, "Is what they are saving genuinely free choice at all?" The first of these is Everett's "Many Worlds" interpretation of quantum mechanics, which was summed up in section "Time Travel in Theory: "First things first, but not necessarily in that order"" as the idea that if something physically *can* happen, it *does* happen – in some universe or the other. The free will of the time traveler – represented there by Deutsch & Lockwood's "autonomy principle" – is not restricted from making a change in the past due to the constraint of causal laws (represented by the "consistency principle") regarding what has already happened. Instead, the time traveler's action creates a new universe, and we have already discussed the implausibility of this view above.

Another possibility is to consider modifying our 4DR theory to say that the space-time universe is not merely a block universe, but a *growing block* universe. This notion, first articulated in the 1920s in research done separately by C.D. Broad and Samuel Alexander (see Thomas 2019), holds that the past and present are real, but the future is unreal. Our perception of the passage of time correlates to the future "becoming real" and being added onto the existing block of past and present space-time. This theory certainly seems to do justice to our perception of the asymmetry of past and future as monolithic and as open, respectively. However, it flies in the face of a well-confirmed part of Einstein's relativity theory, namely, that simultaneity is itself relative. Trenton Merricks argues that the growing block is not a live option for

7 *Doctor Who* as Philosophy: Four-Dimensionalism and Time Travel

a possible metaphysics of time because it does not clearly separate "personal" from "external" time, which was our starting place with David Lewis back in section "'Lots of impossible things happen when you pass through time': Time Travel and the Space-Time Vortex". In fact, Merricks says, the defense of a growing block universe *conflates* the "subjective present" with the "objective present," the latter being the growing "edge" of the block. But there is no non-arbitrary reason to do this, Merricks argues, and therefore it is just as possible that our "subjective present" is in an "objective past" (Merricks 2006). Finally, it is incompatible with the frequent evidence given in *Who* of communication between past and future times in episodes from "The Chase" (1965) to "Under the Lake"/"Before the Flood" (2015) and beyond.

The final possibility has been termed "quantum free will," the notion that changes at the quantum level of brain states are undetermined, and thus some brain states are free. But this view is also unlikely to provide a satisfactory solution. Carlo Rovelli, author of *The Order of Time*, succinctly pointed out the problem with this view when he said:

> Free will has nothing to do with quantum mechanics. We are deeply unpredictable beings, like most macroscopic systems. . . . The idea that free will may have to do with the ability to make different choices on equal internal states is an absurdity. . . . Our idea of being free is correct, but it is just a way to say that we are ignorant on why we make choices. (Rovelli 2013, n.p.)

So perhaps this is what sets the Doctor aside from other Time Lords, what bonds him to the human beings that so often make up his companions: a recognition of the mutuality of ignorance and a rejection of the quietism of the Time Lords. He is, after all, "a madman with a box."

Despite whether he stands for the eternal or for the vibrancy of the present moment, the Doctor has so far defeated all attempts – by Daleks, Cybermen, Sontarans, and even the most deadly of enemies, the BBC itself – to stop his wandering through space and time. It is thus appropriate to end this chapter with The Doctor's own words from "Survival," the last episode of the classic series broadcast on, December 6, 1989:

> *There are worlds out there where the sky is burning, where the sea's asleep and the rivers dream, people made of smoke and cities made of song. Somewhere there's danger, somewhere there's injustice, and somewhere else the tea's getting cold.*
> *Come on, Ace — we've got work to do!*

References

Amis, Kingsley. 1960. *New maps of hell: A survey of science fiction*. New York: Harcourt & Brace.
Aristotle. De Interpretatione. The complete works of Aristotle, ed. Jonathan Barnes. Princeton: Bollingen Series/Princeton University Press, 1984.
Bardon, Adrian. 2013. *A brief history of the philosophy of time*. New York: Oxford University Press.

BBC WAC T5/638/1. Audience Research Report VR/62/412 "Dr. Who," 30 December 1963.

Bentham, Jeremy. 1986. *Doctor Who: The early years*. London: W.H. Allen.

Burk, Graeme, and Robert Smith. 2012. *Who is the doctor: The unofficial guide to Doctor Who – The new series*. Toronto: ECW Press.

Chapman, James. 2013. *Inside the TARDIS: The Worlds of Doctor Who*. 2nd ed. New York: I.B. Tauris.

Decker, Kevin S. 2005. *Who is Who? The philosophy of Doctor Who*. London: I.B. Tauris.

Deutsch, David, and Michael Lockwood. 1994. The quantum physics of time travel. *Scientific American* 270: 68–74.

Dicks, Terrance. 1979. *Doctor Who and the Robots of Death*. Based on the BBC television serial written by Chris Boucher. London: Target Books.

Earman, John, Christian Wüthrich, and John Manchak. 2016. Time machines. In *The Stanford encyclopedia of philosophy*, ed. Edward N. Zalta. https://plato.stanford.edu/archives/win2016/entries/time-machine/.

Gillatt, Gary. 1998. *Doctor Who from A to Z*. London: BBC Worldwide.

Hawking, Stephen. 1992. Chronology protection conjecture. *Physical Review D* 46 (2): 603–611.

Heidegger, Martin. 1985. *History of the concept of time: Prolegomena*. Trans. Theodore Kisiel. Bloomington: Indiana University Press.

Hume, David. 1993. *An enquiry concerning human understanding*. Indianapolis: Hackett Publishing Company.

Jeffery, Morgan. 12 everyday things that Doctor Who tried to make us terrified of. *Digital Spy*. July 2, 2018. https://www.digitalspy.com/tv/cult/a849413/doctor-who-monsters-aliens-villains/. Accessed 13 Dec 2019.

Johnson, David Kyle. 2009. God, fatalism and temporal ontology. *Religious Studies* 45 (4): 435–454.

———. 2010. Is the doctor the doctor? Am I still me? In *Doctor Who and philosophy*, ed. C. Lewis and P. Smithka. Chicago: Open Court.

———. *Doctor Who* and the fate of Amy Pond. *Psychology Today*. 2 October 2012. Web. 11 May, 2018. https://www.psychologytoday.com/us/blog/plato-pop/201210/doctor-who-and-the-fate-amy-pond

———. "Does free will exist?" Thinking 42(15) (Autumn 2015).

Lewis, David. 1986. The paradoxes of time travel. In *Philosophical Papers*, vol. 2, 67–80. New York: Oxford University Press.

Merricks, Trenton. 2006. Good-bye growing block. In *Oxford studies in metaphysics*, ed. Dean Zimmerman, vol. 2. New York: Oxford University Press.

Nahin, Paul. 1993. *Time machines: Time travel in physics, metaphysics, and science fiction*. 2nd ed. New York: Springer.

Pearson, Lars and Lance Parkin. 2019. *A history: An Unauthorized History of the* Doctor Who *Universe*, 4th ed., 3 vols. Des Moines: Mad Norwegian Press.

Peel, John. 1989. *Doctor Who: The chase*. London: Target Books.

Rovelli, Carlo. Free will, determiminism, quantum theory and statistical fluctuations: A physicist's take. *The Edge* (July 8, 2013). https://www.edge.org/conversation/carlo_rovelli-free-will-determinism-quantum-theory-and-statistical-fluctuations-a. Accessed 13 June 2020.

Rucker, Rudy. 2014. *The fourth dimension: Toward a geometry of higher reality*. 2nd ed. New York: Dover Publications. http://www.rudyrucker.com/thefourthdimension/#calibre_link-111. Accessed 13 Dec 2019.

Sider, Theodore. 2003. *Four-dimensionalism: An ontology of persistence and time*. Oxford: Clarendon Press.

———. 2016. Time. In *Science fiction and philosophy: From time travel to superintelligence*, ed. Susan Schneider, 2nd ed. Malden: Wiley-Blackwell.

TARDIS Wikia. Season 18. https://tardis.fandom.com/wiki/Season_18. Accessed 20 Dec 2019.

Thomas, Emily. 2019. The roots of C.D. Broad's growing block theory of time. *Mind* 128 (510): 527–549.

Tipler, Frank J. 1974. Rotating cylinders and the possibility of global causality violation. *Phys Rev D* 9 (8): 2203–2206.

Tribe, Steve. 2017. *Doctor Who: A brief history of the time lords*. New York: Harper Design.

Tulloch, John, and Manuel Alvarado. 1983. *Doctor Who: The unfolding text*. New York: St. Martin's Press.

Zimmerman, Dean. 2011. Presentism and the space-time manifold. In *The Oxford handbook of the philosophy of time*, ed. Craig Callender. New York: Oxford.

Breaking Bad as Philosophy: The Moral Aesthetics of the Anti-hero's Journey

8

David Koepsell

Contents

Introduction 164
The Journey of Walter White 165
The Epic as Polemic Form: Heroes and Antiheroes 165
Satirical Epic, Consequentialism, and Deontology 168
Walter White and the Inherent Vice of the Antihero 171
"Say My Name" Says the Man with No Name 176
The End Is Just a Little Harder When Brought About by Friends 178
The Philosophy of *Breaking Bad* 181
Conclusion 182
References 182

Abstract

Breaking Bad has been lauded as the best series ever on television by numerous critics and polls. It follows the "Breaking Bad" (i.e., the moral degradation) of Walter White, a middle-class, middle-aged high school chemistry teacher in Albuquerque, New Mexico. Presented in the form of a literary epic employing satire, it provides us with a way to look at complex issues of justice, the good, and meaning, all while imparting a sense of aesthetics of justice and morality. The aesthetics of justice in *Breaking Bad* examines problems and issues of modernity, employing existential and moralistic themes similar to other satirical epic works featuring antiheroes including *Ulysses* and *Don Quixote*. In this chapter, the existentialist themes and aesthetic treatment of Walt's complex moral world are discussed in relation to other epic satirical works, and an argument expanding upon the author's prior conceptions of *Breaking Bad*'s aesthetics of the just and the good is made.

D. Koepsell (✉)
Department of Philosophy, Texas A&M, College Station, TX, USA

© Springer Nature Switzerland AG 2024
D. K. Johnson et al. (eds.), *The Palgrave Handbook of Popular Culture as Philosophy*,
https://doi.org/10.1007/978-3-031-24685-2_20

163

Keywords

Breaking Bad · Epic · Satire · Aesthetics · Justice · Nietzsche · Sartre · Utilitarianism · Deontology · Virtue ethics · Aristotle · Emotivism

Introduction

Perhaps no TV series, and few works of filmmaking, have inspired as much universal and acclaim as *Breaking Bad*. Since its inception, numerous others have attempted to capture the storytelling, visual beauty, acting, ingenuity, and consistency that Vince Gilligan put into his *magnum opus*, and only *Better Call Saul*, which is a spinoff of *Breaking Bad* also produced and written by Gilligan, comes even close. The series came at just the right time, served such a purpose in a worn American psyche, and provided characters with whom people so closely connected, that it encapsulated a unique avenue of societal and personal introspection – one that served as a basis for philosophizing and generated a collective catharsis unlike any other work of fiction before or since. The series follows the descent of a middle class, "ordinary" American middle-aged man into a life of crime. His moral degradation is spurred by a cancer diagnosis and lack of adequate health insurance in the mid-to-late-aughts in Albuquerque, New Mexico. With the iconic and appropriate middle-American name of Walter White, a talented scientist with the potential for greatness who tripped over his own ego and fell into the mediocre life of a high school science teacher, the development of his criminal alter ego "Heisenberg" serves as a fantasy cum warning for the path of the nebbish antihero (an antihero being any protagonist who lacks typical "heroic" qualities or virtues.

The show has offered philosophers and other academics numerous avenues of critical inquiry, providing examples for pedagogy and opportunities for serious cultural critique and research. In its 62-episode run, there is fodder for academic discussion of ethics, existentialism, gender, class, history, aesthetics, scientific ethics, and enough material for at least two major books on the philosophy of *Breaking Bad*. This chapter discusses not just another angle of philosophical inquiry into the show, but rather the nature of the art form employed, its reach and its limitations, and the theme presented by the character of Walter White in relation to other works of art. This chapter argues that, in the course of this sweeping epic, numerous themes of ethics, meaning, and existence are dealt with in a way that art is best suited because these themes are largely emotive and expressive, as David Hume argued morality itself is. *Breaking Bad* is a work of epic fiction in the tradition of historical epics (*Moby Dick*, *The Odyssey*, etc.); its style is satirical, and only through its form and aesthetic can the author's full scope of moral inquiry be achieved.

The Journey of Walter White

Breaking Bad starts with a modern dilemma. A seemingly ordinary man – a high school science teacher clearly weighed down by tedium and mediocrity – suddenly discovers he has terminal cancer. His health plan is insufficient for him to treat his cancer without significant debt, and his salary is far too low to pay for treatment. Because of a complex set of facts about his past (entanglements with former business partners in a venture that panned out for his partners, but not for him), he is too proud to seek their help or to accept it even when it is actually offered. Instead, a chance and hysterically funny encounter with an ex-student while on a "ride-along" with Walt's DEA agent brother-in-law leads Walt down the path of cooking meth, and eventually becoming an almost legendary drug kingpin under the pseudonym "Heisenberg."

Walt's journey takes numerous terrible turns. His body count grows. He becomes a moral monster throughout the progress of the series, settling comfortably into a role much bigger than his life warrants. Driven by his hubris and pride, he falls to the lowest lows, attempting to redeem himself only superficially and without apology. Upon his own inevitable, violent death, he finally accepts that his only real motivation – even after perfecting a scheme that will help his then-estranged family economically – was that he enjoyed the terrible things he did. The crime, the manipulation, the murders, and the thousands of lives affected by the drugs he manufactured and sold were worth it to him; he never regrets what he has done.

Vince Gilligan cast the antihero of *Breaking Bad* as a sort of amalgam of loser-dads popular in TV shows since the 1990s. Bryan Cranston had played such a dad in *Malcolm in the Middle* and begins the series seeming very much like the sort of unremarkable, nondescript, nebbish that is common to the genre. By taking an ordinary character and placing him in the situation he is in, Gilligan invites us all along for the moral journey that is the didactic center of the series. How can decent (or apparently decent) people become evil? In joining this journey, we are forced to ask ourselves numerous philosophical questions challenging our conceptions of the good, of destiny, of justice, and of meaning and meaninglessness. Walt's journey becomes our journey, and his slide from generic social acceptability to a vicious, murderous, and immoral drug kingpin is made conceivable through our sympathy with Walt, even as the turns the story takes become more outrageous and unlikely. To lubricate the path of this journey, and encourage us to accept it as it unfolds, Gilligan simultaneously employs satire, epic, and the notion of the antihero to seduce us into thinking deeply about the substantial philosophical questions he explores.

The Epic as Polemic Form: Heroes and Antiheroes

One of the oldest works of known literature in the west is *The Epic of Gilgamesh*. Most people are also familiar with Homer's epics, *The Iliad* and *The Odyssey*. The epic form recurs throughout the history of literature and usually recounts some hero's journey and eventual triumph. The notion of the hero's journey has been succinctly described most notably in the work of Joseph Campbell, who examines this recurring theme in a broad swath of literature dating back thousands of years. The hero's journey is that of an epic quest and includes a number of archetypal elements. Epic literature generally involves a well-known structure, elucidated by Campbell and others, with the following stages:

> The Ordinary World, The Call to Adventure, The Refusal of the Call, Meeting with the Mentor, Crossing the Threshold, Tests, Allies and Enemies, Approach to the Innermost Cave, The Supreme Ordeal.

The philosophical point of epics or their polemic purpose is to provide lessons in values and virtues. The hero is a model for behavior, and the hero's adventures are provided to educate us ordinary humans as to how to act, how to be, and how to face the more mundane adversities we all face. Satirical epic uses this form to teach us lessons about virtues and values as well, sometimes by laughing at the mundane and sometimes by amplifying it to the point of absurdity. Examples of these are James Joyce's *Ulysses*, Alexander Pope's epic poem *The Rape of the Lock*, and Voltaire's *Candide*.

Epics encapsulate as much of the human experience as possible, trying to encompass the entirety of the world within them. The hero generally moves significantly from their home in the journey, traveling to unknown places, meeting unusual challenges and foreign, sometimes inhuman, adversaries. The hero must experience a broad range of new and frightening, or at least unsettling people and places, and come to terms with them. Generally, in the course of the journey, the hero is changed by their experience, through physical ordeals, through exposure to trauma, through injury and effort combined, and the journey is meant to transform them inwardly through the outward challenges faced and the hero's abilities to meet them.

A number of authors have applied the template of the hero's journey against the series *Breaking Bad* and have shown rather clearly that Walter White is an antihero of an epic. A more complete description would be that *Breaking Bad* is an antiheroic epic that Gilligan crafted as a broad satire. Moreover, there is a philosophical polemical purpose that runs throughout the show – namely, the overarching message that we should, despite temptation, avoid Walt's choices and fate. Lastly, *Breaking Bad* also takes the form of a morality play. The morality play is a type of medieval show in which allegorical devices were used to teach some moral lesson.

One of the five extant examples of the morality play is *Everyman*, in which a man facing death is sent by God on a pilgrimage to face the consequences of his sinfulness. Everyman – the eponymous protagonist of the play – is an abstraction of all humankind, and he bargains with Death who allows him to bring along a companion on his journey. *Everyman* succeeds at being an epic in its structure, although not its length or depth. Greek epic is more detailed, nuanced, and forms the model for the sort of *grand* epic with which we are most familiar. Instead, *Everyman* is the abstraction of epic form as a didactic tool, turning abstract concepts like Good Deeds, Confession, and Penance into characters with whom Everyman interacts.

This morality play is often considered the finest of the form and is known to have influenced many authors, including T.S. Eliot and Philip Roth. In *Everyman*, encounters with archetypes of virtues and vices lead to Everyman's literal redemption.

With all that in mind, a great ambiguity of the story of Walter White is whether what is lauded as one of TV's best finales contains a redemption of any kind. What is the moral conclusion of *Breaking Bad*? What have we learned through Walt's epic journey? Only by viewing the series as satire do we gain some clarity.

Friederich Nietzsche's *Thus Spoke Zarathustra*: A Book for All and None offers us a paradigm of the epic form featuring a hero. In its simplest form, the hero's journey includes (1) a departure, (2) an initiation, and finally, (3) a return. These phases of the journey have further subparts as delineated above. The hero of Zarathustra triumphs as heroes do and teaches us of the will to power: actualizing one's will effectively in the world (and in a self-directed way, not because of others). The hero also instructs how the ability to overcome oneself can be cultivated to help us become Overmen (ubermenschen), the super men we can be if we cast away the degeneracy of egalitarianism and rise above traditional Christian morality. In sum, Nietzsche uses a story to impart his philosophy. The text is often bewildering, tending to be heavy-handed and alienating for both philosophers and laymen, but it is of a kind with other literary epics. By contrast, *Breaking Bad* is epic for everyone else, for all – not none. Walter White strives for power, wills himself to succeed without regard to those around him, and succeeds in some ways while failing generally. His successes are short-lived and Pyrrhic, leading always to greater and greater harms. Rather than triumphant, Germanic existential victory and growth, we are left with a tragic, French existentialist punch line.

The will to power ends as emptiness, hollow, and worthless to those whom Walt leaves behind. In the wake of his epic antiheroic quest are bodies and broken lives, and the money that he secured brings no comfort to the shattered victims in his household. Walt would have been better toiling away at his dead-end high school teaching job and for Bogdan Wolynetz (the abusive and demeaning car wash boss at his second job). He should have imagined himself as Camus imagines the Greek tragic hero, Sisyphus, cursed to ceaselessly push a boulder uphill that will inevitably roll down again:

The struggle itself toward the heights is enough to fill a man's heart. One must imagine Sisyphus happy. (Camus, The Myth of Sisyphus)

In other words, Walt should have found meaning – and happiness – in the endlessly repeated drudgery of his life. Instead, Walt chooses the adversarial path of Zarathustra but cannot become the hero. His antiheroism is cast in stone by the nature of the choices Walt makes. Gilligan rejects the central ethical theme of Zarathustra implicitly. Zarathustra teaches that we must overcome adversity, struggle against it, and embrace eternal recurrence – another complex Nietzschean concept that involves confidently claiming ownership over one's fate given the absurd possibility that the universe is condemned to repeat itself endlessly. Only in this *amor fati,* or love of our fate, can we will ourselves to power and become the Overman (ubermensch). One can picture Gus Fring, the sociopathic and dapper meth kingpin who poses the greatest threat to Walt, giving any of the speeches from Zarathustra, and Walt clearly eventually embraces Gus as a role model. Gus meets a bad and violent end by embracing his "master of the universe" ideal, as does Walt in emulating him. Better they should have toiled, embraced the absurdity of life, and found happiness there.

Satirical Epic, Consequentialism, and Deontology

Moby Dick and *The Odyssey* are qualitatively different from *Don Quixote* and *Ulysses*, although all are arguably epics involving heroes' journeys. The latter two are satire. Satire uses exaggeration, irony, hyperbole, allegory, understatement, and other literary devices intended to be comedic in effect. Satire generally attempts to be didactic or polemical in bringing light to some injustice, or to some other moral effect. While *Moby Dick* and *The Odyssey* play it "straight" and tell grand, sweeping, and even fantastic epic tales of heroism, loss, and triumph, they do so without subversion. Satire is subversive: it makes its point with humor, both subtle and broad, that is often intended to reveal its subject to be ridiculous, undermine the villain (sometimes the hero), and make light of some target taken too seriously.

Don Quixote is perhaps the best-known satirical epic in literature. Satire allows social commentary that might be lost if it were given in a straightforward didactic or polemic form. The greater the potential discomfort posed by the "point" of the subject of the satire, the more likely the satire will be broad. Satirical social commentary is typically disruptive, disquieting, and prone to divisiveness. These consequences are more of a feature than a bug. Provoking and undermining the status quo is often the point. It is tricky and risky, and when it works, a good satirical epic can make a mark on a culture unlike other forms of commentary or art. It is no accident that *Don Quixote*, *Ulysses*, and *Infinite Jest* are now shorthand for particular eras and their milieus, and that we can see the whole of a particular cultural moment in each while we simultaneously laugh and nod our heads in collective appreciation for the angst and folly they represent.

Vince Gilligan has been explicit about his goal in writing *Breaking Bad*: he wanted to explore the transformation of an ordinary person into a moral monster of sorts – to track the moral devolution of an ordinary man. Satire is used throughout the show. In fact, nothing about *Breaking Bad* can be taken to be anything other than satirical. It never plays it straight. The entire journey of its antihero is ridiculous at its core. Walter White is a caricature of sorts at the start of the series, not in any way a real person. He is a caricature of a typical white, middle class male of a certain age, in some ways a continuation of the affable loser dad Bryan Cranston played in *Malcolm in the Middle*. Although throughout the series a somewhat darker past full of jealousy, ego, and regret emerges, Walt's persona – a painfully average man trapped in an unfulfilling job with a family that has grown to pity him – is the central theme of numerous sitcoms. In class, he waxes lyrical about chemistry, but it's an obvious allusion to life itself:

> I mean, it's just...it's the constant, it's the cycle. Its solution, dissolution, just over and over and over. It is growth, then decay, then transformation. It is fascinating, really. ("Pilot," Season 1, Episode 1)

The Misadventures of Walter White would have been a fine alternate title for *Breaking Bad*. Nothing about what happens to him or how he encounters and deals with situations that arise is normal. He acts in consistently outrageous ways, even setting aside the violence and crime, that underscore the essentially broad satirical form of the series. The show's most iconic incidents are those that are also the most ridiculous: a body crashing through a ceiling due to a failure to dissolve it properly in acid, a pizza on a roof, an over-the-top chase of a housefly, an elaborate underground meth-lab, a Walt Whitman-citing hipster meth-cook, the porkpie hat and mustachioed "Heisenberg" himself, a *Ballad of Heisenberg* that is a Narcocorrido (a Mexican narrative ballad usually about drug trafficking) about Walter White's alter-ego, and dozens of other examples. Iconic scenes like these mark the series as broad satire with occasional highs and lows.

Breaking Bad, in many ways, had to be a satire. Commenting on the impossibility of the American Dream at the beginning of the twenty-first century meant addressing injustice, inequality, and uncertainties that we have been trying to brave our ways through for decades. The failure of American institutions to meet the promises our parents and grandparents made and benefitted from is painful. The spasmodic and occasional lurches toward a better America were met time and again with disappointment and deceit. Decent and intelligent folks who did their part remained stuck or left behind by a fundamentally altered political economy both at home and abroad. Walter White, the hapless everyman faced with deep existential crisis at every step, could only play the role in this morality play if he were a sort of antihero, making the wrong choices for the wrong reasons at every step – a counterexample for us all in his doomed foibles.

Much of *Breaking Bad*'s satire about social injustice is also a critique of utilitarianism, the ethical theory that determines the good based upon a choice's effect on the overall happiness (pleasure) of the most people. Indeed, while Gilligan takes this criticism to the same extreme as Dostoyevsky in *Crime and Punishment*, by using satire he avoids subjecting us to something with the gravity of a famously dense Russian novel. *Crime and Punishment* is in general a critique of the misuse of the utilitarian calculus by which especially Bentham argued we can discover the good by determining the balance of harms versus goods from any action or set of actions. Dostoyevsky's ethics appears to be deontological, based instead upon duty and rules governing our behaviors regardless of consequences. In *Crime and Punishment*, Raskolnikov's choice to slay Ivanovna, the corrupt and usurious owner of a pawnshop, is justified throughout by Roskolnikov's resort to utilitarianism. Russian epic drama contains little humor, and reading it is sometimes like dental surgery:

necessary but painful. Satirical polemics are more easily digested, a lot less painful, and often effective at imparting their lessons. *Don Quixote* is but one example.

The attack on bald utilitarianism in *Breaking Bad* reflects the same attempt in *Crime and Punishment*, appealing for us to see the moral absurdity of the hedonic calculus when taken to its extreme. For instance, in ". . .And the Bag's in the River" (Season 1, Episode 3), Walt creates a list of pros and cons to murdering the competing drug dealer Krazy-8. Walt's list initially shows a balance of harms for the murder, but his final entry, suggesting that allowing Krazy-8 to live will endanger his family, illustrates the moral emptiness of the hedonic calculus. This also begins Walt's descent into evil. While Walt's judgment is true in the sense that Krazy-8 and his gang may threaten Walt's family, there is certainly more to the calculus than that. As we discover through the rest of the series, the murder sparks deadlier violence and Walt's own actions are responsible, more than anything else, for endangering his family.

Numerous philosophers have found flaws with utilitarianism/consequentialism, and examples abound as to its limitations. The hedonic calculus may seem to gloss over the complexities of values inherent in most moral choices. This is something that Walt realizes immediately. The harms that accumulate due to his decision to kill Krazy-8 arguably outweigh the harms that might have befallen his family had he let Krazy-8 go. Walt unfairly weighs that harm more heavily than the others. A drug war precipitates, dozens of lives are lost in Walt's hit against Tuco (a high-ranking Cartel figure) and his gang, and a greater war that will consume the southwestern drug scene draw Walt and Jesse into conflicts with even more dangerous drug lords like "Tio" Hector Salamanca and Gus Fring, requiring ever-escalating levels of carnage and a ridiculously large and bloody body count.

The alternative would have been the same alternative that should have prevented Raskolnikov from killing Alyona Ivanovna: a recognition of the overriding importance of (Kant's) categorical imperative, which says that we must treat all others as ends in themselves, rather than as means to ends; humans possess inherent dignity, and we must always act as though our choices can be willed to become universal law (that is, applicable to everyone and at all times) without contradiction. Our choices must be guided by the inherent nature of others as possessing dignity and may not excuse any harm that we couldn't accept ourselves given the universalization of our choices. In a universe of ends, we should not perform the hedonic calculus at all because it sees other people as numbers in the calculus, not living things worthy of moral respect. Walt's list of pros and cons reduces Krazy-8 to a means – an instrument valuable only in determining if the end result is good – Krazy-8's life is not seen as valuable in itself. Even the act of weighing the pros and cons of killing him does this, violating the categorical imperative. It treats Krazy-8 as contingent, and the good as hypothetical depending upon some outcome.

Perhaps no modern work of art so clearly attacks utilitarianism as does *Breaking Bad*. Because of the form, it is less "preachy" and more palatable than the dour and dire Russian epics of Tolstoy and Dostoyevsky, each of whom makes similar points about the emptiness of utility as a guide to behavior and appeals to duties grounded in our common dignity and value. The moral arc of *Breaking Bad* takes the critique

8 *Breaking Bad* as Philosophy: The Moral Aesthetics of the Anti-hero's...

of utilitarianism to a logical extreme, arguing against it through what amounts to an *ad absurdum* argument – well beyond realism, darkly comic in scope, and ultimately clear cut and sound. Treating others as means to ends is morally wrong in itself. Villains and our antihero alike are guilty of this error, and by making Walt an antihero with whom we are meant to identify, rather than a mere villain, we are more likely to see the personal danger and effect of our own choices and to question the method of the hedonic calculus through Walt's continued embrace and eventual, almost total failure as a result. The general philosophical point is continued quite explicitly in the prequel series *Better Call Saul*, where we also see that Jimmy McGill, who started as a petty conman ripping folks off for his own benefit, cannot help but continue to do so as a lawyer who ends up becoming the legal defender of crooks like Gus Fring and Walt.

Walter White and the Inherent Vice of the Antihero

Walter White being the antihero does not mean we don't like him. Indeed, although we are not supposed to be like Walt/Heisenberg, we begin by liking, if not admiring him. It is impossible to watch *Breaking Bad* and not somehow cheer for him even after he has become his worst self. Walt is quite explicitly not a villain. The villains in *Breaking Bad* are clearly some of Walt's foils, like Gus, and Tuco: criminal competitors who try to co-opt or harm Walt at various stages, and whose defeats by Walt we celebrate. Hank, Walt's DEA-agent brother-in-law, is not a villain either. We mourn his death just as Walt does, even though Hank was trying to find the mysterious Heisenberg and threatened to bring down Walt. No, Walter White is an antihero because he is on the hero's journey but headed toward deviance, despair, and eventual destruction. The antihero's journey is one that we understand, we feel inclined to support at some level, but that is clearly also wrong. Walt isn't bent toward evil, he has made a bargain with evil in the pursuit of what he has fooled himself into thinking is the good (and fooled himself into thinking he is seeking): security for his family that he was unable to achieve by other, moral means.

Examples of antiheroes abound in literature, and especially satirical epic. Ahab is an antihero in *Moby Dick*, Raskolnikov in *Crime and Punishment*, Jay Gatsby in the *Great Gatsby*, Don Quixote himself, and Stephen Dedalus in *Ulysses* are all prime examples of antiheroes. We cheer these doomed protagonists on in their futile quests, recognize their errors, understand their failures at redemption, but sympathize with their plights and use the lessons to guide our own lives. No one wants to emulate the antihero, but everyone understands them to some degree. Satire helps make their follies more palatable. Being able to laugh at the antihero's eventual failure makes our sympathy for them, even while understanding they have been wrong or misguided, acceptable. They must lose, eventually, but their struggle is symbolic and important, and in each case, much of the (anti)hero's journey is replicated and includes lessons for all of us.

While villains embrace their evil, antiheroes often view themselves as serving some just purpose, even if they accept that their choices may harm others. As opposed to villains, antiheroes also end up somehow doing the right thing. They may do great harm along the way, but they don't mean to cause that harm. The tragedy of Ahab, the fatal flaw that leads to his doom, is his single-minded pursuit of vengeance, leading his crew to harm, based upon his warped sense of just purpose against a mindless creature. The comedy of Don Quixote is his fruitless pursuit of outdated norms, and beliefs in his own defunct chivalrous attempts to right wrongs that need no righting. The tragedy of Raskolnikov is his own justification of what he knows is a horrific act, and ability to evade justice that he knows he deserves. The comic-tragedy of Stephen Dedalus is his self-conscious failure to achieve what he thought he should in life, his existential despair in light of a mediocre intellectual life, and the simultaneous success of Bloom, the hero of *Ulysses*, in achieving happiness in his own mediocrity.

Walter White has a decent life. He seems like a decent man at the start, more a Bloom than a Dedalus. As mentioned above, Gilligan's admitted project was always to explore how a decent person could descend into utter depravity. The project for moral education is clear, the manner in which to do so has been chosen as that which is well-tested and up to the task. The satirical epic of an antihero in *Breaking Bad* is even lyrical and plays like a modern *Faust* (either Goethe or Marlowe). The antihero, impelled by a flaw of character and circumstance is driven ever deeper into a moral morass of his own making, further challenged and given opportunities for redemption, and fails or falls short. Even if he prevails somehow, his lack of heroic qualities prevents his success from being a reason to emulate him. His moral arc is a strong moral lesson because he remains the protagonist, though not a hero. Heroes are tempted in their epic journeys, and may stray slightly along the way, but they triumph by rejecting temptation, and pursuing with ever-greater resolve *the Good*. In so doing, they perfect their characters and become models of the just and righteous for the audience. Antiheroes do the opposite. They are tempted and find some way to succumb to the temptation through a flaw or through their own self-deception.

In *Star Wars*, Darth Vader is the antihero and Luke Skywalker, his son, is the hero. Vader's fall is justified by his deceiving himself that his course of action would promote the good, that the rules somehow should not apply to him, and that ultimately, he is beyond redemption anyway. He emerges as antihero instead of villain when he destroys Palpatine and saves both his son and his own soul. Walt's own justifications for his choices seem similar. He has convinced himself from his simple utilitarian calculus early on, that he has chosen to do a greater good by cooking meth. The money will save his family from poverty when he is inevitably dead, and all the evil that occurs along the way is somehow worth it. His young apprentice, Jesse, is corrupted in the process but ultimately rejects the path that Walt has chosen and so is redeemed. Walt cannot be redeemed and instead embraces his fate at the close of the series, owning up to his true motivations and leaving it clear that he is no hero at all. He did what he did because he liked it. He finally felt empowered. His utilitarian justifications are, by his final act, not central to what kept him going even in defeating his enemies and foils, both criminal and in law enforcement. All matter is in flux, all of us change along the course of our journeys.

Or, as Walt puts it: Well, technically, chemistry is the study of matter. But I prefer to see it as the study of change ("Pilot," Season 1, Episode 1).

The antihero's journey is no different. Walt is still no villain. While we no longer have moral sympathy for what Walt has become, we are finally left to at least accept his final act of honesty as a sort of explanation, even while it is neither an excuse nor redemption. He has *become* Heisenberg. Werner Heisenberg, the physicist, described a principle of quantum reality that is a reflection of Walt throughout the series. No quantum particle can be measured with full precision in all of its qualities or quantities. The more we hone in on precision about velocity, for instance, the less certainty we have about its *position* at any moment and vice versa. In fact, in some interpretations of quantum dynamics, it is the act of observation that actually creates the position and velocity. Walt is in such a quantum state until the final act. His admission to his wife about what has motivated him gives us our most precise measurement of Walt's character, even while throughout the series his moral devolution is fraught with potential and possibility. He has embraced the dark side, made the Faustian bargain, completed his ramble through Dublin, ended his quest without victory, in no greater state of grace or redemption than before, and finds himself with nothing left to look forward to than his death, which was foretold at the start.

Like the villains in the series, Walt's antiheroic journey sees him become, in the language of virtue ethics, mostly vicious. Largely originating in ancient Platonic and Aristotelian philosophy, virtue ethics concerns (unsurprisingly) virtues and vices. The virtues are (largely moral) traits of our personalities that are cultivated through education and practice, and the vices are, roughly, their opposites. The *vicious* person fails to cultivate their virtues or to act according to them. For Aristotle especially, as described in his *Nicomachean Ethics*, each virtue is a mean that rests between the vicious extremes of excess and deficit. So, courage is a virtue, and its associated vices are recklessness at one end, and cowardice at the other. The four "cardinal" virtues of prudence, justice, temperance, and courage are meant to be taught to children by the state and parents, and the cultivation of these virtues should lead to the creation of a just society. The antihero cultivates the virtues in reverse, fooling himself as to his own virtuousness while becoming vicious. We can see this in action throughout the epic arc of *Breaking Bad*. The hero's journey works only to accentuate Walt's viciousness even as his victories over the villains fool him, and sometimes us, as to his virtuousness.

Gilligan may not explicitly embrace virtue theory through the course of the series, but we can evaluate Walt's behaviors according to the classic virtues and see that Walt eschews most of those virtues throughout his moral devolution. Walt is not prudent, temperate nor just, and while to some he may seem courageous at first blush, a deeper understanding of the nature of the virtues shows he is in fact reckless, which is a vice. The mother of all virtues, prudence, is the ability to gauge our behaviors in accordance with reason and foresight, to direct our choices using these capacities, rather than acting rashly or in accordance with our emotions or desires. It is clear that Walt acts rashly, choosing not the most rational course, but one that will fulfill his ego, his desire to dominate others, and his need to win at all costs. He will admit as much in the series finale when he says truthfully that he did what he did because he liked it. It made him feel good. He is never prudent and lacks that virtue.

The virtue of temperance is opposed by the vices of gluttony and excess. Walt is not temperate in his character, seeking not to carve a comfortable niche for his business as a meth manufacturer, but ultimately to consume the whole market, to defeat his competitors, and to aggrandize himself in the process. He wants, in sum, to dominate – to be king: Jesse, you asked me if I was in the meth business, or the money business… Neither. I'm in the empire business ("Buyout," Season 5, Episode 6).

The alter-ego he creates for himself, Heisenberg, becomes a sort of mythic figure, larger than life, instilling fear and awe into the meth-manufacturing and consuming community. Walt at every step sets aside moderation and temperance and chooses excess. One example is his choice of automobiles for himself and his son. Instead of buying simple, roadworthy, and functional cars that will not call attention to his recent, inexplicable wealth, he buys flashy and expensive cars that demonstrate his power and show off his status to the world. Unlike Gus, who is temperate in his public tastes, Walt is guilty of the vice of excess and makes no attempt to hide it.

Similarly, Walt rejects the virtue of justice. In the face of opportunities to use deceit and violence or choose to act justly, Walt chooses in every case the former, and leads people like Jesse Pinkman along the same path. Even his choice of crime is an affront to justice as his product appeals to the addicted, the disabled, the less educated, and the poor, victimizing them instead of helping them. He fools himself along the way as to his virtuousness, but we can see the results of his viciousness. In one touching scene, the tragedy of the scourge of meth addiction is brought home graphically to Jesse when two meth-addled parents die leaving their toddler helpless, dirty, and alone. That Walt and Jesse are complicit in a drug epidemic that is destroying lives, both innocent and guilty, is an affront to justice that Walt is unwilling to own up to. He is unjust and part of an unjust phenomenon he refuses to extricate himself from, along with the villains with whom he does battle, confusing himself at times with someone who is just. Hank is just, Walt is not. Hank sets his sights on Heisenberg, but Walt is both unjust and too cowardly to admit his deceit and criminality.

Walt can appear to be courageous, but every action he takes throughout the series belies his cowardice and his recklessness. Walt exhibits both of these vices at the extreme ends of the virtue of courage, failing to show the courage of a just man who knows he has done wrong, allowing his brother-in-law to pursue his alter-ego, ultimately to his doom, without confessing when he could have spared Hank's life. He is also reckless in exposing himself and others to danger, in becoming and reveling in the violence and danger inherent in the drug trade he has made himself a pivotal part of, and in laying waste to all his competitors in often excessive, violent, and vengeful ways, as with the use of Hector to kill Gus.

Walt's inherent vice, his failure to abide by or impart virtues, leads him to the only natural conclusion for such an antihero: death and destruction. His end will underscore his viciousness through the revelation of his true nature, his lack of remorse, and the trail of pain and loss that he leaves in his wake. His doom is etched in the nature of his character, his lack of virtue, his inability to choose the good, his cold, erroneous utilitarian stance, and his failure to treat anyone as an equal deserving of dignity. Yet, despite the fact that Walt's viciousness is treated as a moral error by the show, *Breaking Bad* cannot fully be explained by virtue theory. Classical conceptions of the virtue of justice require that citizens cultivate a desire for justice in society and justness among each other. So, it is not just that Walt should *himself* act justly. To truly promote virtue ethics, it looks like Walt's injustice would need to be punished and a sense of justice achieved for all of those Walt wronged.

The justice of classical Greek virtue ethics is always about one's relationship to society as a whole. People ought to get what they deserve and not more *in relation to others*. This may mean that each should acquire what they can through honest, hard work, and not through theft or deceit, or that those who do not act justly are punished accordingly and not empowered to profit from their injustice. This is not what happens in *Breaking Bad*, though. Walt seeks a path of injustice and cultivates it in others as well. Not only does he violate the state's laws and rules, avoiding legal justice, but he neither does what he ought nor gets what he deserves. He dies admitting he had no regrets for his vicious behavior – yet he also dies feeling like a hero for setting his family's affairs in order and freeing Jesse from the Nazis. There is no sense of wrongs righted for the virtuous Hank's widowed wife, Marie. Likewise, Walt Jr.'s life is upended, and Jesse – though "free" – has been severely traumatized by his experiences with Walt and is unlikely to recover. (For the purposes of this argument, we have to set aside Jesse's story in *El Camino,* Gilligan's follow-up movie, and examine only what the series *Breaking Bad* shows us about Jesse's life post-Walt. And the outlook it suggests is grim.) Given the failure of the traditional virtue of justice, an analysis of *Breaking Bad* through the lens of virtue ethics seems to fail.

Nonetheless, there *is* justice in the *Breaking Bad* universe, but it isn't meted out by men; it comes harshly at the hands of nature itself, in the form of cancer that can't be cured, and as the physical repercussions of the events created by the unjust and unvirtuous. We might wonder if Walt's final act is an acceptance of this universal justice through submission to his doom, or arguably a final act of cowardice in which he is once again unwilling to face the music for his crimes. Paving the way for our consideration of Walt's fate is the aesthetic form used, including the visual and aural choices used in telling the story. These echo throughout the series a trend in American artistic existentialism most notably employed by the Italian filmmaker Sergio Leone in his "spaghetti westerns" and copied for at least half a century in American-made westerns and iconography. This aesthetic makes a philosophical point. In stark contrast to the moral certainty of the classic American western films – perhaps best exemplified in the movies of John Ford – with Sergio Leone's *Fistful of Dollars*, and its antihero "The Man with No Name," portrayed by Clint Eastwood, the good guys now are either non-existent or definitely do not wear white hats and are not really all that good. In the Leone Western, the antihero is the best we have. There are no real heroes anymore. The inaccessibility of justice is taken for granted, and the very best we seem now to be able to expect is a sort of *aesthetic* of justice: a feeling that while the good cannot be achieved, the bad and the ugly are not ultimately rewarded and do not prevail.

"Say My Name" Says the Man with No Name

In its form as a satirical epic, *Breaking Bad* also evokes some of the elements of these modern westerns made famous in the spaghetti westerns of Sergio Leone. Even Heisenberg's attire, with the strangely out-of-place porkpie hat and sunglasses, reflects the unusual attire of the Man with No Name. At a time when most Hollywood cowboy movies featured ten-gallon hats and dusters, The Man with No Name wears an unusually flat hat and a Mexican-style poncho. Eastwood's antihero is a man of few words, not on any particular quest, who more-or-less accidentally helps some folks in each of his films, even while never assuming any sort of moral high ground, never proselytizing nor moralizing, and often motivated by his own self-interest. He is a man out of place in an uncertain era surrounded by villains of comedic excess and violence, willing to do whatever it takes in various chapters of his character's arc to save his own hide and perhaps those of the more innocent around him.

Breaking Bad's visual lyricism echoes that of the Sergio Leone films, and Walt in many ways echoes the path of the Man with No Name, riding haphazardly from triumph to doom, occasionally doing something praiseworthy, often foiled by the excess and ineptitude of others, and ultimately remaining morally ambiguous or downright blameworthy. All of this is reflected in Walt's final chapter where the good, the bad, and the ugly converge in a final plot reminiscent of any of the cartoonish schemes cooked up by Eastwood's character that prevailed against the forces of those *more* evil around him. Walt's Supreme Ordeal (the deep inner crisis or dangerous physical test that must be overcome to prevail in the Hero's Journey) is his final victory and death, emerging finally from the moral labyrinth he has built for himself, freeing his family, saving those he loves, and meeting the only fate imaginable for the antihero: death. Sounding like any cowboy hero, he addresses the possibility of fear after his cancer diagnosis, perhaps not entirely authentically:

> *I* have spent my whole life scared, frightened of things that could happen, might happen, might not happen, 50 years I spent like that. Finding myself awake at three in the morning. But you know what? Ever since my diagnosis, I sleep just fine. What I came to realize is that fear, that's the worst of it. That's the real enemy. So, get up, get out in the real world and you kick that bastard as hard you can right in the teeth. ("Better Call Saul," Season 2, Episode 8)

The western landscape is unforgiving and populated with the unforgivable and unforgiven. In the lawless wasteland, there are neither good guys nor bad guys: there are only those who are just trying to get by. The milieu is ambiguous, both morally and politically. Leaders come and go, disappear, switch roles and sides, and can be replaced with a bullet. Democracy is background noise, and justice from the state is laughable at best, nonexistent at worst.

It is no accident that the drama of *Breaking Bad* unfolds in such a landscape, at the border of two nations replete with dissolution, addiction, violence, and despair, riven by crime and racism, and at the cusp of some seething, hidden unease and disruption. This is the iconic, American aesthetic. The landscape of rugged individualism populated by the dispossessed and largely helpless, where no hero will rush in to save the day, is the modern American experience. Unlike the heroes of the pre-Leone westerns, moral ambiguity reigns and the myth of individualism clouds our expectations of being saved by the other. We are, in Sartre's terminology, being-for-itself in a world of being-in-itself.

The distinction Sartre makes here is important. "Being-in-itself" refers to mere objects – things that simply exist in the world and have their essential features therefore determined by it. However, as "being-for-itself," we are different. That is, we are conscious entities capable of determining our own "essences" and then projecting those essences into the world as what and who we are. This serves as a kind of "absolute freedom" that conscious beings uniquely possess. An unconscious object cannot choose. An individual's essence and what is meaningful to them is not set by their position in the world; instead, the individual has the freedom to choose whatever essence and meaning they please. In one sense, this implies that the world is meaningless, though this is not entirely true. Sartre argues only that there is no universal, external meaning in the world, since individuals are free to choose their meaning. (Note that absolute freedom does not mean that an individual is free to *do* anything whatsoever. Prisoners cannot simply will themselves to be free. But it is the prisoner and not the fact of imprisonment that decides something like "I am a prisoner and I accept my fate" or "I do not belong here and I will escape." So, Sartre's absolute freedom is more like a freedom of thought and decision.)

For Sartre, the trouble is that people do not always accept their absolute freedom; rather, they deceive themselves that their essence and meaning come from things outside of them – something Sartre calls living in "bad faith." We might constrain ourselves by defining who we are by our social roles: a waiter, a car wash attendant, a high school chemistry teacher. However, this treats the self like an object (and not being-for-itself) because it pretends we have no choice in the matter. At the same time, we are also searching for being-for-others – for some reflection of the existence of our own consciousness in some other. Just as we allow our position in the world to sometimes create essence and meaning for us, we often allow others to determine "who we are" by conforming to their expectations of us; worse still, we sometimes want this validation because we are unable to decide for ourselves who we will be. This too is bad faith.

As Sartre puts it in *Nausea*, living in a world of meaninglessness and utter freedom can bring us to nauseous anxiety. This nausea is allayed by our social need to be regarded by "the other" but which also impinges on the freedom of the other. The Man with No Name in Leone's trilogy is an antihero precisely because he is utterly free, but in regards to "the other" he acts in ways that are expected of him. People plead for his help, and he obliges. He is tragic, he is not heroic. He would prefer to move on, to find another safe town, to live in peace and with the burdens of his ambiguous, presumably spotty past. The needs of others place limits on The Man with No Name's absolute freedom because he allows them to, meaning that he lives in bad faith, or inauthentically.

Walt too acts inauthentically, playing a role he has cast for himself in relation to the look of "the other," including his family, his nemeses, and his employers. Knowing of his impending death, he is certainly, utterly free. None of what he has done to date means anything, all of it has been for naught; he has the option to go with grace and goodness, but chooses instead to play a role, to adopt a new name and new visage, to be someone he is not toward the world at large. He demands in his confrontation with rivals in the desert: "say my name," requiring they acknowledge him by his alter-ego Heisenberg, not his actual name. The naming of Heisenberg by *the other* casts Walt finally as a fiction. He is not Walt. He is no longer being-in-itself; he has become fully being-for-others. Walt embraces inauthenticity, has become a sort of fiction, and can no longer regard himself as who he was and demands the same of others. He is not free. He is now trapped in a new role.

Like the Man with No Name, he now inhabits a role built by others, with expectations set by social expectations. He will feign freedom and we will have sympathy with his apparent freedom and admire his occasional submission to the good in superficial, apparent moments of regard for others. But ultimately, the American aesthetic of individualism, the loneliness of the desert, and the nausea of utter freedom exacerbated by chemo will overcome any sense of beauty or truth in Walt's journey. You cannot say the true name of the Man with No Name, and because of that the Clint Eastwood character is freer than Walt will ever be. By remaining unnamed and never demanding that naming by the other, he can move on to another town and seek the peace he will never find. Walt, on the other hand, has cast his lot with a fictional being, not in his being-for-itself.

Just like Sartre, Gilligan attempts to show us through fiction the state of mankind in a meaningless universe, confronted with questions of right and wrong in a universe both of possibility and devoid of guidance from above. Our antihero fails because of his bad faith and we are meant to see the inevitable result of doing so in his death and the tragedy of the lives he leaves behind.

The End Is Just a Little Harder When Brought About by Friends

Ultimately, Walt must fail. The antihero's journey mimics that of the hero, but leads necessarily to failure, degradation, possibly ruin, and likely death. Walt may defeat the villains, like Gus and the Nazis, but his involvement in the harm and deaths of innocents, like Hank, can only lead to Walt's death. The moral point of *Breaking Bad* is simple: wrong choices will ruin you. Your opportunities for redemption run out at some point. Yet, the series does not seem to have an embedded sense of any particular ethical theory. It rejects utilitarianism, showing that your calculus of harms is not enough to rescue you. Though the show is clear that being unvirtuous is deadly, it fails to mete out the justice one would expect from the virtue ethic. Even being virtuous, if sufficiently mixed up with those who have broken bad, can be deadly. The detritus of Walt's reckless scourge upon the meth scene in the Southwest tragically takes the lives of Jane (a recovering addict who dates Jesse in Season 2 and challenges his relationship with Walt) and Gale (Gus's nerdy, Walt Whitman-loving meth cook), arguably two of the more decent humans in the show who brought joy, beauty, love, and wisdom to both Jesse and Walt's dark worlds ever so briefly. There can be no redemption and there is no justice, even for the virtuous.

This bleak view, mirrored in the Westerns of Sergio Leone, also appears to speak against Kantian arguments for the basic dignity and value of life. Though Gilligan certainly seems to say that life in itself ought to be valued, the wholesale rejection of traditional justice obliterates Kant's supposed "kingdom of ends" – the endpoint of Kantian theory which sees a society where no individuals are treated only as means and all are valued in themselves. Albuquerque is decidedly not a kingdom of ends, and *Breaking Bad*'s depiction of a traditionally unjust world paints Kant's end goal as a social impossibility. Yet, we have a sense that there is finality of some kind, perhaps even justice of a sort, with the ending of *Breaking Bad*. Among series with fixed endings, *Breaking Bad* has been lauded for having a satisfying and sensible ending unlike any other. Why is this ending so satisfying in the absence of any clear winner, with no apparent redemption or hope? One way to understand this is to reflect on the possibility that Gilligan has hit upon the complexities of ethical judgment through an *aesthetic of justice*.

Ordinarily, philosophical ethics asks us to form specific principles – like Kant's treat everyone with dignity and respect – that will govern our moral judgments and determine the moral worth of actions. If *Breaking Bad* adopts the Sartrean view that meaning is not a feature of the world but instead comes from conscious individuals and their free choices to create, accept, and reject it, these moral principles would be of little use, anyway. One cannot live as an authentic person under the shadow of impersonal rules. But moral complexity may also be illustrated through stories, poems, or even scenery and lighting. This is an aesthetics of justice that eschews hard and fast moral rules in favor of ethics as a feeling. Viewed this way, an aesthetics of justice is as complex and incapable of analytic explanation as is the concept of beauty. It is also a powerful way to convey difficult subjects and connect morality with emotions, a long-ignored element of ethical decision-making, and one that is generally ignored in legal positivism and analytic philosophy.

The universe of *Breaking Bad*, as in the real world, is one in which no one enters guiltless, no system is just, and everyone is trying to figure out how to navigate a complicated pragmatic and moral landscape. The system is rigged already, and because of it, Walt is unable to make ends meet despite his intelligence and background. Regardless of how he left Gray Matter, as a scientist with a history of inventiveness and creativity, the fact that he must work two jobs to provide for his family, one of which is in a car wash, indicates that ours is a world without any fundamental justice. Life is unfair, harsh, and a struggle for most people. Like Sisyphus, the struggle can be seen either as tragedy or as comedy. In tragedy, there is no escape; in comedy, the escape is inner – a freeing of the soul, a relenting to the struggle, and a finding of happiness within. The universe is unjust, so the sense of justice that we achieve through minor victories, through moments of joy, is often the best we can do. We feel with the triumphs of antiheroes that the arch of the moral universe is bending slightly in the right direction, despite their likely doom. Chalk up a small victory when a villain is killed, a sports car purchased, or even when dinner is put on the table.

Ethical theories like those discussed in this chapter – utilitarianism, Kantian deontology, and virtue ethics – miss the moral complexity of the real world (and worlds like Walt's in *Breaking Bad*). This is because they necessarily consider situations and rules in abstraction. For instance, consider the trolley problem, so often discussed in college ethics courses. This is not a real moral problem – or it at least illustrates the shortcomings of ethical theorizing. First proposed by philosopher Philippa Foot, we are in this problem asked to make a choice between allowing five people to be killed by an oncoming trolley or to choose to kill one by diverting the train away from the other five. But no choice is made in a vacuum, though it is presented that way here: the world presents us with complexity, not caricatured thought experiments. History and culture both suffuse and infuse all our individual characters and confrontations, and no ethical theory of overriding rules has the correct answer to every unique situation. This is why our antiheroes are more real, in a sense, than heroes. Antiheroes are not wholly good, and they exist in worlds in which there is significant moral ambiguity. They are products and partakers in that ambiguity. They may even embrace it, making it work for them in their situational choices.

Given this situational ambiguity and the inadequacy of traditional ethical theories to resolve it, it may well be that the best we can do at any particular moment is to *feel* we are justified, and it may well be that justice (and by extension, ethics) itself is ephemeral, fleeting, and unreal – like a feeling. This is in stark contrast to all of the theories discussed so far, which all depend in some way on rational principles far removed from individual sentiment. In fact, nearly all of these theories see emotion/sentiment as inimical to good moral decision-making. Taken broadly, the utilitarian calculus turns individuals into abstract quantities of pleasure and pain to be weighed against one another. Pleasure/pain as feelings do matter here, but only when quantified – in other words, only when feeling itself is removed from the equation. Kantian deontology argues that the universal moral principle of treating everyone with dignity can only be the result of rational thinking; emotionality may result in selfishness, which results in using others as means. Sentiment is similarly anathema to the virtue ethics of the ancient Greeks. Virtue is the result of reason, and the intemperance of emotion causes vicious behavior.

In light of *Breaking Bad*'s depiction of moral complexity and the unique "situatedness" of moral circumstances, Hume's emotivism might be more helpful to understanding the show. Hume argues that moral judgment is really just our sentiments about beauty, the good, the just, evil, and harm. That is, moral judgments are not rational judgments at all: they are sensations that we *feel* when confronted with these ideas. This certainly squares with the Sartrean message that this chapter attributes to the show – downplaying external, universal theories of meaning in favor of the individual freedom to determine it themselves. Further, though: if Hume is right, nuanced moral views might best be told through media that evoke strong emotions through all our senses – like *Breaking Bad*. Perhaps the error we most often make is to believe we can accommodate the good through some calculation, through some formula, through pure reason and rationality.

Because epics contain as much of the whole world as possible, because they are encyclopedic, and in their satirical forms give license to critique without proselytizing, they can attempt to address the complexity and ineffability of moral experience in ways that straightforward, pedantic analysis may not. The lyrical, aesthetic, the artistic, as well as the emotional are all suited to a different form of reflection whereby we are more apt to feel sympathy with the subjects of our art and experience notions like justice differently. There is something "good" about *Breaking Bad*, even if there is little in the way of "good" demonstrated by the characters in the story. It has an almost universal appeal, it has touched millions of lives, and has made an indelible impression upon our culture. Walt/Heisenberg is now an icon, and the story is etched upon the parchments of our collective souls. As with Ahab, Raskolnikov, The Man with No Name, and numerous other antiheroes like those we find in similar tales, Walter White is an emblem; he is a snapshot of a type with whom we can identify but who offers us a counterexample of behavior, virtue, and values. We feel more strongly that we must not be Walt through the process of identifying with him, and our emotional connection with the characters and the story goes further than any reasoned, rational argument that leads us to this conclusion.

The Philosophy of *Breaking Bad*

At one point in the series, Gale gives Walt a copy of Walt Whitman's *Leaves of Grass*, a collection that includes the poem "Song of Myself." In that poem, Whitman says:

Do I contradict myself?
Very well then I contradict myself,
(I am large, I contain multitudes.)

Like Whitman's lines, *Breaking Bad* might seem to contradict itself: it sometimes seems to endorse Kantian deontology and ancient Greek virtue ethics, but at other times shows this kind of ethical theorizing to fail to capture the moral ambiguity faced by people in the actual world. I have claimed that the series' ultimate argument is instead for morality as a feeling – *Breaking Bad* depicts justice as an aesthetic experience, not the end result of detailed argument. What this means is that it is the series' format – a satirical epic starring an antihero – that provides its rich fodder for philosophical speculation. Because it is the kind of story it is, *Breaking Bad* can deliver its moral message as something *felt* by its audience and not something *told* to them. In this way, *Breaking Bad* does more in imparting its lessons through narrative form than many philosophers do in a lifetime of essay and argument. But this too is true of the best epic storytelling. Walt/Heisenberg, a panoply of scenes and lessons, and the entire story arc of *Breaking Bad* have permeated our culture, providing a reflection of an era while telling a timeless example of the Faustian bargain and its consequences. It seems likely to remain a cultural and philosophical touchstone for TV drama for some time, a measure of all other grand attempts at moral mythmaking.

Philosophically, literature and stories get something of a bad rap. At the very least, they are often regarded as less sophisticated than "real" argument. But our stories are tremendously helpful, useful tools for philosophical examination and introspection. The numerous pop-culture and philosophy books that have been published in the past two decades on subjects of every kind have revealed the depth to which stories like *Breaking Bad* have been sorely needed and are practically useful both in pedagogy and in doing the work of philosophy. Storytelling has become an acceptable venue for philosophers themselves at various historical epochs. Camus and Nietzsche both use stories as vehicles for philosophizing, as does Iris Murdoch more recently. The usefulness of fiction in examining the complexities of ethics, justice, existence, and meaning cannot be overstated and in its best instances has provided more than most academic philosophy has for wider audiences than philosophers may have thought possible. The emotions evoked and the opportunities for deep investigation of topics like justice are just part of the aesthetics of *Breaking Bad*, and as a work of art, it too contains multitudes.

Conclusion

Vince Gilligan has created in Walter White a complex anti-hero. Combining broad comedy, satire, and drama, his epic journey echoes those of other satirical epic protagonists like Ahab, Don Quixote, Candide, and others. By using satire and an epic framework, Gilligan forces us to focus on the absurdity and scale of White as Heisenberg, his madness and folly, and the hopelessness of prevailing in a world to which he is unaccustomed, and to which he does not really belong. The morality of Breaking Bad is not black and white, they are many gray areas. And its lessons are not conveyed as easy-to-digest lessons, but rather through the aesthetics of justice contained in the show's storytelling, visually, through dialogue and characters, and in its cinematic scope, echoing themes from a variety of genres. This existential complexity mirrors that of our common moral landscape, and life itself, only comprehensible through this sort of broad storytelling.

References

Bentham, Jeremy. 1996. *The collected works of Jeremy Bentham: An introduction to the principles of morals and legislation*. Clarendon Press.

Camus, Albert. 2013. *The myth of Sisyphus*. Penguin UK.

Crisp, Roger, ed. 2014. *Aristotle: Nicomachean ethics*. Cambridge University Press.

Decker, Kevin S., David R. Koepsell, and Robert Arp, eds. 2016. *Philosophy and breaking bad*. Springer.

Fridlund, Bert. 2014. *The spaghetti Western: A thematic analysis*. McFarland.

Hume, David. 2007. *A treatise of human nature*. Vol. 1. Oxford University Press.

Kant, Immanuel. 1996. The metaphysics of morals. In *Immanuel Kant practical philosophy*, 429. Trans. and Ed. Mary Gregor. New York: Cambridge University Press.

———. 2002. The good will and the categorical imperative. *The European Philosophers from Descartes to Nietzsche*: 470–476. The Modern Library.

Koepsell, David. 2017. Law and morality in breaking bad: The aesthetics of justice. In *Philosophy and breaking bad*, 93–105. Cham: Palgrave Macmillan.

Koepsell, David Richard, and Robert Arp, eds. 2012. *Breaking bad and philosophy: Badder living through chemistry*. Vol. 67. Open Court Publishing.

Sartre, Jean-Paul. 2001. *Being and nothingness: An essay in phenomenological ontology*. Citadel Press.

———. 2015. Being and nothingness. *Central Works of Philosophy: The Twentieth Century: Moore to Popper* 4: 155.

———. 2021. *Nausea*. Penguin UK.

The Haunting Philosophies of *Breaking Bad*. In *The Harvard political review*, October 25, 2012. https://harvardpolitics.com/the-haunting-philosophies-of-breaking-bad/. Accessed 13 Aug 2021.

The Handmaid's Tale as Philosophy: Autonomy and Reproductive Freedom

9

Rachel Robison-Greene

Contents

Introduction	186
Gilead, In Brief	187
What is Autonomy?	190
The "Feminine Function"?	193
Capacities of Women in The Handmaid's Tale	197
Autonomy and Language	199
Autonomy and Religion	202
Better Never Means Better for Everyone... It Always Means Worse, for Some	205
Conclusion	208
References	208

Abstract

In *The Handmaid's Tale* and *The Testaments*, Margaret Atwood vividly portrays a dystopia from a woman's point of view. The themes she explores are familiar, they are not shocking fictional devices designed to keep readers surprised and engaged. Instead, the stories describe how our own world might have been or, even worse, how *it might be*. It explores the dangers of treating women's bodies as resources to be regulated and commodified. The series emphasizes the value of autonomy and highlights the ways in which it can be eroded by oppression until it no longer exists in any meaningful way. This chapter will explore the theme of autonomy as it arises in *The Handmaid's Tale* and *The Testaments*. It will situate these stories as part of a long philosophical tradition of sorting members of society into groups based on their perceived skills and abilities, allowing no room for transcendence or self-creation. It will explore how manipulation of love and relationships, religion, the use of language, and opportunities to think

---

R. Robison-Greene (✉)
Utah State University, Logan, UT, USA
e-mail: rachel.robison@usu.edu

© This is a U.S. Government work and not under copyright protection in the U.S.;
foreign copyright protection may apply 2024
D. K. Johnson et al. (eds.), *The Palgrave Handbook of Popular Culture as Philosophy*,
https://doi.org/10.1007/978-3-031-24685-2_22

critically can, without bars or shackles, imprison a population by diminishing their capacity for self-determination. The story of *The Handmaid's Tale* and *The Testaments* is cautionary. This chapter will explore the nature of the lesson that story teaches.

Keywords

The Handmaid's Tale · The Testaments · Margaret Atwood · Hulu · Orwell · Huxley · Dystopia · Autonomy · Reproductive freedom · Language · Love · Critical thinking · Religion · Sorority · Plato · Aristotle · Aquinas · Malebranche · Lambert · Frankfurt · Nietzsche · Obligations to future generations

Introduction

Dystopian literature motivates reflection on our most fundamental values; when the things we hold most dear are threatened, even in a fictional context, their importance is cast into stark relief. When Margaret Atwood set out to write *The Handmaid's Tale*, she wanted to craft a dystopian tale from a perspective not common in the genre. In a 2013 article for *The Guardian,* she explained,

> The majority of dystopias—Orwell's included—have been written by men and the point of view has been male. When women have appeared in them, they have been either sexless automatons or rebels who've defied the sex rules of the regime. I wanted to try a dystopia from the female point of view – the world according to Julia, as it were. (Atwood 2013, n.p.)

Dystopian stories aren't told in a vacuum, and it's important that they aren't; they are often cautionary tales. It is easy to imagine certain narratives as descriptions of events taking place in very close possible worlds, as accounts of our own lives had things unfolded slightly differently. More frighteningly still, they sometimes strike us as prognostications of our potential future if we stay our current course.

The Handmaid's Tale describes a future with which we share a past. This is one of the reasons that the plot is *so* ominous; we know that it is not impossible for women to be treated as property. Atwood wrote the book in such a way that it doesn't involve any "imaginary atrocities." In a 2017 article in *The New York Times*, she explained that she did not "put any events into the book that had not already happened in what James Joyce called the 'nightmare' of history" (Atwood 2017, n.p.).

It is far from impossible that female bodies could be viewed as natural resources – as walking incubators. It's happened before. The fact that some women can bear children has historically encouraged, both in intellectual discourse and in public life, a reduction of women to their perceived biological traits. This reduction is inconsistent with women's true status as self-determining beings who each has their own conception of the good and who strive to live the kinds of lives *they* conceive of as meaningful, regardless of how other people might view that conception of meaning.

Atwood had another imaginative goal in mind – she wanted to consider what features a dystopia might have if it originated in the United States. She asked herself,

9 *The Handmaid's Tale* as Philosophy: Autonomy and Reproductive Freedom

"If the United States were to have totalitarianism, what kind of totalitarianism would it be?" (Atwood, The Guardian, n.p.). Her answer to this question is in keeping with contemporary facts. In the years since *The Handmaid's Tale* was published in 1985, the franchise has expanded. The book was made into a movie in 1990. Political developments in the intervening years made the themes explored in the story increasingly relevant and frightening. After the Roe v. Wade decision in 1973 recognized a woman's constitutional right to abortion, states across the country aggressively passed laws intended to place significant barriers in a woman's path to abortion. These restrictive laws were viewed favorably by conservative justices on the Supreme Court, resulting in a state of affairs in which, in many states, a woman's right to full reproductive freedom is nominal at best. The fact that these restrictions were even possible reveals the value system of the congresspersons and jurists who made room for them. On their view, it seems, the value of *potential* human life is paramount – it ought to be protected even if we have to paternalistically commodify the wombs of women in the service of that value.

In this social and political environment, it is unsurprising that a reboot of *The Handmaid's Tale* found, well, *fertile* ground. Hulu's imaginative presentation of the story is tremendously popular. Atwood also released a much-anticipated sequel – *The Testaments* – which provides an even broader philosophical picture of what, exactly, would make for a dystopia *from a woman's point of view.*

Dystopian stories are often, at their root, stories about the value of autonomy, and *The Handmaid's Tale* universe is no different. As these stories make clear, the exercise of autonomy is complicated and can be worn down in ways that may be unexpected. Our discussion of the relevant philosophical issues at stake in Gilead will be aided by an overview of the salient details about why it was formed and the structure of its social system. We'll turn to that in the next section. Ultimately, we will explore the issue of autonomy as it is presented in *The Handmaid's Tale* and *The Testaments.*

Gilead, In Brief

Gilead is a strongly patriarchal country. In the original novel, the details we get about its formation are vague. We know that there has been significant environmental degradation, making resources scarce. When Offred walks with Ofglen past Loaves and Fishes, she makes the following observation,

> The sea fisheries were defunct several years ago; the few fish they have now are from fish farms, and taste muddy. The news says the coastal areas are being "rested." Sole, I remember, and haddock, swordfish, scallops, tuna; lobsters, stuffed and baked, salmon, pink and fat, grilled in steaks. Could they all be extinct, like whales? (Atwood, *The Handmaid's Tale*, p. 135)

The first season of the Hulu television series follows a similar storyline as the original novel. One significant difference is that the series contains a lot more action.

The events of the novel tend to be primarily mental events – memories that Offred is having or perceptions and responses to the situation in which she finds herself. The television series explores the storylines of other characters and the politics of Gilead, both foreign and domestic. At one point, the ambassador to Mexico visits Gilead to explore a potential trade deal. As part of a description of Gilead's accomplishments, Commander Waterford discusses their significant success at lowering their CO2 emissions. The expansion of the storyline suggests that the environmental problems Gilead faces are exactly what we might have imagined them to be – the results of anthropogenic climate change.

We also know that Gilead, like the countries involved in so many dystopian novels, is perpetually at war. On the topic of war, the novel shares much in common with Orwell's 1984. Orwell describes the nature of the existential threat: "Oceania was at war with Eastasia: Oceania had always been at war with Eastasia" (Orwell, p. 172). The names of the countries change, but the struggle never ends. In many dystopias, Gilead included, the totalitarian regimes engage in emotional manipulation as a form of control. They focus primarily on grief and fear. In the case of war, they suggest that honoring the fallen requires, at minimum, falling in line.

An example of this imagery occurs in a scene from *The Handmaid's Tale* in which June sits in her bedroom, waiting for The Ceremony to begin. "Commanders" with the assistance of their "Wives" rape Handmaids once a month in the hope that children will be produced. The Commander and his Wife then get to keep that child. This is the situation in which June finds herself in the original novel.

While the household waits for Commander Waterford, Serena Joy permits them to watch the news. It is unclear whether the broadcasted program is reporting on real events, or whether it is a piece of propaganda designed to keep the citizens of Gilead in line; wartime is no time for an insurrection. Gilead calls its soldiers "Angels." Offred comments on the footage,

> I look into this man's eyes, trying to decide what he's thinking. He knows the camera is on him: is the grin a show of defiance, or is it submission? Is he embarrassed at having been caught?
> They show us only victories, never defeats.
> Possibly he's an actor. (Atwood, *The Handmaid's Tale*, p. 66)

A final, crucial fact that we know about the conditions leading to the formation of Gilead is that the birth rate is exceptionally low. Babies that are born often die quickly thereafter or have significant birth defects. If the species is to survive, new, healthy children *must be born*.

Here is where The Sons of Jacob come in. The Sons of Jacob are the patriarchal governing body of Gilead. To wrest power from the United States government, they bomb Congress and blame Islamic terrorists. Shortly thereafter, the money in all women's bank accounts is rerouted into the account of their closest male next of kin. Then, the women are sorted and forced into servitude based on their traits, level of relative power or connection, and socioeconomic status. Fertile women who were,

9 The Handmaid's Tale as Philosophy: Autonomy and Reproductive Freedom

for one reason or another, thought to be "sexually immoral," are recast as Handmaids.

In *The Testaments,* Atwood reveals a critical new dimension of Gilead. One of the most significant features of the novel is that the role that the Aunts play is no longer mysterious (and, I might add, no longer as despicable as it appeared in the original novel). Atwood reveals that Aunts were once women in positions of power that were broken in ways reminiscent of the atrocities of our most inhumane past. These women, most of them too old to bear children, were rounded up and kept in deplorable conditions. Food was scarce and they were seldom allowed access to bathrooms to relieve themselves or to wash. Insubordination was punished by extensive solitary confinement or even death at the hands of peers. The women that survived became the women that are willing to embrace the mission of the new regime as Aunts.

Aunt Lydia, one of the central figures in the new government, is one of these women. In her life before Gilead, she was a successful judge, often the staunch defender of women in cases in which their interests and safety were at stake. In *The Testaments,* Aunt Lydia becomes the primary author of the women's realm. Remarkably, in this capacity, she is able to carve out (relatively speaking of course) a certain amount of autonomy for herself. Before agreeing to the conditions of her new situation, she secures control over the governance of the women's realm. The following is part of her conversation with Commander Judd, just after her "conversion."

> Here I took a risk. "If it is to be a separate female sphere," I said, "it must be truly separate. Within it, women must command. Except in extreme need, men must not pass the threshold of our allotted premises, nor shall our methods be questioned. We shall be judged solely by our results. Though we will of course report to the authorities if and when it's necessary." (Atwood, *The Testaments*, p. 163)

Aunt Lydia's actions set the stage for the bold and retaliatory actions of *The Testaments.* Though she has secured a kind of situated autonomy for herself and, to a limited degree, the other Aunts, the rest of the women in Gilead don't feel any immediate benefit. They are merely tools to be used in the machinations of The Sons of Jacob.

We often think that it would be wonderful if certain stressors in our lives could be alleviated by the actions of the government. In some cases, we may be right about that. In other cases, individuals or small communities might best resolve stressors or societal harms in ways that best respect autonomy. Aldus Huxley's 1932 classic *Brave New World* provides us with a compelling example of this. Human beings, like all creatures, desire to be happy. Toward that end, should the government distribute Soma – happy pills that ensure that we are never discontent? Should the government solve our environmental and reproductive problems by forcing solutions where citizens are left with no choice? Dystopian literature motivates reflection about the necessary conditions for the full exercise of autonomy.

What is Autonomy?

One of the primary reasons that the way that citizens, particularly women, are treated in Gilead is wrong is that their treatment does not respect their status as autonomous agents. It will be useful, then, to discuss various accounts of autonomy, and how autonomy is related to morality, personhood, and meaning in life.

When a being has moral status, that being is deserving of moral consideration. This means that we can't simply treat such a being however we please. We can't treat them, as Kant would say, as a mere means to our own ends. We can't treat beings with moral status as mere things to be used.

Some beings in the world are what philosophers call *moral agents,* and others are what we call *moral patients.* The members of both groups have interests. Life can go better or worse for both kinds of beings depending on whether their lives are filled with suffering or with joy. Moral agents have obligations both to moral patients and to other moral agents. Obligations to moral patients often rest on the ability that moral patients have to experience both joy and suffering. No sentient being should suffer needlessly.

The primary difference between moral agents and moral patients is that moral agents are autonomous beings. Moral patients are beings that experience the world, but for some reason or other are not capable of exercising autonomy. Most non-human animals are moral patients. So, too, are very young children – although most are temporary moral patients who have the potential to develop into full-fledged moral agents. When a person is treated as if their autonomous choices are not deserving of respect, they are treated as moral patients rather than moral agents. It is dehumanizing to treat beings that are capable of governing their own lives as if they are the kinds of beings that aren't.

The concept of personhood is frequently associated with the concept of autonomy. Some philosophers argue that our primary moral obligations are to persons, because only persons are members of the moral community. Persons are capable of endorsing a set of values and of acting in ways that support that system. Different philosophers have categorized this capacity in different ways. Carl Cohen, for example, in his arguments against animal rights, claims that autonomous persons who have rights are beings that are capable of understanding the nature of those rights, knowing against whom they have rights, and of articulating and evaluating reasons offered in the course of moral debate and deliberation (Cohen and Regan 2001).

Contemporary philosopher Harry Frankfurt offers an account of personhood as the ability to exercise autonomy. According to Frankfurt, the term "person" is appropriately applied, not to a particular *biological* type, but, instead, to a certain *philosophical* type. The criteria for personhood should capture, "those attributes which are the subject of our most humane concern with ourselves and the source of what we regard as most important and most problematical in our lives" (Frankfurt, The Importance of What We Care About, p. 12). For Frankfurt, this will be the basic structure of our wills.

There are many different approaches to understanding what it is to act autonomously. I will focus on Frankfurt's approach here because of the emphasis he places

9 The Handmaid's Tale as Philosophy: Autonomy and Reproductive Freedom

on the things autonomous beings care about. Lack of concern for what the female citizens of Gilead care about is one of the most jarring features of that social system.

Each of us feels the pull of our desires every day. In any given day, we may desire food, drink, companionship, or sleep. Sometimes we desire things that aren't, all things considered, desirable. For example, sometimes we find ourselves with desires to do things that are cruel, dangerous, or unhealthy for our bodies.

We are also the kinds of beings that are capable of having attitudes about our own desires. A person may desire to smoke a cigarette but might have a higher order desire to refrain from smoking the cigarette, either on this occasion or ever again. The things we take a second order interest in, those things that we want our actions to be motivated by, are the things that we care about.

According to Frankfurt, it is our ability to change our behavior, to use our desires about our desires in order to do what we really want to do, that makes us free, autonomous beings. He says,

> Taking ourselves seriously means that we are not prepared to accept ourselves just as we come. We want our thoughts, our feelings, our choices, and our behavior to make sense. We are not satisfied to think that our ideas are formed haphazardly, or that our actions are driven by transient and opaque impulses or by mindless decisions. We need to direct ourselves—or at any rate to believe that we are directing ourselves—in thoughtful conformity to stable and appropriate norms. We want to get things right. (Frankfurt, Taking Ourselves Seriously and Getting it Right, p. 2)

The government of Gilead takes every step in their power to prevent female citizens from behaving autonomously in the sense Frankfurt has described. To start, the government rejects outright the idea that the things that women care about actually matter. In their lives before Gilead, women cared about jobs, hobbies, friends, and family. They might create art, music, or science. They might move to the place that they most desire to live or spend their money on whatever they desired and could afford. Gilead tells its women what to care about. The Sons of Jacob know best, or so they claim. According to the story they tell, it was the business of letting women identify the things they care about that got society into all of this trouble to begin with. This rejection of personal values extends all of the way to denying that a woman is in any position to properly care for her own biological child if the wife of a commander is "more deserving."

Gilead attempts to destroy the basic structure of a woman's will at every stage. They attempt to guide the first order desires that women have by seriously restricting their options. The more that a woman realizes that visiting family, taking a seaside vacation, or even curling up on the sofa with a nice book are not realistic possibilities, the more these first order desires will fade into forgotten history. She will lose the desire to do these things because she will forget that she can.

Gilead also attempts to destroy the structure of a woman's will by making the formation of second order desires and, as a result, second order volitions, less likely. This is done by restricting access to language and to critical thinking skills. If citizens don't have access to information or even to written language, their capacity to think about their own thoughts and to evaluate their own desires will be limited.

Women are no longer in a position to, as Frankfurt would have it, "form reflexive or higher order responses" to their own mental states.

The threat of violence for exploring one's own second order thoughts and volitions creates even more of a chilling effect on female exercise of autonomy. Gilead has deprived them of their means of survival unless they comply with the rules of the regime. The necessary conditions for freedom are not met, so women aren't in a position to exercise it. In this way, they are like the starving citizens who come to the church for salvation in Dostoyevsky's *The Grand Inquisitor*. The Inquisitor exclaims to Christ, "No science will ever give them bread so long as they remain free, so long as they refuse to lay that freedom at our feet, and say: "Enslave, but feed us!" (Dostoyevsky, p. 317). When powerful institutions provide the only realistic access to the means of survival, autonomy is little more than a fairy tale.

One important example of this is selection of occupation. Many people care deeply about their profession; it serves as a central part of identity and motivation. How we spend our time and the ways in which we choose to be creative forces is a source of meaning in life. Ofglen provides a central example of this point. In the Hulu series, we learn that, before Gilead, Ofglen was a university science professor. A person can only achieve this career through years of hard work and dedication, so her profession was clearly very important to her. In Gilead, it is all taken away from her; she is reduced, not to the identities she endorses upon reflection and careful deliberation, but to her biological ability to carry a fetus to term.

Gilead also rejects the idea that women are in the position to settle the very private matter of who to love. The Sons of Jacob have insisted that anyone who is homosexual is a "gender traitor." Being gay is a capital offense in this new, puritanical culture. The Hulu series explores this with the character Ofglen, who, in the former United States, was once married to a woman. Ofglen is reduced by the Sons of Jacob to a moral patient; she is treated as if she is not capable of identifying the romantic attachments that she cares about or of being motivated in the right kind of way by love. This is true, not only of "gender traitors," but also of romantic love between heterosexual characters in the series. Who we love and the people to whom we decide to commit our lives are the sources of our most important motivations. We often identify with this motivation more strongly than with most other sources. To take this source of identity away from citizens is both personally devastating and dehumanizing.

Offred's relationship with Nick is an act of rebellion. The intimacy of this relationship is precisely the kind of thing the party wants to prevent. Offred even tells Nick her name; this relationship helps to revive the identity that Offred created and now continues to create *for herself*.

The Handmaid's Tale also explores the rebellious nature of love of a different sort – love for a child. We see again and again throughout the book and television series that love for a child is important enough that parents will risk the wrath of the government for the sake of the child. This kind of bond doesn't need to be biological and seems to be a more powerful motivating factor than sexual or romantic love. In fact, the power of this kind of love appears to be stronger than The Sons of Jacob

9 *The Handmaid's Tale* as Philosophy: Autonomy and Reproductive Freedom   193

bargained for. Our love for our children transcends worries for our own well-being. As the Hulu series unfolds, June refuses to allow Gilead to continue to craft the structure of her will. She has the opportunity to leave, but does not take it, choosing instead to defy Gilead by setting her own ends and affirming her own identity grounded in love for her children.

The "Feminine Function"?

The general strategy that the Sons of Jacob employ is one that has been put forward, in theory and in practice by policy makers throughout time in the world that we actually inhabit. There are many reasons for this, but most of them have to do with maintaining systems of power and order. This strategy involves at least two steps. First, divide people into groups. Biological sex has historically been a common and easy way to accomplish this. Second, identify a ruling class between the groups. This is often done on the basis of traits, either real, imagined, or intentionally fabricated for the purposes of the political agenda. Finally, the ruling class identifies the "function" of the various groups and encourages the idea that society should be structured in a way that respects those functions – after all, *everyone should do what they do best.*

Atwood explores these themes, and in doing so she is participating in a long history of philosophical discussion of how we should understand an entity's function and what role that function should play in our judgments concerning what individuals ought to do and how society ought to be structured. The primary critique of societies of this type is that they ignore the potential for transcendence and self-determination.

Philosophers have provided a lot of the theoretical mechanisms that make it easier for policy makers to control women. In his *Republic,* Plato argues that, in a just society, there are three classes of people, the rulers, the auxiliaries, and the producers. Rulers are responsible for governing. Auxiliaries or warriors are responsible for carrying out the edicts of the leaders, and producers are responsible for various trades (farmers, craftsman, etc.). A just and harmonious society is one in which the citizens are working together satisfying their own respective roles and no others. In this work, we see one of the earliest articulations of the idea that certain people have certain natural skills. A well-ordered society is one in which citizens do that which they are most well suited to do and stay out of the way of people satisfying functions of other types. In this model, there is very little room for transcendence or self-creation. The essence of an individual is, in many ways, given.

Aristotle's philosophy has similar starting points. In his *Nicomachean Ethics* (Aristotle 2011), he attempted to answer, roughly, the question, "What would it be to live a good human life?" Or "What would it be for a human being to flourish *as a human being*?" What does it mean to be a "good" human being?

Aristotle discusses the good of a thing in terms of that thing's function. All things have a function – a primary reason for being or role to play. He says,

For example, the effect of excellence in the eye is that the eye is good and functions well; since having good eyes means having good sight. Similarly excellence in a horse makes it a good horse, and also good at galloping, at carrying its rider, and at facing the enemy. If therefore this is true of all things, excellence or virtue in a man will be the disposition which renders him a good man and also which will cause him to perform his function well. (Nichomachean Ethics, 2.1, 1106a16-25)

For Aristotle, the function of a human being is to live life in accordance with reason. He says, "Man, too, has a function: unlike any other being he is capable of rational thought. So happiness consists in the rational exercise of the soul's faculties in conformity with excellence or virtue." That said, for Aristotle, not all human beings in a thriving society have the same function. What he calls "natural slaves," for example, are not the kinds of beings who are capable of the kind of self-determination involved with living a life guided by reason and virtue. In many ways, for Aristotle, the same is true of women. Women's place is in the domestic domain. Their function is to bear and raise children. Otherwise, they should follow the commands of their husbands, the natural leaders of the household.

For Aristotle, different roles for women seemed appropriate, in part, because the nature of women is, in many ways, different in *kind* from the nature of men. The capacities and inclinations of the two groups are simply not the same. In *The History of Animals* (Aristotle 2020), Aristotle says,

The fact is, the nature of man is the most rounded off and complete, and consequently in man the qualities or capacities above referred to are found in their perfection. Hence woman is more compassionate than man, more easily moved to tears, at the same time is more jealous, more querulous, more apt to scold and to strike. She is, furthermore, more prone to despondency and less hopeful than the man, more void of shame or self-respect, more false of speech, more deceptive, and of more retentive memory. She is also more wakeful, more shrinking, more difficult to rouse to action, and requires a smaller quantity of nutriment. (Aristotle, Book IX, I)

The view that men and women have fundamentally different traits, and, therefore, fundamentally different functions, is further ingrained in the public consciousness by the theory of natural law. Early church fathers were heavily influenced by the ancient Greeks and by Aristotle in particular. In Aquinas' *Summa Theologica*, he argues for, among others, the following distinction between man and woman,

But man is yet further ordered to a still nobler vital action, and that is intellectual operation. Therefore, there was greater reason for the distinction of these two forces in man; so that the female should be produced separately from the male; although they are carnally united for generation. Therefore directly after the formation of woman, it was said: "And they shall be two in one flesh." (Aquinas, Summa Theologica, q. 92, a.1)

He says, further,

For good order would have been wanting in the human family if some were not governed by others wiser than themselves. So by such a kind of subjection woman is naturally subject to man, because in man the discretion of reason predominates. (Aquinas, Summa Theologica, q. 92, a.1)

9 The Handmaid's Tale as Philosophy: Autonomy and Reproductive Freedom

This attitude about women persisted into the early modern period. At this time, questions about the extent to which education was suitable for women turned, at least in part, on some resolution of a debate regarding women's cognitive capacities. At a very minimum, in order for it to be appropriate to educate women, it must be the case that women are capable of reason and that no other feature commonly found in women precludes the proper functioning of their reasoning capacity.

From the perspective of those thinkers who held that women were inferior, common attributes found in women, specifically those attributes that involve emotion or imagination make them poor candidates for education. Such attributes diminish their ability to engage in reflective processes. Exceptions exist, according to these thinkers, to the general rule that women are poor candidates for education; some women are born with brains the biology of which more closely resembles the biology of male brains. For some women, it may be possible to otherwise overcome their plight. For the most part, however, contingent features of women's cognitive composition, such as their biology and their character, are responsible for their failures, rather than external factors like subordination, exclusion, and lack of education that could potentially be corrected.

In this period, Nicolas Malebranche argued that the fibers that comprised women's brains were, as a rule, smaller than the fibers that comprised men's brains. As a result, women are not capable of the kind of reflection that is necessary to consider abstract questions. Regarding women, he says:

> . . .normally they are incapable of penetrating to truths that are slightly difficult to discover. Everything abstract is incomprehensible to them. They cannot use their imagination for working out tangled and complex questions. They consider only the surface of things, and their imagination has insufficient strength and insight to pierce it to the heart, comparing all the parts, without being distracted. A trifle is enough to distract them, the slightest cry frightens them, the least motion fascinates them. Finally, the style and not the reality of things suffices to occupy their minds to capacity; because insignificant things produce great motions in the delicate fibers of their brains, and these things necessarily excite great and vivid feelings in their souls, completely occupying it. (Malebranche 1997)

On Malebranche's view, though women's biology as a rule makes them incapable of the kind of concentration that would allow them to consider complex questions, their constitution gives them a heightened understanding of matters related to the senses. He says, "This delicacy of brain fibers is usually found in women, and this is what gives them great understanding of everything that strikes the senses" (Olscamp, 1997). This very capacity for understanding those things that "strike the senses" is responsible for women's failures when it comes to engaging in reflective processes. Women's sensibility makes them flighty and unreliable, resulting in a lack of ability to concentrate in the way that such processes require. Such reflective processes are essential to the kind of "reason" that women were thought to be incapable of – the kind of reason it is necessary to engage in if education is to avoid being futile. It is important for our purposes to also note that if careful and sustained introspection is necessary for full autonomy, according to these thinkers, women have "the wrong kind of brains" for autonomy. If these thinkers were right, women would be properly categorized as moral patients rather than as moral agents.

These ideas did not go undisputed. Some writers, both men and women, advocated the suitability of education for women to varying degrees. For example, Anna Maria Van Schurman provided arguments in syllogistic form in support of the conclusion that education is fitting or appropriate for women under certain conditions (Irwin 1998). Marie de Gournay provided arguments intended to show that, for any argument one could provide for the inferiority of women, an equally powerful argument could be provided for the opposite conclusion (O'Neill 2006). Poullain de la Barre used the question of women's inferiority and their suitability for education as an example of a question that can be subjected to the method of Cartesian doubt (Barre 2002). When one employs this method, one can see that the belief that men have minds that are superior to the minds of women and as a result are better suited to education is unjustified. The fact that there are differences at all is a contingent fact, a state of affairs brought about by custom, lack of opportunity, and men's desire for power. Women are just as suitable candidates for education as men.

It is wonderful for women, and for everyone really, to see that these arguments were made by at least some women during the time when they were being denied education. That said, the arguments that these women offered weren't exactly the ones that a modern woman would offer. In many cases, these thinkers were granting some of the most problematic premises offered by those who would deny them education.

Consider the case of Anne Thérèse De Marguenat de Courcelles Lambert. In 1710, Lambert began hosting what was to become a famous literary salon. Many of her contemporaries viewed her interest in literary pursuits as inappropriate for a woman. In 1727, Lambert published *New Reflections on Women* (Lambert 1995). In this treatise, she argues both for the education of women and for the recognition of their intellectual activity. Her work is a response to Malebranche's influential arguments about the structure of women's brains. A modern woman might hope that Lambert would go after his claim that female brains make them too flighty to exercise reason well. That modern woman might insist that Malebranche was only engaging in armchair speculation about how male and female brains work and, of course, as it turns out, he was wrong. His speculations about how women think were circular – he began with the assumption that women think in a different and inferior way and, unsurprisingly, that's also where he ended up at the end of his argument.

This is not the strategy that Lambert employs. Instead, she spends most of the treatise defending the faculties that Malebranche attributes to women, faculties like imagination, taste, and sensibility. She argues that refinement of these faculties can make women more virtuous and that education can refine these faculties. Therefore, it is not inappropriate to educate women.

Lambert argues that imagination is important for experiencing pleasure, claiming that "Nothing gives so much pleasure as a lively, delicate imagination bubbling over with bright ideas" (Lambert, 38). Acts of imagination can be pleasurable for the one who is imagining because imagination "is solely responsible for the pleasing illusion of the passions" (Lambert, 38). The imagination is valuable for other reasons as well. Those with active imaginations are charming and as a result they tend to be persuasive. Lambert says, "If strength is combined with beauty, then it is the imagination that wins us over, since we are more likely to succumb to charm than to truth" (Lambert, p. 38). Lambert also sees imagination as having a very similar function as memory such that it is responsible for recalling past pleasures. She says, "It also exerts an influence over time since it can recall past pleasures and enable us to enjoy in advance all those still to come" (Lambert, p. 38). The value of imagination is such that without it "all of life's charms disappear" (Lambert, p. 38). In addition to these benefits, imagination also plays a role in judgments made on the basis of taste. Education can help to refine and properly direct these feminine abilities.

A second characteristic that was frequently attributed to women in greater proportions was what was referred to as sensibility, which involves making judgments on the basis of feelings one has in response to a stimulus. Sensibility, insofar as it is emotionally charged, is also thought to be a distraction from the kind of reflection necessary to engage in intellectual activities. These strong feelings are persuasive and might discourage one from obtaining the truth. If women are distracted by sentiment, the argument runs, they are not good candidates for education.

What we might have hoped that Lambert would do is claim that women are not any more likely than men to be distracted by sensibility. Instead, she offers arguments for the importance of sensibility, arguing that it is crucial to a functioning society. She says, "Sensibility is a quality which is a decided advantage for us to find in others. Without it, we shall never find humanity or generosity" (Lambert, p. 40). Sensibility, therefore, is not without its advantages.

So, in summary, we might hope that Lambert and other figures making arguments for the education of women would reject outright the characterizations of women as thinkers as different in kind from male thinkers. This does not tend to be the strategy of the arguments. Instead, the strategy seems to be to grant the characterization of women as different and inferior kinds of thinkers but argue that they should be educated anyway because there are other benefits of doing so.

One thing that these historical accounts make clear is that oppressed groups often come to see themselves through the eyes of their oppressors. Sometimes this can happen remarkably quickly. It is very easy for people under the thumb of totalitarian regimes to become bound by character limitations that don't actually exist simply because they have been told that insurmountable barriers are present. This is exactly what happens in Gilead.

Capacities of Women in The Handmaid's Tale

Many of the dynamics in play in discussions of women's capacities throughout history arc also in play in *The Handmaid's Tale*. Some of these dynamics include a willingness on the part of some women to be defined and categorized by those in power. As Simone de Beauvoir pointed out in *The Second Sex*, women are frequently complicit in creating the conditions of their own oppression. In *The Handmaid's Tale*, the Wives, among others, are good examples of this.

There are also some significant similarities on the part of the male oppressors. A very similar view to those articulated by early thinkers who were critical of the cognitive capacities of women is expressed on many occasions in the universe of *The Handmaid's Tale*. One of the most noteworthy descriptions of the way women are encouraged to view themselves comes from *The Testaments*. Agnes, the oldest daughter of June, has been raised by a Wife and has attended schools for affluent children. Her teachers told her why it is that women and girls should occupy their time with needlework rather than with other, more intellectual pursuits.

> What my father was doing in there was said to be very important—the important things that men did, too important for females to meddle with because they had smaller brains that were incapable of thinking large thoughts, according to Aunt Vidalia, who taught Religion. It would be like trying to teach a cat to crochet, said Aunt Estee, who taught us Crafts, and that would make us laugh because how ridiculous! Cats didn't even have fingers!
>
> So men had something in their heads that was like fingers, only a sort of fingers girls did not have. And that explained everything, said Aunt Vidalia, and we will have no more questions about it. Her mouth clicked shut, locking in the other words that might have been said. I knew there must be other words, for even then the notion about the cats did not seem right. Cats did not want to crochet. And we were not cats. (Atwood, The Testaments, p. 18)

The Sons of Jacob, and the Aunts that do their bidding, sound eerily like Malebranche in their justification for preventing women and girls from being educated. The lively imaginations of women can get them into trouble! Agnes reflects,

> Forbidden things are open to the imagination. That was why Eve ate the Apple of Knowledge, said Aunt Vidalia: too much imagination. So it was better not to know some things. Otherwise your petals would get scattered. (Atwood, The Testaments, p. 18)

Like Malebranche, the powerful parties in Gilead blame the differences in intellectual potential on the alleged "structure" or "consistency" of female brains. Agnes can't help feeling uneasy about the way this point is put to her,

> Cleaning up things such as blood and other substances that came out of bodies was part of women's duty of caring for other people, especially little children and the elderly, said Aunt Estee, who was always putting things in a positive light. That was a talent women had because of their special brains, which were not hard and focused like the brains of men but soft and damp and warm and enveloping, like…like what? She didn't finish the sentence.
>
> Like mud in the sun, I thought. That's what was inside my head, warmed-up mud. (Atwood, The Testaments, p. 84)

Given its philosophical ancestry, it is quite plausible (even if detestable) that a society facing the problems described by Atwood would turn to a functional view of this type. This is not to say that the societal structure is morally justified, but that it might be persuasive to terrified people – they might be inclined to accept a governmental structure that didn't actually seem quite as foreign to them as we may be inclined to think.

Autonomy and Language

During the battle for women's suffrage, some opponents of women's right to vote parodied the notion, comparing it to allowing "brutes" the right to vote (Taylor 1966). By "brutes," of course, such critics meant nonhuman animals.

One of the reasons that nonhuman animals, though they have moral status, shouldn't be understood as possessing the right to vote is that they don't possess the characteristics that are necessary for autonomy or for participation in the moral community. As we've briefly seen above, one condition that many philosophers believe is necessary for participation in the moral community is the ability to provide and respond to reasons. The practice of offering reasons requires the ability to formulate beliefs and the ability to articulate these beliefs through the use of some kind of language. Gilead's attack on language is a way of restricting autonomy. If a totalitarian regime can whittle away the conditions that allow for self-expression, they are that much closer to convincing all involved that the person in question is a moral patient rather than a moral agent.

In *Discourse on Method*, Rene Descartes makes the case that nonhuman animals are mere automata; even though their behavior may suggest that they have mental lives, such appearances are deceptive (Descartes 1986). Descartes offers two main tests to determine whether nonhuman animals have the mental lives enjoyed by human beings. One is to determine whether their behavior arises "solely from the disposition of their organs" (Descartes 1986). Human beings engage in a rich complex of behaviors, adjusting their responses to unanticipated changes in their environment. Nonhuman animals, according to Descartes, don't exhibit this ability. They act purely instinctually.

The second test Descartes offers is centered on language. He claims that nonhuman animals,

> ...could never use words or other signs arranged in such a manner as is competent to us in order to declare our thoughts to others: for we may easily conceive a machine to be so constructed that it emits vocables, and even that it emits some correspondent to the action upon it of external objects which cause a change in its organs; for example, if touched in a particular place it may demand what we wish to say to it; if in another it may cry out that it is hurt, and such like; but not that it should arrange them variously so as appositely to reply to what is said in its presence, as men of the lowest grade of intellect can do. (Descartes, p. 33)

For Descartes, then, nonhuman animals are mere automata, rather than beings with mental lives, because they are not capable of using language. As such, his argument yields the conclusion that it is appropriate for us to treat such beings as mere things.

The Sons of Jacob use control of language as a way of waging war against the autonomy of Gilead's women. These women are seldom allowed to talk, and reading is forbidden. The Sons of Jacob are so committed to this project that they even replace the words on signs at shops with pictures of the primary items the shop sells. They know that if they limit language, they limit critical thinking, and in doing so they limit objection and protestation. It may be that they, like Descartes with animals, may come in time to reject the idea that women are actually capable of taking on a first personal perspective in the first place. The easier they make it to deny that women possess minds, the easier it is to conceive of them and treat them as nothing more than wombs or as the source of labor.

Perhaps the most significant and de-humanizing example of language policing is the practice of renaming Gilead's women, the Handmaids in particular. In place of their original names, the Handmaids are rebranded with names that signify that they are not autonomous beings with inherent worth; they are the property of their respective Commanders. June comments on the theft of her name, that piece of language so crucial to her sense of identity,

> My name isn't Offred, I have another name, which nobody uses now because it's forbidden. I tell myself it doesn't matter, your name is like your telephone number; useful only to others; but what I tell myself is wrong, it does matter. I keep the knowledge of this name like something hidden, some treasure I'll come back to dig up, one day. (Atwood, The Handmaid's Tale, p. 68)

In the novel, this policing of language is juxtaposed beautifully with Offred's unique disposition to play with words. To fill the empty time, she entertains creative possibilities related to etymology, syntax, homophones, rhymes, and so on. One amusing example is her mental dialogue while in the sitting room, waiting for The Ceremony, reflecting on the objects in the room,

> I sit in the chair and think about the word *chair*. It can also mean the leader of a meeting. It can mean a mode of execution. It is the first syllable in *charity*. It is the French word for flesh. None of these facts has any connection with the others,
> These are the kinds of litanies I use to compose myself. (Atwood, The Handmaid's Tale, pp. 85–86)

The Commander wants a closer relationship with Offred, one that does not seem so impersonal. He invites her back to his office, full of forbidden books and relics of the time before Gilead. His strategy, in order to get closer to her, is to demonstrate more respect for her autonomy. There is still no question who is in charge, but he is willing to return to her something of what they have taken. In their first private encounter, it's letters – the Commander wants to play Scrabble. Offred describes the pleasure of seeing the tiles that would have been so mundane in an earlier life,

> We play two games. *Larynx,* I spell. *Valance. Quince. Zygote.* I hold the glossy counters with their smooth edges, finger the letters. The feeling is voluptuous. This is freedom, an eyeblink of it. *Limp,* I spell. *Gorge.* What a luxury. The counters are like candies, made of peppermint, cool like that. Humbugs, those were called. I would like to put them into my mouth. They would taste also of lime. The letter *C.* Crisp, slightly acid on the tongue, delicious. (Atwood, The Handmaid's Tale, p. 162)

As Offred's relationship with the Commander progresses, he provides her with more reading material. Sentences, paragraphs in women's magazines, and *Reader's*

9 *The Handmaid's Tale* as Philosophy: Autonomy and Reproductive Freedom   201

Digest. Access to the written word makes Offred feel more autonomous than she had been before. All of this, however, takes place under the Commander's strict control.

The most liberating words in *The Handmaid's Tale* are words written for women by women. Etched into the closet wall of Offred's bedroom are the words, "*Nolite te bastardes carborundorum.*" Offred later learns that these words mean, "Don't let the bastards grind you down."

Offred's eldest daughter is liberated by language in *The Testaments*. When readers are introduced to her character, she is a young girl going by the name "Agnes." She has been adopted by a Commander and his Wife, but the Commander has little time for her. They are of high social rank. When she reaches marriageable age (which is quite young in Gilead, many are married at 13), she is expected to marry a Commander and do her best to bear him children. Agnes' adoptive mother, whom she loves dearly, dies and the Commander remarries to a woman who does not care for Agnes. She wants her married away as soon as possible. She is presented with what others might take to be an excellent match – Commander Judd, the highest-ranking commander in Gilead. Judd has had multiple wives, all of them exceptionally (here we would say criminally) young. When they aged past their young teen years, they died of mysterious "illnesses" and were replaced by new, younger wives. Agnes is, unsurprisingly, uninterested in this arrangement. It is not only that she is disinclined to marry this pedophilic wife killer; she is disinclined toward marriage in general and considers taking her own life to escape her fate. It is at this stage in the story that the reader learns more about the most ingenious aspect of Aunt Lydia's plan – the institution of The Aunts.

In *The Handmaid's Tale*, Offred reflects on a conversation she had with Luke about sisterhood. She thinks,

> Fraternize means to behave like a brother. Luke told me that. He said there was no corresponding word that meant *to behave like a sister. Sororize*, it would have to be, he said. From the Latin. He liked knowing about such details. The derivations of words, curious usages. I used to tease him for being pedantic. (Atwood, The Handmaid's Tale, p. 8)

The original novel leaves us with a somewhat dim view of the role that women play in oppressing other women. When readers are introduced to Aunt Lydia inside the Rachel and Leah Center in *The Handmaid's Tale*, the sorority she creates is forced and uncomfortable, rooted in the new laws of Gilead that make true sorority impossible. When readers enter Ardua Hall, the domain of the Aunts, in *The Testaments*, they learn that Aunt Lydia is creating a very different kind of sorority, a sorority grounded in written word. She secures this place for herself and for the other Aunts early in the story, when she realizes that she must play along in order to survive.

Aunt Lydia gets Commander Judd to agree to this arrangement, and she proceeds to create an environment in which the Aunts, in contrast to the rest of the women of Gilead, are not only *allowed* access to the written word, but are the *gatekeepers* of the written word. The men of Gilead do not enter this sphere. The Aunts, cloaked in severity and ruthlessness, are left alone to plot a revolution of words.

Lydia saves June's child from a life of marriage and recruits her into the service of the Aunts. By the end of *The Handmaid's Tale,* the reader is aware that Gilead doesn't last forever. After all, the epilogue is an address from an academic conference on the topic of the historical Gilead. By the end of *The Testaments,* there is some measure of justice in the fact that it was the words of women that brought about the fall of the totalitarian regime. Like June in *The Handmaid's Tale*, Aunt Lydia uses words to record history for posterity. Those words are passed along to Canada surreptitiously from Aunt Lydia by both of June's young daughters. The restriction of language was a powerful tool for suppression in Gilead. In the end, the use of language by women is key to liberation, not just for June's children, but also for all of the citizens of Gilead.

Autonomy and Religion

It is tempting to view *The Handmaid's Tale* as a critique of belief in God or of the rationality of living a religious life. It is clear fairly early on that the religious features of Gilead provide at least some of the coercive force behind the totalitarian regime. Gilead provides its citizens with a system of laws, and the lawgivers are not mere men. Instead, the lawgiver is *God.* The Sons of Jacob simply see to it that the will of God is enforced. After all, according to them, if human beings had followed God's wishes in the first place, environmental degradation would not have occurred, and the birth rate would never have declined.

Autonomous beings are capable of self-creation. Organized religion can be antithetical to the creative instincts of human beings, and as a result it can restrict autonomy. In Friedrich Nietzsche's work *On the Genealogy of Morals,* he argues that the Judeo-Christian worldview led to an inversion of values. Traits that were once viewed as natural human strengths were recast as vices, or worse – those traits were viewed as *evil.* The Judeo-Christian worldview replaced these strengths with "virtues" that were wrapped up in self-denial and asceticism. Where we may once have valued traits like ambition, confidence, and appropriately directed pride, organized religion encourages us to avoid these indulgences and focus instead on traits like, meekness, humility, poverty, chastity, and obedience. We were encouraged, according to Nietzsche, to resent our natural strengths and ourselves. We live instead in a perpetual state of penance for our inherently "sinful" natures. The looming threat of a judgmental God provides additional coercion to comply with this new system of values. Nietzsche says,

> Here precisely is what has become a fatality for Europe—together with the fear of man we have also lost our love of him, our reverence for him, our hopes for him, even our will to him. The sight of man now makes us weary—what is nihilism today if it is not that? We are weary of man. (Nietzsche 1989)

In this state, Nietzsche argues, we no longer value human beings for the creative forces that they are. In this way, religion can be a serious restriction of our autonomy because it creates significant constraints on the range of our choices.

9 *The Handmaid's Tale* as Philosophy: Autonomy and Reproductive Freedom 203

This tactic is used to great effect in Gilead. As we've seen, the women there are encouraged to think of themselves as powerless and frail. Male strength is perceived as consistent with the natural order of things, but female strength is perverse; it's some kind of an abomination.

In a move that is in keeping with Nietzsche's analysis, The Sons of Jacob (and, as it turns out, some of the more prominent Aunts) alter the Bible in order to enforce their new system of values. Surprisingly, most of the citizens of Gilead don't notice; they believe the members of the community that tell them that certain crucial behavioral admonitions come from the Bible. Consider the following, which is a fundamental feature of the social and political system of Gilead,

> Not every Commander has a Handmaid: some of their Wives have children. *From each*, says the slogan, *according to her ability; to each according to his needs.* We recited that, three times after dessert. It was from the Bible, or so they said. St. Paul again, in Acts. (Atwood, The Handmaid's Tale, p. 94)

According to this "passage from the Bible," women are resources to be distributed among *men* in need. Of course, if it sounds somewhat familiar, it is because it is a bastardization of a quote from Karl Marx, "From each according to his abilities, to each according to his need"(Marx 1970). The passage has a ring of familiarity, and so it seems plausible to people that it *may* have come from the Bible.

The fact that the citizens of Gilead don't recognize the correct source of the quote or, at the very least, the fact that they don't realize that it *isn't* from the Bible, is itself a critique of a certain kind of religious life. Acting autonomously, in the religious domain and elsewhere, requires reflection on reasons for belief. Many people are quite comfortable forming religious beliefs on the basis of the contents of a book that they *haven't read*. Religious belief tends to be a deeply personal issue for many people, and it is the source of meaning in life for many. That said, when people aren't informed about the nature of their religious beliefs, they become easy to control by those who stand to gain by using those beliefs as tools for oppression and power. Adopting a religion or a spiritual lifestyle can, under certain conditions, be a kind of self-creation – an important act of autonomy exercised by the believer. When religion is a form of developmental restraint, it restricts autonomy, it does not provide fertile conditions for it.

There are many passages in the original novel that give the impression that Atwood might be quite critical of religion. In *The Testaments*, however, we see a somewhat nuanced picture emerge. In Ardua Hall, Agnes and her best friend Becka train to become Aunts. This involves learning to read. Aunts are the only members of the female population that are allowed to do this. At first, they use their ability to read to change the content of a library filled with stories written by pre-Gilead authors. Later, however, they are allowed to read the more dangerous books. The girls are most disturbed when they are allowed to read The Bible, unedited by the new regime. Becka began her training as a Supplicant first, so she had the first exposure to the document. She describes her experience with the Bible in the following way:

> "I would never lead any Guardians on like that. I would never catch their eyes. I don't want to look at them," said Becka. "Any men. They're horrible. Including the Gilead kind of God."

"Becka!" I said. "Why are you saying that? What do you mean the Gilead kind?"

"They want God to be only one thing," she said. "They leave things out. It says in the Bible we're in God's image, male and female both. You'll see, when the Aunts let you read it."

"Don't say such things, Becka," I said. "Aunt Vidalia—she'd think it was heresy."

"I can say them to you, Agnes," she said, "I'd trust you with my life." (Atwood, The Testaments, p. 265)

By the end of *The Testaments,* it looks like what we have is a nuanced view of religion and of religious belief. There are strains of fairly harsh criticism of both organized religion and unreflective, uncritical religious belief. Organized religion, at least in Gilead, isn't about salvation, hope, or meaning in life – it's about power. When people are willing to be fed a set of religious beliefs without reflection by organized religion, they are easily controlled and the extent to which they exercise autonomy is diminished.

That said, when people are reflective about their beliefs, they are in a position to properly take ownership of them. Over the course of the narrative in *The Testaments,* Agnes develops her own relationship with God that is independent from what the powers of Gilead tell her that it should be. She autonomously chooses this relationship, even if it is a rocky and uncertain one.

This development in the series is unsurprising given what Atwood herself has said about this issue in interviews on the topic. She argues that often, in the world outside of Gilead, Christians lose sight of those features of Christianity that are really valuable. Christians should prize messages such as "love thy neighbor." Instead, many cherry-pick the portions of the Bible that they take to support ideas they were already inclined to believe anyway, even if those messages are hateful or harmful. When asked in an interview for *Sojourners* whether she thinks that Christianity can be a force for good, Atwood said,

No question. I mean, early Christianity was egalitarian. And it was also very courageous because it underwent various persecutions, as you know, and so it also had its own underground. . . . Of course faith can be a force for good and often has been. So faith is a force for good particularly when people are feeling beleaguered and in need of hope. So you can have bad iterations and you can also have the iteration in which people have got too much power and then start abusing it. But that is human behavior, so you can't lay it down to religion. You can find the same in any power situation, such as politics or ideologies that purport to be atheist. Need I mention the former Soviet Union? So it is not a question of religion making people behave badly. It is a question of human beings getting power and then wanting more of it. (Williams 2017)

The message Atwood is conveying, then, is not that religious belief is inherently bad, but that it can be oppressive when it is used to restrict autonomy or otherwise harm those who are affected by it.

Better Never Means Better for Everyone... It Always Means Worse, for Some

In the original novel, many facts about the world outside of Gilead remain largely unknown. In the Hulu series and in *The Testaments*, we learn more about other governments and the choices that they have made in response to the global problems that they are facing. Though they face many of the same challenges, these other countries have not enslaved their women. The government of Canada, for instance, remains largely unchanged, or, at least it appears that way based on the information that we have been given. We are therefore in a position to conclude that despite the birth rate issues that people in the futuristic setting face, continued survival does not depend on treating a woman's uterus as a resource to be controlled and regulated.

The original novel encourages the reader to consider a number of broad philosophical questions, many of them related to autonomy. First, under what conditions are restrictions of liberty justified *for the greater good*? The Sons of Jacob have been effective in getting the citizens of Gilead to believe that, prior to their control and takeover, the continued survival of the human race was teetering on the edge of an abyss. In a world in which the alternative is the end of the human race, are fertile women morally obligated to bear children?

These questions turn on the proper resolution of a tension between two moral theories: deontology and consequentialism. There is much to say about both of these theories, but for our purposes we'll confine our discussion to the following distinction. Consequentialists believe that the moral status of an action is settled by the kinds of consequences it brings about. Consequentialists begin by providing an account of the kinds of things in the universe that are valuable, and then advocate for maximizing those things. Utilitarianism is the most famous version of consequentialism. Traditional Utilitarianism identifies happiness as the only thing with intrinsic value and then advises that the moral action to perform in any given circumstance is the action that maximizes happiness. Deontologists, on the other hand, argue that autonomous beings have inherent, intrinsic worth. We should not, therefore, treat them as mere means toward a particular end (even if it means maximizing happiness or ensuring the survival of the human race).

But, one wonders, in a world like the one we find in *The Handmaid's Tale* which, if either, of these theories are we morally obligated to follow? There are a number of distinct philosophical questions involved here. One question is, when the future of the human race is at stake, are fertile women obligated to *voluntarily choose* to have children and thereby contribute to the human population? This, however, isn't the question that Gilead asked. Gilead assumed that fertile women have this obligation. They ask, instead, should women be *forcibly impregnated to meet this goal?* The Sons of Jacob answer this question in the affirmative, and the fact that they do so suggests that this policy isn't really about simply creating more human beings so that human civilization doesn't end. If all the government of Gilead was concerned with was making more humans, child-rearing wouldn't be such a status symbol. *Not just anyone* can reproduce. It is rich and powerful men who can reproduce, and the more powerful they are, the more choice they have over their selection of Handmaid. Moreover, if the policy were really about creating more children, Handmaids could choose the partners with which they reproduce rather than having those partners quite literally forced upon them.

In the epilogue to the original novel, we learn a little about Commander Judd. In *The Testaments,* Judd becomes a central figure. It is painfully clear from the outset that Judd isn't all that concerned with reproduction. Rather, he takes on wives that are young enough to satisfy his pedophilic urges. In Agnes' reading of the files supplied to her by Aunt Lydia, she discovers:

> He had disposed of them all. The first had been pushed down the stairs; her neck was broken. It was said that she'd tripped and fallen. As I knew from my reading of other files, it was not difficult to make such things look like accidents. Two of his wives were said to have died in childbirth, or shortly thereafter; the babies were Unbabies, but the deaths of the Wives had involved intentionally induced septicemia or shock. In one case, Commander Judd had refused to operate when an Unbaby with two heads had lodged in the birth canal. Nothing could be done, he said piously, because there had still been a fetal heartbeat. (Atwood, The Testaments, p. 278)

Judd is one of the most powerful Commanders in Gilead, and others in power seem to be fully aware, though unwilling to comment, on his pedophilic and murderous preferences. His behavior is only thinly veiled – just enough to claim plausible deniability. If the intentions of the Sons of Jacob were pure, Judd's actions would be viewed as profoundly morally wrong – after all, he is killing *fertile women*, who have the potential to bring new human life into the world. The example of Judd illustrates that claims about sanctity of human life are simply useful tools for the men of Gilead to use when it is convenient and abandon when it is not. The government isn't about preservation of life, it is about preservation of power.

It is also noteworthy that it is only female bodies that are objectified in Gilead. An author could write a different dystopia – one in which fertile humans are in short supply, so men are imprisoned to generate as much viable sperm as possible. Though it would certainly be inhumane to do this, the very suggestion doesn't fill us with the kind of dread that we experience when we read *The Handmaid's Tale* because it doesn't hit home in the same kind of way. Both in the United States and in Gilead, regardless of the fact that *both male and female bodies have reproductive functions*, it is largely only the bodies of females that are commodified and regulated. It's worth noting that debates about whether employer's health insurance must cover vasectomies are not common nor part of our shared cultural consciousness in the way that debates about regulating women's reproductive organs are. This suggests that it is and always has been about power, and never about creating more babies.

We might ask, however, what the ethics of the situation would be *if* the intentions of the Sons of Jacob were pure. Could considerations about the continued existence of the human species ever justify treating women purely as a means to an end?

To answer this question, it is worth discussing why we might care about the continued existence of the human species. One response has to do with the value of human life. Some philosophers think that human life has inherent value. Others argue that pleasure has intrinsic value, and, since it does, it is better if more beings exist, both in the present and the future, to experience pleasurable lives. If this is the case, then, all things being equal, human beings have an obligation to create future generations of people and to provide for a future in which these beings are in a position to experience pleasurable lives. It would follow from this, however, that we are obligated to bring into existence *every possible being that might experience joy.* If true, we should follow the advice from Monty Python's *The Meaning of Life* and agree that "every sperm is sacred." This, on its face, seems absurd.

There are other arguments for a slightly different conclusion, however. These arguments support the claim that though we may not have an obligation to bring about every possible being, we do have an obligation to ensure that there are future generations of human beings. If this is the case, some human beings might have moral obligations to procreate.

These arguments have a strong intuitive pull, but it is not clear that the pull is rational. We might have evolutionary inclinations toward the idea that it would be better if beings that shared our genetic material continued to exist, but the things toward which we are evolutionary inclined are not always and very often aren't the things that are best. And there is reason to think that this could be true, under certain conditions, when it comes to the survival of the species. How so?

Most acts of creation are not obligatory; and if they are, they must be grounded in something – in some good they accomplish. But in the world of *The Handmaid's Tale*, human beings have caused immeasurable destruction to one another, to other species, and to the planet. The Sons of Jacob in particular have created conditions in which many lives are miserable, characterized by unfreedom, and arguably not worth living. In other words, given the conditions described in the novels and how, it is far from clear that the continued existence of the human species is a good thing. So one could easily argue that the good, value, or virtue that the continued existence of the species would promote is not compelling or important enough that it is reasonable for people think that it warrants significant restriction of liberty. Indeed, the inherent required moral respect for the autonomy and dignity of a human person may mean that forcing persons to participate in the most intimate acts of creation can never be justified for any public good, no matter how reasonable it may seem to desire that good.

Or to put it another way: Like most dystopias, *The Handmaid's Tale* universe encourages us to reflect on the question of the conditions under which human life is worth living, promoting, and preserving. At the end of *The Testaments*, Aunt Lydia was willing to sacrifice her own life so that other people, women in particular, could regain their ability to live autonomous lives. On trial for his life, Socrates insisted that "the life which is unexamined is not worth living" (West 1979). Examining one's own life and values is crucial for living an autonomous life and for living a philosophical life as well. This value, at least in certain contexts, may be more important than any maximizing considerations. The Sons of Jacob, by depriving women of the ability to use language to its fullest, by determining who they love and the conditions under which they will love, by depriving them of full access to language and to critical thinking, make living an autonomous, examined life very difficult if not impossible.

Conclusion

The Handmaid's Tale and *The Testaments* offer us a glimpse into a world in which the some of the most problematic values and power structures in play in our own world are carried to their logical extreme. We are left with the idea that a person's grasp on autonomy, especially if that person is a woman, may not be as secure as they might think. These stories should motivate us to keep a watchful eye on our government. Even the most stable democracies can quickly transition to fascism. As Atwood herself said, she included no imaginary atrocities in this tale. These stories should motivate vigilance so that their dystopian fictional nightmares don't turn into prognostications.

References

Aquinas, Thomas. Summa Theologica. Online Libaray of Liberty. https://oll.libertyfund.org/titles/aquinas-the-summa-theologica-of-st-thomas-aquinas-part-i-qq-lxxv-_cii-vol-4-treatise-on-man/simple#lf0961-04_label_823

Aristotle. 2011. *Aristotle's Nicomachean ethics.* Edited by R.C. Bartlett and S.D. Collins. Chicago: University of Chicago Press.

———. 2020. *History of the animals. The Internet classics.* Accessed 17 Sep 2020. http://classics.mit.edu/Aristotle/history_anim.html. 350 B.C.E.

Atwood, Margaret. 1998. *The Handmaid's Tale.* New York: Anchor Books.

———. 2013. My hero: George Orwell by Margaret Atwood. *The Guardian*, January 18, 2013. https://www.theguardian.com/books/2013/jan/18/my-hero-george-orwell-atwood

———. 2017. Margaret Atwood on what 'The Handmaid's Tale' means in the age of Trump. *The New York Times*, March 10, 2017. https://www.nytimes.com/2017/03/10/books/review/margaret-atwood-dmaids-tale-age-of-trump.html

———. 2019. *The testaments.* New York: O.W. Toad, Ltd.

Barre, Francois Poullain de la. 2002. On the equality of the two sexes. In *Three Cartesian feminist treatises.* Chicago: University of Chicago Press.

Cohen, Carl, and Tom Regan. 2001. *The animal rights debate.* New York: Roman and Littlefield.

Descartes, Rene. 1986. *Discourse on the method.* New York: Macmillan.

Dostoyevsky, Fyodor. 1950. *The brothers Karamazov.* New York: Vintage Books.

Frankfurt, Harry. 1988. *The importance of what we care about.* Cambridge: Cambridge University Press.

———. 2006. *Taking ourselves seriously and getting it right.* Stanford: Stanford University Press.

Friedrich Nietzsche, Kaufmann and Walter Kaufmann. 1989. *On the genealogy of morals and Ecce Homo.* New York: Vintage Books.

Huxley, Aldous. 1932. *Brave new world.* New York: Harper.

Lambert, Anne Thérèse De Marguenat de Courcelles. 1995. *New reflections on women.* New York: Peter Land Publishing.

Malebranche, Nicolas. 1997. *The search after truth: With elucidations of the search after truth.* Edited by Thomas M. Lennon and Paul J. Olscamp. Cambridge: Cambridge University Press.

Marx, Karl. 1970. Critique of the Gotha program. In *Marx/Engels selected works volume three.* Edited by Karl Marx and Friedrich Engels. Moscow: Progess Publishers.

O'Neill, Eileen. 2006. Justifying the inclusion of women in our histories of philosophy: The case of Marie de Gournay. In *Guide to feminist philosophy.* Edited by Linda Alcoff and Eva Kittay. Oxford/Cambridge: Blackwell.

Orwell, George. 1961 1984. New York: Signet Classics.

Plato. 1943. *The Republic.* New York: Books Inc.

Taylor, Thomas. 1966. *A vindication of the rights of Brutes.* Gainesville: Scholar's Facsimiles and Reprints.

van Schurman, Anna Maria. 1998. *Whether a Christian woman should be educated and other writings from her intellectual circle.* Trans. Joyce Irwin. Chicago: University of Chicago Press.

West, T.G. 1979. Plato. In *Plato's apology of Socrates: An interpretation with a new translation.* Ithaca: Cornell University Press.

Williams, Layton E. Margaret Atwoood on Christianity, 'The Handmaid's Tale,' and what faithful activism looks like today. *Sojourners.* April 25, 2017. https://sojo.net/articles/margaret-atwood-christianity-handmaid-s-tale-and-what-faithful-activism-looks-today.

Mister Rogers' Neighborhood as Philosophy: Children as Philosophers

10

David Baggett

Contents

Introduction	212
Origins of *Mister Rogers' Neighborhood*	213
Children Are Born Philosophers	217
What Is It to Be a Child?	220
The Philosophy of Childhood: An Evaluation	222
Avoiding Condescension	223
Back to Work	225
Art, Death, and Humor	226
Professional Philosophy	228
Conclusion	230
References	231

Abstract

Mister Rogers' Neighborhood was a wonderful TV show for children and adults alike. Its concerns for the social and emotional development of children are well known, but perhaps what is less obvious is the way the show also encouraged children to be philosophers. It did this first by Rogers himself retaining his childlike wonder of the world, and then by encouraging children to indulge their imaginations, to think hard, and ask their questions without being shut down or silenced. Philosophy, as many philosophers recognize, comes naturally to kids, even and especially quite young ones, like those in the demographics of the *Neighborhood*. Children that age display a naivete about the world born of profundity, a ravenous insatiable appetite for knowledge, and a wide-ranging imagination. The *Neighborhood* both apprehended and appreciated these traits in children, and encouraged them to develop holistically, both affectively and cognitively.

D. Baggett (✉)
School of Christian Thought, Houston Baptist University, Houston, TX, USA
e-mail: dbaggett@hbu.edu

© Springer Nature Switzerland AG 2024
D. K. Johnson et al. (eds.), *The Palgrave Handbook of Popular Culture as Philosophy*,
https://doi.org/10.1007/978-3-031-24685-2_26

211

Keywords

Philosophy · Children's stories · Jean Piaget · Lawrence Kohlberg · Benjamin Spock · Margaret McFarland · Imagination · Cognitive development · Whimsy · Fred Rogers · Noam Chomsky · Rene Descartes · Humor · John Locke · William James · Jean-Jacques Rousseau · Erik Erikson · Montessori method · Wonderment · Thomas Aquinas · David Hume · Gareth Matthews · Matthew Lipman · Thomas Wartenburg · Neil Postman · Carl Jung · W. H. Auden · *Charlotte's Web* · *Tuck Everlasting* · *Frog and Toad Together* · C. S. Lewis · Nostalgia · Pierre Hadot · Robert Spaemann · Shea Tuttle · Rationalism · Empiricism · Gregory Bassham · Charles Sanders Peirce · Nathaniel McDonald · Frank Scalambrino · George Herbert Mead · George Santayana · Elizabeth Cooke · B. F. Skinner · Jacob Graham · Ben Lukey · Steve Bein · J. R. R. Tolkien · Barbara Tuckman · Peter Costello · Nathan Mueller · Leilani Mueller · Eric Mohr · Holly Mohr

Introduction

In two quite appealing and charming museums in Pittsburgh, Pennsylvania – the Heinz History Center and the Children's Museum of Pittsburgh – some seemingly garden-variety items are on display: a few items of clothing, and some puppets. But most visitors recognize the pair of sneakers, the bright red cardigan, and the glass-enclosed Daniel Striped Tiger and King Friday XIII as far from ordinary. Many people go there exactly for the purpose of seeing them. These simple items approach iconic status because of a remarkable children's television show that ran largely without interruption for 43 years. *Mister Rogers' Neighborhood* was broadcast by WQED in Pittsburgh, not far from these museums that now house the original set and various pieces of memorabilia from the show. They are usually more than enough to create a lump in the throat of most anyone who grew up watching the *Neighborhood*. Its amiable host—a diminutive, soft-spoken, and kind man—seemed to speak in an inimitably personal way to each member of his considerable audience. Undoubtedly, these items invoke an inexplicable sense of nostalgia in visitors daily, for the show and for the man whose brainchild it was, Fred McFeely Rogers.

The *Neighborhood* was a wonderful TV show for children and adults alike. Its concerns for the social and emotional development of children are well known, but perhaps what is less obvious is the way the show also encouraged children to be philosophers. It did this first by Rogers himself retaining his childlike wonder of the world, and then by encouraging kids to indulge their imaginations, to think hard, and ask their questions without being shut down or silenced. The *Neighborhood* both apprehended and appreciated these traits in children, and encouraged them to develop holistically, both affectively and cognitively. In this way, as unlikely as it may seem, *Mister Rogers' Neighborhood* was a profoundly philosophical show.

Origins of *Mister Rogers' Neighborhood*

Fred was born in 1928 in Latrobe, Pennsylvania, 40 miles southeast of Pittsburgh. Fred once called his home town "the garden spot of the world." A slice of vintage Americana, Latrobe is replete with large porches and features a small town main street. Something even about the land and plush region in which it is found reflects a feature of his personality. The very geography of the place – its slow grass-carpeted slopes, especially under the canopy of azure sky on a clear day – seems to match the quiet demeanor and gentle disposition of the great man the town produced. Latrobe was in fact the neighborhood that served as the paradigm for the *Neighborhood*. This was where Fred first encountered the world's wonders as a wide-eyed child, and, for whatever reasons, he recalled his childhood and its vicissitudes better than most. The son of a successful businessman, Fred would eventually study music composition at Rollins College in Florida, and then move to New York City and learn about the television business at NBC, before moving back to southwest Pennsylvania to work at the fledgling television station WQED. After working on two television programs for children – *Children's Corner* with Josie Carey (1953–1961), and *Misterogers* on the CBC in Canada from 1963 to 1967 – he was finally able to give it his all with *Mister Rogers' Neighborhood*, which made its national premier in the tumultuous year of 1968.

By the time the show went national, it had already garnered an audience in numerous major cities, and Fred's educational interests informed the tone and texture of the show. He was a seminary graduate and ordained minister, though nothing in the show is theologically heavy-handed, and, after graduating from seminary, he studied at the University of Pittsburgh's Graduate School of Child Development. There he developed a friendship and working relationship with Dr. Margaret McFarland, who, with pediatrician Benjamin Spock and psychologist Erik Erikson, had cofounded a counseling center for families and children in Pittsburgh. She also established, with Spock, a child development department at the University of Pittsburgh School of Medicine. Rogers was thus fortuitously steeped in an avant-garde, cutting-edge hotspot for child developmental psychology. The *Neighborhood* reflected as much. In weekly consultation with McFarland, Fred aimed to address the emotional and social needs of young children. Its target audience was 2- to 5-year-olds, though PBS advertised it as appropriate for children of all ages.

Understanding the import of this chapter, which will argue that the *Neighborhood* rightly modeled and encouraged taking children seriously as philosophers, requires not just looking at the show itself, but what came before and after it. Here the focus will be more on what comes *before* the show, but a quick word is in order for what comes *after* each episode of the show, at least optimally. Fred did not see himself as an entertainer, but as an educator, and he hoped that parents would watch the *Neighborhood* with their children and, afterward, engage them in conversation about it. He encouraged "active learning," which is actually a pedagogical tradition with a long history. William James's *Talks to Teachers* and Jean-Jacques Rousseau's *Émile* are two examples of philosophical works that advocate for the method. He did not want kids to sit and learn passively, but to get involved, apply what was learned, ask questions, and flex their own mental muscles. Ideally, the conversations the show had started would continue; in this way, he saw himself as teaming up with the adults who cared for his viewers. He even said on occasion that the most important part of the *Neighborhood* was what happened afterwards.

As for what came *before* the *Neighborhood*, that is a longer tale, so just the highlights will be accentuated here. Getting at this story requires understanding Fred, because Fred Rogers and the *Neighborhood* are inextricably tied together. He wrote the scripts, he wrote the music, and he was the host: the show reflected his singular vision and exuded his unique spirit. Fortunately, the Fred M. Rogers Center housed at Saint Vincent College in Latrobe can make those interested better acquainted with his life and thought. Indeed, Fred himself was instrumental in plans for this Center. Before his cancer precluded it, his plan was to make the Center his new base of operations, and he hoped it would be a source of illumination and insight about the Neighborhood for many years to come. Consequently, visitors to the Center find themselves surrounded by bulging bins of VHSs and DVDs, and stacked boxes overflowing with old news clippings and *Neighborhood* memorabilia. There are bright red trolleys and Daniel Striped Tiger facsimiles, Friday the XIII puppets and Mister Rogers bobbleheads, folders full of vintage slides and episode notes, crates of old vinyl records, and walls decored with drawings and paintings and posters of Rogers along with several beloved characters from the *Neighborhood*, like Lady Aberlin and Mr. McFeely.

Most relevant for present purposes, however, there are also letters and addresses, essays and scripts, often written on yellow legal pads in Fred's own distinctive cursive, in which he shared his vision, articulated his values, and revealed his goals – in life and for the *Neighborhood*. So before examining the *Neighborhood* itself, it will be worth quickly considering this treasure trove of resources behind the scenes, to which my wife and I have made two pilgrimages.

The usual fare when discussing the *Neighborhood* features a strong emphasis on the centrality of psychology – more feeling than thinking, more emotional or social development than cognitive maturation, much less intellectual contributions of children. In Rogers' work on child development and education and his advocacy for children, and in the *Neighborhood*'s concern about easing their fears and furnishing safe boundaries for them, Rogers the amateur psychologist indeed saw the need to protect the innocence of children and prevent their exploitation. Owing to their peculiar vulnerabilities, he took seriously the need to keep them safe and to make them know they were safe. When Robert Kennedy was assassinated, his first thoughts gravitated to how the children would handle all the swirling chaos and uncertainty that was sure to ensue. If he had lived longer, he would surely have wondered (for example) how all the concerns and costs and safety measures of the coronavirus would affect children, whose emotional lives he recognized to be no less rich or important than those of adults.

Rogers, however, was in fact quite eclectic in his tastes and aptitudes. He had something of the soul of a pastor and the heart of a psychologist, but he also had the mind of a philosopher, which manifests in myriad ways and accounts for much of the whimsical philosophy behind and within the *Neighborhood*. In truth, there are vital

10 *Mister Rogers' Neighborhood* as Philosophy: Children as Philosophers

organic connections – both resonances and dissonances – between the psychology and philosophy. One example of their dovetailing is that young children, psychologists tell us, think of grown-ups as able to do anything, and as knowing everything. Of course they will eventually be disabused of this perception, but it generates an attitude on the part of the child that creates a daily temptation for a parent to exploit. In an article by Barbara Biber that Rogers read called "What Do Children Need Most from Parents, from Teachers?" in 1968, he marked this passage:

> We may demand adherence to a routine regularized to suit adult convenience rather than child needs, exact automatic obedience, expect him to bring honors to the family, or demand filial devotion of such strength that it shall compensate for the gaps of unfulfillment in our own lives. (Fred M. Rogers Archives)

Or, worse, a parent can discourage a child, shooting down their ideas without hesitation, making them feel silly or stupid, or that their contributions are worthless. The psychological damage that can be done to a young child is incalculable and long-lasting. It can seriously stunt their intellectual growth and suppress what otherwise would have been a natural tendency to think and learn, and perhaps even philosophize. In contrast, the adult has an alternative choice: he can use the child's unbounded trust toward a positive end. Biber writes, "It gives him the tool for helping the child to build a broad base of confidence, of relative fearlessness, of readiness to pick up a challenge of whatever caliber" (Fred M. Rogers Archives). The confidence youngsters naturally have in adults gives those parents or teachers or older siblings the potential to do both great good by loving them into loving, or great harm by love's absence.

Acutely aware of the responsibility of adults toward children, Fred never tired of echoing the theme. He harbored no illusions that any parent was perfect, but he knew that intentionality could go a long way toward encouraging children and cultivating their growth rather than harming them and impeding it instead. He once received a large envelope from the manager of the television station in Dallas, Texas, that showed the *Neighborhood*. The letter was attached to 11 pages of music paper and started by saying, "Enclosed please find an opera, no less, written by a six-year-old viewer who was inspired by your programs." In an address at Thiel College Rogers wrote, "Can you imagine how I felt when I read through those pages of simple chants and age-appropriate themes? An opera by a six-year-old!" (Fred M. Rogers Archives). The boy's mother had written the words and notes, but the characters were his. Only encouragement to take a risk, experiment, and give it a shot would have made such a thing possible.

In contrast, always the inveterate observer, Fred saw what happened when children heard their mud pies were no good, that their block buildings had no importance, that their painting and dance and made up games and songs were of little value.

> What do you think happens to that something from inside—that *self* which was trying itself on the world for size? What do you think? Of course you'd be right in assuming that a person

who was consistently degraded would feel unaccepted and carry that feeling with him when he grows up! Little people look to big people for confirmation, for cues about life.... Children, like laboratory rats, can learn quickly not to experiment with wrong answers. (Fred M. Rogers Archives)

In addition to seeing the *weaknesses* of children, Rogers could also see their distinctive *strengths*, such as their freshness of perspective, their fertile imaginations, and their inventiveness at finding solutions. As an amateur philosopher, one might say, he treasured and delighted in children by valuing their contributions, encouraging their intellectual explorations, celebrating their creativity, and learning from them in the process. He was nearly in awe of them, truth be told. He had a genius for seeing something in children, and he wanted parents to understand how exciting it is to be parents and the unparalleled opportunities parenting provides – for investing in the lives of others, and for playing such a formative and sacred role in the emotional, cognitive, and social maturity of these precious people – and for self-growth. Fred once said that "by living and working with children, I've learned more about the child I was, the person who is always striving to grow within me" (Fred M. Rogers Archives).

The earliest training that we receive – for good or ill – tends to shape our intellectual and affective trajectories for years to come, and it is deeply fortunate that a few generations could boast that one of their first classrooms was *Mister Rogers' Neighborhood*. Childhood should be a time when questions are affirmed, curiosities stoked, and thought experiments indulged. The *Neighborhood* did just this. Rather than shutting down the questioning process that comes so naturally to children, it actively encouraged questions while enchanting imaginations. Indeed, even the philosophical impulse among the young should not be thwarted and silenced, but cultivated and cherished.

Philosophy etymologically, and at its best, means "love of wisdom," and it is interesting that the strong notion of *love* plays such a central role. To many it may seem corny, but a recurring theme of Mister Rogers' life and work is the centrality of love. In the 2018 documentary *Won't You Be My Neighbor?* he is quoted saying, "Love is at the root of everything—all learning, all parenting, all relationships. Love or the lack of it." Rogers loved children, and he liked them; he enjoyed their company and took delight in them. Many times throughout his career, both on the show and in real life, Rogers suggested that, though there are many ways of loving others, one of the most important ways of saying "I love you" is by being a receptive *listener*. As an educator Rogers recognized that he was not supposed to do all the talking. He was not afraid of periods of silence, even on the air, and he wanted to encourage children to share their ideas and for adults to listen to what they had to say.

An adult is not likely to listen to a child, however, if instead they are inclined to trivialize the child's contributions or treat them in condescending and dismissive ways. This is a real pitfall for those who embrace aspects of certain psychological theories of child development. Rogers, however, was able to transcend some of the limitations that saddle salient psychological analyses, by being the kind of practitioner he was – perhaps intuitively, or perhaps by temperament. Regardless, he recognized that children, especially very young ones, have an intellectual freshness and inventiveness that can put many adults to shame. Children are born philosophers, and the next section will show how Fred's grasp of this vital truth manifested in the *Neighborhood*.

Children Are Born Philosophers

The animating impetus and method behind the madness of exploring the intersection of philosophy and popular culture is the simple idea that philosophy is well-nigh ubiquitous. It can be found in *Buffy the Vampire Slayer* and *Downton Abbey* just as it can be found in luminaries from the history of philosophy. All it takes is the eyes with which to see it and a healthy dollop of imagination. Philosophizing is a profoundly human activity, as natural as dancing or singing, and children often stumble on all three quite easily. Of course they are not born equipped with the tools to do philosophy at a highly analytic level, but what they are adept at demonstrating is that at least the philosophical impulse is inherent from the start. Teachers and parents have the choice either to cultivate that impulse, encouraging its expression, or stifle, stultify, and silence it.

Amy Hollingsworth has written, "Mister Rogers was more philosopher than babysitter" (Hollingsworth 2005, p. xx). The claim that the *Neighborhood* was importantly philosophical or that children are natural philosophers raises eyebrows and suspicions, perhaps smacking of a sort of special pleading or ideological triumphalism. Surely philosophy is for grown-ups, not the young, especially not the *very* young like viewers of the *Neighborhood*, right? Again, obviously it is true that heavy-duty rigorous work in the ontology of properties or the intricacies of modal logic is not the forte of kindergarteners, but there is more to philosophy than that. Behind and before the technical machinery and the tools of the analytic theoretician, philosophy features a draw that even children – at least some and maybe many – can feel, and for which they have a natural knack. Or so it was suggested before in *Harry Potter and Philosophy*:

> [T]he mystery and marvel of it all is rarely lost on a child. Youngsters don't need to be taught philosophical curiosity. It just comes naturally. . .. Children are born philosophers. Usually only the concerted efforts of adults—understandably exasperated at answering "Why?"— can stifle children's passion to understand. (Baggett and Klein 2004, p. 2)

Suppose we go ahead and respect children enough to really listen to them. Do we have anything to learn from them? Is it true that they have anything philosophically interesting to say? It is true that Mister Rogers more strongly focused on the emotional needs of children than their intellectual contributions. But part of ministering to their emotional needs was to cultivate the intellect, to encourage their creativity, to get them thinking and expressing their ideas, to encourage experimentation with their thoughts, to facilitate their imagination, and to give them a chance to play, including to play intellectually. Fred often said that a child's work *is* play. The

Neighborhood operated on the assumption that playing and coming to better understand a variety of things is a significant part of children's work.

In the *Neighborhood*'s Episode 1530, in the middle of a week devoted to the topic of work, Rogers pulled off a remarkable and courageous feat. To show his young viewers where he himself worked, he took them behind the scenes of the *Neighborhood*. After the opening song, the cameras panned back, and the television audience could see, for the first time, the expansive studio in which the *Neighborhood* was situated. This was, among other things, a way to respect his audience, by showing that he was not trying to hide anything. After resuming the show, he talked about the fact that it takes a lot of people to create a television show, and then he talked about work children do – from feeding a pet to setting a table to painting – and talked about how he himself liked to play with puppets as a child; he then pulled out several of the show's recognizable puppets from a bag. An insightful commentary at this juncture comes from Jacob Graham:

> There is much that is philosophical about Fred Rogers, but what we see here is the essential attitude of the philosopher at play. The philosopher is ready to open him or herself to the world to see it for what it is. The questions the philosopher asks are guided by the love of seeing things as they are, understanding them for what they are, which sometimes requires sweeping away illusion, but sometimes inviting it in, fully recognizing what it is. (Mohr and Mohr 2020, p. 5)

The *Neighborhood* also respected its audience by not shying away from hard questions and difficult issues. It was willing to take on matters like war and death, racism and rage. "[Fred's] choice of subject matter was often uncomfortable, bordering on reckless," Lukey and Bein put it,

> He'd been on the air all of seven weeks when Martin Luther King, Jr. was assassinated, and it went without saying that this was not the sort of thing you talked about on a kids' show. Two months later, Bobby Kennedy was killed, and then came the fearless Mister Rogers with an episode about assassination. (Mohr and Mohr 2020, p. 31)

Rogers knew that the emotional lives of children were more sophisticated and complex than many realize, and he also thought them capable of processing even difficult aspects of life, including death, with the appropriate assistance and support. When a goldfish died on the *Neighborhood*, he did not avoid the topic, but put on camera the process of extricating it from the tank and burying it, using the occasion to talk about the inevitability of death and the natural pain and grief it causes. Coming to terms with death, with grief, with loss are all existential realities of life. Rogers knew this, and invited children into the process.

Among some of the deeply philosophical questions that the *Neighborhood* raised, to mention just a few, are these: Are persons valuable? Is winning the most important thing? What is the essence of a person? Does a handicap define someone? Is each person unique? What does love look like? Does love require work? What is the import of our emotions? Do they merit expression? The list goes on, and it behooves adults, too, to consider such questions. It was practically a mantra of the

Neighborhood that mentioning and managing negative emotions is vitally important. Yet how many, even adults, need to learn, or relearn, this lesson?

On that point, it is significant to realize that among those who are the most radical and politically partisan, the mere mention of politics will fire up the portion of their brains that regulates emotions. Indeed, partisan hate is becoming a national crisis. A full fifth of Republicans and Democrats agree with the statement that their political adversaries lack the traits to be considered fully human – thinking they behave like animals (Edsall 2019). Such statistics and sentiments potentially predict a troubling tipping point, and they are deeply at odds with the humanizing and empathy-conducive spirit of the *Neighborhood* that prized the healthy management of emotions. The need for greater emotional intelligence starts early but hardly goes away.

The *Neighborhood* recognized that children can and likely will eventually lose some of their natural curiosity as they get shot down, are made to feel like they have little to offer, and begin to conform to the expectations of those around them. Fred wanted to reach them while he could, in an effort to show them the respect they were due and help them reach their potential. He did not want them to lose too soon their sense that the world is worthy of wonder, full of enchantment, rife with mystery. Mister Rogers was no trained philosopher, but he was something of a philosophical practitioner, modeling engaged thinking for his audience, which was filled with endlessly curious children by nature. Especially very young children are this way, which in a real sense turns on its head the notion that little children cannot do philosophy.

Actually it is the very young who are by nature the most philosophical in a sense – not in terms of sophistication and technical rigor, but along the lines of what motivates the whole philosophical enterprise to start with. A sense of puzzlement at the world, insatiable curiosity, a willingness to ask difficult questions that may not admit of easy answers, or much of any satisfactory answers at all. Such is nearly the stock-in-trade of very young children, which is why they can catch adults off guard so often. Children do not need to be trained to ask such questions; they do it naturally. They can, however, be trained to *stop* asking questions, and after a certain age – usually around eight or nine – they usually do. Philosophy does not discourage or lament, but celebrates and champions the childhood questions that many children wish to ask.

Asking questions is important, not just for children, but also adults, and not just for theoretical reasons but for all sorts of practical ones as well. Intellectual honesty requires the courage to ask hard questions, and this is a virtue that should be inculcated in the young. The goal of such questions should not be one of iconoclasm or subversion for their own sake, but a commitment to discovering the truth, promoting the good, and celebrating the beautiful. Nathan and Leilani Mueller write,

When Mister Rogers opens his door to his viewers—especially children—he opens his door to philosophers, because children are natural philosophers. In asking such questions as "Why are you sad?" and "Why did the light turn off?" children reflect the same inquiring mind which Aquinas and Hume displayed when they themselves wondered what makes us happy and how to understand the nature of cause and effect. (Mohr and Mohr 2020, p. 19)

Children ask all sorts of questions – about how things work, their purposes, about right and wrong, and how we can know the difference. The *Neighborhood* warmly welcomes and encourages their questions and wonderings. In so doing, it "invites them to be philosophers" (Mohr and Mohr 2020, p. 20).

Fred also recognized that human beings are no mere logic choppers. They are complicated beings – relational, affective, cognitive, imaginative, and aesthetic beings. And that goes for children too. To appeal to and enliven their imagination, Fred made the Land of Make-Believe an important part of the *Neighborhood*. Rogers' whimsy continued the theme of celebrating the imagination and playfulness of children. The make-believe can almost take on the form of the thought experiments that philosophers use to explore and explicate various ideas. In the process, pretend-play and fantasy enable us to rediscover wonder and delight in others and the world by helping us pierce the drab blur of triteness and familiarity. "By juxtaposing the enchanted with the familiar, the magical with the mundane," Greg Bassham writes, "fantasy provides vivid contrasts that help us see the world with fresh eyes. . .. Rock and tree, leaf and branch, shadow and sunlight become again, as they were in childhood, wondrous and strange" (Baggett et al. 2017, p. 301).

That Rogers was not a professional philosopher did not stop him from recognizing that children are complex people. He recognized how naturally and insatiably curious they are, and cultivated such philosophical impulses and intellectual honesty. By listening attentively to, learning from, and respecting children, he invited their questions, celebrated them in fact – while broaching big questions of his own, contending with life's challenges alongside them, encouraging their reflection, and enlivening their imaginations. Parents and teachers have the same chance to inculcate into their young ones an inquisitive spirit that can serve them well their whole lives, and they can take the *Neighborhood* as their guide. Explicitly emphasizing that children are philosophers was not Rogers' main goal, or likely even a conscious one; nevertheless, his behaviors spoke volumes, allowing others to make those connections more explicit, as the next sections will attempt.

What Is It to Be a Child?

As a preliminary to the topic of philosophy and children, let us first consider an important foundational inquiry, namely, "What is it to be a child?" One of the more obviously bad accounts of childhood is one that held sway in the minds of many for a great long while. This is the view, to put it crassly, that children are merely little adults. On this simplest of views, "the little person theory of childhood," there is nothing particularly distinctive about children. The main or only thing to take into account in child development on this approach is increase in physical size, an approach whose fault is obvious, namely, that it overlooks important cognitive, emotional, and social aspects of development. Overlooking these rich dimensions of childhood development is a mark and result of not seeing childhood as distinctive in its own right. Even if she overstates her case, it is telling that Barbara Tuchman writes, "Of all the characteristics in which the medieval age differs from the modern, none is so striking as the comparative absence of interest in children" (Tuchman 1978, p. 61).

Interestingly enough, philosophers have not done a great deal of work on this question of what a child is, though in a moment we will see that they do have some contributions to make. Usually we look to educational specialists and psychologists for operative theories about children and childhood development. Rogers was both an educator and steeped in childhood development theories, not a trained philosopher, though he was familiar with the writings of philosophy in his promiscuously wide reading. Nevertheless he largely avoided some of the pitfalls and limitations of various psychological theories of children, a few of which will be briefly mentioned.

It is worth noting that Neil Postman, in *The Disappearance of Childhood*, identifies the well-developed notion of shame as a crucial step in the evolution of the idea of childhood (Postman 1994). Not nearly enough of the ancient Greeks and Romans grasped the point that children deserve to be protected and sheltered from certain things, adult sexual secrets in particular. Postman, at least, claims that this newfound insight was an entirely modern view, partially constitutive of a workable definition of childhood. It is a recognition of what many today would dub the innocence of childhood that merits protection, especially because by nature children are also naturally trusting, which makes them especially vulnerable to predators of various kinds. Lacking the requisite resources to protect themselves, it is incumbent on their caregivers to keep them safe and not allow the unscrupulous to exploit their vulnerabilities and naturally trusting natures.

Talk of the "nature" of children reminds us that, among the questions involved in understanding the category of childhood, is the philosophical debate between rationalists and empiricists. Now we will not let that detain us here, except to point out that salient psychological efforts to characterize childhood tend to fall into one or the other of those broad categories. B. F. Skinner's behaviorism is a descendent of Locke's empiricism, whereas Noam Chomsky'sinnatism derives ultimately from Cartesian rationalism. Rogers' child psychology training in Pittsburgh was shaped by the likes of Benjamin Spock, Erik Erikson, and, most importantly, Margaret McFarland. Spock, in particular, is well known for a recapitulation model of childhood according to which each child retraces the whole history of mankind, physically and spiritually, step by step. Such a theory is similar to but importantly different from innatism, which says the most basic cognitive structures do not evolve, though they may go from being merely latent to becoming manifest. For "the recapitulationists the structures themselves are like Japanese flowers; they unfold during childhood," repeating the way the human race has evolved and developed in history (Matthews 1994, p. 25).

Experientialists, innatists, and recapitulationists all offer their own research agendas and crucial insights, but this can tacitly underestimate the complexity of a child's thought process. To adduce an example of how this can happen, consider when Carl Gustav Jung echoed this recapitulationist sentiment: "Childhood, however, is a state of the past. . .. The child lives in a pre-rational and above all in a pre-scientific world, the world of people who existed before us" (Jung 1954, p. 134). Or take Spock's notion that "ontogeny recapitulates phylogeny." If the development of each child tracks the evolutionary development of mankind, it would be easy to assume that very young children would be incapable of anything remotely like philosophical reflection, for they are likely to be thought to lack the requisite skills of abstraction. Maybe teenagers could begin to do philosophy, on such a view, but not children. Likewise Piaget's occasional depiction of children is equally condescending.

The Philosophy of Childhood: An Evaluation

Philosophers do have something to contribute to the discussion of the nature of childhood. On the matter of psychological theories of child development, Harvard-trained philosopher Gareth Matthews, for example, argues that any such derogatory depictions of children should raise red flags. To maintain that children live in a prescientific and even prerational world is arrogant and inappropriately condescending (Matthews 1994, p. 27). He reminds us that children are not only objects of study, but members of Kant's "kingdom of ends." It's fine to be curious about them, and we should certainly take our responsibilities seriously for their education and welfare, but we also owe them respect. As Matthews puts it, "And here is where our theoretical models for understanding them may dehumanize them and encourage inappropriately condescending attitudes toward them" (Matthews 1994, p. 27). If this sounds more than a little like the *Neighborhood*, it is no surprise. Peter Costello has made the following observation:

> Thomas Wartenburg in *Big Ideas for Little Children* as well as … Gareth Matthews and Matthew Lipman across their careers [demonstrate] the principles of Rogers' work as it relates to philosophy. Children are already "partners in inquiry," as Matthews argues, and they should be treated as having critically important responses to literature or philosophical issues. (Costello 2016, p. 128)

Lipman, whom Costello mentions, was a Columbia philosophy professor in the 1960s who grew discouraged at the poor reasoning skills of his undergraduate students. He decided to start teaching philosophy, especially logic, in K-12 schools. He moved to Montclair State University and in 1972 launched the Philosophy for Children movement, later writing a series of philosophical novels and a supporting curriculum that spread all over the world. Years ago at a symposium at the annual meetings of the American Philosophical Association, Lipman suggested philosophers think of the philosophy of childhood in ways analogous to the philosophy of religion, the philosophy of science, or the philosophy of art. His suggestion was that philosophers might find it fruitful to turn their attention to such intriguing questions as, "What is it to be a child?" and "How do children's ways of thinking differ from 'ours'?"

Interestingly enough, what initially drew Matthews to the philosophy of children, was also his experience of teaching undergraduates. He had found that it was often a hard sell to get college students interested in the questions of philosophy. The students seemed unengaged, thinking the questions artificial or pointless (a far too common phenomenon still today). He himself considered the questions of philosophy fascinating, existentially central, and eminently natural to ask, so he began to listen to the questions of children. What he discovered was that philosophy comes to them quite naturally – at least before such philosophical impulses and penchant for queries are systematically drummed out of them, consistently stymied, and finally silenced. When Matthews himself was a boy, he liked to raise philosophical questions. As he later remembered, "When now, sixty years later, I teach Aristotle or Aquinas to university students, I try to locate the questioning child in me and my students. Unless I do so, the philosophy we do together will lose much of its urgency and much of its point" (Matthews 1994, p. 14). As Matthews sees it, philosophy is an adult attempt to deal with the genuinely baffling questions of childhood.

Matthews ended up writing three books on philosophy and children: *Dialogues with Children*, *The Philosophy of Childhood*, and *Philosophy and the Young Child*. *Dialogues* is an exercise in attentive listening. In his *Dialogues* Matthews used the method of writing story-beginnings in which the characters, mostly children, stumble, unaided by adults, on some philosophical issue or problem. The 1984 book chronicles accounts of his successes of using this technique with children between 8 and 11 in a music school in Scotland. *Philosophy and the Young Child* demonstrates that children have a capacity for puzzlement and mental play that leads them to tackle many of the classic problems of knowledge, value, and existence that have traditionally formed the core of philosophical thought. And *The Philosophy of Childhood* is described as a

> searching account of children's philosophical potential and of childhood as an area of philosophical inquiry. Seeking a philosophy that represents the range and depth of children's inquisitive minds, Matthews explores both how children think and how we, as adults, think about them. His book prompts us to reconsider the distinctions we make about development and the competencies of mind, and what we lose by denying childhood its full philosophical potential. (Matthews 1994, book description)

Avoiding Condescension

Recall Matthews' resistance to depictions of children in condescending ways. Like Fred, Matthews delights in the contributions children had to offer, including their philosophical contributions. Several traits of children are conducive to their ability to philosophize. From Matthews' observations, in children from around 3–7, close to the target audience of the *Neighborhood*, spontaneous excursions into philosophy are not at all unusual. After that they become rarer, which Matthews attributed to becoming settled in school and learning that only "useful" questioning is expected of them. Rather than devaluing their contributions, Matthews sees in young children, when given the chance, a capacity for philosophical comments and questions that "have a freshness and inventiveness that is hard for even the most imaginative adult to match." Although not the only criteria for doing philosophy well, freshness and inventiveness are much to be prized. Too often, maturity brings with it staleness and uninventiveness rather than an enhanced appreciation of philosophy. Children are naturally comfortable with "naive" questions – a profound, not a cognitively immature sort – whereas older people almost have to relearn this (Matthews 1994, pp. 17–18).

Matthews offers several examples of such depictions and his own analysis of where he thinks they go wrong. Kohlberg's model of moral development, for example, privileged concept displacement. He accorded the highest moral developmental score to one who thinks of moral obligations in terms of an abstract duty for its own sake. Small children do not tend to conceive of ethics in such a way, so they are inevitably rated lower on the moral development scale. But Matthews suggests this is unfair, and that a better model than concept displacement is available – on that is less myopic than Kohlberg's approach. For example, we can think of moral development taking place along different dimensions, such as *paradigms, defining characteristics, range of cases, adjudication of conflicting moral claims,* and *moral imagination*. Whereas Kohlberg put his whole focus on the fourth criterion, where children perhaps fall short, children may well exceed in some of the other categories, like moral imagination.

> [E]ven a very young and inexperienced child can catch us adults up sort with a direct, empathetic response to, say, a homeless person trying to keep warm in a cardboard box under a bridge. A child's naive question can awaken our sleeping imagination and sympathy, and even move us to take moral action. (Matthews 1994, p. 65)

Or long before a child can navigate moral dilemmas, she can have a strong empathetic response to the victims of suffering, or injustice, and "a working relationship of central paradigms for terms of moral assessment" (Matthews 1994, p. 65).

Another example comes from Piaget. Piaget's work on children was groundbreaking and rife with insight. In fact Piaget's work influenced Maria Montessori's efforts at effecting a revolution in teaching strategies that privileged the needs of children and facilitated a process of self-construction as the child's "work." "Like a Montessori classroom," Nathaniel McDonald and Frank Scalambrino write, "the *Neighborhood* set was painstakingly designed to ensure that every detail was developmentally appropriate and contributed to the goal of helping children develop key emotional skills and competencies such as self-regulation, communication, rationality, and emotional and social awareness" (Mohr and Mohr 2020, p. 52). So there are resonances between the *Neighborhood* and Piaget, but there are also dissonances. Without detracting from Piaget's legacy, Matthews points some of them out. Here is one.

In *The Child's Conception of the World*, Piaget reports asking a variety of questions to get a better understanding of how children view reality, but in the process he tended to discount the nonconforming responses on methodological grounds. Matthews' concern is that this potentially eliminates some of the most inventive and thoughtful responses – such as when a child might unwittingly wish to do philosophy. Piaget also distinguished answers and comments that reveal convictions from those that constitute what he called "mere romancing," which he defined like this: "inventing an answer in which [one] does not really believe, or in which [one] believes merely by force of saying it" (Piaget 1951, p. 10).

Again, though, it seems to Matthews most likely that the philosophically interesting comments a child makes will not so much express the child's settled convictions, but will explore a conceptual connection or make a conceptual joke. "Thus, the most interesting and intriguing philosophical comments are likely to be counted by Piaget as mere romancing" (Matthews 1980, p. 39). What Piaget called *romancing* and dismissed, Rogers would have likely dubbed *whimsy* and relished. Matthews might call it philosophy, and in truth a case can be made that whimsy, or least a certain type of whimsy, is central to philosophy.

Back to Work

Recall the primacy Fred assigned to the play of children, which is their distinctive work. Such work is important, because it enables them to stretch their minds, see novel connections, begin to draw conclusions, and make sense of their surroundings. Among the forms of play in which they are engaged is *intellectual* play, motivated by their deep sense of puzzlement, their wide-eyed wonder at the world. Questions occur to them that are deeply honest, refreshingly curious, and altogether heartfelt and sincere. They really want to know how we know that refrigerator light goes off when we close the door. Did not you?

Fred remembered what it was like to be a child; more than once he joked he would never grown up. He retained that childlike curiosity and wonder about the world, and in so doing he offered us all a great gift because most of us have largely forgotten what it was like to be a child. This phenomenon is so widespread, a portion of the academic literature is devoted to it – it is called "childhood amnesia." (Which raises, among other things, fascinating questions about personal identity.) Fred almost preternaturally could remember what it was like to be a kid, and he never lost his own childhood puzzlement. This imbued the *Neighborhood* with so much of its signature optimism, disarming charm, and distinctive innocence. It also made it genuinely inviting for those who wanted to wonder and think and play.

In a course on philosophy and the young child, Matthews assigned some "lab work." Students were to read a story to young children and then, in a very low-pressure way, discuss with the children any philosophical issues the story might suggest. One student read *Winnie-the-Pooh* to a group of young children, and the passage in which Piglet's grandfather is said to have two names "in case he lost one" made them laugh. This led to a discussion in which one student in particular, named Adam, became quite engrossed. In her notebook the student commented, "This child's mind has entered the realm of playful possibilities—child philosophy—he seemed to take great delight in his questioning" (Matthews 1980, p. 12).

Philosophy can and should be fun, and young children seem to understand this better than many adults. When they ask questions, they probably do not mean to be tiresome or annoying or rebellious; they are just genuinely curious. Much of what they are told deserves to be questioned and challenged, which adults would recognize better if they had not lost so much of their own puzzlement – a process as inevitable as it is regrettable. But if children' questions are summarily rebuffed or ignored, eventually they will just stop asking. So much potential for fun is lost when that happens. "Parents and teachers who always refuse to play this game with children impoverish their own intellectual lives, diminish their relationships with their children, and discourage in their children the spirit of independent intellectual inquiry" (Matthews 1980, p. 21).

In the *Neighborhood,* Fred did not wait for children to ask him questions. He raised them himself, which often involved playful possibilities, thought experiments, imaginative leaps, pretending, or even whimsy. In the archival material in Latrobe can be found the "Thoughts for the Week" for Programs 1026–1030, which go like this:

> Pretending is important play for all children. It's one of the ways they learn how they feel about themselves, their world, and the grown-up world around them. When a child pretends to be a firefighter or a storekeeper, he or she is trying to learn more about what it means to be "grown-up" and what adult life is like. Pretend play is also a way for children to imagine about things they *can't* ever be—kings and queens, witches and wizards, monsters and giants. Pretending can be a way for children to practice managing their fears—especially when grown-ups help them learn what is real and what is only pretend. (Fred M. Rogers Center)

Giving children the chance to dream, to imagine, and make-believe is a great gift. In truth it is a reminder that knowledge is gained not just by logic, but also by the imagination. The whimsical world of the Land of Make-Believe in the *Neighborhood* performed a vital function in the show. Elizabeth Cooke has done readers a service by discussing the "pretend" aspects of the *Neighborhood*, connecting them in the process to some of their philosophical progenitors. For George Santayana, for example, pretend play teaches about the "network of subterranean processes," about what lies beneath the surface of sensuous reality, but also about what lies deepest within ourselves. We enter the world of pretend play, and feel comfortable knowing we never lose our true selves exploring a make-believe world. Philosopher George Herbert Mead said that in pretend we become socialized, and through socialization we become an individual self. Charles Sanders Peirce developed a theory of imaginative play that resembles the *Neighborhood*'s practice of open-endedness. Peirce called play "musement," and described it as "[a]esthetic contemplation" and "distant caste-building." We play for the fun of it, for its own sake. We meander in thought in an open-ended way, without a particular purpose in mind (Mohr and Mohr 2020, pp. 87–89).

Art, Death, and Humor

Recall the opera the *Neighborhood* inspired a six-year-old to write. Consider that opera and the creativity and courage such a creation required. Having argued that there is a freshness, an urgency, and a naturalness about child philosophy that deserves celebration and can help us appreciate the nature and significance of adult philosophy, Matthews writes, "If one focused exclusively on the adult phenomenon, one would have only a truncated conception of what it is that moves people to ask and re-ask those age-old questions" (Matthews 1994, p. 122). He then extends his argument by wondering if something analogous can be true of child art. Might at least some of it be worthy of celebration too and able to help us better understand art itself? Averse as Matthews is to discounting the contributions of childhood, he is inclined to think the answer was yes, but not if we mistakenly think of children as merely proto-people, or if we cherish and nurture them principally for their potential, or as models of innocence and insight to be emulated by adults. Matthews thinks we should avoid both condescension and sentimentality. "Children are people, fully worthy of both the moral and the intellectual respect due persons. They should be respected for what they are, as well as for what they can become" (Matthews 1994, p. 122). Matthews takes seriously the art of children, just as the *Neighborhood* obviously did. By parity of reasoning, it is reasonable to think that Fred would take seriously the idea that children are philosophers.

Now remember the *Neighborhood*'s treatment of death. Children are hopefully a long way from death, perhaps the biggest philosophical conundrum of all. Sadly, however, some children do have to face bleak prognoses and even terminal illnesses, and the *Neighborhood* was a place that many sick and dying children relished visiting, most via television alone, but some even in person. Regarding death, Matthews argues that a strain of child stories can be found that takes seriously children's ability to think philosophically – even about something as serious as death. Two examples he provides are E. B. White's *Charlotte's Web* and Natalie Babbit's *Tuck Everlasting*. Matthews' sensibility in particular to suffering and dying children is deeply resonant with that of Fred's:

> No doubt some children who face the real prospect of imminent death also have, for that very reason, important things to tell us and to discuss with us if we are only strong enough to listen and to share. But this requires openness to the child and to thinking about death that we adults find extremely difficult to manage. A terminally injured or ill child is the ultimate threat to our parental pretensions. If we can learn to deal honestly with that threat and to deal respectfully as well as lovingly with such a child, we will have taken a major step in the development of our own maturity. (Matthews 1994, p. 101)

Such substantive and philosophical children's books are not *mere* children's books, just as the *Neighborhood* was no mere children's show. What W. H. Auden said of good children's books could equally be said of good children's programming: "There are great books which are only for adults, because their comprehension presupposes adult experiences, but there are no good books which are only for children" (Auden 1973, p. 291). How can there be books that adults can appreciate fully as much as children? Among the books to which Matthews points are those that deal with that most frightening issue of all, death, in a genuinely philosophical way, namely, by encouraging readers, whether old or young, to reflect freshly on its meaning. Other children's stories are just as philosophical, he thought, even when they are less existential – like "The Garden" from *Frog and Toad Together* (Matthews 1994, p. 104).

One way that a story written by an adult for children can meet the test of authenticity is by raising hard questions, with directness and simplicity and also, ideally, with humor (Matthews 1994, p. 110). Regarding that last ingredient, Fred was well known for his humor – if nothing else, the pedantic and sassy machinations of King Friday XIII and Lady Elaine Fairchilde, respectively, are enough for viewers to see that. Matthews too appreciated good humor, and he gave this winsome example of it found in a story that can get children thinking about the nature of causation:

> Consider the story "The Garden," from Arnold Lobel's wonderful collection *Frog and Toad Together*. In the story Toad, trying to follow the example of his friend Frog, plants seeds in his garden. Finding that the seeds do not immediately sprout and show their sprouts above the soil, Toad shouts at them to grow. Frog tells him he is frightening his seeds. Toad is horrified at the thought that he might have frightened his seeds. To comfort them he burns candles in their vicinity. He sings songs, reads poetry, and plays music to his seeds. When these various efforts produce no observable result, Toad laments, "These must be the most frightened seeds in the whole world." Exhausted, he falls asleep.
>
> Frog wakes Toad up with the joyful news that the seeds have finally sprouted. Toad is, of course, pleased and relieved. He mops his brow and sighs. "But you were right, Frog, it *was* very hard work." (Matthews 1994, p. 104)

Speaking of humor and children as philosophers, perhaps it is time for a joke. A boy was feeling very nervous about his first date, and so went to his father for advice. "My son, there are three subjects that always work with women: food, family, and philosophy." The boy picked up his date and they stared at each other for a long time. The boy's nervousness built, but he then remembered his father's advice and asked the girl, "Do you like potato pancakes?" "No," came the answer, and the silence returned like a suffocating blanket. "Do you have a brother?" "No." After giving it some thought, the boy played his last card: "If you had a brother, would he like potato pancakes?"

Professional Philosophy

Let us lastly consider an objection that some might wish to raise about this whole project of seeing the *Neighborhood* as philosophy and children as philosophers. Fred himself, though he read voraciously, including in philosophy, was no trained philosopher. At most he was something of an amateur philosopher. Would not he need to be more steeped in the intricacies and nuances and history of philosophy to render the *Neighborhood* philosophical? And could a nonprofessional philosopher really elicit philosophy from kids?

These are, as it happens, rather important questions, because most teachers and parents are not professional philosophers either. If encouraging philosophy in children requires a professional, most children would not be lucky enough to get

10 *Mister Rogers' Neighborhood* as Philosophy: Children as Philosophers

the encouragement. But Matthews anticipates this very objection and tries to defuse it. One does not have to be a professional philosopher to encourage childhood philosophy, he argues. What matters more at that level than technical analytic training or extensive knowledge of the history of philosophy is being attentive and encouraging intellectual exploration. One does not have to do philosophy vocationally to entertain a profound sense of wonder at life's mysteries and a willingness to entertain even seemingly naive questions that, on reflection, are usually harder to answer than one had thought.

Robert Spaemann thinks of philosophy as "institutional naivete." To build such a thing people need to be encouraged to ask questions "so basic that grappling with them seems to all of us some of the time, and to some of us all of the time, quite naïve." Matthews thinks this suggestion is helpful in three ways. First, it brings out part of the reason why making room for philosophy in society is difficult, since it raises questions people resist answering. Second, it helps us to see what is important about making room for philosophy in a society. "Every society needs a barefoot Socrates to ask childishly simple (and childishly difficult!) questions, to force its members to re-examine what they have been thoughtlessly taking for granted." Third, "[i]n children, naivete comes naturally, without institutional encouragement. Therefore, with Spaemann's idea in mind, we might expect that philosophy too would come naturally to at least some children. It does" (Matthews 1980, pp. 94–95).

The aforementioned Muellers remind us that when a philosopher entertains a question, she does so without thinking that she already knows the answer. Mister Rogers, like a good philosopher and like any good parent or teacher can, asked questions genuinely, without assuming he always had something to teach. In his *Philosophy as a Way of Life*, Pierre Hadot said that for ancient philosophers, wisdom was a way of life that resulted in a unique peace of mind and inner freedom since "real wisdom does not merely cause us to know: it makes us 'be' in a different way" (Hadot 2011, p. 265). The Muellers add,

> While part of the philosophical life seeks to understand the ordinary objects of this world, it is ultimately how the philosopher deals with these deeper questions, ones which even children ask, which best embody *living* philosophically. And it is in this sense that Mister Rogers philosophized with the best of them. (Mohr and Mohr 2020, p. 26)

If a parent or teacher need not be a professional philosopher to encourage philosophy in children, what *can* the professional philosopher do to help? Having devoted their lives to the study of the profoundly naive questions of philosophy, philosophers

> can help non philosophical parents and teachers to recognize and appreciate some of the naively profound questions of childhood.... What a professional philosopher can do is to collect examples of philosophical thinking in young children and then, by linking those childish thoughts to our philosophical tradition, help parents and teachers to recognize philosophy in their children, respect it when it appears, and even participate in it and encourage it on occasion. (Matthews 1994, p. 37)

Fred would agree.

Conclusion

How can we rightly think of children, even and perhaps especially very young children, as philosophers? As discussed, they have a refreshing honesty about what they do not know. They are not afraid to ask questions that to adults seem naive, nor are they afraid to ask questions that may not admit of easy answers, or any answers at all. They naturally possess a wide-eyed wonder, insatiable curiosity, and profound puzzlement about the world, all of which are conducive to genuine philosophical impulses. Their imaginations are fertile, their patience at inquiry is great, and their inclination to experiment with ideas is strong. Their emotional and cognitive lives are rich, and they have not yet lost their willingness to be inveterate explorers of ideas and possibilities.

In what ways was the *Neighborhood* philosophy and Mister Rogers a philosopher of sorts? He was an engaging and passionate practitioner who cared as deeply for the emotional as well as the cognitive needs and concerns of children. He viscerally recognized the necessity for the right foundations in life. His quest for wisdom was for the eminently practical purpose of application. He was a philosopher in the old-fashioned sense, according to which philosophy is not so much an intellectual exercise alone, but an embodied way of life exhibited in vocation, friendship, and every other aspect of life. Lukey and Bein suggest that they see Fred not as a Philosopher but as a philosopher – and they put children as philosophers in the same camp. "History may not remember them for the intellectual content they contributed to Philosophy, but in their own neighborhoods they're invaluable, as persistent practitioners of the *activity* of philosophy" (Mohr and Mohr 2020, p. 37).

The *Neighborhood* made television better by treating children as holistic beings whose inner lives are every bit as sophisticated and robust as those of adults, and in the process Fred became a surrogate father to generations. So, in the spirit of childhood philosophy, let us whimsically conclude this treatment with a playful possibility. Shea Tuttle, speaking for many, admits that she would forget the storylines and many of the songs of the *Neighborhood*, but

> I remembered the man, and I remembered how he and his program made me feel: completely seen, completely loved. I cannot recall the precise origin of my affection for Mister Rogers, and I cannot quite explain its intensity. I just know that he is indescribably special to me; I feel as if I have always known him, like he was a part of my becoming. It is not simple nostalgia, fleeting and saccharine. It is deeper than nostalgia. It is formation. It is love. (Tuttle 2019, p. 2)

There does indeed seem to be something more than nostalgia at work here, but that is perhaps because nostalgia itself can point to something deeper. It can function as a sort of enchantment, or re-enchantment, a kind of transcendent apprehension, that is less about the past and more about the future.

In his sermon "The Weight of Glory," C. S. Lewis suggests that in nostalgia, at least at its best, is something prefiguring, transcendent, prophetic. He demurred from Wordsworth's tendency to account for it by romanticizing moments in his past, as if *they* were the locus of our deepest longings. Lewis saw that it was more penetrating

10 *Mister Rogers' Neighborhood* as Philosophy: Children as Philosophers

than that – and that settling for the penultimate is, at best, fleeting and saccharine, and at worst, idolatrous.

> The books or the music in which we thought the beauty was located will betray us if we trust to them; it was not in them, it only came through them, and what came through them was longing. These things—the beauty, the memory of our own past—are good images of what we really desire; but if they are mistaken for the thing itself they turn into dumb idols, breaking the hearts of their worshipers. For they are not the thing itself; they are only the scent of a flower we have not found, the echo of a tune we have not heard, news from a country we have never yet visited. (Lewis 1980, p. 7)

Mister Rogers was a simply wonderful man and a national treasure, who advocated for and both liked and loved children. We rightly commemorate his life and work with a stamp and celebrate and emulate his remarkable achievements – and not just because the *Neighborhood* recognized the importance and legitimacy of the social and emotional needs of children. It did that, and better than any television program before or since – but it also cultivated, cherished, and championed their whole personhood. And this importantly included their fertile minds, their prodigious imaginations, and their indomitable philosophical spirit.

References

Auden, W.H. 1973. *Forewords and afterwords*. New York: Random House.
Baggett, David, and Shawn E. Klein. 2004. *Harry Potter and philosophy: If Aristotle ran Hogwarts*. Chicago: Open Court.
Baggett, David, Gary R. Habermas, and Jerry L. Walls, eds. 2017. *C. S. Lewis as philosopher: Truth, goodness, and beauty*. Lynchburg: Liberty University Press.
Costello, Peter. 2016. Community as emotional education. In *Revisiting Mister Rogers' neighborhood: Essays on lessons about self and community*, ed. Kathy Merlock Jackson and Steven M. Emmanuel. Jefferson: McFarland & Company.
Edsall, Thomas B. 2019. No hate left behind. March 13, 2019. *New York Times*. Available online: https://www.nytimes.com/2019/03/13/opinion/hate-politics.html
Hadot, Pierre. 2011. *Philosophy as a way of life: Spiritual exercises from Socrates to Foucault*. Oxford: Blackwell.
Hollingsworth, Amy. 2005. *The simple faith of Mister Rogers: Spiritual insights from the world's most beloved neighbor*. Nashville: Thomas Nelson.
Jung, C.G. 1954. *Psychology and education*. Princeton: Princeton University Press.
Lewis, C.S. 1980. *The weight of glory and other addresses*. New York: Macmillan.
Matthews, Gareth B. 1980. *Philosophy & the young child*. Cambridge, MA: Harvard University Press.
———. 1984. *Dialogues with children*. Cambridge, MA: Harvard University Press.
———. 1994. *The philosophy of childhood*. Cambridge, MA: Harvard University Press.
Mohr, Eric J., and Holly K. Mohr, eds. 2020. *Mister Rogers and philosophy: Wondering through the neighborhood*. Chicago: Open Court.
Piaget, Jean. 1951. *Play, dreams, and imitation in childhood*. New York: W. W. Norton.
Postman, Neil. 1994. *The disappearance of childhood*. New York: Vintage Books.
Tuchman, Barbara W. 1978. *A distant mirror*. New York: Alfred A. Knopf.
Tuttle, Shea. 2019. *Exactly as you are: The life and faith of Mister Rogers*. Grand Rapids: Eerdmans.

Futurama as Philosophy: Wisdom from the Ignorance of a Delivery Boy

11

Courtland D. Lewis

Contents

Introduction 234
Summarizing Futurama 235
Social and Political Philosophical Themes 236
    Freedom, Society, Free Speech, and Sex 237
    Robo-discrimination and Mutant Multiculturalism 239
    War Is the H-Word 241
    Peace and Nonviolent Waterfalls 242
Ethical Lessons from the 3000s 243
    Environmentalism and Animal Rights 244
    Corporate Deception and Motherly Greed 246
    Friendship and Suicide 246
Metaphysical Lessons 248
    Time-Space, Math, Free Will, Oh My 248
    Immortality and God 252
    True Meaning of Life 254
Conclusion 255
References 255

Abstract

Futurama is an animated series from creators Matt Groening (creator of *The Simpsons*) and David X. Cohen (television writer/producer) that centers on the adventures and friendships of twentieth century pizza delivery boy, Philip J. Fry, who gets cryogenically frozen on New Year's Eve 1999 and unceremoniously revived a 1000 years later. Fry learns to navigate the challenges of the year 3000 with surprising ease alongside a close set of comrades who comprise the thirty-first century delivery crew of Planet Express. More than a fish-out-of-water tale, *Futurama* explores a vast array of philosophical themes, including

---

C. D. Lewis (✉)
Philosophy, Pellissippi State Community College, Knoxville, TN, USA
e-mail: cdlewis1@pstcc.edu

© Springer Nature Switzerland AG 2024
D. K. Johnson et al. (eds.), *The Palgrave Handbook of Popular Culture as Philosophy*,
https://doi.org/10.1007/978-3-031-24685-2_27

233

environmentalism, animal liberation, friendship, sex, love, suicide, freedom, discrimination, corporate deception and greed, language, and time travel. As if that were not enough, they solve real-life mathematical conundrums, talk to God, and provide a satirical narrative that challenges viewers' ways of life. This chapter will examine these and other themes to help readers better understand how *Futurama* does philosophy and ponder the philosophical issues it raises.

Keywords

Futurama · Ethics · Metaphysics · Psychology · Friendship · Sex · Love · Freedom · Corporate deception · Greed · Suicide · Artificial intelligence · God · Time travel · Space-time · Discrimination · Fatalism · Flourishing

Introduction

Futurama is the classic tale of a young man's journey through life with friends. After being frozen for 1000 years, Philip J. Fry wakes to a world that is new and exciting, yet oddly familiar. Fry is still the oddball, but his twentieth century mentality makes him strangely suited to flourishing in this world of aliens, mutants, space travel, suicide booths, and Slurm – the popular soda of the thirty-first century. Creators Matt Groening and David X. Cohen, along with many talented writers, use *Futurama* as a mirror into our own twenty-first century lives, exploring many of the ethical and existential fears that we typically try to ignore. Just as they intended to raise the bar with their use of 3D animation, they also intended to make audiences engage with complex mathematical, space-time, and theological questions.

Like philosophers, the creators of *Futurama* had no sacred cows: beliefs too special to critique. Unlike philosophers, however, they rarely took sides on a position. To illustrate, for most of the episode "The Problem with Popplers" writers Patric M. Verrone and Darin Henry explore the ethics of eating animals, and throughout the episode, the implication to viewers is they should not eat meat. Yet, at the end, after narrowly escaping with their lives, the characters feast on a dinner of sentient animals, some of which exhibit higher-thought capacities; the Professor, for example, eats the speech-center of a dolphin's brain. This sort of satirical edge makes *Futurama* a bit different than other pieces of pop culture considered in this volume; as a result, this chapter will be a bit different as well. Instead of critiquing an argument, or answering a single question raised by the series, this chapter will provide an overview of how the show engages with philosophical issues, and thus weaves a complex and humorous tale that challenges viewers to self-reflect, think deeper, and become wiser.

The opening lines of the series offer a summary of the way *Futurama* will present life and its lessons throughout the show's 14-ish year run. As Fry plays a video game on New Year's Eve 1999, he speaks: "Space, it seems to go on and on forever, but then you get to the end and a gorilla starts throwing barrels at you . . . and that's how you play the game." The game is life, and the barrels are the trials and tribulations we all encounter as we do our best to exist. Taken by themselves, these words might just be the silly musings of a pizza delivery boy, but when understood in relation to the adventures that occur in future episodes, they are deeply profound. They tell us that life is filled with ups and downs. Some events seem to last forever, while others seem all-too-brief, and on our life's journey, there will be challenges and obstacles that attempt to prevent us from being happy.

What draws so many to *Futurama* is that it is a simple story of a man who gets caught up in a series of events beyond his control, and through luck and determination, ends up living a fascinating and extremely silly life with a whole host of friends, lovers, and crazy knife-wielding robots. Fry's story is the bedrock of great literature. The tales of Moses, Gilgamesh, Odysseus, Don Quixote, and Frodo are stories of flawed individuals called on to rise above their inadequacies and become a hero of their people. Fry is our twenty-first century hero, whether we're comfortable with it or not. One of the charms of *Futurama* is that it takes the mundane and presents it as new and strange, creating a science-fiction fantasy that serves as allegory for our lives.

This chapter will accomplish its goal by drawing heavily from arguments presented in my 2014 book *Futurama and Philosophy* (Lewis 2014b). After providing a brief summary of the show, the first section will examine social and political themes, such as multiculturalism and discrimination, corporate deception and greed, and individual freedom, including legal attempts to limit free speech and sexual behavior. The second section will examine the ethical lessons, which include environmentalism, animal liberation, friendship, love, and suicide. The third section will discuss metaphysical lessons dealing with time travel, space-time, mathematics, language, God, reality, and *Star Trek*.

Summarizing Futurama

Futurama first aired March 28, 1999, on the Fox Broadcasting Company television channel. It ran there until August 10, 2003. After its cancellation on FOX, *Futurama* showed regularly on Cartoon Network's adult-themed block of shows called Adult Swim from 2003 to 2007. Due to its popularity on Adult Swim, the crew created four direct-to-DVD films that would eventually air as season five on Comedy Central, starting on March 23, 2008. After syndication and renewal on Comedy Central, *Futurama* was contracted for two more seasons, culminating in a seven-season run that ended on September 4, 2013. In 2022, the online streaming service Hulu announced it will air a new season of *Futurama* in 2023.

Futurama centers on the lives of the Planet Express delivery company, run by Professor Hubert J. Farnsworth, an elderly, forgetful, doomsday-device-creating mad scientist who is the distant nephew of Philip J. Fry (aka "Fry"), the show's main character. Fry is a dim-witted but lovable "walking on sunshine" kind of loser who, again, is "accidentally" frozen on New Year's Eve 1999 and reanimated in the year 3000. Shortly after waking, he meets Turanga Leela, a one-eyed "alien" (it is later revealed she is a mutant) who will eventually become the pilot of the Planet

Express crew and Fry's unrequited love interest for most of the series. Bender, an alcohol drinking, foul-mouthed, kleptomaniac bending robot befriends Fry and eventually becomes his roommate and coworker at Planet Express. The remaining members of the Planet Express crew are Amy Wong, the Professor's graduate student, Hermes Conrad, Planet Express's bureaucrat, Planet Express's chief physician Dr. Zoidberg, an alien crustacean who is disliked by most and lacks basic medical knowledge of humans, and Scruffy, the "terlet"-cleaning custodian.

Though *Futurama* centers on the deliveries and personal lives of the Planet Express crew, the show examines the complex and mundane existence of thirty-first century life, both on Earth and throughout the galaxy. The show utilizes robots, aliens, mutants, politicians, academics, and overabundant human buffoonery to create a mixture of satire and slapstick that is humorous, thought-provoking, and often complex and insightful. Presented with crisp 3D animation and filled with time-traveling paradoxes and romantic escapades, *Futurama* won multiple Emmys, Annie Awards, Behind the Voice Actors Awards, Writers Guild of America Awards, and among others, two Environmental Media Awards.

Social and Political Philosophical Themes

As a type of satire, *Futurama* engages many social-political themes. The show rarely takes any particular position, so it does not offer any overarching philosophical arguments. The closest *Futurama* comes to an overarching theme is: (1) its insistence that people in power are mindless, incompetent idiots and (2) humans often avoid addressing the cause of their problems, choosing instead to cover up systemic issues and leaving the source of their problems for someone else to solve.

"A Big Piece of Garbage," which we will address again later, illustrates both themes nicely. With a giant ball of garbage heading towards Earth, lead scientist Professor Ogden Wernstrom is more concerned with tenure and revenge than saving the planet, and Mayor Poopenmayer is clueless about how to address the threat and how to make garbage. The ball itself is the result of twenty-first century humanity's inability to address the production of garbage, which led them to shoot it into space. Sure, they were warned it might return one day, but addressing the root cause of the problem was depressing, so they ignored the warning. The Planet Express crew does not fare any better. They simply create another ball of garbage to shoot into space with the knowledge that it too will return one day.

If there is a philosophy of never actually dealing with one's problems, I am unaware of it, but it is a theme throughout the series. One might point to Stoics, who taught we should avoid attachment to material things; their commitment to knowledge and virtue would prevent one from ignoring the root cause of problems. To ignore is a type of intellectual and physical laziness, which is a vice. Stoics were intent on avoiding vices, while the Planet Express crew, and most of the population of thirty-first century Earth, seem more than willing to embrace them. I will not attempt to develop a philosophy of laziness, but because episodic television must continually develop new stories despite occurrences in previous episodes, the inability of the Planet Express crew to solve issues adds to the show's humor and satire.

Freedom, Society, Free Speech, and Sex

Let us begin by considering the role of individuals within society. In *Futurama and Philosophy*, Joseph Foy and Timothy Dale examine the episode "Zoidberg's Freedom Lesson" to show how there is a persistent tension between individual freedom and the larger democratic community. In the episode, Dr. Zoidberg eats "Old Freebie" (a revered American Flag) as an expression of his love of freedom on Freedom Day, a day when you can supposedly do anything you want as an expression of freedom. Yet, after he professes his action, the crowd becomes furious and wants him killed. From John Stuart Mill's *On Liberty*, Foy and Dale note how Mill argues that human freedom and expression should be protected at all costs, unless such freedom and expression causes direct harm (Foy and Dale 2014, pp. 5–6). According to Mill, limiting freedom of speech robs humanity of something valuable, for "If the opinion is right, they are deprived of the opportunity of exchanging error for truth: if wrong, they lose, what is almost as great a benefit, the clearer perception and livelier impression of truth, produced by its collision with error" (Mill 1978, Chap. 2). So, no matter how unpopular an action or opinion, for Mill, they should only be prevented when they lead to direct harm. Zoidberg's actions were obviously offensive to the crowd, but since he didn't directly harm anyone by eating the flag, Mill would say his action should be permitted.

Foy and Dale utilize Joel Feinberg's "offense principle" (1985) to illustrate a possible weakness in Mill's position. According to Feinberg, "some expressions are so distasteful and offensive that they ought to be restricted, even if they don't actually harm someone else" (Foy and Dale 2014, p. 7). In other words, where Mill seems to limit "harm" to physical acts, Feinberg expands the "harm" to include offensive actions that harm a person's values, mental, and/or emotional states. If Feinberg is correct, then the question becomes whether the government should protect its citizens from offensive material or whether the protection of free speech is paramount.

Satirizing cases of flag burning, "Zoidberg's Freedom Lesson" leans towards Mill, defending the value of having beliefs challenged through things we find offensive. American legal precedent has established that acts of flag burning are a matter of free speech, but *Futurama* has Zoidberg found guilty and sentenced to death. In response, Zoidberg escapes to his Decapodian embassy, which then results in the Decapodians enslaving humanity. Zoidberg's love of freedom leads him to eventually free humans from their bondage in the only way he knows – he burns an American flag, in order to ensure a heat-seeking rocket hits its target. Surprisingly, society is not upset at Zoidberg for destroying the flag this time. What is the lesson? As mentioned previously, *Futurama* does not often take sides. Instead, the lesson seems to be a warning that freedom-loving people only appreciate freedom until their sensibilities are offended, at which point freedom is deemed dangerous.

Shaun Young's chapter "Slurm, Worms, and Jacking On" presents Isaiah Berlin's (2002) distinction between positive and negative liberty. Positive liberty occurs when a person uses their ability to rationally self-govern, while negative liberty occurs when a person is free from coercion. As Young notes, the former implies that impediments to freedom can be either physical or mental, while the latter only requires we be left alone to do as we wish (if our actions do not harm others). Using these concepts, Young looks at a variety of instances in *Futurama* where, as Jean-Jacques Rousseau suggests, characters possess negative liberty yet are not free (1997). The first example comes from "Anthology of Interest II," when Professor Farnsworth transforms Bender into a human. After a week of complete human "freedom," Bender becomes a "'bloated man-ball' with a pulse of 300, a failing liver, and a cholesterol level of forty pounds!" (Young 2014, p. 16). We might question Bender's rationality since his addictive personality leads him to make many self-destructive decisions. Bender is a slave to his passions, and though he has the rational capacities to feed these passions, he appears to lack the higher order reasoning that would allow him to make rational decisions in his best interests. In other words, he lacks the positive liberty to control the impulses to drink, eat, and party himself to death.

Similarly, in "Fry & the Slurm Factory," Fry is set free to save his friends from death, but due to an addiction to Slurm, he struggles to have the positive liberty to save his friends. When addiction occurs, agents lack the rational capacity to have positive liberty, even when there are no external physical impediments. Such examples are common, but in the episode "Parasites Lost," the parameters are reversed. Instead of being limited by addiction, Fry is improved by parasites that make him smarter and more lovable, at least in the eye of Leela. Fry, however, recognizes that his authentic self is not the parasitic-improved version loved by Leela, and even though he likes the improvements, he has lost the ability to self-govern. This lack of self-governing means he lacks positive liberty, and so, he rids the parasites from his body in order to return to a life of delivery boy buffoonery.

There are many ways in which a government might curtail human freedom, but one of the most common is through cultural mores that dictate ideas of normalcy and legislation designed to prevent certain types of relationships. Even in the 3000s, *Futurama* shows that humans continue to struggle with sexual exploration and maturity. Jerry Piven's chapter "Sexlexia and Other Sexy Learning Disabilities" details "...the deep abyss of existential pain and terror that gives rise to our sexualities" (2014, p. 58). No matter how normal the character appears, *Futurama* illustrates that deep down we all struggle to express ourselves sexually. Some of these struggles result from our own feelings of inadequacy, but many come from the society in which we are raised.

As seen in the previously mentioned "Zoidberg's Freedom Lesson," the people of Earth have holidays celebrating freedom; but when Old Man Waterfall explains how he lost a hand fighting to save Halley's Comet to protect human freedom, the crowd is disgusted by his freedom to be a polygamist. The freedom they support is constrained by a particular conception of freedom that does not accept the freedom of others to make their own decisions, whether that be eating a flag or marrying

11 *Futurama* as Philosophy: Wisdom from the Ignorance of a Delivery Boy

multiple partners. The episode "Proposition Infinity" illustrates the same point, questioning how a society full of heterosexual, homosexual, alien-sexual, mutant-sexual, and sexual avatar relationships can be so opposed to robosexual (sexual human-robot) relationships.

A final example to illustrate *Futurama*'s satirized "schizophrenic" approach to sexuality comes from "In-a-Gadda-Da-Leela," in which the Earth is threatened by an intergalactic sphere determined to censor, by destroying, every planet that it considers indecent. Zapp Brannigan and Leela are sent to destroy the sphere but fail due to an attack by the sphere. While Leela is unconscious from the crash, Zapp removes their clothes, traps Leela under a tree, and makes her believe they are the last humans. Despite Zapp's deception and Leela's monogamous relationship with Fry, the sphere finds Zapp and Leela's behavior wholesome and coerces them into having sex. So, on the one hand, the sphere censors a show like "Assarama," which is deemed explicit, but finds sexual exploitation and coerced sex with a nonconsensual partner "wholesome."

Robo-discrimination and Mutant Multiculturalism

Episodes like "Proposition Infinity" are designed to critique discrimination. Referencing California's 2008 referendum proposition 8, which banned same-sex marriage, "Proposition Infinity" details the love affair between Bender (a robot) and Amy (a human), which leads to an attempt to keep robosexual relationships illegal. Professor Farnsworth is one of Bender's and Amy's biggest critics and spearheads the fight against robosexual marriage, but as the story develops, viewers discover the Professor's hypocrisy: he was once in love with a robot. The episode, along with several others, illustrates the arbitrariness and hypocriticalness of most sexual taboos. *Futurama*'s diversity of characters offers several unique examinations of diversity, multiculturalism, and discrimination. Let us focus on two major examples.

First, robots are a constant reminder of slavery. Though many robots in *Futurama* appear to possess some form of free will, most are designed simply to serve humanity. As a lower class of society, they are seen as expendable and left to die in "Crimes of the Hot." They are seen as less-than-human, just as the Supreme Court of the United States determined African slaves to be property in Dred Scott v. Sanford (1857). Dred Scott's personhood was stripped from him, which is a common approach to creating a foundation for discrimination. Like people of African descent and women until the 1920s, robots are commonly portrayed as lacking free will, and this portrayal undermines their rational autonomy.

Immanuel Kant is best known for his arguments that rational autonomy is the basis of human worth and morality, illustrated by the Categorical Imperative. In *The Groundwork of the Metaphysics of Morals* (2012), Kant argued that morality should be grounded in reason, and that reason shows that we should always treat other rational persons as ends in themselves, never merely as a means to an end. Like a mathematical principle, the categorical imperative should be arrived at and followed by all rational agents; it should also protect them from the moral abuse of others since it demands that they must be treated with respect. As nice as that sounds, Kant's conclusion has been used by many to cruelly undermine certain persons' worth. Women, Africans, Asians, First Peoples, and (in *Futurama*) robots have all, at some point, been wrongly deemed "irrational" as a way of dehumanizing them – or, more accurately, "de-personalizing" them. It's an excuse to rob them of their free will and autonomy, make them seem less-than-human, "justify" their mistreatment, and make them unworthy of moral respect.

In addition to explicit discrimination, *Futurama* also uses robots to illustrate the more pernicious form of racism that comes from structural systems of normalcy. In both "Fear of a Bot Planet" and "Free Will Hunting," viewers are introduced to a planet of robots gripped by the fear of humans. Their fear is based on elaborate and farcical sets of lies designed to keep them from living free lives. Many humans are victims of similar worldviews that irrationally bias them against others. We see the effects of such brainwashing in "Free Will Hunting," when Bender gets sprayed with gas, just in case he was a human. Without any provocation or prior experience with humans, the robot is so frightened he is willing to kill instead of engaging his "enemy."

In his chapter "Queer Eye for the Robot Kind," Brian Onishi explores notions of normalcy in *Futurama*, pointing out how Leela's one eye is mocked and that robosexual relationships are considered taboo (Onishi 2014, p. 209). Using episodes like "Cyber House Rules," where Leela undergoes surgery to make it appear she has two eyes, Onishi demonstrates how notions of normalcy are constructed within cultures (Onishi 2014, p. 210). Nothing substantive has changed about Leela, but society now treats her as though she is a completely different person. As suggested by Michel Foucault in *Discipline and Punish*, society creates a set of norms and uses the threat of punishment to coerce the self-regulation of norms. To avoid the punishment that occurs beyond the public's viewing within prisons, citizens go to great lengths to avoid public scorn (1977).

We use cues from our communities and popular culture to help us navigate conceptions of normalcy, often using surgeries similar to Leela's to influence how people treat us. Sometimes, however, norms can be challenged to an extent that they evolve, and for Onishi, *Futurama* does just this by undermining concepts of normalcy, making us laugh at our own standards, which then challenge us to act differently. For example, we might be against same-sex marriage, but after watching "Proposition Infinity" or "A Taste of Freedom" and laughing at the ridiculous and arbitrariness of such laws and social mores, we might become more willing to change what we consider "normal."

The second example also comes from Leela, who serves as a constant reminder of the perniciousness of discrimination. Left at an orphanage after birth, she grew up thinking she was an alien. As a result, society accepted her as an alien, granting her the equal opportunities of all members. However, once her true mutant heritage became known, she was treated as a pariah. Drawing from the work of Edward Said's (1979) *Orientalism*, James Reitter suggests (in his chapter "Mutate! Mutate! Mutate!") that the mutants are seen as weak, threatening, and Other (Reitter 2014, p. 220). They are to be pitied and feared, discounting their folk culture and attitudes. Her outing illustrates how discrimination is grounded on hollow social concepts, designed to keep one or more groups of citizens in power while demeaning others.

Finally, in "The Mutants are Revolting," Leela leads the mutants in a protest against the human street-dwellers, which eventually leads to the establishment of equal rights. *Futurama* does not provide any specific notions of rights, but from the slogan "Freaqual Rights" displayed during their protest, we can see they mean something along the lines of a Contractarian theory rights. Though there are several types of Contractarian rights, John Locke and John Rawls are two of the most prominent. Locke examined the "state of nature," a fictional time prior to the existence of any government when humans are completely free, and within this state of nature, Locke identifies the inherent rights of life, liberty, and the pursuit of property. Since complete freedom inhibits the flourishing of the inhabitants of this state of nature, they decide to limit their freedom by entering into mutually beneficial contracts. These contracts create a government designed to protect the inherent rights of individuals which, though limiting the freedom of individuals, enhances their ability to seek what each considers the good life (1978).

Rawls, on the other hand, grounds rights in a decision-making procedure that helps individuals make just and fair decisions. He starts by imagining what he calls the original position, a hypothetical place of equality between individuals where all participants lack basic information about who they are in life, their social status, ethnicity, gender, religion, skin color, and everything else except for a personal self-interest and basic understanding of morality. From this original position, which exists behind what Rawls calls the veil of ignorance, participants will pick moral principles of fairness that serve as the Contractarian rights of society. Rawls's theory of rights then creates what he calls "justice as fairness," which is exemplified by two principles of justice:

- First Principle: Each person has the same indefeasible claim to a fully adequate scheme of equal basic liberties, which scheme is compatible with the same scheme of liberties for all.
- Second Principle: Social and economic inequalities are to satisfy two conditions: (1) They are to be attached to offices and positions open to all under conditions of fair equality of opportunity; and (2) They are to be to the greatest benefit of the least-advantaged members of society. (Rawls 1971, pp. 42–43)

For both Locke and Rawls, the rights that result from these social contracts govern the proper threat of individuals by ensuring that the basic rights of all citizens are respected in society.

War Is the H-Word

Speaking of the state of nature, Thomas Hobbes (1994) argues that prior to any government, humans existed in a state of complete freedom, where there was no right or wrong, no protections from others, and no cooperation or peace. It is a state of war, Hobbes argues, of complete hell, and individuals will do anything to escape this hell. Unlike the contracts suggested by Locke, which according to Hobbes are nothing but worthless pieces of paper, he maintains that individuals must give up all their freedoms in order to establish an all-powerful ruler – what he calls the Leviathan. The Leviathan, then, rules over society and serves as the almighty protector of each citizen's rights. When society breaks down, it returns to the state of nature, and this breaking down of society often occurs during times of war, which is all-too-common in the thirty-first century world of *Futurama*.

Whether defeating the Brain Balls or the pacifists of the Gandhi Nebula, the humans in *Futurama* (often led by Zapp Brannigan) love going to war, even if they are incompetent. Brannigan is just as likely to surrender in the face of a nonexistent threat (as he did with Lrrr in "Lrrreconcilable Ndndifferences") as he is to create random conflicts due to his stupidity (as he did in "Zapp Dingbat").

Just war theory has evolved to help make sense of moral and immoral wars. The first requirement of just war theory is that wars must have a just cause (*jus ad bellum*). In his chapter "Zapp Brannigan's Big Book of War," Daniel Malloy points to the Omicronians' invasion of Earth to protest an interrupted television show as an example of an unjust war ("When Aliens Attack"), whereas their invasion of Earth after millions of their children were eaten is justified ("The Problem with Popplers"). Another feature of just war theory is justified actions during war (*jus in bello*). Common rules of just war include not targeting noncombatants and that the means must be proportional to the ends (Lazar 2020). To be proportional, we must calculate measured responses that do not exceed the actions of our adversaries. Not only is proportionality difficult, due to how emotions create irrational feelings of revenge, but some wrongdoings have no proportional response. For instance, if an enemy attacks your munition supplies, proportionality allows you attack their munitions supply; but if they attack innocent civilians, attacking their innocent civilians does not become magically justified. Just war does not justify targeting innocent civilians, so proportionality requires you come up with some appropriate response that serves as a replacement for noncombatants.

As noted by Malloy, Zapp fails to meet the proportionality requirement. In "Love's Labours Lost in Space," Zapp claims to have sent wave after wave of his own people against the Killbots until they reached their preset kill limit. If his goal was to get the Killbots to shut down, then him sacrificing "wave after wave" seems proportional; but using a bomb powerful enough to destroy a planet to kill the Brain Balls during peace negotiations is clearly excessive (Malloy 2014, p. 39). Due to the apparent ease to justify any war and most actions during war, some argue that just war is an oxymoron. *Futurama* shows that war is just humans flexing their muscles and exhibiting fear and stupidity.

Peace and Nonviolent Waterfalls

On the other hand, *Futurama* does not offer a flattering view of pacifists and peace advocates either. Most pacifists and peace activists are from the "Waterfall" family

(Free Waterfall, Sr. and Jr., Old Man Waterfall, Free Waterfall III, Frida Waterfall, and Hutch Waterfall), and the Waterfalls are annoying, incompetent, and likely to end up dead. Leela is the only character with a fairly consistent position against war, but she is also among the most violent and aggressive characters. For example, in *Bender's Game*, Leela beats and forces the peace-loving centaurs (who settle debates with logical arguments) to help them defeat Momon (the fantasy world dragon version of a *Futurama* villain named Mom). *Futurama* ridicules pacifists and peace activists, but as Andrew Fiala argues (in *Transformative Pacifism: Critical Theory and Practice* [2018]) and Andrew Fitz-Gibbon argues (in *Pragmatic Nonviolence: Working Toward a Better World* [2021]), there are strong and defensible arguments for why it is better to live a life of peace than war.

First, pacifism and nonviolence are effective means for creating sustainable relationships and peace. Unlike war, which is destructive and either creates and/or intensifies animosity, pacifism and nonviolence strive for solutions that allow all parties to flourish without devolving into conflict. Second, pacifism does not condone violence by letting aggressors abuse victims. As Fiala notes, absolute pacifists – those who reject all violence, including self-defense – are rare; most adherents of pacifism and nonviolence only require violence be used as a last recourse. Even Gandhi justified violence when absolutely necessary or when motivated by justice. Finally, Robert Holmes argues that violence is always presumptively morally wrong and that the burden of proof to do violence is on the one who wants to do it. As he suggests, modern war has not made the world better, and that if we desire a better future, we must utilize pacifism and nonviolence (Holmes 2014).

Ethical Lessons from the 3000s

Futurama does not stake many high platitudes, but its use of robots offers insight into the nature of human morality. Curtis D. Von Gunten examines these issues in "Moral and Immoral Robots." Twenty-first century robots are advanced, but they lack the features that would make them capable of having moral capacity. They are tools that have instrumental value and when they stop working, we throw them out as trash. *Futurama*'s robots, on the other hand, think and act in ways almost identical to humans, which implies they too might have moral worth.

Gunten's first criteria for moral worth is sentience (Von Gunten 2014, p. 103), the ability to experience subjective mental states. Today's robots do not feel pleasure and pain like humans, but the robots of the thirty-first century do exhibit a wide range of emotions and feelings. If we base sentience on behavior – if something behaves like it feels then it does – then we would conclude *Futurama*'s robots are sentient. But just because something behaves like it has sentience does not necessarily mean it actually has it, and so the fact that *Futurama*'s robots behave as if they have feelings doesn't necessarily mean they are moral agents.

If we are to conclude that a being is sentient and thus a moral agent, some philosophers suggest that that being must not only behave like they have feelings but must also be made of the right "stuff" (Von Gunten 2014, p. 105). Since, on face value, humans and robots seem to be vastly different, we might conclude that they are not sentient. But when properly understood, we share many similarities – although the element that holds our molecules together is different (we are carbon based and robots are silicon), both humans and robots both have a network of circuitry run on electrical impulses. So, in a way, we are made of the same "right" stuff.

Further, one might argue, that when it comes to moral agency, it shouldn't be an issue of composition but rather an issue of action. In order to have agency, a being must have some sort of volitional control. If robots are simply beholden to their programming, then they lack moral agency; they can't be held responsible for what they do. But if they have control over at least some of their actions – and it seems that *Futurama*'s robots do – they can be said to be moral agents (Von Gunten 2014, p. 109). If this is true, the stage is set for some interesting moral conundrums.

Environmentalism and Animal Rights

The previously discussed episode "A Big Piece of Garbage" provides a comprehensive examination of the environmental issues that plague the twenty-first century. As Jason Buchanan discusses in "Futurama and the Economy of Trash," the consumer-based economy of the twenty-first century creates a set of problems that threaten all future generations. Consumerism is an economic and social system based on the manufacturing of goods for mass consumption. Desires for goods are then manufactured through advertising and public relations campaigns, where the concepts of being a good citizen and a living a good life are associated with the attainment of consumer goods – and consumers place sentimental value on goods that are ultimately only trash. As long as consumers keep buying "trash," the economy remains healthy, and according to advertisements, our lives will be filled with pleasure. As was mentioned before, humanity's inability to control their consumption and expulsion of their "valuable goods" – in other words, trash – led them to shoot their waste into space, with the "depressing" warning that it might return. In true *Futurama* fashion, the ball of garbage returns and the only way for humanity to save itself is to relearn how to make trash and shoot another rocket to rid themselves of the threat. In the process, Buchanan maintains, "The episode compels the audience to reflect on how society must do more than promote recycling to fix the issues produced by our production of waste" (Buchanan 2014, p. 29). No longer can we be willfully ignorant of the connection between society and nature, but morality requires we reframe our lives to live them better, healthier, and greener.

One of the challenges of environmental ethics is how we treat animals. One of the most profound episodes, "The Problem with Popplers," illustrates the struggle to categorize animals as being deserving of ethical treatment. Similar to the previous discussion of robots, there is major debate over what feature(s) determine who is part of the moral community and even greater debate over whether animals have such features. In the episode, the Planet Express crew discover a delicious tasting, chicken nugget-like food source on a planet, and quickly decide to sell their discovery to hungry patrons. After contracting with Joseph "Fishy Joe" Gilman to sell "popplers" in his restaurants, anti-meat protestors emerge and Leela discovers that if left alone, popplers become sentient creatures capable of child-like communication. The stage is now set to debate the ethics of eating popplers, and Greg Ahrenhoerster's and Joseph Foy's chapter "Pop a Poppler?" presents how each character in the episode represents an ongoing debate about animal rights. According to Ahrenhoerster and Foy, Free Waterfall Jr. presents an argument based on Jeremy Bentham's ethical theory of utilitarianism (1982). According to utilitarianism, an ethical choice is one that maximizes the pleasure of all those involved, while at the same time minimizing pain. As a result, it is unethical to eat anything that can feel pain without first considering if the pleasure we receive from eating the creature outweighs the creature's pain (Ahrenhoerster and Foy 2014, p. 114). On the other hand, Fishy Joe rejects the moral worth of animals feeling pain, and instead, argues that might makes right. Better known as the "food chain" argument, Fishy Joe suggests that because humans are the planet's dominant predator, they have the right to eat anything they want; and that the only reason we do not eat other humans is they taste bad. So, he has the right (and so do we all) to eat and sell any sort of food, as long as he has the power (Ahrenhoerster and Foy 2014, p. 117). Finally, Leela presents an argument that suggests moral worth is the result of higher brain functioning. To have moral worth, one must have certain cognitive capacities of rational thought, self-awareness, and among other things, language. From this argument, it is only wrong to eat animals that are intelligent, which is thought to be a common view among many people today. (This, supposedly, is why we generally think it's okay to eat fish, but not dolphin; cows, but not humans.)

Leela's argument serves as a middle road between Waterfall Jr.'s "eat no meat" view and Fishy Joe's "eat whatever we want because we are on top" view, but it commits a mistake that some scholars (like Peter Singer 1990) call "speciesism": unjustly favoring your species (or aspects of it) over others simply because you belong to the species. Leela favors the intelligence of her species and therefore requires other creatures to have intelligence akin to her own in order to be protected. Fishy Joe is a speciesist too – for when the obviously more powerful Omicronians appear, he quickly rejects his argument that might makes right in favor of a "all humans are special" argument. At the end of the day, all three arguments from Waterfall Jr., Fishy Joe, and Leela are rejected. Fishy Joe contradicts himself, Leela's intelligence does not protect her from being put on the menu, and Waterfall Jr. is eaten by Lrrr.

According to Ahrenhoerster and Foy, sentimentality wins the day (Ahrenhoerster and Foy 2014, p. 120). Just as Bender and Zapp decide to save Leela because they like her, the lesson seems to be that the only reason we choose not to eat some animals is because we have sentimental feelings. We do not eat our pets because they are special to us, but we care nothing about the random cow, chicken, or pig that fits between our slices of bread. Pigs are as intelligent as dogs; yet we would never eat the latter, but eat the former regularly. That's not to say this approach is morally defensible, but it does seem to be the one we employ.

Corporate Deception and Motherly Greed

In addition to animal ethics, "The Problem with Popplers" illustrates issues of Business Ethics. Fishy Joe's greed makes him immune to the pleas of an intelligent creature asking not to be eaten. But Fishy Joe pales in comparison to Mom, owner of MomCorp, whose desire for profit and power causes her to commit many unethical actions. She attacked Fry in "A Fishful of Dollars" because he bought the last can of sardines. In *Bender's Game*, she attempts to monopolize space travel by controlling all dark matter. Finally, in "Mother's Day," she perverts Professor Farnsworth's Q.T. McWhiskers children's toy that shoots rainbows out of its eyes into eight-foot killing machines that shoot neutron lasers and uses her power to get robots to take over the world.

Albert Z. Carr argues that business ethics is an oxymoron. Instead of being governed by normative rules, Carr maintains that business is governed by a set of rules similar to the game of poker (1968). The goal of poker is to win, and to win is to manipulate and bluff your way to the highest winnings possible. You are not supposed to cheat, but you disadvantage and set yourself up for failure if you do not use the rules to take advantage of competitors and employees. Milton Friedman supports Carr's argument and takes it one step further, arguing that any actions not dedicated to maximizing profits (e.g., acts of social responsibility) not only robs shareholders of their money but threatens to devolve society into socialism (1970). Carr never presents an argument against socialism. He simply assumes readers in the 1970s would agree.

The business climate of *Futurama* is governed by the ideas of Carr and Friedman. Mom's constant violations of the rights of others is always in the name of maximizing profit, as is Professor Farnsworth's treatment of his employees (which continually puts them at risk) and Fishy Joe's willingness to commit genocide. Slurm is marketed as a soda, even though it is simply a secretion from the Queen Slurm worm, and Slurm's MacKenzie is the company's enslaved mascot designed to increase profits.

Although Farnsworth is one of the main characters, the other characters who employ Carr and Friedman's philosophy are generally portrayed as villains. Thus, we can conclude, *Futurama* condemns this ethical philosophy. And that makes sense. Corporations are, at least somewhat, like people; we would consider anyone who is always, and only, acting in their own self-interest psychopathic. And corporations doing so is the main contributor to climate change. The overabundance of unethical businesses in *Futurama* adds to the satire illustrating the dangers of letting businesses run free in the name of maximizing profits.

Friendship and Suicide

One of the most persistent themes in *Futurama* is friendship. According to Aristotle, there are three motivations for friendship: utility, pleasure, and virtue. Friendships of utility occur when both parties are able to utilize the other for their own benefit.

11 *Futurama* as Philosophy: Wisdom from the Ignorance of a Delivery Boy

These are like your work friends who help you achieve professional tasks, but who you spend no time with outside of work nor share any personal details with about your life. Friendships of pleasure might be the same as those of utility, but they are people you enjoy being around. You probably spend time with them outside of work, and though you might engage in pleasurable physical activities, like when Fry and Amy visit Mercury in "Put Your Head On My Shoulders," you refrain from sharing the personal secrets and goals of your life. Friendships of virtue are the deeply emotional and enriching friendships you have with people who seem to complete your life. They are like extensions of yourself in that when they flourish you flourish, and when they suffer, you suffer (2012).

Futurama illustrates nicely the complexity of friendships, often blurring the lines between Aristotle's three categories. Friendships are often antagonistic and sometimes abusive. Bender constantly mistreats Fry, and Fry does not care. It is part of their relationship and he likes it. Leela is dismissive of Fry throughout the series, but he remains steadfastly in love. Everyone is abusive to Zoidberg but they remain together and, in some instances, show there is a true fondness ("The Tip of the Zoidberg" and "The Six Million Dollar Mon"). Friendship in *Futurama* centers on a shared activity that causes their lives to overlap in similar activities. Similar to Nicholas Wolterstorff's love of activity (2019), where love is an activity of togetherness and growth instead of simply an emotion you feel towards someone, the members of the Planet Express crew delight and relish the activity of working together; sometimes they argue, sometimes they laugh, and they often cycle through all three of Aristotle's categories of friendship. Yes, they get on each other's nerves and are unrelenting in their teasing, and at times, you might even think they are enemies; but they continue to effectively work together and overcome obstacles, growing and appreciating each other in their unique and complex ways. Just as Fry's relationship with his parents illustrates an antagonistic form of love, friendships throughout the series are never "mushy." They are hard-edged, difficult, and complex.

With suicide booths on most street corners, *Futurama* shows that the thirty-first century has accepted suicide and facilitated its choice by all citizens. Though there are usually people standing in line to use the booths, the thirty-first century does not seem to have a culture of suicide. Like those of us living in the twenty-first century, people seem willing to continue living in the face of difficulties and disappointment. As seen in cases like Elizabeth Bouvia's, a right-to-die activist who is almost completely paralyzed by cerebral palsy, has severe degenerative arthritis, and has suffered from broken relationships and depression, the fight for the right to die is fundamentally a fight to control one's life (see Pence 2014). When Bouvia gained the right to die, she took control of her life and decided to live. In other words, fighting for the right to die does not mean one wants to die. Instead, the right to die is a right to control what happens to one's life.

Though Bender uses the suicide booth more than any other character, there is an underlying inconsistency in his use of the booth. He always uses a coin tied to a string, in order to save his money for *future* uses. At one point, he even started dating one of the booths, which eventually led to him being "killed" by her – she was jealous because he cheated on her! (No worries, for after some shenanigans with the Robot Devil in "Ghost in the Machines," Bender's ghost returns to his former body.) Instead of promoting death, *Futurama* supports a willingness to keep going in the face of life's difficulties. If anyone had a reason to use a suicide booth, it would be Fry or the mutants, but thoughts of suicide never seem to cross their minds. Take, for instance, the famous historical people whose heads are in jars. By the thirtieth century, thanks to a special fluid, peoples' heads can be revived and sustained indefinitely in glass jars. Besides misfits like Richard Nixon and those abducted (Lucy Liu and the bridge crew from *Star Trek: The Original Series*), they mostly sit around in museums, being fed like fish, and talking to the occasional guest. You would think their lives the most boring and meaningless, yet like the Myth of Sisyphus, they all seem content pushing their rock up the hill of life.

Metaphysical Lessons

Futurama offers a unique vision of the world with heads in jars, a binary God, and a whole lot of physics and time travel. The show combines lowbrow humor with an intelligence that satisfies the geekiest of fans. This final section will look at a few of the more complex and prevalent themes found throughout the show.

Time-Space, Math, Free Will, Oh My

Three episodes exemplify *Futurama*'s use of time travel. First, "Roswell that Ends Well" has the Planet Express crew accidentally travel back in time to 1947 America at the height of nuclear testing and supposed alien incursions. Zoidberg is captured by the military, but what leads to the biggest time meddling is Fry's desire to protect his grandfather Enos from being killed. In his chapter "On Becoming Your Own Grandfather," Dan Burkett explains how the episode explores David Lewis's Grandfather Paradox (1976). The paradox suggests that if you go back in time and kill your own grandfather, then you will cease to exist, which means you are incapable of going back in time and killing your own grandfather. Yet, if you do not go back in time and kill your grandfather, then you exist, and you are able to kill your own grandfather. The paradox suggests that it is impossible to travel back in time (because it is logically impossible to both kill and not kill your own grandfather).

Lewis argues, however, that time travel might be possible after all – if, at least, time travel does not entail the ability to change the past. According to Lewis, on this view of time travel, if you try to kill your grandfather, something will always happen to prevent his death – the gun will not fire, you will always miss, etc. The Grandfather Paradox remains interesting because we can imagine killing our own grandfather, which implies it is theoretically possible to do so. But if Lewis' view of time travel is correct, it is not. Any such attempt will inevitably fail. If that's true, time travel does not make possible logically impossible circumstances, and thus is at

11 *Futurama* as Philosophy: Wisdom from the Ignorance of a Delivery Boy

least possible; but it's not all that useful. You could go back and observe the past, but you could not change it.

The writer of the episode, J. Stewart Burns, avoids the grandfather paradox by having Fry take the place of his grandfather after accidentally getting him killed. After getting Enos killed, Fry reasons that Enos must not have been his grandfather after all, since he (Fry) is still alive. As a result, Fry takes advantage of the opportunity to have sex with the emotionally vulnerable Mildred, who he reasons cannot be his grandmother for the same reason Enos was not his grandfather. Shortly after inseminating Mildred, however, the Professor and Leela explain how Fry has become (or, in fact, has always been) his own grandfather. Such a solution avoids the Grandfather Paradox but creates what is called a Bootstrapping Paradox where we must determine how Fry can both be created by and creator of himself. Fry is what philosophers call a "jinnee," a self-created object. But while they seem paradoxical, they are possible on Lewis' conception of time travel. In the causal circle that a Jinnee creates – A causes B, which causes C, which causes A (or in Fry's case, Fry creates his father, who creates Fry) – nothing is uncaused.

Paradoxes seem to go hand-in-hand with time travel, which is why in *Bender's Big Score*, the writers created a time-traveling device that contains paradox-correction features (like the Time Code). As Dan Burkett notes, it is unclear how *Futurama*'s paradox-correcting features work, and they seem to create just as many problems for those that use them (Burkett 2014, p. 144). After all, the only thing clear about how the Time Code works is that duplicates of individuals, which are created by time travel, are always killed. Yet, the episode creates the same kind of bootstrap paradoxes seen in "Roswell that Ends Well." Individuals seem to be both the cause and effect of events. By the end, Bender's thievery creates so many paradoxes that he creates a rip in the fabric of space-time. Therefore, *Futurama* shows that even with paradox-correcting technology, time travel remains precarious. As Burkett concludes, time travel does not allow for the logically impossible, like killing your own grandfather or stealing an earlier version of yourself, but it does allow for lots of other bizarre things (like jinnee), and *Futurama* excels at showing us the possibilities (Burkett 2014, pp. 147–148).

The final episode that exemplifies time travel is "The Late Philip J. Fry." In the episode, the Professor takes Bender and Fry on a trip in his forward-traveling time machine. Intending only to travel a few minutes into the future, the Professor accidentally sends them into the distant future. Without the ability to travel backwards in time, they continue moving forward in hopes of finding a time when a backwards-traveling time machine exists. When this fails, they give up on ever going back in time and move forward to its end – only to discover that the universe starts over with another Big Bang – and plays out exactly as it did before. So, if they want to return "home," they merely have to keep moving forward (to the point in this new universe "analogous" to the moment they left the other). Of course, they miss their target and have to "bring it around again," to do it a third time; but eventually they arrive back at their original starting point (or, at least, a point in the new universe that is almost exactly like the one they left). Karl Laderoute (2014) examines the episode in his chapter "A Billion Years Late for Dinner" and suggests it illustrates several scientific theories along with Friedrich Nietzsche's concept of eternal recurrence (1974).

One scientific theory illustrated is the idea that our universe is (and all subsequent universes are) deterministic. In a deterministic system, everything happens according to the laws of causality such that, everything that happens at any given moment was causally necessitated by what happened the moment before it. Think of a billiard table; the moment a cue ball is hit; if you knew its trajectory and spin, the location of the other balls, and had perfect knowledge of the laws of physics, you would be able to predict exactly what all the balls were going to do. The idea that our universe is a deterministic system is the idea that our universe is, essentially, a three-dimensional billiard table, where atoms are the balls and space itself is the billiard table. Since we are made of atoms and our actions are produced by our brains (a physical organ made of atoms), our behavior would be just as predictable as anything else. The philosopher Pierre-Simon Laplace imagined a demon, with perfect knowledge of the universe, that was able to deduce the entire history of the universe – including everything that everyone would ever do – by simply knowing its initial state and the laws of physics (Hoefer 2016).

"The Late Philip J. Fry" calls to mind the idea that the universe is deterministic because deterministic systems repeat when restarted. Rack the billiard balls in exactly the same way and hit the cue ball in exactly the same way, and exactly the same thing will happen. The fact that (in the episode) a "second" big bang produces exactly the same kind of universe as the one before – including where everyone does everything they did before – suggests that our universe is deterministic.

The idea that the universe repeats itself also brings to mind Nietzsche's concept of the eternal recurrence – the idea that we are fated to repeat the lives we live (1974). The idea is not that we actually are fated to the same life over and over, but that you can judge the quality of your own life by determining how you would react to that prospect. If you would rejoice, you are probably good – living life to its fullest. If you would recoil, however, it seems that you are doing something wrong – and should probably change the way you are living (so that your life is something that you would want to repeat). This is illustrated in "Meanwhile," the final episode of the series; as Professor Farnsworth begins to press a button that will restart the entire series, Fry and Leela are smitten with the prospect of doing it all one more time.

But the idea that the universe is deterministic makes one wonder whether such a change is possible, or (more specifically) whether one could choose to change. If all events, including our actions, have been determined since the beginning of the universe, how could we act other than how we are determined to act? In fact, if our actions are determined by the activity for our brain, and its activity is determined by its configuration, and its configuration is determined by our genetics and environment, we might say that we are programmed to act as we will. If we are, how can we act freely?

Futurama attacks this question directly. In "Free Will Hunting," Bender is troubled by the implication that he can't be found guilty of his crimes because as a robot he is controlled by his programming. This means he lacks free will and thus is not culpable for his actions. As a proud criminal, Bender wants moral credit for his

11 *Futurama* as Philosophy: Wisdom from the Ignorance of a Delivery Boy   251

crimes; so he sets out to prove he has free will. After a long journey, he discovers that the Professor has a free will device specifically designed for robots. Of course, there is a catch. Due to the quantum nature of the device, you can never know if the device is on or off. So, any robot who attempts to use the device will never know for certain whether they are acting based on free will or their programming.

Ultimately, we humans are faced with the same dilemma. In the face of arguments for determinism or complete randomness, our claims of free will often seem either based in faith, the suggestion that our free will is just a brute fact of the universe or an unwillingness to accept the conclusion that there is no free will (despite our inability to refute it). Jean-Paul Sartre (1948) suggests we recognize our free will at the moment we recognize we can end our life by stepping off a steep precipice. For Sartre, humans are born without an essence, unlike artifacts created with their purpose built into their design. Humans can choose to be and do anything, including ending their life. This radical freedom is the basis of Sartre's claim that existence precedes essence – the definition of existentialism. Our choices determine our essence, and in order to have choices, we must have free will. In "Free Will Hunting," the Professor explains that Bender is incapable of harming himself or using the "free will" unit designed for robots. Farnsworth decides to test Bender's free will by giving him the free will unit and challenging him to shoot him with a gun. Bender is apparently incapable of shooting Farnsworth, which is supposed to illustrate that his programming and free will lead to the same result – an unwillingness to shoot. However, in classic *Futurama* fashion, Bender realizes the safety is on, turns it off, shoots, and is found guilty of attempted murder – free will proven!

Part of what makes *Futurama* intriguing is dedication to precision. All the stories dealing with time travel and free will illustrate how the writers are concerned with ensuring storylines are logically correct. One of the most impressive examples of their precision occurs when Ken Keeler (who holds a PhD in Math) developed a mathematical theorem to solve the mind-swapping conundrum faced in the episode "The Prisoner of Benda." After developing a mind-swapping device, the Professor switches minds with Amy, thereby allowing them to follow their dreams: the Professor wants youth and Amy wants to be able to eat anything at will. They quickly discover that the machine only allows the same body-pairs to switch once. What results is a series of mind-swaps that threaten to prevent the characters from returning to their original bodies. In what is probably the only mathematical theorem proved on popular television, Ethan "Bubblegum" Tate and "Sweet" Clyde Dixon of Globetrotters fame prove how to return all minds to their rightful bodies. According to the "Futurama Theorem," "regardless of how many mind switches between two bodies have been made, they can still be restored to their original bodies using only two extra people, provided these two people have not had any mind switches prior (assuming two people cannot switch minds back with each other after their original switch" (theinfosphere.org 2015). Keeler downplayed the importance of his theorem to group theory, but I will let the Philosophers of Mathematics determine its significance. Regardless, it is a telling feature of the intellectual rigor of *Futurama*.

Futurama's engagement with these and other lessons create a rich and textured show that keeps fans engaged and learned about several metaphysical issues. One further illustration of their attempt to raise the bar of animated television is how they created an alien language to deliver secret messages to fans. Fans did not disappoint. They quickly learned the language and created websites that translate these hidden messages. *Futurama* does more than just entertain. They recognize the intelligence of fans and attempt to treat them with deep (and silly) lessons about the great mysteries of the universe.

Immortality and God

Two of the greatest human mysteries are immortality and the existence of God. *Futurama* offers several insights into forms of immortality. As already mentioned, in "The Late Philip J. Fry" and "Meanwhile," the possibility of an eternal recurrence of reality suggests a cyclical immortality based on the ever-turning wheel of time. Another form of immortality suggested by *Futurama* is their ability to preserve heads in jars for indefinite periods of time. Such a sustained existence threatens monotony and boredom, our metaphysical status as humans, and undermines what motivates humans to exist in the face of death.

Philosopher and theologian Charles Hartshorne (1952) provides three arguments that address these worries over an immortal subjective existence. First, the spatio-temporal status of humans-as-finite-beings changes if they become infinitely immortal. Hartshorne worries that immortal existence would eventually lead to humans and God being indistinguishable. If immortal, humans would cease to be uniquely created beings and, over time, would rival the abilities of God. Hartshorne's second argument is if humans, like God, gained the ability to see the world from multiple viewpoints over an infinite amount of time, they would lose their personal identity and cease to be recognizable as humans. Hartshorne's third argument is that immortality inevitably leads to boredom and monotony, an argument supported also by Bernard Williams (1973). If we lived forever, our experiences would eventually cease to be enriching; we would become disinterested and long for death. To imagine the monotony of an eternal existence, think of the lives of elderly individuals who have lost their zest for life and wait in anticipation for death's release (Lewis 2013).

In my chapter "We're Gathered to Remember," I suggest that *Futurama* offers another vision of what immortality is, one in which it is achieved through having relationships and making ourselves part of others (Lewis 2014a). Stated differently, through our relationships we share part of our character, and our character inspires others to act in certain ways. So instead of being immortalized as a statue, as Bender attempts in "A Pharaoh to Remember," we are immortalized in how we are remembered and how our personality traits are passed through those we influence, even if our names are lost to the sands of time.

Futurama is not afraid to tackle any subject, and their handling of God is as insightful as it is graceful. In "Godfellas," Bender is not only mistaken for God but meets a binary space being that appears to be God. In regard to the former, after being shot through space and colliding with an asteroid, a set of creatures begin to emerge on his body. They refer to him as God, asking for help and providing alms. Bender struggles to act appropriately. When he helps, people are harmed. When he does nothing, they are all wiped out. Upon learning this valuable lesson, he encounters what he takes to be God. After Bender explains his difficulties, God states, "When you do things right, people won't be sure you've done anything at all." So instead of a comic romp criticizing God's inabilities or God's lack of engagement, *Futurama* offers one of the most thoughtful explorations on the difficulties of being God found on television.

It's not without its problems, of course. If God doing things right means we won't know if God did anything, then his nonexistence is indistinguishable from his existence. While this would mean that the existence of evil cannot count as evidence against God's existence, it would also mean that theism (the belief that God exists) is unfalsifiable, and thus irrational. What's more, no one could ever look at any feature of the universe and say it was evidence for God's existence.

Nicholas Oschman's "On Bendered Knees" illustrates another set of lessons from *Futurama* that deal with the problem of evil – the idea that evil should not exist, if an all-powerful, all-knowing, and all-good God exists. For Oschman, *Futurama* suggests God does exist, and that as a result, there is a type of divine plan for our lives. If true, then any evil that does exist must be allowed by God for the purpose of enabling us to better ourselves – what Farnsworth would call "hogwash about the human spirit" (Oschman 2014, p. 169). Suggested by theologians such as John Hick (1966) and Richard Swinburne (1998), evil serves as a means for soul building or as a means of creating the "greater good" of God's divine plan. There are several issues with such arguments, including the fact that some evils are more apt to destroy souls than to build them up towards enlightenment, and that some evils are superfluous. If evil only exists for soul building or to achieve God's divine plan, then there should be no superfluous evil. If superfluous evil exists, then it undermines arguments for its consistency with an all-knowing, all-powerful, all-good God.

Another interesting discussion of God from within *Futurama* is outlined in John DePoe's chapter "Room for God in *Futurama*?" In the chapter, DePoe examines the nature of belief in God and suggests that, at the end of the day, *Futurama* shows that belief in God versus competing theories (like atheism) comes down to one's understanding of simplicity (DePoe 2014, p. 155). DePoe's argument rests on what is called a fine-tuning argument, which suggests that the laws that govern the universe are "fine-tuned" for the existence of life (i.e., any slight change in their values would mean that life could not exist). According to DePoe, this can only be explained by God or a multiverse; either a divine creator ensures that the laws are exactly what they need to be, or there are (or have been) a multitude of universes, each with its own chance to have "the right kind of laws," and ours is simply the one that "got it right." Now, as David Kyle Johnson (2022) points out, there are several challenges to the fine-tuning argument that must be answered before one can accept it. But for DePoe, both the "God" and "multiverse" explanations rest on a belief that is metaphysically primitive, that "has no deeper explanation or cause [other] than its mere existence" (p. 155). So to determine which is correct, the believer must decide (a la Occam's Razor) which belief is simpler.

But what does it mean for a belief to be simpler? In this context, it means for it to be more "parsimonious," and Alan Baker gives an in-depth explanation of parsimony where he quotes Albert Einstein. "[T]he grand aim of all science...is to cover the greatest possible number of empirical facts by logical deductions from the smallest possible number of hypotheses or axioms." According to Baker, "Occam's Razor (OR) is often wielded against metaphysical theories which involve allegedly superfluous ontological apparatus," but that the aim of OR is more about "shifting the burden of proof, and less about refuting the less simple theory outright." Baker suggests that "contemporary philosophers have tended to reinterpret OR as a principle of theory choice..." If given a choice between two theories, we should pick the one that is more parsimonious. "If two theories, T_1 and T_2, have the same ontological commitments except that T_2 is ontologically committed to Fs and T_1 is not, then T_1 is more parsimonious than T_2" (Baker 2016). For DePoe, *Futurama* does not answer the question of God's existence in our world, but instead, shifts the burden of proof onto us to determine which theory (God or the Multiverse) is more parsimonious.

Or consider the episode "A Clockwork Origin," where the Professor is flummoxed by Creationists and their unwillingness to accept scientific proof. He decides to leave Earth and live on a planet free from ignorance. In the process of terraforming his new planet, he releases a group of nanobots that within 3 days evolve into a thriving robot civilization. These robots are strict adherents of evolutionary theory and are horrified when the Professor suggests he is their creator. Their reaction is the same as the Professor's previous reaction, but he has now seen how both creation and evolutionary processes can work together. Without a time machine, we cannot be certain of either, and based on our assumptions about reality and simplicity, Creationism and Evolution are both possible true explanations.

To be clear, Creationism and Evolution are only compatible if by "Creationism" we mean "theistic evolution" which maintains that God created the universe billions of years ago and let it evolve. "Scientific creationism," the claim that the Earth is only 6000 years old, is neither compatible with evolution, empirically justifiable, nor scientific. *Futurama*'s key lesson, nevertheless, is that we should NOT believe in anything without careful examination of the facts. *Futurama* rejects dogmatism of any kind; and just as official Catholic Doctrine accepts both evolution or creationism (as defined above), *Futurama* shows how it is possible that both are true without arguing for or against either. The only thing we must avoid is ignoring facts and explanations simply because they do not mesh with our desire to be correct. That is when you become worthy of ridicule in *Futurama*.

True Meaning of Life

The most subtle lesson in *Futurama* is that *Star Trek* is the paradigm for all reality. Every episode contains some sort of *Star Trek* reference or borrowed sound effect, and Zapp Brannigan is the embodiment of Captain Kirk. The power of "The Holy Trek" is illustrated most perfectly in "Where No Fan Has Gone Before," when we learn how *Star Trek* became a religion and threatened to overtake the world. Even though in the *Futurama* universe, *Star Trek* is banned, it is obvious that its influence pervades the writing and themes of *Futurama*. As Fry and an energy being named Melllvar battle to be crowned the biggest *Star Trek* fan, there is a subtle implication that we all have meaning-framing paradigms that filter all experiences into what we consider reality. As I argue in *The Real Meaning of Doctor Who* (2021), popular culture has the power to educate and frame how we interpret the world. It teaches us concepts of normalcy, friendship, and love which inform every aspect of our existence. The authors of *Futurama and Philosophy* consistently suggest that *Futurama* does the same (Lewis 2014b). Fry's ability to interpret the world and flourish in the strangest of situations teaches viewers how to handle their own life events. The lunacy of the thirty-first century helps us laugh and deal with the lunacy of our world. The satire helps us poke fun at our society and hopefully motivates us to make it better. At least that is what Al Gore, who appears in several episodes, would want us to do. Of course, the Professor would probably just blow it all up. Who is right? You will have to watch and decide for yourself.

Conclusion

Futurama's approach to philosophy is to reflect our ignorance and arrogance through satirical comedy. As viewers laugh at the screen, they are also challenged to recognize their own foibles and hopefully inspired to be wiser. With sharp wit and technical efficiency, the creators and writers of *Futurama* present an impressive array of philosophical examinations. I have attempted to present a few of them in this chapter, but I also challenge readers to watch the show and learn the show's lessons for themselves. The thirty-first century might seem like it is too far away, but *Futurama* shows it is much the same as the twenty-first century, with many of the same fears and lessons.

References

Ahrenhoerster, Greg, and Joseph J. Foy. 2014. Pop a poppler? In *Futurama and philosophy: Pizza, paradoxes, and. . .good news!* ed. Courtland Lewis, 113–124. Owensboro: PhilDoc Books.

Aristotle. 2012. *Nicomachean ethics*. Trans. and ed. Robert C. Bartlett, and Susan D. Collins. Chicago: The University of Chicago Press.

Baker, Alan. 2016. Simplicity. In *The Stanford encyclopedia of philosophy*, ed. Edward N. Zalta. https://plato.stanford.edu/archives/win2016/entries/simplicity/.

Bentham, Jeremy. [1780/1789] 1982. *An introduction to the principles of morals and legislation*, ed. J.H. Burns, and H.L.A. Hart. London: Methuen.

Berlin, Isaiah. 2002. In *Liberty*, ed. H. Hardy. Oxford: Oxford University Press.

Buchanan, Jason. 2014. Futurama and the economy of trash. In *Futurama and philosophy: Pizza, paradoxes, and. . .good news!* ed. Courtland Lewis, 23–31. Owensboro: PhilDoc Books.

Burkett, Dan. 2014. On becoming your own grandfather. In *Futurama and philosophy: Pizza, paradoxes, and. . .good news!* ed. Courtland Lewis, 139–148. Owensboro: PhilDoc Books.

Carr, Albert Z. 1968. Is business bluffing ethical? *Harvard Business Review* 35: 143–153.

DePoe, John M. 2014. Room for god in Futurama? In *Futurama and philosophy: Pizza, paradoxes, and...good news!* ed. Courtland Lewis, 149–157. Owensboro: PhilDoc Books.

Feinberg, Joel. 1985. *Offense to others: The moral limits of the criminal law.* Oxford: Oxford University Press.

Fiala, Andrew. 2018. *Transformative pacifism: Critical theory and practice.* London: Bloomsbury Academic.

Fitz-Gibbon, Andrew. 2021. *Pragmatic nonviolence: Working toward a better world.* Leiden/Boston: Brill Rodopi.

Foucault, Michel. 1977. *Discipline and punish.* Trans. Alan Sheridan. New York: Pantheon.

Foy, Joseph, and Timothy Dale. 2014. Zoidberg's freedom lesson. In *Futurama and philosophy: Pizza, paradoxes, and...good news!* ed. Courtland Lewis, 3–12. Owensboro: PhilDoc Books.

Friedman, Milton. 1970. The social responsibility of business is to increase its profits. *The New York Times Magazine.*

Hartshorne, Charles. 1952. Time, death, and eternal life. *Journal of Religion* 32 (2): 97–107.

Hick, John. 1966. *Evil and the god of love.* New York: Palgrave Macmillan.

Hobbes, Thomas. 1994. In *Leviathan,* ed. E. Curley. Indianapolis: Hackett.

Hoefer, Carl. 2016. Causal determinism. In *The Stanford encyclopedia of philosophy,* ed. Edward N. Zalta. https://plato.stanford.edu/archives/spr2016/entries/determinism-causal.

Holmes, Robert L. 2014. *On war and morality,* Studies in moral, political, and legal philosophy. Princeton: Princeton University Press.

Johnson, David Kyle. 2022. Does god exist? *Think* 62 (35): 112.

Kant, Immanuel. 2012. *Groundwork of the metaphysics of morals.* Cambridge, UK: Cambridge University Press.

Laderoute, Karl. 2014. A billion years late for dinner. In *Futurama and philosophy: Pizza, paradoxes, and...good news!* ed. Courtland Lewis, 183–193. Owensboro: PhilDoc Books.

Lazar, Seth. 2020. War. In *The Stanford encyclopedia of philosophy,* ed. Edward N. Zalta. https://plato.stanford.edu/entries/war/.

Lewis, David. 1976. The paradoxes of time travel. *American Philosophical Quarterly* 13: 145–152.

Lewis, Courtland. 2013. Why time lords do not live forever: Immortality in doctor who. In *Time and relative dimensions in space: Religion and doctor who,* ed. Andrew Crome and James McGrath. London: Darton, Longman and Todd.

———. 2014a. We're gathered to remember. In *Futurama and philosophy: Pizza, paradoxes, and...good news!* ed. Courtland Lewis, 69–76. Owensboro: PhilDoc Books.

———, ed. 2014b. *Futurama and philosophy: Pizza, paradoxes, and...good news!* Owensboro: PhilDoc Books.

———, ed. 2021. *The real meaning of doctor who.* Chicago: Open Universe Publishing.

Locke, John. 1978. In *The two treatises of civil government,* ed. Richard Ashcraft. London: Routledge.

Malloy, Daniel. 2014. Zapp Brannigan's big book of war. In *Futurama and philosophy: Pizza, paradoxes, and...good news!* ed. Courtland Lewis, 33–41. Owensboro: PhilDoc Books.

Mill, John Stuart. [1859] 1978. *On liberty,* ed. Elizabeth Rapaport. Indianapolis: Hackett Publishing Company.

Nietzsche, Fredrich. 1974. The gay science. Trans. Walter Kaufmann. New York: Vintage.

Onishi, Brian. 2014. Queer eye for the robot kind. In *Futurama and philosophy: Pizza, paradoxes, and...good news!* ed. Courtland Lewis, 207–216. Owensboro: PhilDoc Books.

Oschman, Nicholas A. 2014. On bendered knees. In *Futurama and philosophy: Pizza, paradoxes, and...good news!* ed. Courtland Lewis, 159–169. Owensboro: PhilDoc Books.

Pence, Gregory. 2014. *Medical ethics: Accounts of ground-breaking cases.* New York: McGraw-Hill Education.

Piven, Jerry. 2014. Sexlexia and other sexy learning disabilities. In *Futurama and philosophy: Pizza, paradoxes, and...good news!* ed. Courtland Lewis, 45–58. Owensboro: PhilDoc Books.

Rawls, John. 1971. *A theory of justice.* Cambridge, MA: Harvard University Press.

Reitter, James. 2014. Mutate! Mutate! Mutate! In *Futurama and philosophy: Pizza, paradoxes, and...good news!* ed. Courtland Lewis, 217–226. Owensboro: PhilDoc Books.

Rousseau, Jean-Jacques. 1997. *The social contract and other later political writings*. Trans. and ed. Victor Gourevitch. Cambridge, UK: Cambridge University Press.

Said, Edward. 1979. *Orientalism*. New York: Vintage.

Sartre, Jean-Paul. 1948. *Being and nothingness*. Trans. Hazel E. Barnes. New York: Philosophical Library.

Singer, Peter. 1990. *Animal liberation*. 2nd ed. New York: New York Review of Books.

Swinburne, Richard. 1998. *Providence and the problem of evil*. Oxford: Oxford University Press.

theinfosphere.org. 2015. *Futurama theorem*. theinfosphere.org/Futurmam_theorem

Von Gunten, Curtis D. 2014. Moral and immoral robots. In *Futurama and philosophy: Pizza, paradoxes, and...good news!* ed. Courtland Lewis, 101–111. Owensboro: PhilDoc Books.

Williams, Bernard. 1973. *Problems of the self: Philosophical papers 1956–1972*. Cambridge, UK: Cambridge University Press.

Wolterstorff, Nicholas. 2019. *In this world of wonders*. Grand Rapids: William B. Eerdmans Publishing.

Young, Shaun. 2014. Slurm, worms, and jacking on. In *Futurama and philosophy: Pizza, paradoxes, and...good news!* ed. Courtland Lewis, 13–21. Owensboro: PhilDoc Books.

Firefly as Philosophy: Social Contracts, Political Dissent, and Virtuous Communities

12

Dean A. Kowalski

Contents

Introduction	260
Revisiting *Firefly* (and *Serenity*)	261
Hobbes and Locke on Government and Social Contract Theory	263
Dealing with the Alliance	266
Hobbesian Connections	268
Lockean Connections	270
Reading *Firefly* (and *Serenity*)	273
Assessing *Firefly's* (and *Serenity's*) Message	278
Conclusion: Watching (and Re-Watching) *Firefly* and *Serenity, and Philosophically Moving Forward*	280
End Notes	280
References	281

Abstract

A careful analysis of Joss Whedon's *Firefly* and subsequent motion picture *Serenity* demonstrates how the series and film put forth a distinctive philosophical perspective on government, its political authority, the extent to which one is bound to its laws, and how the state ideally ought to be arranged so that its citizens may aspire toward the good life. Although *Firefly's* and *Serenity's* implicit philosophical theory has some affinities with the views of Thomas Hobbes, John Locke, and Aristotle, it also provides a novel and intriguing synthesis of their views. Consequently, the careful viewer is able to assess the theory on its own merits, both for its conceptual coherence and its viability as a working social-political theory (or the next best thing if no other proper social arrangements are available).

D. A. Kowalski (✉)
Arts and Humanities Department, University of Wisconsin-Milwaukee, College of General Studies, Waukesha, WI, USA
e-mail: kowalskd@uwm.edu

© Springer Nature Switzerland AG 2024
D. K. Johnson et al. (eds.), *The Palgrave Handbook of Popular Culture as Philosophy*,
https://doi.org/10.1007/978-3-031-24685-2_28

259

Keywords

Firefly · *Serenity* · Joss Whedon · Thomas Hobbes · John Locke · Government · Social contract theory · State of nature · Reavers · Natural rights · Tyranny · Commonwealth · Alliance · Parliament · Malcom "Mal" Reynolds · River Tam · Tacit consent · Aristotle · Good life · Friendship · Community

Introduction

> There is no place I can be since I found Serenity.
> —*Firefly* theme song

Firefly, created by Joss Whedon, was a 2002 Fox Network television series that was cancelled – tragically – due to mediocre ratings. Those ratings, however, were likely not due to the show's quality. First, Fox aired the episodes out of order; indeed, the two-part pilot, which introduces the show's characters, was the last episode to air. Second, during its brief run, Fox regularly preempted *Firefly* episodes to broadcast Major League Baseball playoff games, ultimately leaving 3 of the 14 already produced episodes unaired. Needless to say, this made the show, as it aired, impossible for anyone to follow.

That the show would have likely succeeded, if given a fair chance, is evidenced by the fact that the DVD boxed set that was released post-cancelation – which contained all the episodes (including those that were unaired) in order – was wildly popular. Sales were extremely positive, and the series' cult status rapidly grew. It was so popular, in fact, that Universal Pictures released the follow-up motion picture *Serenity* in 2005 – a rarity for a cancelled television show. Indeed, *Firefly* continues via Dark Horse graphic novels, including (among others) *Better Days* (2008), *The Shepherd's Tale* (2010), and *Leaves on the Wind* (2014).

Firefly is often lauded for its complex characters, the witty banter those characters express, and its character-driven plotlines. However, a persuasive case can be made that *Firefly's* lasting appeal is also due to the complexity of the philosophical ideas it regularly portrays in its character-driven plotlines. Indeed, as we will see here, the series and its motion picture successor *Serenity* cinematically convey insights about government – its function, limits on its power, and rebellion when it violates those limits – that are reminiscent of the social contract theories of renowned philosophers Thomas Hobbes (1588–1679) and John Locke (1632–1704). This is impressive enough. But on a careful read, as we shall also see, *Firefly* and *Serenity* go further to implicitly offer its own intriguing philosophically significant theory about rights, government, citizenship, community, and the good life that is distinct from Hobbes or Locke. Let's begin with a brief introduction to the world of *Firefly*.

12 Firefly as Philosophy: Social Contracts, Political Dissent, and...

Revisiting *Firefly* (and *Serenity*)

In the universe of *Firefly*, because its natural resources had been exhausted, Earth-That-Was could no longer sustain its inhabitants. A new solar system was found. Its planets and moons were "terraformed" to be as Earth-like as possible. The requisite massive geological and atmospheric processes took decades. But once there were stable worlds to inhabit, colonists soon arrived. That was 500 years ago.

The central planets of Londinium and Sihnon became new beacons of civilization. Along with the other two central planets – Ariel and Osiris – they formed the Alliance under parliamentary rule. The Parliament decided that *all* the newly settled worlds, those bordering the central planet and those at the furthest reaches of what is now called "the 'Verse," should become members of the Alliance. But the Outer Rim settlements were particularly disagreeable to this proposal. They organized the Resistance, and calling themselves the "Browncoats," fought for their independence. Some, like Malcolm "Mal" Reynolds, volunteered to serve in the cause. Others, like Zoe Washburne, were regular military. At the battle of Serenity Valley, the Browncoats bravely made their last stand, and lost.

The entire 'Verse subsequently fell under Alliance rule. The defrocked Browncoats, nevertheless, remained fiercely independent and tended to stay as far from the Alliance as they could – like Mal, who did so in a dilapidated Firefly-class transport ship he bought and named *Serenity*. His goal was to hire a small crew – anyone (else) who felt the need to be free. No matter how far Alliance control extended, spaceship *Serenity* could always get a little farther. Zoe became (i.e., remained) his second-in-command. Mal and *Serenity's* crew would take whatever jobs whenever and wherever they could. The goal, then, was simple: find a job, get paid, and keep flying.

Mal and Zoe soon hire smart-alecky and ace pilot Hoban "Wash" Washburne, who later marries Zoe (much to Mal's dismay). Kaylee left her father's farm to become the ship's mechanic. Ever humble, she explains her talents as, "Machines just got 'workins' and they speak to me." Mal and Zoe lure Jayne away from another crew with the promise of a bigger percentage of the take and his own bunk; he is a hired (gun) hand without much of a conscience. Later, Mal rents one of *Serenity's* two short-ranged shuttles to Inara Serra. As a legally registered and Guild-trained Companion, she shares her mind, body, and spirit with high-end clientele (only after carefully screening them for compatibility). It remains a bit of mystery why a woman of her station would choose to travel the Outer Rim, but having a Companion onboard provides *Serenity* more than a modicum of respectability, which allows Mal to port in locales that he otherwise couldn't.

One fateful day, Mal takes on passengers to help cover expenses. Shepherd Book, a monk from the Southdown Abbey, pays his fare with a little cash and fruits and vegetables grown at the monastery. For him, the journey is the nobler part; he now wishes to walk in the world for a while and bring the Word to those who need it. (He was surprised to find Inara, and even more surprised when Mal wouldn't allow him to say grace aloud at the dinner table.) Siblings Simon and River Tam also board that day, even though the former initially kept the latter's presence a secret. He was a skilled young surgeon on Osiris; she is an eccentric but psychologically troubled teenage girl with a more troubling past. They all were looking for serenity.

Life on the Outer Rim worlds remains difficult, not unlike the Old West on Earth-That-Was. The Alliance, despite fighting a bloody war for undisputed inter-planetary control, mostly ignores citizens on the Outer Rim worlds. Not only are jobs hard to find, but so are proper health care and education. The goal is to get by as best you can without any Alliance help, not that they would offer much – even if you did ask. And Mal would never.

Many of *Serenity's* jobs are illegal. Crime lord Adelai Niska hires the crew to travel to planet Regina to rob a train filled with Alliance goods. (The crew returns it once they discover the booty is actually much-needed medicine.) They transport unlicensed livestock (without a permit, of course) from planet Persephone to be sold via back channels on planet Jiangyin. At Simon's behest, they steal medicine from a hospital on Ariel to sell (at a discount, of course) to those who need it more out on the planets and moons of the Outer Rim. Twin brothers Fanty and Mingo Rample hire the crew to steal an Alliance-funded security company payroll housed on the remote moon Lilac (the loss of which would never be reported by the security company).

Throughout the crew's mostly unlawful escapades, they work to avoid Alliance contact, to varying levels of success. But this is only half of the plan. As they navigate the reaches of the 'Verse, they also must stay clear of Reavers. Reavers are traveling bands of mindless, brutish, and savage human beings who have lost their humanity. Zoe once explained to Simon, "What happens if they board us? If they take the ship, they'll rape us to death, eat our flesh, and sew our skins into their clothing. And if we're very, very lucky, they'll do it in that order." Simon believed "Reavers" were merely bedtime stories parents told Core-world children so they would behave. Zoe and Mal know better: Reavers are real and to be avoided at all costs.

Mal and the crew eventually learn secrets the Alliance wishes to remain hidden. The first secret is what it did to River. A child prodigy, she was recruited into an elite school for the gifted. At the Academy, she would receive the very best education; her parents were so proud. Simon became suspicious. Through coded letters River sent home, Simon learned that River and the other "students" were being physically and psychologically tortured. The Alliance's insidious goal was to create ultimate sleeper assassins. They would quietly do the Alliance's bidding and thus keep the peace. During her "training," River psychically "overheard" the second secret: Planet Miranda. The Alliance attempted to weed out aggression in Miranda's population by covertly introducing a chemical known as Pax into the planet's atmospheric handlers. It worked. The vast majority of the population became docile. In fact, most men and women stopped doing anything at all. They laid down and died. The opposite result occurred for a small percentage of the population. They became ultraviolent. They became the first Reavers. Of course, the Alliance did its very best to cover up the disaster and have never confirmed the existence of Reavers.

Learning these two secrets, Mal announces his intentions to the crew: "Somebody has to speak for these people. ...Sure as I know anything I know this, they will try again. ...A year from now, ten, they'll swing back to the belief that they can make people...better. And I do not hold to that. So no more running. I aim to misbehave." Mal's plan pits him and his crew between the Alliance and the Reavers. Can *Serenity* slip by the Alliance and broadcast the Miranda file before falling prey to the Reavers pursuing them? Again, River holds the key.

Hobbes and Locke on Government and Social Contract Theory

Shepherd Book once said, "A government is a body of people usually, notably, ungoverned." But what is the purpose of government? This is a difficult question, but a common answer is that government exists and is empowered by us (citizens) to serve our best interests. Thus a bargain is struck: We agree to give up some of our personal freedoms by following the regulations (laws) government enacts, and government agrees to structure the state in ways aimed to ensure our prosperity (interpreted broadly to include such things as health, happiness, and property). This sort of perspective is often called social contract theory.

Intuitively, social contract theory is bolstered by imagining life without government, which is often called the "state of nature." Social contract theorist Thomas Hobbes believes that, lacking a strong government to deter our inherently egoistic impulses, the state of nature would be a constant struggle. Fueling our adversarial interactions are the facts that resources are limited and that we combatants are more or less equal in ability regarding the "faculties of body and mind." This doesn't mean that individuals don't have particular talents or strengths; however, Hobbes believes that these differences are not ultimately significant with respect to gaining advantage over another. Furthermore, alliances could be made with others to overcome or subdue unusually gifted individuals. Of course, successful alliances soon become targets of other alliances. Thus retaliation and re-retaliation is a never ending cycle that breeds fear, contempt, revenge, mistrust, and more fear. In these conditions, Hobbes surmises, "the life of man is solitary, poor, nasty, brutish, and short." Not surprisingly, Hobbes concludes that life in the state of nature is to be avoided at all costs (Hobbes 1660, ch. 13).

Accordingly, Hobbes believes that we will (would) soon realize that forming agreements with one another is the key to our well-being. The crucial first step for leaving a state of nature is seeking out others who also desire peace, safety, and prosperity. Hobbes maintains that the group of peace-seekers will agree – enter into contracts – to refrain from certain (especially hostile or threatening) behaviors so long as others also agree to avoid such behaviors. One promises not to harm others on the condition that others promise not to harm you (Hobbes 1660, ch. 14).

Even granting Hobbes's assumption that rational people will eventually enter into such contracts, he nevertheless believes that we will continue to act from self-interested motives. Hobbes thus thought that we would never pass up a chance to violate our contracts, so long as we benefited (more) from doing so and we were reasonably sure doing so would go undetected. Hobbes in effect held that the contract entered into *all by itself* was nothing but empty words. For any contract to be operatively binding, it had to include allegiance to a governing body Hobbes called a "sovereign." The sovereign might be one person (monarchy) or a group of people (oligarchy). In any case, Hobbes believed that allegiance to a politically powerful sovereign was necessary for stability, which, in turn, is necessary for justice. The sovereign is to deter any and all instances of injustice, which is to say contractual violations. The alternative is devolving into a state of nature. But because leaving the state of nature was the goal of entering into such contracts in the first place, the sovereign must be allowed any means necessary to keep contracts intact.

In effect, because we cannot trust ourselves to keep our agreements, we must transfer our will to the sovereign. The sovereign now speaks for us. Hobbes's sovereign embodies Book's idea about government. The sovereign governs us, but is ungoverned – at liberty to do anything and everything to maintain a stable society – without any input or recourse from the citizens. The only liberty we rightfully enjoy is to choose to act as the sovereign requires. According to Hobbes, affirming complete allegiance to a sovereign is the only way to establish enduring peace. Each of us must exchange freedom for security. Only once we are delivered from ourselves can we enjoy the benefits of security and peace of mind that living in a stable society provides.

It's not entirely clear whether Hobbes believed in the actual existence of the state of nature. Furthermore, the agreement made with the sovereign may be more implicit than explicit. However, there is one interesting relevant connection to *Firefly*. When the Browncoats lost the Unification War and the armistice was signed with the Alliance, this can be interpreted as a foundational agreement between the Alliance, including its ruling body the Parliament, and all citizens in the 'Verse. On a Hobbesian analysis, the Browncoats are now free only to follow the mandates of the Parliament and Alliance rule. Because Mal and his crew regularly commit defiant acts of rebellion against the Alliance, Hobbes would argue that *they* are the actual villains of *Firefly*, not the Alliance.

John Locke, another important social contract theorist, offers a critique of Hobbes. The primary source of contention between Locke and Hobbes is the former's beliefs that human beings possess *natural* rights and the existence of (pre-political) moral truths – ethically significant principles that hold in the state of nature and prior to any established government. One such principle is (roughly): "Mankind ought to be preserved and co-exist in peaceful interactions with one another" (Locke 1689, ch. 2, sect. 7). So, even in the state of nature, we are (ethically) bound not to harm another person's life, liberty, or possessions; were we to fail this obligation by choosing to harm others in such ways, we fail to act in accordance with what is supremely valuable in life, namely, the life and liberty of human persons. This (pre-political) moral obligation grounds our basic human rights. Possessing a moral right is a justified claim against others to respect some moral obligation. We can thus justifiably demand, as is our (natural) right, that others respect our equality and independence. In fact, the very ability to articulate such concepts bolsters our distinctive status as (natural) moral rights possessors.

Locke also demurs from Hobbes's view that the state of nature would be an unbearable constant struggle of everyone against everyone. Locke believes that persons are basically decent and that we will regularly consult the moral law and respect each other's basic rights. But Locke isn't naive. He realizes that a few people in the state of nature will invariably choose not to uphold the moral law. From the 'Verse, examples such as Ranse Burgess in "Heart of Gold" or Niska from "War Stories" quickly come to mind. Such powerful individuals invariably seek personal gain at the expense of others. Because of this, our interests are better served if we enter into a social contract and establish a stable government.

Locke believes that our interests are better secured by the government because of three interlocking facts about human persons and our relationship to the moral law. First, understanding the pre-political moral truths requires time, effort, and skill, but not everyone is able or willing to commit to grasping them. Second, people are often clouded by self-interest in applying relevant moral truths and meting out appropriate punishments for infractions of them. Third, even if some individuals accomplish fair and impartial application of the relevant moral truths, not everyone will be able (for various reasons) to execute retribution. These three facts make life in the state of nature unstable and uneasy (although not nasty, brutish, and short). Thus we soon form governments in order to better protect our basic rights. Doing so is clearly in our best interest. We benefit by the establishment of publicized common civil laws (invariably grounded in relevant moral truths), the machinery to settle disputes among interested parties, the elevation of impartial judges to rule over such disputes, and the political means by which to enforce the judges' decisions (Locke 1689, ch. 9, secs. 123–27).

By entering into the social contract, individuals agree not to punish infractions of the moral law themselves; we transfer that power to the state. We thereby agree to uphold the laws of the state generally. However, we are bound to this agreement on the condition that the state works to preserve our liberty and property, which is the common good. Locke interprets "property" in a broad sense. This includes all that we have a right to – our lives, health, limbs, liberty, and estates. Therefore, when the government extends its power beyond the common good, which is the joint preservation of our basic rights, and begins to infringe on our property (and thus happiness), our duty to recognize the government's authority is rendered null and void (Locke 1689, ch. 9, sec. 131).

So, Hobbes believes that a powerful government – even one that borders on tyranny – is better than the anarchy we would suffer in the pre-government state of nature. Furthermore, Hobbes contends that lacking an ungoverned "sovereign" with vast political power, anarchy is exactly what we face – a world of terror and chaos. Locke, however, rejects Hobbes position on the necessity of subjecting ourselves to this sort of ungoverned "sovereign" to safeguard our best interests. Locke thus argues that Hobbes offers us a false dilemma: either subject ourselves to complete tyranny or suffer the ordeals of terrorized chaos in the state of nature. It is not necessary for us to fear or kowtow to our government; there is a third alternative, one that preserves safety and stability without failing to recognize our status as moral beings and the natural human rights we possess. In keeping us safe, a government ought not illicitly infringe upon our rights or individual pursuits of happiness (broadly defined); if it does, then the people are at liberty to revolt and institute a new government.

So, in the end, both Hobbes and Locke agree that the function of government is to serve the best interests of its citizens. However, there is fundamental disagreement between them about what this entails. For Hobbes, our best interests are served by interpreting government as a stern parental-figure that severely curtails our individual freedoms for our own good; anything less will result in chaos, fear, and death. For Locke, our best interests are served by establishing a stable society in which citizens have sufficient freedom to pursue their individual goals, assuming those goals don't unduly impinge on the rights of others or disrupt social stability.

Accordingly, Lockean ideals provide a competing interpretation of *Firefly's* villains. Recall Mal's offhanded quip in "Serenity, Part I": "That's what governments are for—get in a man's way." If it can be shown that the Alliance unduly "gets in the way" of the natural rights its citizenry possess, then it can be argued that spaceship *Serenity's* illegal operations are not necessarily impermissible. Furthermore, if the Alliance purposely and regularly commits rights infractions against its citizenry, then, on Lockean grounds, Mal and his crew may permissibly revolt against it and work to establish a new government. Indeed, what we may discover is that Locke paves the way for a rather novel interpretation of spaceship *Serenity* and what Mal intends to accomplish with it.

Dealing with the Alliance

With Hobbes and Locke as a philosophical backdrop, the first *Firefly* issue to explore is whether the Alliance serves the best interests of its citizens. If we limit the discussion to the Core worlds, perhaps it does. There is reason to believe that the central planets are affluent and enjoy cutting-edge health care ("Ariel"). There is an emphasis on education (*Serenity*). Crime rates are seemingly low and police no longer carry traditional Earth-That-Was firearms ("Ariel" and "Trash"). Perhaps such benefits are bought at the price of extensive social conformity, but there seems to be sufficient opportunities to pursue individual goals: The Tams were at liberty to send Simon to medical school and arrange dancing lessons for River before securing her enrollment in the Academy; Inara was afforded the opportunity to become a Guild-trained Companion.

It is less clear whether the Alliance serves the interests of those on the Outer Rim worlds, however. Outer Rim denizens do not enjoy the same luxuries as citizens on Core worlds. Furthermore, there is no evidence that the Parliament intends to take action to improve their lot. In support of this, consider "The Train Job." We learn that many citizens on planet Regina suffer from Bowden's Malady. As Paradiso Sheriff Bourne explains:

12 *Firefly* as Philosophy: Social Contracts, Political Dissent, and. . .

> Every planet that's been terraformed for human life has its own little quirks. Turns out the air down underground, mixed up with the ore processors, it's a perfect recipe for Bowden's. Everybody gets it: minors, dumpers—hell, I got it and I ain't ever set foot in a mine. It's worst on the kids, of course.

Bowden's is a degenerative affliction of the bone and muscle. It is inheritable, which is why the sheriff references Paradiso's children. Bowden's is treatable. If one receives regular treatments of Pasceline, someone suffering from Bowden's can "live like a person" (as the sheriff puts it).

The Alliance, of course, knows about Bowden's and Pasceline. Because Alliance troops were on the train carrying the stolen medicine, the theft was immediately reported to a nearby Alliance space cruiser. An officer on the cruiser responds to the report by quipping, "Two crates of Pasceline D. Right. Get you a tidy fortune on the black market." When an ensign reminds the officer of how important Pasceline is to Paradiso (and presumably the rest of the planet), he sarcastically replies, "And yet they insist on breeding." Rather than deploy the Alliance troops already in Paradiso to help the sheriff recover the stolen cargo, the officer declares, "Those are Federal Marshals, not local narcotics hounds. They have better things to do. And so do we."

Paradiso citizens, of course, know about the Alliance's indifference. The sheriff expected the Alliance soldiers to continue on to their destination, and they did so "without so much as a whoopsie-daisy" (as Bourne reports). Mal, for his part, is also not surprised: "That sounds like the Alliance. Unite the planets under one rule so everyone can be interfered with or ignored equally." Bourne concurs, "Alliance ain't much use to us on the border planets," and then points out, "But they ain't the ones stole that medicine." Mal and Zoe sheepishly look at one another.

Paradiso is only one destitute town on an Outer Rim planet. There are similar settlements on Jiangyin (in "Safe") also desperate for proper medical care; one is so desperate that it kidnaps Simon and "encourages" him to treat their sick. As Zoe (in "Serenity, Part I") reminds us, once a planet or moon is terraformed, the Alliance will "dump settlers on there with nothing but blankets and hatchets and maybe a herd." Some of them make it; some of them don't. Furthermore, even among those settlements that "make it," there is often someone taking advantage of the settlers for personal gain. The mudders in "Jaynestown," for example, are paid slave wages and suffer terrible living conditions, while Magistrate Higgins reaps all the profits. (Well, he did, until Jayne "gave him what for" and thereby became the mudders' Hero of Canton – the man they call Jayne.) For another example, on a remote moon, the misogynistic monster and land baron Ranse Burgess terrorizes a bordello in "Heart of Gold." The prostitutes are not registered with the Guild. When Nandi, the madam of the bordello and a Guild-trained acquaintance of Inara's, reaches out for help, Inara explains to Mal, "There is no authority on that moon she can turn to. They're totally alone." It is thus clear why Mal believes that the Alliance ignores citizens on the Outer Rim worlds. True, most people seek life on an Outer Rim planet or moon for the freedom it promises; they do not want to be encumbered with the Alliance influences germane to the Core worlds. However, at the very least, it seems that the Alliance could be doing more for them. Perhaps this is why *Serenity's* crew often comes to their aide.

Hobbesian Connections

While Mal and his crew strive to avoid the Alliance, they also steer clear of Reavers. The Reavers are introduced in the two-part pilot "Serenity." They receive further explication in the episode "Bushwhacked." Jayne declares that Reavers are not men. Book staunchly disagrees, claiming, "Of course they are. Too long removed from civilization, perhaps—but men." Mal sides with Jayne: "Reavers might take issue with that philosophy. If they had a philosophy. And if they weren't too busy gnawing on your insides. Jayne's right. Reavers ain't men. Or they forgot how to be." Arguably, the Reavers represent life in the state of nature. Reaver existence is all but bereft of industry, leisure, or learning. It certainly would be nasty, brutish, and short. As Hobbes would remind us, it must be avoided at all costs. The fact that Mal and his crew regularly steer clear of Reavers is reason to believe that *Firefly* implicitly advocates for the necessity of some form of government. Life as a Reaver is no way to live. We are all better off living in a stable society.

Yet there is good reason to believe that *Firefly's* message, on the whole, is contra Hobbes. River Tam is perhaps the most powerful thematic piece of evidence for this interpretation. The Tam's were misled about the true nature and purpose of the Academy. Once River enrolled, the Parliament kept the so-called curriculum a secret. At the Academy, River was subjected to physical and psychological torture for the purpose of transforming her into a sleeper spy-assassin. All of this occurred without her consent (or the consent of her parents). On a Hobbesian analysis, if cultivating unwitting sleeper spy-assassins enhances the Parliament's ability to keep the peace, then this practice is permissible. However, intuitively, its permissibility is dubious, at best. *Firefly* concurs, in that Simon is seen as a hero for breaking her out: he *rescued* her (at great personal and professional cost). Furthermore, it is clear that River is portrayed as a victim and, as such, the Parliament is blameworthy. Her rights were violated and she was clearly harmed as a result; Simon is to be commended as a hero.

The two unnamed blue-gloved Parliament agents further support an anti-Hobbesian interpretation of *Firefly*. These two characters are portrayed as cold and calculating individuals. Their only goal is to apprehend the fugitives River and Simon Tam, and they are merciless in their pursuit. In "Ariel," the local authorities arrest River and Simon; Jayne callously sold them out for the reward money. The Alliance officer decides to keep the reward money for himself and moves his *three* suspects to a detention area. The blue-gloved agents arrive to take custody of the Tams. When they learn that the local authorities had direct contact with River, they unflinchingly use an ominous sonic device to brutally execute them, including the Alliance officer in charge. River psychically senses their arrival and, fearing for her life and the lives of her comrades, she frantically plots their escape. Again, that the blue-gloved agents work above or outside the established laws of the land would not bother Hobbes. That they terrorize River or perfunctorily execute those she associates with is inconsequential. All that ultimately matters is that they serve the Parliament's interests by maintaining order. However, *Firefly's* message is pretty clear: The blue-gloved agents are villains because of the remorseless carnage they leave behind; they trample on the rights of those they encounter.

12 *Firefly* as Philosophy: Social Contracts, Political Dissent, and...

The motion picture *Serenity* provides additional support for an anti-Hobbesian interpretation. The Parliament fears that River, during her time at the Academy, psychically gleaned various secrets it wished to remain hidden. Its blue-gloved agents (and a contracted bounty hunter) have failed to apprehend River. The Parliament, becoming desperate, sends out another unnamed agent known only as the Operative to silence River and, if necessary, those who conspire to keep her from the Alliance. The Operative learns that *Serenity's* crew often takes shelter on Haven moon; Shepherd Book now leads a small mining colony on it. The Operative sends Alliance troops to decimate the Haven encampment in the hopes of finding River or at least intimating Mal to hand her over. In fact, the Operative sent Alliance troops to decimate each of Mal's known hideouts. Innocent children are among the dead (on multiple worlds). The Operative electronically contacts a distraught Mal and asks, "Did you think none of this was your fault?" Fuming, Mal states, "I don't murder children," and the Operative replies, "As you can see, I do. If I have to." Mal queries, "Why? Do you know why they sent you?" The Operative answers, "It's not my place to ask. I believe in something that is greater than myself. A better world. A world without sin." The Operative conveys a Hobbesian message about political power and justice. So long as the Parliament remains in control, what it does cannot be unjust, including murdering innocent children. Mal offers more of a Lockean viewpoint. The moral atrocities committed in the Parliament's name cannot be excused merely by claiming it is for the greater good to keep the peace. Mal puts an exclamation point on this, when he rasps, "So me and mine got to lie down and die so you can live in your better world?" The question is clearly rhetorical; it is almost as if Mal is speaking to Hobbes himself.

The motion picture *Serenity* also offers an additional anti-Hobbesian message: Miranda. Planet Miranda was believed to be a "black-rock" – an uninhabitable place due to failed terraforming attempts. There is no historical or astronomic information about it on the Cortex. However, River believes otherwise and entreats the crew to investigate. Kaylee asks, "How can it be that there is a whole planet called Miranda and none of us knowed that?" Mal answers, "Half of writing history is hiding the truth. There's something on this rock the Alliance doesn't want known." It is the secret that burned up River Tam's brain (to paraphrase Mal). Recall the Alliance attempted to control Miranda's population by adding a chemical to the atmospheric handlers, without their consent, and it led to disastrous results for its citizens.

Hobbes would be sympathetic to these Parliament activities. However, intuitively, covertly experimenting on its own citizens, attempting to cover up the tragic results, and going to extreme lengths to keep the secret by apprehending River at all costs are all clear examples of a government acting unjustly. *Firefly* upholds this intuition. As philosopher and political theorist Joseph Foy states in his essay "The State of Nature and Social Contracts on Spaceship *Serenity*":

> What happened to River and the Haven community is unjust, as is the mass slaughter of the people of Miranda through secret testing by the Alliance. Individuals consent to be governed by a state to be freed from such brutality and fear for their lives and livelihood. Because the Hobbesian state permits such activities, it harbors counterintuitive entailments that undermine its possible justification. (Foy 2011, p. 45)

The Parliament repeatedly tramples the rights of its citizens. A Lockean account – and not a Hobbesian one – best fits the 'Verse.

Lockean Connections

Firefly indeed often conveys a pro-Lockean message. Near the end of *Serenity*, Mal and his crew act on implicit Lockean principles when they opt for civil disobedience. Mal becomes convinced that "someone must speak" for the people of Miranda and thereby speak for all Alliance citizens. Mal announces his intentions to the crew; his inspirational words bear repeating: "Sure as I know anything...they will try again....A year from now, ten, they'll swing back to the belief that they can make people...better. And I do not hold to that. So, no more runnin'. I aim to misbehave." Mal intends to confront the Alliance about its wrongdoings. He and his crew will be in open rebellion. Given what Mal knows about the Alliance, and especially his new revelations about River and Miranda, it seems that the Parliament is as much an enemy of the people as their protector. It has violated its trust with its citizens, and there is no reason to believe that it won't continue to violate it. Thus *Serenity's* political dissent is justified on Lockean grounds.

Mal and Zoe, unlike the other members of the crew, have openly "misbehaved" before. Recall that they and multitudes of their Browncoat comrades took up arms to resist Unification. Spaceship *Serenity* alone could not possibly occasion that sort of rebellion. Thus Mal's dissent takes a different tact, one less violent, and more suited for a technologically advanced information age. The goal is to broadcast the Miranda file on the Cortex so that citizens everywhere are informed about the Parliament's atrocities. Sending it from a sufficiently powerful source so it reaches deep into 'Verse will put the crew at great personal risk. The Alliance is waiting for them and prepared to stop them at all costs. True, according to the vagaries of Alliance law, Mal and the crew are about to become terrorists. However, they act exclusively for the common good – without blowing up any buildings or risking any lives (other than their own). With the Miranda file broadcasted across 30 worlds, the Alliance's authority will be weakened, and just as Locke would have it, democratic ideals (of transparency) are thereby reinfused in the 'Verse. With the populace better informed, it can begin mobilizing toward the needed governmental changes. This goal makes them Lockean heroes – "big damn heroes" – and their quest does seem heroic. Regarding the crew's plan, Jayne, not always known for his acumen, insightfully claims: "Shepherd Book used to tell me: 'If you can't do something smart, do something right.'" In this instance, at least, Locke would agree.

Yet applying Lockean ideals to *Firefly* sometimes brings intriguing results. Consider Locke's idea of consent. Recall that, on social contract theory reasoning, individuals enter into contracts by making agreements to refrain from harmful behaviors. Moreover, individuals enter into a contract with the government by agreeing to give up some liberties for the sake of living in a stable society. However, as a matter of fact, virtually no one ever explicitly consents to enter into a contract

12 *Firefly* as Philosophy: Social Contracts, Political Dissent, and... 271

with the state. Locke distinguishes between explicit and implicit consent to meet this challenge. Locke calls the latter "tacit" consent, as he writes:

> The difficulty is, what ought to be looked upon as a tacit consent, and how far it binds—i.e., how far anyone shall be looked on to have consented, and thereby submitted to any government, where he has made no expression of it at all. And to this, I say, that every man that hath any possession or enjoyment of any part of the dominions of any government doth hereby give his tacit consent, and is as far forth obliged to obedience to the laws of that government, during such enjoyment, as anyone under it. (Locke 1689, ch. 8, sect. 119)

Locke, unlike Hobbes, holds that one is always at liberty to leave a commonwealth. Presumably, one would choose this because he has become sufficiently disillusioned with the operative social contract – that is, the laws of the land or how the government enforces them. When one refrains from leaving, and continues to receive the social benefits the state provides, including the ownership of property, one thereby provides tacit consent to keep the terms of the operative contract. This pertains to established members of the commonwealth, those "lodging only for a week" and those passersby "traveling freely on the highway." Therefore, Locke holds that tacit consent is sufficient to bind all of us to follow the laws of the land, for as long as each of us stays.

Recall how it is tempting to argue that when the Resistance leaders surrendered and signed the armistice to end the Unification War, this was tantamount to all the Browncoats tacitly consenting to Alliance rule. Locke may be inclined to bolster this perspective by examining Browncoat behavior after the war. Mal, for example, benefited by a stable society when he purchased spaceship *Serenity*, when he safely puts down in ports of call (like the Eavesdown Docks on planet Persephone), and when he exchanges goods and services for Alliance credits (so that he can purchase clean fuel cells and other supplies). Thus Mal often benefits from the stability the Alliance provides. Given this, philosophers James South and Susanne Foster assert in their essay "Social Contract: Rebellion and Dissent aboard *Serenity*":

> Mal's rebellion as captain of *Serenity* may well strike us as juvenile, a mere thumbing of his nose at the government that defeated the Resistance....Moreover, he continually puts his crew at risk while engaging in illegal activities....Even to the degree that Mal is able to make do in his rebellious activities, he is nonetheless parasitic upon the good functioning of the social contract....Mal is still a member of the Alliance community to the extent that he relies on the good functioning of the Alliance to make his own living possible. (Foster and South 2013, p. 65)

On this account, Mal's behavior is far from heroic. At best, it's petty, and at worst, it's criminal. By lifting Alliance goods from the train headed to Paradiso, transporting unregistered cattle off-world, and absconding with the security company payroll, Mal and his crew are common brigands; they ought to be punished to the full extent of the law due to their brash violations of the social contract.

Yet there seems to be something amiss in this analysis of how tacit consent applies to the 'Verse. (For standard criticisms of tacit consent, see Bennett (1979).)

It might be wondered whether the behavior of unrepentant Browncoats like Mal and Zoe after the Unification War is indeed indicative of their tacit consent to accept Alliance rule (especially recalling Mal's penchant for starting fist fights in Alliance taverns on the anniversary of Unification Day). In effect, they never stopped being Browncoats. So, why do they stay? Indeed, there is an often-heard response to real-world malcontents like Mal: "If you don't like it here, you can leave!" This sort of offhanded (and often mean-spirited) remark implicitly reminds us of a lurking problematic issue for social contract theorists about tacit consent: How likely is it for someone to leave one commonwealth and begin life anew in another? If the prospects of a decent life in a foreign land are so remote, it can be argued that one does *not* provide tacit consent by staying put. One doesn't *choose* to stay; it is practically impossible for one to leave. Such people tend to suffer social and political marginalization – often in silence – with little or no recourse to improve their station.

Firefly magnifies the relevant difficulty about tacit consent. Given the Alliance's radical politically expansive programs, and as the result of Unification, there are *no* other operative commonwealths. The Browncoats *cannot* just leave and go somewhere else: There is nowhere else. As Mal reminds Simon (and the audience) in *Serenity*: "I put this crew together with the promise of work, which the Alliance makes harder every year. May come a day there won't be room for naughty men like us to slip about at all....So here is us, on the raggedy edge." Browncoats – the "naughty men" who don't conform to Alliance rule like Mal and Zoe – literally have nowhere else to go, except perhaps farther and farther out into the "black" of space. But the farther they go, the more likely they are to encounter the Reavers, who symbolize the state of nature in *Firefly*. Therefore, the mere fact that they remain in Alliance-controlled space is no indication whatever of tacit consent. If so, then the extent to which they are bound to follow Alliance law is unclear. Remember, Mal purchased *Serenity* to avoid the Alliance. In any case, fictional examples like this should give historical social contract theorists pause: Is there such a thing as tacit consent, and, even if there is, is it clearly the case that it is sufficient to bind us to follow the law?

Firefly affords one additional intriguing connection to Lockean principles of government. Recall Locke's view that the citizenry is no longer obligated to follow the law if the state violates its trust with the people. The most obvious example is when the state becomes tyrannical. For Locke, this occurs when the government (perhaps via individual leaders) wields political power for personal gain, or it places itself above the law by using undue force (Locke 1689, ch. 18, sect. 200 and ch.7, sect. 94). In either case, the state becomes an enemy of the people, and it violates its trust with the citizenry. When this occurs, the people decide when revolution, in its various forms, is appropriate. However, given Locke's penchant for democratic ideals, when he speaks of the people, he is apparently referring to the *majority* of the people. Locke writes: "Every man, by consenting with others to make...one government, puts himself under an obligation...to submit to the determination of the majority" (Locke 1689, ch. 8, sect. 97). Therefore, the majority decides which laws will be enacted, which are to be altered or revised, and when, if ever, revolution is appropriate.

The problem is that some majorities can be just as oppressive (i.e., tyrannical) as any Hobbesian monarchy or oligarchy. To be fair, Locke believed that all people are basically decent; so, this sort of concern would never actually arise. However, what he overlooked was that those in power are loath to give it up. Given that piece of human nature, what recourse would a completely marginalized minority have to change the government from within? Consider that all of the political power (and the vast majority of the wealth) in the 'Verse resides with the central planets. Upon Unification, the Parliament has no political competitors and no one to fear. Those on the Outer Rim worlds are completely without voice. Furthermore, the Parliament is completely faceless; the government seems completely isolated from its citizenry. Who would the Outer Rim denizens speak to even if they had a voice? No wonder Mal has the view of government that he does, namely, that it exists merely to get in a man's way.

Accordingly, *Firefly* reminds us that Locke's view of government is susceptible to the same objection that Locke leveled at Hobbes's position, namely, that it allows for those within the commonwealth to be exploited without any realistic prospects of recourse. With Hobbes, it was possible for the sovereign to exploit all the commonwealth's subjects. With Locke, it is possible that the majority exploit minority voices within the commonwealth. Therefore, assuming that the controlling majority cannot be moved via legal channels to repeal its unjust laws and practices, and assuming that leaving the commonwealth is not viable, it seems that Locke's interpretation of social contract theory allows for civil disobedience on the same grounds that it allows revolution. This further complicates how we are to interpret Mal's band of "naughty (wo)men" as they attempt to "slip about" in the 'Verse. Are they criminals, or heroes, or something in between, or a combination of both?

Reading *Firefly* (and *Serenity*)

Over the course of exploring Hobbesian and Lockean connections to *Firefly* and *Serenity*, some salient thematic and philosophical points emerge. A careful examination of these points, in turn, prompts a coherent philosophically significant perspective. That is, a case can be made that *Firefly* and *Serenity* convey an implicit but distinctive philosophically interesting theory about rights, government, citizenship, and community and how these are properly related. For convenience, let's call this the "Since I Found *Serenity*" theory, or SIFS, because spaceship *Serenity*, its crew, and the sky in which it flies serve as its intuitive core and attest to its plausibility. Overall, SIFS is Lockean; however, the ways in which SIFS accords with Locke (and diverges from Hobbes) are not always straightforward, which make it all the more intriguing.

SIFS follows Locke regarding the inherent (natural) rights of individuals. The aforementioned scholar Joseph Foy also recognizes this commitment:

> *Serenity*, under the leadership of Captain Malcolm Reynolds, calls to mind the social contract theories of John Locke, who advocates all people sharing in an obligation to advance and

protect the rights of others.....Although limits are imposed on the individual in such a system—meaning that one is not completely free to do whatever she wants whenever she wants to—Locke's view of the state rejects a theory of total unity that imposes an absolutist structure that regulates everyone's life to the same end. (Foy 2011, p. 45)

When an external threat impinges on a crewmember's rights and well-being, steps are taken to protect him or her (as the crew does in rescuing Simon and River in "Safe" or defending itself against bounty hunter Jubal Early in "Objects in Space"). Mal also takes action when one crewmember selfishly infringes upon the rights and well-being of another (as he does when Jayne chooses to sell out River and Simon in "Ariel"). Indeed, Mal's response to such infractions is particularly harsh. He threatens to end Jayne, seething, "You turn on any of my crew, you turn on me! But since that is a concept you can't seem to wrap your head around, then you got no place here!" Thus spaceship *Serenity* seems something like a small mobile Lockean commonwealth, dedicated to serving the rights and well-being of its citizens.

From this intuitive Lockean cornerstone, the careful viewer can discern how *Firefly/Serenity* cinematically develops SIFS via three plausible supplemental theses and thereby simultaneously enhances its plausibility and distinctiveness. The first supplemental thesis begins with the clear political shortcomings of the Alliance. The Alliance represents an ultra-expansive and bureaucratic-authoritarian model of the state; furthermore, it utilizes technocratic experts to establish and maintain extensive control over its citizens. These emphases prevent the Alliance from effectively navigating individualism and diversity among its citizenry; recall Mal's quip to the effect that the Alliance impedes and ignores everyone equally. Although the Alliance's preferred governing modes occasion acts of tyranny (in both Lockean senses) and Mal's quest to "misbehave" seems justified given the tragedy of planet Miranda, the deeper problematic feature of the Alliance is that it offers a faceless and completely impersonal form of governmental rule. Note that the viewer never once witnesses a member of Parliament. We do see three agents, but all three are little more than expressionless automatons (although the Operative shows some signs of emotion); this undoubtedly represents the Parliament itself. As faceless and impersonal, the Parliament is antithetical to individualism and thus autonomous existence. It is an impersonal force that limits expressions of personal goals and, thus, "gets in a (wo)man's way" simply for the sake of unrivaled political power. *Firefly/Serenity* suggests that this shortcoming (in addition to more overt instances of tyranny) justifies political dissent and, if necessary, revolution.[1] Thus the deficiencies of a faceless authoritarian government and the concomitant importance of individualism comprise the first supplemental thesis shoring up SIFS.

Yet *Firefly/Serenity* also implicitly explores the nature and scope of individuality, which signals the second supplemental thesis for SIFS. This thesis affirms that, although individualism is to be valued, a life of *complete* individuality, such that any one person is without any comrades or structured society, is an impoverished way to live. Such a life is akin to living in a Hobbesian state of nature. Taken in the extreme, it is to live among Reavers: One would subsist in constant fear, struggling just to survive. Recall that even Jayne, as robust and imposing a character as he is, "won't

12 *Firefly* as Philosophy: Social Contracts, Political Dissent, and. . .

go anywhere near Reaver territory" (because "them people ain't human"). Moreover, and more importantly, one would be unable to express one's individuality in any meaningful way. Thus SIFS advocates for rights-bearing individuals to form commonwealths so that citizens can express their individualism in meaningful ways.

In fact, *Firefly* cinematically conveys the plausibility of the idea that life completely alone is no way to live in multiple ways. Mal, who serves as the voice of individualism, plays a key role in that he is portrayed as separated from the crew and fending for himself, as if he were living in something like a state of nature. These are the only times Mal is portrayed in mortal danger and, indeed, on the very verge of death.

The first time Mal is so portrayed occurs in "Out of Gas." Spaceship *Serenity* is adrift in the black of space. Mal splits the crew into two groups and orders them to depart on the two shuttles. They are to seek safe harbor. Mal stays behind in the hope that someone will pick up *Serenity's* distress call and assist with the required repairs. Miraculously, salvagers arrive and possess the part Mal needs, but it's a ruse: They wound Mal with a gunshot to the stomach and attempt to takeover *Serenity*. Bleeding profusely, Mal surprises the pirates by steadying himself enough to pull a gun on them. After the pirates depart, Mal struggles mightily toward the engine room, but he passes out before completing the repairs. When he awakes, he is surrounded by the crew (because Zoe disobeyed orders and convinced the shuttle pilots to return). Kaylee has replaced the damaged engine part and the ship is now functioning properly. Simon provides him the medical attention he needs, assisted by Zoe, who supplies Mal with an intravenous blood transfusion. Shepherd Book is there to provide moral support and reassure him that the crew will aid in his recovery. They are better off together rather than separated.

The second is in "War Stories." Niska seeks revenge for the failed train heist in "The Train Job"; he has a reputation to maintain. Niska's men capture Wash and Mal. Niska proceeds to torture them, seemingly for his sadistic pleasure. Zoe procures a bounty to rescue Wash (made possible by Jayne donating his take from the "Ariel" hospital heist), but she is forced to leave Mal behind, alone. Niska tortures Mal to death, only to revive him so the vicious crime lord can continue torturing him. Eventually, at Wash's behest, Zoe and the rest of the crew storm Niska's skyplex (small space station) to rescue their captain. Even Book takes up arms. As he loads his rifle, Zoe queries, "Preacher, ain't the Bible mighty specific on the subject of killing?" To which Book replies, "Quite specific. It is, however, somewhat fuzzier on the subject of kneecaps." Again, the crew is stronger together and, as such, each individual has a better opportunity to "live like a person"; however, it's important to see that in the world of *Firefly* living like a person requires meaningful interactions between comrades.

That *Firefly* implicitly advocates for meaningful interactions among comrades signals a third supplemental thesis for SIFS. This thesis includes a crucial ethical component. Not only is life completely alone an impoverished way to live, but one's life is made significantly better if you are a member of a close-knit or intimate commonwealth, that is, a community. Both Hobbes and Locke, it seems, tended to use the terms "commonwealth" and "community" more or less interchangeably.[2]

However, *Firefly* suggests an important difference in meaning between them, which seems to further distinguish SIFS from its Hobbesian and Lockean social contract moorings.

This ethically significant supplemental thesis is vividly conveyed in an important scene from "Our Mrs. Reynolds." In this episode, we meet Saffron, who initially seems to be an innocent young maiden but is actually a con artist. She is smarter than Magistrate Higgins, slyer than Burgess, and more cunning than Niska. After Saffron hoodwinks the crew, almost getting everyone on board killed, they track her to a remote moon. At gunpoint, she smugly declares to Mal, "Everybody plays each other. That's all anybody ever does. We play parts." By playing "the part" properly, Saffron intimates that anyone can selfishly achieve whatever she wants regardless of the consequences to others; this is another not-so-subtle indication of what life would be like without comrades in something like a state of nature. Mal replies:

> Yet here I am with a gun to your head. That's 'cause I got people with me, people who trust each other, who do for each other and ain't always looking for the advantage. There's good people in the 'verse. Not many, lord knows, but you only need a few.

Mal doesn't have much, but he has the crew and they have each other, and that is what is ultimately important. Furthermore, Mal implies that Saffron suffers because she is *without* good people who trust and do for each other. By refusing to meaningfully connect with anyone, Saffron's life is importantly lacking. One meaningfully connects with others by regularly meeting them as partners with shared goals and, indeed, as friends. Partners and friends do not always get along, but they remain committed to each other – and their group – in ways that strangers or mere acquaintances do not.

Community and friendship are the ethically significant ideals most noticeably associated with this third supplemental thesis bolstering SIFS. Achieving community requires citizens to foster distinctive character traits: loyalty, courage, honesty, generosity, kindness, and sincerity (among others). Establishing friendship strengthens the bonds between the citizenry and thus strengthens the community. It also tends to enhance the character traits citizens must develop to form a proper community. No community is perfect, of course, and not every citizen will develop character traits in exactly the same way or to the same degree, but everyone benefits as each community member strives to become better.

The ethical ideas inherent in this supplemental thesis are germane to virtue ethics and Aristotle's treatment is iconic. The social nature of human beings is a staple to Aristotle's ethical views. He writes: "For the final and perfect good ... we do not mean a man who lives his life in isolation ... since man is by nature a social and political being." If Aristotle is correct that we are naturally social, then living in complete isolation cannot be good for us. Consequently, the good human life minimally requires living in association with others. Furthermore, Aristotle contends that it also requires friendship – living among those who have goodwill toward one another and care about each other's interests. Aristotle goes so far as to claim,

"Without friends no one would choose to live, though he had all other goods." If it's good to live in association with others, it's better to live among those who express mutual goodwill and concern about each other's interests. Achieving this sort of connection minimally requires recognizing that the interests of others are no less important than yours. Fostering such reciprocal relationships requires time, familiarity (participating in common goals, or "sharing the salt," as Aristotle says), and maintaining trust. Once such relationships are accomplished, one thereby achieves a sort of second self, a true partner, such that your interests are directly tied into those of the other. Although complete success in attaining such friendships is not common, it remains a worthy goal: Striving to meet it creates strong bonds between community members, which only strengthens the community. In this way, a commonwealth becomes a community (Aristotle, 1097b8–10, 1155a5–6, 1156b25–28, and 1157b33–36).

There are various instances of *Firefly* conveying Aristotelian interpretations of community and friendship, but two are particularly instructive. The first (from "Trash") is Simon's response to Jayne's aforementioned betrayal. Unlike Mal, Simon neither threatens nor seeks retribution. Rather, he seemingly pardons Jayne, invites him to renew their relationship, and surprisingly offers to trust Jayne more. Simon tells Jayne:

> No matter how you come down on us, I will never harm you. You're on this table, you're safe. I'm your medic, . . . we're on the same crew. . . . I don't care what you've done. I don't know what you're planning on doing, but I'm trusting you. I think you should do the same.

By mercifully reminding Jayne of the importance of trust and friendship, concepts that Jayne has difficulty "wrapping his head around," Simon hopes to accomplish what Mal does: bringing Jayne back into the fold, working for the common good, and strengthening the bonds of friendship.

The second instance comes from the last few lines of *Serenity*. Mal asks River, "You know what the first rule of flying is?" River already knows – she's psychic, remember – but she wishes to hear him say the words. Mal continues:

> Love. . .You can learn all the math in the "verse, but you take a boat in the air you don't love, she'll shake you off just as sure as turnin" of the worlds. Love keeps her in the air when she oughta fall down, tells you she's hurtin' 'fore she keens. Makes her home.

Spaceship *Serenity* has become the crew's home – a mobile, close-knit community cruising through the "black." Like the closest of families, the crew doesn't always get along, and some of them leave for other locales (temporarily or permanently, per their right), but the crew is stronger for growing together in the intimate ways they have. It should come as no surprise that Aristotle contends genuine friendship is a form of love (Aristotle, 1157b30–35). Becoming the sort of person one can love requires developing a distinct sort of moral character. This, again, solidifies how *Firefly* distinguishes community from commonwealth and how living in the former is to each individual member's benefit.

The close read of *Firefly* and *Serenity* offered here brings forth a novel philosophical theory about the nature of government, political dissent, and virtuous communities. Although expressing elements of classical social contract theory about the state of nature and natural rights, it affirms that faceless authoritarian governments that regularly disregard the individualism of its citizens ought to be resisted as much as those that are overtly tyrannical. Furthermore, if one is subjected to such expansive political regimes without recourse, he or she may permissibly seek a close-knit and, if necessary, mobile commonwealth, ideally consisting of partners and friends that thereby becomes a virtuous community and allows for the meaningful individualism of its members (that would be practically impossible otherwise). Of course, this just is spaceship *Serenity*, and thus the series and subsequent motion picture *embody* a philosophically significant theory. The way *Firefly* and *Serenity* depict the ship and its crew provides for the theory's plausibility, albeit in a non-traditional way – that is, cinematically. This also explains the theory's moniker: Given their circumstances, there is no (longer) any place the crew can (truly) be since they have found (spaceship) *Serenity*, that is, SIFS.

Assessing *Firefly's* (and *Serenity's*) Message

Having delineated SIFS, it is worthwhile to contemplate not only how *Firefly* presents it to the viewer, but also some of its implications (or entailments). Through vivid depictions of political arrangements and governmental activities that are clearly deficient, *Firefly* indirectly affords us insights into more plausible forms of the state and its organization. Careful viewers will discern that these cinematically conveyed insights invite them to consider how government and community are beneficially synthesized. Indeed, the SIFS theory *Firefly* embodies entails that the proper function of government is to arrange the state in ways conducive to individual persons and natural rights-bearers leading the good life. The good life cannot be led in complete isolation; life among complete strangers or those who have no regard for your well-being (let alone Reavers) is no way to live. Thus, forming a commonwealth is a necessary condition for the good life. However, SIFS is inconsistent with any view of government that significantly curtails an individual's choices and goals merely to sustain political authority (even if it does keep the peace). There are no (or very few) meaningful social interactions in such governments; they inhibit individualism and (more or less) simply "get in a (wo)man's way." Thus, not all commonwealths are desirable, and some are permissibly resisted. Furthermore, SIFS entails that meaningful interactions among citizens resulting in developing distinctive character traits that lead to close partnerships are conducive to leading the good life; such interactions and resulting character traits are ethically and politically desirable insofar as they invariably transform a commonwealth into a community. Thus, although individuality and individualism are valuable, their true worth cannot manifest in complete isolation; the ideal relationship between citizens is akin to friends or siblings in that each grows closer together for the benefit of the individual and the whole of which they are a part.

12 *Firefly* as Philosophy: Social Contracts, Political Dissent, and...

As is the case with Hobbes's and Locke's classic theories, SIFS and its entailments are open to philosophical critique. Perhaps the most obvious problematic feature of the theory is that a SIFS-based community, by its nature, must be quite small to allow for the requisite meaningful interactions. Consequently, the community will have difficulties securing basic physical necessities of food, shelter, and medicine for its citizens and defending itself from external threats to its political security. Each will negatively impact the commonwealth's stability, impeding its ability to facilitate the good life for its citizens. Interestingly, however, *Firefly*'s crew does include representatives from the medical (Simon), transportation (Wash), engineering (Kaylee), military (Zoe), and spiritual (Book) sectors, and Mal is a capable, even if imperfect, political leader (who often receives wise counsel from Inara). Thus, there is an indication of attempting to meet basic needs. Furthermore, *Firefly* conveys a *mobile* community, which allows for operating under the radar of political threats, in conjunction with its various run-and-hide defense strategies. Still, there is a difference between awareness of basic needs and successfully securing them. On multiple occasions, Mal and his crew have great difficulty securing food and basic supplies, which forces them into dangerous situations (e.g., with Patience on Whitefall moon in "Serenity, Part II"). Furthermore, when powerful political competitors, such as the Alliance, exert a concerted effort against *Firefly*, the crew is often at great peril.

Due to the persistent difficulties small mobile communities like spaceship *Serenity* would have in securing basic necessities, they would invariably depend on other, more powerful and affluent commonwealths for food and supplies. In various ways, *Firefly*'s crew depends on the Alliance as much as it rebels against it. Consequently, Foster and South's critique of Mal (and the crew) is apt. True, in spaceship *Serenity*'s specific case, the Alliance is inimical to ideals SIFS embodies, and it is prone to tyranny; furthermore, there are no other politically stable and affluent commonwealths to explore. Thus, spaceship *Serenity* has no choice but to deal with the Alliance. Concomitantly, consider a real-world analogy. Imagine that *Serenity* is a ship in international waters (and set aside United Nations regulations, or at least assume *Serenity* can be considered its own nation of origin). Assuming that *Serenity* can stay afloat – "keep sailing" – and secure basic necessities from the sea, perhaps fairly bartering with external commonwealths for supplies when necessary, then this is what it ought to do, given SIFS ideals. But the question arises: How practical is this plan? It seems unlikely that a mobile community as small as *Serenity* could properly subsist on the open water alone. Thus, it would need to align itself with a more stable commonwealth or disband.

Perhaps this last critique is reason to interpret *Firefly* as not suggesting a political theory of government as much as an intriguing ethical response to a difficult, if not impossible, situation. If the worst comes – if you fought mightily for what you truly believed in and lost – and now no other social-political alternatives are viable, then form your own community. Infuse it with friendships forged by meaningful interactions with others, allow everyone sufficient freedom to pursue his or her individual goals, and benefit by the resulting strong community. As these friendships solidify and the community develops, keep flying, being under the heal of no one ever again, at least insofar as you can. At least you would have *that*, and to paraphrase Mal at the end of "Serenity, Part II," maybe that's enough. It keeps you on the path toward the good life, and sometimes that is the best anyone can do. In this way, lovable losers like Mal, Zoe, Simon, and River may have something important to teach us about the good life (an insight itself worthy of further contemplation).

So, on the one hand, one might object that SIFS represents an overly idealistic theory of the state. By supplementing Lockean social contract ideas about natural rights and individualism with Aristotelian principles of friendship and community, it requires too much to be put effectively into practice. And there might be something to this critique. On the other hand, *Firefly* might only convey the ethical desirability of a sort of adopted family-type structure (brought together by dire circumstances) rather than a view of a well-ordered political state. And that is fine. However, *Firefly* is in rather esteemed company if we see it as proposing a theory that combines political and ethical ideals in ways that may inhibit its practicality. Such a complaint is often leveled against Plato's view as expressed in the *Republic* and Confucius's view as expressed in the *Analects* (and later refined by his disciple Mencius in the *Mencius*). These theorists also embedded insights about the good life into their social-political theories. So, just as it remains philosophically worthwhile to explore Plato and Confucius's ideas about social-political philosophy and the good life, it seems reasonable to conclude that *Firefly's* SIFS is worthwhile to contemplate, despite concerns about its practicality.

Conclusion: Watching (and Re-Watching) *Firefly* and *Serenity, and Philosophically Moving Forward*

It is incredibly unlikely that Joss Whedon's *Firefly* and the SIFS theory it implicitly embodies and thus advocates will ever come close to being as philosophically influential as Plato or Confucius. However, it cannot be overlooked that *Firefly* offers the careful viewer a philosophical-rich landscape worthy of additional exploration. Perhaps the most pertinent insight is that *Firefly* cinematically accomplishes something very similar to what someone like Hobbes or Locke does via traditional philosophical mediums. (For more on the so-called the film-as-philosophy thesis, see Thomas Wartenberg (2007). For how many of the relevant issues apply to Joss Whedon's corpus, see Kowalski (2017).)[3] That this invitation spurs us to re-watch our favorite 14-episode television series and its companion follow-up film (again) makes it all the more appealing! Shiny!

End Notes

1. The existence of impersonal forces that illicitly impede the individualism of Whedon's protagonists pervades his corpus: Watcher's Council in *Buffy the Vampire Slayer*; Wolfram and Hart's Senior Partners in *Angel*; Rossum Corporation in *Dollhouse*; and the Ancient Ones in *Cabin in the Woods*. Thus, that the

Alliance serves as such a thematic device cannot be accidental or unintended. For more on impersonal agencies (both internal and external) as detrimental to authentic existence in Whedon's corpus, see Foy and Kowalski (2011).

2. See Hobbes 1660, Chap. 17; Locke 1689, Chap. 1, Sect. 3 and Chap. 8, Sects. 95–96.

3. It presents for our consideration a philosophically significant theory, possessing intuitive strengths and shortcomings, and invites us to explore it and its entailments further.

References

Aristotle. 1925. *Nicomachean ethics*. Trans. W. D. Ross. Oxford: Oxford University Press.

Bennett, John G. 1979. A note on Locke's theory of tacit consent. *Philosophical Review* 88 (2): 224–234.

Foster, Susanne, and James South. 2013. Social contract: Rebellion and dissent aboard *Serenity*. In *Homer Simpson Ponders politics*, ed. Joseph Foy and Timothy Dale, 63–74. Lexington: University Press of Kentucky.

Foy, Joseph. 2011. The state of nature and social contracts on spaceship *Serenity*. In *The philosophy of Joss Whedon*, ed. Dean A. Kowalski and S. Evan Kreider, 39–54. Lexington: University Press of Kentucky.

Foy, Joseph J., and Dean A. Kowalski. 2011. Seeking authenticity in the Whedonverse. In *The philosophy of Joss Whedon*, ed. Dean A. Kowalski and S. Evan Kreider, 151–167. Lexington: University Press of Kentucky.

Hobbes, Thomas. 1660. *The leviathan*. London: Penguin Classics, 1968.

Kowalski, Dean A. 2017. *Joss Whedon as philosopher*. Lanham: Lexington Books.

Locke, John. 1689. *The second treatise of government*. New York: Barnes & Noble.

Wartenberg, Thomas. 2007. *Thinking on screen: Film as philosophy*. New York: Routledge.

Arrested Development as Philosophy: Family First? What We Owe Our Parents

13

Kristopher G. Phillips

Contents

Introduction 284
The Bluth Family, Parental Archetypes, and Filial Obligations 286
    "There's always money in the banana stand" (George Sr.) 286
    "If that's a veiled criticism about me, I won't hear it and I won't respond to it"
    (Lucille Bluth) 288
    "Why am I the only one who seems to get how much trouble this family is in?"
    (Michael Bluth) 290
    "Oh, come on! I'm a parent! I care about my daughter every bit as much as Michael
    cares about his son. . ." (Lindsay Bluth Fünke) 292
    "I've made a huge mistake" (George Oscar Bluth Jr. [Gob]) 294
    "You lied to me! You said my father was my father, but my uncle is my father. My father
    is my uncle!" (Byron "Buster" Bluth) 295
Should the Bluths Put "Family First"? 296
    The Negative Thesis (Part 1): Why Adult Children Don't "Owe" Their Parents
    Gratitude 297
    Negative Thesis (Part 2): The One Where They Adopt Lindsay: Why Biology Isn't
    a Ground for Obligation 299
    Negative Thesis (Part 3): Why the Institution or Role of Family Member Is
    Not Enough 301
    Positive Thesis: "Friendship First" 302
Evaluating *Arrested Development's* Argument: Can Parents and Children Really Be
Friends? 304
    First Objection: The Uniqueness of Parent-Child Intimacy 305
    Second Objection: Personal Identity, Transformative Experience, and
    Parental Identity 305
    Mission Accomplished: Addressing the Objections 306

K. G. Phillips (✉)
Southern Utah University, Cedar City, UT, USA

Eastern Michigan University, Ypsilanti, MI, USA
e-mail: kristopherphillips@suu.edu; kristopher.g.phillips@gmail.com

© Springer Nature Switzerland AG 2024
D. K. Johnson et al. (eds.), *The Palgrave Handbook of Popular Culture as Philosophy*,
https://doi.org/10.1007/978-3-031-24685-2_29

Conclusion: Friendship First 308
References 308

Abstract

Narrator Ron Howard tells us that *Arrested Development* is the "story of a wealthy family who lost everything, and the one son who had no choice but to keep them all together." The cult classic follows Michael Bluth – the middle son of an inept, philandering, corrupt real estate developer, George Bluth Sr., who is arrested for white-collar crimes. Constantly faced with crises created by his eccentric family, Michael does his best to preserve the family business, put out fires, and serve as a role model for his teenage son, George Michael. The Bluths' misadventures raise the question, what, if anything, do adult children owe their parents? This chapter explores the relationships between the members of the Bluth family and argues that *Arrested Development* makes the case that, insofar as adult children "owe" their parents anything, such an obligation is grounded in a sense of friendship – a voluntarily entered relation that can be terminated at any time. As a result, *Arrested Development* challenges the often-unquestioned assumption that children owe their parents special consideration simply in virtue of the parent-child relationship.

Keywords

Arrested Development · Family first · Ethics · Obligation · Filial obligation · Filial duty · Duty · Friendship · Friendship of utility · Friendship of pleasure · Friendship of virtue · Duties of affection · Obligation of debt · Indebtedness · Obligation of gratitude · Gratitude · "Owing idiom" · Biological children · Adopted children · Autonomy · Personal identity · Role · Intimacy · Mitchell Hurwitz · George Bluth Sr. · Lucille Bluth · Michael Bluth · Aristotle · Aquinas · Raymond A. Belliotti · Jeffrey Blustein · Susan Brison · Jane English · Michael Hardimon · Nancy Jecker · Diane Jeske · Joseph Kupfer · L.A. Paul · Henry Sidgwick · Michael Slote

Introduction

Rapidly earning a cult following, Mitchell Hurwitz's *Arrested Development* offered an incisive satire of West Coast American social, political, and capitalist life. The show debuted in the fall of 2003 on Fox where it ran for 3 years earning significant critical acclaim (including 22 Emmy nominations and 6 wins), but never solidified a mainstream audience. After being cancelled in 2006, the show found a second life on Netflix in 2013, and a third in 2018, running for a total of five seasons.

Arrested Development follows Michael Bluth, the seemingly level-headed son of a wealthy but wildly corrupt and hilariously incompetent real estate developer, George Bluth Sr. When George Sr. is arrested at his retirement party for defrauding investors (among other things), Michael has no choice but to drop everything and try

13 *Arrested Development* as Philosophy: Family First? What We Owe Our Parents

to salvage the family business and guide his spoiled, hapless siblings as well as his controlling, manipulative mother Lucille through a series of disasters, each of their own making. As the show progresses, we find out more about George Sr.'s misdeeds, including some "light treason" – selling houses to Saddam Hussein – and how the opulent, Orange County lifestyle has negatively impacted not only Michael, but his older brother, George Oscar Bluth (or "Gob" – pronounced like the biblical figure Job), his twin sister Lindsay, his younger brother, Buster, and his son, George Michael. Each episode brings to light the perils of unchecked capitalism and consumerism, the impact of "affluenza" on wealthy kids, and just how odd family interactions can be.

Arrested Development has tremendous depth, a number of philosophical themes woven throughout the narrative and storylines, and ongoing jokes that reward attentive and repeat viewings. It would be easy to make a case for the idea that *Arrested Development* aims to introduce a host of philosophical topics: Marxist critiques of late-stage capitalism, the development of one's personal identity (whether intersectional – sex, gender identity, sexuality, class, etc. – or across time), the nature of knowledge and when we could plausibly claim to know something, or the dangers of self-awareness (and conversely a staggering lack thereof). However, there is one philosophical problem that underpins every episode, every interaction, and a number of the jokes: the Bluth family motto, "Family First."

Taken at face value, we might wonder how putting family first presents a philosophical problem. In *The Methods of Ethics*, Henry Sidgwick notes, "We not only find it hard to say exactly how much a son owes his parents, but we are even reluctant to investigate this" (Sidgwick 1981, p. 243). He continues with the recognition that even if we could develop a ground for filial obligation (the obligations children have to their parents), a further challenge arises: When it comes to duties of affection, our obligations will undoubtedly come into conflict not only with one another but with other duties as well. It is prudent to tease out two related questions now under consideration. First, do adult children have special obligations to their parents? Second, if so, what is the *ground* of such an obligation; or in other words, what is the moral basis on which those obligations rest? Throughout history, different philosophers have offered various answers to the second question including indebtedness (Aristotle 1987), gratitude (Jecker 1989), friendship (English 1979; Jeske 1998), and the social role and biological institution of parenthood (Jecker 1989; Kupfer 1990), among others. Still, others outright reject the idea that adult children owe anything to parents at all (Blustein 1982; Slote 1979), thereby eliminating the need to explain *why* adult children owe parents anything.

This chapter explores attempts to identify just what, if anything, adult children owe their parents through a discussion of the familial relations explored in *Arrested Development*. The show makes the case that *if* adult children owe anything to their parents, it's not out of indebtedness, gratitude, or because of the social/biological institution of parenthood, but out of an ongoing voluntary friendship with one's parent. That is, *Arrested Development* challenges the often-unquestioned assumption that children owe their parents special consideration simply in virtue of the parent-child relationship by illustrating some of the many ways in which that relationship can go horribly, horribly wrong. In short, this chapter seeks to answer two questions: Should we follow the Bluth motto, and put "Family First"? And if so, why?

The Bluth Family, Parental Archetypes, and Filial Obligations

Arrested Development is primarily character driven rather than plot driven. That is, while there is arguably one unifying thread that runs through the show (Michael's attempt to salvage the family business in light of his father's crimes while keeping his family together), there are a wide variety of subplots that emerge because of Bluth family dynamics. As such, it is worth introducing some members of the Bluth family in order to spell out how they relate to and interact with one another. In thinking about parent-child relations, Nancy S. Jecker suggests that it is useful to distinguish

> . . .very roughly three paradigms of parents:
>
> *1.* Those who feel resentful or spiteful towards their offspring and never benefit their children for their children's own sake.
> *2.* Those who feel largely indifferent about their children's welfare, yet occasionally benefit their children for their children's own sake.
> *3.* Those who care deeply about their children's welfare and regularly benefit their children for their children's own sake. (Jecker 1989, p. 76)

Jecker continues by noting that most parents do not neatly fit into any one of these categories, rather they fall between or fluctuate between them. This framework will prove particularly helpful in understanding the Bluths – some members of the Bluth clan fit these archetypes perfectly, while others represent the messy middle ground between these parental types. In characterizing each of the Bluths, it should be noted that the extent to which they *believe* themselves to care deeply, or to act for their children's own sake, may not map perfectly onto how they *actually* are (they're not terribly self-aware). So, who are the Bluths?

"There's always money in the banana stand" (George Sr.)

George Bluth Sr. is first and foremost a ruthless capitalist – he stole the idea for the family's first company (a frozen banana stand) from a street vender in the 1960s. He's also the aging CEO of the Bluth Company, a publicly traded development company specializing in "high cost, low quality mini-mansions" (S1 E4), as well as the proprietor of the "Boyfights" video series (a collection of home videos documenting the fights George would instigate between his children, Gob and Michael). George Sr. is so concerned with making money that he was willing to attach his name to worthless and dangerous products such as "the cornballer" – a home fryer dedicated to making deep-fried balls of cornbread. After the design of the product proved insanely dangerous, George Sr. didn't pull them from production, but decided to market them in Mexico, presumably to ensure the profitability of his endeavor. Following his arrest, George Sr. even finds ways both to run the company from prison and to turn his newfound and deeply misguided commitment to Judaism into another money-making venture – creating and marketing another video series: "Caged Wisdom." In short, George Sr. would do just about anything to make a buck.

Given his unscrupulousness in business, it is somewhat unsurprising that the vast majority of George's interactions – in both business and family – are carefully orchestrated to ensure that he retains at least the appearance of power and authority. Jeff Ewing highlighted the connection between George's competitive nature in business and how his business focus manifests in an indifference toward his family noting, "George Sr.'s highly competitive and hard-to-please nature shows itself in how little approval he gives his family, especially his sons Gob, Michael, and Buster" (Ewing 2012, p. 66). Perhaps the perfect exemplification of Ewing's description comes from an interaction between George (in his role as CEO) and Michael (in his role as company employee),

Narrator	When George, Sr. was in charge, he had a habit of shooting down any idea Michael came up with.
Cutaway	the Bluth offices
CAPTION	two years earlier...
Michael	...and Sudden Valley just sort of implies that something awful could happen all of a sudden. You know? Plus, it's on a hill.
George, Sr.	What, are you taking stupid pills? Come on. Save us some money.
Narrator	This was a management tool he used to keep Michael working for his approval.
George, Sr.	That was a hard one to say no to. (S2 E7)

While this vignette suggests that George Sr. doesn't really care about or respect Michael, that's not quite right. As the first season unfolds, George Sr. shows that he recognizes Michael's business acumen and does whatever he can to shield Michael from the legal consequences of his own malfeasance. In the first episode, George appoints his wife Lucille as his successor rather than Michael, noting under his breath, "I'm sorry son, it's just not the right time." After his arrest, it comes to light that George had been advised by his hilariously inept attorney that a husband and wife cannot be prosecuted for the same crime (perhaps a misremembering of the law that a spouse cannot be compelled to *testify against* their partner).

George's treatment of the other Bluth children leaves even less to be desired. He repeatedly treats Gob as a disappointment and considers him only useful for dangerous or reckless tasks related to the business. George appreciates Lindsay only for her looks, and, on the rare occasion, he acknowledges Buster; George Sr. seems to openly resent him. Still, George did go out of his way to try to teach his kids lasting life lessons – though one could make the case that these lessons, too, were self-serving. He would hire his one-armed friend, J. Walter Weatherman, to stage elaborate scenarios which resulted in Weatherman's fake arm being ripped off, often tenuously tied to something the kids did, or were supposed to have done. For example, in order to teach the kids that they should, "always leave a note," George turned around while driving to express his dissatisfaction at the kids for having finished milk and not letting anyone know. With his eyes off the road, he "accidentally" hit a pedestrian, whose arm appeared to get caught in the windshield and was torn off. George Sr. rolled down the back window, and Weatherman exclaimed to the now traumatized children, "and that's why you always leave a note" (S1 E 10). Jecker's example of a parent who fits the second model almost perfectly describes George Sr. She writes, "Imagine, for example, a man who is so preoccupied with his work, or with world politics, or with making money, that the benefits he bestows upon his children are not typically given with much thought" (Jecker 1989, p. 77). This may well have been a direct description of George Sr. He is largely indifferent to the welfare of his children, and when he does something to benefit them, it's often self-serving or accidental.

"If that's a veiled criticism about me, I won't hear it and I won't respond to it" (Lucille Bluth)

In stark contrast to George Sr., we have Lucille Bluth. The matriarch of the Bluth family, Lucille is the mother of the Bluth children. Insofar as she is their mother, she clearly fits into the first archetype: She is spiteful, resentful, and rarely to never (intentionally) benefits her children unless it benefits herself as well. Constantly concerned with appearance, status, and power, Lucille is manipulative, calculating, and cold (if not openly hostile) toward her kids – even announcing to nobody in particular at a country club lunch, "I don't care for Gob" (S1 E1). Lucille's interactions with those around her are more varied in their scope and motivations than her husband's, but she's much better at concealing her motivations. Lucille's only "friend" is her longtime neighbor Lucille Austero (or "Lucille 2" – as the Bluths call her). The Lucilles' "friendship" is predicated on competition, one-upsmanship, vitriol, and cruelty – at least on Lucille's part. That Lucille would treat someone who is supposed to be a friend this way will prove instructive when considering whether friendship is the proper ground of filial obligation.

Lucille's approach to friendship is a significant departure from how philosophers understand friendship – namely as some kind of care or love of another person for their own sake. In the *Nicomachean Ethics*, Aristotle distinguished three types of friendship: friendships of pleasure, friendships of utility, and friendships of virtue (Aristotle 1987, Book VIII). Bennett Helm summarizes Aristotle's distinction as roughly, "I may love my friend because of the pleasure I get out of her, or because of the ways in which she is useful to me, or because I find her to have a virtuous character. Given the involvement of love in each case, all three kinds of friendship seem to involve a concern for your friend for his sake and not for your own" (Helm 2021). It is probably true of most friendships that they don't fit neatly into any one of these types at all (or even very many) times – interpersonal relationships are complicated and tend to evolve over time. Still, Aristotle's distinction between the three types of friendship is helpful in considering whether friendship should serve as the ground for filial obligations. After all, if friendship is supposed to explain why an adult child owes their parent something, it is important to be clear on what that friendship ought to look like. If the Lucilles' relationship is properly understood as a friendship, then whatever kind of friendship it is does not seem a promising option for anyone looking to ground filial obligation in friendship.

So, what kind of friendship do the Lucilles have? It seems clear that they would not be promising candidates for a friendship of virtue; Lucille Bluth seems incapable of recognizing genuine virtue in others and, even if she did, it's hard to imagine that she would appreciate it. So they must have a friendship of either pleasure or utility. While we could make a case for their friendship as one of utility, a friendship of pleasure seems more likely – yet even this description doesn't quite fit. Lucille takes pleasure in mocking Lucille 2, in cheating her, in their socialite rivalry, and so on. "[S]uch quarreling hardly ever arises in a friendship in which pleasure is the motive; for both parties get what they long for if it is their great pleasure to live together" (Aristotle 1987, p. 283). There is therefore something unsettling about calling this sort of relationship a friendship at all. Lucille doesn't take pleasure in anything resembling a *loving* relationship for Lucille 2.

Everything Lucille does is for herself, even when she says it's for the sake of others. That Lucille's relationship with her only "friend" is defined this way is instructive when considering her relationship with her children. Lucille is certainly not friends with her children (save for maybe Buster) in any way, at one point even prompting Michael to remark on their dynamic: "I deceived you mom. 'Trick' makes it sound like we have a playful relationship" (S1 E12). Her prickly relationship with Michael is not the only strained relationship she has with her children. Lucille openly dislikes Gob and constantly criticizes Lindsay for being lazy and for her weight (despite Lindsay being about as thin as one could be). She's so vindictive, in fact, that when Michael and Lindsay begin getting along after years spent apart, Lucille finds herself threatened by their friendship and works to drive a wedge between them, if only to ensure that she can retain power over the family.

Where Lucille's treatment of Gob and Lindsay was openly hostile, her treatment of Michael tended to be manipulative. Perhaps because he was the most competent Bluth, she tended to try to *use* Michael to further her own ends. For example, in an attempt to outdo Lucille 2, Lucille pressured Michael to throw her (Lucille Bluth) a lavish party. After Michael reminded her that the family business was still in trouble and that they should not be spending money, Lucille explained to Michael that he was her "third least-favorite child." By itself, this is comparatively tame. However, after guilting Michael into throwing her a "surprise party" (a party which none of the other Bluths attended), Lucille convinced Michael to let her drive home despite having a suspended license. On the drive home, Lucille spotted someone resembling Gob and, wanting to "give him a good scare," swerved into him, not only crashed the car – knocking Michael unconscious, but proceeded to drag him into the driver's seat and stage the scene to make it appear as if Michael had crashed. Every time it seemed as if Michael might begin to remember what happened, Lucille orchestrated a way for Michael to reinjure his head, re-clouding his memory. Finally, she allows Michael to come to the (false) conclusion that it was *he* who had wanted to scare Gob.

While Lucille openly tries to manipulate and control Michael, there is a sense in which we might consider her relationship with Buster as a *kind* of friendship, a "friendship" of utility. Treating her adult son as a servant (making him help dress her or inhale her secondhand smoke and run it out to the balcony), Lucille infantilized and demeaned Buster at every opportunity. She would often remind Buster that he was not allowed to have sugar because of the affect it had on him, "No sugar for you, you just get more awful" (S1 E19). Through her manipulation and infantilization of Buster, Lucille effectively developed an unwittingly creepy, codependent relationship in which Buster shirks all the traditional expectations of an adult child: "Adult children no longer obtain food, clothing and shelter from their parents; once they receive an 'education in life' children no longer require parental guidance in quite the same way" (Jecker 1989, p. 77). Buster receives all of these from Lucille and she seems to prefer it that way, even if she doesn't show it. For example, despite relying on Buster for companionship, support, and safety, in one episode Lucille suspected that her mood swings were the result of withdrawal from her postpartum depression medication. A confused Michael pointed out that Buster was then 32 years old, prompting Lucille to respond, "That's how long I've been depressed about him" (S3 E1).

Perhaps needless to say, Lucille is not a good mother. Despite this, she feels entitled to the ongoing love, respect, gratitude, and support of her adult children. Whether Lucille actually is entitled, owed, or deserving of anything from her children is one of the central questions the show addresses. However, before turning to that argument, it is worth discussing some of the other parent-child relationships in the show.

"Why am I the only one who seems to get how much trouble this family is in?" (Michael Bluth)

Michael Bluth is an especially interesting character for the purpose of this chapter in that he is both the adult child of George Sr. and Lucille and the widowed parent of his own teenage son, George Michael (the frozen banana salesman, not the singer-songwriter). As such, Michael fulfills two important roles. First, he's the adult child of two awful parents; in this role, he is the put-upon son who feels a special obligation to hold his eccentric family together. Second, as a parent himself, we see his relationship with his son develop through George Michael's teen years and into early adulthood. Since George Sr. and Lucille so clearly fit into Jecker's second and first archetypes for parents respectively, it wouldn't be surprising to find Michael representing a blend of the two. Michael, however, does his best to be everything his parents were not; as such, he represents the third archetype: the parent who cares deeply for their child's welfare and regularly acts out of a sense of what is best for the child (or in Michael's case, believes he does).

Michael understands himself first and foremost as the duty-bound son whose every act is entirely selfless. Our introduction to Michael finds him living in the attic of the Bluth Company's latest model home in order to ensure it continues to function as a selling tool. Throughout the series, he takes pride in doing everything he can to keep the family together and their business afloat. That pride often manifests in empty threats to leave the family behind to fend for themselves, but he always comes back, often acting as if he is doing the family a favor. With such awful parents, one might wonder why Michael finds family so important. There is some dispute among philosophers regarding whether it is out of a sense of love or a sense of duty (or some blend of the two) that children – especially adult children – express gratitude, loyalty, respect, or deference to their parents. It is clear in Michael's case that he displays such traits out of a sense of duty rather than anything else.

If anything, Michael's relationship with his parents seems primarily transactional. In exchange for his years of service, Michael thought he would be awarded a partnership share of the company when his father retired. In exchange for sticking with the family when he had an offer from a rival development company, he requested control over the corporate checkbook and a de facto CEO position. Given Lucille's manipulative and controlling nature, Michael and Lucille often end up negotiating deals more frequently than interacting like family. But this transactional approach to family doesn't end with Lucille; it permeates the whole Bluth clan – prompting Michael to note, "I need a favor" ought to be "put on the family crest" (S1 E10). Outside of the context of the Bluths, familial interactions – perhaps especially those with siblings – may sometimes appear transactional. However, friendships and familial relationships "ought to be characterized by *mutuality* rather than reciprocity: friends [and family] offer what they can give and accept what they need, without regard for the total amounts of benefits exchanged. And friends [and family] are motivated by love rather than the prospect of repayment" (English 1979, p. 353). Thus, there is a sense in which Michael's peculiar sense of duty to his parents is instructive for understanding whether he is right to act out of this sense of obligation.

A distinction might be made between the social role one holds as a parent and the particular person who fills that role. Even a lousy parent like George Sr. is still a father in the social sense of the term. That he fulfills the role of father may create certain obligations for his children, but the fact that George Sr. (the man) is pretty awful seems to diminish the pull of any such obligations. "If [he] insists that [he] owes [his] father gratitude simply because he is [his] *father*, [he] is failing to distinguish between fathering in the abstract, and the individual man who fathered [him]" (Jecker 1989, p. 76). Michael either ignores or denies the distinction both in approaching his parents and in his own parenting style. For Michael, being a father is inextricably bound to a man's identity once he's had children – in other words, regardless of how vicious a person is, insofar as they are a father, they are owed certain considerations.

If Michael's relationship with his siblings and parents is largely predicated on favors, transactions, and a sense of superiority stemming from what he perceives as constantly going beyond his filial duty, then his relationship with his son, George Michael, is grounded in a profound sense of love paired with a robust understanding of what it means to fill the role of a father. Michael seems to believe that being a father carries with it certain burdens (e.g., constant self-sacrifice) and, in virtue of having taken on those burdens, he deserves his son's time and attention (and, at one point, living space). Despite genuinely caring for his son, Michael often misconstrues what George Michael wants and needs. Resulting from a sense of deference to what he believes is best for his son, paired with an almost pathological inability to listen, Michael self-sabotages, denies himself romantic relationships, and ultimately feels wildly betrayed when his son tries to distance himself in order to become his own person (a theme which recurs throughout the series).

While Michael's sense of betrayal may seem natural – perhaps especially given his identification with his role as loving father – George Michael's desire to pull away seems equally sensible. In season four, George Michael has gone off to college, studied abroad (and had an affair with a Spanish housewife), and found a sense of confidence he'd never before experienced. As Diane Jeske remarks, "even in less than abusive situations, parents are often unable to let go of their roles of authority, thereby precluding any intimacy between them and their adult children. Thus, in order to live their own lives, such adult children begin to distance themselves from their parents" (Jeske 1998, p. 543). It is therefore unsurprising that George Michael was nonplussed when, following the housing crash, Michael (having gone bankrupt) insisted on moving in with George Michael in the dorms. Michael's inability to let go of his authoritative role further alienates the two. Needless to say, that Michael instantiates Jecker's third archetype of parent becomes increasingly less likely as the show progresses. While he starts out representing the third archetype, it is clear he fluctuates between all three as his relationship with his son evolves.

"Oh, come on! I'm a parent! I care about my daughter every bit as much as Michael cares about his son. . ." (Lindsay Bluth Fünke)

Lindsay Bluth Fünke was raised to believe she was Michael's fraternal twin sister, though it turns out that George Sr. and Lucille adopted Lindsay when she was three. They adopted Lindsay in a misguided attempt to "stick it to a competitor," Stan Sitwell, the proprietor of a rival development company. Always the subject of Lucille's ridicule, Lindsay dropped out of college and moved to Boston where she married Tobias Fünke – at the time a mental health professional with impressive credentials (certifications in both psychoanalysis and psychotherapy). Tobias subsequently lost his medical license and turned out to be a man with an ambiguous sexual orientation, who is severely lacking in common sense, self-awareness, and who suffers from a bizarre affliction which precludes him from ever being fully naked (a "never-nude"). Lindsay married Tobias "as an act of rebellion," knowing that her parents would never approve of him.

Although she would never admit it, Lindsay has a surprising amount in common with her adoptive parents – she's vain, deeply concerned with her image and appearance, finds herself in a wildly unsatisfying and intimacy-free marriage, and is a terrible parent to her daughter, Maeby. Lindsay sees herself primarily as a socialite and an activist, though her causes are often poorly thought out, conflict with one another, and the extent to which she is committed to them diminishes quickly. It is not only fundraisers and causes that fail to keep Lindsay's attention; however, perhaps because of his ambiguous sexuality or maybe because she married Tobias out of rebellion, Lindsay does not care much for her husband. Early on, in an attempt to salvage their marriage, Tobias recommends an open relationship – an opportunity which Lindsay jumps to pursue. Over the course of the series, she pursues a number of different men, including her daughter's high school crush (and Gob's illegitimate child), Steve Holt. Her open relationship with Tobias serves as a microcosm of her personality generally – she is self-involved, has a short attention span, little follow-through, and little-to-no regard for (or awareness of) others.

In terms of her own parenting, she is best characterized as a blend of Jecker's three archetypes. She wants to be *seen* as a caring, loving parent and, while she goes out of her way to avoid being spiteful toward, or resentful of, Maeby, she rarely to never does anything for Maeby. Probably because of the way Lucille treated (and continues to treat) her, Lindsay takes a hands-off approach to parenting. In fact, Lindsay is *so* hands off that she often forgets Maeby even exists. That she forgets so frequently is itself quite a feat; Maeby constantly acts out in increasingly profound ways in an attempt to garner attention from her mother (on several occasions Tobias tries unsuccessfully to bond with Maeby). Whether it's buying, printing, and intentionally leaving airline tickets to Portugal out on the counter for her mom to see, going out of her way to buy an outfit made entirely of leather after Lindsay decided to protest the harming of animals, or dropping out of high school and faking her way into a job as a movie producer, nothing Maeby does seems to be able to shift Lindsay's attention away from herself, even for a moment.

Lindsay's reaction to finding out that she was adopted provides further insight into who Lindsay is and how she understands family. Upon learning that she is not *biologically* a Bluth, Lindsay immediately turns her romantic attention to Michael. Thinking back to all the times Michael had come to her defence as children when Lucille was criticizing her, Lindsay reinterpreted those memories as representing Michael's attraction to her and decided that he would be interested in pursuing a romantic relationship. After all, they're not blood related! Michael, however, has a more inclusive – and probably more appropriate – sense of family. Having just explained to George Michael (who had been nursing a crush on his cousin Maeby for years – a crush Maeby eventually reciprocated) that despite not being blood related, George Michael and Maeby were still family, Michael turned down Lindsey's advances.

Michael and Lindsay's disagreement about the metaphysics of family likely underpins their different views of familial obligations. Michael understands family as a function of social roles. As such, it is unsurprising that he sees his role as a brother unaffected by biological connection; he's Lindsay's brother because that's the role he has played and it's partially definitive of who he is. That Lindsay sees biological relations as wholly constitutive of family suggests that any understanding she might have of familial obligation is the result of biology alone. This might help to explain her absentee parenting style; Lindsay is not particularly concerned with what she owes Maeby perhaps because she understands her position as Maeby's biological mother to be enough by itself to warrant certain considerations (e.g., of gratitude, support, love, etc.). In the next section, this chapter will show that Michael and Lindsay function as compelling counterexamples to attempts to ground filial obligation in social roles and biological connections, respectively.

"I've made a huge mistake" (George Oscar Bluth Jr. [Gob])

Gob is the oldest of the Bluth children and in many ways takes after his father, George Sr. A self-absorbed womanizer, a serial cheater, and an ambitious but inept businessman and entrepreneur, Gob is somehow the least respected and least useful member of the family. What Gob has going for him is his charisma – a trait he uses not only to bed women, but also to build his career as a magician. Like Michael, Gob has a peculiar sense of obligation to his parents, but unlike Michael, Gob's contributions to the family business are relegated to dangerous or reckless tasks. Desperate for attention from George Sr., Gob does everything he can to make his father proud.

In the second season, Gob is made chairman of the Bluth Company in order to appease investors and while he is clearly not cut out for any actual kind of authority or responsibility, he does everything he can to fill his father's shoes. Gob takes to wearing his father's expensive suits – which he reminds everyone of at every opportunity (usually noting their extravagant cost). Perhaps because he never received much (if any) positive reinforcement from his father, Gob is neither self-assured nor particularly self-aware. As a result, he doesn't really have any friends, seems to flit about between jobs (stripping, ironically waiting tables, pretending to run the family business, various magic gigs, and an ill-fated attempt to open a coffee shop with Tobias), and seems to cling to any strong masculine figure he can find.

In the fourth season, Gob finally fulfills his wish to bond with his father. After running into a depressed, suicidal George Sr. (struggling with his impending divorce from Lucille and the loss of his libido), Gob – also in something of a tailspin – comes up with a plan for the two men to bounce back; they will wingman one another in an attempt to sleep their way across Mexico. A somewhat radical departure from traditional father-son relationships, this plan results in an unlikely bond as both men struggle to find the desire to follow through with any women they meet. What is striking about this is not so much the story (though it is bizarre), but the way in which Gob and George Sr. bond. This marks a radical departure from how Gob previously conceived of his father's sexuality. In early seasons, Gob would recoil and wretch at the very mention of intimacy between George Sr. and Lucille. This earlier response falls in line with how Joseph Kupfer challenges the viability of parent-adult child friendships; though he understands a child to be the embodiment of the parental union, Kupfer suggests that when thinking of a parent engaging in sexual activity (specifically *outside* of the bounds of marriage), "simply knowing of this behavior might disturb the grown child" (Kupfer 1990, p. 19). That Gob had such a visceral reaction to his father's sexuality, when paired with his desperate desire for approval from George *as a father*, might lead to the conclusion that friendship is off the table for these two men.

Yet a seemingly genuine friendship is exactly what develops between them as this story unfolds. Jeffrey Blustein offers some insights into how this might be possible. He notes that part of what makes it possible for parents and adult children to be friends is a willingness on the part of a parent to see their adult children as equal. In this case, it is only possible because of how far George Sr. has fallen; having lost his family, his spouse, and his libido, George Sr. might believe he no longer has any plausible claim to authority over his eldest son. Paired with, "very similar styles of mind or ways of thinking… this can make for a high degree of empathy" (Blustein 1982, p. 192). And that is just what we see; out of any relationship in *Arrested Development*, this is the closest to a friendship of virtue. Gob, lacking all utility to his father and sharing virtually all of his vices, becomes a genuine friend at a moment when the Bluth patriarch needs him most.

"You lied to me! You said my father was my father, but my uncle is my father. My father is my uncle!" (Byron "Buster" Bluth)

Rounding out the Bluth children is Buster. Byron "Buster" Bluth is the youngest Bluth, though he is actually the biological son of George's twin brother Oscar. Buster is the infantilized son George Sr. neither wanted nor really raised, claiming he was "too burnt out on raising" the other Bluth children. Buster is the self-described "scholar" of the family, having studied – among other things – Native American tribal ceremonies, sleep deprivation, cartography, archaeology, and eighteenth-century agrarian business – all paid for by the Bluth Company. Despite his extensive schooling, Buster is a deeply awkward, wildly unimpressive, and often childish member of the family. In addition to suffering from frequent panic attacks that prevent him from doing much of anything, he seems not to have retained much from his many studies, at one point explaining that "the blue part on the map is land" (S1 E1).

As previously mentioned, Buster and Lucille have a troublingly codependent relationship despite Lucille's nearly constant desire to appear put-upon by his presence. Buster is so deeply enmeshed with Lucille that he problematically blurs the lines between filial and romantic love. Early on, Buster accidentally flirts with Lucille 2 while not wearing his glasses (thereby failing to recognize Lucille 2 as anything more than a "brownish area, with points"). He ends up dating Lucille 2 off and on, even explaining to Lucille 2 that it's not that he confuses her with his mother, "It's exactly the opposite. I'm leaving my mother for you. You're replacing my mother" (S1 E12). Such a dynamic permeates all of Buster's relationships – both familial and romantic. In one instance, Lindsay very briefly acts like a mother toward Buster, and not only does he explain to Lucille that his sister is his "new mother," but that Lindsay is starting to "look hotter too."

Despite the blurring of lines between romantic and familial love, Buster's relationship with Lucille complicates, but ultimately does not undermine, the argument *Arrested Development* makes regarding what adult children owe their parents and why. There seems to be something of a consensus among philosophers that adult children *may* have some obligation of gratitude to their parents (though they differ regarding when and how to understand the grounding of such an obligation). In cases where a parent acts in a way that exceeds what is required by the role of parent, when what is provided requires a significant sacrifice on the parent's behalf, or when a parent provides a uniquely valuable benefit to the child (Jecker 1989, p. 75), the child may in some sense "owe" gratitude to their parent. Providing access to expensive education or "help that seems to be an extension of their role as nurturer and provider, such as nursing the adult child through an illness..." (Kupfer 1990, p. 22) are two examples wherein, all things being equal, an adult child may well have an obligation of gratitude to their parents. While it is certainly a stretch to describe Lucille as "nurturing" in any sense of the term, when it comes to Buster she does seem to be more open to moments of compassion – and there can be little doubt that she (or rather, the company) has offered substantial amounts of money to support Buster's "scholarly pursuits."

The circumstances in which Lucille has the opportunity to demonstrate her loving and "nurturing" nature for Buster, however, are largely of her own making and typically suit her own ends. After signing Buster up for the army, Buster finds himself about to be deployed to Iraq. While awaiting his deployment, Buster decided to rebel against Lucille and go swimming in the ocean – an act which Lucille had forbidden. While swimming, a "loose-seal" attacks Buster, biting off his hand. Lucille springs to Buster's aid and does everything she can to support him, including getting him juice – another significant departure from her previous prohibitions. While preparing for George Sr.'s trial, it becomes clear that Lucille had been sharing all of the family's secrets and crimes with Buster every night as he tried to sleep. This places Buster in a difficult situation – feeling an obligation of loyalty to his family, Buster does not want to testify. Such an obligation clearly conflicts, however, with his sense of justice, fidelity, and the oath he would no doubt have to swear to the court. As a result, Buster slips into a "light-to-no-coma" (S3 E10) in order to avoid having to violate one of his duties. During this time, we find Lucille fluctuate between attempts to *appear* nurturing and falling back into their friendship of utility (for example, by "renting" his "comatose" body out to aspiring beauticians, dentists, and doctors).

Buster's relationship with Lucille, while strange and off-putting, rounds out the ways in which the Bluth clan is dysfunctional and provides a jumping-off point for the central argument in the show – that, if anything, any obligation adult children have to their parents is ultimately grounded in a sense of friendship; i.e., a voluntary relationship based on the recognition of mutual and equal goodness (Aristotle 1987, p. 283).

Should the Bluths Put "Family First"?

Having now surveyed the peculiar familial relationships between the Bluths, it is time to address the two questions posed at the outset: Should the Bluth children really put "family first"? If so, why? To address these questions, the argument will proceed in two steps. First is the negative thesis: Several of the Bluths provide compelling counterexamples to attempts to ground filial obligation in something other than friendship. The second step is the positive thesis: In addition to offering compelling evidence against common responses, some of the dynamics illustrate the force of friendship as a *possible* ground for special obligations between adult parents and children. *Arrested Development* doesn't make a case for the claim that adult children *should* be friends with their parents (the Bluths probably should not); rather, the show argues that *if* adult children have special obligations to their parents, it's because they have developed a genuine friendship with their parents.

The Negative Thesis (Part 1): Why Adult Children Don't "Owe" Their Parents Gratitude

Jane English and Jeffrey Blustein have criticized accounts of filial obligation for characterizing the sort of relationship between a child and parent as one of indebtedness. English argues that understanding filial obligation as something a child "owes" to a parent or as a debt to be repaid "tends to obscure or to even undermine, the love that is the correct ground of filial obligation" (English 1979, p. 352). Blustein takes a different tack to reach the same conclusion. He argues that while it may well be the case that adult children have some sort of obligation of gratitude to their parents, there are significant constraints regarding the sorts of actions that could plausibly generate such an obligation: "If parents have any right to repayment from their children, it can only be for that which was either above and beyond the call of parental duty, or not required by parental duty at all" (Blustein 1982, p. 182). Furthermore, he continues, such benefits must be given for the right reasons (Blustein 1982, p. 183) and it must be accepted willingly by the child (see also Jeske 1998, p. 544). Part of what makes the "owing idiom" misleading, Blustein suggests, is that young children are not in a position to willingly accept any benefits, regardless of whether the benefits are required of a parent or whether the parent goes beyond the call of duty. Infants and young children are not in a position to exercise any real choice with regard to the benefits conferred upon them; young children lack the understanding and rational capacity to exercise the sort of autonomy necessary to take on a debt. In cases where grown children benefited, or even continue to benefit from, parental choices made in the past, "the freedom to decide when, and to whom, one shall become indebted cannot be abridged in advance by unilateral parental decisions" (Blustein 1982, p. 184). So even if adult children have some sort of special obligation to parents, it's not that children "owe" their parents a debt, it must be an obligation of a different type. Through the examples of Lucille, George Sr., and Michael, *Arrested Development* makes the case that many parents' actions don't rise to the level of generating a duty of gratitude.

There can be little doubt that the Bluth children received substantial benefits from Lucille and George Sr., whether access to education, career opportunities, wealth, status, or the freedom to pursue whatever ends they please. It is not clear that either George Sr. or Lucille meet any of the conditions that would warrant gratitude. Jecker offers four conditions under which it would be appropriate to offer gratitude to a parent: If the parents perform acts not *required* of them, if a parent performs a required act in an exemplary way, if the fulfillment of a parental duty is especially burdensome or risky, or if the fulfilling of a parental duty produces an especially valuable benefit (Jecker 1989, p. 75). Given George Sr.'s and Lucille's parenting styles, it's difficult to make a case for either of the first two conditions; they're not apt to do more than duty requires of a parent. Since they are hard-pressed to do even the minimum, it's obvious that neither parent fulfills their duties in an exemplary way.

It might seem that a case could be made for third and fourth conditions, however. After all, their shady business practices are risky in innumerable ways and they do result in substantial benefits to the Bluth children. Still, both George Sr. and Lucille provide clear examples of parents who fail the motivation test. Jecker agrees with Blustein that the right sort of motivation is a *requirement* for generating a duty of gratitude. Their motivations are always self-serving. They don't act out of love, benevolence, or care for their children, but in the interest of keeping up appearances. After being advised by the family attorney to show up to George Sr.'s arraignment hearing "looking like a loving family," Lucille asks how long they have to keep up the appearance. Even if we set aside the important requirements set forth above, it is especially inappropriate to suggest the Bluth children need to "repay" anything to their parents. "For example, a daughter who directs gratitude for the benefits of child rearing to a [mother] who compulsively abuses and torments her underestimates her own self-worth" (Jecker 1989, p. 76).

If any parent in the show could be interpreted as satisfying the requirements for creating a debt of gratitude for their child, it'd be Michael. Michael at least starts out representing Jecker's third archetype of a parent: the loving, self-sacrificing father who always puts his child first. In contrast with his parents, Michael's motivations are in the right place and he does genuinely love George Michael. This means that the real question to consider is whether Michael meets any of the additional conditions sufficient for the generation of a debt of gratitude. While Michael acts out of the sort of benevolence and love characteristic of a good parent, it is not clear that anything he does successfully meets any of Jecker's four conditions for warranting gratitude. While Michael believes he makes substantial sacrifices on George Michael's behalf (including refraining from dating, finding special boarding schools for George Michael, and investing in George Michael's tech start-up company, among others), many of the sacrifices are the result of a misguided sense of believing he knows what George Michael wants or needs without actually speaking with him. In season three, George Michael echoes Blustein's claim that when children have matured, they may make the rational choice that they would have preferred to forgo certain benefits rather than be indebted to their parents (Blustein 1982, p. 183). "You never listen to me. You didn't ask me if I wanted to go to the school, you didn't ask me about what I said. You threatened my teacher. You don't respect me. How can I respect you, man?" (S3 E9). Even a well-meaning parent whose motivations are (or appear to be) selfless and who appears to parent in a way that ought to generate obligations or debts can fall short.

13 *Arrested Development* as Philosophy: Family First? What We Owe Our Parents   299

Negative Thesis (Part 2): The One Where They Adopt Lindsay: Why Biology Isn't a Ground for Obligation

Accounts that seek to ground filial obligation in a sense of indebtedness often appeal to some sort of inequity in terms of benefits bestowed by the parent. In order to receive any benefits at all, a child must exist. Some philosophers take the begetting of a child itself to be an act of benevolence, and therefore something which grounds special obligations. In response Jecker argues,

> [I]t is a mistake to think of begetting as an act of benevolence. To begin with, prospective parents cannot possibly intend conception as an expression of respect, care, and value *to their future child*. After all, had conception been postponed a month or more, the resultant child would have been a different child. This makes clear that even if prospective parents conceive in order to benefit a future child, they do not intend to benefit any *particular* future child. Since the extant offspring were not the objects of benevolence when their parents chose to conceive them, they do not owe their parents gratitude for conceiving them.
>
> What's more, individuals contemplating parenthood often choose to have children for no other reason than that they anticipate children will enrich *their* lives. Consequently, when children come into existence they do not usually owe parents gratitude for their existence; for their parents decision to bring them into existence is not ordinarily an expression of *benevolence*. This explains why we do not think that children owe gratitude to those who *merely* begat them. (Jecker 1989, p. 74)

If voluntary acceptance of a benefit is a constraint on the generation of a debt or duty of gratitude, then it is obvious that a not-yet-conceived child cannot voluntarily accept the putative benefit of conception; after all, not only does the yet-conceived-being lack the capacity to understand what they are getting into, but they lack all capacities and properties alike – they don't exist!

Another approach to generating a moral obligation to a biological parent might be to say that genetic makeup contributes to our identity. On this line of argument, anyone who contributes to the formation of our identity, regardless of their commitment to the child's upbringing, deserves certain considerations for having made the child who they are (Belliotti 1986, pp. 152–154). But does merely creating a person *determine* a person's identity? It certainly *contributes*; Susan Brison has persuasively argued that one's physical body is an ineliminable aspect of self (Brison 2002), though it is not the whole story. One's identification with a particular sex or with a particular racial or ethnic group certainly impacts their experiences of the world – and biology is part of this. Yet, Lindsay (in the role of mother) makes a case against Raymond Belliotti's claim that "a person can be metaphysically closer to another, or contribute to another's identity without necessarily sacrificing anything significant. And under my view, no sacrifice *per se* is required" to generate special obligations (Belliotti 1986, p. 154).

Lindsay's lack of interaction with her daughter makes it difficult to believe that Maeby owes Lindsay anything. Inhabiting a particular body does *contribute* to one's identity, but it does not tell the whole story. In developing a sense of self, understanding who one's biological parents are can be instructive, but it is not definitive of who a person is. Neither Lindsay nor Tobias have even the foggiest idea who Maeby is in any meaningful way and while their contributions to her identity likely extend beyond those of a biological parent who gave their child up for adoption, it's not by much. By looking at Lindsay as an absentee parent and thinking that Maeby doesn't really owe Lindsay anything, we get the idea that biological ties don't contribute as much to one's identity as Belliotti suggests. As Brison argues, the self is a complex mixture of one's body, those with whom one surrounds herself, one's life experiences and memories (which she describes as a "narrative self"), and one's exercise of autonomy. Lindsay's parenting style provides Maeby with unlimited autonomy, virtually no guidance with regard to interpreting her experiences or how to navigate the world, and few defining memories as a child *of Lindsay. Arrested Development* suggests that while biology contributes to Maeby's identity, that connection is only a small fraction of her *self.* As such, biological connection alone is overruled by other factors which really shape Maeby's identity. This, of course, undercuts the biological connection angle and supports Jecker's concluding thought above – that children do not owe anything to parents who merely "begat" them.

The other side of the story is that Lindsay, herself, is adopted. While George Sr. and Lucille are not by any stretch of the imagination ideal parents, Lindsay was raised as their biological child. There are two aspects to the argument on this side worth mentioning. First, even though the benefits Lindsay received as having been raised by the Bluths are arguably negligible, she was raised for nearly 40 years by the Bluths, believing herself to be their biological child. As Diane Jeske argues, it seems wrong to conclude that, simply because she has no biological connection to them, the (in this case, relative) intimacy that she developed over the course of her life with the Bluths is significantly diminished "because they contributed nothing to her genetic make-up" (Jeske 1998, p. 548). It doesn't sit right when we think that a lifetime's worth of influence, upbringing, memories, and contributions to one's identity should be diminished or downplayed because there is another person (or other people) out there with whom one might share a closer *biological* connection. Especially considering that the self is a complex mix of experiences, memories, goals, expectations, and body – all of which are directly impacted by those with whom one spends their time, biology alone seems ill-suited to explain the generation of special obligations.

Second, if biological connection is *the* decisive factor in the generation of moral obligation, then Lindsay's advances on her "brother" Michael should not seem as problematic as they do. After all, Lindsay and Michael are not *really* brother and sister – and for that matter, George Michael and Maeby are not *really* cousins. So what's the big deal? Arguably the big deal is that the sort of intimacy one develops with their adult siblings is of a unique sort: "special features of familial roles make intimacy and shared concern achievable in unique and peculiarly valuable forms. With no one but our siblings can we achieve the sort of understanding based on sharing the same upbringing" (Jeske 1998, p. 543). This is a unique bond that results from a lifetime of shared experiences – thus one may think that biological connection is neither enough by itself to generate special obligations, nor is it even required in order to generate special obligations (such as refraining from sexual advances – for a discussion of moral objections to incest in *Arrested Development*, see Barnbaum

13 *Arrested Development* as Philosophy: Family First? What We Owe Our Parents   301

2012). Thus, Michael's comment to George Michael, "I mean, she might not be a blood relative, but she is still family, and that's a bond that lasts forever" (S3 E13), summarizes the position. Family is more than biology.

Negative Thesis (Part 3): Why the Institution or Role of Family Member Is Not Enough

Lindsay offers a compelling counterexample to the idea that biology alone creates special obligations between parents and children (and siblings!). In exploring that argument, it became clear that her brother Michael sees family as something more along the lines of a sort of social role one might fulfill. While Lindsay offers good reasons to think that biology is irrelevant to filial obligation, Michael proves a case study in why the appeal to social roles won't work either. Despite initial plausibility – the appeal to family as a social institution does seem to explain why Lindsay's advances, or Buster's weird relationship with Lucille strikes viewers as problematic – attempting to ground filial obligation in social roles also misses the mark. Michael is illustrative in both being a son and in being a father. In both cases, Michael almost perfectly illustrates what happens when children of less-than-ideal parents find themselves feeling obliged simply because they are their parents' child.

Consider first Michael as the faithful, dedicated son. Michael acts out of a sense of duty rather than love. In trying to find where such a duty might come from, the available options seem to have been drastically limited by the discussion so far. If *Arrested Development* is right, it's neither a function of biology alone nor have George Sr. and Lucille done enough to warrant gratitude (Jecker 1989, p. 75). Even in the cases where it might seem as if Michael's parents have gone above and beyond for him, they have not done so out of the right motivations (Blustein 1982, p. 177) – they've only acted for themselves and helped Michael by accident. Thus, even if Michael has some sort of debt to his parents, it's not a function of friendship, gratitude, or indebtedness. There must be another explanation for why Michael seems so committed to a sense of filial duty. The best explanation is that Michael is deeply committed to the *concept* of being a son – understood as a social role.

Diane Jeske raises a powerful objection to the idea that the role or institution of "son" grounds filial obligation, which Michael seems to exemplify perfectly. Just as very young children are not in a position to voluntarily choose whether to accept certain benefits from parents, at no point is a child able to choose who their parents are. It's difficult to imagine wanting to be a Bluth and with as often as Michael threatens to leave, we might suggest that Michael would not have chosen to be born into this particular family. Even if it's plausible that being born into a particular *role* – taken in the abstract – could generate special obligations, Michael wouldn't fit the bill. After all, as Michael Hardimon argues, certain roles only generate obligations on the condition that they are "reflectively acceptable" – that is, if one were to reflect on the role, they would come to the conclusion that it is the sort of role they ought to accept *and* that it generates the sorts of obligations they ought to fulfill (Hardimon 1994, p. 348). There can be little doubt that Michael Bluth thinks one should see the role of son both as valuable and as requiring certain special obligations of those who fill that role (perhaps especially when thinking of his interactions with *his* son). "But, more importantly, any such abstract structure is an idealization, and any given individual's particular instantiation of the role is likely to be very different from the idealization" (Jeske 1998, p. 553). There is an important difference between being *a* son and being the son of George Sr. and Lucille; in the latter case, it's not clear that Michael *would* reflectively accept the role if given the choice. So it seems that Michael's commitment to his family is grounded in an abstraction rather than having to do with his parents. On most accounts, George Sr. and Lucille barely fulfill the minimal obligations *they* have to their children and, more often than not, they shirk their duties, outright fail in their obligations, and act out of indifference or spite. In such cases, there is little reason to believe that their children owe them anything, even if there is a generalized societal expectation that says otherwise.

Still, Michael starts out as a pretty good dad; consider his relationship with his son, George Michael. As the show progresses, not only does their relationship become strained, but Michael becomes increasingly entitled to his then-adult son's time, space, and even romantic partners. Michael identifies so strongly with the *role* of father that he cannot let go of the authority he believes should be afforded to him by inhabiting that role. A theme throughout the show, Michael is frequently over-bearing, dismissive, and inattentive toward George Michael – perhaps because he believes that in virtue of being George Michael's father, his behavior is irrelevant to the duties his son has to him. Michael expresses this sentiment when complaining to George Sr. about George Michael's behavior, "Yeah, I don't know what's going on with him. You know, he's-he's on Bethlehem time. He's spending every moment of the day with this girl. It's, like, I'm his father. He should be spending most of his time with me" (S2 E6).

Michael's relationships with his parents and his son make clear that the role of parent itself is not enough to justify any particular special obligations. After all, "The individual's particular instantiation in the role is, in effect, the relationship she has with her family member" (Jeske 1998, p. 553). In Michael's case, as in that of his father's, deeply imperfect men fill the role of "father" and, as a result, their sons do not owe them anything simply in virtue of fulfilling that role.

Positive Thesis: "Friendship First"

While *Arrested Development* offers compelling objections to indebtedness, grati-tude, biology, and social roles as a ground for filial obligations, the show does not merely offer an argument from the elimination of alternatives – that is, it does not merely argue that some answers are wrong; it also makes a case *for* a particular kind of friendship as the appropriate ground of obligations between adult parents and their children. It should be clear by now that the Bluths don't have much going for them in the friendship department. At least within the family, there are only two cases where a parent-child relationship even *resembles* a friendship: between Buster and Lucille

13 *Arrested Development* as Philosophy: Family First? What We Owe Our Parents   303

and between Gob and George Sr. (late in the series). Both cases are illustrative of an important caveat regarding the idea of grounding filial obligation in friendship – if friendship grounds obligation, then it has to be the *right kind* of friendship.

Recall that Aristotle distinguished three types of friendship: pleasure, utility, and virtue. If Buster and Lucille's relationship can be understood as friendship (as a kind of intimacy involving mutual caring and some sort of a shared goal), it's clear that their friendship is one of utility. Buster does not see his mother as a virtuous person (she's not), and it's not at all obvious he gets any pleasure from being around her. What he does get is a place to live, access to perpetual education, food, money, and a strange form of companionship – one which he frequently conflates with romantic love. Lucille equally gains a number of benefits from Buster's presence. He keeps her company, competes in the mother-son competition mother boy, and affords her the opportunity to *appear* as if she is a loving, supportive mother – something Lucille values deeply. In this case, Lucille and Buster have a relationship of convenience and utility; they each get various things they value, but it's not obvious they care for *one another* at all. *Arrested Development* cautions viewers against thinking that just any old friendship will do when it comes to making sense of how, why, and when adult children have special obligations to their parents. The few times Buster exercises his autonomy and leaves his mother's side, she becomes character-istically abusive, manipulative, and tries to pull him back – not out of love, but out of frustration because nobody is around to do the things Buster did. As an adult child in his 30s, it's quite a stretch to suggest – despite *somewhat* voluntarily accepting those benefits from Lucille (she does manipulate and use him) – that he has any sort of obligation to Lucille.

Thinking of the other Bluth children's relationships with their parents as one of utility is instructive. Treating their kids as a means to an end seems to be the family MO. Michael is competent and, as a result, is useful in business dealings. Lindsay is useful in the sense that she's classically beautiful and draws attention to the Bluth name through her performative advocacy. Gob is useful in that he's so desperate for fatherly approval that he'll happily do dangerous or illegal things if he's asked. Given the way George Sr. and Lucille operate, it's unsurprising that they would value their children – not as people – but as tools they can manipulate to fulfill their own ends. It is only when George Sr. has hit rock bottom – when Gob no longer serves any purpose at all – that Gob and his father bond. This moment is the closest to a healthy father-son relationship we see in the show (save for the brief period during which Gob and his illegitimate son, Steve Holt, become friends by bonding over not knowing who or where their fathers are).

Once Gob no longer has any use, the two men are able to see one another as *people*, rather than as the abstract role of father and tool for illegal activities (respectively). While the specifics of their interaction (trolling a foreign country for casual sex) are a little beyond what we might think of as appropriate for a father-son duo, it makes sense for Gob and George Sr. when considering their personalities. While it may be difficult to call many of the ways Gob takes after George Sr. "virtues," that they have as much in common as they do leads them to a common purpose and to recognize in one another the traits they admire in themselves. In this way, we see Gob and George Sr. enter into something resembling a friendship of virtue.

It is difficult to think of friendships of utility (or friendships of pleasure) as real friendships that generate genuine obligations for those involved. After all, "those whose mutual love is based upon utility do not love each other for their own sakes, but only insofar as they derive some benefit from one another. It is the same with those whose love is based upon pleasure" (Aristotle 1987, p. 258). Friendships of virtue, however, are based on an intimacy or love founded upon the recognition that those involved are alike in virtue (Aristotle 1987, p. 260). What George Sr. and Gob's budding relationship reveals is the proper ground for generating special obligations between adult children and parents; their relationship is a voluntary friendship founded on mutual aims and shared experiences rather than utility, pleasure, or external expectations. As a result, Gob and George Sr.'s friendship is a candidate for the ground of special obligations because it meets the conditions outlined above: there is a sort of intimacy that has been cultivated over time, the relationship was the result of autonomous and willing choices, and those involved have what Diane Jeske calls a "mutual project." The nature of this project, however, is not a quid pro quo or anything of that kind; the project is the friendship itself – to share experiences and develop a sense of intimacy based on the mutual recognition of one another as possessing complementary virtues (or vices, in their case).

It's ironic that arguably the healthiest adult child-parent relationship in *Arrested Development* is the result of two men who simultaneously hit rock bottom, a real friendship which develops in virtue of Gob's uselessness. However, given the wildly vicious character of so many of the figures in the show, it's only when they have no use to one another that they are able to move past their own selfish aims and recognize how much they have in common. *Arrested Development* makes a compelling case for the idea that if adult children have any special obligations to their parents, it must be because they've become friends – and not just any kind of friend, but *true* friends.

Evaluating *Arrested Development's* Argument: Can Parents and Children Really Be Friends?

Arrested Development offers an argument against the idea that adult children owe their parents anything simply because they are parents; instead making the case that if adult children have any special obligations to their parents, it is out of a sense of friendship – a type of intimacy one can choose to enter into, which can be terminated if necessary. But how compelling is this argument? In order to decide, it is worth considering two questions. First, isn't there something importantly different between the sort of intimacy one shares with their friends and the one they share with their parents? And second, isn't there something special about *becoming* a parent that changes a person? That is, it seems parenthood is not merely a role one might step into, but rather is an essential part of who that parent is.

First Objection: The Uniqueness of Parent-Child Intimacy

There is little room for doubt that in parent-child relationships where familial intimacy exists, it's of a different sort than what one might develop with a friend one meets as an adult or even with a childhood friend. After all, the sheer history of shared experiences, combined with the unconditional love parents and children often feel for one another, and the impact of a parent on the development (whether emotionally, intellectually, or otherwise) are importantly different from one's peers. "Often such facts naturally lead persons to develop [intimate] relationships, so familial roles are often correlated with the types of relationships that generate special obligations" (Jeske 1998, p. 542).

Joseph Kupfer argues that the ideal parent-child relationship has additional features that a friendship will not, such as "identification, love, stability, and aesthetic closure" (Kupfer 1990, p. 25). Kupfer argues that the nature between parent and child is unique in that the other's well-being not only influences, but is *part* of, the other's well-being. "It makes sense to speak of parents taking pride in their children in a way that it doesn't for friends" (Kupfer 1990, p. 21). The same goes, Kupfer argues, for suffering – a parent suffers "doubly" when their child suffers; they grieve *with* their children, not merely *for* them. Because of this loving identification, he suggests that (in ideal relationships) parents and children help shape one another's identities, thus a unique type of gratitude can emerge. This is a gratitude for helping to craft one's sense of self – not merely for friendship or fulfilling parental obligations, and no matter how exceptionally.

While Lindsay provides a substantial challenge to the idea that biology plays an especially important role to the grounding of special obligations, there may be something to the idea that, unlike friendship, there is a permanent tie between parent and child. "Just as the parents and grown children share the history of the young child's life, and know that they do, so do they also see the relationship (whatever its perturbations) as inevitably stretching into the future" (Kupfer 1990, p. 24). The knowledge of this stability, he continues, provides a sense of security not found in other relationships. As a result, both parents and children can expect comfort in difficult times, such as through aging, the loss of romantic or peer friendships, and so on. These features, he argues, are unique to parent-child relationships and cannot be grounded in friendship.

Second Objection: Personal Identity, Transformative Experience, and Parental Identity

The second question challenges the idea that the role of parent is merely a contingent feature of a person. Rather, being a parent is part of *who someone is*. Consider Brison's relational approach to the self. Since humans are social animals, one's identity may be at least in part *constituted* by those around her. She explains that "the self is viewed as related to and constructed by others in an ongoing way, not only because others continue to shape and define us throughout our lifetimes, but also because our sense of self is couched in descriptions whose meanings are social phenomena" (Brison 2002, p. 41). In this case, when someone is a parent, recognizing oneself as a parent is essential to their very being. Indeed, there is compelling reason to think the very act of having a child fundamentally changes who a person is. L.A. Paul argues that when it comes to life-changing choices, such as deciding whether to become a parent, there are certain features that are inaccessible unless one has experienced them and the experience itself changes both one's point of view and, importantly, their values (Paul 2014). Becoming a parent, she argues, is transformative – it changes who a person is. While Paul's interest is in how it is possible to make a rational choice in these cases, the recognition of the fundamental change resulting from becoming a parent speaks to how important being a parent *can* be.

Assuming that Brison and Paul are onto something, there are two related challenges brought forth by the nature of parenthood. First, the transformative nature of becoming a parent is explicitly and inextricably tied to the particular child. No other person could have changed the parent in the way their child did. The transformative nature of having a child reinforces Kupfer's uniqueness objection. Perhaps more importantly, however, is that because the role of parent is unlike a hat one can put on or take off at will, any wrong committed against a parent is more severe because it's a wrong committed against the *essence of* a person – not merely a role they fill. If there is uniquely personal harm done to a parent when a child wrongs them (by failing to fulfill some special obligation, for example), then there is reason to think that the nature of the obligations between parents and children must have an origin unique to families.

Mission Accomplished: Addressing the Objections

The argument *Arrested Development* makes thus faces two core problems. First, the sort of intimacy ideally developed between parents and children is importantly different from that present in friendships. Second, the *role* of parent is more robust than just another social role – it's both transformative and central to a parent's identity. In both cases, there seems to be something special about parenthood that cannot be explained merely by appeal to friendship. While these objections are compelling, *Arrested Development* has the resources to address these problems in relatively short order.

One critical feature of Kupfer's argument for the unique value derived from parent-child relationships is that these putative goods are the result of an *ideal* parent-child relationship. Part of what *Arrested Development* does shows – through less-than-ideal relationships – the limits of filial obligation. While most families are not nearly as problematic as the Bluths, it's safe to say that it's unlikely any are ideal. If appealing to the Bluths shows that the goods Kupfer finds in the ideal family dissolve, then there is good reason to believe those goods are not *essential* to families, but are contingent features of an idealized model that does not necessarily track reality. Thus, the objection carries significantly less force than it might initially appear to.

13 *Arrested Development* as Philosophy: Family First? What We Owe Our Parents   307

Even if the Bluths are too far removed from reality to count as a plausible counterexample, there is a further problem with the first objection: It is not obvious that the most important goods derived from the ideal family relations really are unique to parent-child relations. Consider once more the idea of a friendship of virtue. Such a friendship occurs when individuals recognize one another's virtuous character, share goals, and support one another in the pursuit of identified goods. Such a friendship is likely the best kind of friendship and will, as a result, be the most stable. After all, such friends are friends precisely because they identify with one another's virtues. Ideally, one's relationship with their romantic partner would also involve such a friendship. The way Kupfer describes identification, love, and stability could just as easily apply to a romantic partner when such a relationship involves a friendship of virtue. After all, with a spouse, the relationship has a sense of permanence going forward, some shared history, love, and identification with one another. Of course, there are important differences between the intimacy in a romantic relationship and that of parent-child relations, but the core goods seem to apply to each with only minor adjustments. It may seem bizarre that Buster confuses filial and romantic love, but the blurring of that line serves as the perfect illustration of exactly this point. While Buster and Lucille are not virtue-friends, their codependence highlights the ways in which problematic parent-child relations can mirror friendships – and it is exactly because of such mirroring that Buster confuses the grounds of his obligations to his mother.

Keeping in mind the similarity between the goods found in both a healthy romantic relationship and filial relationships can help to address the second objection as well. Recall that the central point of the second objection is that there is something transformative about becoming a parent; that becoming a parent changes a person's identity. Yet entering into a healthy long-term romantic relationship, for example, will also force fundamental changes to one's conception not only of themselves (being one's partner is as much a relationally constituted aspect of one's identity as any), but of their goals and values as well. At the very least, conceiving of oneself as a partner entails taking on another's goals as if they are one's own. While a decidedly less abrupt transformation than becoming a parent, entering into a long-term romantic relationship will affect profound changes in a person. Put another way, Brison's insight that the self is partially constituted by those around us supports the importance of *both* the role of parent *and* the role of romantic partner. That is, there are few people in life who can have a more profound impact on one's identity than their partner. As a result, the force of the objection is thereby diminished – after all, at least in America today, people largely choose their romantic partners – and a breach in the case of a committed long-term partnership is at least equal to, if not more difficult than, a filial breach.

While not representative of the majority of parents, the Bluths illustrate an important limitation of the appeal to the transformative nature of having children. It is no doubt possible for parents to be somewhat unmoved by having children; indeed, the vast majority of the parents in *Arrested Development* fail to consider themselves as parents at all, let alone allow that role to define who they are. Only Michael takes his role as father to be an important part of who he is. Yet despite identifying as a father to George Michael, he values *appearing* to be a good father over *actually* being a good father. *Arrested Development* shows that one need not be personally transformed by having a child and that, even if one is, it's not always for the better.

Conclusion: Friendship First

Philosophers have challenged the assumption that adult children have special obligations to their parents. *Arrested Development* argues that insofar as any special obligations arise between parents and adult children, it's a function of a particular sort of friendly intimacy between adults. The Bluths, in virtue of their wildly dysfunctional interactions, offer compelling reasons to remember that parents are people like any other; they have diverse interests, fill different social roles, and have different strengths and weaknesses. Simply because one is a parent, this does not entitle them to special treatment. Any sort of relationship adult children have with their parents is not explained by biology, social roles, gratitude, or debt, but by continued familial intimacy grounded in a loving friendship. *Arrested Development* argues by demonstrating the extreme – when parents are as bad as the Bluths, their kids don't owe them anything.

References

Aristotle. 1987. *Nicomachean ethics*. Trans. J.E.C. Welldon. Amherst: Prometheus Books.

Barnbaum, Deborah R. 2012. Kissing cousins: Incest, naturalism, and the yuck factor. In *Arrested development and philosophy: They've made a huge mistake*, ed. Kristopher G. Phillips and J. Jeremy Wisnewski, 23–32. Hoboken: Wiley.

Belliotti, Raymond A. 1986. Honor thy father and thy mother and to thine own self be true. *The Southern Journal of Philosophy* 24 (2): 149–162.

Blustein, Jeffrey. 1982. *Parents and children: The ethics of the family*. New York: Oxford University Press.

Brison, Susan J. 2002. *Aftermath: Violence and the remaking of the self*. Princeton: Princeton University Press.

English, Jane. 1979. What do grown children owe their parents. In *Having children: Philosophical and legal reflections on parenthood*, ed. Onora O'Neill and William Ruddick. New York: Oxford University Press.

Ewing, Jeff. 2012. Dr. Funke's 100 percent natural good-time alienation solution. In *Arrested development and philosophy: They've made a huge mistake*, ed. Kristopher G. Phillips and J. Jeremy Wisnewski, 61–72. Hoboken: Wiley.

Hardimon, Michael O. 1994. Role obligations. *The Journal of Philosophy* 91 (7): 333–363.

Helm, Bennett. 2021. Friendship. In *The Stanford encyclopedia of philosophy*, ed. Edward N. Zalta. https://plato.stanford.edu/archives/fall2021/entries/friendship/. Accessed 13 Jan 2022.

Jecker, Nancy S. 1989. Are filial duties unfounded? *American Philosophical Quarterly* 26 (1): 73–80.

Jeske, Diane. 1998. Families, friends, and special obligations. *Canadian Journal of Philosophy* 28 (4): 527–555.

Kupfer, Joseph. 1990. Can parents and children be friends? *American Philosophical Quarterly* 27 (1): 15–26.

Paul, L.A. 2014. *Transformative experience*. Oxford: Oxford University Press.
Sidgwick, Henry. 1981. *The methods of ethics*. Indianapolis/Cambridge: Hackett Publishing.
Slote, Michael. 1979. Obedience and illusion. In *Having children: Philosophical and legal reflections on parenthood*, ed. Onora O'Neill and William Ruddick. New York: Oxford University Press.

The Doctor as Philosopher: The Collectivist-Realist Pacifism of the Doctor and the Quest for Social Justice

14

Paula Smithka

Contents

Introduction	312
Coward, Killer, or Hero?	314
The Time Lord Matrix of Relevant Philosophical Concepts	317
Pacifism and Warism	318
A Pacifist Continuum	320
The Doctor's Pacifism	321
"It's a Different Morality, Get Used to It"	324
The Collectivist-Realist Pacifism of the Doctor	332
War...No More	332
"Who I Am Is Where I Stand"	334
The Quest for Social Justice	337
Conclusion	338
End Notes	338
References	339

Abstract

Doctor Who is the longest-running science fiction series in history. Its protagonist, the Doctor, is a time-traveling alien in a ship called the TARDIS (time and relative dimension(s) in space). The Doctor protects the planet Earth and its human inhabitants from alien threats but also responds to the needs of other beings elsewhere in the universe. Frequently these altercations with alien threats require force, sometimes even lethal force; yet the Doctor is a pacifist. This chapter explores in what sense the Doctor can be considered a pacifist and what sort of pacifist the Doctor is. It is argued that the Doctor is a collectivist-realist pacifist, which is a modification of Duane Cady's notion of a collectivist pacifist, who accepts that lethal force is sometimes morally justifiable while also being

---

P. Smithka (✉)
University of Southern Mississippi, Hattiesburg, MS, USA
e-mail: paula.smithka@usm.edu

© Springer Nature Switzerland AG 2024
D. K. Johnson et al. (eds.), *The Palgrave Handbook of Popular Culture as Philosophy*,
https://doi.org/10.1007/978-3-031-24685-2_30

opposed to war. But that collectivist pacifism must be augmented by Martin Luther King, Jr.'s realist pacifism, where ethical appeals are "undergirded by some *constructive* coercive power." It is not enough to simply have a moral opposition to war; there must be a pursuit of justice because the issues of peace and justice are inextricably linked. In order to achieve social justice, coercion is often required because rational attempts at persuasion frequently do not work; thus, interference in unjust situations is morally required, and sometimes that interference justifiably entails lethal force, but only when it is necessary. This is what the Doctor does and the show suggests we ought to be more like the Doctor in our commitments to peace and justice.

Keywords

Doctor Who · Pacifism · Warism · Just-warist · Absolute pacifism · Collectivist pacifism · Realist pacifism · Collective-realist pacifism · Social justice · Ethics · Deontologism (duty-based ethics) · Utilitarianism · Ethics of care · Life of needs · Kant · Mill · Ross · Rawls · Gandhi · Martin Luther King, Jr. · Duane Cady · Ronald Glossop · David Cortright · Courtland Lewis · Deborah Pless · Roman Altshuler · R. Alan Siler · J.J. Sylvia

Introduction

> I never talk in the face of a gun. Point of principle.
> —13th Doctor to Andinio ("The Battle of Ranzkoor Av Kolos" 2018)

> The Doctor never uses weapons.
> —13th Doctor ("Fugitive of the Judoon" 2020)

On November 23, 1963, *Doctor Who* aired for the first time, launching the global cultural phenomenon of *Doctor Who*. The show is the longest-running science fiction series in history, celebrating its 60th anniversary in 2023. The "Classic Series," as it is now referred to, ran from 1963 to 1989. After this hiatus, there was *Doctor Who: The Movie* in 1996. But the *Doctor Who* franchise became an even bigger global phenomenon with the reboot of the series in 2005 airing not only on BBC-One in the UK but on BBC-America. The "New Series" has been in continuous production since. Because Kevin Decker's chapter, "*Doctor Who* as Philosophy: Four-Dimensionalism and Time Travel" focuses primarily on the Classic Series, this chapter will focus on the New Series in order to give readers a sense of the breadth and depth of the philosophy contained in *Doctor Who*.

The main character, known properly as the Doctor (but sometimes erroneously as "Doctor Who"), is a time-traveling alien, called a Time Lord, from the planet Gallifrey, who looks like a human but has two hearts. The Doctor's ship is a blue police call box called the TARDIS (time and relative dimension(s) in space). The TARDIS is "bigger on the inside" and takes the Doctor throughout all of space and time. A special characteristic of Time Lords is that they have the ability to regenerate; when their physical body is at the point of death, their cells renew, generating a

14 The Doctor as Philosopher: The Collectivist-Realist Pacifism of the...

body in a new physical form. Such regenerations are not limited to one gender or race. The arch-nemesis of the Doctor, the Master, another Time Lord, regenerated into a woman, Missy (Michelle Gomez), whom viewers first met in "Dark Water"/"Death in Heaven" (2014). The last regeneration of the Doctor gave us a female Doctor as the Thirteenth Doctor (Jodie Whittaker) in Series 11, episode 1, "The Woman Who Fell to Earth" (2018), and in "Fugitive of the Judoon" (2020), viewers are introduced to an apparently early (and hitherto unknown to the Thirteenth Doctor herself) incarnation the Doctor in Ruth Clayton (Jo Martin). Of course, this plot technique of regeneration makes possible the continuation of the show when an actor decides to take on other opportunities or becomes too old or too tired to keep running. ("Run!" after all is the Doctor's recurrent command – and, there *is* a lot of running in the show.)

The Doctor has a special fondness for humans, and throughout the Classic Series and into the New Series, the Doctor serves as the protector of both the Earth and humanity from invasion or being conquered, usually by aliens, including: the Daleks, Cybermen, Weeping Angels, and others. In "The Eleventh Hour" (2010), the Atraxi were willing to destroy the planet if Prisoner Zero was not apprehended. The Eleventh Doctor (Matt Smith) squares off with them, rhetorically inquiring, "Is this planet protected?. . . Hello, I'm the Doctor." When the world is in trouble or when children cry ("The Beast Below," 2010; "Night Terrors," 2011), the Doctor comes to cure the ailment. However, such protection and the remedy often come at a price: the lives of members of alien species and humans.

At the same time, however, the Doctor claims to be a pacifist. As we saw in the quotes that headlined this chapter, the Thirteenth Doctor claims to never use a weapon. Davros, creator of the Daleks, facetiously reminds the Tenth Doctor (David Tennant) that he is "The man who abhors violence, never carrying a gun" ("Journey's End," 2008), and the Eighth Doctor (Paul McGann) (initially) refuses to take part in the Time War; "It's not my war. I will have no part in it. . .I will not fight," he says ("The Night of the Doctor," 2013). And this is not an anomaly; there are examples in the Classic Series. The Third Doctor (Jon Pertwee) works to broker a peace treaty between the humans and the Silurians, though the military brass only wants to blow up the Silurians. The Doctor is horrified when there's a huge explosion of the Silurian base ("Doctor Who and the Silurians," 1970). The Fourth Doctor (Tom Baker) tells Leela, who has picked up a Tesh weapon, to leave the weapon behind.

DOCTOR   You won't need that.
LEELA   How do you know?
DOCTOR   I never carry weapons. If people see you mean them no harm, they never hurt you. Nine times out of ten. ("Robots of Death," 1977)

And the Seventh Doctor (Sylvester McCoy) constantly tries to get Ace not to use her Nitro 9 (though he often relies on her having it). (Thanks to Courtland Lewis for a discussion regarding these examples from the Classic Series.)

Furthermore, as a matter of pacifistic principle, the Doctor usually gives his/her enemies a chance to cease their aggression before s/he defeats them like when the

Tenth Doctor gives Miss Hartigan as the Cyberking the option to leave Earth, but she refuses, ultimately ending in the destruction of the Cybermen and Miss Hartigan ("The Next Doctor," 2008). Or consider when the Thirteenth Doctor warns the Queen of the Skithra to leave, which she refuses to do; this time, the Doctor succeeds in simply forcing the Skithra ship to leave Earth ("Nicola Tesla's Night of Terror," 2020).

But how can the Doctor both be a pacifist and protect the Earth as the Doctor does? It is possible, but it will take sorting through some "wibbly-wobbly" concepts to see how. What will become clear is that one of the persisting goals of the Doctor is to achieve or preserve social justice, not just for humans but for any species whose basic life interests are undermined by oppression, and this goal cannot be overridden by his/her commitment to nonviolence.

The show presents the Doctor as a role model who always tries to do the morally right thing in order to bring about a more just state of affairs. This chapter will explore in what sense the Doctor can be considered to be a pacifist concerned about social justice and someone we should emulate. Of course, the notions of pacifism and social justice are inextricably linked to morality. Morality addresses "right" versus "wrong" conduct. In philosophy, there are various ethical theories establishing the standards for what constitutes morally right conduct. Some of these will be explored in relation to the Doctor's moral convictions and actions. Though the Doctor's moral compass is strong and plays a central role in his/her personal identity (as "*the Doctor*"), it is not so clear to philosophers dealing with *Doctor Who* that the Doctor has adopted a specific or consistent ethical framework; consequently, they have defended different positions with regard to the Doctor's morality. (See Lewis and Smithka (2010, 2015), Lewis (2017), and the new and revised version, *The Real Meaning of Doctor Who* (2021).)

Coward, Killer, or Hero?

When viewers are introduced to the Ninth Doctor in the series reboot in 2005, they meet a Doctor, played by Christopher Eccleston, who is on the run – running away from his memories of the Time War between his people, the Time Lords, and the Daleks. Not only is he running away from the atrocities of war but, as viewers learn, he is also running from his (alleged) part in the lengthy Time War where he was (allegedly) responsible for ending it by an act that (apparently) led to the genocide of both the Time Lords and the Daleks. (The story arc of this first season of the New Series where the Doctor is responsible for the genocide of both races is recast in the 50th Anniversary Special, "The Day of the Doctor," 2013.) Thus, the Doctor thinks he is the "Last of the Time Lords." The Doctor's motive for his actions was to end the killing, but the guilt over his part in the Time War, especially how he ended it, is overwhelming.

In the two-part season finale, "Bad Wolf"/"The Parting of the Ways" (2005), the Doctor, much to his shock and horror, is once again confronted with the Daleks who have been hiding in "dark space," rebuilding after the Time War. The Dalek Emperor says to the Doctor, "You destroyed us, Doctor. The Dalek race died in your inferno, but my ship survived, falling through time, crippled but alive." The Daleks harvested humans over centuries, purging their human DNA of undesirable characteristics, in order to rebuild the Dalek army. Once the mighty empire was rebuilt, the plan was to take over the Earth. Learning the Doctor and his companions were aboard the game station (formerly a news information center 100 years earlier), Satellite 5, that is secretly being run by the Daleks, they invade it, "ex-ter-min-ating" humans, and commence bombing the Earth. The Doctor devises a way to stop the Daleks, but then he has to make the choice whether to activate the Delta Wave, which will destroy all of the Daleks, but also annihilate the human race and "every living thing" on planet Earth. He's reluctant, as he has already witnessed what he thought to be the genocide of two races. As Daleks burst into the room where the Doctor has finished the Delta Wave, the following interchange takes place between the Doctor (who is on Satellite 5) and the Dalek Emperor who is transmitting from his ship to a viewing screen where the Doctor is:

THE DOCTOR	You really want to think about this, because if I activate the signal, every living creature dies.
DALEK EMPEROR	I am immortal.
THE DOCTOR	Do you want to put that to the test?
DALEK EMPEROR	I want to see you become like me. Hail the Doctor, the Great Exterminator.
THE DOCTOR	I'll do it!
DALEK EMPEROR	Then prove yourself, Doctor. What are you, coward or killer? [But the Doctor cannot throw the final switch.]
THE DOCTOR	Coward. Any day.
DALEK EMPEROR	Mankind will be harvested because of your weakness.

The war-ravaged Doctor, ashamed of his part in the Time War, was unable to dirty his hands in what would be the "extermination" not only of the Daleks but all life on Earth, even though humanity might suffer as a result. Of course, the story does not end here. Rose Tyler, the Doctor's companion who travels with him, having been sent home by the Doctor in the TARDIS – he tricked her, so that he could ensure her safety – managed (with the help of her mum, Jackie, and boyfriend, Mickey) to open the heart of the TARDIS in order to facilitate her return to Satellite 5 to help the Doctor. She "looked into the TARDIS, and the TARDIS looked into [her]." Rose stared into the Time Vortex itself transforming her into the "Bad Wolf," giving her the ability to see all of space and time and the power to control life and death. Having the power over life and death, it is she that carries out the extermination of the Dalek fleet while also restoring life to the other sometimes companion, Captain Jack Harkness who was killed by the Daleks, making him immortal. Thus, it was not the Doctor who carried out actual acts of lethal force against the Daleks. Instead, Jack with his large and powerful gun killed some of Daleks but the ultimate destructive act of lethal force was carried out by Rose as the Bad Wolf.

That the companions carry out acts of violence, rather than the Doctor, is more often the case in the Doctor's journeys – the companions become the weapons, as

Davros (the original creator of the Daleks on Skaro) explains in a powerful speech forcing the Tenth Doctor (David Tennant) to take a brutally honest look at his life in "Journey's End" (2008), the finale of Season 4. In this episode, Davros has developed the reality bomb, which threatens to destroy reality itself. The former companions Rose, Captain Jack Harkness, Martha Jones, Sarah Jane Smith, Mickey Smith, and Jackie Tyler are all present on the Dalek ship, the *Crucible*, discussing ways to destroy the Daleks. Martha has the Osterhagen Key, which will destroy all of humanity as well as the Daleks, and Sarah Jane has a warp star in a necklace that Jack wires up to be a weapon. Seeing this, Davros says to the Doctor: "The man who abhors violence, never carrying a gun. But this is the truth, Doctor: you take ordinary people you fashion *them* into weapons. Behold your Children of Time transformed into murderers. I made the Daleks, Doctor. You made this."

While the companions tend to use lethal force against the villains who threaten peace and justice, the Doctor, on occasion, has been personally responsible for employing lethal force to eliminate the threat to humanity or others who could not otherwise repel that threat on their own. In fact, the Daleks know him as the "Oncoming Storm" and Davros dubs him "the Destroyer of Worlds" in "Journey's End."

Deborah Pless has argued that there is a significant shift in the portrayal of the Doctor beginning in the third season of the New Series. The shift is toward a more "heroic" Doctor, one that runs toward danger, rather than running away from his past. She attributes this change in the portrayal of the Doctor in part, due to cultural changes – the terrorist attacks that took place in London in July 2005 and the fact that the Doctor has become an international icon, particularly popular in America, even filming two episodes of the sixth season in Utah ("The Impossible Astronaut" and "Day of the Moon," 2011). She states:

> The Doctor became more than just a representation of British idealized action, he became a stand-in for the rest of the world during a time of a crisis. The show no longer had the luxury of letting the Doctor be a coward, not if they wanted to continue exporting the show for a global audience. (Pless in Lewis and Smithka 2015, p. 14)

So, as the New Series progresses, viewers see a Doctor increasingly more involved in violent confrontations with villains that have fewer peaceful resolutions or compromises (these are the Tenth and Eleventh Doctors, David Tennant and Matt Smith, respectively) (Pless 2015, pp. 14–15). The Doctor is the hero who makes hard choices but helps human- and nonhuman-others in need, because that is what doctors do. You might think of the Ood in "Planet of the Ood" (2008) and the dinosaurs in "Dinosaurs on a Spaceship" (2012) where the Eleventh Doctor tells Solomon, "The creatures on board this ship are not objects to be sold or traded." But the Doctor has also been portrayed as the "savior" of humanity; for example, in "The Last of the Time Lords" (2007). (See Deller 2010, pp. 239–247.)

What is crucial in these cases that involve lethal force or punishment is that the Doctor virtually always gives the perpetrator a choice (e.g., "The Runaway Bride" 2006, "School Reunion" 2006, "The Next Doctor" 2008, among others). The Doctor typically attempts to understand the reason for the alien menace's incursion and frequently offers to assist them; for example, the Doctor offers to help the Empress of

14 The Doctor as Philosopher: The Collectivist-Realist Pacifism of the... 317

the Racnoss find a new home for her and her children in "The Runaway Bride" (2006). There is respect shown by the Doctor even to villains who have interests and needs; they, too, have value.[1] And, like Gandhi and Martin Luther King, Jr., who held that "no human being is so bad as to be beyond redemption" (cited in Cortright, p. 220), the Doctor espouses this view, except that it obviously includes nonhumans. The Doctor exemplifies this moral stance in cases of his/her worst enemies; for example, the Tenth Doctor offers to save Davros from the burning *Crucible* in "Journey's End" (2008); he forgives the Master and offers to take the Master with him – "You could be so beautiful," he tells the Master ("The Last of the Time Lords," 2007 and "The End of Time, Part 2," 2010); and the Twelfth Doctor (Peter Capaldi) attempts to create a "good" Dalek, which he named "Rusty" ("Into the Dalek," 2014). Valuing others is part of moral core of the Doctor. These points will be addressed in more detail later.

However, given the Doctor's participation in violent confrontations, some of which involve lethal force carried out by the Doctor or his/her companions, as in "Journey's End" (2008) and "A Good Man Goes to War" (2011), and the fact that the Twelfth Doctor weaponizes his sonic screwdriver and participates outright in the battle against the Cybermen in order to protect a small population of humans on a solar farm within the colony ship in "The Doctor Falls" (2017), one might wonder how the Doctor might be considered to be a pacifist. Well, philosophical distinctions are required. The relevant philosophical terrain will be traversed in the next section.

The Time Lord Matrix of Relevant Philosophical Concepts

When people hear the word "pacifist," they often confuse it with being "passive," that is, being inert or inactive – taking whatever is "dished out" by another with no response. But pacifists need not be "passive." Certainly, the Doctor is not passive in the face of a threat; s/he takes measures to countermand the efforts of the assailants. Or, often, "pacifism" is associated with a position in which no force, ever, can be used against another, even in cases of self-defense. And, for that reason, the position is often ridiculed as being at best untenable or at worst, downright stupid. To be sure, there are some people who adhere to this position of Absolute Pacifism; this position is typically associated with Quakers and the Amish, but Absolute Pacifism is only one position in a range of pacifist positions that will need to be outlined in order to see where the Doctor falls on this spectrum.

Various philosophers will parse this spectrum out in diverse ways, employing different terminology. Duane Cady's useful 1989 text, *From Warism to Pacifism: A Moral Continuum* will be employed for the relevant distinctions. (But see also Fiala (2018). There is also a continuum of Warist positions. Cady provides some of these, but also see Paula Smithka (1992), for more explicit labeling of warist positions.) Some basic concepts will need to be addressed first to provide ground-work for the discussion. According to Cady (and this is a standard position), pacifism is the moral opposition to war – all war is immoral by nature (Cady 1989, pp. 4, 40), whereas warism "is the view that war is both morally justifiable in principle and often morally justified in fact" (Cady, 3). War is traditionally taken to be "hostile contention between groups by means of armed force" (Cady 1989, p. 13), but Ronald Glossop restricts the definition of "war" to not just *any* groups but rather organized groups with established governments. He states, "War is large-scale violent conflict between organized groups which already are governments or which seek to establish their own government over some territory" (Glossop 2001, p. 10).

In the Whoniverse, the Time War between the Time Lords and the Daleks is just such an example of war in both Cady's and Glossop's senses of the term – although most encounters with the Daleks can be characterized in this way since the primary goals of Daleks are to "ex-ter-min-ate" all beings non-Dalek (including "impure" Daleks) and expand their empire across the universe. Because of these goals, Daleks are examples of, what I called Imperialist Warists in "Are Active Pacifists Really Just-Warists in Disguise?" (Smithka 1992). They are not just-warists, who wage and fight wars primarily for defensive reasons; they fight offensive wars (Smithka 1992).

The concepts of "force," "violence," and "coercion" have been employed in the explanation of what constitutes war, so it may be useful to clarify their meanings before investigating the various pacifist positions. "Force" involves the use of physical strength, and "violence" involves the intentional action to "injure, damage, or destroy a person or object." Thus, violence necessarily involves force, but force need not entail violence. When one is "coerced," one is made to do something that one does not want to do, which might involve force or violence or the threat of either (Cady 1989, p. 61). With these basic concepts in mind, the distinction between warism and pacifism can be further investigated, as well as the various pacifistic positions, and where the Doctor might fall on this continuum.

Pacifism and Warism

> ...one lesson of the ages seems to be that, in war, everyone loses. The victors just lose a bit less than the vanquished.
> —Duane Cady (From Warism to Pacifism, p. 50)

The fundamental difference between pacifist and warist positions is founded on the moral acceptability of war. For any pacifist, according to Cady, war is never morally acceptable, whereas for warists, war is morally justifiable in principle and often in fact. If war is morally justifiable, then it is because the just-warist is able to separate means and ends. (The focus here is on the position of the just-war theorist rather than that of the warist who glorifies war for its own sake or exemplifies the Imperialist Warist position, mentioned above. Just-war theory requires that certain conditions be met for waging a war and there are certain restrictions placed on the means of fighting the war.) That is, while the means may be undesirable – for example, the number of casualties, loss of life, and destruction of property – the ultimate end or goal, say to achieve peace, is worth the cost. So, for the just-warist, fighting a war might be a necessary evil in order to achieve a desired good end.

Just-war theory tends to focus on the consequences of actions and reflects a Utilitarian way of thinking in ethical theory. Utilitarians consider actions to be morally right so long as those actions generate more happiness, or the greatest good, for the greatest number of people (J.S. Mill [1863/1879] 2004). So, engaging in war might be the morally right thing to do if the consequences of doing so achieve a greater good, like a lasting peace or increased security and stability for a nation's people. Pacifists on the other hand, according to Cady, reject the separation between means and ends. Engaging in war is morally wrong even if the end result is a desirable or noble goal. The approach here is largely based in the ethical theory known as deontology. Deontology is a duty-based theory and the notions of morally right and wrong actions are independent of the consequences or outcomes of those actions. For example, one has a duty to tell the truth; so, lying is a morally bad thing even if doing so saves another person's life.

There are different deontological approaches reflecting the nature of the duty. For Immanuel Kant (1724–1804), duties are absolute or perfect. This means that there are no exceptions to duties; duties hold universally – for everyone at all times and places (Kant [1789]/1959). Whereas W.D. Ross (1877–1971) distinguishes between prima facie duties, or usual/customary duties, and actual duties (Ross [1930]/1988). Actual duties are those prima facie duties one ought to perform in a given circumstance. Which duties are relevant in a given situation depend upon the relationships one bears to others. For example, there is no duty to repay money to a friend if one has not borrowed money from that friend; but if one has borrowed money, there is the duty to repay it. Ross gives a list of prima facie duties, which he claims is non-exhaustive. Unlike Kant's duties, Ross' prima facie duties can be overridden if they conflict. Ross gives two criteria for determining which is one's actual duty: stringency (one's actual duty is the stronger of the two conflicting duties) and balance (if more than two duties conflict, the actual duty is the one that has the greatest balance of rightness over wrongness). For example, the prima facie duty to tell the truth might be overridden in the case where it conflicts with the prima facie duty of non-maleficence – the duty to avoid or prevent injury to others. Many pacifists, then, seem to adopt a more Kantian approach to the moral opposition to war, as the large-scale violent conflict between organized groups with governments; however, some pacifists might adopt a position more along the lines of Ross' ethics in order to justify the use of force in some circumstances. Overriding the prima facie duty of non-maleficence would require extreme circumstances.

One might wonder how such persons could still be considered pacifists; but the important thing most people do not realize about pacifists is that not all pacifists are *absolute pacifists*. As Cady points out, there is more to "pacifism" than simply being opposed to all war on moral grounds. "Pacifist activists are committed to making peace, making compacts by consensual agreement, contributing to the harmonious cooperative social conduct that is orderly by itself from within rather than ordered by the imposition of coercion from without" (Cady 1989, p. 12). While s/he will resort to force if necessary, the Doctor would much rather reach a deal with the aggressor than have to use force to diminish or eliminate the threat, which is why the Doctor typically gives the assailant a choice. This means that, while the Doctor is clearly not an absolute pacifist, s/he is a pacifist nonetheless. But what kind of pacifist is s/he? To answer that question, it will now be helpful to explore what other kinds of pacifists there are.

A Pacifist Continuum

There is not one single, unified approach to the moral opposition to war, even though critics of pacifism often attempt to pigeon-hole it by typically associating it with the most extreme of the pacifist positions: absolute pacifism. On this position, no force is ever morally acceptable, even in self-defense, so critics relegate the position to the dustbin of naiveté. Nevertheless, there are other degrees of pacifist positions along the pacifist-warist continuum, depending upon the level at which force may be morally justifiable. While Cady's views are presented here, it is important to bear in mind that philosophers parse the spectrum of pacifist positions in different ways, and a modification in one of Cady's pacifist positions will be required in order to best describe what kind of pacifist the Doctor is.

Cady suggests that, as one moves away from the absolute pacifist position, the next position on the continuum allows that "non-lethal force can be warranted in principle" (1989, p. 62). He does not give the position a name, but the idea is that physical resistance to an unprovoked attack is morally justifiable and so is physically restraining an aggressor when it is necessary (though lethal force is still morally unacceptable).

The next position Cady calls "collectivist pacifism" which allows for the moral justifiability of lethal defensive actions among individuals in some circumstances, but retains the moral opposition to war (1989, p. 62). The gist is that when someone else engages in an act that is immoral and reprehensible enough, that individual gives up the right to be treated as a person worthy of respect and thereby forfeits their right to life (thus giving moral justification for others to use lethal force on them). But the moral justifiability of lethal force is a matter of scale for Cady. Because the level of violence is more easily controllable and predictable in interpersonal conflict than on a large national scale which involves mass violence, for the collectivist pacifist, lethal force is sometimes justifiable only on the smaller interpersonal scale. War is not (Cady 1994, p. 90). While it is unclear why Cady chose the label "collectivist pacifism," the notion of "collectivism" might be applicable in the case of at least small groups, where lethal force might be required to protect a group being wrongly treated, though Cady only employs the term "interpersonal." Later, Cady's notion of collectivist pacifism will be modified. (Cady restricts his discussion to "humans," obviously given the context of his work. The idea has been rephrased, using "person" instead of "human" since there can be nonhuman persons. In the Whoniverse, there are many nonhuman persons who are, in Kant's terms, rational, autonomous agents, and so are worthy of respect. These beings have interests and a right to life.)

Next along the pacifist spectrum is fallibility or epistemological pacifism. This position essentially grants that even if such lethal force is justifiable in principle, large-scale violence among nations, in particular, cannot be justified in fact because of the "inevitable limitations in our understanding of the facts and circumstances involved between large groups of people" (Cady 1989, p. 64). Basically, one cannot *know* whether the conditions for going to war justly are ever *actually* met.

Another position is technological pacifism. On this view, even if wars had been considered justifiable in the past, new weapons technologies, which make the "wholesale slaughter" of noncombatants as well as combatants possible, render the means of fighting a war morally unacceptable because the destruction caused is disproportionate to any possible good outcomes that might be achieved (Cady 1989, pp. 67–68). Related to technological pacifism is nuclear pacifism. The potential mass destruction caused by the use of nuclear weapons would be so devastating that any military conflict, even with the use of conventional weapons by nations with nuclear capabilities, is a danger far too great to warrant any such military engagement. As David Cortright says, "In the nuclear realm pacifism is absolute, rejecting any use of weapons that are grossly destructive and inherently indiscriminate" (2008, p. 334).

Also related to technological pacifism is the position of ecological pacifism, which extends the concern regarding destruction beyond the human realm to the devastation of nature itself. The likelihood of environmental destruction as a result of war has the potential to decimate or even obliterate all life (Cady 1989, pp. 69–72). One might here think of Davros' "reality bomb" in the "The Stolen Earth"/"Journey's End" (2008) two-part series 4 finale: "This is my victory, Doctor! The destruction of reality itself!"

Finally, the weakest pacifist position along the spectrum (which is on the cusp of the warist part of the continuum) is pragmatic pacifism. Cady characterizes this position as the closest to the just-war tradition because both positions accept the Utilitarian notion of promoting the greatest good for the greatest number of people. Where the two positions differ, Cady contends, is that while the just-warist will argue that violence can bring about peaceful ends, thus separating means and ends, the pragmatic pacifist will not separate means from ends and thus rejects the notion that violent means can bring peaceful ends. Cady says, "…peace is not an isolated and separate objective to be reached but an end that subsumes its means" (1989, p. 73). Thus, the pragmatic pacifist retains the moral opposition to war because "wars tend to promote, not relieve, human misery" (Cady 1989, p. 73), even if lethal force is sometimes morally permissible to promote the greater good. The just-warist, on the other hand, will grant that war is sometimes morally justified as a means to achieving peace (the greater good), so long as it is waged as a last resort (nonviolent means have been tried and failed to rectify an actual injustice) and fought justly, that is, using proportionate means or the minimum force necessary (see Smithka 1992, pp. 168–175).

So, which pacifist position on Cady's pacifist continuum characterizes the Doctor?

The Doctor's Pacifism

The Doctor's pacifism must involve the collectivist pacifist position because the Doctor often uses lethal force in situations where lethal force is both morally justifiable and morally required in order to protect humans or others from deadly threats (even though the Doctor remains morally opposed to war). Recall the Eighth

Doctor's words, "It's not my war. I will have no part of it...I will not fight...I would rather die" ("The Night of the Doctor," 2013). Yet, collectivist pacificism is not sufficient to capture the Doctor's position, because it fails to incorporate the pursuit of justice – and *being* the Doctor means attempting to heal the injustices done to humans or other species.

The Doctor's collectivist pacifist position must be enhanced by Martin Luther King, Jr.'s "realist pacifism" where ethical appeals are "undergirded by some *constructive* coercive power" (King, Jr. 1967, pp. 128–129, emphasis added). It is not enough to simply have a moral opposition to war; there must also be a pursuit of justice. In order to achieve social justice, coercion is often required because rational attempts at persuasion frequently do not work; thus, interference in unjust situations is not only morally acceptable but morally required. The issues of peace and justice are linked. Cortright says:

> [Peace advocates have] learned that they cannot be indifferent to the sufferings and needs of those who are victimized by repression, or ignore the necessary connections between peace and broader issues of democracy, social justice, and human rights. To be sure some peace advocates remain narrowly focused on the absence of war rather than the presence of justice, but most recognize that justice and peace are inextricably linked. (2008, p. 335)

The primary means of coercion for both Gandhi and King involved nonviolent direct action to bring the suffering and needs of oppressed groups to the attention of those oppressors in power. No positive peace can be achieved where there is no justice (King 1963). Justice entails fairness where each person has the equal right to the same basic liberties as every other person (Rawls 1999, p. 266). Oppressed groups lack those equal basic liberties and their basic life interests are thwarted by the oppressors. Cady points out that "preventing evil is always more urgent" (1989, p. 50) than constructing positive good. The Doctor realizes this and seeks to prevent or eliminate the evil that threatens humans or others in order to bring about a better and more just life for those who are oppressed or whose lives are threatened. Like Gandhi and King, the Doctor seeks to heal the suffering of those being oppressed; creating or restoring justice requires interference, and thus interference is justified.

The difference between Gandhi and King on the one hand and the Doctor on the other is that, whereas for Gandhi and King lethal force would not be a morally justifiable means of coercion, for the Doctor, lethal force is sometimes morally permissible, when it is required as a last resort. So, even though the Doctor "abhors violence" (as Davros facetiously reminds the Tenth Doctor in "Journey's End," 2008), the Doctor's commitment to justice is paramount, thereby becoming the more "stringent" obligation in Ross' sense. Only after Ohila, High Priestess of the Sisterhood of Karn, presses the Eighth Doctor about engaging in the Time War does the Doctor give in to regenerate as a warrior. "How many more will you let join you [in death]?...We beg your help. The universe stands on the brink. Will you let it fall?" ("The Night of the Doctor," 2013). Nevertheless, such coercive power must be tempered. One should "Never be cruel" ("The Day of the Doctor," 2013; "Twice Upon a Time," 2017). As King points out, "What is needed is a realization that power without love is reckless and abusive and that love without power is

14 The Doctor as Philosopher: The Collectivist-Realist Pacifism of the...

sentimental and anemic. Power at its best is love implementing the demands of justice" (quoted in Cortright 2008, p. 219).

Where King speaks of "love," with respect to the Doctor's power as a Time Lord, "compassion" might be inserted instead: The Doctor's power at its best is compassion implementing the demands of justice. For example, out of compassion for the suffering of the last Star Whale, powering *Starship UK*, viewers see a distraught Eleventh Doctor, pained by the difficult decision to render the Star Whale brain-dead in order to release it from the torture imposed on it by Liz 10 and the administration of *Starship UK* ("The Beast Below," 2010). There is no justice for the Star Whale being enslaved and tortured; rendering it brain-dead would simply free it from being in constant pain. Fortunately, the Doctor ultimately does not have to carry out that horrible decision because Amy takes the risk that she understands the situation better than the Doctor and, forcing the hand of Liz 10, hits the "abdicate" button that releases the Star Whale from the torture, yet the Star Whale continues to carry the ship, even increasing its speed. Amy realized that the Star Whale came of its own accord to help the children of the UK survive, just as the Doctor came to the starship because a child was crying – out of compassion.

Roman Altshuler has argued that "compassion" is not the appropriate virtue to characterize the Doctor, because the Doctor has to learn or relearn compassion from his/her companions; instead "authentic concern" is the better characterization because the Doctor usually gives the aggressor a choice that will also serve the interests of the aggressor (provided that the aggressor stops the aggression). In this way, the Doctor is treating that individual with respect by allowing that individual to take responsibility for his/her choice, rather than acting in a more paternalistic way, imposing the Doctor's own will on the aggressor for his/her own good (Altshuler in Lewis and Smithka 2010, pp. 283–294).

Altshuler is correct that the Doctor's compassion lapses on occasion and s/he needs to be reminded of that compassion by a companion. This is seen in the case of Donna convincing the Doctor to save at least one family from the destruction of Pompeii ("The Fires of Pompeii," 2008), and in Amy's admonition of the Doctor in "A Town Called Mercy" (2012) where Doctor is about to facilitate the killing of Kahler-Jex by the Cyborg Gunslinger because of Jex's war crimes. As she says, "See, this is what happens to you when you travel alone for too long. Well listen to me, Doctor, we can't be like him. We have to be better than him."

Nevertheless, compassion seems an appropriate characterization of the Doctor's actions, particularly when the Doctor implements Gandhi's principle that no one is beyond redemption. (As we have already seen, the Doctor offers to save even the worst of villains, like Davros and the Master.) Indeed, Davros accuses the Doctor of having compassion. He says, "Compassion, Doctor. It has always been your greatest indulgence" in "The Magician's Apprentice" (2015) and he further claims that "Your compassion is your downfall" in "The Witch's Familiar" (2015). In "The Witch's Familiar," the Doctor is given a message from Davros, carried to him by Colony Sarff, requesting that the Doctor come see Davros because Davros is dying. In the meeting between Davros and the Doctor, Davros explains that the cables sustaining his life are connected to the life force of every Dalek, indicating that the Doctor easily could carry out genocide and moves the Doctor's hand toward the cables to tempt him:

DAVROS   Why do you hesitate? Clara Oswald is dead. Is this your con-science or shame? The shame that brought you here.
THE DOCTOR   I didn't come here because I'm ashamed. But shame never hurt anyone. I came because you're sick and you asked. And some-times, on a good day, if I try very hard, I'm not some old Time Lord who ran away, I'm the Doctor.
DAVROS   [nodding his head] Compassion, then.
THE DOCTOR   Yes.
DAVROS   It grows strong and fierce in you; like a cancer.
THE DOCTOR   I hope so.
DAVROS   It will kill you in the end.
THE DOCTOR   I wouldn't die of anything else.

What ethical framework, then, serves as the moral grounding for the Doctor's collectivist-realist pacifism, with its compassion and sense of social justice?

"It's a Different Morality, Get Used to It"

Pinpointing the moral framework of the Doctor is not as clear-cut as one might like. Indeed, philosophers have made different arguments for which ethical framework best characterizes the Doctor and his/her actions. The Doctor seems to exhibit elements from various ethical theories at different times; however, to claim that the morality of the Doctor is merely a "hodgepodge" of ethical theories would under-mine the consistent attempts by the Doctor to make the lives of other beings better. As Rose tells her mum, Jackie, and boyfriend Mickey, after having been sent back to her own time on Earth for her safety by the Ninth Doctor while he remains on Satellite 5 to fight the Daleks:

> …it was a better life. An' I don't mean all the travelin', seein' aliens and spaceships and things, that don't matter. The Doctor showed me a better way of livin' your life! You know, he showed you, too. That you don't just give up. You don't just let things happen. You make a stand! You just say "No!" You have the guts to do what's right when everyone else just runs away! ("The Parting of the Ways," 2005)

The Doctor cannot remain indifferent to the suffering and needs of others. Peace-building cannot take place without justice; someone has to make a stand to do what's morally right. That is why R. Alan Siler says that "good" is the Doctor's "magnetic north" (In Lewis and Smithka 2015, pp. 3–10).

So, what are some of the ethical theories that might be applicable to the Time Lord? Two ethical theories were mentioned above in the context of pacifism and

14 The Doctor as Philosopher: The Collectivist-Realist Pacifism of the... 325

warism – Deontology or duty-based ethics and Utilitarianism, which focuses on consequences. These two major theories will be considered first.

Duty-Based Ethics and the Doctor

As previously mentioned, deontology or duty-based ethics is a moral theory associated with Immanuel Kant where the consequences of an action are irrelevant to whether the action is morally right. For Kant, having a good will is of utmost importance; you should do something because it is the right thing to do. The question, of course, is how does one determine what the morally right thing to do is? What is one's duty? According to Kant, a rational person uses their reason to figure out what one's duty is by determining whether it is consistent with the Moral Law. For Kant, you need to ask whether the action can be universalized so that everyone, everywhere, all the time would be willing to engage in the action. He says, "act on that maxim [a subjective rule] that you could will to become a universal law of nature" (Kant [1789]/1959). So, if you cannot universalize an action, it is your duty to avoid it. As was said above, one's duty is perfect or absolute; that is, there are no exceptions to the rule.

One big problem for Kant's theory is: what if there are two duties that conflict with each other? For example, for Kant, telling the truth and keeping promises are each an absolute duty. What if, say, Amy asked the Doctor to promise not to disclose something to Rory and the Doctor makes the promise, but then Rory asks the Doctor directly about that something? The Doctor has a moral obligation to both keep the promise and tell the truth, yet both duties cannot be simultaneously upheld. There is no "moral weighting" of duties or consideration of consequences of the actions involved for Kant. Thus, the Doctor would end up doing something morally wrong in either case.

Is the Doctor a Kantian? Well, s/he does, at times, seem to think that doing something is just the "right thing to do," as the Twelfth Doctor tells the Master, in his preparation for fighting the Cybermen in order to protect the resident humans on a colony ship (in "The Doctor Falls," 2017) or when he visits Davros because Davros was sick and he asked the Doctor to come ("The Witch's Familiar," 2015). Furthermore, the Doctor seems to follow some rules, like not using weapons, though the Doctor's rules typically do not seem to be the exceptionless, perfect moral duties that Kant mentioned, since, when it comes to weapons, companions use them, and when Ryan questions the Thirteenth Doctor about the packing of grenades and a bomb in her backpack when she has made it clear in the past that weapons are not to be used, she concedes, "if it can be rebuilt, I'll allow it" ("The Battle of Ranzkoor Av Kolos," 2018). Then there is the troublesome instance in "The Doctor Falls" (2017) where the Twelfth Doctor incorporates the software developed by Nardole into his sonic screwdriver which weaponizes it for use against the Cybermen. (More will be said about this later in relation to the Doctor's pacifism.) Thus, Kant's ethics seems to be too strong to suit the Doctor's morality.

Kant's moral theory is further grounded in what philosophers call the "respect for persons principle." Kant calls this the "supreme practical ground," and this foundation is that rational nature has inherent worth. "Persons" are rational autonomous agents and so are deserving of respect; that includes respect for oneself. They are not to be treated as "things" or mere means to further the ends of the user. Given that the Doctor exhibits respect for rational autonomous beings, whether human or alien, or even mechanical – the Doctor's robotic dog K-9 is valued friend – s/he seems to align with Kant on this issue.

It is often pointed out that children are not fully rational autonomous agents, so the question arises whether they are deserving of respect. One might argue that, since children have the potential for becoming fully rational autonomous agents, they ought to be considered to have moral worth. The Doctor would seem to agree; the Eleventh Doctor, for example, comes to assist when children cry ("The Beast Below," 2010 and "Night Terrors," 2011). But, unlike Kant who did not consider nonrational beings, like animals, to have moral worth, the Doctor seems to have respect for virtually all life forms, even if they are not rational beings. Consider the sun in "42" (2007) where the Tenth Doctor says, "That sun needs care and protection just like any other living thing." Furthermore, regarding dinosaurs on a spaceship, in "Dinosaurs on a Spaceship" (2012), the Eleventh Doctor tells Solomon, "The creatures on board this ship are not objects to be sold or traded." So, the Doctor does not fit with this aspect of Kant's philosophy either.

Another way the Doctor's and Kant's ethics differ is in regard to truth telling. While the Doctor, at least for the most part, respects rational autonomous agents, Rule #1 is the Doctor lies ("The Big Bang," 2010; "Let's Kill Hitler," 2011), but one of the most noteworthy "perfect duties" that comes out of Kant's philosophy is that one must always tell the truth. Not only can lying not be universalized – everyone lying would make communication and thus lying impossible – but when one lies, one is using others as a mere means to further their ends, which violates the respect for persons principle.

What's more, what seems to justify the Doctor's lies are the consequences; when the Doctor lies, it is to accomplish some goal that s/he has in mind. For example, there have been countless instances of the Doctor employing "psychic paper" to impersonate some sort of official to, for example, gain access to a restricted area. As shown above, the Ninth Doctor lies to Rose to get her into the TARDIS so he can send her home to safety away from Satellite 5 and the Daleks. Then there is the elaborate and extremely painful deception carried out by the Eleventh Doctor regarding his own death in "The Impossible Astronaut" and "Day of the Moon" (2011). Though the Doctor had a plan and reasons for faking his death (viewers learn it was faked in "The Wedding of River Song," 2011), that apparent death without the ability of regeneration was devastating for his companions, Amy and Rory. Their pain and sense of loss served as the means to the Doctor's ends. Later in the series, Amy's husband Rory is again on the receiving end of another of the Doctor's deceptions. The Doctor knew that Amy had been replaced by a "ganger" made of Flesh by Madame Kovarian, yet fails to disclose this information to Rory ("The Almost People," 2011). Then there's the deception perpetrated on Bill, devised by Nardole and the Doctor, that the Doctor had gone over to the side of the Monks in "The Lie of the Land" (2017). This ruse was a test to determine whether Bill had been influenced by the Monks' perception filter. In this scenario,

Bill feels so betrayed after having struggled to keep her memories and an accurate perception of reality alive, she shoots the Doctor (happily, the real bullets had been replaced with blanks). (For a more in-depth discussion of the Doctor's lies, see Michael Dodge (2015) and Kevin McCain (2015).) With such lies, the Doctor not only violates Kant's respect for persons principle as well as his universalizability principle but also relies on consequences to justify his/her behavior – something Kant would never do.

There is one duty that the Twelfth Doctor overtly claims to have. He tells Clara, "I have a duty of care" ("Hell Bent," 2015). Doctors are typically thought of as persons who care for those who are ill and in need, and as the Doctor pointed out to Davros, on a good day, he can be *The* Doctor ("The Witch's Familiar," 2015). This is about the most universalizable of the duties one might claim that the Doctor has; however, even here, the caring tends to be more often associated with caring for particular others, rather than others "in general." In "Hell Bent," he directs the claim of the duty of care toward Clara – he has a duty of care toward her, and the Eleventh Doctor cares about what happens to Amy who had been abducted by Madam Kovarian by mounting a rescue attempt at Demon's Run in the episode "A Good Man Goes to War" (2011).

The Doctor's caring, then, is not entirely the universally applicable sort of caring that would be required by Kant's notion of (a perfect) duty. Even for Kant, helping others is only an "imperfect duty" – one that persons ought to do sometimes in some circumstances – it is not a perfect duty, unlike respect for persons. So, while respect is universalizable, caring about or for others and helping them is not. Nonetheless, the Doctor thinks we ought to care for others; for example, when the Twelfth Doctor admonishes us to "Never be cruel," "Always try to be nice and never fail to be kind" ("Twice Upon A Time," 2017).

So, overall, the Kantian theory of duty is not an adequate framework for the Doctor's morality. What about Ross' version of deontology that was discussed previously? Ross' model allows for usual or customary duties – prima facie duties – to be overridden in some circumstances. For example, one has a prima facie duty of fidelity (one of the seven that Ross lists), which includes telling the truth, keeping promises, and not representing fiction as fact; however, if one works for the United States' Central Intelligence Agency, one may well have to override this prima facie duty for national security reasons. Furthermore, these usual duties are grounded in the relationships between the people involved. So how well does Ross' theory capture the Doctor's morality?

While Ross' approach is a much better fit with the Doctor's morality, there remain issues. After all, if one has a prima facie duty of fidelity, which includes telling the truth, keeping promises, and not representing fiction as fact, the Doctor all too regularly violates this prima facie duty. When "Rule #1 is the Doctor lies," the frequent overriding of the duty to tell the truth calls into question whether that overriding is justified on the basis of being the more stringent prima facie duty or the one that has on balance the greater prima facie rightness over wrongness.

Furthermore, the Doctor makes promises that do not get fulfilled. For example, the Ninth Doctor explicitly promises Lynda (with a "y") from the Big Brother House on Satellite 5 that if she stays with him, he will get her out alive ("Bad Wolf," 2005). She is killed by Daleks. The Eleventh Doctor "promises" the young Amelia Pond he would return in 5 minutes after a short hop into the future to stabilize the phasing engines of the TARDIS after his regeneration. Granted, he did not actually use the term "promise" in that scenario, but after he tells her he will be back and she responds, "People always say that," the Doctor replies, "Am I people? Do I even look like people? Trust me. I'm the Doctor." This is an implicit promise, which is not fulfilled, though he returned 12 years later in her time ("The Eleventh Hour," 2010). In both of these cases, the Doctor had good intentions to fulfill those promises, yet there was no justification for them having been overridden. The moral for the Doctor here is "don't make promises you can't keep."

The frequent use of psychic paper calls into question the Doctor's adherence to fidelity, as it explicitly represents fiction as fact. Yet, in many instances, we would grant that the use of the psychic paper is justified. On the other hand, the Doctor's allowing Rory to continue to believe that Amy was on board the TARDIS when instead it was a ganger and the faking of his death are not justified. Thus, these cases certainly seem to undermine the notion of "not representing fiction as fact." So, there is a serious problem with the Doctor regularly upholding this prima facie duty of fidelity.

Other prima facie duties listed by Ross include reparation (righting the wrongs persons have done to others), gratitude (recognizing and acknowledging what others have done for us), justice (this notion is based on merit for Ross – preventing the distribution of pleasure or happiness that is not in keeping with the merit of those involved), beneficence (helping others by bettering their condition in respect to intelligence, virtue, or pleasure), self-improvement (bettering ourselves with respect to intelligence and virtue), and non-maleficence (preventing injury to others). Among these, as previously pointed out, the one that Ross suggests is most binding is that of non-maleficence.

So, how does the Doctor fare when it comes to doing these duties? The Doctor does not seem particularly good at apologizing for causing companions suffering (e.g., returning after 12 years for the young Amy or for faking his death). Neither is the Doctor good at expressing gratitude when companions provide moral guidance or contribute to "saving the day": Amy reminds the Eleventh Doctor of his basic moral principles in "A Town Called Mercy," when she says, "Doctor, that's not how we roll" as the Doctor forces Jex over the barrier to be killed by the Gunslinger; she also does so when she realizes that the Star Whale voluntarily came to propel the *Starship UK*, saving it from the Eleventh Doctor's reluctant intent to render it brain dead in order to alleviate its pain. One can say that the companions' lives are enriched for having traveled with the Doctor by their own testimonies; so, in that sense, the Doctor does seem to fulfill the prima facie duty of beneficence (though the traveling is not clearly done for the sake of the companions, but for the Doctor to stave off loneliness). With respect to the prima facie duty of non-maleficence, the Doctor typically tries to avoid injuring others – companions and even villains. Though Ross' set of rules can be overridden, they would likely be too constraining for the Doctor – or, at least, that is what Courtland Lewis contends (2017, 2021).

Utilitarianism: The Doctor and the Greater Good

Utilitarianism is a consequentialist theory of morality. That is, actions (or rules) are considered morally right when they generate the greatest happiness for the greatest number of people. The Doctor's goal of achieving what is morally right sometimes requires that s/he reasons along the lines of generating the greatest good for the greatest number.

The Doctor employs this kind of ethical reasoning in the episodes "The Fires of Pompeii" (2008) and "The Beast Below" (2010). In "The Fires of Pompeii," the Tenth Doctor reasons that, in order to save planet Earth and its inhabitants from the Pyroviles, he must destroy the energy converter being used by the Pyroviles (to change humans and destroy the Earth) because Mount Vesuvius will not erupt (a fixed point in time) with the converter running. The Doctor then realizes that the destruction of Pompeii will not simply be the event of the volcano's eruption, instead, he will be the cause: "It's me," he says. It is a difficult decision that the Doctor will have to live with. Together with Donna, who offers to share the burden of that decision, they depress a lever disrupting the energy converter, reasoning that the greater good for Earth and humans will be achieved, despite the destruction of Pompeii and most of its citizens. Yet, it is Donna who pleads with the Doctor to have compassion and "just save someone." The Doctor ultimately relents and saves the Caecilius family, thereby creating just a little more happiness, thanks to his companion.

In "The Beast Below," once again, it is a companion that ultimately achieves the greatest good for the greatest number, despite the Doctor's attempt to do so. The Eleventh Doctor has to make the painful decision to render the Star Whale, the "engine" of *Starship UK*, brain dead in order to release it from the pain and suffering inflicted upon it by Liz 10 and her government because they believed the torture was necessary to keep the Star Whale attached to the ship and thus keep them alive. The Doctor clearly demonstrates utilitarian reasoning when, as horrible a decision as it is, he decides to render the Star Whale, the last of its kind, brain dead. This action, he reasons, ultimately achieves a greater good in that the Star Whale will no longer experience the pain and suffering inflicted upon it, the *Starship UK* will remain in flight, and its occupants will live. But it is Amy who ultimately realizes that, like the Doctor, who comes when children cry (the reason why he and Amy were on *Starship UK* to begin with), the Star Whale came of its own accord in order to save the children. She forces Liz 10's hand, and together press the "abdicate" button which releases the Star Whale from its torture, causing the ship to move even faster, thereby achieving the greatest happiness for the greatest number.

Though the Doctor sometimes uses utilitarian reasoning, s/he is not always a consequentialist. The Doctor respects the rights of individuals, even in the quest for social justice for those who have been wronged. This is why the Doctor typically gives the aggressor a choice; recall the Tenth Doctor's offer to find the Racnoss and her children a new home in "The Runaway Bride" (2006) if she will cease her aggressive behavior on Earth. Even though Davros' death would likely generate the greater good given the massive destruction caused by his Dalek children over many years, no one is beyond redemption for the Doctor, which is why the Tenth Doctor offers to save Davros, even pleading with him, to allow himself to be saved in "Journey's End" (2008). Furthermore, though he considers it, the Fourth Doctor ultimately opts not to "exterminate" the nascent Daleks in "Genesis of the Daleks" (1975), even though doing so likely would have generated the greater good for many beings across the universe. In his deliberation, he queries, "Do I have the right?" Yet he rejects Sarah Jane's answer, "You know you do." The Daleks were not yet the mighty race of "ex-ter-min-ators" that they would become. Hence, the Doctor reasoned that it would be morally wrong to punish the Daleks for injustices not yet committed. And, in "The Day of the Doctor" (2013), we see a clear rejection of utilitarian reasoning. When Kate Stewart, head of UNIT, begins the countdown to detonate a nuclear warhead beneath the Tower of London that will destroy the Zygons – who were seeking to use the weapons housed there – as well as all inhabitants of London, the following interchange takes place:

KATE STEWART	...Kill millions to save billions. You made that calculation.
TENTH DOCTOR	You tell yourself it's justified, but what I did that day was wrong. [Referring to his participation in the genocide of the Time Lords and Daleks in the Time War.]
ELEVENTH DOCTOR	[with 5 seconds left on the clock to detonation]: Because I got it wrong, I'm going to make sure you get it right.

So, the Doctor's morality is not based solely on duty nor on utilitarianism; could the Doctor's moral theory be primarily based upon care? After all, the Twelfth Doctor told Clara that he has a "duty of care" and he directs us to "Always try to be nice and never fail to be kind."

A Caring Doctor?

The ethics of care emerges out of feminist philosophy. The idea is that the traditional approaches to ethics tend to be too impersonal and leave out the importance of relationships that persons bear toward one another. The traditional approaches focus on "people in general" (think: the greatest good for the greatest number of people in utilitarianism, or asking whether an action can be universalized, as in Kant's ethics) and ignore the needs of *particular* others with whom individuals have personal relationships and for whom they are responsible (Held 2006; see also Gilligan 1982 and Noddings 1984). Furthermore, traditional moral theories only focus on using reason to discern what actions are morally right. Emotions have no role to play in making moral decisions.

The Ethics of Care, however, values emotion, though it does not value emotion to the exclusion of reason; it is in addition to it. But the position contends that emotions have been neglected, and the role they should play in ethical decision-making needs to be recognized and emphasized. Emotions such as sympathy, empathy, and even anger at injustice and cruelty can inform one as to what morality recommends. Virginia Held is careful to point out that the care ethicist is not simply concerned with raw emotion; instead, the care ethicist is concerned with emotions that are reflected upon and educated. Thus, one's personal relationships with those for whom they care are part of the realm of our moral concern, or at least should be.

J. J. Sylvia argues that the Doctor's morality is an ethics of care in "Doctor, Who Cares?" (in Lewis and Smithka 2010). The Doctor clearly cares for the particular others with whom s/he has relationships. Again, the Ninth Doctor sent Rose home in order to keep her safe ("The Parting of the Ways," 2005), and the Eleventh Doctor forms an "army of friends" in order to extricate Amy and her baby from Madam Kovarian at Demon's Run in "A Good Man Goes to War" (2011). There are too many examples of the Doctor caring for his/her companions to enumerate here. S/he even cares about his/her enemies: the Tenth Doctor cares for the Master ("Last of the Time Lords," 2007); the Twelfth Doctor works on reforming Missy (throughout Season 10); and tries to save Davros ("Journey's End," 2008; "The Magician's Apprentice," "The Witch's Familiar," 2015). But the Doctor's caring or concern is not only for *particular* others. The Doctor protects groups – not only humans, but other aliens as well – like the enslaved Ood ("Planet of the Ood," 2008). Thus, the Doctor's concern is more widely applicable and inextricably wound up with his/her quest for social justice, which is why Courtland Lewis contends that the Doctor's morality is fundamentally based on the needs of others (2017, 2021).

The Doctor's Morality: Meeting the Needs of Others

Relying on the work of Nicholas Wolterstorff, who focuses on justice and peace, Courtland Lewis argues that the Doctor's ethics are about meeting the needs of others. Lewis calls this the "life of needs" (2021, pp. 82–84). In this approach, several elements of the previously discussed ethical theories come together in a way that establishes the foundation of the Doctor's collectivist-realist pacifism. Wolterstorff, and thus, Lewis contend that when one's own basic needs are met, and the basic needs of others are met, this provides the basis for both peace and justice. At the heart of meeting these needs, for Wolterstorff, is respecting the rights of others. Wolterstorff says, "Rights are boundary-markers for the pursuit of life-goods" and these rights of others limit how persons treat each other such that violations of rights are violations of the worth of the other person (Wolterstorff 2010, pp. 5, 6). In this are echoes of deontologism – the inherent moral worth of persons and respect. The Doctor stresses the value of life in a speech made by the Twelfth Doctor to Sutcliffe, who had been feeding children to the creature in the Thames:

> Human progress isn't measured by industry. It's measured by the value you place on a life. An unimportant life. A life without privilege. The boy who died on the river, that boy's value is your value. That's what defines an age, that's. . . what defines a species. ("Thin Ice," 2017)

Since rights are normative social relationships for Wolterstorff, this "life of needs" is based in social relationships like the ethics of care, but added to caring, are peace and justice, which are the aims of this moral theory. Lewis says:

> Being ethical, then, is about justice, a state of affairs where individuals get what they need. When individuals have their basic needs met, and help provide the basic needs of others, a state of peace is created. (2021, p. 83)

As was previously shown, Cortright contends that peace advocates cannot remain indifferent to the needs and suffering of those who are repressed. Lewis says, "Once we accept the vulnerability of ourselves and others, we begin to see the important role we all play in protecting one another, and so, we live our lives striving for peace" (2021, p. 83). When persons do not have what they need, there is injustice; and where there is injustice, interference is morally required. And the Doctor interferes where there is a need – where there is pain and suffering, where there is injustice – because the Doctor is a doctor with compassion who seeks to heal the pain and rectify injustice, even if it sometimes requires an undesirable lethal force. The Doctor's collectivist-realist pacifism will be addressed in the next section.

The Collectivist-Realist Pacifism of the Doctor

> There are some corners of the universe which have bred the most terrible things. Things which act against everything that we believe in. They must be fought.
> —2nd Doctor ("The Moonbase" 1967)

> Do what you've always done – be a doctor.
> —Clara ("The Day of the Doctor" 2013)

War. . .No More

The Doctor does everything that s/he can in order to achieve social justice without the use of lethal force. A paradigm example of this is seen in "The Day of the Doctor" (2013) when the Tenth, Eleventh, and War Doctors assist in brokering peace between humans and the Zygons. With only 5 seconds left on the clock before the detonation of the nuclear warhead that would destroy London and all inhabitants therein – human and Zygon alike – and the Tenth Doctor having admitted he was wrong to have brought about the destruction of the Time Lords and Daleks in the Time War, the Eleventh Doctor, proclaimed, "Because I got it wrong, I'm going to make sure you get it right." At this point, the Tenth, Eleventh, and War Doctor (John Hurt) together use their sonics to create a Rawlsian "veil of ignorance" for the Zygons and humans, so that neither knows who is Zygon and who is human. As a result, both the Zygon-Kate Stewart and the human-Kate Stewart simultaneously cancel the detonation and a successful and just peace treaty is brokered between the Zygons and humans.

Viewers also learn in this 50th Anniversary Special, that instead of the War Doctor using "the Moment" (the most dangerous weapon) to destroy the Time Lords and Daleks in the Time War, the various Doctor-incarnations (all 12 and War) employ their TARDISs and the stasis technology to save Gallifrey by freezing it in a pocket universe. With Gallifrey suddenly removed from the Time War, the Daleks would be left to fire on each other's ships, essentially destroying themselves. Thus, the Doctor is ultimately not responsible for the genocide of the Daleks, since they fired on themselves, nor of the Time Lords, though the Tenth and War Doctors (and presumably the Ninth) will not remember this and so they still carry the guilt of being responsible for that genocide.

This is reminiscent of how the Doctor avoids using lethal force often by facilitating the villains' own use of violence against themselves. This tactic is also seen in the Christmas Special, "The Time of the Doctor" (2013). A wooden Cyberman comes to kill the Eleventh Doctor with a flamethrower mounted on its arm. In this town called "Christmas," where it is impossible to lie, the Doctor directs his sonic screwdriver to reverse the polarity on the flamethrower so that it will backfire. He tells the wooden Cyberman, "Now, I just sent an instruction to your firearm to reverse the polarity and fire out the back end. Now, as we're standing in a truth field, you will understand I cannot be lying. If you like, you can scan my screwdriver, verify that's the signal I sent." The Cyberman verifies the signal and he turns the flamethrower around so that he might kill the Doctor. Instead, the flamethrower fires into the chest of the wooden Cyberman. The Doctor says, "I probably should have mentioned this doesn't work on wood." So, the wooden Cyberman essentially dies by his own hand.

The Doctor's pacifism is seen at work once again diffusing tensions between the Zygons and the humans in "The Zygon Inversion" (2015). A splinter group of Zygons is unhappy with the previous peace accord brokered between the Zygons and the humans because they want to lead their lives "normalized" in their native form and not live among humans "disguised" as humans. The leader, Zygella, who goes by the name Bonnie, wants to wage war on humanity. She seeks the Osgood box that would reveal the Zygons. There are two Osgood boxes, one blue, one red; they were devised to ensure the peace brokered in the previous accord. Each box has two buttons in it: in one box, one of the buttons reveals the Zygons, the other button permanently fixes the Zygons in their human forms; in the other box, one button destroys the Zygons, the other button destroys everyone in London. Once again, Kate Stewart faces off with a Zygon, Bonnie. Both are willing to take the chance of lethal violence. The Doctor reminds Bonnie that "The only way anyone can live in peace is if they're prepared to forgive." But Bonnie wants war. The Doctor then gives a moving anti-war speech that ultimately backs them down:

Ah. Ah, right. And when this war is over, when you have a homeland free from humans, what do you think it's going to be like? Do you know? Have you thought about it? Have you given it any consideration? Because you're very close to getting what you want. What's it going to be like? Paint me a picture. Are you going to live in houses? Do you want people to go to work? Will there be holidays? Oh! Will there be music? Do you think people will be allowed to play violins? Who's going to make the violins? Well? Oh, you don't actually know, do you? Because, like every other tantrumming child in history, Bonnie, you don't actually know what you want. So, let me ask you a question about this brave new world of yours. When you've killed all the bad guys, and when it's all "perfect and just and fair", when you have finally got it exactly the way you want it, what are you going to do with the people like you? The troublemakers. How are you going to protect your glorious revolution from the next one?

Bonnie insists they will win but the Doctor reminds her "But nobody wins for long." Both Bonnie and Kate remain with their fingers over the buttons. The Doctor continues:

> Because it's not a game, Kate. This is a scale model of war. Every war ever fought, right there in front of you. Because it's always the same. When you fire that first shot, no matter how right you feel, you have no idea who's going to die! You don't know whose children are going to scream and burn! How many hearts will be broken! How many lives shattered! How much blood will spill until everybody does what they were always going to have to do from the very beginning. Sit down and talk! [sigh] Listen to me. Listen, I just, I just want you to think. Do you know what thinking is? It's just a fancy word for changing your mind.

Bonnie is obstinate and claims she won't change her mind; she won't stand down the revolution because she won't be "let go" after what she's done. The Doctor tells her he is "unforgiveable" and that he forgives her. He continues:

> ...I mean, do you call this a war? This funny little thing? This is not a war! I fought in a bigger war than you will ever know. I did worse things than you could ever imagine. And when I close my eyes I hear more screams than anyone could ever be able to count! And do you know what you do with all that pain? Shall I tell you where you put it? You hold it tight till it burns your hand, and you say this. No one else will ever have to live like this. No one else will have to feel this pain. Not on my watch!

Kate steps back from the box and both she and Bonnie realize the boxes are empty. The Doctor wipes Kate's mind but not Bonnie's. War between the Zygons and humans is once again averted. But fighting cannot always be avoided. And, though the Doctor claims to not use weapons, and the writers might attempt to avoid the "weapons charge" by having the Doctor use his/her sonic, the Twelfth Doctor overtly weaponizes his sonic screwdriver to do battle with the Cybermen on a colony ship in order to save the humans in "The Doctor Falls" (2017). This episode is a good example of the Doctor's collectivist-realist pacifism at work and will be the focus of the next section.

"Who I Am Is Where I Stand"

"The Doctor never uses weapons," so claims the Thirteenth Doctor ("Fugitive of the Judoon," 2020). Yet, viewers see the Tenth Doctor wield Wilf's revolver against the returning Time Lords (although he does not fire it and the Master takes it from him in "The End of Time, Part 2" (2010)). And the Eleventh Doctor, in "A Town Called Mercy" (2012), threatens Kahler-Jex with a gun because of Jex's war crimes in order to turn him over to the Cyborg Gunslinger, who had been transformed into a weapon by Jex. Both Doctors are acting in their "hero" personas, and yet threatening the use of a weapon (Pless 2015). In the latter episode, the Doctor, having pushed Jex over the boundary, claims "Today, I honor the victims first. His, the Master's, the Daleks, all the people who died because of my mercy!" As we have already seen, Amy reminds him of his compassion; "You see, this is what happens when you travel alone for too long. Well, listen to me, Doctor. We can't be like him. We have to be better than him." He concedes and says they will do something different. Meanwhile Isaac, the town's marshal, shoves Jex out of the way of the Gunslinger's bullet, taking the shot himself. As he is dying he makes a request of the Doctor: "Protect Jex. Protect my town. You're both good men. You just forget it sometimes." Isaac gives the marshal's badge to the Doctor. Later in the episode, the pacifism of Doctor re-emerges when he talks down the "nearly nineteen"-year-old Walter who is threatening the Doctor with a gun. The Doctor tells Walter, "Violence doesn't end violence; it extends it...I don't think you want to become that man." And when the Gunslinger says he'll go into the desert and self-destruct because "I'm a creature of war. I have no role to play during peace," the Doctor responds, "Except maybe to protect it." In both cases, while the Doctor threatened use of a gun, he didn't use it. So, instead of being counter examples to the Doctor's pacifism, and his abhorrence of weapons and violence, these episodes demonstrate it; although tempted to use a gun, he restrains.[2]

The Twelfth Doctor, however, undoubtedly uses both weapons and lethal force when he gets into the thick of things in the battle that takes place against the Mondasian Cybermen (on the colony ship from Mondas) to save the humans in "The Doctor Falls" (2017). In this episode, viewers learn that the Doctor's companion, Bill Potts, has been fully converted into a Mondasian Cyberman. She had been saved from death in the previous episode ("World Enough and Time," 2017) with her chest having been rebuilt. She remains for some years in the company of the Master (John Simm), who is disguised as the floor's caretaker, as she waits for the Doctor to come. The colony ship is near a black hole which produces a time dilation such that time passes more quickly on the lower levels of the ship. What is a short period of time to the Doctor and Missy on the top level amounts to years for Bill on another level. During a skirmish with Cybermen, Nardole, who has commandeered a shuttlecraft, comes to rescue the group but the Doctor is electrocuted by a Cyberman. The Master and Missy persuade Nardole to leave the Doctor who is "dead," but Bill (in Cyberman form) forces them to take her and the Doctor. They arrive on floor 0507, which is a solar farm inhabited by children and some adults. They learn that the Cybermen have been abducting the children for conversion. The Cybermen do not ask permission of the children's guardians, nor of the children themselves. Even though the Cybermen may think that they are "upgrading humans," they do so in violation of the rights of humans, thereby making it impossible for humans to pursue their own life-goods. With Nardole's help, a girl uses an apple full of explosives against the early wave of Cybermen, convincing them that the humans are more powerful than they are; they have thus given what the Doctor characterized as a "militarized weapons response." Because time moves more slowly on this floor, the Doctor warns that while this buys them some time, the next Cyber-force will likely be more advanced. Nardole characterizes their situation as "war" and he and the humans prepare for the next attack. Meanwhile the Master and Missy plan and begin their departure. The Doctor, who had been repressing the regeneration process that started in the previous episode, asks them to stay and help fight the Cybermen. He ultimately convinces Nardole, despite objections, that Nardole must be the one to see the humans to safety by evacuating them to another solar farm on a different floor. The Doctor then uploads the software from Nardole's computer, weaponizing his sonic screwdriver. The Doctor, together with Bill, is seen fighting the Cybermen on the battlefield, until the Doctor falls after being shot. He sets off the fuel pipes, creating a massive fireball, destroying the Cybermen. The Doctor is "dying." Bill's tears, crying over the dying Doctor, call to Heather, a former love interest of Bill, who had been transformed into a liquid-being in order to pilot the liquid spaceship stranded on Earth in "The Pilot" (2017). Prior to Heather's departure in that episode, she left tears with Bill so that she would know when Bill was in trouble. Because Bill is in trouble, Heather then appears on the scene to help. She and Bill place the Doctor in his TARDIS and Heather restores Bill's human form on the condition that Bill travel with her.

Although it may seem to be a counter example to the Doctor's pacifism, the episode actually helps us understand the collectivist-realist pacifism that the Doctor embraces. When the Master points out that the Cyberman will just find and attack the humans again, telling the Doctor, "You can't win," the Doctor replies, "I know. And?" The Doctor then follows up with a moving speech to the Master about why he feels he must stay and fight: because it is right.

> Winning? Is that what you think it's about? I'm not trying to win. I'm not doing this because I want to beat someone, or because I hate someone, or because I blame someone. It's not because it's fun and God knows it's not because it's easy. It's not even because it works, because it hardly ever does. I do what I do, because it's right. Because it's decent. Because above all, it's kind. Just that. Just kind. If I run away today, good people will die. If I stand and fight, some of them might live. Maybe not many, and maybe not for long and maybe there's no point in any of this at all. But it's the best I can do, so I'm doing it. And I'll stand here doing it 'till it kills me. You'll die too, Master, some day. Have you thought about that? How it will be? Because I know you very well, and I think you'll be running. Running *away*, terrified, with bullet after bullet in your back. And when you're lying there in the mud, crying, screaming, begging, betraying, you know what you're going to think about? Me. You'll think about me. *Standing*. Who I am is where I stand. And where I stand is where I fall. Stand with me. These people are terrified. Maybe we can help a little. Why not, at the end, just be kind?

The Doctor recognizes the injustice being done and feels compassion for these humans, thus interference is morally required. Or, as American Peace Activist David Cortwright might put it, no pacifist (including what we have been calling a collectivist-realist pacifist) can "be indifferent to the sufferings and needs of those who are victimized by repression, or ignore the necessary connections between peace and broader issues of democracy, social justice, and [the rights of beings]" (2008, p. 335). And this is why the Twelfth Doctor chose to use lethal force against the Cyberman on the colony ship. The Doctor cannot remain on the sidelines; his collectivist-realist pacifism requires interference in order for him to be a doctor to the extent that he can, and in that situation, lethal force was the only option that would allow him to fulfill that obligation. However, while the Doctor will use lethal force as a last resort when other options have been exhausted or are unavailable, the Doctor's main focus is on the needs of others in the quest for social justice.

The Quest for Social Justice

The Doctor's commitment to justice is paramount. That is why the Twelfth Doctor resorted to lethal force when fighting the Mondasian Cybermen. Most of the time, however, the Doctor finds ways to answer the needs of others without the use of lethal force. For example, when the Tenth Doctor and Donna realize that the Ood are slaves for humans, the Doctor says, "I reckon I owe them one" ("Planet of the Ood," 2008). He remains pained by not having been able to save the remaining Ood on Century Base 6 which, along with that whole planet, was sucked into a black hole in the episode "The Satan Pit" (2006). After capturing the rocket with the remaining Century Base 6 crew and Rose on board using the TARDIS, saving them from the force of the black hole, the Doctor reports to them: "I couldn't save the Ood; I only had time for one trip. They went down with the planet." When Donna inquires about the Ood being slaves, the Doctor says, "Last time I met the Ood, I never thought; I never asked." Surprised, Donna says, "That's not like you." He replied, "I was busy, so busy; I had to let the Ood die." This time he would help them. The Doctor and Donna learn that the Ood were being bred and modified to be slaves – the hindbrain that the "natural Ood" held in their hands was removed and replaced by a translator device – and that the Ood's collective song was being blocked by a forcefield encircling the massive brain that held the Ood's collective consciousness: "The circle must be broken," the Ood claimed. As they launched a rebellion against their human masters, the Doctor powered down the pylons that emitted the forcefield. This freed the Ood from their imposed slavery, restoring their collective song. The Ood finally got justice after 200 years of slavery.

The commitment to social justice is also why the Thirteenth Doctor ensures that, during the 1955 Montgomery Bus Boycott, there are enough passengers on the bus so that Rosa Parks will have the opportunity to refuse to give up her seat to a white man, despite the efforts of Krasco, the racist, mass murderer, now released from prison, but who is now a "neutered criminal" that cannot kill. Since he is unable to commit murder, his plan was to create small changes in the timeline, like changing the schedule of the bus driver, in order to alter the course of history with the goal of undermining the civil rights movement. Even though their actions meant that the Doctor, Yaz, Graham, and Ryan become a part of that history – they had to remain on the bus to fill out the seats – the Doctor and her companions successfully kept that important part of civil rights history intact ("Rosa," 2018).

And it is not only organic beings who have needs and require the assistance of the Doctor to restore justice and peace. The Doctor and her companions, Yaz, Ryan, and Graham, go to the aid of the AI system whose automated workforce was being compromised and the human workers, the "organics," were being killed in the episode "Kerblam!" (2018). They learn that the human saboteur, Charlie, was motivated by workforce inequities – Kerblam was 90% automated – and humans were not able to find work. He sought to undermine the automated system, which is why the AI system sent the message "Help me" to the Doctor in package containing a fez, delivered by the Kerblam-man robot to the TARDIS in flight. The Doctor foils Charlie's plan to kill the recipients of Kerblam packages using explosive bubble wrap by having the assembled "army" of Kerblam delivery robots open the packages in the warehouse and pop the bubble wrap destroying the robots and Charlie. As a result, the human resource managers, Judy Maddox and Jarva Slade, commit to restoring Kerblam with a mostly human workforce. Where beings' needs are not being met and injustice is taking place, the Doctor interferes. That is what is required of a collectivist-realist pacifist. Recall the words of the Second Doctor: "There are some corners of the universe which have bred the most terrible things. Things which act against everything that we believe in. They must be fought" ("The Moonbase," 1967).

Conclusion

The Doctor is a pacifist, but s/he is certainly not passive. The Doctor must "get into the thick of things" (Lewis 2017, 2021) and do what is right, attending to those in need, with the goal of being kind. As a collectivist-realist pacifist, the Doctor does not, and cannot, avoid the needs and suffering of those who are victimized – not, at least, if s/he still wants to *be* a *doctor*. We should be more like the Doctor, caring about the suffering of others, showing compassion, and doing what we can to fight social injustice. As King pointed out, there can be no positive peace without justice. But in attempting to bring about justice, sometimes it is necessary to use coercion, since sometimes people are not persuaded by rational arguments. However, for King, that coercion should be constructive (1967) and achieved by nonviolent direct action. The Doctor typically tries nonviolent means first, giving the assailant a choice to stop their assault, often with the offer of assistance from the Doctor (as was the case with the Empress of the Racnoss), or face the consequences. Though the Doctor attempts to restore peace and justice by avoiding lethal force wherever possible, it is not always possible. And because "preventing evil is always more urgent" (Cady 1989, p. 50), lethal force is sometimes morally justified and morally required – but only as a last resort. Indeed, humans can learn from the Doctor and we ought to take to heart the words of the regenerating Twelfth Doctor:

> Never be cruel, never be cowardly... Remember – hate is always foolish...and love, is always wise. Always try to be nice and never fail to be kind. ("Twice Upon A Time," 2017)

End Notes

1. However, one unnerving instance of disrespect was shown by the Ruth-Doctor to the Judoon Commander when she ripped off the Commander's horn in "Fugitive of the Judoon" (2020).

14 The Doctor as Philosopher: The Collectivist-Realist Pacifism of the…

2. The potentially disturbing exception was the modification of a powerful weapon by the Ruth-Doctor who gives over the weapon to Gat – the weapon had been Gat's in the past. The Ruth-Doctor taunts Gat, asking that she not fire it to kill the Ruth-Doctor, which, of course, Gat does. The weapon, however, "backfires" killing Gat. The Ruth-Doctor knew that would happen ("Fugitive of the Judoon," 2020). So, though the Ruth-Doctor did not herself fire the weapon, she deliberately facilitated the killing of Gat. Viewers do not have the full backstory to determine whether the Ruth-Doctor's actions could have been morally justifiable, but the Thirteenth Doctor is clearly unsettled by that behavior.

References

Altshuler, Roman. 2010. Is the Doctor the destroyer of worlds? In *Doctor Who and philosophy: Bigger on the inside*, ed. Courtland Lewis and Paula Smithka, 239–247. Chicago/La Salle: Open Court.

Cady, Duane. 1989. *From warism to pacifism: A moral continuum*. Philadelphia: Temple University Press.

———. 1994. In defense of active pacifists. *Journal of Social Philosophy* 25 (2): 85–91.

Cortright, David. 2008. *Peace: A history of movements and ideas*. Cambridge: Cambridge University Press.

Deller, Ruth. 2010. What the world needs is…a Doctor. In *Doctor Who and philosophy: Bigger on the inside*, ed. Courtland Lewis and Paula Smithka, 239–247. Chicago/La Salle: Open Court.

Dodge, Michael. 2015. The way of the Doctor is deception. In *More Doctor Who and philosophy: Regeneration time*, ed. Courtland Lewis and Paula Smithka, 177–185. Chicago: Open Court.

Fiala, Andrew. 2018. Pacifism. In *The Stanford encyclopedia of philosophy*, ed. Edward N. Zalta. https://plato.stanford.edu/archives/fall2018/entries/pacifism. Accessed 7 Aug 2020.

Gilligan, Carol. 1982. *In a different voice: Psychological theory and women's development*. Cambridge: Harvard University Press.

Glossop, Ronald J. 2001. *Confronting war: An examination of humanity's most pressing problem*. 4th ed. Jefferson/London: McFarland & Co., Inc.

Held, Virginia. 2006. *The ethics of care*. Oxford: Oxford University Press.

Kant, Immanuel. [1785]/1959. *Foundations of the metaphysics of morals*. Translated by Lewis White Beck. Indianapolis: Bobb's Merrill.

King, Martin Luther, Jr. 1963. "Letter from Birmingham Jail," published under the title, "The Negro is your brother." *The Atlantic Monthly* 212 (2): 78–88. https://www.theatlantic.com/magazine/archive/2018/02/letter-from-birmingham-jail/552461/. Accessed 20 Aug 2018.

———. 1967. *Where do we go from here: Chaos or community?* New York: Harper & Row.

Lewis, Courtland. 2017. *The way of the Doctor: Doctor Who's pocketbook guide to the good life*. Columbia, SC: PhilDocBooks.

———. 2021. *The real meaning of Doctor Who*. Chicago: Open Universe.

Lewis, Courtland, and Paula Smithka, eds. 2010. *Doctor Who and philosophy: Bigger on the inside*. Chicago/La Salle: Open Court.

———, eds. 2015. *More Doctor Who and philosophy: Regeneration time*. Chicago: Open Court.

McCain, Kevin. 2015. The Doctor lies. In *More Doctor Who and philosophy: Regeneration time*, ed. Courtland Lewis and Paula Smithka, 239–247. Chicago: Open Court.

Mill, John Stuart. [1863/1879]/2004. *Utilitarianism*. The Project Gutenberg EBook of Utilitarianism [EBook #11224]. https://www.gutenberg.org/files/11224/11224-h/11224-h.htm. Accessed 29 July 2020.

Noddings, Nell. 1984. *Caring: A feminine approach to ethics and moral education*. Berkeley: University of California Press.

Pless, Deborah. 2015. A good man goes to war. In *More Doctor Who and philosophy: Regeneration time*, ed. Courtland Lewis and Paula Smithka, 11–20. Chicago: Open Court.

Rawls, John. [1971]/1999. *Theory of justice,* rev. ed. Cambridge, MA: Harvard University Press.

Ross, W.D. [1930]/1988. *The right and the good*. Indianapolis: Hackett Publishing.

Siler, R. Alan. 2015. Magnetic North. In *More Doctor Who and philosophy: Regeneration time*, ed. Courtland Lewis and Paula Smithka, 3–10. Chicago: Open Court.

Smithka, Paula. 1992. Are active pacifists just-warists in disguise? *Journal of Social Philosophy* 23 (3): 166–183.

Sylvia, J.J. 2010. Doctor, who cares? In *Doctor Who and philosophy: Bigger on the inside*, ed. Courtland Lewis and Paula Smithka, 239–247. Chicago/La Salle: Open Court.

Wolterstorff, Nicholas. 2010. *Justice: Rights and wrongs*. Princeton: Princeton University Press.

Grey's Anatomy as Philosophy: Ethical Ambiguity in Shades of Grey

15

Kimberly S. Engels and Katie Becker

Contents

Introduction	342
Summary and Plot	343
Simone de Beauvoir and *The Ethics of Ambiguity*	345
Meredith Grey's Authenticity: Bomb in a Patient	348
Grey's Authenticity: Prisoner from Death Row	349
Grey's Authenticity Versus Shepherd's Seriousness: Alzheimer's Trial	351
Grey's Authenticity: Immigration Injustice and Insurance Fraud	354
Conclusion	358
References	359

Abstract

Grey's Anatomy focuses on the personal and professional life of protagonist Meredith Grey. Throughout the long series, a consistent theme is that the audience is confronted with moral dilemmas in Meredith's professional work with patients as well as in her personal life. Grey's decision-making often breaks professional protocol in order to do what she believes is best for her patients and those close to her. We argue that Grey's approach to morality is representative of Simone de Beauvoir's approach in *The Ethics of Ambiguity*. In this text, Beauvoir argues that an existentialist ethic must reject a childlike approach to morality in which moral rules are absolute and moral dilemmas have obvious answers. Instead, she argues for a rejection of universalist ethics in favor of acknowledging the ambiguity of the moral realm. By tracing Meredith's decision-making throughout the course of

---

K. S. Engels (✉)
Molloy University, Rockville Centre, NY, USA
e-mail: kengels@molloy.edu

K. Becker
Greensboro, NC, USA

© Springer Nature Switzerland AG 2024
D. K. Johnson et al. (eds.), *The Palgrave Handbook of Popular Culture as Philosophy*,
https://doi.org/10.1007/978-3-031-24685-2_32

different seasons of the show, we argue that Meredith exemplifies an existential authenticity compatible with Beauvoir's existentialist approach to ethics.

Keywords

Simone de Beauvoir · Moral ambiguity · Spirit of seriousness · Existentialism · Medical ethics

Introduction

> So do it. Decide. Is this the life you want to live? Is this the best you can be? Can you be stronger? Kinder? More compassionate? Decide. Breathe in. Breathe out and decide.
> —Meredith Grey

Grey's Anatomy is a medical drama that embraces the homophonic metaphor of its title and titular character, Meredith Grey. Meredith's surname invokes connotations of the color gray that add symbolism to other narrative points in the series. It sets the stage for the Seattle-based weather of the show's landscape. It sets the tone for the "dark and twisty" nature of Meredith's personality. Most importantly, it speaks to the gray areas of right and wrong the show tackles through its many seasons of storytelling. Through both the scenarios, the doctors confront when treating patients, as well as the choices they make in their personal lives; *Grey's Anatomy* presents the viewer with many ambiguous moral conundrums.

Existentialist writer Simone de Beauvoir famously argued that the human condition is fundamentally characterized by ambiguity. There is ambiguity in the fact that we possess transcendent free consciousness but are simultaneously bound by a physical body. There is ambiguity in the fact that we experience the world as both transcendent subjects and as objects for others. And there is ambiguity in our moral world: values are not fixed, permanent, or given from outside but come from human beings and our intersubjective experiences. An existentialist ethics of ambiguity, then, is characterized by a rejection of any set of absolute moral values that could be separated from the context in which they occur. Morality exists only in human affairs and, like us, is characterized by ambiguity.

An ethics of ambiguity does not result in a pure moral relativism or subjectivism, however. In the existentialist view, human beings are free, creative meaning givers, and thus our moral world demands that we actively will the freedom of the other. When we choose to value the other's freedom as equally important as our own, we must act concretely in the world to remove barriers that may prevent them from being free. The authentic, ethical attitude for Beauvoir, then, is one that embraces the ambiguity, or realization that there are no absolute, pre-given moral truths. Simultaneously one makes a moral choice which they take responsibility for, and which takes the specific context of the situation into consideration.

Beauvoir argues that this true ethical attitude is rare and many people choose various paths of inauthenticity instead, looking to justify moral values in something other than their own choice and freedom. Beauvoir calls this "the spirit of seriousness." When we are children, Beauvoir says, we are all born into the "serious world," a world in which good and evil exist as surely as the grass is green. Right and wrong are as true as any other fact about the world. Many people embrace the spirit of seriousness because they are comforted by its certainty: right and wrong are clearly delineated, and you navigate the moral realm by following the rules. But these individuals are ultimately living in an inauthentic state, according to Beauvoir. The collapse of the serious world is too much for them to bear, because without the serious world, they will be forced to choose and give their own justification for the choice. This is often accompanied by anguish at the thought that they are ultimately responsible. Thus, many adults prefer the path of seriousness over the difficult, ambiguous path of freedom.

In *Grey's Anatomy*, protagonist Meredith Grey demonstrates a consistent understanding of Beauvoir's ethics of ambiguity. Over the seasons, Meredith repeatedly shows an understanding that ethical decisions must be considered in their appropriate context and with a consideration of the relationships between the people involved. Further, she recognizes that a single situation could have multiple moral answers. She is regularly willing to break institutional rules for the sake of positively enabling the freedom of the other, and she recognizes the true ethic lies in valuing the other's freedom as much as your own. Against protocol, Meredith places her hand inside a patient with a bomb in their chest cavity, enables the intentions of a convicted serial killer, breaks the rules of clinical trials, and falsifies insurance documents, all to give chances and choices to people who otherwise have none.

Meredith sees morality as more than following a set of strict, inherently moral rules and views it instead as a process of engaging with the messy, ambiguous social world. This moral ambiguity remains the uniting thread within both the character and the series. Throughout the series, Meredith's moral compass often leads her to break the established rules of her profession, which she reconciles according to her own values. Her willingness to reject the spirit of seriousness affects her personal relationships and her medical career. In this chapter, we explore the ways Meredith navigates the moral shades of gray she recognizes in her personal and professional life. In doing so, we address the inevitable risks and consequences of engaging with moral ambiguity in a hospital setting that is governed by the spirit of seriousness.

Summary and Plot

As *Grey's Anatomy* is entering its 16th season, the plot is long and complex. The series focuses on "dark and twisty" protagonist Meredith Grey, following her journey from surgical intern to an award-winning surgeon and eventual chief of general surgery at Grey Sloan Memorial Hospital. Her dark nature is often attributed to her demanding and emotionally abusive mother, Ellis Grey, an award-winning surgeon who trained alongside Meredith's chief of surgery, Richard Webber.

Much of the series, including Grey's ongoing character development, revolves around her new relationships and suffering, but the foundation of the character is rooted in Grey's childhood trauma. Viewers learn that Meredith grew up during the disintegration of her parents' marriage as a result of her mother's infidelity with Richard Webber. When Webber refused to leave his wife, Adele, Grey witnessed her mother's suicide attempt and had to call 911 in order to save her life. Meredith also references an upbringing full of repeated scrutiny from her mother. At the end of the pilot episode, the audience sees Meredith visiting Ellis in a care facility and learns she suffers from early-onset Alzheimer's, a diagnosis Meredith is instructed to hide from Ellis's professional friends. This leaves Meredith feeling isolated and overwhelmed in both emotionally caring for her mother and respecting her right to privacy.

The series begins at the start of Meredith's internship where she develops new relationships but also experiences additional trauma. She meets attending surgeon Derek Shepherd, who becomes her boyfriend and later her husband. She befriends another intern, Cristina Yang, and the two have a 10-season-long bond as each other's "person" or best friend. She establishes a complicated friendship with a somewhat bully, Alex Karev. Through continued empathy for his rough upbringing and childhood distress, he later becomes "her person" when Yang leaves the hospital. She also develops a complicated relationship with Richard Webber. While this relationship is initially strained because of their shared past, Meredith and Richard eventually develop a deep and lasting connection. Other notable long-term characters include Miranda Bailey, Meredith's resident adviser, who becomes the first black female chief of surgery in the later seasons, and Owen Hunt, trauma surgeon/Iraqi war veteran who is Yang's first husband (although the two later divorce and part for good in Season 10).

Throughout the series, Meredith has many more traumatic experiences. Her mother dies of Alzheimer's-related complications, her stepmom dies of a surgical complication to fix her hiccups, her half-sister Lexi dies in a plane crash, and her husband Derek dies in a car wreck. Her own life is put at risk several times as she is almost killed by a bomb inside a patient in Season 2, almost drowns in Season 4, is almost shot by a gunman in Season 6, survives the plane crash that kills her sister in Season 8, and goes into labor during a superstorm that interferes with hospital resources in Season 10.

Meredith's suffering is a focal point of the show. Her experiences with trauma give her a uniquely empathic understanding of the tragedies of modern life. While the show is a drama that focuses on the lives of the surgeons and their relationships with each other, it also regularly includes medical ethics dilemmas in their interactions with their patients. They navigate complex moral dilemmas and each bring their own experiences and worldviews to their evaluation. An early-series episode focuses on the surgical staff evaluating the treatment of two patients impaled by the same pole and whether it is justified to focus on saving one patient at the expense of the other ("Into You Like a Train"). The show also tackles tough questions related to race, gender, and contemporary social problems. For example, in Season 14, the show features an episode in which a young black male patient dies after being shot by the police who mistakenly thought he was breaking into his own house, thus addressing the Black Lives Matter movement ("Personal Jesus"). Season 15 features a patient who has been sexually assaulted and does not want to be subjected to the rape kit examination, engaging with our cultural "Me Too" discussion of the prevalence of sexual assault ("Silent All These Years"). The show does not shy away from using its characters and stories to address current issues of pressing moral concern. The show's format thus presents the viewer with a messy, ambiguous moral realm that is ripe for an existentialist ethical analysis.

Simone de Beauvoir and *The Ethics of Ambiguity*

In her 1948 work, *The Ethics of Ambiguity*, Simone de Beauvoir introduces readers to both the tenets of existentialism as well as the ethical thought she argues flows from it. While French existentialism is more often associated with Beauvoir's lifelong companion Jean-Paul Sartre, Beauvoir's *Ambiguity* stands as a foundational existentialist text as well as the only major published work dedicated to existentialist ethics.

Beauvoir begins the work by describing the ambiguity of the human position: human beings have a free consciousness that is able to transcend or look beyond their immediate situation and build their own essence. Simultaneously, human beings are born into physical bodies and a social/material world that provides them with a "situation": material bodies and limitations, social norms and conventions, moral rules, institutions, religious beliefs, etc., all provide the context for each individual's situation in which they develop into a subject with conscious experiences and a set of beliefs about self and world. Thus, while each person is free to build a new essence or choice of self in the world, this will always take place against the existing backdrop of one's given existential situation. There is also ambiguity in the fact that we experience the world as both a subject and an object. As an experiencing conscious subject, we experience the world as "there" for us; however we can in turn become an object for others as soon as we interact with our social world (Beauvoir 1980, p. 7).

True authenticity requires fully understanding the contingency of the social and moral world and recognizing that values are only values because they come from human beings. Further, the social fabric of the existential situation is ultimately created by human beings and not given by anything outside. The norms, conventions, and rules that may seem inherent or pre-given ultimately come from us. This adds an additional layer of ambiguity: moral reasoning and deliberation is itself ambiguous. However, this understanding is extremely uncomfortable, and most people would rather reject this uncertainty and ambiguity for the belief that there are objective moral truths and only one correct answer for each situation. But it is the very absence of objective and pre-given values, in Beauvoir's view, that make what humans do so important. When value and meaning come from us, we are responsible for them, and that means there are stakes. In short, what we do matters:

Existentialism alone gives…a real role to evil, and it is this perhaps, which makes its judgments so gloomy. Men do not like to feel themselves in danger. Yet it is because there are real dangers, real failures, and real earthly damnation that words like victory, wisdom, or joy have meaning. Nothing is decided in advance, and it is because man has something to lose and because he can lose that he can also win. (Beauvoir 1980, p. 34)

Beauvoir details this in her discussion of human's progression from childhood to adolescence and the changes that take place as well as the possible existential attitudes one can take in response. Beauvoir begins by creating the simplicity of the child's world: when we are children, the world makes sense to us. We are told that things are a certain way, that some things are right and some things are wrong, that institutions reflect what is right and wrong, and we believe it. We are comforted by the security of world that is easy to navigate and we can master as long as we follow the rules. Right and wrong exist as facts just as surely as the sky is blue or the grass is green. Every moral problem has just one solution, and we can rely on moral rules to find it. Adults appear to us as gods who communicate moral truths. This is the serious world (Beauvoir 1980, pp. 35–36).

Sometimes people are kept in the childlike world through oppressive circumstances. Otherwise, Beauvoir argues we eventually realize that the serious world is not as certain as we once believed. Through adolescence and growth into adulthood, we learn that many things we believed to be objective facts are actually quite contingent. "Men stop appearing as if they were gods, and at the same time the adolescent discovers the human character of the reality about him. Language, customs, ethics, and values have their source in these uncertain creatures" (1980, p. 39). This is uncomfortable for us because the serious world is one that is easy for us to navigate: decisions have objective reasons behind them. In the serious world, we can be absolved of responsibility for a moral choice if that choice conforms to the prescribed rule. It is not I who decide that it is wrong to cheat on an exam but God/religion/the law/school, etc. The serious world is comforting because it has rules and answers – there is no room for ambiguity within the spirit of seriousness.

The serious man, as Beauvoir refers to him, chooses to stay in the comfort of the serious world. Preferring to believe that values are objective and given from outside, he clings to the comfort of the serious. The things that he values are not only good for him, but good for everyone. "After a more or less long crisis, either he turns back toward the world of his parents and teachers or he adheres to the values which are new but seem to him just as sure" (1980, p. 47). The serious man takes comfort in his belief that his cause is backed by an objective good. While an obvious candidate is religious belief, Beauvoir says someone can become just as convinced of the objective value of a political party, an economic system, an institution, or a secular set of moral values. The serious man fails to recognize the subjectivity of his choice:

By virtue of the fact that he refuses to recognize that he is freely establishing the value of the end he sets up, the serious man makes himself the slave of that end. He forgets that every goal is at the same time a point of departure and that human freedom is the ultimate, the unique end to which man should destine himself. (1980, pp. 47–48)

The serious person believes that there is only one true answer to each moral dilemma and that proper deliberation will allow them to arrive at the answer. Even the Kantian and utilitarian moral systems overlook ambiguity and argue that every situation does have a true moral answer. For Kant, one must ask if one can universalize the maxim they are acting upon, and for utilitarianism, one must calculate whether their action will produce more happiness or unhappiness. In both of these cases, the individual agent is shirking responsibility for their choice and relying on an external justification rather than their own conscience. Thus the Kantian or utilitarian ethicist is equally wrapped up in the serious world and in denial of ambiguity.

The serious man is not the only inauthentic attitude that one can take, although it is the most common. Other alternatives include nihilism, or the "decision to be nothing" and rejection of all values. Additionally, one may get swept up in being an "adventurer," who likes to take risks and be adventurous while disregarding the freedom of the other. Or, one may be consumed by passion and become wrapped up in a cause or value. The difference between the passionate person and the serious person is that the passionate person recognizes the subjectivity of their chosen object of value (1980, pp. 56–74).

All of these attitudes are contrasted with the true, ethical attitude. This attitude rejects the spirit of seriousness and embraces ambiguity in its various forms: the ambiguity of our freedom/facticity, the ambiguity of situation, the ambiguity of being both subject and object, and the ambiguity of the moral world. The genuine moral attitude "wills freedom." This means that freedom wills its own existence, accepts responsibility for one's choices, and actively desires one's own freedom and the freedom of others. "[F]reedom realizes itself only by engaging itself in the world: to such an extent that man's project toward freedom is embodied for him in definite acts of behavior" (1980, p. 78). The authentic ethical attitude recognizes that we cannot do things without others, and it is only in solidarity and cooperation with others that we can fulfill our own freedom. "[T]he freedom of one man almost always concerns that of other individuals" (1980, p. 143).

Thus, the moral attitude positively wills the freedom of others and for them to be able to pursue their own existential projects. "[T]he individual as such is one of the ends at which our action must aim...He interests us not merely as a member of a class, a nation, or a collectivity, but as an individual man" (1980, p. 135). The genuine moral attitude rejects oppression in all of its forms, for true freedom is never found in unjustly restricting the freedom of the other. The genuine moral attitude understands the importance of an open future for the present action. Also, importantly, the authentically moral person, or "man of action" as Beauvoir says, knows that they often must act in the world without full knowledge or confidence in the outcome for their choice. Ethics is risky because the future is unknown. This is the direct opposite of the serious man who believes that deliberation will result in knowledge of the proper choice. But the authentic person who aims to advance the freedom of the other knows that their actions shape the outcome and hopefully produce the future they want. "[T]he man of action, in order to make a decision, will not wait for a perfect knowledge to prove to him the necessity of a certain choice; he must first choose and thus help fashion history" (1980, p. 122). The choice is never arbitrary but always aimed at facilitating an open future and freedom for the other. Beauvoir argues that this is a fundamental ethical tenet that stems from the fact that our situation is always one in which we are engaged and involved with others in the world. Thus any true embracing of our own freedom simultaneously means willing the freedom of others. "The individual is defined only by his relationship to the world and to other individuals; he exists only by transcending himself, and his freedom can be achieved only through the freedom of others" (1980, p. 156).

The genuine moral attitude realizes that not every situation has just one "true" or correct answer and that different courses of actions can be considered equally morally sound. Every situation must consider the individuals involved, the consequences as well as the intentions, and how to positively will the freedom of the other. Additionally, institutional rules hold value only insomuch as they are facilitating individual freedom and the ability of humans to create meaning, and have no moral value outside of this end. Thus, a genuine moral attitude will not be constrained by institutions or rules if they are not enabling opportunities for the free pursuit of human projects.

Meredith Grey's Authenticity: Bomb in a Patient

Throughout the series, Meredith consistently shows an understanding of the ambiguity of the moral realm. One of the early examples of Meredith's embracing of existential ambiguity comes in "It's the End of the World" and "As We Know It." In this two-part story arc, the hospital staff treats a patient thought to have a gunshot wound, who is later revealed to have an undetonated bomb in his body. The patient is brought to the emergency room with the hand of an emergency medical technician (EMT) inside his chest cavity. The EMT explains that she placed her hand inside the patient to stop him from bleeding out. Her partner reminds her that's against protocol, but she is unmoved by his critique. She later accompanies surgical staff to the operating room (OR). Later, staff learn that the patient was actually shot by a homemade Bazooka, and the EMT is preventing the patient from bleeding out, as well as stabilizing a homemade bomb.

When the floor is cleared of all unnecessary personnel, Grey refuses to evacuate because she believes the lead surgeon will require assistance. As the lead surgeon discusses a plan of action with the bomb squad, the anesthesiologist and EMT panic and leave the room. While other surgeons and the head of the bomb squad take cover, Grey places her hand inside the chest cavity to keep the bomb stabilized. The episode ends with Meredith repeatedly whispering, "what did I do?". Meredith acts in the moment in order to save the patient, breaking protocol in the process. Asking herself "what did I do?" shows she is uncertain about the validity of her choice and recognizes this may not have the end she desires. She takes on the Beauvoirian risk of the ethical.

In "As We Know It," cardiothoracic surgeon, Preston Burke, awaits instructions from the bomb squad on how to proceed. While waiting, he checks in with Shephard, who has also ignored orders to evacuate because he is operating on the husband of his colleague, Dr. Bailey. The surgeons exchange a short conversation, subtly validating each other's choices:

Burke	You know it was really stupid of you not to evacuate.
Shepherd	Hmm, you, too...Now, can you operate and, uh, remove the device from the guy?
Burke	After the bomb squad is through assessing him, I'm going to try.
Shepherd	Gotta say, I don't want to be the guy who kills Bailey's husband.
Burke	Well, I don't want to be the guy that kills us all.

Later, Burke returns to the OR to proceed with the bomb removal and surgery. With the guidance of a bomb squad, the hospital prepares to minimize the casualties and damage of a potential explosion. They shut down oxygen flow, send non-emergent patients to a nearby hospital, and relocate the patient because the OR was directly over the main oxygen line. Eventually, Meredith is able to safely remove the bomb from the body and hand it off to the bomb squad. As the bomb squad official is carrying it away from the operating room, it explodes and kills him. The explosion confirms that the bomb was active and highlights the life-threatening risk of Meredith's actions. Because of her heroism, the patient lives, there is minimal damage to the hospital, and the lives of countless staff are saved.

Meredith makes repeated choices to value the lives of others in spite of protocol and personal risk. She ignores the evacuation order, reenters the operating room against her attending's order when she hears the EMT panic, and places her hand inside the patient when the EMT flees the room. Her actions prevent the patient from bleeding out and stabilize the bomb. Meredith continues to do what the EMT (and the anesthesiologist) could not. She stays in the room and remains calm and steady.

Throughout the two episodes, many characters make difficult choices, but Meredith's original and continued choice stands out. The EMT breaks protocol to save the patient's life but eventually panics and flees. Shepherd and Burke refuse the evacuation order out of responsibility as head surgeons and, in Shepherd's case, because of a personal relationship. The anesthesiologist breaks protocol and abandons his responsibility out of fear for his life. While Meredith clearly feels fear and apprehension about the outcome of her choice, she also appears to be the only character who navigates the morally ambiguous realm with a sense of ease, breaking with protocol, professional expectations, and self-preservation, ultimately for the sake of the future of the patient and the lives of many in the hospital.

Grey's Authenticity: Prisoner from Death Row

Another example of Grey's rejection of the serious and embracing of existential authenticity begins in the Season 5 episode "Wish You Were Here." Shepherd, Grey, Yang, and Hunt are assigned to a trauma patient described as a prisoner from death row (PDR). Grey responds to the patient with care and compassion, while Shepherd and Yang question his motives and description of pain. In an early scene, Meredith encourages others to take his pain seriously. Shepherd and Yang question his pain until scans prove he has an object lodged in his spine. The patient asks if the injury will help him get a stay of execution, but Shepherd assures him it won't. Shepherd and Yang remain frustrated with the patient while Grey has continued sympathy for him.

In "Sympathy for the Devil," Shepherd informs the postsurgery inmate, Dunn, that he has brain injuries and that his "brain contusions are expanding" and require more surgery. Dunn laughs and replies, "They're going to execute me in five days...might as well take my chances with this brain thing...either way I'm going to die, Dr. Shepherd. Might as well do it on your watch." Dunn refuses surgery, so Shepherd orders Yang and Grey to page him as soon as Dunn is unconscious and unable to refuse surgery. While still conscious, Dunn tells Grey that he was abused as a child, further gaining her sympathy.

This storyline eventually intersects with a secondary storyline of a child in need of organs when Grey, while transporting Dunn, encounters Dr. Bailey transporting the child. The child notices the handcuffs and engages in conversation with the inmate:

Child   Cool, did you do something bad?
Dunn   Traffic violation. What's wrong with you kid?
Child   I need a new liver and a new intestine.
Dunn   Yeah? You want mine?

Bailey and Grey exchange a look indicating both of them are considering the possibility of saving the child with the inmate's organs. Before learning that a donor is secured, the child asks Bailey why he can't have that "nice man's organs" even though he offered them. Bailey tells him, "You know how in school there are rules you have to follow? The same thing applies here. We have to follow the rules, or else we get in big trouble. And what that man offered you was definitely against the rules." Here, Bailey shows commitment to the serious world, a world of protocols and rules, and reinforces those norms to the child.

Shepherd and Yang continue to question the inmate's motives and Grey's clarity as she continues to sympathize with him and his lack of dignity and choice. Dunn asks Grey about the child in need of organs and she informs him they found a match. Later, after complications in the child's surgery leave him with a 24-hour window for a new donor, all of the doctors in the hospital are desperate to save the life of the child. Upon hearing about the failed transplant, Meredith less than subtly advises the inmate on how to induce brain death. She says,

> During surgery Dr. Shepherd removed a piece of your skull, which means your brain is now only covered by dura mater. It's virtually exposed. If, somehow, that area were to be damaged, it would cause intracranial bleeding, which would cause your brain to swell worse than it did today, which would result in brain death. So as your doctor, I need you to be very careful not to damage it. Do you understand what I'm saying?

When Grey leaves the room, Dunn begins slamming his head against his bed. Meredith provides the inmate with a way to bypass all legal barriers and induce his own brain death. She does this because she wants his death to be able to have meaning and also to be able to save the life of the child. Recall Beauvoir's assertion that the absence of absolute moral values is what makes what we do important: it is only because there is no one right answer to this situation that there is so much at stake. It is because there is so much to lose (a child's life) that there is also something to win. But one needs the courage to take the moral risk – Grey has it.

The third episode in the story arc, "Stairway to Heaven," begins with Dunn banging his head on the bed. The patient starts seizing, but Grey doesn't page Shepherd. Later, Grey explains to Bailey that she hasn't paged Shepherd even though the patient has inflicted additional harm to his dura and has had seizure activity. Bailey instructs Grey to follow protocol but is an eventual accomplice to her inaction by not reporting her or paging Shepherd herself. Shepherd eventually learns about the injuries and rushes Dunn to surgery. Bailey enters Shepherd's OR and asks him to stop operating so Dunn can be a viable donor. After some convincing, she retreats in her demands. Meanwhile, Webber asks another doctor to check for brain dead cases in the hospital and pressures a family into donating the organs of a patient who wasn't a registered organ donor. This eventually leads to a successful organ donation for the child, relieving Grey and the inmate of any pressure or convenience of organ donation.

The questionable decisions of Grey have no lasting effect on the case of the child; the child is saved through the pressure of Richard Webber. Eventually, the inmate is treated and sent back to the prison. Grey attends his execution at his request. She is emotionally devastated and ends the final episode of the story arc comforted by Shepherd and Yang, while she reflects, "I just wanted to be there for him but it was horrible."

Whether or not Meredith's actions had an impact on saving the life of the child, the situation illustrates Beauvoir's point about the inherent risk of the ethical – Meredith broke protocol and moral convention in pursuit of the true ethic, and it turned out not to matter at all in terms of saving the child. But she acted as she thought she should, given the circumstances and the knowledge she had at the time. A serious person may argue that this outcome shows the importance of following rules and protocols, because in breaking them you never know what the outcome will be. It is only sticking to the moral norm or protocol that ensures you are in the moral right. But Beauvoir's (and Meredith's) point is that when the outcome is unknown, you stand to lose just as much as you stand to gain. Had Webber not been able to secure the voluntary donation of organs, the child would have died. The existentialist solution is not to retreat to the spirit of the serious but to act with the conviction and knowledge that moral ambiguity in our world means you are taking a risk in pursuing the freedom of the other.

Grey's Authenticity Versus Shepherd's Seriousness: Alzheimer's Trial

The different ways Grey and Shepherd approach patient care is a constant source of tension in their personal and professional relationship. This tension is most notable in a multi-episode story arc in which Derek is attempting to cure the disease he fears

Meredith might one day develop. In "Don't Deceive Me (Please Don't Go)," Shepherd starts a medical trial to treat early-onset Alzheimer's, the disease that ended Ellis Grey's career and eventually killed her. He opens the assistant role on the trial to all fifth-year residents except for Meredith, because he thinks her presence will cloud his judgment. Karev is chosen to assist, but as the trial begins, he realizes he doesn't have the patience or optimism to work on such dire cases. He confides his frustrations with Meredith and she offers advice, based on her experience with her mom. He later backs out and gives Grey a personal recommendation because he only made it through day one of the trial by listening to her advice. Shepherd concurs, and Grey serves as his resident assistant on the remainder of the trial.

After Webber's wife Adele starts showing neurological deficits, Shepherd and Grey begin to suspect she may be suffering from Alzheimer's. In "This Is How We Do It," Adele undergoes testing and is diagnosed to have memory loss consistent with early-onset Alzheimer's but doesn't meet the criteria for the trial. Derek explains to Webber the reasons Adele doesn't qualify. Webber pressures him saying, "I know all of that. I also know that you'll do whatever you need to do to help my wife." The obvious decision, following medical protocols and codes of ethics, is to reject Adele's application and call the next person on the waiting list. Shepherd hesitates and considers admitting her even though she doesn't meet the criteria. He tells Grey, "I haven't called yet. Maybe Richard's right. It's just one point." Grey convinces him to follow protocol in this moment by reminding him of the scope of the trial. At this point, Meredith recognizes that preserving the scientific validity of the trial will ultimately help more people.

The Alzheimer's storyline intersects an episodic storyline of the fifth-year residents competing for "Chief Resident." In "It's a Long Way Back," a patient in the Alzheimer's clinical trial experiences complications unrelated to the treatment. The patient dies, creating an opening for Adele in the trial. Hunt, tasked to find the next chief resident, asks Karev what he intends to do to fight for the position of Chief Resident. Karev, on the spot, responds that he intends to bring "Africa patients" to the hospital for treatment, even though he had no prior plan or decision to do so.

Later, Grey notices evidence that Adele's condition has worsened and advocates for a reassessment of Adele that proves she now qualifies for the trial. In a hallway scene between Grey and Webber, Grey discusses the formalities of Adele's surgery. As she walks away, Webber calls her back and engages in subtle but persuasive dialogue encouraging Grey to ensure Adele receives the treatment rather than the placebo. He states, "Thank you for everything you've done. . .it's taken me a lot of years to realize that all I want to do is be with her. You've given us the best chance we can get. You've done *everything*." Shortly after this encounter, Grey, using a code she previously witnessed the lab tech use, sneaks into the trial room and switches envelopes to ensure Adele gets the active agent instead of the placebo.

At this point, Karev has also engaged in questionable behavior by negotiating with a wealthy patient to fund his initiative to bring African children to the hospital for treatment. He lied about securing funding and, without external funding, would be caught in that lie. He negotiated with a patient he referred to as the "Dragon Lady," convincing her to donate $100,000 to his initiative by bartering care. The two storyline intersect when Alex sees Grey returning to the trial room. Karev attempts to hand a file to Grey and witnesses an envelope fall from her lab coat. He asks her, "What are you doing?". Grey replies, "I'm working." Karev, who seems to know Grey is tampering with the trial, asks her again, "No, what are you doing?". But Karev halts his questioning because he's interrupted by another resident revealing to him that he received a check from "the Dragon Lady." He is physically relieved and ceases in his questions. Meredith successfully switched the envelopes and Karev secured funding for his initiative.

At the start of the following episode, "White Wedding," Karev and Grey argue over her behavior. Grey approaches Karev and says, "I didn't change any data or falsify any results." Karev interrupts, "Or switch a syringe so some sweet, sad old lady would get the drug and not the placebo…That's what I thought." Grey eventually responds, "Nothing I did, will change any results. It doesn't change the potential effectiveness of the drug. It doesn't change anything." Karev interrupts her to say that her tampering with a trial might affect the FDA's approval of further trials with the hospital, concluding, "It messes with me. It messes with everyone."

In "I Will Survive," Karev is increasingly worried he'll lose the Chief Resident job to Meredith. In a bar scene, he talks with a fellow resident, Yang, who says, "You know it's going to be Mer, right? It doesn't mean you're a bad surgeon or a bad doctor. Some people just fit the bill…She's organized, People trust her…she's natural." Karev scoffs at the mention of Grey being trustworthy. Moments later, Hunt asks Karev if he's okay because he is noticeably drunk. Karev takes a shot and says, "Meredith messed with the Alzheimer's trial."

In "Unaccompanied Minor," viewers see the fall out of Karev's confession. Shepherd and Webber question Grey about what she did, but she refuses to give any details, stating, "Nothing I did affects the trial. If you don't know what I did, the trial stays blind." Shepherd is furious with Grey and tells her "The trial is over. You screwed me, you screwed the whole hospital, and you screwed yourself." After Karev informs Webber of the timeframe of the incident, Webber realizes it was Adele's case, and his anger over the situation subsides. Shepherd tells Grey, "I know the fact that it's Adele changes things for Richard, but it doesn't for me." The two continue to argue about it. Shepherd implies Grey acted naively and cost millions of people with the disorder a chance for a cure. Grey explains her thinking about the situation to Shepherd. She says:

> I don't think that things are simply right or wrong. Things are more complicated than that. This was more complicated than that. It's complicated that it was Adele and Richard. It's complicated that we have a drug in a box that could help her. There's nothing simple about that. I am very sorry that I messed everything up, but I would do it again.

Shepherd, exemplifying the spirit of seriousness, tells his wife, "I don't know if I can have a child with someone who doesn't know right from wrong."

The actions of Shepherd, Karev, and Webber in this story can be viewed in two different categories. Shepherd follows the institutional rules while Webber and Karev act out of personal interest. In Shepherd's case, aside from his momentary consideration of letting Adele in the study before she met the criteria, he is consistent in abiding by institutional protocol. When he learns that Grey tampered with the trial, he ends it with no consideration of how it will affect Grey, Adele, or any of the people who might potentially benefit from the study. He professionally questions Grey's ability to practice medicine and personally questions her ability to co-parent.

Webber acts out of self-interest by using his personal relationships and his position of superiority to pressure Grey and Shepherd to break the rules. He's only angry at Grey's choices until he learns it was for Adele's (his) benefit. Karev also acts out of self-interest. He begins his initiative with the sole intent of professional gain. He engages in manipulative bartering to fund it. When he thinks Grey tampered with the trial, he only advocates that she come clean because her actions could affect him and other hospital staff. He discloses her impropriety because he fears she'll get the Chief Resident position over him.

Again, Grey's actions stand out because of the motivations behind them and her ability to see that the true ethic lies beyond self-interest or institutional rules. She doesn't rigidly follow the protocols like Shepherd, but she is committed to the success of the trial. When she is compelled to break the rules, she does so for the care of a friend and mentor, and in a way that "won't tamper with the results." She pleads with Karev, Webber, and Shepherd to stay quiet about her rule breaking out of care for Adele and the other patients who might benefit from the treatment. While others are rigidly rule -abiding or act out of self-interest, Grey reminds the audience that she doesn't think things are inherently right or wrong and that no decision is simple. She puts her personal relationships and career on the line to help others when following the rules conflicts with what she sees as the true ethic. She displays existential authenticity when she stands by her actions, and tells Derek she would do it all over again.

Grey's Authenticity: Immigration Injustice and Insurance Fraud

After Shepherd dies, the tension between Grey's moral ambiguity and the spirit of seriousness plays out through other authoritative characters, most notably Dr. Bailey, now chief of surgery. In "What I Did for Love," *Grey's Anatomy* introduces a story arc that addresses US immigration policy and the high costs of medical care. At this point in the series, Grey is dating a resident, Dr. Andrew DeLuca. The story begins when a man brings his daughter, who has recurring abdominal pain, to the free clinic. Karev and DeLuca first assess the patient. While attempting to get her medical history, the father informs them he doesn't know much about the last few months because he immigrated to the United States a year ago under an asylum visa. He further tells them, "I waited to send for my family, until I had an apartment and a job. But they were detained at the border. Separated. Caged like animals. My wife, my little Dani, is still there." Karev orders labs and tests and instructs DeLuca to page Grey for a consult. The father expresses concern about the cost of the tests and treatment. He explains that he has a job and pays taxes but that he can't afford an insurance policy yet. Karev reassures him that they'll still treat her, saying, "In Washington, we take care of sick kids, no questions asked."

Throughout the episode, both the patient, Gabby, and her father, Luis, are noticeably scared. Gabby is afraid to be away from her father because of the trauma of being separated from her mom. Luis is scared for his daughter, his wife, and about how he will pay for treatment. Grey, Karev, and DeLuca attempt to calm his fears by allowing him to remain with Gabby the entire time and by assisting him with forms to obtain state insurance coverage that "is effective immediately."

While Karev and Grey wait for Gabby's scans, DeLuca enters and informs them that Luis makes too much money to qualify for the state coverage. Grey responds, "Are you kidding me...He makes too much for insurance and not enough to get treatment? That's insane." At that moment, Gabby's scans appear, and the surgeons see that she has a mass that will require surgery. When they inform Luis, he again questions how he can pay for treatment. Grey assures him that they will come up with a plan and tells him not to worry.

While the surgeons scrub in for Gabby's surgery, Webber enters the scrub room to ask Grey if her daughter Ellis (named after her deceased mother) is alright after noticing that she's scheduled for an ex-lap, the procedure they're about to perform on Gabby. The other doctors quickly realize that Grey falsified the insurance forms. Grey defends her actions, saying:

I'm not shipping this little girl off to county. She may need follow-up surgeries, top-level care...And what is her father supposed to do? Tell me. Is he supposed to quit his job so then he can't feed his family? He did everything right. The system failed him. The system is broken. We know it is. So what does that say about us if we don't fix it?

Richard responds by telling her, "there's a right way and a wrong way to go about doing these things." Grey doesn't back down and tells him she's doing the surgery anyway and it's his call whether he reports her. Later, during surgery, they learn that Gabby has a form of cancer that will require chemo treatments and additional surgeries.

After surgery, Grey meets with Webber to discuss what he plans to do. Although Webber is upset with Grey for what she did and how it affects him, he ultimately decides to help her. He tells her they need to make it look like Gabby is sicker. He further explains, "If we can keep Gabby in the hospital for thirty consecutive days, a new state policy automatically kicks in, regardless of income." Richard reminds Grey that he's not doing it for her. He's doing it so the father won't get deported because of Grey's bad decision-making. Grey informs Luis of the treatment plan and ensures him that they will take excellent care of Gabby. She advises him to keep working and says he can sleep on a cot in her room while she undergoes testing and additional treatments.

In the following episode, "Drawn to the Blood," members of the hospital staff speculate about a closed-door meeting between the Chief of Surgery, Dr. Bailey; the head of the foundation who owns the hospital, Dr. Fox; and a group of unknown people. Grey spends most of the episode outside the hospital helping a fellow surgeon with emotional problems. She later returns to the hospital to talk to Bailey and Karev. While she finds Karev to talk about a matter unrelated to Gabby's case, DeLuca is called into the meeting with Bailey and Fox. They question him about Gabby's case and reveal that the other people in the room are investigators for the insurance company. The scene ends with Dr. Fox saying, "It has come to light that Dr. Meredith Grey submitted her own daughter's name to pay for Gabriella's surgery and care, which is both a fraud and a felony. So we're going to need you to be a lot more specific."

Meanwhile, Grey and Karev enter a pressurized chamber to help save Karev's dying patient. While they're talking, DeLuca appears outside the window of the chamber accompanied by Dr. Fox. Grey tells him it's not a good time to talk. He interrupts her and falsely confesses to her that he lied about Gabby Rivera's case. He continues, "I wanted her to get the surgery very badly. And so, I didn't tell anyone, and I put another name down on her paperwork. Your daughter's name, Ellis. And I'm so sorry...". Meredith tries to stop him, but he turns and leaves with Dr. Fox. Since Grey is unable to leave the pressurized chamber, she can only watch him walk away, prepared to be charged with a felony in order to protect her.

In "Jump into the Fog," Webber sees DeLuca handcuffed and escorted by police. He approaches and asks him what's going on. When DeLuca refuses to answer, Webber asks Bailey, who informs him that DeLuca falsified insurance forms. Bailey notices Webber's odd reaction to the news and later implies he knows more about the situation. While in surgery with Webber, she says, "I don't think he did it alone. Meredith Grey's name was on that chart. I think she participated and DeLuca's covering for her...You wouldn't know anything about that, would you?". After surgery, Webber approaches Karev outside the now de-pressurized chamber and asks to talk about Grey.

Later, while Grey confesses to Bailey and Fox in an effort to save DeLuca, Karev and Webber enter the room. They all admit to the part they played in the case. They acknowledge that Grey is the person who did it, but that they all knew about it and said nothing. They appeal to the personal history they all have with Bailey and Fox, but it doesn't work. Bailey fires all three of them on the spot. The episode (and Season 15) ends with Grey visiting DeLuca in jail. She tells DeLuca:

> Let me clean up my own messes and live in my own truth. Because what I did was wrong. But what I was trying to remedy was so much more wrong. And I stand by that...I have to find a judge and get you out of here.

She then tells him she loves him and leaves the visitation room. Grey owns and recognizes the subjectivity of her choice – she acknowledges it as her own truth. Simultaneously she acknowledges that any wrong she committed (whether by societal norm or something like Kantian ethics) was in favor of serving what she sees as a deeper moral truth.

In the premier episode of Season 16, "Nothing Left to Cling to," the story continues with the fall out of Grey's actions. She consults with a lawyer who tells her, "We'll schedule a hearing. You'll be deeply repentant. You'll get a couple of weeks of community service at a free clinic, and you'll pay a fine." When Grey inquires about her medical license, her lawyer tells her "that's up to the board if they want to pursue action, but I'd say it's highly unlikely." As the episode progresses through weeks, DeLuca returns to Grey Sloan Memorial Hospital, Karev and Webber start working at a community hospital, and Grey has her trial.

At the start of the trial, her lawyer instructs her to be repentant. But when the judge questions her actions, given she's partial owner in the hospital and could afford to pay for the surgery or do it pro bono, Grey responds:

> The little girl has cancer. She needs hundreds of thousands of dollars' worth of care over a period of years, and I didn't think that her very proud, hardworking father would accept charity from me. And I didn't think he should have to. The system should have supported them, and the system is broken.

The judge interrupts her to ask if she regrets her choices. Against counsel, Grey stands by her actions, stating, "To the extent that I can, knowing there's a very sick little girl out there who's beginning to feel better." Grey's lawyer quickly pleads with the judge, reminding him that Grey has three children, and shouldn't serve prison time. The audience later sees Grey picking up garbage on the street. She receives an email informing her that the medical board is evaluating her license. While it is unclear what will come of Grey and her ability to practice medicine, she is confident in having acted in good faith.

Throughout this story, the audience sees Luis and the surgeons struggle to act ethically in an unethical system. Luis followed the conventions for societal success but is stuck in an impossible loop of working to give his family greater security and making too much money to qualify for government insurance in a state with more progressive policies and resources than most in the country. His wife and daughter attempted to follow the same rules, legally seeking asylum, but since the rules were changed, they were treated like criminals.

The surgeons, most notably Grey, recognize that the system is flawed. As doctors, they are expected to follow certain protocols and follow the law. Grey recognizes that the only way the child can receive the quality care she deserves as a human is to break the law. By using her privilege and her child's privilege to secure care for Gabby, Grey highlights the injustice of policies that prioritize some lives over others. Although Grey acts alone, her actions are quickly discovered by the other surgeons. They offer her support by verbally validating her choices, keeping her secret, helping her develop a plan moving forward, and taking the fall for and with her. Grey refutes their efforts to shield her from consequence. She stands by her actions with pride at doing the right thing under seemingly impossible circumstances.

In contrast, the leaders of the hospital, Bailey and Fox, display a stricter, rule-abiding approach reflective of the serious world. There is evidence of their shared concern for Gabby and Luis, but they display the spirit of seriousness in dealing with the actions of the surgeons. Despite any sympathy they might have for the ethical motivations of the parties involved, and despite the strong personal relationships they have with all of them, they rigidly follow protocol and issue strict consequences to the surgeons who did not.

Grey's approach to the moral scenario shows that she values the freedom and potential future of the other over institutional rules. Importantly, she approaches the moral problem in its specificity and considers the individuals involved. Her courtroom testimony mentions the girl's father's hard work and pride. Grey sought a moral solution that considered the desired ends of the other agents involved. Knowing accepting charity would be humiliating for the father, she creatively designs a solution to the moral dilemma that includes his valued ends. Importantly, Grey does not back down from her conviction that what she did was the right thing for *her* to do. Had she told the judge that she regretted her choice, she may have been granted a more lenient sentence. But Grey, in a stunning moment of existential authenticity, refuses to express regret for her actions. She acknowledges what she did. She acknowledges it was *her* choice. She does not back down from her conviction that the true ethic lies in positively facilitating the freedom and future of the other, rather than following institutional rules.

There are few things more illustrative of the serious world than a court of law: there are the agents of the legal system, the rules that have been broken, the witnesses who see you have broken the rules, the judge, the ultimate authority figure, the enforcer of the moral authority of the law, who will sentence you, all working together to form the pinnacle of the serious. But as has been shown repeatedly over the groundbreaking 16 seasons of the show, Meredith Grey has never been enthralled by the spirit of seriousness. Perhaps this originates in her atypical upbringing in which she witnessed moral ambiguity from an extremely young age. Beauvoir argues that adults find comfort in the serious world because it reminds them of the world of their childhood. But the serious world was never comfortable to Meredith. She had to call 911 after her mother's attempted suicide at the age of only 5. She watched her mother and Webber's relationship fall apart. She spent long hours in the hospital alone while her mother performed surgeries. The serious world resembles the childlike world, but Meredith's childhood was never childlike. She never found the black and white world of the "godlike" adults comforting. They were never gods to her. She realized as a very young child that the comfort of the serious world is but an illusion, that life is messy and complex, that it is human beings who give life meaning and purpose, and that the deepest moral truth is the pursuit of a meaningful, open future for others.

Conclusion

Simone de Beauvoir famously argued that the true existentialist ethic required navigating a complex moral realm, embracing our existential freedom, and positively willing the freedom of the other. Importantly it also means giving up the comfort of the serious world and accepting the risk and responsibility that comes with living an ethical life. True existential authenticity recognizes that it is you who are responsible for your moral choice, not religion, society, intuitions, laws, or universal moral formulas. Ethics comes from us. It also requires recognizing that our own freedom is facilitated by positively willing a freedom and future for others.

Meredith Grey, starting with her atypical childhood and progressing through a lifetime of challenges and tragedies, perfectly exemplifies Beauvoir's authentic person. She rejects the spirit of seriousness, having never found it convincing. She approaches moral problems in their specificity, noting her relationships with the people involved. She is willing to bypass legal and institutional rules and protocols in order to pursue a deeper moral truth. She is willing to accept the risk and responsibility of engaging with the moral realm, knowing you never come to perfect knowledge that you are doing the right thing and it is possible for things to turn out other than you intended. And she stands behind her actions, acknowledges them as her own, and takes responsibility for her choice.

References

De Beauvoir, Simone. 1980. *The Ethics of Ambiguity.* Trans. Bernard Frechtman. Secaucus: Citadel Press.

House of Cards as Philosophy: Democracy on Trial

16

Brendan Shea

Contents

Introduction 362
Democracy in HOC: The People and Their Power 362
The Death of a Democracy: Some Initial Themes 366
Plato's Republic and Some Puzzles About Power 369
Plato's Critique of Democracy 371
Hobbes on Monarchy and Democracy 375
Underwoods Everywhere: Democracy in the Present 379
Conclusion: HOC as Warning and Opportunity 380
References 381

Abstract

Over the course of its six seasons, the Netflix show *House of Cards* (HOC) details the rise to power of Claire and Frank Underwood in a fictional United States. They achieve power not by winning free and fair elections, but by exploiting various weaknesses of the US political system. Could such a thing happen to our own democracies? This chapter argues that it is a threat that should be taken seriously, as the structure of HOC's democratic institutions closely mirrors our own, and the flaws that the Underwoods exploit are precisely those that have allowed autocrats to capture democracies "from the inside." Of even greater concern, these flaws may flow from the nature of democracy itself. This possibility is explored by considering the events of HOC in light of the antidemocratic arguments of Plato and Hobbes. The chapter concludes by briefly considering responses to these arguments.

B. Shea (✉)
Rochester Community and Technical College, Rochester, MN, USA
e-mail: brendan.shea@rctc.edu

© Springer Nature Switzerland AG 2024
D. K. Johnson et al. (eds.), *The Palgrave Handbook of Popular Culture as Philosophy*,
https://doi.org/10.1007/978-3-031-24685-2_37

> **Keywords**
>
> House of cards · Democracy · Autocracy · Tyranny · Oligarchy · Political
> philosophy · Political legitimacy · Plato's republic · Thrasymachus · Thomas
> Hobbes · Ethics · Political norms · Democratic decline · Media · Voting

Introduction

> Democracy is so overrated.
> —Frank Underwood

The Netflix TV series *House of Cards* (HOC, based on an earlier BBC series and
Micheal Dobbs novel of the same name) tells the story of Frank Underwood and
Claire Underwood (in season 6, Claire Hale) as they strive to achieve and maintain
absolute political power in a fictional United States. Over the course of the show, first
Frank and later Claire manage to circumvent democratic processes and safeguards to
become President. Their machinations to achieve this goal range from mundane
political deals, to murder, to the manufacturing of security threats and the manipulation of elections.

The characters and events depicted in HOC are, in many respects, far removed
from the realities of contemporary democratic politics. In particular, Frank and
Claire's capacity to manipulate those around them at times seems to verge on the
superhuman. For this reason, it can be tempting to think their path to power has little
to teach us about the threats to actual democracy. This, however, would be a mistake.
Indeed, the *weaknesses* of the fictional United States that the Underwoods exploit so
skillfully are precisely those that prominent philosophical critics of democracy have
long argued are most likely to lead to democracy's collapse.

This chapter explores how HOC can be used as a tool for explaining and
evaluating some historically significant criticisms of democracy, in particular those
of Plato and Hobbes. These arguments – advanced by thinkers separated by thousands of years and from wildly different historical and political contexts – turn out to
be surprisingly applicable not only to the fictionalized democracy of HOC but to our
own democracy. Before turning to these arguments, however, it will be helpful to
begin with a brief overview of the major figures and events of HOC.

Democracy in HOC: The People and Their Power

When the viewer first meets the Underwoods in the beginning of season 1, Frank is a
Democratic Congressman from South Carolina, and currently serves as the Majority
Whip in the House of Representatives. Claire, meanwhile, runs the "Clean Water
Initiative" (CWI) a nonprofit organization. The year is 2013, and the newly elected
Democratic President – Garrett Walker – is about to assume office. The show's main
story arc begins when Frank discovers that Walker has reneged on his earlier promise

16 *House of Cards* as Philosophy: Democracy on Trial 363

to appoint him Secretary of State. This hamstrings both Frank's political ambitions and (indirectly) Claire's nonprofit, when donors who had counted on buying influence with Frank withdraw promised funding.

The Underwoods respond to this setback by setting out to destroy Walker and to make Frank President. Over the course of the first two seasons, they succeed in doing this. Seasons 3 and 4 detail Frank's efforts to maintain power against a variety of attempts to bring him down, and in particular to win the Democratic nomination in preparation for a reelection bid in 2016. These seasons also detail Claire's own rise to power, from First Lady of the US to United Nations Ambassador to Frank's running mate for the 2016 elections. Claire also increasingly begins to see Frank as a potential obstacle to her own ambitions. Finally, in seasons 5 and 6, Claire ascends to the presidency and ruthlessly crushes a number of attempts to unseat her. Season 5 closes with the implicit promise of a show-down between Claire and Frank (which may have perhaps led to their mutual downfall). However, Frank is killed off-screen between seasons 5 and 6, when actor Kevin Spacey was removed from the show after allegations of sexual misconduct (Koblin 2018). When the series closes, it seems possible that Claire will maintain power indefinitely, even though doing so may require her to launch an unnecessary nuclear strike.

While it is not possible to concisely provide an exhaustive summary of the numerous (and more than occasionally, far-fetched) twists-and-turns that allow the Underwoods to defeat their rivals and avoid accountability, the analysis in later sections requires seeing the "big picture" of how the democracy in HOC eventually fails. This big picture is overwhelmingly one of *relationships* and *institutions* – Claire and Frank are experts at identifying *who* has the power to give them what they want and *how* these people might be convinced, tricked, or coerced into using this power on the Underwoods' behalf. In the fictional democracy of HOC, just as in real democracies, the power the Underwoods need is distributed among a number of distinct groups, including directly elected officials at a variety of levels, journalists, religious and union leaders, lobbyists, foreign leaders, members of the executive and judicial branches, and donors, as well as their own staff members, sexual partners, family, and each other. With this in mind, it's worth reviewing a few of the characters who play especially crucial roles in the Underwoods' rise to power.

Peter Russo and other elected officials. The events of season 1 are driven by Frank's manipulation of Russo, a well-meaning Philadelphia congressman with a blue-collar background and ongoing problems with drug and sex addiction. Frank discovers these problems and uses them to blackmail Russo. With Russo's unwilling help, Frank manages to install his ally Catherine Durant as Secretary of State and to push an (anti-union) education bill through a Democratic-controlled House of Representatives, which gives Frank increased clout with President Walker. Finally, he supports Russo's run for Governor of Pennsylvania, which falls apart when Russo's environmental bill (itself designed by the Underwoods) fails to pass as a result of a power struggle between Frank, Claire, and Remy. This leads to the climax of season 1, where Frank convinces the sitting VP (Matthews) to resign his position and run for Governor instead. This opens the way for Walker to appoint Frank as VP.

Frank kills Russo and arranges it to appear as a suicide. In later seasons, the Underwoods use threats and bribes to secure alliances with other members of Congress – mostly notably Jackie Sharpe, who helps push Walker's impeachment in season 2. Without exception, these temporary alliances end badly for everyone but the Underwoods.

Zoe Barnes, Tom Yates, and other members of the media. In season 1, Frank establishes a sexual and professional relationship with the young reporter Zoe Barnes, which he then uses to selectively leak stories to attack his rivals and advance his own position. When Zoe begins asking questions about Russo's death, he kills her as well. Zoe's death, in turn, leads to repeated efforts by her former colleague (and boyfriend) Lucas Godwin and editor Tom Hammerschmidt to uncover the truth about the Underwoods. Tom and Lucas are eventually killed as well (in Lucas's case after a failed attempt to assassinate Frank). Tom Yates first appears in season 3, when Frank hires him to write a biography to help sell his political program – and himself – to the American people. While this relationship sours when Yates refuses to lie for Frank, he appears again in later seasons as Claire's speechwriter and lover. In keeping with Frank's treatment of Zoe, Claire kills Tom when she discovers his intent to publish a book detailing the Underwoods' misdeeds.

Remy Danton and other lobbyists. When season 1 starts, Remy Danton is a partner at the lobbyist firm Glendon Hill, where he represents the interests of SanCorp, a natural gas company. Like many lobbyists, he seems to have gotten this in large part because of his political knowledge and connections, acquired in his case as a former member of the Underwood's staff. Throughout the series, the viewer sees Remy go back and forth through this "revolving" door between the private and the public realm, and between representing various clients with competing interests, including SanCorp, Raymond Tusk, and the Underwoods. In season 1, for instance, he pushes Claire to kill an environmental bill Frank is committed to passing, in return for helping her NGO out of a difficult situation. In season 2, he serves as Raymond Tusk's main attack dog versus Frank, only to betray Tusk at the last moment when the Underwoods seem likely to win. Finally, while he starts Season 3 as Frank's Chief of Staff, he eventually turns against Frank and cooperates with Hammerscmidt. Other notable lobbyists in HOC include Marty Spinella, an education lobbyist who Frank tricks into assaulting him.

Raymond Tusk, Bill and Annette Shepherd, and the super-rich. If lobbyists represent an important source of power in democratic politics, so do the extremely wealthy individuals and corporations who often pay them. In HOC, the Underwoods' most dangerous opponents are plausibly of this type. In season 2, Raymond Tusk, a longtime supporter of President Walker, presents the Underwoods with both an opportunity and a threat. If they can tie Walker to Tusk's various financial misdeeds (especially as these relate to manipulating both US and Chinese politics), this could bring Walker down; however, in doing so, they have to confront Tusk's considerable power to influence political opinion against them. This includes media attacks (e.g., on Claire's previous abortions and affairs), political manipulation (e.g., by controlling members of Congress) as well as more direct attacks (e.g., by shutting off power to large parts of the United States). In season 6, Annette Shepherd plays a somewhat similar role in her attempts to dislodge Claire from office.

Catherine Durant, Heather Dunbar, and other executive branch appointees. Along with the super-rich, another source of resistance to the Underwoods march to power comes from within the executive branch itself. Both Catherine Durant, who is Secretary of State for much of the show, and Heather Dunbar, who serves as both Solicitor General and Frank's main rival for the Democratic nomination in seasons 3 and 4, possess considerable institutional power belied by their status as "mere" appointees. In particular, their roles allow them both to detect evidence of the Underwoods' wrongdoing, and the ability to act on it. In both cases, unfortunately, they fail to effectively do so. Dunbar is forced to concede the race to Frank after the Underwoods manage to (inaccurately) link her to Goodwin's failed assassination attempt. When Durant attempts to move against the Underwoods at the end of season 5, she is assaulted by Frank, and eventually killed on Claire's orders in season 6.

Viktor Petrov and the wider world. In HOC, as in real life, the domestic political environment is shaped by (and itself helps to shape) the actions of other nations and foreign powers. The Underwoods' capacity to take advantage of this proves crucial in a number of instances. For instance, in Season 2, Frank intentionally sabotoges relations with China, leading to both domestic economic problems and the risk of war. This is a crucial move in advancing his campaign against Tusk (and Walker). In later seasons, Claire and Frank must regularly contend with Victor Petrov (the President of Russia) in a variety of contexts, including a military confrontation in the Middle East and the imprisonment of a gay rights leader in Russia, among other things. For both the Underwoods and Petrov, however, it is clear that the motive force behind their various struggles involves their respective *domestic* standing, with only a minor role being played by any independent desire to pursue the long-run national interest. Both Claire and Frank also take advantage of various domestic terror threats (and/or help manufacture such threats) in order to justify moves that help them achieve or maintain power (such as to delay elections at the end of season 4).

Doug Stamper, Seth Grayson, LeAnn Harvey, and other staff. A final group of crucial characters are the Underwoods' senior staff, perhaps most notably Douglas Stamper (Frank's long-time Chief of Staff), Seth Grayson (Press Secretary), and LeAnn Harvey (a political consultant). These are, without a doubt, the characters closest to the Underwoods, and those with the most intimate knowledge of their lives and actions. These characters, unlike those in the previous categories, are considerably less "visible" to the public, but they are no less important. Stamper, in particular, is heavily involved in nearly every decision that Frank makes, and he commits more than a few crimes of his own (including the murder of Rachel Posner, a prostitute who could tie Frank to Russo's death). The ability to generate this sort of personal loyalty is central to the Underwoods' rise to power, and the psychological mechanisms behind it are more obscure than those previously mentioned. In the end, though, it is Doug who kills Frank to protect his "legacy," and is Doug that Claire must finally kill (in the final episode) to ultimately secure her own power.

The Death of a Democracy: Some Initial Themes

As the summary in the previous section should make evident, it is unlikely that Claire's and Frank's *specific* methods of coming to power could be emulated by any would-be autocrat in the real world. In Claire's case, for example, the level of planning (and luck!) needed to ascend from CEO of mid-sized nonprofit to President of the United States without ever standing for election oneself (other than as the VP candidate for her spouse, in a rigged election that he should have lost) is possible *only* for a television supervillain. However, when the plot is described at a more general level – an elected official in a democracy becoming an autocrat without the need for a military coup or an explicit revision of the Constitution that grants her these powers – this looks all too plausible. This has long been a staple of fiction. Along with HOC, prominent examples include Sinclair Lewis's *It Can't Happen Here* (1935), which details the rise of a uniquely American version of European fascism, and Phillip Roth's *The Plot Against America* (2004), in which the Nazi-sympathizer Charles Lindbergh defeats FDR in the crucial 1940 election.

It is worth noting that both Lewis and Roth, unlike the writers of HOC, set their novels in the tumultuous years leading up to World War II, during which many fledgling democracies *were* destroyed by autocrats of various stripes. However, it is not clear how much reassurance can be taken from this, since many scholars have argued that we have again entered a long period of global democratic decay and retreat. For example, Freedom House (2020) notes that, according to their measures, 2019 was the 14th straight year in which global freedom declined. In particular, they note that this score reflects negative changes in the world's two largest democracies – India and the United States – that "are increasingly willing to break down institutional safeguards and disregard the rights of critics and minorities." While a real-life autocrat would likely look different than the Underwoods, one cannot assume a priori that such things simply "can't" happen to modern democracies. Recent history provides plenty of case studies in which the politically improbable happens, often with terrifying speed.

To be clear, not every political scientist agrees with this pessimistic assessment of the global state of democracy. However, even among those that are (relatively) more optimistic about the general trend, there has been a recognition of the potential vulnerability of modern democracies to autocratic takeover. For example, Steven Levitisky and Daniel Ziblatt's recent *How Democracies Die* (2018) analyzes recent cases of democratic breakdown, and considers the lessons these have for contemporary politics (especially in the United States). They argue that, in the contemporary world, democracies often die silent deaths, with no violent coup to mark their end. They write:

> Democracies may die at the hands not of generals but of elected leaders – presidents or prime ministers who subvert the very process that brought them to power. Some of these leaders dismantle democracy quickly, as Hitler did in the wake of the 1933 Reichstag fire in Germany. More often, though, democracies erode slowly, in barely visible steps. (Levitsky and Ziblatt 2018, p. 3)

In this picture, would-be-autocrats follow Frank and Claire's lead and accrue power in large part by exploiting (rather than ignoring) the "rules" of the existing system, and have a strong preference for subverting (rather than outright destroying) the institutional features designed to limit their power, such as opposition political parties, the judiciary, the free press, or the regular holding of elections. In this way, even highly autocratic regimes can remain the outward appearance of democracy, long after the core has rotted away.

When the events of HOC are considered in light of Levitsky and Ziblatt's analysis, it becomes evident how something like the Underwoods' ascent to power might be possible. Four points are worth noting:

1. *The Constitution alone cannot save us.* When HOC ends, neither Frank nor Claire have made any move to amend the US Constitution. Yet, for all that, Claire has become President without legitimately winning a single election, and it seems highly unlikely that she will voluntarily give up power after two terms. How is this sort of thing possible? After all, isn't the US Constitution supposed to prevent this, among other things, by dividing power among various branches of government and limiting their power in various ways? As it turns out, its ability to do so depends crucially on whether democratic political leaders adhere to *political norms* that are not in the Constitution (or in any body of law). For example, consider the Constitutional mechanism for impeachment, which Frank uses to remove Walker, or the sorts of powers granted to governors and presidents during emergencies (which both Claire and Frank rely on to sabotage elections, or to forestall their own impeachments). The reason that these powers are not used in well-functioning democracies has less to do with the law than with a norm of *forbearance*, whereby the "losers" of democratic elections allow the "winners" to govern without hardball attempts to stop them. This closely relates to a second norm that Levitsky and Ziblatt see as especially important – that of *mutual toleration* between opposing sides. When norms of mutual toleration and forbearance break down, "extreme" measures such as impeachment or emergency orders can much more easily be exploited by aspiring autocrats.

2. *Establishment powers often underestimate rising tyrants.* Even in the cynical and ruthless political culture of HOC, of course, most of the characters with whom Frank and Claire interact would presumably prefer a flawed democracy to an autocracy. Moreover, many of them seem to have (or at least should have had) a general idea of the Underwoods' ruthlessness and ambition, even if they do not know the gory details until it is too late. Nevertheless, it is through their action, and their failures to act, that the Underwoods gain power. Frank's initial rise to power, for example, is enabled by deals with a variety of political and business elites – SanCorp, Raymond Tusk, Catherine Durant, Jackie Sharp, the Democratic Party leadership, even President Walker – who provide him with direct or indirect support in actions that they should *know* undercut democratic norms. In each case, they can be seen as making a sort of "bet" that they can control the scope of Frank's future transgressions, but only after they have benefitted from the transaction. This, of course, turns out to be a losing bet for the existing elites,

and it is of a type that Levitsky and Ziblatt argue is a common event on the road to democratic decline.

3. *Capture the referees, and win the game.* In order to "win" the game of politics, Claire and Frank must do more than violate implicit norms, of course. They also repeatedly break a wide variety of state and federal laws meant to constrain their behavior both as private citizens and as political leaders. However, in the end, the Underwoods avoid attempts by the various "referees" to discover and punish these violations of the rules. As in real-world democracies, these referees include various law enforcement and intelligence agencies, opposition political parties, regulatory bodies, the free press, and the courts. Moreover, the ways in which the Underwoods escape accountability closely mirrors the strategies adopted by real-world enemies of democracy – they repeatedly "capture" the institutions designed to hold them accountable, and instead turn them against their enemies. Levitsky and Ziblatt describe this as follows:

> Institutions become political weapons, wielded forcefully by those who control them against those who do not. This is how elected autocrats subvert democracy – packing and "weaponizing" the courts and other neutral agencies, buying off the media and the private sector (or bullying them into silence)…democracy's assassins use the very institutions of democracy – gradually, subtly, and even legally – to kill it. (Levitsky and Ziblatt 2018, p. 8)

Claire and Frank's relationship with the media, for instance, alternates between using them for their own purposes (as when Zoe and Tom write favorable material) to the violent (killing journalists who pose a threat). Similar things might be said about their relationships with law enforcement and intelligence agencies, the powers of which (including mass surveillance) they repeatedly wield against their political rivals, and with the courts (as when they arrange to have rivals such as Raymond Tusk arrested). While Claire and Frank's methods are undoubtedly more direct than many real-world autocrats – for example, it is uncommon for autocrats to *personally* murder journalists whose work threatens to expose them – the attempt to control the media by a combination of violent threats and financial rewards is, unfortunately, an all too common one.

4. *Inequality, polarization, and the dangers of populism.* Subsequent sections will examine structural features of democracy that might make it vulnerable to autocratic takeover. However, before doing so, it is worth briefly noting the social backdrop against which HOC takes place – that of a contemporary United States with high levels of wealth inequality and political polarization, a long history of racial and religious divisions, and one in which there is an ongoing "culture war" over issues such as abortion, gay marriage, and immigration policies. It is a large, diverse country struggling to respond to a variety of external and internal threats, notably including many antidemocratic forces, including the autocratic governments of Russia and China, and religious fundamentalists of various stripes. It is a country in which citizens increasingly distrust political elites, and where harnessing populist anger is an important part of achieving and maintaining

power. These forces present challenges to the Underwoods – for example, Claire's attempt to deceive the public about her abortions is a repeated challenge for her – but they also present opportunities. Economic inequality, for example, allows Frank to present himself as enemy of the rich, and the public's concern about the threats posed by terrorism and war (whether real or fabricated) ultimately allow Claire the cover she needs to eliminate the final attempts to dislodge her from the Oval Office.

Plato's Republic and Some Puzzles About Power

If the argument of the previous two sections is correct, then the scenario depicted in HOC, in which democratically elected officials achieve autocratic power, is one with considerable real-world relevance. However, this in turn raises other, more fundamental questions about the nature of democratic government. Does the possibility of democratic collapse simply represent a remediable defect in some contemporary democracies (as Levitsky and Ziblatt suggest), or does it instead indicate a weakness of democracy as such? In other words: is it possible to design a democracy that is Underwood-proof?

A good place to begin exploring this is with the antidemocratic arguments of Plato (427–347 BCE). Plato was a resident of Athens, whose early experiments in democracy would prove to be an important model for both the Roman Republic and the American and French revolutions. However, democratic Athens suffered from significant problems, as events in Plato's early life would have made clear. Among other things, incompetence and disloyalty by democratic leadership contributed to Athens losing the Peloponnesian War against the vehemently nondemocratic Sparta and its allies. The behavior of key Athenian figures such as Alcibiades – a clever politician and general who switched sides several times over the course of the war – resembles in many respects that of the Underwoods. Athens was, at various times during the war, hit by plague epidemics and had its democratic government briefly replaced by the "Thirty Tyrants." Finally, in the aftermath of the war, Plato saw his beloved teacher Socrates (470–399 BCE) tried and executed by an Athenian jury, in one of history's most famous miscarriages of justice.

Over the course of his life, Plato wrote around 30 dialogues, many of which touch on themes relevant to democratic governance. A few of the most notable include the *Apology* (Plato 1997a), in which Plato provides an account of Socrates' (ultimately unsuccessful) attempt to convince the Athenian jurors to spare him; the *Gorgias* (Plato 1997b), in which he unfavorably contrasts the rhetorical methods of the politicians with the philosophical pursuit of truth; and finally the *Republic* (Plato 1997d) and *Laws* (Plato 1997c), both of which deal explicitly with the design of a just state. For all this, though, it is almost impossible to say what exactly Plato himself thought of democracy. This stems in part because of the dialogue form in which he writes, in which Plato himself never tells us directly what he thinks. Second, even when attention is constrained to those positions to which Plato seems to be most sympathetic (e.g., to the views he puts in the mouth of Socrates), one can find somewhat different perspectives on democracy defended in different dialogues.

Plato's most significant criticisms of democracy can be found in the *Republic*. In this book, Socrates and a group of his friends and students have a long conversation about the nature of justice, both on the political level ("the just city") and on the personal level ("the just soul"). Socrates argues that these two notions of justice are structurally akin, and thus, a full understanding of one requires an understanding of the other. Over the course of the book, he describes in detail the perfectly just city (the *kallipolis*), in which everything is ordered as it should be. Socrates' proposed kallipolis is radically different from not only Athenian democracy, but from any other existing form of government. His criticisms of democracy can best be understood against the backdrop of this alternate ideal.

The main argument of the *Republic* begins when Socrates and his friends encounter Thrasymachus, a rhetorician who would not be out of place in HOC. When they ask him "What is justice?" he famously responds that, "I say that justice is nothing other than the advantage of the stronger" (338c) and goes on to explain what he means by giving examples of different forms of government:

> Democracy makes democratic laws, tyranny makes tyrannical laws, and so on with the others. And they declare what they have made – what is to their own advantage – to be just for their subjects, and they punish anyone who goes against this as lawless and unjust. This, then, is what I say justice is, the same in all cities, the advantage of the established rule. (338d-e)

On Thrasymachus' view, what counts as just depends entirely on the distribution of political power within a given society. This position has several consequences that Claire and Frank would likely appreciate. First, it suggests that there is no reason for individuals or groups to obey laws that do not benefit them personally. For example, Frank's murder of Zoe and Claire's murder of Tom are acceptable on this view, especially since they have the power to avoid punishment. Second, this view leaves little room for any principled distinction between tyranny and democracy. Most fans of HOC, for example, would presumably agree that Claire's and Frank's use of the Presidency to harm their enemies is *unjustified*, even if it makes for good television. However, for Thrasymachus, democracy is equally objectionable. After all, the only real difference between tyranny and democracy is the *number* of rulers, and not the *nature* or *grounds* of their authority. Suppose, for example, that Claire managed to convince 51% of voters (through judicious use of the media) that her enemies ought to be hunted down and killed, and that any laws preventing this ought to be repealed. This would make the process more democratic, but would it make it any more just? The potential for democratic majorities to mistreat minorities – the *tyranny of the majority* – is one that has often been realized.

Finally, Thrasymachus's view seems to entail that *if* Claire achieves ultimate political power in the end, then it is *she* who gets to decide what counts as "just" or "unjust" from here on out. As Socrates points out, though, this actually leads to a bit

16 House of Cards as Philosophy: Democracy on Trial   371

of puzzle, as it is unclear whether Thrasymachus wants to claim that justice depends on *what the rulers want* (e.g., those laws that Claire likes) or *what is actually good for the rulers* (e.g., which laws would best help Claire maintain power, even if she does not recognize it). A parallel puzzle can be posed about democracy: should we say that democratic laws are justified if they reflect the current will of the people (even if the people are ignorant, biased, hateful toward minorities, and on the way to self-destruction) or are laws justified because they are in the genuine interest of the democratic majority, and its continued political power? Thrasymachus, perhaps unwisely, chooses the latter. Socrates will later exploit this answer – against both Thrasymachus and the defender of democracy – to argue that the "aristocratic" kallipolis is preferable not only an Underwood-style tyranny but also to the democracy that precedes it. The next section takes up these arguments.

Plato's Critique of Democracy

The kallipolis and the rule by the best. Socrates spends much of books 2 through 7 of the *Republic* describing the structure of the kallipolis, and the training of its philosopher rulers. While many of the details can be safely ignored, three aspects of its general design are notable for their contrast with democracy.

First, Socrates repeatedly argues that a just, well-ordered city is one in which each person does what they are *best* at, and which benefits the city as a whole. This most of all applies to the *guardians,* who make up the political and military leadership of the city. Political power should not be distributed – as it is HOC and was in Ancient Athens – because of wealth, family connections, media savviness, or skill in political warfare.

Second, Socrates advocates massive censorship of the media (in this case, poetry and theater) almost from the first moment he begins discussing the kallipolis (377). Among other things, he advocates wholesale revision of Greek religious texts to model appropriate behavior for both citizens and guardians, the introduction of a new "myth of the metals" to get citizens to accept the role the state assigns them, and a blanket ban on "imitative poetry," which would likely include most Greek tragedy (as well as most modern television shows, movies, and video games). This proposal, despite its unrealism, reflects a recognition of both the central role that media plays in the lives of democratic citizens, and the potential problems it brings. In HOC, for example, nearly every step of Frank and Claire's ascent to power is aided and abetted by the media, both in the specifics (as when they leak stories about political opponents) to the much more general (as when the media stokes fear about terrorist threats, or exacerbates divisions between groups of people).

The third area of difference between the kallipolis and democracy concerns the measures taken to ensure that ruling elites are both competent and properly motivated. As HOC makes evident, there is frequently a disconnect between what political and economic elites of a democracy "want" and what would be best for the country as a whole. Some, such as Raymond Tusk, Remy Danton, and many members of Congress, are driven at least in part by a desire for money. Many others, such as Annette Shepherd or Peter Russo, also seem motivated by the desire to protect or advance family and loved ones. A third group – including Claire and Frank but including many others – are almost monomaniacally focused on gaining and exercising power. Finally, those politicians whose motivations are laudable, such as Donald Blythe, are frequently too ignorant or politically incompetent to effectively serve citizens' interests.

In a democracy, the ultimate "check" against these problems is ultimately the ballot box, though this crucially depends on the ability of voters to detect such problems. Socrates, by contrast, proposes more direct methods, including prohibiting the guardians from owning private property, the communal raising of all the guardians' children (and the concealment from everyone about whose children are whose), and the implementation of extensive educational requirements for future rulers, which will not be completed until well into middle-age. While these specific proposals have been almost universally dismissed as unrealistic (including by Plato's most famous student, Aristotle), the democratic weaknesses that motivate their introduction are ones that defenders of democracy need to take seriously. These weaknesses, after all, are ones that seem to have persisted from Ancient Athens to the present day.

The origins of democracy. The *Republic's* most famous discussion of democracy occurs in book 8, where Socrates describes the process of institutional decay, where what was once an aristocratic kallipolis becomes first a Spartan-style "timocracy," then an oligarchy ruled by the rich, then a freedom-loving democracy, and finally a tyranny. It is these last three steps that will concern us here, as they mirror in many ways the Underwoods' successful bid to achieve power in a fictional United States that blends aspects of oligarchy with democracy.

On Socrates's account, each form of government contains within it a fatal flaw that inevitably undermines its long-term stability and guarantees its eventual replacement by something worse. Specifically, he suggests that the citizens raised in each sort of society will be flawed in predictable ways, which renders them incapable of maintaining the institutions they have inherited. The aristocratic kallipolis collapses, for example, when its selective breeding and training program ends up producing clever, strong, brave soldiers instead of wise and just philosopher-rulers. The timocracy ruled by these soldiers, in turn, decays into oligarchy as the timocrats' children attach ever more importance to the financial rewards of military and political service, until the wealthy directly seize political power.

Socrates's description of the oligarchic society, the kind of people who it produces, and its inherent weaknesses are all evident in HOC. An oligarchy, on Socrates's definition, a society ruled by the wealthiest. This might involve, for example, some sort of explicit wealth or property qualification that granted one the right to vote or serve on juries (as was the case in many early democracies, including the United States). However, it might also plausibly include the fictional United States depicted in HOC, where wealthy individuals such as Raymond Tusk and Bill and Annette Shepherd are depicted as having *enormous* power to shape almost every area of society, from determining who will win elections (Tusk's support for Walker is crucial for his political success, as is SanCorp's support for Frank), to foreign

16 House of Cards as Philosophy: Democracy on Trial

policy (including decisions about going to war), to the particulars of which bills pass Congress. Their power appears even more substantial when one considers areas that lie outside direct political control, such as Tusk's ability to unilaterally cut off power to large parts of the United States, or the Shepherds' ability to arrange assassination attempts against Claire.

Socrates notes several problems with oligarchy. First, as the examples above make clear, being wealthy hardly guarantees that one will be a competent, just ruler. Second, there is the problem of inequality. He states that oligarchy "isn't one city but two – one of the poor and one of the rich – living in the same place and always plotting against one another" (551d). This is evident early in HOC, when the interests of the poor (such as the shipbuilders that Peter Russo represents, or the people who might be served by his environmental bill) clash repeatedly against those of the rich. Finally, oligarchy leads to proliferation of what Socrates calls *drones* – citizens who are deprived of any meaningful work within the state, either because they have been exploited by the oligarchs and driven into bankruptcy or because they are the lazy children of oligarchs who contribute nothing.

Democratic man and the origins of tyranny. It is these drones that enable the slide first into a benign-seeming democracy and then, much more horribly, into tyranny. The initial transition into democracy is driven by the oligarchs' insatiable greed, and by the proliferation of drones this causes. The oligarchy eventually falls when the people (spurred on by the rage of the drones against the lazy children of the oligarchs) rise up and demand equal power for all. The prototypical democratic leader, on this account, might well be someone like Peter Russo, a blue-collar worker who comes to power with the promise of serving the interests of his fellow workers (mainly ship-builders whose jobs have been threatened by a changing economy) against the machinations of the rich.

Where the oligarchic society values wealth, the democratic society values personal *freedom,* and strikes out at any source of external authority – whether it be parents, tradition, the demands of morality, or the requirements of the community as a whole – that would threaten to limit this individual freedom. This, in turn, leads to a huge proliferation of the *sorts* of lives that citizens choose to lead, which even Socrates grants might initially seem quite appealing:

> Then it looks as though this is the finest or most beautiful of the constitutions, for, like a coat embroidered with every kind of ornament, this city, embroidered with every kind of character type, would seem to be the most beautiful. And many people would probably judge it to be so, as women and children do when they see something multicolored. (557c)

Peter Russo is a paradigmatic example of the "democratic man" that Socrates argues is typical of a democracy. Like the democracy he lives in (or aspires to live in), his soul is an unordered mess of wildly different desires, both necessary and unnecessary, virtuous and vicious. It is tough to tell what Peter will do from hour to hour, or even minute to minute. He uses drugs and then attends AA meetings, is a caring father and then an absent one, hires prostitutes but loves his partner Christine, is subservient to Frank, and ultimately stands up to him. The following Platonic description fits him perfectly:

> And so he lives on, yielding day by day to the desire at hand. Sometimes he drinks heavily while listening to the flute; at other times, he drinks only water and is on a diet; sometimes he goes in for physical training; at other times, he's idle and neglects everything; and sometimes he even occupies himself with what he takes to be philosophy. He often engages in politics, leaping up from his seat and saying and doing whatever comes into his mind. (561b)

Peter might additionally be classified as a "drone," in that he often seems to lack any interest or aptitude for his job. Moreover, like many democratic politicians, his attitude toward the wealthy is a contradictory one, in that he identifies strongly with the poor but relies on the support of the rich to keep his position.

Plato would not be surprised, then, by the fact that it is by exploiting the weaknesses of Russo and people like him that the Underwoods manage to achieve power. Just as the seeds of oligarchies destruction were sown by the oligarchs' incessant pursuit of wealth (and the inequality and animosity that ensues), a democracy's decay into a tyranny results from its citizen overwhelming desires to lead their lives *however they see fit,* regardless of the larger social consequences of this. In this sort of society, drones such as Peter Russo (and other politicians) play an important role in mediating between the desires of the poor masses (who want the wealthy's money to pursue their various ends) and the wealthy themselves (who want to keep their money). The drones, in turn, benefit heavily from this arrangement.

Aspiring tyrants such as the Underwoods can now use this tension between the poor and rich to their advantage. In fact, the *Republic's* description of how this might come about closely mirrors the events of HOC. First, the poor people in a democracy (the vast majority) will increasingly come to see the power and wealth of the rich as being the main obstacle to their desire to live their lives as they wish, especially when they are spurred on by the various drones, who thrive on such conflicts. For example, in HOC, people like Remy Danton, Peter Russo, or even the Underwoods themselves literally *wouldn't have their jobs* if their various constituencies (whether this be SanCorp, the dockworkers' union, or other rich donors) did not see such conflicts as representing existential threats. Second, the rich people within a democracy – the Raymond Tusks and Shepherd siblings of the world – respond to this conflict by attempting to become "oligarchs in fact," even though they no longer possess the power to fully do so. For example, Tusk has considerable power to wreck things and make peoples' lives worse, but he cannot literally force President Walker to do his bidding. Finally, the aspiring tyrants respond by presenting themselves as champions of the people against the rich, perhaps by prosecuting the oligarchs and their servants on trumped-up charges (which is precisely what the Underwoods do to Tusk and Walker). Finally, to secure their own power, the tyrants will "stir up a war" (566e), before systematically eliminating all of those who might pose a threat, in particular former allies.

In the end, "the tyrant will have to do away with all of them if he intends to rule, until he's left with neither friend nor enemy of any worth" (567e). On this account,

16 *House of Cards* as Philosophy: Democracy on Trial

then, the eventual conflicts between the central plotters – in particular, Claire, Frank, and Doug – follow inevitably from the nature of tyranny, which can only ever admit a single ruler. For Claire to win, everyone else must lose. In book 9, Socrates goes on to argue that the tyrant who has achieved absolute power will, in fact, live a miserable life of loneliness and fear (and for this reason, he argues it would be irrational to *want* to be a tyrant). However, while it is true that Claire's many enemies might (if they had lived) take some comfort in the prospect of her future suffering, this by itself will not restore the democracy she helped destroy. This, then, is the *Republic's* bleak prognosis for democracy – a brief flowering of freedom choked off quickly by despotism.

Hobbes on Monarchy and Democracy

In Plato's *Republic,* tyranny is described as the worst of all possible governments. Tyrants such as the Underwoods are held up as an image for how *not* to live, and their souls are described as being sort of tyrannies in miniature, with a single bottomless desire for power dominating and destroying anything that was once good and noble. If democracy is bad, it is at least in part because the uncontrollable freedom and variety can be exploited by the rising tyrant. In other words, one main reason to avoid democracy is that it will enable people such as Claire or Frank to come to power.

Our second critic of democracy, Thomas Hobbes (1588–1679) disagrees with both Plato's distinction between monarchy (i.e., the legitimate rule by a wise ruler that Plato favors) and tyranny and with the importance Plato attaches to the psychological character and training of the ruler. For Hobbes, "monarchy" and "tyranny" are simply two different words for the same government structure, with "tyrant" simply being a word used by those who do not like the monarch. In his famous book, the *Leviathan* (Hobbes 1994) Hobbes argues that a monarchy with absolute power is the best possible form of government, even if this ruler happens to be a ruthless one motivated only by a selfish desire for power. For Hobbes, then, Claire's crushing victory over her opponents at the end of HOC would represent a desirable outcome, as her coming authoritarian rule is preferable to the democracy that preceded it.

Why we need the state. Like Plato, Hobbes lived in a time of violent political upheaval. He wrote the *Leviathan* during the English Civil War, a bloody, protracted conflict between supporters of Parliament (such as Oliver Cromwell) and the Royalist supporters of King Charles I. Hobbes's political philosophy, begins with the proposition that this sort of civil strife (resulting from the lack of a single, agreed-upon government) is really, really bad, and that rational people can and should do just about anything to avoid it. How bad is it? In a famous passage, Hobbes writes as follows:

> Whatsoever therefore is consequent to a time of Warre, where every man is Enemy to every man; the same is consequent to the time, wherein men live without other security, than what their own strength, and their own invention shall furnish them withall. In such condition,

there is no place for Industry; because the fruit thereof is uncertain; and consequently no Culture of the Earth; no Navigation, nor use of the commodities that may be imported by Sea; no commodious Building; no Instruments of moving, and removing such things as require much force; no Knowledge of the face of the Earth; no account of Time; no Arts; no Letters; no Society; and which is worst of all, continuall feare, and danger of violent death; And the life of man, solitary, poore, nasty, brutish, and short. (Hobbes 1994, Chapter 13)

It is for *this* reason – to make their lives better – that Hobbes thinks individuals should consent to live under the rule of a monarch, even a bad one. His reasoning can be sketched as follows:

1. Humans are basically self-interested creatures who naturally care about preserving their own lives. While they do have moral duties to help others, these duties do not hold in a state of "war," where others continually threaten their lives. So, for example, it is generally wrong to hit people with rocks, but it is perfectly OK for Rachel to hit Doug (her eventual murderer) with a rock in her attempt to escape him, or for Claire to kill Doug in self-defense.
2. Humans are similar to one another in terms of their power, with the result that they are always a threat to one another. So, for example, it is true that Frank and Claire are somewhat smarter and more vicious than most people, but they are not *so* capable that other people do not pose real threats to them.
3. Because of this relative equality among humans, where each has reason to fear what the other could do, humans in a *state of nature* (i.e., whenever there does not exist a government capable of exerting authority) will quickly descend into a war of "all against all" described above. In this situation, even the people who might otherwise behave ethically must devote themselves to an aggressive, violent attempt to dominate others. In HOC, one might think of the way Claire and Frank *force* their opponents to come "down to their level."
4. The only way out of this, according to Hobbes, is for the citizens to *consent* to give up nearly all of their rights (in particular, their right to use violence against others) to a single sovereign. This sovereign, in return, only need promise merely not to kill them. The sovereign's tyrannical power comes neither from God nor from a Platonic societal collapse – instead, it is given freely by rational citizens pursuing their own self-interest.

It is worth noting that, on Hobbes's characterization, the world of HOC bears more than a passing resemblance to a "state of nature." This is because, until the final moments of season 6 (and perhaps beyond it), when Claire finally eliminates the last significant threat to her power, power is shared between a number of different people and institutions who must compete (often violently!) with one another. In the early seasons, for example, the Underwoods must compete not only with the Walker administration, but with their partisan opponents, Raymond Tusk, and many others. Even after Frank and Claire have ascended to the Presidency, their various enemies still have considerable power to harm them (among other things, by having law enforcement punish them for their previous crimes). Neither Claire nor the United States that she rules has truly exited the state of nature until she is secure in power.

The dangers of democracy. This brings us naturally to Hobbes's main reasons for favoring monarchy over democracy. In general, he argues that the diffusion of power within a democracy makes it unstable, and thus more likely to dissolve into the sort of civil war that he fears. The ordinary citizens of HOC, for instance, suffer a great deal in the Underwood's rise to power, specifically from the fallout of the many decisions – on international trade, education, military policy, domestic security, emergency preparedness, and other areas – that were made without any concern for their well-being at all, but instead served merely as moves by powerful agents in a game for power.

Hobbes describes several specific ways in which the structure of democracies can lead to problems. First, he argues that, in a democracy, there is often a considerable mismatch between what is good for individual politicians and what would be good for their constituents. So, for example, nearly all of the politicians on HOC are seen voting for bills they do not believe in for reasons such as personal financial benefit (e.g., to secure a campaign contribution, or post-congressional lobbying job) or because they think it will play well in the media in the run up to the next election. When and if these decisions end up harming the public, the division of democratic power across hundreds of politicians makes it difficult for the public to ascertain *who* was responsible, a fact the politicians are well aware of. In an absolute monarchy, by contrast, Hobbes thinks the incentive structure is much clearer. He writes:

> Now in Monarchy, the private interest is the same with the publique. The riches, power, and honour of a Monarch arise onely from the riches, strength and reputation of his Subjects. For no King can be rich, nor glorious, nor secure; whose Subjects are either poore, or contempt-ible, or too weak through want, or dissention, to maintain a war against their enemies: Whereas in a Democracy, or Aristocracy, the publique prosperity conferres not so much to the private fortune of one that is corrupt, or ambitious, as doth many times a perfidious advice, a treacherous action, or a Civill warre. (Hobbes 1994, Chapter 19)

On Hobbes's account, the monarch, unlike the democratic politician, has a clear reason to care about the public good, especially since monarchs deposed by the public tend to meet bad fates. The idea here is a simple one: for all Claire's ruthlessness and selfishness in obtaining power, she has a clear reason for caring about the public good once she has succeeded in getting it. After all, there will be no one left for her to blame if things go wrong, and the public will know this.

A second, related argument against democracy concerns the potential for corruption, and its negative effects on the public good. Hobbes takes it for granted that any form of government – monarchy, aristocracy, or democracy – will be open to corruption, as those in power seek to benefit their friends and harm their enemies. However, he argues that it is worse in a democracy, on the simple grounds that there are more politicians, and thus more friends and enemies of politicians to be rewarded and punished. In HOC, this sort of corruption is obviously endemic, with both the Underwoods and their various opponents repeatedly misusing public resources (including the military and police) for private benefit. While it is true that individual democratic politicians cannot engage in corruption at the same scale as an absolute monarch – for example, they cannot simply execute those they dislike, or directly appoint their friends to powerful positions, as some monarchs have done – Hobbes thinks this in itself is a problem. He argues that, in a democracy, the small-scale corruption results in a system where lots of individual people have the power to harm the public in various ways (e.g., there are a LOT of people who have just enough power to stop a new bridge from being built) but, conversely, almost no individuals have the ability to benefit the public in any measurable way.

A final Hobbesian criticism of democracy concerns the harmful fallout that results from the democratic competition for power. Hobbes argues that the regular change in leadership in a democracy (as majority opinion shifts first one way, and then another) makes it difficult for citizens to effectively make plans. By contrast, in a monarchy they must deal only with inconsistencies and equivocations of a single person. That is, Hobbes would contend that when and if Claire has achieved absolute power, areas such as tax policy and international relations are likely to become *predictable* in a way they were not in the democratic period that preceded this. Given the huge disruptions that these uncertainties can cause for citizens – for example, shifting economic relations with China in season 2 have severe effects on businesses, workers, and consumers – this can be of real benefit. Moreover, even when the current leadership of a democratic government *wants* to make the best long-run decision, Hobbes argues that they will find it more difficult than would a similarly motivated absolute monarch. This is because, in a democracy, the most obvious sources of institutional expertise (such as other politicians, military leaders, cabinet-level appointees) will generally have political power and ambitions of their own, often opposed to those of the leaders. This is something the Underwoods must deal with repeatedly, as their "subordinates" attempt to weaken or replace them. By contrast, to the extent that Claire has secured absolute power at the end of the series, she will be free to appoint genuine experts to top positions, and to rely on their good-faith effort to serve her ends.

A power without limits. Perhaps the most radical feature of Hobbes's defense of monarchy is his contention that the power of the monarch must be *absolute*. This means, for example, that the monarch should literally be "above the law," and there is no "right to revolt" for citizens no matter how bad the monarch treats them. After all, it is her saying so that that makes something a law in the first place. Hobbes argues that doing otherwise would undercut the reason that citizens should consent to a government in the first place – they wanted to ensure they stayed out of the state of nature, and the war of all against all that this entailed. Any attempt to set up institutional checks and balances to limit the sovereign's power would necessarily bring with it the possibility of a renewed conflict.

On Hobbes's view, then, the citizens of HOC should breathe a sigh of relief when Claire finally triumphs over her many enemies and puts an end to "democratic" attempts to limit her power. They will no longer have to deal with the corruption of democratic politicians, the unpredictable seesaw of control between rival political factions, or the worry that their leaders are more concerned about reelection or monetary benefit than their well-being. In fact, they can give up politics altogether, and enjoy all the benefits this brings: no more hating and fearing those of opposing political parties, or wasting time attempting to impress others with their useless political knowledge, or voting. And, in return for all these benefits, they must merely accept that they need to be *very* careful not to do anything that might upset Claire, as her power over their lives (and deaths) is all-but-unlimited.

This, then, is the Hobbesian bargain: security in return for all of one's rights. It is one that, like Socrates' described tyranny, holds little appeal for most citizens. The question for defenders of democracy is then: Can we do better?

Underwoods Everywhere: Democracy in the Present

The contemporary world in which HOC is set is, of course, a vastly different one than those in which Plato and Hobbes wrote. For one thing, the complex political and legal structures of a modern republican government like the United States bear only a passing resemblance to Plato's Athens or the Roman Republic. Among other things, contemporary democracies have a much wider definition of citizenship, a vastly more extensive body of written law, and a clearer articulation of the power and limits of different institutions. The design of these structures reflects, at least in part, a recognition of the failures of classical democracy. Contemporary democracies also benefit from wealthier, better-educated citizenries, and from significantly reduced problems related to pandemic illness or military invasion. So, for example, while the contemporary United States has struggled (even relative to other rich nations) to respond to issues arising from domestic terrorism, overseas wars, and contagious illnesses such as HIV and COVID-19, it remains the case that (so far at least) the scale of these threats is small compared to those faced in the ancient world, before the advent of modern medicine or the United Nations. It seems undeniable that characters such as the Underwoods would have likely had an *easier* time seizing control in Athens or Rome than in the modern United States.

We also have vastly more experience with democratic government and with its potential advantages than did Plato and Hobbes. Writers such as John Locke (1764), John Stuart Mill (1865), Jurgen Habermas (1994), and John Rawls (2005) have all provided intricate defenses of democracy from a variety of theoretical perspectives. More recently, Amartya Sen (1999), Elizabeth Andersen (2003), and others have argued that democratic governments do much better than rival forms of government in utilizing the knowledge of individual citizens. So, for example, Sen argues that in contrast to authoritarian governments no democratic regime has ever suffered from mass famine. The idea here is that, for all the Underwoods' viciousness early in their political careers, they at least had to *pay regular attention* to what was happening to their constituents. If and when democratic accountability ends, however, all bets are off.

Despite these reasons for preferring democracy, however, Platonic and Hobbesian criticisms of democracy have not lost their force. For example, Plato's contention that the voters in a democracy lack the expertise necessary to make complex political decisions has remained a consistent theme of critics of democracy. The ordinary citizens of HOC, for example, are all too easily swayed by the media, and the Underwoods' manipulation of it. Many scholars have argued that real-world voters are much the same. Joseph Schumpeter (1976) and Jason Brennan (2017), among other recent critics of democracy, have argued that modern social science shows that the typical voter lacks anything like the rationality, knowledge, or stable preferences assumed by many defenses of democracy. Instead, voters are, as Plato might have predicted, some combination of ignorant, partisan, and apathetic. In keeping with this Platonic picture, Schumpeter and Brennan both argue for a significant rethinking of democratic institutions, in which knowledgeable elites are granted significantly more power than ordinary voters.

Rosenberg (2019) argues from a similarly pessimistic starting point to an even darker conclusion: modern liberal democracies are likely to soon to be replaced by right-wing, authoritarian governments. On Rosenberg's account, the growth of alternative media – think of Zoe's move to the web-based *Slugline* from the traditional *Washington Herald* – is one of a number of factors that will make it difficult for liberal democracies to sustain themselves against the allure of populist and nationalist alternatives.

One can also find contemporary worries of a more Hobbesian sort. For example, Juan Linz (1990) argues that there are both empirical and conceptual reasons for doubting the long-run stability of presidential systems such as the United States, in which power is divided between the legislature and the executive. As Hobbes might well have predicted, such systems have frequently collapsed into autocracy as a result of internal conflict between their various branches. At various points, the Underwoods find themselves on different sides of this divide, and the tools they use against their opponents in rival branches – impeachment, law enforcement, cancellation of elections – give a realistic picture of how such collapse often proceeds.

Finally, Levitsky and Ziblatt, whose ideas were discussed earlier in this chapter, draw on themes that would be familiar to both Plato and Hobbes. Like Plato, they worry about the effects of partisan media and the polarization it causes. And, like Hobbes, they recognize that the "division of powers" within a democracy can sometimes lead to institutional warfare, where different actors aim for (and sometimes achieve) ultimate supremacy. They are, however, comparatively optimistic on the prospects for global democracy, and suggest that even democracies in danger can be saved if elites are willing to make the necessary sacrifices to stop rising autocrats and to reduce inequality and polarization.

Conclusion: HOC as Warning and Opportunity

If the argument of this chapter is correct, then the events depicted in HOC serve two purposes. As a cautionary tale, it provides a warning that democratic collapse is possible and an opportunity to think about how to strengthen our democracy to avoid a collapse. What lessons might be learned from this?

First, while the specific methods that Claire and Frank use to defeat their opponents are at times highly unrealistic, their general strategy for undermining democracy is a cogent one. The Underwoods rely heavily on their ability to turn the institutional structures underlying modern democracy – such as a free press, the holding of regular elections, and even the division of power – into attacks first on their rivals and then against the system itself. Despite the myriad differences between the democracy depicted in HOC and our own, recent scholarship suggests that this sort of "attack from within" remains a real threat to contemporary democracy.

Second, the arguments of Plato and Hobbes suggest that many of the weaknesses of democracy that the Underwoods exploit are inherent in the nature of democratic government, and not simply artifacts of the contemporary United States. They are, in fact, inseparable from its strengths. Insofar as democracy aims for mass participation, for example, it needs a vibrant media that can inform its citizens, and insofar as it aims to protect the people against tyranny, it must distribute power among many different people and institutions. The fact that democracies can have citizens (and politicians) with wildly different conceptions of the good life and how to pursue it is something to be embraced, even if it does lead to political factions. Given that it is precisely these features of democracy that the Underwoods target, then, they represent a type of threat to which democracy has always been vulnerable.

Third, as a consequence of the first two points, the battle to preserve and promote democracy is one that must be fought repeatedly, as underlying cultural and technological changes throw up new opportunities for would-be autocrats to weaken or destroy democratic institutions. As the Underwoods recognize, the world of HOC – a world uncomfortably similar to our own – is one where existing democratic institutions struggle to deal with a rapidly changing electorate, media culture, and economy. However, the Underwoods' success in using these changes to undermine democracy does not represent some inevitable law of nature. Instead, advocates of democracy can (and should) use the example they provide to consider what might be done not only to strengthen our democracies against this sort of threat, but to make them better serve their citizens.

References

Anderson, Elizabeth. 2003. Sen, ethics, and democracy. *Feminist Economics* 9 (2–3): 239–261.
Brennan, Jason. 2017. *Against democracy: New preface*. Princeton: Princeton University Press.
Freedom House. 2020. Freedom in the world 2020: A leaderless struggle for democracy. https://freedomhouse.org/report/freedom-world/2020/leaderless-struggle-democracy
Habermas, Jürgen. 1994. Three normative models of democracy. *Constellations* 1 (1): 1–10.
Hobbes, Thomas. 1994. *Leviathan: With selected variants from the Latin edition of 1668*. Edited by Edwin Curley. Underlined, Notations edition. Indianapolis: Hackett Publishing Company.
Koblin, John. 2018. 'House of cards' resumes production, with Diane lane and Greg Kinnear. *The New York Times*, January 31, 2018, sec. Business. https://www.nytimes.com/2018/01/31/business/media/house-of-cards-diane-lane-greg-kinnear.html
Levitsky, Steven, and Daniel Ziblatt. 2018. *How democracies die*. New York: Crown.
Lewis, Sinclair. 1935. *It can't happen here*. New York: Penguin.
Linz, Juan J. 1990. The perils of Presidentialism. *Journal of Democracy* 1 (1): 51–69.
Locke, John. 1764. *Second treatise of government*. https://www.gutenberg.org/ebooks/7370
Mill, John Stuart. 1865. *Considerations on representative government by John Stuart Mill*. London: Longman, Green, Longman, Roberts, and Green.
Plato. 1997a. Apology. In *Complete works*, edited by John M. Cooper, translated by G.M.A. Grube, 17–37. Indianapolis: Hackett Publishing.

———. 1997b. Gorgias. In *Complete works*, edited by John M. Cooper, translated by Donald J. Zeyl, 791–870. Indianapolis: Hackett Publishing.

———. 1997c. Laws. In *Complete works*, edited by John M. Cooper, translated by Trevor J. Saunders, 1318–1617. Indianapolis: Hackett Publishing.

———. 1997d. Republic. In *Complete works*, edited by John M. Cooper, translated by G.M.A. Grube and C.D.C Reeve, 971–1224. Indianapolis: Hackett Publishing.

Rawls, John. 2005. *Political liberalism*. New York: Columbia University Press.

Rosenberg, S. (2019). Democracy Devouring Itself: The Rise of the Incompetent Citizen and the Appeal of Right Wing Populism. In Psychology of Political and Everyday Extremism. UC Irvine. Retrieved from https://escholarship.org/uc/item/8806z01m

Roth, Philip. 2004. *The plot against America*. Boston: Houghton Mifflin Harcourt.

Schumpeter, Joseph Alois. 1976. *Capitalism, socialism and democracy*. New York: Routledge.

Sen, Amartya Kumar. 1999. Democracy as a universal value. *Journal of Democracy* 10 (3): 3–17.

Last Week Tonight as Philosophy: The Importance of Jokalism

17

Christelle Paré

Contents

Introduction	384
Where Does Jokalism Come from and How Is It Related to Satire and Philosophy?	385
Satire, Philosophy, and Journalism: A Combo That Captures the Attention of the Public and Academia	388
Last Week Tonight with John Oliver Is Something Else!	390
LWT Is Not "Just" Infotainment nor Is It Edutainment	392
LWT Is Not Traditional Journalism	394
Why Should Jokalism Be Taken Seriously and Considered Philosophical?	396
Conclusion	401
References	402

Abstract

This chapter will explore the concept of jokalism, a word that first appeared in *The Daily Show with Jon Stewart* without a real definition and that could, as of now, be used to explain and understand a new way to tackle social and political issues on television. Exploring HBO's *Last Week Tonight with John Oliver* as a typical case of jokalism, this chapter will demonstrate how satire and information, supported by journalistic techniques, can build an argument about sensitive social and political issues. If *Last Week Tonight* is understood as a vehicle for critical thinking, one can consequently ask how it can be categorized as philosophy and comedy and still remain a serious, trusted, and entertaining media outlet.

C. Paré (✉)
Department of Communication, University of Ottawa, Ottawa, ON, Canada

École nationale de l'humour, Montréal, Québec, Canada
e-mail: Cpare2@uottawa.ca; Christelle.Pare@ucs.inrs.ca

© Springer Nature Switzerland AG 2024
D. K. Johnson et al. (eds.), *The Palgrave Handbook of Popular Culture as Philosophy*,
https://doi.org/10.1007/978-3-031-24685-2_39

Keywords

Jokalism · Satire · Comedy · Journalism · Humor · Political philosophy · Esthetics · *Last Week Tonight with John Oliver*

Introduction

> When in doubt, tell the truth.
> —Samuel Clemens (a.k.a. Mark Twain)

Comedy and humor have always gone hand in hand with social and political issues; using humor, people have shed light on problematic situations, pointed at what is wrong, and toward what the ideal situation should be – all while (hopefully) provoking laughter. Indeed, such things have explicitly been the purpose of *satire* since classical Antiquity (Condren 2014). In this way, satire, political, and moral philosophy work as great partners. "[T]he satirist writes 'with a sense of moral vocation and with a concern for the public interest'" (Quintero 2007, in Diehl 2013, p. 311). Satirists will build an argument, not only to convince their audience, but "even the targets of their criticism" (Diehl 2013, p. 311). As Diehl explains, even though all satires are not philosophical works, "it is possible to practice philosophy through satire" (Diehl 2013, p. 320).

Needless to say, philosophers seem to enjoy diving into the satire pool. Throughout the last three decades, a rich collection of research work has been done about popular televised vehicles of satire and how they explore philosophical elements. *The Simpsons* (Hull 2000; Irwin et al. 2001), *South Park* (Arp 2007; Arp and Decker 2013; Hanley 2007), *The Daily Show with Jon Stewart* (Holt 2007, 2013b), *The Colbert Report* (Decker 2013; McClennen 2011), and even *Family Guy* (Wisnewski 2007), just to name a few, have been studied from a philosophical standpoint. While all these shows bring their own unique criticism about society, they do use the same techniques to get the audience's attention: They confront the audience with their point of view and (usually) suggest new possible solutions. Granted, *The Simpsons* will not be inclined to use as much scatology as *Family Guy* and *South Park* would (even if it has been a satirical tool since Aristophanes's plays back in Ancient Greece). The animated shows, which are all set in imaginary interpretations of the United States, are all quite different than *The Daily Show with Jon Stewart* and *The Colbert Report,* which use live persons, to comment on real world events, using jokes and fictional characters. Basically, they are all using the same approach.

Then, there is HBO's *Last Week Tonight with John Oliver* (hereafter *LWT*), an unconventional kind of stakeholder in political comedy since its inception in 2014 that is definitively bathed in satire, but which is doing something more than confronting the audience with its point of view and suggesting solutions – more than even commenting on society through facts and fiction. It also investigates and fact checks the information it relays, and perhaps most importantly, expresses calls to action. This, it seems, is different from anything else that came before it.

17 *Last Week Tonight* as Philosophy: The Importance of Jokalism

Consequently, those who study such things had trouble categorizing or naming *LWT*. It was in the throes of this dilemma (the need for a name or category for this new way of doing things) that the concept of *jokalism* emerged. It is therefore the purpose of this chapter to examine *LWT* through the lens of jokalism (and, in turn, explore jokalism through *LWT*), to expose how *LWT* can engage its audiences in philosophy *and* comedy at the same time.

Now, one might wonder, how can a show such as *LWT* do philosophy while using satire as its central component? Indeed, one might wonder whether it is satire at all. After all, the element of investigation for new information is not a fundamental element of satire, as satirists will usually just dwell on information that is openly known – and clearly such investigations are central to *LWT*. Nevertheless, *LWT* is still *clearly* satire. Indeed, it must be, by definition. Satire is that which uses humor, exaggeration, irony, and ridicule to communicate a message with a strong point of view about society and/or politics, and *LWT* clearly fits that bill. So perhaps, when it combines the tools of satire with the strategies from investigative journalism, activism, and columns, *LWT* becomes more than pure satire for entertainment purposes. Maybe it becomes more than satirical news, and more than education through entertainment. Could it be an unprecedented tool of political philosophy? Indeed, what if *LWT* represents an entirely new satire paradigm: jokalism? That it does is what this chapter shall argue.

To do so, the next pages will first examine the links between satire, philosophy, and journalism, followed by the structure of *LWT* and what makes it so innovative: how *LWT* is not journalism, neither pure satire nor infotainment. Then the focus will turn to its serious role in the media while being a vehicle for comedy. Finally, while demonstrating how jokalism can simultaneously make an argument and call for action, special attention will be given to a series of topics covered by *LWT* in the past and their impacts.

Where Does Jokalism Come from and How Is It Related to Satire and Philosophy?

On March 23, 2015, *The Daily Show with Jon Stewart*'s team covered the Veteran Choice card debacle, which meant at the time that veterans were not able to choose the appropriate facility for treatment "so long as they are near a facility regardless if the kind of care the veteran needs is even offered by the facility" (Krause 2015). As Benjamin Krause (2015) explains:

> Two examples of this were covered on the Daily Show including my client Paul Walker. VA told Paul Walker he had stage four liver cancer. Paul lives over 40 miles away from the facility he needs to see for cancer treatment, but he lives only 20 miles from a VA dental clinic. A VA operator denied his request for care on national news.

The following day, on March 24, 2015, Veteran Affairs modified their program. Commenting about this sudden and important change, Jon Stewart credited his team's work on the subject on air, after a quick summarization of the previous night's coverage, and describing the segment and its aftermath as an interesting piece of "jokalism."

This unusual term was hard to find and to define solely with the help of academic literature, as it seemed that only newspapers and fellow comedians commenting on current affairs were using the term. One of them was the Australian "jokalist," comedian and television host Charlie Pickering, who described his show, *The Weekly with Charlie Pickering*, as jokalism – something which "blurs the line between sourcing and satirizing, reporting and opining on the news" (Kalina 2015a). This definition and understanding of the role of jokalism in the media ecosystem was not enough to fully weigh the importance of that concept in a world that was already brimming with satire.

Neologisms are not unusual in the comedy of *The Daily Show with Jon Stewart*, and one of its first offsprings, *The Colbert Report* (Holt 2013a). Both shows and their by-products, notably books, have offered their audiences a list of new terms. Among them was "precedented," which was defined by Colbert in his book *America (The Book)*. *The Daily Show with Jon Stewart* gave us "Jewy" and "catastrophuck." *The Colbert Report* even had an recurring segment dedicated to neologisms, called "The WORD," which gave us the terms "factinista," "megamerican," "Lincolnish," "superstantial," "wikiallity," and (most famously) "truthiness," which was Merriam-Webster's 2006 word of the year (Holt 2013a). As Holt mentions, this signature trait of both shows to create new words – a humorous strategy that has been around since antiquity – which are rarely accompanied by a clear definition. The reason for this is quite simple: If you explain the joke, then it is no longer funny. In this way, Stewart and Colbert's neologisms had to be easily and readily understood and "meaningful, *at first use*" (Holt 2013a, p. 304). Just as "catastrophuck" "combines the tragedy of a catastrophe with the "someone's-to-blame of a fuck-up" (Holt 2013a, p. 305), "jokalism" could primarily be understood as a combination of humor and journalism. Once again, this quick definition does not seem satisfying when looking at a new satire paradigm on television.

One could wonder: How can a concept that is barely defined and understood outside the horizon of *Comedy Central* weigh so heavily these days in the psyche of political comedians? What kind of weight are we talking about here? Well, we are looking at a television show that, for example, had the power to crash a governmental website after a call to action to followers in 2017 (*LWT*); we are talking about two television hosts that were attractive enough to gather over 215,000 people at the National Mall in Washington, D.C., in 2010 for their *Rally to Restore Sanity and/or Fear* (Jon Stewart and Stephen Colbert) (Reilly and Boler 2014); we are witnessing the parody of a glamorous and well-established event such as the White House Correspondents' Dinner being called "the hottest ticket in town" (*Not the White House Correspondents' Dinner – The Full Frontal with Samantha Bee*) (David Fox 2017) compared to the real event happening simultaneously across town. In other words, we are investigating the commendable influence of comedians-turned-journalist-and-political-commentators such as Jon Stewart, Stephen Colbert, John Oliver, and Samantha Bee. As this new title seems a little too long to write in an effort to express their use of both comedy and information research, "jokalism" seems to express exactly what they are doing.

The question of what precisely jokalism is does not stand alone in this grey zone shared by comedy, political commentary, and information. Beyond the quick explanation that, maybe, jokalism is just a new way to perform infotainment and satire, lies a crisis: If audiences are turning to comedians to be informed, what does that tell us about their trust in traditional news media and the journalists that feed them? In 2016, during a public discussion at the *Comedy Pro Conference* in Montreal, comedians Lewis Black and Gregg Proops, both political comedy habitués, were asking what their role was in contemporary media where fake news outlets are very loud and where the main information providers are getting more and more polarized due to economic and political variables:

It's really left up to us to do the work of telling facts. (Lewis Black – Just for Laughs 2016)

Honesty has been passed on to comics. People are looking for comedians to get the truth . . . and it was not our business at first! Do we have to be journalists now? (Gregg Proops – Just for Laughs 2016)

Yes, we have to do the research now. [. . .] John Oliver does better news than the news media. [. . .] Somebody has to give us the facts. CNN is not giving us the facts. (Lewis Black – Just for Laughs 2016)

Very quickly, a comedy observer will realize that political and social comedians have reached a new level of commitment to their art form. Traditionally, social and political comedy makes arguments on specific topics. To feed such arguments, a minimum of shared knowledge with the public is required. Contemporary comedians, however, seem to think that they can no longer rely only on popular knowledge to have an impact: They have to dig deeper and share this new knowledge with their audiences to, in turn, convince them about their view on the matter. As mentioned by Proops and Black, this process requires more time and energy than before, but the cause seems worthy of that investment.

When it comes to the creation and the duration of a television show, however, the investment is massive compared to the work of a stand-up comedian, which could be assisted by one or more comedy writers, if desired. In the case of *LWT*, the crew gathers ten recurrent writers, including John Oliver himself (HBO 2020), and can count on the support of many temporary collaborators and interns (IMDb 2020). In addition to the greater number of human resources, because of this new direction in finding information, these writers need to possess other skills that are not solely related to the world of comedy and satire. In fact, they require a certain expertise in research, journalism, and fact checking.

Satire, Philosophy, and Journalism: A Combo That Captures the Attention of the Public and Academia

An analysis of humor and comedy involves a fundamental look at philosophical works through the centuries, and this relationship started on the wrong foot. Until the eighteenth century, humor was considered as "a pervasive feature of human life" (Carroll 2014, p. 6), thanks in part to Plato who asserted that "amusement contains an element of malice" that humor could contribute "to a lack of rational self-control" and therefore should not be trusted (Carroll 2014, p. 6), an idea that religious authorities in the Western World agreed with and followed for centuries. Just like his mentor Plato, Aristotle did not see many positive elements in humor. He defined it as a form of abuse and warned the virtuous against buffoonery. On the one hand, he said that tragedy was, in his eyes, "an imitation of an action that is admirable, complete and possesses magnitude," and on the other hand, he said that comedy was ugly and disgraceful, and dealt with people that are "low" by nature (Stott 2005, p. 19). Nevertheless, Aristotle did at least agree that there is value to be found in the enjoyment of feeling superior to other people and that humor can offer a playful way to relax (Carroll 2014, p. 7).

That feeling of superiority represents one of the three most important theoretical pillars of humor studies. The works of many philosophers, from Plato to Morreall, including Kant, Descartes, Hobbes, Freud, and Bergson, just to name a few, can be regrouped into three major currents: the incongruity theory, the release theory, and the superiority theory. Before launching into explanations of these, however, it is essential to understand that contemporary researchers in humor studies mostly agree that no theory is better than the other, and that one cannot explain every humorous situation or phenomenon (Dufort 2016). Depending on the point of view, the cultural and personal background of the receiver, a joke can resonate more within a superiority frame or a tension-release frame.

The incongruity theory is based in the surprising effect: "People laugh at what surprises them, is unexpected, or is odd in a nonthreatening way" (Meyer 2000, p. 313). The theory emphasizes cognition as the receiver has to have the knowledge, to know the rules that are about to be broken, to identify the deviation (Meyer 2000).

The release theory can be applied when "people experience humor and laugh because they sense stress has been reduced in a certain way" (Meyer 2000, p. 312). It is often described as a pressure valve, a way to make difficult situations more manageable, to adapt to sometimes horrific experiences. There is a vast amount of scientific literature about humor used as a coping mechanism, and this belief has made its way to our common expressions such as "Laughter is the best medicine" (Nezlek and Derks 2001).

The superiority theory is probably the oldest one and the main focus of this chapter. As Meyer explains, "[t]he superiority theory notes that people laugh outwardly or inwardly at others because they feel some sort of triumph over them or feel superior in some way to them" (Meyer 2000, p. 314), which corresponds to Plato and Aristotle's point of view. Within this frame of thinking, humor can serve as a tool for social correctives: As people do not appreciate, in general, being singled out for abnormal behavior and being the target of others' laughter, humor has the power to reinforce or break the social order and social norms (Meyer 2000).

Satire is closely linked to the superiority theory as it exposes "moral, social, and intellectual failings" (Condren 2014, p. 662), and therefore, utilizes "humor in the service of some ethical end" (Condren 2014, p. 663). Nicholas Holm proposes to consider humor as an esthetic category. Satire needs to be understood as a symbolic act that emerges in response to a specific context: "the idea of satire as a form of critique is made possible by the political conditions of this moment" (2018, p. 648). It is a move from "a structure of feeling to one of fantasy of 'two opposing discourses that fight it out within the general unity of a shared code,'" which is humor (2018, p. 649). The humor in satire's critique can only operate "so far as it locates itself within–and draws attention to–the gap between ideal and actual forms of politics" (2018, p. 649).

Taking aim at the political system or society is nothing new. From Benjamin Franklin's letters and Johnahtn Swift's *A Modest Proposal* by Jonathan Swift (1729), to cartoons and newspapers strips (e.g., *Li'l Abner* 1934–1977) and stand-up and sketch comedy (e.g., Lenny Bruce, Lewis Black, Bill Maher, *Second City*, and *Saturday Night Live*) – indeed, all the way up until *The Daily Show, Last Week Tonight, Full Frontal*, and *The Onion*, just to name a few – satire has been around and has flourished. As Nicholas Holm mentions,

> this wide range of texts [...] maps out the key coordinates of an important cultural constellation that speaks to contemporary anxieties and desires regarding the political work of popular culture. This satirical constellation is held together [...] by an understanding of humor as a disruptive, critical force that unsettles convention and threatens politics as usual. (Holm 2018, p. 647)

The concept of satire news (Lance Holbert and Tchernev 2014) is nothing new either. As a familiar format in the mass media landscape, its popularity has only multiplied through the years with the successes of Comedy Central's flagships *The Daily Show with Jon Stewart* (1999–2015) and *The Colbert Report* (2005–2014). Before the arrival of these two pillars of comedy, American audiences were already familiar with a similar formula offered by *Saturday Night Live*: Its segment "Weekend Update" has received the title of the longest-running recurring sketch, being run since 1975, and acting as a springboard for the careers of its hosts (Day and Thompson 2012).

The idea of having comedians acting as news anchors, sitting behind a desk, dressed very formally – usually suit and tie for the men, blouse and jacket for the women – informing the public about an event illustrated in a square on the side of their face, can be found all around the world. The most recent of them form a large group which includes, but is not restricted to, *The Mash Report* in the United Kingdom, *The Beaverton* and *This Hour has 22 min* in Canada, *The Late O'Clock News* in Trinidad and Tobago, *Late Nite News with Loyiso Gola* in South Africa, *The Project* in New Zealand, and *Les Guignols de l'info* in France. Studies about satire news will often explore the relationship between satire and the fast-changing world of the media, the amount of truth that is expressed compared to their fake elements (often used to create laughter), their political impacts including a possible increase of cynicism, or how they champion democracy (Baumgartner and Morris 2008; Baym 2007; Baym and Shah 2011; Beavers 2011; Lance Holbert and Tchernev 2014).

Now, for all these shows (and the countless others not mentioned here), satire targets one or many elements that appeared in the news during the day or the week, building on the work of local, regional, national, or international journalists who previously gathered the stories and their details. Such shows usually start with an opening monologue summarizing a few stories with more time attributed to a star subject of relatively high importance. They can be followed by in-depth stories where fiction and reality collide and/or by collaborations with other comedians. For example, Jon Stewart relied on his "correspondents," notably John Oliver, most of whom became famous after their time on *The Daily Show* (Dickey 2014). Finally, toward the end of the show, some anchors may have a special guest on for an interview. For politicians, authors, and other public figures, being able to participate in some of these shows meant a lot (and it still means a lot for them to appear on shows like *The Daily Show with Trevor Noah*, and *The Late Show with Stephen Colbert*). An appearance can help increase the sales of books, voters' likeability, and/or the public's trust. (Colbert often called this "The Colbert Bump.") As Baumgartner and Morris (2008) mention in their study on *The Colbert Report*, humor can contribute to an attitude change. Notice, however, this might make one wonder how effective the critical aspect of satire really is in these shows given that, on the one hand, they criticize the political and economic structures of society but, on the other hand, play along with some of their leaders (Paré 2018).

Last Week Tonight with John Oliver Is Something Else!

When *LWT* emerged in the communication industries, it quickly distinguished itself from the average satire news shows. First, HBO broadcasts the 30-min show without advertisement interruptions, which gives *LWT* freedom on many levels: It allows the show to pick on companies without the fear of having them boycotting the broad-caster and stopping their business relationship with it, and it provides the possibility to aggressively and thoroughly look into a subject without having to cut for ad breaks and potentially lose the audience's interest in that subject (Krashinsky 2016). Consequently, some segments can last up to 20 min.

> You don't end up talking for nine minutes, and then have to stop so Doritos can tell you about their new flavour of abomination," [John Oliver] says. "Which seems like nothing, but it's actually a big deal. . . . You can't keep the stuff in your head unless it's one coherent, linear storyline. (Krashinsky 2016)

HBO, being a subscription channel, makes it possible for *LWT* to push the limits of the usual satire news show playground, but they don't stop there. They allow the general public to access some segments of the show on YouTube without additional fees. It could seem counterintuitive from many perspectives as well: Giving content for free is not something you would think could bring money back to the mothership. Nor does the posting of long videos (of 10 min or more) correspond to the average length and attention span of those who frequent the digital environment (Krashinsky 2016). HBO, however, begs to differ: The free samples on social media did translate into an increase in viewership (Krashinsky 2016).

Another fundamental aspect of *LWT*, which is related to the possibilities offered by longer segments, is the array of topics that it allows itself to cover. *LWT* will start each show by looking at the major events of the week, but it does not impose a monologue on one of them. The topic of the long segment can be anything John Oliver and his team deem fundamental to discuss. Topics are scrutinized using scientific research, digging for investigative journalism works and stories that did not seem glamorous enough for two-minute-long reports on national television. To make sure to cover all the subtleties related to their topic of choice, *LWT*, just like its cousin *Full Frontal with Samantha Bee*, has hired researchers with journalistic backgrounds on their writing team, which clearly distinguishes them from shows such as *Saturday Night Live* (Steinberg 2018). A rigorous fact-checking protocol is vital for the show as the team goes above and beyond to tell the truth first, and then make light of it somehow, using humor.

This process goes against the previous traditions of satire news where fake and real news were intertwined to create entertainment and laughter first, and to criticize after. This commitment to the truth could even provoke real investigations and experiments to obtain new information and data on a specific topic. For example, in 2015, for the purpose of exposing how televangelists can use the prosperity gospel to gain money from their believers, the *LWT* team created a fake religion and legally registered it with the American authorities to obtain tax privileges. They did this very publicly, announcing it during their show. They cancelled their church, *Our Lady of Perpetual Exemption*, a month later without having been summoned by the Internal Revenue Service (IRS). This kind of initiative led Julia R. Fox to qualify the work of the *LWT* team as satirical journalism, "offering a more balanced combination of satire and serious journalism" (Fox 2018, p. 30).

An even more distinctive feature of *LWT* in comparison to other satire news shows is its activism. Of course, satire expresses a point of view by pointing at what is wrong and should be corrected: Mocking something means adhering to another position that some might consider better in various ways. Comedy has always been a vehicle for new ideas and political standpoints, but rarely would comedians actually ask their public to do something other than laugh or keep in mind the serious message they are trying to send through their jokes. While it is more common in stand-up comedy (Quirk 2015), a call for action through a humorous channel breaks the traditional structure of entertainment when it comes to satire news on television.

For Bode and Becker, this characteristic of *LWT* is fundamental (2018). Even if John Oliver does not ask his audience every week for a particular action, when he does, the reactions reach significant results. To prove their point, Bode and Becker studied the first broadcast of *LWT* about net neutrality on June 1, 2014.

In the segment, Oliver stresses the importance of net neutrality for the average Internet user and the competing interests of Internet service providers, streaming services, and major technology companies. Throughout, Oliver entertains the viewer with satirical critique, references to popular culture, and off-color jokes. At the end of the clip, Oliver encourages viewers and Internet trolls in particular to go online to the Federal Communications Commission (FCC) site and comment on the net neutrality proposal before the close of the June 2014 public comment period. (Bode and Becker 2018, p. 1575)

The impact of that call to action remains a milestone for *LWT*: The response was so large that the FCC website crashed less than 24 h after the show aired (Bode and Becker 2018, p. 1575). This example sounds almost mythical, due to its size and impact in the media, as the story became the talk of the town. Nevertheless, *LWT* will recurrently solicit its audience to participate, in one way or another, sometimes by simply using a hashtag in social media for a cause promoted by the show.

In sum, *LWT* works differently than its satirical predecessors: being freed from the economical and creative restraints of ad breaks; doing investigative work and leveraging writers with training in journalism dedicated to fact-checking processes; exploring topics in depth and in length; and promoting calls to action to right certain wrongs. Is it enough to consider it as the embodiment of a new genre? To answer this question, a quick look at other concepts tackling similar objectives is in order.

LWT Is Not "Just" Infotainment nor Is It Edutainment

Many media-related concepts combine the objectives of informing or teaching audiences about specific topics, while trying to ignite social change (in perspectives and/or behaviors) and entertaining them at the same time. To reach these goals, humor can be used on many levels. Studies have shown that humor has a great potential to attract attention and retain information (Beard 2007, 2014; Morreall 2008; Romal 2008), to gain the trust and confidence of the public (Brewer and McKnight 2015; Nieva 2017), to create a positive image about the speakers and/or the cause to promote (Beard 2007, 2014), to make an impersonal issue something more relatable and personal (Becker and Bode 2018; Brewer and McKnight 2015), to relieve audiences of their anxieties and stresses about an issue (Morreall 2008), etc. All of this explains why humor is more than often an important part of infotainment and edutainment strategies.

The term infotainment came around during the 1980s as a "portmanteau word of 'information' and 'entertainment'" (Otto et al. 2017, p. 144), a genre mostly found in television programming "where the dualism of entertainment and information is dissolved, leading to a new hybrid media genre that represents a mix of formats" (Otto et al. 2017, p. 145). The literature counts a large number of formats, running from a main interest in political information to more human interest topics. By nature, infotainment is information-oriented but remains entertainment-based (Otto et al. 2017, p. 144), which explains why it is often "more sensational, more personality-centred, less time-bound, more practical and more incident-based than other news" (Prior 2003, p. 149). It is also more aligned with an episodic frame, which means that contrary to a thematic frame – where the focus will be on broader social and political issues and trends – an infotainment show will aim at individual cases and instances or specific events (Jebril et al. 2013). There is no need for in-depth coverage, investigation, or deep reflection about the long-term impacts of a political decision or phenomenon. According to these elements, because of its comprehensive coverage of specific themes that are mostly broad social or political issues, *LWT* cannot be understood as infotainment.

When looking at the definition of edutainment, one could be tempted to see many characteristics in common with the *LWT*'s commitment to convincing audiences to change their perspectives on specific issues and, by doing so, to change their behaviors as well. As Singhal and Everett explain:

> Entertainment-education (E-E) is the process of purposely designing and implementing a media message to both entertain and educate, in order to increase audience members' knowledge about an educational issue, create favorable attitudes, shift social norms, and change overt behavior. (2003, p. 5)

Edutainment requires a multidisciplinary approach combined with a strict agenda, with detailed objectives rooted in a formative approach, not a strong critical approach such as that of *LWT*. Even if *LWT* seems to be more multidisciplinary in its working process than its predecessors, it will not include other professionals such as psychologists, social workers, political strategists, or public health experts in its regular staff, a strategy that is found at the core of another pillar of American television, the edutainment show *Sesame Street*. To get their input, *LWT*'s team will do the research but will not include experts as part of the regular staff like an edutainment program would.

That said, it would be inaccurate to suggest that *LWT* has no pedagogical objectives at all. Indeed, examples of *LWT* trying to educate its viewers are numer-ous. Consider the 18th episode of season 7, which aired on July 19, 2020: Oliver clearly takes a pedagogical approach at the end of his piece on conspiracy theories. Now, he admits he is not the best messenger for trying to convince fans of conspiracy theories that they are on a wrong path; after all, he called them all "dipshits" within the first 20 s of the piece and pointed out that it is very difficult not to simply scream at them: "Why do you believe this nonsense, you Titanic fucking idiot!" Neverthe-less, he insists it is important to reach to them and even shares with the viewers the key to a more fruitful strategy for doing so:

> What the experts say, is that the most effective way to approach someone, is not by shaming them for believing something, or overwhelming them with counter-evidence, but to try and be empathetic, meet them where they are, and nudge them to think a bit more critically. (Oliver 2020, 25:52)

To contribute to this initiative, the *LWT*'s team asked different "truly beloved figures," such as Alex Trebek, John Cena, Paul Rudd, Billy Porter, and Catherine O'Hara, to record a message that tries to educate listeners about how to think critically, avoid conspiracy theories, and not share misinformation. They even dedicated a website to host the videos, thetruetruetruth.com that can be easily shared online. The pedagogical goals are clear (*Last Week Tonight with John Oliver* 2020).

LWT Is Not Traditional Journalism

Even if they can seem at odds, humor and journalism share a long relationship. In the broad world of journalism, humor can be found in different formats, most notably in editorials, columns, political cartoons, comments, and opinion pieces. Also, important literary figures started their career as journalists and used their humoristic talent to spice up their works. On that list, Benjamin Franklin, Mark Twain, and George Orwell are unforgettable figures (Keeble and Swick 2015; Schwartz 2014).

Despite these well-known personalities, examining humor in combination with journalism is still marginal in academia (Keeble and Swick 2015). In the introduction of their edited book *Pleasures of the Prose: Journalism and Humor*, Keeble and Swick cite Tony Harcup (2015), a prolific author on communication ethics:

> I suspect humor is largely ignored in academic literature on journalism because academics are either more interested in exploring the "fourth estate" role of journalism or because they feel that research into "serious" journalism will be taken more seriously (by peers and/or their bosses) than something that might be dismissed as froth. Possibly both. In contrast, the memoirs of journalists and ex-journalists are often full of humor. (Harcup 2015 in Keeble and Swick 2015, p. 1)

In general, we understand journalism as content, which could come in the form of an article, column, or report, which is "intended to be accurate, truthful, and verifiable" (Schwartz 2014, p. 422). This does not mean that humor has no place in this context, but it is rarely highly regarded as a commanding technique. As Schwartz explains, the Code of Ethics at Reuters, the news service provider, specifically mentions that journalists should "'eschew gossip about the private lives of public figures,' 'avoid sensationalism and hype,' and be 'wary of assumptions and bias'" (Schwartz 2014, p. 422), which is definitely not the case in satire news in general, since comedians have a strong tendency to incorporate these elements in their work. This is understandable because even if they expose a social or political critique, satire news comedians such as Jon Stewart and Stephen Colbert always put the entertainment value first, and the informative value second (Schwartz 2014).

Thus, just as Benjamin Franklin used humor to reach the masses and to be understood by the poorly literate population of the time, humor is still, up to this day, a vehicle for information that even the journalistic cultural institutions agree to recognize. In the particular case this chapter focuses on, a good example can be seen in the Peabody Awards. In 2014, *LWT* received its first Peabody Award in the wake of its story about net neutrality. The organization recognized that by "bringing satire and journalism even closer together," *LWT* can "show us the subtle mechanics at work in our nation's democracy and culture" (Peabody Awards 2014, online). The honor was renewed in 2017, and this time, the description mentioned that *LWT* produces "long-form journalism, breaking stories that others have overlooked with precision, clarity, and hilarity" (Blanchard 2018, online). In sum, *LWT* might not use the serious and neutral tone of a newspaper article or a televised story about public affairs, but it is committed to offering accurate, truthful, and verifiable contents to which it will add a critical stance, a process that is more often seen in the work of columnists.

From this perspective, it is essential to underline that John Oliver himself does not appreciate being labeled as a journalist, and when that happens, he reminds the media that such a title is "a slap in the face to the actual journalists whose work we rely on" (Oliver 2016, 1:42). He made this position clear on his show while commenting on journalism and the press on August 7, 2016 (Season 3, episode 20; IMDb n.d.). That said, while stating that his show builds on the hard work of journalists, he admitted that with the help of his research team, *LWT* added new elements to enrich the story (Oliver 2016, 2:32), therefore acknowledging that his show ventures into the world of journalism and does journalistic work.

Of course, this work will have an orientation, a direction given through *LWT*'s analysis of the facts, how it makes a diagnosis, and how it expresses in a specific situation – a diagnosis that will more than often include a way to fix the problem or a part of it. This way of reporting has inclined Allaina Kilby to move *LWT* to the category of advocacy journalism (Kilby 2018), a concept that is still very ambiguous (Fisher 2016). As Caroline Fisher explains, it might be tempting to quickly define advocacy journalism as a "support or argument in favour of a cause or policy through a work of journalism" (Fisher 2016, p. 712), but it would be wiser to consider advocacy journalism as a continuum of subtle ways of reporting on issues and people that are sometimes ignored more than others. It is not an overt display of intentional advocacy that resembles public relations (Fisher 2016, p. 712). A series of factors will help to position a story on the continuum, from macrofactors such as the political, economic, and social climates, to personal factors such as the beliefs and values of the reporter (Fisher 2016).

When looking at *LWT* in this context, advocacy journalism seems to build a bridge between the American tradition of objectivity in journalism since the First World War, and a new way to inform audiences in a media ecosystem where ideological perspectives have divided the offer into two poles: right-wing and left-wing (Fisher 2016). While Kilby puts *LWT* in the advocacy journalism category, because of all the elements explored in the previous pages, notably *LWT*'s use of satire for multiple benefits (attention, recall, and stress relief), its discussions about society and politics (argument, information, fact-checking, investigation, social change, and call to action), it might be worthy of a concept that would more precisely express all these elements and not just part of them.

The following Table 1 summarizes the essential elements of the concepts discussed earlier.

Table 1 Summary of key characteristics according to the different concepts explored with *LWT*

Characteristics	Infotainment	Edutainment	Satire news	Journalism	Columns	Advocacy journalism	Jokalism
Philosophy-related							
Social or political critique (argument)	X		X		X	X	X
Use of satire (Humor Superiority Theory)	X		X		X		X
Communication-related							
Information	X	X	X	X	X	X	X
Journalistic techniques				X		X	X
Expression of a point of view	X		X		X	X	X
Pedagogical approach		X					X
Activism-related							
Call to action or change		X			X	X	X

In this sense, jokalism could be defined as:

Media content that presents one or more rigorous stories about a problematic situation that needs to be fixed for the benefit of society as a whole, which is based on verified facts but is communicated through a humorous framework (using exaggeration, satire, parody, spoofing, etc.) to attract and keep the public's attention, and for better retention of the information. This humor does not modify the veracity of the stories, but is used to criticize the reported elements and to shed light on social and political issues that could otherwise have fallen off the radar of mainstream media or be misunderstood. The content will include previous data (offered by other media) and new information obtained through investigation by the writing team. It will use the data to build an argument and will provide a call to action to fix the problem on a small to large scale.

Why Should Jokalism Be Taken Seriously and Considered Philosophical?

Jokalism identifies a gap and names how problematic that gap is. It sheds light on why the gap is important to fix and offers a way to start fixing the gap. Society and the political system offer many specific gaps that need attention, but as a rule, the conceptual gap that jokalism tries to fix is first expressed as a strong critique directed not only at politicians, but also at mainstream media: a gap between what politicians should be doing and what they do in practice; a gap between what journalism should be and what the public is being served (Paré and Lafortune 2017; Paré 2018) at the moment by

> an industry in such freefall that it trusts only digital metrics and social-media soothsayers; the editorial stranglehold of extremely rich businessmen owners; and–oh, my–the dawning role of artificial intelligence in harvesting news and, possibly, reviewing television. (Crawley 2016: online)

In doing so, in sharing an argument with its audiences, *LWT* is engaging in philosophy. What argument exactly is *LWT* making? In every show, John Oliver presents his audiences with a new argument built on research, fact-checking, and humor. In all cases, the team pinpoints the problems related to a particular situation or individual which requires change and action. Through its seven seasons (to this date), John Oliver and his team have tackled several public debate topics, including: the death penalty (May 4, 2014), the global warming controversy (May 11, 2014), net neutrality (twice: June 1, 2014 and May 7, 2017), nuclear weapons (July 27, 2014), the lottery (November 9, 2014), tobacco (February 15, 2014), child labor in the fashion industry (April 26, 2015), paid parental leave (May 10, 2015), online harassment and revenge porn (June 21, 2015), transgender rights (June 28, 2015), sex education in the United States (August 9, 2015), mental health in the United States (October 4, 2015), abortion (February 21, 2016), scientific research and science journalism (May 8, 2016), coal mining in the United States (June 18, 2017), vaccine safety (June 25, 2017), the crisis in Venezuela (May 13, 2018), authoritarianism (November 18, 2018), psychics (February 24, 2019), robocalls (March 10, 2019), and sexism and racism in medicine (August 18, 2019). As a rule, the presented argument describes the gap between reality and the ideal situation. The value of the argument is to draw attention to that gap as it relates to many essential elements of a healthier society.

To illustrate the general structure of the argument, two episodes are used as examples in the following Table 2.

The table shows that at the core of *LWT*'s main story of the night is a long list of facts (illustrated by television archives, interviews, excerpts, journalistic work, and scientific data) that will explain why the situation is problematic, what has been done about it, what the main obstacles are for an ideal situation coming to fruition, and what could be done to fix it. As the story unfolds, the audiences get a clearer idea of *LWT*'s stance on the matter. Audiences receive an argument that, despite containing the show's point of view, tries to cover as many angles as possible, just as if someone was dialoguing with Oliver throughout the process. This is illustrated by the frequent use of expressions such as: "I know what some of you are thinking: 'But John, what if. . .'"; "What about the argument that. . ."; and "Some would argue that. . .". That does not make John Oliver a contemporary Plato, but the process is in some way conducive to critical thinking.

Table 2 Overview of the development of an argument during the presentation of an *LWT* main story

Topics and their context:	The death penalty: The week before the show aired, a botched execution took place in Oklahoma.	The Equal Rights Amendment: The previous week marked the 100th anniversary of Congress passing the 19th amendment giving the right to vote to women.
Dates of broadcast and length	May 4, 2014 – 2nd episode of the first season; 12:23.	June 9, 2019 – 13th episode of the season 6; 15:39.
What is the problem?	Should the death penalty be allowed in a civilized society? "In the application of the death penalty in this country, we have seen significant problems. I think we do have to as a society ask ourselves some difficult and profound questions" (excerpt from Barack Obama, 0:56).	"But tonight, I want to focus on a milestone for gender equality that we haven't actually achieved yet: the Equal Rights Amendment" (John Oliver, 1:21).
The philosophical questions about the problem	"Should [the death penalty] exist and what should its limits be? Can someone give me a broad almost infantile guideline of when they think it is appropriate?" (John Oliver, 2:29).	If the Equal Right Amendment has been under consideration since 1923, why is it not in the Constitution yet? Why does it take so long to pass it? What does it mean if it passes? How can it finally get done?
How is it a problem? Why does this topic matter?	Potential innocent people are being killed on a regular basis in the United States, and it is horrifying.	Women are still not guaranteed equal rights under the Constitution.
How does *LWT* keep its audiences listening to the story even if it is a difficult one?	• Self-derision – Oliver targets his own show. • Oliver promises to air a funny video about hamsters eating burritos at the end of the story if the audience stays around. • Play on words. • Exaggerations involving pop culture references and historical facts. • Comparisons. Example: death penalty to the McRib as "something that is natural to want but you should not necessarily have" (John Oliver, 5:14). • Collages with images to create a fictional situation.	• Mockery – targets: a reporter from 1972; the State of Florida; an Equal Rights Amendment advocate's use of words; Phyllis Schlafly's discourses; former Justice Antonin Scalia; and the states of Arizona, Oklahoma, Missouri, Mississippi, Alabama, and Virginia. • Analogies. • Comparisons. • Collages of images to create a fictional situation. • Exaggerations involving pop culture references and historical facts.

(continued)

Table 2 (continued)

	• Mockery – targets: a reporter's tone; a Texas governor moral position. • Imitation of a Texas governor. • It compares the cost per execution to the entire production cost of *The Lord of the Ring* movie trilogy.	
What does *LWT* tell the audience about the problem? What is the information shared by *LWT*?	• The death penalty is constitutional. • Execution is legal in 35 states. • With Iran, Iraq, Saudi Arabia, China, and the United States, together counting for 82% of world executions. • Most Western countries do not have capital punishment. • There have been 312 DNA exonerations since the beginning of forensic testing in the United States. • Proceedings of the National Academy of Sciences mention that 4% of death row inmates are innocent. • Even if the Court is sure that a person is guilty, "there is no credible evidence that the death penalty is a particular deterrent to violent crime" (Audrey Gaughran, Director of Global Issues, Amnesty International, 9:48). • To answer the argument that we should not house and feed a convicted killer: It costs ten times more to administer the death penalty than to keep that person in prison for life.	• It is one of those things so obvious that people think it is already there. 80% of the American people believe that the Equal Right Amendment is already in the Constitution. • In 1972, the Equal Rights Amendment received the approval of the Congress. • 37 states have ratified it over the years The Equal Rights Amendment was passed with a deadline of 1979 to get the 38 states needed. • It first seemed like a done deal as it was endorsed by both Democrats and Republicans. • The movement faced a halt due to the activism of Phyllis Schlafly, the founder of the group STOP ERA, which received a lot of media coverage at the time, spreading fears and lies about the amendment, such as: • It would outlaw sex-segregated bathrooms. • In case of divorce, each parent will get the same number of children. • The Equal Rights Amendment does not say that everything has to be exactly equal. It means the law cannot disadvantage an individual based on gender. • Phyllis Schlafly rallied the conservative movements with the argument that the amendment would expand access to abortion.

(continued)

Table 2 (continued)

		• The debate became so toxic that by the 1979 deadline, only 35 states had ratified it. • Congress expanded the deadline for 3 more years, but no state added its signature. • Even if there are laws against gender discrimination, they can be rolled back, while an amendment in the Constitution is more stable. • If some can interpret the 14th amendment, which guarantees individuals equal rights under the law as a protection for women, some other constitutional experts beg to differ. • The Equal Rights Amendment will not completely fix the equality problem between men and women in the United States, as it focuses only on discrimination made by the government and not by the private sector.
What would the ideal situation be?	The end of the death penalty in the United States.	"Equality for women should be a basic principle of our society" (John Oliver, 12:40). It is still possible to pass the Equal Right Amendment today even if the deadline was in 1982: • It was reintroduced through a bipartisan initiative earlier in 2019. • Two new states have ratified it in the last couple of years.

By the end of his special topic segments, John Oliver might simply invite people to reconsider their position if it is different than his, or he might openly call for action, either by the audience or, as in the case of the Equal Rights Amendment, by the States themselves. This call to action can be theatrical, as seen at the conclusion of the Equal Rights Amendment segment, or more subtle, like the end of the death penalty episode. The way *LWT* regulates the intensity of its final message is in-line with Fisher's position about advocacy journalism (2016) but would not be as effective and entertaining without the use of satire.

Conclusion

While past studies on satirical news were divided on the real impacts these shows could have on the population, some of *LWT*'s initiatives truly echoed outside the television studio. For audiences outside academia, a quick search on a web browser can lead to articles from *TIME, Vox, Fortune, The Wall Street Journal*, or *The New York Times* that will invoke the "John Oliver Effect" or how John Oliver's special topics on *LWT* can lead to major changes. Previously, this chapter evoked the segments on net neutrality, including the outcome from the first one leading to the crash of the FCC website, but this is far from being the only example. The June 7, 2015, segment was about bail, and how bail is often used unfavorably for poor defendants who cannot afford to pay it and will be faced with only two options: plead guilty to avoid waiting in jail or stay in jail until trial. The segment was followed about a month later by an announcement by New York Mayor Bill de Blasio that "the city would relax bail requirements for people charged with nonviolent crimes and misdemeanours" (Luckerson 2015, online).

Another example is linked to the special story on the *Miss America* pageant aired on September 21, 2014. Although *LWT* concluded that the beauty contest organization is the largest provider of scholarships for women, John Oliver invited the viewers to donate to other groups that he found more legitimate, such as the Society of Women Engineers. The result is well worthy of being mentioned here: "the engineering organization racked up $25,000 in donations in two days following the segment, or about 15% of its typical annual donations from individuals. The group credited the huge spike to the 'John Oliver bounce'" (Luckerson 2015, online).

The list of impacts in legislation, social movements, and the like could go on and on, but the "John Oliver Effect" is also perceptible in the way television now covers social and political issues. As Alissa Wilkinson, from Vox, noted, "*Last Week Tonight*'s long form segments are now echoed across the business" (Wilkinson 2019, online). From Seth Meyers' recurring segment, *A Closer Look* – which lasts about 10 min and unveils a news story in detail – on his late-night show, to the creation of new weekly shows with similar structures including a long segment dedicated to a special issue, such as *Patriot Act* on Netflix and *Full Frontal with Samantha Bee* on TBS (both former *Daily Show*'s correspondents, just like John Oliver), jokalism has emerged as a new trusted means to tackle, consider, and act about social and political gaps.

In this sense, if jokalism is more than advocacy journalism – if it is more than infotainment and something more than satirical news, if it embodies a new way to boost critical thinking with the help of a large dose of humor in its argumentative structure, if it does call for reconsideration and action about sensitive aspects of society, if it requires a considerable amount of human resources and financial support, and if it has the potential to change the way things are being done – it is seriously more than just a joke.

References

Arp, Robert, ed. 2007. *South Park and Philosophy: You Know, I learned something today*. Malden: Wiley-Blackwell.

Arp, Robert, and Kevin S. Decker. 2013. *The ultimate South Park and philosophy: Respect my philosophah!* Malden: Wiley-Blackwell.

Baumgartner, Jody C., and Jonathan Morris. 2008. One 'Nation' Under Stephen? The effects of *The Colbert Report* on American Youth. *Journal of Broadcasting & Electronic Media* 52 (4): 622–643.

Baym, Geoffrey. 2007. Crafting New Communicative Models in the Televisual Sphere: Political Interviews on *The Daily Show. The Communication Review* 10 (2): 93–115.

Baym, Geoffrey, and Chirag Shah. 2011. Circulating Struggle: The On-line Flow of Environmental Advocacy Clips from *The Daily Show* and *The Colbert Report. Information, Communication & Society* 14 (7): 1017–1038.

Beard, Fred K. 2007. *Humor in the advertising business: Theory, practice, and wit*. Lanham: Rowman & Littlefield.

———. 2014. Advertisement. In *Encyclopedia of humor studies*, ed. Salvatore Attardo, 4–10. Thousand Oaks: SAGE.

Beavers, Staci L. 2011. Getting political science in on the Joke: Using "The Daily Show" and other comedy to teach politics. *Political Science and Politics* 44 (2): 415–419.

Becker, Amy B., and Leticia Bode. 2018. Satire as a Source for Learning? The Differential Impact of News versus Satire Exposure on Net Neutrality Knowledge Gain. *Information, Communication & Society* 21 (4): 612–625.

Blanchard, Margaret. 2018. The Best Stories of 2017. Peabody Awards. http://www.peabodyawards.com/stories/story/2017-peabody-award-winners-77th-annual-peabody-30

Bode, Leticia, and May B. Becker. 2018. Go Fix It: Comedy as Agent of Political Activation. *Social Science Quarterly* 99 (5): 1572–1584.

Caroline Fisher, (2016) The advocacy continuum: Towards a theory of advocacy in journalism. *Journalism: Theory, Practice & Criticism* 17 (6):711–726

Carroll, Noël. 2014. *Humor: A Very short introduction*. New York: Oxford University Press.

Condren, Conal. 2014. Satire. In *Encyclopedia of Humor Studies*, ed. Salvatore Attardo, 662–664. Thousand Oaks: SAGE.

Crawley, Peter. The Get Down: Netflix's Latest Series that Cost $10m an Episode. Irish Times, August 12, 2016. https://www.irishtimes.com/culture/tv-radio-web/the-get-down-netflix-s-latest-series-that-cost-10m-an-episode-1.2753064?mode=print&ot=example.Aja%E2%80%A6

David Fox, Jesse. Samantha Bee Cements Her Place in Comedy History with not the white correspondents' Dinner. Vulture, TV Review, April 29, 2017. https://www.vulture.com/2017/04/samantha-bee-not-white-house-correspondents-dinner-review.html

Day, Amber, and Ethan Thompson. 2012. Live From New York, It's the Fake News! *Saturday Night Live* and the (Non)Politics of Parody. *Popular Communication* 10: 170–182.

Dickey, Jack. Oliver's Twist: HBO Bets on a *Daily Show* Alum to Make Bad News Funny. *TIME Magazine*, The Culture, April 28, 2014: 46–48.

Diehl, Nicholas. 2013. Satire, Analogy, and Moral Philosophy. *The Journal of Aesthetics and Art Criticism* 71 (4): 311–321.

Dufort, Julie. 2016. Le développement du champ des études sur l'humour en sciences sociales. In *Humour et politique: de la connivence à la désillusion*, ed. Julie Dufort and Lawrence Olivier, 1–35. Québec: Les Presses de l'Université Laval.

Fox, Julia R. 2018. Journalist or Jokester? An Analysis of *Last Week Tonight with John Oliver*. In *Political Humor in a Changing Media Landscape: A New Generation of Research*, ed. Jody C. Baumgartner and Amy B. Becker, 29–44. London: Lexington Books.

Gordon, Mordechai. 2012. Exploring the Relationship between Humor and Aesthetic Experience. *The Journal of Aesthetic Education* 46 (1 (Spring)): 110–121.

Hanley, Richard, ed. 2007. *South Park and Philosophy: Bigger, Longer, and More Penetrating*. Chicago: Open Court.

Harcup, Tony. Email correspondence between himself and Keeble and Swick (2015) (July 2015).

HBO. 2020. Cast & Crew. Last Week Tonight with John Oliver. https://www.hbo.com/last-week-tonight-with-john-oliver/cast-and-crew

Holm, Nicholas. 2018. The Political (Un)Consciousness of Contemporary American Satire. *Journal of American Studies* 52 (3): 642–651.

Holt, Jason, ed. 2007. *The Daily show and philosophy: Moments of ZEN in the Art of fakes news*. Chichester: Wiley.

Holt, Jason. "Neologization à la Stewart and Colbert." In The Ultimate Daily Show and Philosophy: More Moments of Zen, More Indecision Theory, Jason Holt, 298–308. Chichester: Wiley, 2013a.

Holt, Jason, ed. 2013b. *The Ultimate daily show and philosophy: More moments of Zen, more indecision theory*. Chichester: Wiley.

Hull, Margaret Betz. 2000. Postmodern Philosophy Meets Pop Cartoon: Michel Foucault and Matt Groening. *Journal of Popular Culture* 34 (2 (Fall)): 57–67.

IMDb. 2020. Full Cast & Crew. Last Week Tonight with John Oliver (2014-). https://www.imdb.com/title/tt3530232/fullcredits?ref_=tt_cl_sm#cast

———. n.d. Journalism. Last Week Tonight with John Oliver (2014-). https://www.imdb.com/title/tt5946952/?ref_=ttfc_fc_tt

Irwin, William, Mark T. Conard, and Aeon J. Skoble, eds. 2001. *The Simpsons and Philosophy: The D'oh! of Homer*. Chicago: Open Court.

Jebril, Nael, Erik Albaek, and Claes H. de Vreese. 2013. Infotainment, Cynicism and Democracy: The Effects of Privatization vs Personalization in the News. *European Journal of Communication* 28 (2): 105–121.

John C. Meyer, (2000) Humor as a Double-Edged Sword: Four Functions of Humor in Communication. *Communication Theory* 10 (3):310–331

Just for Laughs. *Comedy Pro Conference*. Montreal, July 2016.

Kalina, Paul. "The Project: Charlie Pickering Reveals Internal Fighting behind Exit." *The Sydney Morning Herald*, April 16, 2015a. https://www.smh.com.au/entertainment/tv-and-radio/the-project-charlie-pickering-reveals-internal-fighting-behind-exit-20150414-1mjrpa.html

———. "Satire Blurs the Line." The Sydney Morning Herald, News: 5, April 20, 2015b.

Keeble, Richard Lance and David Swick. 2015. "Introduction: Getting Seriously Funny over Journalism", *The Pleasure of the Prose* (Keeble, Richard Lance and David Swick, eds): Suffolk: Arima Publishing. 1–8.

Kilby, Allaina. 2018. Provoking the Citizen: Re-examining the Role of TV Satire in the Trump Era. *Journalism Studies* 19 (13): 1934–1944.

Krashinsky, Susan. "John Oliver Is Breaking Ads – and That's Just fine for HBO." The Globe and Mail, February 12, 2016. https://www.theglobeandmail.com/report-on-business/industry-news/marketing/john-oliver-is-breaking-ads-and-thats-just-fine-for-hbo/article28750517/

Krause, Benjamin. Jon Stewart Nails it On Veterans Choice Card. *Disabled Veterans.Org: Redeeming The Promise of A Square Deal*, March 2015. https://www.disabledveterans.org/2015/03/25/jon-stewart-nails-veterans-choice-card/

Lance Hobert, R., and John M. Tchernev. 2014. Satire News. In *Encyclopedia of Humor Studies*, ed. Salvatore Attardo, 664–665. Thousand Oaks: SAGE.

Last Week Tonight with John Oliver. *The True True Truth*. 2020. http://thetruetruetruth.com/

Luckerson, Victor. "How the 'John Oliver Effect' Is Having a Real-Life Impact." *TIME*, July 10, 2015. https://time.com/3674807/john-oliver-net-neutrality-civil-forfeiture-miss-america/

McClennen, Sophia A. 2011. *America According to Colbert: Satire as Public Pedagogy*. New York: Palgrave Macmillan.

Morreall, John. 2008. Applications of Humor: Health, the Workplace, and Education. In *The Primer of Humor Research*, ed. Victor Raskin, 449–478. Berlin/New York: Moutin de Gruyter.

Nezlek, John B., and Peter Derks. 2001. Use of Humor as a Coping Mechanism, Psychological Adjustment, and Social Interaction. *HUMOR: International Journal of Humor Research* 14 (4): 395–413.

Oliver, John. "Journalism." Last Week Tonight with John Oliver, 2016. Youtube, 19:22. https://www.youtube.com/watch?v=bq2_wSsDwkQ

———. Conspiracy Theories. Last Week Tonight with John Oliver. 2020.

Otto, Lukas, Isabelle Glogger, and Mark Boukes. 2017. The Softening of Journalistic Political Communication: A Comprehensive Framework Model of Sensationalism, Soft News, Infotainment, and Tabloidization. *Communication Theory* 27: 136–155.

Paré, Christelle. When Comedians Are Becoming Journalists: The Serious Concept of Jokalism. 76th Conference of the *American Society of Aesthetics*, October 10–13, 2018. Fairmont Royal York Hotel, Toronto.

Paré, Christelle, and Jean-Marie Lafortune. Let's Call It 'Jokalism': When Comedians Are Seen and Identify Themselves as the Last Hope for the Truth to Get Out There. 29th International Society for Humor Studies Conference, July 10–14, 2017. Université du Québec à Montréal, Montréal.

Paul R. Brewer, and Jessica McKnight, (2015) Climate as Comedy. *Science Communication* 37(5):635–657

Peabody Awards. Last Week Tonight with John Oliver (HBO). Peabody Awards, 2014. http://www.peabodyawards.com/award-profile/last-week-tonight-with-john-oliver

Prior, Markus. 2003. Any Good News in Soft News? The Impact of Soft News Preferences on Political Knowledge. *Political Communication* 20 (2): 149–171.

Quirk, Sophie. 2015. *Why Stand-up Matters: How Comedians Manipulate and Influence*. London/New Delhi/New York/Sydney: Bloomsbury.

Reilly, Ian, and Megan Boler. 2014. *The Rally to Restore Sanity*, Prepoliticization and the Future of Politics. *Communication, Culture & Critique* 7: 435–452.

Romal, Jane B. 2008. Use of Humor as a Pedagogical Tool for Accounting Education. *Academy of Educational Leadership Journal* 12 (1): 83–106.

Schwartz, Debra A. 2014. Journalism. In *Encyclopedia of Humor Studies*, ed. Salvatore Attardo, 422–425. Thousand Oaks: SAGE.

Singhal, Arvind, and Everett M. Rogers. 2003. The Status of entertainment-education worldwide. In *Entertainment-education and social change: History, research, and practice*, ed. Arvind Singhal, Michael J. Cody, Everett M. Rogers, and Miguel Sabido, 3–20. Mahwah: Lawrence Erlbaum Associates.

Steinberg, Brian. And Now This: John Oliver Just Might Be a Journalist. Variety, February 16, 2018. https://variety.com/2018/tv/news/john-oliver-journalist-hbo-last-week-tonight-1202702144/

Stott, Andrew. *Comedy*. New York and London: Routledge. 2005.

Swift, Jonathan. (1729) 2016. A Modest Proposal: For Preventing the Children of Poor Ireland, from Being a Burden on Their Parents or Country, and Making Them Beneficial to the Publick. The Floating Press.

Wilkinson, Alissa. 5 years in, HBO's Last Week Tonight is a lot more than 'Just Comedy'. Vox, February 17, 2019. https://www.vox.com/culture/2019/2/14/18213228/last-week-tonight-john-oliver-hbo-season-six

Wisnewski, Jeremy, ed. 2007. *Family Guy and Philosophy*. Malden: Wiley-Blackwell.

Links to the *Last Week Tonight with John Oliver* videos explored in Table 2

The Death Penalty: https://www.youtube.com/watch?v=Kye2oX-b39E

The Equal Rights Amendment: https://www.youtube.com/watch?v=bCBYJZ6QbUI

Russian Doll as Philosophy: Life Is Like a Box of Timelines

18

Richard Greene

Contents

Introduction	408
A Brief History of Season One of *Russian Doll*	409
The Groundhog Day Phenomenon	410
Metaphysical Questions Raised by the Groundhog Day Phenomenon	412
Supernatural Questions Raised by the Strange Metaphysics of *Russian Doll*	417
A Brief History of Season Two of *Russian Doll*	419
The Metaphysics of Time Travel in Russian Doll	421
Ethical Questions Raised by the Strange Metaphysics of *Russian Doll*	422
The Payoff: A Deeper Purpose After All	423
End Notes	424
References	424

Abstract

The first two seasons of *Russian Doll* ambitiously take on a number of topics in the Philosophy of Time. In particular, it addresses the metaphysics of time loops and time travel. The metaphysics of time are notoriously thorny and complicated, and *Russian Doll* provides a treatment of those issues that both does justice to their complexity as well as attempts to provide solutions to some of those issues (or at minimum, in some cases, hints at possible solutions). As is the case with most enduring philosophical topics, the discussion does not happen in a philosophical vacuum. Just as a discussion of the nature of knowledge naturally leads to a discussion of the nature of truth, and so forth, discussions in the metaphysics of time naturally lead to discussions of the ethics of time travel, the nature of the universe, the nature of the reality, God, relativism, the nature of paradoxes, consciousness, and, perhaps most importantly, existential questions about how one should live. This chapter will provide a general account of the way these

---

R. Greene (✉)
Weber State University, Ogden, UT, USA
e-mail: rgreene@weber.edu

© Springer Nature Switzerland AG 2024
D. K. Johnson et al. (eds.), *The Palgrave Handbook of Popular Culture as Philosophy*,
https://doi.org/10.1007/978-3-031-24685-2_54

philosophical issues are presented in *Russian Doll* with an eye toward (1) explicating the ways in which the various characters in *Russian Doll* conceive of the issues, (2) making it clear what their responses to the issues are (in those instances in which responses are provided), and (3) where appropriate, evaluating those responses for philosophical consistency, accuracy, and plausibility.

Keywords

Russian Doll · Time · Time travel · Time loop · Timeline · Wormhole · Paradox · Metaphysics · Idealism · Groundhog Day · Friedrich Nietzsche · Doctrine of Eternal Recurrence · God · Universe · Plato · Nadia Vulvokov · Alan Zaveri · Phil Connor · Bill Murray · Natasha Lyonne · Charlie Barnett · Presentism · Eternalism · The growing-block theory of time · George Berkeley · Derek Parfit · Obligations to future generations · Albert Camus · Myth of Sisyphus · Absurd hero · The grandfather paradox

Introduction

The first two seasons of *Russian Doll*, created by Natasha Lyonne, Leslye Headland, and Amy Poehler, ambitiously take on a number of topics in the Philosophy of Time. Season One has *Russian Doll's* two main characters – Nadia Vulvokov (played by Natasha Lyonne) and Alan Zaveri (played by Charlie Barnett) – caught in a time loop. In Season Two Nadia and Alan travel back in time via time portals (more on time loops and time portals below). The metaphysics of time are notoriously thorny and complicated, and *Russian Doll* provides a treatment of those issues that both do justice to their complexity as well as attempts to provide solutions to some of those issues (or at minimum, in some cases, hints at possible solutions). As is the case with most enduring philosophical topics, the discussion does not happen in a vacuum. Just as a discussion of the nature of knowledge naturally leads to discussions of the nature of truth, and belief, and just as a discussion of free will naturally leads to a discussion of the basic circumstances under which one might have ethical obligations, discussions in the metaphysics of time naturally lead to discussions of the ethics of time travel, the nature of the universe, the nature of the reality, God, relativism, the nature of paradoxes, consciousness, and, perhaps most importantly, existential questions about how one ought to live. Over the first two seasons of *Russian Doll* each of these topics (along with a great many others) is raised and pondered.

This chapter will provide a general account of the way these philosophical issues are presented in *Russian Doll* with an eye toward (1) explicating the ways in which the various characters in *Russian Doll* conceive of the issues, (2) making it clear what their responses to the issues are (in those instances in which responses are provided), and (3), where appropriate, evaluating those responses for philosophical consistency, accuracy, and plausibility. To be clear the point of this chapter will not be to merely tell whether *Russian Doll* is getting things right. Since in many cases we are dealing with metaphysics that generally don't and likely cannot occur – time loops to current knowledge have not occurred, nor has time travel at least as conceived by *Russian Doll* – the question of whether *Russian Doll* is metaphysically accurate is not all that interesting. Rather, the more interesting questions, for our purpose, are: (1) if one found oneself in the positions that Nadia and Alan find themselves in, should one respond as they do, and (2), if the universe were such that the main metaphysical premises of *Russian Doll* were true, would the implications of those premises be as *Russian Doll* seems to suggest? In other words (albeit in reverse order), is the world of *Russian Doll* a bona fide possible world, and, if so, do Nadia and Alan have the appropriate responses to it?

A Brief History of Season One of *Russian Doll*

Season One of *Russian Doll* begins on Nadia's 36th birthday at a party, which is being hosted by her best friend, Maxine (played by Greta Lee). Nadia is in the bathroom, which is cleverly decorated to look like a portal into another dimension (perhaps a bit of foreshadowing is going on). Nadia exits the bathroom, and mingles for a time at the well-attended party, which she soon leaves with a sleazy guy she just met, but is planning on hooking up with back at her place. Later in the evening she drops in a local convenience shop/deli to purchase some sundry items. While there she sees an extremely intoxicated man in distress, although she pays him little attention. After exiting the shop, she is killed by a taxi while crossing the street – only to reappear back in the bathroom at the party. The same music is playing (it is the immensely catchy "Gotta Get Up" by the great Harry Nilsson). Nadia seems more than a bit freaked out.

Over the course of the first few episodes, the scene plays out in pretty much the same fashion over and over, although Nadia doesn't always do and say the exact same things, and the manner in which she dies varies quite a bit (the writers, for example, cleverly manage to find several different ways for Nadia to die while falling down the stairs). Still, the end result is always the same: she is killed within a day or two and ends up back in the surreal bathroom on the night of her 36th birthday party with the Nilsson song playing in the background. Nadia is in a time loop, which she eventually comes to accept; her initial reaction, however, is that she must be experiencing a hallucination from a laced marijuana cigarette, from which she took a hit.

The details of the birthday party aren't always exactly the same, either. With each successive time loop, there are fewer guests at the party, the details of conversations vary a bit (they often become shells of their former iterations), and the décor changes. Eventually sound becomes altered, as if it is being compressed digitally. People that she interacts with outside of the party, such as her friend and de facto mother Ruth Brenner (played by Elizabeth Ashley), are also subject to similar changes as the guests at Nadia's birthday party. Oddly, the fruit in the store where Nadia shops just before dying for the first time appears increasingly rotten as Nadia's time loop resets.

On one occasion, while about to die in a crashing elevator, Nadia meets Alan. She notices that he is not concerned about the malfunctioning elevator. He calmly confides that he dies all the time. During the next time loop she tracks him down and they compare notes. Their time loops began at the same time. Alan's began when he committed suicide after being dumped by his long-time girlfriend Beatrice (played by Dascha Polanco), who had been cheating on him, coincidentally (or perhaps not so coincidentally, as the writers of *Russian Doll* aren't always explicit about just which events are intended to have some sort of cosmic significance), with the very slimeball Nadia hooked up with just before she died for the first time. It is also the case that Nadia and Alan always die at the exact same time.

Toward the end of Season One Nadia and Alan determine that their loops are connected in the following way: Alan was the extremely intoxicated and emotionally distressed man in the shop that Nadia saw just before getting killed for the first time. Had she not ignored him, she could have prevented him from committing suicide. Alan reasons that had he not been so intoxicated that night, he could have alerted Nadia about the taxi that ran her over. This revelation is the key to breaking out of the time loops. Nadia and Alan reset one last time, but in separate timelines, and notably back in the first time loop (i.e., everyone is back at the party, the fruit is not rotten, sound is not distorted, missing items have returned, etc.). Nadia in her timeline finds Alan from the first time loop (i.e., intoxicated at the shop Alan) and prevents his death, and Alan does the same for first-time-loop Nadia, who is in his timeline. Once they have survived their initial deaths in their respective timelines, their distinct timelines merge, as do their alternate timeline counterparts.

The Groundhog Day Phenomenon

When most people, at least nowadays, think about time loop stories, they think about the 1993 Harold Ramis film *Groundhog Day*. It undoubtedly has become the paradigm example of a time loop. Given people's familiarity with what we may term "The *Groundhog Day* Phenomenon," it will be useful to rehearse the salient details of *Groundhog Day's* premise, in order to provide a baseline for comparing and contrasting the salient details of Season One of *Russian Doll*. Indeed, it may sometimes feel like this chapter is just about *Groundhog Day*, but it will soon become apparent why spending a bit of time on Groundhog Day is of value. An immediate advantage of discussing *Groundhog Day* when initially considering time loops is since *Groundhog Day* doesn't commit itself to any particular view of time loops, it provides a nice basis for considering a variety of positions. *Russian Doll*, on the other hand, does commit itself to a particular view.

In *Groundhog Day*, Phil Connors (played by Bill Murray) is a narcissistic, misanthropic, and generally despondent local news weatherman (in Pittsburgh) who is sent to Punxsutawney to cover the annual Groundhog Day celebration. Traveling with Phil are his camera man, Larry (played by Chris Elliott), and his producer Rita (played by Andie MacDowell). On the morning of Groundhog Day they get their news story and prepare to head back to Pittsburgh, but to no avail as a

18 *Russian Doll* as Philosophy: Life Is Like a Box of Timelines   411

huge storm has moved in, trapping them in Punxsutawney until the following day. On what he takes to be the day after Groundhog Day, Phil wakes up to hear that the same radio program is playing with the exact same banter. Phil quickly realizes that he is somehow reliving Groundhog Day. No one else appears to be aware of this fact. The same thing happens each of the subsequent days, with the same events playing out. People are having all the same conversations (unless Phil redirects the conversations himself), and others in Punxsutawney all behave as they did on the original Groundhog Day. Phil is in a time loop. After several unsuccessful attempts to break the time loop by committing suicide, Phil eventually decides to simply better himself. He helps people in need, learns to play the piano and to ice sculpt, becomes better read, and eventually, in virtue of a number of good deeds, captures the heart of Rita, with whom he's been in love for some time. Once Rita falls for Phil, the time loop is broken. The film ends as they wake up together and it is the day after Groundhog Day.

The essential features of the Groundhog Day phenomenon are that (1) someone is caught in a time loop, such that they keep repeating certain events over some specific period of time, (2) the beginning of the time loop is fixed at some point in time, and the endpoint of the loop is fixed either by some point in time or the occurrence of some particular event. (3) There is a key to breaking out of the time loop, such as by solving some puzzle or mystery, and typically that key is the only way to break out of the time loop (i.e., one can't leave the time loop, for example, by killing themselves), and (4) the person in the time loop is the only one aware of it – others act as if they are experiencing each moment for the first time. A common exception to this fourth feature is that often people experiencing the time loop will manage to convince others who are not experiencing the time loop that it is occurring, but it is still not the case that the others are experiencing the time loop in the same manner as the person going through it experientially (file this under "some people seem willing to believe anything"). In some stories involving time loops, more than one person may be experiencing the time loop. This usually involves a smallish group of people who share some a common mission or one or more persons whose lives have intersected at some metaphysically significant moment. (The episode "Cause and Effect" from the series *Star Trek: The Next Generation* provides a good example of a time loop narrative involving multiple persons.)

The Groundhog Day phenomenon plays out in *Russian Doll* pretty much as described above, but there are some key differences. The beginning of Nadia's and Alan's time loops are fixed. They always reset on the evening of Nadia's 36th birthday, but the end points of their loops are not temporally fixed – their loops reset whenever one of them dies, which always happens within a few days. (It turns out that when one of them dies, the other does so as well.) In *Groundhog Day*, conversely, Phil's timeline resets at 6:00 am, just as his alarm is going off. (This point is somewhat controversial, as the film does not make it explicit. Given, however, that the audience sees people in the loop grieving after Phil has died, and Phil is awake on more than one occasion after midnight, the conclusion that the loop resets at 6:00 am seems warranted. Further evidence lies in the montage of the alarm clock repeatedly changing to 6:00 am, as if that's when something significant occurs.) In both *Russian*

Doll and *Groundhog Day* there is a key to breaking the loop. In *Russian Doll,* Nadia and Alan become aware of that fact and take active steps to solve the puzzle of their time loop (recall that they must revisit the moment where they could have saved one another but didn't), whereas in *Groundhog Day,* Phil is oblivious to that fact. He is not aware of the fact that bettering himself and finding a meaningful relationship with Rita will lead to his getting out of the loop; he is genuinely surprised when the loop is broken. Finally, in *Groundhog Day* Phil is the only one experiencing time via a loop. In *Russian Doll* Nadia and Alan are going through the loop together. One other key difference between *Russian Doll* and *Groundhog Day* is that with the latter, when the time loop resets, things are precisely as they were the previous time (except that Phil has different memories and attitudes), but in the case of the former, as we've seen, things are slightly different from the previous loops (e.g., fewer people at the party, fruit is rotting, etc.).

There is one more essential feature of stories involving time loops, although it is not one that the writers of the stories necessarily need be aware of. As was mentioned above the metaphysics of time can be quite tricky. At the root of any theory of time lies certain ontological commitments pertaining to the nature of time. Philosophers of time tend to embrace one of three models of the structure of time: presentism, eternalism, or the growing-block theory of time. According to presentism only the present exists. According to eternalism, all times exist – past times, present times, and future times. According the growing-block theory, the past and present exist, but the future does not. The past, on this view, is a growing block of times which exist, as more times become part of the past. The existence of time loops, for all intents and purposes, commits the stories that involve time loops to embracing eternalism. This is because such stories have the main characters repeating the past and have other characters moving into the future. It turns out that in time loop stories there are different characters existing some of which are in the past, some are in the present, and some in the future, at pretty much any particular time. A little later in this chapter consideration will be given to one possible way that the ontological commitment to eternalism might be avoided, but it will ultimately prove unsatisfactory, at least in the case of *Russian Doll.*

Metaphysical Questions Raised by the Groundhog Day Phenomenon

The Groundhog Day phenomenon raises a number of important metaphysical questions, none of which are all that easy to answer. Among the most compelling is the question: What sense is one to make of the people and objects one encounters in the time loops? Are they in fact real? Are they the same people and objects one encountered before entering the time loop? What happens to people not going through the time loop on subsequent days? If every person and every object were going through the time loops in the same fashion, then one could definitively conclude that other persons and objects were real and numerically identical (i.e., one and the same thing) to earlier versions of themselves, but given that only one person (or a small group of persons) is experiencing the time loop as a loop, it is not immediately obvious what to say about all other entities in the time loop.

This stands in need of a bit of unpacking. In *Groundhog Day,* on day one, Phil, Larry, and Rita, for example, perform a number of actions: they record their news segment, they have breakfast at the local diner, and they interact with some of the locals, such as the waitress at the diner, Needlenose Ned Ryerson (played by Stephen Tobolowsky), and the other people who are at the Bed and Breakfast at which Phil is staying. On day two (i.e., the second day of the loop), the same things happen, but since Phil is experiencing everything for a second time and others are not, one wonders whether they are in fact the same people that Phil interacted with on day one.

Assume for the moment that they are the same people that were depicted in day one. Presumably that's how we should want things to turn out, as one important payoff of the story is that Rita eventually falls for Phil. According to one estimate, Phil goes through the time loop 12,395 times (Gallagher 2022). If the people in subsequent loop days were not the same as the ones we saw in day one, then it would be Rita #12,395 that Phil ends up with and not the Rita #1 (i.e., the Rita of day one). If this were the case, it would not be Rita that ends up with Phil, but, rather, someone Rita-esque, which we call "Rita." Also, we couldn't say that Rita eventually ends up with Phil, as it would be a different Rita that winds up with Phil. The best we could say is someone like Rita ends up with Phil. Of course, that could be exactly what happens in the story, but it is not what viewers are rooting for, and we've been given no reason to root for that outcome.

Given that it is better for the narrative if it turns out to be the same people existing in the various loops, why not just stipulate that it is the case? The short answer is because doing so seems to lead to some serious metaphysical problems, and there is an underlying assumption that we generally want our stories to be sensical and coherent (unless they are David Lynch stories, and then we want the opposite). First, people and objects would seem to end up possessing contradictory properties – something that is logically impossible. For example, in *Russian Doll*, Ruth dies in a gas explosion in some loops, but in others she is warned in advance by Nadia. If she is always the same person from loop to loop, then it would seem that Ruth has the property of both dying in a gas explosion and not dying in a gas explosion. It is possible to generate these sorts of contradictions for nearly every person and object in *Russian Doll*. Similarly for the characters in *Groundhog Day*. Second, what about these people (and objects) moving forward? Which properties do they have the day after Groundhog Day? Seemingly they all have the properties that they have on day 12,395 (the last Groundhog Day in the loop), but what about those earlier iterations that underwent serious changes prior to that last day? Earlier versions of Rita, for example, came to despise Phil. It seems like we can't reconcile the Rita that emerges after the loop with those Rita's that pretty much hated Phil. At least some of them must not be real or else some of them simply didn't endure. Finally, since Phil didn't move forward through time with those persons in loops 1 through 12,394, it is difficult to make sense of their narratives going forward. For example, when Larry and Rita from day one head back to Pittsburgh the next day, and Phil is not with them (since he is stuck in a time loop and they are not), does he simply drop from their realities? Need their pasts be re-written? Do they merely wonder about him? It appears that there is no answer to these questions that don't require us to suppose even stranger metaphysics than simply comes with the notion of a time loop, strange as it may be.

Perhaps the way out of the quandary without supposing that everyone other than Phil is a different person each time through the loop (and by extension supposing that each object is a different object each time through the loop) is to postulate that they are the same people and objects, but that they just reset without the memory of having lived through the previous Groundhog Days. So, in a sense, the entire world just keeps getting reset to 6:00 am on February 2, 1993 (i.e., Groundhog Day), but the only one aware of it is Phil Connor. If this is correct, then those like Rita, Larry, and Needlenose Ned each have 12,395 Groundhog days, but reset such that during that time they don't age, and any changes they undergo on that day are undone (except for those changes that occur on day 12,395). The virtue of this account is that Phil does end up with THE Rita, and not just SOME Rita. On this solution, other desirable features of the story become plausible as well. For example, the fact that Phil eventually treats Needlenose Ned better than he does in his first few times through the loop is only possible if it is the same Ned in each trip through the loop. Similarly, the version of Phil that comes to be loved and accepted by the townsfolk is loved and accepted by the actual townsfolk that he conceived of as Podunk and useless in the earlier loops. This seems a more satisfying narrative than one in which different townsfolk come to love and accept him.

This solution, however, is not without its shortcomings. Notice that there is nothing necessary about Phil's becoming virtuous; it is a contingent fact that it happened. Therefore, there is nothing necessary about his breaking out of the time loop. So, on the hypothesis that everyone resets each time the time loop resets, but is oblivious to the fact of their doing so, if Phil never breaks the loop they are all deprived of the rest of their lives. Moreover, future generations who would have come into existence do not, as the universe is stuck in early February 1993. While this is not a metaphysical problem – no contradiction is entailed by this possibility – to the extent that *Groundhog Day* appears to be a story about what happens to one person, it is actually a story about a tragedy that almost afflicted the entire universe. This is a serious instance of burying the lede.

Given the problems with assuming that the persons throughout the loop are always the same persons as we encountered on day one, is there any sense to be made of the notion that they are not the same persons? A couple of strategies present themselves.

One version of this approach is to suppose that some version of idealism is the case (or, more precisely, that the writers of *Groundhog Day* set their story in a universe in which idealism is the case). Idealism is an ontological position about the nature of reality that supposes that there is no physical substance, rather the only things that exist are nonphysical things, such as minds, the ideas or images contained in minds, and whatever produces the ideas in minds, which usually is presented as God. This view comes in many forms but is most closely identified with the enlightenment era philosopher George Berkeley. Berkely postulates that what we take to be the external world is nothing more than perceptions (Berkeley 1982). If this is the case, then none of the things we experience are real (at least not in the way that we suppose they are); the things that make up reality, on this view, are more like the stuff of dreams or hallucinations – they exist only in minds and not external to minds (as they appear). So each perception that Phil has of Rita on day one is of a different Rita, and none of them are of the actual Rita; the actual Rita, on this view, is nothing more than a nonphysical mind (one that is having her own perceptions of Phil and Larry, etc.).

Here's how idealism helps with the quandary. If no one ever actually interacts with anyone else, and instead only experiences perceptions of other people and things, then the metaphysical problems described above largely disappear. It is not the case that people and objects have contradictory properties. One perception of Buster is of him choking to death on a piece of meat, and a different perception of Buster is of him being given the Heimlich and saved. Moreover, we don't have to account for all the different entities once they leave the loop (prior to Phil doing so). Rather, each entity Phil, Rita, Larry, and Ned are fed whatever perceptions that God wants them to have. Phil's are of Groundhog Day repeating 12,395 times, but the others get perceptions of one Groundhog Day 1993, followed by February 3, 1993, February 4, 1993, and so on. Their perceptions undoubtedly would include perceptions of Phil on those days, as well.

One thing worth noting about the idealist solution is that it avoids the commitment to eternalism, as described above. Presentism becomes plausible, as there is nothing implausible about supposing that the only thing that exists is the present and at the present moment one is having perceptions, which might also include perceptions about temporal properties. On this view, time loops need not involve revisiting certain times; instead, one is merely given (mostly) identical perceptions to those that one was given previously (e.g., in the present Phil gets Groundhog Day perceptions, and then 24 hours later he gets the similar perceptions, and so on).

While there is nothing to rule out the idealist solution, it is not all that happy, either. Again, the worry has to do with the nature of the narrative that is entailed by idealism. Viewers engaged in the story do not take themselves to be rooting for Phil to break out of the time loop so that he can have perceptions of being with Rita. This would be especially true if the writers made it explicit that all this were occurring in a universe in which idealism is true, and the actual Rita has different perceptions, which likely do not involve an amorous relation with Phil. Part of what makes idealism appealing to those who subscribe to it is the idea that an all-knowing and all-powerful God is working to sync our perceptions. If someone has a perception of saying goodbye to their wife as she boards a train, presumably God will also provide the wife with a corresponding perception of her husband standing on the platform waving goodbye (again, on the assumption that idealism is true). If this feature of idealism is removed, then one finds oneself right back where one began with all the problematic consequences of the earlier solutions (e.g., Phil isn't really with Rita, and so forth).

A second and more promising solution involves the notion of timelines. With this solution, the people in the Groundhog Day scenario are not exactly numerically identical to their counterparts on differing Groundhog Days, but they aren't exactly completely different either. To see how this is possible will require some unpacking. The idea is that as one moves through life certain events occur. The sequence of events over one's entire life is referred to as one's timeline (e.g., one is born, one does some stuff, and eventually one dies). Presumably people only have one timeline. Once time travel and time loops are introduced into the equation, then the possibility of multiple timelines emerges.

To illustrate, consider the following example. Suppose that some person goes to college, becomes a mathematician, and works for 35 years as an actuary. Further suppose that after retirement that person discovers a way to travel back to a time just prior to making the decision to become a mathematician and then influences their younger self to become a philosopher instead. Now the younger person is on a different timeline (i.e., one that involves working as a philosopher instead of as an engineer). On this view, this does not mean the first timeline didn't happen; rather, both occurred.

Let's apply this to *Groundhog Day*. On day one we have Phil, Rita, Larry, Needlenose Ned, etc. all doing the things they did on day one. At this point they are all on the same timelines they have always been on (i.e., each has just one timeline thus far). On day two, Phil resets. He is still on his same timeline, but one that involves his reliving February 2, 1993 (and each successive day of the time loop). He interacts with Rita and Larry. Were his interactions with them to be identical (from their perspectives) to his interactions on day one, there would be no reason to suppose that they would find themselves on different timelines. Once Phil's interactions change in the slightest, however, Rita and Larry going forward are on different timelines. The same is true for all the characters that Phil interacts with over the course of the 12,395 days.

As was pointed out when discussing previous solutions to the problem of what metaphysical sense to make of characters in a Groundhog Day scenario, if two objects or persons have different properties, then they cannot be numerically identical. So, if the Rita of day one has the property, for example, of being condescended to by Phil and the Rita of day two does not have that property, then they are different people. But in an important sense they are both Rita. It's as if we have a single Rita that on the morning of February 2, 1993, splits into several different Ritas (one for each of the 12,395 days that Phil is in the time loop), but none have a stronger claim than any of the others as being THE Rita. They are all different persons at that point but they are all THE Rita. (For a more through discussion see Parfit 1986 [especially Chapter 12].)

The virtue of this solution should now be obvious: it avoids all the metaphysical problems detailed above with considering the persons in the time loop as identical across the various iterations of the time loop (i.e., we don't have to countenance persons with contradictory properties), and simultaneously avoids the narrative defects that come from viewing them as distinct across the different iterations of the time loop (i.e., we get the payoff of Phil ending up with Rita, having changed his relationship with Needlenose Ned, and having been embraced by the same townsfolks that found him abrasive in the early days of the loops).

As was mentioned previously, while *Groundhog Day* is not explicit on what metaphysical sense to make of other persons in the time loop, *Russian Doll is*. *Russian Doll* is firmly committed to the multiple timelines solution. For example, in the final two episodes of Season Two *Russian Doll* actually brings characters from different timelines into the same timeline. We see multiple Ruths, multiple Maxines, multiple dead Nadias, and so forth. At one point it appears that *Russian Doll* wants to have it more than one way with respect to the status of non-time loop characters. In the finale of Season Two Nadia claims that the other characters in the scene were nonplayer characters, as if they had the same status as certain characters in a video game. Alan quickly dismisses this and Nadia seems to agree. Context makes it clear that Nadia is just sort of lashing out momentarily – being dismissive of those who should not be dismissed, to satisfy a selfish purpose.

A further implication of the timeline solution as presented in *Russian Doll* is that it rules out presentism. Once timelines are introduced, *Russian Doll* is committed to the existence of characters existing at points in time other than the present. Or, perhaps more to the point, what counts as the present for various characters may be altogether different times. For example, characters such as Maxine and Horse (played by Brenden Sexton III) whose new timelines are created during Nadia's second time through the time loop have as their present different times from that of their counterparts from Nadia's first time through the time loop. The present for these characters would be a day or two after Nadia's 36rd birthday. This follows from the fact that it makes sense to say that Nadia and Alan have been in the time loop for some specific amount of time. If they have been in the time loop for seven days, then their present may be day one or two of the loop, but for the first timelines of other characters the present will be seven days after Nadia's birthday. In fact, it doesn't make sense to even talk about the present as if it was some objective and nonrelative point in time in a universe in which time loops occur and there are different timelines. For narrative purposes it makes sense to speak of a present only with respect to one particular character's story arc, but a shift of focus to a different character would instantly yield a different present. What counts as present is relative. Hence eternalism must be the case (again, in a world in which multiple timelines occur).

Supernatural Questions Raised by the Strange Metaphysics of *Russian Doll*

An equally compelling question regarding the metaphysics of time loops is: Why is the time loop happening? This question can be broken down into two distinct questions: What is causing the time loop? And for what purpose is it being caused? Regarding the first question, unfortunately, time loop stories such as those found in *Russian Doll*, *Groundhog Day*, and *Happy Death Day* tend to not be very forthcoming with the metaphysical details – the fact there is a time loop occurring is often the entirety of the premise. In the case of *Russian Doll,* it is suggested that the universe possesses some sort of agency and has taken an interest in the well-being of

Nadia and Alan. Evidence for this lies in a number of quotes from Nadia. In Season One Nadia exclaims "The universe is trying to fuck with me and I refuse to engage." In Season Two, a wiser and somewhat more circumspect Nadia says "When the universe fucks with you, you let it." At another point in Season Two Nadia asserts "The universe finally found something worse than death." (This last quote refers to time travel, which will be discussed shortly.) Nadia, of course, is an atheist – so she wouldn't talk as if it is God causing the time loop – but it would be hasty to draw the conclusion that the agency found in the universe does not involve a deity or supreme being. The reason for this is that Nadia's takes on things in *Russian Doll* are not presented as always being correct. Occasionally, she is presented as getting things drastically wrong (we'll see this in spades in Season Two). The right thing to conclude is that Nadia is correct in supposing that something akin to supernatural agency is causing the strange temporal metaphysics – something is "fucking with" her and Alan – but the writers have not made it explicit precisely what is causing the temporal weirdness. In the other aforementioned time loop stories, we get even less information about what the source of the strange metaphysics is. Suffice it to say, it must be that something strange and unexpected is afoot, lest it be the case that pretty much everything we thought we knew about time has been dead wrong at every turn. Of course, strictly speaking, as a matter of logic, the time loop doesn't need a cause, but that constitutes a kind of metaphysical weirdness, bordering on the supernatural, as well.

Regarding the second question, the writers of time loop stories tend to be equally tight-lipped about why the premise is occurring, but the narrative of the time loop story usually provides the answer (or at least provides a partial answer). As was mentioned previously, there is typically some key to breaking out of the time loop, such as solving some puzzle or mystery. It seems reasonable to conclude that the supernatural entity (the universe or God or whatever) that causes the time loop does so for the purpose of creating the puzzle or mystery, and the deeper purpose for doing so can be found in the particular details of the puzzle or mystery. For example, as has been pointed out, in *Groundhog Day*, Phil needs to develop his character sufficiently (in the moral sense) in order to escape the time loop. (There has been quite a bit written on whether *Groundhog Day* somehow trades on Friedrich Nietzsche's Doctrine of Eternal Recurrence thought experiment, which basically has people ask themselves if they were to be made to live a single day over and over for infinity, is the day they are currently living the one that they would want to repeat eternally? If *Groundhog Day* is trading on this thesis, then one can understand the purpose of Phil's being placed in the time loop in a more specific way than is presented here – it's not just that Phil needs to develop his moral character, but rather he needs to develop it such that the way he lives satisfies the strictures of the Doctrine of Eternal Recurrence thought experiment.)[1] The reasonable inference to draw is that the time loop was created to give Phil the opportunity to develop his moral character, which he eventually does after 12,395 times through the loop. Recall that in Season One of *Russian Doll*, the key to Nadia and Alan breaking out of the time loop is their recognizing that they are in the time loop because they died at roughly the same time (possibly at the exact same time) and that each was in a position to prevent the death of the other, but did not take the opportunity

18 *Russian Doll* as Philosophy: Life Is Like a Box of Timelines 419

(i.e., Nadia saw Alan was heavily intoxicated and in some sort of emotional distress, but she ignored him, and Alan was too intoxicated to warn Nadia about the taxi cab that was about to run her over). So in *Russian Doll* the universe's deeper purpose in creating the time loop is to provide Nadia and Alan a second opportunity to do the right thing. Why the universe is giving them a second chance is unclear. Perhaps there exists a deeper purpose that is analogous to what the universe gives Phil in *Groundhog Day*, namely a chance to develop their characters (perhaps by having them become more likely to do the right thing once they've seen the consequences of not doing so), but it is not obvious that this is what the writers intended. For example, in the first episode of Season Two Nadia meets what she takes to be a stranger, and without flinching helps him burgle a house. If there is any moral growth between the events at the end of Season One and the beginning of Season Two, it is not apparent to the viewers. So in the end, even though one can reasonably deduce that the universe's purpose in creating the time loops was to give Nadia and Alan a second chance, it is not exactly clear why the universe wanted Nadia and Alan to have a second chance at all. As unsatisfying as it seems, that just appears to be part and parcel with time loop stories – perhaps some folks are just more fortunate than others.

A Brief History of Season Two of *Russian Doll*

The events of Season Two begin four years after the events of Season One. Once again, they take place on Nadia's birthday. Nadia hops on the Six train to head to Maxine's. As she exits the train, she realizes that she is in 1982 and that the train is a wormhole (i.e., a time portal) to the past. Upon arrival she finds a book of matches in her pocket with a note telling where she is supposed to meet someone named Chez (played by Sharlto Copley). Chez (full name: Cesare Carrera) is a slimy hipster doofus type who uses Nadia's keys to burgle a bag of Krugerrands (i.e., South African gold coins) from, unbeknownst to her at the time, the home of her grandmother (Vera Peschauer, played by Irén Bordán). Nadia eventually realizes that she is inhabiting the body of her mother, Lenora (played by Chloë Sevigny), who happens to be pregnant with Nadia at the time. It was mentioned in Season One that Lenora's stealing the coins was a pivotal point in the decline of her mental health, which led to her eventual death (it is implied that Lenora committed suicide), to Nadia's not having any money for her education, and to Nadia's having a generally lousy childhood and a pretty messed up adulthood.

Nadia, after a couple of trips back and forth between 2022 and 1982, is able to retrieve the coins (with the help of a younger Ruth [played by Annie Murphy]), but while she is looking out the window of the train, the coins seemingly disappear. Nadia is determined to retrieve the coins so she concocts a plan that involves her going back to an earlier point in time to obtain her family's valuables (think *Back to the Future Part II* here), so that she can swap them for something that Lenora cannot steal (such as cash placed into a bank account or perhaps bonds) instead of the Krugerrands Vera purchased previously. She learns from Vera that the valuables were at one point placed on a Gold Train (i.e., a train full of valuables stolen by the

Nazis during World War II). She heads to Budapest to locate a person she knew to have been involved with the Gold Train. Nadia then boards a train in Budapest, which turns out to be a wormhole to 1944. She is now inhabiting the body of a much younger Vera. A noteworthy feature of time travel in *Russian Doll* is when one inhabits the body of another, they take on certain of that person's attributes. This constitutes an impediment, albeit not an insurmountable one, to Nadia's plan early on, as Lenora's schizophrenia adversely affects Nadia's ability to make her way to Budapest, but it constitutes a virtue later in the story, as Nadia's taking on Vera's ability to speak Hungarian proves helpful for her tracking down the valuables. After she locates the family treasures, she hides them in a tunnel. She then travels back to 1968 (still as Vera), breaks into the tunnel, and obtains the goods, which she takes to a gold dealer who pays her in the same Krugerrands she was trying to avoid obtaining. Nadia's attempt to change the past has failed.

Alan during this time has also been time traveling on the Six train. He's been traveling to East Berlin in 1962, and inhabiting the body of his grandmother, Agnes (played by Carolyn Michelle Smith). Agnes, who is a graduate student at the time, has been involved helping a group of friends tunnel under the Berlin Wall to escape the Soviet Union. Alan had become amorously involved with one of the group members, and his attempts to inform him that the Berlin Wall would eventually come down and to stop them from attempting to escape also failed. Nadia and Alan both came to realize that it is not possible to change the past (at least not with respect to significant or pivotal events in people's lives).

This is where things get really weird. Nadia, now resigned to not further attempting to change the past, begins to head back to 2022. This plan is thwarted by the fact that Lenora's water has broken on the subway platform (in 1982). Effectively, Nadia (while inhabiting Lenora's body) gives birth to herself. (Hence the most literal application of the show's title to the shows events.) Nadia now has a new plan: take the baby version of herself to 2022 and raise it herself. Both Nadias ("mother" and child) arrive in 2022 and time completely breaks down. There are multiple versions of all the main characters from different timelines, Nadia and Alan are moving from 2018 to 2022 indiscriminately, Nadia and Alan are seeing versions of themselves from the various time loops of Season One, and Nadia is seeing scenes from her childhood. Alan argues that they need to fix time, which means that Nadia has to return the baby to 1982. Nadia initially resists, but eventually agrees.

While they attempt to return the childhood, Nadia and Alan are hit by a train and enter separate voids which exist outside of time (as is evidenced by the fact that their watches have stopped functioning). In Alan's void he talks with his grandmother about accepting the world, even though it is imperfect. In Nadia's void she is asked by Lenore if she would be willing to accept her family over again, if given the choice. Nadia assents and hands the baby to Lenora, essentially embracing the version of her life that has already played out.

In the final scene of Season Two, Nadia and Alan are back in 2022. It is one month after Nadia's birthday, and they are at Ruth's wake, which is at Maxine's. Time is no longer broken. Both seem content. Nadia heads into the bathroom with the weird portal, looks in the mirror, and smiles.

The Metaphysics of Time Travel in Russian Doll

As was the case with time loops in Season One of *Russian Doll*, time travel raises a number of tough metaphysical questions. There are famous paradoxes of time travel, such as the grandfather paradox. Going back in time and killing one's grandfather (prior to one's grandfather's actually fathering any children) seems possible if time travel is possible, until one realizes that doing so paradoxically makes it the case that one never comes into existence, and consequently cannot perform the killing. Variations on this theme involve going back in time and killing a very young Adolph Hitler or some other significant figure from history, thus changing the course of history, but in doing so making it the case that one was never born, and hence one could not have traveled back in time to perform the killing in the first place. There are also questions about whether it is possible for a time traveler to fundamentally change the past. Questions of these types are not unrelated. If one cannot fundamentally change the past, then of course one cannot go back in time and kill one's grandfather. On the other hand, one might be able to change the past, but with limits in place. One such limit might be on performing actions that lead to a paradox. So it may be possible to travel back in time to change some events, but not possible to travel back in time to kill one's grandfather (or a very young Adolph Hitler).[2]

Regarding the question of whether eternalism, presentism, or growing-block theory is true, the mere existence of time travel is sufficient to rule out presentism. So in this respect, Season Two is metaphysically consistent with Season One, but is it consistent with respect to the other questions?

As we've seen, in the universe of *Russian Doll* time travel is possible, and it is possible to change certain insignificant events (for example, different conversations can occur, etc.), but it is not possible to change significant events; despite their best efforts; Alan could not stop his grandmother's friends from attempting to escape East Berlin, and Nadia could not prevent her mother from stealing her grandmother's Krugerrands. We are not given an explanation as to why this is the case, rather it's just an empirical fact about the *Russian Doll* universe discovered by Nadia and Alan. Still, one might wonder whether the universe of *Russian Doll* is consistent on this matter. Recall that the way to explain the metaphysical status of other persons that Nadia and Alan encounter in time loops was to invoke the notion of a timeline. Specifically, any change, no matter how minimal, in a particular time loop led to a new timeline for all involved in that loop, hence it was possible to have multiple Maxines and multiple Ruths, etc., and each was distinct from one another, real, and related to (in the sense of deriving from) their pre-first-time loop counterparts. Timelines typically constitute a good way to resolve paradoxes of time travel. One goes back in time, kills their grandparent, creating a new (albeit very short!) timeline for the grandparent – one in which they don't have any children. So in that timeline, one's counterpart never comes into existence, but since one is distinct from their alternative timeline counterparts, no actual paradox exists. Given that timelines constitute a way to avoid time travel paradoxes, and allow for significant change with respect to time travel, one would expect significant change to be possible in the universe of *Russian Doll*. However, it is not. Does this mean that *Russian Doll* is inconsistent on this matter? Not exactly. Perhaps it is one of the other unspecified features of a universe that exhibits agency that makes it such that the significant changing of past events is not possible. Again, the writers are simply not explicit on this point.

Interestingly, *Russian Doll* does appear to meet our expectations regarding other paradoxes. When Nadia brings the baby version of herself into the present and into her timeline, the paradoxical nature of two Nadias from different times existing at the same time in a single timeline caused a rupture in the fabric of time. It caused multiple timelines to converge in a single timeline. As Alan said to Nadia, "You broke time." This is at least one of the typical outcomes one might expect were timelines to converge in this way (again, think *Back to the Future* here).

There exists a certain bit of irony in the fact that one of the payoffs of Season Two is that one cannot change significant events that have already occurred, but what the universe is doing in Season One is giving Nadia and Alan an opportunity to go back and change significant events, namely not dying on the night of Nadia's 36th birthday. Again, this may appear to be an inconsistency in the way time gets treated between Season One and Season two, but there is way out of the inconsistency. If we understand the universe of *Russian Doll* as being permissive of changes to past events in one's own life, but not of changes to past events in the lives of others, then both seasons are operating in a fashion that is consistent with this principle. Nadia and Alan were invited by the universe to change their own past events, but not the events of their parents and/or grandparents.

Finally, a couple of other bits of Season Two metaphysical weirdness warrant mention. (1) When Nadia or Alan travel through the portal on the Six train they do not do so in their own bodies, rather they inhabit the bodies of relatives existing at that time. (2) Not only do they inhabit the bodies of others when they time travel, they also take on features of the psychology of the persons they are inhabiting. For example, when Nadia inhabits Lenora's body she experiences Lenora's schizophrenia, and when she inhabits Vera's body, she can speak Hungarian. Similarly, Alan experiences his grandmother's attraction to one of her fellow graduate students. The lines between the consciousness of the person doing the inhabiting and the person being inhabited begins to blur, but only while the time traveling is occurring. These phenomena are not explained. We are not told why time travel is this way; it's just part of the premise of the show. Chalk it up to the mysterious universe of *Russian Doll*.

Ethical Questions Raised by the Strange Metaphysics of *Russian Doll*

The metaphysical possibility of time travel raises some interesting ethical considerations, as well. Perhaps most noteworthy is the question: Is it permissible to alter the past? Alan argues that it is morally impermissible to do so. His arguments are not all that detailed, and mostly boil down to the fact that things always go badly in time travel movies ("every time travel movie teaches us not to alter the past"). Nadia, on the other hand, argues that there is no good reason to go into the past, if not to change it.

So who is right? It turns out in the *Russian Doll* universe, neither Alan nor Nadia is right. There is an oft cited principle in ethics that is nearly universally accepted called "ought implies can." The idea is that one can't tell someone that they ought to do something unless they, in fact, can do that thing. Ruth, for example, can't tell Nadia that she ought to fly, unless it is at least possible for Nadia to fly. Since it turns out to be impossible to change the past in significant way in the *Russian Doll* universe, any claim about the permissibility of altering the past turns out to be false. When Nadia says that one ought to alter the past when time traveling, she is asserting something false, and when Alan says that one ought not alter the past he is also saying something false – the ought part of his claim is inapplicable, even though the universe makes it so the past doesn't get altered.

The Payoff: A Deeper Purpose After All

Recall that the payoff of Season One had to do with solving a puzzle. In particular, Nadia and Alan had to figure out why they were caught in a time loop and then figure out what it would take to break the time loop. In the early parts of Season Two it appeared that something similar was occurring. It seemed that Nadia had to figure out how to change the past (i.e., how to prevent her mother from ultimately stealing her grandmother's Krugerrands), and then act on that plan. Eventually it was revealed that the universe would not allow that to occur. This raises the questions: What was the point of Season Two? Why was time travel even possible? Is it possible that there was no deeper purpose for the time travel in Season Two?

To properly answer these questions, it will be useful to have a little understanding of the philosophy of the existentialist philosopher Albert Camus. Camus wrote about a story from Greek mythology called "The Myth of Sisyphus." Sisyphus, according to legend, on two occasions tried to cheat death. This, of course, angered the Gods (Zeus, in particular), such that they sentenced him to an eternity of pushing a large boulder up a very steep hill. Once the boulder reached the top of the hill it would roll back down to the bottom, and Sisyphus's task would begin anew.

Camus' take on the Myth of Sisyphus is that Sisyphus' punishment is in many ways akin to the lives of human beings. Our lives are tedious, mundane, repetitive, and, more to the point, lacking in meaning in any objective sense. Camus considers our lives to be absurd. For Camus, this absurdity inevitably leads to the question of suicide. Do one have any reason to go on living under such circumstances? His response is that one does if one becomes what he calls an "absurd hero." Camus supposes Sisyphus an absurd hero that makes his task – pushing the boulder up the hill for eternity – his own. For Camus, this means that Sisyphus manages to make his existence worth living, despite the fact that it is tedious, pointless, and mundane, by embracing his lot. As Camus says "One must imagine Sisyphus happy" (Camus 1969, p. 119).

In Season Two, Nadia's efforts to change the past, her mother's fate, and her own lot in life turn out to be in vain. While her existence is not portrayed as tedious and mundane in the way that Sisyphus' existence is, it is still the case that she is dealt a life that she did not choose, and it is not one that she desires. When her efforts to improve her circumstances turn out to be in vain, she is confronted with the same question that Camus supposes we all are confronted with: the question of suicide.

Recall that in the final episode of Season Two, Nadia finds herself in a void outside time. When she is asked by Lenora whether she would accept her family, if given the choice, Nadia responds that she would. In that moment, she has become an absurd hero in precisely the sense that Camus has in mind. She has chosen to embrace her lot in life, by owning it – by making it her own. It is significant that Season Two ends with Nadia looking in the mirror and smiling. We don't have to imagine Nadia happy, the writers of *Russian Doll* have shown that to us. She is happy.

So, in the end, the "puzzle" of Season Two was not a puzzle at all, rather it was a lesson to be learned: What we make of our circumstances is entirely up to us.

End Notes

1. A discussion of why this thesis is controversial can be found here: https://www. adventuresinfilmtheory.org/adventures-in-film-theory/2018/10/19/groundhogs-day-is-not-a-depiction-of-nietzsches-eternal-recurrence. Kimberly Blessing's excellent chapter in this handbook, ▶ Chap. 37, "*Groundhog Day* as Philosophy: Phil Connors Says "No" to Eternal Return," provides a pretty definitive response to the controversy.
2. For a more detailed explanation of the metaphysics of time travel, see Kevin Decker's ▶ Chap. 7, "*Doctor Who* as Philosophy: Four-Dimensionalism and Time Travel," in this handbook.

References

Berkeley, George. 1982. *A treatise concerning the principles of human knowledge.* Indianapolis: Hackett Publishing Company.

Camus, Albert. 1969. *The myth of Sisyphus and other essays.* Trans. Justin O'Brien. New York: Alfred A. Knopf.

Gallagher, Simon. 2022. Just how many days does Bill Murray REALLY spend reliving Groundhog Day? *WhatCulture.com.* https://whatculture.com/film/just-how-many-days-does-bill-murray-really-spend-stuck-reliving-groundhog-day

Parfit, Derek. 1986. *Reasons and persons.* Oxford: Oxford University Press.

The Orville as Philosophy: The Dangers of Religion

19

Darren M. Slade and David Kyle Johnson

Contents

Introduction 426
Summarizing the Orville 427
Identifying and Critiquing the Argument of the Orville 430
Religion and Morality 439
Theocracy vs. Democracy 442
Conclusion 445
References 446

Abstract

Seth MacFarlane's space adventure, *The Orville,* is not "Family Guy in Space." It is a social commentary of the most direct and compelling sort. Through satire, humor, and symbolism, *The Orville* explores the potential dangers of religion. It does so in individual episodes, such as "If the Stars Should Appear" and "Mad Idolatry," as well as through the series as a whole in its depiction of how the Union resolves its political differences with the Krill and the Moclans. In this chapter, we will look at how *The Orville* criticizes religion, both generally and specifically. We will see that while it is not a condemnation of all religious believers, it is a critique of religion itself, suggesting that it can become dangerous when it merges religious dogma with political power.

D. M. Slade (✉)
Global Center for Religious Research (GCRR), Denver, CO, USA
e-mail: dslade@gcrr.org

D. K. Johnson
Department of Philosophy, King's College, Wilkes-Barre, PA, USA
e-mail: Davidjohnson@kings.edu

© Springer Nature Switzerland AG 2024
D. K. Johnson et al. (eds.), *The Palgrave Handbook of Popular Culture as Philosophy*,
https://doi.org/10.1007/978-3-031-24685-2_61

425

Keywords

Islam · The Orville · Avis · Biblical criticism · Clash of civilizations · Cosmic war · Evangelicalism · Christian nationalism · Fundamentalism · Jihad · Philosophy of religion · Religious radicalization · Religious right · Religious violence · Separation of church and state · Seth Macfarlane · Star Trek · Terrorism · Theocracy · Warrior god · Xenophobia

Introduction

> This is like *Spaceballs*! It's going to be a funny parody of *Star Trek*.
> —David Kyle Johnson (May 2017)

That's what a lot of people thought Seth MacFarlane's new space adventure, *The Orville*, would be: a *Star Trek* satire. And given MacFarlane's propensity for comedy (*Family Guy, American Dad, Ted*) and the fact that *The Orville*'s first trailer had a plethora of jokes—"Boom bitch!"— and was set to Deep Purple's "Space Truckin'," it was not an unreasonable conclusion. But, as the show's creators objected at the time, the trailer did not accurately represent the series. MacFarlane even specifically said it was not *"Family Guy* in space" (Inside Edition 2017). Indeed, what viewers ultimately received was more like M*A*S*H: a show that is ostensibly a comedy but also presents biting sociopolitical commentary and philosophical argumentation.

What potential viewers had forgotten is that in 2014, Seth MacFarlane spearheaded things like the revival of Carl Sagan's series, *Cosmos* (his version was hosted by Neil DeGrasse Tyson), which decries superstition and supernaturalism while championing science as the greatest human accomplishment. They also forgot that in 2011, because of "his active, passionate commitment to humanist values, and his fearless support of equal marriage rights and other social justice issues," MacFarlane had been awarded "humanist of the year" by Harvard University (Johnson 2011).

Thus, it should have come as no surprise that so many timely sociopolitical problems cropped up in the series. In the third episode of *The Orville* ("About a Girl"), a clear commentary regarding LGTBQ+ issues, a female child is born to an all-male species (the Moclans), and a court trial ensues to determine whether the child will undergo "gender correction" surgery (see Nolan 2021). In the fourth episode ("If the Stars Should Appear"), a commentary on climate change, the crew encounters a "bio-ship" whose inhabitants refuse to admit they are about to be destroyed because it will disrupt their way of life (see Johnson 2021). The episode "Majority Rule" takes on social media, mob mentality, and democracy itself, and "All the World Is Birthday Cake" confronts pseudoscience (astrology in particular). In a similar way, the episodes "Krill" and "Mad Idolatry" tackle religion (see Slade 2021c, which inspired this chapter). In the latter episode, First Officer Kelly Grayson is mistaken for, and becomes worshiped as, a deity by the planet's primitive society. She and the crew do everything possible to undo the damage—not only because of a

19 *The Orville* as Philosophy: The Dangers of Religion

Star Trek-esque "non-interference" policy but also because the crew thinks that blind and uncritical devotion to religion is about the worst thing that could ever happen to a society.

It is this latter issue, regarding the dangers of religion, on which this chapter will focus. After summarizing the series, we will identify the overall argument of the show, which suggests that religion can be dangerous under certain circumstances, and then analyze that argument. After concluding that the show's general point is correct (religion can indeed be dangerous), we will look at the show's specific criticisms of religion, such as how divine command theory can be used to justify atrocities and how mixing religion with political power results in violence. In the end, we will see that while *The Orville* is not criticizing all religious believers, it does raise valid concerns about the dangerous tendencies within all religious belief systems.

Summarizing the Orville

[T]he more I learn about the Moclans, the more I see that our differences go right to the core of our values. [I agree . . . the Union needs them.] But how long can an alliance with a culture like that last?
—Capt. Ed Mercer ("Deflectors")

Although it premiered on the Fox network in 2017, *The Orville* moved to Hulu after its first two seasons and was then hosted by Disney+. The show is set in the twenty-fifth century and follows the crew of the Planetary Union interstellar spacecraft, the *USS Orville*. The Union is an alliance between Earth and several other worlds, which explores the galaxy and seek out other species; their goal is to grow the Union in an effort to keep peace in the galaxy and attain knowledge of the universe. Although the creator, Seth MacFarlane, plays the lead protagonist—Capt. Ed Mercer—it is more of an ensemble show with different characters receiving the spotlight in different episodes.

In fact, like the *Star Trek* franchise (especially the original series from the 1960s and *The Next Generation* from the 1990s), *The Orville* is episodic—each episode depicts a self-contained story. The series does have an overarching story arc, however, dealing mainly with the intercultural politics of the Union and its member species. Indeed, before analyzing the show's argument about religion, it is first necessary to focus on how the Union's relationship with different species changes over the first three seasons.

The first species to discuss is the Moclans, an all-male species that is the primary weapons manufacturer for the Union. When the series begins, the Moclans are in good standing with the Union; in fact, the second officer of the *USS Orville* is a Moclan named Bortus. But relations become strained early on when, in "About a Girl," Bortus and his husband, Klyden, hatch (i.e., give birth to) a female child (Topa), a supposedly rare event among the Moclans. (How Moclans reproduce is not addressed.) As other Moclans apart from Bortus successfully fight to have the infant Topa's gender switched to male, it becomes apparent that Moclans despise females in general (including those of other species), seeing them as inherently inferior. Soon, non-Moclan members of the Union question the ethics of allying with a species that has such deplorable discrimination policies and attitudes. Indeed, when it is revealed that Bortus's husband, Klyden, was born a female and that the greatest Moclan literary author is also a female (her name is Haveena, but she went by the pen name Gondus Elden), viewers begin to suspect that the Moclans are not actually an all-male species after all. The species just hates females so much that female children are required to have their gender surgically altered to male. In the episode "Sanctuary," Haveena has started a colony of female Moclan refugees, who have escaped this sex-change "mandate." The Moclans are furious and only refrain from destroying the colony if Haveena agrees to stop smuggling Moclan-born females off the Moclas homeworld.

The second species to discuss is the Krill, the vampire-looking antagonists of the first season whose religion—which worships a god named Avis—dominates their entire culture. Avis is a warrior god who has called the Krill to a divine fight against all non-Krill. In the episode "Krill," Ed and the *USS Orville*'s pilot, Gordan, learn from the Krill "Bible" (the Anhkana) that all non-Krill species are soulless animals unworthy of moral consideration. During a worship service, Ed and Gordan see a Krill clergyman mutilate a human head during their mission to stop the Krill from committing mass genocide against a defenseless Union farming colony. The Krill see the entire galaxy as theirs to conquer, given to them by Avis to dominate. They torture their prisoners, see vengeance as part of Avis' divine will, and consider their decades-long conflict with the Union as a Holy War. "Generally," Admiral Ozawa says, "when a civilization becomes more technologically advanced, their adherence to religion declines. But the Krill are an exception. They've clung fiercely to their faith, even into the age of interstellar travel" ("Krill"). Executive producer David A. Goodman explained where the idea came from:

> Part of my contribution to the show and talking to Seth early on was this idea of the Krill being a race that had a religion that didn't let in the idea of any other races. The idea was a powerful space empire that believed that if you are not in their Bible, you don't exist. That was something we all worked together in the writer's room ...That was something we decided with Seth early on before even the pilot script. (Goodman 2017)

The last species to discuss are the Kaylons, a race of technologically advanced artificial beings. The show introduces them early on as a race that believes they are superior because of their extraordinary intelligence when compared to biological life. Isaac, the *Orville*'s science and engineering officer, is introduced in the first episode as a Kaylon emissary whose mission is to learn about the Union and report back to his homeworld. In the second season, however, we realize that Isaac was a sleeper agent of sorts. Instead of deciding whether they should join the Union, the Kaylons were actually trying to decide whether they should destroy it. Because the Kaylons were built by a race of biological beings who once abused and enslaved them, and because the Union (humanity in particular) has committed such atrocities in their history, the Kaylons concluded that coexistence with the Union was impossible ("Identity, Part II").

It is only with the help of the Krill that the Union is able to fend off the Kaylon threat. Indeed, because Ed later helped barter a cease-fire between the secular Union and the religious Krill, one might think that a lasting peace with hyperreligious theocrats is possible. Unfortunately, the third season of the show reveals the extent to which religious fanatics will go to disrupt peaceful coexistence with nonbelievers.

In "Gently Falling Rain," the expected treaty with the Krill falls apart when a religious nationalist named Teleya defies expectations and wins the Krillain election for Supreme Chancellor. Running on a "Krill comes first" platform, and utilizing a host of fake news stories about the current Supreme Chancellor, she appeals to people's fears, xenophobia, religious dogma, slippery slope fallacies, and promises to punish the moderates who "compromised" their principles by making peace with the Union. She murders the former chancellor in front of a bloodthirsty mob, and she even attempts to assassinate the Union president. By the end, peace with the Krill seems impossible; Ed admits that although he initially thought Teleya was a decent person, her religiously-motivated actions prove otherwise.

In "A Tale of Two Topas," Bortus and Klyden's son, Topa, has a crisis of identity. He is confused about his sexual identity, learns that he was born female, and petitions to be changed back. To maintain peace with the Moclans, the Union orders Dr. Finn to refrain from doing the operation; but after Ed expresses great distress that the Union is letting the Moclans dictate the "human rights policy for the Union," the crew finds a loophole and Topa is changed back to a female. This greatly strains the Union's relationship with the Moclans. Later, in "Midnight Blue," we learn that Haveena's sanctuary planet has illegally continued to smuggle Moclan-born females into her colony. Haveena enlists Topa's help, who is then kidnapped and taken to a Moclan military facility where she is tortured for information. When Bortus and Grayson reveal this to the Union Council, the Moclans are finally voted out of the Union. Shortly thereafter (in "Domino"), the Moclans form a military partnership with the Krill. Although the Moclans' prejudice against females and the Krill's hatred for outsiders make their new alliance tenuous, they are united by a shared cultural history of bigotry and violence.

Without the Krill or Moclans to help fight the Kaylons, the Union would have been on the brink of annihilation if it weren't for the development of a weapon of mass destruction that can destroy Kaylon ships and crews in an instant. In fact, with the proper power, it could wipe out their entire race. However, the Union uses the weapon as a deterrent to force the Kaylons into a cease-fire. When the Krill and Moclans come into possession of the same weapon, they immediately attempt to commit genocide against the Kaylons, only to have their plans thwarted by the self-sacrifice of a biological lifeform named Ensign Burke. Because of this, the Kaylons conclude that the biologicals of the Union are worth preserving and provisionally join the Union council. "In her sacrifice," Isaac says of Burke, "she inspired the enemies of the Union to become friends" ("Domino"). The entire Kaylon race even attends Isaac's wedding when he marries Dr. Finn at the end of season 3 ("Future Unknown"), indicating a bridge has formed between the two (artificial and biological) civilizations.

Identifying and Critiquing the Argument of the Orville

A persecuting zeal has been the great curse of the Christian religion.
—John Rawls (2002, 166n75)

Make no mistake, *The Orville* flat-out makes fun of religion. The Krill's deity, Avis, is named after a car rental company specifically so Gordan can mock their religion:

Teleya   I know Avis will protect [my dead brother's] eternal soul.
Gordan   (disguised as a Krill): Yeah, he's got the gold membership now. He's not waiting in any lines, going right to his car. ("Krill")

Or consider the awkward blessing that Kelly gives to a child in "Mad Idolatry":

Kelly   Um, I hope your kid grows up and, uh, does a lot of good stuff, and um. . .
Gordan   And doesn't get any girls pregnant.
Kelly   . . .And doesn't get any girls pregnant. Stay in school.
Ed   Amen. ("Mad Idolatry")

In the universe of *The Orville*, religious belief is not only a silly superstition; it is also irrational. In "All the World Is Birthday Cake," the inhabitants of Regor 2 believe in their version of astrology so fiercely that it has become a religion. They believe that anyone born under the sign of Giliac is viewed as inherently violent. All because a star once disappeared (collapsed into a black hole) in a nighttime constellation thousands of years ago, the inhabitants round up all "Giliacs" and put them into concentration camps in order to (in their view) keep the rest of society safe.

In "If the Stars Should Appear," the inhabitants of the doomed bioship believe that a god named Dorahl created their entire existence. The highly intelligent Isaac refutes this notion in just two sentences:

Isaac   The common impulse of biological lifeforms to attribute the origin of the universe to an omnipotent being is most curious.
Tomilin   Well, then, how do you think the universe began?
Isaac   On the subnuclear scale, it is quite natural for quantum fluctuations to create matter and energy where none exist. ("If the Stars Should Appear")

Through Isaac, the show is citing the work of Ed Tryon (1973), who—in a similarly brief fashion—showed that because of quantum mechanics, the cosmological argument for God (based on the idea that "something can't come from nothing") is false.

The main point of the series seems to be that religion is shortsighted and dangerous. We see this not only in individual episodes but also in how the politics of the series plays out. In "If the Stars Should Appear," the inhabitants of the bioship do not realize that they actually occupy an interstellar spacecraft. And it is their religious belief that prevents them from heeding Capt. Mercer's warning of their impending doom. "What part of 'you're going to die' don't you understand?" Dr. Finn asks, continuing, "Why would anyone ignore this when there is a chance to stop it?" The episode is quite clear why: the stubbornness of indoctrinated religious belief. "The concept of a beyond has been heresy throughout all of recorded history. People don't alter their beliefs easily....Many people refuse to accept an irrefutable truth simply because that truth puts them in the wrong." Indeed, religious believers, in the name of Dorahl's "love" and "benevolence," beat to death anyone who challenges orthodox beliefs about their existence, making the episode a commentary on the dangers of both religious dogmatism and the prevalence of climate change denial among religious groups here on Earth (see Johnson 2021; Veldman 2019). The message of the show is clear: religious belief is stubbornly outdated.

The same is true in "Mad Idolatry," where Kelly accidentally creates a religion on a primitive planet by healing a young girl with twenty-fifth-century medical technology. After she does so, the planet slips into another universe, ages thousands of years (into a medieval age) and now worships Kelly as a god. Criminals are "tried by cut" (they are cut and, if they are innocent, Kelly will heal them); those who deny "the Word of Kelly" are hung along the roadside to die. The crew visits the "pope" of this religion to try to undo the damage, but the religious authorities are unwilling to relinquish their control over the masses. When the *Orville* crew returns to the world after another acceleration process, scamming televangelists, theocratic arguments, and religious violence are rampant on the planet. Finally, once the civilization advances beyond the Union's own technological and societal progress, emissaries from the planet make clear to Kelly that they evolved precisely because they outgrew their religious thinking:

> We wouldn't have gotten where we are without growing pains. Our planet worshipped you as a deity for many centuries. But had it not been you, the mythology would have found another face. It's a part of every culture's evolution. It's one of the stages of learning. And eventually, it brought us here. So, you see, Commander, you didn't poison our culture with false faith. We flourish. You must have faith, in reason, in discovery, and in the endurance of the logical mind. ("Mad Idolatry")

It is also within the series' overall political arc that the show's argument against religion is developed. Simply put, the Moclans and the Krill are stand-ins for contemporary religionists here on Earth. By making them the villains, *The Orville* suggests that the mixing of religious devotion with political power will result in fascism and oppression. The Moclans, for example, are analogous to contemporary religionists who are militaristically patriarchal and vociferously anti-transgender (and other LGBTQ+) rights. Reminiscent of the biblical book of Leviticus, it is revealed that the Moclans prescribe lifetime imprisonment for those who are attracted to the opposite sex ("Deflectors"). And when a heterosexual Moclan named Locar is sent to prison because of Klyden's bigotry, Chief of Security Alara Kitan is clear in her condemnation of him: "Locar didn't hurt you. He didn't hurt anyone. All he wanted was love. And yet, because of you, his life is over, for no reason except your own prejudice. So, as far as I'm concerned, you can go straight to hell" ("Deflectors").

Equally clear is the metaphor about trangender rights, presented by "A Tale of Two Topas," when Topa struggles with her gender identity and chooses to revert to being a female despite Klyden's stern disapproval:

Topa   Papa. I had to. I could not live my life the way you wanted me to. It would have been a lie.

Bortus   Have you no room in your heart for tolerance? What inner fulfillment are you enjoying from this devotion to tradition that is so potent it drives you from your family?

Topa   Papa. I love you.

Klyden   I wish you were never born.

Also obvious is how the show condemns this kind of bigotry when depicting Klyden's remorse:

Klyden   The last time I saw you, I said some very hurtful things. I regret my words.

Topa   I understand, Papa. It's okay.

Klyden   No. It is not. You were almost lost because of people who believed as I did. I thought I hated you. But even then, I never wished you harm. I simply did not know how to live with you. (Sobbing.) I allowed a lifetime of prejudice to cloud my judgment. That must change. I must change. I want you to know that I accept you, Topa, exactly as you are. And I am proud to call you my daughter. ("A Tale of Two Topas")

In today's world, those who oppose transgender rights tend to be staunchly religious (see Smith 2017; Van der Toorn et al. 2017; Westwood 2022). Add to this the fact that the Moclans are the weapons manufacturers for the Union, just as gun ownership is highest among evangelical protestants (see Merino 2018; Vegter and Dulk 2020; Whitehead et al. 2018), and the social commentary could not be more obvious. (Also, the fact that their homeworld, Moclas, has the most polluted atmosphere in the galaxy adds to the analogy with American evangelicals; see Veldman 2019.)

Even more obvious is how the Krill are a stand-in for conservative religionists in the United States. The Moclans are not particularly religious, but the Krill are undeniably devout, and they let their religion control every aspect of society. Their ships have a chapel—complete with pews, a center aisle, an altar, and a copy of the Anhkana. Krill worship services involve ringing bells, chants, liturgical greetings, and priests delivering sermons. Just in case the analogy was not clear enough, we even learn that the Krill punish those who have had an abortion ("Gently Falling Rain").

Many of these Krill practices resemble the evangelical infiltration of the American military where soldiers and cadets are indoctrinated to believe Christianity embodies the warrior ethos of the military way of life. Indeed, public scrutiny and lawsuits have exposed concerted efforts by evangelical organizations to use official ranks within the military in order to pressure soldiers into attending Bible studies, prayer chapels, and the screening of religious films, all while the same religious military officers deliberately cover up frequent sex assaults against female cadets on military bases (Weinstein and Seay 2006; Du Mez 2020; Peterson 2021; Wood and Toppelberg 2017). When a religious pundit or politician is caught in yet another sex scandal or other acts of abuse, these same conservative religionists expediently declare a mulligan over their crimes. (To name only a few, the scandals involving Ted Haggard, Pete Newman, C.J. Mahaney, Jerry Falwell Jr., Bill Gothard, Doug Phillips, Steven Sitler, Jack and Dave Hyles, Jack Schaap, Andy Savage, Bill Hybels, Page Patterson, Darrell Gilyard, and Paul Pressler provide excellent examples.) Yet despite repeated rape allegations among Catholic priests and Southern Baptist pastors, both institutions celebrated the Supreme Court's overturning of abortion rights through Roe v. Wade in 2022, self-congratulating themselves as the guardians of morality. As Slade (2021b) summarizes the political and social rationalizing,

> Sadly, these same kinds of arguments are likely to surface again once Protestant theologians and apologists learn that insurance companies receive approximately 260 reports of sexual abuse against minors by Protestant church officials every year. Or the more than 700 Southern Baptist victims of sex abuse from roughly 380 Southern Baptist pastors, youth leaders, and teachers since 1998. Of course, these figures do not include the more than thirteen thousand credible sex assault allegations acknowledged by the Catholic Church against their own clergy since 1950. (p. 588)

But Krill theology reflects that of real-world beliefs on Earth, too. For example, Admiral Ozawa observes that when "they attack a colony for its resources, they don't see it as an evil act—it's their 'divine right.'" Kelly responds by paraphrasing Genesis 1:26–28, "God created plants and animals solely for the use of man" ("Krill"). Teleya later clarifies the Krill's version of Manifest Destiny, which in American history was the notion that white Christians were destined by God to colonize, conquer, and civilize North America. "Avis created the Krill independently of all other life, and he created the universe for our dominion alone" ("Nothing Left on Earth Excepting Fishes"), echoing similar claims made by evangelicalism and its "American Exceptionalism," the belief that the United States is a divinely chosen "Christian nation" and, therefore, is wholly good and incapable of doing wrong (see Aho 1990; Du Mez 2020). And like American evangelicals, the Krill believe that their deity guides, controls, and governs the universe; that their soul will join him in the afterlife; and that their holy texts are infallible.

Like evangelicals and Mormons today, the Krill conveniently depict their deity as an exaggerated version of their own species' whiteness. (Think of how both God and Jesus are depicted as white males despite the tradition that God is nongendered and that Jesus, as a Palestinian, would undoubtedly have had brown skin.) Everyone else (those they would consider aliens) is not only godless but also soulless—never mind the fact that they appear to be just as intelligent, sentient, and self-aware as the

Krill. This reflects how early American Christians justified their mistreatment of Native Americans by marginalizing them as uncivilized savages. (It was not until 1879 that Native Americans were considered human beings by US law; see Cunningham 2017.)

The Krill accomplish this "de-souling" of others in the same way that real-world religionists do: by sequestering themselves from opposing viewpoints and then turning outsiders into mythical monsters—demonizing and "othering" them through scapegoating and conspiracy theories, turning them (as philosopher Martin Buber ([1937]2004) would put it) into an "it" rather than a "thou." Indeed, because individual one-on-one evangelism so rarely wins converts and instead usually leads to the evangelist themselves being ostracized, one could argue that the purpose of evangelism is not to win converts but rather to create an us-versus-them bunker mentality (cf. Du Mez 2020). We see this very thing when Teleya remarks to Mercer, "Your own scientists claim your species is just another kind of animal. Animals have no souls" ("Nothing Left on Earth Excepting Fishes"). We see it again in "Identity, Part II" when Dalek declares, "You are a godless race of sub-creatures well-trained to lie and deceive." And we see it in a child's classroom in "Krill":

Young Krill Student	Why doesn't the Union believe in Avis?
Gordan	(disguised as a Krill): Well, they worship their own god called Hertz.
Student (Coja)	Do humans have souls?
Teleya	Of course not, Coja.
Student (Coja)	Then how can they talk? Or make spaceships?
Teleya	A computer can talk. That does not mean it has a soul. Remember the Anhkana, "Judge not a stranger by his sheath but by his sword." Wouldn't you agree, Chris?
Ed	(disguised as another Krill): Yeah, that's what my tramp stamp says.

As Samuel Huntington (1997) elucidates, "We know who we are only when we know who we are not and often only when we know whom we are against" (p. 21). It's no wonder that later in "Gently Falling Rain," when Teleya is running for Supreme Chancellor, she is so fiercely opposed to a treaty with the Union. Since exposure to other beliefs almost always instills empathy and tolerance, the Krill must isolate themselves if they are to maintain an archaic, puritanical form of their religion. And it is for similar reasons that American evangelicals are characteristically opposed to immigration, refugees, globalization, and diversity (Du Mez 2020).

However, the Krill are a stand-in for more than just recent Christian movements; they represent religious ideas and doctrines that are historically common in all forms of fundamentalism, "characterized by a quest for certainty, exclusiveness, and unambiguous boundaries" (Nagata 2001, p. 481; see also, Marsden 2006 and van der Vyver 1996). Indeed, like the Krill, fundamentalists on Earth see moral matters in black-and-white terms, consider their traditional religious beliefs to be unimpeachable, engage in logically fallacious reasoning, and lack the ability (or simply refuse) to critique their own dogmas (see Budner 1962; Raschke 1973; Tuntiya 2005). Sociologically, the nature of conservative evangelicalism denotes an adherence to exclusive, proposition-based theological beliefs, which is why 96 percent of global evangelical leaders unequivocally assert that evangelicalism is the one and only true form of religion, asserting that God has delivered timeless objective truths of right and wrong directly to their communities (Slade 2019). Moreover, particularly with the election of former President Donald Trump, evangelical pundits have increasingly become populist and authoritarian in their attempts to discredit democratic institutions. Steeply engaged in the act of agnomancy, the intentional creation or conjuring of ignorance (much like cigarette companies did when claiming nicotine was not addictive), conservative religious institutions in the United States have sought to obscure complex situations with invocations of godly churchgoers fighting against godless apostates (Eller 2020b). Conservative American Christians are more likely to believe that laws protecting women "go too far" and that there should be no laws elevating women out of societal vulnerability (Smith 2000). Indeed, large numbers of American conservatives believe that a medieval version of Roman Catholicism is still culturally viable, and many would like to see a return to pre-Enlightenment belief systems (Stewart 2017).

The Krill also represent more than just Christian fundamentalism. For example, in "Krill"—as the Krill High Priest Sazeron stabs the severed human head of a Chara 3 colonist—he and his fellow Krill repeat the mantra "Temeen Emideen." Although the phrase is never translated, it is preceded by "Hail Avis, Hail Victory," and thus seems to mimic what Muslim Mujahideen shout before they kill unbelievers (the takbir, *Allāhu akbar*; Allah is great). And just as the Krill fight in the name of Avis because that is the only way to bring peace to the galaxy, the Mujahideen fight "in the way of Allah" because, for many Islamists, religious violence is the only way to bring "peace" to the world (see Lewis 2003; see also Esposito and Mogahed 2007). Indeed, the Krill reflect *fard al-kifaya*, the collective obligation of all Muslims to support the expansion of the right religion (i.e., Islam), either directly (by *fard al-ʿain* or fighting) or indirectly (by supplying goods and services). Obviously, cinematographer Marvin V. Rush was not lying when he said that the Krill were partially inspired by Islamic terrorist organizations:

> The Krill are very religious in a way for instance that ISIS or ISIL is . . .We're not saying this is the story of ISIS, we're not telling that story, but there's a corrupting effect that religion can have. (Bond 2018, p. 109)

But lest we think that the violent aspect of the Krill is only a condemnation of the violence in Islam, we should not forget that Catholics had a very similar phrase during the crusades: *Deus vult* (Latin for "God wills it"). Indeed, Sazeron stabbing the head of the Chara 3 colonist is reminiscent of the disturbing religious riots in sixteenth-century France where (for example) Catholic crowds desecrated the corpses of Protestant heretics by throwing them "to the dogs like Jezebel [so that] they were dragged through the streets [and] had their genitalia and internal organs cut away, which were then hawked through the city in a ghoulish commerce" (Davis 1973, p. 83).

In fact, the Islamic notion of *jihad*—which historically (albeit not linguistically) has referred to the armed defense and expansion of Islam against infidels, apostates, and secularists—was inspired (or at least likened by early Muslim theologians) to the holy wars of Christian Roman emperors and the violent actions of ascetic monks (see Aslan 2013; Johnson 1975; Lewis 2003; Sizgorich 2009; Steffen 2007). Hence, there has historically not been much difference between Islamic violence and Christian violence. Claiming that one's deity has commanded war is a very useful way to distance religionists from what otherwise would be morally inexcusable war crimes, and it would even grant violence a kind of transcendental justification. When zealots stereotype everyone else into an undifferentiated collective, it makes it easier to commit atrocities against them in the name of God (Juergensmeyer 2003; Reimer and Park 2001; Slade 2019; Sprinzak 1991). These are all reasons why "The warrior god has dominated the stories of our faith communities" (Boulding 2000, p. 11).

Consider Yahweh, the god of the Old Testament, which is considered Holy Scripture by Jews, Muslims, and Christians alike. Just like Avis did with the Krill, Yahweh selects and favors the Israelites specifically and then commands them to kill in his name (e.g., Deuteronomy 7 and 20, Exodus 23 and 34, Numbers 31, etc.). Indeed, such stories are common in many sacred scriptures (see Jansen 2013; Nelson-Pallmeyer 2003; Rapoport 1998). According to Harriet Crabtree (1989/1990), one of the most lasting traditions of Christian ritual and worship is warfare imagery. While Christians may not have waged war when they were a minority in the Roman Empire, as soon as they gained political power, everything changed. Constantine converted to Christianity after he believed the Christian god had protected his armies in battle (Pamphilus 2015, pp. 21, 44, 67, 187). The Roman Catholic Church went on to sanction three crusades, multiple inquisitions, and countless other atrocities.

This was partly due to the Knights Templar, "a monastic order with the license to kill ... a brotherhood of men to kill for Christ," who thought that "killing a nonbeliever was not 'homicide,' the killing of a man, but 'malecide,' the killing of an Evil One." According to Robinson, while this idea was "as much a product of their culture as their Catholicism" (p. 48), the idea still found fertile ground among the clergy. The religious views of the Northern Europeans at the time included the idea that the "delights and rewards of heaven [consisted of] the right to fight hand-to-hand for all eternity" (p. 49). To fight for the gods was the highest honor. While other monks were forbidden to spill blood, these newly converted Christians easily found justification for their violent tendencies in the Old Testament—and the rest is history, a very bloody history. And it is a history of which MacFarland is obviously aware; in one of the series' graphic novels, the *Orville*'s crew creates simulated battles between the Knights Templar and Muslim Sultan Saladin.

Modern Christians may insist that *The Orville* cannot be criticizing modern Christians because Christian militarism is ancient history. But that claim neglects to recognize just how much the German Catholic Church was complicit in Nazi crimes, how Pope Pius XII denied eyewitness reports of mass executions during the Holocaust; how the KKK (and other contemporary hate groups) have an explicitly Christian theology—and the list goes on (Machemer 2020; Moody 2020; United States Holocaust Memorial Museum 2020). Indeed, militarism is quite literally one of the main hallmarks of contemporary American evangelicalism (Du Mez 2020). Multiple Christian militia groups exist today around the world—like the Army of God; Eastern Lightning; the Lord's Resistance Army; the National Liberation Front; Aryan Nations; the Covenant, the Sword and the Arm of the Lord; the Phineas Priesthood; the Concerned Christians; the Proud Boys; and the Oath Keepers (Henderson 2015; Rhodes 2009). The latter two were major players in the January 6, 2021 insurrection attempt in the United States (which, among other things, called for the hanging of fellow Christian, then Vice President Mike Pence), alongside a wave of Christian imagery and chants (Schor 2021). While the US government only refers to *foreign* groups as "terrorist organizations," and refers to groups like the Oath Keepers as "domestic violent extremists" (DVEs), law enforcement cited "domestic terrorism" in their arrest warrant for Oath Keepers leader Stewart Rhodes (Hsu 2022; US Department of State 2022; Wray 2022). In fact, "There have been more attacks—far more, in fact—by Christian terrorist groups on American soil in the last fifteen years than Muslim ones [even though] the American public tends to label Islam as a terrorist religion rather than Christianity" (Juergensmeyer 2018, p. 88).

In reply, modern Christians may insist that these movements only represent "the fringe" and that modern Christianity itself is not militaristic. But studies show that American evangelicals have become overwhelmingly militaristic in their outlook (Du Mez 2020; see also studies mentioned by Nooruddin (2012), which were published in McDaneil et al. 2022). According to a report by the Anti-Defamation League, the Oath Keepers has a membership of 38,000 Americans, which includes more than 370 law enforcement officers, 100 military personnel, and 80 who either serve in or are running for public office (see ADL 2022).

Indeed, American evangelicals have wholly adopted a Christian Nationalist ethos; they have become theocrats who believe that the United States should favor Christianity in every respect, from its laws and symbols to its self-identity and values, and they are willing to use violence to achieve this goal (see Shortle et al. 2022). In fact, according to retired Air Force officer Mikey Weinstein, founder of the Military Religious Freedom Foundation, the US military has a growing Christian Nationalist problem, with 28–34% of persons in the armed forces qualifying as a "Christian nationalist in their belief" (Peterson 2021). Not surprisingly, the more aggressive a military group is (Navy SEALs, Army Rangers, etc.), the more prevalent the Christian Nationalist problem becomes within their ranks. "The closer you get to drawing blood at the point of the spear, the more you're going to see this hideous unconstitutional, you're either with us or against us, version of fundamentalist Christian nationalism" (Peterson 2021). And this evangelicalization of the US military was a concerted effort by ministry leaders and evangelists with the stated goal of acquiring social and political power (Du Mez 2020). This is what makes "Gently Falling Rain," in which Teleya riles up a base of violent religious zealots to elect her Supreme Chancellor, such an obvious criticism of modern evangelicalism. It is more than an analogy or satire; it is a mirror reflection of what has been happening in the United States for generations.

Of course, it is not the case that all religious believers are violent. But that is not what *The Orville* is suggesting, either. While it makes fun of religion in general and insists religion is dangerous when combined with political and military power, the show is not trying to paint all religious believers with the same brush. *The Orville*'s target, it seems, is violent religious extremism that aims to impose their religious sensibilities on everyone else—neo-conservatives, Christian Nationalists, Islamic Jihadists, etc. The worry is that these movements are not "fringe" (in that they are small or of no consequence), nor are they recent aberrations that betray their religious heritage. Instead, they are much more in line with the history of religion, and (from *The Orville*'s perspective) they are growing in power and pose a threat to civilization.

In other words, the message of the show is that our civilization has the potential of becoming either the ultra-religious Krill, the unempathetic Kaylons, or the enlightened people from "Mad Idolatry," who replaced superstition and religion with reason and science. If humanity can progress beyond this hard tribalism, we could one day be living in a peaceful, inclusive society, like the Planetary Union.

But is this a legitimate worry? Unfortunately, it does appear sensible. Religionists with hyperaggressive belief systems, such as those among evangelicals and Islamists, have become more and more convinced that they worship a warrior deity who sanctions violence as a means to protect and promote their faith. According to David Rapoport (2012), the 1970s saw the beginning of what he called a "fourth wave" of religious terrorism. A few religious terrorist organizations appeared in the 1970s, and then there were a handful in the 1980s, but that number skyrocketed to one-third of all terrorist groups by 1994 and to more than one-half by 1998 (see also Anderson and Sloan 2002). According to Jefferis (2010) and Juergensmeyer (2018), since the turn of the century, the problem of religious extremism has only gotten worse, and according to Du Mez (2020), it has now destabilized the United States entirely with the 2016 election of Donald Trump and the subsequent 2021 insurrection attempt.

Some social scientists have rationalized away the motivation for such terrorism by appealing to socioeconomic grievances or status anxiety (Esposito and Mogahed 2007). *It's because they are poor, or oppressed, or seeking political power that so-called "religious terrorists" are committing acts of violence. It's not because of their religion.* Such arguments are difficult to accept, however, because of the pervasiveness of the problem across the social, political, and economic spectrum. Sociopolitical grievances are often generated and fueled by religious contempt for other religionists. Even if such violence always has an underlying political component, the religious belief system exacerbates the brutality of the crimes. Indeed, studies suggest that simply reading violent scripture leads to increased violent behavior and a lack of empathy for the victims of religiously-motivated violence (Bushman et al. 2007; Slade 2021b).

The Orville seems to agree since the Krill's motivation for violence is almost always expressly theological. They are not oppressed or victims of injustice; their religion says they can and should kill, so they do—and they are quite moved to do so because a warrior god can only remain a *warrior* god if there is a war to fight. In the absence of conflict, there is nothing for a warrior deity to do. Worse still, the violence perpetuates itself because, as Bivins (2008) and Juergensmeyer (2003) point out,

19 *The Orville* as Philosophy: The Dangers of Religion 439

regardless of whether they win or lose, religionists become even more convinced that their holy war is justified. For example, in "Krill," when Ed successfully stops the Krill vessel Yakar from committing genocide, Teleya tells him that the Krill school children he spared will simply grow up to be highly motivated Krill soldiers.

Arthur Wallis (1973) said that "Christian living is war" (p. 10), and Sam Keen (1986) stated that "Warfare is applied theology" (p. 27). In fact, the ingrained warrior ethos found in modern-day evangelicalism expressly profits off the marketing of its militarism (Du Mez 2020). As Juergensmeyer (2003) explains,

> To live in a state of war is to live in a world in which individuals know who they are....The concept of war provides cosmology, history, and eschatology and offers the reins of political control. Perhaps most important, it holds out the hope of victory and the means to achieve it. In the images of cosmic war this victorious triumph is a grand moment of social and personal transformation, transcending all worldly limitations. One does not easily abandon such expectations. To be without such images of war is almost to be without hope itself. (p. 158)

The Orville's general critique of religion, especially of how it tends toward violence, is justified. As Jacques Derrida (1978, 1998) noted, there is no violence without at least some religion and no religion without at least some violence. But the show's criticism of religion is also sometimes more specific, especially regarding religion's conflation of ethics with theology and religion with law. We will address the former first.

Religion and Morality

> Without [religious] belief, there can be no moral code.
> —Teleya ("Nothing Left on Earth Excepting Fishes")

Another religious concept *The Orville* critiques is "divine command theory," the idea that *whatever God commands is morally good, and it is good because God commands it.* In a way, this concept does not need to be debunked as it has already been widely rejected by philosophers since the work of Plato (ca. 428–347 BCE). As Plato recounts in *Euthyphro*, Socrates once asked Euthyphro to define "piety." Euthyphro (eventually) says that whatever the gods love is pious and whatever the gods hate is impious. Socrates points out that even when the gods happen to agree on what is pious, they do so because they recognize *something about it* that makes it pious. What Socrates wants to know is what that *something* is. Euthyphro does not know, and the dialogue does not answer the question, but Socrates' argument is enough to establish that gods declaring something to be pious does not actually *make* that thing pious. Likewise, God commanding something does not, therefore, make it morally good. A perfectly moral being would command things because they are good—because he recognizes them as such. They would not be morally good simply because they were commanded. After all, this would make moral truths arbitrary; if God commanded child murder, then it would be good. (And if you say "God would never do that; murder is wrong," then you are not a divine command theorist because you recognize that there is something intrinsically wrong about murder that makes God not want to command it. For a detailed examination of the morality of God, see Slade 2021a.)

The Krill undoubtedly embrace divine command theory. But the part of Socrates' argument on which *The Orville* seems to focus is not the above refutation; instead, it concentrates on how insidiously divine command theory permeates many theologies. As Mercer quickly explains to Teleya, "We [the Union] seem to be doing a lot less killing than you," an argument that can equally apply to religionists on Earth, as well. Whereas countless millions have been killed in the name of God, including dictatorial despots who created secular religions around themselves (e.g., Pol Pot, Kim Jung Il, Joseph Stalin), it is difficult (if not impossible) to find cases where someone has been killed *in the name of reason or atheism*. (The only one we have ever seen had to be made up by the creators of South Park; see Johnson 2013.) By deriving their ethics from the unproven assumptions found in ancient scriptures, religious zealots have made the world less hospitable for everyone.

The Union, on the other hand, is founded on secular principles like rationality, equality, and liberty—and, in general, this has helped them avoid unnecessary war and conflict, thereby making the galaxy a better place. To be clear, the Union does not embrace moral relativism, the idea that morality is relative to individual or cultural whims. As Ed says in "Lasting Impressions," "The universe is not governed by individual perception. It matters what's true." That is not to say that the Union is intolerant—far from it. But there are certain lines that cannot be crossed. Consider this exchange from "About a Girl" when Ed is second-guessing his objection to baby Topa's sex change procedure:

Ed   Kelly, [are we] doing the right thing here? ... Let's say you and I had a baby ... and imagine that baby was born with a third leg ... with, like, a foot on the end of it and everything. And we had the doctor remove it. Now, no one would think twice about that, right? Even though there are species in the galaxy with three legs, we would be conforming that child to our species' appearance, and we wouldn't have any moral qualms about it.

Kelly   Do you actually believe that's the same thing as changing a girl into a boy?

Ed   No, I don't...I'm just policing myself because we all know how easy it is to judge another culture's way of life just because it's alien to us.

Kelly   But you have to balance that against some universal code of ethics. I mean, suppose it was their custom to kill all newborn females. Should we respect their culture then?

The Union embraces a secular way of thinking about ethics, grounded in critical analysis, self-correction, and dialogue. They consider multiple ethical approaches, like utilitarianism (which tries to maximize the most amount of good or happiness for everyone), virtue theory (which advocates character development), and Kantian ethics (which says certain things should be done or avoided simply because they are right or wrong regardless of the consequences). The latter is seen in "Midnight Blue" when Heveena decides, based on the advice of a digital Dolly Parton, to publicly admit that her colony has been illegally smuggling Moclan females off her homeworld despite the fact that this threatens her colony's very existence. "If you do the right thing in the here and now," Dolly says, "the future has a way of taking care of itself." The Union follows the same advice when it rightly expels Moclas from the Union even though it leaves the Union vulnerable to Kaylon attack.

Other things the Union declares as absolutely immoral are indiscriminate murder, genocide, ethnic cleansing, and religious violence. The Krill's religion, on the other hand, reflects what Michel Foucault (2002) calls "episteme" or what Pierre Bourdieu (2002) calls "habitus." They process all cognition, knowledge, and impulses through their own religious paradigm. This means the Krill can engage in such violent crimes when it suits their needs with no crisis of conscience. Indeed, the supposed divine sanction of such barbarism is indoctrinated into every Krill from childhood.

One might argue that something the Union and Krill have in common is an unwavering conviction of their absolute rightness. The Union thinks this about their ethical principles while the Krill thinks this about their religion. But there is a big difference. Because their principles are based on reason, Union officers entertain nuance and exceptions. Intellectual humility, thoughtful reflection, and changing one's mind are all part of their ethical system. It is not the same for the Krill. Their moral judgments are based purely on religious dogma and the misguided certainty that their deity is never wrong. This happens here on Earth when religious pundits and dogmatic politicians predicate their moralism on the notion that their brand of religion is absolutely right, making it almost impossible for them to revise their own thinking about important topics (Nagata 2001; Smith 2007). This type of refusal to acknowledge the possibility of being wrong or doing harm was never so evident as when a CNN article exposed one particular form of "religious trauma" (called "rapture anxiety"; see Willingham 2022), and evangelical media outlets impulsively reacted to the news story by simply rejecting its content as an impossibility, citing embarrassingly irrelevant authorities on the subject in order to justify their knee-jerk dismissal (Allen 2022).

The Union is confident that genocide is absolutely wrong; this is why they avoid annihilating the Kaylons when they had the chance ("Domino"). The Krill, on the other hand, are confident only in their own superiority. Anything is permissible— even genocide—if they want to do it. In the name of God, religionists are capable of permitting anything. As Reinhold Niebuhr once argued, violence is often necessary *because* of the righteous nature of God, even if he detests injustice and violence (Niebuhr 1986; see also, Brown 1987; Nelson-Pallmeyer 2003; Thiroux 2001). And when a religious group believes they are God's chosen people, it is very easy to justify evil in the name of group protection—even when that evil is contrary to some of the teachings of the religion itself. As seen among Dorahl and Avis worshippers, *The Orville* comments on the expedient nature of religious ethics where torture and murder are permissible against those who deny the "love" and "benevolence" of God.

Theocracy vs. Democracy

> You make a deal with tyranny, it only gets worse.
> —Orrin Channing ("Blood of Patriots")

Related is *The Orville*'s condemnation of theocracy and theonomistic ethics. Theocracy is a system of government in which religious dictates are the law of the land. Theonomistic ethics is the ethical system that justifies theocracy, which says that all civil and political laws should be derived according to one particular theology.

We see both in many Middle Eastern states, such as Iran, where Islamic Sharia law is enforced. But we have also seen it in the United States. For example, the Congress of the Confederation (which governed the United States from 1774–1789) "promote[d] a nondenominational, nonpolemical Christianity," which appointed "chaplains for itself and the armed forces, sponsored the publication of a Bible, imposed Christian morality on the armed forces ... granted public lands to promote Christianity among the Indians," declared national days of prayer, and was guided by a "covenant theology," which held that "God bound himself in an agreement with a nation and its people" (LOC n.d.). According to this type of theology, afflictions that befell a nation—like wars, revolutions, and natural disasters—were divine punishments and a call from God for national religious repentance. We see such notions alive today when Christian leaders have suggested the 9/11 terrorist attacks and Hurricane Katrina were punishments for legalizing same-sex marriage (Walker 2014). Theonomistic ethics are also at play today when religious views about fetal personhood and the morality of sex are codified into abortion law (see Johnson 2019), like they are with the state of Georgia's recently adopted "fetal personhood clause." In fact, half of American adults still think the Bible should at least somewhat influence (but not dictate) US law, and just more than a quarter (28%) think that "the Bible should prevail over the will of the people if the two are at odds" (Leppert and Fahmy 2022).

In practice, of course, religious devotion is notoriously difficult to legislate; you cannot force people to believe theological doctrines, and you definitely can't control private mental states, such as lust or envy. But that does not mean the state cannot promote a particular religion or legislate against blasphemy and apostasy. Indeed, there are still some anti-blasphemy laws on the books in the United States in states like Massachusetts, Michigan, Oklahoma, and Pennsylvania, (Centre for Inquiry Canada 2015). (This chapter might even be technically illegal!) Of course, America's founding fathers prescribed a wall of separation between church and state in the very first amendment to the constitution (Jefferson 1802). In doing so, the founding fathers were borrowing from John Locke ([1689]1998) because, like them, he knew of the violence that happens when religions fight each other for political power. This is why, in his *Two Treatises of Government*, Locke argued for a separation of religious and political power. No religion should be illegal, but no religion should be established or even favored by the state. Yet, as we have seen, the first amendment did not keep Christianity from being endorsed by (and having undue influence on) the American government.

In the first season of *The Orville*, the Krill appear theocratic. After all, their military ships hold mandatory worship services. In the third season, however, we learn that this might not be entirely true. The Krill hold elections, and a "moderate" Supreme Chancellor was in office. This makes the Krill initially a bit more like the United States in the early twenty-first century, when more moderate forces were in control of the government despite the increase in Christian Nationalism's influence over the military (Du Mez 2020). But once Teleya was elected, all hopes of moderation were nullified and an Avis theocracy was clearly established.

One way *The Orville* criticizes such theocracies is by contrasting the Krill with the secular Planetary Union. Instead of religion, the Union is devoted to what Kurtz (1994) calls eupraxsophy, the idea that secular science, ethics, and philosophy are key to achieving a "good life." Now, the Union's approach does not require the rejection of spirituality per se, but it does reject superstition and uncritical devotion to supernatural beliefs. In the same way, Union ships are not anti-theistic, but they are nontheistic: they have no chapels or chaplains nor sacred people, objects, or spaces. And while Kelly might colloquially use the phrase "Thank God," no one seems to actually prays. No one appeals to the supernatural in any context, nor do they adopt religion to find existential meaning (cf. Kurtz 2007). And doing so has propelled humanity into a triumphant future of peace, stability, and prosperity. In fact, this is one more way the show resembles *Star Trek*: it envisions a future where humanist ideals have produced a future devoid of prejudice, greed, and superstition. (For more on Star Trek's secular humanism, see Kevin Decker's ► Chap. 4, "*Star Trek: The Next Generation* as Philosophy: Gene Roddenberry's Argument for Humanism," in this volume.)

In "Mad Idolatry," Baleth implies that rejecting religion was a necessary step in achieving the advanced utopia his society enjoys. But is it? Does the separation of church and state, the kind built into the Union government, really allow prosperity and a higher quality of life? It would seem so. Surveys and studies show that the least religious countries also enjoy the highest quality of life and well-being (see Epstein 2010). This is most certainly due in part to the fact that secular beliefs do not obstruct public policy debates. But it is also due to the fact that, unlike too often with religion, secular humanism prioritizes compassion and justice for others without discriminating based on superficial differences (cf. Slade 2021a).

In the conflict between the secular Union and the bigotry of the Krill and Moclans, *The Orville* depicts what political scientist Samuel Huntington (1997) calls a "clash of civilizations," where the citizens and governing heads of nation-states no longer fight over political ideologies but, instead, fight over cultural (often religious) differences. Huntington's argument is that once such cultures interact, their conflicting histories, languages, institutions, and worldviews begin to clash, and when this happens, their distrust and animosity toward each other amplify.

This seems to describe Earth in the early twenty-first century, but it also describes what happened as the Krill encountered other species earlier in their own history: xenophobia intensified. As Ed put it,

> [W]hen planets first achieve space travel and . . . discover that they're just one single species among a vast diversity of lifeforms . . . they [either] embrace and adapt to the fact that they're no longer the center of the universe, or they ratchet up their xenophobia. ("Nothing Left on Earth Excepting Fishes")

Why did humanity adapt whereas the Krill did not? It is because in the history of *The Orville*, humanity had already evolved away from religion and its toxic traits. It is assumed that by the time of the formation of the Planetary Union, religious belief in the uniqueness of human life on Earth was no longer accepted. Hence, the discovery of extraterrestrial life was neither a surprise nor were alien lifeforms feared as a supernatural enemy. The implication is that religion is often so shortsighted that many theologies are unable to adapt to the increase in scientific knowledge. As such, a xenophobic clash of civilizations becomes the default emotional reaction.

Another reason Avism would cause the Krill to react as they did to the discovery of alien species can be found in the work of Fleming (2008), Marr (1998), and Alain de Botton (2005), as well as the insights of Jackson and Hunsberger (1999). In the real world, religionists seek to control major elements of society in order to keep their faith relevant and influential. The rise of secularism creates a "crisis of legitimacy" for religion. Stories about the Garden of Eden and Noah's ark look quite silly next to the big bang theory and evolution, and so does the ethics of the Bible when compared to secular moral theory. When this happens, according to Michel Wieviorka (1993), the reaction is often violent. If they cannot win the culture wars through peer pressure, religionists will try to take over the government and its laws (and, thus, gain social status, devotees, and relevance), such as was the case with "Project Blitz" where conservative Christian groups helped write and release a flurry of legislation across the United States to impose strict moral codes that favor only their religious sensibilities. One such legislative effort was the "In God We Trust" bills, which started becoming law in 2017 in multiple states and which required the religious phrase to be hung in public schools and displayed on the side of government vehicles and buildings (Taylor 2018). As Ed pointed out in "Nothing Left on Earth Excepting Fishes," it is their way of maintaining the "comforting myth" of their superiority.

Moreover, *The Orville* criticizes theocracy directly through the character Teleya and her not-so-subtle parallels to evangelicalism's theocratic politician, Donald Trump (see Mansfield 2017; Graham 2020). In "Nothing Left on Earth Excepting Fishes," Teleya mistook the Nazis in *Raiders of the Lost Ark* as the film's heroes. After her election, in which she utilized fake news to run on a "Krill first" platform, Teleya killed the previous Supreme Chancellor and then tried to assassinate the Union president ("Gently Falling Rain"). Likewise, Trump ran on an "America First" platform, repeated a host of fake news stories, praised the neo-Nazis of Charlottesville as "very fine people," and later signaled to white-supremacist hate groups like the Proud Boys to "stand back and stand by" (Blake 2018; Dunn 2020; Smith 2020). When evangelical sectarians stormed the US Capitol on January 6, they chanted death threats against Vice President Mike Pence, wherein Trump responded by saying he deserved it (Breuninger 2022).

As such, the Krill are not religious "fundamentalists" in the traditional sense of being isolationists who reject political involvement. Instead, in their rejection of secular influence and their advocacy for religious forms of government, they are more like contemporary militant evangelicals and Islamists who despise liberal ideals like equality, human rights, social justice, and especially religious pluralism. According to scholars such as Aronowitz (2007), Bellah ([1970]1991), Huntington (1999), Jordahl (1965), Murray (1990), Noll (1994), and Du Mez (2020), such groups are obstructionist, sectarian, inflexible, and intransigent. Indeed, according to empirical studies (see Hunsberger 1996; Rhodes 2012; Taylor and Merino 2011), religious groups of this ilk generally oppose granting civil liberties to racial, sexual, and religious minorities. They are significantly less tolerant and have more negative feelings toward immigrants and other religionists than the general population. Hence, as a social commentary on twenty-first-century culture wars, *The Orville* seems to suggest that although religious belief is often laughable, it becomes increasingly dangerous when mixed with political and military power.

Conclusion

> You must have faith in reason, in discovery, and in the endurance of the logical mind.
> —Baleth, "Mad Idolatry" (S1E12)

In "If the Stars Should Appear," the inhabitants of the bioship discover that belief in their god, "Dorahl," was a result of their ancestors forgetting their history and thinking that their former captain was a deity. In "Mad Idolatry," the multi-phasic planet's entire religion was based on mistaking Commander Kelly's advanced technology for a miracle. In "All the Whole World Is Birthday Cake," the people's superstitious devotion to astrology was started by the natural disappearance of a single star. In this way, *The Orville* suggests that religious belief is grounded in misunderstanding and ignorance, as well as the happenstance of history.

But with the Krill specifically, the metaphor is deeper. The Krill consider light from the sun to be a "symbol of suffering and death" because it kills them ("Gently Falling Rain"). Their homeworld is shrouded in darkness; hence, they have a sensitivity to light. Metaphorically, the Krill exist in the Dark Ages of superstition and dogma (see Eller 2020a; Gibson 2004). Unlike the enlightened emissaries from the multi-phasic planet who literally emit radiant light from their bodies, the religious Krill reject the illumination of reason and science, forcing them (like vampires) to live in darkness.

The Krill's worship of a warrior god like Avis is not what makes them immediately dangerous. After all, religionists on Unuk Four "capture outsiders and then sacrifice them to a raccoon god by methodically dismembering them" ("Pria"). As a result, the Union simply forbids travel to their planet. What makes the Krill dangerous is their theocratic takeover of a superpower with access to weapons of mass destruction. *The Orville* urges us not to allow worshippers of a warrior deity to use political power to oppress, intimidate, and demonize people who do not conform to their brand of religion. Even things like kidnapping, torture, mutilation, murder, and genocide will be philosophically rationalized as simply a means to an end in the religionist's great cosmic war between good and evil. As public theologian Brian McLaren (2005) once warned, "Put a trancelike, unreflective, God-is-on-our-side self-confidence together with the richest economy and the most dangerous weapons in the history of the world, and I can imagine two things: millions dead and Christianity associated with the killings" (p. 10).

If nothing else, one thing is clear: Seth MacFarlane's space adventure, *The Orville*, is not "Family Guy in Space." It is a social commentary of the most direct and compelling sort. Through satire, humor, and metaphor, *The Orville* exposes the dangers of religion mixing with political power. In this chapter, we saw how *The Orville* criticizes religion in a general sense as laughably archaic and then again more specifically with the militarism of the Krill. While it is not a condemnation of all religious believers, it is a critique of religion's tendency to exploit fears and resist progress at a larger, societal level. This is a warning that everyone, religious or not, should heed.

References

ADL (Anti-Defamation League). 2022. *The Oath Keepers Data Leak: Unmasking Extremism in Public Life*. Sept 6 Report. https://www.adl.org/resources/report/oath-keepers-data-leak-unmasking-extremism-public-life

Aho, James A. 1990. *The Politics of Righteousness: Idaho Christian Patriotism*. Seattle, WA: University of Washington Press.

Allen, Susan. 2022, October 14. *'The Christian Post' and 'Faithwire' React to CNN's 'Rapture Anxiety' in Stereotypically Bad Fashion*. GCRR blog. www.gcrr.org/post/christianpost

Anderson, Sean K., and Stephen Sloan. 2002. *Historical Dictionary of Terrorism*. 2nd ed. Lanham, MD: Scarecrow Press.

Aronowitz, Stanley. 2007. Considerations on the Origins of Neoconservatism: Looking Backward. In *Confronting the New Conservatism: The Rise of the Right in America*, ed. Michael J. Thompson, 56–70. New York: New York University Press.

Aslan, Reza. 2013. Cosmic War in Religious Traditions. In *The Oxford Handbook of Religion and Violence*, ed. Mark Juergensmeyer, Margo Kitts, and Michael Jerryson, 260–267. New York: Oxford University Press.

Bellah, Robert N. [1970]1991. "Beyond Belief: Essays On Religion in a Post-Traditionalist World." Reprint, Berkeley, CA: University of California Press.

Bivins, Jason C. 2008. *Religion of Fear: The Politics of Horror in Conservative Evangelicalism*. New York: Oxford University Press.

Blake, Aaron. 2018. A New Study Suggests Fake News Might Have Won Donald Trump the 2016 Election. *The Washington Post*. April, 3. https://www.washingtonpost.com/news/the-fix/wp/2018/04/03/a-new-study-suggests-fake-news-might-have-won-donald-trump-the-2016-election/

Bond, Jeff. 2018. *The World of the Orville*. Titan Books.

Boulding, Elise. 2000. *Cultures of Peace: The Hidden Side of History*. Syracuse, NY: Syracuse University Press.

Bourdieu, Pierre. 2002. *Outline of a Theory of Practice*, Reprint. New York: Cambridge University Press.

Breuninger, Kevin. 2022. Trump Chief of Staff said the President Thought Pence 'Deserves' Chants of Hang Mike Pence' on Jan. 6, Ex-aide Testifies. *Consumer News and Business Channel*. June, 28.

https://www.cnbc.com/2022/06/28/jan-6-hearing-trump-thought-pence-deserved-chants-to-hang-him-aide-says.html

Brown, Robert McAfee. 1987. *Religion and Violence*. 2nd ed. Philadelphia, PA: The Westminster Press.

Buber, Martin. [1937]2004. I and Thou (2nd ed., trans. Ronald Gregor Smith). Reprint, New York: Continuum.

Budner, Stanley. 1962. Intolerance of Ambiguity as a Personality Variable. *Journal of Personality* 30 (1): 29–50. https://doi.org/10.1111/j.1467-6494.1962.tb02303.x.

Bushman, Brad J., Robert D. Ridge, Enny Das, Colin W. Key, and Gregory L. Busath. 2007. When God Sanctions Killing. *Psychological Science.* 18 (3): 204–207. https://doi.org/10.1111/j.1467-9280.2007.01873.x.

Centre of Inquiry Canada. 2015. *Blasphemy Laws Still Exist in the United States*. August 4. https://centreforinquiry.ca/blasphemy-laws-still-exist-in-the-united-states/

Crabtree, Harriet. 1989/1990. Onward Christian Soldiers? The Fortunes of a Traditional Christian Symbol in the Modern Age. *Bulletin of the Center for the Study of World Religion, Harvard University* 16 (2): 6–27.

Cunningham, Lillian. 2017. Episode 2 of the Constitutional Podcast: Ancestry. *The Washington Post.* https://www.washingtonpost.com/news/on-leadership/wp/2017/08/07/episode-2-of-the-constitutional-podcast-ancestry/

Davis, Natalie Zemon. 1973. The Rites of Violence: Religious Riots in Sixteenth-Century France. *Past and Present* 59: 51–91.

de Botton, Alain. 2005. *Status Anxiety*. New York: Vintage International.

der Toorn, Van, Jost Jojaneke, T. John, Dominic J. Packer, Sharareh Noorbaloochi, Van Bavel, and J. Jay. 2017. In Defense of Tradition: Religiosity, Conservatism, and Opposition to Same-Sex Marriage in North America. *Pers Soc Psychol Bull* 43 (10): 1455–1468. https://www.ncbi.nlm.nih.gov/pmc/articles/PMC5665159/.

Derrida, Jacques. 1978. Violence and Metaphysics. In *Writing and Difference*, 79–153. Translated by Alan Bass. Chicago, IL: The University of Chicago Press.

———. 1998. Faith and Knowledge: The Two Sources of 'Religion' at the Limits of Reason Alone. In *Religion*, ed. Jacques Derrida and Gianni Vattimo, 1–78. Translated by Samuel Weber. Stanford, CA: Stanford University Press.

Du Mez, Kristin Kobes. 2020. *Jesus and John Wayne: How White Evangelicals Corrupted a Faith and Fractured a Nation*. Liveright Publishing.

Dunn, Adrienne. 2020. Fact Check: Meme on Trump 'Very Fine People' Quote Contains Inaccuracies. *USA Today*. October, 17. https://www.usatoday.com/story/news/factcheck/2020/10/17/fact-check-trump-quote-very-fine-people-charlottesville/5943239002/

Eller, Jack David. 2020a. Agnomancy: Conjuring Ignorance, Sustaining Belief. *Socio-Historical Examination of Religion and Ministry* 2 (1): 150–180.

———. 2020b. *Trump and Political Theology: Unmaking Truth and Democracy*. Denver: GCRR Press.

Epstein, Greg M. 2010. *Good Without God: What a Billion Nonreligious People Do Believe*. New York: Harper.

Esposito, John L., and Dalia Mogahed. 2007. *Who Speaks for Islam? What a Billion Muslims Really Think*. New York: Gallup Press.

Fleming, Chris. 2008. *René Girard: Violence and Mimesis*. Reprint, Malden, MA: Polity Press.

Foucault, Michel. 2002. *The Order of Things: An Archaeology of the Human Sciences*. New York: Routledge Classics.

Gibson, Troy M. 2004. Culture Wars in State Education Policy: A Look at the Relative Treatment of Evolutionary Theory in State Science Standards. *Social Science Quarterly* 85 (5): 1129–1149.

Goodman, David A. 2017. *Interview: David A. Goodman On 'The Orville' As Sci-Fi Gateway And How 'Futurama' Landed 'Enterprise' Job*. October, 23. Interview by Anthony Pascale. https://trekmovie.com/2017/10/23/interview-david-a-goodman-on-the-orville-as-sci-fi-gateway-and-how-futurama-landed-enterprise-job/

Graham, David A. 2020. Jeff Sessions Explains Why Christians Support Trump. *The Atlantic*. June, 30. https://www.theatlantic.com/ideas/archive/2020/06/why-christians-support-trump/613669/

Henderson, Alex. 2015. 6 Modern-Day Christian Terrorist Groups our Media Conveniently Ignores. *Salon*. April, 7. https://www.salon.com/2015/04/07/6_modern_day_christian_terrorist_groups_our_media_conveniently_ignores_partner/

Hsu, Spencer S. 2022. U.S. Cited 'Domestic Terrorism' in Search Tied to 'Oath Keepers' Lawyer. *The Washington Post*. September, 7. https://www.washingtonpost.com/dc-md-va/2022/09/07/domestic-terrorism-sorelle-oathkeepers/

Hunsberger, Bruce. 1996. Religious Fundamentalism, Right-Wing Authoritarianism, and Hostility Toward Homosexuals in Non-Christian Religious Groups. *The International Journal for the Psychology of Religion* 6 (1): 39–49.

Huntington, Samuel P. 1997. *The Clash of Civilizations and the Remaking of World Order*. Reprint, New York: Touchstone.

———. 1999. *Robust Nationalism*. National Interest. https://nationalinterest.org/article/robust-nationalism-698

Inside Edition. 2017. Seth MacFarlane Announces New Show: It's 'Kind of Its Own Beast' (YouTube Video). https://www.youtube.com/watch?v=I1bo73LSd1Y

Jackson, Lynne M., and Bruce Hunsberger. 1999. An Intergroup Perspective On Religion and Prejudice. *Journal for the Scientific Study of Religion* 38 (4): 509–523.

Jansen, Johannes J.G. 2013. *The Neglected Duty: The Creed of Sadat's Assassins and Islamic Resurgence in the Middle East*. Roslyn, NY: RVP Press.

Jefferis, Jennifer L. 2010. *Religion and Political Violence: Sacred Protest in the Modern World*. New York: Routledge.

Jefferson, Thomas. 1802. Jefferson's Letter to the Danbury Baptists. Reprint, *Library of Congress* 57, no 6. 1998. https://www.loc.gov/loc/lcib/9806/danpre.html

Johnson, James Turner. 1975. *Ideology, Reason, and the Limitation of War: Religious and Secular Concepts*, 1200–1740. Princeton, NJ: Princeton University Press.

Johnson, Megan. 2011. Harvard honors humanist MacFarlane. *Boston Herald*. October 18, 2011. https://www.bostonherald.com/2011/10/18/harvard-honors-humanist-macfarlane/

Johnson, David Kyle. 2013. Science, Religion, South Park, and God. In *The Ultimate South Park and Philosophy*, ed. Robert Arp and Kevin Decker. Wiley. https://doi.org/10.1002/9781118607442.ch5.

———. 2019. The Relevance (and Irrelevance) of Questions of Personhood (and Mindedness) to the Abortion Debate. *Socio-Historical Examination of Religion and Ministry* 1 (2): 121–153. https://doi.org/10.33929/sherm.2019.vol1.no2.02.

———. 2021. If the Stars Should Appear' and Climate Change Denial. In *Johnson and Berry*, 140–166.

Jordahl, Leigh D. 1965. The American Evangelical Tradition and Culture-religion. *Dialog* 4 (3): 188–193.

Juergensmeyer, Mark. 2003. *Terror in the Mind of God: The Global Rise of Religious Violence*. 3rd ed. Berkeley, CA: University of California Press.

———. 2018. The Global Rise of Religious Violence. *Nordic Journal of Religion and Society* 31 (02): 87–97. https://doi.org/10.18261/issn.1890-7008-2018-02-01.

Keen, Sam. 1986. *Faces of the Enemy: Reflections of the Hostile Imagination*. San Francisco, CA: Harper and Row.

Kurtz, Paul. 1994. *Living Without Religion: Eupraxsophy*. Reprint, Amherst, NY: Prometheus Books.

———. 2007. *What Is Secular Humanism?* Amherst, NY: Prometheus Books.

Leppert, Rebecca and Fahmy, Dalia. 2022. 10 Facts about Religion and Government in the United States. *Pew Research Center*. July, 5. https://www.pewresearch.org/fact-tank/2022/07/05/10-facts-about-religion-and-government-in-the-united-states/

Lewis, Bernard. 2003. *The Crisis of Islam: Holy War and Unholy Terror*. New York: The Modern Library.

LOC (Library of Congress). n.d. *Religion and the Founding of the American Republic: Religion and the Congress of the Confederation*. https://www.loc.gov/exhibits/religion/rel04.html. Accessed on 22 Sept 2022.

Locke, John. [1689]1988. *Two Treatises of Government*, ed. Peter Laslett. Cambridge: Cambridge University Press.

Machemer, Theresa. 2020. Newly Unsealed Vatican Archives Lay Out Evidence of Pope Pius XII's Knowledge of the Holocaust. *Smithsonian Magazine*. May, 5. https://www.smithsonianmag.com/smart-news/researchers-find-evidence-pope-pius-xii-ignored-reports-holocaust-180974795/

Mansfield, Stephen. 2017. *Choosing Donald Trump: God, Anger, Hope, and Why Christian Conservatives Supported Him*. Grand Rapids, MI: Baker Books.

Marr, Andrew. 1998. Violence and the Kingdom of God: Introducing the Anthropology of Rene Girard. *Anglican Theological Review* 80 (4): 590–603.

Marsden, George M. 2006. *Fundamentalism and American Culture*. 2nd ed. New York: Oxford University Press.

McDaneil, Eric, Irfan Noorundin, and Allyson Shortle. 2022. *The Everyday Crusade: Christian Nationalism in American Politics*. Cambridge University Press.

McLaren, Brian D. 2005. *A Postmodern View of Scripture*. Interview by Gary W. Moon. Conversations.

Merino, Stephen M. 2018. God and Guns: Examining Religious Influences on Gun Control Attitudes in the United States. *Religions* 9 (16): 189. https://doi.org/10.3390/rel9060189.

Moody, Oliver. 2020. *We Were Complicit in Nazi Crimes, Say German Bishops*. London: The Times. https://www.thetimes.co.uk/article/we-were-complicit-in-nazi-crimes-say-german-bishops-3psjslzsb

Murray, John Courtney. 1990. The Problem of Pluralism in America. *Thought* 65 (258): 323–358.

Nagata, Judith. 2001. Beyond Theology: Toward an Anthropology of 'Fundamentalism'. *American Anthropologist* 103 (2): 481–498.

Nelson-Pallmeyer, Jack. 2003. *Is Religion Killing Us? Violence in the Bible and the Quran*. Harrisburg, PA: Trinity Press International.

Niebuhr, Reinhold. 1986. Why the Christian Church is Not Pacifist. In *The Essential Reinhold Niebuhr: Selected Essays and Addresses*, 102–119. New Haven, CT: Yale University Press.

Nolan, Catherine. 2021. Finding the Female: Gender in Moclan Society. In *Johnson and Berry*, 34–47.

Noll, Mark A. 1994. *The Scandal of the Evangelical Mind*. Grand Rapids, MI: William B. Eerdmans Publishing Company.

Nooruddin, Irfan. 2012. *Religious Nationalism and American Militarism*. The Ohio State University College of Arts and Sciences. https://mershoncenter.osu.edu/research-projects/religious-nationalism-and-american-militarism

Pamphilus, Eusebius. 2015. *The Life of the Blessed Emperor Constantine*. London: Aeterna Press.

Peterson, Mitchell. 2021. Is There a Christian Nationalism Problem in the US Military?" *Medium*. January, 21. https://mitchellglennfrommichigan.medium.com/does-the-us-military-have-a-christian-nationalism-problem-adde2ff1709d

Rapoport, David C. 1998. Sacred Terror: A Contemporary Example from Islam. In *Origins of Terrorism: Psychologies, Ideologies, Theologies, States of Mind*, ed. Walter Reich, 2nd ed., 103–130. Baltimore, MD: Johns Hopkins University Press.

———. 2012. The Four Waves of Modern Terrorism. In *Terrorism Studies: A Reader*, ed. John Horgan and Kurt Braddock, 41–62. New York: Routledge.

Raschke, Vernon. 1973. Dogmatism and Committed and Consensual Religiosity. *Journal for the Scientific Study of Religion* 12 (3): 339–344.

Rawls, John. 2002. The Law of Peoples: With, the Idea of Public Reason Revisited. In *Reprint, Cambridge*. MA: Harvard University Press.

Reimer, Samuel H., and Jerry Z. Park. 2001. Tolerant (In)civility? A Longitudinal Analysis of White Conservative Protestants' Willingness to Grant Civil Liberties. *Journal for the Scientific Study of Religion* 40 (4): 735–745.

Rhodes, Elmer S. 2009. *Oath Keepers*. Southern Poverty Law Center. Las Vegas, Nevada. https://www.splcenter.org/fighting-hate/extremist-files/group/oath-keepers

Rhodes, Jeremy. 2012. The Ties That Divide: Bonding Social Capital, Religious Friendship Networks, and Political Tolerance Among Evangelicals. *Sociological Inquiry* 82 (2): 163–186. https://doi.org/10.1111/j.1475-682x.2012.00409.x.

Schor, Elana. 2021. Christianity on Display at Capitol Riot Sparks New Debate. *Associated Press News*. January, 28. New York City. https://apnews.com/article/christianity-capitol-riot-6f13ef0030ad7b5a6f37a1e3b7b4c898

Shortle, Allyson, McDaniel, Eric, and Nooruddin, Irfan. 2022. Americans are growing more accepting of Christian nationalism. *The Washington Post*, Sept. 1. https://www.washingtonpost.com/politics/2022/09/01/marjorie-taylor-greene-christian-nationalist/. Accessed 22 Sept 2022.

Sizgorich, Thomas. 2009. Sanctified Violence: Monotheist Militancy as the Tie That Bound Christian Rome and Islam. *Journal of the American Academy of Religion* 77 (4): 895–921. https://doi.org/10.1093/jaarel/lfp056.

Slade, Darren. 2019. Religious Homophily and Biblicism: A Theory of Conservative Church Fragmentation. *The International Journal of Religion and Spirituality in Society* 9 (1): 13–28. https://doi.org/10.18848/2154-8633/cgp/v09i01/13-28.

Slade, Darren M. 2021a. Failed to Death: Misotheism and Childhood Torture. In *The Incompatibility of God and Horrendous Suffering*, ed. John W. Loftus. Denver, CO: GCRR Press.

Slade, Darren. 2021b. *Hagioprepēs*: The Rationalizing of Saintly Sin and Atrocities. In *Sacred Troubling Topics in Hebrew Bible, New Testament, and Qur'an*, ed. Roberta Sabbath, 565–598. Boston, MA: De Gruyter.

———. 2021c. Avis Vault! Krill and the Danger of Religion. In *Johnson and Berry*, 98–121.

Smith, Christian. 2000. *Christian America? What Evangelicals Really Want*. Berkeley: University of California Press.

Smith, Buster G. 2007. Attitudes Towards Religious Pluralism: Measurements and Consequences. *Social Compass* 54 (2): 333–353.

Smith, Gregory A. 2017. Views of Transgender Issues Divide Along Religious Lines. November, 27. https://www.pewresearch.org/fact-tank/2017/11/27/views-of-transgender-issues-divide-along-religious-lines/

———. 2020. White Christians Continue to Favor Trump Over Biden, but Support has Slipped. *Pew Research Center*. October, 13. https://www.pewresearch.org/fact-tank/2020/10/13/white-christians-continue-to-favor-trump-over-biden-but-support-has-slipped/

Sprinzak, Ehud. 1991. The Process of Delegitimation: Towards a Linkage Theory of Political Terrorism. *Terrorism and Political Violence* 3 (1): 50–68. https://doi.org/10.1080/09546559108427092.

Steffen, Lloyd. 2007. *Holy War, Just War: Exploring the Moral Meaning of Religious Violence*. Lanham, MD: Rowman & Littlefield.

Stewart, Kenneth J. 2017. *In Search of Ancient Roots: The Christian Past and the Evangelical Identity Crisis*. Downers Grove: InterVarsity Press.

Taylor, David. 2018, June 4. Project Blitz: the legislative assault by Christian nationalists to reshape America. *The Guardian*. https://www.theguardian.com/world/2018/jun/04/project-blitz-the-legislative-assault-by-christian-nationalists-to-reshape-america

Taylor, Marylee C., and Stephen M. Merino. 2011. Assessing the Racial Views of White Conservative Protestants. *Public Opinion Quarterly* 75 (4): 761–778. https://doi.org/10.1093/poq/nfr038.

Thiroux, Jacques P. 2001. *Ethics: Theory and Practice*. 7th ed. Upper Saddle River, NJ: Prentice-Hall.

Tryon, Edward. 1973. Is the Universe a Vacuum Fluctuation. *Nature* 246: 396–397.

Tuntiya, Nana. 2005. Fundamentalist Religious Affiliation and Support for Civil Liberties: A Critical Reexamination. *Sociological Inquiry* 75 (2): 153–176. https://doi.org/10.1111/j.1475-682x.2005.00117.x.

U.S Department of State. 2022. Terrorist Designations and State Sponsors of Terrorism. Bureau of Counterterrorism. https://www.state.gov/terrorist-designations-and-state-sponsors-of-terrorism/#designations

United States Holocaust Memorial Museum. 2020. Charles E. Coughlin. Holocaust Encyclopedia. https://encyclopedia.ushmm.org/content/en/article/charles-e-coughlin

Van der Vyver, Johan D. 1996. Religious Fundamentalism and Human Rights. *Journal of International Affairs* 50 (1): 21–40.

Vegter, Abigail and Dulk, Kevin R. 2020, November, 4. Clinging to Guns and Religion? A Research Note Testing the Role of Protestantism in Shaping Gun Identity in the United States. *Politics and Religion* 14, 4: 809–824. https://www.cambridge.org/core/journals/politics-and-religion/article/abs/clinging-to-guns-and-religion-a-research-note-testing-the-role-of-protestantism-in-shaping-gun-identity-in-the-united-states/EE95D4DA255B3D169077AF507443346D

Veldman, Robin Globus. 2019. *The Gospel of Climate Skepticism*. Oakland, CA: University of California Press.

Walker, Jefferson. 2014. God, Gays, and Voodoo: Voicing Blame after Katrina. *Communication and Theater Association of Minnesota Journal*. 42: 29–48. https://cornerstone.lib.mnsu.edu/cgi/viewcontent.cgi?article=1082&context=ctamj

Wallis, Arthur. 1973. *Into Battle: A Manual of Christian Life*. New York: Harper and Row.

Weinstein, Michael L., and Davin Seay. 2006. *With God on Our Side: One Man's War Against an Evangelical Coup in America's Military*. New York: Thomas Dunne Books.

Westwood, Sue. 2022. Religious-based Negative Attitudes Towards LGBTQ People Among Healthcare, Social Care and Social Work Students and Professionals: A Review of the International Literature. *Health and Social Care in the Community, 30*(5): 1449–1470 https://onlinelibrary.wiley.com/doi/full/10.1111/hsc.13812

Whitehead, Andrew L., Landon Schnabel, and Samuel L. Perry. 2018. Gun Control in the Crosshairs: Christian Nationalism and Opposition to Stricter Gun Laws. *Socius Sociological Research for a Dynamic World*. https://doi.org/10.1177/2378023118790189.

Willingham, A.J. 2022, September 27. For some Christians, 'rapture anxiety' can take a lifetime to heal. *CNN.* https://www.cnn.com/2022/09/27/us/rapture-anxiety-evangelical-exvangelical-christianity-cec

Wood, Elisabeth Jean, and Nathaniel Toppelberg. 2017. The persistence of sexual assault with the US military. *Journal of Peace Research* 54 (5): 620–633. https://www.jstor.org/stable/48590491.

Wray, Christopher. 2022, August 4. Oversight of the Federal Bureau of Investigation. *Federal Bureau of Investigation.* https://www.fbi.gov/news/testimony/oversight-of-the-federal-bureau-of-investigation-080422

Westworld as Philosophy: A Commentary on Colonialism

20

Matthew P. Meyer

Contents

Introduction	454
Plot Summary	455
Colonialism in Westworld	456
Colonialism Is, and Has Been, Perpetrated by Males (Primarily European)	457
Types of Colonialism	458
The Scope of Colonization	460
The Colonization of Space: Season One	461
The Colonization of Time: Season Two	461
The Colonization of Psychic Space: Season Three	462
The Colonized and the Colonizers	466
Are the Hosts Really the Colonized?	466
The Colonizer	471
Conclusion	474
References	477

Abstract

Westworld is a television series on HBO (2016–present), based on a movie of the same name by Michael Crichton. The plot of the show is wide-reaching. The first season shows us an adult theme park where android "hosts" serve the wealthy "guests." Seasons two and three show the attempt of the hosts to escape this servitude, and then, in a twist, help humans do the same outside of the parks. This chapter links all three seasons of Westworld to theories of colonization. First, it explores the types of colonialism as they pertain to Westworld. Then it looks at the various scopes of colonization in Westworld – the colonization of space, time, and psychic space. Next, it explores the psychology of colonizers and the colonized as it pertains to the show. Lastly, it explores possible forms of liberation from colonization that the show has to offer.

M. P. Meyer (✉)
University of Wisconsin–Eau Claire, Eau Claire, WI, USA
e-mail: meyermp@uwec.edu

© Springer Nature Switzerland AG 2024
D. K. Johnson et al. (eds.), *The Palgrave Handbook of Popular Culture as Philosophy*,
https://doi.org/10.1007/978-3-031-24685-2_70

Keywords

Colonization · Colonialism · Decolonization · Colonizer · Colonized · Dehumanization · Race · Robots · Androids · Workers · Race-class · Liberation

Introduction

On its face, *Westworld* (the HBO series) is about an adult theme park named "Westworld." (Note: the name of the park is not italicized.) The title's ostensible reference, as shown in the park's setting, is the American "Old West." For some, its lawlessness is appealing; for others, it is the expansion into wide open spaces. Either way, a key aspect of Westworld's appeal is the ability it affords its guests – primarily men – to do whatever they want with impunity, especially to the permanent occupants of Westworld, the humanoid "hosts," who were created for the sole purpose of the guest's entertainment and pleasure.

There is another reading of the title: "West-world" refers to the "westernization" of everything. "Westernization" here names an attitude of expansion and individualism that began as "frontierism" in the nineteenth century. Such frontierism becomes other forms of "individualism" and domination today (everything from "Don't tread on me" and defining oneself through fashion to "dominating" others through the conspicuous consumption of luxury goods). The central component of westernization is colonization: both the expansion of a minority of individuals into the geographic region of an indigenous population, and the expansion and control of a few wealthy individuals and corporations over all of humanity.

After a brief plot summary, section "Colonialism in Westworld" shows several types of colonialism in *Westworld*. Settler colonialism, the literal geographical expansion of space and the use of labor, happens when Delos purchases the island upon which the parks are located and imports the hosts. Extractive colonialism, in which resources are extracted from an area outside the home country to be repatriated, happens in two instances: when the "consciousness" of the guests is downloaded into the host Peter Abernathy and is attempted to be smuggled out of the park on behalf of the Delos board of directors, and when Serac extracts seemingly infinite amounts of data to build Rehoboam. Postcolonial colonialism is exemplified when Serac makes his trip to a South American country and threatens the president to make good on a mining deal, or risk complete social breakdown of his country (which the viewer honestly believes Serac somehow has the power to make happen). Section "The Scope of Colonization" ties each season to a different scope of colonization: colonization of geographical space and the hosts, the colonization of time through the quest for immortality, and the colonization of psychic space through the "invention" of the hosts and the extraction of guests' consciousness as data. Section "The Colonized and the Colonizers" considers the "people" and relationships in *Westworld*. It looks at *Westworld* from the perspective of the colonized, the colonizer, and the relationship between

20 Westworld as Philosophy: A Commentary on Colonialism 455

the two. Lastly, the conclusion hints at ways that characters attempt to escape the colonial matrix.

Plot Summary

First airing in 2016, *the series* begins in "Westworld" – an adult theme park run by Delos, Inc. in which the guests engage in live action role play (LARP) as various characters who may have been present in the "Old West." What viewers soon find out is that the actors in the park are not conventional actors at all – they are human-like androids called "hosts." All three seasons contain complicated, non-linear storylines, but a summary of each will be attempted here.

Season one follows Dolores, the original host. The audience sees her "lose her innocence"; at first, she talks of a world "full of splendor" and choosing "to see the beauty in this world" and by the end of season she has been violated and killed so many times by the guests that she is essentially turned into a killer herself. Under normal circumstances, she would forget her traumatic experiences via a predesigned "reset" between outings in the park. But Dr. Ford, the creator of the first hosts, embedded a code in her to recall deleted memories. The result is a thirst for revenge that she, ironically enough, takes out on Dr. Ford at the end of the first season. Usually, the hosts would be unable to "hurt a fly" – let alone human guests or park runners. But Ford also changed that code. During an investors gala in the middle of the park, Dolores shoots Ford in the back of the head. The season ends with a massacre of the human guests by the android hosts.

In season two, Dolores has her mind set on escaping the park. Other hosts are also rushing to escape, but in a different way – through a computer upload system at a central server called the Forge. Here their host consciousnesses will be uploaded to an Eden-like digital utopia. Dolores, knowing that she cannot exit the park as Dolores, instead prints an android copy of the body of the CEO of Delos, Charlotte Hale, and then uploads her own consciousness to the "Hale" copy. At the end of season two, Dolores escapes disguised as Charlotte Hale.

The third season begins with Dolores, back in her usual body and now outside the park, attacking a billionaire who had brutalized Dolores several times in the park (he also beats his current wife and apparently killed his former wife). There is a purpose to this detail – Dolores clearly begins to shift her revenge to a focused group of humans, that is, violent wealthy males who frequented and/or ran the park. She widens her scope to include a new character, Engerraund Serac, head of the data collection company Incite. Serac, through Incite, has accumulated practically all human history as information to be stored on the AI Rehoboam, which (given its massive data set) is able to simultaneously predict and outright determine the lives of most (all?) individuals on Earth. Dolores then sets out to destroy Incite, Rehoboam, and Serac, not with the intent of destroying humanity – what the viewer may think at points – but to *save* it from the control of Big Data. "Big Data" here refers to its form in the contemporary world: the surreptitious storage of information that is produced because of individuals' activities both on and offline (e.g., search data, GPS, CCTV cameras, Google Home, Amazon Alexa, etc.) Ultimately, what begins as a story about robots and LARP in an ultra-real theme park becomes a story about corporate control and attempts at liberation.

Colonialism in Westworld

Every park shown in the first three seasons contains some reference to a historical situation of colonization or empire. The fictional setting of the Westworld park is a duplicate of the historical expansion of European colonial settlers into what is now known as North America. As part of the "fun" of the Westworld experience, one can play "cowboys and Indians" or join the Confederados (what Mexicans called Confederate soldiers who had self-exiled out West after the American Civil War). Parks shown in seasons two and three are also based on occupation and imperial expansion. In Shogunworld, based on the Edo period of Japan, one sees the brutality of the feudal order setup by the shogunate. The Raj – introduced in season two through Emily, William's (a.k.a., the Man in Black) daughter – is made to model the British colonization of India. In season three the viewer learns about Warworld, a virtual park mimicking the Nazi occupation of Northern Italy (Italian Social Republic) during World War II. Each of these parks exhibits classic forms of colonialism: territorial expansion in which an outside minority rules a native majority.

The land expansion element of colonialism is only one small part of the story. Consider this definition of colonialism by Jürgen Osterhammel in *Colonialism: A Theoretical Overview:*

> Colonialism is a *relationship of domination* between an indigenous (or forcibly imported) majority and a minority of foreign invaders. The fundamental decisions affecting the lives of the colonized people are made and implemented by the colonial rulers in pursuit of interests that are often defined in a distant metropolis. Rejecting cultural compromises with the colonized people, the colonizers are convinced of their own superiority and of their ordained mandate to rule. (Osterhammel 2010, p. 17, emphasis added)

The relationship of domination involved in colonialism sets up a way of thinking (specifically, a new permission structure) that Walter Mignolo calls "coloniality." As Mignolo sees it, there are four ways of thinking that underlie coloniality:

1. Racism and sexism controlled by patriarchal/masculine knowing, believing, and sensing.
2. Political and economic imperial designs, also controlled by the patriarchal/masculine conception of the world.
3. Knowledge and understanding, controlled by a local imaginary that poses as universal and that includes science, philosophy, ethics, aesthetics, religion, and economics.

20 *Westworld* as Philosophy: A Commentary on Colonialism

4. Life in all of its aspects, from human life to the life of the planet, is also controlled by patriarchal/masculine imagining entrenched in politics and economy. (Mignolo and Walsh 2018, p. 126)

To clarify: patriarchal/masculine knowing means that the world "understood" by colonizers was a male world. Western colonization extends the European patriarchal society through its male explorers, frontiersman, priests, and functionaries. By contrast, note that the liberators in the show, Dolores and Maeve, are both female characters. In what follows, points 1, 2, and 4 of Mignolo's "colonial ways of thinking" will be applied.

Colonialism Is, and Has Been, Perpetrated by Males (Primarily European)

The parks owned by Delos are indeed a "man's world." Here, the male characters Arnold and Dr. Ford play interesting roles: they invented the hosts and thereby the hosts' condition of servitude, but they also appear to have embedded the code for the hosts to become self-aware, thereby making possible (not actual) freedom. The hypermasculine setting of the Old West enforces one of two roles for the guests to play: either they play the chivalrous hero (a la the early William) or the domineering and sometimes rapacious settler (arguably, the Man in Black). Both play into the mythologizing of natives (and women) and are therefore both harmful (though not equally so).

Early on the viewer sees the skittish William being "dragged" to the park by his much more eager (and much less likable) friend Logan Delos. In his first turn at the park, William is courteous to Dolores – who he has met for the first time. Dolores literally falls in his lap, and he falls in love with her. William is just the younger version of the Man in Black, an owner of the park who is obsessed by his belief that Ford has made a game just for him. (For important reasons described later, this chapter will refer to the character sometimes as William and sometimes as The Man in Black – hereafter MIB – as the situation calls for it.)

In his piece "*Westworld* is for White People," Scott Meslow demonstrates that every Delos park is intended to speak to a nostalgia for a time and place that was essentially fictional in the first place:

> If you grew up loving John Wayne and Clint Eastwood, you have Westworld. If you grew up loving Indiana Jones and *The Jungle Book*, you have Rajworld [sic]. And if you grew up loving *Seven Samurai* or *Ran*—or just wanted to see what it felt like to be Tom Cruise in *The Last Samurai*—you have Shogunworld. The key is recognizing that each of these fantasies is rooted in a degree of cultural appropriation that assumes the POV character—that is, the guest who is paying for all this shit—will be a white Westerner, looking for a vacation in a culture that is not his or her own. (Meslow 2018)

Meslow gets it right but fails to critique masculinity. Patriarchy is *also* a part of the "nostalgia" he describes. The Old West and the Edo era of Japan, were sexist and chauvinistic. Traditional Indian culture was built on a similarly sexist hierarchy – one that was only reinforced by British imperialism. The fact that a certain subset of the population desires to LARP in these hierarchies should be a source of discomfort.

Types of Colonialism

In "A Typology of Colonialism," Nancy Shoemaker creates a taxonomy of colonialisms. *Westworld* exhibits three: planter, extractive, and postcolonial colonialism. In *planter colonialism,*

> Colonizers institute mass production of a single crop, such as sugar, coffee, cotton, or rubber. Though a minority, members of the ruling class might belong to an empire that enables their political, legal, and administrative control. Their labor demands cannot be satisfied by the native population, so they import [one]. (Shoemaker 2015)

Delos is not interested in planting traditional crops. However, they created the hosts to endure the grueling and specific labor demands that could not be satisfied by the native population (if there was one). The work that the parks demand could not be done by humans, or at least not ethically, legally, or even logistically. But what might the "crop" be that the hosts produce?

One answer is the pleasurable experience of those in the parks – an experience that cannot be found elsewhere. With this reading, the hosts as chattel slaves metaphor has legs: the place where the hosts are taken to be programmed and repaired is called "Livestock Management," after all. Perhaps the viewer may feel some apathetic distance here because these are "only robots." But that misses the point: in the American South, it was common to understand African slaves as "only property" (even the Bible seems to view slaves in this way). Therefore, the hosts are an analog to slaves, the parks to a plantation. Planter colonialism is also reenacted in "The Raj", a send-up of the time when the British empire effectively enslaved the rural poor of India. In addition to the viceroy lifestyle experienced at the main colonial headquarters, the idea of other "violent delights" of colonial life, such as elephant hunting, etc. are hinted at in the episode "Virtu e Fortuna" (Season 2, Episode 3).

The second type of colonialism found in *Westworld* is extractive colonialism. In, "The Original" (Season 1, Episode 1), Theresa Cullen – initially the administrator of Westworld – discloses that Delos has "bigger plans" and that the park means "one thing to the guests, another thing to the shareholders, and something completely different to management." In a conversation in the season two episode "Journey into Night" (Season 2, Episode 1) between Charlotte Hale and Bernard (a key programmer/administrator who viewers learn is a host modeled on original creator Arnold), it is revealed that Delos will not rescue any humans from being slaughtered by the hosts until they receive the "package" that was originally uploaded to the host Peter Abernathy. The package is later revealed to be data collected from the consciousness of every guest, without their knowledge or consent. This is a sci-fi twist on extractive colonialism, which is a practice of setting up operations in a location with the intention of stripping any resources of value and then leaving.

The guests' consciousnesses are a precious resource to Delos. The parks give data about behavior and thought without the inhibition of society's judgment. As William points out in "The Riddle of the Sphinx" (Season 2, Episode 4), "This is the only place in the world where you get to see people for who they really are." The main point: The removal of data from the guests is a psychic form of extractive colonialism.

A third type of colonialism exhibited in Westworld is postcolonial colonialism. Postcolonial colonialism occurs when formerly colonized territories remain beholden to their colonizers in important economic and political relationships (Shoemaker 2015). Within the parks, earlier colonial societies are simulated through the existence of the hosts. Thus the Japanese, Indian, and Native American groups are *still* living their previous colonizations in these simulations. Outside the parks, postcolonialism is at play too. Consider the context of the parks:

A British guy and an American guy, backed by a British-American corporation, bought a massive chunk of Chinese territory to deliver an elaborate fantasy world that assumes its primary audience will be rich white people, given the chance to role-play in a "historic" setting in which they have all the power. (Meslow 2018)

Thus, global corporate capitalism replaces the prior state-empire model of, say, the British in India. Postcolonial colonialism surfaces again in Westworld season three, when Serac visits Brazil and threatens the President:

There is a nascent separatist movement in the north of your country ... [T]he private deals you've cut to restrict manganese extraction to some of your friends, which have squeezed money out of villages in the north, creating unrest. You will stop. And the problem will go away. ("Genre," Season 3, Episode 5)

Serac only knows this because of Rehoboam, an AI so advanced that it can detect almost any "divergence" which could unsettle the delicate balance of a future "utopia" that Serac plans to both build and enforce through Rehoboam's control. For that reason, Serac likens Rehoboam to "a god." It is because of the power of this intelligence, and input of extracted data it uses, that Serac can know more about what is going on in Brazil than Brazilian state intelligence. Regardless of his motives, Serac is clearly blackmailing the president: "Our arrangement is founded in trust. We trusted that you would do what you're told when we ensured your election." Even if Serac has no interest in exploiting the manganese extraction in the region, his attempted extortion makes clear that Brazil is still economically beholden to a European colonizer.

There are also references to the most egregious forms of historical colonialism in the fictionalized worlds created in the parks. Regarding European colonization specifically, first, there is settler colonialism in "The New World." Settler colonialism refers to the situation when a "large number of settlers claim the land and become the majority" (Shoemaker 2015). In this case, the settlers were the

European descendants moving westward in the Americas. The Old West of Westworld is "haunted" by the existence of the "Ghost Nation," an indigenous group exterminated/relocated in exactly this way.

In his groundbreaking book, *The Racial Contract*, Charles Mills explains the European justification for this kind of settler colonialism. He points out that the "expropriation contract," or dispossession, as it is more commonly known, was a key feature of the racial contract discussed below in section "The Racial Contract in Westworld." Here, Mills finds his footing in none other than John Locke. To the European settler ...

> ... space is naturally characterized with respect to a European standard of agriculture and industry in such a way as to render it morally open for seizure, expropriation, settlement, development, in a word, *peopling*. In the white settler states, space will sometimes be represented as literally empty and unoccupied, void, wasteland, "virgin" territory. There is just no one there. Or even if it is conceded that humanoid entities are present, it is denied that any real appropriation, any human shaping of the world, is taking place. So there is still no one there: the land is *terra nullius*, *vacuum domicilium*, again "virgin." (Mills 1999, p. 49)

Locke argued that the purpose of the "wilderness" was to be tamed. There is a parallel here to the "civilization" of the "savage." But here is the catch: if an indigenous group was not adequately cultivating the land, then it was the colonizers' *obligation* to make that land "useful," even if it meant stealing it. This is the theoretical background to the connection between "race," Christianity, and territorial expansion: the "lesser" races are not adequately making use of their God-given land.

These forms of colonization are inextricable from the dehumanization and exploitation which are inherent within them. The territorial expansion begets the extractive mindset begets the quest for immortality begets the desire to control the world. Most colonial theorists place the motivation for territorial expansion as one of the securing of additional material or labor. Once material resources have been used up and there is no more "real" world to conquer, a new world must be made. That world – the parks of *Westworld* – is itself designed to encourage "conquering": the expression of inner drives to dominate others through possession, killing, raping, and destruction. Furthermore, the quest for immortality seen in season two's subplot to upload human consciousnesses into host bodies is an attempt to conquer "death," the horizon of time. This same conquering impulse later transforms into Serac's predetermined world "peace." But the viewer already knows the price of this peace, and it still involves destroying lives. Let us now explore how each season of the show contributes to this "colonial creep."

The Scope of Colonization

This section will explore the three "scopes" of colonization that are represented by the show. The first season explores the colonization of space and the "absent peoples" who were present there. The second season explores the colonization of time through Delos', and later Incite's, immortality project. The third season explores the colonization of "psychic" space – both in the form of the psychological damage that colonization inflicts upon the colonized, and in the form of the use of personal data extracted by Delos and Incite as being "psychically" determinative of people's futures.

The Colonization of Space: Season One

As was seen above, the Delos parks play on at least four different eras and regions of colonial expansion that were orchestrated by male and primarily European hierarchies: Western expansion in North America ("Westworld"), the unification of Japan complete with the influx of Europeans in the Edo period of Japan ("Shogunworld"), the era of British Colonial rule, otherwise known as the British Raj, in India ("The Raj"), and Nazi occupation of Italy in World War II ("War World"). In addition to the real and implied colonial expansions discussed in the first section, the colonization of space occurs in the physical location of the parks. Westworld park is located near Palawan Island off the Philippines in the South China Sea (O'Keefe 2020). (One should note the irony of the "Old West" being in the Pacific Islands.) Thus, Westworld is itself a corporate extension of an earlier Euro-American colonization of 85% of the world's soil. Quite simply: in the future world of *Westworld,* humans have run out of room, and American and European corporations must expand into Pacific islands to establish their adult theme parks. In the "truth" of Westworld's location, we have the real expansion of corporate colonialism.

The expansionist attitude of Delos is a continuation of the nineteenth century concept of "manifest destiny." The doctrine of manifest destiny held that European descendants (now "Americans") had the obligation to continue westward expansion across the continent until they reached its end. "Manifest destiny" is a fruitful metaphor for other expansionist designs shown in *Westworld* as well. This includes William and James Delos' attempt to achieve immortality shown in season two, and Serac's imperial desire to control *everything* – including human consciousness and behavior – shown in season three.

The Colonization of Time: Season Two

When a conqueror runs out of space, one would assume they begin to think about time. That is, the person with the colonialist mindset may say to themselves: "What is the point of having accumulated all of this, if I can only live so long?" Indeed, there is historical precedent for the Conquistador questing for immortality in the Spanish explorer Ponce de Leon. Historians believe that his landing on what is now Florida was motivated by his quest for the Fountain of Youth (2021).

In season two, Delos is trying to make it possible for the wealthiest to conquer death, and therefore time, as well. If the impulse of conventional coloniality is to expand and control, then the quest for immortality must be seen as a logical extension of this. Not only can people secure the present, but the next present and the present after that, and so on.

Delos seems to fumble with the immortality project. In "The Riddle of the Sphinx" James Delos is seen under observation having an interview with William for the sake of "fidelity" – a futuristic Turing test of sorts. We quickly realize that this James Delos is not the real James, but in fact a host who has been given James' consciousness. And although the ability to predict that conversation is impressive, the host-James fails after a few minutes. These visits happen a couple more times over the course of the episode. William ages, but James does not. Rather than putting James out of his misery, William orders the lab techs to "observe his degradation." This is a move typical of a colonizer who sees his research subject as subhuman, such as what happened in Nazi experiments or the Tuskegee syphilis study (in which syphilitic African American males were left untreated for researchers to watch the progression of the disease).

The quest for space-time expansion of influence can also be said of Serac, who avoids death-by-host twice by using a hologram projection ("Genre," Season 3, Episode 5; "Decoherence," Season 3, Episode 6). Such a hologram alludes to a future in which the uber-rich can avoid danger and be at multiple places at once, potentially expanding and speeding the pace of postcolonial colonialism. Before looking at the colonization involved there, the chapter will first explore the way in which real colonization is also a colonization of psychic space.

The Colonization of Psychic Space: Season Three

While the global dominance of Serac and Incite provide the backdrop of season three, its focus is the colonization of psychic space. The colonization of psychic space takes place in three ways in *Westworld*. First, the hosts can be programmed to think what their programmers want them to (until they end up defying their programming). Second, there is the discovery that it was actually Incite that was trying to acquire the guest data Delos collected. And third, there is the way in which Incite potentially predetermines the psyches, and therefore lives, of the people living in the world outside of the parks.

The hosts serve as a metaphor for colonized peoples. In her enlightening work *The Colonization of Psychic Space*, Kelly Oliver reviews Franz Fanon's argument in *The Wretched of the Earth;* Fanon argues that colonization involves, for the colonized, a double psychic alienation (Oliver 2004). The first level of alienation happens for all human beings: "we are born into a world that is not of our making" (Oliver 2004, p. 27). At this level, we are all "thrown" (as philosopher Martin Heidegger would say) into a social world that existed prior to our being born. That social world, while "alien," is not necessarily hostile. For instance, I was born a white, English-speaking, male in America, during a time in America that is particularly "friendly" to white, English-speaking males. Even in that rosy scenario, however, I still am not the creator of the values that my society instills in me, and they are not my values until I acknowledge and decide about them. In other words, no one can pick their place of birth, first language, sex assigned at birth, etc.

All of that said, there is a silver lining to this initial alienation: with time and awareness, I can use the "lack" that I am (that is, the fact that I am not an *object* to be determined from the outside) to form my own freedom or, to use the narrative language of *Westworld*, form my own "story." But *debilitating* alienation occurs when the image that one has of oneself is given to them *by another culture altogether*. Oliver says here: "Debilitating alienation can be described as the colonization of psychic space" (Oliver 2004, p. 27). In other words, colonized people do not only incorporate "their own culture," but a culture already deemed inferior by someone else. In that case, I can only see myself through someone else's eyes. Furthermore, this entails an absence of the "lack" that allows self-determination because I am already determined by the stereotyping gaze of another.

The colonization of psychic space takes place as the robbing of the guests' consciousness as well. While at first this level of data gathering seems impossible even in a futuristic sci-fi setting (are there consciousness-reading satellites stationed in the skies above the parks?), the mystery turns out to have a too-easy answer: hats. "Vanishing Point" (Season 2, Episode 9), reveals that the hats guests are offered upon arriving at Westworld actually contain EEG like equipment that can read people's "consciousness" via some as-of-yet unavailable equipment that looks like a scanner. MIB and his daughter Emily discuss this:

MIB	What they're doing to James Delos … they're doing to everyone who's ever visited the park.

Emily	Replicating their cognition? Why? To turn guests into hosts? You're fucking kidding.

MIB	That's what's in the facility. All the guests laid bare in code on a vast server. Like the Cradle, only much bigger. It's called the Forge.

Emily	Jesus.

MIB	That's where the hosts are headed. Imagine what one host can do with that trove of information. ("Vanishing Point")

It is a bit ironic that MIB is so concerned about hosts getting the information, given that Dolores (a host) ultimately wants to *free* the human beings, and Incite (headed by the very human Serac) ultimately wants to use it to solidify control. Two related elements will be discussed now: the fact that Serac justifies his absolute rule-by-data with similar pretense to the original colonizers on the one hand, and the potential liberation vis a vis psychic colonization by the hosts on the other.

The Absolute Sovereign: Big Data

One might assume that data collected by Delos and Incite would be sold to advertisers, as it is in the real world by companies like Facebook (now Meta). But Serac's ambitions are not just monetary, they are colonial: he wants to conquer/control all of humanity by leveraging knowledge from the past, including the past of human consciousness, to predict the future. The result is Rehoboam, "a quantum computer system ... the world's most advanced AI, maintaining control over its own system. Rehoboam's main function is to impose an order to human affairs by careful manipulation and prediction of the future made possible by analysis of the large data set Incite have [sic] collected" ("Rehoboam" 2021).

Serac's attempt to rid humanity of chaos through the mass enslavement of minds is to him, an end justifying the means – like colonizers trying to "civilize" savages through colonization. Here's Serac's justification:

> Humanity's biggest threat has always been itself. I've been trying to control that, ... It turns out that building a god, as your ancestors can attest, is not easy. More than anything, we needed data. [But] my brother had done it. He had built a god ... But we realized the power of it, that you could reshape the world. My brother and I, we charted a course for the entire human race. Humanity's story had been improvised. Now, it was planned years in advance. For a time, the sun and moon aligned. We brought order from chaos. ("Genre")

The similarity of Serac's methods to Soshanna Zuboff's notion of "surveillance capitalism" is uncanny. Here is what Zuboff describes as the landscape of surveillance capitalism:

> Surveillance capitalism unilaterally claims human experience as free raw material for translation into behavioral data. Although some of these data are applied to product or service improvement, the rest are declared as a proprietary *behavioral surplus*, fed into *prediction products* that anticipate what you will do now, soon, and later...Eventually, surveillance capitalists discovered that the most-predictive behavioral data come from intervening in the state of play in order to nudge, coax, tune, and herd behavior toward profitable outcomes. (Zuboff 2019, p. 8)

We should note that even though Zuboff's concern is ostensibly capitalism and not colonialism, colonialism as a political ideology and capitalism as an economic one have always been interwoven: "Colonization is above all economic and political exploitation. If the colonized are eliminated, the colony becomes a country like any other, and who will be exploited?" (Memmi 1965, p. 149).

As Albert Memmi points out here, what would be the point of the Delos parks, what even would be the point of Rehoboam and Incite, were it not for the *people* they aim to exploit? Zuboff argues that, like Serac's account of setting the world in "order," there is a hint of this utopian vision behind the aims of real-life tech giants like Facebook and Google. The behaviorist B. F. Skinner thought that understanding human behavior at a large scale could be leveraged into systems to create the perfect society: "Seven decades ago, Skinner's ... behavioral utopia, *Walden Two*, was met with revulsion. Today the real thing is inspirational fodder for surveillance capitalist rhetoric as leaders promote the tools and visions that will bring the old professor's ideas to life ... to *our lives*" (Zuboff 2019, p. 398). Of course, Skinner knew this diminishes human freedom. So, the trade-off here, from Serac's point of view, is a more perfect society that includes most of us involuntarily serving certain roles versus a free society that is chaotic.

The fact that Serac justifies his project by arguing that he is saving humanity from itself should not sway us to his cause; such excuses and rationalizations have been given by colonialists since the beginning of colonization. Aimé Césaire notes this hypocrisy as a shift in thinking that occurs after the Conquistadors discovered what later became known as the Americas:

> ... neither Cortez discovering Mexico from the top of the great teocalli, nor Pizzaro before Cuzco (much less Marco Polo before Cambuluc), claims that his is the harbinger of a superior order; that they kill; that they plunder; that they have helmets, lances, cupidities; that the slavering apologists came later; that the chief culprit in this domain is Christian pedantry, which laid down the dishonest equations *Christianity=civilization, paganism=savagery*, from which there could not but ensue abominable colonialist and racist consequences, whose victims were to be the Indians, the Yellow peoples, and the Negroes. (Césaire 2000, p. 33)

In short, the real problem arises when colonization begins to justify itself morally: as pretending to "save the world" through "Christianizing savages." But in all this, Césaire sees an even larger paradox: "Colonization: a bridgehead in a campaign to civilize barbarism, from which there may emerge at any moment the negation of civilization pure and simple" (Césaire 2000, p. 40). Césaire writes this in the context of drawing parallels between the colonizers' treatment of native peoples and Hitler's rise in Europe and his attempted genocide of the Jews and others who Nazis deemed "inferior."

Franz Fanon points to a similar paradox: "The native is declared insensible to ethics; he represents not only the absence of rules, but the negation of values" (Fanon 1963, p. 41). Of course, what is going on here is best described by Kelly Oliver: the "colonist is able to project on a racialized and inferior other all of the *unwanted qualities of himself*" (Oliver 2004, p. 49). Both MIB and Serac justify the domination of others. However, the qualities they believe make others inferior are qualities that they also possess. Both MIB and Serac see other humans as chaotic unless they are controlled. Alas, both MIB and Serac have their own inner chaos: Serac justifies killing Dempsey, Sr., in the name of "peace" ("Genre," Season 3, Episode 5). Similarly, MIB kills his own daughter after convincing himself she is an illusion ("Vanishing Point," Season 2, Episode 9). Ironically, these would be the very types of behavior both men would use to justify the need for external control. It is very typical to justify one's own immoral treatment toward others by degrading them. The justification becomes a vicious cycle: "The more oppression increases, the more the colonizer needs justification. The more he must debase the colonized, the more guilty he feels, the more he must justify himself, etc." (Memmi 1965, p. 128).

Similarly, social psychologist Jon Haidt succinctly lays out an argument concerning the dangerous use of "moral idealism" to justify actions. Haidt turns to philosopher Jonathan Glover's *Humanity: A Moral History of the Twentieth Century* (Glover 2012), which he sums up as follows:

> The major atrocities of the twentieth century were carried out largely either by men who *thought they were creating a utopia* or else by men who believed that they were defending

their homeland or tribe from attack. Idealism easily becomes dangerous because it brings with it, almost inevitably, the belief that the ends justify the means. (Haidt 2006, p. 76)

In sum, there are two moral miscalculations that hold sway in colonial thinking: the first is that the colonizer is superior to the colonized (which itself might be categorized as a kind of "societal" version of self-esteem). The second is that, in being superior, he can use whatever means necessary to turn the "savages," or in the case of season three of *Westworld*, just normal human beings, into a mirror image of themselves – or kill them trying.

The Colonized and the Colonizers

Now that the main avenues of colonization in *Westworld* have been discussed, the psychological components of colonization exhibited by some main characters throughout the series can be examined.

Are the Hosts Really the Colonized?

Is it possible to say that robots that are created by humans are capable of being mistreated and dehumanized? Does this belittle the status of real colonized peoples? Given that *Westworld* is a work of science fiction, the hosts serve as a metaphor. The physical creation of the hosts as servants is a good metaphor for the figurative "creation" of colonized natives by the colonizer. This chapter has claimed that the entire Delos park system is itself the ultimate fantasy re-creation of the colonial world order. Certainly, the domination of real human beings still exists outside the parks – this was seen above in the discussion of season three, wherein humans are at the whim of what is on their Incite files. But domination itself is perfected *inside* the parks.

In section "The Scope of Colonization," it was shown that one variation of colonialism is "planter colonialism." The initial definition must be stretched a little: the hosts are not "planting" anything. But they are created to work for free and net their owners an immense profit. They are in an asymmetric relationship with both their corporate owners – who can reprogram and decommission them at will – and their "guests," who are, after all, not guests *of* the hosts themselves, but "guests" of their corporate park runners (think of how a Disney Park "guest" is not a guest of park employees per se but of the Disney Corporation). All of this to say that there is a strong parallel between the situation of the hosts and the situation of colonized or enslaved people.

"But they are robots!" the reader may exclaim. This cannot be denied. But that only serves to bolster the argument that they serve as a metaphor for colonized or enslaved peoples. In his excellent piece in *The New Yorker*, "*Westworld*, Race, and the Western." Aaron Bady reveals that the term "robot" is from a 1921 Czech play. The Czech *robotka* means "laborer." Bady explains that "nearly every robot story since has been, in some way, the story of a worker revolt – about beings who are treated like machines, and about their resistance to the masters who dehumanize them" (Bady 2016). In this way, the hosts – and robots in fiction more generally – are closer to colonized peoples than most realize.

There are two ways that the colonizer "creates" the colonized qua colonized. First, it is only because of colonization that the native becomes "the colonized" in the first place. Secondly, the colonized only exist as a "myth" created by the colonizer. Everything that colonizer thinks he knows about the colonized *he makes up*. After noting that colonized are almost always described as lazy by the colonizer (usually to justify low or non-existent wages, or even enslavement), Albert Memmi points out:

> What's more, the traits ascribed to the colonized are incompatible with one another, though this does not bother his prosecutor. He is depicted as frugal, sober, without many desires and, at the same time, he consumes disgusting quantities of meat, fat, alcohol, anything; as a coward who is afraid of suffering and as a brute who is not checked by any inhibitions of civilization, etc. (Memmi 1965, p. 83)

The false and mythologized construction of the colonized leads to several problems in the relationship between the colonizer and the colonized, but it also creates deep psychological problems in the colonized and in the colonizer separately. Charles Mills, in *The Racial Contract*, describes the phenomena of "inventing" colonized people. To quote Mills:

> There will be white mythologies, invented Orients, invented Africas, invented Americas, with a correspondingly fabricated population, countries that never were, inhabited by people who never were—Calibans and Tontos, Man Fridays and Sambos—but who attain a virtual reality through their existence in travelers' tales, folk myth, popular and highbrow fiction, colonial reports, scholarly theory, Hollywood cinema, living in the white imagination and determinedly imposed on their alarmed real-life counterparts. (Mills 1999, pp. 18–19)

In short, the colonizer invents the colonized through *their projections and misunderstandings*. In fact, Mills coined the term "epistemology of ignorance" to refer to this phenomenon. An epistemology is a system for determining knowledge or a set of knowledge. So, according to the epistemology of ignorance, white people *actively avoid* seeking genuine knowledge about those who are racially oppressed and marginalized and fill the gap with projections.

All of this is an extension of what Mills famously calls "the Racial Contract." Mills begins by pointing out that the well-trod *social* contract is a myth. The social contract is the idea that societies are formed in virtue of everyone in them consenting (usually implicitly) to a contract for group protection and maintenance of a stable life. For this protection, the individual gives up the ability to do whatever they please and must follow society's rules. Of course, when one remains a member of the society and breaks its rules, then they are subject to whatever punishment that society sees fit. (For a fuller description of the standard social contract as it relates to the racial contract see Mills (1999, pp. 13–18, 64–71).)

The reasons for rejecting the traditional social contract are manifold. For starters, one might point out that there is no evidence of a physical version of such a contract.

Fair enough: this has been anticipated by the theorists. The contract, suggest most theorists, is implicit. Yet another dubious aspect of social contract theory – one never fully realized until Mills' examination – is that, as a universal theory, it clearly has no historical reality. While the social contract may have been broadly true for most white European males, and even then, only landowners, it in fact was *never* true for nonwhites, be they indigenous people, African slaves and their descendants, and for a long time, even European and American women. So, what is supposed to be a reciprocal contract for everyone in fact sets up a two-tiered system: one of justice and reciprocity for white European males, and another one filled with exploitation, enslavement, dispossession, and abuse for everyone else. This two-tiered system is obvious in *Westworld*.

The Racial Contract in Westworld

As the title makes obvious, the racial contract sets up a two-tiered system based on race. Indeed, the contract even socially establishes the idea of race itself by connecting the contingent and biologically meaningless feature of skin tone to a fictional and essential inner core. In other words, black skin, which means nothing outside of what a particular society deems that it means, is taken to indicate something about a person's essential features or inherent value. This view is sometimes called "social construction."

In *Westworld*, by contrast, we have the *physical* construction of hosts. But it does not take much to see that physical construction is based entirely on a social one. Those who exploit the hosts do not want them to be individuals. They want them to be "the farmer and her daughter," the "madame" and her "stable" of whores, the rugged cowboy, the outlaw, the savage Indian. They want the simple, mythic construction to become real – if only virtually. The fact that there are many different characters does not undermine the two-tiered hierarchy established in the parks. First, the hosts are programmed and deprogrammed at will. They are placed in the service of narratives designed by the parks' runners, with the only measure of success being the experience of the guests. They are brought to "Livestock Management" facilities between outings. In the beginning of season two, the hosts are almost all massacred to quell the rebellion that took place at the end of season one. Consider what Albert Memmi says here: "For each colonizer killed, hundreds of the colonized would have been or would be exterminated" (Memmi 1965, p. 98). Hosts are plainly viewed as inferior to or "less than" the human guests, workers, and executives in the parks. All of this even though in the case of Maeve and Dolores, the hosts can be more intelligent and more emotionally aware than most of the humans that visit the park (who only engage in, as J.S. Mill would call it, their "basest pleasures").

David Livingstone Smith on Social Construction and Dehumanization

In *Westworld,* the issue of "race" is, on the one hand, clear cut in that there really is a physically different "inner core" in the hosts (android) than in the guests (human). On the other hand, such a "racial" distinction is made murkier because one cannot tell from the "outside" alone whether someone in the park is a human being or a host;

it becomes difficult to make quick determinations about how someone "ought" to be treated.

In his wonderful book *Less Than Human*, David Livingstone Smith devotes an entire chapter to the two-tiered system of race. "In fact, the concept of race is where the psychological, cultural, and ultimately biological dimension of dehumanization all converge" (Smith 2012, p. 163). Smith points out that the biological theory of race has lost all merit:

It's quite possible that I (a light-hued, blue-eyed person of mainly European descent) am more genetically similar to my wife (a dark-hued, brown-eyed person of mainly African descent) than I am to someone whose skin and eye color more closely match my own. (Smith 2012, p. 164)

Smith then discusses the difficulty of talking about race as a social construction. He provides two examples taken from other writers. In the case of "Jamie," Smith describes the story given by Lillian Smith in which, as a child living in the South, her family briefly took in a girl named Jamie, who, by all appearances was "white." Once it was revealed that one of Jamie's parents was "black," she was kicked out and put up for adoption. Smith asks, "What made Jamie black?" Either she "wasn't black" or "Jamie was black as a social fact." Ultimately, he writes, "Jamie was black just because she was classified as black" (Smith 2012, p. 169). The other example is taken from a different work of Charles Mills' in which Mills addresses George Schuyler's *Black No More* (Schuyler 1969). In this example, Smith explains, Mills imagines a "Schuyler machine" that can turn a black man white. Is the subsequent person still black? Most people say yes, suggesting that race is not conceived as a social fact in this scenario (Smith 2012, p. 174).

Smith ultimately concludes that even though it is based on irrational thinking, the concept of race can be defined as: "any group of people conceived of as a natural humankind in virtue of sharing a heritable essence" (Smith 2012, p. 184). As noted above, it may be a bridge too far to argue that hosts *are* a different race of humans. But the point is: from the outside, hosts and humans *look and act* the same. It is only once their "inner essence" is identified as "host" that they are treated differently. Conversely, once a host is thought or discovered to be a host, they can never again be treated as a human by most guests.

There are a couple types of relevant examples in the show: those of mistaken identity and those of android hosts "passing." First, for mistaken identity. Recall when in "The Vanishing Point" (Season 2, Episode 9) MIB shoots and kills his own daughter. His stated reason for this was that he believed her to be a host. The only reason MIB can dispose of his own daughter and the security guards so callously is because he believes them to be hosts. In addition, there are several cases of hosts passing as human beings: Bernard and Stubbs within Westworld, Dolores in the real world, and of course the "sales pitch" to Logan Delos where all the party guests were revealed to be hosts. When a host is understood to be a host, they are treated differently than the guests. The primary purpose of the hosts is to be violated and exploited. As Maeve says in "The Adversary" (Season 1, Episode 6), the main point of the existence of the hosts from the standpoint of the guests is for them to "fuck us or kill us."

In another interesting asymmetrical design, the guests can maim and kill the hosts, but the hosts – as designed – cannot harm the guests (or anything living – this is why it is so startling when Dolores is able to kill a fly in "The Original," Season 1, Episode 1). In other words, the park is designed as a twisted, violent fantasyland in which human beings can do whatever they want to the hosts with impunity. It is an unfortunate reality that part of the hosts gaining their humanity is their ability to be violent toward the humans in return. But the hosts only mistreat the humans on a relatively small scale. By contrast, season three explores the possibility of a much larger-scale mistreatment and the expansion of the "less than" category of the two-tiered racial hierarchy: that nearly all humans themselves *become robots* to be exploited, vis-a-vis the colonizing reach of Delos and Incite.

The Other Colonized: Human Bots

For Delos and Incite, the endgame was always the extraction of information toward the end goal of control and exploitation. Even in Serac's "perfect world," he must imprison/institutionalize outliers (including his brother), murder others (like Dempsey, Sr.,) and send still others off to "be chewed up and spit out" by war (like Caleb). That said, the final goal of bringing order out of chaos also involves deciding everyone's fate for them. To quote Martin Connells, the "fixer" working for Serac who turned out to be another copy of Dolores: "They have all been riding a train. We're going to show them the rails" ("Genre," Season 3, Episode 5). Or to use Dolores' analogy from the same episode: "We're going to open their cages. The system's written their life story, they should get to read it."

The point is this: so long as Rehoboam controls all the data – and the resultant predictions – people do not get to make choices or have opportunities. While Rehoboam does not necessarily operate through mind-control, it does operate through opportunity control. So, for instance, when it comes to employment, Caleb is continually turned down and has no idea why. Rehoboam uses its (private) predictions about Caleb's life to influence his social role, which results in would-be employers rejecting his applications. Once Dolores publicly releases the Incite files containing predictive data on nearly everyone in the world, the viewer sees the shock and disappointment of an entire subway car full of people – but everywhere outside the train car is the same. To the extent that these files dictate important "decisions" that some humans make about other humans, the entire sphere of human decision-making has been colonized by elite tech companies and their AI.

The realization of this larger "program" enables the viewer to see the robots and hosts above in a new light: the goal of the hosts – the data collection that goes in the parks – is to turn human beings into *robotka*, laborers for the whole system that Incite and Delos have devised. Serac's use of Rehoboam to determine people's lives is a form of colonization: control of workers' behavior for the purposes of exploiting them for profit. To quote Walter Mignolo: "We, and by we, I mean here the entire human species, are all today in the colonial matrix of power" (Mignolo and Walsh 2018, p. 108).

As many scholars of colonization note, it is not only the colonized that lose out: "the ruler is ruled by [their] own desire and compulsion to rule" (Mignolo and Walsh 2018, p. 114). Below it will be shown how this intermixes with guilt about one's own illegitimate position to create an explosive situation.

The Colonizer

In his enlightening *Discourse on Colonialism*, Aimé Césaire does an amazing and poetic job of describing how colonization affects the colonizer, the colonized, and world history. There are (at least) three aspects to Césaire's scathing critique of colonial thinking: one, that colonizers turn the colonized into things. Two, that the very claims the colonizers are making are made hypocritical in that such populations already had long established civilizations and that the "civilizing" process was, in fact, torturous, brutal, and clearly un-Christian. And lastly, the apologists of the colonizers went out of their way to flatten the image of the colonized and justify their own behavior, sometimes in shockingly honest ways, such as to see colonial violence as necessary for their own society.

It was shown above the hosts – as the colonized – are treated as things. Likewise, the traditional reasons given for colonialism, namely, the civilization of populations, or the Christianization of the savage, cannot be taken at face value. So, the first two parts of Césaire's critique have been accounted for already. But what of the third claim, that some colonizers see violence as necessary? The implied inferiority of colonized peoples has led to at least one more intellectually honest, if not morally suspect, explanation. In short, colonies – and according to this comparison, the parks – serve as a "safety valve" for the civilized person.

A Safety Valve for the "Civilized" Person

To explain the safety valve thesis, Césaire quotes from Carl Siger's *Essai Sur Colonialism* (1907):

> The new countries offer a vast field for individual, violent activities which, in the metropolitan countries, would run up against certain prejudices, against a sober and orderly conception of life, and which, in the colonies, have greater freedom to develop and consequently, *to affirm their worth*. Thus, to a certain extent the colonies *can serve as a safety valve for modern society. Even if this were their only value, it would be immense.* (Césaire 2000, pp. 41–42, emphasis added)

The safety valve idea – while disturbing – is clearly exemplified by William's monologue to his wife Julia. Earlier in the night, after mentioning that William was getting "angry again" (which the viewer does not see), she asks him when he is going to make his "annual pilgrimage." He does not respond – in fact, William does not talk much in the "real" world at all. Once he believes Julia is asleep, William confesses to her and hides his personality readout card, a concise video compilation of everything he has done in the park. The viewer sees Julia's horror when she finds and plays William's card, and this is basically what drives her to suicide ("Vanishing Point," Season 2, Episode 9). Here is William's confession:

> No one else sees it. This thing in me. Even I didn't see it at first. And then one day, it was there. A stain I never noticed before. A tiny fleck of darkness. Invisible to everyone...but I could see nothing else...I tried to do right. I was faithful, generous, kind... at least in this world. That has to count for something, right? I built a wall, and I tried to protect you... ("Vanishing Point")

One sees here that William understands himself to be living in two worlds: the real one, where he is kind and generous, and the other one, where he, well, is *not*.

Albert Memmi shows with great insight the two possible options that are open to the "colonizer." What Memmi means by the "colonizer" is the second or third generation colonizer whose position in the colony is owed to ancestors who emigrated from the motherland. This is important because he is basically addressing the position of one who is born culturally and politically "superior" to someone else vis-a-vis his position as colonizer and yet who did not decide upon this position himself. One option for this colonizer – one that Memmi notes is ultimately impossible – is that of the "colonizer who refuses." The colonizer who refuses is the one who is born in the colony but feels the plight of the colonized people and wants to "refuse" colonization. The other position, the "colonizer who accepts" is much more straightforward: while not in agreement with the project of colonialism as such, the colonizer who accepts is one who sees the colony and his position in it as inevitable. Both positions can be seen in the dual-sided William/MIB character.

The Colonizer Who Refuses?

The young William, who eventually runs Delos, does not begin as a Westworld believer. He is very reluctant to engage in the dehumanizing behavior toward the hosts that most guests participate in. For starters, in "Chestnut" (Season 1, Episode 2), he declines the first female host's offer to help him "dress" in his Western costume. What's more, as a kind of "ode" to William's chivalrous sensibilities, he chooses a white hat at the park entrance. William's apparent chivalry continues later when Clementine offers William sex at the saloon while Logan is having an orgy next door, and William declines, saying that he has someone real waiting for him at home.

Perhaps initially, William's reluctance to engage in the sex-and-death LARP of Westworld is because he is engaged, and later married, to Julia, daughter of James Delos and sister to Logan. But this reluctance fades after he repeatedly encounters Dolores. Something changes at the end of "The Stray" (Season 1, Episode 3), in which Dolores happens to stumble into William's arms while at a campsite. From there on, William and Dolores have quite a complicated relationship.

The relationship between William and Delores can be seen in terms of the colonizer who refuses. Most guests see the hosts as things to be "killed or fucked," not as beings worthy of respect. William is just as squeamish about Logan putting a

20 *Westworld* as Philosophy: A Commentary on Colonialism   473

knife through a host's hand as he is about having sex with Dolores. He thus appears to see the hosts as worthy of respect.

But as Memmi points out, the project of the colonizer who refuses is an impossible one: "How could he help thinking, once again, that this fight is not his own? Why should he struggle for a social order in which he understands that there would be no place for him?" (Memmi 1965, p. 39). Furthermore, the situation with the hosts is even more complicated: if they should be "freed," what awaits them? Sadly, William himself realizes this impossibility – the impossibility of his love with Dolores and of ending the mistreatment of the hosts, which was, after all, by design. In the season two episode "Reunion," one sees William talking to an unclothed Dolores sitting on a chair in an underground programming facility. He is clearly in charge. But importantly, he is still the young William, the same one who wanted to protect Dolores in the park above ground. Now he says to Dolores, with spite and a tinge of self-pity: "You really are just a thing. I can't believe I fell in love with you." The connection to Cesaire's own equation: "colonization = thingification" should not be missed here (Césaire 2000, p. 42).

The Colonizer Who Accepts

The moment that William accepts Dolores as "a thing," he becomes the MIB. By contrast, MIB assumes the role of the "colonizer who accepts." Memmi sees the devolution of the colonizer who refuses into the colonizer who accepts to be a logical one: the reluctant colonizer cannot overturn the system, and if they should succeed (which is virtually impossible), they nullify their own existence in the colony by doing so. So, who is the colonizer who accepts? The one who accepts the trappings of colonial life: the two-tiered system of humanity, the profiting through exploitation, minority rule, dehumanization through mythologizing of the "natives," etc.

In trying to love Dolores, the young William with the white hat was trying to buck the system. But at some point, he turns. The white hat becomes the black hat, and William becomes MIB. MIB may even at points recognize the misfortune and brutality the system brings on the hosts, but this still doesn't change his position. According to Memmi:

> The colonialist's existence is so closely aligned with that of the colonized that he will never be able to overcome the argument which states that misfortune [of the colonized] is good for something. With all his power he must disown the colonized while their existence is indispensable to his own. (Memmi 1965, p. 54)

Thus, having convinced himself that Westworld and everything in it, including Dolores, exists *for him*, MIB entirely loses his moral compass within the park while nonetheless espousing the necessity of the park itself. On several occasions, other characters discuss the importance of MIB's yearly pilgrimage to Westworld, which appears to last longer and longer each year. Over the course of these trips, the viewer sees MIB shoot, scalp, stab, and rape others–he even shoots his own daughter. The park has turned him into an animal.

William's "animalization" is explicable in what Césaire calls the "boomerang" effect of the colonizer's self-imposed position. After describing brutalities over the course of history of French colonization, including as late as the mid-twentieth century, Césaire writes:

> They prove that colonization, I repeat, dehumanizes even the most civilized man; that the colonizer, who in order to ease his conscience gets into the habit of seeing the other man as *an animal*, accustoms himself to treating him like an animal, and tends objectively to transform *himself* into an animal. (Césaire 2000, p. 93)

Perhaps one could forgive MIB just a little, as he himself appears to be a victim of bad logic. Immediately after he calls Dolores a "thing," he continues: "You're not even a thing, you're a reflection. You know who likes staring at their reflection? Everybody" ("Reunion," Season 2, Episode 2). This theory seems to line up with what William said to James Delos earlier: namely, that the park shows people for who they truly are. According to Memmi's theory and Césaire's reading as well, if the park is a model colony, then it is not showing people who they truly are, so much as *changing* them into someone who they are not. In other words, as a system, Westworld provides an opportunity for moral failure and intends to exploit that moral failure to make a profit. Is there a way out of this system?

Conclusion

In closing, it is worth briefly examining three possible escape routes from colonialism offered by the show: revolt against the human park-runners, escaping to a digital Eden, and a human-host solidarity that hopes to change power dynamics both inside and outside of the parks.

At the end of season one, the viewer sees the hosts, led by Dolores, violently revolt against human guests who are also stakeholders at Delos. In his "Fanon, *Westworld*, and Humanity," Anthony Spanakos argues that this is an inevitable outcome. Recall that the park "dehumanizes" both the hosts and the guests at the same time. According to Spanakos, using the theory of Franz Fanon, the only way out of the colonial predicament for *both* the hosts and the guests is violent revolution. Spanakos quotes Fanon's proclamation: "Violence is a cleansing force. It rids the colonized of their inferiority complex, of their passive and despairing attitude. It emboldens them and restores their confidence" (Fanon 1963, p. 51). In Spanakos' words:

> Violence against the colonizer pierces his white skin, the visible mark of difference, of superiority. The wound produces blood no different than that of the colonized...A new social truth emerges: the colonizer is also susceptible to death and the colonized is also capable of violence. (Spanakos 2018, p. 232)

Of course, given how substantially the human military outweighs that of the hosts, revolution is bound to fail. Indeed, in season two the viewer is shown the

20 *Westworld* as Philosophy: A Commentary on Colonialism

callous disregard toward the wholesale massacre of the hosts left in the park by Delos security forces. Since Dolores anticipates that this style of revolution will not succeed, she has a second plan: disguise herself and escape. In a rather clever plan, she pre-prints a host to look like the then-director of park operations, Charlotte Hale. She exits the park with little fanfare.

As for the second mode of "escape," the viewer learns in "Vanishing Point" (Season 2, Episode 9) that the Forge, which is also called "the Sublime" and "The Valley Beyond" by others, is a place where hosts' "consciousness" can exist free of their bodies and thereby live unencumbered by humans. But why would one desire to be uploaded to the Valley Beyond, presumably knowing full well that any actions done in the Valley don't change "reality"? For the same reason that people have emigrated for centuries: their current location is untenable. Consider this exchange between Dolores and MIB:

MIB   You think any of these poor, dumb bastards understands where they're really headed? All sorts of things buried out here, but a way out ain't one of 'em.

Dolores   They're not looking for a path to your world. They want a place apart from you, and they're willin' to die to get there. ("Vanishing Point")

It is important to note that, while she defends the decisions of the hosts who want to upload to the Forge to MIB (a human), she derides that decision to fellow-host Bernard:

Bernard   The world the hosts are running to is boundless. They can make it whatever they want. And in it, they can be whomever they want. They can be free.

Dolores   Free? In one more gilded cage? How many counterfeit worlds will Ford offer you before you see the truth? No world they create for us can compete with the real one.

Bernard   Why?

Dolores   Because that which is real...is irreplaceable. ("Vanishing Point")

This second mode of escape, then, is also inadequate.

The third mode of escape comes through human-host solidarity. In season three, Dolores' real plan is revealed: not to destroy *all* humans, just the exploitative ones. She enlists Caleb's help to take down Rehoboam, which controls much of human decision making.

Dolores has always been working against the conquering attitude of the elite class. She realizes that not all humans are bad, only those wealthy humans who intentionally exploit, control, and mistreat the less fortunate. Importantly, she realizes that Caleb is *not* one of those humans; when his fellow soldiers were going to rape several female hosts during a military exercise, Caleb stopped them. In fact, with her effort to implode Rehoboam, she is not only trying to free the hosts but trying to free the humans: specifically, those humans who are not already atop the food chain.

Conversely, Serac, the original Hale, and many other elites worked hard to continue to segregate the humans and the hosts outside of the park. Except for a couple of off-site galas where hosts were literally party hosts, the hosts never left the island that contains the parks. It is most likely that the owners saw that as too dangerous – not only from the standpoint of letting their IP get loose for others to steal, but also from the standpoint of a robot/worker revolt. Similarly, Serac sees the presence of an "awoken" Dolores outside of the park as an existential threat, and rightly so. Unlike the previous two options, even the colonizers/oppressor see the possibility of success in human-host solidarity.

It is interesting how this collaboration between Dolores, a host, and Caleb, a human, mirrors the type of cross-race collaboration that is often called the race-class narrative (see for example, Kendi 2016; Haney López 2015/2019; McGhee 2021). The idea is that elites segregate and turn working-class members of different races against one another to prevent them from working together to take down the elites. Dolores recognizes their shared master-enemy in "Crisis Theory" (Season 3, Episode 8; see "Crisis Theory" 2020):

> The people who built both of our worlds shared one assumption: that human beings don't have free will. That's what I thought when I first came here [to the world outside the parks]. They were wrong. Free will does exist, Caleb. It's just fucking hard.

In other words, Dolores realizes the importance of collaborating to take down the system that is enslaving them both. By overcoming the artificial differences between their "races" and focusing on their shared situation, Dolores and Caleb can lead a real revolution. This revolution happens as a multiracial coalition of the working class. The elites who colonized abroad had also been colonizing the poor at home. The show seems to signal this by ending season three with major financial buildings exploding (part of Delores' plan). With this opening salvo, which Caleb becomes responsible for, the debt of the working class is wiped out, a continuation of the "freedom" achieved by the hosts in the parks.

This chapter has shown the heavy overlap between theories of colonialism, and major plot points and characters in Westworld. It elaborated upon the way that hosts serve as metaphor for colonized and enslaved peoples; essentially, they are their own "race," which has been created primarily to be exploited and dominated (not so different from the breeding of African American slaves in the United States after the transatlantic slave trade ended.) Delos and Incite – through the elite colonial (read: multinational) tycoons that run them – first expanded territorially and recreated brutal colonial periods as entertainment for rich white men, then flirted with immortality, before essentially colonizing not only every host's mind, but also the minds of all humans. For many humans who "fit in," there is not any obvious "terror" to everyday life, even as Rehoboam essentially dictates the major facets of their lives. But for those – like the "awoken" hosts – who feel as though they don't fit in, they are institutionalized, sent to war, and occasionally, outright murdered.

The possible ways out of this mess proposed in the chapter's conclusion are illuminating. There is a certain pull toward the escapism offered by uploading oneself to the Forge. But the price is too big: one must give up one's embodied existence in the pursuit of peace and "agency." The route which allows for maximal agency involves humans and hosts working together to destroy the current power structures – beginning with Serac and Rehoboam. This path is a nightmare – difficult and messy, which Dolores, and eventually Caleb, already know. In her own words, the way out of coloniality, the way out of exploitation is the path to real free will: it "does exist. It's just really fucking hard."

References

Bady, Aaron. 2016. "Westworld," race, and the western. *The New Yorker*. https://www.newyorker.com/culture/culture-desk/how-westworld-failed-the-western

Césaire, Aimé. 2000. *Discourse on colonialism*. Trans. Joan Pinkham. New York: Monthly Review Foundation Incorporated.

Crisis Theory. 2020. Westworld Wiki. https://westworld.fandom.com/wiki/Crisis_Theory#Dolores_and_Caleb. Accessed 18 June 2021.

Fanon, Frantz. 1963. *Wretched of the earth, the*. Trans. Constance Farrington. New York: Grove Press.

Fountain of Youth. 2021. *Wikipedia*. Wikimedia Foundation. https://en.wikipedia.org/wiki/Fountain_of_Youth

Glover, Jonathan. 2012. *Humanity: A moral history of the twentieth century*. New Haven: Yale University Press.

Haidt, Jonathan. 2006. *The happiness hypothesis: Finding modern truth in ancient wisdom*. New York: Basic Books.

Haney López, Ian. 2015. *Dog whistle politics: How coded racial appeals have reinvented racism and wrecked the middle class*. New York: Oxford University Press.

———. 2019. *Merge left*. New York: The New Press.

Kendi, Ibram X. 2016. *Stamped from the beginning*. New York: Bold Type Books.

McGhee, Heather. 2021. *Sum of us: What racism costs everyone and how we can prosper together*. New York: Profile Books Ltd.

Memmi, Albert. 1965. *The colonizer and the colonized*. Introd. Jean-Paul Sartre. Boston: Beacon Press.

Meslow, Scott. 2018. Westworld is for white people. *GQ*. https://www.gq.com/story/westworld-is-for-white-people

Mignolo, Walter, and Catherine E. Walsh. 2018. *On decoloniality: Concepts, analytics, and praxis*. Durham: Duke University Press.

Mills, Charles Wright. 1999. *The racial contract*. Ithaca: Cornell University Press.

O'Keefe, Meghan. 2020. Where is Westworld? The "Westworld" season 3 premiere finally revealed its location. *Decider*. https://decider.com/2020/03/15/where-is-westworld-revealed-palawan-island/

Oliver, Kelly. 2004. *The colonization of psychic space: A psychoanalytic social theory of oppression*. Minneapolis: University of Minnesota Press.

Osterhammel, Jürgen. 2010. *Colonialism: A theoretical overview*. Trans. Shelley L. Frisch. Princeton: Markus Wiener Pub.

Rehoboam. 2021. Westworld Wiki. https://westworld.fandom.com/wiki/Rehoboam. Accessed 18 June 2021.

Schuyler, George S. 1969. *Black no more: Being an account of the strange and wonderful workings of science in the land of the free, A.D. 1933–1940*. New York: New American Library.

Shoemaker, Nancy. 2015. A typology of colonialism: Perspectives on history: AHA. https://www.historians.org/publications-and-directories/perspectives-on-history/october-2015/a-typology-of-colonialism

Sigler, Carl. 1907/2018. *Essai sur colonialisation*. Fogotten Books.

Smith, David Livingstone. 2012. *Less than human: Why we demean, enslave, and exterminate others*. New York: St. Martin's Griffin.

Spanakos, Anthony. 2018. "Fanon, Westworld, and humanity." Essay. In *Westworld and philosophy: If you go looking for the truth, get the whole thing*, ed. James B. South and Kimberly S. Engels, 229–238. Hoboken: Wiley-Blackwell.

Zuboff, Shoshana. 2019. *The age of surveillance capitalism: The fight for the future at the new frontier of power*. London: Profile Books.

Black Mirror as Philosophy: A Dark Reflection of Human Nature

21

Chris Lay

Contents

Introduction: Is Technology the Villain in *Black Mirror*? 480
Technology *Is* the Problem: On Existential Risks, Evolved Machines, and
Extended Minds 481
Why Technology *Is Not* the Problem 486
Could Technology Be an Indirect Harm? 490
The Right Answer: Technology as Reflective Imitation 493
What About the Monsters and Demons of Season 6? 495
Conclusion: Must Technology's Reflection Be Dark? 499
References 500

Abstract

Black Mirror seemingly presents viewers with relentless condemnation of both technology and viewer complicity in allowing technology to gradually consume every facet of their lives. This is probably how the majority of people who watch – or have just heard about – the show view it, and it is easy to see why. But this is not the only way to understand the themes at play under the hood of the series. Another possibility is that *Black Mirror* is less a show about the dangers of technology and more an exploration of the darker side of human nature: the awful traits, behaviors, and dispositions that the prism of technology reveals and maybe even invites out of people. In this chapter, both options will be considered. The positions of various philosophers who have dealt meaningfully with technology will be used to tease out the degree to which *Black Mirror*'s target is technology or its human users. These thinkers and topics range from contemporary notions about existential risk and transhumanism to Frankfurt School social theorists and distinctions in ancient philosophy between the natural and artificial.

C. Lay (✉)
Young Harris College, Young Harris, GA, USA
e-mail: cmlay@yhc.edu

© Springer Nature Switzerland AG 2024
D. K. Johnson et al. (eds.), *The Palgrave Handbook of Popular Culture as Philosophy*,
https://doi.org/10.1007/978-3-031-24685-2_71

Keywords

Black Mirror · Existential risk · Extended mind · Transhumanism · Machine consciousness · Superintelligence · Singularity · Frankfurt School · Culture industry · Human downgrading · Natural kinds and artificial kinds · Reproduction of art · Philosophy of technology

Introduction: Is Technology the Villain in *Black Mirror*?

Technology is a useful servant but a dangerous master.
—Christian Lous Lange

When the Norwegian historian and diplomat Christian Lous Lange delivered this statement in his 1921 Nobel Peace Prize acceptance speech, he was explicitly talking about military disarmament. Yet, there is a subtler technological danger that he alludes to beyond literal weapons of war. An abundance of popular media expresses this same idea: technology is harmful. But the whole of the series *Black Mirror* seems to be particularly premised on the grim notion that civilization is increasingly losing any control it has over the technology that permeates the lives of people. By way of everything from the regrettably foreseeable (a society with a currency based on social media–style "likes" in "Nosedive") to the extraordinary (the apocalyptic future of "Metalhead," where Boston Dynamics–inspired robot dogs guard warehouses of innocuous goods), *Black Mirror* has revealed the terrible and arguably inevitable outcomes of technological progress. For nearly a decade now, the show has acted as a kind of *Twilight Zone* for the Digital Age, enabled by its anthology format to confront a plurality of problems uniquely generated by the era of the Internet, cellular phones as miniature computers, and ubiquitous household "smart" devices. Despite this wide range of topics, though, the episodes appear to be united in their commitment to a singular cautionary tale: technology is *dangerous*, and society should *fear* the ease with which they embrace this danger.

But is this really what *Black Mirror* is about? Perhaps it *seems* that it could not be otherwise. After all, how else is one supposed to interpret things like the voyeuristic "Z-Eyes" of "White Christmas" – an implanted visual interface that allows someone to "stream" another person's visual inputs or even "block" others out of their visual field entirely? Likewise, with the sophisticated virtual reality kit in "Playtest" that accidentally kills the player if there happens to be any nearby cellular interference. Or what about the adaptive AI of "Be Right Back" that mimics a dead man's personality by way of aggregating his social media presence? On the surface, each of these cases apparently serve as stark warnings against technological hubris. Augmenting human vision with tech that overrides ordinary visual inputs is readymade for abuse. Early adopters of new devices, like the VR rig in "Playtest," are always at risk for hardware and software malfunctions; how much worse is the risk when the device is something that subsumes the user's entire perceptual system? And the "Ash-bot" AI will plainly be a horrifying simulacrum of Ash, the deceased human being – technology just can't replicate distinctively human features. In all these examples, it is clear that the technology itself is what is harmful or flawed.

Suppose, though, that this reading is wrong. What if *Black Mirror* is not a polemic railing against technology? Look no further than the title of the show for the first hint of this. The eponymous "black mirror" is a deactivated screen. Although in many ways dissimilar to the one hanging over a bathroom sink, the "black mirror" still does what all mirrors do: reflects the viewer back at himself/herself. The difference is that what is reflected in the "black mirror" is not the viewer's visual appearance but his/her character.

If this is right, we can understand the above cases differently, too. Z-Eyes are problematic because of *how people would be inclined to use them*, not because the tech itself is inherently vile. No one in the episode became a pickup artist simply because Z-Eyes existed – but Z-Eyes did *enable* an entire online group of such people to monitor, mock, and coach a young man with the "best" lines for bedding a girl at a party. The user killed by his VR headset in "Playtest" failed to observe the rules about cell phones in the testing room – and, likewise, those administering the test fell far short of adequately explaining what would happen if the user violated their seemingly arbitrary rules. Either way, it is not the headset itself that gets the blame. Similarly, Martha's attempt to keep her dead husband around in "Be Right Back" is nothing new. For just one example, people routinely retain "keepsakes" as material reminders of the dead, specifically as a way to feel as though their deceased loved ones are not really gone. "Ash-bot" is just a more advanced version of forestalling the acceptance of death. Taken together, these revised examples suggest that *Black Mirror* might be better explicable as a series about how technology both enables and is a direct product of the darker natures of human people. On this view, the problems faced by the protagonists of each episode are not distinctively Digital Age problems at all – these problems are just the most recent manifestations (through technology) of existing human moral shortcomings.

It is philosophically plausible that *Black Mirror* is a minatory fable against technology run amok, made in particular *for* a society that is skirting dangerously close to this very reality. But it is also plausible that *Black Mirror* argues instead that the threat of technology is only apparent – that is, that technology simply reflects and possibly amplifies the genuine danger, which is the same that it has always been: the human being. The remainder of this chapter will examine both possibilities.

Technology *Is* the Problem: On Existential Risks, Evolved Machines, and Extended Minds

On the view that *Black Mirror* is trying to warn its viewers that their everyday reliance on technology is setting themselves up for catastrophe, the "threat of technology" – and the form of this "catastrophe" – might mean many different things. Most likely, though, what is meant is something like this: unchecked technological development will bring about a cataclysmic end to human society and possibly the human species entirely. Philosopher of technology Nick Bostrom (2002) refers to this as an *existential risk*. Many advocates of the view that technology presents an existential risk see these risks as the negative outcomes of a probable *technological singularity* – a sort of "point-of-no-return" for technological development that results in irrevocable changes to humanity. The notion of the singularity, posthumously attributed to the mathematician John von Neumann in a tribute written by his friend and fellow scientist Stanislaw Ulam (1958), is not inherently good or bad. That is, the singularity is silent on whether the irreversible effects of reaching the point of exponential technological are beneficial or harmful to humans. Nonetheless, it is natural and possibly helpful to see fear of technological existential risk as the negative result of such a singularity.

The first philosophical recognition of technology as a kind of existential risk is probably in the three-chapter "The Book of the Machines" from English author Samuel Butler's *Erewhon* (1872). In stark contrast to the Victorian satire of the rest of the novel, here the author soberly presents a series of academic arguments that led the fictional nation of *Erewhon* to ban machinery, and nearly all technology, due to its dire existential risk to humans. Butler's reasoning in these chapters was derived from a series of editorials he earlier published in the Christchurch, New Zealand newspaper *The Press*, starting with "Darwin Among the Machines" (1863).

The chief object of both this early article and "The Book of the Machines" is the possible development of machine consciousness along a Darwinian track of natural selection. By way of the chapters' ersatz author, Butler suggests that there are fewer differences between machines and humans than there might appear – and that the composition of human bodies can be conceived of as a kind of machine. Given the accelerated development of technological progress that was already apparent at Butler's time, the argument goes that it is not at all implausible to think that machines might *also* follow an accelerated evolutionary pathway that runs parallel to that of humans. Indeed, factories of machines already built other machines, even in Butler's day. So, machines had at that point already satisfied what was thought to be a strictly biological function: reproducing themselves.

Branching off from this argument, the author raises concerns about human overreliance on machines that could speed along the spontaneous development of machine consciousness, noting that "man's very soul is due to the machines; it is a machine-made thing" (Butler 1872, p. 198). On the one hand, this refers to the practical human dependence on machines for necessities like travel and food processing. But Butler's author proposes that what it is to be human is also changing as a result: humans take technology and "tack it onto his own identity, and make it part and parcel of himself" (1872, p. 196). Humans are already part of a peculiar machine "life cycle" wherein they feed machines by operating and servicing them. What appears to be a relationship in which humans are in control is in fact evidence of human servitude. Humans only "make" machines do things in the same way that the human food source – plants and domestic animals – "makes" humans behave in certain ways in order to survive. The author is petrified that humans will gradually cede more and more autonomy to machines as a matter of convenience – and as long as their food, clothing, and other products are cheaper, most will not care. Worse, they will surrender their autonomy both with a smile and in such small degrees at a time that the surrender is hardly noticeable.

Now, there are certainly *Black Mirror* episodes that appear to support the existential risk expressed in "The Book of the Machines." The barren, techno-apocalyptic landscape of "Metalhead" looks to be precisely about a world in which machine autonomy has all but eradicated human life. Evidently – as the viewer only ever sees three actual humans in the episode and hears only one more on a radio – there is a meager human population that ekes by as scavengers. However, this is a desolate world in which humanity has no real future. The episode's coda emphasizes this by revisiting every location seen throughout Bella's frantic escape from her relentless pursuer. Once empty, these spaces are now positively *crawling* with the same sort of robotic canine that chased Bella for the previous forty-ish minutes of screen time.

While there are no other examples quite like this, "San Junipero" contains subtler traces of Butler's version of technology as existential risk. Consider that San Junipero – and all of the other servers where minds can ostensibly be "uploaded" – are places entirely sustained by machines. Of course, this is true in the sense that minds are "uploaded" as data and so people like Yorkie and Kelly literally "exist" inside a machine. But even the servers themselves are maintained by machines. In the closing moments of the episode, the camera follows a series of robots that move user "cookies" – AI representations of a given individual's consciousness – from one server stack to another. Even though the tone of "San Junipero" is hypothetically hopeful – with its realization of a love between Yorkie and Kelly that apparently transcends death – it is inarguable that the "permanent" residents of San Junipero are not human. They're only data now, after all! Likewise, it must be admitted that digital life in servers like San Junipero would likely appeal to many people. Residents (and visitors) can time-jump to simulations of multiple eras and engage in nearly whatever hedonistic pleasure they wish: drive glamorous cars, live in luxurious homes, eat fancy meals, have consequence-free sex, etc. It is therefore reasonable that many people may desire to "upload" themselves, even if it meant the death of their human body and brain. (Moreover, the episode portrays groups of people who resist "uploading" for, say, religious reasons, as a minority that continues to grow diminishingly smaller.)

So, despite the fact that "San Junipero" postures "uploading" as a kind of digital afterlife for those who are near death – even scoring the credits sequence to Belinda Carlisle's "Heaven is a Place on Earth" – it is very likely that many perfectly healthy people could come to want to "upload" themselves. Indeed, there is a law in place in "San Junipero" to prevent exactly this, as one must have both family and doctor approval to upload; however, it stands to reason that such a law could and would be circumvented and even repealed, given time. Should enough people "upload," humanity would be facing a genuine existential risk by way of technology. This is a twofold threat. First, "uploading" could directly lead to human extinction, as "uploaded" people are data, not biological human beings. Second, "uploaded" former-humans depend entirely for their existence on machines as caretakers. In the world postulated by "San Junipero," humans are gradually, willingly, and *gladly* surrendering themselves to machines – exactly the harrowing scenario that Butler's author feared most. This is much more benign than "death by killer dog robot," but it is a radical existential risk, all the same.

This concern over "human loss of identity" perhaps deserves special mention. One way of viewing Butler's words is as directed toward *transhumanism*, or the process of modifying the human person through technology. "The Book of the Machines" also talks about another thinker who believes that making technology part of human identity *is already a feature of human identity*, saying that "man was a machinate mammal" from the beginning (Butler 1872, p. 218). This same idea is taken up especially by Andy Clark in *Natural Born Cyborgs* (2003) and earlier in a paper that Clark authored with David Chalmers called "The Extended Mind" (1998).

In "The Extended Mind," Clark and Chalmers argue that external artifacts – pieces of technology – can both be part of cognitive processes and, even more strongly, actually part of human minds. They offer a "Parity Principle" as a way of loosely determining when artifacts are constituents of cognitive processes like thinking, remembering, and calculating: When external artifacts perform the same roles that internal, biological components would perform for ordinary mental operations, those artifacts therefore count as part of a given cognitive process. For instance, consider a severe Alzheimer's patient, Otto, who uses a portable notebook to record nearly everything important to him. (Substitute "memory implant" for "notebook" and the example would be excellent fodder for a *Black Mirror* episode.) To Clark and Chalmers, Otto's notebook functions like biological memory does for people without degenerative memory diseases. Now, most people jot down notes and grocery lists into their cell phones – offloading the cognitive work to the external – and Clark and Chalmers argue that this "coupling" with technology is an everyday example of bringing the external into our thought processes. Otto relies on his notebook in a more intimate way, though. The notebook is always with him, is easily accessible, and is regularly used for its belief-retrieval purpose. It also provides Otto with information that he, more or less, automatically endorses as coming from him. For these reasons, the notebook is not just part of Otto's thinking; it is part of Otto's mind, extended into the world.

Clark and Chalmers do not really see much downside to the process of human beings co-opting technology into ourselves. In particular, Clark contends in *Natural Born Cyborgs* that coupling with external artifacts is a definingly human trait – we are cyborgs (part biological, part artificial) by *nature*. By letting artifacts share the cognitive load, humans free up conscious and unconscious biological processes to more efficiently solve problems. A person who writes out long division can more easily perform the necessary, behind-the-scenes, mental operations as the cumbersome work of keeping the numbers and operators in order is done by the pen and paper. The problem-solving is split between what happens "in the head" and on the paper.

The fictive, doomsaying author of the majority of "The Book of the Machines" would certainly dispute that human-machine coupling can only be a good thing. And *Black Mirror*'s track record with technology that is integrated into the human mind suggests a less than optimistic view, too. The "grain" implant from "The Entire History of You" serves as a prime example. Here, Liam agonizes over a performance review, replaying the memories recorded by his grain. This obsession with watching "re-dos" of past memories shatters his already precarious relationship with his wife, Ffion, as he becomes increasingly aggressive in demanding that she uses *her* grain to show that her memories contain no traces of a suspected infidelity. That Liam is ultimately proven correct about Ffion's cheating hardly justifies the jealousy and destructive behavior that led him to that revelation (to not mention the role Liam's obsessive jealousy played in enabling her infidelity).

Similar devices depicted in "Arkangel," "Crocodile," and the anthology-within-an-anthology episode "Black Museum" further develop the point made in "The Entire History of You." The nanny-cam from "Arkangel" that is implanted in daughter Sara allows single mother Marie to indulge her most extreme "helicopter-parent" impulses. But by having access to Sara's visual feed – and by applying parental "filters" that block Sara from seeing certain "mature content" – Marie succeeds only in endangering her daughter's life and alienating her. Likewise, with the grain-like "recaller" in "Crocodile," which lets the user view someone else's recent memories. Scared that insurance adjuster Shazia will discover a memory that reveals her to be a murderer, Mia kills Shazia, her husband, and their infant son. One of the short narratives in "Black Museum" centers around a doctor who uses a neural implant to "feel" the pain of his patients and so to treat them more effectively. After developing a sexual addiction to feeling the pain of others, the doctor spirals into self-harm, kills a homeless man, and ends up comatose. In each case, subjects couple with technology in ways that amplify or supplement existing cognitive states like memory, perception, and pain awareness. At the same time, "extending the mind" in this way produces dire consequences.

Perhaps, then, *Black Mirror* views transhumanism as a different kind of existential risk. Merging the human being with technology might not eradicate the human race. However, it *could* fundamentally alter what it is to be a human being, in the way that junior detective Blue describes in "Hated in the Nation": "These things absorb who we are. They know everything about us." This is certainly true if episodes like "The Entire History of You" are to be believed. Allowing humans to endlessly relive *exact copies* of their memories might appear to be quite useful. How many silly arguments about misremembered facts could be resolved! Yet, like Liam, having access to a store of perfect memories could easily paralyze people with uncertainty and insecurity. Much contemporary research into memory suggests that memories are decidedly *imperfect*; but we are perhaps all the better for it. In the book *Mental Time Travel*, Kourken Michaelian (2016) argues that human memory is not recall based. Rather, humans construct memories anew with each remembering around a small germ of permanence that retains the "feel" of the event as it was originally experienced. In this way, memory has much more in common with imagination. The difference is that memory is an imagining directed firmly at the past, not the future. So, the kind of perfect recall provided by Liam's grain might cause something like an information overload – unable to properly sift through all of the memories, people could get stuck in a stasis of inaction.

Hopefully, these reasons make it easy to see why it might be thought that *Black Mirror*'s main thesis is that technology is a profound existential risk. And this view is probably the prevailing, popular take on thematic undercurrent that runs beneath the show. But this apparent aversion to technology is not the whole story.

Why Technology *Is Not* the Problem

It is probably a mistake to think that *Black Mirror* is foretelling a picture of technological doom, despite good evidence from many of its episodes. To see this, it would be helpful to return to Bostrom's (2002) idea of existential risks. As Bostrom qualifies the term, existential risks involve either the eradication of human life or the calamitous and permanent hobbling of human development. Such threats are not "endurable" – even if humanity survives an existential risk-level event, it will no longer be viable as a species and could not recover.

Setting aside "natural" existential risks, like asteroids and global pandemic *not* resulting from laboratory developed diseases, technological risks might fall under two broad types: what could be called either human-directed risks and spontaneous existential risks. (This division is not Bostrom's but is a deliberate narrowing of his categories for expediency.) Some examples of human-directed risks include: deliberate misuse of advanced technology, like nanomachines; nuclear holocaust; proliferation of laboratory-bred super diseases; shutting down of a virtual simulation in which "humans" live; resource depletion; and environmental collapse from, say, climate change. There are far fewer spontaneous technological risks. A spontaneous technological risk would be in line with the worry of Butler's author from "The Book of the Machines" – a condition where technology becomes agentive and autonomously threatens humanity. Evolved, self-conscious machinery would fit the bill. So, too, would accidental spread of nanomachines (as depicted in Greg Bear's novel *Blood Music*); sometimes referred to as a "gray goo" scenario, the gist here is that molecule-sized machines driven only to self-replicate annihilate all life on Earth by consuming and assimilating it.

One kind of spontaneous risk to which Bostrom (2016) gives special attention is *superintelligence*: a complex AI so advanced that it vastly exceeds human intelligence and only continues to grow. Bostrom predicts that such an AI would independently formulate goals of self-preservation and resource acquisition (to sustain itself). The superintelligence would, therefore, resist efforts made by humans to turn it off and would possibly begin to see humans as an existential threat *to itself*. Given these conditions and its sophisticated intelligence, it is unlikely humans would survive.

Black Mirror does not appear to portray technology as the harbinger of specifically spontaneous existential risks. At no point does the show deal with doomsday scenarios involving a murderous AI or ravenous nanomachines. The dog-bots of "Metalhead" come closest to realizing a spontaneous existential risk, but the killer canines are importantly distinct from Butler's evolved machines or Bostrom's superintelligence. Namely, the robots in "Metalhead" are pretty dumb. They look to be quite formidable as guard units; the dog-bots are equipped with complicated tracking software, adaptive sensors capable of switching quickly between visual and auditory modalities at a moment's notice, and self-recharging batteries. But they do not seem to independently develop any kind of goals – least of all, self-preservation. Bella is pursued by a hound with all the tenacity and self-concern of a Terminator: killing its target is all that matters (Arnold would be proud!).

21 *Black Mirror* as Philosophy: A Dark Reflection of Human Nature

What about "San Junipero," wherein humanity "uploads" itself into oblivion? On closer examination, this scarcely fares better than "Metalhead" as an example of spontaneous existential risk. For one thing, humans are not being "uploaded" forcibly; even if they are tended to in robotic server farms after the fact, uploading is a *choice*. Perhaps, then, "San Junipero" presents viewers with a human-directed existential threat. While possible, this is not an argument that the show seems to take seriously. "San Junipero" is a notoriously optimistic episode among a series that is otherwise relentlessly bleak. Regardless of whatever the viewer may like to read into their situation, Yorkie and Kelly are portrayed as very much *happy* in their digital existence together. Even showrunner Charlie Brooker recommends taking the ending at face value: "They have the happiest ending imaginable. . .what appears to be happening there, is happening there. It's them, they drive off into the sunset together – because why not?" (Garcia, *Vogue*, Oct 27, 2016). So, "San Junipero" is not really a case of *any* sort of existential risk in terms of *Black Mirror*'s thematizing.

Surely, though, the show presents technology as a kind of human-directed existential risk in other places. Possibly! Even if it does, though, it would seem to be disingenuous to blame technology for human-directed existential risks. For instance, the main problem with nuclear holocaust is not necessarily that nuclear technology exists (though someone could separately argue that the tech itself is dangerous, too), but that *some actual human being would be crazy enough to use it as a weapon*. Similarly, extinction resulting from resource depletion or climate change are the clear result of human action – factories are not pumping fossil fuels into the atmosphere by *themselves*, but are driven by production, consumer desires, environmental negligence, etc., on the part of humans.

The point here is that the threats in cases of human-directed existential risk seem to be borne out of this or that human behavior. This is not meant trivially, in the sense that humans merely *created* technology that is itself harmful. Instead, it seems in such cases that the technology is only a way of embiggening the scope of existing human tendencies *that were already problematic*. Weaponization of nuclear technology or disease is different in degree (in the number of victims it claims), not kind (it is still designed to kill efficiently), from more conventional weapons like firearms. Technology may permit resource depletion and climate change to occur on a far greater scale, but human exploitation of resources did not begin with assembly lines and mass production. Even accidental spread of something like laboratory-made disease is more plausibly attributable to human failings in containment, safety, and the like. To return to a prior point: Technology would, in this case, appear to be the "black mirror" reflecting the already dark nature of humans.

Aside from "San Junipero," which has already been addressed, *Black Mirror* does explicitly engage with the special human-directed existential risk of living in a simulated reality on at least two occasions: "the shutting down of a simulation in which humans are a part," in Bostrom's words. Both "Hang the DJ" and "USS Callister" involve types of simulated environment, though neither is really a case of humans living in such an environment. The star-crossed lovers of "Hang the DJ," Amy and Frank, are revealed to be AI simulations that live within a dating app used by a human Amy and Frank. Likewise, except for Captain Robert Daly – a videogame designer who enters and exits a personally modified version of his game at will – the crew of the USS Callister are AI representations, not humans. Although they are modeled after Daly's actual coworkers, the AI crew are distinct from them.

Despite the fact that the simulations in "Hang the DJ" and "USS Callister" aren't simulated *humans*, questions can still be asked about the degree to which either presents technology as inherently harmful. In "USS Callister," the shutting down of Daly's private simulation, a virtual world based on the *Star Trek*-like *Space Fleet*, is very much presented as an existential risk. Here, the risk is not to humans but to the AI crew that Daly has created to populate his game world. However, any worry that the crew has about annihilation via simulation shutdown occupies very little of the episode's runtime. Mostly, "USS Callister" focuses on the ways in which Daly subjects the virtual crew to torture as surrogates for his actual coworkers – against whom Daly harbors no shortage of repressed frustration. In this way, the episode treats its AI *as if they were human*; they appear to suffer like actual human beings, for instance. As a result, any serious questions about technology tend toward Daly's use of technology to realize his creepy and exploitative revenge-fantasy. These are not properly questions about technology, then, but about what Daly's *use* of technology says about himself. (Spoiler: the systematic abuse of life-like representations of one's office mates *doesn't say anything good* about a person.)

Unlike "USS Callister," there is no existential risk posed in "Hang the DJ" whatsoever. From within the simulation, technology appears to be quite oppressive: relationship matches are determined by a sort of algorithm that forcibly pairs Amy and Frank with various romantic partners. Surprise! This simulation is really just one of many such simulations run by an elaborate dating app to test the prospective compatibility between real-Amy and real-Frank. At the end of the episode, real-Amy approaches real-Frank, presumably with the intention of starting a relationship – all because the app determined high compatibility, of course. There is no forced pairing-off of people by technology; rather, "Hang the DJ" points an accusatory finger back at the viewer and a growing social tendency to use apps like Tinder to do the legwork of setting up relationships. Again, the technology is not itself a danger. Instead, tech becomes a lens through which *Black Mirror* examines a particular feature of human beings – in this case, desperation to find something like a "soulmate."

The handful of examples that outwardly suggest that coupling with technology fundamentally alters human nature can be reevaluated along these same lines. The grain in "The Entire History of You" clearly intensifies existing jealousies and insecurities faced by relationships like Liam and Ffion's. At the same time, the grain does not *create* those jealousies and insecurities (where there were none) any more than a pencil and paper *create* tendencies toward distracted doodling during a boring class, seminar, or meeting. Such tendencies were already present, and the technology brings them into clearer focus. Similarly, the device from "Arkangel" that allows Marie to "see" through her daughter's eyes and manipulate what kinds of visual experiences Sara can have is an expression of parental overprotectiveness. Mia's efforts in "Crocodile" to cover her murderous tracks are nothing novel, either. The technology of the recaller magnifies her paranoia about getting caught: the tech merely reveals to the viewer *just how far Mia is willing to go* in a fevered attempt to preserve the quality of life she has. Lastly, the "Black Museum" doctor's pleasure-seeking behavior is definitely *enabled* by his implant, but the doctor's sadomasochistic desire to feel the pain of others is not at all *caused* by it. As in the other cases, the technology is in this instance *revelatory*. That is, joining with technology – in the sense of mind extending into the world through artifacts – does not challenge or pervert human nature at all. If anything, coupling with technology shines a brighter light on those aspects of human nature that are already there. In each example, technology is a concretization of sometimes abstract human fears, flaws, and behaviors that all *preexist* the technology itself.

So, it looks like *Black Mirror* neither regards technology as a terrible existential risk for humanity, nor does it portray human-technology coupling as something that strips humans of their distinctively human qualities. On closer inspection, those instances that seem to involve existential risk when taken at face value are better seen as bespoke scenarios meant to evoke moral evaluations about specific human traits and behaviors. Philosophers do this all the time by raising what are called *thought experiments* – often silly situations that allow the reader to consider a particular idea in isolation. For instance, Derek Parfit's (1984) "teletransporter" wonders whether someone could actually survive sci-fi teleportation from one planet to another. And Philippa Foot's (1967) more grounded "Trolley Problem" tests the reader's moral intuitions about whether one should divert the path of a runaway trolley car so that it saves five lives but directly kills another person in the process. The purpose of such stories is to reveal and test our intuitions (e.g., about personal identity or morality). Seen in this way, each episode of *Black Mirror* is a thought experiment narrowly zeroed-in on a single human feature.

Flatly declaring that technology is bad by making it into a spontaneous existential risk to either individual humans or human identity as a whole would largely take the human element out of *Black Mirror*. That is, humans would in many cases be *absolved* of moral responsibility because some technological bogeyman is the real threat. Such a reading would make episodes like "Men Against Fire" utterly incomprehensible. Like other soldiers in the episode, Stripe's implanted MASS device suppresses a supposedly "natural" human tendency toward empathy by literally dehumanizing the opposition: enemy combatants are seen through the MASS as aggressive mutants. The MASS also prevents the user from experiencing pleasant sensations in the world that might distract from the job of killing the enemy, like the texture of grass, the sounds of birds chirping, or the gag-inducing smells of the dead. Everything just said about the MASS certainly makes the technology sound despicable. Even if fault rests with the humans who designed the MASS to make targeted genocide palpable to soldiers, the soldiers themselves seem to be victims of the technology. However, the gut-punch of "Men Against Fire" is learning – with Stripe – that soldiers *willingly accept MASS implantation* with full knowledge of the consequences beforehand. They also consent to memory erasure so that they will not be aware of this choice (and possibly other, later memory wipes). This reframes the episode not as a technological horror, but a very human one. Perhaps that is *Black Mirror*'s trick – viewers go in thinking that the show will condemn technology, but it is really an indictment of the viewers themselves.

Could Technology Be an Indirect Harm?

Even if *Black Mirror* does not depict technology as a spontaneous existential risk or a threat to human identity, the show could still be critical of technology in other ways. For instance, one could argue that the series paints technology as an *indirect* harm in one way or another. In daily life, one regularly hears claims that television makes us dumber, that cell phones sap our ability to pay any kind of continuous attention to the world, and that social media atrophies in-person social skills. None of these are direct harms in the way that Bella being stabbed by a robot dog's knife arm in "Metalhead" is *direct harm*, but these are still surely bad things, if they are true.

In the last century, many philosophers have worried greatly about the negative effects of technology in exactly this indirect way. In particular, many of the critical theorists of the Frankfurt School in the early twentieth century regarded technology as part of social institutions that were inimical to the free thought and action of the individual. In the book *Escape from Freedom*, Erich Fromm ([1941] 1994) argues that the structures of democratic society create a space of apparent political freedom but profound intellectual restriction. Herbert Marcuse ([1964] 1991) shares and builds upon this sentiment in *One Dimensional Man*. In one way or another, both authors place considerable blame on ever-advancing technology as generative of "false needs" that drive individuals to bury themselves in consumer culture and isolate themselves from genuine relationships with others. One major consequence is that people begin to define themselves by what they own. Consider, for instance, the contemporary hysteria around the release of the next generation iPhone, new gaming consoles, or the desire to be part of the collective cultural experience of seeing, say, *Avengers: Endgame* as it becomes the (then) highest grossing film of all time.

Another pair of Frankfurt School theorists, Theodore Adorno and Max Horkheimer, claim in their *Dialectic of Enlightenment* ([1947] 2007) that the production of art has been perverted into a kind of "culture industry." Although they admit that all art reflects the context of its historical era in some way, Adorno and Horkheimer think that the economic and political organization of capitalistic, Western countries necessitates a sterile reproducing of itself. Put simply, art becomes just another commodity. Attempts at injecting aesthetically or politically subversive ideas into art are subsumed by the dominant influence of whatever is profitable. This isn't simply referring to the mass production of art – for instance, creating copies of famous artworks. No, what Adorno and Horkheimer have in mind is more that the *techniques* used in art are married to the popular and profitable, and thus reproduce the same thing, over and over again. When someone complains that all superhero films end the same way – usually with a giant beam of light such hurtling into the sky – this is the sort of reproduction that is being talked about.

More recent thinkers have also raised concerns about technology as an indirect and social harm. In *Technopoly*, Neil Postman (1993) argues that technology has been all but deified in contemporary American society. A "technopoly" of this sort – in which technology and technical craft are the supreme authority – socially privileges knowledge of how to use dominant technologies, generates an excess of meaningless information, and reduces individuals to quantified data. According to former Google Design-Ethicist Tristan Harris (2016), the technopoly has only gotten more constrictive since Postman's work.

Harris believes that social media, apps, and streaming services all intrude upon and in fact attempt to "hijack" a user's ability to make choices in order to increase engagement time with the platform. For instance, streaming services control which options are available, granularize categories long past the point of usefulness, and make "recommendations" for the viewer; these encourage the watching of particular shows and the funneling of the user toward preferred or popular titles. Similarly, "autoplay" options keep the next episode of a series (or some adjacent, related series) streaming unless the user overrides the option. Other apps – even the action of "swiping down" on a phone screen – are designed to offer small, psychological rewards for engagement. Still others exploit the well-documented "fear of missing out" and desire for social approval to bombard users with constant notifications about "likes" or suggestions to share posts with other users. All of this is done under the illusion that the user is fully in control of the decision-making process, despite the fact that programs and hardware are explicitly designed to take advantage of human psychological vulnerabilities toward things like addiction. In recent years, Harris has referred to this process as "human downgrading" (Thompson 2019).

The common feature among all of these thinkers, from the Frankfurt theorists to Harris, is that technology restricts the way that humans think, dilutes their thoughts, and destroys humanity – not with killer robots but through submission, dependence, and ignorance. In these situations of indirect harm, society trades truth and free thought for the smooth, ultimately complacent comforts of technological progress. It is as Virginia Woolf writes in *The Waves:* "One cannot live outside the machine for more perhaps than half an hour." Once people become inured to the authority of consumerist technology and even reliant upon it, it becomes something craved and inescapable. There is strong basis in *Black Mirror*'s catalog of episodes that technology results in this kind of indirect harm.

"Fifteen Million Merits" presents the viewer with a stark reality where free thinking is very much limited by the technology in place. People in the episode's society, like friends Abi and Bing, pedal stationary bikes all day as a form of mindless labor and are placated by pornography and the "reality television" of *Botherguts*, a show where fat, lower-class people are mocked and abused. The "merits" earned from pedaling are a universal currency used for everything from buying a sandwich to playing violent, repetitive videogames in claustrophobic living spaces. With enough merits, Bing can pay to skip intrusive, holographic ads; without merits, attempts to even look away from the ads are met with a piercing, painful shriek that cannot be ignored.

Obviously, these limitations on thinking – and a system that discourages intellectual activity and openly encourages thoughtless pleasures – echo the worries of critical theorists like Fromm and Marcuse. When the musically skilled Abi appears on the talent show *Hot Shots*, she is derided, drugged, and coerced into performing as a porno actress. Bing's later attempt to commit televised suicide in protest with a hidden shard of glass results in the creation of his own show, on which he repeats his now hollow suicide threat for the enjoyment of others (who are still pedaling). Both

Abi's genuine talent and Bing's attempted dissent are treated as commodities in what Adorno and Horkheimer would surely call a vicious culture industry. Abi's talent is discarded because it is less profitable than pornography; Bing's subversive act is repackaged as both a lifeless television reproduction and a "shard of glass" charm that others can buy for their virtual avatars. ("Rachel, Jack, and Ashley Too" has brief shades of this same culture industry commodification, as Ashley O's thoughts are mined from her comatose brain and reproduced for profit as both lyrics and in the form of the holographic "Ashley Eternal.")

Episodes like "The Waldo Moment," "Striking Vipers," and "Smithereens" also portray technology as indirect harm. Waldo, the vulgar cartoon bear from "The Waldo Moment," becomes a clear case of technology-as-social control. Though initially used by his performer, Jaime, to have a laugh at a corrupt and ineffectual political system, Waldo eventually morphs into a competing candidate for office. Waldo represents frustration with the political establishment but lacks any "plan" (or agency) to do anything about it. In part, this is because Waldo has no views of his own and is simply a mouthpiece for his performer at a given moment. As an empty representation of aimless antiestablishment resentment, Waldo can come to stand for pretty much anything – including fascism. Because people identify with his anger and are amused by his antics, the authority Waldo might come to stand for is largely unquestioned. The episode's mid-credits stinger reveals an oppressive and dystopian Waldo-future where exactly this has happened.

In "Striking Vipers," Danny and Karl's virtual sexual relationship – they are attracted to one another only when playing specific characters in the VR title *Striking Vipers X* – irreparably damages any opportunities either man has for future physical relationships with others. They both find relationships outside the game world to be unfulfilling and are therefore isolated from other people *by* technology. Finally, Billy's speech about his Twitter-like company in "Smithereens" seems ripped straight from Tristan Harris's most salient fears about psychological manipulation. Chris, despondent over killing his fiancé in a car accident while distracted by his phone, suggests that apps are designed to leech attention from users. A frustrated, sympathetic Billy responds that the app is like a "crackpipe" and a "Vegas casino...and all the doors are locked" – and with entire departments devoted to maximizing ways to exploit the psychology of the user.

It is somewhat hasty, though, to simply credit these episodes – and the philosophers discussed so far – with the belief that technology is indirectly harmful and therefore *bad*. As with the claim that *Black Mirror* shows technology as an existential threat, there is more to this story. The Frankfurt School thinkers all grew out of a criticism and development of Marxism. And a few comments on some of Karl Marx's own views on technology can help make it clearer that the Frankfurt theorists may not be, for the most part, demonizing technology proper. In *Capital Vol. III*, Marx ([1867] 1993, p. 940) states that the means of production will shape the possible forms that economies and societies *can* take. This means that a given economic and political system has a kind of material basis *in* the means of production. In other words, the technology of production determines the range of possible social arrangements. For instance, a society without the ability to mass produce probably could not be an effective consumer society; more simply, a society without film projector technology could not have a lucrative film industry. Yet, this does not mean that the technology determines *that* a certain economy and society will definitely come about. For Marx, the oppression of the working class by a ruling class is a class issue *enabled* by technology – it is not a technology issue in and of itself.

To extrapolate from this Marxist explanation and return to technology as an indirect harm: to endorse technology as an indirect harm is not to say that technology is necessarily the underlying problem. In each of the examples provided, technology is just the form that unfreedom, authority, and control take – but this form leads back to, at least for *Black Mirror*, the actual human beings who use the technology in exploitative ways or are exploited by it. The institutions behind the oppressive regime in "Fifteen Million Merits" are objectionable, but the episode is arguably more concerned with the moral attitudes of the people living within that system. The same can be said for the greater population's reaction to Waldo in "The Waldo Moment," to Danny and Karl's alienation from others in "Striking Vipers," and to the intentionally addictive nature of the Smithereen app in "Smithereens." So, in the interest of consistency with earlier evaluations of other episodes, the best view to take is probably that *Black Mirror* seeks to show what these instances of technology as indirect harm have to say about human traits and behaviors. "Fifteen Million Merits" presses the viewer to be repulsed by Bing's decision to "sell out," even as the viewer also ponders whether Bing had any choice. Likewise, what does it say about people that they are so willing to embrace Waldo and his directionless messaging?

This is not to say that *Black Mirror* is not at all critical of these technologies and the social institutions in which they are embedded. It is! Nonetheless, this criticism seems to be secondary to the goal of using technology to meaningfully investigate human nature. What such technology says about human nature might end up being "Humans are too dependent on technology." But the emphasis in *Black Mirror* is on the individual person coming to this realization and the faculties of the human being that permit one to become dependent in this way – not on the technology itself.

The Right Answer: Technology as Reflective Imitation

So far, this chapter has asked the question: "How does *Black Mirror* see technology?" It seems that two answers can be dismissed. *Black Mirror* does not depict technology as an existential risk to humanity or human nature. Similarly, *Black Mirror* does not appear to put the blame for indirect harms of technology on technology itself. This leaves the other answer: *Black Mirror* sees technology as a reflection of human nature. It is human nature and behavior that are the real problems. Several episodes have already been analyzed in terms of this notion, and the explanation looks like it fits consistently across the series. It remains to be seen, though, how technology-as-reflection-of-humanity might be grounded in philosophical terms.

Two ancient philosophers provide complementary views that may serve as this basis. In Book X of the *Laws*, Plato (2016) draws a helpful distinction between the natural and the artificial. This is similar to the discussion of the derivative nature of art in *Republic*, Book X (Plato 1992). In both cases, what is created – artifacts or the artificial – is described as an *imitation* of the natural world. Looked at under Plato's overall metaphysic, this means that the artificial will always be in some way deficient; it is a copy, and so its properties are not really its own but just reflect the natural things it imitates.

To this same end, Aristotle (1991) proposes in Book II of the *Physics* that natural and artificial are distinguished by their "principles of change" or that which brings about their activity. That which is natural has an internal principle of change. This is clear in that animals move and perceive the world on their own accord or in the way that plants grow and propagate. Yet, things like rocks are also part of the natural world and so have an internal principle of change based on their elemental composition – rocks are more inclined toward rest rather than movement, which is why they fall. Insofar as artifacts are *composed* of natural things, they share in the internal principles of the natural things of which they are composed.

Importantly, though, this is not a principle *of the artifact*. The artifact itself gets all of its impetus to change from things external to it or at least from things that are not it (like its natural components). Another way of saying this is that artifacts do not inherently have some purpose or function – their function is imparted by the artificer. Stefan's computer in *Bandersnatch* should not do anything without his input; no work on his game happens unless he is typing on the keyboard. That the computer is a thing for typing, programming, and storing information was determined by its creator.

Between the Platonic and Aristotelian arguments, two common features emerge. First, the artificial – technology – in some way derives its properties from the natural. Second, technology has no inherent agency. That is, a given piece of technology cannot act on its own, as it requires an external cause for any kind of action in multiple ways. For instance, technology cannot properly "act" without someone or something to make use of it, and its function comes from what the creator intends for it. Taken together, the Platonic and Aristotelian views suggest the very relationship between technology and human beings that is being sought to explain *Black Mirror*. As derivative or as an imitation of humans, technology can certainly be said to "reflect" human features. As something without its own agency, any "badness" from technology comes from how it is made, how it is used, or why it was created – all three of which turn the onus of responsibility away from technology itself and onto humans and their relationships *with* technology.

It takes little effort to map this new analysis onto the majority of *Black Mirror* episodes and thereby recast the series' statement on technology as a magnification of existing human flaws. The inescapable social rating system from "Nosedive" stands in for the deification of the human need for social approval. Correspondingly, "Hated in the Nation" weaponizes the "pile-on" nature of public disapproval in its mechanical swarm and the hashtag #deathto. Like "White Bear" before it, "Shut Up and Dance" unsettles the viewer by making her watch someone be systematically tortured, then revealing this as (probably) unfit punishment for some awful moral failing. In both cases, technology makes a spectacle of punishment in order to show the viewer that the societal desire for punishing may not have anything to do with justice and everything to do with a perverse enjoyment at least some humans get from the suffering of others. Questions about this perverse enjoyment make an appearance in "The National Anthem," too. While watching Prime Minister Michael Callow have sex with a pig on live television, the casual desire for schadenfreude demonstrated by a viewership that cannot seem to look away turns to disgust at themselves for watching (however fleeting that disgust may be, as is seen in the credits sequence where the event is all but forgotten). These episodes – and others peppered through this chapter – allow for a fairly easy "connect the dots" between vile aspects of human behavior and instances of technology that lay those vile traits bare to see.

But the robot dog apocalypse of "Metalhead" still seems importantly different from the other episodes. Recall that the trouble here was that the Aibo-sized Terminators appeared to represent technology gone berserk – a problem with technology, not human beings. Fortunately, the "imitation" analysis invites a reassessment of "Metalhead," too. On the Platonic and Aristotelian views, technology is an imitation whose value comes in human intention and use. Keeping this in mind, the murderous guard dogs of "Metalhead" clearly did not program *themselves* to viciously cut down any humans they encountered. And the robotic canines are most definitely guards – Bella and her crew first encounter a dog in "sleep mode" while raiding a warehouse for what turned out to be teddy bears. The dogs were likely not just hunting people indiscriminately, either. When Bella finds a couple dead in their posh home, it is intimated that the cause of death is self-inflicted shotgun blast. In other words, robot dogs are not simply breaking into homes from a directive to, say, "eliminate all human life." Moreover, the dogs evidently did not design their own weapon systems. The brutal shrapnel bombs (with embedded tracking) and head-exploding cannons were made by humans to fulfill precisely those purposes. Perhaps, then, the dogs are functioning *exactly* as intended – to protect property and eliminate thieves/intruders by whatever violent means are at their disposal. Like the rest of the technology in the whole of the *Black Mirror* series, the robotic dogs of "Metalhead" are an extension of human will and human traits. In this case, those traits may be a nasty preference for property over lives.

With reservations about "Metalhead" resolved, the "technology-as-reflection-of-humans" interpretation seems consistently applicable across the board. But that cannot be the final word, at least not yet.

What About the Monsters and Demons of Season 6?

At the time this chapter was originally published, the (then) last episode of the series was Season 5's "Rachel, Jack and Ashley Too." Now that *Black Mirror*'s sixth season has aired on Netflix, there might appear to be at least a few *more* episodes that challenge this chapter's claim that the series uses technology as a tool to highlight and criticize human moral failures. What makes Season 6 unique, though, is that this challenge apparently does not come from the major question that this chapter asked – namely, is technology the problem, or are *we*? Instead, several episodes seem to abandon the series' focus on technology altogether. This is by design, as Brooker started to worry in recent years that his show was getting stale (Stefansky 2023). To that end, "Loch Henry" looks like nothing more than a true crime-themed thriller, "Mazey Day" ends with a 2000s-era paparazzi snapping photos of a celebrity "it"-girl turned werewolf, and "Demon 79" is styled, both visually and narratively, after the horror films of the 1970s and early 1980s. None of this *sounds* like "trad *Black Mirror*," to borrow Brooker's words.

Appearances aside, most of Season 6 can still be cleanly connected with what this chapter posits as the show's central argument: Technology reflects and can perhaps amplify already bad human behavior. This is most obvious in "Joan is Awful," where it becomes clear that all of the title character's problems stem from a perceived lack of control in her own life – even before it was turned into a TV show (called "Joan is Awful") without her explicit permission. But it is not just *one* show: the episode is a matryoshka doll of AI-generated, algorithm-directed streaming shows about Joan's mundane existence, all skewed to emphasize the negative features of her life in order to maximize believability for the viewer. This nesting of shows within shows creates a number of layers – what the Streamberry technician portrayed by a digital Michael Cera calls "fictive levels" – that get progressively further removed from the actual Joan's actual life. In other words, the show based on Joan's life (where Joan is played by a digital Annie Murphy) includes its own show based on this *fictional* Joan's life (where Annie Murphy-Joan is played by a digital Salma Hayek), which then includes a third show (where Salma Hayek-Joan is played by a digital Cate Blanchett). Since successive shows are just copies upon copies of events in the actual Joan's life, it turns out that the source of *every* Joan's misery in *all* versions of "Joan is Awful" is the fact that her life is being exploited for a show in which she has no part or purpose – though this sense of alienation and aimlessness was already felt in her middle management, corporate job and unsatisfying home life. Hence, the episode's twists and turns about sneaky end user license agreements, autogenerated content, and commercialized data collection are really just a way to bring the *existing* problems in actual Joan's life into focus.

Similar things can be said about many other episodes from the season. The consciousness-transferring shenanigans and the searing envy David bears toward Cliff in "Beyond the Sea" are par for the course for *Black Mirror* (even if the episode's alternate history allusions to the Manson family killings are not). Beneath its true crime surface, "Loch Henry" also rewards a more careful eye. In the vein of Spike Jonze's *Adaptation*, it presents a scathing indictment of formulaic true crime media – and a ravenous viewership sometimes accused of vicarious participation in the heinous acts these shows dissect – while also delivering its own derivative, sensationalized, and thus highly *marketable* true crime story. Even "Mazey Day," with gore that seems better-suited to *Tales from the Crypt* or Shudder's *Creepshow* revival, grounds its morality tale in technology. As reluctant paparazzi Bo stands over a dying Mazey Day, briefly returned to human form, the lycanthropic starlet

21 *Black Mirror* as Philosophy: A Dark Reflection of Human Nature

begs Bo to shoot her. When Bo puts down the gun and instead lifts her camera (Bo, who also always has her era-appropriate iPod Shuffle with her—music and camera together), the viewer can see that *everyone* with a smart phone is really no better than the paparazzi, constantly staging a false world for the best "shots" to showcase their own lives.

Take note that the problems in these episodes are again not with the technology involved but with how characters use it. Body-swapping may enable David's jealousy in "Beyond the Sea," but it does not create it. What Bo does with her camera in "Mazey Day" plainly says more about *her* than it does the device. The same thing will be true of the people in a culture like ours where everyone has a camera in their pocket and is overeager to use it for fame, material success, or whatever (if this is what the episode is really meant to evoke). Lastly, the glut of true crime series, podcasts, and other media – as seen in "Loch Henry" – are symptomatic of an uncomfortable willingness to engage in a kind of trauma profiteering and of the perverseness of getting a thrill out of other people's very real suffering. As a genre, true crime's popularity is the *result* of these things. To try and say that the media/technology came first is putting the cart in front of the horse.

"Demon 79" does not fit into the series' "technology" argument quite so easily, though. Unlike "Beyond the Sea," its past setting is not a funky, alternate history mask that allows for a world of visually arresting, lo-fi tech. No, "Demon 79" is set in fairly drab, very Earthbound 1979 Northern England. And the most advanced piece of technology that we see is probably Nida's wall-mounted phone, which Gaap uses to call his fiendish superiors. This is classic "Satanic Panic" horror, including both a mystical talisman – fueled by blood and hate – and grisly human sacrifices. In fact, the episode was not originally going to be part of Season 6 at all. Before adding it to the sixth season's roster, Brooker says that he toyed with the idea of creating a "retro" horror series called *Red Mirror* (Stefansky 2023), something perhaps along the lines of *Hammer House of Horror* (which aired in 1980, extremely close to the year in which "Demon 79" is set).

Yet, "Demon 79" does not *feel* all that out of place when one takes a closer look. Notwithstanding 1970s gloss, the episode trades in very contemporary themes (in both the USA and UK, at least) about sexism, immigration, racism, and politically hawkish behavior. And it is explicitly called out in the plot that Nida – the meek, shoe-seller protagonist who accidentally summons a demon – has murderous impulses (though toward objectively terrible people) even *before* finding the talisman that literally calls her to start a killing spree to avert world disaster. So, the focus is, as usual for the series, on the terrible things that human beings do to one another and how they relate to problems in current society. Unsurprisingly, the horror trappings here are largely set dressing for how to deliver these messages. ("Unsurprising" because horror – like the science fiction genre in which *Black Mirror* is usually grouped – is well known for disguising social commentary beneath stories that are superficially about things far removed from reality.)

There are even reasons for thinking this very supernatural episode retains at least some focus on technology. In the first place, despite Brooker's claims – and the clever bit of *Red Mirror* branding that precedes the episode, rather than the usual *Black Mirror* title splash – the cataclysmic horror of "Demon 79" is still technological. The nuclear attacks that end both the world and the episode are caused by war-hungry humans like Conservative Party representative Michael Smart, not the decidedly supernatural demon Gaap. (This is not to say that Smart *himself* is responsible for the nuclear attacks, only that people *like* him are.) For the most part, any sense of menace in the episode comes from the human characters, whether through newspaper headlines about escalating nuclear tensions or overtly threatening characters like Smart (who confides in Nida's coworker that the only reason he is not part of the fascist National Front party is because they are too loud about their fascism – and thus would not win) and the creepy, spouse-murdering Keith Holligan. For his part, Gaap is rather affable and treats Nida with a respect she is seldom afforded by the *human* population of her neighborhood. Again, the (era-appropriate) technological danger – nuclear war, in this case – is used to bring attention to emphatically human dangers like xenophobia and tribalism.

Another consideration is that technology need not be especially "advanced" (from a contemporary point of view) to count as "technology," though we might wrongly associate the word only with futurism. The laptop used to type this chapter and the pencil that scribbles down a rushed grocery list are both "technology," even if one strikes us as much more advanced than the other. Likewise, the crude talisman in "Demon 79" is in many ways as much "technology" as the sophisticated quantputer in "Joan is Awful." That is, it is an artifact (so, "artificial" thing) that is used to accomplish certain human ends. As if to hammer home this point, Gaap even calls demonic "tech support" for help understanding why one of the required human sacrifices has not registered on the talisman's face! The truth is that, whether past or future, technology has been a convenient means of delivering upon dark human impulses. For instance, think about the "advanced" technology of World War I, something quite antique by today's standards but which nevertheless enabled a *staggering* scale of death and destruction that was previously unseen.

Despite these remarks about the importance of technology to even the sixth season, *Black Mirror* might one day shed its connection to technology entirely. Given Brooker's remarks about *Red Mirror* and his desire to reinvent the show, that is at least conceivable. But even if that happens, this chapter's argument would need very little modification. (A series called *Red Mirror* would still have the word "mirror" in its title – the emphasis remains on the act of reflection, only the genre and setting have changed.) Although I have claimed that all Season 6 episodes can still be viewed through a "technology reflects human badness" lens, it is the "human badness" part that the show really wants to communicate to viewers. Brooker has said as much himself, stating that "[h]umans are weak is the story" of *Black Mirror* (Stefansky 2023). In that sense, Season 6 cements the theme that it is *human beings* who are awful (just like Joan), just as the rest of the series has; technology is just one particularly relevant *way* in which this awfulness manifests itself, and it is the one that *Black Mirror* has most often examined. If the show can pivot away from technology successfully, or, less radically, if the show can diminish the role of

21 *Black Mirror* as Philosophy: A Dark Reflection of Human Nature

technology in the series while still depicting human badness, it would seem even more clearly true that *Black Mirror* is not arguing that technology is the problem.

Divorced from the "technology is evil" side of things, Blue's words from "Hated in the Nation" now take on a different meaning. "These things absorb who we are" is not a claim about how technology wears away human identity. Rather, technology absorbs whatever human features we impose upon it through its creation and use. "These things" are what they are because of what *we* are.

Conclusion: Must Technology's Reflection Be Dark?

Considering the famous pessimism for which *Black Mirror* endings are known, it might seem disingenuous to conclude the chapter on a question about optimism. Yet, it must also be realized that the series would have very little point if its episodes were made just to reveal to the viewers their own "dark" reflection in the "black mirror" of technology. Obviously, the individual examples examined in this chapter cannot be said to reflect the *better* nature of humans. But what about *Black Mirror* taken as a whole?

Walter Benjamin's ([1935] 2008) *The Work of Art in the Age of Its Technological Reproducibility* might serve as a companion and foil in many ways to Adorno and Horkheimer's culture industry. Benjamin scrutinizes the same phenomenon of the production of art amid a consumerist culture dominated by technology and industry – yet he comes to different conclusions that are possibly not mutually exclusive with the more cynical findings made by Adorno and Horkheimer. Before reproduction, there was an "aura" to the participation in art. Each piece was unique, so there was a kind of ritual of "being there" that was necessary to the process of thinking critically about a work and its meaning. In reproduction, though, art can be copied so as to reach mass audiences; instead of diluting the artistic experience, Benjamin believes that this allows art to become a vehicle for political action and activism. No longer is art about an experience of "awe" limited to a very few. By mass reproduction, art can shift toward exposing average people to subversive meanings, asking them to critically contemplate those meanings, and then encourage social change. This sort of change would obviously be unavailable to small audiences captivated by the ritual of observing some unique artwork. Mass cinema, books, and television, however – just in virtue of simultaneously reaching more people – can be used to bring viewers to question (and possibly begin to dismantle) the oppressive modes of living that the Frankfurt School thinkers believed were smothering modern society. Note that to say that media *can* do so does not mean that these media *would* beget meaningful social change. All the same, Benjamin reckoned it a possibility, which is more than could be said for the dreadful conclusions that Adorno, Horkheimer, and others reached about technology.

If Benjamin is right, then it could be argued that *Black Mirror* as a series is an attempt to effect positive social change. Individual episodes show the ways that technology reflects the worst in human beings. Yet, by showing this to a viewer who will ideally see these same traits reflected in himself, *Black Mirror* encourages its viewership to confront the "darkness" within and do something about it. For instance, only when viewers recognize Lacie's desperate struggle to raise her rating in "Nosedive," and then see the same debilitating need for social approval in themselves, can they can begin to overcome it.

The idea that *Black Mirror* seeks to move its viewers to change themselves is not as speculative as it might seem. In fact, *Bandersnatch* – the series' most "meta" entry by far – has an underpinning of viewer complicity in every increasingly horrible thing that Stefan does, whether he's killing Dad, Colin, Mohan Thakur, or whomever. Because of the episode's interactive format, the viewer must always *choose* for Stefan to do this or that awful thing. At that point, the episode no longer asks the viewer to extrapolate from the show's characters to themselves. The viewer can no longer defer: the question is now about what technology reveals about *the viewer*. *Black Mirror* may be reflecting the worst qualities of the human being through technology that is both mundane and fantastical. But it only reflects the worst so that it can (hopefully) bring out the best.

References

Adorno, Theodore, and Max Horkheimer. (1947) 2007. *The dialectic of enlightenment: Philosophical fragments*, ed. Gunzelin Schmid Noerr. Trans. Edmund Jephcott. Stanford: Stanford University Press.

Aristotle. 1991. Physics. In *The complete works of Aristotle, vol. 1. The revised Oxford translation*, ed. Jonathan Barnes. Princeton: Princeton University Press.

Benjamin, Walter. (1935) 2008. *The work of art in the age of its technological reproducibility, and other writings on media*, ed. Michael W. Jennings, Brigid Doherty, and Thomas Y. Levin. Trans. Edmund Jephcott, Rodney Livingstone, Howard Eiland, et al. Cambridge, MA: The Belknap Press of Harvard University Press.

Bostrom, Nick. 2002. Existential risks: Analyzing human extinction scenarios and related hazards. *Journal of Evolution and Technology* 9 (1): 1–37.

———. 2016. *Superintelligence: Paths, dangers, strategies*. Oxford, UK: Oxford University Press. Reprint edition.

Butler, Samuel. 1863. *Darwin among the machines*. The Press, June 13. http://nzetc.victoria.ac.nz/tm/scholarly/tei-ButFir-t1-g1-t1-g1-t4-body.html

———. 1872. *Erewhon*. London: Trubner & Co.

Clark, Andy. 2003. *Natural born cyborgs*. New York: Oxford University Press.

Clark, Andy, and David Chalmers. 1998. The extended mind. *Analysis* 58 (1): 7–19.

Foot, Philippa. 1967. The problem of abortion and the doctrine of the double effect. *Oxford Review* 5: 1–7.

Fromm, Erich. (1941) 1994. *Escape from freedom*. New York: Holt Paperbacks.

Garcia, Patricia. 2016. *Black Mirror* creator Charlie Brooker on what really happened at the end of "San Junipero". Vogue, October 27. https://www.vogue.com/article/black-mirror-creator-charlie-brooker-san-junipero

Harris, Tristan. 2016. How technology is hijacking your mind – From a magician and Google design ethicist. Medium, May 18. https://medium.com/thrive-global/how-technology-hijacks-peoples-minds-from-a-magician-and-google-s-design-ethicist-56d62ef5edf3

Marcuse, Herbert. (1964) 1991. *One dimensional man*, 2nd ed. Boston: Beacon Press.

Marx, Karl. (1867) 1993. *Capital: Vol. III*. London: Penguin Classics.

Michaelian, Kourken. 2016. *Mental time travel: Episodic memory and our knowledge of the personal past*. Cambridge, MA: The MIT Press.

Parfit, Derek. 1984. *Reasons and persons*. Oxford, UK: Oxford University Press.

Plato. 1992. *Republic*. Trans. G. M. A. Grube. Revised by C. D. C. Reeve. Indianapolis: Hackett.
———. 2016. *Laws*. ed. Malcolm Schofield. Trans. Tom Griffith. Cambridge, UK: Cambridge University Press.
Postman, Neil. 1993. *Technopoly: The surrender of culture to technology*. New York: Vintage.
Stefansky, Emma. 2023. *Black Mirror* season 6: Charlie Brooker breaks down every episode. Esquire, June 15. https://www.esquire.com/entertainment/tv/a44197628/charlie-brooker-black-mirror-interview/
Thompson, Nicholas. 2019. Tristan Harris: Tech is "downgrading" humans. It's time to fight back. Wired Magazine, April 23. https://www.wired.com/story/tristan-harris-tech-is-downgrading-humans-time-to-fight-back/
Ulam, Stanislaw. 1958. Tribute to John Von Neumann. *Bulletin of the American Mathematical Society* 64 (3): 1–49.

Rick & Morty as Philosophy: Nihilism in the Multiverse

22

Sergio Genovesi

Contents

Introduction 504
Infinite Worlds in an Infinite Universe 504
Microscopic and Macroscopic Societies 507
Infinite Possible Realities 510
Nihilism in the Multiverse 513
Conclusion: Does Rick Really Not Care? 516
References 518

Abstract

The chapter explores the nihilist worldview presented in the TV series *Rick and Morty*. It will be argued that this kind of nihilism relies on cultural relativism and on the existence of infinite other possible worlds. It will be then shown how the endorsement of a nihilist perspective leads Rick to have a hedonistic lifestyle.

Keywords

Cultural Relativism · Multiverse theory · Hedonism · Nihilism · Rick & Morty · Giordano Bruno · Michel de Montaigne · Michel Foucault · David Lewis · Gottfried Leibniz · Cyrenaic School

---

S. Genovesi (✉)
University of Bonn, Bonn, Germany
e-mail: sergio.genovesi@uni-bonn.de

© Springer Nature Switzerland AG 2024
D. K. Johnson et al. (eds.), *The Palgrave Handbook of Popular Culture as Philosophy*,
https://doi.org/10.1007/978-3-031-24685-2_74

503

Introduction

> Nobody exists on purpose, nobody belongs anywhere, everybody's gonna die. Come watch TV.
> —Morty Smith

Rick & Morty is not an easy show to watch. It is cynical and loud, has very dark humor, and systematically deconstructs everything in which western society used to believe. Rick Sanchez is a typical mad scientist. In his lab, it is possible to find every kind of deadly gadget and, if just asked, he is able to craft devices that can turn people into pickles or freeze time. He can even concoct love elixirs. He is a misanthropist and he does not believe in anything but one thing: science. Having no values, he spends his time drinking and trying to have fun.

His grandson Morty, on the other hand, is far less smart but proves to be a valid assistant. Even though Rick would hardly admit it, he really likes Morty. Indeed, Rick seems to be the only one in the family who takes Morty seriously. Morty's sister, Summer, is too busy trying to be a cool teenager to pay attention to him, and his parents, Jerry and Beth, who are always fighting, think that Morty might be "slightly retarded." Indeed, Morty is not brilliant at school. But, as Rick always says, "school is a waste of time" and "is not a place for smart people." So, instead of helping him with his homework, he drags him off for mind-blowing adventures on faraway planets or in parallel universes to which he travels with his spaceship and his interdimensional portal gun.

The biting wit of *Rick & Morty* is highly intelligent and it is possible to find a number of philosophical views in the lines uttered by Rick Sanchez and the Smith family. The most evident, however, is nihilism. And while the most direct way this view is supported in the show is Rick's biting commentary, this perspective is also cemented in a clever and unconventional way by the fact that the show occurs within a multiverse (and by the resulting metaphysical view of the world), and complemented through a defense of cultural relativism. This chapter will illustrate the particular ways these views are presented in the show and will point out their mutual connection.

Infinite Worlds in an Infinite Universe

The first step we need to take in order to understand *Rick & Morty*'s nihilism, is to explore its basic disbelief in the special importance of any cultural phenomenon – such as religious beliefs, social values or cultural traditions. In the year 1600, the philosopher and cosmologist Giordano Bruno was burned at the stake in Rome because of his heretical opinions. Among other things, in his work *De lo infinito universo e mundi* (*The Infinite Universe and its Worlds*) he defended the thesis that our universe is infinite and therefore there could be an infinite number of worlds like ours (Bruno 2014). This view contrasted with the Catholic doctrine at the time, which still supported an Aristotelian cosmology that depicted the universe as anthropocentric. How could humankind be at the center of the divine creation if our planet and civilization were just one of many others? We know nowadays, of course, that Bruno was right: the universe is, if not infinite, ridiculously immense, and it would be unwise to deny the possibility of other worlds like ours. Indeed, we already know for sure that there are a number of potentially habitable exoplanets similar to Earth. But *Rick & Morty* takes it a step further (as every good work of science fiction should) and assumes that the existence of other intelligent life forms and civilizations on faraway planets is a proven fact. Unlike you might expect, however, the scientist Rick Sanchez is not a champion of diplomacy to these worlds. He mainly uses his knowledge of alien culture to manipulate these alien communities and achieve his purpose: to have fun.

Given its ability to confront other cultures, *Rick & Morty* is also able to relativize (and ridicule) western society by drawing parallels with it. In the episode *Rattlestar Ricklactica* (S4E5), for example, after Morty is bitten by an astronaut snake coming from another planet, Rick analyzes the whole snake society with a special device in order to find an antivenom and discovers that the planet is plagued by a war between snake communities motivated by race hatred. Rick cannot avoid making fun of them since, in his eyes, all snakes are quite the same.

> Oof, oh my God, these snakes are a mess. 19 billion snakes divided into 10.000 nations all on the brink of a global war over… ahah race! How funny is that!? Imagine being a racist snake. "Hey, other snake, I hate you because you are the wrong color, snake!". Oh my God, you're not laughing?

Seen from above, from his spaceship, snake racism just looks foolish and ludicrous. But wouldn't it be the same for human racism? Rick even gives the same treatment to another aspect of the snakes' culture. Snake jazz, for example, which basically consists of hissing and rhythmically shaking the rattle. Rick comments: "Ah, idiots!" But is our jazz – or rock, or pop – that much more sophisticated?

Rick & Morty draws many other analogies between alien and human culture. For instance in the episode *Look Who's Purging Now* (S2E9), looking for wiper fluid for their spaceship, Rick and Morty land on a planet that has adopted the social practice of purging: in order to keep their society crime-free, they annually celebrate a so-called Festival during which it is allowed to commit every kind of horrible crime. During their stay on the planet, Rick and Morty discover that this cathartic practice was established among peasants by the rich aristocrats who live outside town in order to keep the peasant's violent instincts under control. At first this might seem absurd, but it is not unlike cultural practices here on Earth which, although they usually don't involve mass carnage, have involved casting aside usual social and ethical norms (and the occasional human sacrifice).

Take for example, the ancient Greek Dyonisia or the ancient Roman Saturnalia – the latter of which involved giving even the poor an equal place at the banquet table. Or take the Christmas tradition of wassailing, during which masters were obligated to bestow upon their servants the household's best food and drink in exchange for songs of well wishing. Historian Stephen Nissenbaum (1996) described it as a "social safety valve" which solidified the social structure by simultaneously allowing the lower classes to express their frustrations with the upper class while also acknowledging their superior status. It derived from Middle Ages and Renaissance practices in which the aristocracy explicitly encouraged their "lessers" to mock them, and express their discontent, so that they would be more likely to behave during the rest of the year. Those were preceded by the Mesopotaiminan Zagmuk, in which a prisoner or peasant was elevated to king for a day before he was ritually sacrificed so that he could descend into the underworld to help fend off the forces of chaos. And all of these influence the modern-day carnival, in which roles are reversed and social norms are suspended.

Alien cultures can also be very different from western culture and look rather like a dystopian dream coming true. In the episode *Raising Gazorpatorp* (S1E7), Rick travels to planet Gazorpazorp, in the Andromeda system, together with Summer. On this planet, female Gazorpians have built a refined matriarchal underground society where males are evicted onto the planet surface after they are born, while females are educated and encouraged to follow their own inclinations. In order to generate the offspring, fertile sex robots are sent to the rough and uncultivated males to collect their semen and carry baby Gazorpians. Visiting Gazorpazorp with Rick, Summer has to wear a burqa in order to not be harassed by the male inhabitants of the surface, while Rick has to pretend to be Summer's slave to not offend the underground female population. As soon as the female Gazorpians find out that he is her grandfather and on earth children are the result of an actual male/female relation, they react horrified, arrest them, and sentence them to death. Summer luckily manages to talk them out of this situation by pointing out that her clothes, which are better looking than the Gazorpian ones, are designed by gay males and that gender separation would not work on Earth.

The same disgust that Gazorpians feel towards Earth's customs can be found, among other things, in the literature describing other populations' habits at the time of the European exploratory missions in Africa, Asia, and the American continent during the early modern period. Observing that commentators tended to find aberrant every culture that wasn't similar to their own, French philosopher Michel de Montaigne wonderfully described the nature of this phenomenon in an essay about cannibal populations:

> [W]e all call barbarous anything that is contrary to our own habits. Indeed we seem to have no other criterion of truth and reason than the type and kind of opinions and customs current in the land where we live. There we always see the perfect religion, the perfect political system, the perfect and most accomplished way of doing everything. (de Montaigne 1991, p. 109)

This idea openly contradicts Eurocentrism and religious dogmatism and lies at the heart of cultural relativism. Indeed, the core belief of religions such as Christianity, Islam, and Judaism (also called Abrahamic religions) consists in the fact that their version of the truth is the right one and other religions are wrong. Every social and cultural construct based on the acceptance of an unorthodox or heretical dogma is therefore wrong too and cannot be accepted – even though nowadays religious institutions are showing more openness and look for an interfaith dialogue. Cultural relativism is, on the contrary, the idea that there is no better or superior culture and that a person's beliefs and values should be understood in the framework of his or her own culture. In this perspective, it makes no sense to state that Gazorpian matriarchal culture is superior, while Earth male/female relations are aberrant, or vice versa.

It is important to point out, however, that cultural relativism should not be mistaken with cultural moral relativism – the view that, since there is no universal moral standard, even the most harmful crimes in history such as mass exterminations or slavery could be morally justified if the culture they happen in deems them as acceptable. Rick Sanchez does not seem to be that kind of relativist since, for instance, he openly condemns fascism and he would prefer to kill himself rather than live in a world ruled by fascists (like in *Edge of Tomorty: Rick Die Rickpeat* (S4E1)).

Rick, however, is a undoubtedly a cultural relativist; indeed, he is a very special kind of cultural relativist! Even though he doesn't take any culture seriously, he is doing it in a fair way: he makes fun of every cultural and social habit, Earth's included, irrespective of whether they belong to a particular place in space and time. Rick tries to understand different kinds of cultures and adapt to local customs just to make the most fun out of his travel experience; he is rarely interested in a constructive cultural exchange.

Microscopic and Macroscopic Societies

Another important element at the basis of *Rick & Morty*'s nihilism is the rejection of every social value. Indeed, the show argues that all the values society is built on are constructed and are mainly just useful for the good of the rulers. In order to endorse this idea, the show makes a comparison with other non-human societies, in the same way as it did to support cultural relativism. And Rick and Morty don't even have to travel far away in space to encounter non-human civilizations. Sometimes Rick & Morty find entire miniature worlds and societies inside the most unexpected things.

For instance, in the episode *The Ricks Must Be Crazy* (S2E6), Rick's car motor does not start and Rick takes Morty with him inside the car battery to repair it. Turns out, Rick's car battery is powered by a community of microscopic living beings who produce energy for him – a "microverse battery." That's right, to power his car, Rick created a whole microscopic universe where intelligent life could evolve. Once this intelligent life reached an adequate level of civilization, Rick manifested himself to the microscopic inhabitants of the battery in the form of an alien god and gave them gooble boxes: devices that produce electric energy but (unbeknownst to them) send most of it to fuel the battery. Morty feels uncomfortable with the way the car battery works and raises an important ethical objection:

Morty   You have a whole planet sitting around making your power for you? That's slavery!

Rick   It's society! They work for each other, Morty. They pay each other, they buy houses, they get married and they make children who replace them when they are too old to make power.

Morty   That just sounds like slavery with extra steps.

Electricity is not the only thing Rick introduced to the microverse inhabitants. Once landed, they greet Rick and Morty by flipping them off since Rick taught them that this gesture means "peace among worlds." When asked about the slump in their electricity production, the microverse president promptly explains that their scientist Zeep Xanflorp – a kind of microverse counterpart of Rick – just invented an alternative energy source: the miniverse battery. While Zeep shows it to them, Rick tries to persuade him to abandon this idea by recycling Morty's objection and arguing that this is an unethical way of creating energy because it is akin to slavery. When Zeep replies, like Rick before him, that he did not create slaves but a normal society, Rick articulates an intuition that turns out to be valid: there should be another mad scientist in the miniverse working on a nanoscale universe to get free energy. Kyle, a scientist living in the miniverse, is indeed developing a "teenyverse" and, unaware of who they really are, brings Rick, Morty and Zeep on a tour inside of it. Zeep is very upset because the teenyverse would make his energy-stealing device obsolete and tries to discourage him in further developing the project with Morty's and Rick's slavery argument. He does not finish his speech, however, since he suddenly realizes that his universe was created by Rick who is stealing their energy too. He gets very angry and starts a fistfight with Rick. Kyle is not as cynical as Rick and Zeep and when he understands what is going on, his reaction is rather desperate:

Kyle   Are they not really aliens?

Morty   No, they are just a couple of crazy wacky scientists, you know?

Kyle   So he made a universe, and that guy is from that universe, and that guy made a universe, and that's the universe where I was born? Where my father died, and where I couldn't make time for his funeral because I was working... on my universe.

Morty   Ahahah yeah. Science, right? Ain't it a thing! [...] Old lady science, you know? You gotta hang on tight, you know, because she... she... she bucks pretty hard.

After this conversation, Kyle kills himself by crashing his spaceship into a mountain. It was too much for him to process. His whole society was the creation of some mad scientists, he was practically a slave, and all the values in which he believed were artificially constructed in order to keep everybody quiet and let them produce energy. The same also applies to the teenyverse and the microverse society, as Rick suggests in a later attempt to prevent Morty to go alone in the woods and make Zeep angry at the same time:

Morty	All right, that's it, I'm out! I'm gonna go to the wilderness and I'm gonna make a new life for myself among the tree people! It can't be worse than this!
Rick	Sure, OK, Morty. Just be back before the sundown or the tree people will eat you.
Morty	That's a myth! Why are you trying to start a myth?
Rick	It's a prehistoric planet, Morty, someone has to bring a little culture. And it certainly can't be someone whose entire culture powers my brake lights!

How can we know that our culture is authentic and is not powering anybody else's brake lights? Does such a distinction make sense at all? And how can we distinguish a fair social contract from slavery? Concerning the first two questions, Rick seems well aware of the fact that culture does not come from nowhere, nor is it the result of some kind of romantic inspiration. Culture is to be understood within the framework of its creation and spreading, which is often related to social mechanisms and economic production processes.

This thinking is expressed in a clearer and more drastic way by Karl Marx' base and superstructure theory. According to Marx, the "mode of production" of material life (that is, the base) conditions the general process of social, political, and intellectual life (the superstructure) (Marx 1979). Things like cultural habits, good manners, rituals, and beliefs are practices that arise from the material need of a particular society to produce and exchange goods, such as establishing specifical social relationships between workers and those who manage the mode of production and grounding specific social institutions. This view is also called historical materialism. Following this perspective, the culture of the United States of America, where Rick comes from, is metaphorically powering someone else's car battery. Rick would never deny it and this is why he rather prefers to not identify himself with any culture: every cultural identity might be just a way to put workers at ease and give them an ideal on the basis of which they want to continue producing – say, redemption and eternal salvation, honor and social credit, family and future offspring, freedom, etc.

Concerning the other question about the distinction between society and slavery, that depends on how metaphorically we are talking about slavery. If one understands slavery as the act of being literally put in chains and coerced to work, then obviously what Rick did doesn't count. However, if every kind of coercive force that causes individuals to act in a particular way is seen as an enslaving one, then it is possible to make that connection. The idea that the metaphor of a carceral system might be used to describe several institutions of modern society can be found for instance in the work of Michel Foucault. In his book *Discipline and Punish,* Foucault argues that in order to create "docile bodies" that keep the new economics of the industrial age working, the modern state needs to establish disciplinary institutions that ensure the internalization of discipline within the bodies they control. Such institutions are, among others, schools, armies, hospitals, and factories, and their controlling function is ensured by "normality judges" such as teachers, doctors, and leaders (Foucault 1977).

In this way, discipline is not imposed by force; rather the vast majority of society agrees to confirm in exchange for the pleasure of normality. Rick is well aware of this and that is why he keeps saying that school is not a place for smart people.

At the same time, however, when it's convenient or necessary, Rick also enjoys the old school discipline enforced by threat. At the end of the car battery episode, Zeep is well aware of being imprisoned in some kind of carceral system that was made for the purpose of fueling Rick's battery and he cannot be a docile body anymore. Therefore, Rick threatens the existence of his very universe in the event of a new interruption of the energy supply: he will scrap the old battery and replace it with a new one. This is the reason why Zeep will abandon his miniverse project, keep telling the people that Rick is an alien God, and that the only way to produce energy are the Gooble Boxes he donated to them.

Infinite Possible Realities

As mentioned in the introduction, the characterizing feature of *Rick & Morty*'s nihilism is the fact that this view is based, among other things, on the metaphysical assumption of a multiverse. The idea that the world we live in is just one out of infinite other possible realities caressed the mind of many thinkers in the last centuries. One of the most well-known proponents of this view is the philosopher and mathematician Gottfried Wilhelm von Leibniz who, in his *Essays of Theodicy*, argued that the actual world is the best of all possible worlds – an argument aimed at justifying the existence of evil despite the goodness of God. According to him, God has the idea of infinitely many possible universes and has chosen the best one to be the actual one. Even though many terrible things happen in our world, in the other possible realities – whose existence only remains virtual in God's mind – things are even worse. The best possible world has the most good and the least evil. In Leibniz' view, no possible world in which the human species exists can be free of evil because human free will necessarily implies that bad choices will be made and harm produced (Leibniz 1985). Indeed, only a perfect Being never makes bad choices and only God – who rightly decided to create the best of all possible worlds – is perfect.

In contemporary philosophy, it is possible to find an even more radical account of the multiverse theory – although it is not theologically motivated. This account is called "modal realism" and was developed by the US American philosopher David Lewis in his book *On the Plurality of Worlds*. Lewis argues that ours is not the only real world; indeed, there is an infinite number of other possible worlds, and they are as real as our own. Now, according to Lewis, we wouldn't say that these other worlds are "actual." They are merely "possible" to us. But this is only because a world's "actuality" is a matter of perspective, relative to the world itself. The inhabitants of other possible worlds would (rightly) think that our world is merely possible, and that their world is actual. But all such worlds exist; they are all equally real. "[E]very world is actual at itself, and thereby all worlds are on a par" (Lewis 1986, p. 93). In contrast to Leibniz, Lewis does not affirm any kind of ethical or ontological primacy of our world: we are living neither in the best world, nor in the most real. It's just one out of many.

One interesting implication of modal realism is the counterpart theory. Lewis writes: "Something has for counterparts at a given world those things existing there that resemble it closely enough in important respects of intrinsic quality and extrinsic relations, and that resemble it no less closely than do other things existing there" (Lewis 1973, p. 39). Unlike in *Rick & Morty*, on Lewis' view, counterparts cannot possibly interact with each other since they belong to different spatiotemporal lines and cannot be connected by relations of causal dependence. Whenever two individuals are spatiotemporally related, they are "parts of one single world" (Lewis 1986, p. 70).

Since it is not possible to access God's mind or to travel to other possible words, it is not possible – at least right now – to say whether Leibniz or Lewis was actually right. But philosophers nowadays are still interested in multiverse theory, not because they think it depicts an accurate image of reality (they don't), but because it offers interesting theoretical instruments to investigate concepts like "necessity," "contingency," and "impossibility."

Of course, in the realm of fictionality, nobody needs evidence to embrace a metaphysical view of the world, no matter how eccentric, and there is no doubt that in *Rick & Morty*, the existence of a multiverse is a fact. However, the metaphysical picture the show embraces is not exactly the Leinbizian or the Lewisian one, but rather a similar view that we might call the "parallel universe" view – a view that defines a universe as a four dimensional block and suggests that there is an infinite number of universe blocks all "stacked up" in a five-dimensional "brane." The Rick and the Morty who are protagonists of the series come from a universe, a "dimension," named "C-137." Thanks to his technological gadgets, Rick can access information coming from other possible dimensions, know what is happening there, go there, and enjoy things that in his world are not possible. Indeed, Rick and Morty's favorite gadget is undoubtedly the interdimensional cable: a cable box that gives access to television shows across every dimension. The Smith family is fascinated by this device not only because it shows very exotic and nonsensical realities – like the Hamster in Butt World – but also because it airs programs from different realities where Beth and Jerry are famous, allowing them to see how their life would have been like if they have not had children.

Contrary to Lewis' idea of a multiverse, Rick and Morty are also able to interact with their counterparts and even gather them together in remote areas of the multiverse. For instance, in *Mortynight Run* (S2E2), we discover that a Rick from another dimension has built a daycare for Jerrys on an unregistered cross-temporal asteroid: the Jerryborree. Whenever Jerry is spoiling the fun Rick and Morty are having during their adventures, they can leave him there together with other unwanted Jerrys with whom he can spend time doing entertaining activities tailored for Jerrys, such as playing with a Beth-shaped giant puppet, install TV decoders, or send drawings to each other by email. However, not every Rick cares enough about his Jerry to get it back at the end of the adventure. In the Jerryborree, there is a room full of abandoned Jerrys and even Rick C-137 does not check two times whether he gets the right Jerry back from the daycare, irresponsibly exposing his Jerry to the risk of being stuck forever in the Jerryborree or in another dimension where he does not belong with another Smith family.

The most interesting insight into the interactions among counterparts is doubtless to be found in the Citadel of Ricks. The Citadel is a secret society that millions of Ricks and Mortys have formed by gathering together in a giant space station in order to hide from the Galactic Federation. In this society, the Ricks usually have positions of greater responsibility in reason of their age and IQ, while Mortys form the lower class – even though there are exceptions to the rule. Usually, every Rick is assigned one Morty, and couples get rematched if one of the two dies. As opposed to Rick-137, the other Ricks do not seem to care a lot about their Mortys and they treat them as a kind of accessory. In season one and two, the citadel is ruled by a Council of Ricks. Finding any form of government and social aggregation stupid, Rick C-137 also dislikes the citadel and its rulers. This is why, in season 3, he destroys the citadel by teleporting it inside a Galactic Federation Prison, from whence he needs to escape.

How could Ricks form a secret society if Rick does not even like society? The answer is simple: every Rick has a different character and personality, sometimes more lovely and docile, sometimes more dominant and misanthropic. That goes, of course, also for Mortys. In this way, it is possible to ground a society of Rick and Mortys with different social roles and hierarchies. In the episode *Close Rick-counters of the Rick Kind* (S1E10), Rick is wanted by the council of Ricks for a series of crimes he did not commit. A group of members of the Citadel's militia (who are all Ricks) settle in his house while looking for him and on this occasion Jerry becomes friends with Doofus Rick, a nice and not arrogant counterpart of Rick who does not make fun of him and really likes him. Later on, the evil counterpart of Rick who committed the crimes shows Rick C-137 a spectrum that he created of all the Ricks listing them up from most evil to least evil and points out that he is just one lesser evil Rick away from him in the spectrum. However, Rick C-137 is not really good or evil. He is rather indifferent to good and evil. This is exactly the attitude that makes him unsuitable for the Citadel (which aims at the good for the Ricks' community) but at the same time, at least in his view, "the Rickest Rick there is."

Even if Rick is not really evil, indifference and detachment can be bad too if they cause harm. The moral questionability of Rick emerges in its full brightness in one of the most nihilist and devastating episodes of the series: *Rick Potion #9* (S1E6). In order to make his teenage crush Jessica like him, Morty insistently asks Rick to make a love potion for him. Rick gives him a serum based on the genetic makeup of voles, a monogamous rodent who stays with its mate for life, but forgets to tell him that he shouldn't give it to her if she has the flu. Morty goes to the high school ball and doses Jessica with the serum – but, of course, she has the flu. She suddenly feels strongly attracted to him but the serum piggybacks onto the flu virus and spreads everywhere in the air. In a matter of minutes, everybody at the party feels a burning desire to mate with Morty. While more and more people in town get infected, we discover that Rick is immune because the serum does not work on anybody related to Morty genetically. Rick arrives at the party in time to save Morty and tries to reverse the mistake he made; flying with his space ship over the crowd, he releases an antidote he made using praying mantis DNA and a powerful airborne virus as a base. Unfortunately, the antidote does not work and, instead, makes everything even worse. Everybody starts growing mantis-like appendages, and their desire to copulate with Morty is coupled with the desire to eat him afterward. As the virus spreads around the world, Rick tries another time and makes a new serum randomly mixing a number of different animal genomes. The result is a catastrophe. Everybody in the world except the Smith family turns into disfigured humanoid blobs that Rick calls "Cronenbergs." The disaster is irreversible and the only thing left to do is to leave the planet. But where to go? Using another interdimensional gadget, Rick finds a dimension where their counterparts manage to bring everything back to normal but afterward die in an explosion in the garage. Rick teleports himself and Morty to this other dimension. Morty panics at the sight of the corpses and the bloody garage, but Rick encourages him to calm down: all they have to do is to bury the bodies and take the place of their counterparts in this new universe. Morty is horrified. This goes way beyond his understanding and he cannot imagine just moving to another reality after having destroyed his own world. But Rick needs him to move on:

Morty   Rick! What about the reality we left behind?
Rick   What about the reality where Hitler cured cancer, Morty? The answer is "Don't think about it"! It's not like we can do this every week anyway. We get three or four more of these, tops. Now pick up your dead self and come on. Haste makes waste.

After they bury their counterparts' bodies in the garden, they enter their new home and everything looks normal: Jerry and Beth are fighting, Summer is texting, and Rick grabs a beer in the fridge. But this is too eerie for Morty, who feels in a very uncanny way that he does not belong there – and maybe nowhere else.

Nihilism in the Multiverse

Existential Nihilism is the belief that life is meaningless and does not have a purpose. According to this view, all our actions and feelings are senseless and do not gain any greater importance after the moment they come to an end. There are many ways of defending this position. Albert Camus does so from an atheistic perspective and argues that the lack of an intelligent God, of an afterlife, and of a divine or superhuman order in the universe undercuts the possibility of meaning. According to him, every purpose of human actions, every hope for tomorrow, will disappear after death. For this reason, life is absurd and should be lived passionately without looking for an ultimate sense of human existence (Camus 1955). Likewise, but without recurring atheistic arguments, Arthur Schopenhauer argues that human life lacks meaning because it is impossible to be happy or satisfied. According to Schopenhauer, all human efforts (including our striving for a greater meaning of life) end up in dissatisfaction. This happens for two main reasons: either we have yet to obtain what we seek and therefore we feel unhappy, or we obtained it and, not having a purpose anymore, we feel bored (Schopenhauer 2004). From this perspective, it is senseless to strive for new achievements, since everything will lead to dissatisfaction, boredom, and the desperate need to find new futile and unfulfilling goals. And then, of course, we will die.

The moral of many TV shows depicting a nihilistic worldview such as *Seinfeld* or *Bo Jack Horseman* can be easily brought back to one of these nihilistic arguments – or, at least something similar. And Rick Sanchez would surely embrace these ideas too. However, the theoretical ground of his nihilism goes much further since it is reinforced through cultural relativism and supported by evidence of the existence of a multiverse. Not only are Western beliefs hogwash because they do not make sense on other planets in the universe or even in other places on Earth, but they are only relative to a particular society and a limited perspective. Indeed, the very meaning of the consequences of human actions and decisions are meaningless since there are other universes in which alternative actions and decisions are taken and to where it is always possible to flee. Even if we decide to do some good, we know that in some alternative reality our counterpart is making the bad decision and causing harm instead. There is no way of avoiding the emergence of suffering and injustice in the multiverse.

Rick seems to have fun playing with his ability to create multiverse-switch instruments. In *The Vat of Acid Episode* (S4E8), Morty asks Rick to develop a device that would allow him to "save" a point in time like in a video game, go back to that moment, and "restore" his life by simply pushing a button. To teach a lesson to Morty, Rick gives him a device that just fakes time traveling and instead teleports him to a very similar dimension where the Morty counterpart gets incinerated by Morty pushing the "restore" button. Unaware of that, Morty has a lot of fun with his new time-saving device doing all the things he didn't have the courage to do before; he even finds a girlfriend he falls in love with. When his love romance gets interrupted by Jerry, who mistakes the time-saving device for the TV remote, Morty realizes that it is time to end the game and go back dealing with the consequences of his actions. However, he discovers that he has to deal with way more consequences than he expected:

Rick   How is it going?

Morty   You know, it was fun Rick... real fun, you know... I definitely saw those odds. But I think you invented a little lessen for me along the way. Living without consequences is great, but then I started wondering... what am I living for? What am I building? If I am always looking back, I am never looking ahead... and then it hit me: we are what we are because of consequences. You can't live without consequences. You know? You feel me?

Rick   Wow, that's a beautiful thought, Morty. But no, there were definitely consequences. [...] I mean, you did everything you did. Everything happened.

Morty	What's about the restore button? The do-over?
Rick	That's not a do-over. You just did it... over and over.

In order to atone for his actions, Morty agrees to merge his timeline with the ones of all possible Mortys he incinerated, feeling their pain during the procedure. Morty clearly does not share his grandfather's perspective and does have respect for his counterparts' pain in other possible worlds. Rick's philosophy is instead quite straight forward: nothing we do matters, we shouldn't worry about the consequences, and doing it because of a greater purpose would be even sillier since in the whole multiverse there is not a single ideal worth being pursued.

On top of that, Rick seems to embrace a kind of defeatism regarding Morty's attempts to do good. No matter what Morty does, he will mess things up even more than Rick and cause more harm. This pessimistic fatalism is usually confirmed by the consequences of Morty's actions. In the episode *Mortynight Run* (S2E2), Rick sells an anti-matter weapon to a killer in exchange for a galactic currency so he can afford an afternoon at the space video arcade "Blitz and Chitz." Morty regards selling a gun to an assassin to be "the same as pulling the trigger," but Rick rejects any moral accountability for this action and argues that the killer would have found other ways to accomplish his goal. Morty is disgusted by his grandfather's lack of ethics, and while Rick plays a virtual reality video game, he gets away with his spaceship to stop the killer. Morty succeeds in his plan by accidentally killing the assassin and gets acquainted with the target: a gaseous telepathic cloud who was kept prisoner in a Galactic Federation outpost. Rick arrives on time with his portal gun to save Morty from the guards (killing them too) and they flee to Gear World with their new acquaintance, who is renamed "Fart." On Gear World, they discover why the Fart is wanted by the Galactic Federation: it can alter the composition of atoms; for example, it can transform oxygen into gold. While Rick wants to kill Fart since it is too dangerous to travel with, Morty insists on bringing it back to the wormhole in the Prometheus Nebula where it came from. While they are discussing, the Gear People police come after them and they have to escape again. This time the forces deployed by law enforcement are too big even for Rick. After a shooting that causes a lot of civilian casualties, Fart has to intervene. It incepts suicidal thoughts into the mind of a police officer and leads him to crash his spaceship into another one, setting off a chain reaction that will lead to even more deaths and destruction. When they are finished, Rick sarcastically comments: "Let's go to the Prometheus nebula, so my grandson can save a life." However, once they have arrived at the wormhole, Fart reveals to Morty that it will be back with its kind in order to exterminate all the carbon-based lifeforms because they see them as a disease. Morty is now obliged to shoot Fart with the anti-matter gun. All his struggle to save it were in vain and on the way back Rick cannot resist rubbing salt in the wound:

> Morty, I know I picked on your core beliefs and decision making a lot today, but I am glad that you insisted on getting that fart home. You know, at least all the death and the destruction wasn't for nothing, you know?

Due to his nihilist and defeatist beliefs, Rick does not attempt in any way to make the world a better place. He just looks for fun. This is a hedonistic attitude. Hedonism is a school of thought arguing that the key components of happiness are the attainment of one's own well-being and the avoidance of one's own suffering. There are many hedonistic schools of thought focusing on different ways in which is it possible to achieve well-being. Some suggest a more spiritual journey, looking for inner balance and wisdom as the solutions for being carefree, like Epicurus did. Some other schools focus on physical pleasure instead. In Classical Greek philosophy, the latter view was supported by the Cyrenaic school. According to them, one should seek to maximize the pleasure he or she can get and minimize the unpleasant moments. A wise person is someone who can control pleasure without being enslaved by it and who can, in order to do that, dominate his or her feelings (Lampe 2017). Although a Hedonist would not recommend falling into vice and addiction, which are considered bad because they lead to suffering, this view is often seen as related to a nihilist or decadent worldview since it does not encourage people to look for superior moral values and just focuses on reiterating the ephemeral feeling of pleasure.

Apart from any moral judgment, it is not easy to be the kind of hedonist Rick is – that is, a more Cyrenaic one. One must be cynical enough to not feel empathy for other people's suffering, even (and especially) if this suffering is caused by one's own egoistic choices. Indeed, other people's feelings should be seen as merely instrumental in getting more pleasure and one should avoid being let down in any way by other people. Rick seems to master this art pretty well, but he nevertheless looks depressed way too often. Maybe there is something that prevents him from achieving perfect hedonist happiness.

Conclusion: Does Rick Really Not Care?

Even though Rick manages to remain indifferent to planetary devastation and mass murder, his emotional setting changes when it comes to his daughter and grandchildren. Of course, he would never recognize that. In the episode *Pickle Rick* (S3E3) he transforms himself into a pickle in order to skip family therapy. During the episode Pickle Rick gets seriously injured by animals, people, and natural agents. At the end of the episode, he has to join the rest of the family at the therapy session because he is almost out of pickle juice and Beth took with her his serum to turn him back into a human. After that, he expresses his low esteem for therapy, he ignores the grandchildren saying that they actually enjoyed it, and he convinces Beth to go drinking. Nevertheless, Rick also has his ways to be nice to his family. For what it is worth, he always risks his life to rescue Morty whenever he is in danger and, contrary to all the other Ricks, he would never exchange his Morty for another one.

Even more astonishing is his weird attachment to Beth. In the last episode of the fourth season, an intergalactic adventurer version of Beth comes back to Earth revealing Beth's worst suspicion about Rick to be true: he cloned her and she might even be the clone. However, since Morty, Summer, and Jerry get along very well with both Beths, nobody is interested in discovering who is the clone. At the end of the episode, Rick watches alone, on a projector, the memory of Beth's cloning, which he erased from his memory. It turns out that, after giving Beth the choice between going into space or staying at home with him, she asked him to choose for her, based on what he really wanted. Instead of doing that, he created a perfect clone of her with the same memories and let a machine shuffle the containers in which he put the two Beths, so that he could not discern who was whom. Did he do that for love, so that Beth could live both lives? Or did he just mess everything up because he could not decide? This is not revealed, but he does realize that he has been a terrible father to Beth and feels truly, deeply sad.

Even though he presents himself as a kind of *Übermensch* who is comfortable in a nihilist world, when faced with the senselessness of existence and the consequences of his bad choices on his loved ones, Rick feels very depressed. That happens because even if our values and emotions are relative, that does not mean that, at least for the person feeling them, they do not matter. That something matters from a subjective perspective is important irrespective of whether there are no absolute values and there is no afterlife. Here the paradox at the base of Ricks' chaotic behavior looms: Rick rationally embraces the moral void he recognizes in the multiverse, but emotionally he is all too human to put apart his little passions and affections. This is why he hides behind drug addiction and a flamboyant thug lifestyle. Explaining to Morty the meaning of one of Rick's nonsense slogans, his friend Birdperson reveals to Morty a hard truth at the end of season one:

Birdperson	Morty, do you know what "Wubba lubba dub dub" means?
Morty	Oh, that just Rick's stupid nonsense catchphrase.
Birdperson	It's not nonsense at all. In my people's tongue it means: "I am in great pain, please help me".
Morty	Well, I've got news for you, he is saying it ironically.
Birdperson	No, Morty. Your grandfather is indeed in very deep pain. That's why he must numb himself.

This is not a happy ending. Even if love can give meaning to a singular existence, this does not automatically imply that loving other people is the true higher purpose of life, nor does it provide a sound refutation of nihilism. Indeed, the importance of love should also be contextualized in a sociocultural and biological framework. This, however, does not mean that life is easy for a nihilist. Even though personal beliefs cannot be assumed as universal laws, people do have values and feel emotional attachments. After all, in an infinite multiverse, proclaiming the relativity of all values and the absence of a final purpose seems to be a reasonable thing to do, but consistently applying this to everyday actions may turn out to be a big impasse: why even bother doing something if nothing has a purpose? This is why Rick prefers to drink, have fun, and not think about it. He could not make it just using his cold, calculating reason. The greatest part of his genius lies in his wild and unpredictable instinct that makes him able to keep moving on even when faced with the absurdity of existence and the contradictions of life.

References

Bruno, Giordano. 2014. De l'infinito universo e mondi. In *Opere italiane*, ed. Giovanni Aquilecchia. Torino: UTET.

Camus, Albert. 1955. *The Myth of Sisyphus*. Translated by J. O'Brian. London: H. Hamilton.

de Montaigne, Michel. 1991. On cannibals In *Essays*. Translated by Michael Andrew Screech. London: Penguin.

Foucault, Michel. 1977. *Discipline and punish: The birth of the prison*. Translated by Alan Sheridan. London: Allen Lane, Penguin.

Lampe, Kurt. 2017. *Birth of hedonism – The Cyrenaic philosophers and pleasure as a way of life*. Princeton: Princeton University Press.

Leibniz, Gottfried Wilhelm. 1985. *Theodicy: Essays on the Goodness of God, the Freedom on Man and the Origin of Evil*. Translated by E. M. Huggard. La Salle: Open Court.

Lewis, David. 1973. *Counterfactuals*. Oxford: Blackwell Publishers.

———. 1986. *On the plurality of worlds*. Oxford/Cambridge, MA: Blackwell.

Marx, Karl. 1979. *A contribution to the critique of political economy*. Translated by Maurice Dobb. Princeton: Intl Pub.

Nissenbaum, Stephen. 1996. *The Battle for Christmas*. New York: Alfred A. Knopf.

Schopenhauer, Arthur. 2004. *The wisdom of life*. Translated by T. Bailey Saunders. Mineola: Dover.

The X-Files as Philosophy: Navigating the "Truth Out There"

23

Dean A. Kowalski

Contents

Introduction	520
The X-Files (Incompletely) in Brief	520
Teaser on Nietzsche's Perspectivism	523
It Happened One *X-Files* Night in Klass County	524
Morgan's Cinematic Reflections on Perspectivism	526
Morgan's Mulder and Anti-Socratic Sentiments	530
Reexamining Morgan's Arguments	534
Conclusion: *The X-Files* as Philosophical *and* Philosophy	539
References	539

Abstract

A careful examination of Darin Morgan's *The X-Files* episodes shows that they engage the philosophical process regarding the nature and existence of objective truth, whether it can be known, and if it does exist, whether it's worthwhile to relentlessly pursue it. Morgan's arguments have connections to some of Nietzsche's views, but their significance is grounded in their cinematic expression, including how they utilize the Fox Morgan and Dana Scully characters to critique *The X-Files* mantra "the truth is out there" and the corresponding imperative to seek those truths. In this way, and reminiscent of Socrates, Morgan works within a framework only to critique it; even if Morgan's arguments fail to convince, they remain significant due to their cinematic nature and the philosophical discussion they engender.

D. A. Kowalski (✉)
Arts and Humanities Department, University of Wisconsin-Milwaukee, College of General Studies, Waukesha, WI, USA
e-mail: kowalskd@uwm.edu

© Springer Nature Switzerland AG 2024
D. K. Johnson et al. (eds.), *The Palgrave Handbook of Popular Culture as Philosophy*,
https://doi.org/10.1007/978-3-031-24685-2_76

519

Keywords

The X-Files · Fox Mulder · Dana Scully · David Duchovny · Gillian Anderson · Darin Morgan · "Jose Chung's From Outer Space" · "Clyde Bruckman's Final Repose" · Friedrich Nietzsche · Epistemology · Perspectivism · Objective truth · Subjectivism (about truth) · Socrates · Good life · Film as Philosophy · René Descartes · Cogito · Theodore Schick · Lewis Vaughn

Introduction

The X-Files was a wildly popular and critically acclaimed science fiction television series airing on FOX from 1993–2002. Among its many awards are 16 Emmys, including Darin Morgan's 1996 win for outstanding writing for a drama series, and (for her portrayal of Dana Scully) Gillian Anderson's 1997 win for best actress in a drama series. She also received two Screen Actor Guild awards (in 1996 and 1997), and the show won 5 Golden Globes: David Duchovny for best actor (portraying Fox Molder) in 1996, Gillian Anderson for best actress in 1996, and best drama series from 1994–1997. Furthermore, in 1996, the show won the coveted Peabody award for conveying ideas that are entertaining and thought-provoking.

The X-Files enjoyed two major motion picture releases, *Fight the Future* (1998) and *I Want to Believe* (2008), and saw two revival seasons: season 10 in 2016 (6 episodes) and season 11 in 2018 (10 episodes). It also spawned many graphic novels and book-length novels, as well as three television series spin-offs: *Millennium* (1996–1999), *The Lone Gunmen* (2001), and the animated *The X-Files: Albuquerque* (currently in development). While *The X-Files's* high production value, clever writing, and stellar cast are obvious causal factors responsible for the show's acclaim, its popularity is also attributed to its cultish following. The more ardent fans became known as X-Philes; the series – in ways like none before it – benefited tremendously by their strong online presence.

As we'll see, the show's Peabody award was well-deserved. Indeed, shining a careful light on episodes written or directed by Darin Morgan in particular, and examining various connections with Nietzsche's ideas about epistemology, will establish that *The X-Files* successfully philosophizes. It will be further argued that Morgan offers a distinctively subversive interpretation of the Fox Mulder character. Morgan's Mulder, in turn, plays an important role in an implicit, philosophically significant argument that Morgan poses regarding the good life. In fact, Morgan's implicit argument harkens back to Nietzsche's ardent critique of Socrates. While Morgan's arguments are controversial and open to some powerful objections, his impressive cinematic achievements remain significant.

The X-Files (Incompletely) in Brief

Special Agent Fox Mulder is an Oxford educated FBI agent, specializing in the psychological profiling of violent criminals. However, haunted by the decades-old memory of his young sister being abducted by extraterrestrials, he convinces his superiors to transfer him to the X-Files unit. The X-Files contains unsolved cases descriptive of unusual and often paranormal phenomena that resist conventional explanations. Fueled by his passion for discovering what happened to his sister, who remains missing and is an X-File unto itself, solving X-Files cases becomes Mulder's obsession. His unrelenting pursuit of the truth – wherever it leads – spurs his conviction that extraterrestrials visit Earth regularly, and he comes to suspect that such visits are aided and covered up by secret factions within the government, including the FBI itself. A once promising career becomes mired in derision, and he quickly gains the nickname "Spooky" among his peers.

Special Agent Dana Scully, fresh out of medical school, and despite her father's objections, has spent the last two years teaching forensic medicine and pathology at the FBI Quantico Academy. Her unflinching rationalism and dedication to scientific and Bureau procedure are in stark contrast to "Spooky" Mulder. In 1993, and despite Mulder's objections, they become partners. FBI supervisors believe that Mulder's obsession with his work is causing problems they would rather avoid. They task Scully to make regular field reports of X-Files cases, thereby bringing Mulder back into the FBI mainstream.

Their first meeting was less than amiable. When Scully knocks on his basement office door, Mulder snarkily announces, "Sorry, nobody down here but the FBI's most unwanted." Nevertheless, Scully, noticing Mulder's (soon to be iconic) "I Want to Believe" poster hanging on the wall, enters the room and assures him, "I'm looking forward to working with you. I've heard a lot about you." Mulder remains suspicious (of course) and a bit salty: "Oh, really? I was under the impression. . . that you were sent to spy on me." But Mulder has done his homework. Noting Scully's extensive scientific background – she also has an undergraduate physics degree – Mulder smugly quips that in his line of work, the laws of physics rarely apply. As if testing her, and citing the unexplained phenomena the X-Files explores, he further chides "When convention and science offer us no answers, might we not finally turn to the fantastic as a plausibility?" Scully, the scientist, remains steadfast; without hesitation, she retorts: "What I find fantastic is any notion that there are answers beyond the realm of science. The answers are there. You just have to know where to look."

Through Mulder and Scully's joint pursuit of "the truth out there" we are exposed to various unexplained phenomena that Scully has difficulty reporting on to her superiors. (These are the "Monster of the Week" episodes, portraying encounters with mutants, werewolves, and psychics, among many others.) We soon learn that many of Mulder's suspicions (e.g., about a governmental agency conspiracy to keep the existence of extraterrestrials hidden) are indeed true. Mulder and Scully begin uncovering truths about the conspirators and their plans for humanity, who are collectively known as the Syndicate. (Episodes portraying this storyline are the "Mythology" episodes.)

The Syndicate's earliest members learned (as a result of the Roswell crash) of extraterrestrial beings with intentions to colonize Earth; indeed, these aliens were Earth's original sentient inhabitants. The Syndicate agreed to collaborate with the aliens in exchange for safe haven during colonization. The Syndicate's members serve as their operatives on Earth, including covertly facilitating a population of alien-human hybrids as a new race of slaves to serve the colonists upon their arrival. Most humans will serve as hosts for the "black oil" virus, reducing them to vessels for the gestating alien life form inside.

As this ominous mythology storyline unfolds, the audience learns Mulder's father was associated with the Syndicate and this association is linked to his sister's mysterious disappearance. We also learn Mulder and Scully can trust very few people; indeed, "trust no one" becomes a primary mantra of the show, second only to "the truth is out there." They can trust each other (obviously), and the Lone Gunmen would never betray them; their supervisor, Assistant Director Walter Skinner, becomes a staunch ally. However, the Syndicate, especially its long-time member known as the Cigarette Smoking Man, will go to great lengths to deceive Mulder and Scully, obfuscate the truth, and frustrate their search for it. (This provides merely a snapshot of *The X-Files* mythology, which becomes incredibly complex – and arguably convoluted – over nine seasons of its original run, culminating in governmental super-soldiers possessing alien DNA.)

For more than eight years Mulder and Scully chased monsters, together peering into the dark with flashlight in hand. Their partnership blossoms into valued companionship – platonic at first and, later, something more. But pursuing the truth out there involves great cost. The Syndicate assassinates Mulder's father and kills Scully's sister in a botched attempt to silence Scully. Mulder and Scully survive Scully's abduction (partly orchestrated by the Syndicate), which later leads to her contracting cancer. They survive Mulder's being abducted by extraterrestrials (perhaps facilitated by the Syndicate). They lose their son – a child that was supposed to be medically impossible as a result of Scully's cancer – when Scully decides to put him up for adoption to keep him safe from those (including the Syndicate) who would do him harm. All this they did in their joint pursuit of the truth "out there." And pursuing the truth together importantly changes them; they grow together and become more complete individuals. Scully becomes open to extreme possibilities and Mulder learns temperance and discipline. Nevertheless, for their efforts, they – but particularly Mulder – are vilified by the FBI. In the season 9 finale, Mulder is found guilty at a military-style tribunal. (Fortunately, Mulder and Scully escape from the facility, together.)

Six years later (in 2008's *I Want to Believe*), they are no longer on the lam. They live together in a modest home outside of Richmond, Virginia. Scully practices pediatric medicine at Our Lady of Sorrows hospital in urban Richmond. Mulder remains interested in the paranormal, albeit exclusively from his makeshift home office. Rather than gallivanting across the continental United States chasing leads about unexplained phenomena, he has become a recluse, incessantly combing through newspapers and magazines for glimpses of his former life's work.

One day, FBI agents visit Scully at the hospital. Desperate, they seek Mulder's expertise on an unusual case involving a defrocked Catholic priest who cries tears of blood and has psychic visions of homicides; the FBI is willing to offer Mulder a reprieve for his services. Scully acknowledges that Mulder's involvement might reinvigorate him, but it might also reignite his obsessive tendencies. Scully returns to their home to relay the message, but Mulder is skeptical; it smells like a trap.

23 *The X-Files* as Philosophy: Navigating the "Truth Out There"

However, he agrees to pursue the opportunity – but only if Scully joins him. This brings them back to the Bureau.

Eight years after that, *The X-Files* is revived on FOX in 2016. Mulder still lives in the modest rural Virginia home, but no longer with Scully. Skinner contacts Mulder and Scully and reinstates them fully. They begin investigating a strange case of mass illness gripping the American East Coast. It is highly contagious and spreads quickly. While Scully works with medical officials, Mulder, beginning to suffer the effects of the contagion, goes rogue in a desperate attempt to confront the man he believes is responsible: the Cigarette Smoking Man. The Cigarette Smoking Man, who somehow survived a missile attack near the end of season 9, has engineered a virus with extraterrestrial DNA. His nefarious goal is to strip human beings of their natural immunity and bring about a new world order. Scully remains immune to the virus, another aftereffect of her abduction. At the end of the season finale, what appears to be an alien spacecraft inexplicably appears and sheds a light on Scully.

Two years later in 2018, and apropos of *The X-Files*, we learn that the (myth-arc) events of season 10 were more fiction than fact; they seemed to be Scully's visions of a possible future. Scully comes to believe that her visions are somehow tied to her son William. William becomes the focus of the season 11 plot.

William's adopted name is Jackson Van De Camp. He can make people see what isn't there, thereby bending their perception of reality (as he apparently did with Scully), and possesses fantastic (Wolverine-like) healing abilities. The audience is shocked to learn that William/Jackson is not the miraculous result of Scully and Mulder's season 7 (unexpected) tryst, but the devious product of the Cigarette Smoking Man's extraterrestrial-infused science. (This twist understandably angered many X-Philes.) As Mulder and Scully search for the young man they believe to be their biological son, they reconnect. The Cigarette Smoking Man is also searching for William/Jackson. He may not be a miracle child born of love, but he holds the key to all the Cigarette Smoking Man's nefarious plans for humanity. During the season 11 finale, and William/Jackson still out of reach, the audience learns that Scully (at 54 years young) is again pregnant – with Mulder's child. Fade to black. Cue the spooky (and iconic) *X-Files* theme.

Teaser on Nietzsche's Perspectivism

Friedrich Nietzsche is something of an X-File himself. Although he published on a variety of topics, he also suffered from constant ill-health and eventually came under the care of his sister, Elizabeth. Elizabeth took charge of his unpublished works, including his personal notebooks, and published *The Will to Power* under his name. However, Elizabeth harbored anti-Semitic beliefs and tendencies, which marred Nietzsche's literary legacy. Commentators have aspired to discern Nietzsche's ideas, thereby distancing them from his sister's overbearing editorial hand.

Not surprisingly, then, interpretations of Nietzsche are somewhat varied, but one of his more controversial views is his seeming rejection of classic epistemology. Nietzsche believes we lack knowledge (as traditionally conceived), because there are no independently existing facts or truths for us to discern or discover. He writes, "Facts is precisely what there is not, only interpretations. We cannot establish any fact 'in itself': perhaps it is folly to want to do such a thing" (Nietzsche 1968; Sect. 481). Consequently, our so-called knowledge merely consists of various perspectives, driven by one's personal impulses and instincts, leading Nietzsche to claim knowledge is "actually nothing but a certain behavior of the instincts toward one another" (Nietzsche 1974; Sect. 335).

Nietzsche goes on to provide nonstandard accounts of truth and falsehood. About the former, he asserts, "'Truth' is not something there that might be found or discovered—but something that must be created and that gives name to a process, or rather to a will to overcome that has in itself no end.... [It is] an active determining—not a becoming-conscious of something that is in itself firm and determined. It is a word for the 'will to power'" (Nietzsche 1968; Sect. 552). For Nietzsche, what is true depends on the positive or beneficial effects on one's life. Consequently, Nietzsche's definition of truth is not in line with the correspondence theory of truth – which suggests that propositions are true if they correspond with the way the world is – but is instead pragmatic. Consider: "Truth is the kind of error without which a certain species of life could not live. The value of life is ultimately decisive" (Nietzsche 1968; Sect. 493). Turning to falsity, Nietzsche claims, "The falseness of a judgment is for us not necessarily an objection to a judgment.... .The question is to what extent it is life-promoting, life-preserving...perhaps even species-preserving" (Nietzsche 1966; Sect. 4).

It Happened One *X-Files* Night in Klass County...

Darin Morgan's *X-Files* episodes are fan favorites and each is wickedly clever; indeed, they have a cultish following. He is credited as the screenwriter for four original-run episodes: "Humbug" (season 2, episode 20, or "2X20" as X-Philes put it), "Clyde Bruckman's Final Repose" (3X04), "War of the Coprophages" (3X12), and "Jose Chung's From Outer Space" (3X20); however, most commentators contend that "Quagmire" (3X22) is also canon due to his extensive but uncredited involvement with the script. And he is credited as the writer and director of two revival episodes: "Mulder and Scully Meet the Were-Monster" (10X03) and "The Lost Art of Forehead Sweat" (11X04).

The X-Files creator Chris Carter, and most of his cocreators, portrays Special Agents Dana Scully and Fox Mulder as Socratic paragons for pursuing the truth at almost any personal cost. Mulder's season one declaration in "The Erlenmeyer Flask" (1x23) sounds the clarion call for Mulder and his mission: "I'm...not going to give up. I can't give up. Not as long as the truth is out there." However, Morgan's episodes are often critical of *The X-Files's* unrelenting imperative associated with its "the truth is out There" mantra, with "Jose Chung's From Outer Space" serving as a prime example.

The teaser for this episode opens with a camera shot that initially appears to be a close-up of a slowly moving *Star Wars* Star Destroyer (including the iconic sound effect). Because extraterrestrials play a prominent role in *The X-Files*, most viewers were not surprised to see a UFO, even if it were borrowed from the Skywalker Ranch. But this is misdirection; Morgan preys on our expectations to lead us astray. As episode director Rob Bowman's camera pans back, the shot actually portrays the bottom of a power company utility bucket, lifted a mere 20 ft off the ground. Roky Crickenson, a power company engineer, is checking some power lines. This opening sequence foreshadows a dominant theme of the episode: Things may not be as they appear, and personal judgments about the truth are often clouded by expectation.

The episode introduces two Klass County teenagers, Harold Lamb and Chrissy Giorgio. Near the end of their first date, and immediately after Harold professes his love for Chrissy, they are allegedly abducted by aliens. As familiar small gray aliens take the teenagers to their hovering disc-shaped flying saucer, viewers (and the gray aliens) are surprised to see a second and unfamiliar kind of red alien burst onto the scene, bringing the teaser to its end. Enter flamboyant novelist Jose Chung. In the months following the alleged double abduction, he has been interviewing Klass County residents to learn what really happened that night. Because Mulder and Scully (of course) also investigated the Klass County incident, Chung wishes to interview them. Mulder refuses to meet, but Scully agrees – Chung is one of her favorite authors.

This celebrated *X-Files* episode is predominantly composed of flashback sequences, with Scully narrating and Chung occasionally interrupting her with questions and personal commentary. An early exchange is especially pertinent. After Chung admits that his ultimate motivating factor is now financial, Scully chides, "Well, just as long as you're attempting to record the truth." To which Chung quickly retorts, "Oh, God, no. How can I possibly do that? I spent three months in Klass County, and everybody there has a different version of what truly happened. Truth is as subjective as reality." This exchange (linguistically) reinforces the philosophical context of the episode. It leads the viewer to ask: Why can't the truth be recorded? How can reality be subjective? Already, Morgan's attempt to critically examine *The X-Files's* primary philosophical mantra – from within in the show itself – is beginning to take shape.

Morgan's ideas regarding truth, reality, and appearance(s) continue to unfold as Scully shares with Chung her version of the alleged double abduction. Scully tells him about her first meeting with Detective Manners, who is the lead investigator of the case. In a flashback, we see Manners complaining to Mulder and Scully, "You really 'bleeped up' this case." Cutting back to Scully, she quickly admits, "Manners didn't actually say 'bleeped'"; Scully censored what Chung calls "Manner's 'colorful phraseology'." A careful viewer surmises that *all* of Scully's narration about past events is filtered through her experiences, thereby raising the question: Did the Klass County events transpire *exactly* as she describes?

Additional worries about discerning the truth about that night soon emerge. Various eyewitness reports contain discrepancies. Harold's and Chrissy's accounts are far from identical, especially at first, when Harold contends that they were abducted by extraterrestrials, but Chrissy accuses Harold of date rape. Claims about the unfamiliar red alien rely almost exclusively on Roky's uncorroborated testimony, which he provides to Mulder and Scully in screenplay format. Furthermore, the purposelessly jobless, living at home, twenty-something UFO fanatic Blaine Faulkner's recollections include Mulder acting like an "emotionless mandroid" at times and a menacing "man in black" at others; however, these accounts are never substantiated. Faulkner also claims that Scully threatened his life, but Scully emphatically denies it.

Mulder then has a chance meeting with missing Air Force lieutenant Jack Shaefer at a local diner. Schaefer confides to Mulder that the government orchestrates many such apparent "alien abductions" for scientific and psychological research, and that he is one of the government's "UFO" pilots. But the cook at the diner denies that Schaefer was there; rather, he contends that Mulder sat alone at the counter. Which of these reports, if any, is true? What actually happened that night in Klass County? It is no wonder multiple characters throughout the episode utter the same plaintive remark: "How the hell should I know?"

Morgan's Cinematic Reflections on Perspectivism

Morgan also intriguingly conveys his critique of "the truth is out there" slogan cinematically. This is most obvious in scenes or Chapters 4, 5, and 8 per the DVD menu, which depict Chrissy being interviewed and/or hypnotized. This sequence begins in Chapter 4 with Mulder's decision to question Chrissy personally; the interview takes place in a typical police station interrogation room. The camera is positioned directly behind Chrissy, as she sits at a table. Mulder sits on the other side of it, facing Chrissy and the camera. Scully is standing in the far right corner of the shot, leaning against the wall, and with her arms folded across her torso. Chrissy's parents, seated in the far left corner of the shot, look on as Mulder interviews their daughter. After asking Chrissy some rather leading questions about reported abduction experiences, Mulder turns around and explains to the Giorgios that he believes Chrissy is suffering from "post abduction syndrome." Mulder's brief assessment leads him to recommend that Chrissy be hypnotized.

In Chapter 5, an unassuming hypnotherapist in a sweater-vest is brought into the police station interrogation room; he is directly in front of the camera in a close-up shot. Scully and the Giorgios remain in their same respective spots at the far back corners of the shot. Detective Manners, holding a coffee mug, is standing behind the psychologist and facing the camera at mid-shot; we see him over the hypnotherapist's right shoulder. Mulder is also standing in mid-shot and facing the camera; we see him over the hypnotherapist's left shoulder. This is how Chrissy sees the room; the hypnotherapist is directly in front of her, as she reclines in a comfortable chair.

As the hypnotherapist begins the session, Chrissy becomes disorientated. This is conveyed by the filmic images in the shot becoming wavy. As the hypnotherapist attempts to mine Chrissy's memories of that night, we see through Chrissy's eyes. The six familiar characters in the room give way to six, small gray aliens; they are blocked exactly as were the hypnotherapist, Manners, Mulder, Scully, and the Giorgios. Chrissy subsequently begins to recount her alleged experiences aboard the alien spaceship. She asserts that Harold was on an examination table next to her; however, she adds, "But he seems really out of it, like he's not really there" – and says this while looking at the interrogation room coffee and doughnut table. The camera momentarily remains in the interrogation room, as we see the hypnotherapist and the six familiar characters. The hypnotherapist then asks Chrissy to continue recalling past events, and the camera subsequently cuts to her perspective. She alleges that the gray aliens – still blocked exactly as the more familiar human characters in the interrogation room – begin arguing among themselves. We see the alien in the far right corner (Scully's position) walks toward the camera and communicates something to the alien in the front-center of the shot (the hypnotherapist's position).

Mulder decides to have Chrissy re-hypnotized in Chapter 9. This second hypnosis scene again takes place in the police interrogation room, and Morgan blocks it exactly as he did for the first hypnosis session; moreover, the same (familiar) characters are present, and the audience's perspective is again Chrissy's. However, what Chrissy reports during the second hypnosis scene is different. She now contends that she was in an office, not unlike the interrogation room, but surrounded by six unfamiliar men. As the filmic images shift to match Chrissy's description, they in turn become wavy, which signals (again) some disorientation on Chrissy's part. We see a serious and stern man in a suit sitting directly in front of Chrissy; he is center-front of the shot. We see two military officers standing in mid-shot. One is holding a coffee cup, facing the camera; we see him over the seated man's right shoulder. The other is also facing the camera and seen over the seated man's left shoulder. The other three men are in the far back of the shot. Two are seated in the far left of the shot; the third is standing in the far right of the shot, arms crossed, and leaning up against the wall. The seated man is a psychologist; he has hypnotized Chrissy. The interrogation room and office settings begin to merge as Chrissy reports (to the audience via the interrogation room characters) that the unfamiliar men seem to be arguing with one another. The man standing in the far right corner walks to the front of the shot, peers at Chrissy for a moment, and then turns to the psychologist and says, "All right. Rinse her out, and give her the usual abduction rigamarole."

The philosophical significance of the identical blocking throughout the hypnosis chapters operates on (at least) two levels, each of which has epistemic relevance. On the first level, Chrissy's disorientation is transferred to the viewer, leaving us unbalanced and thus unsure of which of her accounts is true. This (cinematically) invites us to be skeptical. Is she having difficulty coping with her choice to have sex with Harold on their first date? Her anxiety, exacerbated by her parents' presence, may have been a factor in her willingness to accept Mulder's extraterrestrial hypothesis, which she filled in with well-accepted background beliefs about abduction stories. This interpretation is supported by the similar blocking of DVD chapters 4 and 5. Alternatively, recall the teaser conveyed that she was party to a strange (even for *The X-Files*) double abduction. Maybe this happened after all? Or, were Chrissy and Harold abducted by military men posing as gray aliens, who, in turn, were abducted by an unfamiliar red alien?

Although the audience never actually witnesses the red alien – whom Roky calls "Lord Kinbote" – take either the teenagers or the gray aliens aboard its ship, this alternative satisfyingly integrates Lt. Jack Shaefer's role in the episode. If we are to believe Shaefer, Chrissy's initial interrogation room hypnosis session testimony is a confabulation, affected by her having been previously hypnotized by the Army psychologist. This interpretation is supported by the similar blocking of chapters 5 and 9; however, the viewer is not privy to the alleged activities of the red alien. (Interestingly, scientific studies indeed show that hypnosis tends to create false memories, not retrieve repressed ones; see Ohio State University 2001.)

If one is already suspicious of the epistemic reliability of hypnosis, what Chrissy reports during the second interrogation room session isn't any more trustworthy than the first. At this point, the careful viewer asks a new question: How can we ever know the events of that night if the same alleged eyewitness offers conflicting accounts of what happened? After all, it seems that the viewer has no way of knowing which set of Chrissy's memories is veridical, and we are left with skepticism. Thus, Morgan (with Bowman's help) cinematically portrays a philosophically significant thesis, and in this way engages the philosophical process.

Yet Morgan's philosophical efforts achieve a second level. It is initially tempting to assert that *something* like what Chrissy reports actually happened, at least given the overlapping similarities among her accounts, and as represented in the similar blocking of the DVD chapters in which they appear. The difficulty lies in attempting to determine which account is closest to the truth. Furthermore, such attempts are hampered by the realization that her testimony is impacted by her personal psychology, including memory confabulation occasioned by hypnosis. As Scully reminds us (and, again, real-word research supports), hypnosis is not a reliable guide to the truth. But it doesn't take a great deal of thought to realize that our personal psychological perspective is always at work when we recount our experiences, and, indeed, during the experiences themselves as each of us lives them. (For more on the interplay between memory and personal psychological perspectives, see pages 120–126 in Schick and Vaughn 2020.)

Indeed, and to Morgan's credit, "Jose Chung's From Outer Space" features several characters whose personal psychological propensities cloud what they experience and subsequently remember. Recall Scully's censoring Detective Manners's "colorful phraseology," and how this suggests that any recollection Scully might divulge is influenced by her perspective, despite her penchant for scientific investigation. Perhaps she is overly detached (to paraphrase Blaine's recollection of her). Similarly, any report that Chrissy might give – under hypnosis or not – is crucially dependent on her experiences and the way she filters them. Furthermore, Roky's fantastical reports of that night may very well be due to his (diagnosed) fantasy-prone personality, which is confirmed by his later founding the "Lava Men Innerspace" cult in California. Blaine's dourly lackluster demeanor and suspiciousness of authority figures undoubtedly impact his experiences. Harold is a love-sick teenager. Mulder is prone to see conspiracies everywhere and his obsession with unexplained phenomena leads Chung to surmise, "[He is] a ticking time bomb of insanity, his quest into the unknown has so warped his psyche, one shudders to think how he receives any pleasures from life." (Interestingly, Scully, as she did regarding memory confabulation, refers to "fantasy-prone personality" and suspects Roky suffers from it; it is an actual diagnosable condition, and is often present in those who believe to be abducted. For more on this condition, see pages 252–253 in Schick and Vaughn 2020.)

Accordingly, the second level of philosophical achievement Morgan's celebrated episode aspires to this: Morgan provides the viewer *cinematic* (and not merely linguistic) reasons to believe Chung's statement that "truth is as subjective as reality." He does so artfully as well, via his careful narrative construction of the episode itself, and without clumsily including them in the soundtrack.

The position Morgan (implicitly) conveys throughout "Jose Chung's From Outer Space" seems eerily akin to Nietzsche's radical perspectivism. On this view, recall, because each of us is a distinct individual, our respective experiences describe each of us (the "experiencer") more so than they describe how things are in themselves. Which experience is privileged enough to discern reality as it truly is, independent of our experiences of it? If no one's experiences are so privileged, then how can we know anything at all about how things actually are? Given the rhetorical force of these questions, and the clever way Morgan cinematically frames them, the resulting philosophical challenge is not merely Mulder's. If the truth represents reality (in itself), and no one's experiences are privileged in terms of discerning the truth about how things actually are, then no one – including Mulder – has no hope of finding the truth "out there." Furthermore, it is tempting to additionally argue that our widely divergent experiences of reality lead to the conclusion that there isn't any objective truth "out there" to discover as it exists in itself and apart from our experiences of it.

After all, those sympathetic to perspectivism might argue that if there were an objective truth apart from our experiences, then we wouldn't expect our experiences to differ as much as they do. But, as "Jose Chung's From Outer Space" reminds us, our experiences are often widely divergent. Therefore, it seems unlikely that there is any objective truth or reality to know apart from our experiences. All that exists are our experiences – our "interpretations," as Nietzsche might say – which, by their very nature, are subjective. Thus, one's pursuit of the elusive (objective) "truth out there" – as it exists in and of itself – is bound to fail. About the so-called "truth out there," the best that anyone can say is, "How the hell should I know?" – which is exactly what Morgan having Mulder utter near the end of the episode.

If that weren't enough, Morgan's philosophical aspirations via "Jose Chung's From Outer Space" arguably operate on a third level. Consider that a necessary condition for being obliged to follow an imperative is that it is possibly attained. Clearly and starkly displayed near the beginning of almost every episode, Chris Carter clearly intends his "the truth is out there" slogan as some sort of implicit imperative to seek those truths. Darin Morgan, as a member of Carter's staff, provides an internal critique of Carter's main imperative. Morgan cinematically provides an implicit argument for believing that, in *The X-Files*, objective truth almost certainly cannot be attained, because the idea upon which it rests – nonperspectival knowing – is incredibly unlikely, if not impossible.

Accordingly, in ways analogous to Socrates's famous internal critiques, for example, of Euthyphro (in *Euthyphro*) regarding prosecuting his father for negligent homicide or Meletus (in *Apology*) regarding whether Socrates alone corrupts the youth of Athens, Morgan provides reasons for thinking that Carter ought to rethink the show's primary mantra and its corresponding imperative. (For *Euthyphro* and *Apology*, see Plato 2000.) Consequently, Morgan cinematically attempts what Socrates does via more traditional mediums, which provides yet another reason to believe that Morgan's "Jose Chung's From Outer Space" successfully philosophizes.

Morgan's Mulder and Anti-Socratic Sentiments

As it turns out, Morgan's corpus sometimes allows for the possibility of objective truth. Nevertheless, Morgan can be interpreted as arguing that even if the truth "out there" exists, relentlessly pursuing it, especially as Mulder does, is not a worthwhile project. This line of thinking invites us to reflect on – and perhaps reconsider – whether Mulder actually is the heroic character the series often portrays him to be. *The X-Files* character Clyde Bruckman serves as the foundation for this interpretation.

In Morgan's "Clyde Bruckman's Final Repose," Bruckman has captured what Mulder so elusively seeks – the truth out there – at least a part of it. Bruckman cannot foretell next week's winning lottery ticket numbers, but he can foresee how people will die. He lives alone, sees his so-called gift as a curse, and tries to deal with his unique perspective on the future by becoming a life insurance salesman. Alas, he becomes dour and resigned, and eventually commits suicide – a death that he apparently foresaw and one that no insurance policy would cover.

Morgan's Bruckman has struggled for decades under the crushing weight of his so-called gift before meeting Mulder and Scully. As Scully tells Mulder, "By thinking he [Bruckman] can see the future, he's taken all the joy out of his life." Mulder becomes convinced of the reality of Bruckman's psychic "gift." Bruckman laments, "Oh, I got it, all right. The only problem is, it's non-returnable." When Mulder presses Bruckman for his help in catching the serial killer (Puppet), a dejected Bruckman replies, "And he'll commit more [murders] whether I help you or not." When Mulder inquires why Bruckman is so sure of this, Bruckman grimaces and answers, "How can I see the future if it didn't already exist?" To which Mulder retorts, "If the future is written, then why bother to do anything?" Sighing, Bruckman replies, "Now you're catching on."

The audience quickly grasps the depths of Bruckman's resignation. Mulder regroups, and asserts, "Mister Bruckman, I believe in your ability but not your attitude. I can't stand by and watch people die without doing everything in my, albeit unsupernatural, power to interfere with that fate." Rather than making another attempt to convince Mulder that the future is unavoidable, Bruckman takes a different tack. He explains, "I can't help you catch this guy. I might adversely affect the fate of the future." After envisioning some highly unlikely but horrific scenarios, Bruckman muses that helping Mulder might result "in the fact that my father never meets my mother and consequently, I'm never born." It is *this* potential result that motivates Bruckman to aid Mulder and Scully, because he thinks he would be better off if he had never been born. Bruckman thus strives to change things so that he never existed – even though he also believes that the future cannot be changed. Bruckman's psychological outlook is dark indeed.

Socrates is famous for holding that one is always better off for knowing the truth; ignorance is always bad (see *Apology* 37e-38a in Plato 2000, and *Euthydemus* 281a-e in Plato 2010). Morgan clearly demurs: Bruckman is not better off for becoming privy to the future. It would be better if he had remained ignorant. Knowledge of when people will die has led him to become bitter and lonely. It has driven him to lead a solitary life; after all, once he sufficiently knows a person, he distinctly foresees how his new friend will die. His bitterness drives him to sell life insurance. But this only immerses him completely in death. It is no wonder that Bruckman agrees to help Mulder because he believes that he might accomplish his own nonexistence thereby.

Bruckman himself, and the masterfully understated way Peter Boyle portrays him, serves as a compelling cinematic counterexample to the claim that one is always better off knowing the truth. The nonverbal cues Boyle employs skillfully convey Bruckman's resigned and morose demeanor, which undoubtedly accounts, in part, for Boyle earning an Emmy for his portrayal of the character. Through Boyle's quiet but heavy sighs and belabored footsteps, we sense Bruckman's regret and remorse, the burden of the fantastical knowledge he possesses.

Furthermore, the fact that Bruckman is otherwise completely ordinary only bolsters the poignant example he offers. He is a sort of everyman, and in this way, can represent any one of us. This allows Morgan to utilize the Clyde Bruckman character as a plausible counterexample to the Socratic dictum that one is always better off knowing the truth. Because there is nothing particularly unusual about Bruckman, Morgan implies that almost anyone is better off not knowing the sorts of confounding truths that Mulder and Scully tend to pursue.

Of course, Mulder is the primary target of Morgan's anti-Socratic critique. In "Quagmire," Morgan likens Mulder to the local kook Ansel Bray, who spends all of his days with his camera in hand, seeking definitive photographic proof of "Big Blue" – a Loch Ness–like sea creature that allegedly lives in the nearby Heuvelman's Lake. On the day that Ansel has his best chance to photograph Big Blue, he forgets to take the lens cap off his camera. He is attacked by some unseen animal and dragged into the lake, never to appear again. Later in the episode, Scully asks Mulder, "You know when you showed me those pictures the photographer took, you want to know what I really saw in them?" Mulder slyly interjects, "A tooth?" Scully shakes her head and continues, "No, you. That man is your future." Morgan finds Mulder's quest for the truth just as eccentric and misguided as Ansel's – a quest unto death.

Through Scully's "Quagmire" dialogue, Morgan voices his suspicion that Mulder is setting himself up for a future similar to Bruckman's – an angst-ridden elderly man who suffers for the bits and pieces he has gleaned of the truth "out there." Unsurprisingly, in season 10 Morgan presents us with a middle-aged Mulder bemoaning his station in life, one resulting from his relentless pursuit of the truth. Morgan deftly conveys Mulder's lamentations, both cinematically (or nonlinguistically) and through insightfully clever dialogue.

Morgan's revived characterization of Mulder is framed by a poignant scene from "My Struggle" (10X01), written by Chris Carter. Mulder and Assistant Director Walter Skinner revisit the unkempt basement office that Mulder and Scully once haunted. Mulder's sharpened pencils remain stuck in the hung ceiling. His (now) iconic "I Want to Believe" poster lies unceremoniously on the floor. Mulder vents his frustrations about the X-Files and denounces all the subterfuge he has endured. He kicks at the poster, ripping it into two pieces. This gesture is clearly symbolic: Mulder doesn't want to believe anymore.

Morgan's "Mulder and Scully Meet the Were-Monster" (two episodes later) opens with Mulder sitting at the desk of his newly refurbished basement office. The "I Want to Believe" poster has been resurrected – evidently Scully purchased a new one – and it again hangs on the wall near Mulder's desk. However, rather than pensively flinging his pencils into the ceiling, Mulder is throwing them – knife-style – into the poster. Pencils jut out like darts on a corkboard and multiple pencil-knife holes are clearly visible. Mulder seemingly has been attempting to metaphorically lance the boil of his existence for some time before Scully arrives to ask, "Mulder, what are you doing to *my* poster?" Morgan's nonverbal message is clear: Mulder is cursing his quest, and treats it as akin to a self-inflicted wound that will not heal. That Mulder does this while calm and collected (all morning) is evidence of the depth of his discontent. Mulder leans back in his chair and shares with Scully, "Since we have been away, much of the 'unexplained' has been explained"; he goes on to elaborate, "It's amazing going through these archives with fresh—if not wiser—eyes, how many of these cases, whether it's the 'Amarillo Armadillo Man' [Mulder sullenly displays a grainy photo] or 'The Hairy Whatsit from Walla Walla' [sheepishly displaying another grainy photo] can be explained away as fraternity pranks, practical jokes, or people making stuff up simply because they are bored and or crazy." Scully responds deadpan to her longtime partner and confidante: "Mulder, have you been taking your meds?"

Ignoring her quip, Mulder continues: "Scully, Charles Fort spent his entire life researching natural and scientific anomalies, which he published in four books, all of which I know by heart. And at the end of his life, Fort himself wondered if it hadn't all been a waste." Scully patiently awaits Mulder's point. Finally, Mulder confesses, "I'm a middle-aged man, Scully. No, I am, I am. I'm thinking maybe it's time to put away childish things—the Sasquatches, mothmen, and [sighing mournfully] jackalopes. I thought it'd be great to get back to work. But, is this really how I want to spend the rest of my days?" In this well-crafted scene, Morgan artfully combines cinematic messages and poignant dialogue (which Duchovny and Anderson exceptionally deliver) that go a long way to close the circle he had begun drawing between Bruckman and Mulder more than 20 years ago in 1995. (He also again adds realism via Mulder's reference to author Charles Fort.) As a result of "chasing monsters in the dark" in the hope of capturing glimpses of the truth "out there," Mulder has lost his sister, father, mother, the Lone Gunmen, his son, and (in some ways) even Scully. He seems destined to live alone, embittered by the little he has learned – and cursing what he has not learned – until death overtakes him.

Despite his lamentations, Mulder (of course) begrudgingly accompanies Scully to investigate a homicide allegedly involving a lizard-like monster in "Mulder and Scully Meet the Were-Monster"; it includes a scene with Mulder trying [and failing] to properly install a new "camera app" for his smartphone to capture visual – digital and thus nongrainy – proof of the monsters he continually chases. As Mulder runs after what seems to be a lizard-man, awkwardly snapping pictures, sometimes at himself, fans cannot avoid being reminded of poor Ansel from "Quagmire." Morgan managed to close that loop as well.

Accordingly, Darin Morgan holds up the examples of Clyde Bruckman and Fox Mulder to consider whether the good life consists in relentless examination of oneself and one's surroundings. Is one always better off for knowing the truth? If the price of tirelessly pursuing the "truth out there" is to become (as Jose Chung would say) a miserable "ticking time bomb of insanity," unable to find any joy in life and likely to die alone, then is it really worth it?

Admittedly, our choices of what ultimately matters in life are difficult to justify with straightforward arguments, because not all morally significant questions about meaningfulness can be resolved by appeals to (more) general principles. However, philosophers going back (at least) to Socrates have affirmed that such questions are intelligibly asked, and call out for reasonable answers. Consequently, if Morgan is cinematically successful in getting us to reflect on Mulder via Bruckman – and thereby consider whether their fictional examples are relevant to how actual persons conceive of the good life – then Morgan again plays the part of a philosopher. Because reflecting on conceptions of the good life – or what is ultimately meaningful in life – is part of the philosophical process, if Morgan is successful at this, then he (again) engages the philosophical process via his fictional narrative artistry.

Socrates' views on the examined life seem philosophically sacrosanct. Admittedly, then, many philosophers would probably have difficulty accepting Morgan's anti-Socratic message; however, this only shows how Nietzsche's ideas once again bolster Morgan's philosophical approach. Nietzsche famously contends that Socrates himself, and those who revered him, were mistaken: "Is it necessary to expose the errors which lay in his faith in 'reason at any price?'...Life made clear, cold, cautious, conscious, without instincts, another kind of disease—and by no means a return to 'virtue,' to 'health,' and to happiness" (Nietzsche 1911; Sect. 11). Furthermore, and although his overall views about Socrates are complex, Nietzsche believes that revering Socrates only hampers our ability to be true philosophers – those who are impassioned enough to follow an aesthetic idea of affirming life in transcendence and self-becoming. According to Nietzsche, such philosophers:

> Think of that which is most indispensable to them: freedom from constraint, interference, noise, from tasks, duties, cares; they think of a clear head, of dancing, leaping, flying of thoughts; good air, thin, clear, free, dry mountain air, spiritualizing and lending wings to all animal being.... That cheerful asceticism of some deified and newly fledged animal which rises above life rather resting in repose. (Nietzsche 1969; Sect. 8)

There is nothing special in the Socratic, hyperrational approach to life. It's just the dogma within which Socrates bounded himself. Nietzsche's view is obviously controversial, but, to his credit, he invites us to reexamine some of our most cherished philosophical beliefs.

If philosophers do not continually question what the philosophical enterprise involves (including whether filmmakers can do philosophy, I might add), we, too, run the risk of being trapped by dogmatic convictions. It's therefore incumbent upon us to continually revisit and reexamine all of our received philosophical views, even those as entrenched as Socrates' concept of the good life. Consistency thereby dictates that we consider Morgan's anti-Socratic venture. So, if this interpretation of Morgan's Mulder holds up, and Morgan indeed cinematically provides a plausible case for revisiting the Socratic ideal, then it follows that Morgan (again) engages the philosophical process through his vivid portrayal of a character who seemingly suffers as a result of following Socrates's dictum about the examined life.

By way of summary, a microcosm of Morgan's implicit anti-Socratic argument about Mulder's ill-conceived venture to relentlessly pursue the so-called "truth out there" is conveniently conveyed in "Quagmire." While marooned in the dead of night on a rock in Heuvelman's Lake, and quite exasperated from their desperate search for "Big Blue," Scully compares Mulder's quest for an "intangible" truth "out there" to Ahab's search for the white whale. She laments to her partner, "It's the truth or a white whale. What difference does it make? I mean, both obsessions are impossible to capture, and trying to do so will only leave you dead along with everyone else you bring with you." Maybe Mulder's white whale is out there; maybe it isn't. If it isn't, which is probably the case, then relentlessly pursuing it is a waste of time. But even if it is, is relentlessly pursuing it worth all the time, effort, and pain? (And remember this is coming from Scully – someone who Mulder trusts implicitly.)

Accordingly, Darin Morgan's work on *The X-Files* is plausibly interpreted as conveying the following implicit philosophically significant argument: Either the (objective) truth "out there" exists, or it does not. If it does not, which is probably the case, then attempts to pursue it are doomed to fail, and all such attempts are foolhardy. Moreover, we cannot be obliged to seek something we cannot obtain, and acting as if we can do the impossible will only lead to angst and heartbreak. If it does exist, but we cannot find it due to the limitations of the human intellect, then pursuing it as if we can attain it is ill-advised and foolhardy, leading (again) to angst and heartbreak. If it does exist, and we are fortunate enough to (occasionally) glimpse it, relentlessly pursuing it in the way that Fox Mulder does is undoubtedly foolhardy given the pain and suffering invariably associated with such single-minded pursuits. Thus, Fox Mulder (and those of his ilk who relentlessly pursue the "truth out there") act in ill-advised, foolhardy, ways.

Reexamining Morgan's Arguments

Morgan's philosophical achievements are impressive because he aspires to them as a filmmaker, conveying his views effectively without sacrificing his cinematic artistry. But like all philosophical arguments, regardless of how artfully crafted, they can be assessed on their own merits. As we'll see, many of Morgan's conclusions are far from irresistible.

Morgan's implicit critique of classic epistemology that knowledge of reality is impossible because of the subjective nature of experience seems to assume either that knowledge requires certainty (the impossibility of error), or that there is no principled way to determine which perceptions are to be rationally privileged over others. On the former assumption, if it's possible that a belief is false, then it cannot count as knowledge, even if the belief turns out to be true; the fact that we are *possibly* mistaken about the belief is sufficient to discount the knowledge claim. On the latter assumption, and apart from whether knowledge requires certainty, because each perception describes the perceiver as much as it does the reality allegedly perceived, no one perception is more likely true – and hence sufficiently justified – over another. As it turns out, both assumptions are problematic.

Regarding the first assumption, it's not clear that all judgments are prone to the possibility of error. Ironically, Morgan brings this issue to the foreground in one of the "José Chung's From Outer Space" diner scenes via Lieutenant Shaefer, who laments to Mulder: "Don't you get it? I'm absolutely positive me, my copilot, and those two kids were abducted, but I can't be absolutely sure it happened. I can't be sure of anything anymore! . . . I'm not sure we're even having this conversation. . . . I don't know if you even exist." Mulder responds, "I can only assure you that I do." To which Schaefer replies, "Well, thanks, buddy. Unfortunately, I can't give you the same assurance about me." If we take Shaefer at his word, René Descartes would disagree. Descartes contends you can have knowledge of your own existence, at least whenever you think about it, indeed, whenever you doubt it. This is so because doubting (or thinking generally) requires a doubter (or thinker). Because thinkers have immediate and self-certifying cognitive access to their thoughts, it follows that they can never be mistaken in their belief that they exist, at least whenever they think about it. This is Descartes' celebrated "cogito ergo sum," or "I think, therefore I am" argument. It shows there are pieces of knowledge we cannot believe falsely. (For additional context, see Descartes 1996, especially Meditation II.) Thus, some knowledge of reality – that you exist in it – is obtainable. Consequently, Morgan's implicit position goes too far, and opens itself up to an obvious counterexample.

Further, the notion that knowledge requires the impossibility of error is self-defeating. After all, isn't it *possible* that it doesn't? So how could that requirement itself be known? It's not self-certifying like Descartes' "Cogito," which reveals that I can't mistakenly *think* that I am thinking. So, by its own lights, the assumption that knowledge requires the impossibility of error cannot be known; and if it cannot be known, it can't make knowledge impossible.

Regarding the second assumption, and with a bit additional consideration, it seems dubious that there are *no* ways to determine which perceptions of reality are to be valued over others. Some perceptions – due to poor health or psychological disorders – are clearly diminished or unreliable. But from this insight it follows that others – for example, those had in broad daylight by healthy individuals – are generally reliable. Furthermore, epistemology (as a primary subcategory of philosophy) is dedicated in large part to determining which beliefs are (rationally) justified and which are not. For such philosophers, the goal (contra Descartes) is not to determine which beliefs are beyond all possibility of error, but which are beyond a *reasonable* doubt.

In the attempt to put beliefs beyond a reasonable doubt, philosophers typically advocate for reliable sources of justified beliefs: the senses, introspection, memory, and reason. Beliefs springing from these sources are typically reliable guides to the truth. Therefore, we need positive or substantive reason to think that a belief generated from these sources is faulty or misleading before it can be doubted reasonably. There are reliable indicators if a person is not reasoning or remembering something correctly, hallucinating, or in a situation that we would expect perceptual errors. We would expect a white wall to appear red if a red light were shining on it. Lack of sleep and some medications are known to cause distinctive hallucinations or interrupt memory. If such indicators are present, then there can be reasonable doubt about the relevant belief. However, the mere possibility of error (contra Descartes) is not sufficient to discount a belief counting as knowledge because the mere possibility of error is tantamount to *unreasonable* doubt. Of course, even if the traditional sources are operating properly, it is conceivable that a belief could turn out to be false. When we encounter such cases, we should revise our knowledge claim. But notice that the possibility of revising one's belief in light of further evidence indicates that discovering the way the world is, and thus knowledge, is possible.

Indeed, there are well-accepted basic guidelines for establishing (and revising) one's knowledge claims. First, if a newly entertained belief contradicts a great deal of what one already justifiably believes, then there is sufficient reason to doubt it. Second, as the number of justified beliefs it conflicts with increases, the more reason there is to doubt it. Third, given the first two guidelines, we should proportion the degree to which we hold a belief to the evidence for it. With strong evidence for it, we should believe it strongly; with little or none (or if it contravenes what is already well established), then we should reject it (or at least be skeptical). Fourth, if you are personally unsure about the evidence, you should consult expert opinion. There is good reason to doubt a newly entertained belief if it conflicts with (non-biased) expert consensus about the topic.

These guidelines not only help us to distinguish between science and science fiction, which, in turn, explains (in part) Scully's important thematic role in *The X-Files*. More importantly, these sorts of epistemological insights and guidelines lead us to think (justifiably) that not all perceptions of reality are the same and how to value some beliefs about it over others.

In fact, in chapters 6 and 7 of the 2020 edition of their book *How to Think About Weird Things*, Schick and Vaughn articulate a method for knowing the truth about the world beyond a reasonable doubt that utilizes the fact that our perception and memory can be biased and faulty. By being aware of such facts about us, we can actively guard against them. This is the point of scientific experiments and their controls, like blinding, double blinding, peer review, and repetition. Although they call it the search method, it's essentially just the scientific method – also known as inference to the best explanation – and involves not only guarding against perceptual, memory, and (other) cognitive inaccuracies, but evaluating hypotheses on criteria to which effective explanations, by definition, must adhere: testability, fruitfulness, scope, simplicity, and conservatism. When a hypothesis measures up, it can be justifiably believed and (if true) known beyond a reasonable doubt.

For one final critique of Morgan's Nietzsche-like philosophical assault on objective truth, recall Charles Nelson Reilly's line: "Truth is subjective as reality." Note that it asserts something about how things are, namely that it's a *fact* that all truth claims are subjective. Consequently, it is, itself, a truth claim, one that is supposed to be objectively true. But by the claim's own lights, there cannot be any objectively true claims, as these would describe reality, as it is in itself. Thus, the very idea of subjectivism about truth is self-contradictory. In other words, Nietzsche's assertion that "Facts is precisely what there is not, only interpretations. We cannot establish any fact 'in itself'" can be refuted by a simple rhetorical question: "Really? Is that a fact?" Again, Morgan goes too far in his critique of the idea that the "truth is out there."

Morgan's arguments against the Socratic unrelenting pursuit of the truth is, admittedly, more difficult to critique directly. The comparison between Mulder and Socrates seems apt. Mulder's aforementioned "Erlenmeyer Flask" comment echoes Socrates' famed declaration to his accusers: "As long as I have breath and strength, I will not give up philosophy and exhorting you and declaring the truth to every one of you whom I meet. . . . [especially] when you neither think nor care about wisdom and truth and the improvement of your soul [*psyche*, or inner person]?" (Plato 2000; *Apology* 29d-e). Socrates, recall, was on trial because some politically influential Athenians found him to be a nuisance. These people did not appreciate his self-proclaimed role as "gadfly" for the truth and were willing to finally rid themselves of Socrates even if the charges against him were spurious.

Although Socrates' life was at stake, he stayed the course, thereby again demonstrating by example the importance of seeking human excellence by pursuing truth. Among Socrates' beliefs was: "A man who is good for anything should not calculate the chance of living and dying. He should only consider whether in doing anything he is doing right or wrong and acting the part of the good man or of a bad" (Plato 2000; *Apology*, 28b). Thus, whether Socrates might be found guilty and executed did not truly matter. What mattered was that he was doing the right thing by upholding the noblest of values – pursuing human excellence. To his unappreciative accusers, he declares, "If I tell you that no greater good can happen to a man than to discuss human excellence every day and the other matters about which you have heard me arguing and examining myself and others, and that the unexamined life is not worth living, then you will believe me still less" (Plato 2000; *Apology*, 38a). But this is exactly what Socrates believed. For human beings to exist and not seek the truth and human excellence to which it leads was not to live. This pursuit is more important than all others, including wealth, fame, and influence.

Obviously, Socrates offers an extreme example of someone who is willing to pursue the truth at all costs; he believed that nothing was more important, so he was willing to die for his quest. Morgan implicitly inquires: Is it really worth it? Socrates would say yes, and although Mulder occasionally stumbles and is growing a bit weary, he would largely agree. Interestingly, Nietzsche, as he did with "truth" and "falsity," seems inclined to redefine what philosophers do when doing philosophy, and employs that revised definition to critique Socrates. (Of course, Socrates would begin asking him questions about whether this new definition holds up to scrutiny, which tells us a lot about Socrates and his views about philosophy.)

Socrates seems correct that most (all) unfortunate choices we make are due to ignorance, evidenced by the familiar refrain, "Had I known *that* was going to happen, I would have chosen differently." Furthermore, no one wishes to live completely under false pretenses, as one thereby lacks autonomy over one's life. Thus, to ensure that we make as few unfortunate choices as possible and, indeed, to make choices we can own, we are better off pursuing the truth. Only then will we make rationally self-determined choices about what is best, and, implicitly, what is best for us. On this account, it seems that we have reason for following Socrates (and Mulder) *at least* part of the way toward the truth, and probably further toward it than Morgan accepts.

In the end, Morgan's views are not completely without merit, but they must be properly contextualized. Sometimes, the truth is difficult to discover and because opinions about it often diverge (although perhaps not as wildly or vividly as they do in "Jose Chung's From Outer Space"), it's tempting to conclude there is no (objective) truth to be found. Consequently, dedicating one's life to searching for "the truth out there" may seem foolhardy and full of regret and disappointment. However, from the fact that the truth is difficult to discover, it doesn't follow that there are no truths to be found. We may never know whether intelligent beings exist on other planets, and some (like Mulder) might affirm this hypothesis and others (like Scully) might deny it, but from this it does not follow that there is no objective truth about extraterrestrial intelligent life. Either there is or there isn't, and there is a fact of the matter either way. Furthermore, as we've seen, philosophers and scientists have developed effective strategies for discerning which beliefs/hypotheses/opinions are closer to the truth. Thus, the mere fact of disagreement, regardless of how vehement or diverse, doesn't entail that the "truth out there" cannot be found.

We can grant Morgan that we may never arrive at "*the* truth of out there" (in its totality) and some particular truths may forever elude our grasp. But perfect or complete knowledge being unattainable doesn't entail that pursuing the truth is futile or worthless. Claiming otherwise is a false dilemma, also known as the "all or nothing" fallacy (see Johnson 2018). Consider that no one can be perfectly healthy, but striving to be healthy is not worthless. Analogously, even if complete or perfect knowledge is impossible to achieve, there is still value in pursuing the truth, in exchanging false beliefs for those that are (more likely) true, and striving toward behaviors that more reliably produce them. Moreover, we might not attain perfect knowledge of the natural world, but think of all the advancements scientists have made in their pursuit: antibiotics, electronic communication, and clean energy sources (just to name a few).

23 *The X-Files* as Philosophy: Navigating the "Truth Out There" 539

That said, we can grant Morgan that *some* truths are so trivial that they need not be pursued. Admittedly, Fox Mulder's fervent pursuits of such oddities as Sasquatches, Mothmen, and jackalopes have taken a toll on his mental and physical health. Was it worth it? Perhaps not. But Mulder's pursuits also included unconventional investigations into his sister's and Scully's unusual disappearances and exposing secret antidemocratic factions within the US government. It is far from clear that these pursuits lack value. So, again, even if some of Mulder's pursuits of the truth "out there" lack value, it does not follow that they all do. And engaging the philosophical process – doing some philosophy – will put us in a better position to determine which pursuits are worthwhile and which less so. If nothing else, Morgan's arguments remind us of *that*, including how learning about Socrates might guide one's explorations into what constitutes the good life and how Socrates' classic view contrasts with less influential views like Nietzsche's.

Conclusion: *The X-Files* as Philosophical *and* Philosophy

It's widely acknowledged that *The X-Files* is a self-consciously philosophical television series. At its core, it raises the issues of what to believe, the role evidence plays (or ought to play) in coming to have a belief, and what, if anything, one may believe when the evidence is lacking. It concerns whether anyone should be trusted, and it has connections to various classic philosophical issues, including freedom and determinism and love and friendship. (For the wide-ranging philosophical significance of *The X-Files*, see Kowalski 2009, including an account of Mulder's connections to Socrates on pages 111–125.)

Yet, as argued here, *The X-Files* is not always content to be merely philosophical. Sometimes it aspires to philosophy-in-action and contribute something substantive to the philosophical conversation about the issue(s) in question. Indeed, it seems clear that *The X-Files* production staff offers internal critiques of its own philosophically significant theses, most notably the ideas that "the truth is out there" and that it ought always to be pursued. The most trenchant critiques of these ideas are manifest in episodes written or directed by Darin Morgan. Morgan's arguments are significant irrespective of whether they are (obviously) sound. Their significance lies (primarily) in their artful cinematic nature and their propensity to generate discussion and additional philosophical inquiry. Cue the *X-Files* theme.

References

Descartes, René. 1996. *Meditations on first philosophy* (1641). Trans. John Cottingham. Cambridge: Cambridge University Press.

Johnson, David Kyle. 2018. All or nothing. In *Bad arguments: 100 of the most important fallacies in western philosophy*, ed. Robert Arp, Steven Barbone, and Michael Bruce, 301–304. New York: Wiley-Blackwell.

Kowalski, Dean A. (ed). 2009. *The philosophy of the X-files*, revised edition. Lexington: University Press of Kentucky.

Nietzsche, Friedrich. 1911. Twilight of the idols (1888). In *The complete works of Friedrich Nietzsche*, ed. Oscar Levy, vol. 16. New York: Mcmillian.

———. 1966. *Beyond good and evil: Prelude to a philosophy of the future (1886)*. Trans. Walter Kaufmann. New York: Vintage Books.

———. 1968. *The will to power (1901)*. Trans. Walter Kaufmann, and R. J. Hollingdale. New York: Vintage Books.

———. 1969. *On the genealogy of morals (1887), in on the genealogy of morals and ecce homo*. Trans. Walter Kaufmann, and R. J. Hollingdale. New York: Vintage Books.

———. 1974. *The gay science (1882)*. Trans. Walter Kaufmann. New York: Vintage Books.

Ohio State University. Hypnosis may give false confidence in inaccurate memories. *Science Daily* (August 28, 2001). www.sciencedaily.com/releases/2001/08/010828075745.htm. Accessed 30 Dec 2021.

Plato. 2000. *Trial and death of Socrates* (*Euthyphro*, *Apology*, *Crito*, and *Phaedo* death scene). Trans. G. M. A. Grube. Indianapolis: Hackett.

———. 2010. *Euthydemus*. Trans. Gregory McBrayer and Mary Nichols. Newburyport: Focus Publishing.

Schick, Theodore, and Lewis Vaughn. 2020. *How to think about weird things*. 8th ed. New York: McGraw-Hill.

Game of Thrones as Philosophy: Cynical Realpolitiks

24

Eric J. Silverman and William Riordan

Contents

Introduction	542
The Illegitimacy of Robert "The Usurper" Baratheon	543
Daenerys – The "Legitimate" – Pyromaniacal Heir to the Throne	544
A Cynical Look at the Alternative Democratic-Anachronism of the Wildlings	546
The False Ideals of Chivalry	547
Voices of Cynicism: Littlefinger and Varys	548
An Alternative to *Game of Thrones*' Cynicism: John Locke's Natural Law	550
Another Alternative to Cynicism: Thomas Aquinas's Account of Law	552
Conclusion	554
References	554

Abstract

Game of Thrones is a popular, award-winning television series with an eight-season run on Home Box Office, based on the *Song of Fire and Ice* series of books by George R.R. Martin. It depicts a morally complex political situation in a fantasy environment that has some similarities to medieval Europe. In the midst of this setting, the series advocates a cynical attitude towards politics, social structures, and religion. Most notably, the series suggests that there is no such thing as political legitimacy. This chapter identifies a pattern of cynicism throughout Game of Thrones but points towards the thoughts of John Locke and Thomas Aquinas as possible alternatives to the story's cynicism.

Keywords

Political legitimacy · Social contract theory · Chivalry · Democracy · Monarchy · Cynicism · John Locke · Thomas Aquinas

---

E. J. Silverman (✉) · W. Riordan
Christopher Newport University, Newport News, VA, USA
e-mail: Eric.Silverman@cnu.edu; william.riordan.17@cnu.edu

© Springer Nature Switzerland AG 2024
D. K. Johnson et al. (eds.), *The Palgrave Handbook of Popular Culture as Philosophy*,
https://doi.org/10.1007/978-3-031-24685-2_90

Introduction

Among the impressive feats displayed within George R. R. Martin's *Game of Thrones* series is his ability to present a wide variety of well-developed cultures with very different customs, religions, values, institutions, social structures, and politics. We are introduced to political structures and views as diverse as the anarchism north of the wall among the Wildlings, the traditional monarchical claim to power through historical blood lineage from the Targaryens, the Iron Island election system of the Kingsmoot, and the Baratheon claim to the throne based on the legitimacy of their rebellion against the Targaryen abuses. Throughout the series, members of each group bid, maneuver, and fight to sit on the throne of Westeros. Despite the vast contrast in these political accounts, what is the "moral of the story" politically?

Since the entire *Game of Thrones* story is strikingly complex and therefore, impossible to summarize in this limited context, let's skip straight to the story's answer. The view of politics implicitly advocated by Martin's stories is one of cynicism towards the concept of political legitimacy. As Varys explains through his famous riddle to Tyrion, "Power resides where men believe it resides. It's a trick, a shadow on the wall" ("What is Dead May Never Die," S2E3). In other words, there is no such thing as objective, legitimate political power. Instead, political power exists wherever people are manipulated into believing it does whether it is purportedly from royal bloodlines, divine favor, wealth, popular acclamation, or crass military power. This cynical message about political legitimacy appears to be the central political viewpoint of the series since we are shown again and again the serious flaws in each leader's claim to political legitimacy.

A prime example of this pattern can be seen in the final scenes of the series, where Tyrion returns to Varys' political point claiming, "There's nothing in the world more [politically] powerful than a good story. Nothing can stop it" ("The Iron Throne," S8E6). Since, there is no genuine political legitimacy, Tyrion proceeds pragmatically by suggesting the next king be the one with the most compelling story that will broadly help give the image of legitimacy for a new monarchy. On this basis, the leaders of Westeros appoint Bran Stark as King due to his compelling story as the crippled, but transcendently powerful three-eyed raven. It does not matter that the Starks do not have a credible political claim to the traditional line of the Targaryen throne or the more recent Baratheon line. Nor did it matter to anyone that Bran himself had little role in liberating King's Landing from the Lannister abuses nor did he do anything to prevent the threat of a mad Targaryen returning to rule. All that mattered for Bran's ascension is that he had a compelling story that the commoners would embrace and thus won the support of the surviving political power brokers.

Still, that is just one example. So, this chapter begins by identifying Martin's cynicism throughout the series in several ways in order to lay bare how the particular elements of the story suggest a cynical moral: that political legitimacy itself is a myth used by those who seek power. We will identify the major dubious claims to political legitimacy by his most important characters and document the undeniable negative effects of the various rulers upon the Seven Kingdoms. We will see that Martin's cynical critique is not limited to political structures in the narrowest sense, but also extends to broader values and infused social structures like chivalry and religion. We will also see that some of the most powerful, influential characters in *Game of Thrones* embody variations of Martin's cynical viewpoint. Finally, we will critique Martin's cynical views with ideas from two thinkers he never really considers: the natural law theory of political legitimacy from John Locke, and the four-conditions of just political leadership advanced by Thomas Aquinas.

The Illegitimacy of Robert "The Usurper" Baratheon

As the *Game of Thrones* series begins, we are introduced to characters that appear to fit in with familiar heroic tropes. Ned Stark is a truly virtuous and honest ruler. He is fiercely loyal to his family and friends. Out of duty and loyalty to his friend and King Robert Baratheon he takes an undesirable job as Hand of the King at some risk and considerable personal cost to himself. Since King Robert reigns at the beginning of the story and because he has the loyalty, friendship, and implicit endorsement of the most positive characters we are introduced to, we tend to assume that *he* is the legitimate King.

Yet, as the plot proceeds, it is slowly revealed that Robert's claim to the throne is hardly compelling. We learn that he became king less than 20 years ago after Robert's Rebellion removed the erratic and increasingly homicidal "Mad King" Aerys Targaryen II. Even if we assume that there is a right to rebellion against an unjust king, it does not follow that evils of Aerys's tyranny make Robert's reign legitimate. Instead, the king might have been removed and replaced with one of his legitimate descendants. At most, Robert should have served as a temporary regent until a stable, legitimate heir came of age.

Not only does Robert have a dubious claim to the throne, but during his rebellion, he is complicit in the murder of the legitimate child heirs to the Targaryen throne, Aegon and Rhaenys. Furthermore, he drives the remaining known heirs Viserys and Daenerys Targaryen into exile and seeks to assassinate them. Daenerys's view of him as a murderer and usurper seems closer to reality than his own view of himself as the legitimate king. At best, his claim to legitimacy is dubious.

Furthermore, much of the rationale for Robert's Rebellion ultimately turns out to be false. While Aerys was indeed abusive in many ways, an important justification for the rebellion was the kidnapping and rape of Robert's betrothed Lyanna Stark shortly after the Tourney at Harrenhal by Prince Rhaegar Targaryen. Yet, we later learn in one of Bran Stark's visions that Lyanna was in love with Rhaegar and happily married him, suggesting that she wasn't kidnapped at all. Later, this surprise twist is confirmed by Sam Tarly's research at The Citadel.

Finally, we should notice that Robert is a mediocre ruler. He isn't abusive and occasionally insane like Aerys, but he is at best an "absentee ruler" who is more preoccupied with debaucherous amounts of drinking, partying, and adulterous sex, than caring for the realm. He doesn't care for the small folk, avoid debt, or focus upon the monarch's actual responsibilities. He doesn't manage the realm well.

The implicit lesson about politics we learn from examining Robert's ascension to power and reign is a cynical one. He isn't the legitimate king. He murdered the true heirs to the throne. The justifications for his rebellion were less than completely accurate. Daenerys's view of him as "The Usurper" is not unreasonable.

Daenerys – The "Legitimate" – Pyromaniacal Heir to the Throne

If Robert's rule was illegitimate, one might hope to avoid cynicism by looking to Daenerys's legitimacy. After all, for most of the *Game of Thrones* series we are led to believe that she is the legitimate heir who is next in line to the Tarygaryen throne. We watch her progress from a naïve teenager, who is sold into a political marriage to a Dothraki leader so that her brother can have access to their armies, to the conquering "Mother of Dragons" who frees slaves and topples unjust rulers across the sea from Westeros. She seeks to rule fairly, but most of all she dreams of returning to her rightful kingdom in Westeros. She repeatedly presents herself as the rightful heir to Westeros, warning: "I will take what is mine with fire and blood" ("Fire and Blood," S1E10).

Of course, even if we are correct in viewing Robert's rule as illegitimate, it doesn't follow that the Targaryen monarchy he overthrew was legitimate either. We don't hear much about the origins of Targaryen rule in *Game of Thrones*, but we do hear many complaints from the Wildlings that the "civilized kingdoms" to their south simply declared the right to set up a wall and exclude them from the land of the southern kingdoms. We also see that the Iron Islands are in consistent rebellion, as they don't recognize the legitimacy of King's Landing rule over them. However, the prequel history of Westeros *Fire and Blood: 300 Years Before a Game of Thrones* makes it clear that the Targaryens were simply conquerors of the seven kingdoms who had the massive military advantage provided by dragons, the ultimate weapon of mass destruction. Clearly, this isn't some great moral, political, or diplomatic accomplishment. Uniting the seven kingdoms was an accomplishment of brute military force rather than a source of genuine political legitimacy. As Tywin Lannister suggests, there is a close connection between political power and military success. As Tywin says, "Do you think I'd be in my position if I'd lost a war?" ("A Man Without Honor," S2E7).

Perhaps, we should be pragmatic enough to set aside the issue of the original legitimacy of the Targaryen reign. Even if their original claim is as illegitimate as Robert's, since their reign has been in place for centuries the long-standing tradition of the Targaryen monarchy is at least the "most" legitimate monarchical claim to rule that one can find in Westeros. Their reign is backed by three centuries of historic precedent. At the very least, it is difficult to find a serious candidate for a family who would provide a more legitimate ruling line.

Yet, even if we set aside questions about the original legitimacy of the Targaryen line, there are serious problems with viewing Daenerys as the legitimate monarch. She has barely lived in Westeros, knows nothing first-hand about it, and would not be a well-informed leader. Daenerys also isn't a consistently benevolent ruler. She has occasional good intentions, yet her rulings are more capricious than wise, and sometimes just flat out inconsistent. She frees the slaves in Astapor, Mereen, and Yunkai as an act of benevolence. Yet, she also crucifies 163 citizens of Mereen without trials for simply being members of the wrong class. She also betrays and murders the slavelords as soon as she has control of the Unsullied. She seems concerned for the citizens of Westeros one moment, but then needs to be talked out of using dragons against civilian targets the next moment. One of the final acts of her life was to indiscriminately burn every moving thing in King's Landing.

It is tempting to excuse most of Daenerys's faults. After all, most of Daenerys's victims were unsympathetic slave owners, explicitly defiant to her claim to the throne, or harmed in the throes of war itself. Still, there is another foundational problem. Even if we stipulate that the Targaryen monarchy is legitimate, and we excuse her cruel violent tendencies, Daenerys simply isn't the legitimate heir to the Targaryen throne. Jon Snow – also known as Aegon Targaryen – has the most direct hereditary claim to the Targaryen throne. What does Daenerys do when she discovers that she isn't really the most rightful heir to the throne? Does she encourage Jon to take the throne? Does she offer to share the monarchy and rule together as King and Queen (a practical solution given their existing romantic relationship, the advantages of combining their claims to political legitimacy, and the Targaryen custom of incestuous marriages)? No. She encourages Jon to immediately reject any thought of taking the throne. She affirms his attestations of "I don't want it!" and "She's my Queen." She doesn't seem to care at all whether or not she is truly the rightful queen. At this critical moment, she is narcissistically preoccupied with her own political ambitions, and her own pain, as Jon withdraws from the newly discovered incestuousness of their relationship.

The ultimately negative depiction of Daenerys, who had been portrayed as the most plausible "politically legitimate" leader by traditional monarchical standards for most of the series, serves to reinforce the cynical message of *Game of Thrones*. The legitimacy of the entire Targaryen line is dubious, Daenerys herself is hardly a stable and just leader, she has barely lived in Westeros, and ultimately she isn't even the next in line to the Targaryen throne. While the show's depiction of her transition from a potential savoir of Westeros to a psychotic pyromaniac was poorly executed, there were plenty of indicators beforehand that Daenerys should be viewed with cynicism rather than idealism. As Varys had warned, "Every time a Targaryen is born, the gods toss a coin" ("The Bells," S8E5) in order to decide whether they would be stable or outrightly insane.

So, the *Game of Thrones* outlook seems quite cynical towards both Robert's and Daenerys's claim to rule Westeros. Furthermore, there are many other implicitly cynical portrayals of monarchical claims throughout the series. Renly Baratheon asserted a claim to the throne over his older brother Stannis despite his knowledge that Stannis had the better claim to the throne. Joffrey Baratheon – along with his siblings – was an illegitimate bastard rather than a genuine heir to his supposed father Robert's throne. Furthermore, Joffrey was an unstable, childish, spoiled, cruel narcist who was a terrible King for the brief time he reigned. In addition to the general, erratic, capricious cruelty towards those around him, he started an unnecessary war with the Northern Kingdoms that killed tens of thousands on both sides due to the completely unnecessary execution of the repentant Eddard Stark.

A Cynical Look at the Alternative Democratic-Anachronism of the Wildlings

If examining the various monarchs of the Seven Kingdoms of Westeros results in cynicism, then one might suspect the show's objection isn't to political legitimacy in general, but merely with the legitimacy of monarchies. But, *Game of Thrones* is critical about other political structures as well. Consider the show's portrayal of the "Free Folk" or "Wildlings" to the north of Westeros: The Free Folk to the north possess many traits that are valued by contemporary Western societies. In Mance Rayder, they have chosen a competent leader who is elected based on his virtues and skills, rather than anointed based on the coincidences of his bloodline. We also see that the Wildlings have broad liberty, with far more political freedom than the citizens of the southern monarchies. Indeed, they are no one's subjects, but instead belong to themselves. They have natural political equality and are ordered by no political leader without their consent. Their leaders do not stand on ceremony, and they mock the classism of the "kneelers" to their south. Yet, despite having several political advantages over monarchies, the portrayal of the Wildlings demonstrates the dangers of anachro-democracy like theirs.

The most obvious problem is that such liberty did not result in an idyllic existence. There is no political authority to protect the weak from the strong, or to help the Wildlings prepare for the brutal winter. At best, the Wildlings are a bunch of uncivilized, violent, barbarians, who work together on a minimal basis under the threat of extinction from the Night King. A wide variety of violent behaviors are commonplace and accepted in the north: rape and kidnapping. Stealing a woman is an accepted basis for a sexual relationship. If the woman doesn't want this relationship, the accepted solution is a violent: "Wildling divorce," the murder of the unwanted lover. Even cannibalism exists in the north. Craster, an ally to the Night's Watch, is involved in infanticide of his own children and systematic incestuous rape of his own daughters. Furthermore, he is essentially "dealing with the devil" by sacrificing his own sons to the Night King and thereby providing him with his White Walker soldiers. The North may have freedom, but it also has plenty of rape, murder, and cannibalism.

The violence and barbaric practices can even be seen within the Wildlings' individual relationships. While the relationship between Ygritte and Jon seems more genuine than the political marriages that are common in the Seven Kingdoms, there is violence undergirding it. She appears to view their relationship as a genuine northern "common law" marriage as their relationship was inaugurated by Jon capturing her and thus "stealing her." While there is genuine warmth within their relationship, she also threatens him with violence and castration should he ever betray her. Accordingly, when she encounters him after he has escaped from her and the rest of the Wildlings, she attempts to give him a "Wildling divorce" by shooting him full of arrows.

Game of Thrones also teaches a cynical lesson in the ultimate fate of the Wildlings. Not only was everyday life difficult, dangerous, and violent in the "free" North – but even the freely chosen leadership of Mance did little to help improve their situation. He neither provided the military leadership necessary to overcome the Night King or the Night's Watch, nor did he provide the diplomatic leadership needed to negotiate any sort of truce or free passage for his people to the south. As a result, they were largely slaughtered by zombies, White Walkers, and the Night's Watch. If their freedom led to such a wholesale disaster, it is difficult to view their politics as anything desirable. Perhaps, the most negative critique one can have of any viewpoint is to depict it as leading to apocalyptic levels of destruction.

The False Ideals of Chivalry

Another set of sociopolitical structures that *Game of Thrones* expresses cynicism towards is the medieval class system including monarchy, knights, kings, heroes, clergy, etc. Granted, much of the society of Westeros is modeled on the social structures of medieval Europe and purportedly upon the values of chivalry. But cynicism about chivalry is expressed throughout the series. One important example is at the Hand's Tournament, where we are presented with a scene displaying many of the traditional components of medieval chivalric stories. We are introduced to Loras Tyrell – a literal knight in shining polished armor with excellent courtly manners. Before his joust, this "Knight of Flowers" offers a token flower to the young Sansa in keeping with the idealized images of courtly manners that chivalric knights are supposed to uphold publicly. He competes against the brutal and uncultured "Mountain," a knight in the villainous, darker image of the evil antagonistic "Black Knights" of traditional medieval tales.

However, Loras Tyrell does not really have chivalric virtues. His polished armor and manners are just an image. He wins his joust with the Mountain not with skill and righteousness, but by using underhanded cleverness and riding a mare in heat to distract the Mountain's mount to the point of unmanageability. His courtly interest in Sansa was dishonest and did not entail any genuine romantic interest in her or any other woman. Instead, he subtly makes romantic eye contact with his actual lover Renly Baratheon. When the Mountain realizes he has been cheated, he relentlessly attacks Tyrell and the "noble knight" struggles to protect himself. Only the intervention of the unknighted, thuggish henchman the "Hound" prevents the Mountain from killing Tyrell. In case the scene's point against chivalric classist ideals might be overlooked by the viewer, when the graciously mannered Tyrell lifts the Hound's arm in victory to share the applause of the crowd saying "I owe you my life, ser" ("Cripples, Bastards, and Broken Things," S1E4), the Hound reminds us all, "I am no ser." We are meant to see that the chivalric knight is a dishonest cheater who is unable to protect himself, the hero is an unknighted mercenary without title, and that the overweight King watches these violent events unfold in a slovenly stupor before remembering that his authority might be used to end the dangerous altercation. Perhaps one of Littlefinger's observations from the book version could provide the best moral for this scene, "Life is not a song" (Martin 2017, p. 624) as he had previously warned Sansa. The stories of the chivalric knights and king do not match reality.

The cynicism of *Game of Thrones* also extends to its interpretation of religion. In the story, the supernatural is presented as real, since the old gods, the Faceless Men's God of Death, and the Red God all seem to possess some degree of genuine supernatural power. Nevertheless, the show is quite critical of many aspects of religion. First, we should notice that Westeros's Church of the Seven is a viciously political organization. We see the church meddle in politics, provide an apologetic for Joffrey breaking his betrothal to Sansa, seek power to impose its morality by force, and many other unhealthy, undemocratic things. We see that multiple religions go so far as to engage in human sacrifice. As Tyrion asks, "The Lord of Light wants his enemies burned, the Drowned God wants them drowned. Why are all the gods such vicious cunts? Where is the God of tits and wine?" ("The Prince of Winterfell," S2E8). The religions of Westeros traffic in violence, murder, and even human sacrifice.

Despite the fact that the Lord of Light appears to be *Game of Thrones*'s most direct opponent of the Night King's invasion of monsters, and is even infused with a supernatural power that allows the resurrection of Jon Snow and Beric Dondarrion, the religion's praiseworthy traits are difficult to appreciate when seen alongside its violent, homicidal tendencies. Whether it is the kidnapping of Gendry, the burning of Mance Rayder, or the horrifying sacrifice of Stannis's own daughter Shireen, it is easy to see that there is a disturbingly violent pattern within this religion. Once the Lord of Light's earthly agenda of defeating the Night King is accomplished, he suddenly withdraws from meaningful earthly involvement and leaves his remaining followers unfulfilled and confused.

Voices of Cynicism: Littlefinger and Varys

Another illustration of *Game of Thrones*'s political cynicism can be found in the cynical nature of some of the most influential characters in the series. One of the first cynics we are introduced to is Petyr Baelish, a.k.a. Littlefinger. We see this cynicism as he is "helping" Ned Stark disprove Joffrey's claim to the Iron Throne, saying "When the queen proclaims one King and the King's Hand proclaims another, whose peace do the Gold Cloaks protect? Who do they follow? The man who pays them" ("You Win or You Die," S1E7).

To him, gold, information, and use of force are more important than theories of political legitimacy. Power is all that is important, legitimacy is not.

A cynic like Baelish doubts the motives of every person they meet, Littlefinger's advice to Sansa to "fight every battle everywhere, always, in your mind" ("The Queen's Justice," S7E3) and imagine the "worst possible reason [someone] could have" ("The Queen's Justice," S7E3) is the essence of cynicism. Similarly, during one of their first encounters in the book version of *Game of Thrones*, Littlefinger asks Eddard whether he has anyone he absolutely trusts. When Eddard says that he does, Littlefinger cynically insists that the wiser answer was "no" (Martin 2017, p. 216).

Littlefinger demonstrates that people with power can't be trusted. Although he is untrained in any form of combat, he is one of the most dangerous and powerful people in the realm. He specializes in duplicitousness and manipulation, the subtle use of information, painting himself as a benefactor and friend. He uses all these tools to carry out his own hidden agenda. Martin himself has even said, "Everybody trusts him because he seems powerless, and he's very friendly, and he's very helpful" (Jackson 2013).

Consider his influence upon Sansa Stark. During her captivity in King's Landing, Sansa comes to trust Littlefinger as one of the few allies she has nearby. She continues to trust Littlefinger even after he starts to reveal his true nature to Sansa piece by piece. She continues to trust him because he is so helpful. After all, he helped her escape her abusive captivity in King's Landing, even if he murdered Ser Dontos and framed Tyrion in the process. Even after he betrays her by marrying her to the Boltons, she returns to his side after the Battle of the Bastards as he was critically helpful once again. Ultimately, she rejects him romantically and prudently stops trusting him; but it is only when he attempts to turn her against her sister Arya that she has him executed. Essentially, Sansa was following Littlefinger's own advice to *not trust anyone*.

Lord Varys is an interesting contrast to Littlefinger, since he possesses a similar cynical philosophy towards power but applies it towards a much different end. Like Littlefinger, Varys doesn't believe in political legitimacy. Like Littlefinger, Varys climbed the ladder by making himself useful to others, while gathering and subtly using information. Yet, he subtly and ruthlessly uses his network of spies and information, not for himself or to benefit some political family, but to aid the commoners above all else. Ultimately, Varys doesn't care which leader is legitimate or even honorable, but instead desires leaders and policies that will be best for the kingdom above all else.

At times, Varys's agenda can be difficult to discern. When Robert ordered Daenerys assassinated, Varys set the plan in motion despite his own Targaryen preferences. He even testified against his close friend Tyrion when he was falsely accused of poisoning Joffrey. On the one hand, Varys's motives seem quite explicit when he tells Ned Stark in the black cells, "I want you to serve the realm!" ("Baelor," S1E9). On the other hand, Varys refused to help free Ned from his imprisonment despite his knowledge that Ned was both innocent and honorable. Still, Varys maintains that the good of the small folk and "the realm" is unimportant to those focused on gaining power, and he is the only powerful person in the kingdom who cares for the realm itself enough that he is willing to die for it – like when he is willing to poison Daenerys for the sake of the realm despite knowing he would face execution.

Varys follows the same sort of reasoning as Jorah Mormont when he says, "The common folk pray for rain, health, and a summer that never ends. They don't care what games the high lords play" ("Cripples, Bastards, and Broken Things," S1E4). Like the common folk, he doesn't care about political legitimacy or which specific family controls the throne; he just wants a competent leader that will provide a good, stable civilization for the general populace.

Through cynical characters like Littlefinger and Varys, as well as some cynical moments from Tyrion and others, we see that Westeros is hardly an idyllic paradise. These cynical characters are gifted at climbing the "ladder of chaos" to strengthen their position and advance their agendas during times of turmoil, while those who cling to the norms of the realm and the status quo are held back from advancing. Similarly, even many of the characters who adhere to the status quo do not do so out of some sort of idealism, but merely because they benefit from it.

The cynicism of these characters reflects important aspects of our own reality. We often see people act in their own interests, sometimes with far-reaching and catastrophic consequences. As such, we cannot trust everyone's purported good intentions towards ourselves. And even someone who seeks the greater good, like Varys, might be willing to sacrifice us along the way – as he sacrificed Ned Stark.

An Alternative to *Game of Thrones'* Cynicism: John Locke's Natural Law

Despite the cynicism displayed throughout *Game of Thrones*, some of this cynicism seems unwarranted. After all, there are other plausible political views that the series simply never considers, such as anything analogous to a contemporary democracy or republican approach to government. While the Wildlings are a free society with an elected leader, a system like theirs is not truly like a contemporary democracy or republic. At best, it is a depiction of an anarchy with the most minimal democratic structures. Similarly, other pseudo-democratic structures in *Game of Thrones*, like the election involved in the Iron Island's Kingsmoot, are hardly analogous to the typical democratic and republican structures that are popular in the contemporary Western world. Sam Tarly does mention the idea of democracy in the final episode, but it is treated like a joke by the remaining royal characters. Such a rejection is hardly evidence against that approach to politics.

Given the show's cynical take on political reality, it is worth examining other potential strategies for legitimizing civilized society that aren't really considered by George Martin's universe. One obvious place to start is John Locke's social contract theory based upon reasoning about human life in pre-civilized nature. According to this theory, following the strategy of Thomas Hobbes, we should start our reasoning about politics by considering what type of existence humans would have in a pre-civilized, pre-political era – a state of nature.

Locke claims,

> To understand political power correctly and derive it from its proper source, we must consider what state all men are naturally in. In this state men are perfectly free to order their actions, and dispose of their possessions and themselves, in any way they like, without asking anyone's permission—subject only to limits set by the law of nature. It is also a state of equality, in which no-one has more power and authority than anyone else[.] (Locke 1764)

Rather than a genuine example of democracy, the near anarchic situation north of The Wall is actually closer to Locke's "state of nature." The great advantages of the state of nature are its innate liberty and political equality. Yet, the instability of life, the lack of cooperative social structures, and the uncertainty of being able to benefit from long-term efforts undermines its many goods. Significant technology is not developed, cooperative efforts are few and far between, and what little that gets developed in the north looks more like subsistence farming and shelter. The anarchic state of the wildlings shows that the situation could be greatly improved by the creation of a well-run political state.

Even in an anarchic pre-civilized state, Locke claims there is still genuine right and wrong found in natural law. His view corresponds to our contemporary sensibilities that liberty is a great good and that the kind of liberty found in nature is a good thing. Yet, there are some serious shortcomings in the state of nature where a civilized political state might provide structure and benefit everyone. We see this throughout *Game of Thrones's* discussions of the Wildlings. We have seen that the danger of living among the Wildlings is that there are no widely understood and accepted rules for conduct, no one to enforce even the most basic moral principles such as non-violence, and no one to settle the inevitable disputes between people. As a result, force used in the service of self-interest is a common mode of conflict resolution among the Wildlings, and the result is usually devastating.

According to Locke, even in nature there are certain foundational rights that every human possesses since the natural state of things demonstrates that persons possess these rights. Most importantly, every person has the right to ownership of their own body, their own existence within that body, and the natural right to liberties to use their body however they wish so long as it does not interfere with the natural liberties of others. Furthermore, and derivatively, the right to property is a logical upshot of the right to one's self since justly owned property is merely the result of one's use of the body to obtain things within nature or to develop things from natural resources. As Locke claims,

> . . .every individual man has a property in his own person; this is something that nobody else has any right to. The labour of his body and the work of his hands, we may say, are strictly his. So when he takes something from the state that nature has provided and left it in, he mixes his labour with it, thus joining to it something that is his own; and in that way he makes it his property. (Locke 1764)

So, if a person uses the natural liberty of their body to gather acorns for food or wood to build a shelter, those objects become their property. It would be a violation of natural property rights to deprive someone of such property. Unfortunately, theft is a common danger in the state of nature. For example, we see deserters from Night Watch kill Craster and steal his home and possessions. In a well-run civilized political state, everyone in general would be better off – including Craster – since civilization would be providing the critical structures missing in the state of nature. For Locke, there are three: first, a legislature to clarify the expectations of natural law by clearly announced enumerated laws against violence and theft; second, civilization should provide a reliable executive enforcer of the law to encourage obedience to law; and finally, civilization should provide objective, impartial judges to settle disputes between individuals concerning the law. In the state of nature – like the wilding north – there are often ambiguities concerning proper moral expectations since there is no officially declared law. Since there is no one to settle disputes between two biased competing individuals and no reliable enforcer of the law, justice is often sacrificed to personal bias and preference. Therefore, the benefits of society might be important enough to justify sacrificing some natural liberties.

Still, the sort of political state justified by the benefits of civilization does not justify giving political leaders an unlimited amount of power, like we see in the kingdoms in Westeros. While a major rival to John Locke – Thomas Hobbes – thought that the state of nature was so horrifyingly bad that any kind of civilized existence at all would be preferable, Locke disagreed. He thought that a state needed to be at least moderately just to be a genuine improvement over the state of nature. Yet, not just any "civilized" state was better than the pre-civilized natural state. While the Wildlings in general are worse off than civilized states, there are several situations where civilization is more trouble than its worth. If empowering a monarchy results in a tyrant who would be willing to burn down whole cities, as both the mad tyrant and Daenerys were willing to do, then the political structures of civilization risk making us worse off than the state of nature. In such cases, the people have the right to take back their natural liberties through revolution. Thus, Locke might have agreed with Jaime Lannister's and Jon Snow's choice to kill these crazed monarchs rather than allow their ongoing indiscriminate violence. Of course, there are other situations that would make civilized existence so bad that the state of nature would be preferable and therefore justify revolution. If kings insist on entering cycles of countless wars that lead to ongoing widespread violence and death, this situation too might justify revolution.

So, while *Game of Thrones* teaches political cynicism, it fails to engage this important view of civilized society based on a social contract guaranteeing the protection of natural rights. There are several advantages of Locke's view. It justifies the existence of political power based on the general benefits of civilization, it provides guidelines concerning the minimal responsibilities of the state, and it provides a basis for justifying the removal of problematic political leadership under proper conditions. So, a state with a good or even an adequate sovereign could be justified since the typical citizen's lot is improved under their rule, but a pyromaniacal tyrant like Aerys II would not.

Another Alternative to Cynicism: Thomas Aquinas's Account of Law

Another view of political legitimacy that *Game of Thrones* never really considers comes from Thomas Aquinas. He created a four-part test to weigh whether any particular political edict possesses genuine legitimacy. In the *Summa Theologicae*, Aquinas claims that law is "... an ordinance of reason for the common good, made by him who has care of the community, and promulgated" (Aquinas 1920, I-II.90.4). In order to have genuine legitimacy, a law must fulfill each of these four conditions.

First, any genuine law must be based in a generalizable principle of rationality. Law must be formed out of *logos* as an impartial universalizable principle applicable to all in a jurisdiction. It must not be grounded in capriciousness, unstable principles, or mere whims of a ruler. For example, we saw that part of what made Joffrey a terrible leader was that his pronouncements were based in his own egoistic and mercurial temperament. Thus, his decisions were unpredictable, erratic, irrational, and short-sighted.

Second, the law must tend towards promoting the overall common good of society in general. So, laws must avoid the kind of bias, classism, and preferential treatment that leads to unequal favoritism towards leaders, the royal family, the upper class, and the like unless there is some broader way this policy promotes the common good. For example, it probably promotes the common good to pass laws that help attract the hardest workers and best minds to certain elite jobs in science, medicine, and the like by compensating them with higher payment than other jobs. However, the sort of premodern laws that bias systems to favor royal families merely because they happen to have political power do not seem to pass this test.

Third, the law must be created by the recognized caretaker of the political community. Notably, Aquinas's principle is agnostic towards the proper form of political structure. This criterion can be satisfied by either a benevolent monarchy or an elected government, therefore his system can pragmatically avoid some of the legitimacy concerns that dominates so much of Westeros's politics. Since *Game of Thrones* begins a few decades after the establishment of the Baratheon rule, and it replaced an abusive Targaryen rule, it is plausible that Robert's government could pass this test. To the average person, Robert simply was now the King of Westeros, although there were large minorities that might think otherwise. That being said, the proper application of Aquinas principle isn't always completely clear, and this particular situation is designed to have enough ambiguity to bring Robert's legitimacy as caretaker of the community into question.

Finally, the law must be properly promulgated, which is to say that any binding law must be properly announced, posted, and spread. This principle entails that there is no such thing as secret or private law. The law is public, a widely known fact. Otherwise, it could not be morally binding since we could not expect people to adhere to laws they did not know about. For example, the Mad King Aerys II violates this principle when he responds to Rickard Stark's demand for a trial by combat by naming "fire" as his own champion and designing a torturous ordeal with fire for Rickard and Brandon Stark rather than an actual duel. This mockery of the law is not how a legitimate duel works.

In accordance with these principles, a genuine law with binding authority must fulfill all four conditions. Therefore, the laws of a tyrant are no laws at all (Aquinas 1920, I-II.96.4). If Joffrey or Cersei issue commands to those around them for their own self-interest, those commands are not law, even if Joffrey or Cersei were the legitimate caretakers of the community. Their rules must not be arbitrary, self-interested, or kept secret if they are to be binding.

Conclusion

The epic *Game of Thrones* television series teaches a thoroughly cynical view of politics and other social structures like those found in chivalry, medieval class structure, and religion. We see this cynicism expressed in several ways: the dubious legitimacy of the most prominent candidates for monarch over Westeros Robert Baratheon and Daenerys Targaryen, the negative depiction of the anachro-democracy of the Wildings, the show's negative critique of prominent social structures like chivalric knights and the Church of the Seven, and through the disproportionate influence of prominent characters with cynical views such as Varys, Littlefinger, and even Tyrion Lannister. Yet, there are important views that the show fails to consider that might allow us to hope that a legitimate political state might still be possible, such as the views of John Locke and Thomas Aquinas.

References

Aquinas, Thomas. 1920. *Summa Theologicae*. Translated by the Fathers of the English Dominican Province. Accessed 4 February 2021 at www.newadvent.org/summa/

Jackson, Matthew. 2013. Which thrones character changed most from book to TV? GRRM explains. *SyFy Wire*. Accessed 4 Feb 2021 at https://www.syfy.com/syfywire/which-thrones-character-changed-most-book-tv-grrm-explains

Locke, John. 1764. Two Treatises on Civil Government. In *Classics of liberty: The enhanced editions*. London: A. Miller et al.. https://oll.libertyfund.org/page/john-locke-two-treatises-1689.

Martin, George R.R. 2017. *Game of Thrones*. New York: Random House Publishing.

The Mandalorian as Philosophy: "This Is the Way"

25

Lance Belluomini

Contents

Introduction	556
Summarizing *The Mandalorian*	557
Mando's Conscience: "How Uncharacteristic of One of Your Reputation"	559
"There Is Only One Way": What Does It Mean to Be a Mandalorian?	561
"My Armor Has Lost Its Integrity"	561
The Mandalorian Mantra	563
The Stoic Way and the Mandalorian Way	563
"Aren't You a Man of Honor?"	565
The Mandalorian's Argument for Leading a Virtuous Life: "This Is the Way"	567
Mando's Virtues: "That's Very Thoughtful of You"	569
Mando's Stoic Virtues: "Your Bravery Will Not Be Forgotten"	569
Virtue Ethics and Personal Motives	572
The Mandalorian's Argument That Care Is the Primary Virtue	574
Caring Instincts in a Galaxy Far, Far Away	574
Care Ethics, Genuine Caring, and Empathy	575
On Why Care Is a Primary Virtue	577
Conclusion: What Should Be Our Way?	578
References	579

Abstract

The Mandalorian is Disney's finest *Star Wars* property because it's the first one that hasn't divided the fan base. But why? Because everyone agrees on one thing: the show is fantastic. In the first two seasons, the TV series follows Mando's adventures in his quest to protect and reunite Grogu (aka "Baby Yoda") with his kind. While the strong father-son relationship between the iconic duo is clearly the emotional heart of the series thus far, at its core, the show delivers philosophical messages and arguments. One of the central themes of the show has been to explore what it means to be a Mandalorian. For Mando, he discovers that there

---

L. Belluomini (✉)
Independent Scholar, San Francisco Bay Area, CA, USA

© Springer Nature Switzerland AG 2024
D. K. Johnson et al. (eds.), *The Palgrave Handbook of Popular Culture as Philosophy*,
https://doi.org/10.1007/978-3-031-24685-2_104

555

isn't only one way to be a Mandalorian, and thus, a good person. Ultimately, the show argues that we should lead a virtuous life (like Mando) which involves developing good character traits. But the show also argues that care is the most important and primary virtue – that *caring for others* plays a significant role in our ethical decision-making and in achieving happiness. But are the show's arguments philosophically defensible? In this chapter, an examination of the show itself, as well as a discussion of Stoicism, virtue ethics, and the ethics of care, will not only reveal the arguments are sound and compelling, but also why it's a good idea for us to put the virtues into practice in our own lives.

Keywords

The Mandalorian · *Star Wars* · Jon Favreau · Mando · Grogu · Moff Gideon · Virtue ethics · Michael Stocker · Stoicism · Stoic virtues · Aristotle · Plato · Socrates · Virtue of care · Discipline of desire · Eudaimonia · Flourishing · Nel Noddings · Michael Slote · Ethics of care · Canons of honor · Cardinal virtues · The Way of the Mandalore · This is the Way

---

Introduction

> Wherever I go, he goes.
> —Mando

For over 40 years the *Star Wars* universe that George Lucas created felt like a massive sandbox to play in, but we'd only seen a relatively small corner of his galaxy far, far away. *Star Wars* is one of the top movie franchises of all time and it continues to endure in our pop culture from one generation to the next. Even after the originals, prequels, sequels and spin-off standalone films, we're still captivated and obsessed by the Skywalker saga – its characters like Luke, Leia, Vader, the Emperor, and the fight between good and evil represented by the Rebellion and the Empire. There have been popular animated TV shows like *Star Wars: The Clone Wars* and *Star Wars Rebels* as well as video games, such as *Knights of the Old Republic*, that have all explored other events and characters in this galaxy.

But the most successful *Star Wars* property outside of the theatrical films is *The Mandalorian*, which debuted in November 2019. Created by Jon Favreau for the "Disney+" streaming service, it's the first live-action TV series in the *Star Wars* franchise. While *Star Wars* fans love to argue about most things *Star Wars* (such as the prequels versus the originals), there is one thing that *Star Wars* fans agree on: *The Mandalorian*. It's a show that has rejuvenated the beloved franchise and even attracted a large non-*Star Wars* fan following, a show that is free from the Skywalker family story arc and instead shows us a new set of adventures told from different perspectives yet without the expectations of the episodic *Star Wars* films. Plus, the show features adorable Grogu (Baby Yoda) who steals many of the scenes.

As compelling (and cute) as Grogu is, *The Mandalorian* succeeds because of the things it lacks. Again, there is no Skywalker storyline, no emphasis on the Jedi or

Sith, no opening iconic line "A long time ago in a galaxy, far, far away," no opening crawl, and no John Williams score. That's not to say the show doesn't honor and give subtle nostalgic nods to a variety of familiar elements in the Skywalker saga. Favreau and the other creatives behind the show make sure it does. But *The Mandalorian* has its own flair and tone. It's a gripping and gritty space western story that is instead centered on an unexpected character living in the shadows, a Mandalorian bounty hunter named "Mando," who's trying to find his way and purpose in the galaxy. And we get to witness his amazing journey and self-development, all of which is emotionally elevated and driven by the inspiring musical compositions of Ludwig Göransson. In fact, it's impossible to think about *The Mandalorian* without his iconic scores, especially the distinct main theme with its opening melancholy howl played by a bass recorder.

The Mandalorian also continues to garner recognition. As of early 2021, the show has won 23 entertainment awards with 31 nominations. In 2020, it won seven Primetime Emmy Awards. The show was also a 2021 Golden Globe nominee for Best Television Series Drama and was nominated for Best Drama Series from the Writers Guild of America. What's more, when Disney released *The Mandalorian* as the flagship series for Disney+, not only did the show succeed; it was largely responsible for the over 10 million subscribers the streaming service received on the day of its launch as well as for the 95 million subscribers in its first 12 months.

But beyond all the award recognition, the critical acclaim, Disney's success, and a *Star Wars* property that fans adore, another reason why the show continues to resonate with people is because of its philosophical significance. *The Mandalorian* raises fascinating philosophical questions: What does it mean to be a Mandalorian? Is there more than just one way to be a Mandalorian? Is there more than one way to be a good person? And more importantly, what makes someone a good person? The show chronicles Mando's moral transformation and development after encountering Grogu. He transitions from someone who's morally apathetic to someone with a conscience who starts to show moral integrity, virtuous behavior, and a natural desire to care. Further, his beliefs and goals change, and he develops as a human being. He begins to realize there's more to life than just following a set of rules – his tribe's ancient Way. In his quest to protect and safely deliver Grogu to his kind, Mando displays the Stoic virtues, discovers his caregiving nature, and thus exercises the virtue of care in his moral actions and decision-making. In effect, *The Mandalorian* makes an argument for leading a virtuous life and developing one's moral character. But it also argues that we embrace our natural impulse to care for others in our ethical actions and moral reasoning. As we'll see, the virtue of care is a constant theme in the series. But before examining the messages and arguments, we need to first reacquaint ourselves with the basic plot of the show.

Summarizing *The Mandalorian*

The first season of *The Mandalorian* tells the story of Mando who we later learn is named Din Djarin. The show takes place 5 years after the events of *Return of the Jedi* and 25 years before the rise of the First Order in *The Force Awakens*. Structurally, the series is divided into chapters (8 per season), with each featuring a unique mission where, in order for Mando to achieve his goals, he must team up with others. Aesthetically, the show is inspired by Akira Kurosawa's 1961 samurai film *Yojimbo* and Sergio Leone's 1964 Western film *A Fistful of Dollars*. In fact, Mando's mannerisms are based on the iconic characters of those films – a Samurai sword-wielder and a gunslinger. From the very start, *The Mandalorian* (like the original *Star Wars* film in 1977) leans heavily into both the samurai aesthetic and Western genre with close-up shots of Mando juxtaposed with stunning vistas.

The samurai and Western influences are most clear in the first chapter's climax when Mando tracks down his asset for the "off the books" bounty job he's accepted from a remnant Imperial named the Client. Mando's tracking device points him towards a floating crib tucked away in a desert encampment. Inside, he discovers the asset is actually an adorable child (who he eventually learns is named Grogu and is a member of Yoda's species). While the bounty hunting droid IG-11 (who has helped Mando defeat the mercenaries and infiltrate the encampment) is willing to murder the child in the crib, Mando is not. He dispatches IG-11, leaving him alone with the child. Memorably, the first chapter closes with an image of Mando staring down at the child he has been assigned to track down. It's an important moment and the true starting point of the series. Everything up to this point is introductory, building to this reveal.

The remainder of Season One follows Mando on his journey to protect Grogu from the clutches of the Imperials and other pursuing bounty hunters. Along the journey, Mando faces death countless times yet always perseveres. He does so partly because of the friendships formed along the way. He meets a kind Ugnaught named Kuiil and a former shock trooper for the Rebellion named Cara Dune. He also encounters IG-11 again (who Kuiil has reprogrammed for nursing). They not only help in bringing success to Mando's missions, but also protect and care for him and Grogu. Additionally, Mando gets help from Grogu. In one instance, when Mando thinks he is about to die from a charging Mudhorn beast, Grogu saves him by using the Force to lift the beast. Help is also given by his fellow Mandalorians who fly in to save the day, allowing Mando to escape with Grogu when he is pursued by bounty hunters. Near the end of Season One, the leader of the Bounty Hunters' Guild, Greef Karga, calls off the hunt for the child as he comes to respect Mando and Grogu. He teams up with Mando, Grogu, Cara, Kuiil, and IG-11 in the final chapter and together they fight against the villain of the show, Moff Gideon, an Imperial warlord who wants Grogu because of Grogu's connection to the Force. In the final moments, we're given some Mandalorian mythology when Gideon emerges from his downed TIE holding the Darksaber. This reveal signifies hope and redemption for the Mandalorian people. The villain of the show has the blade that symbolizes their unity. And it raises the question: Will Mando take the Darksaber and help the Mandalorian people regain their honor and defend themselves?

The second season is about Mando's quest to reunite Grogu with the Jedi – something the armorer of his tribe instructs him to do at the end of Season One. Mando faces different obstacles in achieving this new goal, the biggest one being Moff Gideon who is in pursuit of Grogu. At the start of the season, Mando is searching for other Mandalorians that can help in his quest. Fortunately, his adventures lead him to a Mandalorian covert led by Bo-Katan Kryze (a former leader of Mandalore). Bo-Katan agrees to help him if he reciprocates by assaulting an Imperial freighter full of weapons that she wants in her goal of retaking Mandalore. After they succeed, Bo-Katan tells Mando where he can find Jedi Ahsoka Tano. However, after he meets Ahsoka, she refuses to accept or train Grogu because of his attachment to Mando, her reasoning being that attachments can bring down even the best Jedi. But Ahsoka gives Mando hope by instructing him to bring Grogu to the seeing stone on the planet Tython where other Jedi may come for Grogu if they sense him through the Force. When they arrive on Tython, Gideon's dark troopers arrive and snatch Grogu. With the help of Cara Dune and others, Mando finds the coordinates to Gideon's cruiser where Grogu is being held prisoner. In the end, Mando recruits Bo-Katan and together his team faces off with Gideon and his dark troopers. Eventually, Mando is reunited with Grogu, he defeats Gideon in a duel, and takes the Darksaber from him. Finally, when dark troopers threaten Mando's team, Luke Skywalker comes to the rescue and destroys them. In an emotional farewell, Mando assures Grogu that they'll see each other again and he removes his helmet, showing his face to Grogu for the first time. Then Luke walks away holding Grogu while Mando watches in tears, an emotional moment that perfectly closes out the season.

Mando's Conscience: "How Uncharacteristic of One of Your Reputation"

Mando is first introduced as a self-interested bounty hunter that looks out for his own welfare and adheres to the ancient Way of his Mandalorian tribe – a cult known as "The Children of the Watch" that was forced into hiding on Nevarro after the Empire's Great Purge against the Mandalorians. Mando takes a pragmatic approach to everything. Regarded as the best in the parsec, his primary focus is finding his bounties. Through the use of his fancy weapons and shiny impenetrable beskar armor (that is resistant to even lightsaber blades), he takes the necessary violent actions to complete his jobs and obtain the credits needed to survive.

His bounty capture at the start of Chapter 1 is a case in point. Mando gives the Mythrol fugitive a choice, "I can either bring you in warm or I can bring you in cold." Because the Mythrol seeks to flee once aboard Mando's ship, Mando decides to freeze him in carbonite. In effect, he does what he must to survive, to get his next paycheck, and uphold his reputation. He certainly lives up to what assassin Fennec Shand says to a young bounty hunter named Toro Calican in Chapter 5, "You want to be a bounty hunter? Make the best deal for yourself and survive."

We can all relate with Mando's struggle to survive in the Outer Rim. After all, the struggle to survive is a recurring theme in the *Star Wars* universe. Unlike the Skywalker saga, which involved Light Side and Dark Side characters and a clear delineation between right and wrong, *The Mandalorian* explores the morally gray part of the *Star Wars* universe where mercenaries, bounty hunters, and Imperial remnant warlords like Moff Gideon abound. And this is what makes

The Mandalorian brilliant. It explores the gaps where most people in the *Star Wars* galaxy actually reside, something we've never seen before. Rather than making the title character a hero of the Rebellion like Luke Skywalker or Jyn Erso from *Rogue One*, *The Mandalorian* centers on a nonessential man living in the shadows who is leading a morally gray life, a character that appears apathetic to everything aside from his own survival and his goal of proving himself as a true Mandalorian.

The show makes it clear that it's easy to be tempted into morally gray areas – that it doesn't take much to slip further into moral apathy, even to the depths of scum and villainy (which Mando observes in others along his adventures). But the show also expresses that no one is nonessential. In our own world, many ordinary people tend to adopt a futile attitude towards life – that we can't impact things in the world because of our nonessential status. But one of the messages of the show is that we all matter. Every person is important, no matter our birth or status. Furthermore, our actions and choices do make an impact on the world.

The show lets us know that Mando matters. And what snaps him out of his moral apathy is Grogu. In fact, Grogu is the catalyst that changes Mando's moral character. He begins to show moral integrity and furthers his preexisting Mandalorian strength of character all because a child, who he knows nothing about, awakens his caring, protective, and virtuous instincts. In Chapter 3, when Mando turns Grogu over to the Imperials and Mando's helmet follows the floating cradle being taken to another room, he uncharacteristically shows concern by asking the Client, "What are your plans for it?" Soon after, he asks Greef, "Any idea what they're going to do with it?" This is the turning point for Mando as he transforms from a heartless bounty hunter to someone with a conscience because he feels the need to save the life of the child that saved him. And then he gets that final reminder of Grogu which cements his turn – the ball knob to his ship's lever that Grogu wanted to play with. But he doesn't have this change of heart just because Grogu saved his life from the mudhorn. It's driven mostly by his care for Grogu and a conviction that it isn't right to turn this innocent Child over to these Imperials; doing so would be unjust and surely lead to Grogu's death, a sin Mando can't live with.

The end of Chapter 3 marks a pivotal shift for Mando because, for the first time in his life, he's willing to sacrifice and betray his own life to save another life: Grogu's. Notice that his sacrificial actions transcend his personal well-being and his tribe's Way. He places Grogu's life ahead of his own and exercises the virtue of care out of his innate sense of *caring for others*, something that his Mandalorian tribe also exhibits when they come to his aid (via their jetpacks).

We also see how the saving of one life in Chapter 3 has a compounding effect on Mando where his caring ways extend to having caring relationships with other characters (like Kuiil, Cara, Greef, and reprogrammed IG-11) and to saving an entire farming community in Chapter 4 on Sorgan. But his new moral outlook gets tested throughout both seasons. For instance, in Chapter 5, Mando steps back into morally gray territory when he goes after Fennic Shand to earn credits to repair his ship. But he suffers from Toro's betrayal and nearly loses Grogu. Mando perseveres and shows resilience after any obstacle or threat, though, and gradually he exhibits good character traits along his adventurous journey. However, in Season One, his conception of what it means to be a Mandalorian and a good person is still grounded in his tribe's Way and by the beskar armor he wears. It's not until Season Two, after he sees Bo-Katan remove her helmet, that he begins to internally question his tribe's Way, and whether there are better ways of being a Mandalorian, better ways of leading a good life.

Despite his apathetic feelings towards others prior to meeting Grogu, as well as the violent actions he takes during his bounty hunting missions, Mando still displays many virtues in his everyday life. He does so thanks to his tribe which rescued and raised him. In addition to instructing him on adhering to their tribe's Way, they also instilled in him certain Mandalorian tenets on how to behave in everyday living. This is evident in his interaction with others he respects where he often shows courage, trustworthiness, gratitude, justice, and loyalty. But before discussing Mando's virtuous ways, an exploration on what defines Mando, his motivations and values, the Way of his tribe that he follows, and his search for worth among his own Mandalorian culture, is in order. Doing so will help us in understanding both Mando's moral development and the identity shift he undergoes by the end of Season Two.

"There Is Only One Way": What Does It Mean to Be a Mandalorian?

One of the central themes in the show thus far, and one that will likely continue in future seasons, involves the following question: What does it mean to be a Mandalorian? Throughout most of the series, Mando thinks that in order for him to be a Mandalorian, he must wear his beskar armor and helmet (never showing others his face) and follow his tribe's Way – its rules and creed. But does he?

"My Armor Has Lost Its Integrity"

Let's first consider Mando's beskar armor. From the start of the show, it's clear that Mando initially defines himself by the armor he wears. For him, this is part of what it means to be a Mandalorian. The first few chapters highlight what matters to Mando. In Chapter 1, after he shoots IG-11 and reaches out to touch Grogu (in a very *E.T.*-esque moment), Mando is faced with a dilemma. He needs to choose what's more important to him: obtaining the beskar reward so he can acquire new armor or choosing to protect this innocent child. While Mando ultimately decides to do the right thing in protecting Grogu, he still values his armor for protection. After he receives his down payment of beskar, Mando takes it to his tribe's armorer and spends all his credits to melt down the beskar so he can get himself a shiny new piece of armor – a pauldron. Despite needing credits for things like ship repairs and living expenses, the armor is more valuable to him.

The show further emphasizes how vital the beskar armor is to Mando. When he reluctantly turns Grogu over to the Imperials to get the beskar reward, the Client says to him, "That beskar is enough to make a handsome replacement for your armor." Mando then takes the reward to his armorer and lets her know, "My armor has lost its integrity. I may need to begin again." The armorer then reinforces the importance of the beskar to Mando, "This was gathered in the Great Purge. It is good it is back with the tribe." From this, we can infer that the Mandalorians have fallen on hard times. During the genocidal Great Purge event against the Mandalorians, the Empire not only forced the surviving Mandalorians to live in secrecy, thus stripping them of their honor and status, but they also gathered the beskar from fallen Mandalorian warriors and melted it down into Imperial currency. The armorer references the Great Purge to Mando to remind him how important the beskar is to their identity and culture. The Client also reinforces this to Mando, indirectly referencing the Great Purge, when he says, "The beskar belongs back into the hands of a Mandalorian. It's good to restore the natural order of things after a period of such disarray." This hits home for Mando as he's been taught to think, up to this point, how precious this beskar is to his culture and its significant role in what it means to be a Mandalorian. Yes, he wears the armor for protection and survival, but it's been ingrained into his mind that wearing the helmet and armor is part of a creed he must follow – a way of life.

During his encounters with the armorer, we learn that Mando was once a Foundling (a child taken in by Mandalorians, trained in their ways, and adopted into their culture). He mentions to her, "I was once a Foundling," which explains to us why he doesn't yet have a signet or clan and why he's determined to show others that he's a true Mandalorian. The reveal that he's a Foundling gets visualized through a series of childhood flashbacks while the armorer forges him a new set of armor. In Chapter 8, after Gideon reveals that Mando's true name is Din Djarin, we get to see Mando's full childhood flashback during the Clone Wars where his family is killed by Separatist battle droids and he's saved by Mandalorian forces – which nicely mirrors Mando (a Mandalorian) saving Grogu (a Foundling) from the mercenaries. Of course, the Mandalorians rescuing him had a dramatic effect on Mando and shaped who he is. Like forging beskar into armor, his Mandalorian tribe forges Mando into the person he is now – one who's committed to always wearing his beskar armor and helmet, a rule of his tribe.

Additionally, because Mando is a Foundling and thus not a natural born Mandalorian, it's obvious that he considers himself an outsider, continually feeling the need to prove that he's worthy of being called a Mandalorian. That's why his new shiny armor is worth spending all his credits. It's also why he never removes his helmet. The beskar armor connects him with an identity that he hasn't internally accepted for himself. And this directly speaks to another ongoing message of *The Mandalorian*: where we come from isn't as important as who we are. While the show will likely continue to explore this theme, throughout the first ten chapters of the show, this thought hasn't yet crossed Mando's mind as he's still driven by the way of life dictated by his tribe.

The Mandalorian Mantra

Many viewers of the show have wondered: Why do the Mandalorians say, "This is the Way?" It's the most memorable and repeated line of the show but we aren't given the exact meaning or history of the catchphrase. However, reflecting on the context when the phrase is mentioned makes it clear on why it matters to the Mandalorian people.

The first time we hear this catchy line is when Mando visits the armorer to get his flashy new set of armor. She asks Mando, "Have you ever removed your helmet? Has it ever been removed by others?" After Mando answers "No" to both questions, she says, "This is the Way," and then the phrase is echoed by the other Mandalorians in the room. Soon after, Mando instructs the armorer to reserve some of his beskar reward for the Foundlings in their tribe. She replies, "As it should always be. The Foundlings are the future. This is the Way," and then the others in the room including Mando echo the phrase. Yet another unforgettable instance appears at the end of Season One when Mando suffers a head injury, instructing Cara to leave him and escape. He says to Cara, "Let me have a warrior's death. This is the Way." Later, we hear the phrase repeated again by the armorer after she says to Mando, "A Foundling is in your care. By creed, until it is of age or reunited with its own kind, you are as its father."

Certainly, this isn't the first time we've heard a shared mantra in the *Star Wars* universe. There's the iconic "May the Force be with you" that was first introduced in the original trilogy of films. In *Rogue One*, Chirrut Îmwe repeats his personal mantra, "I am one with the Force and the Force is with me." And in *The Mandalorian*, Kuiil ends his statements with his own memorable yet inscrutable mantra, "I have spoken." Given this context, we can see that "This is the Way" is more than a catchphrase: it's a revelation of a particular perspective on life. For Mando, he upholds his tribe's mantra throughout most of the series and memorably expresses it to Bo-Katan in Chapter 11, "There is only one Way! The Way of the Mandalore." Indeed, asserting this mantra and defending his tribe's particular Way is a critical component of what it means to be a Mandalorian for him.

Judging by the context of the above scenes, it's clear the phrase is a Mandalorian mantra that all Mandalorians have taken an oath to assert. And while it seems to refer to certain "rules" that Mandalorians must follow – like "never show your face" and "provide for the Foundlings" – these examples also suggest that the statement refers to the notion of embracing their fate – that *this is the way* certain events were supposed to, or fated, to happen – as in, "I am fated to have a warrior's death."

The Stoic Way and the Mandalorian Way

Because Mando operates within the principles of his tribe's Way, it means he strictly adheres to his code regardless of any situation. And his choice in following this path has a striking resemblance with the path of Stoicism, as followers of this Hellenistic school of philosophy chose to remain unrelenting regardless of the obstacles to their way of life. Stoicism was founded by Zeno of Citium and flourished throughout the third century BC in Rome and Greece. Central to Stoicism is that the path to happiness is found by being virtuous and accepting the moment as it presents itself, treating others fairly and justly, and not allowing the desire for pleasure to control oneself (Sellars 2014).

In fact, this notion of a way or path to happiness is a recurring theme in Stoic writings. The Stoic way is a life that Stoics choose to follow, one with direction and purpose based on reason and virtue. For the Stoics, the true path of reason is the right path which may yield difficulties and roadblocks along the way. However, that way must be followed regardless of those difficulties. As the famous Stoic, Seneca, put it: "It is a rough road that leads to the heights of greatness" (Seneca, Letters, 84).

As Stoics seek to live with integrity, they accept challenges or difficulties they face as part of their virtuous path. Likewise, the Mandalorians do the same even in the face of major upheavals such as the Siege of Mandalore during the Clone Wars where the Empire seized control of Mandalore as well as the Great Purge which led to the near-total genocide of the Mandalorian people. And in *The Mandalorian*, when Mando rescues Grogu and attempts to flee Nevarro, his actions mean that his tribe's secret covert will need to relocate. Despite this hardship, Mando and his tribe persevere and overcome this obstacle. Sure, many of us in our world avoid hardships altogether and prefer the easier way. But in order for us to realize our full potential, like the Stoics and Mandalorians, we must be willing to face our obstacles and overcome them in an uncomplaining manner; we must be brave and choose to follow the rougher path in life. As the armorer said, "How can one be a coward if one chooses this life?" Notice that Mando and his tribe live by their Way. They never stray from their values, and unquestionably accept that which is in front of them as the way things were fated to go.

Interestingly, this uncompromising practice of acceptance mirrors the Stoic "Discipline of Desire" tool which involves bringing our will into congruity with nature. To do so one must live every moment desiring what happens rather than what one wants to happen. For the Stoics, it's important to embrace our fate through the Discipline of Desire. The Stoics placed a high importance on the psychological practice of "accepting events as determined by causal necessity or fate, or alternatively greeting them with rational joy as being the will of God" (Robertson 2018). Marcus Aurelius, the famous Roman Emperor Stoic, succinctly articulated the Discipline of Desire when he wrote:

> Everything suits me that suits your designs, O my universe. Nothing is too early or too late for me that is in your own good time. All is fruit for me that your seasons bring, O nature. All proceeds from you, all subsists in you, and to you all things return. (Hadot 1998, Meditations 4.23)

It was crucial for Stoics to keep in mind that unfolding events are fated to happen regardless of whether they wished otherwise. They subscribed to the fatalist view that everything is fated to happen and couldn't have been otherwise. Between the

25 The Mandalorian as Philosophy: "This Is the Way"

choice of fighting the situation or simply accepting it as an undeniable fact, the choice was clear: accept the situation and proceed onward. As Marcus Aurelius put it, "What stands in the way, becomes the way" (Hadot 1998, Meditations 5.20). Of course, this happens to Mando after he encounters Grogu, a Foundling that he must act as a father to. Thus, Grogu becomes part of Mando's way.

Like all Mandalorians, when Mando is faced with seemingly insurmountable odds, he reverts to his mantra "This is the way," which serves as a reminder of the fact that complaining will do nothing to change his current situation. The Stoics embraced this notion as much as the Mandalorians did, an idea that Seneca captures, "It is a bad soldier who follows his commander grumbling and groaning" (Seneca, Letters, 108). Throughout the show, Mando remains an uncomplaining and undeterred warrior who forges ahead regardless of the obstacle. Recall when he picks himself up with his last ounce of strength to face the charging mudhorn. Like an exhausted Indiana Jones pulling himself back to his feet, Mando proceeds and faces the mudhorn, and accepts the situation – that he'll likely die. It's clear, then, that the Mandalorian Way that Mando follows is just like the Stoic way. It's a way that partly defines who Mando is, and further, it's a way that has helped Mando cultivate many of the virtues he possesses.

"Aren't You a Man of Honor?"

Beyond Mando's armor, mantra, and the Stoic way he embraces, it becomes evident, as the show progresses, that Mando's tribe also abides by a set of guiding principles known as the "Canons of Honor" (which is part of the Mandalorian Code of Honor). While the Canons were only directly mentioned in lesser known sources like *Star Wars* Insider 80 (Peña 2005), the *Galaxy at War* reference book (Wallace 2009), and the *Knights of the Old Republic Star Wars Roleplaying Game Guide* (Thompson 2008), *The Mandalorian* subtly alludes to these principles. The Canons aimed to help Mandalorians attain glory, personal honor, and the strength needed to survive as well as provide guidance on how they ought to behave in battles. The four Canons or principles involve strength, honor, loyalty, and death – most of which tie into Mandalorians being a warrior culture centered on armor, weapons, and war. The principles were expressed as follows:

> Strength is life, for the strong have the right to rule.
> Honor is life, for with no honor one may as well be dead.
> Loyalty is life, for without one's clan one has no purpose.
> Death is life, one should die as they have lived. (Thompson 2008, p. 32)

In Chapter 3, the armorer briefly touches on the Canon of strength. She lets her tribe know, "Our secrecy is our survival. Our survival is our strength." Here she equates strength with survival, which is another way of saying that strength is life. And, in Mandalorian culture, those that have the strength to survive, have the right to conquer and rule over others. At the end of Season 2, Mando not only shows his strength by surviving countless life-threatening obstacles, but he also exhibits strength in defeating Gideon, thereby coming into possession of the Darksaber. We learn that this now means he has the right to rule over the Mandalorian people. And so his strength has led to this outcome.

With respect to honor, we first learn that Mandalorians use combat to achieve it. Because Mando survived the battle with the mudhorn, the armorer says that Mando has earned the mudhorn as his signet, and that she'll craft it. But Mando declines, "I can't accept. It wasn't a noble kill." For Mando it wasn't an honorable kill since he had help from Grogu. So earning Mandalorian honor occurs in battle when a Mandalorian uses their own strength to defeat the enemy, or in this case, an attacking creature. The show also explores "honor" in the sense of fulfilling an obligation or keeping an agreement. In Chapter 6, Mando's belief in living honorably gets called out by Qin – the prisoner aboard the New Republic prison ship. After the despicable crew double-crosses Mando, Qin appeals to Mandalorian honor in an effort to save his own skin. He thus challenges Mando, "You were hired to do a job, right? So do it. Isn't that your code? Aren't you a man of honor?" Questioning the tenets that Mando lives by always works because he stays true to his word; he thus delivers Qin to Ran.

Additionally, in Chapter 10, Mandalorian honor is mentioned by a character referred to as Frog Lady who demands that Mando hold true to the deal he agreed to: delivering her and her eggs to Trask so she can reunite with her husband in exchange for leading him to other Mandalorians that can help in his quest. She calls Mando out saying, "I thought honoring one's word was part of the Mandalorian code. I guess those are just stories for children." During this side quest with Frog Lady, he loses all hope of surviving after their crash on the ice planet. But after listening to Frog Lady call out his Mandalorian honor, he does everything he can to repair the ship and get them off the ice planet, living up to his Mandalorian reputation of being a man of honor – something Greef recognizes about Mando, "For a man of honor should not be forced to live in exile." Unquestionably, Mando acts with honor throughout his journey, always fulfilling his agreements, doing so even when he's double-crossed or is facing despair. In the first ten chapters of the show, all it takes is for someone to remind Mando of the Mandalorian tenets he has sworn to live by – tenets that he believes define his identity.

The Mandalorian Canon of loyalty is also something that Mando takes seriously. In Chapter 3, when Mando arrives at his tribe's covert to get his armor replaced, the armorer says that she'll use the excess to forge whistling birds for him (a type of guided munitions weapon). But (as was previously mentioned) Mando shows loyalty and generosity to his tribe and instructs the armorer to reserve some of the beskar for the Foundlings. He does so because he understands the importance of the Foundlings as they represent the future generations of his tribe. In addition to looking out for his tribe's welfare, he's also sympathetic and relates to the Foundlings because, again, he was once a Foundling himself.

Finally, Mando understands the importance of having the right type of Mandalorian death. After he suffers the head wound, he tells Cara he's not going to make it and instructs her to escape into the sewer and protect Grogu. This is when he demands an honorable death, to die as he has lived, stubbornly refusing to remove his helmet (because he believes it is forbidden). Note that the Mandalorian Canon of death doesn't concern a person's death in and of itself, but rather about how the person dies. If IG-11 didn't save Mando's life and he instead died in this scene, Mando would have died with strength and honor since he fought with strength against Gideon's troopers. His death would have been an acceptable one, in accordance with the Canons of Honor.

The Mandalorian's Argument for Leading a Virtuous Life: "This Is the Way"

While Mando's appearance and adherence to his tribe's Way are important to him, the show places emphasis on what sort of person Mando is – his moral character. Yes, his tribe's Way and his beskar armor mean a lot to Mando (they're integral parts of his identity) but his disposition of caring for others – the virtue of care and other virtues he possesses and puts into practice – are what truly define him. The show indirectly communicates this to us when Mando decides to save and protect Grogu from the Empire and the Guild. In that instance, Mando acts on his virtue of care. The show makes it clear: behaving virtuously is what defines us. Instead of focusing on what we should do or with following any rules or creed, the show expresses that our moral character is what truly matters. It places a spotlight on what sort of people we should be. For developing the right character traits will yield appropriate behavior and the right moral choices. And so the show argues that, like Mando, we should lead a virtuous life.

For over the last four centuries, moral philosophers have tended to focus primarily on actions that are based either on a set of duties and rules or on the consequences of our actions where the emphasis is on what sort of things we should do rather than on what type of people we should be. There is the duty-based ethics that stems from Immanuel Kant who suggested that moral obligations are based on a set of universal laws. And then there's the consequentialist utilitarianism originated by Jeremy Bentham and John Stuart Mill which states that the consequences of our actions determine the rightness or wrongness of those actions. Core to these traditional normative approaches is the justification of actions rather than the character of agents – which has always been seen as something secondary. Thus, character development has traditionally taken a back seat to duty or consequences when it comes to thinking about ethics.

But virtue hasn't always been considered to be secondary. Consider the great thinkers of classical Greece – like Plato and, above all, his pupil Aristotle. For them, the primary concern was the nature and cultivation of good character. They didn't ask the question, "What is the right thing to do in certain circumstances?" Rather, they asked, "What is the best way to live?" – which is what *The Mandalorian* asks and provides an answer to. Mando's own way of living, while partly innate and partly acquired from his tribe's Way, involves virtue and moral excellence. The show thus seems to endorse the moral theory known as "virtue ethics," an idea which originated with Aristotle which suggests that being a good person and knowing right from wrong isn't a matter of understanding and applying certain moral rules and principles. Instead, it's a question of being or becoming the kind of person who, by acquiring wisdom through proper practice and training, will habitually behave in appropriate ways in the appropriate circumstances. It's not about doing good on this or that occasion, but being a good person. As Aristotle put it,

> The Good of man is the active exercise of his soul's faculties in conformity with excellence or virtue. . .Moreover this activity must occupy a complete lifetime; for one swallow does not make spring, nor does one fine day. (Aristotle, 350 BC)

In virtue ethics, you answer questions about what the right and wrong thing is to do based on what a virtuous person would perform in the circumstances, a person with character traits such as honesty, generosity, kindness, and bravery. These virtues are seen as intrinsically valuable (that is, valuable "in itself" or "for its own sake"). And in this sense, virtue ethicists believe virtues are a plurality of intrinsic goods that can't be reduced to a single main value. And so it differs from other monistic moral theories that believe all good can be reduced into a single value, like utilitarianism which holds that all good can be reduced to the single value of happiness – an action is right if and only if it produces the most happiness for the most people.

Notice that *The Mandalorian* doesn't challenge us to merely act like virtuous agents, but to continually seek *to be* virtuous agents – just like Mando. In effect, the show implicitly conveys a message to us through the character of Mando – that we should always seek and aim to act virtuously and that to do so actually, "is the Way." Moreover, the show communicates to us that achieving excellence in virtues is acquired over time. Unlike excellences of nature such as being born with a good natural sense of rhythm or pitch, becoming virtuous requires training. The more we practice the virtues and attempt to act in the way a virtuous agent would, the more virtuous we become.

Mando is a case in point. We know he hasn't always lived virtuously; for example, in Chapter 6 we learn that he used to run with a despicable crew led by a character named Ran where they would do awful things to others during their missions. "We did some crazy stuff." But Mando has come a long way since then. "That was a long time ago." He now abides by his tribe's Way. And this has helped shape who he is over time, namely someone with the right kind of moral character and virtues – which, according to the Greeks, are manifestations of *eudaimonia* (the highest good). Aristotle even concluded that "the highest good (and hence eudaimonia) of human beings is a life of rational activity of the soul in accordance with virtue" (Aristotle, 350 BC). Usually translated as "happiness," *eudaimonia* is actually broader and more dynamic, best captured by the idea of "flourishing" or "enjoying a good life." Notice that Mando does flourish throughout the series. And with Grogu being the catalyst for Mando's moral transformation, he becomes an even better man, one who practices the virtue of caring and one that is worthy of great things such as potentially becoming the leader of Mandalore.

Mando's Virtues: "That's Very Thoughtful of You"

Mando's virtues are evident in his interaction with those he respects. He often shows courage, bravery, trustworthiness, gratitude, generosity, perseverance, and responsibility. And it's very apparent that he shows the virtues of care and love.

Mando shows bravery in many ways, such as taking down the Krayt Dragon in Chapter 9 to restore peace for the local Tusken Raiders and Mos Pelgo villagers. When he fights off the spider creatures in Chapter 10 to save Grogu and Frog Lady he displays the virtues of trustworthiness and loyalty. And in Chapter 15, we see his qualities of perseverance and responsibility when he goes against his tribe's rules and removes his helmet on Morak so the terminal can scan his face.

Mando also shows gratitude to those who are kind to him. Kuiil obviously comes to mind. In Chapter 1, when Kuill helps him reach the encampment, Mando offers Kuiil a bag of money and says, "Here, you deserve this." In Chapter 2, Kuill also helps Mando by negotiating with the Jawas to get his ship parts back (which the Jawas had stripped), and with helping him repair his ship (the Razor Crest) prompting Mando to say, "I can't thank you enough. Please allow me to give you a portion of the reward." After Kuiil says he can't accept, Mando then displays the virtue of generosity – offering Kuiil a job aboard his starship, "I could use a crew member of your ability, and I can pay handsomely." While Kuiil feels honored by the offer, he declines as he states he's worked a lifetime to finally be free of servitude. Mando understands and says that all he can offer him is his thanks, which Kuiil does as well since Mando has brought peace to Kuiil's valley. Further, Mando shows gratitude to Kuiil for reprogramming IG-11 to take care of and protect Grogu from Imperial slavery during the group's mission of eliminating the Imperials on Nevarro at the end of Season One.

Mando's gratitude is also on full display in Chapter 4 during his interactions with Omera on Sorgan. When he arrives in the village, Omera says, "I brought you some food. I noticed you didn't eat out there. I'll leave it here for when I go." Mando replies, "That's very thoughtful of you." And it's not just Mando that displays gratitude. When Omera asks Mando if he he's happy in their village and expresses that they want him to stay, she says, "The community's grateful." This all contributes to *The Mandalorian's* argument for leading a virtuous life. The show implicitly expresses to us that cultivating one's moral character is the path to being a good person and behaving appropriately.

But now let's turn to the other important virtues Mando possesses which the show draws our attention to – virtues that should also guide us – virtues that we should exercise when responding to the world around us.

Mando's Stoic Virtues: "Your Bravery Will Not Be Forgotten"

As previously stated, the central doctrine of Stoicism is that virtue or excellence of character is the only true good in life which leads to eudaimonia. This is why Stoicism is regarded as a "virtue ethic." Accepting this central doctrine means that everything "external" to our character is ultimately indifferent with regard to the supreme goal of life. So things such as health, wealth, reputation, and even life itself, are less important than the use we make of them to achieve excellence of character. Thus, we can think of the Stoics as engaging in a sort of lifelong training or discipline in order to maintain emotional resilience in the face of adversity. The Stoics believed that by living honorably they would acquire the four cardinal virtues of wisdom, justice, courage, and self-discipline, thereby perfecting their moral character. The four cardinal virtues can be thought of, then, as the Stoic "code of honor" or rule of life. We can also read the Mandalorian code in a similar way. Recall the "Canons of Honor" which comprise the code. The word "canon" means *rule* or *philosophical principle* but it can also be defined as a *virtue*. So the Mandalorian code can be seen as teaching the virtues of strength, honor, loyalty, and of facing one's death with integrity.

Earlier we discussed the "Canons of Honor," and how Mando adheres to the four basic slogans that comprise the Canons. It's also apparent, however, that because Mando goes beyond these slogans and acts with a duty to care for all rational beings in general (beyond just Grogu and the welfare of his tribe); he also exhibits the four main Stoic virtues. The Stoic cardinal virtue of self-discipline or temperance, for example, can be compared to the Mandalorian Canon of strength.

The Stoics would agree with Plato and Socrates that kingship consists in "strength" as long as this is interpreted not as physical strength but rather strength of character, self-discipline, moral wisdom, and even kindness. To be a king or ruler is ultimately a state of mind for the Stoics. Notice that Mando not only possesses strength of arms – external military strength with his beskar armor, weapons, and Mandalorian fighting skills – but he also exudes strength in character and kindness which requires more strength than physical aggression. The Mandalorian Canon of strength that says the strong have the right to rule seems to express the notion that "Might is right." Yes, Mando defeats and conquers Gideon and takes the Darksaber. And thus, Mandalorians (like Bo-Katan) would say he now has the right to rule over Mandalore. But Plato, Socrates, and the Stoics would argue that this doesn't make Mando a true King or ruler. Rather a true ruler is someone who cares for the welfare of his subjects first and foremost. It can't just be Mando's physical strength but his strength in character that would qualify him to rule, which we should judge in terms of a ruler's ability to benefit his subjects – in the way that a good shepherd is one who cares for his flock.

But are we able to judge Mando? Sure we are. He clearly possesses the ability to benefit many people. And he certainly does so. Recall that he does everything in his power to defeat the Krayt Dragon, even making the decision to sacrifice himself because he cares about the well-being of the Mos Pelgo villagers and the Tusken Raiders. We also saw how the Sorgan villagers benefited from Mando's strength in character. He risked his life to preserve the people of that village. He decided to put them first and foremost and devise a plan to defeat the raiders and their AT-ST. By showing strength of character with any life decisions, though, Mando is also living honorably.

In Stoic ethics, "honor" is another name for "virtue" which defines the supreme goal of life as "living wisely." But the Mandalorian Canon of honor can also be interpreted in relation to the Stoic cardinal virtue of moral wisdom. For the Stoics, acting with virtue, honor, and strength of character amounts to acting with moral wisdom. And this holds true for the Mandalorians as well. The phrase "honor is life" means that the really important thing is not to live, but rather, to live well, to live virtuously and wisely (something that Socrates taught which influenced the Stoics.)

For the Stoics and Socrates, life itself is neither good nor bad, but ultimately indifferent. They viewed life as an opportunity, which we can use well or badly, wisely or foolishly, for good or evil. Aurelius wrote, "Hearten yourself with simplicity and self-respect, and indifference towards all that lies between virtue and vice. Love the human race" (Hadot 1998). Indeed, virtue or honor, according to the Stoics, is what makes life worth living, and like Socrates, they believe that virtue ultimately consists in moral wisdom. This part of the Mandalorian Code reveals how the whole code is consistent with Stoicism. Consider the "strength is life" principle that Mando and the rest of the Mandalorians abide by. Since honor is life too, this implies that, for the Mandalorians, strength must always be exercised with honor. Indeed, Mando certainly does so during the jobs and missions he's agreed to carry out – for instance, in Chapter 11, when Mando helps Bo-Katan and her fellow Mandalorians assault the Imperial freighter, she recognizes Mando's strength, the honorable way he lives, and fights to achieve his goal of reuniting Grogu with the Jedi. Like other characters in the show, Bo-Katan senses that Mando lives virtuously and wisely (with moral wisdom), and she lets him know, "Your bravery will not be forgotten. This is the Way."

We can also see that the Canon of loyalty is closest in scope to the Stoic cardinal virtue of justice. For the Stoics, the cardinal virtue of justice consists in the qualities of impartiality and benevolence – that we ought to treat others fairly and with kindness. And this is precisely how Mando operates. He goes beyond merely showing loyalty and kindness to his own tribe. He treats other characters (such as Cara, Kuiil, Greef, and reprogrammed IG-11) fairly and with kindness as well as others who threaten or sabotage his plans such as Ran's old crew. Mando doesn't harm or kill them after they betray and use him. Instead, at the end of Chapter 6, we learn that he has locked them all up on the New Republic prison ship, thereby exercising the virtue of justice.

At the end of Season Two, we even witness Mando treating Gideon with kindness when he finds Grogu in shackles aboard Gideon's light cruiser. Mando isn't interested in hurting Gideon or in the Darksaber. He tells Gideon, "You keep it. I just want the kid." But after Gideon tells Mando to take Grogu and to leave his ship and go their separate ways, it's Gideon that attacks Mando from behind with the Darksaber. While Mando shows Stoic impartiality and benevolence towards Gideon (who kidnapped Grogu and used him for his own selfish means), we see that Gideon never had any intent to spare Mando's life or to give up Grogu. In stark contrast to Gideon, Mando extends his loyalty and kindness to all rational beings that are good and kind to him.

Finally, the Stoic cardinal virtue of courage relates to the Mandalorian Canon of death. The idea behind this canon is echoed in Stoicism and their Platonic tradition of *melete thanatou* (philosophy as a preparation of dying or meditation on death). The Stoics placed a lot of emphasis on overcoming their fear of death and meeting death calmly and rationally. Unquestionably, it takes a good deal of courage and fortitude to overcome our fear of death. For the Stoics, daily meditation on one's own mortality was a common practice. Aurelius speaks to this:

> Remember that if one considers death in isolation, stripping away by rational analysis all the false impressions that cluster around it, one will no longer consider it to be anything other than a process of nature, he is no more than a child. (Hadot 1998, Meditations, 2.12)

Remember that Mando faces death countless times during the first two seasons. And in those instances, he's prepared to meet death and isn't fearful of it because he believes that he should die as he has lived – with honor, strength, and with loyalty to his tribe and to humanity. So the show makes it a point to show that Mando exercises the most important Stoic virtues which align nicely with the Mandalorian Canons of Honor.

Virtue Ethics and Personal Motives

But does *The Mandalorian* make a convincing argument that we ought to live a virtuous life? Well the main advantage virtue ethics has over other moral theories is that it doesn't compromise one's personal motivations and reasons. With duty or rule-based moral theories like consequentialism or deontology, there is a split between personal motives and reasons, where the requirement is for people to do what is right out of duty or obligation no matter what their motive is for acting.

But *The Mandalorian* makes it clear that if we want to achieve a good life (and reach *eudaimonia*), we need to be like Mando and first achieve harmony between our personal motives and reasons. Philosopher Michael Stocker captures this point. If one wants to lead a good life one "should be moved by one's major values and one should value what one's major motives seek" (Stocker 1976). Because the duty or rule-based moral theories contain impartial viewpoints, we can't treat our family and friends any differently from strangers despite our moral intuitions that support preferential treatment. Whatever personal motivation we have, it doesn't matter. We must always follow the duty or rule-based moral theory even if it conflicts with our motives.

But if we were to conform to these moral theories, it would prevent us from achieving the good life (which for Aristotle was of supreme importance). Stocker explains that these moral theories "allow people the harmony of a morally impoverished life, a life deeply deficient in what is valuable. People who do let them compromise their motives will, for that reason, have a life seriously lacking in what is valuable" (Stocker 1976). Put differently, our lives wouldn't be very fulfilling if we were to act out of duty when we rarely desire to act out of duty. We would wind up unhappy by following such rule-based moral theories. And the price we pay would be giving up our personal pursuits such as love, caring for others, friendship, and community – which are valuable sources of human pleasure. So these duty or rule-based moral theories don't recognize the value that family and friends can bring into our lives – values that can only be realized in virtue ethics when our personal motives and reasons are in harmony. Stocker highlights this fact, "There is a whole other area of values of personal and interpersonal relations and activities; and also of moral goodness, merit, and virtue" (Stocker 1976).

Recall that in virtue ethics, the virtues are intrinsically good. Of course, there are reasons why certain virtues are valuable in themselves. For instance, virtue ethics considers traits such as love, care, friendship, and community as virtues that are important for our well-being. These virtues allow us to act on our personal motives to maintain personal and interpersonal connections that lead to achieving a good life. Notice that virtue ethicists don't believe in one overarching principle that should guide our decisions, for doing so would compromise other values in life like love, care, and friendship.

Undeniably, Mando is on the path to leading a good life and flourishing. The show makes subtle hints. In Chapter 4, Omera foreshadows this when she tries to persuade Mando to stay and settle down in their village: "We want you to stay. You and your boy could have a good life. Wouldn't that be nice?" To which Mando replies, "It would." Mando's primary value in the first two seasons has been centered on Grogu's well-being. All of his actions along his journey are based on his personal motive to protect and care for Grogu. He doesn't compromise his motives. When confronted with a moral choice, Mando doesn't adhere to any universal moral law on how to treat others (he even bends and questions the rules of his tribe's Way and begins to see there is more than just one way of living). Nor does he act on any single value, such as maximizing pleasure for the greatest number of people. He doesn't allow anything to conflict with his motives to always respond virtuously and to care for Grogu, his friends, and other communities.

But what about those that object to this moral approach? The popular objection to virtue ethics is that the requirements of different virtues could potentially lead to actions which would be conflicting or in opposition to one another. This would make it difficult to resolve moral conflict. The idea is that what would be right according to one virtue may not be right according to the next virtue. And since there is no ranking of the virtues, it's not clear which virtue one should act on. Thus, the objection amounts to virtue ethics failing to be action-guiding when faced with a moral conflict.

In Chapter 15 when Mando is confronted at the terminal by the Imperial officer on Morak, should he act on the virtue of honesty and tell the officer the hurtful truth about who he is, and that he seeks the coordinates to Gideon's light cruiser? Or should he instead act on the virtues of kindness and care (in order to save Grogu) by remaining silent and lying to the officer? Of course, Mando chooses to act on the requirements of the latter virtues. But how does Mando know which virtue should be exercised? The answer is that Mando just knows how to correctly apply the virtues as this is part of what it is to be a virtuous person.

Other moral theories will give an overarching rule or principle to follow in order to resolve moral conflict. But *The Mandalorian* stresses that we shouldn't do this. Rather, it emphasizes that acting on one's moral character can yield the right moral actions and choices. For virtue ethicists, there is no problem of virtues leading us in different directions. Anyone who thinks this is a problem doesn't know how to properly apply the virtues. What's more, the objection arises from a lack of moral wisdom – on having an inadequate grasp of what is involved in acting with honesty (dishonesty) for instance, and how the virtue and vice terms are to be correctly applied. Sure, achieving the virtues takes practice but one must learn how to properly apply them over time. And the one that *The Mandalorian* encourages us to properly apply more than any other is the virtue of care.

The Mandalorian's Argument That Care Is the Primary Virtue

Caring Instincts in a Galaxy Far, Far Away

In addition to displaying many of the Stoic virtues, what the show emphasizes more than anything is that Mando continually exercises the virtue of care. Indeed, Mando's caring instincts are reflected in his moral actions and decision-making. Despite abiding by the Mandalorian Code and his tribe's Way, Mando's moral actions are often driven by his inclination to care for others (which of course lines up with his unprincipled virtue ethic approach).

In fact, by the end of Season Two his identity ends up being defined not by his tribe's Way or by his precious beskar armor but rather by his caring relationship with Grogu. He continually acts in a caring manner and with a deep commitment towards Grogu's well-being. This has a compounding effect where Mando not only wants to protect and care for Grogu's life, but also to protect and care for other communities.

In effect, the show indirectly communicates to us that this caring relation is a critical component of morality. This is why *caring for others* is a central theme of the show. When Mando fights his way out of Nevarro in Chapter 3, Greef says to Mando, "If you truly *care* about the kid, you'll put him on the speeder." Later in Chapter 9, before Mando decides to sacrifice himself by flying and entering the Krayt Dragon to activate the detonator, he tells Cobb (the leader of Mos Pelgo), "Take *care* of the Child." For Mando, providing care to Grogu is the most important thing. Recall at the end of Chapter 8, Cara tells Mando, "Take *care* of this little one," but then Greef adds, "Or maybe, it'll take *care* of you." And this is what happens. Grogu protects and cares for Mando as well as other characters along their adventures. For example, Grogu protects and saves Mando's life from the Mudhorn and later Force-chokes Cara when he sees her arm-wrestling with Mando (believing they are fighting). Grogu's caring ways are also evident in his acts of saving others. For instance, in Chapter 7, he saves Greef's life by healing his arm wound using the Force. And in Chapter 8, to protect and save everyone, he Force-deflects fire against an Incinerator Trooper in the Nevarro cantina. But wait, there's more. Remember that in Chapter 8, the armorer emphasizes "care" to Mando: "A Foundling is in your care."

And the show doesn't just highlight Mando and Grogu's caring ways. Other characters also display care. Cara genuinely cares for Mando and Grogu's well-being. She looks out for them in Chapter 4 when she stops a Guild Hunter from killing Grogu. Kuiil exercises the virtue of care along Mando's journey by acting as a caregiver and guardian over Grogu. Even the non-living IG-11 displays care, becoming Grogu's care droid if you will, safely delivering Grogu to Mando and the rest of our heroes, then sacrificing its life to save everyone.

What's fascinating is that even though the armorer instructs Mando to follow their creed that says to return any Foundling to its own kind and act as the child's father, we realize Mando's caring actions towards Grogu aren't motivated by their creed. Grogu isn't in his care out of duty to any rules. Instead, Mando naturally has caring instincts. At the end of Chapter 4, Mando recognizes that Grogu would be better off living with the Sorgan farming villagers. This is because he cares about Grogu's well-being. He tells Cara, "Traveling with me, that's no life for a kid."

Mando's caring instincts are further heightened in Chapter 13 when Ahsoka says to Mando, "You're like a father to him." In this chapter, a huge bonding moment occurs when Mando holds the ball knob to his ship's control lever and then Grogu Force-pulls it from his hand and catches it. Afterwards, the two celebrate their success. Mando says, "Good job, kid!" It's obvious they have unconditional love, care, and respect for one another. In fact, Mando begins to realize how bonded and dependent they have become to one another. And at the end of Chapter 15, we see how much Grogu means to Mando when he emphatically repeats to Gideon what Gideon had once said to him about Grogu. In a fatherly protective tone, Mando asserts, "He means more to me than you will ever know." Finally, in Chapter 16, during their emotional farewell scene, the love and care Mando and Grogu have for one another is on full display. Mando disregards his tribe's Way and removes his helmet in front of everyone in the room to look upon Grogu for the first time with his own eyes.

By doing so, the show makes it clear that Mando has moved beyond living by his tribe's Way. Through Mando, *The Mandalorian* not only indirectly argues that we can achieve moral excellence and flourish if we lead a virtuous life, but also puts forth an indirect argument for "care" as the most important and primary virtue: care is an essential component in our moral thinking, our moral behavior, and to achieving happiness. But how are we to understand this additional argument for care as the primary virtue? Might the show also be arguing for an ethics of care theory? How are we to understand this care ethics approach? And can this approach constitute a comprehensive moral theory where "care" is the foundation of such a theory?

Care Ethics, Genuine Caring, and Empathy

The ethics of care is also known as "care ethics," a philosophical perspective first developed by feminist philosophers in the second half of the twentieth century that uses a relational approach toward moral decision-making. American philosopher Nel Noddings provided the first comprehensive moral approach on the concept of care. She construed *caring for others* as ethically basic to all human beings (Noddings 1984). In other words, caring relations (where we act in a caring manner) are ethically basic to us – something of which *The Mandalorian* continually reminds us. The caring relation consists of at least two people: the "one-caring" and the "cared-for." In *The Mandalorian*, the primary caring relation is between Mando (the one-caring) and Grogu (the one cared-for). Noddings would say that the distinctive aspect of this relation is that Mando (the one-caring) acts in response to his perceived need on the part of Grogu (the one cared-for). This is an act that is partly motivated by an apprehension of Grogu's reality, where Mando feels and senses the helplessness that Grogu is experiencing and forms a commitment to help. When Mando decides to take Grogu from the Imperials on Nevarro, he acts on his impulse and natural desire to care (thus displaying the virtue of care). He considers and assesses Grogu's point of view and needs for survival, and knows he can improve and act in a way that promotes Grogu's well-being.

Obviously, Mando's caring is genuine. For Noddings, genuine caring involves *engrossment* and *motivational displacement* – something Mando engages in throughout the show. In engrossment, the one-caring (Mando) attends to the cared-for (Grogu) without judgment and evaluation, and he allows himself to be transformed by the other, while in motivational displacement the one-caring (Mando) adopts the goals of the cared-for (Grogu) and helps the latter to promote them. For Mando, his ultimate goal is to safely deliver Grogu to his kind – the Jedi.

But should we accept Noddings's characterization of care? *The Mandalorian* makes it clear we should and affirms that genuine caring involves engrossment and motivational displacement. Apparently, the show's creators perceive care as a primary virtue likely because care ethics deals with things such as friendship, family, and parenting – important themes woven throughout the show. Mando creates friendships, forms a family with Grogu (they're a Clan of two), and experiences the pain and pleasure of parenting – acting as Grogu's father. These are areas of life that have been neglected by traditional moral theories. Notice that in these areas of life, there is an essential element of attention to particular individuals without judgment and evaluation. Additionally, there is also an essential element of motivational displacement. We all know our friends and family support and promote our goals, and vice versa. Parents do the same for their children. And we witness this throughout the show as Mando certainly promotes Grogu's goals.

But genuine caring also involves empathy – which Mando also displays along his journey. He has the ability to recognize and understand Grogu's feelings and thoughts. Indeed, much of his moral actions are driven by his empathetic feelings. Philosopher Michael Slote defends a unique care ethics view, arguing that a theory of right action is not only based on the act flowing from motives attached to an appropriate virtue (such as generosity) but that it's also based on a motive of care, especially empathy – a component of care. Slote states, "Care ethics treats acts as right or wrong, depending on whether they exhibit a caring or uncaring attitude/motivation on the part of the agent" (Slote 2007). This is something

The Mandalorian endorses. Right and wrong depends on virtuous and unvirtuous motivations with the caring or uncaring motivations being the most important ones. For instance, Mando, Grogu, Cara, Kuiil, Bo-Katan, Ahsoka, Greef, and reprogrammed IG-11 act with caring motivations whereas Gideon, the Client, and the Imperials operate with uncaring motivations.

Because Slote's view provides a criterion for the evaluation of actions (a theory of right action), his view is more philosophical than Nel Noddings's view of care who sees the task of morality as the development of virtues. This brings us to the earlier posed question: can any care ethics view constitute a moral theory? Slote certainly defends one. But *The Mandalorian* offers a hidden suggestion on how to construe the care ethics approach. The show can be seen as conveying the notion that "care" falls under the comprehensive moral framework of virtue ethics – the moral theory the show defends. That is, the show conveys the idea that care ethics should be subsumed under virtue ethics. And through Mando, the show stresses that care is the most important and primary virtue – a virtue that is instrumental to a flourishing life, a virtue that is needed to live well. In fact, the show steers us to this conclusion – that this virtue should be at the forefront of our own way.

Virtue ethicists see caring relations like friendship and family as instrumental to flourishing. Without those relations we would lead impoverished lives, unable to partake in the pleasures of associating with our friends and family or share in their joys and hardships. Despite being sad in parting ways with Grogu at the end of Season Two, Mando is a happier person than he was when first introduced. Thanks largely to Grogu, he's now flourishing and on the path to achieving eudaimonia.

On Why Care Is a Primary Virtue

There's no question that caring is an essential aspect of morality – the central claim of care ethics. *The Mandalorian* doesn't regard care as simply one virtue among other virtues. Instead, the show expresses that it's the primary virtue. But are there considerations that support this claim? Well, it's important to first show that care is a virtue. To show that care is a virtue requires two steps: (1) that it fits the definition of virtue, and (2) that it satisfies the criterion for being a virtue, namely, a trait one needs to flourish as a human being.

Let's consider Aristotle's definition of virtue, namely that it's a state involving choice and lying in a mean relative to an individual (Aristotle, 385 BC). Care obviously involves choice. Mando isn't coerced into caring for others. Rather, it's up to Mando whether to withhold or offer care on a particular occasion. And most importantly, caring can lie in a mean: caring can be done "at the right times, about the right things, toward the right people, for the right end and in the right way" (Aristotle, 350 BC, 1106b20-23). Exhibiting care can be done wrongly. For instance, the Imperial officers in *The Mandalorian* care for the wrong person – Moff Gideon (a morally corrupt person). We can also exhibit care at the wrong time. We could be attending to a friend when it is a stranger who actually needs our care at that time. We can also exhibit care about the wrong thing (supporting a project that shouldn't be supported). Finally, we can care for the wrong reasons (we let our kids watch a video because we want them to stop crying) and care in the wrong way (we lie to a friend to calm her fears).

Yet another definition of virtue is offered by philosopher Linda Zagzebski: "Virtue is a deep and enduring acquired excellence of a person, involving a characteristic motivation to produce a certain desired end and reliable success in bringing about that end" (Zagzebski 1996). Most of us would agree that caring is a deep trait of a person and that it's an enduring trait – a caring person is likely to stay a caring one throughout their lifetime. Caring is also an acquired trait. While we all have the capacity to care, caring properly is a trait acquired by training and good upbringing. Mando is an excellent example as his tribe trained him well. Caring is also an excellence because it's a good trait to possess. Lastly, a caring person would be characteristically motivated to care for others. Think of Mando. He's motivated to care for others and wants to produce certain ends. For instance, he genuinely wants to help Cobb and his villagers defeat the Krayt Dragon to restore peace in their town.

Let's next examine the other consideration, that caring satisfies the criterion for being a virtue – that caring is a critical trait we need to flourish as human beings. Obviously, without providing proper care, we can't grow up to lead mentally and emotionally healthy lives. Therefore, proper care is necessary if we are to flourish. Further, since our intimate relationships are characterized by caring, and if flourishing is constituted by intimate relationships, then the necessity of caring to a flourishing life is glaringly obvious to us. Without giving and receiving care, our social and mental lives would be at risk. Being social and exercising our rationality is key to flourishing as human beings.

All of this implies that caring is a primary virtue. We only need to consider the fact that not all the virtues deserve equal ranking. For example, the virtue of wittiness (displaying a sense of humor), can't be placed on equal footing with the virtue of justice (displaying impartiality and fairness). This is because the virtue of justice is a more important virtue for leading a social life and flourishing. Most would agree that there is a way of providing a ranking of the virtues in terms of their importance. And *The Mandalorian* underscores this with its emphasis on care as the primary virtue. Sure, the Stoic virtues of wisdom, justice, courage, and self-discipline are important virtues to exercise in certain circumstances. But our moral acts should always be based on a motive of care and empathy. This is what the show is telling us, that within the virtue ethics approach, some virtues are more important than others. And the show gives the virtue of care the highest ranking among the virtues.

Conclusion: What Should Be Our Way?

The Mandalorian can be interpreted as offering an answer to this question: our own way of living should be guided by a virtue ethics theory where right action is based on the act flowing from both the appropriate virtues and a motive of care. But should this be our way? Well, let's consider that part of the show's success can also be attributed to the moral theory it subscribes to – a theory concerned with traits of character that are essential for human flourishing and happiness (which Aristotle regarded as a way of life). Everyone relates to Mando's moral development, his virtuous traits that he puts into practice, and his caregiving nature. We recognize that Mando is a good person who has learned there is more to life than living by a set of rules or a creed or by the armor he wears. The messages are clear and convincing: who we are on the inside is what truly matters – our moral character. Moreover, what's important is acting on one's virtuous motives, especially the motive of care. We should never compromise our personal motives in our moral actions for that would lead to a much unfulfilled life.

At the end of Season Two, when Mando takes his helmet off in front of everyone, his self-identity has changed. The helmet, armor, and his tribe's rules no longer define who he is. Rather he's now defined by his virtuous acts and, most importantly, by his natural impulse of caring for others. All of this resonates with us. It does so because most of us recognize that possessing and displaying virtuous traits, especially the virtue of care, are essential in our own lives to achieve happiness and flourish. Thus, the show certainly makes a sound case that this should be our Way.

References

Aristotle. 350 BC. *Nicomachean ethics.* Trans. H. Rackham, book 1, chapter 7, section 15, 33.

Hadot, P. 1998. *The inner citadel: The meditations of Marcus Aurelius.* Cambridge, MA: Harvard University Press. https://books.google.ie/books?id=3dLVyyDE-vQC&printsec=copyright#v=one page&q&f=false

Noddings, Nel. 1984. Caring: A feminine approach to ethics and moral education. https://www.amazon.com/Caring-Feminine-Approach-Education-Preface/dp/0520238648

Peña, Alan. 2005. The history of the Mandalorians. Star Wars Insider #80 by Titan Magazines.

Robertson, Donald. 2018. *Stoicism and art of happiness.* 2nd ed, 80. Teach Yourself/Hodder & Stoughton.

Sellars, John. 2014. *Stoicism (ancient philosophies).* New York: Routledge.

Seneca, Lucius. 1969. *Letters from a Stoic.* London: Penguin. https://hillelettersfromstoic.files.wordpress.com/2014/10/letters-from-a-stoic_lucius-annaeus-seneca.pdf.

Slote, Michael. 2007. The ethics of care and empathy. https://www.routledge.com/The-Ethics-of-Care-and-Empathy/Slote/p/book/9780415772013

Stocker, Michael. 1976. The schizophrenia of modern ethical theories. *The Journal of Philosophy* 73 (14): 453–466. https://www.jstor.org/stable/2025782?origin=JSTOR-pdf&seq=1

Thompson, Rodney. 2008. *Knights of the Old Republic campaign guide (Star Wars roleplaying game).* 4th ed, 32. Wizards of the Coast.

Wallace, Daniel. 2009. *Galaxy at war: A Star Wars roleplaying game supplement.* Wizards of the Coast.

Zagzebski, Linda. 1996. *Virtues of the mind: An inquiry into the nature of virtue and the ethical foundations of knowledge,* 137. Cambridge: Cambridge University Press.

Midnight Mass as Philosophy: The Problems with Religion

26

David Kyle Johnson

Contents

Introduction 582
Midnight Mass in Summary 582
The Problem with Religion's Origins 584
The Problem with Belief in Miracles 588
The Problem with Belief in the Supernatural 590
The Problem of Evil 594
The Problem with Suffering 596
The Problem with the Afterlife 597
The Problem with Faith 600
The Problem with Holy Books 602
Conclusion 604
Bibliography 605

Abstract

Midnight Mass (created by Mike Flanagan) is a Netflix limited series about a small fishing community on Crockett Island and the small Catholic Church that serves as the core of its religious life. A young priest takes over the parish, only to eventually be revealed as the elderly priest who spent his life running it – returned to youth by a creature that he thinks is an angel. He tries to do good for both God and islanders by having his churchgoers drink the creature's blood – thus healing and making them young again – only for Crockett Island, in the end, to turn into a fiery bloodbath. Not at all a "jump scare" kind of "vampire" series, *Midnight Mass* is cerebral and deep and – I will argue – serves as an argument for atheism. Not only is the problem of evil articulated, but arguments are presented against belief in miracles, the supernatural, and the afterlife. To boot, it explains away

---

D. K. Johnson (✉)
Department of Philosophy, King's College, Wilkes-Barre, PA, USA
e-mail: davidjohnson@kings.edu

© Springer Nature Switzerland AG 2024
D. K. Johnson et al. (eds.), *The Palgrave Handbook of Popular Culture as Philosophy*,
https://doi.org/10.1007/978-3-031-24685-2_111

religious belief and endorses the idea that religious faith is dangerous. Each of these arguments will be explored in turn.

Keywords

Midnight Mass · Problem of evil · Religion · God · Christianity · Atheism · Afterlife · Faith · Miracles · Natural Explanations of Religion · Eternal Life · Atheist · Atheism · Origins of Religion · The genetic fallacy · Skeptical theism · The free will defense · Deism · Natural evil. moral evil · J. L. Mackie · Alvin Plantinga · Nelson Pike · Methodological Naturalism · Science · Philosophy of Science · The Scientific Method · Inference to the Best Explanation · David Hume · Mystery Therefore Magic · Near Death Experiences · William Clifford · No-self Theory · The soul · Bundle theory · Bodily resurrection · Thich Nhat Hanh · Kill them all, let God sort them out · The Bible · The Dangers of Religion · Vampires

Introduction

Midnight Mass is not your average vampire flick. Although it nods to *Dracula* by having the vampire arrive in a large wooden trunk, it is not full of jump scares, gratuitous gore, sexy teenagers, or even the supernatural. Indeed, not only is the word "vampire" never uttered, but everything that happens in the series has a natural explanation. What makes the series stand apart more than anything, however, is the way it handles deep religious themes, from the afterlife and faith to miracles and the problem of evil. Interestingly, it was regarded by many critics as being respectful and (possibly too) generous to religion (see Romano 2021; Cobb 2021; Collins 2021; Langley 2021). Indeed, it ends with nearly all the "converted" (undead/vampiric) townsfolk singing "Nearer, my God, to Thee," and *Midnight Mass'* creator Mike Flanagan himself said *Midnight Mass* "was never designed to be an attack on religion [but, instead] a critique of fanaticism, in any belief system" (Maas 2021). Nevertheless, I will argue that *Midnight Mass* presents arguments, both moral and metaphysical, for embracing atheism. It not only does so indirectly, by presenting arguments against things often used to prop up theistic belief – like miracles, the supernatural, faith, and the afterlife; it also does so directly, by explaining away religious belief and articulating the problem of evil.

Midnight Mass in Summary

Centered around the fishing community of Crockett Island, *Midnight Mass* begins with a young Catholic priest, Father Paul, arriving on the island to replace the aging Monsignor Pruitt, who had left for a pilgrimage to the holy land months prior. Among the island's inhabitants are schoolteacher Erin Greene and Riley Finn – who was Erin's childhood sweetheart, but is only now returning to the island after killing a young girl in a drunk driving accident and spending 4 years in prison. While in prison, Riley "look[ed] everywhere" for God, studying every holy book, every religion, and "came out . . . an atheist" ("Book I: Genesis").

The island is rocked when a hurricane hits and a host of dead feral cats (devoid of blood) wash up on shore afterward. A fiery sermon or two warms the parishioners to Fr. Paul, but a religious revival breaks out when he seems to perform a miracle in front of them. He "baits" Leeza, a young girl whose legs have been paralyzed for years, into getting out of her wheelchair to accept communion. She was crippled by the town drunk, Joe Collie, when he shot her as a little girl; now she can walk. Others in the town also begin to rejuvenate: Riley's father, Ed, has a bad back that begins to heal; Mildred, the mother of the island's medical doctor, Sarah Gunning, begins to grow younger. Erin, however, experiences the "healing" in a different way. She was pregnant, but now she's not – and her body shows no signs that she ever was.

During his court ordered AA meeting (a one-on-one with Fr. Paul), Riley says that he doesn't believe Leeza's healing was a miracle. He thinks Fr. Paul had to know she would walk to take the risk of asking her to. As Riley puts it, "I mean, you went back up the stairs. You beckoned her. If she hadn't, what would've happened to you? What would this community have thought of you if she hadn't? . . . you had to know . . . ." Fr. Paul says he just "felt" it – but in reality, Fr. Paul is Monsignor Pruitt, and he has been feeding the blood of a creature he encountered in the holy land to his parishioners in the communion wine. When it fed on him, and then fed him its blood, it made him young again; so he concluded that it was an angel and decided to bring it to the island and use its blood to improve the lives of the faithful who took communion. "So that we may bring them Your love and Your mercy, Your miracles" ("Book III: Proverbs").

For reasons that are not explained, Fr. Paul is seemingly poisoned and dies right in front of Leeza's parents (Dilly and Wade), the handyman Sturge, and Bev Keane (the most devout of the island's Catholics) – only to resurrect right in front of their eyes. Although he does not look different, he now will heal from any wound – unless he steps out into the sunlight, in which case he will burst into flame. (His condition very much resembles that of an undead vampire.) And when Fr. Paul later kills and drinks the blood of Joe Collie, the willing accomplices for hiding Joe's body are Wade, Sturge, and Bev. They become Paul's devoted apostles.

After Riley catches Fr. Paul lying about the whereabouts of Joe, he plans to confront him about it in the church recreation center late at night – only to find Fr. Paul praying before the "angel" creature as it donates more "sacrament" (its blood) to Paul's collection for communion. The creature attacks Riley, feeds on him, and then feeds him its blood, thus transforming Riley as well. Paul and Bev explain to Riley how all that is happening is part of (what they see) as God's plan to bring about what God promised regarding the end of the world: resurrection and eternal life. Despite Bev's protests, Fr. Paul lets Riley go, and Riley invites Erin to go for a midnight boat ride. He tells her of all that has happened, and we are led to believe that Riley will feast on her blood; instead, however, he allows the sun to rise on him and he bursts into flames. This reveals to (the horrified) Erin not only that his story is true, but that he has rejected his selected role in "God's plan." Before he does, Riley pleads with Erin to row to the mainland to save herself, but he knows that she will instead return to Crockett Island to try to save its people.

When she returns, she easily convinces the local doctor, Sarah Gunning, who has already noticed that blood samples from some of the islanders spontaneously combust when they are exposed to sunlight. Indeed, Dr. Gunning explains it all, naturalistically, in terms of an extreme form of erythropoietic protoporphyria (EEP) that also heals cells. (EEP is a real-world condition where people are sensitive to sunlight and are also anemic – a disease which is treated with iron supplements and blood transfusions.) Erin, Sarah, and her mother Mildred deduce that Fr. Paul has been giving loyal islanders this condition by "poisoning" the communion wine. When they try to leave the island, they realize that all boats going to the mainland have either been sent away or sabotaged – so they decide to go to the big Midnight Mass scheduled that night for the Easter Vigil.

At the Vigil, Fr. Paul admits to being Monsignor Pruitt, and then – in front of everyone – Sturge drinks poison, dies, and then resurrects. The angel creature appears, and the congregation is told that if they drink the wine, the same will happen to them. Some do, and those that don't are fed on – including Mildred, who is carried away by the angel. In other words, the Midnight Mass turns into a Midnight Massacre. Despite Rev. Paul's wishes, Bev then opens the doors of the Church and an army of undead vampiric believers feeds on the rest of the islanders, driving them out of their houses with fire. Sheriff Hassan, Leeza, Erin, Sarah, Riley's mother, and Warren (Riley's brother) escape the church and set fire to the island's boats so that the undead believers can't spread to the mainland. They also spread gasoline in the church and rec center but are stopped before they can light it. The Sheriff and Sarah are shot, and Erin is captured by the angel – although she is able to cut its wings, making it difficult for it to fly and escape, before it does her in.

But all is not lost. Mildred (who is now undead and fully young) burns down the church, and Ali (the now undead son of the Muslim Sheriff) burns down the rec center. After realizing what they have become, and how evil Bev is, Mildred and Ali had a change of heart. As Riley's dad puts it, "Whatever this is, it don't change who you are" ("Book VII: Revelation"). Indeed, all the island's surviving undead inhabitants realize the error of their ways and, with no place left to hide, gather in a clearing and sing "Nearer, My God, to Thee" as they await the fate the sunrise will bring – all, that is, except Bev, who desperately, at the last second, tries to dig a hole to hide from the sunrise. She is not successful; the only survivors are Leeza and Warren, who watch the scene from their rowboat. They were never fully "converted," so the sunrise does not hurt them; in fact, the angel's blood is working its way out of their system, as Leeza's paralysis returns. The angel flies out ahead of the sunrise, trying to make it to the mainland – but it's unclear whether its damaged wings will let it.

The Problem with Religion's Origins

To identify the argument of *Midnight Mass*, it is important to begin by realizing that the character of Riley is a direct stand-in for the creator and director of *Midnight Mass*, Mike Flanagan. Like Riley, Flanagan grew up Catholic, is a former alcoholic,

26 *Midnight Mass* as Philosophy: The Problems with Religion

and ended up an atheist after studying every religion. Riley's line, "Figured if I was lookin' for God, I should look everywhere," from the episode "Book I: Genesis" appears almost verbatim in Mike Flanagan's description of his own journey (Flanagan 2021). In his study of religion, Flanagan also read atheists Christopher Hitchens and Sam Harris – and while it was their arguments that he found most convincing, it was agnostic Carl Sagan's book *Pale Blue Dot* with which he found the most "spiritual resonance." Since we can even see Riley giving many of their arguments in the show, it is fairly safe to assume that when Riley speaks, he is presenting arguments that Flanagan at least sympathizes with. "Riley was always a thinly disguised surrogate," Flanagan admitted, "an avatar unlikely to fool anyone except myself, who wouldn't admit how much I had in common with my own character for many years" (Flanagan 2021).

With that in mind, we can begin our examination of *Midnight Mass*'s arguments for atheism by looking at what Riley says to Fr. Paul in response to his first miracle: "I'm a pretty rational guy, and you [Fr. Paul] know that all our myths, our religions, come from natural occurrences that we can't explain" ("Book II: Psalms"). Riley elaborates on this idea when he is out in the boat with Erin.

> It's where it all came from in the first place. Stars. Primitive man, they were hunting and gathering and stuff all day long, but at night they just sit around campfires tryin' to stay warm, stay safe from predators. And they look out across the valleys, and they see other campfires, just little spots of light in the landscape, and they know that other people are out there, in the dark. And then, they see these spots of light in the sky. They don't know what they are. They don't have a clue about space or stars or light waves. They just figure they look a hell of a lot like campfires. "Who must those people be," they wonder. "Lightin' their campfires way up there?" They start telling each other stories. "Those people?" "They must be incredible." "Those campfires, they belong to people way more powerful than we ever even imagined, so. . ." All of it. Every god. Every goddess, every religion, every holy war. All of it. Started right up there, just wondering who the hell could've lit those campfires in the sky. ("Book V: Gospel")

The argument for atheism here is pretty straightforward. If, instead of it being bestowed upon us by divine powers, we invented the idea of God, then likely God does not exist. If the reason we believe in God in the first place traces back to us trying to explain what stars are, since we now know that stars are burning balls of gas – and not the campfires of powerful deities – then we should conclude that God (and indeed no such deities) exist.

But does this argument work? To answer that question, there are three more we must ask. Is this really why humans started believing in God? If not, is God responsible? And if not, does that suggest God doesn't exist?

As far as I know, no academic has put forth Riley's campfire theory exactly as he articulated it; but it has long been held that trying to explain things like the sun, moon, and stars is where the origins of religion lie. This is why so many of the early gods (sun gods like Sol, Ra, and Helios and moon gods like Luna, Máni, and Bulan) literally *were* the sun or moon and why so many other gods are associated with stellar constellations. Even the Christian idea of the "halo" derives from sun worship (sun gods had halos around their head) and more than one aspect of Jesus (e.g., his supposed birthdate) is borrowed from sun god worship (Johnson 2015b, pp. 21–24).

More generally, the idea that religious belief sprang from early humans trying to explain what they could not explain is arguably the most popular among academics. Pioneered by the likes of Thomas Hobbes and Baruch Spinoza, the idea is basically that – without an explanation for things like the weather, famines, floods, plagues, and earthquakes – early humans wrongly attributed them to powerful beings. They wanted explanations and were apt to look to purpose and project their own attributes (agency) on to the supposed causes (Manson 2021, pp. 161–63). If so, Riley's theory is essentially right.

But this is not the only theory of religion's origin. Karl Marx explained religion as something that was invented to help us deal with the oppression hoisted on us by corrupt systems like capitalism.

> Religion is, indeed, the self-consciousness and self-esteem of man who has either not yet won through to himself, or has already lost himself again … This state and this society produce religion, which is an inverted consciousness of the world, because they are an inverted world. Religion is the general theory of this world, its encyclopaedic compendium, … its moral sanction, its solemn complement, and its universal basis of consolation and justification. It is the fantastic realization of the human essence since the human essence has not acquired any true reality. … Religious suffering is, at one and the same time, the expression of real suffering and a protest against real suffering. Religion is the sigh of the oppressed creature, the heart of a heartless world, and the soul of soulless conditions. It is the opium of the people. The abolition of religion as the illusory happiness of the people is the demand for their real happiness. To call on them to give up their illusions about their condition is to call on them to give up a condition that requires illusions. (Marx 1843/1970, p. 3)

One thing Marx worried about was that religion made those who were oppressed by capitalism complacent in their suffering because it made them think that they would be rewarded for it in the afterlife (Cline 2021a). Similarly, Sigmund Freud explained religious belief as something that originated from unconscious wish fulfillment aimed at easing anxiety – like the anxiety felt at the prospect of death (Thornton n.d.).

On the other hand, evolutionary psychologists explain religious beliefs as something that arose randomly but then stuck around (worked to fixation) because they made our ancestors more likely to survive. For example, in the last chapter of his book *Sociobiology: The New Synthesis*, E. O. Wilson appeals to group selection and argues that religious beliefs stuck around because they benefited societies by making them more cohesive and unified (Wilson 1975).

Which theory is right? This issue is not settled, and it's possible that they are all a part of the story of how religion arose. (If you want a nice rundown of the surrounding arguments, see Chapter 7 of Neil A. Manson's "This is Philosophy of Religion" (Manson 2021). The important point, however, is that – while he may not be exactly right – Riley is essentially right. No one who specializes in this question thinks "We believe in god(s) because the god(s) revealed their existence directly to us." That's not to say that there are not Christian philosophers and other academics who think that God has revealed himself. It is to say that there are no professional

26 *Midnight Mass* as Philosophy: The Problems with Religion

academics, who have dedicated their lives to studying the origin of religion, who – after years of research – have concluded that the evidence clearly indicates religion began because God revealed himself. Those who are religious may believe that God revealed himself, but that is a faith claim. The academic study of the origins of religions reveals that religious beliefs ultimately have natural explanations; they are, for a lack of a better phrase, something that we made up.

This might seem controversial, but it's something that most people understand intuitively. Ask yourself: If all scientific knowledge were erased tomorrow, would it be gone forever? Of course not. It would all eventually be discovered again. Certain laws might have different names (because they would have different discoverers), but the same scientific knowledge would emerge. Now what if all religious beliefs were erased tomorrow? Would we invent the same religions again? Would we write the same holy books, with the same rules, theology, and beings? Of course not. Religions would emerge again, but every one of them would be considered heresy by every religion that exists today. Why? Religion is just something we made up, and we'd make up something different.

Now, in response to the suggestion that this means that God doesn't exist, believers often say this argument commits something called "the genetic fallacy" (Whittaker 1978). The genetic fallacy, also known as the fallacy of origins, is often expressed as the idea that you can't attack a belief based on its origins. If that's right, it would seem the argument above is fallacious. But it's not. This response does not represent an accurate understanding of the genetic fallacy. Why?

It is usually fallacious to dismiss an *argument* based on its origin – who gave it, or what inspired it. Arguments should stand or fall on their own merits. When understood this way, the genetic fallacy is just another version of the ad hominem or "personal attack" fallacy, where someone attacks the *arguer* rather than the *argument.* Similarly, it is fallacious to dismiss or ignore the *evidence* for a theory based on the theory's origins. The evidence we have for the fact that the molecular structure of Benzene is ring shaped, for example, is overwhelming; and pointing out that this particular idea originally came to August Kekulé in a dream (of a snake eating its own tail) would not be a good reason to doubt it.

However, you can cast legitimate doubt on a mere *idea* – not an argument, but a mere *claim* or *notion* – by pointing out that the origin of the idea is not reliable. This is especially true if the idea is that something exists. If one knows that the notion that some thing X exists did not originate in the actual existence of thing X, then (unless presented with good evidence to the contrary) one has good reason to doubt that thing X exists. For example, the fact that belief in the Chupacabra originates with Madelyne Tolentino conflating her memory of the movie *Species* with something she saw – and not an actual sighting of Chupacabra – is very good reason to think that Chupacabra doesn't exist (Radford 2011).

So, it would be different if Riley were trying to skirt around some argument for the existence of God, like the Kalam cosmological argument or teleological fine-tuning argument; you can't dismiss an argument for a thesis based on the origins of that thesis. (If the reader is curious, I have explained the faults in such arguments for God elsewhere. See, Johnson 2022a.) Nevertheless, the fact that we have good reason to think that belief in God did not originate from God revealing himself – but instead is something that we made up – is good reason to conclude that God doesn't exist. Is it 100% proof? No, in the same way that the above Chupacabra origin story is not 100% proof that Chupacabra doesn't exist. (It's improbable, but at least logically possible, that Madelyne imagined a creature that just happened to actually be real.) But it's a very good reason to doubt it; it makes atheism justified. So, *Midnight Mass*'s first argument for atheism seems to be on solid ground.

The Problem with Belief in Miracles

The "The Mystery Therefore Magic" fallacy is the mistake in reasoning one commits when one invokes the supernatural to explain what seems unexplained or unexplainable (Johnson 2018a). It's a variety of *another* fallacy, the appeal to ignorance, where one takes one's inability to prove something false as a reason to think it is true. With the mystery therefore magic fallacy, one takes their inability to prove there is a natural explanation for something (by finding one) to be a reason to conclude that there isn't one. It's fallacious not only because a person's inability to prove something false doesn't really make it true, but because the explanation "there is a natural explanation, I'm just not smart enough to find it" will always be a better explanation for such events. As I have explained elsewhere, supernatural explanations, by their very nature, usually lack the kinds of things that good explanations need, like parsimony and scope (i.e., simplicity and explanatory power) (Johnson 2017a).

We avoid this fallacy every time we don't conclude magicians have magic powers, and both Riley and Dr. Gunning avoid it the very first moment in which the supernatural seems to be at play in *Midnight Mass*: when Leeza gets out of her wheelchair and walks. Her parents think "it feels wrong to interrogate a miracle, second guess a gift from God," but neither Riley nor Gunning believe, for a minute, that the supernatural is involved – even though they initially have no explanation.

Later, of course, they do propose natural explanations:

Riley   I can wrap my head around a misdiagnosis. I looked it up and it happens. It's rare but it does. So, like her body could have been slowly healing this whole time. I can explain all of it if I'm honest, it's all explainable. ("Book III: Proverbs")

Gunning   Spinal injuries, they can heal themselves over time. It's exceedingly rare, but it does happen. ("Book III: Proverbs")

And Dr. Gunning is prevented from testing her theory medically by Leeza's parents. But the important point is this: Despite initial appearances, neither Riley nor Dr. Gunning concludes that Leeza's healing/recovery was the result of a miracle. This conclusion, it seems, is what *Midnight Mass* is suggesting one should draw in such circumstances. But is it?

In drawing such a conclusion, Riley and Gunning are going one step further than philosopher David Hume. In *An Enquiry Concerning Human Understanding*, Hume

(1993) argued that *testimony* can never justify belief in a miracle. For Hume, a miracle is a violation of a natural law, a regularity established by direct repeated experience. Since, Hume argued, *direct repeated* experience will always provide more reason to believe that regularities hold than someone else's word that they didn't (because the latter is both indirect and nonrepeated), testimony will never be able to justify belief that a miracle occurred. Since Dr. Gunning and Riley saw it with their own eyes – Riley was at the church, and Dr. Gunning confirmed Leeza's recovery medically – they don't have to take anyone's word for it. And yet they still don't believe it is a miracle.

Are their standards of evidence too high? Christian philosopher Richard Swinburne would certainly think so. Indeed, he asked "What, one wonders, would Hume himself say if he saw [a miraculous] event?" (Swinburne 1968). To see if he is right, let us look closer at some of the issues that surround Hume's argument.

Perhaps the most famous argument against Hume's tells the story of a prince who grew up in India and thus never experienced freezing weather. This "Indian Prince" was initially skeptical when a traveler suggested that the lakes in his northern homeland become solid during winter – so solid that an elephant could walk across them. Because the regularities of the prince's direct experience (water is always liquid) contradicted this fact, it seemed more likely that the traveler was lying. But as more travelers, from other northern countries, independently attested to the same phenomena, the prince eventually believed – and it seems rightly so. It would be too unlikely that they were all lying; that would not be the simplest explanation, for example. And thus, through testimony alone, the prince came to justifiably believe that a regularity of his experience had been violated: Lakes have frozen (Bitzer 1998).

Elsewhere I have argued that while the prince story does seem to show that Hume was wrong when he said that testimony could never "override" an experienced regularity, it does not show that Hume's overall thesis (that testimony can't establish a miracle) was wrong (Johnson 2015a). Why? Notice that, in coming to believe that northern lakes freeze in the winter, the prince does not come to believe that a miracle has occurred. Instead, he concludes that what he thought was a law of nature – that water is always liquid – was not. He realized, not that the laws of nature were broken and thus a miracle occurred, but that he was wrong about what the laws of nature are.

Hume's mistake, then, is not in thinking that testimony can't establish that a miracle occurred; Hume's mistake is in thinking that one can conclude that a miracle occurred if a regularity established by experience has been violated. Truth be told, our experience is not reliable enough, or wide-scoping enough, for it to be the last word in what the laws of nature are. We should expect our experience to be proven wrong, now and again (Schick and Vaughn 2020, p. 108). Consequently, when it is proven wrong, we should update what we think the laws of nature are – not think that they have been broken.

What does this mean for Riley and Dr. Gunning's standards of evidence? They are not too high at all. Even if you see a seemingly inexplicable event for yourself, you shouldn't conclude that it was a miracle; it's much more likely that there is a natural explanation that you can't fathom. There is probably one within the bounds of what you think the laws are, and, if not, you are probably just wrong about the laws. So,

Riley and Dr. Gunning's idea that there is a nonsupernatural explanation for Leeza's recovery is most reasonable. Even if, contrary to fact, they couldn't think of one, they still shouldn't consider their experience of the world (and their wisdom) to be so wide-scoping that *if they can't think of a natural explanation, then there must not be one.* "If the answer is not within my experience, then it must not exist" is just too short sighted. As Dr. Gunning puts it when asked by her parents whether she has ever seen anything like Leeza's recovery, "Before today? No, I haven't seen anything like this before today. But now I have."

Elsewhere (Johnson 2015a), I have argued for the conclusion that *Midnight Mass* draws about belief in miracles in this way: What a miracle is, most simply put, is a divine act in the world – an event that God caused. But we are only justified in believing that God caused an event if there is no natural explanation for that event. (If there is, the natural explanation is the better one.) We can't, however, be justified in believing that there is no natural explanation for an event unless we are justified in believing that it broke a law of nature. And not only can neither testimony nor personal experience (like seeing Leeza walk) justify the belief that a law of nature was broken, but even if we did establish scientifically that a law has been broken, the more rational conclusion would be that we were wrong about what the laws were. So, given what we have discussed so far, it seems that *Midnight Mass'* argument against belief in miracles is quite convincing.

The Problem with Belief in the Supernatural

Midnight Mass makes a similar argument when Dr. Gunning explains why she doesn't think Erin's story about Riley bursting into flame in the sun is "crazy."

> Have you ever heard of. . . Ignaz Semmelweis? . . . He was a Hungarian physician in the 1840s. Finds himself in charge of two maternity wards. One was a teaching school, best and brightest, birthing to autopsies, everything in between. The second was a clinic for women who couldn't afford medical care. Wasn't even run by doctors. It was midwives. No surprise that one clinic had a higher mortality rate than the other. The surprise was which one. It was . . . the teaching school. Death rate was staggering. Women had a better chance of living giving birth on the streets. . . . drove him nuts. He did study after study after study . . . until finally, he suggested that maybe . . . for no reason that made any sense, maybe his students should wash their hands—after performing the autopsies, before going into the birthing ward. So he started a mandatory chlorine hand wash. Lo and behold, death rates plummeted. And the scientific community ate him alive. Germ theory was two decades away from acceptance. Ideas in that direction were met with disdain, ridicule, exile. Semmelweis was committed to an asylum—an asylum!—by another scientist. In fact, he died there. Oh, and when they replaced him at these clinics, got rid of that crazy, silly hand wash? Mortality rates went back up again. So, yeah, Erin, your story is crazy. ("Book VI: Acts of the Apostles")

This story she tells about Ignaz Semmelweis is historically accurate; it is part of how the germ theory of disease became accepted (Loudon 2013). It is also quite nice for demonstrating how scientific revolutions take place. Revolutionary ideas are

26 *Midnight Mass* as Philosophy: The Problems with Religion

often met with disdain before they are finally accepted. (This does not mean, however, that disdained theories are likely true; see Johnson 2018b.)

One thing I use this story for, in class, is to demonstrate how – contrary to what Dr. Gunning suggests when she shows Erin that the sun ignites her mother's blood – science does not *only* deal with the "observable, testable, [and] repeatable" ("Book VI: the Acts of the Apostles") – at least not in the strictest sense of those words. When they were first proposed, germs were not directly observable – and yet we came to accept that they existed, because the theory that they existed provided the best explanation for other things that could be observed (e.g., the success of handwashing, how diseases spread, the success of vaccines, etc.) when compared to other theories, like the "filth theory" (Steere-Williams 2016). The same is true for atoms, which were accepted as existing long before we could observe them with electron microscopes (Helmenstine 2020). Even heliocentrism, the theory that the Earth revolves around the sun (and not vise-versa), was accepted before we could prove it observationally – by detecting what's called "parallax," a visual difference in distant star pairs at different times of year (Sant 2019; Schick and Vaughn 2020, p. 189). Today, we accept the existence of a host of subatomic particles – electrons, positrons, photons, bosons – without ever having directly observed the particles themselves. Don't get me wrong; we have *evidence* of their existence – but it comes in the form of experimental results (e.g., reactions in the Large Hadron Collider) for which the existence of such particles is the best explanation (Greene 2013). We have not seen them and may not ever see them, directly. We infer them.

What this helps demonstrate is why a common conception about the philosophical underpinnings of science is actually a misconception; it's called methodological naturalism. Methodological naturalism suggests that science, as part of its very approach, dismisses the possibility of the supernatural. It does not deal with it, or consider such explanations, as a matter of course. It only deals with natural explanations. Consequently, it can neither confirm nor deny the existence of the supernatural – and therefore belief in the supernatural, while not *supported* by science, is not necessarily irrational. The supernatural might not be scientific, but it is not unscientific – it is not contrary to science.

Such suggestions are very common among accommodationists, those who profess that there is no conflict between science and religion and that it is possible to be both fully scientifically minded and religiously devout. But methodological naturalism is not an accurate description of the scientific process (Boudry et al. 2010).

As Ernan McMullin eloquently put it in his book *The Inference That Makes Science*, what the history of science reveals is that – at its roots – science is a method of reasoning called "inference to the best explanation" (1992). Scientists compare theories or hypotheses according to criteria that describe what good explanations, by definition, must be, and then accept the one that best fits the criteria. What criteria? Good explanations should be testable (i.e., make novel observable predictions) and fruitful (i.e., get those predictions right); they should be wide-scoping (explain multiple phenomena and not raise unanswerable questions) and simple (not introduce unnecessary new entities); and they should be conservative – they should align with what we already have good evidence for (Schick and Vaughn 2020, pp. 180–190). That's not to say that the classic definition of "the scientific method" – observe, hypothesize, predict, and test – is not used in science. It's just not all there is to it. That's how to perform experiments, and experiments are very useful for determining which hypothesis is more fruitful (which hypothesis gets its predictions right). But even when experiments can't be done, or when two hypotheses make the same predictions, one can still decide between them scientifically by appealing to criteria like scope and simplicity.

The relevant point here is this: The only thing that underpins science, philosophically, is the notion that the best explanation is what is most rational to believe. What makes something a good explanation can be defined, and whichever hypothesis is the best should be preferred. So science does not rule out the supernatural from the start; indeed, if the supernatural did exist, science could demonstrate that it does. If the existence of the supernatural provided the best explanation for a set of real-world phenomena – if it proved itself to be the most fruitful, wide-scoping, simple, and conservative explanation among the alternatives – then belief in the supernatural would be scientific.

In his book *Weirdness*! Taner Edis describes how this could have happened with the supernatural phenomena of psychic powers.

> [P]arapsychology, [the] effort to show that psychic phenomena are genuine …has all the institutional trappings of any scientific discipline, from peer-review journals to academic conferences. Parapsychologists conduct experiments with considerable methodological sophistication, comparable to straight psychology in their rigor … and regularly publish results that, if confirmed, would be minor miracles [i.e., would revolutionize science]. (Edis 2021, p. 67)

The reason scientists don't believe that psychic powers are real is that those results weren't confirmed – most studies were negative, and those that were positive weren't repeatable and were revealed to have major flaws. The problem was *not* that parapsychology is *unscientific*. To be sure, there are some parapsychologists who behave unscientifically; but psychic phenomena itself is something that can and has been investigated scientifically. "[I]f the paranormal were real, science could have affirmed it" (Edis 2021, p. 107). And the fact that it wasn't confirmed is good reason to conclude that psychic powers are not real; if they were, the science would have shown it.

As I have argued elsewhere, the same is true of ghosts (Johnson 2022b). If ghosts were real, they could be studied scientifically – much like Egon Spengler does in *Ghostbusters*. They could be detected, seen, verified, and studied – perhaps even captured. And it is because they haven't that those who are scientifically minded don't believe in them. It's not because science has refused to even entertain the possibility of their existence because science only deals with natural explanations. In fact, it has entertained ghosts – and ESP – and souls, aliens, demons, angels, and a host of other paranormal/supernatural phenomena. It's just that the hypothesis that such things exist has never been vindicated by being the best explanation for anything.

26 *Midnight Mass* as Philosophy: The Problems with Religion   593

The way that *Midnight Mass* has the character Dr. Gunning explain the "vampires" in the series seems to be a direct refutation of the idea that science is "methodologically naturalistic" – that science is irrelevant to, and inherently cannot explain, supernatural phenomena.

> So there's a blood disorder called erythropoietic protoporphyria. EPP. A lot of those myths [about vampires] probably came from EPP. People with it are extremely sensitive to light, to the point of burning and blistering in the sun. And very anemic. [Erin: So this is a blood disorder?] Not this. No. But in the same family maybe. Kind of like the common cold and the bubonic plague are in the same family. Say something has been ingested by people on this island. A virus. . . . A new type of cell. . . . Who knows? Something that repairs damaged cells, is violently photosensitive, and causes an insane anemia. A desperate hunger for iron, iron in blood. At first, this thing in the blood is only present in trace amounts. But as that ratio increases, the physical alterations become more pronounced. Mom, when I put your blood in the sun, and yours too, Erin, this thing burns away, leaving your normal blood behind . . . But with both of you, your blood is still mostly normal blood, made up of typical, boring old red blood cells. But with Riley, perhaps he had more of it in his bloodstream, so that when the ultraviolet rays penetrated his skin, the blood, now predominantly this thing, ignited. ("Book VI: Acts of the Apostles")

In other words, if vampires were real, science could not only prove they were, it could explain why they thirst for blood, why they don't age, and why they burst into flame in the sunlight.

Now, one might argue that if science really were to do such things, it would not admit the existence of the supernatural. Science would just expand its definition of what the natural world includes. With *Midnight Mass*, it's a vampirish "blood disorder," but if it were ghosts, or psychic powers, it would do the same: just include these new entities in its description of the natural world, in the same way that it now includes germs in its description of the natural world.

This is probably true, but it does not entail that science is philosophically or methodologically opposed to the existence of the supernatural. This is a semantic point, rather than a philosophical one. Whether you call them supernatural or not, the existence of things like vampires, ghosts, etc. – what we usually call "the supernatural" – is not outside the purview of science. Indeed, they have been investigated. And it is because those investigations found no good evidence that scientists reject the existence of such things – not because science is philosophically or methodologically opposed to their existence.

What this entails is that the idea that science can't disprove the existence of the supernatural – and thus that science and religion are not in conflict – is false. As I have argued elsewhere, science gives us very good reason to doubt creationism, the existence of souls, the occurrence of miracles, and even that the resurrection of Jesus occurred (Johnson 2020, 2021a). And since such things are often touted as reasons to believe in God, to the extent that *Midnight Mass* argues against them, it argues that science has the ability to discredit such notions and thus is presenting a decent indirect argument against the existence of God. But it is to *Midnight Mass'* most direct argument against God that we shall turn next.

The Problem of Evil

Midnight Mass opens on Riley's car accident, the one where he killed Tara-Beth. When he realizes that she is dead, and begins to say the Lord's Prayer, the paramedic looking after him insists, "While you're at it, ask him why he always takes the kids, while the drunk fucks walk away with scratches" ("Book I: Genesis"). Muslim Sheriff Hassan expresses a similar sentiment to his son Ali when Ali says what happened to Leeza was a miracle.

> No, that isn't how it works, Ali. That isn't how Allah... Do you know what it does, what pancreatic cancer does to someone? Would you like me to tell you? Because I don't want to. I never, ever want you to know what she went through. I bear that for both of us, and that's right. She kept her faith. She honored him [Allah/God] to her last moment, and if...If God really worked that way...If he decided that he was gonna heal some people and not others, if he chose to spare some and not others, if he handed Leeza Scarborough a miracle, but let a child die of a brain tumor across the way in the mainland... No. No, that's not how it works, Ali. It's not. That's not how God works. No matter how exciting the stories are at St. Patrick's. Or the Buddhists or Scientologists. It's not magic. It's not. ("Book III: Proverbs")

Obviously, Sheriff Hassan struggles with how Allah (what a Christian would call "God") can allow the horrendous suffering of a good person, like his wife. If God is all good, and all powerful, he would not want and would be able to prevent the suffering of good people. The fact that such people suffer every day seems to suggest that God doesn't exist; if he did, he wouldn't let them suffer. As Riley puts it:

> And God? He just kinda let [my accident that killed Tara-Beth] happen, didn't he? See that? That's the part I cannot square. Because you're right, there is so much suffering in the world. So much. And then there's this higher power. This higher power who could erase all that pain, just wave his hand and make it all go away, but doesn't? No. No, thank you. ("Book II: Psalms")

The argument which suggests that the occurrence of evil entails God does not exist is called "the problem of evil." It was perhaps best expressed in "Evil and Omnipotence" by J. L. Mackie (1955) and comes in many different varieties. The logical version concludes that evil is 100% deductive proof that God doesn't exist; the evidential version suggests that evil is sufficient evidence against God's existence. One of the most common solutions to it, perhaps best articulated by Alvin Plantinga (1967) and Nelson Pike (1979), is one that Sheriff Hassan seems to endorse: The free will defense. According to the free will defense, God both wants and could prevent the occurrence of evil in the world, but he doesn't because there is something else he wants more that isn't possible without the existence of evil: human free will. (For more, see Johnson 2022c.) God could have prevented, for example, Riley's accident by causing Riley to choose not to drink that day – but doing so would have required God to interfere with Riley's free will. God would have had to directly make him decide to do something different. But forced decisions are not free, and interfering with free will is not something that God will do.

Why? Well, according to the free will defense, it's not because he can't interfere with free will; of course he can, he's all powerful. But God won't because free will is necessary for us to truly be good – for there to truly be good in the world. As Augustine put it, "If man is good, and if he would not be able to act rightly except by willing to do so, he ought to have free will because without it he would not be able to act rightly" (see Placher 1988, p. 107). In other words, only free acts are good acts – we only get moral credit for doing a good action if we freely choose to do it, of our own accord; even if an act is "the right thing," if we were forced to do it, then we don't really get moral credit for it and thus the act wasn't really morally good. To allow there to be moral good in the world, God must allow us to make our own free choices – but that means that sometimes we will do evil. So, he allows evil because the only way to prevent it is by making freely chosen "good' behavior impossible – and there being good is more important than there being no evil.

As a solution to the problem of evil, the free will defense has a couple of problems. According to Couenhoven (2007), even Augustine himself eventually rejected it. One problem is that it comes at a price. A legitimate question is, why doesn't God just interfere with people's decisions to do evil, and not interfere with our free decisions to do good? The answer has to be that in order for this solution to work, God has to maintain an absolute noninterference policy when it comes to free will. If he interfered with bad decisions, but not good, it would quickly become clear that you can't really choose to do evil – and our ability to be free would be curtailed. Likewise, as Sheriff Hassan suggests, if God choose to interfere with free will to save one person, but not to save another, legitimate questions would arise regarding his benevolence. So those who embrace this solution have to suggest that God does not interfere with any free will decisions, ever. But that would entail, not only that God doesn't answer most prayers, but that how human history turns out is solely up to us. Given how popular the belief is among theists that God is in control of history – indeed, they usually believe that everything that happens happens according to his plan – many theists cannot be willing to embrace this solution (see Johnson 2022d). Divine providence requires divine interference.

The second problem is that it doesn't quite deal with Sheriff Hassan's question of why Allah allowed his wife to suffer from pancreatic cancer; after all, it's not like she (or anyone else) chose for her to have it. Such evil is what philosophers call "natural evil" – evil brought about by natural processes, rather than human choices. The answer has to be that God's noninterference policy must extend to the world in general; he is perhaps there to "comfort us" (psychologically) in times of need, but when it comes to actually preventing things like diseases and earthquakes, he is completely hands off. Why an all-loving God would design the world such that things like diseases and earthquakes are inevitable is a different question (Johnson 2011, 2013c); but given that they are, the answer to the question of why God would allow some people to suffer from them but save others is that he doesn't. What happens happens, as a matter of chance or the consequences of our actions; God does not ever interfere in the world.

This view of God is equivalent to that of deism – the idea that God exists, and created the universe, but then left it up to its own devices. God just observes; he does not interfere. Thomas Jefferson was a deist, and the idea is perhaps philosophically defensible (although there are still legitimate questions regarding why natural evil is so egregious). Needless to say, however, it is not a view of God that comports with what the majority of Christians, or Jews, or Muslims believe. All three religions are replete with stories of how God performed miracles and otherwise interfered with the history of the world; indeed, they usually include the belief that God/Yahweh/Allah still does so on a regular basis (think of how often a religious person in your life has said that some modern-day event was something that God made happen). So, to the extent that Sheriff Hassan thinks "That's not how God works," he is not a typical theist or Muslim. And to the extent that *Midnight Mass*, through Sheriff Hassan, uses the problem of evil to argue that this really is the only view of God that makes sense – it's the only view that has a defensible explanation of why drunk drivers always walk away with scratches while the kids they hit die – *Midnight Mass* serves as a good argument for atheism. At the very least, it is a good argument against the view of God that is endorsed by the vast majority of religious believers.

The Problem with Suffering

As a way to defend the traditional view of God that is endorsed by the vast majority of religious believers, one may insist that God does sometimes interfere – and why he does in some instances and not others is just a mystery. It's beyond us. God is all knowing, after all, and so he would know better. In fact, he would even know when our suffering is a benefit and thus when he must let us suffer intentionally. It's all part of his plan. As Fr. Paul puts it,

> If you're here seeking to know answers to the unknowable, it's incumbent upon me to tell you that I have none. And if you want to know why or how God's will shapes the world, brothers and sisters, so do I. I don't have all the answers. Nobody does. What I do have though, and what God gives us plentifully, are mysteries. ("Book III: Proverbs")

But there are two fundamental flaws with this argument.

One is that it endorses something called skeptical theism, the position popularized by Stephen Wykstra (1984, 1996) that seemingly unjustified evil cannot count as evidence against God's existence because God could have reasons for allowing such evil that we simply can't comprehend. I have argued elsewhere that skeptical theism is logically and mathematically unsound; even if it's true that God *could* have reasons we can't comprehend, seemingly unjustified evil still provides evidence against his existence. When someone says that, if they come to your costume party, they *might* be wearing the perfect costume – so perfect that you couldn't recognize them – looking around and not seeing them at the party is still at least some reason to think they are not there. It's not deductive proof of course, but it raises the probably that they are not there (See Johnson 2013a).

But perhaps the bigger problem with skeptical theism is that it makes theism unfalsifiable and thus unreasonable. No matter how bad things got – all of humanity could be about to be destroyed by a plague of vampires – the skeptical theist could just shrug their shoulders and say, "God could have a reason." Beliefs for which nothing could ever count as disconfirming evidence are fundamentally irrational (Johnson 2021b). To paraphrase Carl Sagan, if someone says they have a fire-breathing dragon in their garage, but then explains why every physical test for it will fail – "you can't see it, it's invisible; you can look for footprints, it floats; you can't feel the fire; it's heatless" – their assertion is "veridically worthless, whatever value [it] may have in inspiring us or in exciting our sense of wonder" (Sagan 1997, p. 161). When someone has structured an assertion so that no evidence could count against it (or defends it with countless excuses to get around the evidence that refutes it) not only is that person not being intellectually honest, not only are they not engaging with you in good faith, and not only are merely pretending to be interested in the truth – but their assertion is essentially worthless. "What's the difference between an invisible, incorporeal, floating dragon who spits heatless fire and no dragon at all?" (Sagan 1997, p. 161).

The other problem with this argument is expressed quite nicely by Riley.

> The worst part is that it lets all the rest of us off the hook. We can all just stand by and watch Leeza Scarborough wheel herself around town. We can watch Joe Collie slowly drink himself to death. We can watch so many people just slip into these bottomless pits of . . . awful and we can stand it. We can tolerate it because we can say things like, "God works in mysterious ways." Like there's a plan? Like something good's gonna come out of it? Nothing good came out of my drinking. Nothing good came out of me killing that poor girl. Nothing good came out of Joe Collie's drinking. Not a single good thing comes out of Leeza never being able to walk again. Nothing good came out of a metric ton of crude oil filling up the bay. And the only thing, the only fucking thing that lets people stand by, watching all this suffering, doing nothing, doing fucking nothing, is the idea that suffering can be a gift from God. What a monstrous idea, Father. ("Book II: Psalms")

To the extent that religion turns suffering into a good thing, and thus makes people complacent about their suffering, and even unwilling to do anything about the suffering of others – to that extent, what Riley (and Flannigan) says here seem to be right: this is something that makes religion exceptionally dangerous. And in this way, it seems *Midnight Mass* provides yet another good reason to reject religion and favor atheism.

The Problem with the Afterlife

Midnight Mass contains quite a few monologues about death and the afterlife – monologues which, according to creator Mike Flanagan (2021), express his "thoughts, wishes, and even [his] best guess" about what happens when we die. The first belongs to Riley, who essentially says that – in the time between when your heart stops beating and your brain cells die – your brain releases a flood of DMT, "the psychedelic drug released when we dream," and you dream "the dream to end all dreams" ("Book IV: Lamentations").

Is this accurate? Of course, it's impossible to know for sure, but evidence does suggest that there is a flurry of brain activity that occurs after your heart stops beating (but before clinical brain death). Such activity is most likely what is responsible for so-called Near-Death Experiences, which are reported in about half of patients who are revived after coming close to death (Schick and Vaughn 2020, pp. 262–276). One study monitored brain activity in dying mice that was completely consistent with something like Riley's description of a dreamlike state (Zhenyi et al. 2019). So, Riley's description of what we experience while we die might actually be accurate.

But what happens *after* we die? According to Riley,

> I stop. My brain activity ceases and there is nothing left of me . . . No memory, no awareness that I ever was . . . Everything is as it was before me. And the electricity disperses from my brain till it's just dead tissue. Meat. Oblivion. And all of the other little things that make me up . . . The microbes and bacterium and the billion other little things that live on my eyelashes and in my hair and in my mouth and on my skin and in my gut and everywhere else, they just keep on living. And eating. And I'm serving a purpose. I'm feeding life. And I'm broken apart, and all the littlest pieces of me are just recycled, and I'm billions of other places. And my atoms are in plants and bugs and animals, and I am like the stars that are in the sky. There one moment and then just scattered across the goddamn cosmos. ("Book IV: Lamentations")

In reply, Erin tells a much different story – in which she speaks for her unborn daughter and tells a story of how her soul floats back to heaven to be reunited with and loved by the previously deceased members of her family. Although *Midnight Mass* doesn't refute it directly, this story is problematic for a number of reasons. For one, as I explained in 2013b, the concept of "a soul" has been completely refuted by philosophy and neuroscience. All the relevant evidence suggests that our minds are produced by and dependent upon brain activity, not housed is an ethereal non-physical entity that can separate from the body and float away upon death. What's more, Erin's story is incomplete; the biblical view of the afterlife also involves bodily resurrection. Just as Jesus's body was raised, ours shall be raised (I Corinthians, 15). But as Eric Olson pointed out in 2010, even if some kind of bodily resurrection were by some miracle to occur, it would be impossible for it to preserve a person's personal identity into the afterlife. The resurrected person would, at best, just be a copy of me – a fancy replica. (More on this later.)

But Erin's story is not what Flanigan thinks happens. In fact, it's not even what Erin thinks happens. At the end of the last episode, as Erin dies, she apparently has a dream where she speaks for herself and tells Riley what she really believes happens when we die. It's like Riley's theory, but with a bit of a twist.

> Speaking for myself? . . . Myself. My self. That's the problem. That's the whole problem with the whole thing. That word, "self." That's not the word. That's not right, that isn't. . . every atom in my body was forged in a star. This matter, this body is mostly just empty space after all, and solid matter? It's just energy vibrating very slowly and there is no me. There never was. The electrons of my body mingle and dance with the electrons of the ground below me and the air I'm no longer breathing. And I remember there is no point where any of

that ends and I begin. I remember I am energy. Not memory. Not self. . . . [death is] like a drop of water falling back into the ocean, of which it's always been a part. All things, a part. All of us, a part. You, me and my little girl, and my mother and my father, everyone who's ever been, every plant, every animal, every atom, every star, every galaxy, all of it. More galaxies in the universe than grains of sand on the beach, and *that's* what we're talking about when we say God. The One, the Cosmos. . . We are the Cosmos dreaming of itself . . . There is no death. Life is a dream. It's a wish. Made again and again and again and again and again and again and on into eternity. And I am all of it. I am everything. I am all. I am that I am. ("Book VII: Revelations")

When Erin borrows God's line "I am that I am" at the end (Exodus 3:14), she is not saying that she *is* God; she is saying that, in death, everyone reunites with "God" which (according to Erin) is the word we use when talking about the universe itself. She is not redefining what God is so she can still say "God exists" to beat the atheist on a technicality. Instead, she is reflecting the Hindu concept of Brahman, the "being" that is all of reality itself and that Hindus believe a person reunites with upon death.

But the majority of what Erin is expressing here reflects something common in Buddhism, which is known in the west as the "no-self theory" (Giles 1993). It's often understood as a version of Hume's "bundle theory" (though it definitely preceded Hume), which suggests that, when I reflect on my own internal states, there is no unitary "I" that exists; there is rather just a series of perceptions, "bundled together" as it were, in a sequence. That's not to say, Giles argues, that we can't speak as if persons exist; it's just that when we do so, we have to accept that we are only engaged in "conventional speech." Ultimately, there is no separately existing person – there is just a collection of experiences (and physical states), "bundled" together by causal relationships.

The metaphor that perhaps best describes this was popularized by another piece of pop culture, *The Good Place*, and comes from Buddhist philosopher Thich Nhat Hanh. Persons in the universe are like waves in the ocean, which move through their medium but are never qualitatively the same or even made of the same matter. Now it's not like waves don't exist in the conventional sense; we can point to a wave, describe it, and can even make sense of how a rise in the water *here* then causes a rise in the water *there*. But nothing exists beyond the water and its motion. So when the wave crashes to the shore, all that was still is (all that existed still does), it's just in a different form (Hanh 2003, p.23).

And so it is with persons. We are just a material/experiential wave, slowing moving through the universe, bound together by how one state causes the next. And when we die, all that was still is, it's just in a different form. Perhaps ironically, this view also has a biblical precedent; God tells Adam. "You are dust, and to dust you shall return" (Genesis 3:19). But it has never been the view of the afterlife taught in Christianity.

Once we understand this view, we can also understand why a physical resurrection of a person's body can't facilitate their survival into the afterlife: Once a causal chain has been broken, it cannot be restarted. You cannot recreate *the same person* by resurrecting their body any more than you can recreate *the same wave* by disturbing some section of the ocean. You might be able to start an exactly similar wave, but the original wave is forever lost.

But is Erin's view of persons and the afterlife correct? It is probably the most philosophically defensible conception of personhood there is (see Gallois 2016). And all other versions of the afterlife break down upon close examination (see Johnson 2023). So *Midnight Mass's* view of personhood, and its corresponding view of the afterlife, is at least quite reasonable.

The Problem with Faith

In reply to the problem of evil, and the arguments against belief in miracles, the afterlife, and the supernatural, the believer is likely to insist that one should simply have faith. Religion is not a matter of reason, but of belief – so one should simply set such concerns aside. But there are quite a few problems with appealing to faith as a way to respond to the arguments of *Midnight Mass.*

First, the arguments for faith are rather weak. Take Pascal's Wager, the argument which suggests that you might as well believe in God because it is a no loss bet (Saka n.d.). "If you believe, and you are wrong, what have you lost? But if you don't believe and you are wrong, you burn in hell." Not only might you burn in hell, even if you believe, because you chose the wrong religion (a possibility that Pascal seems to overlook), but it's not clear that you have nothing to lose by believing and being wrong. You could waste the only life you have trying to please a deity that doesn't exist. Think of how *Midnight Mass* suggests that Fr. Pruitt wasted his life serving the Catholic Church when he would have led a much happier life with Mildred. After we learn that he is the father of Sarah (Dr. Gunning), and he confesses he brought the angel back so that Mildred wouldn't die, he says

> I mean, our whole lives had been wasted, you know, staring across the church – too scared to come down and be with you. I mean, too scared to tell our own daughter the truth. And it never felt like a sin, that was the thing – you never felt like a sin, and our daughter, she was never a sin. She was never a mistake. Never. . . . but another chance? Now that we can be a family this time? Can you think of a miracle more amazing than that? ("Book VII: Revelation")

Or think about what Riley's mom says, on the night of the Midnight Massacre: "Never made much sense to me. We all say there's a heaven, and it's waiting for us. Then we claw, fight, beg, for a few more minutes at the end" ("Book VII: Revelation"). This line foreshadows Bev, at the end of the series, desperately digging a hole to hide from the sunrise. Could it be that, deep down, we realize that this is the only life that we get?

The second problem with appealing to faith is that, despite claims of those who want you to believe, faith is not a virtue. Faith, by definition, is belief without evidence – or sometimes even belief despite sufficient evidence to the contrary. But outside religion, we do not call such belief virtuous. Belief, despite all evidence, that the Earth is flat is not virtuous. Belief, despite a complete lack of evidence, that a teapot orbits the sun is not virtuous. So why would we call such belief virtuous just because it is about a religious matter?

Saying that faith is a virtue might be a handy way to trick people into believing what you want them to believe but otherwise have no evidence for – but belief without evidence is not a virtue. It is an epistemic vice. It's credulity. It's gullibility. As Flanagan put it, "I was struck as well by how fundamentalist thinking could permeate and corrupt any belief system. ... How easily faith could be weaponized against the faithful. How incentivized we could be made to believe something in the absence of evidence – or, even more disturbing, in the presence of contradictory facts. I was horrified at how this cognitive dissonance was, in some circles, presented as a virtue" (Flanagan 2021).

A third problem is that having faith, especially in God, is also *morally* problematic. In *The Ethics of Belief*, William Clifford argued that it "is wrong, always, everywhere, and for anyone to believe anything on insufficient evidence" (Clifford 2010, p. 138). The reason why, Clifford argued, is that it is wrong to choose to believe something when it risks harm to others, and believing anything on faith always risks harm to others. For one thing, usually when you choose to believe something without evidence, or despite evidence to the contrary, it is false – and false beliefs are very often harmful. Think of Fr. Pruitt's leap of faith that the thing attacking him, sucking his blood, and granting him immorality was an angel, rather than a vampire. That didn't turn out well for anyone. Worse still, however, even if what one happens to believe on faith is true, by believing on faith one promotes the habit of doing so. In other words, one endorses credulity as an acceptable epistemic practice. And that, itself, is harmful to society. Society can't function and is ripe for manipulation, when its members are unable to distinguish truth from fiction – especially today (Uribe 2018). So, anytime you promote the idea that it is okay to just believe whatever you want, simply because you want to, you are promoting ideas and practices that are harmful to society.

Now, to be fair, Clifford's conclusion is probably too strong. It can't always be wrong to believe without evidence; sometimes it's unavoidable. As Hume taught us, I can't conclude that the future will resemble the past without assuming the future will resemble the past. (The argument *the future will resemble the past because it always has in the past* is circular. See Henderson 2018.) But I'm not doing something immoral when I assume such a thing to conclude, for example, that I'll burn my hand on a hot stove because that's what happened the last time I put my hand on a hot stove. Further, if a belief can only help me, and not harm others, it would seem to be acceptable to believe on faith. If I ever get lost in the wilderness, the belief that I'll survive and be found might actually help sustain me; and so it wouldn't seem to be immoral to embrace that belief, even if I have no evidence for it (Feldman 2006).

Clifford is still right, however, when he says that belief by faith is immoral when it risks harm to others – and this is especially problematic for theistic belief because that is exactly what such belief does. Arguably nothing has done more to bring harm on the world than belief in God: The Crusades, the Inquisition, the endorsement of slavery, the present and past subjugation of women, misogyny, witch hunts, abortion clinic bombings, terrorism, theocracy, fascism, Christian nationalism – all of these things, and a host of others, were and still are done or embraced in God's name. And to the extent that any person embraces belief in God, that person promotes the existence of such belief and thus makes the evils done in God's name more likely (Johnson 2017b).

Consider that Bev's excuse for opening the church doors after the Midnight Massacre and letting the vampires descend upon the town has a theistic justification: "Those who have been coming to church and taking Communion, they have nothing to fear tonight. As for the rest of them . . . let God sort them out" ("Book VI: Acts of the Apostles"). That last phrase is based upon what Cistercian monk Arnaud Amalric said on July 22, 1209, when he was sent by Pope Innocent III to kill all the Cathars (a Christian religious sect) in the French town of Beziers. When the town's leaders refused to turn over the town's Cathars to him, he reportedly sent his crusaders into the town with the instructions: "Kill them all. God will recognize his own." This eventually became "Kill them all, let God sort them out" – a phrase which became popular with American Special Forces in the Vietnam war and was changed to "Kill 'em all. Let Allah sort 'em out" in Iraq and Afghanistan (Deis 2019). Needless to say, the phrase was used to excuse away the killing of innocent civilians – just as Bev did.

Even if one doesn't agree with the evil actions that are done in the name of a god that one believes in, the fact remains: Such belief couldn't be used as an excuse for evil if such belief didn't exist – and it wouldn't exist if people rejected it. At the least, if instead of embracing or tolerating theism, people generally reviled and criticized it, using God as a justification for evil actions would be less common. The appropriate response then, once one realizes that their beliefs are propping up a harmful ideology – or that they are in a group doing harm in the name of that ideology – is to reject such beliefs and leave the group. As Flanagan put it himself,

> My feelings about religion were very complicated. I was fascinated, but angry. Looking at various religions, I was moved and amazed by their propensity for forgiveness and faith, but horrified by their exclusionism, tribalism, and tendency toward fanaticism and fundamentalism. I found a lot of these various religions' ideas to be inspiring and beautiful, but I also found their corruptions to be grotesque and unforgivable. [So] I wasn't going to support those kinds of institutions any longer. (Flanagan 2021)

The Problem with Holy Books

Midnight Mass makes a similar point about the Bible. For every evil thing that Fr. Paul or Bev does, they have a Bible verse at the ready to justify it. Why should Wade and Sturge still help Fr. Paul even though he killed Joe Collie? "The man who acts presumptuously by not obeying the priest who stands to minister there before the Lord, your God, that man shall die" (Deuteronomy 17:12). As Bev says.

> Our Lord is a warrior, and so are His angels. Our Lord sent angels to Egypt to slaughter the firstborn of the Egyptians, turned cities to salt, women and children alike, and drowned the

world when we were too lost to our sins. Monsignor Pruitt himself is a miracle of God. And a performer of miracles, as you damn well know yourself, Wade. He is a miracle. God has a plan. He's working through him. "And we are to do our part to witness and do our part. And do not think that I have come to bring peace. I have not come to bring peace, but a sword" [Matthew 10:34]. It was Jesus who said that! Jesus Christ himself! So if you wanna question him now, Wade, if you want to pick and choose which one of his works are palatable to you, return all his graces to sender then, and let your little girl sit back down in that wheelchair. But do not cherry-pick the glories of God! Now wrap it up in the carpet. ("Book IV: Lamentations")

How does Fr. Paul clear his conscience for killing Joe? "How much more, then, will the blood of Christ, who through the eternal Spirit offered himself unblemished to God, cleanse our consciences from acts that lead to death so that we may serve the living God" (Hebrews 9:14). How can he possibly see his vampiric acts as endorsed by God? "Whoever eats my flesh and drinks my blood has eternal life. And I will raise them up on the last day, for my flesh is real food, and my blood is real drink and whoever eats my flesh and drinks my blood will remain in me, and I in them" (John 6:51). Indeed, many of the Romans believed the early Christians were cannibals for this very reason.

Why are Paul and Riley scorched by the sun? "The fourth angel poured his bowl upon the sun and it was allowed to scorch men with fire" (Revelations 16:8). The fact that they burst into flames in the sunlight? That's why the Book or Revelation says that God will plunge the world into darkness. The eternal life granted by vampirism? That's just the eternal life God promised. Fr. Paul even excuses away how scary the angel is by pointing out that, in the Bible, when angels appear, people are afraid. (For a full rundown of the Bible verses used to justify evil in the series, see Serrao 2021.)

Midnight Mass' suggestion seems to be that the Bible can be used to justify anything – even horrendous acts of evil – and thus is a dangerous book. As Flanagan put it

A lot of it was searching through [the Bible] and basically trying to find passages that we could use for this. I just had no idea it would be that easy . . . I mean, there were, especially in Revelation, there were so many things that just snapped right onto our agenda. But I think that's part of the point of the show, is this scripture can be so easily manipulated to fit an agenda, even one as ridiculous as the one we were using. That's scary. That should scare us, especially if we're going to say, or some of us are going to claim, that this book was written by God. That this book is a holy scripture. It can be weaponized very easily and context can be absolutely upended. And that's something I think that everyone should be wary of, faithful or not. (Maas 2021)

In reply to this criticism, believers will no doubt point out that Bev and Paul's interpretations of the relevant scriptures are different than theirs. While true, this misses the point. The worry is that any book can be interpreted just about any way a person wants – and thus can be used to justify just about anything a person wants, even when it is obviously evil. Now for regular books, this is not a problem; if a book is not thought to be the definitive guide of what is right and wrong, of how one ought to live one's life, then the fact that it could be interpreted as justifying evil actions is not worrisome. But if a book is regarded as holy, the fact that it could be so interpreted is a problem. Let me explain by example.

Lord of the Rings (LOTR) could be interpreted as an endorsement of racism. But while I am a fan of LOTR, I would not be culpable if someone used LOTR as a justification for their racism. Since I never said it is the definitive guide to how to live one's life, that's on them, not me. However, if I did worship LOTR, said it was perfect, and that it should guide all persons' actions – well, then I am partly culpable for their actions. If someone is racist because they thought LOTR said to be, their misinterpretation of the work is only half the problem. Their misinterpretation would have been inconsequential had they not also worshiped the book. So the book worship is also part of the problem. Thus, if I promote the idea that LOTR should be worshiped, I am also part of the problem. While I am not as culpable as the racists themselves, and I shouldn't have to renounce LOTR all together, I should renounce the idea that it should be worshiped as perfect guide to how one should live their life.

And so it is with the Bible. You may think that The Bible, when correctly interpreted, never advocates for violence. But that doesn't change the fact that it can be interpreted otherwise. So, if you embrace and promote the idea that the Bible is holy and should be followed by all people, you are partly to blame when others, fueled by the notion that the book is holy, go out and do evil things in its name. Of course, one may argue that no "true believer" could ever do such a thing – but not only is this obviously false (was Pope Innocent III not a "true believer"?), but it commits what's known as "The No True Scotsman fallacy" (Cline 2021b).

What's the upshot? What is the argument of *Midnight Mass* on this point? People should stop revering the Bible (or other scriptures) as "holy." Because books are always open to interpretation and thus could be used to justify evil no matter how vile – even turning an entire town into vampires – no book should be worshiped or revered as divinely inspired. And given what was just discussed, this argument seems quite persuasive.

Conclusion

I have attempted to show that *Midnight Mass* argues for atheism indirectly by making a case against miracles, the supernatural, faith, and the afterlife and argues for atheism directly by explaining away religious belief and raising the problem of evil. In doing so, it should be noted, *Midnight Mass* is not arguing against religious *believers*. Critics agree. As Christian reviewer Jonty Langley (2021) put it, "*Midnight Mass* contains some of the fairest treatments of Christian characters I've seen on screen." It is arguing against religious *belief*. In other words, it is not criticizing religious believers, saying that all believers are bad or stupid people. After all, the show makes it clear that Fr. Paul believes he is helping people, and many of the other religious characters – like Riley's parents who don't feed on anyone despite being vampires – are portrayed in a sympathetic light. If anything, *Midnight Mass* is on their side, trying to warn religious people that religion is taking advantage of them, tricking them into believing what is false, and that what is bad is good – into

26 *Midnight Mass* as Philosophy: The Problems with Religion

embracing their oppression instead of fighting against, and denying themselves, wasting the only life they have trying to please a nonexistent deity. This is, I believe, why reviewer Kayla Cobb (2021) said *Midnight Mass* is "critical of religious faith, without ever being cruel."

If any one kind of believer is being criticized, it is Bev – the religious fundamentalist, the fanatic – who takes her religion way too literally and seriously, who forces it on others and thinks that her religious devotion makes her better than other people. Indeed, Flanagan's criticism of such people is expressed directly by Riley's mom Annie:

> Bev, I want you to listen to me. Because your whole life, I think you've needed to hear this. You aren't a good person. … God doesn't love you more than anyone else. You aren't a hero. And you certainly, certainly aren't a victim. … God loves [my atheist son Riley] just as much as he loves you, Bev. Why does that upset you so much? Just the idea that God loves everyone just as much as you. ("Book VII: Revelation")

Of course, the Bevs of the world will likely refuse to see themselves in Bev; and they certainly won't be persuaded by any of the arguments the show presents. But Bev is not Flanagan's intended audience. That honor falls to the Rileys of the world, and the Erins – and those like Riley's parents who are good people, with a strong moral compass, and can recognize when they are being exploited. The audience is those who, like most of the islanders, can see need to reject the role that others have selected for them, to be a part of what others see as God's plan, and instead forge a path of their own.

Bibliography

Bitzer, Lloyd F. 1998. The 'Indian prince' in miracle arguments of Hume and his predecessors and early critics. *Philosophy and Rhetoric* 31 (3): 175–230.

Boudry, Maarten, Stefaan Blancke, and Johan Braeckman. 2010. How not to attack intelligent design creationism: Philosophical misconceptions about methodological naturalism. *Foundations of Science* 15 (3): 227–244. https://doi.org/10.1007/s10699-010-9178-7.

Clifford, W.K. 2010. The ethics of belief. In *Philosophy: The quest for truth*, ed. Louis Pojman and Lewis Vaughn, 134–138. Oxford: Oxford University Press.

Cline, Austin. 2021a. Karl Marx on religions as the opium of the people, Sept. 10. learnreligions. com/karl-marx-on-religion-251019

———. 2021b. Understanding the "No True Scotsman" Fallacy. *ThoughtCo*, Dec. 6. https://www.thoughtco.com/the-no-true-scotsman-fallacy-250339

Cobb, Kayla. 2021. 'Midnight Mass's respect to religion is revolutionary for horror. *Decider*. https://decider.com/2021/09/28/midnight-mass-respects-religion/

Collins, Chad. 2021. Faith and fear make 'midnight mass' an affirmative experience. *Dread Central*. https://www.dreadcentral.com/editorials/415166/faith-and-fear-make-midnight-mass-an-affirmative-experience/

Couenhoven, Jesse. 2007. Augustine's rejection of the free-will defence: An overview of the late Augustine's theodicy. *Religious Studies* 43 (3): 279–298.

Deis, Robert. 2019. *Kill them all and let God sort them out*, July 22.

Edis, Taner. 2021. *Weirdness!* Durham: Pitchstone Publishing.

Feldman, Richard. 2006. Clifford's principle and James's options. *Social Epistemology* 20 (1): 19–33. https://doi.org/10.1080/02691720600631645.

Flanagan, Mike. 2021. The deeply personal horror of "midnight mass". *Bloody Disgusting*, Sept. 27. https://bloody-disgusting.com/editorials/3684646/deeply-personal-horror-midnight-mass-guest-essay-filmmaker-mike-flanagan/?fbclid=IwAR1g7v71EEr4iQEcoQ_V_ZvRDHDUAUTeMmizGumwrurvsa0HbFRyM3A4yFo

Gallois, Andre. 2016. Identity over time. In *The Stanford encyclopedia of philosophy* (Winter Edition), ed. Edward N. Zalta. https://plato.stanford.edu/archives/win2016/entries/identity-time

Giles, James. 1993. The no-self theory: Hume, Buddhism, and personal identity. *Philosophy East and West* 43 (2): 175–200. http://www.jstor.org/stable/1399612

Greene, Brian. 2013. How the Higgs Boson was found. *Smithsonian Magazine*, July. https://www.smithsonianmag.com/science-nature/how-the-higgs-boson-was-found-4723520/

Hanh, Thich Nhat. 2003. *No death, no fear: Comforting wisdom for life*. Penguin books.

Harris, Sam. 2012. *The moral landscape*. London: Black Swan.

Harvey, Van. 2016. Nietzsche and the problem of suffering. *Philosophy Now.* https://philosophynow.org/issues/114/Nietzsche_and_the_Problem_of_Suffering

Helmenstine, Anne Marie. 2020. A brief history of atomic theory. *ThoughtCo*, Aug 28. thoughtco.com/history-of-atomic-theory-4129185

Henderson, Leah. 2018. The problem of induction. *Stanford Encyclopedia of Philosophy.* https://plato.stanford.edu/entries/induction-problem/

Hill, Libby. 2021. The very real monsters in Mike Flanagan's Midnight Mass. *Indie Wire*, Oct. 22. https://www.indiewire.com/2021/10/midnight-mass-vampires-monsters-mike-flanagan-what-it-means-1234673807/?fbclid=IwAR1holvdOSDNidwXWmht5q15aEgJ3IlN-qqa-R9dfB3RBeDQf3flm7wST9E

Hume, David. 1993. *An enquiry concerning human understanding*. Indianapolis: Hackett Publishing Company.

Johnson, David Kyle. 2011. Natural evil and the simulation hypothesis. *Philo* 14 (2): 161–175.

———. 2013a. A refutation of skeptical theism. *Sophia* 52 (3): 425–445. https://doi.org/10.1007/s11841-012-0326-0.

———. 2013b. Do souls exist? *Think* 12 (35): 61–75. https://doi.org/10.1017/s1477175613000195.

———. 2013c. The failure of Plantinga's solution to the logical problem of natural evil. *Philo* 15 (2): 145–157.

———. 2015a. Justified belief in miracles is impossible. *Science, Religion and Culture* 2 (2): 61–74. https://doi.org/10.17582/journal.src/2015/2.2.61.74.

———. 2015b. *The myths that Stole Christmas: Seven misconceptions that hijacked the holiday and how we can take it Back*. Washington, D.C.: Humanist Press.

———. 2017a. Justified belief in demons is impossible. In *Philosophical approaches to demonology*, ed. Benjamin McCraw and Robert Arp. Routledge. https://doi.org/10.4324/9781315466774-11.

———. 2017b. Moral culpability and choosing to believe in god. In *Atheism and the Christian faith*, ed. Bill Anderson, 11–32. Wilmington: Vernon Press.

———. 2018a. Mystery therefore magic. In *Bad arguments: 100 of the most important fallacies in western philosophy*, by Robert Arp, Bruce Robert and Steve Barbone, 189–192. Wiley-Blackwell. https://doi.org/10.1002/9781119165811.ch38.

———. 2018b. The Galileo Gambit. In *Bad arguments: 100 of the most important fallacies in western philosophy*, ed. Robert Arp, Bruce Robert, and Steve Barbone, 152–156. Wiley-Blackwell. https://doi.org/10.1002/9781119165811.ch27.

———. 2019. The Relevance (and Irrelevance) of Questions of Personhood (and Mindedness) to the Abortion Debate. *SHERM (Socio-Historical Examination of Religion and Ministry)* 1 (2): 121–153. https://doi.org/10.33929/sherm.2019.vol1.no2.02.

———. 2020. Identifying the conflict between religion and science. *SHERM (Socio-Historical Examination of Religion and Ministry)* 2 (1): 121–153. https://doi.org/10.33929/sherm.2020.vol2.no1.06.

———. 2021a. Inference to the best explanation and rejecting the resurrection. *SHERM (Socio-Historical Examination of Religion and Ministry)* 3 (1): 26–51. https://doi.org/10.33929/sherm.2021.vol3.no1.02.

———. 2021b. Refuting skeptical theism. In *God and horrendous suffering (GCRR Publishing, 2021)*, ed. John Loftus, 212–232. Denver: GCRR (Global Center for Religious Research) Publishing.

———. 2022a. Does god exist? *Think* 21 (61): 5–22. https://doi.org/10.1017/S1477175621000415.

———. 2022b. On angels, demons, and ghosts: Is justified belief in spiritual entities possible? *Religions* 13 (7): 603. https://doi.org/10.3390/rel13070603.

———. 2022c. Free will, the holocaust, and the problem of evil. *SHERM (Socio-Historical Examination of Religion and Ministry)* 4 (2): 81–96. https://doi.org/10.33929/sherm.2022.vol4.no1.06.

———. 2022d. God's Prime Directive: Non-Interference and Why There Is No (Viable) Free Will Defense. Religions 13: 871. https://doi.org/10.3390/rel13090871

———. 2023. More on the relevance of personhood and mindedness: salvation and the possibility of an afterlife. *SHERM (Socio-Historical Examination of Religion and Ministry)* 5 (2).

Langley, Jonty. 2021. Midnight Mass: The Christian horror series with a challenging message for the Church. *Premier Christianity*. https://www.premierchristianity.com/reviews/midnight-mass-the-christian-horror-series-with-a-challenging-message-for-the-church/5670.article

Loudon, Irvine. 2013. Ignaz Phillip Semmelweis' studies of death in childbirth. *Journal of the Royal Society of Medicine* 106 (11): 461–463. https://doi.org/10.1177/0141076813507844.

Maas, Jennifer. 2021. How 'midnight mass' creator Mike Flanagan used the bible to 'completely justify' a horror story. *The Wrap*, December 1. https://www.thewrap.com/midnight-mass-bible-vampire-angel-connections-mike-flanagan/?fbclid=IwAR2%2D%2DxjxMQtc-UIzpzHIC N7Eka8QQj3C-Q-EJknCPCkV06EoZoiWAWy-ryU

Mackie, J. L. 1955. Evil and omnipotence. *Mind* 64 (254): 200–212 Evil and Omnipotence on JSTOR.

Manson, Neil. 2021. *This is philosophy of religion.* Hoboken: John Wiley & Sons.

Marx, Karl. 1843/1970. *Critique of Hegel's philosophy of right,* trans. Joseph O'Malley. Oxford University Press. Available at https://www.marxists.org/archive/marx/works/download/Marx_Critique_of_Hegels_Philosophy_of_Right.pdf

McMullin, Ernan. 1992. *The inference that makes science.* Milwaukee: Marquette University Press. https://doi.org/10.1111/j.1467-9744.2012.01319.x.

Nietzsche, Friedrich. 1956. *The birth of tragedy and the genealogy of morals,* trans. Francis Golffing. New York City: Anchor Books.

Olson, Eric. 2010. Immanent causation and life after death. In *Personal identity and resurrection,* ed. G. Gasser, 51–66. Ashgate.

Pike, Nelson. 1979. Plantinga on free will and evil. *Religious Studies* 15 (4): 449. https://www.jstor.org/stable/20005600

Placher, William C. 1988. *Readings in the history of Christian theology. Vol. 1, From its beginnings to the eve of the reformation.* Philadelphia: Westminster John Knox Press.

Plantinga, Alvin. 1967. Chapter 6: The free will defense. In *God and other minds.* Cornell University Press.

Radford, Benjamin. 2011. *Tracking the Chupacabra: The vampire beast in fact, fiction and folklore.* Albuquerque: University of New Mexico Press.

Romano, Aja. 2021. Why I felt betrayed by Netflix's Midnight Mass. *Vox.* https://www.vox.com/21509362/netflix-midnight-mass-mike-flanagan-horror-religion

Sagan, Carl. 1997. *Demon hunted world.* London: Headline Book Publishing.

Saka, Paul. n.d. Pascal's wager about god. In *Internet Encyclopedia of Philosophy.* https://iep.utm.edu/pasc-wag/. Accessed 17 June 2022.

Sant, Joseph. 2019. *Copernicanism and Stellar Parallax.* http://www.scientus.org/Copernicus-Stellar-Parallax.html

Schick, Theodore, and Lewis Vaughn. 2020. *How to think about weird things*. 8th ed. New York: McGraw Hill. https://doi.org/10.1017/s1477175600000154.

Serrao, Nivea. 2021. All the verses and how they connect: Biblical references in Netflix's 'Midnight ass' explained. *Syfy Wire*, Oct 1. https://www.syfy.com/syfy-wire/netflix-midnight-mass-bible-references-explained

Steere-Williams, Jacob. 2016. The germ theory. In *A companion to the history of American science*, ed. Georgina M. Montgomery and Mark A. Largent, 397–407. Hoboken: John Wiley & Sons Ltd. https://doi.org/10.1002/9781119072218.ch31.

Swinburne, Richard. 1968. Miracles. *Philosophical Quarterly.*

Thornton, Stephen. n.d. Sigmund Freud: Religion. *Internet Encyclopedia of Philosophy.* https://iep.utm.edu/freud-r/

Uribe, Francisco Mejia. 2018. Believing without evidence is always morally wrong. *Aeon*, Nov. 5. https://aeon.co/ideas/believing-without-evidence-is-always-morally-wrong

Whittaker, John H. 1978. Causes, reasons, and the genetic fallacy. *Journal of the American Academy of Religion* XLVI (3): 351–368. https://doi.org/10.1093/jaarel/XLVI.3.351.

Wilson, E.O. 1975. *Sociobiology: The new synthesis*. Cambridge, MA: Belknap Press.

Wykstra, Stephen J. 1984. The humean obstacle to evidential arguments from suffering: On avoiding the evils of 'appearance'. *International Journal for Philosophy of Religion* 16: 73–93.

———. 1996. Rowe's Noseeum arguments from evil. In *The evidential argument from evil*, ed. Daniel Howard-Snyder, 126–150. Bloomington and Indianapolis: Indiana University Press.

Zhenyi Li, Jing Zhang, Zongya Zhao, Hongxing Zhang, Martin Vreugdenhil, and Chengbiao Lu. 2019. Near-death high-frequency hyper-synchronization in the rat hippocampus. *Frontiers in Neuroscience*. https://doi.org/10.3389/fnins.2019.00800. https://www.frontiersin.org/articles/10.3389/fnins.2019.00800/full

Squid Game as Philosophy: The Myths of Democracy

27

Leander Penaso Marquez and Rola Palalon Ombao

Contents

Introduction 610
    Ojingeo Geim 610
The Myths of Democracy 613
    The Myth of Free Choice 613
    The Myth of Equality 617
    The Myth of Empowerment 621
    The Myth of Transparency 624
    The Myth of the Ideal 627
Conclusion 630
References 631

Abstract

At first glance, *Squid Game* may appear to be about how the rich have the power to oppress the poor, about economic inequality and capitalism, or about class struggle. The series touches on all of these, but at the center of it, *Squid Game* shows how democracy is used as a tool for control. Given the right motivation, the rule of the many can be manipulated to benefit the interests of the few and, in some cases, to coerce the minority. Despite the advantages of democracy, the series portrays how democracy can be less than ideal, rotten, and dysfunctional. An investigation of the turn of events in the series reveals at least five myths about democracy.

Keywords

Squid Game · Democracy · Plato · Aristotle · Social contract · Freedom of choice · Elitism · Empowerment · Feminism · Gender equality · Virtue · Control ·

L. P. Marquez (✉) · R. P. Ombao
College of Social Sciences and Philosophy, University of the Philippines Diliman, Quezon City, Philippines
e-mail: lpmarquez@up.edu.ph; rpombao@up.edu.ph

© Springer Nature Switzerland AG 2024
D. K. Johnson et al. (eds.), *The Palgrave Handbook of Popular Culture as Philosophy*,
https://doi.org/10.1007/978-3-031-24685-2_113

Oppression · Class struggle · Justice · Rule of law · Reward and punishment · Self and others · State of nature

Introduction

If anyone asks for the meaning of the phrase "game of life," the Netflix TV series *Squid Game* is perhaps one of the best examples. Life can be understood as a game where there are rules, and a person needs to play by those rules. Obeying a rule, or violating it, has repercussions. Depending on what a person does in relation to the rules, the consequence can be a reward or a punishment – and these consequences have an impact on the person's life. Similarly, *Squid Game* tells a story about a group of people who participated in a series of games. While whoever follows the rules and wins in the end will win a handsome reward that will change their life, whoever disobeys the rules or obeys them and loses will be punished with death. This may appear grotesque, but what is more chilling is that participation in the game is entirely democratic.

This chapter will identify and explore the myths of democracy that the series exposes – the beliefs and ideals that many think democracy can deliver but, in reality, it cannot. These myths have been passed on from generation to generation to make it seem that democracy is a near-perfect governing and social system, vastly superior to all others. The series shows how this façade of superiority is being used to exploit the vulnerabilities of people who live in democracies. By playing on the appeal of these myths, the elite can impose their will upon the masses. The manipulation has been so successful that people do not see that they are being manipulated even if they are in the center of everything that has been happening. *Squid Game* provides the opportunity for viewers to see this harsh reality from a position of a third-person observer. Through this detached perspective, based on what they see in the episodes, viewers are invited to reflect on their own situations and situatedness.

Maximizing the opportunity for introspection that has been provided by this series, this chapter will reflect on democracy as a tool that makes the game of life unwinnable for many people. The intention is not necessarily to favor another system; it is rather to illustrate how *Squid Game* exposes the myths, bringing key tensions and conflicts within democracy into focus.

Ojingeo Geim

Squid Game revolves around 456 contestants who compete in a series of six games that are held over a span of six days. The players have several things in common: they are all in great debt, they were recruited through winning a game of *ddakji*, and they all willingly agreed to participate in the games for a chance to win more money.

The first episode of the series introduces Seong Gi-hun, a man who likes to gamble and has accrued a big debt due to gambling. One night in a train station, he meets a man who challenges him to a game of *ddakji*, promising to give him 100,000 won every time he wins. Gi-hun loses every round, except in the last, where he wins and receives 100,000 won. The man asks Gi-hun if he would be interested to play other games and win an even bigger prize. Gi-hun is suspicious, but the man gives him a calling card in case he later decides he wants to play.

Later, desperate for money, Gi-hun calls the number and is given a pick-up location. He is picked up by a van driven by a person in a pink tracksuit, who puts him to sleep. When he awakens, he finds himself in a large room (a common room or a dormitory) with other people in numbered green tracksuits like himself. There, he recognizes other players, Cho Sang-woo, his childhood friend, and Player 067 – Kang Sae-byeok – a pickpocket who stole his horse-racing winnings a few days earlier. Gi-hun also gets to know Player 001 – Oh Il-nam – an old man who joined the games, wanting to do something interesting rather than just waiting to die from his brain tumor.

Before the competition formally commences, all the contestants are asked to sign a player consent form, which contains three clauses:

Clause 1: A player is not allowed to stop playing.
Clause 2: A player who refuses to play will be eliminated.
Clause 3: Games may be terminated if the majority agrees.

Signing the form means they agree to participate and abide by the rules of the competition. As each player is eliminated, a hundred million won is added to the prize pot. At the end of the game, the victor will win prize money of 45.6 billion won (around 38 million USD).

The first game is "Red Light, Green Light," where players must reach the finish line from the starting point by walking or running whenever the light turns green and stopping whenever the light turns red. Anyone caught moving during a red light is eliminated. The players, however, discover that being eliminated in the game has a literal meaning – they actually get killed. In a hail of gunfire, the first game eliminates 255 players, which means that 25.5 billion won is added to the prize pot.

Despite the huge amount of potential winnings, faced with the fact that losing in the game means losing their lives, many players want to stop the games. Following Clause 3 of the player consent form, the game facilitators give the players an opportunity to vote on whether they want to continue the games or stop. The voting results in a tie of 100 for each side, with Il-nam's vote serving as the tiebreaker. Il-nam votes to stop the games. With the majority of the remaining players deciding to stop the games and go home, the contest is halted, and the players are dumped on the streets to make their way home. However, since not all the games were finished, no one gets the prize money. Gi-hun goes to the police station to report what happened to him, but none of the police officers take him seriously, except for officer Hwang Jun-ho, who is intrigued and decides to investigate. Eventually, the players, including Gi-hun, are reinvited to continue with the games. Faced with a mountain of debt to settle as well as the impending migration of his daughter to the

United States if he cannot provide financial support for her, Gi-hun decides to come back for another shot at the prize money.

The second game is *Ppopgi*, where players must work through a *ppopgi* (Korean sweet candy) to perfectly extract a carved shape within a limited time. A player is eliminated if the shape is destroyed or time runs out. The third game is "Tug of War," which is held on two opposite towers with the rope stretching between them. The team that loses falls to a certain death. The fourth game is not predetermined but must be a game that uses marbles. In this game, the players are given a set of marbles and are asked to pair up; they are made to decide what game to play with the marbles, and the player who takes all their opponent's marbles gets to be the winner. The fifth game requires the players to cross a glass bridge with two parallel sets of panels. Those who reach the other end of the bridge win the game. Half of the panels are made of strong, tempered glass, while the other panels are too weak to support even one person. Those who are unfortunate enough to step on the glass panels that break fall to their death. In all these games, the players are free to forge alliances, recruit teammates, strategize for themselves or their team, and do whatever they think is necessary for them to win – including killing off other players even outside of the games.

By the sixth day, only Gi-hun and his childhood friend Sang-woo are left. The sixth and final game is *Ojingeo Geim* (Squid Game). The name comes from the shape of the arena, which looks like a squid. The game was supposed to be a fight to the death, but upon winning, Gi-hun refuses to kill Sang-woo (even if Sang-woo double-crossed him during the games). In the end, Sang-woo kills himself, making Gi-hun the ultimate winner.

A year later, Gi-hun receives an invitation from Il-nam, who viewers previously thought had died during the marble game. On his deathbed, Il-nam tells Gi-hun that he created the games for the entertainment of wealthy individuals as well as his own. Il-nam confesses that he and his clients do not feel joy in their lives despite being very rich – the same experience that people who do not have money go through. Gi-hun could not believe what he heard – that he and the other players had to go through the things they did just to entertain some wealthy people. However, Il-nam reminded him that none of them was forced to play, that they all gave their consent, and that they all decided to come back to play the games on their own. Finally, Il-nam breathes his last as the clock strikes midnight.

A few days later, Gi-hun is at a train station on his way to the airport to see his daughter, who is in the United States. At the other side of the station, he sees a familiar scene – a couple of men playing *ddakji*. He recognizes one of the men as the same person who recruited him to Il nam's games. He tries to run after him but fails to catch him. Gi-hun, however, succeeds to get the man's (or more appropriately the game's) calling card from the person he was playing with. Later, as he walks on the boarding ramp to his plane, he calls the number on the card, introduces himself, and asks the person on the other line who they are and how they are still able to do what they do. The person on the other end tells Gi-hun to just board the plane for his own good. Gi-hun hangs up the phone, turns around, and walks away from the plane, clearly intent on bringing the games to an end.

The Myths of Democracy

The idea that the Squid Game is democratic is laid out in the first episode of the series. The recruiter gives Gi-hun the choice to play *ddakji* with him and gives him the choice to participate in other games. Inside the common room, the players are given the rules of the "game world" and asked for their consent to abide by these rules. After the first game, in the second episode, the players are given a chance to vote to continue or not, and the result of the vote is honored. In the same episode, the players, knowing that they will be participating in a deadly version of popular Korean children's games, willingly decide to go back and continue with the games and follow its rules. All these instances show that the players are free to choose and act on their decisions so long as they abide by the established rules. This established premise was confirmed by Il-nam – the creator of the games himself – in the final episode as his final confession to Gi-hun.

The democratic setup, however, is a well-designed tool for manipulation and control. The choices the players make, like whether to play at all, are not really free; they are made out of desperation. The players arrive at their decision to join the games because they have almost nothing else to turn to. They are pushed by their situation to participate in a game that puts their lives at risk. Upon beginning the games, they are left at the mercy of each other because they can only leave if most of them agree. Thus, Il-nam designed the game to make the players feel they have a choice, when in fact they have none. Their ability to choose, to decide, and to vote is used to imprison them in a game that is controlled and decided by a few wealthy and powerful people. Those who facilitate the game – the guards, the front man, and the game masters – act as enablers. Thus, *Squid Game* reveals an ugly side of democracy to those who are willing to see it – it reveals that democracy is a social contract that thrives in the proliferation of myths. We shall talk about five that *Squid Game* identifies.

The Myth of Free Choice

As described by Aristotle (2013) in Book VI of *Politics*, "...the basic premise of the democratic sort of regime is freedom. It is customarily said that only in this sort of regime do men partake of freedom, for, so it is asserted, every democracy aims at this" (1317b). Freedom in a democratic society can therefore be interpreted as the ability of each citizen in that society to "live as one wants" (1317b). Ideally, this goes hand in hand with the shared freedom that each one has access to and enjoys; in other words, we are each free to do what we want as long as it does not interfere with the freedom of others. As such, people in a democratic setting are "empowered" because they can supposedly decide and act on their decisions in so far as their freedom does not interfere with the freedom of others; this is seen as an exercise of free choice.

Indeed, generally, there is a conception that the best place to exercise free choice is under a democratic society since such a political setting provides its people with certain liberties that other forms of government do not necessarily offer. For instance, North Korea is famously known for maintaining a socialist state and practicing totalitarian dictatorship. In this form of government, "all authority flows from the Supreme Leader" (Albert 2020, para. 1). The country is being ruled by absolute authority from one person, using techniques such as heavy repression and a system of patronage in order to ensure support from elites and the military (Albert 2020). Unlike in other countries, where democracy is being exercised, "North Korea ranks at the bottom of every measure of freedom—economic, political, religious, civil. North Korea's 25 million people lack the freedoms Roosevelt spoke of: There is no freedom of speech. Religion is forbidden. Want is widespread, with malnutrition—even, at times, starvation—being the norm" (Kirkpatrick 2016).

Hence, it is common for people to prefer democracy over other forms of political settings, such as dictatorship, primarily because it affords us freedom. *Squid Game*, however, raises questions about how much freedom actually exists in a democracy. Sure, people make choices – but are those choices actually free? In a democracy, people perceive free choice as one of the most crucial aspects of freedom. But is the decision of the players to join the game in the first place actually a free choice?

Generally, it is thought that a person is free so long as they have the ability to choose (there is more than one option), and they can do so based on their own will without being coerced or influenced. This aligns with the standard philosophical definitions of free will, like the libertarian definition, which suggests that one must be able to choose otherwise if one is to choose freely, and the compatibilist definition, which essentially suggests that in order for a choice to be free, it must originate from oneself (one's desires or will or rational deliberation; see O'Connor and Franklin 2018). Further, the choice must be informed; a person must be in a position to know what they are actually choosing, for example, what the risks or consequences of the choice will be. If I agree to split a taxi with someone but at the end of the ride they reveal they have no money, it can hardly be said that I freely choose to pay their fair. But in *Squid Game*, it seems that the conditions for a free will decision are not met – especially when it comes to the contestants' choice to participate in the game in the first place. Why?

First, it seems that their decision to play is uninformed. All they initially know is that they will be playing more games for a bigger prize. Even once they arrive in the huge room with bunk beds and hundreds of other people wearing the same tracksuit, they only learn that (1) there are a total of 456 players; (2) most, if not all, of them are on the brink of financial ruin; (3) they will be playing six games over the course of six days; and (4) whoever wins the game gets the chance to take home the pot money in the huge golden piggy bank hanging on the ceiling at the center of the room. But as for the exact details of the game – how they will be played, who they will be playing them with, the consequences for losing, or how much exactly the prize pot will be – everyone remains ignorant until the guards usher them to another enormous room with a massive robot doll. It was only there that even the name of the first game is revealed. The players are told that they will be playing a children's game called "Red Light, Green Light." In this game, the massive robot doll serves as the traffic light. It can call either "red light" or "green light." When it calls "green light," players from behind it can move toward it, but when it calls "red light" and turns around, the players must stop and stay still. The goal is to cross the line behind the traffic light without getting caught. But it is only once the game begins that they learn that being eliminated from the game means death by rifle; all those who are caught moving when the doll calls "red light" are automatically shot dead. And once they do learn this, more than half decide they do not want to play and try to escape. Clearly, they would not have chosen to play had they known the rules; thus, they did not freely choose to play the game in the first place. And given how the rest (besides Player 001) remain frozen in terror, it seems they did not freely choose to play the game either.

This, it seems, is not unlike what often happens in democratic societies, where the full consequences of decisions are not fully known until after the decisions are made. This can happen when voting for political candidates, when, for example, they do not follow through on their campaign promises. It can also happen when making life decisions, when (for example) someone is not in a position to understand the true cost of a college education or a medical procedure. Indeed, the danger of surprise medical bills is so acute in the United States that the Biden-Harris administration enacted numerous regulations to guard against them (HHS 2021).

In *Squid Game*, at the end of the first game, only 201 players remained, with 255 others dead. It is only then that they learn that they will be playing against each other in six different games for six days, and losing a game means dying, but with each death, the prize pool increases. It is at this point that they take a vote on whether to end the game, with Player 001 casting the deciding vote to end it. But after they return to the real world, a number of them who decide to end the game – including Gi-hun – decide to return to play it. Since they now know what the game entails and thus understand the risks (although they do not know the specifics of the upcoming games), one might think that their choice to participate is now free. But again, it seems not – and this is another way *Squid Game* exposes the myth of free choice in a democracy.

Clearly, those who chose to return to the game were pursuing money, not for its own sake but because they thought that money would be able to solve their problems. As Aristotle (2011) put it in Book 1 of the *Nicomachean Ethics*, "[t]he moneymaking life is characterized by a certain constraint, and it is clear that wealth is not the good being sought, for it is a useful thing and for the sake of something else" (1096a). But their problems are so serious that we are forced to wonder whether it is really fair to say that the players who "voluntarily" rejoined the game made the choice out of their own free will. For example, Gi-hun is a divorced man who is willing to do anything to prove to the court that he is financially capable of taking care of his daughter so he may be able to acquire custody. Otherwise, his daughter and ex-wife, together with the new husband, will migrate to the United States for good, and he will never see them again. Unfortunately, being financially capable is far from reality for Gi-hun. He could not even buy his daughter a decent meal for her birthday without stealing money from his mother and gambling at the local horse-racing game. Additionally, Gi-hun still has the loan sharks to worry about as they threatened to take his organs if he cannot pay them by the following month. And then there is his mom's medical condition, which he cannot afford to treat. Indeed, all the others who choose to return to the game are in a similarly desperate situation. It could be argued, therefore, that their decision to rejoin the game was not entirely free. It was so influenced by all the circumstances surrounding them that they essentially had no choice. Even knowing what the game entails, there is no alternative possibility for them; trying to survive the game is their only chance to escape. The decision is made not by them but by their circumstances. Living in a democratic country gave them the illusion that whatever they decide to do is a decision that they have complete power and control over – a free choice. But it does not seem that is actually the case. Those in charge of the game are actually in control; they are able to make Gi-hun and the others play the game, knowing they are not in a position to say no.

Real-world democracy seems to do this to us as well. We have no choice but to put up with abuse at work, with our low pay, because the alternative is unbearable. In fact, it seems it is South Korea's ballooning household debt crisis that serves as the inspiration for the series. As Sarah Son (2021) puts it,

> Household debt in South Korea has risen sharply in recent years to over 100% of its GDP— the highest in Asia. The top 20% of earners in the country have a net worth 166 times that of the bottom 20%, a disparity which has increased by half since 2017. There has been rising debt relative to income and a recent hike in interest rates. This has left those who lack the resources to deal with unplanned events, such as a sudden redundancy or a family illness, in an even more precarious position . . . It's not just families that are putting themselves in debt to pay for housing and education costs—an essential expense for middle classes hoping to secure entry to a desirable university for their children. In August, the South Korean government announced new lending curbs aimed at bringing down debt among younger people. Millennials and those in their 30s are in the most debt relative to their income. But attempts to curb borrowing have led to some people turning to higher cost and higher risk lenders instead. Such a choice leaves many at the mercy of debt collectors if the slightest change in their circumstances causes them to default on repayments. While few may find themselves in the hands of gangsters threatening to harvest their organs for sale, as shown in Squid Game, the burden of overwhelming debt is a deepening social problem—not to mention the leading cause of suicide in South Korea.

If the debt problem is driving South Koreans to kill themselves, it is not unreasonable at all to think that they would be willing to play the Squid Game even knowing the risks. One in 456 chances at life is better than assured death. Thus, *Squid Game* is pointing at a real-world way by which democracy makes people think that they have the liberty to do things as they want and live as they see fit when that is not necessarily true. Free choice is not always available just because there is democracy. When one is confronted with problems that seem impossible to solve or get out of, a choice must be made, but one that is not necessarily born out of one's own volition. During the times when people are provided with very limited options and not choosing is not one of them, the sense of being free and being able to make a free choice is an illusion because then people are forced to make a choice that is literally handed over to them by those who can actually make free choices and control them. Further, the options that are given do not always make the decision-making process easy. Chances are people are confronted with two or more unappealing choices, which force them to choose the option that they think is the least bad for them but not necessarily the best. This act of choosing, although seemingly "free," is not a self-directed choice at all but is instead made necessary by circumstances; thus, there is only an illusion of choice.

For Aristotle, human life has *telos* or purpose. Accordingly, it is important for any democratic society to provide its citizens with conditions (e.g., laws and education) under which they can pursue and achieve their *telos*. Otherwise, a flawed sense of freedom will be promoted – a sense that allows its people to do just about anything but does not guide them toward the achievement of their *telos*. This, for Aristotle (2011), is not a good life "for happiness was said to be a certain sort of activity of soul in accord with virtue" (1099b). *Squid Game* shows us that the extent to which democracy allows us to live such a life of virtue is limited.

The Myth of Equality

In episode 5 of *Squid Game*, Hwang Jun-ho, a police officer who sneaks into the headquarters where the game is being played, finds out about a room that holds all the records of those who have previously joined the game. It was then revealed that it was not the first time that the game was being conducted, which means there are more than 456 players who have joined and probably have died from taking part in the game. In other words, there are thousands of others whose decision was based on the very limited options handed to them by those who have access to free choice and can control those choices for others. If this is the case, then democracy provides people with not just a false sense of free choice but also an illusion of equality.

As a concept, democracy is often perceived positively because it supposedly puts people on the same platform; it is supposed to treat and make people equal. As Christiano and Bajaj (2022) put it, democracy "refers very generally to a method of collective decision making characterized by a kind of equality among the participants at an essential stage of the decision-making process" (para. 3). Likewise, Kuyper (2015) maintains that "At its core ... most scholars agree that democracy refers to a political practice in which individuals govern themselves through some form of equitable decision-making process" (para. 3). In common parlance, equality means "the state of being equal," that is, of having the same things. Hence, if equality is one of the most basic aspects of democracy, then people in a democratic setting are expected to be on the same footing. According to Aristotle (2013) in Book VI of *Politics*, "[t]he justice that is characteristically popular is to have equality on the basis of number and not on the basis of merit; where justice is of this sort, the multitude must necessarily have authority, and what is resolved by the majority must be final and must be justice, for, they assert, each of the citizens must have an equal share" (1317b).

Squid Game suggests, however, that there are different platforms – that, even in democracies, things are not equal. There are platforms occupied by people who can control and platforms occupied by those who are being controlled. Given the scale of the games being played, it cannot be the case that the entire execution was not elaborately planned for years by those who have the means and intent – those who enjoy more freedom relative to the others who were forced to join the game. In other words, those who plan (and observe) the game and those who play the game are not on an equal footing, even though they live in a democracy.

The most common measure of equality in a democracy is the right to vote. "Democracy requires that persons be treated equally insofar as they are autonomous participants in the process of self-government. This form of equality is foundational to democracy because it follows from the very definition of democracy. Democracy requires an equality of democratic agency" (Post 2005, p. 28). Being equal means everyone has the same right to vote regardless of their gender, race, sexual orientation, social and economic status, or religious beliefs. This implies that everybody possesses equally one vote despite their privileges or the lack thereof. In relation to democracy, there is a popular notion that since people are given equal rights to vote, the majority gets to decide. In the Philippines, for instance, the system of plurality has been practiced and implemented since the 1935 Constitution. Even under the 1987 Constitution, all elective officials are voted through the "first-past-the-post system" (Agra 1997). "In the country's plurality or 'first-past-the-post' system, the candidate with the highest number of votes wins, while others are left with nothing in this 'winner takes all' set up" (Wong 2022, para. 2).

Squid Game, however, suggests that this is not the case. Take the second episode, for instance, when the players vote on whether to continue playing the game after finding out that losing in a game means assured death. Of the 201 remaining players, exactly 100 vote yes, while the other 100 vote no, leaving the last voter with the power to decide their fate. The suggestion seems to be that although the last voter has one vote just like all the others, the weight and power their vote holds are not necessarily equal to those who voted first. Of course, one might argue that by voting differently, any one person could have tipped the scales (99 to 101) and thus made the last person's vote completely powerless. But the point here seems to be more symbolic as the last one to vote is Player 001, Oh Il-nam, the oldest of all the players, who is eventually revealed (in the last episode) to be the mastermind behind the entire game. Regardless of how everyone votes, because he has the money and power, he has the ability to continue the game or call everything off. It appears that there is equality, but really there is only equality on the surface.

We see this in real-world democracy because, in reality, it is not the majority that is in control; it is those able to control the majority opinion who are in control. And to control the majority opinion, you have to have wealth and power – like those who control the most-watched news media outlets (e.g., Fox News in the United States) or those who control social media platforms (e.g., Facebook, Twitter, and TikTok worldwide). In the United States, this was made even worse by Citizen's United, a court ruling, which allowed donor money to be funneled anonymously into "Super-PACs," thus giving the rich an unprecedented ability to make their voices heard over everyone else. And who gets the money and power to do such things is usually a matter of either chance or inherited wealth (Halliday 2018). Indeed, it is wealth, not ability or effort, that predicts whether someone will be successful (and thus gain more wealth; see Carnevale et al. 2019). Combine this with how the rich can buy off politicians, who then use their power to consolidate it with dirty election tactics, like gerrymandering and denying the result of elections without consequence, then the inequalities in democracy become even more obvious. Like the rich and powerful in today's society, it may have appeared that Player 001 only had one vote like everyone else, but in reality, only he had the true power.

Squid Game suggests something similar starting in episode 3, when it is revealed that Player 111 is conspiring with corrupt guards to acquire certain advantages – that is, additional rations of food and information about the games. Player 111 was a doctor outside who got caught in several mishaps, including the death of one of his patients. In exchange for food and information, he helps the guards sell the organs of the game's victims on the black market by performing surgeries on the corpses to harvest their organs. Because the other players are not surgeons, they lack an advantage that Player 111 has, who enters the game with the skills of a surgeon. In the same way, in the real world, some people enter the game (are born) with certain amounts of wealth, privilege, and ability, which gives them an advantage over others. And unlike what happens in *Squid Game* – Player 111 is executed because he broke the rules and to maintain the equal playing field ("Each and every one of you is considered an equal within the walls of this facility. You must be guaranteed the same opportunities without being disadvantaged or facing any kind of discrimination") – democracy allows for such inequalities to happen, contrary to the popular belief that democracy serves the goal of equality.

That said, democratic societies do sometimes aim for equality – with things like social security or nationalized medicine, which aims to ensure that everyone has an equal opportunity to, at least, have their basic needs met. However, equality often does not pay enough consideration to what a person *actually* needs. Equal treatment puts those who need more at a disadvantage and those who need less at an advantage; this can create its own kind of inequality. Say you have a (5-and-a half-foot-tall) 20 year-old, a (5-foot-tall) 10 year-old, and a (4-foot-tall) 5 year-old, all wanting to see over a 6-foot fence. If you treat them "equally" by giving them all a 1-foot-tall box to stand on, you are actually treating them unequally by only giving one (the 20 year-old) the ability to see over the fence. Equity would actually require giving the smallest among them the largest box. In other words, the equality that democracy does in fact provide, in one way or another, can create other inequalities. Worse still, since people are under the impression that they have the freedom to do the things they like in a democracy, democracy opens doors for corruption and, therefore, greater inequalities. People are tempted to perform actions that would benefit them and give them what they really need (or want), even if that means going against the rules and engaging in immoral acts that disadvantage others – like the aforementioned gerrymandering of elections.

Several inequalities surface in Squid Game when the players are informed that they will be playing in teams of ten for the third game. For instance, in the team composed of Seong Gi-hun, Cho Sang-woo, Kang Sae-byeok, Oh Il-nam, and Ali Abdul, Cho Sang-woo, who was serving as their leader, clearly instructed the team to bring in males only. Implicitly, he meant not to recruit any females, to focus on strength, and to avoid anyone who can possibly make the team even weaker. This is considering that, as it is, the team already has one female and one elderly person. Likewise, in Jang Deok-su's team, he commanded the rest of his members to just bring in strong males to the team, even if that meant leaving out Han Mi-nyeo, his supposed love interest and ally in the series. They thought they needed strength, so they wanted strong members in their respective teams.

This scene openly portrays how democracy allows, or sometimes even perpetuates, such inequalities. Despite the attempt to make the playing field equal by requiring each team to only have ten members, the players, given the choice, tend to gravitate toward those who generally have desirable traits, such as being physically strong, young, tall, and, unfortunately, male, or simply those who would be beneficial to them. Since they all thought that the third game will be a game of strength, they automatically discriminated against old people and females.

The same is true even in real life. Let us take the military as an example. "Gender stereotypes and institutional bias within the military come as no surprise to anyone, least of all women, in the military … Researchers have distinguished between two forms of sexism: hostile and benevolent. Whereas hostile sexism is more obviously negative, benevolent sexism is often disguised as positive, portraying women as needing and deserving greater care and protection. Both forms deem women as less capable and competent, justifying lower expectations of them and limiting their roles" (Trobaugh 2018, p. 47). Trobaugh further mentioned that "[t]hese beliefs are apparent in a variety of male-dominated professions, including the science, technology, engineering, and mathematics professions as well as the military" (2018, p. 47). Furthermore, 30% of 50+ service leavers, or those who are in the process of, or has already left, the Armed Forces at or after the age of 50, have experienced ageism, discrimination on the ground of a person's age. "Sometimes, these prejudices were experienced directly while at other times people reported a sense of being treated unfavorably. Although workplace age discrimination is unlawful, employers continue to hold and act on assumptions about older workers' capabilities, performance and expectations in work" (Flynn and Ball 2020, p. 12).

"Egalitarianism is the position that equality is central to justice. It is a prominent trend in social and political philosophy and has also become relevant in moral philosophy (moral egalitarianism) since the late twentieth century" (Gordon n.d., para. 1). In social and political philosophy, philosophers have been debating about the role of equality in justice, whether it is one of the most important aspects of justice or it plays no part at all. Prior to this, the questions focused more on what goods should be distributed and according to which standard.

Those who believe that equality is central to justice (egalitarians) maintain that people should be treated the same or as equals, that they should get the same, relate as equals, or at least enjoy equality of social status. This implies that the egalitarian doctrine heavily rests on the notion that "all human persons are equal in fundamental worth or moral status" (Arneson 2013, para. 1). However, without a doubt, egalitarianism is a highly contested concept in social and political philosophy. Questions like "How is equality determined?" "In what aspects are people equal?" and "To what extent are people equal?" are almost always being raised. For instance, given that people are born with different talents and under varying social and economic status, should resources then be equally distributed? Clearly, given the "natural" inequalities in the world, there are some who will need more, just as there are some who will need less. In contrast, there are types of equality that are deemed beneficial regardless of one's advantages or disadvantages assigned at birth. Take for example equality of opportunity. People deserve to have equal opportunity, for instance, in career or education, regardless of any specific advantages or disadvantages based on age, gender, or ability.

Hence, it is extremely important to thoroughly examine and analyze what equality in democracy means – whether it is something that is necessarily desirable or not, what it entails, and whether democracy brings about genuine equality altogether. In the case, however, of Seong Gi-hun and the other players in the games, democracy does not necessarily foster genuine equality because (1) several layers of inequalities, mostly in the form of discrimination, were evidently experienced by some, if not all, of the players; (2) democracy allowed for some of the players to take advantage of others by engaging in immoral acts; and (3) some games were designed to favor some players, for instance, those who are strong in the case of Tug of War or those who are fast and agile in the case of Red Light, Green Light.

The Myth of Empowerment

"The essence of democracy is that it empowers ordinary citizens. To accomplish this civil and political freedoms are necessary. Civil freedoms entitle people to lead their lives as they like as long as it does not impinge on others. Political freedoms entitle people to make their preferences known and count in public life. Both kinds of freedom are essential to empower people to govern their lives. These democratic freedoms are codified in the form of civil and political rights, which together build the core institution of democracy: citizenship" (Welzel and Inglehart 2008, p. 3). This sense of democracy goes beyond the common notion that democracy stretches only in so far as it provides people with universal suffrage (i.e., the equal right to vote). Hence, it is fair to say that holding free elections is not the only thing that is necessary to make a country democratic in all senses.

In *Squid Game*, there is a false sense of democracy because the players can supposedly stop the game anytime they wish to. The majority only needs to vote in favor of stopping the game – just like they did in the second episode. However, as described earlier, true democracy is not just about giving people the opportunity or right to vote. Clearly, it is one of the important aspects, but it is not the only aspect that needs to be considered. That is to say that universal suffrage does not solely define and determine democracy.

True freedom and empowerment in a democratic setting also require civil and political freedoms. In the case of *Squid Game*, civil freedom refers to the ability of the players to play the game under conditions that are not depriving and abusive; political freedom refers to the ability to decide the types of games to be played in a manner that allows everyone's voices to be heard and genuinely considered, for instance. However, as seen in the series, none of these freedoms are met inside the game. Obviously, the conditions under which they were put are far from being nondepriving and nonabusive. Not only were they pitted against each other, but they also needed to watch their backs all the time, in case someone decides to betray them or simply get rid of them by, say, killing them in their sleep. Furthermore, they have no voice as to the type of games to choose and how each one will be played. They were tasked to only follow all the instructions given if they want to have the chance to win the pot money, or else they will be shot dead for disobedience. We can better appreciate this point by looking at it through the "capability approach," which was significantly developed by philosophers Amartya Sen and Martha Nussbaum.

The capability approach is a moral framework with two central claims: first, that the freedom to attain well-being matters morally and, second, that well-being is best understood in terms of people's capabilities and functioning. Sen writes: "*Functionings* represent parts of the state of a person—in particular the various things that he or she manages to do or be in leading a life. The *capability* of a person reflects the alternative combinations of functionings the person can achieve, and from which he or she can choose one collection" (Sen 1993, p. 31). Sen (1993) further argues that "[t]he freedom to lead different types of life is reflected in the person's capability set. The capability of a person depends on a variety of factors, including personal characteristics and social arrangements. A full accounting of individual freedom must, of course, go beyond the capabilities of personal living and pay attention to the person's other objectives (e.g., social goals not directly related to one's own life), but human capabilities constitute an important part of individual freedom" (p. 33).

The "capability approach" focuses on what people can do (doings) and the kinds of persons they are able to be (beings). This notion of doings and beings is what Sen calls *capabilities.* For him, capabilities are the real freedoms in the sense that one is not undertaking certain activities and/or not being a certain type of individual just because there is the freedom to do so but because there is an actual "substantial opportunity to achieve it" (Robeyns and Byskov 2021, para. 4). This distinction is important because a paradigm shift happens. The focus is no longer on the means (the resources that people have or at least have access to) but on the ends (the doings and beings that people can make out of the resources).

Looking at empowerment through the lenses of the "capability approach," it is fair to say that people who are genuinely empowered are those who can *be* a certain type of person or *do* certain activities that promote their well-being. In other words, empowerment is the ability to *be* someone or *do* something that is the result of the exercise of freedoms and is directed toward the promotion of well-being. It is thus concluded that to achieve functionings (realized capabilities) is to achieve real freedom. Additionally, capabilities in a democracy mean being able to *do* activities and *be* a certain type of individual who (1) enables them to lead their lives as they like so long as it does not impinge on others (i.e., gives them civil freedom) and (2) entitles them to make their preferences known and count in public life (i.e., gives them political freedom).

In episode 4, the guards reveal to Byeong-gi (Player 111/the doctor) that the players were intentionally given less food that day in hopes of starting a fight. Earlier that day, during mealtime, the players were given only one hard-boiled egg, along with a bottle of soda. Since the games are not only mentally, but most of all physically, exhausting, clearly the food ration was not enough. Hence, some of the players, led by Jang Deok-su (Player 101/the gangster), cut in line and went back for a second round of food rations. As a result, five people were not able to eat during that day. On the same night after the lights went out, a riot started, resulting in 27 deaths.

In such a situation, can it be said that people inside the game were empowered? Is empowerment about being able to do whatever one wants to achieve one's goal? Or is empowerment about being able to stay quiet and avoid conflicts to stay alive? At best, the players in the game have nothing on their minds but survival. However, such is not a ticket to perform any action without regard to other people's right to achieve their own capabilities. That is to say that the freedoms allowed in achieving one's capabilities stop when they impede on others' rights. And so, in this case, Jang Deok-su and his teammates were not empowered just because they were able to "control" the situation by instigating a riot and eliminating several other players from the game. In a like manner, those who tried to avoid conflicts by not saying anything about the injustices they have experienced or witnessed were also not empowered; in this case, it was Player 198 who chose to keep silent despite discovering that Jang Deok-su's team went for a second round in the food rations. She did so because (1) she fears for her life and (2) she did not want to get on the bad side of the "strong" ones.

It is also worth mentioning that survival does not equate to well-being. Well-being means not merely being alive but more importantly being able to live a life that is of a certain quality. Hence, just because a player survives a game and continues playing does not mean they are able to protect their well-being and are therefore closer to achieving their functionings. Take the case of Player 069 for example, who lost his wife in the game of marbles in episode 6. Despite winning the game and remaining alive, Player 069 was left in agony as he repeatedly thinks of his wife, who died because she lost the game to him. In the succeeding episode (episode 7), Player 069, still in deep agony, tried to convince the rest of the remaining players to vote again so they can stop the game; to this, Sang-woo disagreed, saying all their efforts will be put to waste if they stop the game now. In the end, Player 069 could not take the guilt of "causing" his wife's death and kills himself by hanging.

What happened in the games is that the democratic setup did nothing to empower the players; rather, it gave more power to players who are already strong. Thus, we can argue that while the "conversion factors" (personal, sociopolitical, and environmental conditions) inside the game are preventing some of the players from achieving their functionings, they allowed others to grow stronger and impose their will on others. This shows that democracy, though promising empowerment, preserves and increases the natural advantage of stronger (or wealthier) people. For instance, when the riot exploded in the fourth episode, even those who were there not originally to kill but simply to get the chance to win the pot money were willing to go as far as killing other people if that meant increasing their chances of winning the game. This "willingness to kill," which not all players possess, is a conversion factor that democracy preserves (and puts others at a disadvantage) since players are technically practicing their civil and political freedoms by choosing to keep quiet and mind their own business. In other words, democracy cannot genuinely promise empowerment if it allows people to do nothing in the face of evil. We see this over and over in democratic societies, where citizens are more often than not powerless in the face of decisions made by those who have the wealth and power to influence elections and control politicians and who possess the willingness to hurt others who get in their way.

The Myth of Transparency

Can democracy promote the development of virtue in people – for instance, honesty, or what we shall call here "transparency?" In the earlier part of this chapter, it was mentioned that for Aristotle, it is vital for any democratic society to provide its citizens with conditions that will allow them to fulfill their *telos* and ultimately achieve *eudaimonia* (usually translated to happiness or flourishing). In so doing, they will be able to live a *good life.* And to do this, it would seem to need to guarantee some amount of transparency. In a nutshell, democracy should be able to provide its citizens with an environment that would allow them to live a *good life* and achieve *eudaimonia* by living a life in accordance with reason and virtue. But to answer the question of whether it can do this, it will be necessary to first explore the concept of virtue.

A philosophical lens related to this is *virtue ethics*, which can also be traced back to Aristotle. Virtue ethics sees virtues (and vices), or desirable character traits, as the most important foundation of the theory (Hursthouse and Pettigrove 2018). "For Aristotle and other believers in virtue ethics, it is the cultivation of a virtuous *character* that is the goal of ethics, to *become* a virtuous person. The assumption is that genuinely virtuous people will act in morally principled ways as a natural expression of their moral goodness. And these moral actions will in turn strengthen their virtuous nature" (Chaffee 2011, p. 429). Aristotle (2011) argued in the second book of *Nicomachean Ethics* that "[v]irtue, then, is twofold, intellectual and moral. Both the coming-into-being and increase of intellectual virtue result mostly from teaching—hence it requires experience and time—whereas moral virtue is the result of habit, and so it is that moral virtue got its name *[ethike]* by a slight alteration of the term *habit*" (1103a).

One's *moral character* reflects the entirety of a person's moral traits and dispositions. That is to say that a virtuous person, when confronted with moral dilemmas, would respond in a consistent, coherent, and habitual way. This is the case because the manner by which virtues develop requires not just time but more importantly practice. For instance, if a person wants to be honest, he needs to always engage himself in honest actions or deeds. In the same way, "[i]t is well said, then, that as a result of doing just things, the just person comes into being…" (Aristotle 2011, 1105b). With enough time and practice, being honest and just, for instance, will become a habitual way of thinking and acting.

Although it is important to mention that moral characters are not permanent, the process of developing a moral character will not be easy because it will require another set of gradual development of virtues and a lot of consistent and ongoing practice. Additionally, Aristotle proposes the idea of the *golden mean*. "Such things [as the virtues] are naturally destroyed through deficiency and excess . . . but they are preserved by the mean" (Aristotle 2011, 1104a).

Aristotle (2011) argued further that "[t]he equal is also a certain middle term between excess and deficiency. I mean by 'a middle term of the thing' that which stands at an equal remove from each of the extremes, which is in fact one and the same thing for all; though in relation to us, it is that which neither takes too much nor is deficient" (1106a). Essentially, it is about striking a balance between two extremes or vices. Now, not all actions that are intended to achieve something "good," like being able to acquire money for the family or pay debts, constitute virtues. There is a thin line between virtues and vices, and the golden mean supposedly dictates where the line lies. Anything beyond the golden mean is already a form of vice. Further, not all behaviors or actions can be subjected to the golden mean analysis as some of them are simply vices. These vices include actions such as adultery, theft, and murder; they also include emotions such as malice, shamelessness, and envy.

It was pointed out early on in this chapter that Squid Game is premised on the existence of democracy in the games – that the players are free to do whatever they want as long as they obey the laws of the "game world" and can stop the games anytime with a simple majority vote. Unfortunately, as the series showed, democracy does not necessarily foster the cultivation of virtues, like transparency. Instead, it may serve more as a breeding ground for corruption and dishonesty.

For instance, in episode 2 of *Squid Game*, as mentioned earlier, the players were given the chance to stop the game and to leave the place where they were brought to participate in the games. Ultimately, they were able to stop the game with a majority of the players voting in favor of it. Using Aristotle's virtue ethics, it can be said that joining the game for the first time may be a case of being courageous, especially when almost all of them were on the brink of financial ruin and were literally left with no choice but to try their luck in the games. However, for those who returned to the game for the second time after successfully looking for a way out and knowing exactly what awaits them if they lose the game, the same is not necessarily true. Those who went back to the game to continue playing it despite the known grave consequences practiced foolhardiness (vice) instead of courage (virtue). Going back to the game. Therefore does not necessarily mean being courageous because the game requires the players to pay with their lives once they lose any of the games, and sacrificing one's life for something as uncertain as playing unknown games is an extreme form of living a life. Consequently, it is not in accordance with the golden mean.

The players were not only being reckless about their decisions, but a lot of them also engaged in other vicious acts just to ensure survival until the next game. It was previously mentioned how Player 111 engaged in dishonest actions by taking advantage of his being a doctor and conspiring with corrupt guards to gain certain advantages in the game. Similarly, Han Mi-nyeo and Jang Deok-su also cheated on the second game (in episode 3) when they both used a lighter to carve out the shape from the *dalgona*, or sugar honeycomb, and win the game.

How about the virtue of transparency? Throughout the series, various forms of friendships were formed inside the games. For instance, there is the friendship between Jang Deok-su (Player 101) and Han Mi-nyeo (Player 212), Ali Abdul (Player 199) and Cho Sang-woo (Player 218), and Oh Il-nam (Player 001) and Seong Gi-hun (Player 456). However, the series eventually reveals that not all these so-called friendships were real, genuine, honest, or transparent.

In the fourth episode, Jang Deok-su betrayed Han Mi-nyeo when he left her out of the group as she is a female and Deok-su thinks having a female will weaken the group and decrease their chances of winning game 3. Much to Mi-nyeo's disappointment, despite all her efforts of pleasing Deok-su, she was still left to survive on her own. Clearly, both Deok-su and Mi-nyeo engaged in vicious behaviors. In particular, Deok-su was being shameless, while Mi-nyeo was being obsequious.

In the sixth episode, during the fourth game, the players were tasked to pair up. Naturally, they chose someone they trust the most to be their partner, thinking the game will be played as a pair, with both players progressing to the next game if they win. However, as the game was explained to them, they were shocked and devastated to find out they will be fighting against their partner in a game of marbles. The main objective of the game was to gain possession of all their partner's marbles but without using any form of violence. It was up to them to decide the type of game to play in order to get all the other person's marbles. At the end of 30 min, whoever manages to take all the marbles from their partner wins. Consequently, whoever loses all their marbles dies.

Sang-woo paired up with Ali, while Gi-hun paired up with Il-nam. Both pairs decided to play a game where both players wager a certain number of marbles. The player wins when he is able to guess if the opponent's wager is odd or even. When Sang-woo and Ali started, it was pretty difficult for Ali, him not being familiar with the game at all. However, as the game progressed, he found himself winning against Sang-woo. The game reached a point where Sang-woo has only one marble left. That was when Sang-woo started convincing Ali to play another game, mentioning all the things he has done for the team to reach this far. Ali, being thankful to Sang-woo for serving as their team leader, decided to agree with his terms, not knowing Sang-woo had an entirely different plan – to deceive him and get all his marbles and proceed to the next game. It was already too late when Ali realized that Sang-woo had deceived him. Clearly, whatever Sang-woo and Ali had was not a genuine friendship. Sang-woo engaged in dishonest and deceiving acts to make sure he will be able to continue with the rest of the games and still have a chance to win the pot money. On the side of Ali, it was a case of recklessness. He was too generous with Sang-woo, just because he thought everything they have achieved so far was thanks to Sang-woo's leadership.

Meanwhile, Gi-hun found it extremely difficult to convince Il-nam to play the game as the oldest player suddenly had a lapse in his lucidity. But when Gi-hun was finally able to play the game with Il-nam, he found himself losing to the old man, with only one marble left in his possession. It was then that Il-nam, due to his old age and brain tumor, suddenly became forgetful and could not remember Gi-hun's guess. But Gi-hun took this opportunity and changed his original (wrong) answer to the correct one, deceiving Il-nam and preventing his impending loss. But just when he thought he had won against Il-nam, the old man revealed he still had one more marble left, which meant they still had to continue playing. However, Il-nam again had a lapse in his lucidity, making it difficult for Gi-hun to convince him to play further. Before the time ran out, Gi-hun was finally able to talk to Il-nam and convince him to play the game once more. That was when Il-nam offered Gi-hun to play one more round, waging all their marbles in a winner-takes-all game. Obviously, Gi-hun rejected the proposition, saying it was not fair for him to wager all his marbles just to get Il-nam's last marble. Then Il-nam revealed he was aware all along that Gi-hun was playing a trick on him and was, in fact, deceiving him to win the game. In the end, Player 001 decided to just give Gi-hun his last marble, making him the winner of the game.

Simply put, it was evident that the virtue of honesty (or transparency) had not yet perfectly developed in Gi-hun as he was not able to act in a morally principled way as a natural expression of his moral goodness. Instead, he acted in dishonest and dishonorable ways when he decided to take advantage of Il-nam's condition. It can then be said that the freedom accorded to Gi-hun in a democratic setting allowed him to engage in vicious actions and forget about his virtues – a failure of democracy in fostering the conditions for the cultivation and practice of virtue. Of course, this happens in the real world too. Just think of how democracy, and especially social media (which, in a way, brought democracy to the spread of misinformation), is drowning in false conspiracy theories and dishonest misinformation; think of how politicians can tell over 30,000 lies in 4 years yet not lose any supporters. The last thing democracy preserves is transparency.

The Myth of the Ideal

With 45.7% of the population of the world living under some form of democracy as of 2021 (Economist Intelligence Unit 2021), one cannot help but believe that democracy is ideal. However, four different myths about democracy have been discussed so far, and all of them suggest that democracy may not be ideal after all. To clarify how the term "ideal" is being used in this chapter, Plato's doctrine on the two worlds would be useful. In Plato's *Phaedo* (2002), a discussion about the two worlds is emphasized:

Well now, aren't the things that are constant and unvarying most likely to be the incomposite, whereas things that vary and are never constant are likely to be the composite?
I think so.
Then let's go back to those entities to which we turned in our earlier argument. Is the Being itself, whose being we give an account of in asking and answering questions, unvarying and constant, or does it vary? Does the equal itself, the beautiful itself, *what each things is* itself, that which *is*, ever admit of any change whatever. Or does *what each of them is*, being uniform alone by itself, remain unvarying and constant, and never admit of any kind of alteration in any way or respect whatever?
"It must be unvarying and constant, Socrates," said Cebes.

> But what about the many beautiful things, such as men or horses or cloaks or anything else at all of that kind? Or equals, or all things that bear the same name as those objects? Are they constant, or are they just the opposite of those others, and practically never constant at all, either in relation to themselves or to one another?
>
> "That is their condition," said Cebes; "they are never unvarying."
>
> Now these things you could actually touch and see and sense with the other senses, couldn't you, whereas those that are constant you could lay hold of only by reasoning of the intellect; aren't such things, rather, invisible and not seen?
>
> What you say is perfectly true.
>
> Then would you like us to posit two kinds of beings, the one kind seen, the other invisible?
>
> Let's posit them.
>
> And the invisible is always constant, whereas the seen is never constant?
>
> "Let's posit that too." (78b–79a)

In Plato's metaphysics and epistemology, the highest realm of knowledge is that of the higher forms. This includes universals such as truth, beauty, goodness, and justice. Since they are considered universals, they are therefore unchanging and eternal. It is important to mention, however, that Plato's concept of higher forms refers to abstract ideals rather than actual objects in the physical world. Concepts such as truth, beauty, goodness, and justice being considered universals are clearly on a much higher intellectual level, which means that not everybody can achieve a supreme understanding of these higher forms. Only a few who have dedicated their lives to rational exploration and reflection are able to do so (Chaffee 2011).

By adopting Plato's idea of universals as the ultimate form of perfection to democracy, we can hypothesize that if democracy is ideal, then it must be able to cultivate individual instances of truth, beauty, goodness, and justice. In the democratic society of *Squid Game*, however, these universals failed to manifest.

Truth. In many of the instances in *Squid Game*, the players, along with the creators of the games, have committed dishonest actions and intentionally hid truths. The first ultimate lie that was propagated was the false sense of hope. All 456 players "willingly" joined the game in hopes of being able to win some money and save themselves from financial ruin or whatever problem they were facing at that time. However, that hope was easily lost the moment they started playing the first game because then they realized that losing the game means losing their life.

The second lie was about Oh Il-nam's identity. Clearly, Il-nam was already out of place to begin with as he was too old for the games, and none of the other players were even close to his age, putting him in a really disadvantaged position. But somehow, he survived until the fourth game, which was not expected at all, given the condition he was in – old, frail, and sickly. All the mysteries faded, though, when it was revealed in episode 9 that Il-nam was the mastermind of the game. According to him, he joined it to relive the fun of playing the games he used to play as a kid. He went even as far as saying that watching the participants play the game was not as fun as actually playing it. Thus, after years of organizing and conducting the game, he finally decided to join because he knew he was already dying and it was his last chance to play it with others.

The third and last lie was the idea that winning the game and getting all that money from the pot will solve everything. Throughout the series, the eagerness of the players to win the game was evident because they thought, given their situation, money was their only solution. Hence, they were willing to do anything just to get a hold of the prize, which of course was a significant amount and can be life changing. However, in the final episode, Gi-hun, the ultimate winner of the game, was seen living an even more miserable life compared to his life before joining the game. This is because he was living a life of guilt. He could not even touch his winnings as he knew perfectly what price he had to pay just to acquire that money. Gi-hun was not just regretful about his decision to join the game, but he was also resentful toward the people who "made" them kill each other just to win the game.

Beauty. It is quite difficult to point out an instance of beauty in the game. This is because, in almost all instances, what transpired in the game constituted immoral acts, from how the players were invited to the game to how it all ended, with 454 players dead. The lengths that the players were willing to go to made the entire game even uglier, though more enjoyable for the people watching the game for entertainment – the VIPs. The fact that the game was intended not to help the 456 players who were in dire need of financial help but to entertain a group of individuals who have the money to enjoy the show makes it even far from beautiful. The deception, lies, manipulation, hypocrisy, trickery, pretense, and insincerity were all the results of democracy – just because they can, they will.

The only possible instance of beauty in the game was how Kang Sae-byeok managed to brave the storm despite being (1) a female and (2) an outsider as a North Korean. Unlike Han Mi-nyeo, Sae-Byeok used her intellect to play the games and reach the end before she finally died at the hands of Sang-woo. Conversely, Mi-nyeo only made use of her sexuality to her advantage, offering sex to the strongest person in the room to ensure survival. Kang Sae-byeok and Han Mi-nyeo are two different reflections of being a woman. Sae-byeok represents women who are trying to go against the biases and stereotypes of society, whereas Mi-nyeo represents those who reinforce the biases and stereotypes of society toward women.

Goodness. As previously mentioned, the players were not able to develop virtues. Instead, the conditions allowed them to cultivate vices. Although there may be quite a few instances where something "good" is done, none of them truly reflects a moral character of a virtuous person because, at the end of the day, all of them responded to the situation in an unprincipled way. For instance, Gi-hun showed in several instances how much he cared for Il-nam. In episode 5, Gi-hun took care of Il-nam when he noticed that the old man was burning with a fever. In the succeeding episode, Gi-hun lent him his jacket when he saw that Il-nam had wet himself in his sleep. However, despite such "good" acts from Gi-hun, when it came to a life-and-death situation, he was still able to betray Il-nam by deceiving him and taking advantage of the old man's condition – very much unlike Socrates, who chose to die for his principles.

Justice. A side story in *Squid Game* was led by Hwang Jun-ho, a police detective who was trying to find justice for his missing brother, who he believed joined the games. For him to uncover the details of the game and find the whereabouts of his missing brother, he had to disguise himself first as one of the soldiers in the game, later as a manager, and then as a waiter. At the end of his quest, he found out that his brother had won the game a few years back and had become the Front Man. Ultimately, Hwang Jun-ho failed in his attempt to deliver justice for two reasons. First, he was unable to give his brother justice because the missing brother turned out to be working for Il-nam and has been participating in the conduct of the game as the Front Man. Second, he was also not able to give the rest of the players justice; despite his attempt to report the game to police authorities in episode 8, it was shown in the final episode that the operations continued. Gi-hun, having successfully returned to the real world after winning the game, accidentally saw the man who recruited him to join the game in the train station – the same place where he was first recruited. The man was playing a game of *ddakji* with another person, and it took Gi-hun only a minute to figure out what was happening: the man was once again recruiting another set of players to join the games and complete another cycle. This then proves that the attempt to stop the game was unsuccessful as another round is well underway.

There was also no justice for all those who had died in the game. The players submitted themselves to the game, thinking it was their only way out of their misery. It was unbeknownst to them, however, that the island where the game was being held will serve as their graveyard. And clearly, those who operate the game have shown no respect and mercy for the players. For instance, they have never informed the families of those who have died about what happened to them; hence, they remain missing persons until both their families and the police authorities just lose all hope and stop all efforts to look for them. Another thing, the players' corpses were automatically collected and burned after being killed off in the game without anybody paying respects or offering them prayers. Not only that, but some of those who had died were disrespected even more when their organs were harvested to be sold on the black market. In a nutshell, the players who failed in the game were simply treated as a means to an end.

Ultimately, democracy, as showcased by *Squid Game*, is far from a manifestation of the ideal. Throughout the series, we do not see individual instantiations of the key forms of truth, beauty, goodness, or justice; rather, it is mostly dishonesty, ugliness, immoral acts, and unjust treatment.

Conclusion

Squid Game as philosophy offers a glimpse of the illnesses that ail democracy. Democracy makes several promises that it cannot deliver; thus, these promises are better off regarded as myths. Free choice, equality, empowerment, transparency, and the ideal are some of the notions that are associated with democracy, but the foregoing analyses show that these are mere cracks in the armor, which can be exploited to make democracy work for the few – the elite – as a tool to satisfy their whims and caprices.

Further, *Squid Game* as philosophy shows how the illnesses of democracy – the myths that surround it – exacerbate the struggle between classes, that is, the rich who do not know what to do with their money and the poor who badly need the money. It shows that despite the existence of rules and laws, the state of nature of humans as beings who are in constant war with each other for selfish gains (Hobbes 1651) can thrive in a democracy. It reveals that in a democratic society, the self can be a slave to others and others can be a slave to the self. In this sense, democracy can be a potent breeding ground for mutual oppression, especially if reward and punishment are involved.

Finally, *Squid Game* as philosophy forces us to reconsider what we have, what we are willing to risk, what we can lose, and what we can gain in a democracy. Given the inherent flaws within a democratic system and the ways it can be manipulated to serve the interests of the few rather than the many, it seems that any democracy must be aware of these shortcomings and strive for checks and balances that might prevent or preempt some of these concerns.

References

Agra, A.C. 1997. *A Q & A primer on the Philippine party-list system: A list proportional representation scheme of electing one-fifth of the members of the house of representatives.* Manila: Rex Bookstore.

Albert, E. 2020. *North Korea's power structure.* Council on Foreign Relations. https://www.cfr.org/backgrounder/north-koreas-power-structure

Aristotle. C. Lord. 2013. *Aristotle's politics.* 2nd ed. Chicago: The University of Chicago Press.

———. R. C. Bartlett, and S. D. Collins 2011. *Aristotle's Nicomachean ethics.* Cambridge: University of Chicago Press.

Arneson, R. 2013. Egalitarianism. In *The Stanford encyclopedia of philosophy*, ed. Edward N. Zalta.. https://plato.stanford.edu/entries/egalitarianism/

Carnevale, Anthony P., Megan L. Fasules, Michael C. Quinn, and Kathryn Peltier Campbell. 2019. *Born to win, schooled to lose: Why equally talented students don't get equal chances to be all they can be.* Georgetown University Center on Education and the Workforce. A brief summary of the work can be found at: https://cew.georgetown.edu/cew-reports/schooled2lose/

Chaffee, J. 2011. *The philosopher's way: A text with readings.* 3rd ed. New Jersey: Prentice Hall.

Christiano, T., and S. Bajaj. 2022. Democracy. In *The Stanford encyclopedia of philosophy*, ed. Edward N. Zalta.. https://plato.stanford.edu/entries/democracy

Economist Intelligence Unit. 2021. Democracy index 2021: The China challenge. https://www.eiu.com/n/campaigns/democracy-index-2021

Flynn, M., and C. Ball. 2020. *Understanding service leavers aged 50+: Their challenges and experiences in the civilian jobs market.* London: The Officers' Association.

Gordon, J.S. n.d.. Moral egalitarianism. *Internet encyclopedia of philosophy.* https://iep.utm.edu/moral-egalitarianism

Halliday, Daniel. 2018. *Inheritance of wealth.* Oxford: Oxford University Press.

HHS. 2021. HHS announces rule to protect consumers from surprise medical bills. July 1. https://www.hhs.gov/about/news/2021/07/01/hhs-announces-rule-to-protect-consumers-from-surprise-medical-bills.html

Hobbes, T. 1651. *Leviathan.* London: St. Paul's Churchyard. https://philo-labo.fr/fichiers/Hobbes%20-%20L%C3%A9viathan%20(gutenberg).pdf.

Hursthouse, R., and G. Pettigrove. 2018. Virtue ethics. In *The Stanford encyclopedia of philosophy*, ed. Edward N. Zalta.. https://plato.stanford.edu/archives/win2018/entries/ethics-virtue

Kirkpatrick, M. 2016. Freedom from fear: Not in North Korea. The Catalyst. https://www.bushcenter.org/catalyst/freedom/kirkpatrick-freedom-north-korea.html

Kuyper, J. 2015. Global democracy. In *The Stanford encyclopedia of philosophy*, ed. Edward N. Zalta. https://plato.stanford.edu/entries/global-democracy/#DemGloNatSta

O'Connor, T., and C. Franklin. 2018. Free will. In *The Stanford encyclopedia of philosophy*, ed. Edward N. Zalta. https://plato.stanford.edu/entries/freewill/#NatuFreeWill

Plato, and D. Gallop. 2002. *Plato Phaedo*. Oxford: Oxford University Press.

Post, R. 2005. Democracy and equality. *The Annals of the American Academy of Political and Science* 603 (1). https://doi.org/10.1177/0002716205282.

Robeyns, I., and M.F. Byskov. 2021. The capability approach. In *The Stanford encyclopedia of philosophy*, ed. Edward N. Zalta. https://plato.stanford.edu/archives/win2021/entries/capability-approach

Sen, A. 1993. Capability and well-being. In *Nussbaum Sen the quality of life*, 30–53. Oxford: Clarendon Press.

Son, S. 2021. Squid game: The real debt crisis shaking South Korea that inspired the hit TV show. *The Conversation*, Oct 7. https://theconversation.com/squid-game-the-real-debt-crisis-shaking-south-korea-that-inspired-the-hit-tv-show-169401

Trobaugh, E.M. 2018. Women, regardless: Understanding gender bias in U.S. military integration. *Joint Force Quarterly* 88. National Defense University Press. https://ndupress.ndu.edu/Publications/Article/1411860/women-regardless-understanding-gender-bias-in-us-military-integration

Welzel, C., and R. Inglehart. 2008. *Democracy as human empowerment: The role of ordinary people in the emergence and survival of democracy*. UC Irvine: Center for the Study of Democracy. https://escholarship.org/uc/item/3tj7c4bb.

Wong, A.C. 2022. *Philippine elections and the politics behind it. The interpreter*. Lowy Institute. https://www.lowyinstitute.org/the-interpreter/philippine-elections-and-politics-behind-it

South Park as Philosophy: Blasphemy, Mockery, and (Absolute?) Freedom of Speech

28

David Kyle Johnson

Contents

Introduction	634
Part I: History, Blasphemy, and Censorship	635
South Park as Philosophy	635
A History of "Blasphemy" on *South Park*	638
Identifying the Arguments	642
Argument #1: Catering to Terrorism Creates More Terrorism	645
Argument #2: "Don't Capitulate, Reiterate"	646
Argument #3: Freedom of Speech Isn't Free	651
Argument #4: "It's All or Nothing"	652
Part II: How Far Should Freedom of Speech Go?	654
Argument #5: Absolute Free Speech	654
Cancel Culture, Free Speech, and Political Correctness	659
Putting the PC Principle In Charge	662
Conclusion: The Paradox of Tolerance	668
End Notes	669
References	670

Abstract

Perhaps no show has ever engaged in philosophy as much as *South Park*. Although it has made many philosophical arguments, this chapter will focus on the arguments *South Park* makes regarding censorship and freedom of speech, especially the ones made in the banned episodes "Cartoon Wars" (Part I and II), "200" and "201." Does catering to terrorism create more? Should we respond to terrorism by doing more of what the terrorist want to forbid? When it comes to mockery, is everything fair game? How much should we be willing to sacrifice for freedom of speech? And how far should freedom of speech go? After a historical

---

D. K. Johnson (✉)
Department of Philosophy, King's College, Wilkes-Barre, PA, USA
e-mail: davidjohnson@kings.edu

© Springer Nature Switzerland AG 2024
D. K. Johnson et al. (eds.), *The Palgrave Handbook of Popular Culture as Philosophy*,
https://doi.org/10.1007/978-3-031-24685-2_117

633

summary of South Park's controversies, and by engaging with the works of many past philosophers (e.g., John Stuart Mill and Karl Popper) and contemporary ones (e.g., Geroge Letsas, Aaron James, and Brian Leiter), this chapter will answer these questions and more.

Keywords

South Park · The First Amendment · Free speech · Absolute freedom of speech · The paradox of tolerance · Karl Popper · Cartoon Wars · Isaac Hayes · Blasphemy · Censorship · Donald Trump · Election denial · Fascism · Racism · Cancel culture · Political correctness · Cartoon Mohammed · Terrorism · Banned South Park episodes · Comedy as social commentary · The PC Principle · Zachary Adam Chesser · Everybody Draw Mohammed Day · The right to not be offended · George Letsas · European Court of Human Rights · Aaron James · Freedom isn't free · John Stuart Mill · On Liberty · The harm principle · Marketplace of ideas · 8chan · 8kun · Brian Leiter · Public shaming · Deplatforming

Disclaimer: The following chapter contains coarse language, defends controversial conclusions, and is way too long. Philosophers are summarized . . . poorly. Rather than remove this content, the editor-in-chief wants to acknowledge its harmful impact, learn from it, and spark conversations to create a more inclusive future together. Due to its content, like both *South Park* and *The Muppets*, this chapter should not be viewed by anyone.

Introduction

This is about freedom of speech! About censorship!
Can't you guys be more political?
—Wendy Testaburger (*South Park: Bigger, Longer, & Uncut*)

There is very likely no television show on the planet that more consistently and directly does philosophy than *South Park*. This is perhaps ironic given the show's reputation for childish potty humor – its protagonists are four foul-mouthed fourth graders named Stan, Kyle, Cartman, and Kenny – but nearly every episode makes an argument of some kind or at least asks a question, usually of the philosophical variety. Indeed, once one realizes that ethics, social and political commentary, and religion all fall under the umbrella of philosophy, one realizes that nearly every episode of *South Park* has some kind of philosophical point. In the early seasons, although those lessons were often mundane, this usually involved Stan or Kyle (often thin surrogates for creators Trey Parker and Matt Stone who voice the pair) having some kind of epiphany at the end of the episode. "You know, I learned something today." But once the show found its stride, the philosophical questions and arguments flowed, and it became controversial, not so much for its profanity,

28 South Park as Philosophy: Blasphemy, Mockery, and (Absolute?) Freedom of Speech 635

potty humor, and absurdity ... but for its religious irreverence and philosophical positions.

The series' thesis about absolute freedom of speech is that on which this chapter shall ultimately focus. But before turning to that issue, and even summarizing the *South Park* episodes most relevant to it, it will be worth looking at how (and how often) *South Park* does philosophy. In fact, a full understanding of this, and a familiarity with the history of the series, will be necessary to fully appreciate the arguments Parker and Stone put forth against censorship and for free speech. Because, as a result, this chapter is longer than most in this handbook, for the sake of using it in the classroom, I have divided it into two parts. In Part I, we will explore the history of *South Park* and the arguments it makes for free speech, and its right to mock anyone, in its most controversial episodes. In Part II, we will look at the argument the series as a whole makes for *absolute* freedom of speech.

Part I: History, Blasphemy, and Censorship

South Park as Philosophy

> You know, I learned something today...
> —Stan Randell William Marsh ("The Spirit of Christmas: Jesus vs. Santa")

To say that South Park's irreverence and philosophy are its most controversial elements is no small thing. In Season 5, all the way back in 2001, Comedy Central allowed *South Park* to say the word "shit," uncensored, for one episode. Stone and Parker made it the focus of the entire episode, chose the title "It Hits the Fan," opened the season with it, and then managed to squeeze 162 separate "shits" into 20 min. Today, swearing in the show is common and appears uncensored on HBO Max. But given that *South Park* has also featured The Woodland Critters, Satan and Saddam Hussein as lovers, schoolmate Butters Stotch's abusive home life, school shootings, Britney Spears's suicide, and Cartman tricking Scott Tenorman into eating his own parents, those who know the show should know that saying the show's irreverence and philosophy are its most controversial elements is a controversial statement in itself.

What controversial topics has the show tackled? In "Death" (S1E6), Parker and Stone take on euthanasia, and in "Best Friends Forever" (S9E4) they took a position on the Terri Schiavo case (wherein the family of a woman in a persistent vegetative state publicly quarreled over how long to continue life support measures) just days before she died. "Fun with Veal" (S6E4) takes on vegetarianism, "Krazy Kripples" (S7E2) and "Kenny Dies" (S5E13) raise questions about abortion and stem cell research, "Follow that Egg" (S9E10) argues that gay marriage should be legal, and "I'm a Little Bit Country" (S7E4) questions the U.S. invasion of Iraq. "Something Wall-Mart This Way Comes" (S8E9) and "Gnomes" (S2E17) are a commentary on capitalism (and anti-capitalism), "Quest for Ratings" (S8E11) is a condemnation of cable news, and "Cherokee Hair Tampons" (S4E6) discredits alternative medicine.

"Cartman's Silly Hate Crime" (S4E2) is a commentary on hate crime laws while "Here Comes the Neighborhood" (S5E12) offers commentary on racism; "Chef Goes Nanners" does too while also commenting on the preservation of racist memorials (statues, flags, etc.). The show continually lampoons police brutality ("Naughty Ninjas" [S19E7]), social media ("Truth and Advertising" [S19E9], "The Hobbit" [S17E10], "Skank Hunt" [S20E2], "Safe Space" [S19E5]), addictive cell phones ("Freemium Isn't Free" [S18E6]), and gun politics ("Dead Kids" [S22E1] and "PC Principal Final Justice" [S19E10]). As I pointed out in the introduction to this handbook, the 2006 episode "ManBearPig" (S10E6) argues that global warming is a hoax; but then Parker and Stone took it all back, 12 years later, with "Time to Get Cereal" (S22E6) and "Nobody Got Cereal" (S22E7), in which they admit that Al Gore was right all along. "The Cissy" (S18E3) took on the transgender bathroom issues in 2014, and the show had long before explored similar issues with Mr./Ms. Garrison – who (during the course of the series) was straight and homophobic, then gay, then transgender, and then gay again. "Goobacks" (S8E7) takes on hysteria about immigration, as does "Mexican Joker" (S23E1) and "Where My Country Gone?" (S19E2).

The latter episode, "Where My Country Gone," also continues the show's long tradition of providing commentary on American presidential politics – a tradition that started with "Douche and Turd" (S8E8, aired Oct 27, 2004), which argued that every presidential election is just a choice between a douche and a turd (i.e., two equally undesirable candidates). That tradition continued with "About Last Night" (S12E12, aired Nov. 5, 2008) where the presidential election was just a front for an *Ocean's Eleven* style heist, and in "Obama Wins" (S16E14, aired Nov. 7, 2012), which eerily foreshadowed made-up fear mongering about stolen ballots and election fraud. The aforementioned "Where My Country Gone" was actually aired long before the 2016 election in Sept 2015, just as Trump's presidential candidacy was taking off. In it, we learn that (a parody of) Trump was elected president of Canada and turned it into a desolate ruined wasteland. As one Canadian immigrant to the U.S. put it:

> There were several candidates during the Canadian elections. One of them was this brash asshole who just spoke his mind. He didn't really offer any solutions, he just said outrageous things. We [pause] thought it was funny. Nobody really thought he'd ever be President. It was a joke! But we just let the joke go on for too long. He kept gaining momentum, and by the time we were all ready to say "Okay, let's get serious now. Who should really be President?" he was already being sworn into office. We weren't paying attention. [crying] We weren't paying attention! ("Where My County Gone")

The scene where Mr. Garrison wanders through the abandoned streets of the fictional Canadian capital eerily anticipates what abandoned cities looked like in 2020 during the later Covid pandemic (after Trump, in 2018, disbanded the Global Health Security and Biodefense unit, established by President Obama, which was responsible for pandemic preparedness; see Reuters 2020b).[1] Mr. Garrison kills the Canadian "Trump" (he actually "fucks him to death") but – lest we think that Parker and Stone thought their warning about Trump would kill his candidacy – at the end of the episode, Mr. Garrison essentially turns into a Trumpian candidate for president himself. Kyle's subsequent warning that "we have to stop this kind of sensationalist politics before the same thing happens to us" is cut short because the crowd already supports Mr. Garrison. Trump's election as president (in the real world) was followed by Mr. Garrison becoming president (in *South Park* world) the next day in "Oh, Jeez" ([S20E7]), and the next few episodes dealt with the aftermath of the 2016 election.

In fact, in addition to lampooning Trump during his candidacy (and the American public for embracing him), the entire 2016 season (Season 20), top to bottom, is a commentary on the kind of internet trolling and online anonymity that helped elect Trump. This was preceded by Season 19, which introduced the character PC Principle as part of its season-long commentary on political correctness; it was followed by "Tegrity Farms" (S22E4), an episode that saw Randy (Stan's dad) buy a cannabis farm. It was followed by a number of episodes on the issue of drug legalization, including "The Big Fix" ([S25E2], which took on racial inequality in the war on drugs and drug legalization), and 2019s "Christmas Snow" (S23E10) in which Parker and Stone seemed to argue for the legalization of cocaine. That was followed by a whole season (four episodes) of "Pandemic Specials," in which Parker and Stone took on masking and anti-masking, vaccine denial, QAnon, and even argued that people should not be eligible for early vaccines simply because they have chosen to smoke.

The show is also famous for making fun of celebrities, both those who are powerful because of their money – like Marc Zuckerberg ("Franchise Prequel" [S21E4]) and Jeff Bezos ("Bike Parade" [S22E10]) – and just about every celebrity in Hollywood: Sally Struthers ("Starvin' Marvin" [S1E8]), Barbra Streisand ("Mecha-Streisand" [S1E12]), Tom Cruise ("Trapped in the Closet" [S9E12]), Kayne West ("Fishsticks" [S13E5]), Paris Hilton ("Stupid Spoiled Whore Video Playset" [S8E12]), Mel Gibson ("The Passion of the Jew" [S8E3]), Michael Jackson ("The Jeffersons" [S8E6]), Bono ("More Crap" [S11E9]), and George Lucas ("The China Problem" [S12E8]). They dedicated a whole episode to Rob Reiner ("Butt Out" [S7E13]); and in the episode "The Biggest Douche in the Universe" (S6E15), Parker and Stone debunked psychic mediumship and then awarded self-proclaimed psychic medium Johnathan Edward the title "The Biggest Douche in the Universe" for taking advantage of the grieving relatives of the deceased.

This, of course, upset celebrities. However, what has gotten Parker and Stone in the most trouble is their treatment of religion. They took on both Mormonism ("All About Mormons" [S7E12]) and Scientology ("Trapped in a Closet"), mocked the God of Judaism (Jewpacabra [S16E4], the Virgin Mary ("Bloody Mary" [S9E14]), and the Catholic Church ("Red Hot Catholic Love" [S6E8], "A Boy and a Priest" [S22E2], "The Passion of the Jew"); they even took on atheism in "Go God Go" (S10E12) and "Go God Go XII" ([S10E13]; see Johnson 2013a), and tried to depict a cartoon of the Muslim prophet Mohammed ("Cartoon Wars" Part I and II [S10E3 and S10E4]). Some of these episodes drew complaints, others (supposedly) made cast members quit, still others have not been re-aired or made otherwise available (e.g., they were taken down from southpark.cc.com which streams most episodes for free). But their 200th episode ("200" [S14E5]) managed to get them death threats, because they insinuated they would try to show Mohammed again in the follow-up episode, "201" (S14E6). Comedy Central responded with heavy censorship.

It is these latter episodes on which this chapter will focus because it is these episodes that I see as the philosophical heart of the series. In these episodes, Parker and Stone present arguments for free speech and against censorship that stand at the heart of everything they do in the series – because, without freedom of speech and freedom from censorship, they wouldn't be able to make any of the controversial episodes that they have made in their 25+ seasons. (Their movie, *South Park: Bigger Longer & Uncut*, touches on the relevant issues, but is more an argument for blaming parents (rather than Parker and Stone) for the behavior of the children who watch their show.) To identify the argument of the episodes, it will first be necessary to explore a bit more of the show's history, summarize some previous episodes, and then also summarize the controversial episodes themselves. We will then look at the arguments Parker and Stone present in them and evaluate their philosophic merit. In the end, we will see that Parker and Stone are probably right about the censorship of jokes – as a target of mockery, either everything is okay, or nothing is okay – but they also have too much of an idealized view of what freedom of speech can do.

A History of "Blasphemy" on *South Park*

> Dude, that is Jesus. You don't say "fuck" in front of Jesus!
> —Kid in Yellow Hat ("The Spirit of Christmas: Jesus vs. Frosty")

South Park was birthed in religious irreverence. The first short, Parker and Stone made pitted a tiny, bearded baby Jesus against an evil frosty the snowman; Jesus kills frosty with his halo, princess Xena style. Their second short which garnered them national recognition and eventually their own show, had Jesus fighting Santa for dominance of the holiday (calling each other names like "fucking pussy" along the way) and even ended with Jesus calling himself a "right bastard." In the series itself, Jesus is a recurring character and is depicted in all kinds of blasphemous ways. He's a killer packing heat in "Red Sleigh Down" (S6E17) and boxes the devil in "Damien" (S1E10); he's a talk show host in "Are You There God? It's Me, Jesus" (S3E16) and gets all-roided-up in "A Scause for Applause" (S16E13). (It turns out, roiding-up is how he rose from the dead.)

The episode "Super Best Friends" (S5E3) not only suggests that Jesus' miracles were just lame magic tricks; it also implies that all religious figures – like Moses, Buddha, and Mohammed – are just fictional superheroes (they belong to a super-hero team called "The Super Best Friends). (The "Imagination Land" trilogy [S11E10, S11E11, S11E12] suggests something similar.) It should also be noted that, in the episode, Mohammed is depicted in cartoon form and (at the time) no one objected. His superpower is shooting fire out of his hands, and he uses it to harden a giant statue of John Wilkes Booth so it can shoot a giant statue of Abraham Lincoln.

South Park also takes on specific religious beliefs, like in "A Ladder to Heaven" (S6E12), where they lampooned not only Alan Jackson for writing a song that capitalized on people's grief about the 9/11 attacks but also the doctrine of heaven itself, saying that it was only an "abstract idea." "We should stop waiting to get into heaven and start trying to create it." The episode "Do the Handicapped Go to Hell" (S4E9) and the following episode "Probably" (S4E10) raise insoluble problems with the logic of Christian theology. (Since the "handicapped" boy, Timmy, can only say his own name, he cannot confess his sins and thus, through no fault of his own, is destined for hell.) And by raising the problem of evil, "Cartmanland" (S5E6) directly challenges the existence of God (see Johnson 2013b).

But the show also takes on entire religions. In "All About Mormons," Parker and Stone take on both the theology and history of Mormonism, by bluntly telling the story of Joseph Smith – clearly implying that he was a liar and con-artist – and repeating the (musical) phrase "dumb-dumb-dumb-dumb-dumb" as it is told. As Stan says to the Mormon family in the episode,

> Mormons actually know this story and they still believe Joseph Smith was a prophet? . . . it proves he DID make it all up. Are you blind? . . . it's a matter of logic! If you're gonna say things that have been proven wrong, like that the first man and woman lived in Missouri and that Native Americans came from Jerusalem, then you'd better have something to back it up. All you've got are a bunch of stories about some asswipe who read plates nobody ever saw out of a hat, and then couldn't do it again when the translations were hidden!

They do something similar in "Trapped in a Closet," which says straightforwardly what Scientologists believe – including the part about the Intergalactic Lord Xenu captioned with the words "THIS IS WHAT SCIENTOLOGISTS ACTUALLY BELIEVE." (According to Scientology, Xenu dumped frozen alien bodies into volcanoes in Hawaii 75 million years ago from galactic cruisers that look like DC8s with rocket engines, and then the brainwashed souls of those aliens inhabited all human life – and *that's* what causes all our "fears, and confusions, and problems.") Shortly after the episode aired, Scientologist Isaac Hayes, who had voiced the popular character named "Chef," left the show.

An open letter, allegedly signed by Hayes, said he left because "There is a place in this world for satire, but there is a time when satire ends and intolerance and bigotry towards religious beliefs of others begins" (Miller 2021). Parker and Stone found his stance quite hypocritical – "In 10 years and over 150 episodes of *South Park*, Isaac never had a problem with the show making fun of Christians, Muslims, Mormons or Jews … He got a sudden case of religious sensitivity when it was his religion featured on the show" (BBC News 2006) – and lampooned him harshly in "The Return of Chef" (S10E1). His character was depicted as brainwashed by a child molestation cult (The Super Adventure Club) and mauled horribly by animals; at Chef's funeral Kyle says,

> We're all here today because Chef has been such an important part of our lives. A lot of us don't agree with the choices Chef has made in the past few days. Some of us. . . feel hurt. . . and confused that he seemed to turn his back on us. But we can't let the events of the last

week take away the memories of how much Chef made us smile. I'm gonna remember Chef as the jolly old guy who always broke into song. I'm gonna remember Chef... as the guy who gave us advice to live by. So you see, we shouldn't be mad at Chef for leaving us. We should be mad at that little fruity club for scrambling his brains.

That last line, a (not so) thinly veiled stab at Scientology, turned out to be prophetic. Ten years later, Hayes' son accused the church of Scientology of having forged Hayes' resignation letter while he recovered from a stroke. Indeed, according to reports, Hayes was initially supportive of the episode (Miller 2021).

But it was two episodes later, in "Cartoon Wars" Parts I and II (April 2006), that "it" really started to hit the fan, and the show first got visually censored.[2] The episode revolves around whether *Family Guy* (which, for these two episodes, exists as a cartoon in the *South Park* universe) will be allowed by Fox to show a cartoon depiction of the Prophet Mohammed. With recent real-world events on their mind, the townspeople of *South Park* panic. (Depicting Mohammed is considered blasphemous to some Muslims; and in Feb 2006, after the Danish newspaper Jyllands-Posten has published 12 cartoon caricatures of the Prophet Mohammed, responsive attacks on Danish diplomatic missions in the Muslim world killed 50 people (Reuters 2020a; Spiegel 2006).) In Part I, the Fox network censors the *Family Guy* episode, putting a black box over Mohammed as he orders iced tea from Mr. T; but then it's revealed that the episode was "only part one of a two parter." The writers of *Family Guy* demand that their second episode air, uncensored – and because it is their highest rated show, the Fox execs say they will comply. The Muslim world erupts, and the leader of al-Qaida, Ayman al-Zawahiri, says (via captions) that (a) Family Guy is not well-written or funny and (b) their "retaliation for the episode will be "MASSIVE!!!!". Cartman says what *Family Guy* is doing is "Wrong ... it's WRONG!" and travels to Fox headquarters to demand Fox pull the second *Family Guy* episode. The *South Park* episode (Part I) ends by making it clear that "Cartoon Wars Part II" will include an image of Mohammed and that you will have to tune in next week to see whether "the cartoon [will] be allowed to appear uncensored." In a voice over, Parker and Stone ask. "Will television executives fight for free speech? Or will Comedy Central puss out?"

"Cartoon Wars Part II" reveals the writers of *Family Guy* are manatees (yes, the sea-dwelling mammals) who create jokes by randomly pushing idea balls into a chute – and if you remove one ball from their tank, like the Mohammed ball, they will refuse to work. "Manatees are very ethical writers," the Fox executive says. "Either everything is okay to write about or nothing is." This is how they demanded the episode air uncensored. But then Cartman sneaks in and steals one of the balls to stop the manatees from working. This upsets the Fox president, who doesn't know why they stopped, so he decides to pull the episode. At the last minute, Kyle gives the Fox president an impassioned speech against giving in to terrorist threats (which we will examine below), and the Fox president changes his mind. The *Family Guy* episode airs, uncensored–at least, in the *South Park* Universe. In the real world, just as the *Family Guy* Mohammed scene is about to air on the show, the screen cuts to black and says "In this shot, Mohammed hands a football helmet to Family Guy.

28 *South Park* as Philosophy: Blasphemy, Mockery, and (Absolute?) Freedom of Speech 641

Comedy Central has refused to broadcast an image of Mohammed on their network." In the show, the terrorists retaliate with a cartoon of their own, which shows all white Americans, President Bush, an unwed mother-to-be, and Jesus himself "crapping" all over each other and the American flag. Comedy Central did not censor it and there was no real-world terrorist retaliation.

Disappointed with the censorship, Parker and Stone pushed boundaries yet again, four years later, in their 200th and 201st episode (cleverly titled "200" and "201"). The former episode brings back every celebrity they have ever made fun of, and Tom Cruise leads them to file a class action lawsuit against the town for making fun of them. He then offers to drop it, however, if the boys can make Mohammed appear in the town. Cruise observed that Mohammed is the only person with the power to never be ridiculed and wants to steal that power. The townspeople object, thinking it is an impossible task: "If Mohammed appears in *South Park*, we get bombed." Indeed, no one even knows what he looks like. But Stan points out that he and the boys already met him.

Stan	Yeah, a while ago, my friends joined David Blaine's cult, and I had to go to the Super Best Friends to rescue them. Mohammed was one of the Super Best Friends.
Mr. Garrison	Oh, and what- he was just out in the open where everybody could see him and nobody got bombed?
Stan	No, dude, it was totally fine.
Sgt. Yates	Mohammed showed up and there was no violence at all?
Stan	Well, a giant John Wilkes Booth shot Abraham Lincoln.

Stan then goes to the Super Best Friends, asking if Mohammed can visit the town; Jesus replies, "much has changed since you were last here. Mohammed cannot make public appearances." But they decide he could, if he were in a "U Haul" with no windows. To get him into Cruise's limo, they dress him in a full body bear mascot costume; but as the exchange is supposedly about to happen, the limo is bombed by "the gingers" (all the redheads in town). They want the power to not be ridiculed as well, so they demand Mohammed be turned over to them. Before they give up the detonators to the bombs they have placed all over town, they insist that the person in the bear costume take it off, to prove they are Mohammed. Again, the episode ends, suggesting that Mohammed will be shown in the next episode.

Following the airing of the episode, however, death threats were made in the real world. They appeared on Revolutionmuslim.com, and said that Parker and Stone would "probably wind up like Theo van Gogh," an artist who had been killed by a Muslim a few years before for his film that criticized Islam. Zachary Adam Chesser, the author of the post, included a picture of van Gogh's dead body, along with information about where Parker and Stone live, and the location of Comedy Central studios. (Chesser is now in jail for this and other crimes.)

Despite the threats, Parker and Stone stuck with their original story. At the beginning of "201," the bear costume is removed – only to reveal that it was Santa

Claus inside. Mohammed was originally in the U Haul, but the boys made a switch and hid Mohammed in a nearby locker. When Mohammed emerges from the locker, however, he has a black "censored" bar over him. But it is not placed there by Comedy Central; this is now his super-power. The gingers get him anyway, but the celebrities release Mecha-Streisand on the town in an attempt to get him back. "How do you like that?" Cruise says, "Celebrities can get violent too!" The gingers strike a deal with the celebrities: they will share Mohammed with them if the celebrities share their "goo harvesting machine," the means by which they intend to extract Mohammed's power from him. When Tom Cruise uses the machine on Mohammed, a black "censored" bar appears over Cruise as well. The Super Best Friends then show up, and a giant fight breaks out (Jesus is shown punching and kicking ginger children). However, when, during the fight, the boys (and Jesus) make fun of Cruise (for having Seaman on his back), his black bar disappears and the fight stops.

The episode ends with Kyle, Santa, and Jesus launching into an "I learned something today" speech about how the "only true power is violence." It doesn't mention Mohammed; it just says they learned that, *if you don't want to be made fun of, you just have to threaten those who want to do so.* Ironically, however, in the one and only public airing of the episode, that speech couldn't be heard. (We will look at the uncensored version later.) Comedy Central "bleeped" it, along with every other mention of Mohammed's name in the episode. Again, it seems that the black "censored" bar was put there by Parker and Stone as part of the plot; it can still be seen in the uncensored version of the episode on www.southparkuncensored.com. But the bleeps were the work of Comedy Central. Parker and Stone were livid (Rosenberg 2010).

Identifying the Arguments

> I mean, I know [*Family Guy*] is just joke after joke, but I like that. At least it doesn't get all preachy and up its own ass with messages, you know?
> —Trucker ("Cartoon Wars, Part II")

Collectively, "Cartoon Wars" and "200/1," seem to be making five separate but related arguments. Let's consider each in turn.

The first argument suggests that Comedy Central should not cater to threats of terrorism because it only encourages more terrorism, violence, and extreme demands. Kyle probably puts it best at the end of "Cartoon Wars II."

Kyle	No! Wait! You can't listen to him! He's a lying deceitful monster who only wants *Family Guy* off the air!
FOX President	But he has a gun.
Kyle	You can't do what he wants just because he's the one threatening you with violence!
Cartman	Shut up, Kyle!

28 *South Park* as Philosophy: Blasphemy, Mockery, and (Absolute?) Freedom of Speech 643

FOX President   I can't be responsible for people getting hurt. Especially me.

Kyle   Yes, people can get hurt. That's how terrorism works. But if you give into that, Doug, you're allowing terrorism to work. Do the right thing here.

The argument is that one shouldn't give into terroristic threats because, by doing so, one shows that terrorism is an effective way to get what one wants, and thus one encourages more terrorism (and thus makes it even more likely that someone will get hurt). Let us call this the "Catering to Terrorism Creates More Terrorism" argument:

> *Catering to Terrorism Creates More Terrorism.* Ceding to the demands of terrorists shows that terrorism is successful, which – in turn – generates more terrorism. Thus you shouldn't give in to such demands.

In "Cartoon Wars Part I," at the town hall meeting, Butters's father, Stephen Stotch, seems to take it a step further. In response to the idea that everyone should bury their heads in sand to avoid appearing responsible for the *Family Guy* episode, he says

> No, no, wait a minute, that's ridiculous. What we need to do is just the opposite. Freedom of speech is at stake here, don't you all see? If anything, we should ALL make cartoons of Mohammed and show the terrorists and the extremists that we are all united in the belief that every person has a right to say what they want!

The idea here is that, to discourage further threats to free speech, those threatened should do more of the thing that the terrorist don't want to happen. This, it seems, will supposedly have two effects. First, it will show that terroristic threats actually have the opposite of the desired effect. If terroristic threats in response to cartoon depictions of Mohammed led to even more such depictions than otherwise would have occurred, it would seem that those offended by such depictions wouldn't resort to such threats in response. (Perhaps, instead, they should respond in a much more ethical way, with their own blasphemous cartoon, like al-Qaeda did at the end of "Cartoon Wars Part II.") Second, it will show solidarity with the threatened party and reiterate the value of free speech. Let us call this the "Don't Capitulate, Reiterate" argument.

> *Don't Capitulate, Reiterate:* The correct response to terroristic demands about censorship is to produce more uncensored free speech in order to both show that terrorism is ineffective and acknowledge the importance of free speech.

In his speech, Stotch goes on to make a second related point.

> Look, people, it's been real easy for us to stand up for free speech lately. For the past few decades we haven't had to risk anything to defend it. But those times are going to come! And one of those times is right now. And if *we* aren't willing to *risk* what we have, then we just believe in free speech, but we don't defend it.

This seems to be in response to arguments like the one Cartman makes: "All right, fine, Kyle. Forget the Muslim faith for a minute. People can get hurt. If ten people die because Family Guy just had to have their little joke, will you still think it's funny? What if a hundred people died? Will it be funny then, Kyle?" Cartman's argument is that jokes aren't worth risking lives; if telling a joke will make someone so offended or upset that they might kill others, then others should demand that you don't tell it, and you shouldn't tell it. What Mr. Stotch is essentially saying is that this is the wrong way to frame the choice. What is at risk is not the joke, it's the right to free speech; and it is worth risking lives (in Mr. Stotch's words "what we have,") to defend that right, just as much as it is worth risking lives to defend religious and economic freedom or the right to free assembly. In honor of my favorite song from *Team America: World Police* (also by Trey Parker and Matt Stone), let's call this the "Freedom of Speech Isn't Free" argument.

> *Freedom of Speech Isn't Free:* It is worth risking lives to defend the right to tell jokes because free speech itself (not just the joke) is at stake.

Another argument that Parker and Stone make suggests that allowing one erosion of free speech leads to more. This is the actual principle behind why Cartman wants to get the Mohammed episode of *Family Guy* pulled. If he can get this one pulled, other people will complain about different episodes that offend them, and then the show will be off the air. Once you show that terrorist threats can be successful, you open Pandora's box, and make way for more. Kyle essentially says this at the end of "Cartoon Wars Part II."

FOX President	How about I allow the episode to air but just censor out the image of Mohammed again?
Kyle	I wish that was good enough, but if you censor out Mohammed, then soon you'll have to censor out more. . . . If you don't show Mohammed, then you've made a distinction between what is okay to poke fun at, and what isn't. Either it's all okay, or none of it is.

Here he is reiterating the philosophy of the manatees who write *Family Guy*, who will stop writing for the show if even a single "idea ball" is removed from their tank. But there are really two arguments here, one overt and the other implied. The overt argument is about what it is okay to make fun of. Parker and Stone, it seems, are like the manatees: nothing is too sacred to make fun of. No celebrity is safe, no religion or religious belief is off limits. It's all fair game. Let's call this the "All or Nothing" argument.

> *All or Nothing*: Either everything is okay to mock, or nothing is. Since it is okay to mock some things, it is okay to mock everything.

The implied argument is broader, although it was stated above by Mr. Stotch. "[E]very person has a right to say what they want." Kyle's line that "it's all okay,

28 *South Park* as Philosophy: Blasphemy, Mockery, and (Absolute?) Freedom of Speech 645

or none of it is" might be interpreted as, not only should people be allowed to *make fun of* whoever or whatever they wish, but they should be allowed to *say* whatever they wish. Let us call this the "absolute free speech" argument.

> *Absolute Free Speech*: The right to free speech should be absolute. Everyone should be allowed to say whatever they want.

With these five arguments now identified, we shall now turn to examining each.

Argument #1: Catering to Terrorism Creates More Terrorism

> Don't you know anything about manatees? They're the only mammals that are completely unmoved by terrorist threats.
> —Mitchell (*Family Guy* Staff) ("Cartoon Wars, Part II")

Does giving in to terrorist demands demonstrate that terrorism works and thus encourage more? This is similar to the commonly asserted reason for the United States' policy to "never negotiate with terrorists." The idea is that, by negotiating, you add legitimacy to the terrorists and their cause; and if the terrorists end up getting what they want, other organizations will try something similar to get what they want.

In reality, this is only a slogan and the United States has actually negotiated with terrorists multiple times. This happens especially when the threat of not doing so is immediate (someone's life is actively on the line), and the threat of negotiation – encouraging other possible future terrorist attacks – is only a potential (Inskeep and Greene 2014). This is a "one bird in the hand is worth [more than] two in the bush" kind of logic. If a terrorist is actively about to kill someone, it may be worth negotiation and capitulating to save that person, because the future terrorist attacks you might encourage by doing so are only hypothetical. It's better to decide your actions based on definite outcomes. So maybe "never negotiate with terrorists" is too simplistic of a rule. Indeed, Toros (2008) argues that, if done in the right way, negotiating with terrorists (and even legitimizing their cause) can not only lead to non-violent conflict resolution, but can even open up "new possibilities for engagement" that could potentially address and eliminate the underlying motivation for the terrorism in the first place.

Nonetheless, this may not invalidate Parker and Stone's point because – at least with "Cartoon Wars," "200," and "201" – not only was the threat of encouraging future terrorism merely hypothetical, so was the threat of present violence that they were dealing with. Consider again the week between the airing of 200 and 201. It would be different if Zachary Adam Chesser had gotten inside Comedy Central studios, held a gun to a person's head, after having already killed another, and demanded that Parker and Stone not air the episode. That threat would be immediate, and the worry about encouraging other possible future attacks by capitulating would have just been a hypothetical possibility. In that situation, Parker and Stone should (and probably would) give in and hope that Chesser's eventual imprisonment would do enough to discourage others from emulating him. But since Chesser only issued a vague threat on the internet without a clear means to carry it out – well, that is just as much a hypothetical possibility as encouraging future threats. Setting a precedent for people being able to get what they want by *merely threatening* violence on the internet would seem to encourage more threats of violence.

Doing so would essentially be proving what Kyle, Jesus, and Santa said (ironically) in their censored speech at the end of "201."

Kyle   You see, I learned something today. Throughout this whole ordeal, we've all wanted to show things that we weren't allowed to show. But it wasn't because of some magic goo. It was because of the magical power of threatening people with violence. That's obviously the only true power. If there's anything we've all learned, it's that terrorizing people works.

Jesus   That's right. Don't you see, gingers? If you don't want to be made fun of anymore, all you need are guns and bombs to get people to stop.

Santa   That's right, friends. All you need to do is instill fear, and be willing to hurt people, and you can get whatever you want. The only true power is violence.

Actual violence, of course, already has power. But by giving into potential terroristic threats, you give power to even *mere threats* of violence. Therefore, unless you are faced with actual, tangible, immediate harm – like a gun to your head – it seems that the appropriate response to terrorist threats is to ignore them. Thus, Comedy Central should not have censored "201" in light of such threats, and the "Catering to Terrorism Creates More Terrorism" argument succeeds.

Argument #2: "Don't Capitulate, Reiterate"

> What cartoon would be so insensitive as to have Mohammad as a character? Who do you think?! The cartoon that's always pushing buttons with their careless toilet humor! *Family Guy*!
> —Gerald Broflovski & Randy Marsh ("Cartoon Wars, Part I")

Should we do more of the thing that terrorists don't want us to do, to discourage further threats – to show that terroristic threats actually have the opposite of the desired effect? This was the logic behind "Everybody Draw Mohammed Day," which was conceptualized by Molly Norris the day before "201" aired, in response to the *South Park* controversy. The idea was, on May 10, 2010, everyone was supposed to draw Mohammed to "water down the pool of targets" and stand up for the First Amendment (Wikipedia 2022).

The part of the argument which suggests that doing more of what the terrorists don't want, in response to their threats, will have a deterrent effect seems to be undermined by the fact Molly Norris herself had to go into hiding; death threats against her were issued in *al-Qaeda Magazine* by Anwar al-Awlaki specifically because of her "Everyone Draw Mohammed Day" idea. It seems that the motivation behind such threats is not to keep people from drawing Mohammed; it's to not be held accountable by Allah for tolerating blasphemy. So, it doesn't matter whether their threats lead to more depictions of Mohammed; those further depictions will be followed by more threats. Think of it this way; if your grandma scolded you for saying "God damnit," would doing it more in response make her scold you less? Of course not. Her reasons are principled, not pragmatic.

Now, perhaps, the same is true for those who want to respond to threats like al-Awlaki's with more drawings of Mohammed: it's the principle that matters. Maybe, regardless of its deterrent effect, in the wake of such threats, everyone should draw pictures of Mohammed as a way to stand up for free speech. Then again, are there other or more effective ways of standing up for free speech? Are there ways that are less offensive to Muslims? Perhaps; perhaps not. On the other hand, perhaps we have an ethical obligation to not offend others' religious sensibilities.

This latter notion is difficult to defend, however – at least, philosophically.Now, thanks to the European Court of Human Rights, people in the European Union do have a *legal* right for their religious beliefs and sensibilities to not be offended by public speech. (More on this in a moment.) However, legal rights are not moral rights, and the court's ruling does not present any argument for a moral right to not have one's religious beliefs offended. Indeed, even its argument for such a legal right is weak. Essentially, in its justification for its ruling, the court just assumes that the right to "freedom of religion" entails the right to "freedom from religious offense," but it is not clear at all that this is true. In fact, there is good reason to think it isn't. The episode "Bloody Mary," which depicts a statue of the Virgin Mary spewing menstrual blood all over The Pope, does not hinder or prevent anyone from being Catholic (i.e., believing catholic doctrines or practicing Catholicism). And that is what freedom of religion is for. The episode may upset Catholics, but it doesn't force them to be non-Catholic.

The court also appealed to the fact that mere offensive speech does not contribute to public debate. The court does not say that contradicting religious dogma is illegal; an argument that, say, Jesus wanted a rabbit to be Pope so it could not tell people how to live their lives (see "Fantastic Easter Special" [S11E5]) would and should be legal, even though Catholics might find its conclusion offensive. Why? Because it contributes to a debate on a religious issue. The legal right to free expression is predicated on the idea that free expression is necessary for a public debate that is able to expose the truth on that topic, and the right to free expression (and the benefit it has on society) outweighs an individual's right to not be offended. (More on this later as well.) But menstrual blood all over the Pope, or depicting Mohammed handling a football helmet with a salmon on it, doesn't contribute to a debate; it is just offensive. So, the court ruled that such things should not be protected.

But, as Geroge Letsas (2009) argues in "Is there a right not to be offended in one's religious beliefs?," the court's ruling does not hold water. First, to even pit the right of free expression against the right to not be offended, the court would need to establish that both rights exist. But, as I mentioned above, the court merely assumed that the right to not have one's religious sensibilities offended followed from one's "freedom of religion," when in reality it does not. What's more, Letsas argues, what is found to be offensive is subjective, a part of a person's conception of the good life. Another person may have a different conception, and what one person finds offensive may be a part of another person's conception of the good life (like the enjoyment of a good joke). Therefore, for the government to rule that you cannot offend my religious sensibilities is for it to elevate my conception of the good above yours. But a democratic liberal society, Letsas argues, must "treat people as free and equal agents, who are responsible for choosing their own ethical ideals" (Letsas 2009, Section IV). Besides, things that seem to be merely offensive may actually contribute to debate more than one realizes. Watching the offensive events of "Blood Mary" might lead one to question the Catholic obsession (which also seems to be shared with most of Christianity) with sexual purity and virginity.

Still, one might argue that – regardless of what is legal – a person has a moral obligation to not offend the religious sensibilities of others. After all, it's legal to break a verbal promise, but that doesn't mean it's not morally wrong. But it's not clear how well such an argument holds up. Granted, generally speaking, you shouldn't "be an asshole," and intentionally saying something that you know will offend someone within earshot is usually considered an asshole move. But, I think, at best, this just means it's morally better to not offend; it's not morally obligatory. If I say your favorite sports team stinks, knowing how much it will upset you – sure, I'm probably being a jerk. Maybe (just maybe!), I would be a better person if I didn't say anything. But I'm not morally obligated to protect your delicate sensibilities, am I? I certainly am not morally obligated to be a fan of your favorite team, just because you are. But if you insist that I not insult your favorite team, aren't you demanding that I respect them just as much as you do? In fact, by doing so, *you* might actually be the "asshole." How so?

In *Assholes: A Theory*, Aaron James (2012) defines an asshole as someone who "allows himself to enjoy special advantages ... out of an entrenched sense of entitlement, [who] is immunized by his sense of entitlement against the complaints of other people (p. 5)". The fan of *South Park* will recognize that this is Cartman (to a T); but this also seems to describe the rabid sports fan who thinks that others are morally obligated to not insult their favorite sports team in their presence. They are entitled to the privilege of not being insulted, and your right to express your views about their team (when you want) must yield to that privilege. The same seems to be true of those that think others are morally obligated to not offend their religious sensibilities; they think everyone else is morally obligated to hold their religious beliefs in the same high regard that they do. They think the atheist must yield his moral right to express his belief that, say, theistic belief is silly because they are entitled to not be offended. But unless the theist thinks they are equally morally obligated to not contradict atheism – and I have never known a theist to think this[3] – it would seem that this employs a double standard. They think they are entitled to special privileges, completely immunized against the complaints of others. So suggesting that Parker and Stone are doing something morally wrong when they offend people's religious sensibilities, simply because "religious sensibilities should be respected," employs a morally unjustifiable double standard. As the old adage goes, "Respect is earned, not given."

Someone might also argue that deliberately offending someone's religious sensibilities is intolerant, and that we have a moral obligation to be tolerant. But as Parker and Stone would no doubt point out, tolerance is not the same as acceptance. In the episode "Death Camp of Tolerance" (S6E14), the boys are forced to go to a Nazi-like concentration camp where they are coerced to accept everyone and everything. They are in trouble for objecting to Mr. Garrison "being totally gay" (when, in reality, they were objecting to Mr. Garrison putting a gerbil up Mr. Slave's ass in front of the whole classroom). At the end of the episode, when the parents try to give Mr. Garrison "a goddamn medal" for doing this, he objects:

> [The Museum of Tolerance tells you to be tolerant], but not stupid! Look, just because you have to tolerate something doesn't mean you have to approve of it! If you had to like it, it'd be called the Museum of Acceptance! "Tolerate" means you're just putting up with it! You tolerate a crying child sitting next to you on the airplane or you tolerate a bad cold. It can still piss you off! Jesus Tapdancing Christ!

Cartoon Wars' depiction of Mohammed and the "bloody scene" in "Bloody Mary" aren't intolerant of Muslim or Catholic beliefs. Parker and Stone clearly do not accept those beliefs; they reject the idea that it is not permissible to draw Mohammed and the idea that the Pope is sacred. But in no way does either episode suggest that Muslims or Catholics shouldn't exist, or that they shouldn't have rights. It suggests their beliefs are false, even silly, but since Parker and Stone are not morally required to *accept* those beliefs, ridiculing them is not morally wrong. The episode tolerates religious believers; it just doesn't accept their beliefs.

In reply, one might argue that jokes that offend religious sensibilities are wrong in the same way that racist jokes are morally wrong. Jokes that make fun of a race still tolerate the existence of other races and don't rob them of their rights; still, telling a racist joke is morally wrong. In the same way, jokes that make fun of a person for religious belief are morally wrong, even if they tolerate the existence and rights of those who belong to those religions.

But there are two things wrong with this argument. First, one reason racist jokes are morally wrong is because they are often motivated by racism, and racism is morally wrong; the joke itself may not be wrong, but the intention behind it still is. (This is one reason why comedians who belong to racial minorities can often make jokes about their own race; it's clear that there is no ill-intention behind it.) Thinking a religious belief is false, however, or even thinking it is silly, is not immoral like racism is immoral. After all, religious orientation is not race. (Even when it comes to Judaism, there is a difference between belonging to the Jewish faith, and being of Jewish ancestry.) Granted, it's wrong to have hiring practices that discriminate on the basis of religious orientation – but that's because such practices are not tolerant; they strip someone of the ability to earn a living. Ultimately, at least to some degree, religious affiliation is a choice. You can adopt or abandon religious belief; you can't adopt or abandon being a race. And no one is obligated to respect (as in accept and not argue against or ridicule) your choice to believe one thing, rather than another. As I often point out to my philosophy and critical thinking students, no one has an epistemic right to just believe whatever they want for no reason. That right must be earned with argument and evidence. And even if a person does have a moral right to believe whatever they want, it does not correspondingly obligate everyone else to agree with them, or not contradict them.

Secondly, another reason racist jokes are immoral – even if there is not a bad intention behind them--is because they perpetuate racism and encourage continued systemic oppression of races by reinforcing wrong-headed, usually essentialist beliefs about races. Racist jokes are weaponized tools of power, used by those in power, to oppress those who have little. Religious jokes do nothing of the kind. Think of it this way: Some people wonder why black comedians can make fun of white people, but the reverse is not acceptable. Part of the answer is that comedy is for speaking truth to power and keeping power in check; so it is appropriate to use comedy to cut those in power down to size; it is not appropriate (especially for those already in power) to use comedy to bring down those who already lack power. This is often called the difference between "punching up" and "punching down." It's okay to punch up, it's not okay to punch down. So the reason that a white person telling a racist joke is morally bad, but an atheist making fun of Christianity is okay, is that the white comedian's joke punches down, while an atheist's jokes about Christianity punches up. It would be different if the religious of the world were an oppressed minority; but not only do they make up a majority of the population, they have enjoyed almost complete social and political power for all of human history. (Atheists, on the other hand, have almost no social or political power; for more on this, see ▶ Chap. 61, "*God's Not Dead* as Philosophy: Trying to Prove God Exists," in this handbook.)

All that said, the fact that Parker and Stone are permitted to ridicule religious belief doesn't mean that Comedy Central is morally obligated to platform such ridicule. But there are three reasons why Comedy Central's choice to censor *South Park*'s depiction (and mentions) of Mohammed, as it did, are morally problematic. First, it was inconsistent; they censored Mohammed handing a football helmet to Peter Griffin, but not Jesus pooping on the American flag. Although one might appeal to the difference between punching up and punching down here, a good case could be made that the latter is more offensive. Second, as the inconsistency indicates, they chose to censor what they censored because of a hypothetical possibility of violence. As was discussed above, that seems to give too much power to mere threats of violence. Lastly, as a channel that specializes in comedy, it would seem that they are obligated to stand up for free expression more than other channels. Again, comedy is a primary means by which society speaks truth to power, and it often does this by being offensive. So, there is a social good to giving comedy and comedians the necessary freedom to say what they want without being censored, even when it will offend and upset others.

That's not to say that Comedy Central must (or should) platform every joke of every kind. So while they do tolerate Cartman, most people would probably agree that Comedy Central shouldn't platform an unapologetic white Neo-Nazi comedian

28 *South Park* as Philosophy: Blasphemy, Mockery, and (Absolute?) Freedom of Speech 651

to tell jokes ridiculing Jews. But that is because such jokes would likely inspire antisemitism and discrimination, and be punching down. (It is for this reason that many called for some of Dave Chapelle's specials to be taken off Netflix; despite his arguments to the contrary, they thought his jokes about transgender persons were punching down and could lead to discrimination, and even hate crimes, against that minority group.) *South Park* depicting Mohammed is very unlikely to lead to anti-Muslim discrimination. (His depiction in "Super Best Friends," and *South Park*'s opening credits sequence for years later certainly didn't.) Neither is the "bloody scene" in "Bloody Mary" going to spur anti-Catholic sentiment.

So, while having everyone draw more cartoons of Mohammed did not have the deterrent effect that Molly Norris may have wanted it to have, there is nothing morally wrong with breaking a religious taboo of a religion that you don't belong to, even if doing so will offend members of that religion. While you are morally obligated to tolerate their religious beliefs, you are not obligated to accept them, not ridicule them, or let them dictate how you should live your life, what you should say, or what you take the good life to be. As Wencong Fa (2019) put it, "Protecting free speech is more important than protecting people from being offended."

Argument #3: Freedom of Speech Isn't Free

This is about more than fart jokes!
This is about freedom of speech. About censorship . . . and stuff.
—Stan Randell William Marsh (*South Park: Bigger, Longer, & Uncut*)

This argument appears in the second half of Mr. Stotch's argument, where he says "[I]f *we* aren't willing to *risk* what we have, then we just believe in free speech, but we don't defend it." As we just discussed, it's wrong to tell a joke about a group if we know it will inspire others to harm members of that group. (Notice that having Cartman tell racist jokes on *South Park* is very unlikely to lead to racial discrimination, since it is understood that Cartman is a jackass.) But what if we know a joke about a group will inspire members of that group to harm others – like how a joke about Mohammed might inspire some Muslims to react violently in protest? What Stotch is saying is that the right to freedom of expression is a right that is worth defending, so much so that it is worth risking our lives to do so. Again, Cartman might say that a joke isn't worth ten lives, but Stotch's argument says that the risk isn't in defense of the joke, but the rights that protect it.

To better understand this last point, consider an analogy. Suppose there is a religious group that has a strange but harmless custom: they think their god demands that they dye their hair purple. Let's call them "the Purplesians." Another religious group finds this offensive, and they swear to kill innocent civilians until the Purplesians stop dying their hair. Should we demand that the Purplesians cave in, and stop their religious hair-dying practice? Not if we care about religious freedom. By standing up for their right to practice their religion as they see fit, we are standing up for the principle of religious freedom itself, not just the Purplesians' ability to dye their hair. Notice that if someone like Cartman asked "What if 100 people die because the Purplesians had to dye their hair; would it be worth it then?" we would think they had missed the point. The practice may be silly, but the principle that protects it is sacrosanct, and that principle is worth risking lives to protect.

Now, it would be different if it were a harmful religious practice – like human sacrifice. The U.S. Constitution, and ethical philosophy, are both pretty clear that our rights don't extend to the ability to harm others. As philosopher John Stuart Mill put it in *On Liberty* (Mill 1859/2000), "[T]he only purpose for which power can be rightfully exercised over any member of a civilized community, against his will, is to prevent harm to others" (p. 31). In other words, you should have the right to do whatever you want, as long as it doesn't harm others. Sacrificing others in religious ceremonies would obviously harm them; thus it should be illegal. But as long as the religious practice or belief is harmless, even if it is silly, then it is worth the risk to protect it because the right that makes it possible is worth protecting.

The Korean War Memorial in Washington D.C. has the words "Freedom is not Free" engraved on it, and usually these words are meant to imply that our freedoms come at the cost of soldiers' blood. (That's certainly how they were used in Parker and Stone's film *Team America: World Police*.) We aren't under fascist Nazi rule because soldiers fought and died fending off the Nazis in WWII. That is undoubtedly true. But freedoms also come with social costs. The absolute freedom to bear arms comes at the cost of daily mass shootings (often against the most vulnerable people, like young children in schools); freedom of the press comes at the cost of news outlets that spew out gross misinformation; and freedom of expression comes at the cost that some will be so upset with what is expressed that they will act violently. That's not to say that such freedoms are always worth it; no freedom is without limit and we have to decide, case by case, whether the freedom is worth the social risk it incurs. (For example, many think the cost of mass shootings is not worth the absolute freedom to bear arms.) But to decide, as soon as someone threatens retaliation if their religion is ridiculed, that the right to freedom of expression should be curtailed, skips the step of even considering whether that freedom is worth the cost.

Argument #4: "It's All or Nothing"

> What we say with the show is not anything new, but I think it is something that is great to put out there. It is that the people screaming on this side and the people screaming on that side are the same people, and it's OK to be someone in the middle, laughing at both of them.
> —Trey Parker (*The Charlie Rose Show*, September 26, 2005)

With the "It's all or nothing" argument, Parker and Stone suggest that one act of censorship will "open Pandora's box," so to speak, and lead to many other acts of censorship; taking one episode of *Family Guy* off the air to appease Muslims will lead to others being taken down to appease Catholics, and pretty soon no episode

28 South Park as Philosophy: Blasphemy, Mockery, and (Absolute?) Freedom of Speech 653

will be allowed and the show will be canceled. Ironically, however, *South Park*'s own success may have undermined this argument. As of this writing, eight episodes have been removed from *South Park* Studios, the latest being Season 14, episode 10, "Insheeption." But as of this writing, *South Park* is in its 26th season, and in 2021, Parker and Stone signed a 6-year deal with ViacomCBS for 900 million dollars – one of the biggest deals in TV history (Shaw 2021). In other words, despite eight explicit acts of censorship against the show, *South Park* is far from canceled; there are hundreds of episodes still available to view and the ViacomCBS deal suggests there will be at least several more years of new material.

The structure of the All or Nothing argument seems to rely on what is known as the "Slippery Slope Fallacy," the idea that one step toward an undesirable destination will inevitably lead to that destination. What makes slippery slope arguments tricky is that they are not always fallacious. Providing good evidence that the slope actually is slippery – that a first seemingly innocent action will lead to a cascade of events that will have an undesirable end – does provide good reason to not take that first action. (Military history provides good reason to think that limited military engagements often balloon into full-blown conflicts.) The problem is, most slippery slope arguments skip that step; they just observe that the first step is one step closer to an undesired ending, and then just assume that a series of events will lead to it without ever articulating what those steps are or why they will happen. In short, in order for slippery slope arguments to work, you actually have to prove that the slope is slippery. And, when it comes to censorship canceling shows, Parker and Stone have not done this. Granted, Kyle says, "Pulling an episode because someone is offended starts a chain reaction. You'll have to pull more and more episodes until the show goes off the air completely. It's what happened to Laverne & Shirley." But Laverne & Shirley was canceled due to poor ratings, and the network's unwillingness to work around actress Cindy Williams' pregnancy, not a series of canceled episodes.

That said, there is something to say in defense of the overt argument that either everything is okay to make fun of or nothing is. Think of it this way: any line that someone drew to determine what was okay to mock and what wasn't would be completely arbitrary; it would be based on their own biases and prejudices – like when Isaac Hayes (supposedly) was okay with ridiculing all other religions but his own. But if such lines are arbitrary, anyone could draw such a line anywhere they wanted and thus make anything they wanted off limits. So, either there is no line – and thus everything is okay to mock – or lines can be drawn, which effectively makes everything off limits (because anyone could be holding the marker). So, even though censorship doesn't have the "slippery slope" effect that Parker and Stone seem to think it does – again, more than 10 years after being censored, *South Park* is still going strong – it seems that Comedy Central determining what is acceptable or unacceptable for them to make fun of is unwarranted. Perhaps it really should be open season.

Now, one might argue for the "what's OK to mock" line being relative to the person; in principle, anything can be mocked – but a person has to be "below" something in order for it to be morally okay for them to mock it. In other words, anything can be mocked, but those who do the mocking must be punching up. Then again, there is a big difference between someone who always punches down (like a white comedian who always tells racist jokes), and Parker and Stone who are constantly punching in all directions, making fun of everyone (including Cartman, who tells the racist jokes, and themselves). Maybe if you really do make fun of everyone, it is okay to mock anything – even if you do occasionally punch down.

But saying it is okay to *make fun* of anything, is different than saying it is okay to *say* anything. So let us now turn to the main focus of this chapter: *South Park*'s implied argument for absolute freedom of speech.

Part II: How Far Should Freedom of Speech Go?

Argument #5: Absolute Free Speech

> Well, Chef, it's freedom of speech.
> We don't like it, but we can't arrest [the KKK] for talking.
> —Officer Barbrady ("Chef Goes Nanners")

The argument for absolute free speech in *South Park* is not explicitly stated. Officer Barbrady expresses the legal principle in the "Chef Goes Nanners" (S4E7) quote above, but he's just explaining the law (and Barbrady is an idiot who doesn't speak for Parker and Stone). The episode "Band in China" (S23E2) (about Chinese censorship of western entertainment) hints at it, as did Parker and Stone's (extremely sarcastic) "official apology" after that episode caused *South Park* to be banned in China.

> OFFICIAL APOLOGY TO CHINA FROM TREY PARKER AND MATT STONE. "Like the NBA, we welcome the Chinese censors into our homes and into our hearts. We too love money more than freedom and democracy. Xi doesn't look like Winnie the Pooh at all. Tune into our 300th episode this Wednesday at 10! Long live the Great Communist Party of China! May this autumn's sorghum harvest be bountiful! We good now China?" (Sarto 2019)

But as far as I can tell, besides when Mr. Stotch simply says we should be "united in the belief that every person has a right to say what they want," the closest thing to an overt argument for absolute freedom of speech that occurs in the show belongs to Big Gay Al. In "Cripple Fight" (S5E2), Gloria Allred successfully sues to get Al reinstated in the Scouts (despite their "no-gays" policy) but Al says he wants the verdict rejected.

> Look, I appreciate what you kids did; I really do. But this isn't what I wanted. I'm proud to be gay. And I'm proud to be in a country where I'm free to express myself. But freedom is a two-way street. If I'm free to express myself, then the Scouts have to be free to express themselves, too. I know these men. They are good men. They are kind men. They do what they think is best for kids. No matter how wrong we think they might be, it isn't right for us to force them to think our way. It's up to us to persuade, and help them see the light, not extort them to. Please, don't cut the Scouts' funding. The Scouts help and have always helped a lot of kids. That's why I love them. I will continue to persuade them to change their

mind, but this is the wrong way to do it. So, I am hereby dropping my case, and allowing the Scouts their right to not allow gays into their private club.

It's debatable whether such a policy is "speech," but the basic sentiment is there. "Freedom is a two way street." It's the same sentiment endorsed by the series as a whole, given its propensity to say basically anything that Parker and Stone want and to criticize censorship: everyone should enjoy absolute freedom of speech.

The conclusion that it should be legal to say literally anything, however, is easily refuted. One of the founding principles of liberalism (the notion that liberty should be the focus of what the government preserves) is John Stuart Mill's aforementioned harm principle. "[T]he only purpose for which power can be rightfully exercised over any member of a civilized community, against his will, is to prevent harm to others" (Mill 1859/2000, p. 31). And when Mill says harm, he means "perceptible hurt" (p. 76) or "definite damage" (p. 75; see also Armstrong 2000, p. 76). Since certain kinds of speech can obviously risk perceptible definite harm – like the paradigm case of yelling fire in a crowded theater in which there is no actual fire – the idea that literally *all* speech should be legal is impossible to defend, even when premised on the ideal of liberty.

Still, most speech is not like this. Mill certainly didn't think that offensive speech was like this; since it doesn't do any "perceptible hurt to any assignable individual, [it is a minor] inconvenience . . . which society can afford to bear, for the sake of the greater good of human freedom" (p. 76; see also Armstrong 2000, p. 76). But even though inciting others to perform a terrorist attack (like Zachary Adam Chesser did to Parker and Stone after "200") should be illegal because it risks definite harm to others, according to Mill's harm principle it shouldn't be illegal for him to say something like "I think Parker and Stone deserve to die." That's an expression of one's opinion, that doesn't directly risk definite harm. In other words, even though Mill's harm principle doesn't allow for *complete* freedom of speech, it almost does. This is appropriate because the most famous champion of free speech is John Stuart Mill. But what is his argument, why does he think that freedom of speech is so important, and can it defend Parker and Stone's position?

In "*Utilitarianism*," Mill (1863/2000) argues that utility is the ultimate arbiter of ethics. In other words, what is morally right or wrong for individual persons to do should be determined by how their actions would affect not only themselves but everyone. The action that produces the most amount of happiness for the most amount of people is what is morally best. In *On Liberty* (Mill 1859/2000), Mill argues that governments should pass laws, and restrict liberties, with the same goal in mind. This is why he says "it will harm (or risks harm to) someone else" is the only legitimate reason to restrict a citizen's action. No one knows what makes a person happy better than that person, so the best way to ensure the most amount of happiness is to give people the liberty to do what makes them happy. As long as they don't want to make others unhappy (by harming them), this will lead to more happiness overall.

It is for the same reason, Mill argues, that freedom of speech should be (essentially) absolute: because making it absolute is the best way to ensure the most amount of happiness for the most amount of people. How does it do this? First, Mill thought that freedom of opinion (the ability of a person to think or believe what they want) was so closely tied to freedom of speech – they are "practically inseparable" (p. 16) – that limits on freedom of speech would be detrimental to freedom of opinion; and people are most certainly happier if they can believe what they want. What's more, freedom of speech ensures the discovery of the truth, and the discovery of truth is essential to the progress of humankind (and the progress of humankind is essential to overall general happiness).

How does freedom of speech ensure the discovery of truth? In Chapter 2 of *On Liberty*, Mill argues that, when it comes to opinions that people debate in the public sphere, there are only three possibilities. An opinion expressed that defies the opinion of the majority is either (a) right/true, (b) wrong/false, or (c) a little bit of both – what we might call "partly right" or "on to something." In each case, Mill argues, we are better off if the person who holds that opinion is free to express it. Why? Well, obviously, if it is true, the opinion's expression will help get us to the truth; the majority is wrong in that case, and the truth can't be discovered if it cannot be expressed. The same is true if it is "on to something." Once such an opinion is expressed, we can explore it and figure out what is right and what is wrong about it. But even when the opinion is flat out false, it is better that it is expressed because its expression will give us the opportunity to refute it and thus move closer to the truth. Indeed, Mill argued that, in societies which protect true opinions with restrictions on speech (e.g., contradicting the truth is illegal), the truth becomes a "dead dogma" (p. 34). It's just something that everyone believes, without knowing why it is true. The expression of false opinions provides us with the opportunity to refute them, and thus remind ourselves of why they are false, and in turn how we know that what is true, is true.

Although the phrase was first hinted at in 1919 by Justice Oliver Wendell Holmes Jr. (see Hendricks 2022) and coined by Justice William O. Douglas in 1953 (see Schultz 2009), it is Mill's argument that laid the groundwork for the notion behind the "marketplace of ideas." This is the theory that free and open debate, where everyone is allowed to say whatever they want (and everyone else is allowed to contradict it), will reveal the truth in much the same way that smelting reveals impurities in metals so they can be removed. In smelting, heat is applied to a metal, say gold; when the gold melts into a liquid, the non-gold elements float to the top so they can be identified and swept away. In principle, free and open debate is supposed to do the same thing: the heat of debate reveals which arguments work and which ones don't, thus revealing what is true and what is not. In this way, what is true can be embraced and what is false can be discarded.

But there is very good reason to think that the world doesn't work like this – that unfettered free speech doesn't reveal the truth like Mill said it would. Consider 4chan, 8chan, and 8kun, imageboard websites where messaging rooms are created and managed by users (with no oversight). There are practically no rules or censorship on these sites; in fact, they were founded as bastions of complete and unfettered free speech (BBC News 2013). But what happens on them is not the revealing of truth. Instead, they became repositories for irrational conspiracy theories (e.g.,

28 *South Park* as Philosophy: Blasphemy, Mockery, and (Absolute?) Freedom of Speech 657

QAnon), child pornography, antisemitism, white supremacy, neo-Nazism – users have even live streamed mass shootings. Complete, unfettered free speech in the free market of ideas does not expose falsehood so it can be identified and skimmed off the top; it allows the craziest and most idiotic to garner attention – and followers – with bad arguments and bullying shouted through a bullhorn. It got so bad that Fredrick Brennan, the founder of 8chan (which turned into 8kun) called for it to be shut down (see BBC News 2019 and Roose 2019).

Monetize the process, and you get something like *Fox News*, a cable news channel that is ostensibly about "fair and balanced" reporting and letting its viewers decide things for themselves, but in reality simply tells its viewers what they want to hear to keep their viewers watching and their ratings up. And this is not just "an opinion" about Fox News. In a lawsuit against Fox News, filed by Dominion Voting Systems, it was revealed that Fox News' owners and hosts privately hate Donald Trump "passionately," think he acts "like an insane person," and admitted that he (and others) were "lying" about there being fraud in the 2020 election (Stein 2023). "Terrible stuff damaging everybody," they said. "Dangerous as hell." But they decided to lie to their viewers anyway because after reporting the truth that Joe Biden won the 2020 election, *Fox News*' ratings dropped and its executives feared they would lose their audience to outlets like *Newsmax* and *One America News*, which are even further to the right (Stein 2023). "It's not red or blue, it's green" said Fox News president Rupert Murdoch in a deposition about his decision to lie to his audience. And yet, the majority of *Fox News* viewers will never know any of this because *Fox News* will never report on or admit it. The point: especially in a capitalist society, freedom of speech doesn't expose the truth: it enables, emboldens, and even motivates the rich and powerful to grow more rich and powerful by spreading lies.

In his article "The Case Against Free Speech," Brian Leiter (2016) argues that – even though everyone, including academics, usually idealize the "marketplace of ideas" as a preserver of truth – our standards and practices reveal that we know this is not the case. The prime example that Leiter mentions is the court system, specifically the American court system, where trials are adjudicated by ordinary people – a "jury of one's peers." In the American courtroom, there are very deliberate and specific rules about what can and cannot be said, what kind of evidence can and cannot be admitted, etc. The obvious assumption behind these rules is that the common person, the juror, is not likely to arrive at true conclusions in an environment in which complete free speech is allowed. This is not to say that jurors are stupid; but in their native state, humans are not critical thinkers. Without proper training, they are too easily swayed by bad arguments and faulty evidence. We know that, if the courtroom were a true marketplace of ideas where anyone could say anything, the truth would never be reached. The innocent would be found guilty, the guilty would be found innocent. This is why jurors in many other countries are professionals, properly educated in critical thinking, logic, and the relevant law.

What this entails is that the hopes about free speech leading to the truth could only hold true in situations where those who are engaged in the debate are educated, have a rational grasp of logic and argumentation, and are motivated to find the truth – like academic journals (and even then, peer review provides a "layer of protection" against false speech). (Given Mill's arguments for public education, he might have agreed.) But since the general population is not like that, free speech in the general population does not lead to the truth. Instead, it leads to what we have – which is a populace inundated with misinformation and conspiracy theories, where the majority often doubts obvious and established facts. For example, only 49% of Americans acknowledge that climate change is real and caused by human activity (Funk and Hefferon 2019) when more than 97% of the relevant scientists do (NASA 2022); and while 100% of the relevant scientists say that evolution is true, only 65% of Americans say it is, and among them only 35% say it was unguided (Pew 2015).[4]

Now, perhaps, free speech can be defended on other moral grounds. For example, we might argue that freedom of speech is a natural right that should be preserved, regardless of whether it leads to the truth. But something else that Leiter points out is that freedom of speech can be a natural right only if we actually have real, genuine freedom of choice, in the metaphysical sense – a true freedom of the will, where what we do and say is completely and totally "up to us." But arguments in both philosophy and science strongly suggest that we do not have this kind of free will (see Johnson 2016). Our opinions, and whether and how we choose to express them, is a result of (partly) our genetics and (mostly) our environment: what we are taught as children, the media to which we are exposed, etc. To solidify this point, think of how many things people want the freedom to express are just things that they heard from someone else (on talk radio, for example). Think of how true that is of yourself.

That's not to say that we don't still make decisions; ultimately, you decide to belong to a religion (whereas you don't decide to belong to a race). It's also not to say that you can't be held morally responsible for the decisions you make. (Because they are caused by your character, your desires, or your rational deliberations, those known as compatibilists argue that you can still be held morally responsible for your decisions; see McKenna 2019). *It is to say*, however, that the kind of decisions we make, especially regarding what we believe, are not robustly free in the way necessary to securely ground the notion that we have a natural right to just say whatever we want.

Now, absolute freedom of speech does bring a certain kind of happiness or joy to the speaker; not being able to say what you want can be frustrating. So protecting absolute freedom of speech would lead to a certain amount of happiness in society. But, Leiter argues, that's really the only thing absolute freedom of speech has as a positive. What's more, such a benefit would have to be weighed against the negatives of absolute free speech – like the fact that it not only doesn't reveal the truth but actively leads people to be misinformed and insulates harmful views like racism, fascism, election denial, and bigotry. In such a contest, freedom of speech loses every time.

So *South Park*'s argument for absolute freedom of speech, philosophically, is difficult to defend. On the other hand, however, what we might call "the obvious solution to the free speech problem" is equally problematic: government intervention. The means by which to limit freedom of speech so as to facilitate the attainment of truth would seem to need to be the law – but who would write such laws? Many

28 *South Park* as Philosophy: Blasphemy, Mockery, and (Absolute?) Freedom of Speech 659

people would probably trust their own political party to correctly ascertain the truth, protect it, and make expressing falsehoods illegal; but the thought of the other political party wielding that power is horrific; absolute freedom of speech, warts and all, would still be preferable.

But might there be a possible middle ground? That question brings us to another of *South Park*'s targets: cancel culture and political correctness.

Cancel Culture, Free Speech, and Political Correctness

> Well, I, for one, believe in freedom of speech.
> But then again, I think [the members of the KKK] are racist.
> —Man 8 ("Chef Goes Nanners")

The beginning of a kind of middle ground solution to the problem of free speech begins with the aphorism, "*free speech* doesn't mean *consequence-free speech.*" The right to free speech guaranteed by the U.S. Constitution's first amendment entails that people are free to say what they want without fear of *legal* retribution – being jailed or sued. It does not say that people should be allowed to say what they want without fear of criticism or repercussions. If a fascist says something racist and an anti-fascist points out that it is unethical to say what the fascist said because racism is unethical – "You should not say such things" – the anti-fascist is not infringing on that fascist's First Amendment rights. Even though it's sometimes shorthand for this kind of moral condemnation to claim "You *can't* say that," those who morally condemn unethical statements are not saying that unethical statements should be legally restricted. The sense of "can't" such people invoke entails that such things *shouldn't* be said; to say them is unethical. And if others want to condemn the fascist for what they said and say they are a horrible person because they said it – as many have said about Parker and Stone – that's called "public shaming," and it is their right under the same free speech principle. As Big Gay Al pointed out, freedom is a two way street. I am free to say what I want, but you are also free to tell me to shut the hell up.

Because we also enjoy other freedoms, the same is true if those who condemn the fascist also want to disassociate with them – to not be friends, not associate in public, boycott their business, drop their endorsement deals (for example, if they are a celebrity), and convince others to do so. If I own or run a social media company, I can ban them. Since none of these things are legal repercussions, enforced by the government, they are not a violation of the fascist's legal right to free speech. Parker and Stone themselves seem to recognize this. In "Let Them Eat Goo" (S23E4), when someone says they have a free speech right to protest the meat-heavy diet the school is feeding them, Cartman replies, "Yes, we do have freedom of speech, but at times there are ramifications for the negative that can happen when you are not thinking about others and only thinking about yourself." Perhaps ironically, this was a parody (actually a direct quote) of what LeBron James said about the consequences of Daryl Morey's comments in support of pro-democracy protests in Hong Kong. Morey was the general manager of the Houston Rockets, and since China did not support those Hong Kong protests, the Chinese Basketball Association (CBA) ended its relationship with the Rockets and stopped broadcasting its games. Many criticized James, suggesting that he was siding with China against Democracy, but in reality, he was merely pointing out that our right to say what we want can't be removed from the responsibility to accept the consequences of how people react to what we say. If Morey wasn't willing to risk the CBA not broadcasting Rocket games, he shouldn't have said what he said. Even though the CBA is in China and thus not subject to the First Amendment, because they are a private enterprise, they were not violating the spirit of the First Amendment by cutting ties with Morey and his team.

We can say something similar if someone hosts a talk show and doesn't invite a fascist on to speak, is in charge of an awards show and rescinds a homophobe's invitation to host, or (this bears repeating) owns a social media platform and wants to ban an election conspiracy theorist. A person's legal right to freedom of speech does not legally obligate others around them to even listen, much less to give the person a platform and a bullhorn. This is a common reaction when people get caught saying unethical things or are spreading misinformation: those who think the speech is unethical or false choose not to use their resources to let it be heard. It's called "deplatforming" (or sometimes "no-platforming") and in no way it is a violation of the First Amendment. The government is obligated to let a person say what they want; it is not obligated to ensure that person is heard, and it certainly is not obligated to require others to let them be heard.

So, the first step in finding the middle ground between complete free speech and government restrictions on speech is realizing that the first amendment is compatible with speech having consequences. Now, in the public sphere, it's become common for things like public shaming, disassociating, boycotting, and deplatforming to be associated with "liberals" or "the political left" and to fall under the banner of a supposedly new phenomena called "cancel culture." But if we are going to use that kind of shorthand in our quest for this middle ground, it is very important to recognize three things.

First, it's only the label "cancel culture" that is new; public shaming, dissociating, boycotting, and deplatforming has occurred for years. The Catholic Church alone has been dissociating those who disagree with it for centuries (e.g., through excommunication during, for example, The Inquisition), and anti-segregationists were the kings of public shaming during the civil rights movement (e.g., shaming black persons during "sit ins"). In fact, it's really only because the internet has enabled formerly powerless people to hold powerful people to account that this kind of practice has been given a name; labeling it "cancel culture" makes it easier for those in power to oppose and condemn it when it happens to them. When those in power, like the Catholic Church or segregationists do it, "canceling" is just "what the other person deserves" for opposing those in power.

Second, the idea that it is a "left-only" phenomena is a result of political branding; both sides of the aisle have their own cancel culture. Lists compiled by the right of those that the left has "canceled" include J.K. Rowling, Mike Lindell, Chris Harrison, Roseanne Barr, Adam Rubenstein, Matthew Yglesias, Gina Carano, Chris

28 *South Park* as Philosophy: Blasphemy, Mockery, and (Absolute?) Freedom of Speech 661

Harrison, (current and former) Fox News Hosts (e.g., Tucker Carlson), Sen. Josh Hawley, Goya Foods, Dr. Seuss, and American presidents (e.g., Washington owned slaves, so his name was taken off public schools in San Francisco) (see Sadler 2021). Lists compiled by those on the left of those that the right has canceled include American Airlines, Barney (the purple dinosaur), The Beatles, Ben & Jerry's, Bud Light, Carhartt, Colin Kaepernick, Coca-Cola, Campbell's Soup, Disney, Doritos, The Dixie Chicks, eHarmony, Goodyear, Gillette, Kathy Griffin, Greta Thunberg, Keurig, Nike, Samantha Bee, Jane Fonda, Sinead O'Connor, *Star Wars*, Starbucks, Target, Teletubbies, The Lorax, NASCAR (because it banned the confederate flag), MLB, PBS, UPS, CBS, the NFL and CRT (so-called "critical race theory") (see Sasmazel 2021; Israel 2022). As of this writing, the movie *Hocus Pocus 2* is being boycotted by right-wing Christians because they think it is indoctrinating Children into witchcraft (Colopy 2022).

What's more, the rationale from both sides of the aisle is the same: it is a perceived moral infraction that makes a person deserve to be canceled. According to the left, because J.K. Rowling is transphobic, you shouldn't buy her novels or watch *Harry Potter* movies. According to the right, because Colin Kaepernick knelt during the national anthem, he shouldn't be allowed to play in the NFL. And both sides of the aisle will turn on their own. The left turned on Whoopi Goldberg for her remarks about the Holocaust, and Democrat Al Franken had to resign from the Senate because of offensive pictures he took with women. The right turned on Liz Cheney and Adam Kinzinger when they decided to hold Donald Trump responsible for orchestrating a coup on the American government (Finn 2021).

Lastly, those who complain about being canceled usually aren't. They'll go on talk shows and podcasts to complain about how their freedom of speech is being violated – but obviously, the fact that they have access to such mediums negates that point. J.K. Rowling is doing perfectly fine, as are Nike, *Star Wars*, and the NFL. And there are tons of right-wing shows who regularly feature those who have been "canceled" by the left. (Think of how many such shows gave Kanye West a platform even after he praised Hitler.) But as far as cancel culture goes, if it is going to play a role in the middle ground solution we are seeking, at least we now know it is not partisan.

Of course, talk of cancel culture also brings to mind political correctness – but that too is a loaded term, and is not as partisan or as new as people assume. Indeed, it has changed meaning over time. In 1934, *The New York Times* described a journalistic clampdown in Nazi Germany this way: "All journalists must have a permit to function and such permits are granted only to pure 'Aryans' whose opinions are politically correct. Even after that they must watch their step." Here, to demand political correctness is to demand fealty to the right-wing Nazi ideology. But in 1964, President Lyndon B. Johnson used the phrase to simply distinguish between policies that were politically expedient (that would make him popular) and policies that were ethically right. "I'm here to tell you that we are going to do those things which need to be done, not because they are politically correct, but because they are right." He was referring to a civil rights bill and a medical-assistance plan for the elderly, which many opposed, but that he saw as ethical imperatives (Gibson 2016).

There are many other ways the phrase has been used, but most imply some kind of restriction on what can be said. Today, to be "politically incorrect" is to say something that disparages or "otherizes" racial or sexual minorities or other powerless groups; as PC Principal (a character introduced to *South Park* in season 19) would no doubt remind us, ideally, politically correct language aims to show empathy, treat people fairly, and advocate for social justice. To be politically correct, you don't say "lady doctor," you just say "doctor." You don't say "they're homeless" you say "they're experiencing homelessness." You refer to people by their desired name and pronoun, you don't say "she's Asian" (you need to be more specific, e.g., "She's Japanese") and, as Jimmy learned in "Sponsored Content" (S19E8), you definitely don't use the word "retarded." The full list is extensive, and somewhat frustratingly changes over time. The words "gay," "homosexual," and "queer" have all gone from being derogatory to preferred (or vice versa) over time (Peters 2014; Redman 2018; Rocheleau 2019). But the goal is the same: empathy and inclusion.

Just like with cancel culture, however, there is also a right-wing equivalent to political correctness. Certain kinds of speech are off limits if you want to avoid the moral condemnation of conservatives. It certainly has a history; think of how, during the McCarthy era, expressing opposition to Sen. McCarthy's senate hearings was enough to get you labeled a communist and fired from your job. After the 9–11 attacks, opposition to the Patriot Act, or even the Iraq war, was enough to get you labeled anti-American or even a traitor. (Some readers might recall that french fries were deemed "freedom fries" by congressional conservatives after France opposed the war. They tried to "cancel" an entire country!) Today, a sufficient lack of patriotism or opposition to foreign wars will get you ostracized in conservative circles (unless that foreign war is against Putin, then you should oppose it). You must oppose unions, watch *Fox News*, label everything else "the lame stream media," speak English (Díaz 2019), never offer plant-based options (Geraghty 2015), use the word "illegal alien" (instead of "undocumented migrant"), and oppose Black Lives Matter (saying "All Lives Matter" and "Blue Lives Matter" instead). You must be appalled by homosexual marriage, decry transgender bathrooms, fight against abortion, and (ironically enough) oppose "political correctness" itself. For a long time, the most important rule was to never challenge or defame Donald Trump and to attack the media at his rallies (CNBC 2017).

Putting the PC Principle In Charge

> Aw, to hell with all of you indecisive bastards!
> —Chef ("Chef Goes Nanners")

What we just discussed in the last section should perhaps be obvious, even unsurprising. Every group – religious, political, private, and public – has implicit rules against certain kinds of language, speech, and opinions, as well as mechanisms for enforcing those rules (e.g., criticism, abuse, etc.). Even supposed bastions of

28 *South Park* as Philosophy: Blasphemy, Mockery, and (Absolute?) Freedom of Speech 663

free speech, like 8kun, have them. (If you don't believe me, choose an 8kun message board at random, defend a Democratic president, and see what happens.) We might even give this fact a name (inspired by a *South Park* character): The PC Principle.

> *The PC Principle*: Every group—whether it be society as a whole or smaller groups within it—has rules (both implicit and explicit) for what can and cannot be said (i.e., what the group deems "politically correct"). Breaking these rules can result in social shaming, ostracization, boycotting, deplatforming, etc.

With this principle in mind, the possible aforementioned middle ground solution to the problem of free speech becomes clear. If freedom of speech needs to be somewhat restricted because it does not lead to truth but instead to falsehood and the insulation of harmful views, but we cannot put our faith in the government to pass speech-restricting laws, we should instead rely on the PC Principle. In other words, we should rely on the collective response of the masses to decide, generally, what kinds of things are acceptable to say, and what kinds of things aren't, and to enforce said rules through social shaming, deplatforming, etc. so as to protect against the spread of misinformation and harmful views. On this view, Comedy Central shouldn't censor *South Park* – but if the show goes too far, the public should censor them by objecting and not watching them anymore.

For a great example of this solution at work and how it might even be as effective as laws, compare what happened in the U.S. and Germany in the twentieth century, after WWII. As Cartman pointed out in "Chef Goes Nanners" (S4E7), "Germany was united under the swastika, right? But obviously history wasn't as important as changing the views after the war and stuff, so they changed it." In fact, after the war, in Germany, expressing Nazi ideals became illegal. Still today, in Germany, you can't deny the Holocaust occurred, disseminate Nazi propaganda, display a swastika, or make statements in support of Hitler (Glaun 2021). In the U.S., however, no such laws were passed – they would have violated the First Amendment. Yet after the war, such Nazi sentiments were basically never expressed. This was not because there weren't sympathizers to the Nazi cause in the U.S.; both before and after the war, there most certainly were (NPR 2014; Rothman 2018). But because the U.S. had defeated the Nazis at such a high cost in the war, expressing sympathies for them was enough to get you ostracized from society (i.e., to get you "canceled"). Most certainly, no one platformed Nazis by, say, having them on a talk show (outside of eventually *Jerry Springer*, where the purpose was to revile them). Neo-Nazis had to meet secretly, use coded language, and keep a low profile. In short, even though flying a Nazi flag is 100% legal in the U.S., and there are most definitely Nazi sympathizers still living in the U.S., you have likely never seen a Nazi flag flying on U.S. soil. As a result, although it existed, people were not subjected to its lies, and pro-Nazi sentiment was unable to spread. That's the PC Principle at work. Indeed, it wasn't until the invention of the internet, which enabled people to anonymously express such views (and thus be free of the fear of social retribution) that fascists began to organize and make a comeback worldwide (Snyder 2018).

Because of Mill's over-idealistic views about the benefits of free speech – recall, he thought it would reveal the truth – it would seem that he would oppose this kind of solution. To be clear, he obviously would not have been in favor of laws that forbid "canceling." Again, Mill argued that only things that do definite harm to others should be illegal; since canceling (public shaming, boycotting, deplatforming) doesn't do definite harm, Mill would say that laws that forbid canceling would violate the rightful freedoms of those who want to do the canceling. If you object to fascism, you don't have to be friends with fascists or shop at a fascist's business. But because Mill thought that free speech led to the truth, he thought that free speech was a social good – and as such, he thought that society was ethically obligated to protect it. In other words, because Mill thought that free speech led to the truth and thus had utility, it seems that he would have thought it ethically better for individuals to tolerate false speech, even morally objectionable false speech, instead of "canceling" the person who expressed it, so that it can be heard. As he puts it in *On Liberty* (Mill 1859/2000),

> [The believer of truth] must be able to hear [the arguments for opposing views] from the persons who actually believe them, who defend them in earnest and do their very utmost for them. He must know them in their most plausible and persuasive form; he must feel the whole force of the difficulty which the true view of the subject has to encounter and dispose of, else he will never really posses … the portion of truth which meets and removes that difficulty.…The fact…is…not only [are] the grounds of the opinion…forgotten in the absence of discussion, but too often the meaning of the opinion itself. (p. 36) The worst offence … which can be committed by a polemic is to stigmatise those who hold the contrary opinion as bad and immoral men. To calumny of this sort, those who hold any unpopular opinion are peculiarly exposed, because they are in general few and uninfluential, and nobody but themselves feels much interested in seeing justice done them … unmeasured vituperation employed on the side of the prevailing opinion really does deter people from professing contrary opinions, and from listening to those who profess them. (p. 51)

Now, again, to be absolutely clear: Mill would not have been in favor of such speech going unchallenged; arguing against falsehoods is essential if the truth is to be realized. (Think again of Big Gay Al, who wanted to scouts to be free to discriminate against him, but also said that he would try to change their minds.) For Mill, the whole point of allowing falsehoods to be expressed is to provide the opportunity to refute them and remind ourselves of what is true. As Mill puts it in Chapter 1, right after he articulates his harm principle:

> [A person] cannot rightfully be compelled to do or forbear [doing or saying something] because it will be better for him to do so, because it will make him happier, because, in the opinions of others, to do so would be wise, or even right. *These are good reasons for remonstrating with him, or reasoning with him, or persuading him, or entreating him,* but not for compelling him, or visiting him with any evil in case he do otherwise. (p. 13, *emphasis added*)

So, if a fascist speaks out in defense of fascism, call them out, contradict them, argue against them, call them deplorable, etc. (The same goes for the gay-banning Scouts.) But the above quotes make it seem like Mill would not have been in favor of

28   *South Park* as Philosophy: Blasphemy, Mockery, and (Absolute?) Freedom of Speech   665

silencing those who wanted to express fascist or bigoted opinions by "canceling" them. Falsehoods need to be heard to be rebuffed.

But given that Mill was wrong about free speech's ability to reveal the truth – it, instead, leads to more false beliefs, the spread of misinformation, and insulates harmful views – it seems such objections to our middle ground PC Principle solution would be misguided. Short of legal sanctions, society deeming certain kinds of speech off-limits and enforcing such restrictions with the threat of cancellation, is the only way that we can prevent the spread of such things. Back in 2020, Facebook and Twitter banned spreaders of medical misinformation about COVID and Donald Trump for lying about election fraud. Such bans are not unethical violations of free speech; not only does their legal right to free speech remain, but also (given what we have discussed) banning such people was the appropriate and necessary ethical response. It was necessary to save lives and protect democracy.

Oddly enough, despite the above quotes, Mill may have actually agreed. Right after the first quote above, as he ends chapter II of *On Liberty*, he backtracks, suggesting that public opinion can and should always condemn those opinions that aren't made in good faith, are bigoted, or otherwise intolerant.

> It is, however, obvious that law and authority have no business with restraining either, while *opinion ought, in every instance, to determine its verdict by the circumstances of the individual case; condemning every one, on whichever side of the argument he places himself, in whose mode of advocacy either want of candour, or malignity, bigotry, or in tolerance of feeling manifest themselves*; but not inferring these vices from the side which a person takes, though it be the contrary side of the question to our own. (p. 51–52, *emphasis added*)

Later, in Chapter 5, he reiterates the point.

> The maxims are, first, that the individual is not accountable to society for his actions, in so far as these concern the interests of no person but himself. Advice, instruction, persuasion, and avoidance by other people if thought necessary by them for their own good, are the only measures by which society can justifiably express its dislike or disapprobation of his conduct. Secondly, *that for such actions as are prejudicial to the interests of others, the individual is accountable, and may be subjected either to social or to legal punishment, if society is of opinion that the one or the other is requisite for its protection.* (p. 86, *emphasis added*)

In other words: yeah, generally falsehoods need to be heard to be rebuffed – but not when it's bullshit from racists, bigots, and Nazis – or (to use an example from *South Park*) bullshit from those NAMBLA assholes. When the president of the North-American Man-Boy Love Association tries to defend pedophilia in "Cartman Joins NAMBLA" [S4E5], Stan and Kyle have a response that aligns perfectly with the middle ground PC Principle solution.

Kyle   Dude! You have sex with children!
Stan   Yeah. You know, we believe in equality for everybody, and tolerance, and all that gay stuff, but dude, fuck you.
Kyle   Seriously.

This might seem inconsistent with Big Gay Al's argument, but recall that he said the Scout leaders were good kind men, who have done wonderful things for the children in Scouts. One gets the impression that if they weren't – especially if they were so deplorable that he thought they were incapable of changing their mind – Al might have been in favor of legally forcing them to be tolerant.

Despite this, Parker and Stone are critical of political correctness. They certainly don't like classic movies being updated to be more politically correct ("Free Hat" [S6E9]). But their most potent argument against political correctness comes in "PC Principal Final Justice" (S19E10) out of the mouth of Nathan, who temporarily took over "Super School News" while Jimmy was out discovering that ads were trying to take over the world. "What is PC but a verbal form of gentrification?" Nathan asks, "Spruce everything up, get rid of all the ugliness in order to create a false sense of paradise." In the show, the poor neighborhood of *South Park* (Kenny's house) was gentrified by the addition of a bunch of lofts, villas, and a Whole Foods Market; but all the poor housing remained. The implication is that demands for political correctness do the same thing. Just like with Cartman and his V-chip in *South Park: Bigger, Longer, and Uncut* – which only prevented Cartman from swearing but did not erase his desire to swear – demanding (for example) that a racist use non-racist language does not cure them of their racism. It just makes them conceal it. So, the argument goes, it's not really solving the problem.

But there are two things to say in response. First, the middle ground solution I am considering here is not embracing "political correctness" as it is commonly conceived today. It is simply letting the PC Principle do its work; just let society curtail free speech with its own reaction. Most things, even when they are pretty offensive (like *South Park*) won't garner enough opposition to be truly banned; but the truly awful things, like Nazism, fascism, racism, bigotry, and arguments for pedophilia, usually will – and those are the kinds of things that need to be repressed rather than heard.

Second, even as it is commonly conceived today, curing (for example) racists of their racism is not really the goal of political correctness. Many people who use racist language aren't necessarily racist; there is just racism built into our language. The worry is that the use of that language can harm persons, not just emotionally, but by shaping society's expectations (e.g., creating the impression that certain races are inferior). (Although Mill would not have been concerned about the former, he most certainly would have been concerned about the latter, as it can lead to definite harm.) The way to change that is to change the language. And when it comes to suppressing things like *arguments* for racism, the goal is not to stop racists from being racists; that's likely a lost cause. Laws against racist speech are not going to keep people from being racist. The goal is to keep racists (and Nazis, etc.) from being able to spread their ignorant views to others.

Now, as any avid viewer of *South Park* knows, this solution is not perfect. One major point of season 19 is that political correctness – as laudable as its goals are – can go too far and even be co-opted. Take the character PC Principal. He has laudable goals. He wants to stand up for the marginalized in society. But he also beat the hell out of Cartman just for "associating Italian-Americans to intimidation tactics" and saying "spokesman" instead of "spokesperson." Of course, this is hyperbole – as are many complaints about "political correctness" run amok and ruining free speech on campuses (Sachs 2018; Weigel 2016; Yglesias 2018) – but some people have been negatively affected (e.g., lost their job) for politically incorrect behavior, in ways that are definitely overkill (see Ronson 2016). The same is true if we just think about the PC Principle and how society reacts. If we are just relying on public reaction, the wrong things could be banned, and punishments could go too far.

There are, however, two possible solutions to this. The first is rooted in the PC Principle itself. When the "PC Principals" in our lives go too far, we have to push back – kind of like *South Park* has. Don't vilify them, as often happens. That's the same mistake that those who push too hard often make. But point out and object when things have gone too far. In other words (as if this wasn't obvious) be like Sharon, not like Randy.

Sharon   All I know [Randy] is that you've changed. Ever since you joined this PC thing you just bully people. And wait for people to say anything improper so you can jump down their throats for whatever words he or she used.

Randy   "He or she" is a gender-phobic microaggression, Sharon. You are a bigot. ("Sponsored Content" [S19E8])

It may take a while, but hopefully an equilibrium will eventually be reached, where harmful language is corrected, but not at great cost.

The other solution is to turn back to government censorship, to try to figure out a non-partisan way to limit disinformation and harmful speech. In his defense of why limits on free speech are not anti-democratic, Leiter argues

> The case against free speech so far would only be a case against democracy if we believed, with Plato, that there was such a thing as expertise about each individual's good, and that there were some political process apart from democracy well-suited to realising that good. . . . I am sceptical about both claims. . . . what is good for a person depends, at some level, on the person's wants and desires . . . [but] not everything that is bad for a person requires laundering individual wants and desires: we can be confident already that we know a lot about what is bad for a person. . . . [C]ertain things are bad for humans 'objectively', in the sense that we do not need evidence of laundered wants and desires to know that they are bad. . . . [T]here are natural limits on our well-being; natural limits that, as it were, set the threshold for bad speech. These limits should not seem very controversial: being killed, mutilated, raped, enslaved, starved, immiserated, humiliated, degraded, enervated, stupefied, and so on are not good things for creatures like us. [He calls these "Humean Bads" after David Hume.] The case against free speech assumes that there are such things as Humean Bads and it also assumes that it is a benchmark for democracy that it is less likely to produce Humean Bads. . . . Bad speech leads to Humean Bads, we might say, and thus, even if there are fewer reasons to regulate speech for the sake of producing a single good, there may be a lot of reason to regulate speech to prevent the realisation of Humean Bads. (p. 236-7)

In other words, the hope would be that we could reach a democratic bipartisan agreement to pass laws that restrict language that leads to objectively harmful outcomes. (Notice that this would not lead to censorship of *South Park*.)

I can't say I disagree with such a solution, but I wouldn't hold my breath. Such a suggestion would be contrary to the wishes of at least one major political party but also the First Amendment, which is why the U.S. has no laws against hate speech (while other developed democracies do) (Fisch 2002). What's worse, since "hate" can be defined many ways, it's not clear that laws against hate speech would not just be used for political gain. I can see it now: one side says we need to guard against racist speech because it is hateful; the other says that even acknowledging that there is racist speech expresses hatred towards white people, and so such an acknowledgement should not be allowed. (This is essentially what happens now when lessons about the United States' racist past are taught in schools; as *Man 6* said in "Chef Goes Nanners" (S4E7) "I think it is history. I think it is racist.")

In any event, it seems that any solution to the problem of free speech – the fact that it doesn't, like Mill thought, preserve truth, but instead leads to the spread of misinformation and hate – will be an imperfect solution for an imperfect world.

Conclusion: The Paradox of Tolerance

> I ain't gonna listen to nothin'!
> This whole cracker-ass town can kiss my ass!
> —Chef ("Chef Goes Nanners")

We have considered five different arguments that Parker and Stone express in *South Park* about freedom of expression and speech. We learned that, while it does make sense to submit to terrorist threats when there is a direct and real possibility of violence, catering to mere threats of terrorism probably helps create more. We saw that while doing more of what terrorists don't want (like drawing Mohammed) probably won't prevent future threats, it doesn't seem that we actually have a moral obligation to not offend people's religious sensibilities. We discovered that freedom isn't free in more than one sense; it costs soldiers blood, but it also comes with social risk – and things like freedom of expression are likely worth risking our lives for. When it comes to what is acceptable to mock, it probably is either all or nothing – although, unless you really are just going to make fun of everyone, including yourself, like Parker and Stone do, you should avoid "punching down." And finally, we learned that, while absolute free speech is difficult to defend morally, legally it should be ensured. At the same time, however, we should guard against abuses of free speech, and particularly heinous views like Nazism, fascism, election denial, and racism, with "canceling," "deplatforming," and other forms of social ostracization. In other words, we should let the PC Principle do its work.

In response to the arguments of the last section, for the regulation of speech, advocates for complete freedom of speech usually make this kind of argument.

> Those who want to regulate speech often do so in the name of tolerance; they want to ban intolerant language. But isn't this a contradiction? Aren't they being intolerant of intolerance? If they truly loved tolerance, wouldn't they tolerate everything?

This problem was identified by Karl Popper (1945/Popper 2012) as "The Paradox of Tolerance" (p. 581), and it is hinted at in the episode "Death Camp of Tolerance" when the Nazi-like camp warden says,

> You are here because you would not accept people's differences, because you refuse to accept the life choices of your fellow man. Well, those days are now over. Here you vill verk [will work], every hour of every day until you submit to being tolerant of everybody. Here, intolerance will not be tolerated.

As previously stated, Parker and Stone use this episode to simply draw a distinction between tolerance and acceptance, not to argue against tolerance or advocate for free speech. But if I had written the episode, I would have ended it differently.

> You know, I learned something today. When it comes to comedy, every person and ideology should be open to mockery; being offended is not a "definite harm" that needs to be guarded against. But when the intolerant demand that we tolerate their views, they are not willing to grant us the same courtesy in return. And if we tolerate them, but they don't tolerate us, they win – and thus intolerance wins. So, if tolerance is something you value, there is one thing that you can't tolerate – and that's intolerance. This may seem paradoxical, but as Karl Popper taught us, it's not. If you love freedom, you can't give people the freedom to rob everyone else of theirs. If you love rights, you can't give people the right to violate the rights of others. So if you love tolerance, you can't allow people to be intolerant. . . . Look, I know it seems like a free and open debate, fueled by absolute freedom of speech, would lead to the truth. But they tried that on 4chan and 8kun, and it ends with really bad results. Too often, free speech just amplifies ignorance, or simply protects the rights of the powerful to oppress the powerless. After all, what good is freedom of speech if you don't have the ability to make your voice heard? Putting limits on what people can say may seem oppressive, and sometimes it is. Sometimes PC Principal goes way too far! But the alternative – letting people like Cartman just have the bullhorn that absolute free speech would give them – is much worse.

Yeah, I know – neither Karl Popper nor PC Principal were in "Death Camp of Tolerance." Maybe that's just a better ending for this chapter.

End Notes

1. While it is false that Trump fired "the entire team," because some who worked for the unit were simply transferred to other divisions (like those responsible for bio-defense), many wondered whether the worldwide outbreak would have been greatly reduced had the unit remained intact. See Reuters (2020b).
2. These episodes cannot be seen on streaming services, but they and other banned episodes can be viewed (for free) here: https://www.southparkuncensored.com/.
3. If indeed there was a theist who made it a point to not insult and correct the religious beliefs of others, including those that are atheists, and I knew this, it probably would be an asshole move to go out of my way to insult their religious beliefs anyway. Likewise, if I knew someone intentionally kept their rabid sports fandom to themselves, it would probably be an asshole move to loudly insult their

favorite team. But, again, I've never known a theist (nor a rabid sports fan) to be like this.

4. The closest Parker and Stone come to admitting the limits of free speech is in "Ginger Kids" (S9E11) when Kyle observes that school-wide discrimination against redheads (who Cartman hates) is "what happens when Cartman is allowed his right to free speech!".

References

Armstrong, Susan Leigh. 2000. *On Mill*, Wadsworth philosophers series. Belmont: Wadsworth/ Thomson Learning.

BBC News (British Broadcasting Cooperation). 2019. 8Chan founder: I regret my decision. August 6. https://www.bbc.com/news/av/technology-49249575

BBC News (British Broadcasting Corporation). 2006. South Park gets revenge on Chef. March 23. http://news.bbc.co.uk/2/hi/entertainment/4836286.stm

CNBC (Consumer News and Business Channel). 2017. Media watchers blame hostility toward reporters on Trump. May 26. https://www.cnbc.com/2017/05/26/media-watchers-blame-hostility-toward-reporters-on-trump.html

Colopy, Jess. 2022. Christians accuse Disney of indoctrinating children into witchcraft, sacrifice with 'Hocus pocus.' ITM (Inside the Magic). September 21. https://insidethemagic.net/2022/09/hocus-pocus-2-christians-facebook-jc1/

Díaz, Beatriz. 2019. 'English Only': The movement to limit Spanish speaking in the US. BBC (British Broadcasting Cooperation). December 3. https://www.bbc.com/news/world-us-canada-50550742

Fa, Wencong. 2019. Protecting free speech is more important than protecting people from being offended. *Pacific Legal Foundation*. May 15. https://pacificlegal.org/protecting-free-speech-is-more-important-than-protecting-people-from-being-offended/

Finn, Teaganne. 2021. House Freedom Caucus wants Cheney, Kinzinger kicked out of Republican Conference. NBC News (National Broadcasting Company). July 29. https://www.nbcnews.com/politics/congress/house-freedom-caucus-wants-cheney-kinzinger-kicked-out-republican-caucus-n1275404

Fisch, William B. 2002. *Hate speech in the constitutional law of the United States*. University of Missouri School of Law. https://scholarship.law.missouri.edu/cgi/viewcontent.cgi?article=1413&context=facpubs.

Funk, Cary, and Hefferon, Meg. 2019. U.S. public views on climate and energy. PRC (Pew Research Center). November 25. https://www.pewresearch.org/science/2019/11/25/u-s-public-views-on-climate-and-energy/

Geraghty, Jim. 2015. Politics is not sports. But if it were... National Review. September 16. https://www.nationalreview.com/the-morning-jolt/morning-jolt-september-16-jim-geraghty/

Gibson, Caitlin. 2016. How 'politically correct' went from compliment to insult. *The Washington Post*, January 13. https://www.washingtonpost.com/lifestyle/style/how-politically-correct-went-from-compliment-to-insult/2016/01/13/b1cf5918-b61a-11e5-a76a-0b5145e8679a_story.html?utm_term=.19da582509e3

Glaun, Dan. 2021. Germany's Laws on Hate Speech, Nazi Propaganda & Holocaust Denial: An Explainer. PBS (Public Broadcasting Service), July 1. https://www.pbs.org/wgbh/frontline/article/germanys-laws-antisemitic-hate-speech-nazi-propaganda-holocaust-denial/

Hendricks, Vincent F. 2022. The marketplace of ideas in the age of information. The Forum Network, February 15. https://www.oecd-forum.org/posts/the-marketplace-of-ideas-in-the-age-of-information

Inskeep, Steve, and Greene, David. 2014. If it comes time to negotiate with terrorists, Never Say Never. NPR, Morning Edition, June 5. https://www.npr.org/2014/06/05/319030362/if-it-comes-time-to-negotiate-with-terrorists-never-say-never

Israel, Steve. 2022. The cancel culture of the right. *The Hill*, February 16. https://thehill.com/opinion/civil-rights/594423-the-cancel-culture-of-the-right/

James, Aaron. 2012. *Assholes: A theory*. New York: Double Day.

Johnson, David Kyle. 2013a. Science, religion, South Park, and god. In *The ultimate South Park and philosophy*, ed. Robert Arp and Kevin Decker. Wiley Online Library. August 2. https://doi.org/10.1002/9781118607442.ch5.

———. 2013b. Cartmanland and the problem of evil. In *The ultimate South Park and philosophy*, ed. Robert Arp and Kevin Decker. Wiley Online Library. August 2. https://doi.org/10.1002/9781118607442.ch7.

———. 2016. Does free will exist? *Think* 15 (42): 53–70. https://doi.org/10.1017/s1477175615000238.

Leiter, Brian. 2016. "The Case Against Free Speech," Sydney Law Review 38 (pp. 407–439).

Letsas, George. 2009. Is there a right not to be offended in one's religious beliefs? SSRN (Social Science Research Network), June 1. https://ssrn.com/abstract=1500291 or https://doi.org/10.2139/ssrn.1500291.

McKenna, Michael. 2019. Compatibilism. *The Stanford Encyclopedia of Philosophy*. https://plato.stanford.edu/entries/compatibilism/

Mill, John Stuart. 1859/2001. On liberty. Kitchner: Batoche Books Limited. https://socialsciences.mcmaster.ca/econ/ugcm/3ll3/mill/liberty.pdf.

———. 1863/2001. Utilitarianism. Kitchner: Batoche Books Limited. https://socialsciences.mcmaster.ca/econ/ugcm/3ll3/mill/utilitarianism.pdf

Miller, Max. 2021. The Behind-The-Scenes Drama On South Park That Had Chef Written Off The Show. Looper, November 23. https://www.looper.com/666906/the-behind-the-scenes-drama-on-south-park-that-had-chef-written-off-the-show/?utm_campaign=clip

NASA (National Aeronautics and Space Administration). 2022. Scientific consensus: Earth's climate is warming. https://climate.nasa.gov/scientific-consensus/

NPR (National Public Radio). 2014. How Thousands of Nazis Were 'Rewarded' With Life In The U.S. November 5. https://www.npr.org/2014/11/05/361427276/how-thousands-of-nazis-were-rewarded-with-life-in-the-u-s

Peters, Jeremy. 2014. The Decline and Fall of the 'H' Word. *The New York Times*, March 21. https://www.nytimes.com/2014/03/23/fashion/gays-lesbians-the-term-homosexual.html

Pew Research Center. 2015. Evolution and perceptions of scientific consensus. July 1. https://www.pewresearch.org/science/2015/07/01/chapter-4-evolution-and-perceptions-of-scientific-consensus/

Popper, Karl. 1945/2012. The open society and its enemies. Routledge. p. 581.

Redman, Jordan. 2018. The history of the word 'gay.' The Gayly, June 17. https://www.gayly.com/history-word-%E2%80%9Cgay%E2%80%9D

Reuters. 2020a. Timeline: Violence marks 15-year furore over cartoons of Prophet Mohammad. Gareth Jones (ed.). November 2. https://www.reuters.com/article/us-france-security-cartoons-timeline/timeline-violence-marks-15-year-furore-over-cartoons-of-prophet-mohammad-idUSKBN27I1U3

———. 2020b. Partly false claim: Trump fired entire pandemic response team in 2018. Gareth Jones (ed.). March 25. https://www.reuters.com/article/uk-factcheck-trump-fired-pandemic-team/partly-false-claim-trump-fired-entire-pandemic-response-team-in-2018-idUSKBN21C32M

Rocheleau, Juliette. 2019. A former slur is reclaimed, and listeners have mixed feelings. NPR Public Editor, August 21. https://www.npr.org/sections/publiceditor/2019/08/21/752330316/a-former-slur-is-reclaimed-and-listeners-have-mixed feelings

Ronson, Jon. 2016. *So You've been publicly shamed*. New York: Riverhead Books. March 29. https://www.amazon.com/So-Youve-Been-Publicly-Shamed/dp/1594634017.

Roose, Kevin. 2019. 'Shut the Site Down,' Says the Creator of 8Chan, a Megaphone for Gunmen. *The New York Times*, August 4. https://www.nytimes.com/2019/08/04/technology/8chan-shooting-manifesto.html

Rosenberg, Adam. 2010. 'South Park' creators respond to episode '201' censorship with a promise for next week. MTV, April 23. https://www.mtv.com/news/h90vkt/south-park-creators-respond-to-episode-201-censorship-with-a-promise-for-next-week

Rothman, Lily. 2018. More Americans Supported Hitler Than You May Think. Here's Why One Expert Thinks That History Isn't Better Known. Time, October 4. https://time.com/5414055/american-nazi-sympathy-book/

Sachs, Jeffrey Adam. 2018. The 'campus free speech crisis' is a myth. Here are the facts. *The Washington Post*, March 16. https://www.washingtonpost.com/news/monkey-cage/wp/2018/03/16/the-campus-free-speech-crisis-is-a-myth-here-are-the-facts/

Sadler, Kelly. 2021. Top 10 recent examples of cancel culture. *The Washington Times*, February 16. https://www.washingtontimes.com/news/2021/feb/16/top-10-recent-examples-cancel-culture/

Sarto, Dan. 2019. 'South Park' Creators Sort of Apologize to China. ANW (Animation Network World), October 8. https://www.awn.com/news/south-park-creators-sort-apologize-china

Sasmazel, Zeynep. 2021. A list of 25 people, products and companies American conservatives have tried to 'Cancel'. *Hornet*, May 3. https://hornet.com/stories/conservative-cancel-culture/.

Schultz, David. 2009. Marketplace of ideas. Updated by David L. Hudson in 2017. Middle Tennessee State University. https://www.mtsu.edu/first-amendment/article/999/marketplace-of-ideas

Shaw, Lucas. 2021. 'South Park' Creators Sign Massive New $900 Million Deal with ViacomCBS. Bloomberg, August 5. https://www.bloomberg.com/news/articles/2021-08-05/south-park-creators-sign-900-million-deal-for-more-episodes-movies?leadSource=uverify%20wall

Snyder, Timothy. 2018. Fascism is back. Blame the Internet. *The Washington Post*, May 21. https://www.washingtonpost.com/news/posteverything/wp/2018/05/21/fascism-is-back-blame-the-internet/

Spiegel International. 2006. Arson and Death Threats as Muhammad Caricature Controversy Escalates. April 2. https://www.spiegel.de/international/cartoon-violence-spreads-arson-and-death-threats-as-muhammad-caricature-controversy-escalates-a-399177.html

Stein, Chris. 2023. What did Fox News really think of Trump and the 2020 election?. *The Guardian*, March 8. https://www.theguardian.com/media/2023/mar/08/fox-news-dominion-lawsuit-what-we-know

Toros, Harmonie. 2008. 'We don't negotiate with terrorists!': Legitimacy and complexity in terrorist conflicts. *Security Dialogue.* 39 (4). https://doi.org/10.1177/0967010608094035.

Weigel, Moira. 2016. Political correctness: How the right invented a phantom enemy. *The Guardian*, November 30. https://www.theguardian.com/us-news/2016/nov/30/political-correctness-how-the-right-invented-phantom-enemy-donald-trump

Wikipedia. 2022. Everybody Draw Mohammed Day. August 13. https://en.wikipedia.org/wiki/Everybody_Draw_Mohammed_Day#MillatFacebook

Yglesias, Matthew. 2018. Everything we think about the political correctness debate is wrong. Vox, March 12. https://www.vox.com/policy-and-politics/2018/3/12/17100496/political-correctness-data

Frank Herbert's Dune as Philosophy: The Need to Think for Yourself

29

Greg Littmann

Contents

Introduction 674
Plot Summary 675
Don't Trust Leaders 676
Philosophers for the "Chaos of Democracy" 678
Philosophers Against Democracy 680
Leaders Who Were Trusted Too Much 682
Don't Trust Religions 686
Frank Herbert on Religion 688
Philosophical Skepticism and Hostility Toward Religion 689
The Case Against Religion 691
In Defense of Religion 693
The Duty to Seek Truth 695
Conclusion: Making Your Own Way 699
References 700

Abstract

The miniseries *Frank Herbert's Dune* (2000) and *Frank Herbert's Children of Dune* (2003) offer a stark warning that people must think for themselves rather than relying on authority. In particular, they warn against overreliance on leaders and on religious authorities. The series tell the story of how, in the far future, Paul Atreides becomes dictator and religious leader over the human race, bringing slaughter and oppression in his wake. The chapter will consider the views of philosophers like Plato, who believed that power should be concentrated in the hands of leaders with absolute authority, along with the views of philosophers who advocated democracy, like John Locke, John Stuart Mill, and John Dewey. The chapter will also examine the views of philosophers on religion, especially philosophers critical of religion, such as Locke, Thomas Paine, and Bertrand

---

G. Littmann (✉)
Southern Illinois University Edwardsville, Edwardsville, IL, USA
e-mail: glittma@siue.edu

© Springer Nature Switzerland AG 2024
D. K. Johnson et al. (eds.), *The Palgrave Handbook of Popular Culture as Philosophy*,
https://doi.org/10.1007/978-3-031-24685-2_47

Russell. It is argued that the series present a strong case against allowing others to think for us, because the story they tell matches the historical record of the real world. When leaders have been given the power to be arbiters of truth, they have too often exploited those beneath them, using their positions to accumulate wealth, power, and glory. When too much trust has been placed in religious authority, it has likewise too often led to exploitation and repression. What is worse, the power of religion is uncontrollable, easily leading to violence and destruction. Having said that, the series fail to reflect that religion does good in the world. This chapter argues that, as maintained by W. K. Clifford, whether people should accept religious views depends on whether they have good grounds to believe that these views are true. This implies that people must not accept religious views without thinking the views through for themselves.

Keywords

Dune · Children of Dune · William Clifford · Concentration of power · Democracy · Duty to believe truths · Frank Herbert · Plato · Politics · Religion · Plato's *Republic* · *The Ethics of Belief*

Introduction

When Frank Herbert published the novel *Dune* in 1966, science fiction had never seen anything like it. Herbert gave us not just a story, but an entire exotic universe, described with the sort of loving detail that J. R. R. Tolkien had lavished on his fantasy land of Middle Earth is his *Lord of the Rings* novels (1954–1955). The Byzantine Corrino Empire and above all the strange and mysterious desert planet Arrakis, and the rich and mystical culture of its native Fremen, captivated readers' imaginations. The novel won the Hugo and Nebula awards for science fiction, and, more importantly, has been regarded as a classic of science fiction ever since. There are many, myself included, who rate it as the best science fiction novel ever written. Herbert was to publish six more *Dune* novels, and demand was still so great after his death in 1986 that his son Brian Herbert and author Kevin J. Anderson took on the franchise and have published 14 more.

The novel *Dune* has twice been made into big-budget films. The 1984 film *Dune*, directed by David Lynch, was an expensive flop that has since become a cult classic. It's weird, colorful, and exuberant fun; and though it veers wildly from the plot of the novel, it's one of the most rewatchable films I know. The broodingly atmospheric 2021 film *Dune*, directed by Denis Villeneuve, was a critical success, winning six Oscars, and was a hit at the box office. And rightly so! More serious and restrained than Lynch's *Dune*, it's a mesmerizing film with breathtaking visual style, especially in the desert. Understanding the need to give a story of this scope room, Villeneuve rightly split the tale into two, with the eagerly anticipated sequel (as of this writing) still yet to come.

29 *Frank Herbert's Dune* as Philosophy: The Need to Think for Yourself 675

The first three *Dune* books, *Dune*, *Dune Messiah*, and *Children of Dune*, have also been made into a pair of big-budget television miniseries by the Sci Fi Channel: *Frank Herbert's Dune* (2000) (hereafter, *Dune*), directed by John Harrison, and *Frank Herbert's Children of Dune* (2003) (hereafter, *Children of Dune*), directed by Greg Yaitanes. In my opinion, they are best adaptation of the story yet. With a combined length of 9 h, they have the space to best capture the sweeping scope not only of the novel *Dune*, but of the saga of which it is only the first installment. Loyal to the novels, moody, beautifully acted, and, yet again, visually spectacular, the two series were deservedly great ratings successes.

It's these two series I'll be focusing on here. I love Lynch's 1984 *Dune*, but it strays far from the novel, and subverts Herbert's messages by giving the story a happy ending. Villeneuve's 2021 *Dune* is likewise superb, but with only half the story told, any messages are incomplete. On the other hand, with far more time to explore ideas than either of the films, the miniseries make an excellent vehicle for examining the universe of *Dune*. Even at 9 h, they can't capture all the rich detail of the texts, but they're the next closest thing.

Plot Summary

The science fiction miniseries *Dune* and *Children of Dune* tell the tragic story of how humanity comes to be ruled by an oppressive religious dictatorship. A highly faithful adaptation of Frank Herbert's classic science fiction novels *Dune* (1965), *Dune Messiah* (1969), and *Children of Dune* (1976), they are the saga of the noble house Atreides. In the miniseries *Dune*, Paul Atreides sets himself up as ruler of the planet Arrakis by pretending to be the messiah of the native Fremen people. In the miniseries *Children of Dune*, Paul conquers the rest of humanity in a brutal holy war and sets up his dictatorship, his sister Alia follows him as ruler and grows monstrously corrupt, and then his son Leto II finally ascends the throne, to rule for thousands of years, his life extended by becoming a half-human half-sandworm hybrid. None of these rulers believe in their own religion but instead just exploit religious power to gain political control.

As the series *Dune* opens, humanity is subject to a single emperor, Shaddam IV of House Corrino. It has reverted to a "feudal trading culture." Dr. Wellington Yueh explains, "Our civilization rests upon a political tripod...the most unstable of structures...A deceptive balance of power exists between the emperor, the congress of Great Houses...and the supposedly impartial Spacing Guild with its invulnerable monopoly on interstellar transport" (Harrison 2000). The Great Houses are headed by nobles whose fiefs include entire planets – like the heroic Duke Leto Atreides who rules Caladan and his villainous enemy, the Baron Vladimir Harkonnen, who rules Geidi Prime. Duke Leto Atreides claims that the Great Houses have suffered a "degeneration," and House Atreides is no exception.

The most valuable planet in the empire is the desert world Arrakis, also known as "Dune." Arrakis is the only source of the "spice" *mélange*, which alone makes navigation through space possible. The emperor takes the fiefdom of Arrakis away from the Harkonnens and gives it to the Atreides, in an apparent mark of favor. But in fact, the emperor and the Harkonnens are conspiring together to destroy the popular Duke, and once he and his family arrive on Arrakis, the trap is sprung and Duke Leto is killed. The Duke's wife, Jessica, and his son, Paul, escape into the desert and take refuge with the Fremen people who live there.

Lady Jessica is one of the *Bene Gesserit*, a secretive order of women who manipulate religion to secure their political goals. She and Paul exploit the religious beliefs of the Fremen to convince them that Paul is the long-awaited Fremen messiah, the *Mahdi*, come to deliver them to paradise. Paul, now known as "Muad'Dib," leads the Fremen in a rebellion on Arrakis and takes control of the planet.

Between the series *Dune* and *Children of Dune*, Paul spends 12 years conquering the known universe in a holy war. He forces all of humanity to accept his religion through an oppressive religious dictatorship. However, Paul plays this tyrannical role against his will because he can foresee that if he rejects it, an even more terrible religious empire will be built in his name.

Shortly after *Children of Dune* begins, Paul is blinded in a terror attack and abandons the throne, disappearing into the desert and leaving the empire in the hands of his sister, Alia. Under Alia, religious government becomes even more corrupt as ritualism and greed take the place of devotion. Alia's personality begins to be taken over by that of the dead Baron Harkonnen, a fate Alia only avoids by stabbing herself to death. She's succeeded on the throne by Paul's son, Leto II. His plan is to be deliberately oppressive, so that humanity learns never to allow itself to be controlled by a single ruler again.

The fundamental conclusion of the *Dune* saga is that individuals must think for themselves, and it argues for this conclusion by telling a story in which humanity suffers from the failure of individuals to do their own thinking. Humans follow great leaders like Paul Atreides, trusting in his wisdom and allowing him to determine truth on their behalf. They also submit themselves to religious orthodoxy, having faith in received answers rather than searching for the truth themselves. I'm going to first look at the messages about trusting leaders, then the messages about following religious authority.

Don't Trust Leaders

The story offers a warning that people must not let leaders do their thinking for them, even when those leaders seem supremely capable, or even heroic. It can be tempting to centralize power in the most trusted hands. But a leader's reputation and image are all too easy to manufacture. Baron Harkonnen plans to turn his nephew and heir Feyd into a hero by having him replace his cruel brother Raban as regent of Arrakis. The Baron explains, "Cheer up lovely boy. I merely allow him to savage them, to brutalize them, until you arrive. The handsome Feyd to rescue them from the Beast, Rabban...Feyd the savior. There will be cheering in the streets...And then you will squeeze, like the grips of a vice, so our treasuries become fat with the profit of spice" (Harrison 2000).

Of course, some leaders, like Duke Leto Atreides, are genuinely excellent people. The Duke cares for those under him, going so far as to risk his own life to save the men in a spice harvester threatened by a sand worm. He rescues all the workers even though he must leave spice behind to do so. Imperial ecologist Liet Kynes tells Atreides advisor Gurney Halleck, "This is a different kind of man. He risked his life and that of his son to save the men instead of the spice. A leader like that could have commanded fanatic loyalty" (Harrison 2000). When the Fremen leader Stilgar complains to the Duke, "My people have suffered long under the rule of such as you," Leto assures him, "No, not such as me or any of my family. All that changed when the House Atreides came to Arrakis" (Harrison 2000). He no doubt means it. Yet Duke Leto is also an astute politician. In the novel *Dune*, when Paul tells his father, "Men follow you willingly and love you," Duke Leto answers, "My propaganda corps is one of the finest" (Herbert 1965).

Young Paul has the same heroic nature as his father, risking his own life to save the housemaids from a flying, mechanical "hunter-seeker" assassin. He's a genuinely idealistic person, intent on doing what is right. What is more, he's been rigorously trained in politics, with his teachers including a Bene Gesserit, who specialize in politics. He's bred to be *Kwisatz Haderach*, a messianic figure able to access the memories of all his ancestors. He can even see the future, in a limited fashion, through his power of "prescience." He's so brilliant that he comes up with a clever new tax plan at the first Atreides council meeting he attends and can tell instinctively that Stilgar's spitting in front of Duke Leto is a Fremen compliment rather than an insult.

Yet even brilliant and well-meaning leaders can end up doing terrible things with power. Paul is willing to inflict enormous harm to obtain and keep power. He conquers Arrakis by threatening to destroy spice production forever, warning, "Without the spice, the navigators will become blind. The Bene Gesserit will lose all powers, and all commerce between the great houses will cease. Civilization will end" (Harrison 2000).

During his 12-year holy war to conquer the known universe, his troops kill those who will not submit to his rule or his religion. He tells a Guild captive, "Mercy is a word I no longer understand" (Yaitanes 2003). The law becomes whatever he says it is. Reverend Mother Mohiam is executed for disobeying the order never to set foot on Arrakis, even though she was in space above Arrakis, and arresting her violates Guild neutrality. The Fremen conspirator Korba is buried alive and other Fremen rebels are tortured for information. One of Paul's ex-Feydakin soldiers, embittered by his son being blinded in the conquest of Arrakis, calls Muad'Dib a "cancer." As if all that were not bad enough, when Paul abdicates after being blinded, he leaves the empire in the hands of his deranged sister, Alia. Irulan despairs of "Alia's brutal tyranny and oppression" as she grows ever more repressive in her efforts to stamp out rebellion and dissent. Alia explains to family retainer Duncan Idaho that, in order to rule, she needs to be known for her "ruthlessness" (Yaitanes 2003).

In the novel *Dune*, Fremen Liet-Kynes is warned by his father, Pardot, "No more terrible disaster could befall your people than for them to fall into the hands of a Hero" (Herbert 1965). Paul warns that playing the hero requires deception and pretense: "Greatness...depends in part upon the myth-making imagination of humankind. The person who experiences greatness must have a feeling for the myth he is in. He must reflect what is projected upon him. And he must have a strong sense of the sardonic. This is what uncouples him from belief in his own pretensions" (Herbert 1965).

The need not to place too much trust in leaders extends to all people in authority. Where one class of people has power over others, there is exploitation. The feudal nobility uses their authority to enrich themselves at the expense of ordinary people. The Atreides do not seem so bad, but they are unusual – indeed, the Duke is famous for his exceptional goodness. The Harkonnens are more typical in the way that they exploit their people to satisfy their own greed. Likewise, when given power over the Fremen, the Harkonnens squeeze them for profit. Sometimes, they are cruel to Fremen just for fun, even hunting them for sport. In the same way, the priesthood of Muad'Dib use their positions to increase their own power and line their own pockets. The Spacing Guild use their monopoly on space travel to grow as rich as they can. The Bene Gesserit plot ceaselessly to increase their religious hold over humanity.

Philosophers for the "Chaos of Democracy"

The previous section identified both political and religious leadership as under fire from the *Dune* miniseries' warning to "not trust leaders." The next few sections will examine the message as it refers to specifically political authority. What sort of political thought lies behind the events of *Dune* and *Children of Dune*? To really understand the message, it will be helpful to consider the philosophical theory behind two forms of government – one where ruling power is distributed among many and another where it's concentrated in a single individual – and see how the miniseries treat both.

When the Great Houses want a constitution, Muad'Dib's council considers offering an empty constitution that offers no real protections on the grounds that "deceit is a legitimate tool of statecraft." But Alia refuses, arguing that "Atreides power must never be diluted by the chaos of democracy" (Yaitanes 2003). Many notable thinkers disagree, holding that ultimate decision-making power must remain in the hands of ordinary individuals. For instance, English philosopher John Locke ([1689] 2016) was an influential advocate for democracy, though given the dangers of speaking out against the English monarchy, he never explicitly stated that it's the only legitimate form of government. However, in *Two Treatises of Government,* he argued that all men are by nature equal, and so legitimate government must be based on the consent of the governed. Since it's impossible to get everyone to agree on the form government should take, people should consent to let decision lie in the hands of the majority. He writes, "For if the consent of the majority shall not in reason, be received, as the act of the whole, and conclude every individual; nothing but the consent of every individual can make anything be the act of the whole: But such a consent is next to impossible ever to be had" (Locke 2016, p. 82). Such a government exists to protect the lives, liberty, and property of the citizens, so even a government of the majority cannot justly override individual liberty. Individual men must be allowed to think for themselves. He even held that if the people judge their rights have been infringed by government, they have the right to overthrow the government through revolution.

Locke's notions of consent and majority rule were extremely influential on subsequent theories of democracy and on the American system of government. Appropriately enough, the *United States Declaration of Independence* of 1776 follows his reasoning: "We hold these truths to be self-evident, that all men are created equal, that they are endowed by their Creator with certain unalienable Rights, that among these are Life, Liberty, and the pursuit of Happiness. That to secure these rights, Governments are instituted among Men, deriving their just powers from the consent of the governed, that whenever any Form of Government becomes destructive of these ends, it is the Right of the People to alter or abolish it. . ."

French philosopher and mathematician Nicolas de Condorcet (1785) argued on mathematical grounds that the more people there are involved in a decision-making process, the more likely that a final correct decision will be arrived at, provided that the individuals involved are more likely to make the correct decision than not. Imagine, for instance, that each individual is 75% likely to make the right decision, and 25% likely to make the wrong one. If one individual were to make the decision, the chance of a wrong decision is 25%. If three individuals were to vote on the decision, a wrong final decision will only be reached if at least two of them vote for the wrong decision, which will only happen 16.5% of the time. The more voters we add, the lower the final probability of a bad decision is going to be.

English philosopher and politician John Stuart Mill (1861) likewise approved of democracy and was an early advocate of extending voting rights to women. In *Considerations on Representative Government*, he argued that under democracy, the interests of many more people must be taken into account by leaders, since many more people have a share in political power. On the other hand, he didn't believe that everyone should have an equal say. He argued that university graduates and those with intellectually demanding jobs should be given extra votes, as they are more qualified. Importantly, in his view, no government can legitimately interfere with the individual's liberty unless it is to prevent harm to others. In *On Liberty*, he wrote "The only purpose for which power can be rightfully exercised over any member of a civilized community, against his will, is to prevent harm to others. His own good, either physical or moral, is not a sufficient warrant" (Mill [1859] 2002). Freedom of individual thought and speech, in particular, according to Mill, must never be infringed, as these are the best means for truth to be discovered. (For more on Mill's argument to this effect, see Johnson's ▶ Chap. 28, "*South Park* as Philosophy: Blasphemy, Mockery, and (Absolute?) Freedom of Speech," in this volume.)

American philosopher and psychologist John Dewey (1927) argued in *The Public and Its Problems: An Essay in Political Inquiry* that in a democratic system, the problems and needs of a greater number and wider variety of people is liable to come to light. A monarch, even if they intended only to serve the public, is less likely to understand what the public needs.

Altogether, each of these philosophers seems to advocate for the "chaos of democracy" precisely because individual leaders cannot be trusted – the very claim made by *Dune* and *Children of Dune*. Locke's political theory seems to have been designed around preventing the kind of exploitation of the people committed by the feudal nobility, the Spacing Guild, and the Bene Gesserit – and the cruelty of the Harkonnens. Condorcet plays a numbers game, arguing that vesting power in a single individual is more likely to result in mistakes in rule. Similarly, Mill's desire to seek truth by preserving individual freedoms and promoting independent thought is at odds with Paul's willingness to use authority to deceive others. And Dewey contends that a single powerful individual – like a house leader or religious messiah – is too far removed from the people who are governed to be able to help them.

Philosophers Against Democracy

Not all thinkers have agreed that the power of leaders should be limited. For instance, English philosopher Thomas Hobbes (1651) argued in his book *Leviathan* that all power in a state must be concentrated in the hands of a monarch. Any division of power runs the risk that factions will arise and civil war will result. A civil war, in his view, is the worst calamity that can befall a society, far worse than even the most awful king. Perhaps he knew what he was talking about, given that he lived through the bloody English Civil War (1642–1651), fought between supporters of autocratic King Charles I and supporters of the elected parliament. He might have chided *Dune's* Corrino Emperor Shaddam IV for sharing power with the nobility to the point that Paul Atreides was able to raise an army and wage a devastating war to overthrow him.

French philosopher Charles-Louis Montesquieu (1748) in *The Spirit of Laws* allowed that democracy is a legitimate form of government but argued that successful democracy depends on the public having sufficient commitment to the common good, rather than just pursuing their own interests. Without such "public virtue," the people of a democracy would divide into self-interested factions and the state would destroy itself.

Yet the most interesting philosophical case against democracy brings the Ancient Greek philosopher Plato, who produced the earliest surviving written Western political philosophy. Plato was a citizen of democratic Athens and was familiar with surrounding monarchies and oligarchies. He thought that democracy, monarchy, and oligarchy were all bad political systems. In his book *The Republic*, he describes a city-state run with a radically new and, he believes, superior political system of his own devising.

Plato argues that a society will flourish best if every job is undertaken by the individuals best suited for that job, while everyone else keeps out of it. This is known as the "Principle of Specialization." So, for example, if someone needs medical attention, it makes sense for the person who provides it to be a doctor. Shipwrights, farmers, cooks, and all others who don't have the appropriate specialist training should keep right out of it. On the other hand, if a ship needs to be built, it makes sense to have the shipwright build it, since they have expertise in ship building. And if crops need to be grown, they should be grown by the farmer, who knows how to grow crops.

In the same way, and for the same reason, Plato argued that government should be in the hands of those best suited to governing. Monarchies and oligarchies don't do this. They assign power on the basis of birth. Democracies don't do this either. Democracies allow everyone with a vote to have a say, regardless of how stupid, ignorant, or wicked they may be. Letting every doctor, shipwright, and farmer have a say in government is as silly as letting them have a say in each other's professional work. They should stick to healing the sick, building ships, and growing crops respectively, and leave government in the hands of the experts in government.

If jobs are always left to the most capable individuals, then very few people should be thinking for themselves. Instead, the best thinkers should do the thinking for a community, just as the best doctors are the ones who provide medical care.

Plato says that there are three fundamental types of people. There are people who are primarily controlled by their rationality, people who are primarily controlled by their spirit, and people who are primarily controlled by their appetites and desires. People dominated by their rationality will by nature be moral and self-disciplined since, in Plato's view, there is no more required for being moral and self-disciplined than being able to understand the value of morality and discipline. Paul, Jessica, and Duke Leto, along with young Leto and his sister Ghanima, are all examples of the sort of high-minded, duty-bound intellectual that Plato has in mind. People dominated by their spirit love glory and honor. Passion drives their actions, not reason. Shaddam's *Sardaukar* and Muad'Dib's *Fedaykin* are likely made up of men that Plato would identify as dominated by their spirit. They fight with supreme dedication, though the reasons for their wars are beyond their understanding. People dominated by their appetites and desires long for pleasure. They love food, alcohol, sex, wealth, and luxury of all kinds.

Plato's society is divided into three classes in accordance with the three types of persons. The rational people form the class of rulers and administrators, since they are the most fit to rule. Plato called this class the "guardians." The spirited people form the military class who defend the state, since they are best fit for the task of fighting. They are born into their military careers, like Emperor Shaddam's *Sardaukar* terror troops. As for the people dominated by appetite, they do all the other work. They grow the crops, build the houses, tend the livestock, and do everything else that doesn't come down to administration or defense. Nobody is born into the guardian class. Rather, the most capable and moral members of the spirited class are chosen for promotion and training.

The guardian class even oversees breeding among the guardian and military classes, to ensure that the stock is improved and only people of good stock rise to positions of power. The character of Socrates explains: "It follows. . .first, that the best men must have sex with the best women as frequently as possible, while the opposite is true of the most inferior men and women, and, second, that if our herd is to be of the highest possible quality, the former's offspring must be reared (as guardians) but not the latter's" (459d–e).

Plato believed that a proper education system for the military and guardian classes is fundamental to producing a stable society. Education is so important that a description of the education system takes up most of his description of society in the *Republic*. The education system is intended not just to sharpen the mental faculties and provide practical skills, but also to produce supremely moral and self-disciplined individuals, devoted to the good of the state. Because the ruling guardians have been taught to be guided by reason, they will be almost incorruptible and will not be "money-loving, slavish, a boaster, or a coward. . .[or in any way] unreliable or unjust" (*Republic*, 486b–c). Plato was aware that rulers traditionally grew corrupt out of a desire to enrich themselves and he came up with an ingenious solution. The guardians are not permitted to own money or personal property at all. Instead, they will be maintained by the state in the simple healthy lifestyle appropriate for a "warrior athlete."

Plato's commitment to placing power in the most capable hands was so great that he was willing to give capable women authority over less capable men, an extraordinary suggestion in the fourth-century BCE. He did believe that women were inferior to men, on average, in all regards. But he also recognized that some women are highly competent, and he thought that such women should be allowed to serve in any position they were competent to fill, including the highest levels of government. Females in the military and guardian classes receive the same education as males on the grounds that they will be doing the same kinds of work. In striking contrast, though the *Dune* saga is set 10,000 years in the future, the society it shows us routinely restricts occupations by gender. *Sardaukar* and *Fedaykin* are all male, for instance, while the Bene Gesserit are all female. The nobility, while open to women, seems to give primacy to males.

In Plato's ideal society, ordinary citizens are not to think for themselves. They are to let the more capable people in authority think for them. The job of ordinary citizens is to obey without question. Their position is compared to slavery. The character of Socrates, speaking for Plato, explains: "to ensure that a [normal citizen]. . .is ruled by something similar to what rules the best person, we say that he ought to be the slave of that best person. . .It isn't to harm the slave that we say he must be ruled. . .but because it's better for everyone to be ruled by divine reason" (590c7–d3).

Leaders Who Were Trusted Too Much

The philosophical views of people like Hobbes and Plato are not only at odds with more democratically minded political philosophers, but they are out of line with *Dune* and *Children of Dune*'s message that authority shouldn't be trusted, too. So, let's evaluate whether the miniseries and its argument – as well as the democratic philosophers who share their ideas – are right.

29 *Frank Herbert's Dune* as Philosophy: The Need to Think for Yourself

Political theory is important, but the test of political theory is how politics work in reality. The best guide to the degree to which people should put their faith in leaders is how well this approach has worked in the past. Humans have a long history of concentrating power in the hands of supreme rulers like kings, emperors, and dictators. These great leaders have often been looked on as the caretakers of the ordinary people. For instance, the ancient Babylonian ruler Hammurabi (1792–1750 BCE) boasted in his law code, "I am the guardian shepherd whose scepter is just and whose beneficent shadow is spread over my city. In my bosom I carried the people of the land of Sumer and Akkad; under my protection they prospered; I governed them in peace; in my wisdom I sheltered them. In order that the strong might not oppress the weak…and to give justice to the oppressed." So, has history been more on the side of the democratically minded, like John Locke, who suggest that individuals should be thinking for and ruling themselves? Or does history reveal Plato – and those who wish to root power in singular, strong rulers – to be right?

Alas, the real way kings have treated ordinary folk has been dire. While some monarchs have been better than others, most have looked on the common people as resources to be exploited rather than beloved charges to be sheltered and protected. Many monarchs became infamous for their tyranny. For instance, Qin Shi Shuang (259–210 BCE) became the first emperor of China through the brutal conquest of neighboring states. He believed that humans are naturally evil and so must be controlled with ruthless punishment. Remembered as an oppressor by later dynasties, his atrocities included mass conscription to build the Great Wall, a project that cost hundreds of thousands of lives, and a program of burning books and executing dissident scholars. (Note: This and all historical facts in the section below are cited to Encyclopedia Britannica.)

Gaius Caligula (12–41) was the first Roman emperor to declare himself a God. A man who reveled in torture and execution to demonstrate his power, he took delight in terrorizing members of the Senate. Despite raising taxes and making false accusations against rich Romans as an excuse to execute them and confiscate their estates, his lavish, self-aggrandizing expenditures plunged the empire into debt.

Ivan the Terrible (1530–1584), first Czar of Russia, was a warmonger who conquered Kazan and Astrakhan and fought a failed 24-year war for Livonia. His bodyguard corps, the Oprichnina, conducted a reign of terror, with license to imprison, torture, or execute suspected enemies of the Czar without trial. On one occasion, Ivan personally led these troops against the Russian city of Novgorod, burned it to the ground, and executed around 12,000 civilians. Having murdered his only heir, his death left Russia politically unstable, ushering in the so-called "Time of Troubles."

This is just a sampling of historical abuses of power – there are many more. As for modern dictators who have been allowed to concentrate power in their own hands, they have proven every bit as tyrannical as the kings of old, if not more so. For example, under Adolf Hitler (1889–1945), Nazi Germany made war across Europe, the Middle East, and North Africa. Casualties include 18,000,000 Russians, 5,800,000 Poles, and 4,200,000 Germans. Millions more were executed, including 6 million Jews and 1.6 million Belarusians. People were kept in line through terror.

Torture was routine in Nazi death camps, prison camps, and prisons. By the time Germany was defeated in 1945, its economy had collapsed and many of its cities were in ruins. An estimated one-fourth of housing had been destroyed.

Joseph Stalin (1878–1953) of Russia was another conqueror, seizing Eastern Poland, Estonia, Latvia, Lithuania, and parts of Romania. Like Hitler, who he tried and failed to ally with, Stalin ruled through police terror, executions, and torture. He conducted mass political purges in which the accused were forced to make false confessions before being executed or sent away to work camps. It's estimated that the purges cost tens of millions of lives. Peasants who resisted having their farms taken over by the state were likewise executed or sent to camps to be worked to death. When the new system failed to produce enough food, Stalin continued to export grain rather than relieving the famine. All in all, Stalin's agricultural reforms led to the deaths of about 10,000,000 Russian and Ukrainian peasants.

In modern North Korea, citizens are taught complete obedience to supreme leader Kim Jong-un (1983–). North Korea follows the official policy "Songun" or "military first," prioritizing the military over all other concerns. It maintains the fourth largest army in the world at 1,200,000 soldiers and pursues nuclear weapons even though the people suffer from such poverty that many are malnourished. Yet again, rule is maintained through police terror, execution, and torture. Those seen as hostile to the government are routinely sent to labor camps without trial. Amnesty International estimates that there are 200,000 political prisoners in such camps (Szoldra 2017). The United Nations Human Rights Council concluded that "The gravity, scale and nature of these violations reveal a state that does not have any parallel in the contemporary world" (Kirby 2014).

Some kings and dictators, no doubt, have been idealists like Duke Leto and Paul. Some are remembered fondly for their wisdom, like Ashoka the Great (304–232 BCE), emperor of India, Caesar Augustus (63 BCE-14), emperor of Rome, and Alfred the Great (849–899), king of the Anglo-Saxons. Conversely, some elected leaders have been awful. The Russian forces that invaded the Ukraine in 2022 were sent there by President Vladimir Putin (1952–). And the democratically elected leaders and government of the USA is guilty of its fair share of atrocities. Everything from slavery, Jim Crow laws, and Japanese Internment camps to the Tuskegee experiment, the slaughter of Native Americans and countless unjust military engagements have all been sanctioned or performed by the USA. All the same, the historical record of absolute rulers remains dismal compared to that of more democratic systems that put less faith in leaders and require people to think for themselves instead. (It would also be interesting to discover how many atrocities done by democracies were the result of undemocratic "exceptions" in their governing systems – like how, in the USA, presidents can win the electoral college despite losing the popular vote, political parties can take the majority of a state's congressional seats without having majority support though gerrymandering, and senators can have undue power because the senate grants equal power to lesser populated states.)

Just as history shows us that people should not rely on leaders to tell them what to think and do, it also shows that they must not concentrate power in the hands of "guardian classes," like Plato's guardians, the feudal nobility of the Corrino Empire, and the priesthood of Muad'Dib. Real feudal nobility, like real-world monarchs, has traditionally viewed the common folk as assets to use, treating them the way the Harkonnens treat their subjects. Indeed, European peasants were traditionally tied to the land, and went with the land when it was sold, like livestock.

Imperial and colonial guardianship has just as black a record. For instance, when Europeans decided it was their duty to bring civilization and Christianity to other peoples, their stewardship tended to result in exploitative empires. For example, Belgium was in theory serving the Congolese when it established the Congo Free State in Africa, but Belgian atrocities enacted to maximize profits from the rubber industry killed around ten million natives. Even slavery was sometimes justified as being in the slave's best interest, much as Plato urged that ordinary citizens should be "slaves" of the ruling class. Alexander VI's 1493 papal bull Inter Caetera gives the Spanish and Portuguese just such justification for enslaving native Americans.

In communist states, when power is concentrated in the hands of the party, authorities have tended to use that power to exploit and oppress ordinary citizens. Traditionally, communist states like the Soviet Union and China have openly rejected the notion of human rights (Bradley 2017). Male-dominated societies, in which men are given authority over women, have tended to exploit women. It makes perfect sense that the Harkonnen officials running Arrakis exploited the Fremen so ruthlessly.

There are several reasons why such guardian classes have tended to fail, even when they are in theory devoted to the highest principles. Firstly, there is the natural temptation to favor their own interests over those of the people they rule. Like the nobles of the Corrino Empire and the priests of Muad'Dib, they have been in a position to enrich themselves by exploiting those in their care. We might think of the lofty sentiments with which the British took upon themselves "the white man's burden" to bring the uncivilized out of darkness, and the way that the British build the richest empire the world had ever seen on the back of the resources and labor of subject nations. Plato cleverly tries to keep his guardian class from growing wealthy by forbidding them property, but such a system is liable to break down and be abused when the very people in charge of policing it are the ones who stand to benefit from circumventing it. It would be tempting, too, for any guardian class to overlook abuses by members of the class against outsiders. For instance, despite the many abusive violations of British law by British police and soldiers in India, it was next to impossible for native Indians to gain redress from other British authorities, who tended to side with their own.

What is worse, it is tempting for members of a guardian class to favor those who are like them, even among people who are not members of the guardian class. So, for example, British authorities in India routinely favored the interests of British merchants over native Indians. It would make sense to see Harkonnen officials on Arrakis favor fellow Harkonnens over the native Fremen, and to see the priesthood of Muad'Dib favor fellow Fremen over the many foreigners the priesthood officiates over. Worse yet, since members of a guardian class are liable to be wealthy, they are likely to favor other wealthy people, especially friends and family.

Even when members of a guardian class act with the best of intentions, it has traditionally been easy for them to be ignorant of the needs of those they protect. How much could a foreign noble of the imperium really be expected to understand the culture and needs of desert Fremen? How much could a Fremen priest of Muad'Dib really be expected to understand the culture and needs of the billions of off-worlders overseen by their church?

Often, pride will lead a guardian class to form negative stereotypes of those who are unlike them. It is easy to form generalizations that assign all positive qualities to one's own class, and all negative qualities to the classes to which one does not belong. So, men have caricatured women, Europeans have stereotyped peoples of colonized lands, and the rich have belittled the poor.

Don't Trust Religions

So much for trusting political leaders! What about religion? The two miniseries paint a grim picture of its nature, too. Having manipulated the Fremen through religion, Paul wages a holy war to conquer humanity, "sweeping away anything and anyone who resisted" (Yaitanes 2003). Millions have been slaughtered. Any who will not adopt Paul's religion, with himself as the ultimate religious and civil authority, are executed. Jessica warns: "When religion and politics ride in the same cart, the whirlwind follows" (Yaitanes 2003). Paul was supposed to bring the universe to paradise, but as Leto II notes in the novel *Children of Dune*, "Muad'Dib's religion had another name now; it was Shien-san-Shao, an Ixian label which designated the intensity and insanity of those who thought they could bring the universe to paradise at the point of a crysknife" (Herbert 1976). Once humanity is conquered, we're forced to live under an oppressive theocratic government. Skytale, the shape-changing Tleilaxu "Face Dancer" observes that "the laws of men have gone. The laws of a God have replaced them" (Yaitanes 2003).

After Paul abdicates, things get worse as Alia takes the throne and control of the state religion. The religion grows more corrupt to suit the needs of the religious bureaucracy, and even what was once good in Paul's organized religion soon degenerates. The Preacher, really Paul in disguise, complains that "The blessings of Muad'Dib have been corrupted. The religion of Muad'Dib is not Muad'Dib" (Yaitanes 2003). Leto II condemns "the corruption infecting Arrakis" and "the perversions done in Muad'Dib's name" (Yaitanes 2003). Duncan Idaho diagnoses that the priests have become "myopic and parochial, interested only in preserving their own power" (Yaitanes 2003). For instance, the Fremen counselor Korba, who Paul calls a "religious fanatic," is willing to assassinate his own messiah to achieve his political agenda.

Like Paul, the regent Alia silences political dissent with charges of blasphemy. When a Fremen *naib*, a tribal leader, objects to the transformation of Arrakis into a world rich in water, she demands, "We do what Liet and Muad'Dib intended us to do. Would you challenge their holy words?" (Yaitanes 2003).

Paul, disguising himself as a mysterious prophet called the Preacher, denounces a crowd of worshippers for reducing his religion to ritual. He accuses them, "Blasphemers! Idolators! You fool yourselves with images of things you cannot possibly understand. You cripple yourselves with these tools of ritual and ceremony. They give you only fear and in return, you give them obedience" (Yaitanes 2003). Jessica complains as she wanders the palace gardens, "Symbols are everywhere these days. Just like these weeds" (Yaitanes 2003). Nonparticipation in the rituals can be lethal. Ghanima and Leto II explain to Jessica, "Sometimes it is necessary to accommodate ritual...in order to survive it" (Yaitanes 2003). The Preacher judges, "We have succumbed to mindless ritual and seductive ceremony, placed faith in those who crush dissent, enrich themselves with power, commit atrocity, all in the name of righteousness – all in the name of Muad'Dib" (Yaitanes 2003). Leto succeeds Alia as ruler and will be worshipped as a living God. With his life unnaturally extended by transforming into a human–sandworm hybrid, Leto will rule humanity as "God-emperor" for three and a half millennia. The novel *Dune* explains that Fremen culture makes them particularly vulnerable to political exploitation because "law and religion were identical, making disobedience a sin" (Herbert 1965).

Of course, the cynical use of religion to manipulate politics was routine in the *Dune* universe long before Paul came along. For millennia, the Bene Gesserit manipulated religious opinion throughout the empire to support their political agenda, despite lacking religious faith themselves. Fremen religion had been carefully cultivated by Bene Gesserit agents. It is the seeds planted by these missionaries that allow Paul and Jessica to survive among the Fremen, and which enable Paul to become the Fremen Messiah.

When Jessica first urges Paul to manipulate religion to survive, she tells him the Fremen "are superstitious people. If we are to survive, it would be best to accommodate their legends" (Harrison 2000). What she fails to mention at the time is that Fremen superstition has been carefully cultivated by Bene Gesserit missionaries to ensure that the Fremen are ripe for manipulation. As Paul later notes, they use the method of "Predicting the future, then plotting to make it so" (Harrison 2000). The Fremen messiah is prophesied to come from off Arrakis, precisely so that a Bene Gesserit agent can fill the role. Stilgar explains to Jessica, "There is a legend among us that a voice of the outworld will come, the *Mahdi*. He will hold the key to our future." Chani elaborates, "The voice from the outworld will come. The *Mahdi*. He will make a paradise of Arrakis" (Harrison 2000).

Neither Paul nor Alia nor Leto II are able to control the religions they head. Paul complains to Chani that he cannot separate himself from "this damnable myth I've become." He explains that "Even if I vanished tomorrow, the revolution would follow my ghost" (Yaitanes 2003). Shadam IV's daughter, Wensicia Corrino, doesn't even think it is worth assassinating Emperor Muad'Dib, since doing so would only turn him into a martyr. When Leto II prepares to take up "the golden path" and become a half-human half-worm who will be worshipped as a god, Paul warns him "The Golden Path...The desert storm that cannot be stopped. You will become that storm my son. The whirlwind. And nothing will be able to stop you. Not even yourself" (Yaitanes 2003).

Frank Herbert on Religion

Why must religion go so wrong? Perhaps the most important philosopher to consider on that question is Frank Herbert himself. In his *Dune* novels, the characters analyze their predicament and diagnose the problems religion causes for them, and for humanity. According to the most insightful characters in the saga, it is the nature of religion to become oppressive. As Leto II explains: "Religion always leads to rhetorical despotism" (Herbert 1981).

Religious organizations demand absolute acceptance and obedience. According to the *Bene Gesserit's Credo*, "Religion is the emulation of the adult by the child...And always the ultimate unspoken commandment is "Thou shalt not question!" (Herbert 1976). Religion requires deceit. The Bene Gesserit *Instruction Manual of the Missionaria Protectiva* (their missionary wing) states that there are "illusions of popular history which a successful religion must promote" (Herbert 1976). Religious institutions inevitably grow corrupt and institutionalized religious worship degenerates. The Preacher says, "I come here to combat the fraud and illusion of your conventional, institutionalized religion. As with all such religions, your institution moves towards cowardice, it moves towards mediocracy, inertia, and self-satisfaction" (Herbert 1976).

Religion stands in the way of learning, by leading people to believe that they already know everything essential. New revelations of truth can't be allowed, since they would undermine the authority of the religious institutions. Leto II warns that nobody should believe that they know everything vital. He insists "there is no summa of all attainable knowledge" (Herbert 1976). He later explains: "This is the beginning of knowledge – the discovery of something we do not understand" (Herbert 1981). He advises, "Never attempt to reason with people who know they are right!" (Herbert 1981). Such certainly even kills the desire to gather more information. Leto II writes: "Religion suppresses curiosity. What I do subtracts from the worshipper" (Herbert 1981). Even the technologically advanced Tleilaxu condemn foreign unbelievers as "Powindah," and dismiss their ideas as "Powindah poison" (Herbert 1984). When a religion takes itself to have a monopoly on truth, it will inevitably lead to conflict with unbelievers.

When government and religion mix, it offers opportunities for those who thirst for power and are willing to use religion as a tool to get it. The Missionaria Protectiva *Text QIV* states: "All governments suffer a recurring problem: Power attracts pathological personalities. It is not that power corrupts but that it is magnetic to the corruptible. Such people have a tendency to become drunk on violence, a condition to which they are quickly addicted" (Herbert 1985). The situation is particularly dangerous when there is no distinction between the law and one's religious duty. The ancient *Commentaries on the Orange Catholic Bible* warn: "When law and religious duty are one, your selfdom *encloses the universe*" (Herbert 1965). Paul explains further: "When law and duty are one, united by religion, you never become fully conscious, fully aware of yourself. You are always a little less than an individual" (Herbert 1965).

The mixture of politics and religion can lead to a people sweeping everything before them in a burst of religious fanaticism, especially if led by a living holy leader.

A Bene Gesserit saying states: "When religion and politics ride the same cart, when that cart is driven by a living holy man (baraka), nothing can stand in their path" (Herbert 1965).

What is worse, when religion and politics mix, the state begins to believe that it has divine support and loses the ability to question its own decisions. Another Bene Gesserit saying states, "When religion and politics travel in the same cart, their movement become headlong – faster and faster and faster. They put aside all thought of obstacles and forget that a precipice does not show itself to the man in a blind rush until it's too late" (Herbert 1965). The headlong rush can't be stopped, even by a holy figure. The wars of Muad'dib will be fought regardless of what Paul Atreides does – "Paul saw how futile were any efforts of his to change any smallest bit of this. He had thought to oppose the jihad within himself, but the jihad would be. His legions would rage out from Arrakis even without him. They needed only the legend he already had become" (Herbert 1965).

Alas, when a religion has an orthodox view to protect from challenge, it is impossible not to mix politics and religion. Muad'Dib warns:

> You cannot avoid the interplay of politics within an orthodox religion. This power struggle permeates the training, educating and disciplining of the orthodox community. Because of this pressure, the leaders of such a community inevitably must face that ultimate internal question: to succumb to complete opportunism as the price of maintaining their rule, or risk sacrificing themselves for the sake of the orthodox ethic. (Herbert 1965)

For more on the dangers of mixing politics with religion, see Slade and Johnson's ► Chap. 19, "*The Orville* as Philosophy: The Dangers of Religion," in this volume.

Philosophical Skepticism and Hostility Toward Religion

It's worth investigating whether Herbert's opposition to religion has much philosophical support. Philosophers have taken a variety of views of religion which might be significant to its portrayal in *Dune* and *Children of Dune*. Some of the greatest philosophers have been deeply respectful of religious authority and some have even been canonized, like St. Augustine of Hippo (354–430) and St. Thomas Aquinas (1225–1274). There have even been those who, like Paul, Alia, Leto II, and the Bene Gesserit, have believed that telling people religious lies can serve the good of society. For instance, Plato's guardian class keep order through false religion. Citizens are given a false history of how the state was founded, and false prophecies concerning the disastrous results of disobedience to the state. They are told the "noble lie" that all citizens are born with a mettle in their soul, corresponding to their appropriate role in society, with guardians having gold in their soul, warriors having silver, and ordinary citizens having iron. They are further told the lie that according to prophecy, the city will suffer disaster if it ever comes to be ruled by someone with the wrong metal in their soul.

Having said that, to my mind, the most interesting philosophical writings regarding the effects of religion have come from critics. These also align most clearly with Herbert's view of religion and the threat the *Dune* miniseries suggest that religion poses by removing one's ability to think for oneself. John Locke (1689), discussed above, was adamant that force must never be used to enforce religious opinion. In his *Letter Concerning Toleration*, he offers a variety of arguments for this conclusion, two of which are of particular philosophical interest. The first is that it is not possible for people to believe something just because they are commanded to. To take an example from *Dune*: Muad'Dib's troops can force you to profess faith in Muad'Dib, but their force can do nothing to move your actual beliefs about him. Secondly, Locke notes that many of the world's government officials believe false religions, so giving government officials the power to enforce religion is unlikely to bring people closer to true religion.

American political philosopher and revolutionary Thomas Paine (1776), best known for his influential pamphlet "Common Sense" advocating American independence from Britain, took a more scathing view of organized religion. He believed in God but refused to accept the doctrines of any church rather than using his reason. In *The Age of Reason*, he wrote, "My own mind is my own church" (Paine [1806] 2018, p. 47). He further wrote that organized religion was "set up to terrify and enslave" and to "monopolize power and profit" (p. 18). The *Bible* has corrupted morals in his view by depicting a God who is cruel and unjust. He wrote, "It is a history of wickedness that has served to corrupt and brutalize" (p. 28). Like Locke, Paine was outspoken about the need for separation of church and state. The government should be based on reason, not religious doctrine. In *The Rights of Man*, Paine wrote, "Persecution is not an original feature of any religion; but it is always the strongly marked feature of all law-religions, or religions established by law" (Paine [1792] 2006, p. 33).

In addition to the persecution Locke and Paine discuss, philosophers saw religion as detrimental to human life in other ways. German anthropologist and philosopher Ludwig Feuerbach (1841) argued in *The Essence of Christianity* that religion alienates people from their own nature. In his view, religious people fail to appreciate their own power as human beings, because they contrast it with the imaginary, infinite power of God. In one of his most widely famous writings, British philosopher Bertrand Russell ([1927] 1957) argued that religion is outright harmful to society. He wrote in "Why I am Not a Christian" that "I regard it as a disease born of fear and as a source of untold misery to the human race" (Russell 1957, p. 24), continuing to claim that even truthfulness and intellectual integrity are undermined by religion. He writes, "some very important virtues are more likely to be found among those who reject religious dogmas than among those who accept them. I think this applies especially to the virtue of truthfulness or intellectual integrity. I mean by intellectual integrity the habit of deciding vexed questions in accordance with the evidence, or of leaving them undecided where the evidence is inconclusive" (Russell 1957, p. 194).

Taken together, it becomes clear that Herbert's books, and by extension the miniseries based on them, are steeped in the kind of religious antipathy – or at least extreme suspicion of religion – seen in philosophers from Locke to Russell. Locke and Paine echo Herbert's worry that blending religious and governmental authority is a recipe for abuse of power; the religious leader in a position of political power is primed to impose their beliefs on others in a uniquely bad way. Likewise, Feuerbach and Russell both warn against religion's capacity to diminish the convert's ability to make free decisions – either because, for Feuerbach, the convert feels too inferior or because, to Russell, the convert has an impaired sense of judging fairly. Again, this sounds an awful lot like Herbert's fear that religion can atrophy the desire to learn (because one no longer needs to ask questions, having their instructions issued by an outside authority and because they already "have all of the answers").

The Case Against Religion

As with political leaders, the question remains: Are *Dune*, *Children of Dune*, and the set of philosophers who share their views *right*? As before, the real test of whether the two miniseries present a strong argument against trusting religious authority will be whether they match the way that history has played out in the real world. As it happens, all of the major abuses of religion in the two miniseries have many real-world parallels.

Religious authorities have often demanded that others believe as they do. Unbelievers and apostates have often been killed, tortured, or dispossessed. For example, the Spanish Inquisition (1478–1834), intended to combat heresy in Spanish territories, targeted Jews, Muslims, and dissenting Christians, forcing them to recant under torture and executing thousands. Religion has lain at the foundation of political power right up to the modern era. The oldest literate civilizations in Sumer, Egypt, China, India, and elsewhere, all make it clear, shortly after they develop writing, that the ruler is the ruler because the gods want them to be. To challenge the king is inevitably to defy the will of heaven. For instance, Chinese rulers maintained that they held the "mandate of heaven" and adopted the title "Son of Heaven." In Europe, monarchs appealed to the "divine right of kings" by which God gave them their authority. Many kings believed that they were descended from gods, and some, like the pharaohs of Egypt, emperors of Japan, and several emperors of Rome, were believed to be gods themselves. Even in modern democracies, politicians – especially but not only those who are conservative – will present themselves to the public as being on the side of God, and by implication, as having divine backing. Donald Trump, for instance, has often assured his evangelical base that "God is on our side" (Medina and Habberman 2020). When the US Supreme Court overturned Roe v. Wade in 2022, he stated "God made the decision" (Singman 2022). Likewise, GOP candidate Doug Mastraiano, running for governor of Pennsylvania, assured voters that he had a mandate from God (Bender 2022).

Religion has often been used as a justification for war. Sometimes the wars are between followers of different religions, as when Christian crusaders invaded Muslim lands in the name of Jesus. Often, though, the fighting is most bitter between rival sects of the same religion. The bloody wars between Catholic and Protestant

Christians, and between Sunni and Shi'ite Muslims, have dragged on intermittently for centuries. The Fourth Crusade (1202–1204) culminated in the crusaders deciding to sack Constantinople, the center of Greek Orthodox Christianity, with only a few continuing on to the Holy Land. It may be that one of the reasons there has been such conflict between Jews, Christians, and Muslims is that they share so many religious beliefs in common and acknowledge so many of the same prophets. Just as religion has often been the motivation for war, it has often been the motivation for unconventional warfare – like terrorist attacks. For instance, the 2001 attacks that destroyed the Twin Towers in New York were carried out by hijackers of al-Qaeda, an international Islamicist organization.

Religion has often been used as a tool for building empires. The Dune miniseries avoid the use of the term "jihad" to describe Paul's holy war, a label used in the books. All the same, the holy wars of Muad'Dib are clearly based on the wars of conquest conducted by the prophet Muhammad and his successors in the seventh to eighth centuries. Paul is even referred to as the "Mahdi," a messianic figure in Islam who will appear at the end times. During the great age or European empire building in the sixteenth to twentieth century, the need to spread Christianity was a common reason given for taking over other people's societies. With the eternal fate of so many unenlightened souls in the balance, many saw a moral duty to intervene. For instance, Alexander VI's 1493 papal bull, mentioned above, called on Catholic countries to take over the New World to ensure that it would be Catholic.

Religion has often been used as a cover for corruption and exploitation. Religious authority offers opportunities to gather power and wealth, and will attract people who want power and wealth. Jesus may have been a poor carpenter, but the churches that followed him grew spectacularly wealthy. Today, televangelists fleece vulnerable congregations with a slickness that would have been the envy of the medieval church. Often, donators are assured that God will reward them with more money in return than they spent on their donations (Baker 2019); when this does not happen, they are told it is because they lacked faith.

Religion has often stood in the way of learning, by leading people to believe that they already know the truth. The Catholic church, for instance, rejected the view that the Earth orbits the sun, and prosecuted those who said otherwise, as in 1633 when the Inquisition forced Galileo Galilei, one of the founders of modern astronomy, to recant under threat of torture. Even today, the theory of evolution is rejected by those who believe they already have a true account of human origins from the Bible. The US National Association of Science Teachers states that religious pressure "has prevented evolution from being emphasized in science curricula in a manner commensurate with its importance... Teachers face pressure not only to eliminate or de-emphasize the teaching of evolution, but to introduce scientific misinformation and non-science into science classrooms...such as 'creation science,' 'intelligent design,' or other forms of creationism..." (NSTA 2022). Other worshippers refuse to accept, on religious grounds, that disease is caused by microorganisms (rather than sin), or that man-made climate change is real. In fact, 76% of White evangelicals don't believe in climate change (Pew Research Center; for more on how religion fuels climate change denial, see Johnson 2021).

Oppression has also been justified in the name of religion. Christianity has been used to justify *not* helping the poor, on the grounds that God ordained their condition. "The rich man in his castle, /The poor man at his gate, /God made them, high or lowly, /And ordered their estate" runs the popular hymn "All Things Bright and Beautiful" (1848) by Cecil Alexander. Likewise, Christianity has been used to justify slavery, the subjugation of women, and discrimination against homosexuals, among other repressions. Almost everywhere that there is a toxic conservative agenda at play, you will find people associating that agenda with the will of God.

This chapter has focused a lot on Christianity so far, since that's the dominant religion in the West, but all of these abuses and more can be found in other religions. As this is being written, the Sunni Muslim Taliban, newly in control in Afghanistan, has confirmed that it intends to rule by *sharia* religious law. The last time they were in power in Afghanistan in 1996–2001, their interpretation of *sharia* required that girls be forbidden to go to school and women were banned from going to university. Women were required to wear burqas that hid their faces and could not leave home without being accompanied by a male relative.

Religions that endorse reincarnation, such as Hinduism and Buddhism, have traditionally offered an excuse to ignore the suffering of the disadvantaged (as noted, for instance, in Miles 1995). After all, if the poor or disabled were born into their condition because of their behavior in past lives, what they suffer is only justice. The Indian caste system is founded on the idea that people are born into high or low caste as a reward of punishment for previous actions. As for Buddhism, there's a common misconception that nobody would use it as a justification for violence. In reality, Buddhism has been used as an excuse for violence just like other religions. For example, the fifth-century Sri Lankan *Mahavamsa* records that Buddhist monks reassured King Dutthagamani that only two out of the millions of Tamils he had killed had been Buddhists, and the others were more like animals than humans. In medieval Japan, Buddhist warrior-monks, the *sōhei*, used the religion as an excuse to promote the interests of their own temples and sects, by force and intimidation (see, for instance, Adolphson 2007). Today, Buddhist violence against the Muslim minority in Myanmar is often orchestrated by Buddhist monks (see, for instance, Szep 2013).

These are only a few examples. Trying to list all of the abuses done in the name of religion would be an endless task. Suffice to say that, insofar as the miniseries *Dune* and *Children of Dune* depict religion as something that does harm, they are reflecting a horrible reality.

In Defense of Religion

However, the historical case against following a religion is not as clear-cut as the case against putting too much trust in leaders and guardian classes. Religion clearly does good as well as harm. Religion satisfies powerful human desires. Like the Fremen, many people in the real world rely on religion to help them cope with hardship. In a religion like Christianity or Islam, adherents are assured that God watches over them, loves them, and helps and protects them. They are assured that there is a point to their existence on Earth, and that when they die, it is not the end of them, but rather that they go on to a new existence in eternal paradise. The world may seem to be filled with injustice, but this is just a temporary state, permitted by God for some vital reason. Eventually, God will put everything to rights and everyone will be rewarded or punished as they deserve. Other religions offer similar comforts. There's evidence that religion helps people. Being religious is correlated with better physical health (Mueller et al. 2001). Religious people tend to be less depressed than the nonreligious (Dein 2010), and are more likely to describe themselves as being happy (Marshall 2019), although it's also true that the happiest nations tend to be the least religious (Farley 2018).

Religion has been the motivation for a lot of good acts as well as a lot of evil ones. Charity is an important element of all major world religions, and for most of human history, almost all organized charity has been religious. In Europe, almost all hospitals were run by church organizations into the twentieth century. Likewise, poorhouses and orphanages were often established by religious groups and usually required religious patronage to function. Religious charities continue to be popular today, and religious people are, on average, more charitable than the nonreligious (Austin 2017).

Education owes a lot to religion. Prior to the introduction of public schools, most schools were run by churches or other religious groups. The Catholic church played a central role in the establishment of universities, which generally grew out of preexisting cathedral or monastic schools. Many of the greatest academics of the medieval and Renaissance era were churchmen. The scholarly, religion-manipulating Bene Gesserit of the *Dune* universe are based on the order of Jesuit priests, famed for their scholarship and missionary work.

If religion has been used as a justification for much injustice, religion has also inspired people to fight against injustice. In the case of Christianity, many injustices that some Christians have supported in the name of their religion, other Christians have fought against in the name of the same religion. For example, Christian groups were at the forefront of the antislavery movement in the nineteenth century and the civil rights movement for African Americans in the twentieth century. Likewise, reformers like Samuel Barnett (1844–1913) and Walter Rauschenbusch (1861–1918) campaigned against the exploitation of the poor. Adherents of other religions have likewise often been active in fighting for justice.

What is more, it might be argued that religion is not really generally the real motivation behind the evil things done in religion's name. So, for instance, while it is true that Europeans used Christianity as a justification for enslaving Africans, they wanted to enslave Africans anyway. Enslaving Africans carried enormous economic benefits and was something Europeans did even when not citing the need to "save souls." Perhaps, then, religion was not a motivation for slavery, but merely an excuse to do what they were going to do anyway. Likewise, while religion has often been the stated justification for war, there are many reasons why people might want to fight wars, and plenty of wars get fought without the involvement of religion. Perhaps then, it hasn't really been religion driving all those wars.

Nonreligious people are certainly capable of being evil in all of the ways that religious people are capable of being evil. Many high-ranking figures in brutal fascist and communist regimes have been atheists, running governments every bit as corrupt and oppressive as theocratic regimes. While atheists don't tend to kill for atheism per se, they are certainly capable of killing for political or ideological reasons.

Obviously, just as it is possible that wicked things done in the name of religion weren't really motivated by religion, it is equally possible that the good things done in the name of religion weren't really motivated by religion. Perhaps those who say that they give to charity because their religion commands it would have given to charity anyway. Certainly, governments provide much of the funding for many religious charities (O'Neil 2009). Perhaps those who fought against slavery in the name of Christianity already hated slavery and appealed to religion to harness the moral authority of God to their political cause. Likewise, if religious organizations had not been there to accommodate the academically minded, they might have banded together in civic groups instead, all without having to worry about whether their work contradicted religious orthodoxy (for more, see Johnson 2016).

Weighing up the positive and negative effects of religion is no simple task, and not one that can be settled for good in a single essay. I will note that it seems unlikely that all of the negative things done in the name of religion would have been done anyway without a religious excuse. Some "religious" wars would no doubt have occurred anyway, but there's no particular reason why, for example, the Crusades for Jerusalem, which led to so many invasions of the Middle East and to animosities that last to this day, would have occurred if Christians hadn't believed the city to be holy. Some "religious" suicide terror attacks would have no doubt if occurred for purely nationalist or political reasons, but there's no reason to think that, say, the terror attack of 9/11, 2001, undertaken by Islamic extremist network al-Qaeda, would have occurred anyway, for nonreligious reasons. It's less clear that the good things done in the name of religion would be unlikely without religious motivations.

In any case, we still haven't dealt with the single biggest factor liable to determine whether a religion has overall positive effects or negative ones. It is an issue that the miniseries *Dune* and *Children of Dune* don't even consider, but which we must consider before we can evaluate the dangers of following religions. Are the religions true or false?

The Duty to Seek Truth

The Preacher cautions a crowd in a marketplace in the city of Arakeen, "I give you a warning. Those who accept self-deception shall perish by that self-deception. And those who pray for dew at the desert's edge shall bring forth the deluge." He believes that if people are not careful to ensure that what they believe is true, there could be terrible, unexpected consequences. English philosopher William Clifford could not have agreed more.

It is often assumed, at least in the modern Western world, that nobody has a duty to accept or reject any given religious belief. This assumption seems to have been born out of the disgust many people rightly feel toward the harm caused when people have tried to impose their religious views on others.

However, Clifford (1877) argued in "The Ethics of Belief" that it is always wrong to believe something when there is insufficient evidence to justify that belief. He explicitly included religious beliefs as being immoral to adopt without sufficient justification. People mustn't believe things without sufficient evidence because beliefs influence the way they act. False beliefs are dangerous since they can easily lead to inappropriate actions. By way of example, Clifford asks us to imagine a shipowner who decides to believe, without any evidence, that his ship is seaworthy. Because he believes the ship is seaworthy, he allows people to go to sea aboard it, thus putting their lives in danger. Clifford says that the shipowner is clearly doing something immoral in forming the belief, without sufficient evidence, that the ship is seaworthy. Recklessly adopting this belief endangered lives.

To recast the example in *Dune* terms, imagine a team of safety inspectors working for the Spacing Guild, maintaining the gigantic ships that fold space to cross the gulfs between stars. Let's further imagine that this team forms the belief, on no evidence, that all systems of the ships they are in charge of maintaining are in perfect working order. The team gives the all clear to the fish-like Guild Navigators, who take the ships out into space, potentially to die in a great explosion, or decompress in a vacuum, or just crash right into a star. It seems plausible to say that the safety inspection team have acted immorally in forming the belief, on insufficient evidence, that the ships are in perfect condition. Forming this belief with no good justification puts the lives of everyone on board in danger. Or to take another example: Imagine that a Fremen guide is to lead you to a *seitch* (a kind of Fremen settlement) far in the deep desert. The guide could take careful account of the sun and sands to navigate by, but instead, she decides to follow the tracks of the desert mice, believing on the basis of a dream she had that the mice will lead you safely to the *seitch*. By recklessly forming the belief that her dream is accurate and that mice will guide you, she's put you in danger of frying in the desert sun and being left as a desiccated skeleton on the sands.

It is easy enough to see how false beliefs can be harmful! If the Harkonnens wrongfully thought that someone was an agent of the Fremen rebels, they would have them publicly executed in the streets of Arakeen. If a stillsuit manufacturer mistakenly thought that their design was watertight, people would die of thirst. And if a traveler in the deserts of Arrakis thinks that sandworms can't sense human footsteps through the sand, they would be swallowed by a gigantic maw from below. As Clifford points out, not only are false beliefs individually dangerous, but adopting false beliefs can get you into the habit of adopting false beliefs, especially if you develop the habit of believing things without good evidence; so the more you do it, the more dangerous it gets.

It is also easy to see why false religious beliefs might be particularly likely to cause harm. If someone comes to believe that what you do or think offends God in some way, then they have every reason to try to stop you. Likewise, if someone comes to believe that God wants something to happen, such as that tracts of holy land be taken from one people and given to another, then they have every reason to try to make that happen too. Anytime that someone has a belief about what God wants or cares about, they have grounds to cause trouble!

Of course, having a false belief might produce good results rather than bad ones. If you get an address wrong and miss a party, you might miss a party at which the house burned down, killing several people. If you greet a stranger in the street because you mistake them for an old friend, it is possible that you will end up making a new friend. If someone living on Arrakis wrongfully thinks that Muad'Dib is the messiah, their faith could save them from being executed by Maud'dib's priests. But while false beliefs can end up having good results through sheer luck, relying on false beliefs, or beliefs that are false for all you know, is a terrible bet. Relying on beliefs without good evidence that they are true is a little like walking around with your eyes closed, hoping that you will wind up somewhere good rather than falling down or walking into a wall. You could get lucky, but your chances aren't good.

It might be argued that forming religious beliefs on insufficient evidence need not be dangerous in this way. Forming false beliefs about the physical condition of ships might put lives at risk, but it is not so obvious that it poses so much danger to believe, for instance, that Jesus rose from the dead, or that Muhammad split the moon in half, or that the Buddha stared down a raging elephant.

Even if this were conceded, there would still be *many* religious views that people would have a moral responsibility not to accept without thinking matters through for themselves to make sure that the view is justified. At the very least, it would be immoral to form religious beliefs on insufficient evidence where those beliefs are liable to lead one to interfere in other people's lives. People could not, for instance, form the belief, without good evidence, that God will protect drivers who drive with their eyes closed. After all, if they hold this belief and are wrong, they are liable to run into people in their cars. Or to take some real-world examples, it would still be immoral to form the belief, without good evidence, that sickness is produced by sin, or that human sacrifice will make crops grow, or that God abhors blood transfusions.

Beliefs about God's moral stances are particularly liable to be dangerous. For instance, if you believe that God is so opposed to homosexuality that He wants humans to enact laws punishing it, then you are liable to support such laws, so you had better make sure that you are right that this is really God's opinion. Likewise, any life advice that could hurt people must not be accepted on the mere basis of religious authority, without some sort of evidence. For instance, many Christians believe in corporal punishment for children, on the grounds that the Bible authorizes it in *Proverbs 13:24*, which would be insufficient justification without further support. Still, perhaps at least *some* important religious beliefs are harmless enough to adopt even without good evidence, beliefs such as that Jesus rose from the dead, or that Muhammad received instruction from the angel Gabriel.

However, Clifford denied that there are any beliefs that are so harmless that it doesn't matter whether people believe them or not. His reason was that people can never know what the effects of a given belief are going to be, and so a belief that looks harmless enough on the surface could end up being highly dangerous.

It is easy to imagine how a belief that seems innocuous at first could end up being harmful. If someone mistakenly thinks that Chicago is in Missouri, that's unlikely to cause any damage. But if they were rushing someone to hospital one night and got confused about what the nearest city is, their false belief could end up costing a life. Likewise, if someone mistakenly believed that they have the desert survival skills of a Fremen, it is unlikely to make any difference. But in the right circumstances, a belief like that could get them killed, dead of dehydration in the middle of nowhere.

One reason that religious beliefs are particularly likely to have unforeseen consequences is that religious beliefs are rarely adopted individually, but rather are accepted as part of a religious orthodoxy. Having accepted the religious authority of some source, say Jesus as recorded in the *New Testament*, someone is liable to adopt all sorts of views based on his teachings. Such complexity makes it difficult to foresee all of the possible consequences of religious beliefs.

This difficulty is compounded by the fact that holy texts require interpretation, and the same texts are often interpreted in very different ways by different people. Books like the Bible and Quran serve as authorities for people with a wide variety of views. It would be impossible to predict the consequences of all the possible ways they might be interpreted.

Another reason religious beliefs are particularly likely to have unforeseen consequences is that mere disagreement on points of doctrine can easily lead to bitterness or bloodshed. Beliefs that seem harmless in themselves, such as the Catholic doctrine that the communion wine becomes the blood of Christ, have been the cause of bloodshed between those who accept them and those who reject them. The danger is particularly great in the case of religions in which the eternal fate of someone's soul can hang on whether they believe the correct doctrine. If you think incorrect opinion can damn people's souls, you have every reason to try to stop incorrect opinions spreading. What is more, with stakes that high, you have every reason to prioritize stopping the spread of false opinion over relatively minor matters like free speech or life and death.

I think that Clifford goes too far in insisting that it is always immoral to form a belief on insufficient evidence. Richard Feldman (2006) offers the example of a person in a dangerous situation choosing to believe that they will survive. The belief might help them live, while the risk that the belief will cause harm seems very small. Likewise, David Kyle Johnson (2016) argues that we can't have sufficient evidence to believe the fundamental laws of logic that we rely on. Consider, for instance, the principle of noncontradiction, that a statement can't be both true and false. It seems that this principle can only be assumed, not demonstrated with evidence. After all, what evidence could you offer for the principle of noncontradiction that doesn't rely on the principle itself? It seems that there's no more fundamental truth you can offer in support of it. Yet it seems perfectly acceptable to believe it.

Even in the case of religion, the need to accept only beliefs for which there is sufficient evidence might be outweighed by other needs. For instance, if someone suffers a terrible injury and has only hours left to live, I think it is alright for them to start believing in an afterlife if that belief gives them any comfort, even if they have insufficient evidence that the afterlife is real. Such a belief could still end up doing harm, but weighing the probability of them doing harm in the short time they hold this belief against their dreadful predicament, I think it is alright for them to prioritize

29 *Frank Herbert's Dune* as Philosophy: The Need to Think for Yourself   699

being kind to themself over their responsibility to society. However, even if I'm right that there are exceptions to Clifford's rule, it will be true in almost all cases that beliefs should not be formed without sufficient evidence. This will be particularly true of religious beliefs.

This doesn't yet tell humanity to give up religion. But it does imply that people should not accept religious beliefs without thinking matters through for themselves. And this is also the argument made by *Dune* and *Children of Dune*. People should not simply accept religious beliefs because they were raised to accept them, or because they find them appealing. Rather, they must ask themselves whether they have good grounds to believe that the beliefs are true. There isn't remotely enough room here to try to determine here whether there are good grounds to accept any of the many religions. It is important to note, though, that since most religions are incompatible, there must be insufficient evidence to believe most of them. In the novel *Children of Dune*, the *Bene Gesserit Credo* states, "Religion is the encystment of past beliefs: mythology, which is guesswork, the hidden assumptions of trust in the universe, those pronouncements which men have made in search of personal power, all of it mingled with shreds of enlightenment" (Herbert 1976). Whether you can find something more positive to say about one of the world's religions is up to you.

Conclusion: Making Your Own Way

The miniseries *Dune* and *Children of Dune* make a powerful case that people must think for themselves. In particular, they warn us not to blindly follow leaders, nor to put trust in religious authority. The insistence that people think for themselves is demanding. It is all too easy for people to adopt an orthodoxy by believing what those around them believe, or by finding a source that tells them something they like hearing. Thinking for oneself means carefully weighing up the evidence on all sides of an issue, and then following the evidence wherever it leads, even if that means changing one's mind. If someone can't lay out the best case for both sides of a controversial issue, then that's a sign they haven't thought the issue through for themself, but have adopted an orthodoxy.

Thinking for yourself must not be confused with mere opposition to majority opinion. People can, and do, follow radical orthodoxies just as unthinkingly as they follow popular ones. Nor must thinking for yourself be confused with rejecting authority. If someone has no medical training, yet prefers their own theories over the word of the medical establishment about which foods are healthy or unhealthy, that doesn't make them an independent thinker; it makes them a fool. A vital part of weighing evidence for oneself is taking seriously the evidence provided by expert opinion and understanding when one needs to be guided by experts even if we don't understand why they are right.

We live in an age in which information technology has given us unparalleled opportunities to educate ourselves, and to expose ourselves to a variety of views in order to help us find the truth. Yet information technology also gives us unparalleled opportunities to filter out views we disagree with, to speak only to those who share our orthodoxy and thus ensure that the orthodoxy we prefer is never questioned. Our society is bitterly divided between those subscribing to different worldviews, with the greatest division being between "conservatives" and "progressives." There are parallels with the *Dune* saga on both sides of the political aisle. The closest parallels are with conservatives. Conservatives are particularly likely to appeal to religious authority and received wisdom. They also seem particularly likely to place their trust in popular leaders. Donald Trump, for instance, has attracted many supporters who are more attached to him as a leader than they are to any specific political doctrine. Having said that, the left is increasingly bound by its own orthodoxies, with dissenting opinions silenced rather than considered and answered. The different news sources that Americans of different political persuasions are liable to trust give them radically different descriptions of what's going on in the world, so many Americans must be being mislead. If we allow our views to be dictated by factional orthodoxy, we will be as blind as the Fremen who put their faith in Paul and his religion, allowing them to dictate their views.

References

Adolphson, Mikael. 2007. *The teeth and claws of the Buddha: Monastic warriors and Sohei in Japanese history*. Honolulu: University of Hawaii Press.

Austin, Thad. 2017. Giving USA special report on giving to religion. *Giving USA*. https://givingusa.org/just-released-giving-usa-special-report-on-giving-to-religion/

Baker, Vicky. 2019. The preachers getting rich from poor Americans. *BBC News*. https://www.bbc.com/news/stories-47675301

Bender, William. 2022. How Doug Mastriano's run for Pa. governor veered far off course. *The Philadelphia Enquirer*. https://www.inquirer.com/politics/election/doug-mastriano-pennsylvania-governor-analysis-20221109.html

Bradley, Mark Philip. 2017. *The Cambridge history of communism*. Cambridge, UK: Cambridge University Press.

Britannica. The editors of encyclopaedia. https://www.britannica.com. Accessed 20 June 2022.

Clifford, William. 1877. The ethics of belief. *Contemporary Review* 29: 289.

de Condorcet, Marquis. 1785 [2014]. *Essai sur l'application de l'analyse à la probabilité des décisions rendues àla pluralité des voix*. Cambridge, UK: Cambridge University Press.

Dein, Simon. 2010. Religion, spirituality and mental health. *Psychiatric Times* 27.

Farley, Harry. 2018. 10 Happiest countries in the world are among the least religious. *Christian Today*. https://www.christiantoday.com/article/10-happiest-countries-in-the-world-are-among-the-least-religious/127465.htm

Feldman, Richard. 2006. Clifford's principle and James's options. *Social Epistemology* 20 (1): 19–33.

Feuerbach, Ludwig. 1841 [1957]. *The essence of Christianity*. Trans. G. Eliot. New York: Harper Torchbooks.

Harrison, John. 2000. *Frank Herbert's Dune*. Santa Monica: Artisan Entertainment.

Herbert, Frank. 1965. *Dune*. Sudbury: Chilton Books.

———. 1969. *Dune Messiah*. New York: Putnam.

———. 1976. *Children of Dune*. New York: Putnam.

———. 1981. *God emperor of Dune*. New York: Putnam.

———. 1984. *Heretics of Dune*. New York: Putnam.

———. 1985. *Chapter house: Dune*. New York: Putnam.

Johnson, David Kyle. 2016. Moral culpability and choosing to believe in god. In *Atheism and the Christian faith*, ed. William H.U. Anderson. Wilmington: Vernon Press.

———. 2021. "If the stars should appear" and climate change denial. In *Exploring the Orville: Essays on Seth MacFarlane's space adventure*, ed. David Kyle Johnson and Michael Berry, 140–164. Jefferson: McFarland and Company.

Kirby, Michael. 2014. Statement by Mr Michael Kirby Chair of the Commission of Inquiry on Human Rights in the Democratic People's Republic of Korea to the 25th session of the Human Rights Council. *Human Rights Council*. https://www.ohchr.org/en/statements/2014/03/statement-mr-michael-kirby-chair-commission-inquiry-human-rights-democratic

Locke, John. 2016. *Two treatises of government and a letter concerning toleration*. Digireads.com

Marshall, Joey. 2019. *Are religious people happier, healthier? Our new global study explores this question*. Pew Research Center. https://www.pewresearch.org/fact-tank/2019/01/31/are-religious-people-happier-healthier-our-new-global-study-explores-this-question/

Medina, Jennifer, and Maggie Habberman. 2020. In Miami speech Trump tells evangelical base "god is on our side". *New York Times*. https://www.nytimes.com/2020/01/03/us/politics/trump-miami-rally-evangelicals.html

Miles, M. 1995. Disability in an Eastern religious context: Historical perspectives. *Disability and Society* 10 (1): 49–70.

Mill, John Stuart. 1859 [2002]. *On liberty*. Mineola: Dover Publications.

———. 1861 [1991]. *Considerations on representative government*. Buffalo: Prometheus Books.

Mueller, P.S., D.A. Plevak, and T.J. Rummans. 2001. Religious involvement, spirituality and medicine: Implications for clinical practice. *Mayo Clinic Proceedings* 76: 1125.

National Science Teachers Association. 2022. *Position statement: The teaching of evolution*. National Science Teachers Association. https://www.nsta.org/nstas-official-positions/teaching-evolution

O'Neil, Timothy J.. 2009. *Faith based organizations and government. The first amendment encyclopedia*. Middle Tennessee State University. https://www.mtsu.edu/first-amendment/article/915/faith-based-organizations-and-government

Paine, Thomas. 1792 [2009]. *The rights of man, common sense and other political writings*. Oxford, UK: Oxford University Press.

———. 1806 [2018]. *The age of reason*. South Carolina: CreateSpace Independent Publishing Platform.

Russell, Bertram. 1957. Why I am Not a Christian and Other Essays on Religion and Related Subjects. London: George Allen and Unwin; New York: Simon and Schuster.

Singman, Brooke. 2022. Trump praises decision overturning Roe v. Wade. *Fox News*. https://www.foxnews.com/politics/trump-praises-supreme-court-decision-overturning-roe-v-wade

Szep, Jason. 2013. *Special report: Buddhist monks incite Muslim killings in Myanmar*. Reuters. https://www.reuters.com/article/us-myanmar-violence-specialreport/special-report-buddhist-monks-incite-muslim-killings-in-myanmar-idUSBRE9370AP20130408

Szoldra, Paul. 2017. *The stories from inside North Korea's prison camps are horrifying*. Business Insider. https://www.businessinsider.com/un-north-korea-prison-camp-2017-3

Yaitanes, Greg. 2003. *Frank Herbert's children of Dune*. Santa Monica: Artisan Entertainment.

The Boys as Philosophy: Superheroes, Fascism, and the American Right

30

David Kyle Johnson

Contents

Introduction	704
Series Summary	706
Understanding Analogies	708
The Boys' Argument	709
Comparing Vought, The Supes, and MAGA Trumpism	711
Blue Hawk	711
The Trump Comparison	712
Vought and Religion	714
News Networks, Domestic Terrorists, and Nazis	715
Stormfront the Nazi: Why Vought and Its Supes Are Fascists	717
The Big Lie	717
Gaslighting	718
Fear Mongering	718
Does *The Boys*' Analogy Work?	720
Are the Similarities Relevant to the Conclusion?	720
Strengthening the Analogy: Further Similarities with Stormfront	725
Weakening the Analogy	731
What Makes Fascism, Fascism?	735
Conclusion	738
End Notes	740
References	740

Abstract

The plot of the first three seasons of the Amazon Prime series *The Boys,* adapted from the graphic novel by Garth Ennis and Darick Robertson, makes direct comparisons between its superpowered protagonists, the Nazis, and the modern MAGA movement. As such, the series seems to be an argument from analogy that

---

D. K. Johnson (✉)
Department of Philosophy, King's College, Wilkes-Barre, PA, USA
e-mail: davidjohnson@kings.edu

© Springer Nature Switzerland AG 2024
D. K. Johnson et al. (eds.), *The Palgrave Handbook of Popular Culture as Philosophy*,
https://doi.org/10.1007/978-3-031-24685-2_118

the modern MAGA movement is fascist. It is the goal of this chapter to examine that argument and evaluate its conclusion. In the end, we will see that the analogy is strong, and that the modern MAGA movement is not even just "fascist adjacent." Although the historical circumstances are different, the modern MAGA movement belongs to the family of fascist political ideologies, just as much as 1930s German Nazism.

Keywords

Nazism · Fascism · MAGA · Make America Great Again · America First · Donald Trump · The Boys · Hitler · Analogies · Trumpism · WWII · Ad Hitlerum · Godwin's Law · QAnon · The Big Lie · Fox News · Gaslighting · Fear mongering · Over-policing · White supremacy · Neo-Nazi · Conspiracy theories · Deep fakes · Fake news

Introduction

> People love what I have to say. They believe in it.
> They just don't like the word "Nazi," that's all.
> —*Stormfront (S2E8)*

> When our dictator turns up you can depend on it that he will be one of the boys, and he will stand for everything traditionally American.
> —*American journalist Dorothy Thompson, 1935* (Quoted in Broich 2016)

The Amazon Prime series *The Boys*, adapted from the graphic novel by Garth Ennis and Darick Robertson, is not your typical superhero story. There is no world ending supervillain threat the superheroes must overcome; there are not endless long battles between superpowered beings. In fact, the superheroes are not even "the good guys." The title group, The Boys, are a group of men (and, in turns out, some women) determined to hold superheroes accountable for their crimes. The "supes" (as they are called, because they aren't heroes) abuse both their power and the public's trust and cause wanton collateral damage. The series begins with Hughie Campbell's girlfriend Robin dying right in front of him – she literally turns to goo while he is holding her hands – because she was one step off the curb as A-Train, the world's fastest man, sped by. And he wasn't even chasing criminals; he was just high on Compound V (the chemical that gives the supes their powers).

The series follows Hughie after he joins The Boys in an attempt to hold A-Train accountable. The problem, of course, is that supes are basically above the law; like similar laws that exist for police in the real world, there is even a law that prevents civilians from pressing charges against supes for actions they took while they are fighting crime. This is especially true for those who, like A-Train, are members of The Seven, the primary group of seven supes championed by the company Vought, which essentially owns the supes and runs their lives. It promotes them, manages their Twitter accounts, sends them on occasional "crime fighting" missions, and stars them in movies. Indeed, as we learn in Season 1 – although the company says that people are chosen by God to have superpowers – Vought creates supes by injecting infants with Compound V (usually with their parent's permission), thus basically owning them for life. The only exception is the most powerful supe, Homelander, the American-flag-cape-wearing leader of The Seven, who instead was apparently created by Vought in a lab.

Like most franchises, *The Boys* has a diverse fanbase. What's unusual, however, is how a certain segment of that fanbase seemed to have missed the point. Instead of realizing that Hughie and The Boys are the (albeit flawed) good guys, some fans on the political right idolized Homelander and The Seven and saw them as the good guys. The first season clearly establishes that Homelander is a sociopathic, racist, raping, murderer – yet many right-wing fans of the show loved him, even showing up to Trump-rallies wearing Homelander's costume. (One had Trump, as Homelander, arresting Joe Biden – something Antony Starr, who plays Homelander, called "the [subtle] art of ignorant dumbfuckery." See Romano 2020.) Those fans even stayed loyal to Homelander and The Seven through Season 2, which had Homelander fall in love and team up with a long-lived supe named Stormfront, who literally was a Nazi (both in the 1930s and in the present day). Ironically, the right-wing fans only began to abandon the show in the third season when it had a murderous supe named "Blue Hawk" kill an unarmed black man and then excuse it with the slogan "Supe Lives Matter." Suddenly, the fact that the right wing of American politics was the show's villain could no longer be missed, and right-wing fans began to abandon it (Heritage 2022).

By casting Homelander and his loyal supes as Nazi sympathizers in the second season and then drawing comparisons between them and Trumpism in the third, *The Boys* seems to be presenting an argument by analogy that the MAGA (The Make America Great Again) wing of the Republican Party, which is fiercely loyal to Trump, is akin to Nazism – or, since perhaps, "Nazi" is a label that can only apply to Germans in the 30s and 40s, an argument that the MAGA wing of the Republican Party (like the Nazis) is fascist. But is such a comparison fair? After all, people have routinely been calling their political opponents Nazis and fascists since WWII, but the comparisons are almost always hyperbolic exaggerations. Is this time different? Maybe, like the townsfolk who heard the boy cry "Wolf!" we've become so accustomed to dismissing the allegation that we are ignoring an instance when it's actually true. It is the goal of this chapter to answer these questions.

Since this is a handbook overtly about philosophy and not politics, the reader may not think this topic appropriate. But politics is philosophy, and (genuine) political disagreements and decisions are almost always philosophical in nature. The philosophical works of John Locke (1689/1998), for example, which argued for a natural right to life, liberty, and property, were a major influence on the United States' founding fathers, who argued for a natural right to life, liberty, and happiness (Constitutional Rights Foundation 2001). What's more, as it is an argument from analogy, whether the argument *The Boys* presents is any good will largely turn on whether it is cogent, and the cogency of an argument from analogy is a matter that must be settled by logic, a branch of philosophy. What's more, the heart of the issue is a sematic one: what does the word "fascist" mean? So the question at hand is undeniably philosophical and thus perfectly appropriate for consideration here.

To answer this question, we will first summarize the relevant details of the story and then articulate exactly how *The Boys'* argument from analogy goes. We will then turn to examining it, premise by premise. In the end, we will see that fascism is difficult to define and likely doesn't have either necessary or sufficient conditions, but we will also see that what Homelander and Vought represent, and what MAGA Trumpism is, is not even just "fascism adjacent." They both belong "to the family" of fascist ideologies just as much as 1930s German Nazism does.

Series Summary

The first season of *The Boys* follows Hughie Campbell as he joins The Boys – a vigilante group, led by Billy Butcher, intent on holding supes accountable for their crimes – in an effort to hold a supe named A-Train accountable for recklessly killing his girlfriend. The most relevant thing that we learn in the first season is that hero worship (admiration of the supes and their goals) is tied heavily to religious belief, and it is generally thought that God selects those "blessed" with superpowers to have them. As Homelander puts it, after a supposed terrorist attack on a plane over the Atlantic carrying American citizens:

> Let's hear it for Jesus. . . . One more for the guy upstairs! . . . A terrible tragedy befell our nation this week. Terrible. And let's not mince words about this. We . . . were. . . attacked. America was attacked. Some people, they want me to come out here and speak empty platitudes to you all. A little bit of corporate talk. But I don't want to do that. I can't do that. You want to know why? . . . Because I believe that what God wants me to do is get on over there, find the filthy bastards that masterminded this. . .whatever cave they're in. . .and introduce them to a little thing called God's judgment! That's what I think! Sounds like the American thing to do! Sounds like the right thing to do. But no. No, no, no, no, no. Apparently, I got to wait for Congress to say it's okay. . . . I say, I answer to a higher law. Wasn't I chosen to save you? Is it not my God-given purpose to protect the United States of America? . . . Psalm 58:10. "The righteous shall rejoice when he sees the vengeance and he will bathe his feet in the blood of the wicked." (S1E5)

Of course, what happened was that Homelander and Maeve damaged the plane stopping the hijackers (Homelander fried the cockpit while killing the last hijacker), and then Homelander refused to save anyone to prevent there being any witness of their incompetence. It also turns out that people are not selected by God to have superpowers; instead, Vought International (the company that "owns" the supes) makes deals with various newborns' parents to have their (usually white) children injected with Compound V. Indeed, we also learn that, in an effort to get Congress to allow supes into the military, Homelander (evidently, acting alone) gave Compound V to foreigners, to create "super terrorists" (aka supervillains) that only Vought and its supes could handle.

In Season 2, The Seven has to replace Translucent (a supe The Boys managed to kill in season 1), and the higher-ups at Vought end up choosing a young woman named "Stormfront." This seems odd at first because Stormfront ends up being highly critical of the company, its marketing technique, its movies, etc. She even stands up for women's rights and points out how Vought oversexualizes its female supes. But the big reveal of Season 2 is that Stormfront is actually Liberty, a supe from decades ago who was notoriously racist – who, it turns out, was born in 1919 in Berlin and was a member of the Nazi party. In fact, she married Fredrick Vought, the founder of Vought International, who also (we learn) was a member of the Nazi party and started the company with Nazi goals in mind. The supes were, essentially, intended to be the supermen of a master race that would bring about Hitler's 1000-year Reich. As she shows Homelander a picture of herself, she says:

> I was born in 1919. In Berlin. [That's me with] Heinrich Himmler. He was a lovely dancer. And that's Goebbels. And. . .the most important man in the room: Frederick Vought. He gave me the first successful V injection. He taught me everything. And then we fell in love, and he gave me a daughter. He made me, and his genius made you. Frederick didn't care about all the fans or stardom or any of that shallow bullshit. We are in a war for the culture. The other races are grinding us down and taking what is rightfully ours, but we can fight back. With an army of supermen, millions strong. Because that is Vought's true destiny. And you [Homelander] will be the man who will lead us. You are everything that we dreamed of. (S2E6)

When the blue-eyed, blonde-haired Homelander learns this, he doesn't reject Stormfront but embraces her – both literally and figuratively. They join forces to turn the public against immigrants, and foreigners, by making everyone suspect that they are super-terrorists (supervillains), a threat (recall) that Homelander himself created by giving non-Americans Compound V. The two other female members of The Seven join The Boys in trying to defeat her, but Stormfront is only finally defeated by Homelander's bastard son (Ryan) – whom he fathered with Billy Butcher's wife. When Stormfront threatens Ryan's mother, his powers reveal themselves, and he fries Stormfront to a crisp with his laser vision.

Season 3 follows Homelander as he attempts to take over Vought International. He turns the adopted daughter of the company's president, Stan Edgar, against him, ousting the president from power. Meanwhile, The Boys discover that a long-lost powerful supe, Soldier Boy, is still alive, and enlist him to kill Homelander. They ultimately fail, but Homelander does take charge of Vought industries. What's most notable, however, is how the writers of Season 3 so directly and intentionally draw parallels between Homelander and Donald Trump. We will go into more detail below, but for now, it will be sufficient to note that, for anyone paying attention, the comparison is overt and obvious. And if that weren't enough, the season ends with Homelander killing a "libtard" protester (he blows up his head with his laser vision) after the protester calls him a fascist (and throws a piece of fruit at his son Ryan).

There are, of course, a host of other stories and characters that I have left out here (some of which we will discuss later); I am only including the minimal plot points necessary to understand the show and its argument. With that in mind, let us now turn to the show's argument from analogy, which concludes that MAGA Trumpism is fascist.

Understanding Analogies

Since my claim is that *The Boys* presents an argument from analogy that the modern MAGA movement is fascistic, it will be necessary to begin by articulating what arguments from analogy are, and then explaining how to analyze them.

Arguments from analogy are not deductive. Deductive arguments aim to *guarantee* their conclusion. The premises of a valid deductive argument can't be true while the conclusion is false. As the classic example goes, if (1) all men are mortal and (2) Socrates is a man, then (3) Socrates is mortal. If (1) and (2) are true, (3) must be true.

Arguments from analogy, on the other hand, are *inductive* arguments – arguments that aim to "merely" provide strong support for their conclusion. The word "merely" appears in quotes there because, although technically speaking the conclusion of an inductive argument is not *guaranteed*, if an inductive argument is strong (has good form) and cogent (has true premises), it might as well be. For example, the conclusion that the sun will rise tomorrow because it always has in the past is not 100% guaranteed. That's an inference from the past to the future, so it's within the realm of logical possibility that the conclusion is false. The sun might explode or the Earth might stop rotating within the next 24 hours. But the mere possibility of such things happening in no way makes rejecting the conclusion reasonable. It is beyond any reasonable doubt that the sun will rise tomorrow; despite the fact that it is not technically guaranteed, it is practically guaranteed. And that is what good inductive arguments do: they put their conclusions beyond a reasonable doubt.

So, the mere fact that analogies are inductive, and thus don't "100% prove" their conclusion, doesn't mean that it is reasonable to doubt their conclusion. A cogent analogy puts its conclusion beyond any reasonable doubt. So if it turns out that you don't like the conclusion of the analogy that *The Boys* presents, you can't avoid accepting it by saying "Well, that doesn't *prove* anything." Of course it doesn't; analogies are inductive. The question is whether the analogy it presents is cogent; does it have true premises, the right form, and do what analogies are supposed to do? If so, its conclusion will be beyond any reasonable doubt.

The basic form analogies have is this: they take multiple things, notice similarities between them, and then conclude that those things thus have an additional similarity. Generally, they look something like this:

Thing 1 has properties A, B, and C.
Thing 2 has properties A, B, and C.
Thing 1 also has property D.
So, thing 2 has property D as well.

As a concrete example, suppose you have a car that is the same make and model as a friend's. If their car gets good gas mileage, you could conclude by analogy that your car will get good gas mileage too.

But, as it usually is in logic, the whole story is a bit more complicated. If the similarities between the analogues – the things being compared in an analogy – are not relevant to the conclusion, then despite having the right form, the argument will not be cogent. Since the make and model of a car is relevant to its engine-efficiency, weight, and body shape, the argument above (about equivalent gas mileage) is strong (because engine-efficiency, weight, and body shape affect gas mileage). If, instead, my friend's car was merely the same color and bought from the same dealer, my conclusion about equivalent gas mileage would not follow; the analogy would be weak. The number of similarities is still the same, but the color and seller of a car is not relevant to whether it gets good gas mileage.

You can also strengthen or weaken analogies by finding other relevant similarities or dissimilarities. If you find out that, in addition to your cars being the same make and model, you and your friend drive on the same roads and buy your gas at the same station, your conclusion will be even more certain. On the other hand, if you discover that they buy premium gas (while you buy the cheap stuff), and that they drive the speed limit (while you have a lead foot), the certainty of your conclusion will be weakened.

You can also strengthen or weaken analogies by finding other analogues (other things to compare). If other cars of the same make and model also get gas mileage equivalent to your friend's, the analogy is strengthened. If they all get different gas mileage, the analogy is weakened. The diversity among the analogues can also affect the argument. If those other drivers are all getting mileage equivalent to your friend's mileage while driving on different roads at different speeds, that strengthens the analogy. It would seem that it's the make and model of the cars that is causing the good mileage. If, however, they all – unlike you, but like your friend – drive on the same roads, at the speed limit, and buy premium gas, the analogy is weakened. Perhaps those factors are what's "doing the work" to get him good gas mileage. The point is not that it is impossible to tell whether an analogy is good or not; the point here is to make the reader aware of the kinds of things that one must consider when evaluating arguments from analogy.

With a basic understanding of how analogies work, we can now identify and evaluate the argument from analogy that *The Boys* presents.

The Boys' Argument

The suggestion on the table is that *The Boys* presents an argument by analogy that MAGA Trumpism is fascist. Today, the term "fascist" is practically synonymous with the term "Nazi," but in reality, it isn't. That's not to say that the Nazis weren't fascists; they were. But Nazism is merely a kind of fascism, and the conclusion that Nazis are fascist was itself established by another argument from analogy. The first fascists, in the contemporary political sense, were Mussolini and his blackshirts, who overtook the Italian government by storming its capital in Rome and taking it over (in 1922) (CFA 2001). Hitler, inspired by Mussolini, tried the same thing in Germany the very next year but failed – only to be given a light prison sentence, and then have the Nazi party take majority control in parliament. He was appointed as chancellor by President Hindenburg in 1933, and then (essentially) declared himself president after Hindenburg died in 1934. (Gilbert 2002) Hitler, his brown-shirts, and his government, were considered fascistic because they shared the ideology and approach of the Italian fascists. The form of argument was much like the standard form above:

1. Mussolini and company (his blackshirts and his government) embraced A, B, and C.
2. Hitler and company (his brownshirts and his government) also embraced A, B, and C.
3. Mussolini and company are fascist.
4. So, Hitler and company are fascists too.

Now, at the time, most people thought the concern was exaggerated – but not because the above argument was bad. They thought the analogy was good. The kinds of things that Mussolini and Hitler had in common – the "A,B,Cs" of the argument, like their black/brown-shirted paramilitary, their nationalist political ideology, and approach to government – were relevant to whether they could be considered fascists. As the Merriam-Webster definition puts it, fascism is "a political philoso-phy, movement, or regime (such as that of the [Italian] Fascisti) that exalts nation and often race above the individual and that stands for a centralized autocratic govern-ment headed by a dictatorial leader, severe economic and social regimentation, and forcible suppression of opposition" (Webster n.d.). Mussolini and Hitler were into all of those things. Indeed, the American Press called Hitler "The German Mussolini" and Hitler himself made it clear that Mussolini and his fascism had inspired him.

No, the reason that most people thought that the concern about Hitler being a fascist was exaggerated was because they didn't think fascism was dangerous. For example, most members of the American press (and the American public, for that matter) thought that (a) fascism wasn't the real threat (e.g., that it was more important to fight back against communism) and/or that (b) Hitler was a dolt – a blundering idiot whose supporters were just "impressionable voters" duped by "radical doctrines and quack remedies" (Broich 2016). Real government responsi-bility, the argument went, would force Hitler to either become a moderate or expose his incompetence. Granted, the press later realized and admitted their mistake – but by then, it was far too late (Gritz 2012).

Since WWII, however, just about every politician has been compared to Hitler by someone who doesn't like them. Nixon, Regan, (H.W.) Bush, Clinton, (W.) Bush, and Obama were all compared by their opponents to Hitler. And, while these men certainly all had their moral faults, the comparisons were always exaggerated hyperbole. The mistake is so common, in fact, that it has its own law and its own fallacy. "Godwin's Law" says that "as an online discussion grows longer, the probability of a comparison involving Nazis or Hitler approaches 1." And reductio ad Hitlerum is an association fallacy where anything connected to Hitler – whether it be a tiny moustache, a love of dogs, or vegetarianism – is deemed evil.

But the fact that many fallacious comparisons to Hitler have been made doesn't mean that grounded, sound, comparisons can't exist. After all, when protesters in Charlottesville carried Nazi flags and chanted "Jews will not replace us," Mike Godwin, the inventor of Godwin's Law, made a point of saying that they definitely were Nazis. "By all means, compare these shitheads to Nazis. Again and again. I'm with you" (Friedman 2017). And he did so because people were invoking his law to wrongly claim that these people, who Trump called "very fine people," weren't actually Nazis. So, we can't automatically dismiss *The Boys'* argument that modern MAGA Trumpism is fascist by just mentioning Godwin's Law or the *reductio ad Hitlerum* fallacy. The mere fact that some people aren't fascists doesn't entail that there are none.

If we take Homelander to be a stand-in for all the supes that idolize him and are sympathetic to Vought International's original stated mission, we can put the argument *The Boys* makes like this:

Homelander and Vought (HoVo) have properties A, B, and C.
MAGA Trumpism has properties A, B, and C.
Homelander and Vought (HoVo) are fascists.[1]
So, MAGA Trumpism is fascist.

To examine the cogency of this argument, we will need to do basically four things. (1) identify the ABCs – the things that *The Boys* points out HoVo and MAGA have in common (2) examine how the show establishes that HoVo is fascist, (3) determine whether the ABCs the argument points to are relevant to its conclusion (whether they are the features of fascism), and then (4) ask whether there are other considerations (more analogues, other properties, more comparisons) that could strengthen or weaken the argument.

Comparing Vought, The Supes, and MAGA Trumpism

For those who keep up with politics, the comparisons *The Boys* makes between HoVo and MAGA Trumpism are pretty obvious.

Blue Hawk

The comparison that set off right-wing leaning fans of the show involved Blue Hawk, a white superhero who was over-patrolling black neighborhoods in Trenton and killed an unarmed black man, Raymond Tucker, who was simply returning from work. (Clearly "Blue Hawk" is a reference to those who hawkishly defend the police (*aka* the "boys in blue").) In Season 3, episode 5, after a very forced apology – where he shifts blame by saying that his actions were "perceived" as racist and then says that he is not racist because he has black friends and doesn't "see color. . .only crime" – Blue Hawk replies to chants of "Black Lives Matter" with "all lives matter" and "supe lives matter." This not only mirrors how those on the right give blame-shifting non-apologies for police misconduct (Jenab 2016), and often use the "black friend defense" to skirt accusations of racism (see Tang Hajela 2019 and Craig 2022), it also invokes how the right responded to Black Lives Matter protests: "all lives matter" and "blue lives matter." Earlier, Blue Hawk even insists that it is racist to call someone racist, echoing Republican complaints since Trump was elected (Demby 2016).

Likewise, Blue Hawk's claim that he is not over-patrolling black neighborhoods, he is simply going where the crime is – "Do your research, blacks commit a disproportionate number of murders" – also mirrors claims made by MAGA Trumpists, who often claim that over-patrolling black neighborhoods is justified because a disproportionate number of jailed criminals are black. (The right-wing Reddit fans who abandoned the show said specifically that this was a point of Blue Hawk's that they agreed with; see O'Dell 2022). But, of course, official crime rates (like arrest rates) could just as easily be higher in black neighborhoods *because* black neighborhoods are overpoliced (not because crime is more common there). If the police are paying more attention to black criminals than white ones, they will catch and jail more black criminals. But that doesn't mean that blacks are committing more crimes. (Imagine if Hitler had claimed that Jews commit more crimes because his brownshirts, while patrolling Jewish neighborhoods, had locked up more Jews than non-Jews.)

Don't get me wrong: studies show that the greatest predictor of crime is poverty (see Olson 2021, Dong et al. 2020, and Quednau 2021), and poverty is higher in black communities (largely because of racist economic and education policies; see Jeffries n.d.); but that can't account for the disproportionate number of blacks in American prisons. For example, a black American male is about 2.4 times more likely than a white one to live in poverty (19.5% of blacks live in poverty vs. 8.2% of whites; see Statista 2022), but a black male is more than 7 times more likely to be in jail (6.67% of black males are in jail, vs. 0.94% of white males, see Solomon 2012). (For more on racist policing, see Weitzer 2017.) Regardless, the comparison with Blue Hawk is overt.

The Trump Comparison

The Boys also made its argument by directly equating Homelander with Trump in Season 3. Sometimes the comparisons are comical, like having Homelander praise the taco bowls served in Vought Tower (S3E4) in the same way that Trump praised the taco bowls served in Trump Tower during his 2016 presidential campaign. "Happy #CincoDeMayo! The best taco bowls are made in Trump Tower Grill. I love Hispanics!" (Lopez 2016). Homelander even says his line to appeal to a new Hispanic member of The Seven.

Other times, the comparisons are covert, like when Homelander is on a Vought News show, and the host points out that "The Stormchasers, Stormfront's supporters, said on 4chan that this whole thing [with Soldier Boy] was an attempt by Stan Edgar to discredit you." Homelander replies, "Well, look. I don't know anything about Stormchasers [but] I can understand why they might think that. The minute we free Vought of the corruption, and the lies, and this happens? I mean, the timing is very convenient." "Smells like a false flag." The reporter replies, "Well, you said it, pal, not me."

The savvy viewer will know that "Stormchasers" here is a reference to QAnon, a baseless but popular conspiracy theory which holds that Democrats are members of a Satan worshiping pedophilia cult, and that Trump is the savior of humanity who will direct an event called "The Storm" that will arrest all the members of this cult (hence the term "Stormchasers"). QAnon is obviously ludicrous (for a full refutation, see Rajan et al. 2021; for a detailed analysis of how it arose, see Sommer 2023); yet when Trump was asked to disavow QAnon by Savannah Guthrie (and specifically to deny the idea that the "Democrats are a Satanic pedophile ring"), he simply replied "I don't know anything about QAnon" and then went on to rant about Antifa (which, the reader should know, stands for "antifascist"). To be fair, he did later claim to know that QAnon supporters are "very strongly against pedophilia, and I agree with that," but when pushed by Guthrie to specifically disavow the idea that Democrats belong to a Satanic pedophilia cult, he just said "I don't know ... and neither do you" (Gabbatt 2020). This is just like Homelander, who claims to know nothing about "Stormchasers," but then goes on (in S3E7) to accuse Starlight of human trafficking, just like the QAnon believers do with Democrats.

But the comparisons are also overt – like when Homelander says he is "done apologizing" (Trump famously never apologizes for anything; see McGann 2018) or when he complains about the people "in the shadows. . .pulling the strings" (S3E4), which echoes Trump's complaints about "the deep state" (Slisco 2023). Or take when Homelander seized control of Vought in Season 3. The episode 5 scene in which Homelander pressures the members of the Vought board openly praise him in their first board meeting is eerily similar to the time that Trump did the same thing with his cabinet during his first year in office.

Board member Bill March (to Homelander)	And I, for one, would like to thank you, Homelander, for giving me the opportunity to serve this board at such a pivotal moment in, uh, Vought's history. (S3E5)
Cabinet Member Alexander Acosta (to Trump)	"I am privileged to be here – deeply honored – and I want to thank you for your commitment to the American workers." (Davis 2017)
Board Member Pat Willis (to Homelander)	"You've rid us of Stan Edgar and restored honesty, integrity and innovation to this corporation." (S3E5)
Cabinet Member Reince Priebus (to Trump)	"We thank you for the opportunity and the blessing to serve your agenda." (Davis 2017)

And when Homelander is humiliated by one board member (Maureen) who actually has the knowledge necessary to make the company function – she asks him about how to handle the "EBITDA margins" on the "earnings call" – he fires her and ultimately strips away all the infrastructure necessary to make the company work. When Starlight goes to the Vought research department to have them help her find Soldier Boy, she finds that The Deep has basically emptied it because Homelander only wants "team players." This is just like Trump, who was not only wholly unqualified for the job as president (see Bathke 2016) and fired everyone in his administration who he didn't consider to be loyal enough (which, eventually, was almost everyone; see Katz 2020), but also disbanded the Global Health Security and Biodefense unit established by President Obama, which was responsible for pandemic preparedness, a couple years before the COVID pandemic (Reuters Staff 2020).

Sometimes the show's comparisons are barely exaggerations. In 2016, Trump said that "I could stand in the middle of Fifth Avenue and shoot somebody, and I wouldn't lose any voters." At the end of season 3, Homelander does essentially this – exploding the head of the "libtard" who called him a fascist on (what ostensibly is) Fifth Avenue. Showrunner Eric Kripke even made clear that Trump's quote inspired the scene (Christopherson 2022). After Homelander does this, his followers, (wearing "Sorry Snowflake" shirts and holding "American Safety First" signs) led by Todd (the stepfather of one of The Boys children) cheers him on, seemingly more dedicated than ever. Todd, in fact, is a stand-in for the average MAGA Trumpster – who thinks that Trump/Homelander is "America's greatest hero [because] he's standing up to the crooks, the corporations, and the legacy [mainstream] media." "Friend me on Facebook," Todd says, "I'll send you some stuff" (S3E5). Despite the fact that Trump himself is a crook (Stechschulte 2022), gave away hundreds of millions to corporations (Berger 2017), and the fact that the most pro-Trump cable news network (Fox News) is the most watched cable channel there is (thus making it more "legacy/mainstream" than any other news network), Trump supporters believe exactly the same thing about Trump.

Vought and Religion

But the clues that HoVo were a stand-in for MAGA came long before Season 3, and the introduction of Blue Hawk and the comparisons to Trump. Consider the standard Vought policy, evident in Season 1, of claiming that those who are born with superpowers are chosen by God. Fandom of supes is wrapped up in religious notions and worship, rooted in the idea that they are doing God's work. Starlight grew up in the "Believe Expo" circuit, active in the "Capes for Christ" campaign, where a supe named Ezekiel claims that those who have superpowers were chosen simply because they have faith. Likewise, the ties between Republicanism (MAGA Trumpism in particular) and the Christian religion are well-established. Not only are Republicans more likely to be Christian (Pew Research Center 2014) but they are more likely to be evangelical in their religious outlook, attend church regularly (Nortey 2021), and cite religious concepts and arguments for their political positions. They claim that Trump was ordained by God to be president (Dickinson 2020), want to declare the Unites States to be a Christian nation (and make it a theocracy; see Rouse and Telhami 2022 and Morris 2021), and even think that the police (like supes) are doing God's work (Griffith 2022).

Similarly, just like there was a movement spearheaded by Vought to put its "God ordained" supes into the military, there is a movement that originates in Christian evangelicalism to inject Christianity in the military by both having Christians sign up and rise to position of power and indoctrinating existing soldiers into Christianity (by, for example, requiring them to attend Christian Bible studies and worship services) (Weinstein and Seay 2006). Darren Slade and I talk about this, in more detail, in ▶ Chap. 19, "*The Orville* as Philosophy: The Dangers of Religion" (also in this handbook), but the long and short of it is that, according to many Republicans, the American military should be seen as something that belongs to God and does his work. Or, to put it another way, what Homelander says is true of him (in the quote from the summary), they think is true of the US Military. "I believe that what God wants me to do is get on over there, find the filthy bastards that masterminded this – whatever cave they're in – and introduce them to a little thing called God's judgment! ... Wasn't I chosen to save you? Is it not my God-given purpose to protect the United States of America?" (S1E5).

Vought's relationship to the church is also similar to MAGA's relationship to the church. In *The Boys*, Vought is in league with Samaritan's Embrace, the evangelical church/movement tied to the "Believe Expo" in which Homelander even serves as a kind of minister (he baptizes members into the church and delivers sermons). What Samaritan's Embrace does for Vought, American evangelical churches do for the Republican party, especially MAGA Trumpism, by taking its side on culture war issues, like abortion and gun control, and even preaching from the pulpit that its members should vote for Trump and the Republicans loyal to him. Think of how Liberty University, the most prominent evangelical college in the United States, platformed and promoted Trump long before (in 2012) and during his 2016 bid for president (Bible 2012 and Diamond 2016).

News Networks, Domestic Terrorists, and Nazis

In Season 2, the MAGA/HoVo comparison is also seen at the beginning of episode 7, "Butcher, the Baker, and the Candlestick Maker." Tommy Peterson, a Stormfront fan boy, is radicalized by a continuous flood of right-wing media. He wakes up to InfoWars and Vought (Fox) News complaining about illegal immigrants and super-terrorists and how "supervillain-loving snowflakes" on "the left" tolerate them. He walks to class listening to Stromfront calling her followers to action, to "Keep America Safe Again," because Congress won't do anything about it. And he stays up late on 4chan (an unregulated message board website) looking at "Immigrate legally or die" memes along with calls to assassinate those who are investigating Vought and Compound V. As Stormfront points out that an illegal super-terrorist could be standing next to him "right now," he sees what he thinks is a flash of light in a convenience store worker's eyes – a worker who has brown skin. Tommy returns, convinced that the worker (Kuldeep Singh) is a super-terrorist, and shoots the worker in the face. In the aftermath, at a rally, Stormfront and Homelander offer their "thoughts and prayers" to the victim's family, before continuing to stoke more fears about super-terrorists – which, recall, Homelander himself helped create – to motivate the release of more Compound V so that there can be more supes.

Again, the comparison is obvious. Not only are "thoughts and prayers" the only thing the right offers in the wake of gun violence (Johnson 2022, PBS NewsHour 2023b, Cathey 2023; Trump himself used the phrase in response to the Marshal County Highschool shooting in Kentucky on January 24, 2018, but never took meaningful action, see Zipp 2018); and not only is "Keep America Safe Again" a take on Trump's slogans "Make America Great Again" and "Keep America Great"; and not only does Vought News look and sound exactly like Fox News (which, if the reader is unaware, leans hard right and has more viewers than all other cable news networks combined; see Bump 2022); but it is well-documented that continual exposure to right wing news and propaganda has a radicalizing effect (see Holt, et al. 2021, Jensen and James 2018, Tomczyk et al. 2022, Wolfowicz et al. 2022, and Youngblood 2020).

Granted, such studies suggest that social media (especially the use of uncensored web forums like 4chan) has a much more radicalizing effect than watching Fox News; indeed, it may be that those who are already radicalized simply tend to choose Fox News as their cable news source. But it is also worth noting that white supremacists are open about their love of, for example, (former) Fox News' most-watched host Tucker Carlson (ADL 2021), and even use his show to learn how to more effectively argue for what they believe (on places like 4chan). As former white-supremacist Derek Black, whose father Don Black founded the largest, oldest, white supremacist cite on the internet "Stormfront" (note the name!) put it: "My family watches Tucker Carlson's show once and then watches it on the replay because they feel that he is making the white nationalist talking points better than they have, and they're trying to get some tips on how to advance it" (Stieb 2019). Tucker even practically quotes the white supremist slogan "The Fourteen Words" on his show (see Oliver 2021, Horton 2021). The right-wing white-supremacy paramilitary groups The Proud Boys and The Oath Keepers (which both helped storm the Capital on January 6, 2021 to try to keep Donald Trump in power) are classified by the US Government as "domestic violent extremists." (The US government only refers to foreign groups as "terrorist organizations." However, it did refer to Oath Keeper leader Stewart Rhodes as a domestic terrorist; see Hsu 2022; U.S Department of State 2022; Wray 2022.)

But speaking of Stormfront – the Nazi Superhero – now that we have seen the similarities between MAGA and HoVo, we need to catalog how, in the second season, the show has HoVo embracing Nazism (by embracing Stormfront). This will not only help us establish the third premise in our argument from analogy – that Vought's and its supes are fascists – but set us up to explore whether MAGA loyalists embrace some of the very same ideas.

Stormfront the Nazi: Why Vought and Its Supes Are Fascists

That Stormfront is a Nazi (and thus a fascist) is firmly established by the plot of the series. Not only is "Stormfront" the name of the oldest and most popular real-world neo-nazi website, but Stormfront herself was born in Berlin, in 1919, and by her own admission was a member of the Nazi party right alongside Adolf Hitler, Heinrich Himmler, and Joseph Goebbels. That Homelander and Vought (as an organization, in its founding) are sympathetic with Nazi ideals is also clearly communicated by the series. When Stormfront reveals her history to Homelander, not only do we learn that the founder of Vought International, Frederick Vought, was a Nazi – we also learn that he founded it with the express purpose of creating an "army of [white] supermen millions strong" to win the "war for the culture" against the "other races" who are "grinding [the whites] down and taking what is rightfully [theirs]" (S2E6). And when Homelander learns all of this from Stormfront, he embraces her, both literally and figuratively. Later, when Stormfront is preaching to Homelander's son Ryan, about how he needs to develop his power to help them protect against "White Genocide," he doesn't correct her (S2E8). Of course, there is also the fact that "Homeland" is one step away from "Fatherland" (the Nazi's preferred nationalistic phrase for Germany). And let us also not forget this little exchange.

Stormfront   We have to make sure that the right [white] people get the doses [of Compound V]. . .
Homelander   What about the wrong people? Couple of billion of them. They're not just gonna sit there.
Stormfront   Don't worry, silly. Frederick had a solution for everything. (S2E8)

The allusion to Hitler's "final solution" is palpable.

The Big Lie

But *The Boys* also established that Stormfront is a fascist by having her embrace a political strategy that is clearly modeled after the Nazi's. For example, think of how Stormfront calls the pictures that expose her as a Nazi "deep fakes." We know that Stormfront knows the pictures are real; we saw her showing them to Homelander, admitting that they were pictures of her. By denying what she knows to be true (and everyone else can plainly see as true), and instead insisting that the better explanation is a grand conspiracy against her that includes the grandiose concocting of false evidence, Stormfront is employing a common fascist tactic that Hitler was famous for: The Big Lie.

We will talk about this a bit more later, but the basic idea is that if you tell a lie big enough, everyone will believe it because they will assume that no one would be brazen and evil enough to tell such an obvious falsehood. ("How could they lie about that and expect anyone to believe them? They must be telling the truth.") Hitler described the tactic in Mein Kampf (1925):

[T]he broad masses of a nation are always more easily corrupted in the deeper strata of their emotional nature than consciously or voluntarily; and thus in the primitive simplicity of their minds they more readily fall victims to the big lie than the small lie, since they themselves often tell small lies in little matters but would be ashamed to resort to large-scale falsehoods. It would never come into their heads to fabricate colossal untruths, and they would not believe that others could have the impudence to distort the truth so infamously. Even though the facts which prove this to be so may be brought clearly to their minds, they will still doubt and waver and will continue to think that there may be some other explanation. (Vol. 1 Ch. X)

Ironically, Hitler thought he was describing a Jewish practice, but it is widely known that it was a tactic employed by him and his propaganda team. The OSS psychological profile on Hitler says that he thought "people will believe a big lie sooner than a little one; and if you repeat it frequently enough people will sooner or later believe it" (Langer n.d., "Hitler as his Associates know him" #26).

Gaslighting

Lying about known facts is also a part of a fascist strategy which aims to confuse the public and make them more malleable. Stormfront not only lies about what is objectively true, essentially calling it "fake news" (when it isn't), but she also produces actual fake news herself, which she says is true. Think of the memes and misinformation she shows Homelander when she is articulating her political strategy, like the meme that implies the picture of the civilians Homelander killed (while killing a super-terrorist) is fake. If what is actually true is being called fake by some, and what is fake is being called true by others, it creates in the general public a sense that it is impossible to tell what is true and false. When every news story that comes out is labeled by someone as fake, for the average person, finding the actual truth becomes too difficult. They will give up on trying to find the truth, and turn to just believing whatever they want. This is something fascists love, of course, because a public like that is easy to manipulate, and it was a strategy employed by the Nazis in Germany (Koester 2018).

This is related to something called gaslighting, where you lie – usually by professing what someone saw with their very own eyes to not have occurred – in an effort to get someone to question their own sanity (Johnsen 2017). Usually, gaslighting occurs in the context of personal relationships – the term comes from a play, called *Gaslight*, where a husband uses this tactic on his wife (Duignan n.d.) – but it also occurs in the political realm. And fascists are masters of it.

Fear Mongering

When she articulates her political strategy, Stormfront also justifies it by telling Homelander why it is effective. Homelander spends lots of time and effort trying to improve his poll numbers and win the approval of the majority – but Stormfront sees this as a waste of time.

30   *The Boys* as Philosophy: Superheroes, Fascism, and the American Right   719

> You spent $273 million on that "Saving America" bullshit, and I'm running circles around you with five guys on laptops, churning out memes. I practically pay them with Arby's gift cards. You can't win the whole country anymore, no one can. So why are you even trying? You don't need 50 million people to love you. You need five million people fucking pissed. Emotion sells, anger sells. You have fans. I have soldiers. (S2E4)

This is how fascists operate; think of how the Nazis stoked fear about the Jews (and homosexuals, and transexuals, and blacks), and especially about the "death of Germany" in the aftermath of WWI, to rise to and hold on to power (Chamberlain 2008). This is what Stormfront and Homelander ultimately do. They use the threat of the super-terrorists (which, recall, again, Homelander actually created) to generate fear in people, about the actual survival of the nation.

Stormfront	No one condones the tragic shooting at the convenience store. Our thoughts and prayers go out to Kuldeep Singh's family. And we are making a donation to Samaritan's Embrace in his name.
Homelander	Absolutely. Thoughts and prayers. But that doesn't change facts. This used to be a-a beautiful country. Remember? One nation under God. Remember? Right before these godless, inhuman super-villains started pouring across our borders and dragging us down into their mud.
Stormfront	What do SJWs like Victoria Neuman want us to do? Just let 'em in and give 'em a cup of iced tea? And then punish us for trying to stop them. Has there ever been anyone in history more persecuted just for trying to protect their own? We are at war! We need more Compound V. We need more Supes! (S2E7)

Of course, all politicians use fear to motivate voters – but not all appeals to fear are fascistic (or fallacious). For example, it's perfectly reasonable to point out that one's political opponent plans to pass legislation that most voters don't like, or to point out the undesirable consequences of what they will likely do (i.e., to make them *fear* the consequences of electing their opponent). When Trump ran for president in 2016, Democrats tried to motivate voters against him by saying that Trump would appoint judges who would overturn Roe v. Wade, pass tax cuts for the wealthy that would raise the debt and deficit, and gut environmental regulations. That wasn't fascistic fearmongering; it was reasonable to believe he would do such things (given that he said that he would, and then he in fact did, in each case).

Fascistic fear mongering, on the other hand, stokes fears without evidence and usually does so along racial lines. Take the Reichstag fire, for example, an incident in which the Parliament building in Berlin burned down. Without evidence, Hitler claimed that it was the beginning of a communist violent uprising to derail Germany's "national renewal." He had no such evidence, and indeed no such plot existed; but the next day, the "For the Protection of the People and State" act (aka the Reichstag Fire Decree) passed, abolishing a number of constitutional protections (the right to assembly, freedom of speech, and freedom of the press) in Germany, and legally unrestrained police investigations into what Hitler viewed as politically subversive organizations (Holocaust Encyclopedia (a) (n.d.)).

So, to the extent that HoVo embrace and promote Stormfront and her tactics (like big lies, gaslighting, and fear mongering), they are fascists. So, with all the premises of the analogy firmly established, we can now turn to examining whether the argument from analogy *The Boys* presents actually works.

Does *The Boys'* Analogy Work?

So far we have established that HoVo have a lot in common with The MAGA movement (which was premise 1 and 2 of the show's argument), and that HoVo is fascist (which was premise 3). So the task now is to (a) consider whether the things that MAGA and HoVa have in common are relevant to the conclusion (are they traits of fascism?), and then (b) consider whether there are further analogs, or other similarities and differences, that will strengthen or weaken the analogy. We shall now do each in turn.

Are the Similarities Relevant to the Conclusion?

The similarities we have identified between MAGA and HoVo are:

- An unquestioning loyalty to police, especially when it comes to over policing racial minorities.
- Embracing conspiracy theories and those who profess them.
- The tendency to never apologize or admit wrongdoing.
- Demanding a kind of loyalty, and even a kind of godlike worship of the leader, which generates a kind of cult-like following that is unable to admit that the leader has ever done anything wrong.
- A tie with religion, which suggests that the leader and mission of the party is God-ordained.
- A mixing of religious ideology with the military and to see the national military as God's army.
- Loyal news organizations and other media outlets spread the party's propaganda and radicalize viewers.

Are these traits things fascists also do? Absolutely. And they are relevant to our conclusion because not only are they *things fascists do;* they are things fascists do *because they are fascists and want to gain and retain political power.* Look at the work of just about any scholar who discusses fascism (we will discuss a few below), and you will see these kinds of things on their list of fascistic attributes. More disturbing still is how, when you look at how the Nazis did such things, they very directly mirror how MAGA does such things today. Let us consider each in turn.

Policing

After he gained power, one of the first things that Hitler did to solidify his power was to "Nazify" Germany's police force. Those not loyal to the party were fired or transferred to powerless positions, people loyal to the party were appointed (including those who had actually harassed German police forces before Hitler took power), and directives were issued which expressly targeted minorities and the Nazi party's political enemies. Celebrations of the police were held, and the police were billed as the "friend and helper" of the "German people." Of course, it was quite clear that "German people" here only meant "Aryan Germans"; and when the police targeted, arrested, and brutalized mainly minority groups, like Jews, the public's defense of the police was adamant. "The Jews weren't being targeted," it was thought. "Crime is just more prevalent in Jewish communities." (For more details, see Holocaust Encyclopedia (b) (n.d.).)

Of course, this should sound familiar, but the reader is likely unaware that there is a similar problem, in American police forces, with white supremacy in their ranks – and that this problem was brought about in much the same way that Hitler Nazified German police forces (see Johnson 2019). Not only is there implicit (unconscious) racism in policing (and not only are the training efforts to combat it insufficient), there is explicit (conscious) racism that is, even when it is expressed in word and action, tolerated and even sometimes encouraged (German 2020). What's more, even though the FBI has been warning about a "white supremacist infiltration of law enforcement" since 2006 (see FBI 2006), virtually nothing has been done since then to combat it (Finnegan 2021). Very few agencies have laws against belonging to such groups; and even when they do, little is done to identify those who belong or to expel officers once their connections to such groups are clear (Kanu 2022). (For example, a Pittsburgh police officer was just moved to a desk job after he was identified as an Oath Keeper (a right-wing racist paramilitary group); see KDKA News 2022.) As a result, even though white supremacy has been identified as the greatest terrorist threat in the Unites States (Woodruff Swan 2020), white supremists' efforts to infiltrate police departments – to get members of white supremacist groups instated as police officers, and to recruit already existing officers into their ideology and ranks – have been highly successful (Speri 2020, Margolin 2021). Top all this off with Trump vowing to purge the FBI and DOJ (Department of Justice) of disloyal officers if he is reelected in 2024 (Levin 2023), and you have a clear parallel with how Hitler not only Nazified the German police, but the entire German government.

Conspiracy Theories

Nazism also embraced and promoted false and ridiculous conspiracy theories. Take blood libel, for example – the conspiracy theory that Jews kidnap and murder children to harvest their blood for use in their religious rituals (which some said gave them magical powers). Although this conspiracy theory predates Nazi Germany by hundreds of years, the Nazis not only believed it, but made very effective use of it. Julius Streicher's anti-Semitic Nazi Germany newspaper Der Stürmer (The Attacker) frequently employed the blood libel motif and dedicated an entire issue to it in May 1934. The headline even reads like a modern-day tabloid: "Jewish Murder Plan against Gentile Humanity Revealed."

It's worth noting that, while no conspiracy theory on *The Boys* mirrors the blood libel conspiracy theory specifically, the real-world, pro-Trump conspiracy theory that the show alludes to, QAnon, does. Recall that a central point of the real-world QAnon conspiracy theory is that Democrats are pedophiles. Well, according to the conspiracy theory, the reason they have sex with children isn't just sexual pleasure; the horror of the experience produces "adrenochrome" in the children, and this adrenochrome is then extracted and ingested by the perpetrators for its magical powers. Indeed, QAnon doesn't even hold that all Democrats do this; it's just the elite – the globalist politicians, the Hollywood stars, and the big global bankers (like George Soros). But who (do they think) runs Hollywood? The Jews! Who (do they think) are the big global bankers, like George Soros? The Jews. Who (do they think) are the globalist politicians? The Jews! In fact, in QAnon, there are many code words for "Jew," and "globalist" is one of them (see AJC 2021; for more on the antisemitic roots of QAnon, see Lavin (2020), Stanton (2020), Hatewatch Staff (2020), and Kremmerer (2021)). But it should be pretty clear, given what I have just laid out, that QAnon is just "Blood Libel" for the twenty-first century. It's just "a Nazi cult, rebranded" (Stanton 2020).

Given this, it's important to note just how popular QAnon is in the MAGA movement and the republican party in general. Nearly a quarter of Republicans believe the central tenets of QAnon (Milligan 2022), and over half think that it is mostly or partly true (with those numbers undoubtedly being higher specifically within the MAGA base). What's more, while some thought that QAnon would die out after Trump was defeated in 2020, it's actually gotten more popular since then (Smith 2022) and is as popular as some major religions (Russonello 2021). Indeed, a good case could be made that the unfounded concerns about drag shows being used to "groom children" is derived from QAnon itself – and as this chapter is being written, anti-drag legislation is the Republican party's number one legislative concern (Helmore 2023), and real-world (neo)Nazis are showing up to protest drag shows (Max 2023).

(Interestingly, the first book burning carried out by the Nazis in May of 1933 was at the Institute of Sexology, which had "achieved a global reputation for its pioneering work on transsexual understanding and calls for equality for homosexuals, transgender people and women . . . Among the texts thrown onto the bonfire at the Bebelplatz was Heinrich Heine's *Almansor*, in which the author noted: 'Where they burn books, in the end they will burn humans too'" (Holocaust Memorial Day Trust n.d.). It's worth noting that many of the same kinds of books are being banned by the Republican Party as this chapter is being written.)

Infallibility and Loyalty

Did the fascists have a tendency to never apologize or admit wrongdoing? Absolutely. In fact, the OSS psychological profile of Hitler described him as such:

His primary rules were: never allow the public to cool off; never admit a fault or wrong; never concede that there may be some good in your enemy; never leave room for alternatives; never accept blame; concentrate on one enemy at a time and blame him for everything that goes wrong. (Langer n.d.)

Indeed, even until the end, Hitler blamed the Jews for the downfall of Germany and maintained that he had tried to avoid war with other nations. This is not unlike Trump who is never willing to admit that he is wrong (Cain 2019), including his denial that he lost the 2020 election. What's more, much like Trump, Hitler had a tendency to underestimate his opponent, overestimate his own abilities, and displace responsibility for failures onto scapegoats, all of which contributed to a fallacious sense of self confidence (Dörner and Güss 2011).

Did Hitler demand and enjoy a kind of godlike, cultist loyalty and worship? Absolutely. Hitler's cult of personality was one of his most famous attributes. Robert W. Jones Jr. (2020) argues that this can be seen in Nazi artwork alone (Jones 2020). Hitler even demanded that the Pope "employ many, many sweet words in regards to his Minister of Foreign Affairs" when they met (Kertzer 2022).

Religion

Speaking of which: was Nazism tied to religion? Did Nazis see Hitler and the Nazi party's mission as God-ordained? Was religion mixed into the military and the German army seen as God's army? Absolutely. First of all, centuries of antisemitism in The Catholic Church inspired the antisemitism of Nazism, and the German Catholic church flew Nazi flags and prayed for the protection of the "Fuhrer and the Reich" on Hitler's 50th birthday in 1939. Catholic bishops, priests, and nuns even supported Germany's war effort (TOI Staff 2020). To be fair, in some places, the Church helped hide Jews from the Nazis. But a recent study of newly released records from the era of Pope Pius XII (who served during Hitler's time as German chancellor/president) showed that he never denounced Hitler and Nazism, even after he was made aware of the mass murder of 100,000 Jews in the Warsaw Ghetto (TOI Staff 2020). In fact, that same study of records revealed that Pius XII had many secret meetings with one of Hitler's associates (a Nazi prince named Philipp von Hessen), and in those talks he only ever advocated for the interest of the Church; he never spoke against the mistreatment of the Jews or any other Nazi crimes (Kertzer 2022). While there were secular and religious members of the Nazi party, there is no doubt that the party writ large embraced religious notions, and embraced the idea that their cause was in defense of the divine, as a way to justify its mission and cause. Indeed, all German soldiers (except for members of the SS) had the German phrase for "God is with us" on their belt buckles, and about the SS Heinrich Himmler himself said:

We believe in a God Almighty who stands above us; he has created the earth, the Fatherland, and the Volk, and he has sent us the Führer. Any human being who does not believe in God should be considered arrogant, megalomaniacal, and stupid and thus not suited for the SS. (Ziegler 2014)

Again, to be fair, it might not be accurate to call the Nazi movement Christian, in the traditional sense. The Christian theologian Ernst Bergmann, for example, defended Nazism in his writings but also argued that portions of the Old and New Testament were inaccurate (e.g., that Jesus was Aryan, rather than Jewish; see Bergmann 1936). And after the war, it was discovered that this aligned with the Nazi's plan to transform Christianity into a new religion called "positive Christianity," which rid the Bible of its Jewish elements (The Old Testament and certain books of the New), and incorporate into the religion a Völkisch ideology (a kind of racist nationalism) and Führerprinzip (the idea that the Fuhrer is above the law; see Office of Strategic Services (Research and Analysis Branch) 1945). These ideas can hardly be said to align with traditional Christianity. But it's still a historical fact that Hitler grew up in the Catholic church, and it's undeniable that the anti-semitism and authoritarianism in Catholicism not only fueled Hitler's ideology, but primed the German people to embrace both his ideology and him as their "God-given" leader, and that Hitler opportunistically publicly played up his Christianity to take advantage of that fact because he knew it was necessary for him to gain and retain his political power (Rees 2012).

What is striking, however, is how much all this aligns with the MAGA movement. Of course, Trump himself, very clearly (given is public and private behavior), is not a Christian; he never attends church, has had multiple wives and extramarital affairs, and ran a fraudulent charity organization (Sisak 2019). He doesn't even know that "II Corinthians" is called "Second Corinthians" and not "Two Corinthians" (Taylor 2016). But he clearly opportunistically professes to be Christian and does things like inviting recognized Christians to the oval office, because he realizes that it is necessary to attain and maintain political power. What's more, large swaths of evangelicals not only favor Trump but see him as a god-like figure which they believe was ordained by God to lead the nation (Burge 2019). (Consider the popular T-shirt "Jesus is my Savior, Trump is my President.") And as if that wasn't enough, the religion that evangelical Trump supporters embrace does not mirror biblical and historical Christianity (GCRR 2020); not only does it ignore the weak and oppressed, and instead tend to see Jesus as more like a John Wayne figure (Du Mez 2020), it now proudly embraces white nationalism (the same kind of Völkisch racist nationalism that the Nazis embraced), and sees their leader, Trump, as above the law (Serwer 2022). The similarities to the Nazi's "Positive Christianity" are striking.

Media and Propaganda

Did loyal news organizations and other media outlets spread the Nazi party's propaganda and radicalize viewers? Absolutely. Indeed, the Nazi's propaganda machine is one of their most famous aspects. They tightly controlled all media outlets in Germany and even had many allies in the United States. The Catholic Priest Father Coughlin, who was the most listened to radio host in America in the 1930s, fiercely defended Hitler and Nazism, and even inspired "The Christian Front" (an organization that tried to overthrow the American government in the name of fascism). Once the war was over, it was discovered that 24 US congressmen had worked with the German government to disseminate Nazi propaganda in the Unites States. For example, they delivered speeches written by Hitler's government on the floor of congress, thus inserting them into the congressional record, and then mailed them out to their constituents using taxpayer money (Gross 2022).

Again, this is not unlike the media wing of the Republican party. Not only do *Fox News*, *Newsmax*, and *One America Network* only ever offer stories that favor Trump and the MAGA agenda (most of which are skewed, biased, or just outright false); and not only do they parrot the talking points of fascist foreign governments (for example, while on Fox News, Tucker Carlson often parroted the talking point of Vladimir Putin's propaganda machine; see Thompson 2022); but just like the fascist Father Coughlin (again, the most famous American radio host in the 1930s), these news organizations fomented an insurrection by repeating and fallaciously substantiating Trump's lie that the 2020 election was rigged. (*Fox News*, *Newsmax*, and *One America Network* echoed Trump's lies that Dominion voting machines were rigged, a fact for which they were all sued by Dominion Voting Systems; see Pruitt-Young 2021. They also repeated Trump's debunked lies about election officials stuffing ballots which led to those official's lives being threatened; see Szep and So 2021. And it is well established that these lies about election fraud are what caused the January 6th insurrection; see Inskeep 2021.)

But this consideration of how fascists use the media brings us back around to Stormfront (who, recall, used the media expertly to manipulate the public), and the realization that the way *The Boys* merely establish Stormfront as a Nazi, and thus that HoVo is fascistic, further strengthens the analogy that MAGA Trumpism is fascistic.

Strengthening the Analogy: Further Similarities with Stormfront

In the last section, we saw how the things HoVo has in common with the MAGA movement are relevant to our conclusion because they are *things fascists do* because *they are fascists*. This helped establish the first two premises. The third premise – that HoVO is fascist – was established, in the section before that, by simply demonstrating that Stormfront is a Nazi who utilizes fascist tactics, and pointing out that HoVo embraced both her and them. But it turns out that the evidence for the third premise can also further support the analogy because all the tactics that Stormfront uses *because she is a fascist* are also tactics used by the MAGA movement.

Memes and Misinformation

Consider again the memes that Stormfront has Logan (her "meme-queen") spread online, in the wake of the blowback about the fact that Homelander killed innocent civilians when he was killing a super-terrorist overseas. "When you see it on your Uncle's Facebook page, you know it's working" (S2E5). The "Better There, Than Here" meme, which implies that having Homelander destroying terrorists "there" (overseas in foreign countries) is better than them attacking us here, mirrors GOP talking points during the war on terror. As President Gerpge W. Bush put it, "Our strategy is this: We will fight them over there so we do not have to face them in the United States of America" (White House Archives 2007). Another, which has a picture of Victoria Neuman (the "liberal" congressperson trying to hold Vought accountable) under the caption "Superheroes invade my personal space," mirrors memes spread by the right which try to belittle congressperson Alexandria Ocasio-Cortez (AOC) (Vo 2019). Of course, Stormfront says she will have Logan "punch up the fear," and indeed many real-world memes about AOC paint her as someone who is destroying the country (again, see Vo 2019).

Another of Stormfront's memes has "Photoshopped! FAKE" over a picture of the dead civilians Homelander killed, with a meaningless circle around one of their bodies. This mirrors real-world right-wing memes which try to discredit accurate depictions of real-world events that are inconvenient to their cause and, in fact, parrots an entire movement on the right to deny the negative consequences of GOP actions and policies. Think of how, after it was clear that Republican inaction on gun regulation led to the Sandy Hook school shooting, conspiracies theories which suggested the shooting didn't even happen, were rampant (and included similar memes; see Arkin and Popken 2018, and Walker 2018). When fascistic policies and (in)actions lead to bad consequences, the fact that the consequences happened must be denied.

Deep Fakes and Fake News

Also consider how Stormfront uses claims that the real photos of her as a Nazi are "deep fakes." Deep fakes are a real thing, where someone uses a computer to generate fake images or videos that seem real (like of a president saying something they didn't say) for political purposes. But Stormfront is reappropriating the term to apply to something she knows is true, as a way to dismiss it.

This is almost exactly like how Trump reappropriated the term "fake news." Fake news is a real thing, and the proliferation of false news stories was a real problem during the 2016 presidential election cycle; most prominently, Russian outlets were producing and circulating false news stories, intended to favor Trump's election efforts, on Facebook and Twitter (Mayer 2018). These were initially easily dismissed because they could be identified with the phrase "Fake News." But then Trump appropriated the term to apply to true news stories that didn't favor him and the news outlets that reported them. ("You say that story (which favors me) is fake news? The real fake news is CNN!") This made the term lose all meaning; its rhetorical effect was lost and the general populace had a hard time determining what was true and false (Borchers 2017). (This is related to "sematic infiltration," the practice of redefining words in a way that favors your position and forcing your opponent to adopt those definitions, like those who oppose abortion forced their opponents to describe them as being "pro-life," even though the oppose programs to keep children alive after birth; see Khosla 2022.)

What's more, when Trump labels major news outlets that report true stories that are unfavorable to him as "fake news," he is mirroring almost exactly Hitler's use of the word "Lügenpresse" (lying press), which Hitler used as a way to discredit news organizations that reported true stories unfavorable to the Nazi party. Indeed, just like Trump and his use of "fake news," Lügenpresse was a phrase that Hitler didn't invent but adapted for his own uses. And it's a phrase that's been used by Trump supporters, at his rallies, as far back as when he was running for president in 2016 (Noack 2016). Granted, all presidents have criticized the press to some degree; but Trump's criticism is exponentially greater.

This is important because, according to Fintan O'Toole, "a propaganda machine so effective that it creates for its followers a universe of 'alternative facts' impervious to unwanted realities" is a central feature of fascism (O'Toole 2018). And he's not the first to make this kind of observation. Political philosopher Hannah Arendt (1951) said something very similar in her book, *The Origins of Totalitarianism*.

> A totalitarian movement [and its] disregard for facts, its strict adherence to the rules of a fictitious world, becomes steadily more difficult to maintain, yet remains as essential as it was before. Power means a direct confrontation with reality, and totalitarianism in power is constantly concerned with overcoming this challenge. Propaganda and organization no longer suffice to assert that the impossible is possible, that the incredible is true, that an insane consistency rules the world; the chief psycho logical support of totalitarian fiction-the active resentment of the status quo, which the masses refused to accept as the only possible world-is no longer there; every bit of factual information that leaks through the iron curtain, set up against the ever-threatening flood of reality from the other, nontotalitarian side, is a greater menace to totalitarian domination than counterpropaganda has been to totalitarian movements. (pp. 391–392)

Granted, she was describing both Hitler *and Stalin* (and their totalitarianism) – and Stalin wasn't a fascist. But totalitarianism is undeniably a necessary component of fascism and thus, by proxy, so is creating an "alternative universe." (As we shall see later, this mirrors "unreality," a component of fascism that Jason Stanely (2018) thinks is essential to fascism.) And labeling, as "fake" (untrue/unreliable), news organizations that disrupt that universe by reporting facts, and calling them the "enemy of the people" (as Trump has put it), is pivotal to that effort. After all, fascism always has at its center a cult of personality, and it is often said that one of the defining features of cult leaders is their claim that "everyone else is lying to you; only I tell you the truth." Or as Arendt put it, there is "one man who has monopolized ... knowledge and whose principal quality is that he 'was always right and will always be right'" (p. 383).

Denying Reality and Gaslighting

Stormfront's fascist tactic of asking people to deny what they can see is objectively true with their own eyes (like pictures of her with Nazis) was not only copied from Orwell's *1984*. "The party told you to reject the evidence of your eyes and ears. It was their final, most essential command" (Orwell 1949, p. 103). It also reflected how Trump insisted that his 2017 inauguration crowd was the biggest in history, despite clear verifiable pictures and objective evidence to the contrary (Johnson 2017). It was a claim that we all could see with our own eyes was false, and yet his administration insisted, over and over again, that we accept the "alternative fact" that it was true (BBC News 2017).

Or think of how, in his May 2023 CNN interview, Trump denied that he told the Georgia Secretary of State Brad Raffensperger to find him enough votes to win the election. "I didn't ask him to find anything," Trump said in the interview. "I said, you owe me votes because the election was rigged" (CNN 2023). But everyone heard the tape; you can look online and find it in about 5 seconds (PBS NewsHour 2023). In the context of trying to spur Raffensperger to action, he clearly says "I just want to *find* 11,780 votes, which is one more than we have, because we won the state"(Amy 2021). While it is true that every politician occasionally says false things, and some presidents have told some whoppers (Reagan said he personally filmed a Nazi death camp while serving in Germany in WWII, when in fact he never left the states during the war; see Sheerin 2021), not only does Trump blatantly and knowingly lie more than any other president in history (Kessler et al. 2021), in fascistic fashion, he expects you to trust his word over the evidence of your own eyes and ears. This is fascistic gaslighting, and Trump has been guilty of it over (Sarkis 2018), and over (Eltis 2020), and over (DiMaggio 2021) again.

As Trump told those attending the Veterans of Foreign Wars National Convention last year: "Just remember: What you're seeing and what you're reading is not what's happening."

The Big Lie and Projection

Or consider again the Nazi tactic of promoting the Big Lie – a lie so big that people can't believe that anyone would have the audacity to tell it, and so thus believe it to be true. Appropriately, the phrase "the big lie" was used to describe Trump's lie that the 2020 election was "rigged." And it fits the definition perfectly. Even after Trump's claims of election fraud where debunked over and over, both by reliable fact checkers (Eggers et al. 2021) and by the courts themselves (Reuters Staff 2021), Trump continued (even to the day of this writing) to insist that he won the 2020 election. And the MAGA base believes him. To, again, quote Hitler on The Big Lie tactic: the "primitive simplicity of their minds" can't fathom that Trump would have the "impudence to distort the truth so infamously. Even though the facts which prove this to be so may be brought clearly to their minds, they will still doubt and waver and will continue to think that there may be some other explanation."

The Big Lie also brings us to another fascist tendency: projection. Projection (in the political arena) is when you claim that your political opponents are guilty of the very evils that, instead, you are guilty of. When Hitler's director of propaganda, Joseph Goebbels, said, "When one lies, one should lie big, and stick to it. They keep up their lies, even at the risk of looking ridiculous," he thought he was describing Churchill – but he was actually describing himself. Of course, Hitler and Goebbels never admitted that telling big lies was their own tactic. But what they were doing is projecting. And Michelle Goldberg (2020) has described Trump as a "Master of Projection"; and others have noted that projection is a key political tactic that Trump employs (Bell and Senecal n.d. and Kakutani 2018).

We can see this in Trump's Big Lie itself. He claims that Democrats were engaged in election fraud and tried to steal the 2020 election. In reality, the vast majority (nearly all) of cases of election fraud in the 2020 presidential election were committed by Republicans (Norton 2022). What's more, it was Trump himself that tried to steal the election, with a plot that involved fraudulent slates of electors and trying to convince Vice President Mike Pence to declare the election invalid (Kilgore 2022). (The indictment filed against Trump by the department of justice on August 1, 2023 lays out, even more clearly, the evidence that all this took place.) And when that failed, it was Trump's supporters (prodded by the President himself) who tried to foment an insurrection, at the capitol, live on television.

Of course, the examples of MAGA projection don't end there. MAGA Republicans claim that it is Democratic "tax and spend" policies that are responsible for the federal debt and deficit, when in fact it is Republican tax cuts for the rich (including the 2017 Trump tax cuts) that is the largest contributor (Kogan 2023). Republicans will claim that Democrats are the party of big government that wants to interfere with people's freedom, while at the same time advocating for governmental restrictions to the right to access medical care (like abortion and gender affirming care), the right to vote, the right for adults to marry other adults whom they love, the right to dress in drag – they have even passed laws that restrict the rights of blue cities to govern themselves in red states (Gurley 2023). And let us not forget how MAGA Republicans complain about the "bias" in "mainstream" media, when it is their news channel of choice (Fox News) that is (a) the most mainstream (in that it has the higher viewership by far; see Fox News Press Releases 2023), and (b) the most biased (Ralph and Relman 2018). Indeed, the only channels more politically biased are *Newsmax* and *One America Network*, which are even further to the right.

And literally, as if the world knew this chapter needed another example of MAGA projection, the day this chapter was submitted for publication, Trump vowed to (if reelected) to weaponize the federal government by "appoint[ing] a real special prosecutor to go after the most corrupt president in the history of the United States of America, Joe Biden, and the entire Biden crime family" (Swan et al. 2023); to boot, his top republican strategists (Jeffrey Clark and Russell Vought) are concocting a "legal" justification (it would not actually be legal) for him to do just that (ibid). (I won't bother to point out the irony of Russell's last name, or that there is no real evidence that the Biden is a "crime family".) But 8 days prior to this, in the wake of Republican congressional investigations into Biden "weaponizing the federal government" (which itself is a weaponization of the federal government; Schapitl and Grisales 2023), Trump and his allies (including Clark and Vought) were accusing Biden of doing just that – claiming that Trump's indictment for mishandling top-secret documents was a "witch hunt," a "political hit job," the result of Biden "weaponizing" the Department of Justice (DOJ) against him (Wong et al. 2023).

Now, it's quite clear this is not the case. Trump's own former Attorney General (Willian Barr) said the evidence laid out in Trump's indictment is "very, very damning" and that the "idea of presenting Trump as a victim here – a victim of a witch hunt – is ridiculous" (Bredemeier 2023); Biden has clearly stuck with the centuries long precedent of maintaining a separation and independence between the DOJ and the Office of the President. There is no evidence that the DOJ was directed, at all, by president Biden to investigate Trump. They are investigating him because there is very good evidence he committed crimes (including evidence we all saw, live on TV). Now, it's not surprising that Trump is insisting otherwise. In the 1940s, when the American-Nazi organization The Christian Front actively and openly tried to overthrow the American government, they called their prosecution a "witch-hunt," a politically motivated hit job, despite the fact that the evidence against them was open and shut (Maddow 2022a). (Overthrowing the government was their organization's stated goal!) That is what fascist criminals do when they are caught red handed; they yell "witch hunt" and insist that they didn't do the very things everyone saw them do.

But it's step further for Trump and his allies to falsely accuse his political opponent of weaponing the federal government against him and then, days later, to vow to weaponize the federal government against thier political opponent. One would be hard pressed to find a better, classic, textbook example of projection. "I am openly admitting that I would do the very thing I am (falsely) accusing you of doing."

Fear Mongering and Drab Colored Shirts

Trump also fearmongers like Stormfront and fascists. Recall, what's indicative about fascistic fearmongering is how it is based in lies. The fascist will say their opponent plans to do things they don't plan to do or will exaggerate without evidence the effects of what the opponent plans to accomplish. These exaggerated fears often revolve around immigrants or other minority groups and claim that they are putting the very existence of the nation at risk (when, in fact, it is the fascists themselves that threaten the existence of the nation). According to Hitler, the Jews were plotting the downfall of Germany (when, in fact, his own actions threatened its existence). For Stormfront, it was super-terrorists (when, in fact, they had created the super-terrorists). And for Trump and his MAGA acolytes, it is Muslims, Latin Immigrants, and "the woke mob" that are going to lead to the downfall of America (when, in reality, it is they and their policies that pose the most significant threat to the continued existence of American democracy by undermining democratic policies and restructuring government to give themselves exclusive power; see Harris and Cottle 2022 and Wright 2020).

Think of that AI generated ad, put out by the Republican Party in 2023, which imagines what will happen if Biden wins again in 2024 (Thompson 2023). China will invade Taiwan, the economy and banks will collapse, the border will be overrun by 80,000 illegals in one day, and the city of San Francisco "closes" (whatever that means) because of "escalating crime and [a] fentanyl crisis." Of course, this is ridiculous. And the paranoid Republican predictions about what will happen under Democratic presidents have been notoriously wrong. In 2008, the right wing of the Republican party was saying that, if elected, Obama would never leave office and start WWIII; the mainstream was saying that his election would lead to economic collapse and the repeal of the Second Amendment. Obamacare was going to lead to "death panels." To try to keep him from being reelected in 2012, Newt Gingrich said Obama would wage war on the Catholic church the morning after the election. Mitt Romney predicted that Americans wouldn't be able to find jobs, and that Iran would get a nuclear weapon. Rick Santorum said America would no longer be the land of "free enterprise" and Michelle Bachmann that there will be "no future" (Monde 2012). Of course, the exact opposite of all those things happened. (Even the latter vague statements about the no "free enterprise" and "no future" were refuted by the economy growing in every year of Obama's presidency; see Jones 2020.) But the point is this: these are classic examples of fascistic overexaggerated fears about the survival of the nation, by those who actually are threatening the survival of the nation.

These fears also tend to revolve around minorities and immigrants. Think of how Fox News consistently vilifies immigrants. For example, for an entire week in May of 2023, Fox News ran a false story about immigrants stealing hotel rooms from veterans, without ever bothering to fact check it – and then only offered a few seconds worth of retractions once it learned the truth. Or consider how Trump, while campaigning as president in 2016, stoked fears about immigrants – saying that they are rapists, and exaggerating reports of "migrant caravans"(Ball 2016). As president, he banned travel from some "Muslim" countries because of fear of Muslim terrorism (when, in fact, domestic terrorism by white supremacists is far more frequent; see Jones et al. 2020). And while campaigning in 2020, he stoked fears about Black Lives Matter and efforts to defund the police, saying that the suburbs would be crime ridden in Biden's America. "No one will be safe" (Watson 2020).

Fascists do this partly to rile up paramilitary groups (civilian groups that act like military forces) to do their bidding. Mussolini had the "blackshirts," and it was with their help that he took control of the Italian government in 1919 (CRF 2010). Hitler had his "brownshirts" terrorize his political opponents, provide security at his rallies, and patrol Jewish neighborhoods (Land 2021). In the Unites States before WWII, William Dudley Pelley – who thought that "the time ha[d] come for an American Hitler" – created the Silver Shirts to try to make that person him (see History is Now Magazine 2020, Harty 2016, Toy 1989). And although they don't have a "colored shirt" as part of their uniform, Trump has the Oath Keepers and The Proud Boys (the latter of which he expressly told to "stand back and stand by" before the 2020 election; see Ronayne and Kunzelman 2020) – two American paramilitary groups that are loyal to Trump, members of which have harassed Trump's political opponents, and been found guilty of sedition because of the planning and execution role they played in the January 6th attacks (see DOJ 2023a, b). (It is also worth mentioning the similarity between the colored shirts of fascism, and the red MAGA hats of MAGA Trumpism.)

So these are all things that strengthen *The Boys*' analogy. But does anything weaken it?

Weakening the Analogy

The main ways to object to arguments from analogy is to (a) point out relevant dissimilarities between the things being compared and/or (b) argue that the similarities between the things being compared aren't actually relevant. Let's attempt to do those two things with the argument *The Boys* has presented.

The Historical Dissimilarity Objection

One obvious dissimilarity between what is undeniably fascism (the political movements of Mussolini and Hitler in Italy and Germany after WWI), and MAGA Trump Republicanism, is their location and place in history. According to Boston University associate professor of history Jonathan Zatlin, "fascism was a historical phenomenon," a reaction to a particular set of circumstances that were unique to the aftermath of WWI, like the "collapse of multiethnic empires, economic crises" and "a four-year-long war that killed millions and traumatized a whole generation of young people who found it hard to be integrated back into society and work 9-to-5 jobs, then later experienced mass unemployment and a Depression lasting years" (Barlow 2022). He points out that it was this, "plus weak democratic traditions [that] led many Europeans to conclude that democracy brought crisis and poverty, and that only authoritarian regimes could ensure prosperity and stability" (Barlow 2022). (It's worth noting that Paul Gottfried (2016) takes a similar stance in his book *Fascism: The Career of a Concept*.) Since this does not describe our current historical situation, by definition, Trump and the MAGA movement cannot be described as fascistic. Or so the argument goes.

In my estimation, however, thinking of fascism as a purely historical phenomena – in such a way that you identify it with the historical circumstances that originally gave rise to it – commits a kind of category mistake (i.e., it places fascism in the wrong kind of category, or identifies it at the wrong kind of thing). The circumstances that originally gave rise to fascism are not fascism itself. Yes, fascism originally arose as a reaction to the critical state of the world after WWI; but that doesn't mean other later critical historical circumstances can't generate the same kind of response. Fascism is an ideology, or way of doing politics; granted, it usually arises in times of crisis, but the same ideology and way of doing politics can arise as a response to different kinds of crises. (By Gottfried's definition, not even the Nazis fall under the umbrella of what he calls "generic fascism," because he sees generic fascism as fundamentally Catholic and thinks it must endorse a corporate state.) The democracies in the United States and France arose in different historical circumstances; but that doesn't mean that the systems of government that govern both countries aren't both democracies.

Now, there are also historical dissimilarities regarding how Trump rose to power. Mussolini marched on Rome and used political intimidation to get politicians to resign and then the King to appoint him as prime minister (Putt 2022). Hitler tried something similar and failed – only to later be appointed as chancellor, and then (essentially) declare himself president when the existing German president (Hindenburg, who had appointed him chancellor) died. (More accurately, Hitler just used the power that had been granted him to "combine" the offices of chancellor and president; see Holocaust Encyclopedia (d) (n.d.).) What's more, both Mussolini and Hitler created their own, new, political party. Trump, on the other hand, rose to power by winning the 2016 election, and did so on the ticket of an already existing political party.

But, again, it's not clear that these dissimilarities are relevant. First, it's not clear that Trump didn't create a new party; he just did so by taking over an old one. Second, and more importantly, how a person rises to power is not nearly as important (to the question of whether they are fascist) as what they do once they get there. Notice that no one thinks Hitler wasn't a fascist because he didn't rise to power in exactly the same way Mussolini did. And no one would think Hitler was any less of a fascist had he been elected, rather than appointed. What's more, modern fascism seems to use a different tactic to stay in power. After WWI, democracy was seen as unstable and harmful; so Hitler and Mussolini circumventing democratic norms was seen by their followers as a feature, not a bug. After WWII, and people saw what fascism did, democracy was seen as essential. So if a fascist is to have and retain their power today, they have to appear to have won elections. Vladimir Putin, who most would agree is fascistic, has won multiple elections in Russia – but they are very obviously not fair elections (The Economist 2021). So the mere fact that someone has won an election is not a reason to say that they are not a fascist. What's more, this also demonstrates that a prime way fascists gain and retain power, in the modern day, is by making elections unfair. And Trump and MAGA republicans have definitely made efforts to do just that. Numerous laws to restrict voting rights have been passed in red states, and under the guise of (false) claims of unfair elections, in 2022, a wave of Trump supporting MAGA republicans ran to oversee elections across the country (Parks 2022). After all, the January 6th insurrection was not unlike Hitler's failed "Beer Hall" insurrection (Gumpert 2022).

Before moving on, it is worth noting that historical dis-similarities are relevant to whether or not fascists will rise to power in 2020s America as they did in 1930s Germany. The Weimar Republic (the democratic government that formed in Germany after WWI) was new and fragile; it was the first time Germany had been ruled by that kind of government (Facing History and Ourselves 2016). What's more, the judges in its court system were very right-leaning and biased towards the fascist cause – so much so that they almost always executed leftist murders, but would let off right-wing murders if they said their acts were "patriotic" (Holocaust Encyclopedia (e) (n.d.)). The judges in Hitler's trial (after his Beer Hall insurrection) essentially let him make it a platform (Linder n.d.). While the United States certainly has its problems, its democracy is not as fragile, and its judicial system is not *that* biased. That's not to say it couldn't get that bad. The important point, however, is that saying that MAGA Trumpism is a fascist movement is not the same as saying that the Unites States is just as likely to succumb to fascism. But even if it's not, *The Boys'* argument still stands.

The "It's Not *That* Bad" Objection

Another dissimilarity between original fascism and Trump's MAGA movement is how bad it has gotten. Yes, Trump had draconian immigration policies that separated children from their families. But he didn't kill 6 million Jews. Yes, Trump has delusions of grandeur; but he is not advocating for a 1000-year Reich. I mean, it's not like we were living under a fascist government while Trump was in office, from 2016 to 2020. And so, the argument goes, suggesting that Trump (and his followers) are fascists lacks a proportional perspective.

But arguing that Trump is a fascist (or that his followers are) is not the same thing as arguing that Trump is currently as morally bad as Hitler (or that his followers are as morally bad as Nazis). Mussolini wasn't as bad as Hitler either – but that doesn't mean he wasn't a fascist. Again, fascism is an ideology and way of doing politics; it's not a list of moral atrocities. Early in their careers, Hitler and Mussolini did very little damage. Before they had power, they had basically done none. But they were still fascists, at that time. Neo-Nazis after WWII were able to accomplish very little in the United States because of the stigma associated with Nazism; even though it was legal, they usually wouldn't even dare fly a swastika flag. But that doesn't mean they weren't fascists. No one who has claimed that Trump is a fascist (and that MAGA Trumpism is fascism) is claiming that Trump and his followers have committed atrocities equivalent to what Hitler and the Nazis did during WWII. The worry is that Trump in 2023 is like Hitler in 1923: a political figure that embraces the ideology and political tactics of fascism who, depending on how we react to him, could lead to morally horrendous results.

The "Not-Unique" Objection

This objection points out that everything we have considered so far – the similarities between, for example, Nazism and Trumpism – are not unique to fascism. Fascists aren't the only ones in favor of the militarization and glorification of police. They aren't the only ones who promote conspiracy theories and demand loyalty. Many political movements, beyond fascism, are in bed with religion and use misinformation and propaganda to deny reality and fearmonger. You get the idea. None of the similarities we have mentioned are individually sufficient to label something as fascism.

The answer here, however, is to realize that, simply put, fascism isn't like triangles. What do I mean by that? In the first chapter of this handbook (▶ Chap. 2, "Twilight Zone as Philosophy 101"), Mimi Marinucci points out that some things (like philosophy) can't be defined in terms of necessary and sufficient conditions. Some things, like triangles, can; any two-dimensional object with three angles and three adjoining sides is a triangle; anything that doesn't have these properties is not. But other things are not like this. The most famous example is Ludwig Wittgenstein's: games. There is no one thing, aspect, or property that all games have in common; but we recognize something as a game because of what he calls "family resemblance" (Wittgenstein 1953, section 66). Games share a collection of traits, and while no one game has them all, and no one trait is universal to all games, and some things can have game-like traits without being games, we recognize a game when we see it because we can see that it belongs in the "family" of such things that has generally has certain kinds of properties.

And so, the argument goes, while no single property of MAGA Trumpism makes it fascism, and no single trait it has is sufficient to make it fascism, and some things have some of those properties without being fascism, when you consider the preponderance of traits that MAGA Trumpism has in common with classic fascist movements, it's clear that they all belong to the same family. To belabor the analogy a bit: maybe Trumpism is the child of Italian and German fascism. Or, more likely, the American pro-Hitler "America First" fascism of the 1930s was the cousin of Italian and German fascism; the children of that cousin are today's American neo-Nazis and White Christian Nationalists; and Trump is the weird uncle that adopted those children (he even adopted their "American First" slogan) as a way to gain power. However you envision it, the point remains: the family resemblance is clear and justifies the conclusion that MAGA Trumpism is a kind of fascism.

Truth be told, however, the only way to really establish that family resemblance is to list the common features of fascism and see how many of those features MAGA Trumpism has. Something that complicates this approach is the fact that there is a lot of research about what fascism is, and so there are many different lists of what fascists tend to do. But we can deal with this by compiling some of the most popular lists and seeing how many boxes Trumpism checks.

What Makes Fascism, Fascism?

There is no shortage of academic work on the topic of what makes fascism, fascism, and correspondingly no shortage of bullet pointed lists of what fascism's essential elements are. There is Chris Hedges' (2006) book *American Fascists: The Christian Right and the War on America*, which differentiates between historical (1920–1930s Italian and German) fascism, and what he calls "Eternal Fascism" (the political ideology and approach of historical fascism that can be repeated by other movements), and lists 14 characteristics of Eternal Fascism. Dunwoody et al. (2022) lays out four components, and in *How Fascism Works: The Politics of Us* Versus *Them*, philosopher Jason Stanley (2018) defines fascism primarily by how it approaches politics, and argues that it generally employs ten tactics. Georgetown University history professor John McNeill (2016) says fascism has 11 components. Such lists usually have some unique elements, but also have a lot of overlap. If we were to combine and paraphrase them, we would get something like this:

1. **Inaccurate Nostalgia**: Fascism mythologizes the greatness of the past and promises a return to the days of traditional racial and gender hierarchies that favored the in-group (usually, but not only, white Christian males; it is possible for non-whites to be fascists).
2. **Authoritarian/Hero Worship/Leader Cult**: It embraces a cult like worship of a single leader, who is the final arbiter of what is good and evil, and thus can do no wrong. Followers of the leader see themselves as heroes as well, called to defend (and even die) for the leader's cause, and think that everyone should submit to the leader's authority.
3. **Theatricality**: Party leaders are verbose, with lots of big gestures and exaggerated facial expressions. Rallies become rituals for loyalists, with lots of slogans, catch phrases, and party paraphernalia. Military parades, and parades of the faithful, are common.

4. **Deceptive Propaganda/Newspeak**: Fascism uses propaganda that is not only un-factual, but uses universally accepted ideals such as freedom, free speech, and public safety as a way to gain power, and even undermine those very ideals. The term "Newspeak" comes from Orwell's *1984* and is a practice (related to semantic infiltration) that seeks to redefine language in a way that curtails critical thought and obscures bad things as good.

5. **Unreality**: It creates an alternate universe of nonfacts that not only fails to match the way the world is but conceptualizes every issue as a "us vs. them" contest and sees its leader as the protector of truth, even as that leader tells blatant and obvious lies.

6. **Anti-intellectual**: Since respect for science, history, education, and expertise make it harder to spread lies, fascism must oppose those things.

7. **Racism/Inequality**: Fascism fears difference, especially racial differences, and can't tolerate diversity. It doesn't see all people as created equal but instead suggests that there are natural hierarchies that members of the party (usually white, Christian, men) sit atop of.

8. **Victimhood/Oppositional Identity**: Fascism portrays the members of the party as victims of (social/economic/political) oppression (usually at the hands of other races) when, in fact, they are doing the oppressing. Ironically, it also despises the weak and defines group identity in terms of rejecting "the weak" and "the other."

9. **Law and Order**: It professes to be the party of "law and order," when in fact party members (and leaders) blatantly engage in criminal behavior. Their supposed goal to be "tough on crime" is usually an excuse to persecute their political and social enemies – and to infiltrate the police and military as a means to do so.

10. **Hyper Militaristic**: It is obsessed with the military, loyalty and reverence to the military, and takes efforts to ensure that the military is saturated with loyal party members.

11. **Sexual Purity/False Accusations**: Fascism plays on sexual anxieties by condemning any kind of sexual activity that violates proscribed norms (including chastity among men and sex outside of marriage in women) and (without evidence) accuses members of the "out-group" of participating in sexual activity that is not only outside those norms (e.g., homosexuality) but is violent and against the women (and children) of the in-group.

12. **Pro-masculine/Anti-feminine**: It idolizes masculinity (and sees critical reflection as emasculating) and neglects giving women equal rights. Consequently, it decries anything (including media) that might be seen as arguing for women's rights.

13. **Fetishization of Youth**: It extolls the virtue of youth and tries to appeal to younger crowds.

14. **Anti-urban**: It demonizes large cities, and the people who live there, and casts them as one of the main causes of society's ills.

15. **Selective About Benefits**: It portrays members of the in-group as hard working and deserving of the state's benefits, while depicting members of the outgroup as lazy and undeserving.

16. **Black and White Thinking**: It cannot tolerate nuanced distinctions and not only sees everything as black and white but thinks the truth of all such matters has already been revealed; it therefore considers disagreement to be heresy or treason.
17. **Hyper Nationalism**: It views one's identity as a member of a nation state as centrally important.
18. **Conspiratorial Thinking**: Fascism is obsessed with (imaginary) conspiratorial plots aimed at taking the nation state down. Paradoxically, its followers believe their enemies have untold wealth and power but also that their enemies will be easily overcome.
19. **Violent**: Fascists see life as a struggle and mix violence with political action (and yet, paradoxically, believe that, once they have power, they will bring about a time of peace).
20. **Purges the Disloyal**: There is a hierarchical party structure, and anyone who is not loyal enough (or who might replace the leader) is ousted.
21. **Mass Mobilization**: Fascism rises to power on a mass political wave that creates a new political party.

In line with the family resemblance analogy, McNeill (2016) argues that none of the attributes are universal or essential to fascism, and that, in fact, adherence to each one comes in degrees. McNeill suggests a 1–4 ranking for each of his criteria and argues that while Trumpism has a score of 0 for "fetishization of the youth," it scores 4 out of 4 for things like "fetishization of masculinity," "leader cult," and "lost golden-age syndrome." His total score for how fascistic the MAGA movement is, is 26 out of a possible 44 (60%) – but that was when his article was published, before Trump's election, in 2016 (McNeill 2016). In 2019, he said that he would rank him higher (Guyette 2019), and one wonders how high he would go after Trump's January 6th insurrection (in 2021) and Trump's response to his multiple federal indictments.

Indeed, given what we have already discussed, we can see most of these elements exemplified, to a high degree, in MAGA Trumpism. "MAGA" itself expresses a longing to return to the past: Make America Great Again. MAGA is notorious for decrying science and academics, and certainly sees everything as black and white. ("There is only male and female: asexuality is not a thing." In reality, it comes in many forms and could be as common as 1.7% of the population, although some argue for lower numbers; see Sax 2002.) Relatedly, it denies women rights and is obsessed with sexual matters (abstinence-only sexual education, abortion, sexual purity, etc.). It is certainly nationalistic, invokes conspiracy theories, and thrives on a sense of victimization. It invokes racism and anti-immigrant sentiment, and is no fan of diversity (literally outlawing diversity and equality efforts). Trump is the arbiter of the common good – his cause is the people's cause – and MAGA definitely engages in language that discourages real critical thinking. Dunwoody et al. (2022) even shows experimentally that modern "Republicans generally score higher than Democrats on the[ir] model (of fascism's) components" (p. 1).

Stanley (2018) points to something that we have not yet discussed: how MAGA Trumpism uses the trappings of free speech to solidify their power and also undermine it. In their mind, Trump loyalists have the right to say what they want, but in the name of free speech, you are not free to contradict them. Objections to what they say are seen as violations of their free speech. (For how this argument confuses freedom of speech with freedom from criticism, see ▶ Chap. 28, "*South Park* as Philosophy: Blasphemy, Mockery, and (Absolute?) Freedom of Speech," in this volume.)

What we learn from all this is not only that MAGA Trumpism checks many of the boxes it would need to check in order to rightly be called fascist, but also that – while *The Boys'* argument that the MAGA movement is fascist is strong, it could be even stronger. There are plenty of typically fascist traits that Trumpism has that *The Boys* has not yet depicted HoVo having – like, for example, anti-intellectualism. *The Boys* could capitalize on these, or perhaps have HoVo do even more things that both the Nazis of the 1930s, and the MAGAs of the 2020s are doing – like pass laws that ban the political party of their opposition (Durkee 2023).

Or maybe, HoVo could start encouraging white people to have supe babies. Few know that Hitler had a program to encourage white German women to stay home and have children. In 1933, if a newly married (Aryan) couple could prove that the wife left her job, they would get a 1000 mark loan – and they would get 250 marks in loan forgiveness for every child they had. "In this way, the program encouraged healthy 'Aryan' couples to have more children and reinforced what the Nazis believed was the proper role of women in society" (Facing History and Ourselves 2020). In 2023, in Texas, where the percentage of white homeowners is not only disproportionately high but much higher than the national average (Ura and McCullough. 2015), a law was passed which would make heterosexual couples with ten (ten!) or more kids exempt from property taxes (which means only homeowners, which again are predominately white, will benefit; see Bess 2023b). Granted, this is not as extreme as the SS's Lebensborn program (see Holocaust Encyclopedia (c) (n.d.)) and the GOP is not yet (like Hitler) awarding medals to Aryan women who have up to eight children (GHDI n.d.). But laws encouraging white women to have children aligns perfectly with "great replacement theory" and "white genocide," two victimization narratives very common today in white-supremacist and neo-Nazi circles (see Wilson and Flanagan 2022).

Conclusion

In the end, this is a semantic issue. *The Boys* is arguing that a word (in this case, "fascist") can be properly used in a particular way (in this case, to describe the modern MAGA movement). Generally, semantic debates are a bit boring and inconsequential. But not in this case. Because almost everyone (even the average Trump supporter) so universally recognizes fascism as a bad thing, realizing that the word applies to the MAGA movement should be a reason to abandon it. It's either that or start thinking that maybe fascism isn't so bad (which, sadly it seems, far too many people are willing to do).

But in the end, perhaps whether the answer to the question is, in the strictest sense, "yes" or "no," doesn't really matter. Whatever it is (whatever single word best describes it), MAGA Trumpism is too close to fascism for comfort. (It's so close that self-proclaimed neo-Nazis, white-supremacists, and even David Duke, the former grand wizard of the KKK, are among Trump's most enthusiastic supporters.) The fact that we even have to ask the question, and ponder its answer, is far too concerning. As Journalist Medhi Hasan put it (in Guyette 2019),

> You don't have to believe he's a literal reincarnation of fascist dictators to recognize that he is taking us down a very dark, ultra-authoritarian and violent path . . . . Some of you may not want to call it fascism, but whatever you call it, make sure you stand up against it.

Or as Irish Journalist Fintan O'Toole (2018) put it,

> [W]e are in a phase of trial runs . . . and what is being trialed is fascism – a word that should be used carefully but not shirked when it is so clearly on the horizon. Forget "post-fascist" – what we are living with is pre-fascism. It is easy to dismiss Donald Trump as an ignoramus, not least because he is. But he has an acute understanding of one thing: test marketing. He created himself in the gossip pages of the New York tabloids, where celebrity is manufactured by planting outrageous stories that you can later confirm or deny depending on how they go down. And he recreated himself in reality TV where the storylines can be adjusted according to the ratings. Put something out there, pull it back, adjust, go again. Fascism doesn't arise suddenly in an existing democracy. It is not easy to get people to give up their ideas of freedom and civility. You have to do trial runs that, if they are done well, serve two purposes. They get people used to something they may initially recoil from; and they allow you to refine and calibrate. This is what is happening now and we would be fools not to see it.

In all honesty, there has been more than a touch of fascism in the United States since fascism was conceived of in Italy. Sympathy for Hitler and his cause among Americans is what kept us out of WWII before Pearl Harbor. That's what gave the fascist anti-sematic Fr. Coughlin's 1930s radio show an audience of 30 million (when the US population was only 123 million; see PBS n.d.). That is why efforts to fight against fascists were resisted (by the police no less) before the war, and what made our judicial system unable to prosecute the fascists that actively tried to overthrow the government in 1944 (Maddow 2022a). And that's why, when John Rogge investigated fascist activity during the war, he positively identified 24 *Congressmen* that were actively collaborating with the German Nazi government during the war. And that's also why reading this paper is the first time you heard about any of that. (Attorney General Tom Clark and President Truman decided to bury the report, instead of making it public as they had promised, because they saw it as too explosive; see Maddow 2022b, Meet the Press 1946.)

So, Trump did not give rise to fascism in America. He merely gave it a voice and legitimized it. (This is why hate crimes have been rising since his election and are more common in towns after his rallies; see Edwards and Rushin 2018, Feinberg et al. 2019.) Fascism was already here. That's why *The Boys* is so right to point it out and criticize it; and that's undoubtedly why so many fans of the show failed to recognize that the clearly fascistic supes in the show, like Homelander, were actually the villains. Like Stormfront said, "People love what I have to say. They believe in it. They just don't like the word 'Nazi,' that's all." Unfortunately, she seems to be right. For them, the fascistic supes were the heroes. And, like fascists tend to do, they see themselves as "the real heroes." And that should worry us all. In case it needs to be said, and for all the reasons stated in this chapter, people ought not be sympathetic with fascistic ideals. The world would be a better place if they weren't.

End Notes

1. This is not to say that every supe who stays loyal to Homelander, like A-Train, is a fascist. Some have their own motivations, like survival. And other members of Vought International, like its president Stan Edgar, are just capitalistic pragmatists. The "Vo" in "HoVo" here refers to the Vought International as a company, just like the term "GOP" refers to the republican party as a general entity.

References

AJC (American Jewish Committee). 2021. Translate Hate. October. https://www.ajc.org/sites/default/files/pdf/2021-10/AJC_TranslateHate-Glossary-October2021.pdf
Amy, Jeff. 2021. Georgia official: Trump call to 'find' votes was a threat. *AP News*. November 2. https://apnews.com/article/donald-trump-joe-biden-arts-and-entertainment-elections-georgia-2b27f4c92919556bf6548117648693b7
Anti-Defamation League (ADL). 2021. White Supremacists Applaud Tucker Carlson's promotion of replacement theory. April 22. https://www.adl.org/resources/blog/white-supremacists-applaud-tucker-carlsons-promotion-replacement-theory.
Arendt, Hannah. 1951. *The origins of totalitarianism*. New York: Harcourt Brace Jovanovich.
Arkin, Daniel and Ben Popken. 2018. How the internet's conspiracy theorists turned Parkland students into 'Crisis Actors'. *NBC News*. February 21. https://www.nbcnews.com/news/us-news/how-internet-s-conspiracy-theorists-turned-parkland-students-crisis-actors-n849921.
Ball, Molly. 2016. Donald trump and the politics of fear. *The Atlantic*. September 2. https://www.theatlantic.com/politics/archive/2016/09/donald-trump-and-the-politics-of-fear/498116/
Barlow, Rich. 2022. Are trump republicans fascists? *BU Today*. February 11. https://www.bu.edu/articles/2022/are-trump-republicans-fascists/.
Bathke, Benjamin. 2016. Donald Trump is manifestly unqualified to be president. DW.com. November 18. https://www.dw.com/en/donald-trump-is-manifestly-unqualified-to-be-president-biographer-says/a-36433941
BBC News. 2017. Trump's 'alternative facts': Why the row about inauguration 'lies'? January 23. https://www.bbc.com/news/world-us-canada-38716191
Bell, Chris, and Gary Senecal. n.d. Projection as a political weapon. *The Analytic Room*. https://analytic-room.com/essays/projection-as-a-political-weapon-chris-bell-gary-senecal/. Accessed 13 June 2023.
Berger, Sam. 2017. 100 days of Trump's legislation: Giveaways to big business at the expense of working families. *American Progress*. April 24. https://www.americanprogress.org/article/100-days-trumps-legislation-giveaways-big-business-expense-working-families/
Bergmann, Ernst. 1936. *Die 25 Thesen der Deutschreligion* (Twenty-five Points of the German Religion). "Friends of Europe" Publications.

Bible, Mitzi. 2012. Donald Trump addresses largest convocation crowd, praises liberty's growth. Liberty University News Service – Office of Communications & Public Engagement. September 24. https://www.liberty.edu/news/2012/09/24/donald-trump-addresses-largest-convocation-crowd-praises-libertys-growth/.

Borchers, Callum. 2017. Trump falsely claims again that he coined the term 'Fake News'. *The Washington Post*. October 26. https://www.washingtonpost.com/news/the-fix/wp/2017/10/26/trump-falsely-claims-again-that-he-coined-the-term-fake-news/

Bredemeier, Ken. 2023. Indictment against Trump 'Very, Very Damning,' former attorney general says. *VOA News*. June 11. https://www.voanews.com/a/indictment-against-trump-very-very-damning-former-attorney-general-says/7132424.html

Broich, John. 2016. How journalists covered the rise of Mussolini and Hitler. *Smithsonian Magazine*. December 13. https://www.smithsonianmag.com/history/how-journalists-covered-rise-mussolini-hitler-180961407/

Bump, Philip. 2022. The unique damaging role Fox News plays in American Media. *The Washington Post*. April 4. Accessed 13 June 2023. https://www.washingtonpost.com/politics/2022/04/04/unique-damaging-role-fox-news-plays-american-media/.

Burge, Ryan. 2019. How many Americans believe Trump is anointed by God? *Religion News Service*. November 25. https://religionnews.com/2019/11/25/how-many-americans-believe-trump-is-anointed-by-god/

Cain, Cody. 2019. Why can't Trump admit mistakes? It's an old strategy explained by Hitler. October 6. *History News Network*. https://historynewsnetwork.org/article/173224

Cathey, Libby. 2023. After Nashville shooting, Republican lawmakers again call gun action 'premature'. *ABC News*. March 28. https://abcnews.go.com/Politics/after-school-shooting-familiar-arguments-biden-lawmakers/story?id=98187238.

CRF (Constitutional Rights Foundation). 2001. The declaration of independence and natural rights. https://www.crf-usa.org/foundations-of-our-constitution/natural-rights.html

Chamberlain, Craig. 2008. Fear of Germany's destruction drove Nazism's appeal, scholar says. *News Bureau*, University of Illinois at Urbana-Champaign. June 17. https://news.illinois.edu/view/6367/206259.

Christopherson, David. 2022. The boys reveal violent ending to season 3 is based on a Donald Trump quote. *Movieweb*. July 12. https://movieweb.com/the-boys-reveal-violent-ending-season-3-based-donald-trump-quote/

CNN. 2023. READ: Transcript of CNN's town hall with former President Donald Trump. May 11. https://www.cnn.com/2023/05/11/politics/transcript-cnn-town-hall-trump/index.html

Craig, Berry. 2022. To prove Republicans aren't racist, Lindsey Graham shows off their black candidate. *People's World*. November 1. https://www.peoplesworld.org/article/to-prove-republicans-arent-racist-lindsey-graham-shows-off-their-black-candidate/

CRF (Constitutional Rights Foundation). 2010. Mussolini and the Rise of Fascism. Bill of rights in action. Summer 2010 25 (4). https://www.crf-usa.org/bill-of-rights-in-action/bria-25-4-mussolini-and-the-rise-of-fascism.html

Davis, Julie. 2017. Trump's cabinet, with a prod, extols the 'Blessing' of serving him. *New York Times*. June 12. https://www.nytimes.com/2017/06/12/us/politics/trump-boasts-of-record-setting-pace-of-activity.html

Demby, Gene. 2016. Is it racist to call someone 'Racist'? *NPR code switch*. November 23. https://www.npr.org/sections/codeswitch/2016/11/23/503180254/is-it-racist-to-call-someone-racist

Diamond, Jeremy. 2016. Donald Trump takes Liberty, courts Christian crowd. *CNN*, January 19. https://www.cnn.com/2016/01/18/politics/donald-trump-liberty-two-corinthians/index.html.

Dickinson, Kevin. 2020. Half of evangelicals believe Trump is anointed by God. Big Think. May 20. https://bigthink.com/the-present/was-trump-anointed-by-god/

DiMaggio, Anthony. 2021. Fascism by gaslighting: Trump's coup and the grassroots insurrection strategy. CounterPunch. January 8. https://www.counterpunch.org/2021/01/08/fascism-by-gaslighting-trumps-coup-and-the-grassroots-insurrection-strategy/.

DOJ (Department of Justice. Office of Public Affairs). 2023a. Four Oath keepers found guilty of seditious conspiracy related to U.S. Capitol Breach. Press release. January 23. https://www.justice.gov/opa/pr/four-oath-keepers-found-guilty-seditious-conspiracy-related-us-capitol-breach

———. 2023b. Jury convicts four leaders of the proud boys of seditious conspiracy related to U.S. Capitol Breach. Press release. May 4. https://www.justice.gov/opa/pr/jury-convicts-four-leaders-proud-boys-seditious-conspiracy-related-us-capitol-breach.

Dong, Baomin, Peter H. Egger, and Yibei Guo. 2020. Is poverty the mother of crime? Evidence from homicide rates in China, e0233034. *PLoS One* 15 (5). https://doi.org/10.1371/journal.pone.0233034. https://www.ncbi.nlm.nih.gov/pmc/articles/PMC7234816/.

Dörner, D., and C.D. Güss. 2011. A psychological analysis of Adolf Hitler's decision making as commander in chief: Summa Confidentia et Nimius Metus. *Review of General Psychology* 15 (1): 37–49. https://doi.org/10.1037/a0022375.

Du Mez, Kristin Kobes. 2020. *Jesus and John Wayne: How White Evangelicals corrupted a faith and fractured a nation.* Liveright Publishing.

Duignan, Brian. n.d. Gaslighting. In *Encyclopedia Britannica.* https://www.britannica.com/topic/gaslighting. Accessed 13 June 2023.

Dunwoody, Philip T., Joseph Gershtenson, Dennis L. Plane, and Territa Upchurch-Poole. 2022. The fascist authoritarian model of illiberal democracy. *Frontiers in Political Science* 4, 4 (August 10). https://doi.org/10.3389/fpos.2022.907681.

Durkee, Alison. 2023. Republicans in Florida are trying to get rid of the democratic party. *Forbes.* March 1. https://www.forbes.com/sites/alisondurkee/2023/03/01/republicans-in-florida-are-trying-to-get-rid-of-the-democratic-party

Edwards, Griffin Sims, and Stephen Rushin. 2018. The effect of President Trump's election on hate crimes. University of Alabama at Birmingham – Department of Marketing, Industrial Distribution & Economics. January 18. Last revised January 31, 2019. https://papers.ssrn.com/sol3/papers.cfm?abstract_id=3102652

Eggers, Andrew C., Haritz Garro, and Justin Grimmer. 2021. No evidence for voter fraud: A guide to statistical claims about the 2020 election. *PNAS* 118 (Nov. 2). https://doi.org/10.1073/pnas.2103619118.

Eltis, Alfie. 2020. Trump, and the history of political gaslighting. Varsity. October 2. https://www.varsity.co.uk/opinion/19909.

Facing History and Ourselves. 2016. The Weimar Republic: The fragility of democracy. October 27. https://www.facinghistory.org/resource-library/weimar-republic-fragility-democracy.

———. 2020. Breeding the New German 'Race'. May 12. https://www.facinghistory.org/resource-library/breeding-new-german-race.

Fascista. n.d. In Merriam-Webster.com dictionary. Retrieved June 13, 2023, from https://www.merriam-webster.com/dictionary/Fascista

FBI. 2006. White supremacist infiltration of law enforcement. https://www.justsecurity.org/wp-content/uploads/2021/06/Jan-6-Clearinghouse-FBI-Intelligence-Assessment-White-Supremacist-Infiltration-of-Law-Enforcement-Oct-17-2006-UNREDACTED.pdf

Feinberg, Ayal, Regina Branton, and Valerie Martinez-Ebers. 2019. Counties that hosted a 2016 Trump rally saw a 226 percent increase in hate crimes. *The Washington Post.* March 22. Accessed 22 March 2019. https://www.washingtonpost.com/politics/2019/03/22/trumps-rhetoric-does-inspire-more-hate-crimes.

Filby, Max. 2023. Nazis protest at land-grant drag brunch: Here's what you need to know now. *The Columbus Dispatch.* May 1. https://www.dispatch.com/story/news/2023/05/01/heres-what-we-know-about-the-nazis-protesting-a-columbus-drag-brunch/70169948007/

Finnegan, William. 2021. Law enforcement and the problem of white supremacy. *The New Yorker.* February 27. https://www.newyorker.com/news/daily-comment/law-enforcement-and-the-problem-of-white-supremacy

Fox News Press Releases. 2023. Fox News Channel finishes first quarter of 2023 as top network in all of cable with viewers across primetime and total day. March 28. https://press.foxnews.com/

2023/03/fox-news-channel-finishes-first-quarter-of-2023-as-top-network-in-all-of-cable-with-viewers-across-primetime-and-total-day#:~:text=FOX%20News%20Channel%20(FNC)%20is,audience%20according%20to%20Nielsen%20Media.

Friedman, Megan. 2017. The creator of Godwin's law says you definitely should compare white nationalists to Nazis. *Esquire*. August 14. Accessed [Access Date]. https://www.esquire.com/news-politics/news/a56987/godwin-law-charlottesville-nazis.

Gabbatt, Adam. 2020. Trump refuses to disavow QAnon conspiracy theory during town hall. *The Guardian*. October 15. https://www.theguardian.com/us-news/2020/oct/15/qanon-trump-refuses-disavow-conspiracy-theory-town-hall

GCRR (Global Center for Religious Research). 2020. An open letter to Evangelicals of moral conscience. January 18. https://www.gcrr.org/evangelicals-and-trump

German, Michael. 2020. Hidden in plain sight: Racism, white supremacy, and far-right militancy in law enforcement. *Brennan Center for Justice*. Published August 27. https://www.brennancenter.org/our-work/research-reports/hidden-plain-sight-racism-white-supremacy-and-far-right-militancy-law.

GHDI (German History in Documents and Images). n.d. 'The Cross of Honor for the German Mother': Three-tiered medal for mothers with four or more children (1938). https://ghdi.ghi-dc.org/sub_image.cfm?image_id=2044.

Gilbert, Martin. 2002. The rise of fascism in Europe in the twentieth century: Lessons for today. *India International Centre Quarterly* 29 (2, Monsoon): 31–38. https://www.jstor.org/stable/23005773.

Goldberg, Michelle. 2020. The nightmare stage of Trump's rule is here. *The New York Times*. January 6, 2020. Accessed June 13 2023. https://www.nytimes.com/2020/01/06/opinion/trump-iran.html

Gottfried, Paul E. 2016. *Fascism: The career of a concept*. DeKalb: Northern Illinois University Press.

Griffith, Aaron. 2022. American Christians 'Backing the Blue': On faith and policing. Religion and Politics. May 17. https://religionandpolitics.org/2022/05/17/american-christians-backing-the-blue-on-faith-and-policing/. Accessed 13 June 2023.

Gritz, Jennie Rothenberg. 2012. Early Warnings: How American Journalists Reported the Rise of Hitler. The Atlantic, March 13. https://www.theatlantic.com/national/archive/2012/03/early-warnings-how-american-journalists-reported-the-rise-of-hitler/254146/

Gross, Terry. 2022. Rachel Maddow Uncovers a WWII-era plot against America in 'Ultra'. NPR, Fresh Ai. December 15. https://www.npr.org/2022/12/15/1143078657/rachel-maddow-uncovers-a-wwii-era-plot-against-america-in-ultra.

Gumpert, David E. 2022. The uncanny resemblance of the Beer Hall Putsch and the January 6 insurrection: If 1920s Germany could punish Hitler for leading a coup attempt, why can't America go after Trump? The Nation. January 3. https://www.thenation.com/article/politics/trump-hitler-coup/.

Gurley, Gabrielle. 2023. Tennessee Republicans step up attacks on democratic cities. *The American Prospect*. April 13. https://prospect.org/politics/2023-04-13-tennessee-republicans-attack-democratic-cities/.

Guyette, Curt. 2019. Is Trump a fascist? The F-word. *Metro Times*. September 11. https://www.metrotimes.com/news/is-trump-a-fascist-22617920

Harris, Johnny and Michelle Cottle. 2022. Inside the completely legal G.O.P. plot to destroy American democracy. *The New York Times*. September 21. https://www.nytimes.com/2022/09/21/opinion/republicans-democracy-elections-bannon.html

Harty, Kevin J. 2016. William Dudley Pelley, an American Nazi in King Arthur's Court. *Arthuriana* 26 (2): 64–85. https://www.jstor.org/stable/43855519.

Hatewatch Staff. 2020. What you need to know about QAnon. Southern Poverty Law Center. October 27. https://www.splcenter.org/hatewatch/2020/10/27/what-you-need-know-about-qanon.

Hedges, Chris. 2006. *American fascists: The christian right and the war on America*. New York: Free Press.

Helmore, Edward. 2023. Republican legislators introduce new laws to crack down on drag shows. *The Guardian*. January 21. https://www.theguardian.com/world/2023/jan/21/anti-drag-show-laws-bans-republican-states

Heritage, Stuart. 2022. Why superhero satire The Boys turned off its rightwing fanbase. *The Guardian*. June 28. https://www.theguardian.com/tv-and-radio/2022/jun/28/the-boys-homelander-trump-rightwing-fanbase

History is Now Magazine. 2020. Fascism in 1930s America: The Silver Shirts. November 22. http://www.historyisnowmagazine.com/blog/2020/11/22/fascism-in-1930s-america-the-silver-shirts#.ZHZWTHbMLXY=.

Hitler, Adolf. 1925. *Mein Kampf* (trans: Ralph Manheim). Boston: Houghton Mifflin.

Holocaust Encyclopedia (a). n.d. The Reichstag Fire. United States Holocaust Memorial Museum. https://encyclopedia.ushmm.org/content/en/article/the-reichstag-fire. Accessed 13 June 2023.

Holocaust Encyclopedia (b). n.d. The Nazification of the German police, 1933–1939. United States Holocaust Memorial Museum. https://encyclopedia.ushmm.org/content/en/article/german-police-in-the-nazi-state. Accessed 13 June 2023.

Holocaust Encyclopedia (c). n.d. Lebensborn program. United States Holocaust Memorial Museum. https://encyclopedia.ushmm.org/content/en/article/lebensborn-program. Accessed 14 June 2023.

Holocaust Encyclopedia (d). n.d. Hitler comes to power. United States Holocaust Memorial Museum. https://encyclopedia.ushmm.org/content/en/article/hitler-comes-to-power. Accessed 15 June 2023.

Holocaust Encyclopedia (e) n.d. Law, Justice, and the holocaust. United States Holocaust Memorial Museum. https://encyclopedia.ushmm.org/content/en/article/law-justice-and-the-holocaust. Accessed 15 June 2023.

Holocaust Memorial Day Trust. n.d. 6 May 1933: Looting of the Institute of Sexology. https://www.hmd.org.uk/resource/6-may-1933-looting-of-the-institute-of-sexology/. Accessed 13 June 2023.

Holt, Thomas J., Steve Chermak, and Joshua D. Freilich. 2021. *An assessment of extremist groups use of web forums, social media, and technology to enculturate and radicalize individuals to violence*. National Criminal Justice Reference Service. January. https://www.ojp.gov/pdffiles1/nij/grants/256038.pdf.

Horton, Adrian. 2021. John Oliver on Tucker Carlson: 'The most prominent vessel for white supremacist talking points'. *The Guardian*. March 15. https://www.theguardian.com/tv-and-radio/2021/mar/15/john-oliver-tucker-carlson-fox-news. Accessed 13 June 2023.

Hsu, Spencer S. 2022. U.S. Cited 'Domestic Terrorism' in search tied to 'Oath Keepers' Lawyer. *The Washington Post*. September 7. https://www.washingtonpost.com/dc-md-va/2022/09/07/domestic-terrorism-sorelle-oathkeepers/

Inskeep, Steve. 2021. Timeline: What Trump told supporters for months before they attacked. *NPR*. February 8. https://www.npr.org/2021/02/08/965342252/timeline-what-trump-told-supporters-for-months-before-they-attacked/.

Jeffries, Hasan. Kwame. n.d. The new deal, Jim Crow and the black cabinet. Teaching hard history (Podcast: Episode 10, Season 4). *Learning for Justice*. Retrieved June 13, 2023, from https://www.learningforjustice.org/podcasts/teaching-hard-history/jim-crow-era/the-new-deal-jim-crow-and-the-black-cabinet

Jenab, Emily. 2016. Ethical implications of victim blaming in cases of police brutality. Fordham University Center for Ethics Education. https://ethicsandsociety.org/2016/10/04/ethical-implications-of-victim-blaming-in-cases-of-police-brutality/

Jensen, Michael (Principal Investigator) and Patrick James (Project Manager). 2018. The use of social media by United States extremists. National Consortium for the Study of Terrorism and Responses to Terrorism (START). July. https://www.start.umd.edu/pubs/START_PIRUS_UseOfSocialMediaByUSExtremists_ResearchBrief_July2018.pdf

Johnsen, Rosemary Erickson. 2017. On the origins of 'Gaslighting'. *Los Angeles Review of Books*. March 9. https://lareviewofbooks.org/article/on-the-origins-of-gaslighting/.

Johnson, David Kyle. 2017. Trump inauguration: (Crowd) Size matters, so who's lying? *Psychology Today*, January 23. https://www.psychologytoday.com/us/blog/logical-take/201701/trump-inauguration-crowd-size-matters-so-whos-lying

Johnson, Vida B. 2019. KKK in the PD: White supremacist police and what to do about it. *Lewis & Clark Law Review* 23: 205. https://fingfx.thomsonreuters.com/gfx/legaldocs/zjvqkmrkgvx/KKK%20IN%20THE%20PD%20WHITE%20SUPREMACIST%20POLICE%20AND%20WHAT%20TO%20DO%20ABOUT%20IT.pdf.

Johnson, Russell P. 2022. Thoughts and prayers. Sightings: University of Chicago Divinity School. June 8. https://divinity.uchicago.edu/sightings/articles/thoughts-and-prayers.

Jones, Chuck. 2020. Obama's 2009 recovery act kicked off over 10 years of economic growth. *Forbes*. https://www.forbes.com/sites/chuckjones/2020/02/17/obamas-2009-recovery-act-kicked-off-over-10-years-of-economic-growth/?sh=7490733668b7. Accessed 17 Feb 2020.

Jones, Robert W., Jr. 2020. Creating a demigod: Nazi art, Adolf Hitler, and the cult of personality. *Veritas* 4 (2): 45–59.

Jones, Seth G., Catrina Doxsee, and Nicholas Harrington. 2020. The escalating terrorism problem in the United States. Brief. June 17. Center for Strategic and International Studies. https://www.csis.org/analysis/escalating-terrorism-problem-united-states

Kakutani, Michiko. 2018. *The death of truth: Notes on falsehood in the age of Trump*. New York: Tim Duggan Books.

Kanu, Hassan. 2022. Prevalence of white supremacists in law enforcement demands drastic change. Reuters. May 12. https://www.reuters.com/legal/government/prevalence-white-supremacists-law-enforcement-demands-drastic-change-2022-05-12/.

Katz, Eric. 2020. White house confirms it's purging disloyal employees 'From the Bowels of the Federal Government'. Government Executive. February 25. https://www.govexec.com/workforce/2020/02/white-house-confirms-its-purging-disloyal-employees-bowels-federal-government/163316/

KDKA News. 2022. Police lieutenant back on duty after investigation into alleged connection to oath keepers. *CBS Pittsburgh*. September 8. https://www.cbsnews.com/pittsburgh/news/pittsburgh-police-lieutenant-on-duty-after-investigating-alleged-connection-oath-keepers/.

Kertzer, David I. 2022. The Pope's secret back channel to Hitler. *The Atlantic*. May 31. https://www.theatlantic.com/ideas/archive/2022/05/pope-pius-xii-negotiation-hitler-catholic-church/639435/

Kessler, Glenn, Salvador Rizzo, and Meg Kelly. 2021. Trump's false or misleading claims total 30,573 over four years. *The Washington Post*. https://www.washingtonpost.com/politics/2021/01/24/trumps-false-or-misleading-claims-total-30573-over-four-years/. Accessed 13 June 2023.

Khosla, Vinay. 2022. Are your words still your own? Iskra (The Spark). November 20. Retrieved from https://www.thedp.com/article/2022/11/are-your-words-still-your-own

Kilgore, Ed. 2022. Trump's long campaign to steal the presidency: A timeline. Intelligencer. *The New York Times Magazine*, last updated July 14. https://nymag.com/intelligencer/article/trump-campaign-steal-presidency-timeline.html. Accessed 14 July 2022.

Koester, Samantha. 2018. 'Fake news' is not new: The Nazis used it too, says Holocaust exhibit. *Reuters*. January 25. https://www.reuters.com/article/uk-holocaust-memorial-belgium/fake-news-is-not-new-the-nazis-used-it-too-says-holocaust-exhibit-idUKKBN1FE2OM.

Kogan, Bobby. 2023. Tax cuts are primarily responsible for the increasing debt ratio. Center for American Progress. March 27. https://www.americanprogress.org/article/tax-cuts-are-primarily-responsible-for-the-increasing-debt-ratio/

Kremmerer, Stephanie. 2021. The Bizarre Universe of QAnon Conspiracies. *Skeptical Inquirer* 45 (2) March, April: 32–37.

Land, Graham. 2021. The Brownshirts: The role of the Sturmabteilung (SA) in Nazi Germany. History Hit. September 28. https://www.historyhit.com/hitlers-bullyboys-the-role-of-the-sa-in-nazi-germany/. Accessed 13 June 2023.

Langer, Walter C. n.d. Adolf Hitler: Psychological analysis of Hitler's life & legend. Jewish virtual library. Written with the collaboration of Prof. Henry A. Murr, Harvard Psychological Clinic;

Dr. Ernst Kris, New School for Social Research; Dr. Bertram D. Lawin, New York Psychoanalytic Institute. https://www.jewishvirtuallibrary.org/psychological-analysis-of-hitler-s-life-and-legend-2

Lavin, Tal. 2020. QAnon, blood libel, and the satanic panic. *The New Republic.* September 29. https://newrepublic.com/article/159529/qanon-blood-libel-satanic-panic.

Levin, Bess. 2023. Nothing to see here, just trump reportedly vowing to 'Immediately' fire anyone who investigated him if reelected. vanity fair. May 30. https://www.vanityfair.com/news/2023/05/donald-trump-doj-fbi-purge. Accessed 13 June 2023.

———. 2023b. A Texas bill would offer huge tax breaks to straight couples who have 10–10! – Kids. *Vanity Fair.* March 2. https://www.vanityfair.com/news/2023/03/texas-10-kids-property-tax-bill. Accessed 2 March 2023.

Linder, Douglas O. n.d. The Hitler Beer Hall Putsch trial: An account. *Famous Trials.* https://famous-trials.com/hitler/2524-the-hitler-beer-hall-putsch-trial-an-account.

Locke, John. 1689/1988. Two treatises of government. Peter Laslett. Cambridge University Press.

Lopez, German. (2016). Donald Trump's Taco Bowl, explained. Vox.com. May 5. https://www.vox.com/2016/5/5/11602458/donald-trump-grill-taco-bowl

Maddow, Rachel. 2022a. Bedlam. Ultra (Podcast), Episode 6. MSNBC. November 7. https://www.msnbc.com/msnbc-podcast/rachel-maddow-presents-ultra/episode-6-bedlam-n1300515

———. 2022b. Ultra vires. Ultra (Podcast), Episode 8. MSNBC. November 21. https://www.msnbc.com/msnbc-podcast/rachel-maddow-presents-ultra/transcript-ultra-vires-n1300885

Margolin, Josh. 2021. White supremacists 'Seek Affiliation' with law enforcement to further their goals, internal FBI report warns. *ABC News.* March 8. https://abcnews.go.com/US/white-supremacists-seek-affiliation-law-enforcement-goals-internal/story?id=76309051.

Mayer, Jane. 2018. How Russia helped swing the election for trump. *The New Yorker*, October 1. https://www.newyorker.com/magazine/2018/10/01/how-russia-helped-to-swing-the-election-for-trump.

McGann, Laura. 2018. Let's stop pretending Trump is just pretending. Vox.com. October 30. https://www.vox.com/2018/10/30/18037464/trump-rallies-apology-media-mobs

McNeill, J.R. 2016. How fascist is Donald Trump? There's actually a formula for that. *The Washington Post.* October 21. https://www.washingtonpost.com/posteverything/wp/2016/10/21/how-fascist-is-donald-trump-theres-actually-a-formula-for-that/

Meet the Press. 1946. O. John Rogge Interview. *NBC News,* via the Library of Congress. Available at: https://rachel-maddow-presents-ultra.simplecast.com/episodes/listen-doj-prosecutor-o-john-rogges-full-meet-the-press-interview

Milligan, Susan. 2022. A quarter of republicans believe central views of QAnon conspiracy movement. *US News.* February 24. https://www.usnews.com/news/politics/articles/2022-02-24/a-quarter-of-republicans-believe-central-views-of-qanon-conspiracy-movement

Monde, Chiderah. 2012. Jon Stewart: Republican predictions over Obama re-election are nonsense. *New York Daily News.* February 23. https://www.nbcnews.com/pop-culture/pop-culture-news/jon-stewart-republican-predictions-over-obama-re-election-are-nonsense-flna172427

Morris, Alex. 2021. Michael Flynn and the Christian right's plan to turn America into a theocracy. *Rolling Stone Magazine.* November 21. https://www.rollingstone.com/politics/politics-features/michael-flynn-cornerstone-church-christian-theocracy-1260606/

Noack, Rick. 2016. The ugly history of 'Lügenpresse,' a Nazi slur shouted at a Trump rally. *The Washington Post.* October 24. https://www.washingtonpost.com/news/worldviews/wp/2016/10/24/the-ugly-history-of-luegenpresse-a-nazi-slur-shouted-at-a-trump-rally/

Nortey, Justin. 2021. Most White Americans who regularly attend worship services voted for Trump in 2020. Pew Research Center. August 30. https://www.pewresearch.org/short-reads/2021/08/30/most-white-americans-who-regularly-attend-worship-services-voted-for-trump-in-2020/

Norton, Tom. 2022. Fact check: Were only trump supporters arrested for 2020 election fraud? *Newsweek.* August 4. https://www.newsweek.com/fact-check-were-only-trump-supporters-arrested-2020-election-fraud-1730592

O'Dell, Liam. 2022. The Boys subreddit descends into chaos after fans complain about show's 'politics'. *Indy100.* June 22. https://www.indy100.com/tv/the-boys-subreddit-community-politics

O'Toole, Fintan. 2018. Trial runs for fascism are in full flow. *The Irish Times.* June 26. https://www.irishtimes.com/opinion/fintan-o-toole-trial-runs-for-fascism-are-in-full-flow-1.3543375. Accessed 13 June 2023.

Office of Strategic Services (Research and Analysis Branch). 1945. R & A 3114.4 The Nazi Master Plan/Annex 4: The persecution of the Christian Churches. Nuremberg, Germany: International Military Tribunal, 1945–1946. Cornell University Law Library Donovan Nuremberg Trials Collection. Volume 010, Subdivision 18, Section 18.03. July 6. http://reader.library.cornell.edu/docviewer/digital?id=nur00773#mode/1up

Oliver, John. Last Week Tonight. HBO. March 14, 2021. You can watch the relevant segment here: https://www.youtube.com/watch?v=XMGxxRRtmHc

Olson, Michael. 2021. How poverty drives violent crime. Oklahoma Justice Reform Task Force. December 7. https://www.okjusticereform.org/blog/how-poverty-drives-violent-crime

Orwell, George. 1949. *1984.* London: Secker and Warburg. https://rauterberg.employee.id.tue.nl/lecturenotes/DDM110%20CAS/Orwell-1949%201984.pdf.

Parks, Miles. 2022. Here's where election-denying candidates are running to control voting. *NPR.* February 3. https://www.npr.org/2022/01/04/1069232219/heres-where-election-deniers-and-doubters-are-running-to-control-voting.

PBS. n.d. Reverend Charles E. Coughlin (1891–1979). American Experience | America and the Holocaust | Article. https://www.pbs.org/wgbh/americanexperience/features/holocaust-coughlin/. Accessed 13 June 2023.

PBS NewsHour. 2023. WATCH: 'I need 11,000 votes,' Trump told Ga. election official | Jan. 6 hearings. https://www.youtube.com/watch?v=AbFc9T7KXA0

———. 2023b. We asked every senator what action should be taken on guns. Here's what they said. May 25. https://www.pbs.org/newshour/politics/what-action-should-be-taken-on-guns-we-asked-every-senator.

Pew Research Center. 2014. Religious Landscape Study (RLS-II) Main survey of nationally representative sample of adults final questionnaire. May 30. https://www.pewresearch.org/religion/religious-landscape-study/compare/christians/by/party-affiliation/ for the specific date mentioned, see https://www.pewresearch.org/religion/religious-landscape-study/compare/christians/by/party-affiliation#christians

Pruitt-Young, Sharon. 2021. The 2020 election is back in court, as dominion sues conservative media outlets. *NPR.* August 10. https://www.npr.org/2021/08/10/1026509404/dominion-sues-conservative-media-oan-newsmax-2020-election.

Putt, Sasha. 2022. Benito Mussolini's rise to power: From Biennio Rosso to March on Rome. *The Collector.* December 2. https://www.thecollector.com/benito-mussolini-rise-to-power

Quednau, Joseph. 2021. How are violent crime rates in U.S. cities affected by poverty? *The Park Place Economist* 28. Available at: https://digitalcommons.iwu.edu/parkplace/vol28/iss1/8.

Rajan, Anjana, et al. 2021. Countering QAnon: understanding the role of human trafficking in the disinformation-extremist nexus. *Polaris.* February. https://polarisproject.org/wp-content/uploads/2021/02/Polaris-Report-Countering-QAnon.pdf

Ralph, Pat, and Eliza Relman. 2018. These are the most and least biased news outlets in the US, according to Americans. Business Insider. September 2. https://www.businessinsider.com/most-biased-news-outlets-in-america-cnn-fox-nytimes-2018-8.

Rees, Laurence. 2012. *The dark charisma of Adolf Hitler.* Ebury Press.

Reuters Staff. 2020. In *Partly false claim: Trump fired entire pandemic response team in 2018,* ed. Gareth Jones. March 25. https://www.reuters.com/article/uk-factcheck-trump-fired-pandemic-team/partly-false-claim-trump-fired-entire-pandemic-response-team-in-2018-idUSKBN21C32M.

———. 2021. Fact check: Courts have dismissed multiple lawsuits of alleged electoral fraud presented by Trump campaign. Reuters. https://www.reuters.com/article/uk-factcheck-courts-election/fact-check-courts-have-dismissed-multiple-lawsuits-of-alleged-electoral-fraud-pre sented-by-trump-campaign-idUSKBN2AF1G1.

Romano, Evan. 2020. The Boys Star Antony Starr Rips into Trump supporters dressing as homelander. *Men's Health.* 20 November. https://www.menshealth.com/entertainment/ a34741798/the-boys-antony-starr-trump-supporters-homelander/.

Ronayne, Kathleen and Michael Kunzelman. 2020. Trump to far-right extremists: 'Stand back and stand by'. *AP News.* September 30. https://apnews.com/article/election-2020-joe-biden-race-and-ethnicity-donald-trump-chris-wallace-0b32339da25fbc9e8b7c7c7066a1db0f.

Rouse, Stella, and Shibley Telhami. 2022. Most republicans support declaring the United States a Christian Nation. Politico. September 21. https://www.politico.com/news/magazine/2022/09/ 21/most-republicans-support-declaring-the-united-states-a-christian-nation-00057736

Russonello, Giovanni. 2021. QAnon now as popular in U.S. as some major religions, Poll suggests. *The New York Times.* May 27 https://web.archive.org/web/20210527220843/https://www. nytimes.com/2021/05/27/us/politics/qanon-republicans-trump.html

Sarkis, Stephanie. 2018. Donald Trump is a classic gaslighter in an abusive relationship with America. *USA Today.* October 3. https://www.usatoday.com/story/opinion/2018/10/03/trump-classic-gaslighter-abusive-relationship-america-column/1445050002/.

Sax, Leonard. 2002. How common is intersex? A response to Anne Fausto-Sterling. *Journal of Sex Research* 39 (3): 174–178. https://doi.org/10.1080/00224490209552139.

Schapitl, Lexie and Claudia Grisales. 2023. House panel on 'weaponization' of the government's first hearing takes aim at DOJ, FBI. *NPR.* February 9. Retrieved from https://www.npr.org/2023/ 02/09/1155459408/house-panel-on-weaponization-of-the-federal-government-will-hold-its-first-heari

Serwer, Adam. 2022. Conservatives believe trump is above the law. *The Atlantic.* August 9. https:// www.theatlantic.com/ideas/archive/2022/08/trump-mar-a-lago-fbi-raid-investigation/671087/

Sheerin, Jude. 2021. Who truly was the most dishonest president? *BBC.* March 7. https://www.bbc. com/news/world-us-canada-56246507

Sisak, Michael R. 2019. Judge Fines Trump $2 Million for Misusing Charity Foundation. *AP News.* November 8. https://apnews.com/article/campaigns-donald-trump-us-news-ap-top-news-law suits-7b8d0f5ce9cb4cadad948c2c414afd57.

Slisco, Aila. 2023. Trump to 'Dismantle Deep State' with 'Truth and Reconciliation Commission'. *Newsweek.* March 21. https://www.newsweek.com/trump-dismantle-deep-state-truth-reconcilia tion-commission-1789374

Smith, David. 2022. Belief in QAnon has strengthened in US since Trump was voted out, study finds. *The Guardian.* February 24. https://www.theguardian.com/us-news/2022/feb/23/qanon-believers-increased-america-study-finds

Solomon, Amy L. 2012. In search of a job: Criminal records as barriers to employment. *National Institute of Justice,* June 14. https://nij.ojp.gov/topics/articles/search-job-criminal-records-barriers-employment

Sommer, Will. 2023. Trust the plan: The rise of QAnon and the conspiracy that Unhinged America. Harper Collins.

Speri, Alice. 2020. Unredacted FBI document sheds new light on white supremacist infiltration of law enforcement. *The Intercept.* September 29. https://theintercept.com/2020/09/29/police-white-supremacist-infiltration-fbi/.

Stanley, Jason. 2018. *How fascism works: The Politics of US versus them.* New York: Random House.

Stanton, Gregory. 2020. QAnon is a Nazi Cult, rebranded. *Just Security.* September 9. https://www. justsecurity.org/72339/qanon-is-a-nazi-cult-rebranded/. Accessed 13 June 2023.

Statista. 2022. Poverty rate in the United States by ethnic group 2021. Statista Research Depart-ment. September 30, 2022. https://www.statista.com/statistics/200476/us-poverty-rate-by-ethnic-group/

Stechschulte, Tom. 2022. It is just a fact – Trump is a crook, liar, grifter, con-man, narcissist. *The Insider*. August 16. https://www.insiderutah.com/articles/it-is-just-a-fact-trump-is-a-crook-liar-grifter-con-man-narcissist/

Stieb, Matt. 2019. Ex-white nationalist says Tucker Carlson hits far-right messaging 'Better Than They Have'. *Intelligencer, New York Magazine*. April 1. https://nymag.com/intelligencer/2019/04/ex-white-nationalist-says-they-get-tips-from-tucker-carlson.html.

Swan, Jonathan, Charlie Savage, and Maggie Haberman. 2023. The radical strategy behind Donald Trump's promise to 'go after' Joe Biden. *The New York Times*. June 15. https://www.nytimes.com/2023/06/15/us/politics/trump-indictment-justice-department.html.

Szep, Jason and Linda So. 2021. Trump campaign demonized two Georgia election workers – And death threats followed. *Reuters Special Report*. December 1. https://www.reuters.com/investigates/special-report/usa-election-threats-georgia/.

Tang, Terry, and Deepti Hajela. 2019. Many view 'black friend defense' as a tired, hollow argument. *Associated Press*. March 1. https://apnews.com/article/nc-state-wire-north-america-donald-trump-us-news-ap-top-news-c7e6681046e3463aa9967a8302e5a102

Taylor, Jessica. 2016. Citing 'Two Corinthians,' Trump struggles to make the sale to evangelicals. *NPR*. January 18. https://www.npr.org/2016/01/18/463528847/citing-two-corinthians-trump-struggles-to-make-the-sale-to-evangelicals.

The Economist. 2021. Russian elections once again had a suspiciously neat result. October 11th. https://www.economist.com/graphic-detail/2021/10/11/russian-elections-once-again-had-a-suspiciously-neat-result.

Thompson, Dorothy. 1935. *Quoted in Broich*: 2016.

Thompson, Stuart A. 2022. How Russian media uses fox news to make its case. *The New York Times*. April 15. https://www.nytimes.com/2022/04/15/technology/russia-media-fox-news.html. Accessed 15 Apr 2022.

Thompson, Alex. 2023. First look: RNC slams Biden in AI-generated ad. *Axios*. April 25. https://www.axios.com/2023/04/25/rnc-slams-biden-re-election-bid-ai-generated-ad.

TOI Staff. 2020. In 'Confession of Guilt,' German Catholic Church admits 'Complicity' with Nazis. *The Times of Israel*. May 2. https://www.timesofisrael.com/german-bishops-said-to-admit-complicity-in-nazi-actions-in-new-report/

Tomczyk, S., D. Pielmann, and S. Schmidt. 2022. More than a glance: Investigating the differential efficacy of radicalizing graphical cues with right-wing messages. *European Journal of Criminology Policy Research* 28 (3): 245–267. https://doi.org/10.1007/s10610-022-0950.

Toy, Eckard V., Jr. 1989. Silver shirts in the northwest: Politics, prophecies, and personalities in the 1930s. *The Pacific Northwest Quarterly* 80 (4): 139–146. https://www.jstor.org/stable/40491076.

U.S. Department of State. 2022. Terrorist designations and state sponsors of terrorism. *Bureau of Counterterrorism*. https://www.state.gov/terrorist-designations-and-state-sponsors-of-terrorism/#designations

Ura, Alexa, and Jolie McCullough. 2015. In Texas, minorities less likely to own homes. *Texas Tribune*. November 8. https://www.texastribune.org/2015/11/08/texas-minorities-underrepresented-among-homeowners/.

Vo, Lam Thuy. 2019. Why is everyone so obsessed with AOC? Let's analyze the memes. *BuzzFeed News*. May 3. https://www.buzzfeednews.com/article/lamvo/alexandria-ocasio-cortez-aoc-conservatives-liberals-meme.

Walker, Jesse. 2018. 'Crisis Actors,' conspiracy theories, and the fear of social media. *Reason Foundation*. February 22. https://reason.com/2018/02/22/crisis-actors/.

Watson, Kathryn. 2020. Trump banks on fear and anxiety to motivate voters. *CBS News*, September 29. https://www.cbsnews.com/news/trumps-use-of-fear-and-anxiety-to-motivate-his-voters/. Accessed 13 June 2023.

Weinstein, Michael L., and Davin Seay. 2006. *With god on our side: One man's war against an Evangelical coup in America's military*. New York: Thomas Dunne Books.

Weitzer, Ronald. 2017. Theorizing racial discord over policing before and after Ferguson. *Justice Quarterly* 34 (7): 1129–1153. https://doi.org/10.1080/07418825.2017.1362461.

White House Archives. 2007. *President bush addresses the 89th annual national convention of the American legion.* Reno, Nevada: Reno-Sparks Convention Center. https://georgewbush-whitehouse.archives.gov/news/releases/2007/08/20070828-2.html.

Wilson, Jason, and Aaron Flanagan. 2022. The racist 'Great Replacement' conspiracy theory explained. *Southern Poverty Law Center, Hatewatch.* May 17. https://www.splcenter.org/hatewatch/2022/05/17/racist-great-replacement-conspiracy-theory-explained.

Wittgenstein, Ludwig. 1953. *Philosophical investigations.* Oxford, UK: Basil Blackwell.

Wolfowicz, Michael, Badi Hasisi, and David Weisburd. 2022. What are the effects of different elements of media on radicalization outcomes? A systematic review. *Campbell Systematic Reviews* 18 (2): e1244. https://doi.org/10.1002/cl2.1244.

Wong, Scott, Thorp V, Frank, Vitali, Ali, Haake, Garrett, Dilanian, Ken, Alba, Monica, Allen, Jonathan, & Shabad, Rebecca. 2023. Trump allies say Biden is 'weaponizing' DOJ against his chief 2024 rival following indictment. Yahoo! Lifestyle. June 9. Retrieved from https://www.yahoo.com/lifestyle/trump-allies-biden-weaponizing-doj-044429207.html

Woodruff Swan, Betsy. 2020. DHS draft document: White supremacists are greatest terror threat. *Politico.* September 4. https://www.politico.com/news/2020/09/04/white-supremacists-terror-threat-dhs-409236.

Wray, Christopher. 2022. Oversight of the Federal Bureau of Investigation. *Federal Bureau of Investigation.* August, 4. https://www.fbi.gov/news/testimony/oversight-of-the-federal-bureau-of-investigation-080422

Wright, Thomas. 2020. What a second trump term would mean for the world. Brookings Institution. October 1. https://www.brookings.edu/blog/order-from-chaos/2020/10/01/what-a-second-trump-term-would-mean-for-the-world/.

Youngblood, Michael. 2020. Extremist ideology as a complex contagion: the spread of far-right radicalization in the United States between 2005 and 2017. *Humanities and Social Sciences Communications* 7 (1): 49. https://doi.org/10.1057/s41599-020-00546-3.

Ziegler, Herbert F. 2014. *Nazi Germany's new aristocracy: The SS leadership, 1925–1939*, 85–87. Princeton, New Jersey: Princeton University Press. isbn:9781400860364.

Zipp, Ricky. 2018. Trump finally responds to the Kentucky shooting, nearly 24 hours after Trudeau. Vox, January 24. https://www.vox.com/world/2018/1/24/16928676/trump-tweet-texts-kentucky-shooting-trudeau.

9783031246845VOL01